ISBN 978-1-334-05458-7
PIBN 10721607

This book is a reproduction of an important historical work. Forgotten Books uses
state-of-the-art technology to digitally reconstruct the work, preserving the original format
whilst repairing imperfections present in the aged copy. In rare cases, an imperfection in
the original, such as a blemish or missing page, may be replicated in our edition. We do,
however, repair the vast majority of imperfections successfully; any imperfections that
remain are intentionally left to preserve the state of such historical works.

1 MONTH OF
FREE
READING

at

www.ForgottenBooks.com

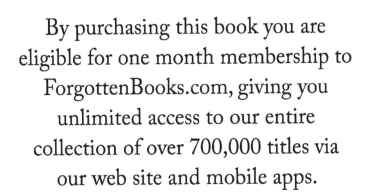

By purchasing this book you are eligible for one month membership to ForgottenBooks.com, giving you unlimited access to our entire collection of over 700,000 titles via our web site and mobile apps.

To claim your free month visit:

www.forgottenbooks.com/free721607

Counties of England

EDITED BY WILLIAM PAGE F.S.A.

A HISTORY OF
CUMBERLAND

VOLUME II

A HISTORY OF CUMBERLAND
EDITED BY JAMES WILSON, M.A.

THE

I

F THE COUNTIES
OF ENGLAND

CUMBERLAND

665.42
28/9/05.

ARCHIBALD CONSTABLE
AND COMPANY LIMITED

This History is issued to Subscribers only
By Archibald Constable & Company Limited
and printed by Butler & Tanner of
Frome and London

INSCRIBED
TO THE MEMORY OF
HER LATE MAJESTY
QUEEN VICTORIA
WHO GRACIOUSLY GAVE
THE TITLE TO AND
ACCEPTED THE
DEDICATION OF
THIS HISTORY

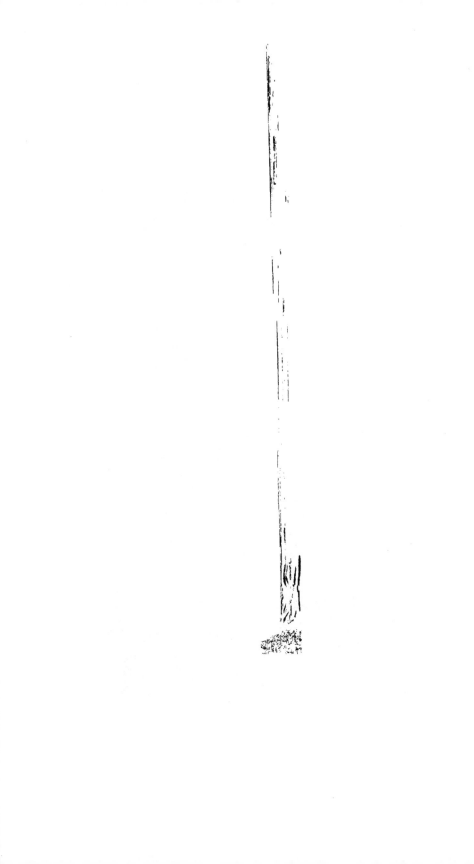

Carlisle

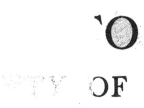
'O

TY OF

THE
TORIA HISTOR
OF THE COUNTY OF

EDITED BY JAMES WILSON, M.A.

VOLUME **TWO**

HAYMARKET
1905

CONTENTS OF VOLUME TWO

LIST OF ILLUSTRATIONS

LIST OF MAPS

xi

EDITORIAL NOTE

No claim to exhaustiveness is made for the lists of abbots and priors of the religious houses. It is probable that as the contents of private muniments and the public records become more accessible, new names will be added. Since the article on the religious houses was completed, the name of John, abbot of Holmcultram, in 1406, was brought to light by the publication of the *Calendar of Papal Letters* (vi. 77) : John, prior of St. Bees, was witness to a deed, dated 1330, at Cockermouth Castle, and Nicholas de Warthill was prior of the same place in 1387, as stated in a charter at the British Museum.

During the time of the preparation of this volume death has removed two esteemed colleagues—the Rev. H. A. Macpherson, a zoologist of distinction, and Mr. William Steel, a keen sportsman as well as an experienced writer.

The Editors wish to express their obligation to Mrs. Henry Ware for the loan of her valuable collection of casts of episcopal seals ; to the Cumberland and Westmorland Archaeological Society for the use of blocks ; to the Mayor and Corporation of Carlisle for liberty to photograph the initial letter of one of their royal charters ; to the Director of the Public Library, Carlisle, for the loan of engravings for reproduction ; to the Bishop and Chapter of Carlisle, the Earl of Lonsdale, and Lord Leconfield, for access to their muniments ; to the Rev. Dr. Greenwell, Mr. W. Farrer, Sir E. T. Bewley, Dr. George Neilson, Mr. William Brown, and Dr. Haswell, for advice and assistance readily given.

Abbrev. Plac. (Rec. Com.)	Abbreviatio Placitorum (Record Commission)
Acts of P.C.	Acts of Privy Council
Add.	Additional
Add. Chart.	Additional Charters
Admir.	Admiralty
Agarde	Agarde's Indices
Anct. Corresp.	Ancient Correspondence
Anct. D. (P.R.O.) A 2420	Ancient Deeds (Public Record Office) A 2420
Antiq.	Antiquarian or Antiquaries
App.	Appendix
Arch.	Archæologia or Archæological
Arch. Cant.	Archæologia Cantiana
Archd. Rec.	Archdeacon's Records
Archit.	Architectural
Assize R.	Assize Rolls
Aud. Off.	Audit Office
Aug. Off.	Augmentation Office
Ayloffe	Ayloffe's Calendars
Bed.	Bedford
Beds	Bedfordshire
Berks	Berkshire
Bdle.	Bundle
B.M.	British Museum
Bodl. Lib.	Bodley's Library
Boro.	Borough
Brev. Reg.	Brevia Regia
Brit.	Britain, British, Britannia, etc.
Buck.	Buckingham
Bucks	Buckinghamshire
Cal.	Calendar
Camb.	Cambridgeshire or Cambridge
Cambr.	Cambria, Cambrian, Cambrensis, etc.
Cant.	Canterbury
Cap.	Chapter
Carl.	Carlisle
Cart. Antiq. R.	Cartæ Antiquæ Rolls
C.C.C. Camb.	Corpus Christi College, Cambridge
Certiorari Bdles. (Rolls Chap.)	Certiorari Bundles (Rolls Chapel)
Chan. Enr. Decree R.	Chancery Enrolled Decree Rolls
Chan. Proc.	Chancery Proceedings
Chant. Cert.	Chantry Certificates (or Certificates of Colleges and Chantries)
Chap. Ho.	Chapter House
Charity Inq.	Charity Inquisitions
Chart. R. 20 Hen. III. pt. i. No. 10	Charter Roll, 20 Henry III. part i. Number 10
Chartul.	Chartulary
Chas.	Charles
Ches.	Cheshire
Chest.	Chester
Ch. Gds. (Exch. K.R.)	Church Goods (Exchequer King's Remembrancer)
Chich.	Chichester
Chron.	Chronicle, Chronica, etc.
Close	Close Roll
Co.	County
Colch.	Colchester
Coll.	Collections
Com.	Commission
Com. Pleas	Common Pleas
Conf. R.	Confirmation Rolls
Co. Plac.	County Placita
Cornw.	Cornwall
Corp.	Corporation
Cott.	Cotton or Cottonian
Ct. R.	Court Rolls
Ct. of Wards	Court of Wards
Cumb.	Cumberland
Cur. Reg.	Curia Regis
D. and C.	Dean and Chapter
De Banc. R.	De Banco Rolls
Dec. and Ord.	Decrees and Orders
Dep. Keeper's Rep.	Deputy Keeper's Reports
Derb.	Derbyshire or Derby
Devon	Devonshire
Doc.	Documents
Dods. MSS.	Dodsworth MSS.
Dom. Bk.	Domesday Book
Dors.	Dorsetshire
Duchy of Lanc.	Duchy of Lancaster
Dur.	Durham
East.	Easter Term
Eccl.	Ecclesiastical
Eccl. Com.	Ecclesiastical Commission
Edw.	Edward
Eliz.	Elizabeth
Engl.	England or English
Engl. Hist. Rev.	English Historical Review
Epis. Reg.	Episcopal Registers
Esch. Enr. Accts.	Escheators Enrolled Accounts
Excerpta e Rot. Fin. (Rec. Com.)	Excerpta e Rotulis Finium (Record Commission)
Exch. Dep.	Exchequer Depositions
Exch. K.B.	Exchequer King's Bench
Exch. K.R.	Exchequer King's Remembrancer
Exch. L.T.R.	Exchequer Lord Treasurer's Remembrancer
Exch. of Pleas, Plea R.	Exchequer of Pleas, Plea Roll
Exch. of Receipt	Exchequer of Receipt

TABLE OF ABBREVIATIONS

Exch. Spec. Com.   Exchequer Special Commissions

Feet of F. . . .   Feet of Fines

Feod. Accts. (Ct. of Wards)   Feodaries Accounts (Court of Wards)

Feod. Surv. (Ct. of Wards)   Feodaries Surveys (Court of Wards)

Feud. Aids . . .   Feudal Aids

fol. . . . . .   Folio

Foreign R. . . .   Foreign Rolls

Forest Proc. . .   Forest Proceedings

Gen. . . . .   Genealogical, Genealogica, etc.

Geo. . . . .   George

Glouc. . . . .   Gloucestershire or Gloucester

Guild Certif. (Chan.) Ric. II.   Guild Certificates (Chancery) Richard II.

Hants . . . .   Hampshire

Harl. . . . .   Harley or Harleian

Hen. . . . .   Henry

Heref. . . . .   Herefordshire or Hereford

Hertf. . . . .   Hertford

Herts . . . .   Hertfordshire

Hil. . . . . .   Hilary Term

Hist.   History, Historical, Historian, Historia, etc.

Hist. MSS. Com.   Historical MSS. Commission

Hosp. . . . .   Hospital

Hund. R. . . .   Hundred Rolls

Hunt. . . . .   Huntingdon

Hunts . . . .   Huntingdonshire

Inq. a.q.d. . . .   Inquisitions ad quod damnum

Inq. p.m. . . .   Inquisitions post mortem

Inst. . . . . .   Institute or Institution

Invent. . . . .   Inventory or Inventories

Ips. . . . . .   Ipswich

Itin. . . . . .   Itinerary

Jas. . . . . .   James

Journ. . . . .   Journal

Lamb. Lib. . .   Lambeth Library

Lanc. . . . .   Lancashire or Lancaster

L. and P. Hen. VIII.   Letters and Papers, Hen. VIII.

Lansd. . . . .   Lansdowne

Ld. Rev. Rec. . .   Land Revenue Records

Leic. . . . .   Leicestershire or Leicester

Le Neve's Ind. .   Le Neve's Indices

Lib. . . . . .   Library

Lich. . . . .   Lichfield

Linc. . . . .   Lincolnshire or Lincoln

Lond. . . . .   London

m. . . . . .   Membrane

Mem. . . . .   Memorials

Memo. R. . . .   Memoranda Rolls

Mich. . . . .   Michaelmas Term

Midd. . . . .   Middlesex

Mins. Accts. . .   Ministers' Accounts

Misc. Bks. (Exch. K.R., Exch. T.R. or Aug. Off.)   Miscellaneous Book (Exchequer King's Remembrancer, Exchequer Treasury of Receipt or Augmentation Office)

Mon. . . . . .   Monastery, Monasticon

Monm. . . . .   Monmouth

Mun. . . . . .   Muniments or Munimenta

Mus. . . . . .   Museum

N. and Q. . . .   Notes and Queries

Norf. . . . .   Norfolk

Northampt.   Northampton

Northants . . .   Northamptonshire

Northumb. . . .   Northumberland

Norw. . . . .   Norwich

Nott. . . . .   Nottinghamshire or Nottingham

N.S. . . . . .   New Style

Off. . . . . .   Office

Orig. R. . . .   Originalia Rolls

Oxf. . . . . .   Oxfordshire or Oxford

p. . . . . .   Page

Palmer's Ind. . .   Palmer's Indices

Pal. of Chest. . .   Palatinate of Chester

Pal. of Dur. . .   Palatinate of Durham

Pal. of Lanc. . .   Palatinate of Lancaster

Par. . . . . .   Parish, Parochial, etc.

Parl. . . . . .   Parliament or Parliamentary

Parl. R. . . .   Parliament Rolls

Parl. Surv. . . .   Parliamentary Surveys

Partic. for Gts. .   Particulars for Grants

Pat. . . . . .   Patent Roll or Letters Patent

P.C.C. . . . .   Prerogative Court of Canterbury

Peterb. . . . .   Peterborough

Phil. . . . . .   Philip

Pipe R. . . . .   Pipe Roll

Plea R. . . . .   Plea Rolls

Pope Nich. Tax. (Rec. Com.)   Pope Nicholas' Taxation (Record Commission)

P.R.O. . . . .   Public Record Office

Proc. . . . .   Proceedings

Proc. Soc. Antiq. .   Proceedings of the Society of Antiquaries

pt. . . . . .   Part

Pub. . . . . .   Publications

R. . . . . .   Roll

Rec. . . . .   Records

Recov. R. . . .   Recovery Rolls

Rentals and Surv. .   Rentals and Surveys

Rep. . . . . .   Report

Rev. . . . . .   Review

Ric. . . . . .   Richard

Roff. . . . .   Rochester diocese

Rot. Cur. Reg.   Rotuli Curiæ Regis

Rut. . . . . .   Rutland

Sarum . . . .   Salisbury diocese

Ser. . . . . .   Series

Sess. R. . . . .   Sessions Rolls

Shrews. . . . .   Shrewsbury

xvi

TABLE OF ABBREVIATIONS

Shrops	Shropshire
Soc.	Society
Soc. Antiq. . . .	Society of Antiquaries
Somers.	Somerset
Somers. Ho. . .	Somerset House
S.P. Dom. . . .	State Papers Domestic
Staff.	Staffordshire
Star Chamb. Proc.	Star Chamber Proceedings
Stat.	Statute
Steph.	Stephen
Subs. R. . . .	Subsidy Rolls
Suff.	Suffolk
Surr.	Surrey
Suss.	Sussex
Surv. of Ch. Livings (Lamb.) or (Chan.)	Surveys of Church Livings (Lambeth) or (Chancery)
Topog.	Topography or Topographical
Trans.	Transactions
Transl.	Translation
Treas.	Treasury or Treasurer
Trin.	Trinity Term
Univ.	University
Valor Eccl. (Rec. Com.)	Valor Ecclesiasticus (Record Commission)
Vet. Mon. . . .	Vetusta Monumenta
V.C.H.	Victoria County History
Vic.	Victoria
vol.	Volume
Warw.	Warwickshire or Warwick
Westm.	Westminster
Will.	William
Wilts	Wiltshire
Winton. . . .	Winchester diocese
Worc.	Worcestershire or Worcester
Yorks	Yorkshire

ECCLESIASTICAL
HISTORY

T HE early ecclesiastical history of the county of Cumberland is
enveloped in a dark cloud which the efforts of modern research
are unable to penetrate. In the absence of satisfactory evidence,
the story of the early missions, as far as it relates to our district,
must be accepted with considerable hesitation. The monumental
remains of the Roman occupation, though of great variety, give no
indication that Christianity was accepted by the Roman legions or the
auxiliary forces which guarded the great wall and colonized the country
in the immediate vicinity. About the time of the departure of the
Romans, it is said that Ninian pushed his evangelical mission beyond
the Solway. As bishop of the nation of the Picts who dwelt south of
the Grampians, his missionary sphere extended throughout the south-
west of Scotland, and his cathedral church was built at Whithern or
Candida Casa on the south coast of Galloway.[1] Bede tells us that he
was a most holy man of the British nation who had been instructed at
Rome in the faith, by whose instrumentality the Picts on this side of
the mountains were led to forsake idolatry.[2] Though the historian gives
no hint that he ever preached in the dales of Cumberland, the opinion
of Geoffrey Gaimar cannot be overlooked when he identifies the Picts
baptized by Ninian with the people of Westmorland.[3] If Ninian
was born on the shores of the Solway,[4] the saint must have passed
through Cumberland along the great military roads on his way to and
from Gaul and Rome. As his father was a Christian, and as Ninian
was baptized in infancy, the faith must have been accepted in the
neighbourhood of Carlisle at an early date.

When the protection of the Roman power was withdrawn the
Britons were torn asunder by internal dissensions and hardly pressed by
external invasion. For a century and a half all matters connected with
the religious history of the district are in hopeless confusion. The
events which led up to the battle of Ardderyd in 573 bring upon the

---

[1] *Anglo-Saxon Chronicle* (Rolls Series), i. 31–2.
[2] *Hist. Eccles.* iii. cap. 4.
[3] *Mon. Hist. Brit.* (Rec. Com.), 776.
[4] The life of Ninian by Ailred, abbot of Rievaulx, written between 1147 and 1167, contains little of
value in addition to the well-known passage in Bede with which he opens his narrative. It may be
taken, however, as the tradition prevalent in the twelfth century that the coast of the Solway was the
birthplace of the saint.

II

scene the great apostle of the Cumbrian region. When we come to the labours of St. Mungo or Kentigern we catch a glimpse of what appears to be genuine history. In the opinion of Jocelyn, one of his biographers,[1] Kentigern was the prominent figure in the revolution which evangelized the district. Some portions of the scenery of Kentigern's life can be identified in districts of modern Cumberland. Flying from Glasgow to escape the persecution of the pagans, he resolved to seek refuge among the Christian Britons of Wales, and arriving at Carlisle, where he heard that many among the mountains were given to idolatry, the saint turned aside, says his biographer, and, God helping him, converted to the Christian religion very many from a strange belief and others who were erroneous in the faith. For some time he remained in a thickly wooded place, and he erected a cross, from which the place took the English name of Crossfield—that is, *Crucis Novale*—where a new basilica was erected in Jocelyn's time and dedicated in the name of the blessed Kentigern. When his work in Cumberland was accomplished the saint pursued his journey by the seashore, scattering the seed of the Divine word wherever he went till he reached Wales.[2] It was in 573, during Kentigern's absence, that the establishment of Christianity was secured by battle at a place which has been identified as the plains of the Esk near Arthuret. The new king, who had been brought up as a Christian in Ireland, recalled the saint. On his return the people flocked to meet him at Hodelm or Hoddom in Dumfriesshire, where he placed his see for a time till he transferred it to his own city of Glasgow. For many years he ruled his vast diocese, which is said to have stretched far enough south to include the present counties of Cumberland and Westmorland.

In tracing the footsteps of St. Kentigern on his missionary journey through Cumberland the churches entitled in his name have been pointed out as witnesses of his triumph over the paganism of the district. Within the modern county there are eight such dedications, seven of which belong to parish churches which date at least from the twelfth century. The narrative of Jocelyn, compiled about the year 1185, agrees with the distribution of Kentigern churches in the county, and from it we may gather that these dedications were in Jocelyn's mind when he discoursed on the saint's wanderings in the neighbourhood of Carlisle. The churches of Irthington and Grinsdale are on the line of the Roman wall, the supposed route taken by Kentigern on his flight from Glasgow. Of the others, Caldbeck, Mungrisdale, Castlesowerby and Crosthwaite lie at the roots of the mountains which form the northern boundary of the Lake District. It was to the people living among the mountains that he is said to have directed his steps after his arrival in Carlisle. The two remaining churches of Aspatria and Brom-

---

[1] Two biographies of St. Kentigern are known to have been compiled in the twelfth century. A portion only of the earlier, written by an unknown author at the suggestion of Herbert, bishop of Glasgow, remains to us, and has been printed in the *Registrum Episcopatus Glasguensis* by Mr. Cosmo Innes. The complete Life, written about the year 1185 by Jocelyn, a monk of Furness, exists in two manuscripts: one in the British Museum, and the other in Archbishop Marsh's Library in Dublin.

[2] *Historians of Scotland*, v. 74.

field are within short distances of the sea, situated *in locis màritanis*, to which the saint was obliged to digress from the direct route to his destination in Wales. It has been claimed that these churches occupy sites hallowed by the presence of Kentigern.[1] None of them are mentioned in Jocelyn's biography with the exception of Crossfield, which must be Crosthwaite. A church was built in Jocelyn's day on the site where it was believed that Kentigern erected the cross as the sign of salvation and as a witness to its triumph in the district. As no other Kentigern dedications are known in England, the tradition which ascribed the evangelization of Cumberland to his agency is deserving of the highest respect.

Nothing seems to be known for a long period of Kentigern's successors or the fortunes of the Christian church in the diocese of Glasgow, which he founded and over which he ruled. The Inquest of David,[2] a document ascribed to the year 1120, which deals with the history of the see, so far as it could be ascertained by 'the elders and wise men' of Cumbria at that date, points to a serious state of affairs. The narrative of the Inquest is worthy of attention. The king of the province, the jurors said, co-operated with the magnates of the kingdom in founding, in honour of God and of St. Mary the Blessed Mother, the church of Glasgow as the pontifical seat of the bishop of the Cumbrian region. That church flourished in the holy faith, and by divine direction received Kentigern as its first bishop. But after Kentigern and his many (*plures*) successors were gathered to God, insurrections, arising everywhere, not only destroyed the church and its possessions, but wasted the whole country and drove the inhabitants into exile. When a considerable time had elapsed, tribes of different nations poured in and took possession of the desolated region. These tribes, differing in race and language and custom, clung to heathenism rather than the worship of the faith. Looking back from the beginning of the twelfth century on the early history of the diocese of Glasgow, the Cumbrian jurors could see nothing but anarchy and confusion after the death of Kentigern. Several successors the saint is said to have had in his diocese, but neither their names nor the dates at which they lived have come down to us. The district was the battle ground of conflicting races—Britons, Picts, Scots and Angles. Until the middle of the seventh century the confusion lasted, when the Anglian race obtained the mastery and absorbed at least the southern portion of the country into the kingdom of Northumbria.

When we pass from the dark period during which the Britons

---

[1] Bishop Forbes first called attention to the dedications in Cumberland in connexion with Kentigern's missionary journey (*Historians of Scotland*, v. pp. lxxxiii.–lxxxv.). Others have followed in the Bishop's steps (*Trans. Cumb. and Westmorl. Archæol. Soc.* vi. 328–337, vii. 124–127). But such methods of argument are very unsafe. Jocelyn evidently constructed his narrative from the Kentigern dedications existing in his time.

[2] *Registrum Episcopatus Glasguensis*, No. I., printed at the joint expense of the Bannatyne and Maitland Clubs in 1843. Haddan and Stubbs, *Councils and Eccles. Doc.* ii. 17. In 1901 it was issued in facsimile as a tract in Glasgow.

struggled for their independence, we obtain a few glimpses of real history. The first light comes from the pages of two historians to whom we are indebted for much of our knowledge of the early history of northern England. Bede comes first in point of time, and it must have been from his pages that the anonymous author erroneously identified with Symeon of Durham, some centuries later, wrote the first authentic chapter of the religious history of Carlisle and the country around it. From these well-known and trustworthy authorities we learn that it was about the year 685 that the Church of the English became established beyond the Pennine range on the shores of the western sea. It is not known at what precise date Cumbria had been severed from British dominion, but in the year above mentioned Ecgfrid, king of Northumbria, gave to St. Cuthbert, who had been recently consecrated bishop of the Anglian diocese of Lindisfarne,[1] the city of Luel, that is, Carlisle, and the country for fifteen miles around it as a portion of the territory with which he endowed the see.[2] In that city Cuthbert placed a community of nuns under the rule of an abbess and founded a school. From Bede[3] we learn that the abbess was a sister of the Northumbrian king. When Ecgfrid set out on his fatal expedition against the Picts, Cuthbert came to Lugubalia, which was corruptly called Luel by the English, to speak to the Queen, who was there in her sister's monastery awaiting the result of the war. It was during that visit that the citizens of Carlisle conducted him to see the walls of the town and the remarkable fountain built by the Romans. It is of importance to notice the condition of the church within the borders of Cumberland at this date, so far as it can be ascertained from these northern chronicles. That some portion of it, if not all, was included in an organized diocese is undoubted. Cuthbert was bishop of Lindisfarne, a diocese which had been in existence for half a century with a succession of Scottish or Irish bishops. The points of difference between the English and Celtic rites had been fought out at the famous conference of Whitby in 664, when the Celtic Church was dispossessed of its hold on Northumbria. Lindisfarne was an English diocese from this time onwards, and Carlisle was included as an outlying portion of it, in which the royal family of Northumbria took a special interest. The bishop of the ecclesiastical province in which the city was situated paid occasional visits to this part of his spiritual charge. While Cuthbert was in Carlisle preparing the Queen for the disaster which he foresaw on the moors of Nectansmere he was called to a neighbouring monastery to dedicate a church.[4] The name of the church consecrated has not been recorded,

---

[1] Bede, *Hist. Eccles.* iv. 28. Bishop Stubbs dates St. Cuthbert's consecration on 25 March 685 (*Reg. Sacrum Anglicanum*, Ed. 1897, p. 7).

[2] Symeon of Durham, *Historia de S. Cuthberto*, p. 141; *Relatio de Sancto Cuthberto*, pp. 230–1, Surtees Society. The Lives of St. Cuthbert ascribed to Symeon are by an earlier author, probably in the tenth century.

[3] *Vita S. Cuthberti*, cap. xxvii. It is clear from the language of Bede that the Abbess of Carlisle was Ecgfrid's sister, and not the sister, but the sister-in-law, of the Queen. Freeman has taken this view of the passage (*Trans. Cumb. and Westmorl. Archæol. Soc.* vi. 256).

[4] Bede, *Vita S. Cuthberti*, cap. xxviii.

but we know that it was not far from Carlisle, as he had undertaken to rejoin the Queen next day. Not long after he was called to the same city to ordain priests and to give benediction to the Queen herself, who had taken the veil in that monastery. It was on the occasion of this visit that the venerable priest and friend of St. Cuthbert, Herebert by name, came from his seclusion in an island of the large marsh in which the Derwent rises, the lake now called Derwentwater, as he used to do every year to receive from the saint admonitions in the way of eternal life. Bede's narrative supplies a beautiful picture of the state of the Church as it existed in the district towards the close of the seventh century, and rests on the surest historical basis, for Bede was recording events which had happened in his boyhood, and his account of St. Cuthbert was submitted for revision to men who had been well acquainted with what had taken place.

It was political wisdom on the part of the Northumbrian rulers to use the organization of the church as the basis on which the many races of the kingdom might be united into one nation. For this reason, no doubt, local usages, such as the incidence of the Easter festival and the mode of tonsure, were abandoned in favour of a more universal custom. Whatever sort of submission was involved by the compromise at Whitby in 664 it did not obliterate the essential features of the Scottish Church. The whole tone of the church in the northern kingdom was Celtic. The early associations of the bishops of Lindisfarne, the training of St. Cuthbert in the Celtic monastery of Melrose, the well-known objections of the King and Queen to the claims of Wilfrid, need not to be repeated here. The old features of the Celtic Church were retained, and chief amongst them was missionary monasticism. We have no trace of a parochial system in this portion of Cumbria before the Norman settlement in the twelfth century. The centres of ecclesiastical work were monastic rather than parochial while the district remained under English rule. The monastery of Carlisle and its school were centres of educational effort, in which clergy no doubt were trained, and from which they were sent forth to minister in the surrounding district.[1] In Bede's day there was also a monastery near the river Dacore or Dacre,[1] not far from Penrith, which was ruled by Abbot Thridred. The Celtic character of the Church in Cumberland about the eighth century is still further illustrated by the legendary life of St. Bega, who is said to have landed in a certain province of England called Coupland, and to have taken up her abode in a dense forest, where she spent many years in solitary devotion.[2]

[1] *Hist. Eccles.* iv. c. 32. There seems to be no doubt that the Dacre in Cumberland is the place meant here, and that it was a monastery of considerable importance. It must have been in existence as late as 926, in which year it appears to have been the scene of the famous agreement between the three kings, when Eugenius, Ewen or Owen, king of the Cumbrians, and Constantine, king of Scots, made submission to king Athelstan. William of Malmesbury calls the place of meeting Dacor (*Gesta Regum* [Rolls Series], i. 147), but the *Anglo-Saxon Chronicle* (i. 199) says that the peace was confirmed at a place called Eamont. The collocation of names, seeing that Dacre and Eamont are so close together, is sufficient to identify the place as belonging to Cumberland.

[2] Cotton MS. Faustina B. iv. ff. 122-39.

5

A HISTORY OF CUMBERLAND

By the defeat of Ecgfrid the kingdom of Northumbria was de-prived of some of its dependencies, for Bede[1] states that the strength of the English Crown from that time began to waver, insomuch that the Picts recovered their land and some of the Britons their liberty ; but it must not be taken that the ecclesiastical relations of our district with the see of Lindisfarne were disturbed by the catastrophe. Though the events which followed are shrouded for a long time in darkness, so late as 854, when Eardulf was consecrated bishop, Carlisle was a portion of that diocese.[2] During this episcopate came the Danish invasion, which swept every organization in church and state into the abyss of paganism. The whole kingdom of Northumbria was overrun and desolated by the Danes. The church was in dire jeopardy and its rulers hesitated whether to stand their ground or to flee. Eardulf on consultation with his clergy determined on flight. He summoned Eadred, abbot of Carlisle, surnamed Lulisc, from Luel the ancient name of the city, with whom he took counsel about the shrine of St. Cuthbert.[3] After an exchange of views it was deemed more agreeable to St. Cuthbert's wishes that his bones should not be left to the danger of desecration. Raising the holy and uncorrupt body of the father, says Symeon,[4] they placed beside it the relics of the saints, such as the head of St. Oswald, some of the bones of St. Aidan, together with the bones of those revered bishops Eadbert, Eadfrid and Ethelwold, successors of St. Cuthbert, and fled, abandoning the mother church of the Bernicians, which had been the residence of so many saints. No sooner had Bishop Eardulf departed with his sacred burden than a fearful storm burst over the whole province of Northumbria. Every-where did the Danes burn down the monasteries and churches, and carry fire and sword from the eastern to the western sea. For this reason the bishop of Lindisfarne and those who were guardians of St. Cuthbert's relics found no place of repose, but going now forward, now backward, hither and thither, they fled from the face of the heathen invader. Crossing into Cumbria they made their way to the mouth of the Derwent at Workington, with the hope of taking ship to Ireland. But as a storm prevented them leaving the haven, they bent their steps towards Gallo-way, where they stayed till the death of Halfdene, the Danish king, emboldened them to return.

---

[1] *Hist. Eccles.* iv. cap. 26.

[2] *Symeon of Durham* (Surtees Society), i. 67.

[3] Ibid. i. 73. *Ancient Monuments, Rites and Customs of Durham* (Surtees Society), pp. 55–6.

[4] The story of the translation of St. Cuthbert's relics has been handed down as a precious tradition in the northern church. To the writings of Symeon (*Opera et Collectanea* (Surtees Soc.), i. 162–4), and Reginald (*Libellus*, Surtees Soc. pp. 16–19, 20–1), two of the historians of Durham, we are chiefly indebted for the details. Attempts to trace the course pursued by the fugitives, who carried the sacred burden, have been often made. John de Wessington, prior of Durham from 1416 to 1446, compiled a list of places where they rested, and hung it over the choir door of the church of Durham. The original compilation in the prior's handwriting has been found (Eyre, *History of St. Cuthbert*, pp. 98–9). The list includes as resting-places in Cumberland and Westmorland such parishes as St. Cuthbert's, Carlisle, Edenhall, Great Salkeld, Plumbland, Embleton, Lorton, and Cliburn, to which have been added, from other versions, Bewcastle and Dufton. In recent years all of the sixteen churches in the two counties which bear the dedication of St. Cuthbert have been added to the list (*Trans. Cumb. and Westmorl. Archæol. Soc.* ii. 14–20 ; vii. 128–31).

It has been supposed that the country lay in ruins after the inroad of the Danes, and that no remnant of church organization was allowed to exist for two centuries from that date. The ecclesiastical history of the period from the Scandinavian invasion till the conquest of the district in 1092 is confused and uncertain. Florence of Worcester tells us that the city of Carlisle which Rufus conquered in 1092, like some other cities in these parts, had been destroyed by the pagan Danes two hundred years before, and had remained deserted up to the time of its recovery ; but we cannot think that the Christian faith was totally obliterated from a district in which it had once taken so deep root, as we know it had done in the neighbourhood of Carlisle while the Northumbrian kings ruled from sea to sea. Whatever may have been the vicissitudes through which it passed, no history exists.[1] The state of the church of Cumbria south of the Solway between the invasion of the Dane and the conquest of the Norman is one of the great puzzles of our early history.[2]

When the district of Carlisle was added to English dominion by William Rufus in 1092, as a matter of course it would fall under the jurisdiction of the metropolitan to whose province it was adjacent. Twenty years before the annexation, a compact was made between the two archbishops at the council of Windsor in 1072, whereby the primacy over Scotland was assigned to York.[3] In these circumstances, whatever pleas were put forward by way of claim to the ecclesiastical oversight of the new province, the metropolitan had the determining voice in its ultimate bestowal. As a matter of fact the land of Carlisle became an integral part of the metropolitan diocese from the date of its conquest[4] till the time arrived for the creation of a new see in the northern province. It will be seen that subsequent events assume this to have been the case. No certain information has been preserved to tell us the nature of the plans employed for the ecclesiastical organization of the district during the remaining years of William's reign. It is perhaps too much to expect.

The first act for the supply of ecclesiastical institutions in the district has been ascribed to one of the followers of the Conqueror, who is said to have been placed in Carlisle by William Rufus shortly after the annexation. A story of the origin of diocesan institutions, which has been handed down by tradition from a remote period, is worth consideration, though we may not be able to accept it. It is

[1] It would be a mere romance to build up a narrative from the remains of Christian monuments with which the modern county abounds. From these lapidary evidences only one conclusion can be drawn. The Church had embraced the seaboard and penetrated the plains. Beyond this nothing more definite can be said. For these monumental remains, see *V.C.H. Cumb.* i. 253–84.

[2] Freeman, *William Rufus,* i. 315.

[3] Haddan and Stubbs, *Councils and Eccles. Doc.* ii. 12, 159. By this agreement the jurisdiction of York extended from the boundaries of the diocese of Lichfield over the whole region northwards ' usque ad extremos Scotiae fines,' including the bishopric of Durham or Lindisfarne.

[4] Rival claims to the spiritual sovereignty of the new district were put forward by the bishops of Durham and Glasgow, but they were disallowed. For a discussion of these matters, see Haddan and Stubbs, *Councils and Eccles. Doc.* ii. 10–27.

the King of Scotland that he retired in disgust to a monastery.[1] Thurstin had no difficulty in satisfying the interested parties as far as English law was concerned. The archdeacon of Richmond was compensated for the loss of jurisdiction by the bestowal of such privileges as the right of institution to and the custody of vacant churches within his archdeaconry, these privileges having been granted at the request and by the confirmation of the King. In fact many of the ecclesiastical immunities, which the famous archdeaconry enjoyed, may be traced to this period when a new diocese was carved out of its ample limits.[2]

In furtherance of the scheme for a new bishopric Henry had recourse to his old policy, when he set about the completion of the priory, of selecting a rich man as the first bishop. Among the royal chaplains he had a wealthy Yorkshire landowner,[3] Adelulf by name, who had taken the religious habit, and had become prior of St. Oswald's, Nostell, an Augustinian house near Pontefract. The difficulties of founding the bishopric were not insuperable when little or no provision had to be made for the maintenance of the office. The poverty of the see of Carlisle for the first century after its creation is well known. When Adelulf died in 1156 the bishopric remained derelict and vacant for about fifty years till adequate provision could be found for the support of the dignity. At first the separate endowment was ridiculously small. Though the priory of Carlisle was first founded, gifts of real property came in but slowly till the new foundation was raised to the dignity of a cathedral church in 1133. For some years after that date political events were not favourable to religious enthusiasm among the local magnates. Three years after its foundation the diocese passed under the sovereignty of the Scottish king while it remained subject to the

---

[1] Fordun, *Scotichronicon*, ed. Goodall, i. 449–50 ; Haddan and Stubbs, *Councils and Eccles. Doc.* ii. 27.

[2] When John of Hexham was describing the limits of the bishopric which Henry I had set up at Carlisle, he assumed the York oversight when he stated that the churches of Cumberland and Westmorland which belonged to a York archdeaconry (*quae adjacuerunt archidiaconatui Eboracensi*) were bestowed on the new creation (*The Priory of Hexham* [Surtees Soc.], i. 109, 110 ; Twysden, *Decem Scriptores*, col. 257). In 1201 Honorius in his appeal to Pope Innocent about the archdeaconry of Richmond stated 'quod cum inclytæ recordationis primus Henricus, rex Angliæ, apud Carleolum sedem episcopalem vellet de novo creari, quia ex hoc archidiaconatus Richemundiæ lædebatur, rex ipse a bonæ memoriæ quondam Éboracensi archiepiscopo postulavit, ut in recompensationem cuiusdam partis, quæ subtrahebatur archidiaconatui memorato, ei predictas concederet dignitates' (Hoveden, *Chronica* [Rolls Series], iv. 177–8). Whitaker has described the privileges of this archdeaconry in some detail (*Hist. of Richmondshire*, i. 34–6). From a description of the archbishopric of York in an Arundel manuscript Hinde has quoted the following statement about the diocese of Carlisle : 'Alterum Cardolensum, scilicet Carduel vel Carlel, qui fuit subtractus ab Eborascensi, non tamen demptus ab episcopatu' (*Symeon of Durham* [Surtees Soc.], i. 221). In his 'mappa mundi,' Gervase of Canterbury has enumerated such places as 'Holm Cotram,' 'Woderhall,' 'Egremunt,' 'Carduil,' and 'Ingelwde' under 'Richemuntsire' for ecclesiastical purposes (*Gesta Regum* [Rolls Series], ii. 441).

[3] Selden has printed a charter out of his own collection whereby Bishop Adelulf, while Henry I still lived, endowed the deanery of York and William the dean and all his successors in the deanery with the tithes of the mills of Pokelinton and of his domain and of all his soch (*decimas molendinorum de Pokelinton et de dominio meo et de tota socha*), for so it had been provided and appointed by King Henry (*Historie of Tithes*, ed. 1618, pp. 337–8). The inference is obvious. Had Adelulf been exercising the right as prior of St. Oswald, the deed of gift would not have run in the name of 'Ael. Dei gratia, Carleolensis episcopus.' Besides, we have yet to learn that the priory of Nostell owned the manor of 'Pokelinton' at this date. It is certain that the manor did not belong to him as bishop of Carlisle.

metropolitical jurisdiction of York. It is this which makes the early history of the church of Carlisle so unique. For almost the whole of his episcopate Adelulf was an English bishop beneficed in the kingdom of Scotland. After his death in 1156, though the district reverted in the following year to English sovereignty,[1] no successor was appointed for almost half a century. During this long vacancy the diocese was reckoned a unit of the northern province administered by an archdeacon, with the assistance of a suffragan of York for the performance of pontifical offices.[2] While Adelulf lived he must have resided at his cathedral church, of which he was the head and in which he had his 'stool' or 'cathedra.' Owing to the peculiar vicissitudes of the see at this time, the early growth of the capitular institution at Carlisle is involved in no little obscurity. But there can be no question, as we shall learn from subsequent proceedings, that throughout the first episcopate the endowments of the bishopric and the priory were held to be indivisible, and that the bishop had no real property distinct from his cathedral church.[3]

The King of England was fortunate in his choice of the first bishop of Carlisle. Of all the prelates who have ruled the northern diocese Adelulf is pre-eminent, not only as a great churchman gifted with the will and the power to organize the new foundation, but also as a wise statesman and diplomatist capable of reconciling the many conflicting interests arising from his political position. Before he was raised to the see he was a personage of considerable influence at the English and Scottish courts. It is said by Eadmer that Henry I would not put an Englishman even at the head of a monastery; but if it be true that Adelulf was not a Norman, as we may fairly infer from his name, the historian's rule may be regarded as affording the usual exception. In any case it must be confessed that his qualifications eminently fitted him to fill with distinction the difficult post to which he had been nominated. Though his diocese had been incorporated with the kingdom of Scotland, he was often employed on English affairs, and attended the English court on its peregrinations in various parts of England and on the continent. It is, however, a matter of doubt whether Adelulf was able to take up the administration of his diocese immediately after his consecration. The retirement of John, bishop of Glasgow, to the monastery of Tyron as

---

[1] *Roger de Wendover* (Rolls Series), i. 16.

[2] Though there was no bishop of Carlisle, the district retained a separate existence as a diocese, and did not become an archdeaconry of Carlisle within the archdiocese of York. When Uctred, son of Fergus, conferred the church of Torpenhow on the abbey of Holyrood, the canons of that place were empowered to hold it as freely ' sicut aliqua ecclesia in toto episcopatu Karloliensi ' (*Liber Cartarum Sancte Crucis* [Bannatyne Club], pp. 19, 20). Christian, bishop of Candida Casa, often ministered in the diocese of Carlisle, while it was vacant, as suffragan of York. He was present at the foundation of the priory of Lanercost about the year 1169 (Reg. of Lanercost, MS. i. 1). In 1159 and 1160 the sheriff of Cumberland allowed him 14s. 8d. in each year, no doubt as a reward for his services (Pipe Rolls [Cumberland], 5 and 6 Hen. II.). Bishop Christian died at Holmcultram in 1186 (*Chron. de Mailros* [Bannatyne Club], 95).

[3] There were of course endowments of a spiritual nature which belonged to the bishop alone. For example, Archbishop Thurstin gave him the prebend of St. Peter's, York (*Cal. of Papal Letters*, i. 91). The Pipe Roll of 1188 gives an account of the episcopal revenues apart from those of the priory at that date. ●

a protest against the creation of the bishopric is significant. As soon as Stephen had seized the throne, Pope Innocent II reminded him of the project of raising 'the place of Carlisle to the rank of episcopal dignity which Henry his royal predecessor had laboured to accomplish till his decease,' at the same time urging the King to supply what was lacking in the original foundation.[1] Whatever may have been the obstacles in the way of completing the formation of the see they were surmounted in 1138 when Alberic, the papal legate, held a provincial council of Scottish bishops at Carlisle. David, king of Scotland, was present with the bishops, abbots and barons of his kingdom. The council was also attended by Robert, bishop of Hereford, and Adelulf, bishop of Carlisle, who formed the legate's suite as he journeyed through England. By this synod John, bishop of Glasgow, was ordered to leave his retirement and return to his cure, and Adelulf was admitted to the favour of King David and established in his diocese.[2]

When the diocese had become finally absorbed into the English kingdom in 1157 the ecclesiastical sympathies of the local magnates upon whom the church depended for the support of its ministrations were not completely diverted into English channels. The church in the twelfth century was not insular or national, belonging to one race or one kingdom : it claimed an universal sovereignty over all nations. For this reason no doubt the political frontier which marked off the English from the Scottish kingdom was scarcely recognized at the outset among the benevolent landowners who first endowed religious institutions in this part of the country. But apart from religious considerations there was a community of feeling as well as an identity of aim among the people on both sides of the national boundary. By ties of property, intermarriage and old associations, the inhabitants of ancient Cumbria remained practically one people for a long period after they had become politically separated. The needs of the church knew no political barriers. Religious houses in Scotland received grants from the lords of Cumberland after the severance of the diocese from Scottish rule. National prejudice did not hinder Scottish laymen from extending their benevolence to institutions on the English side of the Border. Turgis de Russedale, the baron of Liddel, appropriated the church of Kirkan-

[1] *The Priory of Hexham* (Surtees Soc.) i., Appendix No. viii. This letter of Pope Innocent II to King Stephen, taken from the Great White Register of York, is dated at Pisa on 22 April; and as the Pope was there on that day in 1136, and apparently not in that month of any later year, Haddan and Stubbs say that 1136 is almost certainly the date (*Councils and Eccles. Documents*, ii. 30). In this letter Innocent reminded Stephen that the see had been created 'ex dispensatione Apostolica.' Prynne had overlooked this fact when he took the formation of the diocese of Carlisle as the basis of his argument to show that the King had an inherent power without the Pope to create new bishoprics, alter dioceses, and curtail the privileges of archbishops, bishops, and archdeacons, so as to bind their successors thereby (*Chronological Vindication*, ii. 232).

[2] The two Hexham historians, Richard and John, give identical accounts of this provincial council of Scottish bishops under Alberic the legate in 1138, John adding that 'Aldulf' the bishop was received to the favour of King David and admitted to his bishopric by the intercession of the legate (*The Priory of Hexham*, i. 96–100, 121). The chronicle of Melrose, under date 1138, mentions Alberic's visit to David at Carlisle.

WALTER MALCLERC (1224–1246).

WALTER MALCLERC (1224–1246)
COUNTERSEAL.

BERNARD (1204–1214).

SYLVESTER EVERDON (1247–1254).

SYLVESTER EVERDON
(1247–1254)
COUNTERSEAL.

drews or Arthuret[1] to the abbey of Jedburgh, a monastery which was also enriched with the church of Bassenthwaite by the gift of Waldef son of Gospatric.[2] The church of Torpenhow[3] was granted to the abbey of Holy Rood, Edinburgh, by Uctred son of Fergus in right of Gunnild, daughter of Waldeve, his wife. The abbey of Kelso enjoyed a pension issuing out of the church of Lazonby[4] by the gift of Hugh de Morvill. The favours conferred on Scottish monasteries by Cumberland landowners were reciprocated from the other side. On the western border alone many instances might be given wherein the great lords of Annandale and Galloway were equally considerate to English institutions. No small portion of the endowments of the abbey of Holmcultram was situated in Galloway and on the northern shore of the Solway.[5] The family of Brus, the owners of the great fief of Annandale, were among the foremost benefactors of the priory of Gisburn in Yorkshire.[6] The priory of Lanercost had rent charges in Dumfries.[7] It is true that family ties or national sentiment had much to do with several of these endowments. One might expect that the abbey of Holmcultram should possess strong claims upon Scottish liberality, seeing that it was of Scottish foundation and the only institution left in the district as a relic of the Scottish occupation. Making due allowance for considerations of this sort, we should not forget the strong international sentiment which pervaded the people of both kingdoms,[8] and which had done so much to forward the interests of the church in the diocese of Carlisle.

Though the establishment of churches cannot be ascribed exclusively to Norman agency, we are not left altogether in ignorance of the progress that church extension had made under the first Norman settlers in the new province. If we take the barony of Burgh by Sands, there is a strong presumption that the church of that place was founded by one of its early Norman owners. At the close of the twelfth century, when Hugh de Morvill made a grant of the church to the abbey of Holmcultram, a schedule was drawn up of the lands with which it was endowed. From the circumstances of the transaction, it is clearly seen that the origin of the institution was a matter of common knowledge. The foundation of the church was spoken of; the first priest was named; the portion of land with which the church was endowed 'at its first foundation' was set out. If Swain, the first priest, on his appointment

[1] *Facsimiles of National MSS. of Scotland*, No. 38; Morton, *Monastic Annals of Teviotdale*, pp. 57–9; Carl. Epis. Reg. Ross, MS. f. 262; Inq. ad quod damnum, 2 Edw. III. No. 3.
[2] *Pedes Finium* (Rec. Com.), 10 John, p. 10.
[3] *Liber Cartarum Sanctae Crucis*, Bannatyne Club, 19–20.
[4] *Liber de Calchou*, Bannatyne Club, ii. 351; Reg. of Lanercost, MS. xiii. 25, 26; xiv. 1.
[5] Reg. of Holmcultram MS. ff. 66–7, 91–125.
[6] *Cart. Prioratus de Gyseburne* (Surtees Society), ii. 340–52.
[7] Reg. of Lanercost, MS. ix. 13. See also a grant of Robert de Brus, lord of Annandale, of pasture in Gamelsby and Glassonby (Ibid. xiv. 4).
[8] The close communion between the canons of Carlisle and the canons of Holyrood in Edinburgh may be estimated by the 'confederacio' for the purposes of prayer which existed amongst them on the death of one of their number (*Liber Cartarum Sanctæ Crucis*, Maitland Club, p. cxxxv.; *Liber Vitæ Eccl. Dunelm.* (Surtees Society), p. xvi. The 'confederation' is written in a comparatively modern hand in the Ritual Book of Holyrood.

to the new church, had only one acre of land on the south side of the village for his support, the worldly possessions of his benefice were not destined to remain long at that figure. As other gifts of real property soon came in, it cannot be said of the landowners of Burgh that they were backward in making suitable provision for the maintenance of religious ministrations in that parish.[1] But we are not dependent on the example of Burgh alone to support the view that the parochial system was not fully established in Cumberland at the period when charter evidence furnishes us with guidance. If we look from the north to the south angle of the county as it now is, we shall find that a church was founded there and a parish formed so late as the pontificate of Henry Murdac, archbishop of York, that is, between 1147 and 1153. Copsi, the first lord of Corney on record, founded a church in his manor and gave it with its appurtenances at the date named to the priory of St. Bees, to which house it was confirmed by Roger, his son, and by other members of his family at a later date.[2] It was owing, no doubt, to the wildness and isolation of the place that provision had not been already made, for the parish is situated on the side of a ridge of fells which forms the eastern boundary of that portion of the county and terminates in Black Comb. Of the ancient parish churches, that is, of those founded before the close of the twelfth century, Corney occupies the singular position that it is the only church in Cumberland whose founder's name is at present known.

Church extension throughout the county can be more easily understood by reference to its progress in the royal forest, which had not been split up into parishes till a late date. This is what might be expected, for in many places the need could not have been pressing : with the exception of the officers of the forest, the population within its bounds must have been very small. Penrith, on the southern limit, had its church at an early period, no doubt of royal foundation, as the King transferred it to the bishop when he created the diocese in 1133.[3] As all the churches within the forest were in the gift of the Crown in the first instance, we may take it that the King was in no way behind his subjects in making spiritual provision for his tenants in proportion to the property held in his own hand. All the unenclosed land in the forest was extra-parochial. When assarts were made and became inhabited, the tithes accruing from the cultivated land were the right of the Crown. Upon this point a notable case was heard in 1290 in a dispute about the tithes arising in certain enclosed lands called Linthwaite and Curthwaite. The King's attorney claimed them because these places were within the bounds of the forest, where the King alone could enclose lands, build

---

[1] Harleian MSS. (Reg. of Holmcultram), 3911, f. 28b, 3891, f. 32b.
[2] Reg. of St. Bees MS. (Harl. MS. 434), ii. 3. In the same Register are preserved the confirmation charters of Roger son of Copsi, Orm son of Roger, Benedict de Pennington, and Christina de Coupland and Waldeve her husband (Ibid. ii. 2). Christina de Coupland was probably the daughter of Copsi (Pipe Roll [Cumberland], 31 Hen. II.).
[3] Close, 3 Hen. III. m. 11d; Pat., 3 Hen. III. m. 5d; Prynne, *Chronological Vindication*, ed. 1665, ii. 376.

houses, found churches,[1] and assign the tithes to whom he pleased. The prior of Carlisle based his claims on former royal grants ; the parson of Thursby asserted that the enclosures were within his parish ; the Bishop of Carlisle put forward the singular plea that they were in the parish of Aspatria, the advowson of which belonged to him.[2] After much litigation the tithes were awarded to the King, who afterwards granted them to the prior.[3] The church of Carlisle had many chartered privileges[4] in the forest of Inglewood, and the burden of providing spiritual ministrations eventually devolved upon the prior and convent.

The practice of founding chapelries or district churches arose gradually as the need began to be felt in large parishes. It was usual for the owner of property at some distance from the parish church to obtain the bishop's licence to have an oratory in his house or to build a chapel on his estate, due regard being had to the rights of the mother church. The method of founding a chapel of ease differed but slightly from that of the parish church, except in the ecclesiastical status of the establishment. As far back as records carry us in Cumberland, the custom of erecting chapels was contemporaneous with the founding of parish churches. One of the earliest and most interesting of these foundations is the chapelry of Treverman in the parish of Walton, founded by Gilmor, son of Gilander, during the episcopate of ' Edelwan,' the first bishop of Carlisle, 1133–56. As lord of Treverman and Torcrossoc he caused a chapel to be constructed of wattlework (*de virgis*) at the former place and appointed his kinsman Gillemor to the chaplaincy, at the same time assigning him a certain parcel of land, afterwards called Kirkland, for his sustenance. It is particularly noted that the inhabitants had the benefit of all divine offices of religion, with the exception of baptism and burial, before the parish church on which it was dependent had been appropriated to the priory of Lanercost.[5] In later instances the ecclesiastical authorities were more particular in

---

[1] In the lordship of Penrith, which belonged to the Crown, a chaplain was maintained out of the revenues issuing from that place. Richard III. directed a warrant to his receiver ' of the lordship of Penryth in Cumberland that now is or for the tyme shalbe to content and paye yerely unto the same S⟨r⟩ William (Bellendre, priest) the sum of fourty shillinges to thentent that the same S⟨r⟩ William shall syng masse in the chapell of o⟨r⟩ lady of grace at Amotbrigge. Yeven etc. at Notingham the xxth day of Marche a° primo ' (Harleian MS. 433, f. 166b)

[2] *Rot. Parl.* (Rec. Com.), i. 37, 38, 48 ; ii. 44–5 ; Ryley, *Placita Parliamentaria*, ed. 1661, pp. 49–51. A compressed account of this suit was cited by Sir Edw. Coke in support of his explanation of the word ' assert ' or ' assart ' (4 *Institutes*, ed. 1648, p. 307).

[3] Pat. 22 Edw. I. m. 27.

[4] These privileges originated with the following charter of Henry I.: ' Henricus, Rex Angliæ, justiciariis, vice-comitibus, baronibus, forestariis et ministris suis et fidelibus de Cumberlanda, salutem. Precipimus quod Canonici sanctæ Mariæ de Karl[eolo] bene et in pace et quiete habeant et teneant diuisas suas de foresta sicut eis dedi et concessi in elemosinam et sicut eis perambulari et demonstrari precepi et omnia aisiamenta sua in bosco et pascuis et omnibus rebus sicut in suo dominio. Et nullus eos vel homines siue res eorum inquietet super hoc super forisfacturam meam, set omnes res eorum in pace sint sicut elemosina mea. T[este] Nig[elo] de Alb[iniaco] apud Waltham ' (Chart. R. 6 Edw. III. pt. i. No. 30, by *inspeximus*). This charter, together with the grant of the lands of Walter the priest, was recited and confirmed by Henry II.

[5] Reg. of Lanercost MS. ff. 260–1. The internal evidence of this deed is conclusive that the bishop referred to by the jurors was Adelulf of Carlisle, and not Æthelwin of Durham (1056–1071).

defining the relationship of the district chapel to the parish church. When Patric, son of Thomas de Workington, founded the chapel of Thornthwaite about the year 1240, the abbot and convent of Fountains, rectors of the parish of Crosthwaite, in which the new chapel was built, made a stipulation that all the chaplains should give obedience to the mother church and relinquish all claim to tithes, great and small, and to all oblations and obventions, due and accustomed.[1] Though the rights of the parish church were always jealously safeguarded, it did not prevent the occurrence of parochial troubles. When Thomas, rector of Dean, induced the inhabitants of Clifton to bury their dead in his churchyard, the rector of Workington, in whose parish the chapelry was situated, appealed in 1219 and forced the rector of Dean to discontinue the practice.[2]

In course of time chapels attained to a position of independence, but it was frequently a long process. For various causes, as the need was felt, parochial rights were granted by the ecclesiastical authorities. The right of burial in the chapel yard was a crucial stage in the development, and the concession was considered of such high moment that every precaution was taken to maintain the supremacy of the mother church. The chaplain on his appointment was obliged to swear subjection to the rector, by whose will he was always removable ; the inhabitants entered into an agreement to continue their contribution to the repairs of the mother church as well as to keep the chapel and all its belongings at their own charges. In all cases the consecration of the chapel yard was a necessary feature of the transaction ; in some cases the dedication of the chapel is mentioned. In 1534 the right of burial was granted to the chapel of Ennerdale by reason of its distance from St. Bees and the great inconvenience occasioned at funerals by the badness of the roads.[3] About the same time a similar privilege had been given to the chapel of Loweswater on the petition of Henry, earl of Northumberland, the good friend of the church in that neighbourhood. In a deed of extraordinary length[4] the relative position of chapel and mother church was set out with a minuteness which showed what a firm grip the monks kept over their subordinate churches. It was given with its endowment of two oxgangs of land to St. Bees by Randulf de Lindesay and Hectreda his wife soon after the foundation of the priory.[5] Many of the independent cures in Cumberland have attained their present position by this process of development from district chapels.

---

[1] Reg. of Fountains (Cotton MS. Tiberius, C. xij), ff. 97-8. Patric son of Thomas had a grant of 'Tornthayt in Derwentfelles' from Alice de Rumelli, daughter of William fitz Duncan, in the early part of the thirteenth century, which place he undertook to assart and cultivate. It is noteworthy that as soon as the estate became inhabited, the owner set about at once to provide a chapel for his tenants. A late copy of the deed, by which Patric was enfeoffed, remains with his descendant at Workington Hall.

[2] Reg. of St. Bees (Harl. MS. 434), ii. 15. In the Register of Glasgow there are several documents illustrating the origin and privileges of parish churches, and the jealousy with which their incumbents watched the tendency of chapels to interfere with the offerings and dues of the mother church which were only of inferior importance to its tithes (*Reg. Epis. Glasguensis* (Bannatyne Club), i. pp. xxiii. 41, 48, 61, *et passim*).

[3] Reg. of St. Bees MS. viii. 13.   [4] Ibid. ix. 6.   [5] Ibid. i. 12, 29.

The prolonged vacancy of the see, extending over nearly fifty years after the death of Bishop Adelulf in 1156, was so unprecedented that writers of distinction were driven to hazard various guesses to account for it. The tradition among the antiquaries of the sixteenth and seventeenth centuries that a certain Bernard, indiscriminately styled Archbishop of Ragusa and Archbishop of Sclavonia, immediately succeeded Bishop Adelulf, was transmitted to our own day and accepted without hesitation till recent years. In fact, two Bernards in succession were often conjured from the shades to supply the missing links and preserve the continuity in the roll of bishops. But the witness of the chronicles alone, without the aid of charter evidence, is conclusive that no bishop had accepted the see of Carlisle during the reigns of Henry II. and Richard I., though the former king, notwithstanding his well-known habit of keeping the ecclesiastical revenues of vacant dignities in his own hand, made a genuine attempt to remedy the scandal in Carlisle. So great was the injustice to the diocese that Gervase of Tilbury, a chronicler who wrote at the close of the reign of Richard I., while describing the condition of the northern province, stated that the archbishop of York had only two suffragan sees, Durham, which enjoyed so many privileges from the Roman church, and Carlisle, which by reason of its prolonged vacancy was relegated to oblivion more than to subjection.[1] When Robert de Torigni was accounting for the absence of some of the bishops from Prince Henry's coronation in 1170, he mentioned this fact among others that Adelulf, bishop of Carlisle, was dead and that his *cathedra* up to that date had remained without an occupant.[2] In 1186 the king, being in Normandy, dismissed Hugh, bishop of Durham, from his attendance on the court, and sent him back to his diocese to celebrate the Easter festival, as there was no bishop in the northern province at the time, York with many other bishoprics in England being vacant, one of which was Carlisle, which had been without a bishop for almost thirty years.[3]

There can be no question about the sincerity of Henry's intention in 1186 to fill the vacancy by the appointment of a bishop. Many things occurring at that time contributed to bring about this desirable work. Christian, bishop of Whithern, who had been acting as suffragan to the archbishop in his administration of the diocese of Carlisle, had died at Holmcultram in that year.[4] The King reached Carlisle about the same time on his expedition to punish Roland, lord of Galloway. There is reason to believe that Archdeacon Robert, the local head of

---

[1] The words of Gervase, in his *Otia Imperialia*, are important in this connexion—'Eboracensis Archiepiscopus hos duos tantum habet suffraganeos : Durhamensem, qui tot gaudet privilegiis Romanæ ecclesiæ, quod jam in plenam se recepit libertatem : et Carleolensem, qui sæpissime tanto tempore vacat, quod oblivioni potius datur quam subjectioni' (Leibnitz, *Scriptores Rerum Brunsvicensium* (Hanover, 1707), i. 917).

[2] *Chron. of Stephen, Henry II. and Richard I.* (Rolls Series), iv. 245.

[3] Benedict Abbas, *Gesta Hen. II. et Ric. I.* (Rolls Series), i. 344.

[4] *Chron. de Mailros* (Bannatyne Club), 95 ; *Pipe Rolls* (Cumberland), 5 and 6 Hen. II. ; Reg. of Lanercost MS. i. 1.

the diocese during the vacancy, had died also in 1186, or had become so hopelessly crippled with debt that he was obliged to resign his charge. The occasion was opportune, as the King was in Carlisle, and as the need was urgent the canons of St. Mary's petitioned him for licence to elect a bishop. The choice of the chapter fell upon Paulinus de Ledes, master of the hospital of St. Leonard's, York, who was known as an honest, prudent and accomplished man. The election was very popular in the city and diocese, and great rejoicing was manifested everywhere, for the see had been so long bereft of the consolation of a chief pastor, the vacancy having continued since the death of Adelulf, the first bishop, in 1156. But unfortunately Paulinus was not willing to accept the nomination, though the King urged him to it by the offer of an annual rent charge of three hundred marks issuing from the churches of Bamborough and Scarborough, from the chapel of Tickell, and from two of the royal manors near Carlisle.[1]

It may be taken that King Henry did not despair of ultimately filling the vacancy, in spite of the abortive attempt in 1186, for a reversion to the old condition of ecclesiastical government by means of an archdeacon was not permitted for at least two years. The custody of the bishopric was kept in his own hand, and no archdeacon was appointed to the office vacated by Robert during that period. On no other supposition can be explained the singular entry in the Pipe Roll of 1188 when the sheriff accounted to the Exchequer for the issues of the archdeaconry as well as the bishopric for the two years in question. The sheriff's return gives a welcome insight into the episcopal revenues at this early period. The sources of receipts from 'the bishopric of Carlisle for two years' are set out as the fees of two synods in the diocese and archdeaconry, oblations at Whitsuntide, issues of the churches of Carleton, Melburn, Dalston and the school of Carlisle, besides the pleas and perquisites of the diocesan court. It will be seen that at this date the bishopric, as distinct from the priory, was not endowed with any real property, the total revenue, which amounted in two years to £52 19s. 6d. being exclusively of spiritual obligation. While the custody remained with the King, the whole of the issues, with the exception of a balance of 50s., was spent on building operations, then in progress at the great altar and pavement in the cathedral church and the dormitory of the canons. The only expenses of a purely episcopal or archidiaconal nature amounted to the small sum of 14s., which was the cost of holy oil for the Easter sacrament and its carriage from London, the archbishopric of York being then vacant. The King's attempt to fill the bishopric having failed, the old system of administration through an archdeacon was revived in 1188–9, when Peter de Ros was appointed

---

[1] *Benedict Abbas* (Rolls Series), i. 349, 360 ; *Hoveden* (Rolls Series), ii. 309 ; *Walter of Coventry* (Rolls Series), i. 340. Paulinus de Ledes was afterwards mixed up in an interesting plea about the advowson of the church of Clifton between Richard de Marisco and the Canons of Wartre in 1199 (*Rot. Curiae Regis* [Rec. Com.], ii. 32–3).

to the archdeaconry and also to the custody of the See.[1] For this reason, there is little doubt, the sheriff ceased to account for the revenues. It is probable that the archdeacon was appointed shortly before or soon after the death of Henry II. on 6 July 1189, when the project of an immediate filling of the vacancy was abandoned.

The fateful journey of King Richard from the Holy Land in 1192 seems to have been the indirect cause of bringing the long vacancy in the diocese to a close. Touching at Ragusa[2] on the shores of the Adriatic, the King made the acquaintance of Bernard, the archbishop of that district, who perhaps befriended him in his sorry plight. Bernard came to England with King Richard,[3] or if he did not actually attend him on his homeward journey, it is known that he was in England a few years after the King's return. Bernard, archbishop of Ragusa, was present at the coronation of King John in 1199, and witnessed the homage of the King of Scots at Lincoln in the same year.[4] For some time after this date he was in constant attendance at the English court, with the probable intention of obtaining preferment in England. Meanwhile, Pope Innocent was unable to account for the truancy of the archbishop, who, with characteristic temerity, had forsaken the church of Ragusa. In 1202 he directed a bull to the chapter of that place, informing them, as their pastor had been absent for more than four years and had not returned to his cure notwithstanding frequent expostulation, that they should proceed to elect a successor within one month from the date of receiving his licence.[5] The position of Archbishop Bernard was critical, as his tenure of the church of Ragusa had determined and no charge had been found him in his adopted country. The bishopric of Carlisle was still vacant, and though it possessed few attractions, even for a needy archbishop, Bernard was induced at last to accept it.

The archbishop of York did not relish the prospect of importing another archbishop into his province, as if two suns could not be expected to shine in the same firmament. The pope, however, disarmed the prejudice of Archbishop Geoffrey by the undertaking that Bernard should lay aside his archiepiscopal dignity, exercise the episcopal office in the diocese of Carlisle without the use of the pall, and pay due

---

[1] Errors about Robert's tenure of the archdeaconry have arisen from a misunderstanding of the ways of the Exchequer. The archdeacon was a debtor to the estate of Aaron the Jew of Lincoln, who died before 1189 (*Mag. Rot. Pip.* 1 *Ric. I.* [Rec. Com.], 219, 226). These debts appear in the sheriff's accounts of Cumberland from 1191 to 1195, the Jew's estate being in the King's hand. From the continued mention of Robert's indebtedness, it has been concluded that he remained archdeacon of Carlisle. Peter de Ros was archdeacon in January, 1190 (Reg. of Holmcultram MS. f. 51), and held that office till his death in 1196 (Hoveden, *Chron.* [Rolls Series], iv. 14).

[2] Hoveden, *Chron.* (Rolls Series), iii. 185–6.

[3] *Annales Monastici* (Rolls Series), iii. 450.

[4] Hoveden, *Chron.* iv. 89, 141.

[5] Migne, *Patrologiae*, ccxiv. 970–1. By all accounts Bernard was very unpopular in his diocese of Ragusa, and Innocent III. was glad to get rid of him. He told the archbishop of York, when he was begging the see of Carlisle for him, that Bernard had been unable to live safely at Ragusa, and if he returned again, 'mortis sibi periculum imminebat' (ibid. ccxv. 58–9). William of Tyre, who brought up his *Historia Rerum* to 1184, has drawn a woeful picture of the inhabitants of Ragusa at this period—'populo ferocissimo, rapinis, et caedibus assueto inhabitata.' (ibid. cci. 266–7).

reverence and obedience to his metropolitan.[1] On 10 January 1203–4 King John intimated to the archbishop of York that he had confirmed the arrangement, and at the same time he had directed his letters to the clergy of the diocese of Carlisle to receive Bernard and obey him as their bishop.[2] Thus closed one of the strangest chapters in the history of the northern church, for from this date the irregularity in the episcopal succession may be said to have ceased. Perhaps there is no diocese in England which presents so many curious features of ecclesiastical vicissitude. If we consider the political difficulties which confronted the first bishop, the lengthy vacancy which followed · his death owing to the poverty of the see, the attempts which were made to remedy the deficiency, the personality of the second bishop as primate of a foreign province whose allegiance to the papal chair was so slender that he forsook his charge without permission, we can in some measure estimate the early struggles of our ancestors in building up the church in this portion of the kingdom, and the sacrifices they were called on to make before such a glorious heritage could be handed on to their children.

Soon after the episcopate of Bishop Bernard it was found possible to put the tenure of the diocese on such a financial basis that a return to the old state of things which existed before his arrival was not likely to occur. The time had come for a partition of the property of the church of Carlisle between the priory and the bishopric. During the

[1] This letter of Innocent III. to the archbishop of York is interesting. In the first place the pope expressed the fear that Bernard's poverty would bring the ministerial office into disrepute. He acknowledged also the source from which the grant of the bishopric of Carlisle was derived, for it was conferred on Bernard, not by the pope himself, but ' de munificentia et liberalitate clarissimi in Christo filii nostri, Johannis regis Anglorum illustris,' for his maintenance. It is important, too, in explaining Bernard's future position in the diocese of Carlisle, that is, the tenure of a suffragan see by an archbishop. Bernard's ecclesiastical status in relation to his metropolitan is thus set out—' Nos enim ei de sedis apostolicae benignitate concessimus, ut in ipso episcopatu, absque usu pallii, officium episcopale valeat exercere, tibi tanquam metropolitano reverentiam et obedientiam impensurus ' (Migne, *Patrologiae*, ccxv. 58–9). Bishop Stubbs must have overlooked this letter, as he does not acknowledge him to have been one of the bishops in regular succession. In one place he says that the see had not been ' filled up until 1219, although administered for a time by Bernard, ex-archbishop of Ragusa ' (Benedict Abbas, i. 344): in other places he calls him ' the administrator of Carlisle ' (*Registrum Sacrum*, p. 51, new edition ; Hoveden, iv. 89). It is evident that Stubbs had been misled by the phraseology of some writs of Henry III. For instance, on the restitution of the temporalities to Bishop Hugh in 1218, the sheriff is commanded to give such seisin as ' Bernardus, Archiepiscopus Sclavonie, quondam custos ejusdem Episcopatus inde habuit cum custodiam inde recepisset per dominum Johannem Regem patrem nostrum ' (*Rot. Litt. Claus.* [Rec. Com.], i. 369). There can be no doubt that Bernard was as much bishop of Carlisle as any of his successors.

[2] *Rot. Litt. Pat.* (Rec. Com.), pp. 37b, 38 ; Rymer, *Fœdera*, new edition, i. 90 ; Migne, *Patrologiae*, ccxvij. 110–11 ; Prynne, *Chronological Vindication*, ii. 241. But Bernard must have had the offer of Carlisle some years before 10 January 1203-4, the date of his nomination and acceptance, for King John granted the see to the archbishop of Sclavonia in 1200 till he could provide him with a better benefice (*Rot. Chart.* [Rec. Com.], i. 96b). Bernard was evidently holding out in hope of more important preferment, for in 1202 the diocese was still vacant (*Rot. Litt. Pat.* [Rec. Com.], i. 7), and in 1203 Alexander de Lucy had the archdeaconry and custody of the bishopric (ibid. i. 30b, 35b). King John endeavoured to supplement the slender income of the northern diocese. In 1206-7, he granted to ' Bernard, bishop of Carlisle,' an annual pension of twenty marks for life (*Rot. Litt. Claus.* [Rec. Com.], i. 67b ; *Rot. Litt. Pat.* [Rec. Com.], i. 76). As the bishopric was again vacant in 1214 (ibid. i. 118, 138b, 142, 142b), Bernard ruled the diocese from 1204 to 1214. Fordun states that in 1212 he was ' aetatis decrepitae, et infirmitatis continuae, sicque mortem in januis ei cerneret imminere,' and that he afterwards died as bishop of Carlisle—' episcopo Karliolis mortuo ' (*Scotichronicon*, ed. Goodall, ii. 12–13).

long period while the diocese was without a bishop the endowments were at the sole arbitrament of the prior and convent, and the canons came to regard them as belonging exclusively to the priory. In due course they were disillusioned. While the nation was torn asunder by the indefensible conduct of King John, political feeling in Cumberland was on the side of the barons, who invited the Scottish king to espouse their cause, and offered to deliver up the city of Carlisle and the castles of the county to him.[1] When Alexander seized the county the bishopric was vacant by the death of Bishop Bernard. The canons not only received the King to communion, though he was in a state of excommunication, but also committed the dark deed of electing a Scotsman to the vacant bishopric at Alexander's suggestion.[2] The act of treason brought a doom on the priory. On complaint of King John and the bishops to Rome, the papal legate in England was instructed to take extreme measures for the punishment of the offenders. The canons were forthwith expelled from Carlisle in 1218 and placed in other regular churches; their election of a bishop was declared void; and other canons, faithful to the English king, were appointed in their room.[3]

It is evident that the treason of these unfortunate churchmen was made the occasion of effecting a radical change in the relation of the bishop of Carlisle to his chapter. The time was opportune, as the see was vacant. Not only were the offending canons to be sent into exile, but the possessions and rents of their church were to be distributed between the bishop and the new canons, the complainants having urged that such measures would tend to tranquillity, as the priory, being near the Border, exercised much influence either for or against the King and realm. The papal mandate came into force soon after the consecration of Bishop Hugh de Beaulieu, which took place in February 1218–9. From this time onward through the episcopates of Hugh, Walter and Silvester de Everdon, a sordid controversy raged between those bishops and the canons on the division of the property of the church. Two legates in succession, Gualo and Pandulf, were arbitrators between the parties, with the assistance of local commissioners to arrange the details. The burden of the partition fell chiefly on the abbot of Holmcultram and the prior of Hexham, but various officials, lay and clerical, from the sheriff of the county to the rural deans, were employed from time to time to bring about an amicable arrangement.[4] It is unfortunate that

---

1 Ayloffe, *Calendar of Ancient Charters and Scottish Rolls*, pp. 327–8 ; *Chron. de Lanercost* (Maitland Club), pp. 17–18, 25.
2 *Chron. de Lanercost*, p. 27.
3 *Cal. of Papal Letters*, i. 48, 57, 68, 81. The King's complaint to the pope will be found on Pat. 1 Hen. III. m. 3d. The pope's mandate for the expulsion of the canons has been printed by Rymer (*Fœdera* [new edition], i. 147).
4 Honorius III., in May 1223, confirmed to Bishop Hugh and his successors, 'in accordance with letters of Popes Innocent and Adrian, the bishopric and parish of Carlisle, as defined by Turstin, archbishop of York, at the request of the chapter, with the consent of King Henry ; namely the episcopal see in St. Mary's church, Carlisle, called of old ' Lugubalia,' in which are to be observed all the customs of other bishoprics in England ; the prebend of St. Peter's, York, granted by Turstin ; the church of Meleburn ; the land of Barou-on-Trent ; 5s. daily by gift of the said King ; and all other lands, houses, and goods granted or that shall be granted by kings of England or others ; also the ordinance of possessions and

the first award made by Gualo has not been found, though fairly accurate schedules could be compiled from the evidences of later history. The second distribution made by Pandulf the legate while Hugh was bishop and Bartholomew was prior, and the final agreement between Bishop Silvester and Prior Ralf, are happily on record by *inspeximus* in a Charter Roll of 1290.[1] The unpleasantness of this thankless duty fell chiefly to the lot of Bishop Hugh. For this reason we can well understand the acrimonious language used by the author of the 'Chronicle of Lanercost' in reference to this bishop, for that anonymous scribe took the side of the canons throughout the dispute, alleging that they were coerced by fear of death into celebrating divine offices with the King of Scotland. When Bishop Hugh met with a fatal accident at the abbey of Ferte in Burgundy on his return from the Roman court in 1223, the chronicler saw in his death the just judgment of God for the expulsion of the canons and the fraudulent division of their property.[2]

The name of Walter Mauclerk will rank among the foremost of the early bishops of Carlisle who have contributed by their exertions and influence to the endowment of the bishopric. As a young man he was appointed one of the king's clerks in the reign of John,[3] and was often employed on the King's business in that and the succeeding reign. His connexion with Cumberland commenced before his consecration as bishop of Carlisle. He had been constable of Carlisle castle and sheriff of Cumberland in 1222, and was engaged in that year on the special business of the King in the district.[4] It is probable that he was a canon of Carlisle as well as a canon of Southwell when he was elected to the see in 1223, for the King intimated to the archbishop of York that he had not assented to the election, and until that assent was given the archbishop was forbidden to confirm the choice of the canons.[5] During his episcopate the division of the property between the bishopric and the priory had advanced almost to completion. In 1244 Bishop Walter made an important concession[6] to the prior and convent of certain

rents made by G(ualo) cardinal of St. Martin's, papal legate, and their divisions made between the bishop and the prior and convent of Carlisle' (*Cal. of Papal Letters*, i. 91). In 1226, by order of the same pope, another report was made on the local conditions of the ordinance (ibid., i. 112).

[1] Charter Roll 18 Edw. I. (83) No. 26. The date of the first ordinance by Pandulf is about 1220, and the final agreement was made in 1249. Innocent IV. issued a bull, 17 January, 1248, on the *materia questionis* between Bishop Silvester and his chapter about the division of the possessions of the Church of Carlisle (Add. MS. 15,356, f. 239; *Cal. of Papal Letters*, i. 256).

[2] *Chron. de Lanercost*, pp. 27, 30. Bishop Silvester, also concerned in the division of the property, 'transit eciam sed horribiliter ex hoc mundo, equo lapsus et fractus cervicibus' (ibid. p. 62). Matthew Paris (iii. 333, ed. Madden) tells the same story that on 13 May 1254 this bishop died 'supinus corruens de equo et ossium dissolutis compagibus expirans.' Bishop Walter did not fare so badly, though he had many troubles.

[3] *Rot. Litt. Claus.* (Rec. Com.), i. 20b.   [4] Ibid. i. 490b, 502b, 513.

[5] *Chron. de Lanercost*, p. 31; *Cal. of Papal Letters*, i. 57; *Reg. of Abp. Gray* (Surtees Society), 134; *Rot. Litt. Claus.* (Rec. Com.), i. 560b, 573b; Pat. 7 Hen. III. m. 2d. The profession of subjection made by Bishop Walter to Archbishop Gray of York is as follows: 'Ego Walterus, Carleolensis electus episcopus, profiteor sanctæ Eboracensi ecclesiæ, et tibi, Waltere, Ebor. archiepiscope et Angliæ primas, et successoribus tuis canonice substituendis subjectionem et canonicam obedientiam, et propria manu confirmo et subscribo' (*Reg. of Gray* [Surtees Soc.], p. 144).

[6] Bishop Walter's concession to the canons of Carlisle is recited in the *Inspeximus* charter of 6 Edw. III., the original of which still remains among the archives of the bishop of Carlisle. The deed was dated at Carlisle on 3 April, in the twenty-first year of his pontificate.

liberties and privileges which had been previously granted to them jointly by Henry III. From the same king he obtained the manor of Dalston[1] in 1230, which has afforded the principal residence of the bishops of Carlisle almost from that date. The grant was afterwards extended by the addition of ample privileges in the neighbouring forest. As patron and benefactor of the Friars from their first coming to England, he was instrumental in importing colonies of the Dominicans and Franciscans into his cathedral city.[2]

As a courtier and diplomatist the fortunes of Bishop Walter shared in the vicissitudes of success and defeat according as he pleased or displeased his royal master. At one time he held the highest offices in the state, and at another he was under arrest or in flight. In 1233 he went into exile beyond the sea for no other reason, in the opinion of the chronicler of Lanercost,[3] than for the wrong done by the King to him and his church of Carlisle. The quarrel must have been acute, for on his flight the diocese was put under an interdict on the first Sunday in Advent, and the regular and secular clergy were obliged to say the divine offices in a low voice with closed doors. The estrangement, however, did not last long, for in 1234 the same authority reported that the bishop had become reconciled to the King. There can be little doubt that Bishop Walter had been harshly treated. The King gave him the treasurership of the Exchequer in 1232 to hold during life, but by the influence of Peter de Roches, bishop of Winchester, he was dismissed in a summary manner.[4] Intending to cross the channel from Dover, with the view perhaps of laying his grievances before the pope, he was seized by the King's messengers. The bishop of London, being an eye-witness of the indignities inflicted on the distressed bishop, threatened to excommunicate all who had laid violent hands on him, and repaired immediately to the court to submit the matter to the King.[5] The bishop again visited the court and took part in the baptism of Prince Edward in 1239.[6] Though he was joined with some of the other bishops in a commission to discuss the affairs of the church in 1241,[7] his relations with the King were not as cordial as they were before the rupture. King Henry sent him a reprimand in 1243 commanding him not to intermeddle in affairs of state, as it was high time that he attended to the health of his soul.[8] Galling as the rebuke must have been to the old favourite, it was not till three years afterwards

---

[1] Chart. R. 14 Hen. III. pt. ii. m. 10.

[2] *Chron. de Lanercost*, p. 42. We are told in the Annals of Bermondsey that in 1206 St. Francis instituted the rule of the Friars Minors, and in that year was made the translation of the first prior, Petreius, by the lord Bernard, formerly archbishop of Ragusa, who had come to England with King Richard, from whom he had received custody of the bishopric of Carlisle (*Annales Monastici* [Rolls Series], iii. 450).

[3] *Chron. de Lanercost*, pp. 42–3.

[4] Charter 16 Hen. III. m. 4; Madox, *History of the Exchequer*, 1711 edition, pp. 568–9; M. Paris, *Chronica Majora* (Rolls Series), iii. 240.

[5] M. Paris, *Chronica Majora*, iii. 248; *Historia Anglorum*, ii. 358.

[6] Ibid. iii. 539–40; *Historia Anglorum*, ii. 422.

[7] *Chronica Majora*, iv. 173.

[8] Close 27 Hen. III. pt. i. (Vasc.) m. 13d.

that he took the King's hint and retired from the see of Carlisle. Divinely inspired, as it was thought at the time, Bishop Walter resigned his bishopric in 1246, and took refuge among the Friars Preachers at Oxford, where he did many memorable things before his death.[1] Matthew Paris puts a different complexion on the cause of his resignation, ascribing it to qualms of conscience, as the bishop feared his entry on the episcopate in the first instance had not been legitimate.[2] It would be nearer the truth perhaps to accept the bishop's own statement that the causes of his retirement were old age and weakness of body, which rendered him incapable of doing his work. Archbishop Walter Gray, before releasing him from the pastoral care of the diocese, bore a willing testimony to his loyalty to the church of York and to his diligence in the exercise of the episcopal office.[3] Before he left the diocese the King gave him licence to make his will.[4] He died at Oxford in 1248,[5] in the religious society of those whom he favoured and endowed before he had embarked on the stormy sea of temporal affairs.

Few striking events of diocesan interest took place during the episcopates which covered the latter portion of the thirteenth century. Like Bishop Walter, his predecessor, Bishop Silvester de Everdon had held high office in the state before his election to the see of Carlisle. Matthew Paris, who always spoke in admiration of this bishop, in describing his nomination in 1246, said that he had been king's clerk and sometime chancellor of England, a man of great fame and conversation, well versed in legal forms, specially in matters relating to chancery, but that he was unwilling to accept the proffered honour, not so much on account of his riches, as his reluctance to undertake the burden of the episcopal office.[6] At last, under pressure, though he considered himself unworthy, he consented. During the few years of his episcopate he was much engaged in legal[7] and political affairs, and took part in the stirring contests between the church and the crown. The memorable struggle on the right of free election to bishoprics is well known. Bishop Silvester was one of the four prelates chosen by the lords spiritual to wait on the King at the parliament held in London in 1253 for the purpose of demanding those liberties he had sworn to maintain, the most fundamental of which and the most pressing at that moment was the right of election. It was only on that condition they would consent to supply him with the money he asked for. The King turned upon the prelates, and with an unusual display of indignation asked them individually where they would have been had he not exercised his discre-

---

[1] *Annales Monastici*, ii. 337 (Annals of Waverley) ; iii. 170 (Annals of Dunstable) ; iv. 94 (Chronicon Thomæ Wykes).

[2] M. Paris, *Chronica Majora*, iv. 564 ; *Historia Anglorum*, iii. 11.

[3] *Reg. of Abp. Walter Gray* (Surtees Society), 98.

[4] Nicolson and Burn have printed this licence (*Hist. of Cumberland*, ii. 255-6).

[5] *Chronica Majora*, v. 16; *Historia Anglorum*, iii. 40.

[6] *Chronica Majora*, iv. 569-587 ; *Historia Anglorum*, iii. 30, 302.

[7] Bishop Silvester was a justice itinerant with Roger de Thurkelby at York at Michaelmas, 1251 (*Cal. Doc. Scot.* [Scot. Rec. Pub.], i. 336 ; Foss, *Biographia Juridica*, p. 242). See also *Fine Rolls* (Rec. Com.), ii. 130 ; and the *Guisbro' Chartulary* (Surtees Society), i. 216.

tion in the filling of their sees. His ironical reference to the bishop of Carlisle, as he addressed him, was bitter in the extreme. 'And you, Silvester of Carlisle,' he said, ' who have been licking my chancery as the clerkling of my clerks, I have raised to a bishopric, and I have made you a somebody at the expense of many divines and great men whom I have passed over in your favour.' But personal rebuke was not enough. The King called on them to resign, as they had been so unjustly elected, and promised that his partiality in their favour would put him on his guard in future, and prevent him from preferring any person to a bishopric without due merit. The bishops pleaded, in their embarrassment, that the past might well be overlooked, if security for the future was guaranteed. It was a drawn battle. The King obtained his subsidy, and the bishops were satisfied with the assurance that the liberties of the church would be respected.[1] Bishop Silvester was killed by a fall from his horse[2] in 1254.

The effect of the bishops' remonstrance with the King was visible on the election of a successor to Bishop Silvester. The choice of the canons of Carlisle fell on Master Thomas de Vipont, rector of Greystoke, no doubt a member of the well-known local family of that name, though the King urged the claims of the prior of Newburgh. The canons, however, maintained their right, and Thomas was consecrated in February 1255 by the bishop of Durham.[3] As his short episcopate terminated in October 1256,[4] little remains of his episcopal acts in the diocese except a few confirmation charters to the religious houses of no general interest.[5] On his death, Walter de Kirkham, bishop of Durham, successfully pleaded his right to the sequestration of the benefices in his diocese belonging to the bishopric of Carlisle while that see was void. After inquiry in the king's court, the profits arising at that time and also on the previous vacancy were assigned to him by the King's writ, for which the bishop paid a thousand marks.[6] Again and again in after years the same claim was made and the same decision was given. In 1279, on the avoidance by the death of Bishop Robert de Chause, when the custody of vacant bishoprics formed one of the *articuli cleri* proposed before the King in parliament, the King acknowledged his charter to Bishop Walter above mentioned, and awarded the fruits of the bishop of

[1] *Chronica Majora*, v. 374. Bishop Silvester joined with the other bishops on this occasion in pronouncing the sentence of excommunication on all violaters of charters (Rymer, *Fœdera*, i. 289-293; Hemingburgh, *Chron.* (Eng. Hist. Soc.), i. 285; Stubbs, *Select Charters*, edition 1870, pp. 364-5. A corrupt version of the ' sentence ' is on record in *The Whitby Chartulary* (ii. 509-10), which has led Canon Atkinson into grievous miscalculations.
[2] *Chron. de Lanercost*, p. 62; *Chronica Majora*, v. 431; *Historia Anglorum*, iii. 333.
[3] *Chronica Majora*, iv. 455; *Historia Anglorum*, iii. 337; *Chron. de Lanercost*, p. 62.
[4] *Chronica Majora*, v. 588.
[5] *Reg. of Wetherhal* (Cumbld. and Westmorld. Archaeol. Soc.), p. 61; Reg. of Holmcultram MS. f. 25. One of the earliest acts of Bishop Vipont was a licence to Alan de Berwise to build a private chapel in Berwise. The deed is dated ' Apud la Rose vij Kalend. Marcij, pontificatus nostri anno primo,' i.e. 23 February 1255 (Machel MSS. v. 255; *Reg. of Wetherhal*, p. 319). He had been consecrated only sixteen days (*Chron. de Lanercost*, p. 62).
[6] Nicolson and Burn have printed the King's writ (*Hist. of Cumberland*, ii. 257-8) from Prynne (*Chronological Vindication*, ii. 970). The letters patent will be found on *Pat. R.* 44 Hen. III. pt. i. m. 5.

Carlisle's churches in the diocese of Durham to Bishop Robert of Durham, and a writ was issued to Robert de Avenel to make livery accordingly and not to meddle with them further.[1]   A different rule was applied to the custody of the spiritualities situated within the vacant bishopric ; these were adjudged to the primate of the province by order of Parliament.   A test case arose in 1328 after the death of Bishop Halton, when Robert de Barton, keeper of the bishopric, was ordered by Edward III. to cause the fruits and obventions of the churches of Penrith and Dalston, which were appropriated to the bishopric, to be delivered to William, archbishop of York, then keeper of the spiritualities, in accordance with the agreement in the late Parliament at Westminster, that the keepers of void archbishoprics, bishoprics, abbeys, and priories should only intermeddle with the temporalities and not with appropriated churches, prebends and other spiritual things.[2]   Precisely the same mandate was sent to the prior and convent of Carlisle, who had been appointed keepers of the temporalities on the death of Bishop Ross in 1332.[3]   But this did not touch the right of the bishop in whose diocese the spiritualities of other bishops were situated.   It was natural that these should revert to his custody and not to that of the primate.   The bishop of Durham had custody of the churches within his diocese in the patronage of the bishop of Carlisle ; the spiritualities within the diocese of Carlisle were the perquisites of the archbishop of York.   If this distinction be borne in mind, much confusion will be avoided.

A new type of bishop succeeded on the death of Silvester de Everdon, not a politician engaged in statecraft, not a justice on circuit, but a bishop who devoted his energies to the duties of his office.   When Robert de Chause[4] was elected by the canons in 1257, Archbishop Sewall, who, according to the annalist of Dunstable, made him fair promises and ill returns, temporized in confirming the choice, with the supposed intention of securing the appointment of a certain master John, thus causing a delay which obliged the bishop designate to appeal to the pope for redress.[5]   On taking over the charge after two short episcopates, Bishop Chause was confronted with many difficulties, occa-

---

[1] The date of the *articuli cleri* found in the register of Archbishop Wickwaine (*Letters from the Northern Registers* [Rolls Series], 70–8) must be about the year 1279, the only possible year to make Article xiij intelligible.   The see of Carlisle was vacant from 1278 to 1280.   In 1279 the King addressed letters to his northern officers to deliver the sequestration to Bishop Robert de Insula (Close, 7 Edw. I. m. 3 ; Pat. 7 Edw. I. m. 5).

[2] Close, 2 Edw. III. m. 20.   [3] Ibid. 6 Edw. III. m. 23.

[4] Though this bishop is found under various names, we have adopted that of Robert de Chause, the name given to him by Matthew Paris (*Chronica Majora* [Rolls Series], v. 678).   As Robert de Chauro he was rector of Stanton in the diocese of Ely in 1254, when by request of the Queen, whose clerk he was, permission was given him to hold additional benefices (*Cal. of Papal Letters*, i. 307) ; he was dispensed by Pope Innocent IV. on account of illegitimacy, and while Archdeacon of Bath, as Robert de Chaury, an indult was granted in 1257 that he might receive episcopal dignity (ibid. i. 347).   A local chronicler, who ought to know best, calls him Robert de Chalize or Chalise (*Chron. de Lanercost*, pp. 101, 145).   In the annals of Dunstable he is named Robert de Chawre (*Annal. Monast.* [Rolls Series], iii. 205).   His name was given as Robert Chaury in 1290 by one of the clerks in the Court of Chancery (Pat. 18 Edw. I. m. 20), and he was styled 'archbishop' of Carlisle by another (ibid. 5 Edw. I. m. 3).

[5] *Annales Monastici* (Rolls Series), iii. 205.

sioned probably by a previous slackness in the administrative work of the diocese. During the whole term of his episcopate from his consecration in 1258 till his death in 1278, his life was engrossed with a succession of disputes, sometimes acting as mediator in local differences, often standing out in defence of the rights and traditions of his see. As a reformer he met with determined opposition in the highest quarters. Yielding in his dispute with the abbey of St. Mary, York, in 1266, he relinquished his claim to the custody of the priory of Wetheral during a vacancy, as well as to the institution and removal of the priors, in exchange for the remission of an annual pension due to that priory from one of the churches in his patronage.[1] The King of Scotland failed to deprive him of the church of Great Salkeld[2] in 1261, though he was not so fortunate in his defence of the patronage of the church of Rothbury in Northumberland, claimed by King Edward.[3] Richard de Crepping, who succeeded the bishop as sheriff of the county in 1272, unjustly charged him before the lord chancellor with urging his tenants to refuse the oath of fealty to the young king, a groundless allegation, which caused much bitterness in the district.[4] The last four years of the bishop's life were troubled by a long and expensive suit promoted by Michael de Harcla, who claimed that the manor of Dalston and the advowson of the church were his by right of hereditary succession, a suit which was still undecided at the bishop's death.[5] He did not flinch from what he conceived to be the duties of his calling on account of the frowns of kings and magnates, but steadily worked for the rights of his diocese and the welfare of his spiritual subjects. With Robert de Chause the series of bishops who resided in the diocese and gave themselves wholly to local administration may be said to commence. The chronicler of Lanercost has left us a beautiful picture of the piety and amiability of the bishop's character, his zeal for the honour of God, and the good of His people, which he said would never fade while the world lasted.[6]

The informalities attending the election of a successor to Bishop Robert involved the prior and convent of Carlisle in serious trouble with the Crown. In due course two of the canons were deputed to carry the news to London and obtain the necessary *congé d'élire* for the election of a new bishop.[7] The choice of the house fell on William de Rothelfeld, dean of York, who renounced the election and died soon after. With-

---

[1] *Reg. of Wetherhal*, pp 73-7.

[2] Close 46 Hen. III. m. 12d ; Rymer, *Fœdera*, i. 417.

[3] Close, 6 Edw. I. m. 15d ; Pat. 18 Edw. I. m. 20; *Chron. de Lanercost*, p. 102 ; *Rot. Parl.* (Rec. Com.), i. 6b, 22b.

[4] Nicolson and Burn, *Hist. of Cumberland*, ii. 258.

[5] De Banco Rolls No. 6 Mich. 2 and 3 Edw. I. m. 64d ; No. 11, 3 and 4 Edw. I. m. 77d ; No. 17, 4 and 5 Edw. I. m. 3d ; No. 36, 8 and 9 Edw. I. m. 43d. An account of this interesting series of pleas will be more appropriately given under the manorial history of Dalston.

[6] *Chron. de Lanercost*, pp. 101-2.

[7] Pat. 6 Edw. I. m. 3. The licence to elect is dated 27 October, 1278. The name of the prior of Carlisle in 1282 was Robert (Carl. Epis. Reg. Halton MS. f. 14), though perhaps not Robert de Everdon as stated in Nicolson and Burn (*Hist. of Cumberland*, ii. 259). .

but petitioning for a fresh licence, the canons appointed a committee of the convent to proceed to election, and they chose Ralf de Ireton, prior of Gisburn in Yorkshire, and apparently a member of the well-known family of Ireton in Cumberland, and presented their choice to William, archbishop of York, who died before confirming it. The chapter of York refused confirmation, and the King also withheld his consent in high indignation that a second election should have been made without his licence. The convent appealed to the pope, and Prior Ralf repaired to Rome to support the petition. The pontiff appointed three cardinals to examine the election, and on account of the informality that they discovered, he cancelled it. Then on his own authority, in consideration of the character and learning of Prior Ralf, as he said, he appointed him bishop of Carlisle, and had him there and then consecrated by the bishop of Tusculum. Without further parley he intimated what he had done to the prior and convent of Carlisle, to the clergy and people of the diocese, to the archbishop of York and to the King.[1] Though the King compromised with the pope for the sake of peace and accepted the provision,[2] he did not forgive the convent for the second election, for they were forced to pay the greater part of five hundred marks, of which they had been amerced in satisfaction of the irregularity.[3]

Bishop Ireton lost no time in taking up the threads of diocesan work, which had fallen from the fingers of his predecessor. It would appear that building or improvement was in progress at his cathedral, and that money was needed to complete it. Bending his energies at once in this direction, he summoned his clergy in synod for consultation, and made request for a subsidy. Though he only landed in England on 30 May, the synod was held in the following October, when the clergy granted him a tenth of their ecclesiastical revenues payable in two years on the basis of the true valuation. It was a drastic measure for a new bishop, and gave rise, of course, to much grumbling. The levy on the monastic house in which the chronicler of Lanercost was domiciled amounted to £24 of the new money for one year, and drew from the poet of the establishment a caustic screed of Latin verse on the ill-doings of the shepherd who ought to feed rather than fleece the flock so long bereft of a pastor's care. As the chronicler distinctly says that funds were needed *ad fabricam culminis majoris ecclesiae suae sedis*, we should not wonder at the poor estimation in which the bishop was held by some of those who were called upon to supply them. In their eyes he was crafty,

[1] *Cal. of Papal Letters*, i. 461. The dean of York was elected 13 December, 1278 (*Chron. de Lanercost*, p. 102). Nicolson and Burn notice an assize roll quoted by Prynne (*Chron. Vindic.* iii. 1230), in which the prior of Carlisle pleaded that he and his convent did not understand that they had done any contempt or prejudice to the King by the second election, for that having obtained leave to elect and the person elected disagreeing thereto, they thought it was *res integra*, and that they might proceed to choose again; but if it was contempt, they submitted themselves to the King (*Hist. of Cumberland*, ii. 258–9). The annalist of Dunstable was in error when he stated that the prior of Gisburn appealed to the pope against the metropolitan (*Annales Monastici* [Rolls Series], iii. 283).

[2] Pat. 8 Edw. I. m. 10.

[3] Ibid. 10 Edw. I. m. 18; Close 10 Edw. I. m. 7.

RALPH IRETON (1280–1292) COUNTERSEAL.

RALPH IRETON (1280–1292).

JOHN HALTON (1292–1324).

JOHN ROSS (1325–1332).

JOHN KIRBY (1332–1352).

THOMAS APPLEBY (1363–1395).

THOMAS APPLEBY (1363–1395).

THOMAS APPLEBY (1363–1395) COUNTERSEAL.

i

subtle, and very greedy, using his visitations as the means of wringing contributions from the simple-minded clergy of his diocese.[1] In the latter years of his life the bishop was often employed by his sovereign on political and other missions, chiefly in connection with Scottish affairs.[2] But the end was drawing near. In April 1291 he received a faculty from Pope Nicholas IV. to dispose by will of his personal property (not belonging to the service of the altar or to the Augustinian order of which he was a member) in funeral expenses and remuneration of servants and kinsmen, his debts being first paid.[3] On the last day of February 1292 he died at his house of Linstock after the fatigue of a journey in deep snow from London, where he had been attending Parliament, and was buried in his cathedral church.[4]

A most dreadful calamity befell the city of Carlisle a few months after Bishop Ireton's death, the desolation of the flock following closely on the removal of the pastor, as the chronicler of Lanercost pathetically described it. For the space of a whole day and night towards the end of May 1292 a tempest raged on sea and land. The winds blew with such terrific fury that travellers on foot and horseback were overthrown or driven from the track; the sea was forced inland to a greater distance than ever was known by the oldest inhabitant, inundating the maritime districts and destroying crops and cattle. When the hurricane was at its highest, an incendiary, in a moment of malicious rage against his father for disinheriting him, set fire to certain houses without the city walls to the west of the cathedral, that a stranger might not enjoy his inheritance. The city and neighbourhood were soon in flames, and the devastation was universal. The chronicler of Lanercost, who was an eye-witness of the conflagration, has left behind him a vivid picture of the destruction. Streets, churches, municipal buildings, houses, muniments, organs, bells, wood, glass and stalls were burnt to ashes. The only houses of note left standing were the conventual buildings of the Jacobins or Black Friars on the west walls, which were saved with the greatest difficulty. It was particularly noted that the flames devoured the tomb of Bishop Ireton in the cathedral, *mausoleum improbi exactoris*, as the chronicler, retaining his old grudge against the bishop, referred to it, though that of his predecessor, Robert de ' Chalix,' escaped untouched. The culprit, at least the young man on whom suspicion had fallen, was taken, tried and hanged.[5] The destruction of the city was not altogether an unmixed evil. The fire taught the citizens the dangers to which they were exposed by the employment of wood in the construction of their houses. With the co-operation of the King, who granted them charters in place of those that were burnt, and in supplying stone for

[1] *Chron. de Lanercost*, pp. 102–6.
[2] Rymer, *Fœdera*, new edition, i. 734–6, 738, 762, 766–8, 774.
[3] *Cal. of Papal Letters*, i. 534–5.
[4] W. de Hemingburgh, *Chron.* (Eng. Hist. Soc.), ii. 40; *Chron. de Lanercost*, pp. 143–4. The latter authority puts the bishop's death on the following day, 1 March.
[5] *Chron. de Lanercost*, pp. 144–5, 147; Walter de Hemingburgh adds that the culprit was found, tried, and hanged (*Chron.* ii. 40).

the building of their houses, the city again rose to its ancient dignity and importance.[1]

It was fortunate that a prelate of the courage and resource of Bishop Halton ruled the diocese at the close of the thirteenth century. His election took place about the time of the calamity which laid the cathedral in ashes.[2] Four years afterwards the war with Scotland broke out with all its attendant miseries and disasters to the inhabitants of the Border counties. For almost three centuries from this date the history of the diocese, owing to Scottish invasions, is coloured by the troubles and devastations arising from its geographical position. The bishops of the period in question were sometimes military commanders, mostly north-country born, often natives of the county, not unfrequently cadets of great feudal families. Some of them, like Halton and Kirkby, controlled the garrison of Carlisle Castle, and, not content with acting on the defensive, went into Scotland more or less in a military capacity, at one time as diplomatists to effect a peace, and at another to carry fire and sword into the enemy's territory. Bishop Kirkby was held in particular detestation (*summo odio*) by the Scots for commanding in person on various expeditions in 1337, and the enemy was not slow in retaliating on the bishop and all his belongings.[3] A visit to the bishop was a feature of almost every Scottish invasion. They sacked Rose Castle again and again, killed his deer, and emptied his fishponds.[4] Nearly all the bishops before the Reformation were employed in the adjustment of diplomatic relations and the arrangement of truces between the two kingdoms, and sometimes little thanks they got for their pains. After nearly thirty years of conspicuous service to the State, Bishop Halton on one occasion in 1321, after a period of unexampled suffering among his tenants and dependants, petitioned the Crown for relief, and asked that his expenses should be allowed for the nine weeks he spent at Newcastle-upon-Tyne with other magnates on an embassy to the Scots, but it seemed to the King and the council that since the bishop went for the good of the realm in general and his own diocese in particular, and since his journey from Carlisle to Newcastle was not far, he must bear . his own expenses.[5]

---

[1] On the petition of the citizens of Carlisle in 1304, the King granted leave to take stone without hindrance in the forest of ' Inglewode ' for the building of their houses and the restoration of the same vill after the late fire (*Rot. Parl.* [Rec. Com.], i. 166b ; Ryley, *Placita Parliamentaria*, p. 255). In their petition for a new charter with all their former privileges, the citizens stated ' quod carte sue per quas eandem villam tenuerunt combuste fuerunt' (ibid. i. 166–7). A new charter was granted in 1293, wherein it is testified that their late charters were burned by misadventure in a fire in the city of Carlisle (Pat. 21 Edw. I. m. 8). This confirmatory charter has been printed (*Royal Charters of Carlisle*, ed. R. S. Ferguson, pp. 10–11).

[2] Hemingburgh states that Bishop Ralf de Ireton died on the last day of February and the burning of the cathedral took place on the feast of St. Dunstan the archbishop (May 19) 1292 (*Chronicon*, [Eng. Hist. Soc.], ii. 40). Another account of the fire fixes the date on 30 May (*Chron. de Lanercost* [Maitland Club], 144). As the election of John de 'Halghton,' canon of Carlisle, to the vacant see was made on 9 May, and the King's confirmation was given on 26 May (Nicolson and Burn, *Hist. of Cumberland*, ii. 262 ; Pat. 20 Edw. I. m. 12), it may be taken that the calamity to the cathedral church had no influence on the choice of the canons.

[3] *Chron. de Lanercost*, pp. 291–3.   [4] Close, 13 Edw. II. m. 19, m. 21.

[5] Ancient Petition, No. 5117.

ECCLESIASTICAL HISTORY .

A few words will be sufficient to indicate the miserable condition of the diocese during the progress of hostilities between the two kingdoms. Seldom had the land absolute rest from the fear of invasion. There is little occasion to turn to the pages of chronicles for adequate language to describe the sufferings of clergy and laity on both sides of the Border in those barbarous struggles. From the pens of the Bishops of Carlisle pictures of woe and desolation have been handed down to us which no chronicler could imitate, unless he was a witness of the miseries he described and a sufferer in the spoliation. In pleading for an indulgence in the payment of a royal tenth in 1301, Bishop Halton pointed to the miserable state of the diocese for the past four years and more, owing to the depredations of the treacherous Scots. Some of the religious were scattered, as their monasteries were destroyed, and several of the churches with their parishes were reduced to ashes, insomuch that the clergy were unable to live on the fruits of their benefices, but were forced to beg alms from place to place.[1] In 1318 the same bishop bewailed the dreadful injuries which his diocese had suffered for more than twenty-four years from cruel invasions. The Scots had slain men and women, old and young, orphans and widows, burnt nearly all the churches, houses and buildings, driven off their cattle, carried away their treasure, ornaments and every movable of value, and destroyed the whole country, so that the lands of the bishopric lay uncultivated, the sources of his revenues were wasted, and he himself was reduced to a state of indigence and want. For the relief of his urgent need he begged the pope to sanction the appropriation of the church of Horncastle in Lincolnshire to his see.[2] Afflictions of this nature afforded a common theme of complaint to the bishops of Carlisle in the fifteenth century as well as the fourteenth, though of course the frequency of hostilities and the amount of damage depended on the recurrence of international disputes. Few indeed of the medieval bishops escaped losses or troubles from the Scots. The remains of the ancient defences at Rose Castle, their official residence, about seven miles to the south-west of Carlisle, are a witness to the present day of its former strength.[3]

The poverty of the diocese, caused chiefly by the Scottish wars, drove the bishops and the monastic corporations to cast covetous eyes on the wealthier of the parish churches, with the view of encompassing their appropriation. It was no new policy, for the religious houses had ample experience of this method of increasing their revenues. Priories, like Carlisle, Wetheral and St. Bees, were endowed with advowsons and

---

[1] Carl. Epis. Reg. Halton MS. f. 59; *Letters from the Northern Registers* (Rolls Series), 151. In 1309 Bishop Halton excused his attendance at parliament 'propter distanciam, temporis brevitatem, timorem invasionis Scottorum, necnon corporis infirmitatem qua affligimur' (Carl. Epis. Reg. Halton MS. f. 120).

[2] Carl. Epis. Reg. Halton MS. f. 211; *Letters from the Northern Registers*, 282–3. The bishop had obtained licence from the Crown to appropriate the church in 1314 (Pat. 8 Edw. II. pt. i. m. 17).

[3] John de Kirkby, the warrior bishop, had a licence to crenellate his house of 'La Rose' in 1336, and the same liberty was repeated to Bishop Welton at a subsequent date (Pat. 10 Edw. III. pt. i. m. 27, 29 Edw. III.).

had obtained rectories as early as the reign of Henry I.   All the early bishops granted licences for appropriations, though the custom of the ordination or taxation of vicarages was not completely established till the reign of Henry III. and the episcopate of Walter, the fourth bishop. If we glance at the process by which the revenues of a parish church became the property of a religious house, it will be seen how step by step the monks gained their end.   The advowson of the church of Crosthwaite, for example, was granted to the monastery of Fountains by Alice de Romelli, daughter of William fitz Duncan, about the year 1212.   Bishop Bernard confirmed the appropriation of the whole of the revenues, except an annual stipend of one hundred shillings, which he reserved for a vicar who should be elected by the monks and presented to the bishop for institution, the said vicar being answerable for all episcopal dues and having the cure of souls.   The appropriation had the sanction of the pope, the metropolitan, and the prior and convent of Carlisle, but its completion was delayed by the resignation of the rector, who retired on an annual pension of five marks.   Though this arrange-ment lasted through two episcopates and received the confirmation of Bishops Hugh and Walter, it was not brought to a successful issue till Henry de Curtenay had resigned his pension in 1227, and till Adam de Crosthwaite, the first vicar, had died some years afterwards.   All the complications, however, were cleared away in 1250, when Bishop Silvester made a definite ordination of the vicarage by declaring particu-larly the various sources of the vicar's stipend, assigning him a vicarage house, certain tithes and other revenues.[1]   In the taxation of vicarages after appropriation, unless the sources of the vicar's stipend were care-fully set out, quarrels with the impropriators were likely to ensue. When Adam, son of Adam de Levington, granted the church of Kirk-andrews on Eden to the nuns of St. Andrew of Marrig, though Bishops Bernard and Hugh in succession confirmed the appropriation of the church to their use, Ralf the chaplain succeeded in forcing a composition in 1263 whereby the nuns should receive a pension of sixty shillings a year, and that he and his successors should have peaceable possession of the residue *nomine personatus*.[2]   But ordinations were drawn up with the greatest care, so that the vicar was independent of the individual or corporation to whom the appropriation belonged.   The division of the parochial revenues was so arranged that the incumbent was answerable to the bishop in spiritualities and to the impropriator in temporalities, yielding to the latter no other service than that which was due from any tenant of a lay fee.

This policy of robbing parishes for the support of religious corpora-tions, some of which had no connection with the diocese or the county, though it had fallen to some extent into decay towards the close of the thirteenth century, was resuscitated after the outbreak of the Scottish wars and the impoverishment of the local monastic houses by the con-

[1] Reg. of Fountains MS. ff. 101, 323-330.
[2] *Collectanea Topographica et Genealogica*, v. 235-6.

centration of the national host on the Border for the invasion of Scotland. Edward I. was often the guest of the bishop and the local monasteries. The expenses of entertainment of the King and his court were a severe burden on their resources. But for a couple of centuries the losses caused by Scottish incursions were the reasons pleaded for the appropriations.[1] In 1230 Henry III. had bestowed the manor of Dalston with the advowson of the church on the see,[2] but none of the bishops, though resident within the parish, had intermeddled with the fruits of the rectory till Bishop Halton had obtained a royal licence in 1301 for its appropriation,[3] and in later years he had no difficulty in getting the sanction of successive archbishops of York, when the way was made clear by the death or cession of the rector in possession.[4] The archbishop gave elaborate reasons for his consent, such as the burning of the cathedral church, the losses caused by the international troubles, the daily goings and comings of magnates on the Border, and the crippling expenses incurred by affording hospitalities on these occasions.[5] He contented himself by sketching out the broad principles on which the appropriation should be carried out, and the bishop of Carlisle filled in the lines. The last attempt at appropriation that need be mentioned was made by Bishop Lumley, who obtained a licence in 1441 to annex to his table the churches of Caldbeck and Rothbury on the old pretext that he was unable to support his episcopal dignity owing to his losses from the daily inroads of the Scots,[6] but this appropriation never took place.

One of the first chantries in the diocese was founded in 1300 at Bramwra by Thomas de Capella, vicar of Kirkbystephen. With the King's licence the founder alienated three messuages and seventy-two and a half acres of land in Newbiggin, Raughton, and Bramwra, for the purpose of maintaining one priest to celebrate in a chapel *de novo con-*

---

[1] On 8 July 1304 the King issued licences to the prior and convent of Carlisle for the appropriation of the churches of Addingham and Edenhall 'in compensation of the burning of their houses and churches, and divers plundering by the Scots,' both churches being of their own patronage (Pat. 32 Edw. I. m. 11 ; Inq. p.m. 32 Edw. I. No. 130). When the same king gave his consent for the appropriation of Castlesowerby in 1307, the grant was made 'out of devotion to the Virgin Mary, and in consideration of the relics of Thomas the Martyr and other saints being in the church of St. Mary, Carlisle, and of the losses of the prior and convent by invasions and burnings of the Scots' (Pat. 35 Edw. I. m. 17). The appropriation took place on the death of the rector, Henry de Ritter, in 1309 (Carl. Epis. Reg. Halton MS. f. 124).

[2] Chart. R. 14 Hen. III. m. 10.   [3] Pat. 29 Edw. I. m. 29.

[4] The ordination of Archbishop Corbridge, which recites the licence of King Edward, was made on 29 March 1301, 'cedente vel decedente rectore ipsius ecclesiæ qui nunc est,' but the rector held out for some years. Archbishop Greenfield completed the ordination on 19 February 1306-7. In the record it is entitled 'Acceptacio et approbacio W. Archiepiscopi Eboracensis super appropriacione ecclesie de Dalston.' The deed by which Bishop Halton assigned the stipend to the vicar—'Assignacio vicario de Dalston '—is dated 4 July 1307 (Carl. Epis. Reg. Halton MS. ff. 107-9).

[5] These were the reasons alleged by Bishop Kirkby in 1334 why his diocese was unable to pay the royal tenth demanded from the clergy (Carl. Epis. Reg. Kirkby MS. f. 308). In 1341 the same bishop absolved the diocese 'ab onere visitationis ' in consequence of their impoverishment by the Scottish wars, and pleaded his great charges in guarding the Marches, in which their churches were situated, that the clergy might give him a subsidy, specially as he foresaw a renewal of hostilities (ibid. f. 430).

[6] Pat. 21 Hen. VI. pt. 2, m. 22 ; Tanner, *Notitia Monastica*, ed. J. Tanner, p. 75 ; Nicolson and Burn, *Hist. of Cumberland*, ii. 273.

struenda at the latter place for the souls of himself and his ancestors.[1] But the fashion did not take hold of the public mind till a much later date, when it became a rule to found chantries in parish churches. We have a notable example of this when it became necessary to transplant the chantry of Bramwra to the church of Hutton in 1361. Owing to the depreciation in the value of land caused by the scarcity of tenants and labourers after the great pestilence,[2] the endowments of the chantry were quite insufficient to maintain a chaplain at Bramwra. The chapel had been vacant for a long time and no priest was willing to undertake the duty. In these circumstances Thomas de Hoton in the Forest, upon whom the right of the founder had devolved, reconstituted the chantry in the church of St. James in Hutton, and gave, in addition to the old endowment, land in the vill of Hutton to sustain a perpetual chaplain to celebrate at the altar of the blessed Mary there for the souls of himself and his wife, Isabel, and for the souls of their parents and all their predecessors. It was stipulated that the advowson and patronage of the chantry should be vested in Thomas de Hoton and his heirs. In giving confirmation to the transference of the institution, Bishop Welton ordained that the chantry priest should sing or say (*dicat cum nota vel sine nota*) the Canonical Hours daily with the rector or parish chaplain of Hutton and celebrate at St. Mary's altar on Sundays with special commemoration of all souls above mentioned, using on other days of the week the office of the dead with *Placebo* and *Dirige*. It should be mentioned that the chaplain of the chantry was subject to the rector in all canonical and lawful demands.[3] The subjection of the chaplain to

---

[1] Inq. p.m. 28 Edw. I. No. 133. On 20 October 1302 a writ *ad quod damnum* was issued to the sheriff to inquire if Thomas de Capella may alienate to the bishop of Carlisle a messuage and forty acres of land in Newton Reigny (Carl. Epis. Reg. Halton MS. f. 62). The founder made an addition to the endowment of the chantry in 1310–1311 (Orig. R. 4 Edw. II. m. 19; Inq. ad quod damnum, 4 Edw. II. No. 66), and the bishop of Carlisle obtained the appropriation of the chapel in the following year (Orig. R. 5 Edw. II. m. 21). John de Capella, a burgess of Carlisle, founded a chantry in St. Katherine's chapel in the church of the Blessed Mary, Carlisle, the chaplain of which was obliged to celebrate for his soul and for the souls of all the faithful departed for ever. In 1366 some of the tenants of the burgages, with which the chantry was endowed, withheld the rents from J. de Galwidia, the perpetual chaplain, to ' the peril of their souls and the prejudice of the said chaplain and chantry' (Carl. Epis. Reg. Appleby MS. f. 156).

[2] We have little local information about the havoc made among the clergy by the great pestilence or Black Death of 1349 in this diocese. There is an ominous gap in the diocesan registers between 1347 and 1352. When the plague attacked the province of York, the pope sent the archbishop an indulgence allowing every one to choose his own confessor with a proviso that the privilege should not be abused. A copy of this brief was sent to the bishop of Carlisle on 28 April, 1349 (*Letters from the Northern Registers* [Rolls Series], 399–400). There is more explicit evidence of the devastation among the clergy caused by the second visitation, which was the cause of the removal of the chantry from Bramwra to Hutton. In 1363 Bishop Appleby complained to the pope of the lack of priests in his diocese owing to the late pestilence, and prayed for the necessary faculties to promote forty persons, secular and regular, of the age of twenty to all the holy orders that they might minister in the same, and also to dispense twelve persons of illegitimate birth or illegitimate sons of priests or illegitimate sons of married men, so that they might be ordained and hold benefices with cure of souls (*Cal. of Papal Petitions*, i. 437).

[3] Carl. Epis. Reg. Welton MS. ff. 78–9. There is an account of a very curious dispute about the patronage of a chantry in the church of Brigham in 1532. Sir John Lamplugh had the King's letters to induct one Richard Robinson, clerk, but the church was held by force in the interests of the Earl of Northumberland. The parish priest was obliged to go ' to his chamer to say his mattens' as ' the chirche dorrys was shett upe ne culd hawe entres in the chirche bot at such tymys as he was lattyne in.' The earl's servants abode day and night in the church ' and hawd meytt and drynke and a bed within the sayd

the rector or vicar of the church in which the chantry was established was a prevailing feature of these foundations. When Lady Margaret de Wigton conferred the rectory of Wigton on the monastery of Holmcultram in 1332 on condition that four monks should be added to the inmates of the convent and two secular priests should be maintained by the monastery in Wigton church for the purpose of celebrating masses for the souls of her ancestors and all the faithful departed, the Bishop of Carlisle in ordaining the chantry made provision that the chaplains should be under the control of the parochial vicar.[1]

The bishop presided in the diocesan synod[2] unless prevented by sufficient cause, in which case he commissioned a deputy, often the official or the prior of Carlisle, to act in his place. Though several of these commissions are recorded, one only need be mentioned. Bishop Welton, wishing to have counsel and advice from his clergy on arduous business, issued a mandate in 1353 to the Abbot of Holmcultram, recently made his official, and John de Welton, learned in the law, empowering them to summon together the prior and chapter of the cathedral church, abbots and priors exempt and not exempt, the archdeacon, rectors, vicars, and other ecclesiastical persons within the diocese, and to expound to them when so assembled the business in hand. At the Michaelmas synod in the following year, the prior of Carlisle was commissioned to convocate the clergy, and to preside in the bishop's absence ; also to certify by his letters the result of their deliberations.[3] By virtue of their appropriate churches, abbots and priors of religious houses not situated in the diocese were obliged to attend the Carlisle synod in person or by proxy unless the obligation was remitted by special grace. Bishop Welton was very considerate in granting these remissions. In 1354 he issued licences to Richard, prior of Wartre ; Thomas, abbot of Whitby ; and John, prior of Connishead, excusing their personal presence in synod during their tenure of office.[4] Mulcts (*multe*) were not unfrequent for non-appearance. In 1402 the abbot of Whitby was amerced in 20*s*. because 'in no manner' did he appear in the synod held after the feast of Michaelmas, and the abbot of Fountains was fined 10*s*. in 1469 for a like offence. The mulcts of the parochial clergy were naturally smaller than those of abbots and priors, and varied considerably, perhaps according to the richness of the benefice or the contumacy of the offender. The rector of Greystoke had to pay 6*s*. 8*d*., and the rector of Brough under Stainmore, 10*s*. for non-appearance in 1402. The bishops were not very exacting in the levy or recovery of these fines. In 1494 the arrears amounted to the very respectable sums

---

chirch and chantre.' With the help of the parishioners the intruders were finally expelled by force and possession was given (*L. and P. of Henry VIII.*, vol. v. 1433).

[1] Carl. Epis. Reg. Kirkby MS. ff. 280–1.

[2] The holding of synods and the payment of synodals seem to be coeval with the formation of the diocese. The acts of the early bishops of Carlisle assume the one and the other (*Reg. of Wetherhal* [Cumbld. and Westmld. Arch. Soc.], 44–5, 210–12 ; *Reg. of Lanercost*, MS. viii. 3, 6).

[3] Carl. Epis. Reg. Welton MS. ff. 1, 10 ; Ibid. Kirkby MS. f. 403.

[4] Ibid. Welton MS. ff. 9, 10.

in each of the deaneries as follows :—Carlisle, 107s. 4d. ; Cumberland, 115s.; Allerdale, 88s. 10d. ; and Westmorland, 143s. 10d.[1] In the matter, however, of the payment of synodals, the mandates of the bishops gave no uncertain sound. Bishop Appleby issued a monition to the dean of Cumberland in 1379 to warn those clergy, with whose names he had supplied him, that they must pay the respective sums at which their benefices were rated within twenty days from the date of the monition.[2]

The most interesting document connected with diocesan synods in Carlisle may be found in the second of the ancient registers of the see bound up between the acts of Bishops Welton and Appleby. It has no date and little internal evidence upon which to found a conjecture as to the episcopate in which it was originally drawn up.[3] The compilation is made up of an introduction and sixty-two canons or constitutions on subjects of ecclesiastical work and administration. The statutes[4] embrace a wide range of subjects dealing with diocesan and parochial work. There are directions for the administration of the sacraments and the instruction of the people ; rules for the custody of churches and churchyards ; injunctions about sequestration, wills, tithes, litigation, excommunication and punishment ; regulations for the guidance of archdeacons, rural deans, and executors, for visitations, rural chapters and the recovery of debts. Several of the constitutions were drawn up with special reference to the clergy in all their private, social and public relations, domestic life, association with nuns, taverns, secular business, offices and courts, their ordination, learning, residence, amusements, and goods. Few of these diocesan regulations are without local colour. Though nearly all of them may be found among the institutes of other dioceses, they have been so adapted to the needs of Carlisle that they

[1] These facts are taken from the original *Compoti* of registrars and rural deans now in the Bishop's Registry at Carlisle.

[2] Carl. Epis. Reg. Appleby MS. f. 312. Lists of the ' denarii synodales ' payable at various periods by the benefices of the diocese, arranged under deaneries, may be found among the diocesan muniments. For the fourteenth century, see ibid. Halton MS. ff. 501-2, and ibid. Appleby, MS. f. 340 ; for the seventeenth century, the manuscript Rental of Bp. White ; and for the eighteenth century, the MS. Schedule of Bp. Osbaldiston. The synodals *pro utroque termino* were 4s. or 2s. for each benefice in the fourteenth century and only half of these sums in the seventeenth, but the custom of the eighteenth century reverted back to the payment of the full quota. Such churches as Stapleton, Eston, Cambok, Carlatton, and others were excused payment in the fourteenth and fifteenth centuries owing to the destruction caused by Scottish invasions. The payment of synodals and procurations was abolished in the diocese of Carlisle by the Ecclesiastical Commissioners for England by virtue of ' an instrument which has been sealed by the Board and which was published in the *London Gazette* on the 31 July, 1876.'

[3] The copy of the constitutions entered in the diocesan register of Carlisle (Welton MS. ff. 129-140) must have been made long after they had been enacted in synod and published by the bishop. The scribe, when adding marginal notes, was sometimes in doubt about the true meaning of an article and placed *ut patet* as a warning to the reader not to take his summary as absolute. The articles of greater importance and more frequent use are scored with index fingers. These constitutions probably belong to the great episcopate of Bishop Halton.

[4] The Carlisle constitutions were framed on the model of the statutes of the councils mentioned in the preamble. The Lateran council was held in 1215 under Pope Innocent III. The canons of the council of Oxford, held for all England under Archbishop Langton in 1222, were published in conformity with those of the Lateran. The bishop of Carlisle followed closely the canons of Oxford in many particulars. The council of London, celebrated in 1237 under Otto the papal legate, the archbishops of Canterbury and York sitting with him, was also for all England.

may be regarded as characteristic of northern ecclesiastical life and morals. The constitutions on the decline in popular esteem of the feasts of St. Cuthbert and on the prevalence of perjury in the diocese may be taken as examples of independent legislation. Few will withhold a word of admiration for their high religious tone and far-reaching usefulness. No one can read these diocesan constitutions without the conviction that the public worship of God had been conducted with a reverent solemnity and magnificent splendour capable of engaging the senses and impressing the hearts of the people of that distant age.[1]

There does not appear to have been any ritual uniformity in Cumberland and Westmorland before the promulgation of the Book of Common Prayer as the national use in the sixteenth century. By an enactment of the diocesan synod in the fourteenth century the Archdeacon of Carlisle was obliged, when on visitation, to inquire whether the canon of the mass was celebrated in churches correctly and distinctly according to the use of York or Sarum.[2] From this it may be gathered that either 'use' could be selected according to the predilection of individual incumbents. When Sir Robert Parvyng attempted to found a college in the church of Melmerby in 1342, it was ordained that the master and chaplains, vested in surplice, amice and black cope, should sing matins and prime daily at sunrise according to the use of the church of Sarum.[3] On the other hand, in 1369, Richard de Aslacby, vicar of St. Michael, Appleby, bequeathed to his son John a psalter and a breviary of the use of York.[4] In this respect Carlisle seems to have followed the custom of the metropolitan diocese of York, where the uses of York and Sarum were employed at discretion.

The diocese of Carlisle was too compact to need the permanent employment of a bishop suffragan. Neighbouring bishops, or sometimes the suffragans of York, were called in to perform the necessary

---

[1] For a century and a half after the Submission of the Clergy in 1534, when the diocesan synod was emptied of its legislative functions, the bishops of Carlisle continued to call their clergy together twice a year as aforetime, viz. soon after Easter and about Michaelmas, the traditional dates on which synods had been held in previous centuries. Bishop Robinson celebrated his *sacrosancta synodos* in 1606, the record of which still exists. At the Easter session, Chancellor Dethick presided, and at Michaelmas the bishop presided in person. In 1627, during the episcopate of Bishop White, there were 'two Synods in the yere on Thursdaies after Low Sunday and Michaelmas.' The total of the synodals paid at each session was £6 9s. 8d., of which sum 7s. 6d. was 'due to the fouer Rural Deans; to the archdeacon, £1 19s. 9d. So there remains due to the Lo. Bishop every synod, £4 2s. 5d. So this is pd. twice in the yere, scilicet, yerely, £8 4s. 10d.' (*Rental of Bp. White*, MS.). In 1686 Bishop Smith issued a monition for holding a synod. He intimated to his apparitor-general that he purposed doing so for the whole of the diocese on Thursday, 19 August, in the consistorial place (*loco consistoriali*) of his cathedral church at nine o'clock in the forenoon. To this holy synod were called the Dean and Chapter of Carlisle, and all rectors, vicars, curates, and stipendiaries who were wont to be summoned *ab antiquo*. The clergy were required to pay 'the annual synodals and all other sums of money due and payable to us by reason of the said synod' (Carl. Epis. Reg. Smith MS. ff. 87-8). Records of the diocesan synod should be carefully distinguished from those of synods *ad eligendum*, that is, meetings of the clergy of the archdeaconry to elect proctors for convocation (ibid. ff. 186-7).

[2] Carl. Epis. Reg. Welton MS. f. 135.

[3] Ibid. Kirkby MS. f. 459.

[4] Ibid. Appleby MS. f. 178. In 1342 the Vicar of Morland, *vultum lugubrem exhibens*, complained to Bishop Kirkby that on his way from Morland to Penrith he lost his book, called a *Journal*, which he carried with him for the purpose of saying the Canonical Hours either on the road or in the vill of Penrith (ibid. Kirkby MS. f. 451).

functions when the see was vacant or in cases of illness or absence. On several occasions during the latter portion of the twelfth century the bishop of Whithern, probably under commission from the archbishop, was employed in Carlisle, and remunerated for his services out of the Exchequer.[1] When Bishop Appleby was unable, owing to illness, to cope with the work entailed on him in preparation for the Eastertide of 1371, he issued a commission to William, bishop of Sodor, solely for the consecration of holy oil and the confection of chrism, naming Maundy Thursday and Dalston church as the time and place for the performance of the function.[2] If a considerable time elapsed between the death or translation of one bishop and the enthronement of another, the services of a suffragan were requisitioned to do what was necessary. When William Raa, diocesan registrar, rendered his account to Bishop Story in 1464–5, he reported that he had nothing to answer in the matter of dimissory letters, as they had been issued without charge, no suffragan having been engaged before his incoming. The costs of employing a suffragan during a vacancy were charged to the revenues of the bishopric. In 1478–9 Robert Whelpdale, the registrar, paid to the lord suffragan of York 20s. in part of a greater sum due to him by Bishop Bell. The same prelate, through his registrar, Richard Stanley, paid a sum of 40s. on 27 August 1489 for a like purpose.[3] It may be taken that the institution was not known in the diocese before the Reformation, and that when outside bishops were employed they were remunerated according to the services rendered.[4]

The frequent mention in the episcopal records of the occurrence of bloodshed and violence in churchyards arose partly no doubt from the practice of holding fairs and markets in such places during the medieval period.[5] Though the statute of 1285 (13 Edw. I. st. 2. cap. 6) alleged ' the honour of the church ' as the reason for prohibiting the custom,

[1] Pipe R. 5 and 6 Hen. II. An allowance of 14s. 8d. was made by the sheriff of Cumberland in each of these years, 1159 and 1160, to this bishop.

[2] Carl. Epis. Reg. Appleby MS. f. 247.

[3] Accounts of the diocesan registrars, MS. 1464-90.

[4] The parliament of Henry VIII. (26 Hen. VIII. cap. 14), providing for the appointment of suffragans, specified the names of several towns which should ' be taken and accepted for the sees of Bishops Suffragans to be made in this realm and in Wales.' As ' Pereth ' is one of the towns mentioned in the Act, it was confused with Penrith in Cumberland, a pardonable error when it is remembered that the Cumbrian town was often written ' Perith,' and is often so pronounced at the present day. At no period, perhaps, was the confusion more inconvenient than in 1888, when the bishop of Ripon selected the town of Penrith as the titular see of his suffragan. The consecration led to a protest from the diocese of Carlisle, which contributed to the change of title to that of Richmond by Royal warrant in 1889. To this controversy we owe the ' Suffragans Nomination Act ' (51 & 52 Victoria, c. 56) and the subsequent consecration of the Rev. H. Ware, on 11 June 1889, as the first bishop suffragan of Carlisle with the title of Bishop of Barrow-in-Furness.

[5] For the origin of fairs and markets in churchyards, see Spelman, *Glossarium*, s.v. Feria. Causes of blood were forbidden to be heard in churches or churchyards by a constitution of Archbishop Langton in 1222 (Lyndwood, *Provinciale*, Oxford edition, p. 270). Markets were prohibited in churches (and in churchyards according to the gloss of John of Athon) by the constitution of Othobon in 1269 (Lyndwood, *Constitutiones Legatinae*, p. 136). The penalties for striking or drawing weapons in sacred places are set out in the statute of 5 Edw. VI. cap. 4. The 88th canon of 1603 rigidly insisted on the inviolate character of churches and churchyards. Breaches of the seventh commandment or other uncleanness as well as the shedding of blood, were held to cause desecration (Carl. Epis. Reg. Welton MS. f. 5).

there is good reason to believe that the real motive was of a different nature. In 1300 Isabel de Fortibus, countess of Albemarle, was summoned to show by what right she held a market at Crosthwaite without the King's licence, to which charge she replied by her attorney that she held no market and exacted no toll, stallage, nor any other profit, but that the men of that neighbourhood were accustomed to meet at the church there on festival days for the sale of flesh and fish.[1] As the practice was continued, the people of Cockermouth complained to Parliament in 1306 that the congregation of Crosthwaite bought and sold every Sunday in their churchyard corn, flour, beans, peas, linen, cloth, meat, fish and other merchandise to the detriment of the Cockermouth market, and in contravention of the rights of the Crown therein. In response to this petition the sheriff of Cumberland was ordered to stop the holding of the market in Crosthwaite churchyard on Sunday or any other day.[2]

If the interests of commerce weighed with Parliament in forbidding Sunday markets in churchyards, another consideration altogether was present in the minds of the clergy of Carlisle. By a fourteenth century constitution of the diocesan synod, pleas and markets were forbidden to be held in churchyards. The canon declared that as our Lord and Saviour ejected those who bought and sold in the Temple that the house of prayer might not be made into the den of a thief, so it was justifiable for the synod to decree that public markets or pleas should not be held in churches, porches or churchyards on Sundays or other days, and that buildings should not be erected therein unless the time of war demanded it, and if they had been so erected they should be thrown down. Parish priests were also enjoined to forbid lewd dances (*luitas choreas*) or other shameful plays, specially on festivals of the church and vigils of saints, for those who did such things were accounted to sacrifice to demons and desecrate holy places and sacred seasons.[3] But the statute of the diocesan synod was not sufficient to check the custom in Carlisle. In 1379 Bishop Appleby learned that fairs and markets were held on Sundays and festival days in churches and churchyards throughout his diocese, and that owing to the tumult caused thereby it was impossible for rightly disposed persons to attend to their devotions.[4] In the bishop's opinion the time had come for the discontinuance of the custom, and in consequence the machinery of the diocese was put in motion to abate the nuisance. Many centuries were destined to elapse before the bishop's hopes were realized.[5]

[1] *Placita de Quo Warranto* (Rec. Com.), p. 115.
[2] *Rot. Parl.* (Rec. Com.), i. 197; Ryley, *Placita Parliamentaria*, 332–3.
[3] Carl. Epis. Reg. Welton MS. f. 132.
[4] Ibid. Appleby MS. f. 313.
[5] Hutchinson relates a story of Thomas Warcop, Vicar of Wigton 1612–1653, in connection with the butcher market held in that town on Sundays during his incumbency. 'The butchers,' he said, 'bring up their carcases even at the church door to attract the notice of their customers as they went in and came out of church; and it was not infrequent to see people who had made their bargains before prayer began, to hang their joints of meat over the backs of the seats until the pious clergyman had finished the service' (*Hist. of Cumberland*, ii. 479).

The bishops of the fourteenth and fifteenth centuries in the Border diocese were as a rule men of action, either as soldiers and diplomatists or as prelates and pastors. Bishop Halton, not merely by reason of the duration and strenuousness of his episcopate, but on account of his remarkable individuality, may be truly regarded as one of the greatest bishops that has ever adorned the northern see. His untiring energy during the early severities of international troubles, his attentive supervision of the diocese, his independence of papal dictation,[1] his tact as a diplomatist, as well as his courage as a soldier, the trusted counsellor of his sovereign and the resolute defender of his clergy, the rebuilder of his cathedral and the impartial dispenser of justice among his people, qualities such as these shed a lustre on his episcopate and make it memorable for all time. Bishop Ross, his successor, was a prelate of different mould, a mere puppet of the papacy, who was wont to describe himself as bishop of Carlisle 'by divine permission and by favour of the apostolic see.'[2] A local historian called him a man from the south (*homo australis*) imposed on the diocese by the pope.[3] From his subsequent quarrels with the prior and convent about their appropriated churches[4] we may infer that the cathedral body never forgot the manner of his appointment when their own nominee was rejected in his favour. In many respects Bishop Kirkby's tenure of the see was the stormiest on record. When he was not fighting with the Scots in the open field, he was engaged in feuds with the pope, the chapter of York, or his own archdeacon;[5] but he appeared to care as little for the threats of excommunication from Rome as the actualities of invasion from Scotland. When some of his officers were assaulted at Penrith in 1337 and at Caldeustanes in the suburbs of Carlisle in 1341, he issued in each case a general sentence of outlawry against the assailants, and afterwards ordered the body of one of them to be exhumed and cast out of the churchyard. Before the mandate was carried out, however, he was induced to relent on the intercession of Robert Parvynk and to absolve the corpse.[6] His firmness in the exercise of disciplinary powers during a period of unexampled laxity caused by the Scottish wars prepared the diocese for the quiet episcopates which followed. There is

---

[1] Bishop Halton was a signatory to the non-allowance of a papal provision in 1305. Hugh, bishop of Byblus in Syria, presented letters from Benedict XI., appealing to the King for a provision, as Hugh had been harassed by the Saracens and was unable to maintain his dignity. The privy council of King Edward, of which Bishop Halton was a member, replied that the papal request was 'manifestly prejudicial to the king and his royal crown, and therefore could not be granted' (*Rot. Parl.* [Rec. Com.], i. 178b, 179). It was at Carlisle that the first anti-papal statute was passed by the English Parliament, 35 Edw. I. cap. 2 (Ingram, *England and Rome*, p. 99). In 1318 Bishop Halton was selected as one of the peers to be in close attendance on Edward II. (Close 12 Edw. II. m. 22d; *Rot. Parl.* i. 453b). He was present at the great council of Vienne in 1311–12 when the Templars were suppressed (Milman, *Latin Christianity*, ed. 1867, vii. 298–302). His arrangements for the administration of the diocese, while he was 'in remotis,' and several of his acts, while he sojourned 'apud Viennam,' are recorded in his Register, MS. ff. 142–3.

[2] Carl. Epis. Reg. Ross MS. f. 253.

[3] *Chron. de Lanercost*, p. 253.

[4] Carl. Epis. Reg. Ross MS. f. 258.

[5] Ibid. Kirkby MS. ff. 358–9, 362, 367, 453–5, 458, etc.

[6] Ibid. ff. 355, 427, 431.

The Meeting of Richard II. and Bishop Merks with Henry of Lancaster.

no need to dwell on the domestic policy of Bishops Welton and Appleby, for apart from their political services on the frontier, their tenures of the see were chiefly remarkable for devotion to the work of the pastoral office. For almost the whole of his episcopal life, 1353–62, vigorous efforts were made by Bishop Welton to restore and beautify the choir of his cathedral.[1] The long episcopate of Bishop Appleby, 1363–95, was unhappily disturbed by a grievous commotion in his chapter, which threw the diocese into an uproar for several years.[2]

Little need be said of the two bishops whose episcopates brought the fourteenth century to a close. Robert Read was bishop of Carlisle only for a few months in 1396 before his translation to Chichester.[3] Though Bishop Merks cannot have often visited his diocese during the two years he held the see, he is perhaps the most famous of all the medieval bishops of Carlisle. The speech[4] which he is alleged to have delivered in the Parliament of 1399 on behalf of his unfortunate sovereign, Richard II., has played an important rôle in the controversies about the royal prerogative which raged in the seventeenth century. Whether or not he made the speech ascribed to him, it is certain that the bishop was much in the company of King Richard before his deposition, and that he was actually present at the time it is supposed to have been delivered. Moreover, Henry IV. informed the pope in 1400 that he had deprived Merks of his bishopric for high treason and treachery to his royal person. The portrait of this bishop, the earliest portrait of a bishop of Carlisle in existence, is preserved in the British Museum.

None of the bishops of the fifteenth century left a permanent mark on the diocese except Bishop Strickland at the beginning and Bishop Bell at the end of the century. We do not attribute this phenomenon to the disturbed condition of the nation during the historic struggle between the houses of Lancaster and York half as much as to the shortness of the episcopates. No fewer than eleven bishops ruled the diocese

[1] Carl. Epis. Reg. Welton MS. ff. 64, 74, 82, 109, 123. In 1363 the pope granted an indulgence to penitents who visited the cathedral, which had been burned, on the five feasts of the Blessed Virgin, or who would lend a helping hand to the fabric (Cal. Papal Petitions, i. 437).

[2] Carl. Epis. Reg. Appleby MS. ff. 348–53. This disturbance is noticed in the account of the priory of Carlisle.

[3] Bishop Robert Read was translated from Lismore to Carlisle on 26 January, 1395–96, and from Carlisle to Chichester on 5 October, 1396 (Cal. of Papal Letters, iv. 535, 539). In the same year John Frizelle, rector of Uldale, had an indult for seven years to let the fruits of his rectory to farm while engaged elsewhere, as he was unable to reside without danger owing to the whirlwinds of war (guerrarum turbines) which were afflicting the diocese (ibid. iv. 535).

[4] The controversies occasioned by this speech cannot be reviewed here. The speech is ascribed to the bishop by the contemporary author of the Chronique de la Traison et Mort de Rich. II. (Eng. Hist. Soc.), pp. 70–1, though it is not mentioned by another French contemporary authority, the metrical chronicle of Creton (Archaeologia, xx. 99), which states that no word was said in parliament in Richard's favour. Much has been written by the editors of these chronicles for and against the authenticity of the speech. It has been also recorded and embellished by Hall (Chronicle, p. 14, ed. 1809), Holinshed (Chronicles, iii. pt. i. 512), and Shakespeare (Richard II., Act. iv. Scene 1), from whom it passed into English literature. The speech has been often printed in separate form, as may be seen by reference to the catalogue of the library in the British Museum. Bishop White Kennett vigorously attacked the authenticity of the speech in three celebrated but now very rare ' Letters to the Bishop of Carlisle concerning one of his predecessors, Bishop Merks,' published in 1713, 1716, and 1717.

during that period, a larger number than in any other century of its history, several of whom were in possession only for a few years. To the episcopates of Bishop Strickland, 1400–19, and of Bishop Bell, 1478–96, may be traced various diocesan undertakings, some of which remain to this day.[1] But it must not be assumed from the frequent vacancies in the bishopric that the work of the church was altogether impeded, or that there was anything in the nature of lethargy or stagnation peculiar to the fifteenth century. The ecclesiastical machinery continued to move in its destined course : the bishops changed, but the organizations of the diocese went on. The ministers' accounts of the see[2] which have survived for this century show that the diocese was well equipped in all its departments, and that the diocesan officers of all grades were not slow in the performance of their duties. The disciplinary powers of the court were exercised in the cases of clergy and laity as occasion required, and ample provision was made for bringing religious ministrations within reach of the people. The bishops kept a staff of domestic chaplains about them, who seem to have been passed on from one bishop to another, and were always ready to take charge of a parish when the incumbent died or was laid aside by illness. The parochial clergy worked under many difficulties. Licences for non-residence were often issued and pluralities were allowed. At one time the diocese was thrown into a turmoil as the fortunes of war gave success to the Yorkist or Lancastrian faction, and at another it was devastated by an incursion of the Scots.

During the time of the relaxation of hostilities between the two kingdoms, inaugurated by the accession of the Tudor dynasty and the close of the wars between the rival Roses, more settled modes of life became possible and a new era may be said to have commenced. The close of the fifteenth century and the early years of the sixteenth witnessed an astonishing revival of ecclesiastical activity in the diocese of Carlisle. Though many of the parish churches in Cumberland bear traces of architectural alteration at this period, the new spirit is more manifest in the monastic houses. Within a few miles of the Border, three of the most important houses in the north-western county were situated, each of which was exposed to incessant attack. The priory of Carlisle, protected by the walls of the city, was more at liberty to follow its internal development without serious inconvenience, but Holmcultram and Lanercost were destitute of this advantage. As soon as inter-

---

[1] According to Leland, Bishop Strickland ' fecit magnum campanile in cathedrali ecclesia a medietate ad summum, una cum quatuor magnis campanis in eadem, et stalla perpulchra in choro, et co-operatorium cancellae ejusdem. Aedificavit turrim magnam in manerio de Rosa, quae adhuc vocatur Strikelands Towre ' (*Collectanea*, ed. T. Hearne, 1774, i. 346). The same authority states that ' Strikland, bishop of Cairluel did the cost to dig ' the Penrith water supply (*Itinerary*, ed. T. Hearne, 1711, vii. 50–1). In the *compoti* of the diocesan receiver-general for 1488-9, there is a full account of the costs of rebuilding the castle and chapel of Rose. For the decoration of the chapel three images were purchased at York by Bishop Bell.

[2] Too little attention has been given to these diocesan accounts : they are full of the most curious information about the administration of the diocese during several episcopates from Bishop Strickland to Bishop Penny. They consist of numerous rolls of parchment and paper in the Registry of Carlisle.

national matters began to settle down, there is ample proof of activity and vigour in repairing and improving what had been ruinated by neglect and war. The election of Prior Godebowre of Carlisle almost synchronised with the period indicated, and very soon after his appointment his labour in beautifying the priory was begun. It is scarcely possible to exaggerate the value and amount of the work done by him and his two successors within the priory precincts. Their names or initials are found almost everywhere. Turning to Holmcultram, the largest and wealthiest house in the county, the same evidence of vitality and zeal was manifest at this time. Abbot Chamber was a great builder, and the fragments of his work in that church and neighbourhood are monuments of his energy and skill. Meanwhile the religious men of the neighbouring priory of Lanercost were not idle. There is no need to search the ruins for bricks and mortar, inscriptions and dates, as valid witnesses of contemporary facts. We have documentary proof that the prior and his brethren were just as active as their neighbours in bringing up their church and conventual buildings to the requirements of a more peaceful and settled period.[1] That which strikes us in all these improvements and decorations is the evidence it affords, which cannot be contested, that the monasteries on the Border were full of life and vigour at the time that violent hands were laid upon them.

Conspicuous in this movement was the desire to recall the monasteries to their ancient ideals of austere devotion and charity. With the restoration of the outward fabrics of the monasteries there was a corresponding revival of monastic rule and a general transformation of religious life. It was a time of national renascence. Wolsey was its guide. His attempt to save the church of England in its entirety by a judicious reformation has not received the attention it deserves. But we are only concerned with his doings so far as they relate to our own district. Synods of the regular and secular clergy were held and codes of regulations were drawn up and issued to the monasteries and the bishops. We have no certain evidence that any of the local ecclesiastical magnates took part in the deliberations at Leicester and London. Whether they did or not is immaterial; we know their attitude. Prior Simon, whose zeal at Carlisle is well known, did not appear in person or by proxy at Leicester in 1518, but the worst complaint the visitors of his Order could make against him was that he had forwarded his dues with the accustomed liberality of his house.[2] It is fortunate that we have a clear statement, a year or two later, of the views of the bishop of Carlisle on the religious movement of this time. It is a most pathetic

---

1 Additional MS. 24,965, f. 218; *L. and P. of Henry VIII.*, vol. iv. 128.

2 The priors of Kyrkam and Worsthorpe, visitors of the province of York, certified ' quod prior de Carlill nec per se nec per procuratorem comparet, cum quo tamen mitius agitur prematura sua liberalitate loci debita ' (Cotton MS. Vespasian, D. i. 68b). At this Council the Cardinal was admitted a *confrère* of the chapter and commissioned to reform the Order (Ibid. Vitellius, B. iii. 223). Wolsey lost no time in issuing his *ordinationes et statuta*, consisting of eighteen articles, on the internal discipline of Austin monasteries (Ibid. Vespasian, F. ix. 22 *et seq.*). These statutes have been printed by Wilkins (*Concilia,* iii. 683–8). The priories of Carlisle and Lanercost would be affected by these injunctions.

letter[1] from an old man just recovering from a severe illness, unable to undertake a journey to London. He deplored the obvious vices and errors which were beginning to spread without check through Christendom, and wished Wolsey success in their repression—a task which the aged prelate acknowledged to be difficult. That was in 1520, be it remembered, several years before the domestic affairs of Henry VIII. had brought him into conflict with the papacy. This movement was a spontaneous effort of the English church to purge herself of the *egregia vicia et errores* and to bring herself into line with the requirements of a more enlightened age. In the hands of a prelate like Bishop Penny the new injunctions must have made a change in the religious houses and among the clergy within his jurisdiction.

The ecclesiastical movement was continued with considerable vigour during the early portion of the episcopate of John Kite, who succeeded Bishop Penny in 1521. Wolsey had little faith in non-resident bishops. A few months after his translation from Armagh[2] my lord of Carlisle was requested with other prelates to be personally within his diocese on an appointed day. Lord Dacre, the steward of the episcopal manors, pleaded with the cardinal for delay owing to the scarceness of provisions in Cumberland, of which, he said, there was not enough to sustain the people without the help of the other northern counties.[3] There is abundant evidence that Bishop Kite was the firm ally of Wolsey in the reformation of the church, and an earnest prelate in the pastoral care of his people. ' I beseech you of pity,' he wrote to the cardinal in 1523, the year after his coming, ' to have mercy of many good men, women, and children of the parish of Bewcastle within my diocese, who, since before Easter last past, have had neither sacrament nor sacramental that I know of, though many of them have been often with me for redress. There are both aged and young who have not offended and yet are in like punishment.'[4] The diocese of Carlisle had its share in the reforming movement of this period.[5] The

---

[1] *L. and P. of Henry VIII.*, vol. iii. 77. The letter of Bishop Penny is the earliest known document connected with the Reformation in the diocese of Carlisle. It has been printed in full by the present writer in *The Monasteries of Cumb. and Westmor. before Dissolution*, App. i., Carlisle Scientific and Literary Society, 1899.

[2] John Kite, archbishop of Armagh, who had been employed on the King's business in Spain, was named among the bishops to attend Henry VIII. to ' The Field of the Cloth of Gold ' (Rymer, *Fœdera*, xiii. 710). In the summer of 1521 he was translated to Carlisle through Wolsey's influence. The cost of the papal bulls amounted to 1,790 ducats, but for Wolsey's sake 275 ducats were remitted. It was considered a great compliment, as the pope was in great need of money at the time (Cotton MS. Vitellius, B. iv. 132, 136 ; *L. and P. of Henry VIII.*, vol. iii. 1430–1, 1477). Kite had restitution of the temporalities of the see on 12 November, 1521 (Pat. 13 Hen. VIII. pt. 1, m. 11 ; Rymer, *Fœdera*, xiii. 759) ; the papal bull, authorizing the preferment, bears date 12 July (*L. and P. of Henry VIII.*, iii. 1757). Bishop Penny must have died early in 1521.

[3] Cotton MS. Caligula, B. ii. 252.

[4] *L. and P. of Henry VIII.*, vol. iii. 34, 36. The bearer of this letter to Wolsey was ' a clerke of my dyocesse, my servant and offycyall (who) hath licence of me, in as moche as my power is, for iij yeres to goo to his booke at some unyversite ' if necessary beyond the sea.

[5] Bishop Kite's friendship with the cardinal is well known. He was one of the bishops with whom Wolsey was accused of taking secret counsel in Lord Darcy's impeachment (*L. and P. of Henry VIII.*, iv. 5749). After his fall, the cardinal and his attendants ' continued for the space of three or four weeks without beds, sheets, table cloths, cups and dishes to eat our meat or to lie in.' He was ' compelled to

MARMADUKE LUMLEY
(1430–1449).

RICHARD BARNES (1570–1577)
AD CAUSAS.

NICHOLAS CLQSE
(1450–1452).

RICHARD SENHOUSE
(1624–1626).

JOHN KYTE (1521–1537).

JAMES USSHER (1642–1656).

bishop's association with the cardinal was the means of supplying him with a subordinate who was perhaps a more famous man than his diocesan. William Byrbanke, the friend and correspondent of Erasmus, became archdeacon of Carlisle about the same time that Kite became its bishop. With the art of a courtier, which earned for him the sobriquet of the 'flatteryng Byshope of Carel,'[1] Kite told Wolsey that he had delayed Byrbanke's return from Rose Castle, as he wished to entertain him for the favour he bore to the court he came from.[2] There is little evidence of the archdeacon's personal residence in the diocese, but his appointment and his tenure of office may be taken as symptomatic of what was going on. Byrbanke was in the constant employment of Wolsey, acting as his agent in all the schemes in which that prelate was engaged.[3] A notable feature in the archdeacon's life was his friendship with Erasmus. From the pen of that illustrious man we have a picture, as he only could sketch it, of what Byrbanke was, the *vir integerrimus* of all his friends. The archdeacon of Carlisle was one of a constellation of brilliant men who dreamt of reforming ecclesiastical abuses without disturbing the unity of the church. Of this band of scholars Erasmus was the sun and the strength. While writing of these men he exclaimed to Byrbanke : ' *O vere splendidum Cardinalem, qui tales viros habet in consiliis, cujus mensa talibus luminibus cingitur !* ' Even in the remote diocese of Carlisle two of Wolsey's friends were posted to carry out the policy of reformation in parish church and monastery with which his great name is identified.[4]

borrow of the bishop of Carlisle and Sir Thomas Arundell both dishes to eat his meat in, and plate to drink in, and also linen cloths to occupy ' (*Life of Cardinal Wolsey*, ed. Singer, pp. 225, 257-8).

[1] This nickname was given to Bishop Kite by the Earl of Northumberland in a letter to ' his beloved cosyn Thomas Arundel, one of the gentlemen of my lord legates prevy chambre ' (Cavendish, *Life of Wolsey* [ed. Singer], p. 463).

[2] *L. and P. of Henry VIII.*, vol. iii. 2566.

[3] Archdeacon Byrbanke appears to have been of Cumbrian extraction (*Trans. Cumbld. and Westmorld. Archaeol. Soc.* xv. 38). We find him as early as 1488 in the service of Bishop Richard Bell as his chaplain. In 1508 he was nominated by the Austin priory of Conishead in Lancashire as one of their proctors to the diocesan synod of Carlisle by virtue of the appropriation of the church of Orton in Westmorland to that house (*Hist. MSS. Com. Rep.* [Rydal MSS.], xii. App. vii. 5). He accompanied Archbishop Bainbridge to Rome as one of his secretarial staff. In Rome he made the acquaintance of Erasmus, which afterwards ripened into a life-long friendship. In 1512 he was appointed prebendary of Fenton in the church of York, which he held till he resigned in 1531 (Hardy, *Le Neve*, iii. 185). On the death of Cardinal Bainbridge, he acted as one of his executors, and wrote some letters to Henry VIII. accusing the Bishop of Worcester of poisoning the cardinal (Cotton MS. Vitellius, B. ii. ff. 94-97 ; Ellis, *Orig. Letters*, 1st ser. i. 99-108). Bishop Silvester rewarded his traducer by defaming him in turn among his friends as ' that scoundrel Burbanke,' or again that ' he does not know under heaven a greater dissembler ' (Ibid. Vitellius, B. iii, f. 172). Pope Leo X. acted as peacemaker, absolving the bishop *sub plumbo* of all knowledge of the crime, and creating Byrbanke a prothonotary apostolic with a strong recommendation, on his departure from Rome, to the King's favour (*L. and P. of Henry. VIII.*, vol. ii. 13 ; *Dep. Keeper, Rep.* ii. App. p. 190). At least six impressions of his seal exist, and all of them of the same date in February, 1524-25. They are attached to the deeds of survey and surrender of certain monastic houses taken by Byrbanke as commissioner for Henry VIII. and Wolsey (*L. and P. of Henry VIII.* vol. iv. 1137). The illustration of this archdeacon's seal given above is the only seal of an archdeacon of Carlisle known to exist, and has been reproduced from the impression attached to the Tonbridge surrender. The seal now used by archdeacons of Carlisle is a *sede vacante* seal of uncertain date, procured at some date for the keeper of the see, when vacant, and has no connexion with the archdeaconry (*Trans. Cumbld. and Westmorld. Archaeol. Soc.* xv. 35-42).

[4] *Erasmi Epistolae*, lib. xvi. 3, p. 725 ; xviii. 41, p. 806 ; xxi. 57, p. 1124 ; Jortin, *Life of Erasmus*, i. 150 ; *L. and P. of Henry VIII.*, vols. ii.-iv. *passim*.

But events travelled fast in these days. The church was not left to recover herself in her own way. The clouds were gathering around the monastic institution, not for the purpose of purgation but of extinction. When the storm broke, reform was not mentioned. The destruction of the monasteries was not conceived, matured and carried out in a day. The actual suppression was the outcome of long years of agitation, distress, calumny, bitterness, in which the sacred name of religion itself was imperilled. There is no trace in the diocese of Carlisle at this time of any opposition to the exercise of the traditional rights of the Crown in ecclesiastical affairs. The renunciation of papal authority was an easy matter in the diocese. The parish clergy followed their bishop,[1] and none of the regulars are known to have dissented either in Convocation or elsewhere. But the agitation and unrest which led up to all this had a serious effect on monastic communities.

At this juncture cases arise in one of our local houses which throw out as in a mirror a picture of what was going on in the nation at large. In 1533 a monk of Holmcultram, Thomas Grame by name, was possessed of a procuratorial office in the neighbouring church of Wigton, a church appropriated to that monastery. As the profits of the office were spent on his own amusements to the detriment of the house, the seal was called in, but the monk remained obdurate and appealed to the Roman pontiff, who 'without consent or counsel of our chapter nor yet having licence from the visitors of the Cistercian Order' pronounced him *capax beneficii* and overruled all objections. The monks must have felt now, if they had never felt before, the inconvenience of a foreign authority exercising jurisdiction in the internal affairs of English houses. At all events, the attachment of this monastery to Rome must have been very slender indeed, when the secular arm was invoked to set aside the papal decree.[2]

In the same year much more serious matters were brought to light in the monastery of Holmcultram, which caused no small stir among the friends and enemies of the monastic order. A short time before, Gawyn Borudall or Borradale, an inmate of the house, was a candidate for the vacant abbacy, but he was rejected in favour of Matthew Deveys, whose election was duly confirmed. In a brief space Abbot Deveys died after a short illness, which recalled to the monks the threats of Borradale in the hour of his defeat. Foul play was freely discussed, and the suspicion of poison rested on the rejected candidate. Borradale was arrested and confined in the dungeon of Furness Abbey, where he lay for nearly six months.[3] The uproar brings out many things which show us how matters were working up to the desired end. The Abbot of Furness,[4] the monk's gaoler, told Cromwell, the minister who had the King's business in hand, that Borradale was a 'masterful man' with

---

[1] Bishop Kite's declaration of the Royal Supremacy in 1534 is one of those still surviving at the Record Office (Chapter House, *Acknowledgments of Supremacy*, s/a i. 27, Bp. of Carlisle). It is in beautiful condition with an undamaged impression of his seal.
[2] *L. and P. of Henry VIII.*, vol. vi. 781.
[3] Ibid. vi. 986.   [4] Ibid. vi. 1557.

'secret bearers.' The notorious Dr. Legh, the future scourge of the monasteries, one of the secret bearers of the accused monk, interceded in his behalf and reminded Cromwell that he was capable of doing the King good service in that house and on the Border.[1] When we know that this was the monk, who was subsequently chosen Abbot of Holmcultram for the purpose of surrendering the monastery into the King's hands, the scandal assumes a new magnitude and the intrigues of the royal agents come into view. We can now understand why it was that Borradale's name was omitted in after years from the infamous charges which blackened the characters of the rest of his brethren, when Legh and his associates made their reports to the King and Parliament on the eve of the suppression.

Cromwell was now master of the monasteries. Every religious house in England was entangled in his net. There was no room in his system to distinguish between their virtues and their vices ; the hour for their complete overthrow had come. But the tales of his agents must be arranged in formal language and invigorated with official sanction. With this view, royal commissioners[2] were despatched to visit the monasteries and bring back a report for the information of the King and Parliament. It is of some interest to know that Thomas Legh, the most diligent of these visitors, was a native of Isell in Cumberland. His associate, Richard Layton, was also north country born. These two men were the chief commissioners for the north. In their petition[3] to Cromwell begging for the post, it is stated that they knew 'the fassion off the countre and the rudenes of the pepull' and that through 'owre frendes and kynsfookes dispersyde in thos parties ther ys nother monasterie, selle, priorie nor any other religiouse howse in the north but other doctor Lee or I have familier acqwayntance' with it. Ready tools like these could not be disregarded by a minister who was a matchless judge of men. With astonishing quickness they accomplished their task. From a study of their movements, not more than a few days could have been devoted to the visitation of all the houses in Cumberland and Westmorland. It is absurd to suppose that the commissioners had any intention to make a *bona fide* report on the condition of individual monasteries. There was no time to hold a serious investigation, and there is no evidence that any court of inquiry was held or witnesses called. By 28 February 1536, it was announced to Cromwell that 'a clean booke of the compertes' was made and sent to his honourable mastership 'bye yor commissaries Doctor Layton and Doctor Lee' and 'a duble thereof' would be brought to him shortly.[4]

[1] *L. and P. of Henry VIII.*, vol. vi. 985, 986.

[2] The instructions to the commissioners for the county of Westmorland have been printed in *Trans. Cumbld. and Westmorld. Archaeol. Soc.*, xiii. 385–8, from the original book (*L. and P. of Henry VIII.*, vol. v. 721 (2). General instructions will be found in Burnet (*Collection of Records*, Oxford, 1816, i. pt. ii. 24–26).

[3] Layton's petition on behalf of Legh and himself has been printed by Wright (*Suppression of the Monasteries*, Camden Soc., pp. 156–7) from Cotton MS. Cleopatra, E. iv. f. 10. The business he was so desirous to undertake appeared so light, that he proposed 'to ryde downe one syde' of England 'and cum up the other.'

[4] *L. and P. of Henry VIII.*, vol. x. 363.

A HISTORY OF CUMBERLAND

Notwithstanding the indignation with which the King's declaration on the contents of the 'Black Book'[1] was received in parliament, the arts of diplomacy counselled prudence in framing the Act of Suppression. In order to allay the fears of the bishops and mitred abbots in the House of Lords, it was resolved to suppress only the smaller monasteries with a revenue under £200 a year. The preamble of the Act (37 Henry VIII. cap. 28) sets out the reason for parliamentary interference with the property and organization of the church. The monasteries, marked out for destruction, are stated to have been guilty of 'manifest synne, vicious, carnall and abhominable lyvyng' on the evidence of 'the compertes' of the late vysytacions as by sondry credyble informacions.' But the larger houses, which were for the present exempted, were equally plunged in nameless infamy by the 'compertes' of the late visitation, though, according to the same Act, 'relygyon is right well kept and observed, thankes be to God, in the great solempne monasteryes of this realme.' It is manifest that the statutory reasons for parliamentary action were fraudulent and that the court party had got up the alleged irregularities for the purpose of passing the Bill through both houses. In our own district the exemption of the Act affected only the abbey of Holmcultram and the priory of Carlisle, but all the other smaller communities, Lanercost, Wetheral, St. Bees, Calder and Shap, the nunneries of Armathwaite and Seton, and the friaries of Carlisle, Penrith and Appleby were swept away.

The dissolution of the smaller houses of religion caused unrest and indignation throughout the country. Insurrection broke out in Lincolnshire and soon spread to the north. The rising in Yorkshire assumed such alarming proportions that the King was advised to treat with the rebels in a conciliatory spirit. An account of the Pilgrimage of Grace, as the rebellion was called, may be read in any history. But the notable feature of the rebellion in Cumberland was the entire absence of men of position from the movement. The rabble had no leaders. Even the parish clergy stood aloof. It is probable that the monks secretly fomented the disaffection ; but if so, with the exception of the abbot of Holmcultram, they did not show themselves in the open field. The indifference of the clergy provoked the commons to a white heat of exasperation. It was openly discussed 'that they shuld never be well till they had striken of all the priestes heddes, saying they wold but deceave them.' A special grudge was felt against two or three of them. Chancellor Towneley, who was rector of Caldbeck, though his parishioners were

[1] The Black Book does not exist in its entirety, but supposed fragments of it may be found at the Record Office and British Museum (L. and P. of Hen. VIII., vol. x. 364 ; Cotton MS. Cleopatra, E. iv. 147 ; Lansdowne MS. 988, f. 1). The portion relating to Cumberland and Westmorland has been often printed (Trans. Cumbld. and Westmorld. Archaeol. Soc., iv. 88–90 ; Monasteries of Cumb. before Dissolution, pp. 45–7).

[2] For various reasons some writers have doubted whether the contents of the Black Book were ever read in parliament. There is now no doubt upon the point. Bishop Latimer says that 'when their enormities were first read in the parliament-house, they were so great and abominable that there was nothing but "down with them"' (Sermons, Parker Soc., p. 123). In the Act of Suppression 'the compertes of the late vysytacions' hold a prominent place.

up, did not join the insurgents till a missive was sent threatening to hang him on the highest tree of the diocese. Roland Threlkeld, the pluralist vicar of Melmerby, Lazonby and Dufton, was treated in a similar fashion.[1] Rumours were current in London implicating the bishop of Carlisle, the prior of Lanercost, the vicar of Penrith, and others, but without sufficient reason. The Duke of Norfolk corrected the mistake about the vicar of Penrith, and Chancellor Towneley exculpated his diocesan from any knowledge of the rebellion. As for the prior of Lanercost, there is no evidence of his treason.[2] The only cleric of consequence, who took a prominent part, was Robert Thomson, vicar of Brough under Stainmore, a demented individual, who was regarded as a prophet among the people. When Norfolk 'tied up' his threescore and fourteen of the rebels in the various towns and hamlets of the county, only one ecclesiastic[3] was among the number, a chaplain in Penrith, all the rest being of the labouring or agricultural class.

In many ways the rebellion was an unexpected piece of good luck to the King and his advisers. It furnished them with a pretext to demolish the monasteries root and branch, and they were not long in setting about it. There was no talk now that 'religion was right well kept and observed' in them as the Act of 1536 declared; many of the monks were compromised by siding with the rebels, and the King was determined not to let the opportunity slip. The exemption of the statute in the first instance did not blind the abbot of Holmcultram to the ultimate intention of the legislature. When he joined the insurrection and urged his tenants to follow his example, it was with the conviction that the existence of his abbey was the stake for which he was about to play at the risk of his own life. On the day before the commons laid siege to Carlisle he sent the brethren in solemn procession for a blessing on the enterprise, praying the 'All myghty God prossper them, for yffe they sped not this abbe ys lost.'

The King's agents forwarded to Cromwell indisputable proof of

---

[1] In the confession of Chancellor Towneley and the examination on oath of Robert Thomson, vicar of Brough under Stainmore, two lengthy documents, we get a good account of the insurrection in Cumberland (*L. and P. of Henry VIII.*, vol. xii. pt. i. 687 (1, 2). These and other documents have been printed in *Monasteries of Cumb. before Dissolution*, pp. 50–94.

[2] One of the county histories (Nicolson and Burn, *Hist. of Westmorland*, i. 569) contains a letter from the Duke of Norfolk to the King, correcting the rumour with regard to the vicar of Penrith. This letter is important, as the original does not now exist among the State Papers. It is said to have been procured 'from the lords' answer to the tenants concerning tenant right'—a manuscript in the hands of the editors in 1777. The cock-and-bull-story about the bishop of Carlisle was transmitted by Sir Thomas Wharton to Cromwell (*L. and P. of Henry VIII.*, vol. xi. 319), and demolished by Chancellor Towneley (ibid. xii. 687). There is no evidence known to the writer against the prior of Lanercost, except that he is mentioned in a despatch from the King to Norfolk, ordering him 'to be tyed up' with a number of others. This is not the only mistake made by the King in that despatch. The document has been printed in full by the Surtees Society (*The Priory of Hexham*, vol. i. pp. cl.–cliii.).

[3] It is stated in a document ascribed to 1539 that ten men, chiefly coiners and thieves, were condemned at the Carlisle assizes in the December of that year, but two of them 'for high treason, because they had bruted in those parts that the Comons were up in the South countrey.' One of these was Richard Howthwaite, sub-prior of Carlisle (Cotton MS. Caligula, B. iii. 156; *Monasteries of Cumb. before Dissolution*, pp. 92–4). The name of the ecclesiastic who was 'tied up' with the others was Edward Penrith (*L. and P. of Henry VIII.*, xii. 498).

Abbot Carter's treason.[1] The tenants of the lordship of Holmcultram testified to overt acts of rebellion. Thomas Grame, the monk who had, on the recommendation of Sir Thomas Wharton, previously intrigued for the abbacy on the death of Abbot Ireby, and who had so recently, with the connivance of the pope, defied the monastery in the matter of the Wigton office, came forward to tighten the noose on the neck of his late superior, and did not leave a single loophole through which the doomed man could escape. Before the King's pardon after the first insurrection, and after the King's pardon at the second insurrection, the abbot was at the head of the insurgents. In dealing with the abbot, when his treason was so public, one would have expected at least the ordinary formalities of a regular trial. But justice did not suit the tortuous methods of the royal agents. Sir Thomas Wharton repaired 'sekerethly' with his confederates to the abbey, examined some witnesses procured by Dan Thomas, and afterwards boasted to Cromwell that he was able to depart from the abbey without the abbot's knowledge of his proceedings.[2] As the King had as yet no legal authority to dissolve the abbey, notwithstanding the abbot's treason, Holmcultram being one of the larger houses exempted by the statute, Gawyn Borradale, the late suspect for poisoning Abbot Deveys, was appointed the last abbot with the object of making a free surrender. The final act was not long delayed.

There was little now to be done but to take possession of the houses and granges of the expelled monks. Before the royal commissioners started on their visitation, Cromwell was flooded with applications from all parts of the country for a share of the spoils. To these he paid little heed as long as the King's affairs sped to his liking. When it became necessary, as he told the King, 'to clinch the business and make the settlement irrevocable '—that is, to pass a confirmatory Act and to make legal the surrender of the greater monasteries—the most useful of the large landowners had their applications graciously entertained. To write of the dismantling of the monastic houses in Cumberland, the stripping of the lead roofs, melting the bells, the sale of the contents of dormitories and kitchens, the desecration of the altars, the holy vestments and all the *instrumenta ecclesiastica* of the conventual churches, would be a melancholy chapter of diocesan history. The church of Holmcultram was spared on the supplication of the inhabitants of that district. It was their parish church, they pleaded, and little enough to hold them all, being eighteen hundred ' houselynge' people; and it was their place of refuge as well, their only defence against their Scotch neighbours.[3] Dr. Legh, with infinite magnanimity, allowed the church to stand till the King's pleasure was known.[4] The property of the

---

[1] Cotton MS. Caligula, B. iii. 285, 286.

[2] *L. and P. of Henry VIII.*, vol. xii. pt. i. 1259 (i.).

[3] Cotton MS. Cleopatra, E. iv. 243 ; Ellis, *Original Letters*, 1st ser., ii. 90.

[4] It does not appear that the fabric of the conventual church was hurt in any way at the suppression of the abbey. The dilapidation of the chancel or choir in 1602 was the occasion of certain negotiations between the bishop and the University of Oxford for its repairs. In 1724 a faculty was issued to rebuild

priories of Carlisle and Wetheral was still retained in the service of religion, but the monastic features of the one and the bulk of the buildings of the other went down in the general devastation.

Perhaps the most pathetic scene in the last act of this drama was the condition of the religious men who were driven from their houses. There is little doubt that all of them, or nearly all of them, had received patents for an annual pension, varying from £6 to a few marks according to station or age. It did not suit the royal policy to permit the use of the religious habit for the remaining life of the disestablished clergy. Writing of the surrender of Holmcultram, Dr. Legh told his employers[1] that 'the monks, arrayed in secular apparel, having honest rewards in their purses, are dispersed abroad in the country.' It was a high offence on the part of William Lord Dacre, in the eyes of the court hack who expected the grant of Lanercost, that the expelled monks were allowed to revisit their old home[2] in their 'chanons cotes.' These priests were forbidden to wear the ecclesiastical habit as well as to exercise the sacred function. A whole brood of them was scattered broadcast in the land in laymen's apparel, but unable to do laymen's work. The Duke of Norfolk reported to the King, after the suppression of the monasteries in the northern counties, that he had 300 monks on his hands wanting capacities. A few who had served the King were accommodated here and there, like Thomas Grame, the betrayer of his master, who was appointed by Dr. Legh to 'the chapel called St. Thomas' chapel to make him a chamber there'—one of the several chapels now extinct in the parish of Holmcultram. Some, like Edward Mitchell and Hugh Sewell of the priory of Carlisle, were selected to fill vacancies on the new foundation in order to save their pensions. But the mass of the dispossessed monks remained mere pensioners without clerical employment to the end of their days. They were required to show their patents periodically to their paymasters, as returned convicts are obliged to report themselves to the police. If they left the district where they were known, it was at the risk of losing their pensions. The lists of these pensioners appear year after year with monotonous regularity ; each year they grew fewer in number ; some of them survived the collapse of their houses for almost half a century.

The ecclesiastical legislation of Edward VI. added an important contingent to the multitude of the pensioners. One of the first acts of his reign was to seize the lands and endowments of the chantries, free chapels, stipendiary curacies and collegiate churches throughout the kingdom. It is true that the revenues of many of these institutions had been granted to Henry, his father (37 Hen. VIII. cap. 4) ; but the

---

the nave and sell the materials to be got by dismantling the chancel ; at which date the church took its present shape ; or rather the shape as shown in Buck's print of 1739 with the groins of the chancel arches *in situ.*

[1] *L. and P. of Henry VIII.*, vol. xiii. pt. i. 547, 551.

[2] Ibid. xiii. pt. i. 304.

spoliation was not complete when that monarch died.[1] The new Act (1 Edw. VI. cap. 14) annexed their lands, goods and chattels to the Crown on a pretext of the 'superstition and errors in the Christian religion, brought into the minds of men by devising and phantasying vain opinions of purgatory and masses satisfactory to be done for them which be departed, the which doctrine and vain opinion by nothing more is maintained and upholden than by abuse of trentals, chantries and other provisions made for the continuance of the said blindness and ignorance.' In order to allay public apprehension, there was a sort of promise held out that the money should be used for founding grammar schools, helping the Universities and making provision for the poor ; but these pious intentions were never wholly fulfilled.[2]

As the Act was passed on 4 November 1547, and the commission to survey the spoils was issued on 14 February 1547–8, it cannot be said that much time was lost in putting the new law in force. The commissioners for Cumberland were authorized to survey and examine all colleges, chantries, free chapels, fraternities, guilds, stipendiary curacies, and other spiritual promotions within the county, the revenues of which had been given and ought to come to the King. In a certificate[3] delivered into court on 6 December 1548 by the hand of Allan Bellingham, the surveyor, the commissioners reported on the religious institutions of sixteen different places in Cumberland. Kirkoswald, a

---

[1] The commission for this survey, dated 14 February, 1546, consisted of Robert, bishop of Carlisle, Thomas lord Wharton, Sir John Lowther, knight, and Edward Edgore, esquire. The survey for the two counties was returned on six membranes written (save the last) on both sides, giving in detail the possessions of each chantry with the names of tenants and annual rent. The first three membranes comprise the chantries in the 'Countie of Cumbrelonde,' and the remaining three comprise those in 'Westmerlonde.' The list for Cumberland begins with the 'Rood Chantry' in the cathedral church of Carlisle. It had a total yearly rent of £4 13s. 5d. from tenements, a sum which agrees exactly with the subsequent survey of Edward VI. The 'goodes and cattalles belonginge to the same,' valued at £3 5s. 2d. in the Edwardian survey, are here set forth in detail thus : ' Furst, one messe booke, 3s. 4d. ; foure aulter clothes, 12d. ; thre vestementes, 3s. 4d. ; two aubbes, 12d. ; two candelstykes of brasse, 2d. ; and challes of silver (55s.) parcell gylte weynge 15 ounces at 3s. 8d. the ounce ; a corporax with case, 4d. ; an olde chyste, 10d. ; 2 crewettes, 2d. (Total) 65s. 2d.' This survey, which is of considerable local interest, will be found at the Public Record Office under the official description of ' Rentals and Surveys, No. 846,' but formerly known as ' Exch. Q. R. Ancient Miscellanea, bundle $\frac{7.8}{16}$.' In many parishes there were various small endowments for the perpetuation of obits, lights before the sacrament and other minor parochial institutions, which were plundered at this period. Among the ancient rentals of the see of Carlisle there is a survey of the 'Terre luminarium beate Marie' in the parish of Dalston, of the time of Henry VII., which betokens an adequate provision for that purpose. The endowment consisted of no fewer than seventeen separate parcels, each parcel varying in value from 1½d. to 7s. a year, such as a messuage, a toft, a rood of meadow, an acre of land, a tenement, a cottage, and so forth, up and down the parish. The total rental amounted to 29s. 5d. It is evident that these small parcels were bequeathed by the poorer tenants of the parish.

[2] Strype has given a list of free grammar schools founded by Edward VI. (*Memorials*, edition 1721, ii. 535-7), but if this list be carefully scrutinized, it will be found that very few of them had their origin in the reign of that monarch. The statement of J. R. Green that ' one noble measure, indeed, the foundation of eighteen grammar schools, was destined to throw a lustre over the name of Edward' (*Short History of the English People*, edition 1891, p. 360), has been disputed by Mr. A. F. Leach in an article on ' Edward VI. : Spoiler of Schools ' in the *Contemporary Review*, September, 1892. The preface to the *Yorkshire Chantry Surveys* (Surtees Society) by Mr. Wm. Page should also be consulted.

[3] This certificate, containing the survey of all the chantries in the county, is preserved in the Augmentation Office, Chantry Certificates, No. 11, Cumberland.

parish with a population of five hundred[1] 'howseling' people—that is, of persons old enough to receive the Eucharist—had a college in the parish church of the foundation of Thomas the late Lord Dacre, father of the Lord Dacre that then was. The lands and tenements belonging to the institution were valued at £89 10s. 9d. The college in the parish church of Greystoke, on which three thousand 'howselinge' people were dependent, was 'off the foundation of one Urbane, bishoppe of Rome at the peticon of one Rafe, baron of Graystocke, auncestour to the lorde Dacre that nowe is.' John Dacre, the master, was also parson and served the cure himself, there being no endowed vicar. There were two chapels belonging to the college called 'Watermelike and Threlkett, th' one distant seven miles and th' other six miles from the parish church.' The yearly revenue of the college amounted to £84 19s. 8d., which, after deducting reprises of 57s. 10d., left a rental 'clere by yere' of £82 1s. 10d. These were the only two collegiate churches in the county.

The chantry of Our Lady in Hutton in the Forest was of the foundation of the ancestors of William Hutton to celebrate in the parish church there for ever. There were two chantries in Penrith, one in the castle and the other in the parish church ; the salary to the priest of the former was paid annually at the King's audit, the office being in the gift of the Crown. There were no lands to maintain the service of the priest in the parish church, but the incumbent received his stipend yearly by the hands of Sir John Lowther. The chantry of the Blessed Mary in Skelton and that of St. Leonard[2] in Bromfield were founded to celebrate mass and sing divine service in the parish churches there. The parish of Wigton contained three institutions coming within the purview of the Act, namely, the chantry of St. Katherine in the parish church, the hospital of St. Leonard, and a free chapel 'of the foundation of the ancestors of the late Earl of Northumberland to celebrate there, which was not observed, for it lieth on the Borders and is decayed and destroyed.' Three stipendiary cura-cies were endowed for the purpose of celebrating mass in the parish church of Torpenhow, the incumbents whereof received a salary of £4 each. Though the parish of Crosthwaite contained two thousand 'house-ling' people, there was but one chantry, that of St. Mary Magdalene, for the purpose of celebrating mass in the parish church. In Egremont there was a stipendiary, called a Lady priest, and in Brigham a chantry, both for the purpose of celebrating mass and singing divine service in the parish churches there. The chantries of Cockermouth were of a diversified description. The stipendiary of the parish chantry 'used to kepe and teache a grammer schole there and to pray for the soulle of

---

[1] In another list of the chantries, compiled when they were in the hands of the King, the population of Kirkoswald is set down as 'one thousand howseling people' (Augmentation Office, Chantry Certificate No. 12, Cumberland). In both enumerations, of course, the parish of Dacre, being under the spiritual charge of the college, would be included.

[2] When the revenues of this chantry were sold, it was called the chantry of St. George the Martyr in the church of Brumfeld (Augmentation Office, Miscellaneous Books, lxvii. 148-50).

the foundor for ever.' Rowland Noble, the incumbent and master of the school, enjoyed the revenues, amounting to 116*s*., for his salary. Two stipendiaries were constituted 'of the gifte of the late Prynce of famous memory, Kinge Henrye the eight, to celebrate in the castle there'; there were no lands belonging to these chantries, but the incumbents yearly received their allowances from the King's receiver-general at Cockermouth. In Edenhall there was a chantry for the maintenance of the mass of the Blessed Mary in the parish church; in Great Salkeld, a stipendiary curacy for the celebration of one mass in the parish church, 'off the foundacon of John Worsoppe' with an annual revenue of 40*s*.; and in Mosser, a chantry of Our Lady founded to find a priest to celebrate there for ever, but 'one Thomas Sawkeld Esquier receyvethe the yerlie profittes therof, by what tytle it is unknowne, and gyvethe the priest 4*l*. towardes his fyndinge.' The city of Carlisle had no fewer than six chantries, endowed with lands and tenements affording revenues of varying amounts from 15*s*. 4*d*. to £4 13*s*. 5*d*. In the cathedral were the chantries of St. Katherine, St. Roke, the Rood or St. Cross and Our Lady, the incumbents of which used to celebrate mass there; dependent on the church of St. Cuthbert were the chantry of Our Lady[1] and the chantry of St. Alban. "In all whych colleges, chauntryes, frechappelles, guyldes, fraternytyes, stypendaryes, ther ys no precher founde, grammer scole taught, nor pore people relevyd, as yn ther severall certyfycates yt dothe appere.' The pensions awarded to the priests of the dissolved foundations were about as much or almost as much as the salaries they were in the habit of receiving as incumbents.[2] For this reason the secular priests were more liberally treated than the monks, inasmuch as no rule seems to have been observed in the granting of pensions at the dissolution of the monasteries. The lands and endowments of these institutions were immediately leased or sold, the sale often reaching as many as twenty-four years' purchase. Some of the property was bought by local people, but much of it went to professional jobbers like one 'Thomas Brende of London scryvener.'[3]

As the sale of the chantry lands was insufficient to provide the King with money to meet his pressing debts, a new commission was sent out in 1552 instructing local committees to seize all the goods, plate, jewels, and ornaments of the parish churches and chapels, 'leving nevir the less in every parishe churche or chappell of common resorte

---

[1] This chantry, which had the small revenue of 15*s*. 4*d*. a year, does not appear to have been dissolved. It does not occur in the list of chantries in the King's hand, nor is the incumbent, Henry Blanrasset, mentioned in the list of ejected priests to whom pensions were bestowed. It is odd that the chantry of St. Alban is ascribed both to St. Cuthbert's church and to the cathedral. In the survey made by the local commissioners it is placed under St. Cuthbert's; in the King's list it is catalogued under the cathedral.

[2] These pensions are recorded on the King's list of chantries (Augmentation Office, Chantry Certificates, No. 12, Cumberland).

[3] The particulars of the endowments, the names and rents of the tenants, the conditions of sale, the names of the purchasers, and the amount of the purchase money are all set out in schedules in Miscellaneous Books, Nos. 67 and 68, at the Augmentation Office. The property of the Carlisle chantries lay chiefly within the city, from which it would appear that they had been founded by burghers.

two or more challesses or cupps according to the multitude of the people every such churche or chappell and also such other ornaments as by their discretions shall seme requisite for the devyne servyce in every such place for the tyme.' When the work was finished a certificate was delivered into court, entitled 'A just veue and perfyt inventorye of all the guds, plate, juells, bellis, vestiments, and other ornaments within every pariche churche, chapell, brotherheid, gyld, or fraternitie in the countie of Cumbreland, maide by Sir Thomas Dacre, Sir Richard Musgrave, knights, William Pykerynge, Thomas Salkeld, Robert Lamplughe, Anthony Barwis, esquiers, auctorisid by the Kyngs Majestie's commission heronto datid the vjth day of May in the sext yeir of his Majesties reign.' The commissioners returned the schedules of church goods according to wards, ranging the churches under the wards of Cumberland, Leith, Eskdale, Allerdale above Derwent and Allerdale below Derwent: the Leath ward entries have been divided into two sections. As might be expected in a scattered and poor diocese like Carlisle, the sacred instruments of divine service were neither numerous nor valuable. A chalice of silver, a couple of vestments and a bell or two were the only requisites of some of the churches, but most of them of average wealth and importance possessed two candlesticks of brass and a pair of censers. In larger churches like Carlisle cathedral and Greystoke college the ornaments presented a greater and richer variety. By subsequent mandates directions were given for the disposal of the spoils. Churches were entitled to retain one or two chalices 'to thintent the said churches and chappelles may be furnysshedd of convenyent and comely things mete for thadmynystracion of the holy Communyon'; a proper cover for the 'communyon table' and a surplice or surplices for the minister or ministers, the residue of the linen ornaments and implements to be distributed freely among the poor of the parish; but all copes, vestments, altar cloths and other ornaments, as well as all parcels or pieces of metal, 'except the metall of greatt bell, saunce bells in every of the said churches or chapells,' were ordered to be sold to the King's use.[1] Before the whole of the proceeds of the sale reached the royal coffers, Edward VI. died, and Mary, who succeeded, at once stopped the spoliation of the parish churches. On inquiry in 1556 it was found that much of the plunder, of which the plate alone weighed 265 ounces, was in the custody of the Lady Ann Musgrave, the widow of one of King Edward's commissioners for Cumberland. No doubt, as much of the plate as was recovered and could be identified was returned to the parishes to which it belonged, but the vestments and other ornaments, which had been 'prysed by the sworne men' and sold, were lost or destroyed.[2]

[1] The Rev. H. Whitehead, a most diligent and painstaking antiquary, has printed the instructions of the commissioners for Cumberland and the full text of the survey from the 'Exchequer Q. R. Church Goods $\frac{1}{33}$ and $\frac{1}{34}$ 6 Edward VI.' (*Cumbld. and Westmorld. Archaeol. Soc. Trans.* viii. 186–204).

[2] Mr. Whitehead has written a very interesting appendix on 'Queen Mary's commission of inquiry as to church goods' in *Old Church Plate in the Diocese of Carlisle* (pp. 316–8) from the original documents

If all the parishes of Cumberland felt the scourge when the valuable portion of their church furniture was confiscated, several of them were notoriously wronged in the matter of religious ministrations after the dissolution of the chantries and endowed curacies. The district of Mosser, which had its own chapel and priest, was absorbed into the extensive parish of Brigham. The staff of clergy which served Greystoke and the outlying chapelries, comprising an area of nearly eighty square miles with a population of 3,000 communicants, was reduced from seven priests to three. Of the eight clergy who ministered in the associated parishes of Kirkoswald and Dacre only two were left. The two parishes of Carlisle, embracing large areas around the city, were stripped naked of religious services except what could be afforded by two minor canons of the cathedral. Three stipendiary curacies in Torpenhow and three in Wigton were abolished ; in fact every endowment for the maintenance of assistant clergy in the larger parishes of the county was gathered into the royal treasury.[1]

The religious changes during the reign of Edward do not appear to have troubled the consciences of the clergy of the diocese. At least there is not much evidence to show that they warmly favoured or violently opposed the new Prayer Book. The progressive party was fortunate in securing the compliance of Robert Aldridge, bishop of Carlisle, for though he was not in sympathy with many of the liturgical innovations[2] we may well believe that his scholarly abilities exerted a moderating influence on the extravagances of some of the reformers. There can be little doubt that the bishop reflected the general attitude of the clergy of Carlisle. In 1540 King Henry had ordered him home to his diocese ' there to remain for the feeding of the people both with his preaching and good hospitality,'[3] and if he continued to cultivate in mature age the charm of eloquence which in his earlier years had captivated Erasmus,[4] we may be sure that his advocacy of the Reformation on the old lines must have produced an impression on the northern clergy. We have not met with any cases of deprivation for resistance to the Second Book, but there was one notable figure in the diocese, Lancelot Salkeld, the last prior and first dean of Carlisle, who was unable to accept the new ecclesiastical position. As soon as the religious policy of Edward's reign became manifest, he took the wise step of resigning his deanery. At Christmas 1548, Sir Thomas Smith was appointed to succeed him with the obligation to pay the late dean

in the Public Record Office. The Marian inquiries went back to the spoliation of the lead and bells of cathedrals and monasteries in the reign of Henry VIII.

[1] The Survey of the chantries (Augmentation Office, Chantry Certificate, No. 11, Cumberland) should be compared with Bishop Best's report on the clerical staff of his diocese in 1563 (Harl. MS. 594, f. 9), in order to see how the number of the parochial clergy had been reduced in the intervening period.

[2] Strype, *Memorials*, ii. 466.

[3] *Proceedings and Ordinances of the Privy Council* (Rec. Com.), vii. 88.

[4] Erasmus was much attached to Aldridge when he was master of Eton. In his letters he used such terms as ' Mi Roberte in Christo charissime,' and spoke of him as the ' blandae eloquentiae juvenis ' (*Erasmi Epistolae*, edition 1642, xxi. 26, 55, xxiii. 8). The two friends visited together the shrine of Our Lady of Walsingham (*Life and Letters of Erasmus*, ed. Froude, p. 229).

a pension of £40 a year.[1] But none of the prebendaries followed Dean Salkeld into retirement. The reaction under Queen Mary was attended with few inconveniences. In 1554 Dean Salkeld was restored to the deanery, though Sir Thomas Smith was very loth to yield it to him. ' About May,' he said, ' I gave up *quasi sponte* the provostship of Eton and the deanery of Carlisle, and I had a pension from the queen of £100 a year.' As Dean Smith had never visited his deanery, the return of Salkeld to his old home must have been welcome to his former colleagues. With the exception of a couple of the clergy,[2] who were deprived because they were married men, we have met with no other cases of mishap during Mary's reign. The atrocity of the stake and the faggot, thanks perhaps to the enlightened instincts of Bishop Aldridge, had not gained an entry into the diocese of Carlisle. Owen Oglethorpe who succeeded in 1557 was not the style of prelate, if we may judge him by the part he took in the theological discussions of the late reign, who would willingly consent to the penalty of death as a punishment for doctrinal aberrations.[3]

The intentions of Queen Mary to restore to the church what had been confiscated by the legislation of the late reigns, that is from 20 Henry VIII., are matters of general history. When she could not prevail on her subjects to relinquish the spoils of the religious houses, she determined to set them an example by making a full restitution of all the church property vested in the Crown. With the masterly firmness of Tudor resolve, the Queen informed the privy council that her conscience would not suffer her to retain it, but with all her heart, freely and willingly, she surrendered all the said lands and possessions that order and disposition might be taken of them to the honour of God and the wealth of her realm.[4] Parliament was prevailed upon to pass an Act[5] for this purpose as far as the Crown was concerned. By it, under the direction of Cardinal Pole, all rectories, impropriations, tithes, glebe lands, and other ecclesiastical possessions, which had been perquisites of the Crown since the twentieth year of Henry VIII., were to be employed

---

[1] *Archaeologia*, xxxviii. 97-127. In this paper Mr. J. G. Nichols has collected many additional particulars about the life of Sir Thomas Smith. Writing to the Duchess of Somerset in 1550, Smith stated among other things that the revenue of ' the deanery of Carlisle, paieing 40 *li*. pencion to him that resigned it to me, is 80*l*.' (Harl. MS. 6989, f. 141). Nichols questions the truth of Strype's statement that Sir Thomas ' repaired to his deanery of Carlisle,' as the order of the Council, which he quoted, does not support the inference that Smith ever visited the church of which he was nominally dean.

[2] The names of these incumbents were Thomas Atkinson, rector of Ormside, and Percival Wharton, vicar of Bridekirk, but they were restored by the royal commissioners at the accession of Elizabeth (S.P. Dom. Elizabeth, x. ff. 147, 149).

[3] Fuller, the historian, accounted for the absence of martyrs in Cumberland during Mary's reign by the facts that the people were ' nuzzled in ignorance and superstition,' and that those who favoured the Reformation were connived at by Owen Oglethorpe, the courteous bishop of Carlisle ' (*Worthies of England*, ed. S. Jefferson, p. 8). If we can believe Fox, Isabel Foster, wife of John Foster, cutler, of the parish of St. Bride's in Fleet Street, London, who was burnt on 27 January 1556, was a Cumberland woman—' This foresaid Isabel was born in Greystock, in the diocese of Carlisle ' (*Acts and Monuments*, Ch. Hist. of England, vii. 748).

[4] Fox, *Acts and Monuments*, Ch. Hist. of England, vii. 34.

[5] 2 & 3 Philip and Mary, cap. 4. This Act was repealed by 1 Elizabeth, cap. 4, as that queen had intentions somewhat different from those of her deceased sister.

in the augmentation of small livings, the maintenance of preachers, and the provision of exhibitions at the Universities for poor scholars. The cardinal lost no time in carrying out the intention of the statute and relieving the conscience of his royal mistress. The royal warrant, which restored these ecclesiastical possessions to Bishop Oglethorpe, is still preserved in the diocesan registry of Carlisle.[1] As the document is dated 14 November 1558, its provisions were never carried into effect. The Queen and Pole were dead and the Act was repealed not many months after the arrival of the warrant at the registry of Carlisle. But the Queen has left at least one memorial of her benevolent intentions which is still exercised in the diocese. It was by her gift that the bishops of Carlisle had obtained the right of advowson and collation to the four prebendal stalls in the cathedral,[2] a privilege which experience has proved to be of great moment in diocesan administration.

The legislative changes for the settlement of the church introduced into the first parliament of Elizabeth were vigorously opposed by Bishop Oglethorpe of Carlisle, one of the most moderate and enlightened prelates on the episcopal bench at that time. Though he was the only bishop in England who could be induced to act at the Queen's coronation,[3] his papal sympathies were robust enough to enable him to join in the general resistance of the episcopate to the new departure in ecclesiastical reform. For some reason not specified, he was obliged to enter into recognizance with certain other bishops to appear daily before the lords of the Council, and not to depart from London without licence. In addition he had to pay a fine of £250 for 'contempt of late committed against the Queen's Majesty's Order.' It is a curious circumstance, showing the bishop's hostility to the proposed changes, that day by day as he appeared before 'Lord Great Seal' in obedience to the conditions of his recognizance, he had been most assiduous in his attendance in the House of Lords, opposing the passage of the two great measures, the Supremacy and Uniformity Bills, then before the House.[4] When these measures became law, the bishop of Carlisle refused to take

---

[1] The warrant is endorsed 'A graunte to Bishop Oglethorpe and his successors in the See of Carlisle of certain benefices and advowsons by King Phillip and Queene Mary, viz.: Bampton, Crosby, Millom, Irton, Dereham, Kirkoswald, etc., in Cumberland by Letters Patent; date 5 & 6 Phil. and Mary,' a copy of which has been entered on the Patent Roll of that year. The cord, composed of mixed strands of green and white silk, still hangs from the vellum sheet,but the seal which it once carried is completely gone. The document has been printed by the present writer in *Trans. Cumbld. and Westmorld. Archaeol. Soc.*, xv. 21–6.

[2] Pat. 4 & 5 Philip and Mary; Tanner, *Notitia Monastica* (ed. J. Tanner, 1744), p. 75.

[3] The coronation of the Queen was solemnized with all the ceremonies of the ancient ritual. Bishop Oglethorpe had the use of Bonner's vestments for the occasion. A letter was sent by the Privy Council (*Acts* [New Series], vii. 42) 'to the Bishop of London to lende to the Busshopp of Carlisle, who is appoynted to execute the solempnitye of the Quenes Majesties Coronacion, *universum apparatum pontificium quo uti solent Episcopi in hujusmodi magnificis illustrissimorum regum inaugurationibus.*' The Queen continued to hold Bishop Oglethorpe in kindly remembrance, for she told Bishop Robinson, when he did fealty for Carlisle in 1598, that she was resolved to furnish that see with a worthy man for his sake who first set the crown on her head (Fuller, *Worthies of England*, edition 1684, p. 135).

[4] Compare *Acts of P. C.*, vii. 79, 80, 81, etc., with D'Ewes, *Journ. of the House of Lords*, pp. 19, 21, 23, 26–7, etc. The events of this period have been narrated in chronological order by Rev. Henry Gee (*Elizabethan Clergy and the Settlement of Religion*, 1558–1564).

the Oath of Supremacy, and was deprived on 21 June 1559. But he did not long survive the final overthrow of the papal jurisdiction, for he died on the last day of that year and was buried in the church of St. Dunstan in the West.

When steps were taken to put into operation the Acts of Supremacy and Uniformity as the legislative basis for the settlement of religion, the diocese of Carlisle was bereft of the guidance of its bishop.[1] On the very day that the Prayer Book was to come into use, 24 June, three days after Bishop Oglethorpe's deprivation, letters patent were issued for the royal visitation of the northern province by virtue of the powers vested in the Crown by the Act of Supremacy.[2] The Queen held the English clergy in the hollow of her hand. But it was thought advisable, after the resistance of the episcopate, to proceed prudently and to treat the consciences of the general body of the clergy with as much leniency as possible. The chief duty of the visitors was to enforce the settlement of religion as it was set out in the Prayer Book of 1559. It was the acknowledgment of the *suscepta religio* that played the most prominent part in the visitation of the diocese of Carlisle. Coming so soon after the Marian reaction, when the reforming movement suffered a temporary check, the liturgical changes made so many of the clergy to wince that no one could forecast what would be the result of the visitation. But the unrivalled diplomacy of Cecil in dropping for the present the Oath of Supremacy and fastening attention on the Prayer Book probably averted an ecclesiastical revolt.

The commission which exercised the powers of visitation in the diocese of Carlisle consisted of only three members, Edwin Sandes, S.T.P., Henry Harvey, LL.D., and George Browne, esquire. The first act was to visit the cathedral, and for this purpose the whole capitular body was summoned to the chapter house on Tuesday, 3 October 1559. Prayers having been said and the word of God having been sincerely preached to the people by master Edwin Sandes, the aforenamed visitors, as it is related in the record,[3] sat judicially, and solemnly exercised the royal

---

[1] We have good authority for assuming that Archdeacon Neville was in favour of the liturgical changes then in progress. Soon after the Queen's accession, the following letter was addressed to Cecil by the Earl of Westmorland on the archdeacon's behalf : 'After my vearye hartie comendacons, wheras George Nevell, doctor in devinitie, archedeacon of Carlell, is desirous to be one of the Quenes Ma[ts] chaplins ordenarye to attende one quarter in the yere, thiese are to assure you that notwithstandinge he is of my howsse and kindred, yet if I did not knowe the man to be of honeste conversacon and therwith so well inclined and disposed to set fourthe, in his Cures and ells wheare, all suche good and vertuous doctrine as by the quene her highnes aucthoritie shalbe from time to time set fourthe, so as the procurers of his preferment shall susteine no lack therby, I wolde not voughtsafe this comendacon of him. But consideringe and trusting his service maye be acceptable to that respect, I am bold to desire you to further his sute, wherin yow shall binde me, besides hattie thankes to doo yow the like plesure. And thus fare you well.'.Frome London this xviith daye of December, 1558, by youre asseuryd ffrend, H. Westmirland ' (S.P. Dom. Eliz. vol. i. No. 36).

[2] Ibid. iv. 33.

[3] The record of the Northern Visitation, embodied in a book of 400 pages, is a document of great importance. It is officially known at the Public Record Office as S.P. Dom. Eliz. vol. x. It opens with the commission to the visitors, and contains an account of the visitation of the four dioceses of the northern province (ff. 1–108). Then follow the ' acta et processus habiti et facti coram commissariis—in causis beneficiatorum et restitutionis beneficii, etc.' (ff. 121–205). Further on in the book we get a summary of the *Detectiones et Comperta* and schedules of the absentees from the visitation. As the various

visitation. The venerable dean, Lancelot Salkeld, the last prior of the old foundation, who had passed through all the vicissitudes of this eventful period, appeared personally and subscribed *voluntarie et bono animo* to the articles of the received religion (*suscepte religionis*). Then the commissioners charged him on oath to make a return to the articles of inquiry on the morrow at noon. The four prebendaries also voluntarily and willingly subscribed. Seven out of the eight minor canons appeared and did likewise. The other minor canon was detained in the country by reason of bad health. The commissioners found little to complain of in the internal affairs of the capitular body. The only presentations recorded among the *detectiones et comperta* of the visitation were 'that the Dean, Edward Mytchell and Richard Brandlynge, prehendaries ther, have not byn resident as often as they oughte, nether have theye kepte their quarter sermones accordyng to the statutes. Item, Hugh Sewell, prebendary ther, hath not byn so often resydent as he oughte. Item, Barnabye Kyrkebride hath not byn resident nether kepte his quarter sermones as he oughte to have don.' The success of the visitors in reconciling the dean and chapter to the Prayer Book was a good omen for the rest of the diocese. On the following day, 4 October, the visitors sat in the choir of the cathedral to which the clergy and people of the deaneries of Carlisle and Allerdale were summoned. All the clergy who did not appear were pronounced contumacious. The visitation was continued on Friday in the parish church of Penrith, for the deaneries of Cumberland and Westmorland. During this session the commissioners ordered the fruits, tithes and other emoluments of the rectory of Marton (Longmarton) which William Burye, clerk, then possessed, to be sequestrated, and committed the power of sequestration to John Dudeley, gentleman.[1] Nearly a third of the parish clergy of the diocese absented themselves from the visitation, and were pronounced contumacious.

By one of the provisions of the letters patent directing the visitation, the commissioners were authorized to restore incumbents who were unlawfully deprived during the late reign. Only two cases of restitution to benefices were made by the visitors in the diocese of Carlisle. In the case of the benefice of Ormside (Ormysyde), moved by Thomas Atkynson, rector, against Percival Yates, the commissioners at their session in Penrith on 6 October 1559, adjudged the benefice to Atkinson, and decreed that Yates should be removed from the same. But Atkinson did not enjoy his recovered rectory long, for we read soon after that the church of 'Ormysshed' had been vacant for a whole year by the resigna-

---

sub-sections of this record have been used for the account of the royal visitation of the diocese of Carlisle, it has not been thought necessary to indicate the folio for each statement. The arrangement of the manuscript makes it easy to consult. Strype made use of this book, for he says : 'This commission I saw in the Queen's Paper House bound up in a volume in folio, containing all the inquisitions and matters done and found in this large Northern visitation' (*Annals*, ed. 1709, i. 167).

[1] Bury was not deprived, for he died rector of Longmarton ; and was succeeded by Mr. George Bury, M.A., on 17 April 1562, on the presentation of Henry, Earl of Cumberland (Carl. Epis. Reg., Best, MS. f. 5).

tion of the last incumbent.[1] Marriage was the cause of the deprivation in the other case. The motion was made by Percival Wharton, the former vicar of Bridekirk, against William Graye, the vicar in possession. Both parties appeared before the visitors in the parish church of Kendal on 10 October. Graye stated 'that the sayde Percyvall Wharton was instituted and inducted in the sayd benefice and beynge in possession was depryved for that he was maryed and as to the statutes he doth refer himself to the same.' The benefice was adjudged to Wharton, who enjoyed it till 1563, when he became vicar of Kirkbystephen.[2] The detections or *comperta* presented against the laity were neither specially characteristic of the time nor of a very serious nature. The church-wardens and parishioners of Morland, Great Salkeld, Shap, and Skelton presented that they had no register book; the church of Great Salkeld was in decay ; the parishioners of Warcop lacked a Paraphrase, though they had a box for the poor ; the churches of Skelton and Kirkandrews had no curates; presentations for breaches of morality were made only by the churchwardens of Cliburn and Newbiggin. When we remember that these detections were made in answer to the Articles of Inquiry, the churchwardens having first touched the most holy Gospels of God, it cannot be said that the diocese of Carlisle was in an unsound condition. The notable feature of the visitation was the alacrity with which the main body of the clergy subscribed to the Prayer Book, for though the number of absentees swells to a formidable list, the figures are deceptive, as several of the incumbents were pluralists or non-resident and subscribed in other places.[3] At a later date we shall be able to estimate the value of this conformity to the majority of the clergy and how much of it was due to fear.

The conformity of Dean Salkeld was a great blow to a distinguished personage who was anxiously expecting to obtain his place. For more than two centuries it has been maintained that the dean of Carlisle was deprived by the visitors of 1559, but we have already shown that no fault was found in him at that time. As the error has been so often repeated[4] it may be convenient if we state the efforts that were unsuccessfully made to bring about his ejectment. The following letter

---

[1] 'Item quod ecclesia de Ormysshed in comitatu Westmerland, Carliolensis Dioceseos, vacat in presenti et vacavit per annum integrum per resignacionem ultimi incumbentis' (Exch. Cert. Bishops' Inst. Carl., No. 1). On 20 July 1565 Richard Towlson was collated to the rectory on the death of Christopher Parker, the last incumbent (Carl. Epis. Reg., Best, f. 19).

[2] Percival Wharton was appointed to the free chapel in the castle of Penrith in 1552 (Memo. R. Records, East., 5 Edw. VI. m. 33). He vacated the incumbency in 1554, when he had an exoneration of £23 exacted from him for the fruits of the said chapel (ibid. Mich., 1 and 2 Phil. and Mary, m. 194).

[3] For instance, George Nevell, rector of Bolton in Alderdale, was preconized at Carlisle, and, as he did not appear, was pronounced contumacious, but he must have appeared and subscribed at Penrith as rector of Great Salkeld, for his name does not find a place in the black list for the deanery of Cumberland in which his benefice was situated.

[4] It seems that Hugh Todd was the first to start the theory of Dean Salkeld's ejection in 1559 for refusing the supremacy (*Notitia Ecclesie*, p. 8). To Todd may be traced the error in Le Neve (*Fasti*, ed. Hardy, iii. 246), and in all the local histories. It is worthy of note that early controversialists like Nicholas Sander, Bridgwater and Dodd did not claim Dean Salkeld as a papist, for his name does not appear on their lists.

from Sir Thomas Smith, addressed to Cecil and dated 9 September 1560, throws a much needed light upon a very strange transaction.

S[r]. As I have bene ever so I praye yow let me be now bolde to troble yow in my small cawses. How be it I do not thinck this small. Ye know in Quene Maries tyme, as from diverse other whome they did not favor they toke away all spirituall livinge, so from me they toke the provostshippe of Eaton and the Deanery of Carleill. Eaton in dede I was content *quasi nolens volens* to resigne and did resigne. But the deanerie of Carleill I never did resigne nor was therof deprived, and to saie the truth they never made matter of yt, but gave it streight to one S[r] Launcelot Salkeill. Now in this tyme emongs other I partlie at your advice put my peticon up before my Lord of Caunterburie and other the Commissioners to be restored. Citacon was decrede and sent downe and not aunswerid, for the waye beinge so farre and those contrey men have all the shiftes in the worlde to avoide the lawe. Well, another was decreed and sent downe, enclosed within a Lettre directed from my Lords the Commissioners to the Maior of Carleill to se it servid. Yet wolde he not aunswer nor make a procter, but sent to me another excuse of sicknes, and that he wold either come or sende one to me to satisfie me out of hande. Now this Salkeld is dede, and I know nothinge dothe let whie I shold not enioie my Deanery of Carleill as frelie as ever I did. And therefore I am so bolde as to declare this unto yowe, that if eny labor be made to the Quenes Majestie for it, ye wold be so good as to show my right unto it, and to requier hir Highnes to be so gracious unto me as to let me enioie that w[ch] is myne owen, and w[ch] no man can take fro me by the lawe. Or if ye will be so good, though no labor be made, yet to shew this to hir Highnes lest it shold be graunted unwares, for if it shold be given to eny other (as I trust her highnes, being enformid of my right, will not) I must enter my sute against hym as an usurper, as I did against this Launcelote Salkelde, who, although he did enioie it all Quene Maries tyme, yet being now cited, neither wold nor could have aunswerid me. And after all kiend of delaies, now this Michaelmas I dowted not to have had hym deprivid and removid, one of the prebendaries there, a verie honest man, and whom the said Salkeld did sende unto me to entreate me to staie the sute against hym for a tyme, sent his man unto me with certaigne word of the said Salkeld's deth, w[ch] was on Tewisday the thirde of this moneth, willinge me to tak the Deanery uppon me and to declare the same with som open doeinge to the hole Chapitre. Which thinges I did miende to do, but not before I had made yow privie unto it and had furst your aide and advise. I praye yow let me be so bolde as to crave an aunswere of yow by this bearer my servaunt, if it be not to moche troble unto yow. I wold have waited uppon yow myself, but my rewme is now so sore uppon me that it puttith me in feare of an agew, but I trust with good guidaunce it shall rather be feare than daunger. Thus I committ yow to God From Theydon Mount in Essex the ixth of September, 1560. Yowres allwais to commaund, T. Smith.[1]

Amazement is scarcely the word to express our feelings at the audacious perversion of the truth which this pillar of the Reformation had made with regard to Dean Salkeld's connection with the capitular body. But a new anxiety was before him. There was another candidate for the vacant deanery in the person of Hugh Sewell, one of the prebendaries. We must, however, allow Sir Thomas to tell his story to the end. There is another letter from him 'to the right honorable S[r] Will[m] Cicill, knight, principall secretarie to the Quenes Majestic.' It is as follows :—

' S[r]. When I cam fro the Cowrte havyng reposed my trust and confidence in yow after so gratious words of the quenes Majestie, I did so quiet myself that I thought this mater at an eand and me happy. Now I understand by my freend Michel that there is still a broile in it, and that there should be a commission derected out, w[ch]

---

[1] S.P. Dom. Eliz. xiii. 30.

wherfore it should be I can not gesse. Yf for restitucon, I am in possession of the Deanery and so taken and reputed at Carliell as Deane, ffor there thei all know my right. And agayne for that mater it is all ridie before the Commissioners in the consistorie and two citacons were sent from my l(ord) of Cant(erbury) and the rest of the Commissioners to the lat usurper therof in his lief tyme t'apere and shew cawse whie he should not be avoided and I restorid, afore whom, if eny man have eny thyng against me, he may obiect it. Yf y° enquire of Sewell's habilitie, both my l(ord) of London and my l(ord) of Worcester and all the rest of the quenes Majesties visitors there knowes hym well enough, a man most unworthie not onely that but eny such rowme. And even in Quene Maries tyme when I had not myche favor as ye knowe, and mater was so right agaynst me, and partlie as the compleyning of Barnaby Kirkbride and hym, we were all callíd before the cownscell. And when I was fownd innocent, there aperid such fowle matr agaynst them two for spoilyng of the churche and devidyng the goodes therof amonge them selves, and other wise misusyng of the revenues therof that the were comytted to the Flet. But what hath he to do with the Deanery now except to resigne it ? I still must crave of you, seyng I beg no new thyng, but to enioy myne owen, and desire nothyng so myche as quietnes to contynewe as ye have bene myn earnest freende and help that such one as he be not borne agaynst me to make contro- versie in my right where he hath none. For as I am contente with my pore livyng, so methynk's in this world I should not feare that it should be demynisshed. Thus ones agayn and still beyng bolde to troble yow, I comyt yow to God. From Mounthall the xxiii of October, 1560. Y꜀ allwais assuridlie, T. Smith.[1]

It is quite true that Sewell and Kirkbride appeared before the Council on 23 October 1555, in answer to summons, and the charges against them were committed on 10 November following to Sir Edward Hastings, master of the horse, and Bourne, one of the secretaries, for examination, with power to send them to prison if they thought good till the matter was further investigated.[2] Though Bishop Sandes selected Sewell to preach at the Penrith session of the visitation in 1559, he can have had little respect for a man who was a zealous papist in Mary's reign and an ardent reformer as soon as Elizabeth came to the throne. Bishop Grindal, the other prelate to whom Sir Thomas Smith referred, informed Cecil three years afterwards that Sewell was 'discreditted by reason of his inconstancie.'[3]. The importunity of the worthy knight at last prevailed, for Lancelot Salkeld died on 3 September 1560, and Sir Thomas Smith was installed in the deanery on the twentieth of the same month.[4]

The clergy of the diocese had a little breathing time to reflect on the ordeal through which they had just passed before they were again called upon to renew their allegiance to the religious settlement. Mean- while the see had to be supplied with a bishop. As yet Bishop Ogle- thorpe was the only clergyman of the diocese of Carlisle who suffered by the legislative changes made in the first parliament of the Queen. Though there was no legal impediment in the way of filling up the bishopric rendered vacant by the bishop's deprivation, no appointment

---

[1] S.P. Dom. Eliz. xiv. 27.
[2] *Acts of the* P. C. [new series], v. 188, 192.
[3] Lansd. MS. (Burghley Papers, 1562–3), vi. 86. Hugh Sewell was appointed canon of the cathedral on 20 August 1547, on the death of William Florence (Rymer, *Fœdera*, xv. 190). The dean and chapter made him vicar of St. Lawrence, Appleby, in April 1559, and he was instituted to Caldbeck in Decem- ber 1560 (Exch. Cert. Bishops' Inst. Carl., No. 1).
[4] Exch. Cert. Bishops' Inst. Carl., No. 1.

had been made for over a year after his death. It was probably about the time of the northern visitation that Edwin Sandes was nominated to Carlisle, but he gave no reasons for declining it except a general reluctance to undertake the responsibilities of the episcopal office.[1] In urging Bernard Gilpin, the Apostle of the North, to accept the nomination early in the following year, Sandes reminded him that there was no man in that part of the kingdom fitter than himself to be of service to religion. He informed him also that by the Queen's favour he should have the bishopric just in the condition in which Dr. Oglethorpe left it ; nothing should be taken from it, as had been the case with some others. Gilpin is said to have replied that if any other bishopric but Carlisle had been offered to him, he might possibly have accepted it, but in that diocese he had so many friends and acquaintances, of whom he had not the best opinion, that he must either connive at many irregularities, or draw upon himself so much hatred, that he should be less able to do good there than any one else.[2] Ultimately, the see was filled by the consecration of John Best on 2 March 1561,[3] a man who had been a select preacher for the northern visitors, and who had been instituted by them to the benefice of Romaldkirke,[4] in the diocese of Chester, void by the deprivation of Bishop Oglethorpe. There can be little doubt that Sandes was the instrument of his preferment.

In a few months after the see was filled by the consecration of Bishop Best, steps were taken to bring those clergy to conformity who had refused subscription to the *suscepta religio* during the royal visitation of 1559. Early in 1561 the lord president of the north was ordered to inquire into certain secret conventicles of recusants which were reported to have been held in Cumberland and Westmorland and the other northern counties. In the following May a commission, consisting of the civil and ecclesiastical rulers of the northern province, was issued

---

[1] *Zurich Letters* (Parker Society) 1558-1579, No. xxxi. : Burnet, *Coll. of Rec.*, iii. 382-3. In this letter, Sandes told Peter Martyr, on 1 April 1560, that he had returned to London fatigued in mind and body after his labours in the northern parts of England. The see of Worcester had been thrust upon him by the Queen, though he had wished to decline it, as he had done that of Carlisle, to which he had been nominated before. He relates his action in the northern visitation in taking down and burning ' all Images of every kind.' Then he adds significantly : ' Only the popish vestments remain in our church, I mean the copes, which, however, we hope will not last very long.' This hope of the good bishop was never realized. The dean and chapter of Carlisle, replying to Bishop Rainbow's articles of visitation in 1666, stated that ' necessary utensils for the performance of Divine Service we have, and ornaments, as copes, etc., we intend shortly to have. But some of the Church utensils were imbezilled in the late times of usurpation, as the brazen Eagle, upon which ye chapters were read ' (*Statutes of Carlisle Cathedral*, ed. J. E. Prescott, p. 30). In an inventory dated 1 February, 1674, belonging to the same church, there are mentioned ' two wrought and embroidered copes ' which the dean and chapter still possess (ibid. p. 35).

[2] *Mémoirs of Bernard Gilpin*, ed. C. S. Collingwood, pp. 122-5 ; *Life of Bernard Gilpin*, ed. William Gilpin, pp. 58-60 ; Fuller, *Church Hist.*, bk. ix. 63-4.

[3] Strype, *Life of Parker*, edition 1711, p. 67 ; *Machyn's Diary*, Camden Soc., p. 252. Sir John Hayward gives the surname of ' Beast ' to this bishop, the way in which ' Best ' was probably pronounced in the sixteenth century (*Annals of Eliz.*, Camden Soc., p. 27). John Best had been deprived of his benefice in 1555, and afterwards went about privately from place to place in Lancashire and the adjoining counties preaching the Gospel to select companies assembled by assignation, and sometimes giving the Communion (Strype, *Mem.*, ed. 1721, iii. 222, 471).

[4] S.P. Dom. Elizabeth, vol. x.

with the view of tendering the Oath of Supremacy to the clergy.[1] Bishop Best, who was a member of this commission, undertook the first visitation of his diocese, backed up by its protection and armed with its powers. It was during this visitation that the real trial of strength between the Old and New Learning was made in the diocese. The year 1561 marks a memorable period in the history of the reforming movement in which the church of Carlisle passed once and for all from the papal jurisdiction. From the bishop's own pen we have an account of the reception he met with from the clergy and laity of the diocese. After three sermons in the cathedral church, the common people, with much rejoicing, affirmed that they had been deceived. The same thing happened for the next two weeks throughout all his visitation; the gentlemen of the country received him in every place with much civility. He was unable to express his obligations to Lord Wharton and Lady Musgrave, his daughter, who had entertained him ' for ye Gospell's sake.' Lord Wharton was a worthy, wise man, and very well beloved in the country, in whose time, as the Bishop had heard, the country was never so well governed. But he had a very poor opinion of the clergy. 'The preistes,' he reported to Cecil,

> are wicked ympes of Antichrist, and for ye moste parte very ignorante and stubburne, past measure false and sotle : onlie feare maketh them obedient. Onlie three absentid themselves in my visitacon, and fled because they wolde not subscribe, of ye which two belonge to my Lorde Dacres and one to ye Earle of Cumberland. Unto which I have assigned dayes undre danger of deprivation. Aboute xii or xiii churches in Gylsland, all undre my Lorde Dacre do not appeare, but bearyng themselves apon my Lorde refuse to come in, and at Stapilton and sondrye of ye other have yet masse openly, at whome my lorde and his officers wynke ; and althoughe they stande excommunycate, I do no furdre medle with them untill I have some aide frome my lorde president, and ye consaile in ye northe, lest I myght trouble ye contrey withe those yt in maner are desperate, and yet I doubte not but by pollycie to make them obedient at my lorde Dacre commyng into ye contrey.

The bishop perceived that Lord Dacre was

> something too myghtie in this contrey and as it were a prynce and ye lorde warden of ye West marches of Scotland and he are but too great frendes.

It was the prevalent opinion in the district that the lord warden suffered the Scots to do harm in England with impunity and put off the days of march and justice on offenders for the purpose of drawing home Lord Dacre, who had been too long detained in London in the opinion of his friends.[2] As the bishop had been only four months consecrated when he commenced his visitation, he had little opportunity of making the personal acquaintance of his clergy or judging of their feelings and difficulties. At all events, it was determined to make an example of one

---

[1] In the commission it is stated that as certain ecclesiastical persons had absented themselves from the late visitation, the commissioners were appointed to administer the oath to all ecclesiastical persons in the northern province and to certify the reception and refusal thereof into Chancery. The text of the commission has been printed by Dr. Gee (*The Elizabethan Clergy*, pp. 172–3) from Pat. 3 Eliz. pt. 10, m. 34d.

[2] S. P. Dom. Eliz. xviii. 21. This letter has also been calendared under Foreign Papers, *Elizabeth*, 1561–2, No. 323.

of those 'wicked imps of Antichrist' without further delay, and for this purpose the aid of the Council in the north was invoked.

The bishop's success in bringing most of the recalcitrant clergy to a state of passive conformity must have exceeded his expectations. Much had taken place in the two years that elapsed since the royal visitation. There had been sufficient time to discuss the ecclesiastical changes and to make up their minds about their future attitude. It is noteworthy that only two of the clergy of the whole diocese, who had absented themselves from the bishop's visitation, pushed their resistance to the extreme limit and refused to acknowledge the legislative settlement of religion. These men were Hugh Hodgson, rector of Skelton, and Robert Thompson, rector of Beaumont, both churches being in the patronage and under the protection of Lord Dacre, who, as we have seen, was a resolute opponent of the reforming party. As Hodgson had been deprived of his provostship of Queen's College, Oxford, by the royal visitors in 1559, little compunction was felt in proceeding against him at once. Bishop Best had no power as yet to deprive for nonconformity, but as he was a member of the Northern Commission his duty was clear. Hodgson was arrested early in August at Kirkoswald, the house of Lord Dacre,[1] his patron, by the authority of the president and council of the north, and conveyed to York, where the oath was tendered to him, and by him peremptorily and obstinately refused. On 21 August the sentence of deprivation was pronounced,[2] and on 26 November Henry Dacre, bachelor of arts, was instituted to Skelton on the nomination of Lord Dacre, warden of the march.[3] The case of Thompson, rector of Beaumont, did not come on at that time. It was not, however, long delayed, for on 5 May 1562 Henry Haselhead was instituted to the rectory, vacant by the deprivation of Robert Thompson, the last incumbent, who had obstinately refused to take the oath contained in the Act of Parliament. This nomination was also made by Lord Dacre.[4] There can be little doubt that these two recusants were influenced in their resistance by the shelter of the great name of Dacre, a nobleman who, in the words of Bishop Best, was 'something too mighty in this country and as it were a prince.' These were the only victims of the Elizabethan settlement of religion in a diocese which contained at least 120 cures of souls,[5] including curates in quasi-sole charge. If we sum up the whole loss which the diocese sustained by the enforcement of the Act of Uniformity, we cannot count on more deprivations than those of the bishop and two parish priests. It cannot be said that the clergy as a body embraced the liturgical changes with alacrity, but none except those mentioned persisted in their refusal to work the new ecclesiastical system.

---

[1] *Hist. MSS. Com. Rep.* (Rydal MSS.), xii. App. vii. 10. Dacre's influence may be gathered from the fact that the lord president wrote to him, after Hodgson's deprivation, that Richard Dudley might not forfeit his favour in consequence of his having arrested the priest in his lordship's house.
[2] Carl. Epis. Reg., Best, f. 3.
[3] Ibid. f. 4.   [4] Ibid. f. 5.
[5] Harl. MS. 594, f. 9.

When Bishop Best had finished his first visitation and had come to an understanding with his clergy, his difficulties were not by any means surmounted. There was a deep underlying current of disaffection which caused him considerable anxiety for the ultimate triumph of the cause he had espoused. As far as the clergy of the diocese were concerned, the battle of uniformity was fought and won : the papal jurisdiction was shattered : the supremacy of the Crown was treated with toleration : the book of Common Prayer was installed in the churches: the Injunctions were generally accepted and observed. But the clergy alone did not constitute the church ; the laity had still to be reconciled. If it were true, as the Bishop informed Cecil, that the common people heard him gladly, and that some of the gentry had entertained him for the Gospel's sake, yet there was a wide-spread opposition to the principles of the reformed religion among the great magnates of the two counties which forced him to proceed with the utmost caution. Six months after his visitation, on 14 January 1561–2, he opened his mind to Cecil again, and informed him by a secret message of the perilous position in which he stood. First, he said, there are here such rumours, tales and lies secretly blown abroad, partly by writings in French and partly by evil-disposed papists, secretly whispered in corners, that every day men look for a change and prepare for the same. The people desirous of it openly say and do what they wish concerning religion without check or punishment. The rulers and justices of the peace wink at all these things and look through their fingers. When the bishop pointed out these irregularities he only provoked private displeasure. Before the great men came into these parts, he could do more for Christ's Gospel in one day than he could do now in two months. He only wished to punish and deprive certain evil men, who would neither do their office according to the good laws of the realm, nor acknowledge the Queen's supremacy, nor obey him as ordinary. Such men as these were not only supported and tolerated, but also retained as counsellors and brought into open place, whereby those of evil religion were encouraged to be stubborn, and those who embraced the true doctrine were defaced and ignored. These men were kept in private households contrary to the orders of the archbishop of York, the lord president and the commissioners. The bishop dared not to say it was wrong, as he knew the danger thereof; but he assured Cecil that as long as this state of things lasted God's glorious Gospel could not take root there. If he were present to see the rule of Cumberland and Westmorland under the two heads thereof,[1] Lord Dacre and the Earl of

---

[1] Bishop Grindal, writing to Cecil on 21 January 1562–3, besought him to be good to the bishop of Carlisle. There were marvellous practices to deface him ' in my lawless country,' and by him to destroy the cause of religion. If the two noblemen of whom he complained were touched by the authority of the Privy Council, it would be a terror to the rest (Lansd. MS. vii. 57 ; *Remains of Abp. Grindal*, Parker Soc., pp. 267–8). Grindal always maintained a lively interest in the county of his birth, though he had not a very high opinion of its religious condition. In another letter to Cecil, dated 17 May 1563, he said that ' I have offte thowghte to make a generall sute to you for regarde for that litle Angle wher I was borne, called Cowplande, parcell off Cumberlande, the ignoranteste parte in Religion and moste oppressed off covetouse landlordes off anie one parte off this realme to my knowlege. I entende att my

Cumberland, it would cause him to weep. By the hand of a trusty friend he sent him a copy of certain articles in the French tongue which had been circulated in the diocese, causing much talk and great rejoicing among the papists, with such wishing and wager making about the alteration of religion, such rumours and tales of the Spaniards and French landing in Scotland and in the west marches of England for the reformation of the same, alienating the people's hearts which were quieted before. Little wonder that the people, after their experience of the rapid changes in religion under Edward VI. and Mary, were becoming bewildered, and were slow to accept the Elizabethan settlement 'for feare of a shrewid torne.'[1] Time only could give them confidence and wean them from their old ways.

When we turn to Bishop Best's relations with the members of the capitular body of the diocese, we shall find that little help or encouragement could be gained from that quarter. As a matter of fact this good prelate was obliged to fight the battle of the Reformation single-handed; his greatest enemies were the men of his own house. Writing to Cecil on 15 April 1563, he complained that owing to the absence of Dr. Smith, the dean, the church of Carlisle was going to decay; their woods were almost destroyed; the leases of their farms were made to kinsmen for three or four score years, though the limit was twenty-one years by their statutes,[2] the canons themselves taking the profits; where ten pounds were allowed yearly for repairs, nothing was done; almost as little was done where thirty pounds were allotted for the poor and the mending of highways; no residence was kept, no accounts; the prebendaries turned everything to their own gain. The bishop was unable to bring about reform by his visitation, for they were confederate together, and the losses were their own. Three of the

nexte cominge to you to discourse more largely off the state theroff which godde wyllynge shall be shortly. I have no more to saye for this matter, butt only to praye you yff yor graunte be nott fullye paste to take order bothe for the goode education off the Warde and nott to leave the poore tenantes subiecte to the expilation off these countrey gentlemen without some choyse' (Lansd. MS. vi. 51). Twenty years after this date he founded the Grammar School of St. Bees in the 'litle Angle' of Cumberland where he was born.

[1] S.P. Dom. Eliz. xxi. 13. The articles in French, which were circulated in the diocese and caused Bishop Best so much disquietness, were called 'Articles of the Religion,' scheduled under several heads (S.P. Foreign, Eliz. 1561-2, No. 771).

[2] The seventh statute contains the following restriction on leases: 'We will also that no lands shall be let on lease beyond twenty-one years, nor from time to time, as from three years to three years, or from seven years to seven years, or by way of renewal of any term after it shall have expired. Nevertheless, we permit, that houses or buildings in cities and villages may be let on lease for a term of fifty years or at the most of sixty years' (Stat. of the Cathedral Church of Carl., ed. J. E. Prescott, p. 34). These leases were afterwards the source of much trouble. From a statement by Attorney-General Gilbert Gerard, called the 'Case of the Colledge of Carlisle,' drawn up in 1568, we learn that most of the judges, but not all, thought that the leases were valid, though issued by the dean and chapter of Carlisle with a variation from the proper style and title. An authoritative decision in the courts was much needed (S.P. Dom. Addenda, Eliz., xiv. 31, 38). When 'Mr. Wolley, her Highnes' secretary for the Latyn tounge,' was appointed to the deanery of Carlisle in January 1577-8, he was instructed 'to understande the state of that churche, to th'ende that such thinges as were a misse might be reformed.' Certain of the same College remained in deep arrearages to the church; the accounts should be looked into; the tenants backward with their rents should be urged to pay [Acts of P. C. (new series), x. 131-2]. There are three interesting writs from Charles I. on the subject of leases made by the bishop and the dean and chapter of Carlisle in Carl. Epis. Reg. Potter, ff. 286-8.

prebendaries were unlearned and the fourth unzealous. In a word, 'the Citie is decaid by theym, and Godes truth sclanderyled.' As a new warden of the western marches was about to be appointed, he recommended that some wise and grave men of experience should be joined with him in the commission, for it was hard to find a man that should not be quickly corrupted there and buy and sell poor men's goods and lives. The sheriff was vexing him so much about the affairs of the late Bishop Oglethorpe that his estates were of little value to him.[1] Soon after this terrible indictment was delivered, Barnaby Kirkbride, one of the 'unlearned' prebendaries, was gathered to his fathers, and a vacancy in the capitular body was created. The bishop did not spare 'horseflesshe' in order that his own nominee might be appointed. Gregory Scott was posted up to London with a letter to Bishop Grindal in furtherance of his candidature. In a letter to Cecil, begging the appointment of Scott, Bishop Grindal stated that the bishop of Carlisle had often complained to him of the want of preachers in his diocese, having no help at all from his cathedral church. Sir Thomas Smith, his dean, was occupied in the Queen's affairs, as he knew ; all his prebendaries (Sewell only excepted, who was discredited by reason of his inconstancy) were 'ignorante preistes or olde unlearned monkes.' One of the said unlearned prebendaries had lately departed, and the bishop of Carlisle was anxious to obtain the void prebend for Gregory Scott, 'beinge thatt countrie man borne, well learned and off goode zeale and synceritie,' as Bishop Grindal partly knew by his own experience. The prebend was in value just £20 as he had been informed.[2] It is satisfactory to know that Scott, with the help of such distinguished patrons, obtained the appointment and was installed on 2 May 1564, in the presence of Thomas Tukie, the official principal of Carlisle, and six of the minor canons, but none of the prebendaries assisted at the function.[3] Bishop Best, being an advanced reformer of the Helvetian type, kept about him as private chaplains certain refugees, who had returned to England on the accession of Queen Elizabeth, and gradually slipped them into benefices or prebends as they became vacant by the death of the old priests. One of these, a Scotsman called John Mawbraye, Maybraye, or Makebray, a noted preacher at Frankfort in Queen Mary's days, was installed in the cathedral on 18 January 1565–6,

[1] Lansd. MS. vi. (Burghley Papers, 1562–3).

[2] Ibid. vi. 86. Bishop Grindal's letter is dated 'frome my howse att Fulham, 27 Decemb. 1563,' and endorsed ' B. of London for Mr. Scott to be a prebendary of that church.' It has been printed by the Parker Society in the *Remains of Abp. Grindal*, pp. 285–6. Strype has explained that from the bishop's allusion to Sewell's inconstancy we may infer that he was ' a complier under the late religion ' ; indeed Sewell changed his religion on every demise of the Crown. But the same writer misunderstood the reference to the departure of 'one of the said unlearned prebendaries,' as Kirkbride had died, and not ' fled abroad, perhaps to Louvain or some other place, as many of the papists now did ' (Strype, *Life of Grindal*, edition 1710, p. 85).

[3] Carl. Epis. Reg., Best, f. 14. Gregory Scott, the new prebendary, was a writer of verses and published ' A briefe Treatise agaynst certayne Errors of the Romish Church, etc. Very plainly, notably and pleasantly confuting the same by Scriptures and auncient writers. Compiled by Gregory Scot, 1570. Perused and licensed according to the Quene's Maiestie's Iniunction, 1574.' There can be no doubt about the strong Protestant flavour of the poet's sentiments.

on the death of Edward Mitchell, one of the prebendaries.[1] As
time went on, the dawn on the ecclesiastical horizon began to break
before the bishop's eyes, and though he often complained of failing
health and ' paynfull travails,' he lived to see a certain measure of success to crown his efforts. The poor opinion that Bishop Best entertained about the intellectual equipment and administrative ability of his
prebendaries was not altogether justifiable. Charges so sweeping are
seldom upheld. It is true that the state of the capitular body was bad
enough, but we must not overlook the sentiments of Sir Thomas Smith,
the dean, about the conduct of his diocesan and the effect of his intermeddling in capitular affairs. In a letter to Cecil from Toulouse on
10 February 1564–5, he complained of ' that busy Bishop of Carlisle '
who had made such turmoil among the prebendaries of the church
there, and pointed out that the bishop had more ' tongue ' than wisdom
and goodwill. The dean did not wish to excuse the prebendaries, ' as
they have done, so let them have ' ; but there was one Mitchell there,
whom he had left as his vice-dean, who almost alone had held up that
church by his worldly policy, so as to bring it out of debt. Every
prebendary, the dean reminded Cecil, was catching for himself and
his friends what he could in these days of religious changes. He
knew the fashion of these countrymen well enough, that if the presence
of Mitchell was withdrawn from the cathedral, the church would not
stand long ; but what betwixt the bishop and the prebendaries, the
dean was unable to get a penny out of them for a twelvemonth or
more.[2]

The bishop had his diocese in some state of organization at this
period so far as it could be expected from one in his difficult position.
From a memorandum which he supplied to the Privy Council in July
1563 in answer to certain articles of inquiry, we get a good idea of the
condition and characteristics of the ecclesiastical area over which he
ruled. In answer to the first article he replied that the diocese of
Carlisle contained two shires, Cumberland and Westmorland ; but out
of the former Coupland was exempted as being in the diocese of Chester,
and out of the latter the barony of Kendal was exempted, being in the
same diocese. By the second article the Council inquired ' into what

[1] Among the refugees at Frankfort in 1554, Strype enumerates ' the Scotch preacher, John Makebray, who was the first that preached the Gospel to the English there for about a year, and then went
to another church in the Low Country (*Mem.*, edition 1721, iii. 146–7). Makebray appears also in the
list of exiles given by Whitehead in his *Brief Survey of the Troubles begun at Frankfort*, printed in 1575.
In the same list we have the names of such north country men as Edmond Grindal and Edwin Sandes
(Dodd, *Church Hist.*, ed. Tierney, ii. 67). In July 1564 Lord Scrope, reporting to Cecil his conferences
with the Scottish warden at Dumfries, stated that ' a chaplin of the Bishop of Carlisle, called Mawbraye,
and two of the prebendaries of the same church, preached there several days to great audiences who liked
their sermons and doctrine' (Foreign Papers, *Elizabeth*, 1564–5, No. 558). In the record of his collation
to the prebend, to which he was inducted by Sewell, he is described as ' magister Johannes Maybraye,
verbi Dei minister.' Mitchell, who preceded him, was ' in legibus bacchalarius' (Carl. Epis. Reg.,
Best, f. 20).
[2] S.P. Foreign, Eliz., 1564–5, No. 980(7). Strype has much to say on the ' unreasonable leases
in the church of Carlisle ' and the efforts that were made ' to redress the mischiefs the Popish spoilers
of the church now reformed had done, as well out of malice as covetousness ' (*Annals*, ed. 1709, i. 510–1).

72

maner of regimentes' the diocese was divided ; whether the same be archdeaconries, deaneries or such like ; how many there were with their distinct names ; 'who occupieth the same roomes at this present and wher they are to your understanding ?' The bishop answered that the diocese had but one archdeaconry, and that the archdeacon's name was Mr. George Nevell, who was not resident within the diocese, but lived at a place in Richmondshire called Well ; the diocese was divided into one deanery of the cathedral church and four rural deaneries, viz. Cumberland, Westmorland, Carlisle and Allerdale ; the dean of the cathedral, who was always absent by dispensation as he alleged, had under him four prebendaries of the same church, of whom none kept residence there, but lay upon their benefices abroad in the diocese.   In reply to the third question he reported that as yet he knew not of any 'exempte or peculiar places' within the circuit of his diocese where he had not full jurisdiction as ordinary.   The fourth and fifth articles were concerned with the number of churches within each archdeaconry, deanery or other regiment, which of these churches were parochial, how many of them had parsons, vicars or curates ; 'and wheras the parishes are so large as they have divers chappells of ease which have or ought to have curates or ministers in them, to certifie howe manye be of that sort in everie suche parishe, with the names of the townes or hamletts, where the same churches or chapells are so scituate,' and also to state how many households were within every parish or member of any parish that had such churches or chapels of ease.   In the bishop's return of over one hundred parishes, there is no indication that any of the benefices were destitute of curates, or that there was any lack in the supply of clergy.   Extensive parishes like Crosthwaite, Holmcultram and Kirkbystephen had the largest populations, exceeding those of the two Carlisle parishes, and such places as Kirkandrews-on-Eden, Grinsdale, Denton and Rocliffe were very sparsely populated.[1]

The attention of the second parliament of the Queen was turned to the enforcement of the Royal Supremacy among the clergy and laity alike.   The chief provisions of the penal Act[2] of 1563 were concerned with the repression of papal sympathy and the acceptance of the oath of allegiance.   Under this new legislation the justices of the peace were directed to search out defenders of papal authority and certify the presentments into the Queen's Bench under penalty.   Before the justices could be employed on this delicate business, it was necessary to have satisfactory assurances of their loyalty to the religious settlement and their capabilities to administer the Act.   From Bishop Best's return of the justices, dated 18 November 1564, we get an insight into the condition of conformity among the educated portion of the laity of his diocese. As soon as the bishop had received the Council's letter he had a conference with such 'grave wyttye men, good in relligion as favourers of the policie of the realme nowe established,' but with men of contrary

---

[1] Harl. MS. 594, f. 9. Compare also ibid. 595, f. 85.
[2] 5 Eliz. cap. 1.

religion he durst have no conference. A great obstacle to the good success of the ' policies established ' was the perpetual continuance of the sheriffwick of Westmorland, by which means there was always some one in office who by no means favoured 'the true way.' Suspicious people were allowed to pass through the country unapprehended, and some had 'in the wyld mountaynes preached in chappells.' The Queen's receivers and other officers of the lower sort, not being good in themselves, often discouraged such as dared not displease them. The tenants of noblemen in the two counties were afraid to declare themselves in favour of ' that way ' for fear they should lose their farms. The justices of assize, though they made ' a good face of relligion in gevinge of the charge,' in all their talks and acts showed themselves not favourable towards any man or cause of religion, which the people marked and talked much of. The bishop enclosed the names of all the justices of the peace of the two shires within his diocese, with notes of religion, learning and wisdom, both according to his own knowledge, and from what he could learn by conference with trustworthy men ; also the names of such as in religion were sincere and favourable to the settlement, ' most fytt men to be appoynted in place of some of the other.' The value of the bishop's opinions on the religious sympathies of the chief laymen of his diocese at this early period of Elizabethan uniformity cannot be exaggerated in point of interest. Of the justices of the peace already in office he reported as follows : ' My Lord Dacre, butt especially my lady his wyfe, are to be reformed in relligion : Sir Thomas Dacre of Lannercost, knight, *Custos Rotulorum* within the countie of Cumberland, to be admoneshed in relligion, and verie unfytt for that office ; Henrye Curwen of Workington, armiger, William Pennington of Muncaster, armiger, John Lampleugh of Lampleugh, armiger, Thomas Myddleton of Skyrwith, armiger, in relligion good and meat to contynue, and the said Myddleton lerned somethinge in the lawes; John Aglionby of Carlill, armiger, Richard Blannerhasset, deade, armiger, not staid in relligion, but to be admoneshedd, and within the lyberties of the Cetie of Carlill none other able but poore men ; Richard Salkeld of Corby or Rosgill, armiger, not good in relligion ; William Myddleton, gentleman, William Pyckringe, gentleman, in relligion evell and not meatt.' The bishop recommended the following to be appointed : ' Henry lord Scroope, lord warden, Mr. George Scroope his brother ; George Lampleughe of Cockermouth, armiger, Henry Towsone of Brydekyrk, armiger, Thomas Layton of Dalemayne, armiger, Mr. Anthony Twhattes of Unerigg, clerk,[1] men of wysedome and good relligion, experyent and learned but not in the lawes ; Thomas Carleton of Carleton, gentleman, Andrewe Huddlestone, gentleman, in relligion good and wyttye men.' In the bishop of Chester's return for the parcel of

---

[1] Anthony Thwaites, S.T.P., was the only clerical justice recommended. He was an early supporter of the reforming policy of Bishop Best, and was present at Rose Castle on 29 September 1561, when that bishop held his first ordination in the diocese. He was appointed to the vicarage of Aspatria in December 1565, a benefice in the bishop's patronage (Carl. Epis. Reg., Best, ff. 3, 20).

Cumberland within his diocese he stated that William Pennington of Muncaster was favourable and Henry Curwen of Workington and John Lamplugh of Lamplugh were unfavourable to the established religion, but that so far as he knew there were no other persons in that district fit to be made justices.[1] It cannot be denied that the reformed doctrine had met with some acceptance among the educated laity of the north-western counties; and though there is evidence of a strong opposition, active resistance was destined to decline as the new ideas made progress among the clergy, and men became more assured that the settlement of religion was permanent and irreversible.

The uncertainty which prevailed about the permanence of the settlement had a serious effect on the supply of a good class of clergy in the northern diocese. Throughout the years of Bishop Best's episcopate, when the strain of the Reformation was greatest, few men were admitted to holy orders by him for work in his own diocese. Two deacons and one priest make up the sum of his ordinations for the first eight years of his episcopate, 1561–8. The educational equipment of candidates for ordination during the episcopates of his successors, Bishops Barnes and May, appears deplorable in the extreme. The mention of a graduate in long lists of deacons and priests is of very rare occurrence. As a rule the clergy had little education except what they received at the village school. It was no uncommon thing for a candidate to be admitted to the diaconate on one day and to be instituted to a benefice on the day following. Early in the struggle for uniformity, when the want of clergy was most acute, the bishops constituted a new order of 'Reader' to tide over the dearth of the right sort of men. These readers were placed in parishes destitute of incumbents, and were obliged to live according to certain rules laid down by the bishops. The new order was not allowed to preach or interpret, but only to read what had been appointed by authority. The ministration of the sacraments and other public rites was forbidden, except the burial of the dead and the churching of women. To the constitution of this new departure in ecclesiastical order Bishop Best gave his adhesion.[2] The influence of such a staff of parochial clergy for the Christian edification of the mass of the people can be well imagined. From the pen of Bishop Henry Robinson, a native of the parish of St. Mary, Carlisle, successively Fellow and Provost of Queen's College, Oxford, we get an authoritative account of the moral condition of the diocese the year after his consecration to its oversight. Writing from Rose Castle on 26 December

---

[1] These letters are now at Hatfield in the possession of the Marquess of Salisbury, and have been calendared by the Hist. MSS. Com. (*Hatfield House MSS.*, i. 306–312) as ' A Collection of Original Letters from the several Bishops, etc., to the Privy Council, with Returns of the Justices of the Peace and others, within their respective Dioceses,' 1564. Miss Mary Bateson has printed those letters in full for the Camden Society in the *Camden Miscellany*, vol. ix.

[2] This is a very interesting document of date not earlier than 1561. It is called ' Injunctions to be confessed and subscribed by them that shalbe admytted Readers,' and bears the signatures of the two archbishops and nine bishops, including Bishop Grindal of London and Bishop Best of Carlisle (Add. MS. 19,398, f. 59). Strype says that its provisions were enjoined in 1559 and confirmed by the Convocation of 1562 (*Annals of the Reformation*, ed. 1709, i. 306–7).

1599, the bishop told Cecil that the most part of the gentlemen of the country gave good tokens of soundness in religion, and the poorer sort were generally willing to hear, but withal they were pitifully ignorant of the foundations of Christianity, of the corrupt state of man, of the justice of God against sin, the grace of Christ and the resurrection of the dead. As they were without knowledge, so many of them were without all fear of God, adulterers, thieves, murderers. The chief spring of all this wofulness came principally of the weakness and carelessness of the ministry. In divers places of the Borders, the bishop continued, the churches had walls without covering, and they had none to celebrate divine service, save only certain beggarly runners, who came out of Scotland, neither could men of worth be induced to live there, because their maintenance was withholden and their lives were in continual danger. In the more peaceable parts of the diocese there were some clergymen of very commendable parts both for knowledge and conscience, but their number was very small. Others there were that might do much good if they had half that delight in discharging their function which they had in idleness, vain pleasures and worldly cares. The far greatest number is utterly unlearned, unable to read English truly and distinctly. One great occasion thereof was the great facility of his predecessor in committing the charge of souls to such as were presented by those who cared not how silly the clerk was, so long as they themselves enjoyed the fat of the living. But that was not all, for there were divers churches appropriated and served only with stipendiary curates, divers chapels of ease served at the charges of poor people, because the parish churches were too far from them. These places must be wholly unserved, and so let the people grow from ignorance to brutishness, or else such must be tolerated as will be entertained for five marks or four pounds; the greatest annual stipend that any of the clergy had was twenty nobles towards all charges. It was a heavy but too true description of these poor churches, for redress whereof the bishop submitted himself and his service to Cecil's direction.[1] This was not the peevish complaint of a partizan like Bishop Best when he called the Marian clergy of his diocese ' wicked imps of Antichrist,' but the sober judgment of an earnest prelate taking a dispassionate survey of his charge, and estimating the results of what forty years of the new church policy had wrought upon the manners and sentiments of the people.

A new force was about to be introduced which was destined to upset the calculations of those who were working steadily for uniformity throughout the church. The political action of the papacy in denouncing Queen Elizabeth marked a turning point in the history of conformity to the established doctrine and worship. A body of foreign theologians, sitting at Trent, declared unanimously that it was a grievous sin for Englishmen to attend the prayers and sermons of the English church, and the pope, acting on the decision, published his well-known

[1] S.P. Dom. Eliz. cclxxiii. 56.

bull excommunicating and deposing the Queen. On 15 May 1570 a copy of this document was found on the gates of the house of the Bishop of London, placed there by a man named Felton. It was the casting of the die. The pace of the reforming movement was quickened and developed into a struggle between England and Rome. We shall not stop to notice the precautions taken on the English side to protect the Queen and to safeguard the future of the established religion. But one cannot help expressing compassion for the men who were not altogether dissatisfied with the national policy, and yet unable to dissociate themselves from the fascination of the old worship. A new situation was created. Civil allegiance was now declared to be incompatible with papal sympathies. Though Felton's act was known and discussed in Cumberland very soon after the excommunication was set up, and was producing disastrous results in places so near as Lancashire, Bishop Barnes of Carlisle could write on 27 October 1570 that he was most hopeful of his work in his new diocese. Of a truth, he told Cecil, he never came to a place in the land where more attentive ear was given to the Word than in Carlisle, and that if he could receive the aid of the civil power, he could promise ' as faythfull, paynefull (and if God will) effectuall travell as ever poore Bisshoppe did performe within his cure.' For ten years he had acted as bishop in those north parts, and knew the disposition of the people right well, as he persuaded himself. To tell the truth he had found the commonalty of Cumberland and Westmorland far more conformable and tractable in all matters of religion than ever he found in the better sort in Yorkshire. All will most quietly and reverently hear, ' none will reclayme nor feare by deede,' except the lowland men and certain gentlemen, but attentively and gladly seem to hear and yield to the truth. The bishop was sanguine of great and good success in this ' so rude a countrie,' and yet not by far so rude as the people of many places in the south, nor so far from God's religion as they had been thought. But the publication of the papal bull, though it had not the effect its authors expected, was a real danger, and unless precautions were taken in time, a papal reaction might set in which would prove disastrous to the commonwealth. As a preliminary, he enclosed ' a brefe note ' of the gentlemen of his diocese as they showed themselves, and as he found them, in order that the authorities might know how to act in the case of emergency.[1]

---

[1] The bishop's 'brefe note' is as follows: 'Comb'. Simon Musgrave, miles, licet evangelium profiteatur circa religionem tamen negligens, vanus, atheist,' etc. Henricus Curwen, miles, vir multum jurans, nec timens Deum nec religionem ullam curans: domi nescio quid monstri alit. Christoferus Dacre, armiger, pauperum insignis oppressor, ceterum in partes evangelii inclinare potius videtur quam papismi. Cuthbertus Musgrave de Crokedake, armiger, vanus, inconstans, supersticiosus, ac sanguinarius·papista. Johannes Dalston, armiger, vir vafri ingenii, tempori serviens, et qui maxime extinctum cuperet evangelium. . . . Lee, armiger, licet fautor avitæ religionis, corrigibilis tamen ac mansuetus papista, ingenuæque naturæ, virtutis ac justiciæ amans. Anthonius Barwis, armiger, jurisperitus, evangelio inimicus capitalis in quo signa iræ Dei apparent. Thomas Salkyld, armiger, jurisperitus, maximus hostis evangelii. Richardus Salkyld, armiger, (et) Thomas Hutton, armiger, veritati resistunt, quamque qui maxime. Thomas Denton de Warnehill, armiger, papista, Lovaniensium fautor maximus. Johannes Briskoe, generosus, cordis obdurati veritatem odit. Cane pejus et ang. . . . Henricus Denton de Cardewe, generosus, vir timens Deum ac fautor veritatis. ' .Richardus Blaner-

The publication of the bull deposing the Queen appears to have made little difference to the progress of conformity in the diocese of Carlisle, except that it was the means of redoubling the vigilance of the local authorities and urging them on to a more stringent application of the existing law. Bishop Barnes, on a closer acquaintance with the people of the two counties, took an optimistic view of the prospects of religion within his charge. Writing to Burghley on 19 October, 1571 he thankfully recognized that God had reared up the church of his Christ, and mightily prospered His Gospel and the bishop's simple ministry. 'in this angle and utmoste corner amongst these salvage people,' and he doubted not that in a short time his labours would yield great and good fruit to God and the Queen's Majesty. At this juncture the Bishop's opinions on the state of external conformity in his diocese are of considerable interest. He dared boldly to assure Burghley that at that day there was not one known gentleman or other within his little diocese that openly repined against religion, refused to communicate or come to church to hear divine service, or shunned sermons or openly spoke against the established religion or the ministers thereof. There was the insignificant exception of the Lowlands, consisting of the four parishes of Arthuret, Kirklinton, Bewcastle and Stapleton, amongst the people of which there was neither fear, faith, virtue nor knowledge of God, nor regard of any religion at all. Some indeed were not in all things satisfied or reclaimed, but they were in a good way and coming well forward.[1]

hassett, armiger, Maior Carleolensis, vir mitis, justiciæ pacisque studens, licet papista. Johannes Eaglionbye, armiger, justiciarius Carleolensis, vanus, blasphemusque papista, nullum Dei habens timorem, raptor, pestis, perniciesque reipublicæ. Johannes Blanerhassett, armiger, insignis adversarius veritati. Johannes Lamplewghe, armiger, insignis fautor evangelii, veritatis . . . professor pius. Georgius Lamplewghe, armiger, verus Israelita in quo non est fraus. Henricus Towson, generosus, amicus veritatis. Thomas Carleton, generosus, vir timens Deum, evangelio favens. Thomas Laiton, generosus, virpius, zelotes. Westm': Richardus Lowther, armiger, veritatis adversarius insignis, azilum et propugnator pessimorum quorumcunque. Henricus Crakenthorpe, armiger, Blinkensoppe, armiger, Wyber, armiger, Lancastre, armiger, papistæ. Richardus Dudley, armiger, alter Jehu. Thomas Warcoppe, armiger, aulicæ religionis nec inimicus. Clibburne, generosus, spirans minas maliciamque adversus veritatem. Humfridus Musgrave, armiger, amicum veritatis palam se profitetur. Lancelotus Pickringe, armiger, evangelio favet. Gilpyn, generosus, ex animo evangelium profitetur. Qui juxta regulam evangelii incedunt, pax super illos et misericordia et super Israelem Dei etc. His vero qui contentiosi sunt veritatem resistunt, ventura est gravi Dei indignacio etc.' (S.P. Dom. Eliz. lxxiv. 22, i.)

[1] S.P. Dom. Eliz. Add. xx. 84. The savage state of society and the want of adequate religious instruction on both sides of the Border attracted the attention of the commissioners who met at Carlisle in 1596 to discuss the lamentable effects which the lawless and disobedient disposition of the most part of the inhabitants had wrought between the Marches. The first article agreed upon was 'that the princes be most humbly and earnestly entreated to cause God's ministers of the Word to be planted at every border church, to inform the lawless people of their duty, and to watch over their manners, and that the principal inhabitants of each parish shall put in surety to their prince for due reverence to be used towards their pastors in their offices, and the safety of their persons ; and that to this effect, order may be timely taken for reparation of the decayed churches within the bounds' (Nicolson, *Leges Marchiarum*, 151). A presentation was made by a jury of Cumberland gentlemen at Carlisle on 30 April, 1597, 'that the churche of Bewcastle, the churche of Stapleton, the church of Arthred, being within this Marche, have bene decayed by the space of threescore yeares and more, but we certanely knowe not the patrons of the sayd churches, neyther who ought to buyld the same. And the churche of Lanerdcost ys nowe also in decaye and haith so bene by the space of two or thre yeates last past, but by whome the same ought to be repaired we knowe not. And the churche of Kirklinton is also in decaye, and so haithe contynewed the space of twentie yeare, and that William Musgrave esquier, and Edward Musgrave his sonne, are patrons of the same' (*Border Papers* [Scot. Rec. Pub.], ii. 311-2).

Bishop Barnes was not backward in bringing gentle pressure upon those who were halting in their allegiance between England and Rome in order that the national movement might be accelerated in his diocese. With the High Commission at his back he was armed with coercive power sufficient to meet all his requirements. Archbishop Grindal's visitation of the northern province marked a new era in the history of conformity. His injunctions, drastic in substance and detail,[1] were fraught with consequences of great ecclesiastical interest. The bishop of Carlisle adapted them to the needs of his own diocese. The visitation of 1571 appears to have worked a change of considerable magnitude in the ritual of divine service. At the conclusion of his visitation Bishop Barnes issued a mandate to the eighteen men and churchwardens of Crosthwaite, with the authority of the Queen's Commission in the province of York, that the old accessories of the church service, with which the people had been familiar, but which Archbishop Grindal had stigmatized as 'relics and monuments of superstition and idolatry,' should be utterly defaced, broken and destroyed. The mandate was given at Rose Castle under the Bishop's seal on 31 October 1571, and ran in the names Richard, bishop of Carlisle, Henry, lord Scrope of Bolton, lord warden of the Western Marches, Symon Musgrave, knight, Richard Dudley, esq., Gregory Scott and Thomas Tookye, prebendaries of Carlisle, members of the High Commission. As portions of the document are of considerable interest in describing the ritual changes at this period, we do not hesitate to appropriate them.

'We command and decree,' so the mandate recites, ' that the said eighteen men and churchwardens doe buy and provide for the said church of Crosthwait and use' of the parishioners before Christmas next two fayre large Communion Cups of silver with covers, one fyne diaper napkin for the Communion and Sacramental Bread, and two fayre potts or flaggons of tynne for the wyne, which they shall buy with such moneye as they shall receyve for the chalices, pixes, paxes, crosses, candlesticks, and other church goods which they have to sell, yf the some taken for the same will suffice to pay for the said cuppes, table napkin, pewter potts or flagons ; yf not, a levye or taxe to be cesste through the said parish for the provideing and buying of the premisses. And we furthermore enjoyne that the eighteen men and churchwardens do furthwith sell, alienate and put away to the most and greatest commoditye of the said church all and everye such popish reliques and monuments of superstition and idolatrye as presently remaine in the said parish, of the church or parish goodes, converting the prices thereof receyved to the parish use wholly ; and, namely, two pixes of silver, one silver paxe, one cross of cloth of gold which was on a vestment, one copper crosse, two chalices of silver, two corporase cases, three hand-bells, the scon whereon the Paschall stood, one pair of censures, one shippe, one head of a paire of censures, xxix brasen or latyne candlesticks of six quarters longe, one holy watter tankard of brasse, the canopies which

1 These injunctions will be found in full in the *Remains of Abp. Grindal*, Parker Soc., pp. 121-144, and in summary in Strype's *Life of Abp. Grindal*, edition 1710, pp. 167-170. There can be no doubt, as Strype says, that the Archbishop showed a great zeal for the discipline and good government of the church, but it is questionable whether all the ritual practices which he condemned could be described as ' old popish customs.' There is a strong presumption that both Grindal and Parker, the two archbishops, exceeded their powers as metropolitans in the wholesale destruction of church furniture made in the visitations of 1571. The same remark would apply to the visitation of Bishop Barnes, except in so far as he sheltered himself under the autocratic power of the High Commission. The correspondence between the archbishops on this subject may be read in *Remains of Grindal*, pp. 326-8, or in Strype's *Grindal*, pp., 165-6.

hanged and that which was carryed over the Sacrament, two brasen or latyne chrismatories, the vaile cloth, the sepulcher clothes, the painted clothes with pictures of Peter and Paul and the Trinity; and all other monuments of poperye, superstition, and idolatrye remaininge within the said parishe; and this to be done effectuallye before the first daye of December next, and a perfect accompt of the parcels sold and moneye receyved for the same, to be delivered up unto the ordinarye under the subscription of the vicar of Crosthwait, three of the eighteen men, and the three churchwardens before the sixt daye of December next. We also enjoyne that the fower vestments, three tunicles, fyve chestables, and all other vestments belonging to the said parish church and to the chappells within the said parishe be presently defaced, cut in peces, and of them (yf they will serve thereunto) a covering for the pulpitt and quissions for the church made and provided: and likewise the albes and amysies sold, and faire lynnen clothes for the Communion Table, a covering of buckram frynged for the same, to be bought and provided before Christmas next; and that for the chappels in the parish, decent Communion Cupps of silver or of tynne to be provided before Christmas next. We doe also decree and firmlye enjoyne that all and singular the parishioners of this parish of Crosthwait, being of years of discretion and sufficientlye instructed in the grounds and principles of the Christian faith (the examination and approbation whereof we leave and referre to the vicar) shall openlie communicate at least thrise in their parish church yearly, whereof Easter to be one tyme, and at such general Communions the deacons and ministers of chappels of the parish shall come and help and assist the vicar and curate at the ministration of the same. We also decree, ordain and straitlye enjoyne the said eighteen men and churchwardens that this year be, that they before Christmas next prepare, make, erect, and set up a decent perclose of wood wherein the morninge and eveninge prayer shall be read, to be placed without the Quear doore, the length whereof to be twelve foot and the breadth twelve, the height five foot, with seats and desks within the same, the paterne whereof we send you here withal; and that they also see the said church furnished with all books convenient for the same before Christmas next, that is to say, with a Bible of the largest volume, one or two Communion books, fower Psalter books, the two tomes of Homilies, the Injunctions, the Defence of the Apology, the Paraphrasies in Englishe, or instead thereof Marlorate upon the Evangelists and Beacon's Postill and also four Psalter books in metree. We decree also, enjoyne and straitly charge and command that from hencefurth there be no divine service publiquely said in this parish church nor any of the chappels thereunto belonginge, nor any bells runge on any abrogate holidayes, nor any concourse of idle people to the church or chappel on such forbidden days, that is to wette, on the feasts or dayes of Allsowles or the evenning and night before, on St. Katharine, St. Nicholas, Thomas Becket, St. George, the Wednesdayes in Easter and Whitson weekes, the Conception, Assumption, and Nativity of our Ladye, St. Lawrence, Mary Magdalen, St. Anne or such like, which are forbidden to be kept holidaye by the lawes of this realme. And we straitly command that none hereafter use to pray upon anye beads, knots, portasses, papistical and superstitious Latyne Prymers or other like forbidden or ungodly bookes either publiquely or openlye, commandinge the vicar, curate and churchwardens diligently and circumspectly to inquire hereof from tyme to tyme and duely to present without favour all offenders against this injunction from tyme to tyme. We command also that from hencefourth there be no Communion celebrated at the burial of the dead nor for any dead nor any monethes mynds, anniversaryes, or such superstitions used.

These injunctions were 'for ever to be observed within the parish of Crosthwait and chapels thereof' under the heaviest fines and penalties.[1]

---

[1] Before issuing the above orders the commissioners had settled divers disputes in the parish of Crosthwaite and made certain awards about the mode of electing and admitting the eighteen men and churchwardens, the parish clerks' wages, and the school stock. The whole mandate was issued in duplicate, one copy to be kept in the parish chest of Crosthwaite and the other to be deposited among the records of the Commission. The original of the parish copy was brought to Bishop Nicolson by Mr. Clarke, curate of Crosthwaite, from the vicar, eighteen men and churchwardens, and was transcribed by him on 19 July, 1704. The bishop's transcript is now preserved in the *Nicolson MSS.* ii. 189–199, in the custody of the dean and chapter of Carlisle.

After this visitation the sacred instruments of divine service were sold and put to profane uses.[1]

But the work of visitation was not given up wholly to destruction. At his cathedral church, which he visited on 26 October 1571, he took steps to institute a course of preaching throughout the year which in his opinion would contribute to the augmentation of Christian knowledge in that city. The visitation was held in the upper chamber (*in solario eminentiori*) of the chapter house between the hours of nine and eleven in the forenoon, where all the ministers of the church were preconized and appeared, with the exception of Sir Thomas Smith, the dean, who answered by proxy. After the delivery of the charge the Bishop proceeded to unfold his scheme for the greater increase of the church of Christ under his pastoral care. Additional sermons were to be undertaken by the Bishop himself, the dean, archdeacon and prebendaries on stated[2] Sundays and holy days at different times of the year.[3] The adults and children of the city were to receive systematic instruction in the church catechism in the parochial churches of St. Mary and St. Cuthbert on days set apart for that purpose. The lecturer of the cathedral (*sacre theologie prelector*), who had his duties defined as catechist in the choir, was required to supply the place of any of the preachers who might be unavoidably absent when his turn came. All the ministers of the church, including the dean, greater canons, lesser canons, schoolmasters, choristers and bedesmen were counselled to receive the holy Eucharist (*sacram sanctamque synaxim*) at least eight times a year, viz., on the first Sunday of Advent, Christmas Day, the first Sunday of Lent, Easter Day, Pentecost, and on the fifth, twelfth, and nineteenth Sundays after Trinity. The Bishop enjoined the minor canons, who had been suspected of papism (*suspectos papismo*), to repeat the Articles of Religion with an audible voice in St. Mary's church at the time of divine service after the Apostles' Creed, as well as in the presence of the congregations of the churches of which they were incumbents. That there might be no shirking of the duty, appointed days were declared for the purpose.

As yet no trace of nonconformity has been found in the diocese of Carlisle. Within the womb of the church there was a struggle of extreme elements, but their time of birth had not yet arrived. The incumbents of Dacre, Melmerby and Crosby Ravensworth were deprived in 1572 for refusing subscription to the Thirty-nine Articles of Religion,

---

[1] William Fleming of Rydal wrote to his cousin William Lowther of 'Sewborwens,' on 4 June 1576, asking for the loan of plate, as he was expecting a great number of worshipful friends and strangers. A 'chalice' was enumerated in the memorandum of receipt, and Fleming was so pleased with it that he asked for the 'patrone' which belonged to it, in order to make a trencher (*Hist. MSS. Com.* [Rydal MSS.], Rep. xii. App. vii. 11). It is little wonder that so few examples of medieval Communion vessels have survived to the present day.

[2] The visitation took place in the presence of Barnard Aglionby, notary public and principal registrar of the diocese, who made a notarial record of the proceedings, a copy of which will be found in the *Nicolson MSS.* iii. 49–56, in the custody of the dean and chapter of Carlisle.

[3] Henry VIII. did not lay a heavy burden on the dean and canons in the matter of sermons. Each canon was obliged by statute to preach personally or by deputy every year four sermons at least to the people in the cathedral in the English tongue on certain specified Lord's days; and the dean only three sermons a year (*Stat. of the Cathedral Church of Carl.*, ed. J. E. Prescott, pp. 41–2).

and in the same year Percival Kirkbride was ejected trom Asby probably for the same cause. There were two or three other cases of deprivation in 1575, but the record gives no clue of the influences that brought them about.[1] No attempts seem to have been made at this period to organize congregations or to carry on surreptitious ministrations from place to place either in the puritan or papal interest. The two priests who refused the oath of supremacy in 1561 and those others who were unable to accept the Articles of Religion dropped altogether out of view after deprivation. But taking the diocese as a whole, we do not find evidence of external nonconformity, or recusancy as it was then called, till the foreign-bred emissaries from Douay and other seminaries started their secret mission in the northern diocese. None of the old priests had anything to do with the movement. It was a new and alien institution, half religious and half political, glowing with enthusiasm and tainted with treason, bringing disastrous consequences to those who came under its spell. The conspicuous figure in the new crusade was John Bost, son of a Westmorland landowner, a man of undoubted ability and undaunted courage, a dexterous controversialist and a devoted papist. Born of an old family for many centuries settled at Penrith and Dufton, younger son of Nicholas Bost of Wellyng in the latter parish, educated at Queen's College, Oxford, of which society he was elected a Fellow in 1572, he passed over to Douay in August 1580,[2] and was ordained according to the Roman ritual and sent on the English mission in the following year. It was this remarkable man who first laid the foundation of nonconformity in the diocese of Carlisle, and who may in truth be regarded as the father or originator of the Roman Catholic body in Cumberland and Westmorland. If it were possible to stir up a desire for the Roman obedience in the breasts of the people of the two counties or to fan into flame the dying embers of their papal sympathies, no more brilliant agent could have been selected, for his intellectual gifts and family connexions and knowledge of the district invested him with a prestige which the whole hierarchy of Carlisle was powerless to rival or put down.

In 1581, the year in which the chief penal act against papism was passed, the real troubles of those who had papal sympathies may be said to have begun. By this statute (23 Elizabeth, c. 1) it was made high treason to be reconciled to the Roman church, and seminarists saying,

[1] Carl. Epis. Reg. Barnes, MS. ff. 41-3.
[2] *Douay Diaries*, ed. T. F. Knox, i. 10, 28, 168, 173. Nicholas Boste, gentleman, of Wellyng in Dufton, made his will on 3 December, 1569, which was proved at Brougham [Browholme] on 13 February 1569-70. He bequeathed his ' sowle to God Almyghte, trystyng in the mercye of Chryste and throwgh his Passyone yt yt shall be partyner wt. the holye company of Hevyne ' and his body to be buried in the parish church of Dufton. Bequests were made to Janet Boste his wife, Lancelot his son and heir, Elizabeth his daughter, Thomas Warcoppe his godson, Edward, Hugh, and Michael Boste his cousins, Oliver Middleton his right worshipful kinsman, and others of the Hutton and Threlkeld families. To the future seminarist, at that time an undergraduate at Oxford; ' I wyll that my sone, John Boste, shall have fower merks of mony in the yere for thre yeres nyxt to come and yt to be payd by my executors owt of my guds and lands and he to clame no more of my guds for his barne part or other waye.' The testator was possessed of lands and houses, goods and chattels, both at Penrith and Dufton. The will is now lodged in the Probate Registry of Carlisle.

and persons hearing mass were subjected to fine and imprisonment. Further penalties were laid upon those who neglected to attend the church service. The necessity for this oppressive legislation was ascribed to the efforts that were being made at that time to withdraw English subjects from their natural allegiance to the Queen. From this date the conflict between England and Rome became acute. The local authorities were on the alert for the presence of strangers; domiciliary visits were made to the houses of persons suspected of harbouring seminarists; the boundaries of the diocese of Carlisle were watched and notes taken of the personal appearance of suspicious characters who passed in or out; the clergy and justices of the peace were obliged to inform the bishop [1] or the lord warden of what was taking place in the country; the eyes of Walsingham's spies looked into every corner of the two counties. Lord Scrope could report in February 1583–4, that privy search had been made in all suspected places for writings and letters touching 'the present state of religion.' Andrew Hilton, 'a wicked piller of papistrie,' was in the sheriff's close ward; so was Lancelot Bost, brother of the notorious seminarist; and Richard Kirkbride of Ellerton was also safe under good bond. A few days later, in answer to letters from the privy council, Lord Scrope and the Bishop of Carlisle stated that they had failed to apprehend Richard Cliburne and ' one Mouneforde a seminarie Scottes preist,' though diligent search had been made throughout the two counties by Humfrey Musgrave, Thomas Hamonde, chancellor of the diocese of Carlisle, Richard Dudley and Henry Leighe. Damning evidence against Hilton as the associate of Bost and a retailer of news from Scotland to foreign intriguers was transmitted; Richard Kirkbride of Ellerton, brother-in-law of Cliburne, had been apprehended, but they had admitted him to bail as he was an honest conformable man, and although he was a brother of Percival Kirkbride, 'a verie notable papiste,' yet the said Richard was one of the jury that indicted his said brother for not coming to church. Lancelot Bost had also been taken into custody at his mother's house, and by the letters found there it appeared that he was the associate of his brother, the seminarist, who had recently paid him a visit, and of other seminarists like William Hart lately executed at York for high treason.[2] So far nonconformity had made but little progress in the diocese of Carlisle, its chief stronghold being in Westmorland among the kinsfolk of John Bost.

From the letters and papers taken on the persons of Hilton and Lancelot Bost some knowledge is obtained of the tactics of the seminarists in their attempts to promote discontent against the established religion. Bost the priest was very shy of appearing often in his native district, but he had intermediaries through whom his books and writings were distributed among the faithful. The chief scene of his labours was in Yorkshire, where he ' ridd with a cloth bag behinde him, apparelled in a cloake of rattes color, a white frise jerkin laide with blewe lace, and in a paire of buffe lether hose.'[3] For the thirteen years of his mission he

[1] S.P. Dom. Eliz. cclxxviii. 7.   [2] S.P. Dom. Eliz. Add. xxviii. 57, 58.   [3] Ibid. xxviii. 58 (1).

had never been out of England, except for five years in Scotland, when he sojourned at Edinburgh, Lord Seton's, Fernihurst, and other places, but the greater part of his life, since he first arrived at Hartlepool from abroad, was spent in the northern counties.[1] It must be acknowledged that the seminarists as a rule took high ground in their assaults on the church of England. Bost arrayed the whole force of his dialectic in proving that the established religion had none of the marks of a true church, inasmuch as it wanted antiquity, universality, and consent. His writings on the claims of the church of Rome to the sympathies of his brethren were full of earnest piety and eloquence. But the political position which he sought to defend was very curious in view of the papal bull which deposed the Queen as a heretic and usurper. He maintained that he loved the Queen and would take her part if the pope himself should send an army against her majesty, but if the pope by his Catholic authority deposed her as a heretic, then he could not err, nor could the church, and all Catholics were bound to obey the church. It was little wonder that Topcliffe told lord keeper Puckering that the seminarist was ' full of treason as ever wretche was.'[2] It may be mentioned, however, that the burden of the arguments contained in the seized letters and papers belonging to the priests and their Cumbrian sympathizers was chiefly taken up with denunciations of the church of England and with praise of the church of Rome. The main thesis of the controversy was, as Andrew Hilton from his prison in Carlisle urged on his friend Lancelot Bost, that the Roman communion was the ark of God, outside of which there was no salvation. The propaganda went on and the local authorities bent their energies to catch the agents. In time of danger the fugitives were hidden in caves in the ground or secret places where it was impossible to find them. In the opinion of one of Cecil's spies,[3] expressed in October 1593, many were ' converted unto popery ' within the past two years, but especially among tenants in Westmorland. He was able to report the names of twenty-one ' preistes yt ar now in ye North ' and there were many more that he could not name.[4] But the North was getting too hot for the papal sympathizers, and many of them began to withdraw to the Low Countries and elsewhere.

By proclamation in 1580 certain places in each diocese were specially appointed for the restraint of the principal recusants, as the ordinary prisons to which they were accustomed to be committed only rendered them more obstinate in their recusancy.[5] This new policy was no doubt recommended with the view of showing more leniency to those

---

[1] Lansd. MS. 75, f. 22.
[2] S.P. Dom. Eliz. Add. xxviii.58. (viii.) ; S.P. Dom. Eliz. ccxlv. 124.
[3] Ibid. ccxlv. 131.
[4] The examination of Lancelot Bost, Andrew Hilton, and James Harrington, together with the documents found in their houses, may be seen in S.P. Dom. Eliz. Add. xxviii. 58, i. ii. iii. vi. vii. viii. 59, i. ii. iii. The State Papers of 1583-4 contain much interesting matter about recusancy in the diocese of Carlisle.
[5] Peck, *Desiderata Curiosa*, iii. 11-12, 39-40; *Egerton Papers*, Camden Soc., pp. 83-6.

who had conscientious scruples about conformity. At first the castle or citadel of Carlisle was utilized by the sheriff for this purpose, though as a matter of fact few were committed to his custody. After the attainder and condemnation of Philip Howard, earl of Arundel, in 1589, when his estates escheated to the Crown,[1] the castle of Greystoke was used for some years as the special place where the local recusants were lodged, and within the limits of the ample park of which they were confined. Francis Mountain was the keeper of the recusants of Greystoke,[2] at least from 1592 to 1594, the ordinary diet of the Fleet prison being allowed for their maintenance. But the arrangement did not last long, for the Lady Arundel regained possession of Greystoke in 1601, and afterwards became an occasional resident at the castle.

It is worthy of notice that Lord Scrope, warden of the western marches, showed a greater zeal for bringing recusants to conformity than the bishop of Carlisle, his colleague in these matters. In a letter to Walsingham[3] on 8 February 1583-4, he pleaded for the issue of a commission to himself and Bishop May to call before them Francis Dacre and his wife and Thomas Denton of Warnell and his wife, who were ' of late mytche drawne and persuaded from relegyon,' to examine them when they received the Communion during the past six months, and also to make a general call to all suspected persons and their wives within the diocese for a public Communion, in order that a good understanding might be obtained how they stood affected to the church. But some time elapsed before his wishes were gratified. In January 1596-7, the bishop of Carlisle took action through his chancellor to find out from the churchwardens the names of the recusants in the various parishes of the diocese and the dates when they were last presented for recusancy. The return of Chancellor Dethick, endorsed ' recusants in Cumberland and Westmerland in the diocess of Carlisle, dated Januarie 1596, but received May 1597,' is a document of the greatest interest in showing the extent of nonconformity at this period. It is as follows :—

' Jan. 1597. Presentment of recusants in the diocese of Carlisle. The presentment by the churchwardens of the recusants within the dioces of Carlisle in Januarye 1596. Cumberland, Crostwhait : Mr. Frauncis Radcliffe of Darwaine water, esquier, and Issabell his wife, with his tenn children and his servauntes, George Blenkinsopp, Francis Hetherington, Robert White and one Albanye, servingmen, Issabell Hutchinson, Grace Fetherston and one Myrable, with the base begotten daughter of Sr George Radcliffe, knight, the Ladie Katherine Radcliffe (mother to ye said Mr. Frauncis Radcliffe), a verie old woman : xiii moneths. Seburham : Mrs. Anne Denton the wife of Thomas Denton esquier recusant : ii moneths. Wetherall : George Skelton gentleman and Anne his wife, recusants : viii moneths. Warwick : Helene Warwick the wife of Thomas Warwick of Holme yate gentleman, recusant by her own confession : iiii years. Westmerland, Petterdale, a chappell of Barton : Mrs. Fraunces Lancaster the wife of Mr. Lancelott Lancaster, gentleman, recusant : vi moneths. Askham : Mrs. Martha Sanfoorde the wife of Thomas Sanfoord esquier, and Fraunceis Teasdale

---

[1] *The Lives of Philip Howard, Earl of Arundel, and Ann Dacres his wife*, ed. Duke of Norfolk, E.M., 1857, pp. 89-95.
[2] In the parish register there is a record of the baptism of the children ' of Mr. Francis Mountaine then being at that present Keeper of the recusants at Graistoke castle.'
[3] S.P. Dom. Eliz. Add. xxviii. 59.

sometimes his servant, recusant: vi moneths. Warcopp: Andrew Hilton, esquier, endyted long synce, Alice his wife, Wenefrede his daughter, and Mary ye wife of John his sonne, recusants: vi moneths. Dufton: Mrs. Frauncis Boaste the wife of Mr. Lancelot Boaste, recusant, vi moneths. St. Michael's in Appelbie: Margaret Machell the wife of Hugh Machell, gentleman, recusant: xii moneths. Crosby Ravensworth: Mr. Thomas Pickering, gentleman, relapsed, and Ann his wife daughter to ye Lady Radcliff, and John Warriner her servaunt, recusants; iii moneths. Morlande: Jone Sawkell the wife of Oswold Sawkell, a very poore woman, recusant: vi moneths. Burgh under Stanemoore: the wife of Mr. Henry Blenkinsopp of Helbeck esquier, Joane her maide, and William Colling, servauntes, which are said to be gone, Mrs. Margerie Blenkinsopp his mother, an old woman, and her two daughters Maudlin and Joane, Frauncis Blenkinsopp her sonne and Charles Blenkinsop her coosin, recusants every one: vi moneths. The forenamed parties have bene yerelye presented for ye space of these five yeres at the least unto ye graunde juryes at the assises. 'Henry Dethick chancelor to the Lord B(ishop) of Calisle.' [1]

It need scarcely be pointed out that only in four parishes in Cumberland and in eight parishes in Westmorland had the papal agents made any permanent impression. And yet the bishop of Carlisle, Dr. Henry Robinson, on his first acquaintance with the diocese, was not altogether satisfied with its condition in the matter of conformity. On 26 December 1599 he stated that he found in his new charge more popish recusants than he anticipated, yet the number which belonged to that faction within his diocese was far less than within the barony of Kendal and the deanery of Coupland, both of which places were within the jurisdiction or Chester. Of those that had been long faulty in that way, eight or nine had within the past two months reformed themselves. Of the rest who persisted in their separation, the chief people by little and little went out of the country as the Lady Katherine Ratcliffe, Francis her son, Anne Denton the wife of Thomas Denton of Warnell, Henry Blenkinsopp of Helbeck, his mother, wife and children, Thomas Sandford of Askham, a non-communicant, and Martha his wife, a recusant, with all the rest of the recusants of their several families.[2]

In this great effort to produce a reaction in favour of the papacy, the diocese of Carlisle contributed two heroic souls who sought and found martyrdom in the interests of the Roman church. We cannot withhold a word of admiration for the long and splendid services which John Bost rendered to the papal cause. For many years his fame rang through the northern counties as the most dangerous seminary priest in the country. Vain were the efforts of the lord president of the north to arrest him; a whole army of spies was on his track, as the fugitive wandered in disguise from place to place, seldom stopping more than two or three nights in one house. When the time came for him to yield up his life in testimony to the strength of his religious convictions, it was by the treachery of friends that he was delivered into the hands of the civil authorities. Ewbanke had conference once with Bost, said Tobie Matthew, Dean of Durham, writing to Burghley, and was in some hope to have brought him into the lord president's hands, for in their youth they had been chamber-fellows in Queen's College, Oxford, and

[1] S.P. Dom. Eliz. cclxii. 22.   [2] Ibid. cclxxiii. 56.

were countrymen, and had been schoolfellows before in Westmorland. But as Bost grew jealous of his safety, they never met again till the priest was captured. When Bost was taken, Ewbanke was present by the Dean's special direction and behaved himself so considerately that without him and his man the fugitive could not have been secured at that time.[1] In his examination at Durham on 11 September 1593, by the lord president, the dean of Durham, and others of the Council of the North, Bost acknowledged that he was above fifty years of age ; born at Dufton in Westmorland ; left Oxford 'aboute thirteen yeres synce' to go to the parts beyond the seas ; within a year and a half was made priest at Rheims by the Bishops of Laon and Soissons and returned again to England with twenty-eight other priests, including Ballard. After describing his wanderings he further confessed that for the past year he never left Yorkshire, Durham and Northumberland, and during the past five years he was often in Yorkshire for a month at a time, and that it was very much against his will, when he was unable to say mass once every day.[2] During his imprisonment in the Tower he is said to have been 'often most cruelly racked insomuch that he was afterwards forced to go crooked upon a staff.' Of his trial and execution in July 1594, on a charge of treason to his country, we have a graphic description, if genuine, by an eye-witness, Christopher Robinson, a fellow-countryman and seminary priest of the same mission. The execution was carried out according to the barbaric methods of the sixteenth century, when the victim behaved with the greatest fortitude and devotion. In 1597 Robinson himself, a native of Woodside near Wigton in Cumberland, who had been ordained in 1591 at Douay while the college sojourned at Rheims and sent to England in the following year, was executed at Carlisle on the same charge. The bishop of Carlisle is said to have held frequent conferences with him and to have showed him great kindness and consideration while he was in custody, but was unable to shake his papal convictions.[3] Few causes doomed to failure can

---

[1] S.P. Dom. Eliz. xxxij. 89 (latter part). For the academic career of Henry Ewbanke the reader may consult Clarke's *Register*, Oxford Hist. Soc., ii. 56, iii. 81, or Foster's *Alumni Oxonienses*. He is described on the matriculation register of Queen's College as a Londoner by birth, but as Dr. Magrath, the present provost of Queen's, has privately pointed out, 'it is probably a bedel's blunder, as he would not in that case have got a tabardship or a fellowship.' It will be seen from the dean of Durham's statement that Ewbanke was at school in Westmorland with John Bost, probably at Appleby Grammar School. He was afterwards a canon of Durham and had his pedigree and arms enrolled at St. George's visitation in 1615.

[2] A certified copy of his confession will be found in Lansd. MS. 75, f. 22. The *vera copia* is signed by John Bost, and witnessed by 'H. Huntyngdon,' the lord president. The document is endorsed '1593. The examination of John Boste, 11 Septembris, 1593.'

[3] Challoner, *Memoirs of Missionary Priests* (1878), i. 207-9, 239-40, ii. 311-5 ; *Douay Diaries*, i. 15, 31, ii. 223, 232, 239. Bishop May, writing to Sir Robert Cecil on 11 July, 1597, said that 'Thomas Lancaster is the only man that I have trusted or can trust to discover such Jesuits and seminaries as do lurk within my diocese, to the corruption of many of her Majesty's subjects. He was the only man that gave me sure intelligence when and where I might apprehend, as I did, Christopher Robinson, our late condemned seminary, whose execution hath terrified a great sort of our obstinate recusants ; where, nevertheless, there be still harboured three or four more notable seminaries or Jesuits, who pass and repass within my diocese without controlment, such is the careless or partial dealing of some of our justices. Among the said seminaries or Jesuits there is one Richard Dudley, termed by the aforesaid Robinson and other his associates the angel of that profession. He is the only heir of Edmund Dudley, esquire,

number two such disciples. But the enthusiasm for Rome which flamed up brilliantly for a time in the diocese of Carlisle never laid hold of a considerable section of the community and was soon spent.

The episcopate of Bishop Robinson was so remarkable for its success in bringing about conformity to the national religion that the words inscribed on the pastoral staff which forms a feature of his memorial brass in Carlisle cathedral—*Corrigendo, Sustentando, Vigilando, Dirigendo*—may be taken as descriptive of his ministry and not as a mere monumental euphemism. Immediately after his appointment to Carlisle, he petitioned for a special commission ' for the repressing of recusants,' but the archbishop of Canterbury thought the time inopportune until the renewal of the general commission for the province of York. In 1600 he petitioned again on the ground that some of the most disordered of his churches were superstitiously popish and others were impiously licentious, one husband having several wives then living and one wife several husbands. People of that sort took little notice of ecclesiastical censures, but he pleaded that if the principals felt the smart of civil justice, they would be humbled, at least it would prevent the canker spreading as it was then doing to the subversion of many.[1] At the same time he felt that the church of which he was bishop needed the most strenuous exertions in order to raise the clergy and people to a higher moral standard, the want of earnestness in the former and of Christian knowledge in the latter being a real trouble to him.[2] No pains were spared during the eighteen years of his episcopate to bring about the desired result.

It was the tendency of the penal laws to produce outward conformity only, without reference to the religious convictions of the individual. Papists were not agreed at this time on the expediency of attending the church services. Prominent men like Lord William Howard of Naworth, according to Panzani, were in favour of the oath of allegiance and occasional conformity.[3] It was his moderation perhaps which saved Lord William from the troubles of the general persecution. The agents of the government in the north were not slow to bring railing accusations against him on account of his papism, but James I. steadily refused to disturb him.[4] Soon after the King's accession complaints were made that Howard was maintaining one Skelton of Wetheral in his service, the said Skelton being a ' church papist' who came to church only at Easter and was said to have been a harbourer of

whose grandfather, old Richard Dudley, being a good Protestant, did in his lifetime so detest his grandchild's obstinacy that he disinherited him of all his lands and conveyed them to his second brother. It is known to many of our gentlemen that the said angelical Jesuit or seminary is harboured in those parts, yet none of them will, though they see him, lay hands on him. Unless Lancaster can be induced by his persuasion and authorized to apprehend Dudley and his associates, now lurking in this country, they will never be taken ' (*Cal. of Salisbury MSS.* vii. 298).

[1] S.P. Dom. Eliz. cclxxv. 66. [2] Ibid. cclxxiii. 56.
[3] *Engl. Hist. Rev.* xviii. 118.
[4] John Dudley, writing to his brother from London on 12 November, 1616, stated that the information Mr. Salkeld had exhibited against Lord William Howard for recusancy was withdrawn by the King's command (*Hist. MSS. Com. Rep.* [Rydal MSS.] xii. App. vii. 15).

seminary priests and a traitor who fled into Tyrone's camp during the rebellion in Ireland. He was further accused of keeping a priest in his house and trying to revive recusancy throughout the district.[1] But no attention was paid to these reports by those in authority, and Lord William Howard continued to the end of his days a trusted servant of the government in the civilization of the Border counties. As a matter of fact the battle of national religion had been fought and won during the late Queen's reign. Recusancy had become so insignificant that it was no longer regarded as a danger to the State.

When King James visited Carlisle in August 1617, Bishop Snowden presented an address on his own behalf in which he laid before his Sovereign some notice of the civil and ecclesiastical condition of the diocese as he had found it after a study 'for the space of well nere two moneths by my presence in visitations, sessions, and commissions, and by petitions, conference and suggestions.' The state ecclesiastic was hugely weakened, not only by the impropriations served by poor vicars and a multitude of base hirelings, but by compositions contracted in the troublous times and now proscribed, yet there was some show of grave and learned pastors. And albeit many of the clergy in their habits and external ' inconformities ' seemed to be puritans, yet none of them were found of repugnant opinion to the bishop's monitions or the ecclesiastical law. Though the diocese was not infested with recusants so dangerously as the bishoprics of Durham and Chester, yet in his late visitations about eighty persons had been detected and presented, and most of these were confined to a few families, whose conversion or reformation he should strive to effect by gentle persuasion and all other good means to the utmost of his power.' The condition of the diocese was such as we might have expected from its previous history. The succession of bishops of ultra-protestant proclivities, who were more interested in the suppression of papism than in the building up of the clergy and people in the principles of the national religion, had done its work. The standard of clerical education and efficiency had been lowered and the church had fostered within itself those puritan ' habits and external inconformities' which were so soon to break out to the subversion of Church and State.

The true tendency of the old ecclesiastical policy began to be realized when King James addressed a letter to Archbishop Abbot in 1622 on the abuses and extravagances of preachers in the pulpit, and sent him directions to be observed in the composition of sermons. The King's interposition produced much discontent among the clergy, who

1 S.P. Dom. James I. vols. xl. 11, lxxxvi. 34 ; *Lord William Howard's Household Books*, Surtees Soc. pp. 423-4, etc.
2 Bishop Snowden's address to his ' most blessed Soveraigne my great and most gratious Lord and Master ' was dated at ' Rose Castle, August 2, 1617,' by ' your Maties meanest but most obliged and most dutifull subject and servant, Robt. Carlisle.' The document was found about twenty years ago by Mr. Walter Money, F.S.A., among papers collected by John Packer, secretary to George Villiers, first Duke of Buckingham, and printed in the Carlisle newspapers. Chancellor Ferguson has made it more accessible by reproducing it in full in his *Dioc. Hist. of Carl.* (S.P.C.K.), pp. 131-3.

viewed the directions as an unwarranted reflection on their discretion. To smooth matters over and to explain the royal message a supplementary mandate was issued by authority, a summary of which was sent to every bishop and through him to every parsonage in the kingdom.[1] In a letter to Bishop Milburne of Carlisle[2] for the reform of the pulpit, dated 9 January 1622–3, Archbishop Matthew stated that his majesty was grieved to hear almost daily of defection 'from our religion' both to popery and anabaptism, or other points of separation in some parts of the kingdom, and that he was inclined to ascribe the growing leakage to the failure of the preachers. The clergy were enjoined to devote themselves to a simple exposition of the positive teaching of such formularies as the catechism, homilies and articles of religion, giving special attention to the examination of children in the catechism, 'which was the most ancient and laudable custom of teaching in the church of England.' Above all preachers were counselled to leave off bitter invectives against papists and puritans, and to give more attention to the explanation of the doctrine and discipline of their own church.

The diocese of Carlisle was unfortunately situated at this period for carrying out reforms owing to the interruptions in a settled policy caused by frequent changes in the episcopate. During a period of about thirty years, 1616–46, no fewer than six bishops had ruled the see. With one exception there was little opportunity for any of these bishops to make a permanent impression on the diocese. For the whole of the period, though a great effort was made by Bishop Potter to alter the tack, the old ship was steadily drifting towards the rocks. The supply of educated clergy was the problem then, as it had been in the time of Elizabeth. It was the complaint of Bishop White's secretary that 'at our first visitation there was never a doctor of divinitie nor advocate, but eleven or twelve licensed preachers, three or four bachelors of Divinity and eight double beneficed men.'[3] Notwithstanding the academic prestige of Bishop Potter as provost of Queen's College, Oxford, he was unable to attract educated men to seek holy orders at his hands. Though there was general conformity in his diocese, he reported to Archbishop Neile that the wretched stipends of the benefices forced him to admit mean scholars to the diaconate rather than to allow the people to be utterly without divine service. The tendency of the time may be gauged by the further statement that the churchwardens were slow to present absentees from church, and the magistrates were equally reluctant to punish them.[4] The articles of inquiry which the bishop sent to the churchwardens and sworn men at his first visita-

---

[1] Collier has printed these three documents on the reform of preaching (*Eccl. Hist.*, vii. 428–34, ed. Lathbury).

[2] Carl. Epis. Reg. Milburne, ff. 252–4.

[3] The little paper rental-book of Bishop White, from which this information is taken, contains many notes of interest about the diocese from 1626 to 1629 in the matter of the episcopal revenues, leases, subsidies, fees, synodals, patronage and procurations.

[4] Ferguson, *Dioc. Hist. of Carl.* (S.P.C.K.), p. 133.

tion in 1629 are of the comprehensive character that prevailed at that period. They were formulated chiefly, as one might expect, to enforce the canons of 1603. The instruments of divine service which the laity were bound to provide in every parish church and chapel were the Book of Common Prayer with the new calendar, the English Bible of the new translation in the largest volume, two Psalters, two books of Homilies, a decent font, a table of the Ten Commandments, a convenient seat for the minister to sit in, a comely and decent pulpit, with cloth and cushion for the same ; a comely communion table, with a fair linen cloth to lay on the same, and some covering of silk, buckram, or other suchlike for the clean keeping thereof ; a fair and comely communion cup of silver with a silver cover, for the ministration of the Holy Communion ; a chest or box for the poor, and the book of constitutions and canons. The only vestment for the minister supplied at the charge of the parish was a decent large surplice with sleeves, but the churchwardens were required to state whether the minister *usually* wore the surplice when he was saying public prayers and ministering sacraments, and, if he were a graduate, did he also upon his surplice wear such hood as was agreeable to his degree, and such decent apparel as was appointed by the late constitutions.[1] When Potter was nominated to the see of Carlisle by the influence of Archbishop Laud, people were astonished at the selection, as the new bishop was suspected of puritan inclinations. Fuller says he was known at Court as the penitential preacher; he afterwards came to be called the puritanical bishop.[2] But there is no trace of puritanism in his articles of inquiry. One reads them over with the feeling that he was steadfastly loyal to the church as then understood, and wished to see the doctrine and worship as embodied in her constitutional documents accepted and observed by the people.

When it was said of Bishop Potter that organs would blow him out of the church, the satire may have been occasioned in allusion to the revival of more stately and reverent methods of conducting Divine worship with which the name of Archbishop Laud will be for ever associated. But there was less fear in this isolated corner of the kingdom than in any other diocese of a recrudescence of the ancient solemnity in the church service. If the parish churches of the diocese of Carlisle were no further advanced in point of ritual and reverence than the cathedral, it cannot be said that the new ideas which at that time began to fill men's minds had ever reached the northern counties. There is a curious description of Carlisle cathedral in the autumn of 1634, in which three officers of the military establishment in Norwich, whilst on a tour of pleasure from thence into the north, have left us their impressions of its service. The cathedral was nothing so fair and stately as those they had seen, but more like a great wild country church ; and as it appeared outwardly so it was inwardly, neither

---

[1] *Second Rep. of the Commissioners on Rubrics, Orders, etc.* (Blue Book), pp. 506–8.
[2] *Worthies of England*, ed. 1684, p. 841.

beautified nor adorned one whit. The organs and voices did well agree, the one being a shrill bagpipe, the other like the Scottish tone. The sermon in the like accent was such as they could hardly bring away, though it was delivered by a neat young scholar, one of the bishop's chaplains. The communion also was administered and received in a wild and irreverent manner.[1]

Though it cannot be said that church feeling was remarkably strong in the diocese, there was a leaven of devoted loyalty among the clergy to King Charles as the political clouds began to gather around his throne. When events became more threatening the clergy were destitute of the immediate supervision and personal guidance of their bishop. It is true that James Usher, the saintly primate of Ireland, had received the see *in commendam* from the King in 1642, about a month after the death of Bishop Potter. But it is doubtful whether that illustrious prelate ever set foot within the diocese. When Sir Timothy Fetherstonhaugh laid the King's request for a subsidy in his distress before the assembled clergy in the chapter house at Carlisle on 13 April 1643, the attitude of those that were present, though far from sympathetic, cannot be described as disloyal. They acknowledged with thankfulness that 'the honourable bench' had recognized their 'ancient and due libertys' in representing the subsidy as a voluntary contribution, and they were quite willing to admit that a tenth part of the sum of the counties, as far as the diocese extended, was a full proportion if they had enjoyed their entire dues as set out unto them by the law of God. But notwithstanding the fact that every one of them had suffered great diminution in their rights by impropriations and prescriptions, yet they were willing to raise themselves to the proportions suggested, and were of opinion that the same might be expected of their absent brethren. It was not their intention that lay impropriators should be allowed to escape, for they were required to join with the vicars to advance the tenth, or wholly to undertake it where there was no vicar, 'since they are, so farr as concerning the tithes they recieve, ecclesiastical persons.' For once the clergy of Carlisle spoke out in defence of their ancient rights, inasmuch as they stipulated 'that this our acte may be acknowledged as voluntary and not to be drawn into example and so worded by the clerke of the sessions.'[2] Before the year 1643, in which these manly words were spoken, was brought to a close, the diocese of Carlisle, as an administrative unit of the English church, had ceased to

---

[1] 'A Relation of a short Survey of 26 counties, &c., observ'd in a seven weekes journey begun at the City of Norwich and from thence into the North on Monday, August 11th, 1634, and ending at the same place. By a Captaine, a Lieutannant and an Ancient. All three of the Military Company in Norwich' (Lansd. MS. 213).

[2] This document, the earliest in the register of Bishop Usher, is headed 'the humble answere of the clergy within the diocez of Carleill present in the chapter house, April 13th, 1643, to the request brought from the ho.le bench by Sir Tymothy Fetherstonhaugh K.ts,' and is subscribed by 'Isaac Singleton, archdeacon, Frederick Tonstall, Hen. Sibson, Leonard Milburn, Tho. Head, William Fairfax, Christofer Peale, Charles Usher, Will Gregson (?), Parcivall Head, Tymothy Tully, William Head, Richard Sibson, Richard Sharples' (Carl. Epis. Reg. Usher, MS. f. 313).

exist. The last entry in the diocesan register of Bishop Usher is dated 3 November 1643.[1]

There was no serious disturbance of the clergy in their benefices till the city of Carlisle received a Scottish garrison on 28 June 1645, after a protracted siege, during which the inhabitants made a gallant stand, and suffered many privations for church and king. Taken as a whole the clergy and gentry of Cumberland were royalists, and managed to hold their ground till the capital was forced to surrender. The county, says the youthful historian of the siege, was generally free from the seeds of schism and untainted with the present rebellion.[2] Before the city was given up to General Lesley it was stipulated that a livelihood out of the church revenues should be allowed to every member of the cathedral body then resident, until the parliament had determined otherwise, and that no church should be defaced. But the terms of surrender were not observed. In a moment of fanatical fury, the cloisters, part of the deanery, the chapter house and prebendal buildings were pulled down, and the materials were sacrilegiously used to build a main guard and repair the fortifications of the city. The west portion of the cathedral was also demolished, leaving only three bays of the venerable Norman structure standing, and the parliamentary officers were so moved with zeal and something else against magnificent churches that they had intended to pull down the whole cathedral, and to have no church but St. Cuthbert's.[3] Fortunately the intention was not carried out. Though Cumberland was far removed from the headquarters of the destructive party, it had its full share of sufferings in other ways. The Scots had not forgotten their old methods of harrying the country. Hugh Todd told Walker in after years that the clergy suffered more from the Scots than from other people.[4] So great was the destruction about the cathedral that the charters of the capitular body were sold to make a tailor's measures.[5] From the Border church of Rocliffe the parish register and other church requisites were taken away by the Scottish army in 1648.[6] For several years little else but anarchy prevailed in the county, as the fortunes of the opposing forces fluctuated in favour of the King or the parliament. In the sequestrations which

[1] The acts of Bishop Usher were made by commission consisting of the archdeacon and one of the canons, though they ran in his own name; 'James, by divine pity, archbishop of Armagh and primate and metropolitan of all Ireland, also commendatory bishop of the diocese of Carlisle' (Carl. Epis. Reg. Usher, ff. 314–7). Very few of his acts are on record, and only those between 15 April and 3 November 1643.

[2] *Narrative of the Siege of Carlisle in* 1644 *and* 1645, ed. S. Jefferson, pp. 1–48.

[3] The articles of surrender have been preserved by Hugh Todd (*Account of the City and Diocese of Carlisle* (Cumbld. and Westmorld. Arch. Soc.), pp. 23–6). Todd's account of what took place during the Civil War may be accepted as satisfactory, inasmuch as he lived so near the times which he described. He was a Cumberland man, and must have been acquainted with many of the actors in these great events.

[4] *Sufferings of the Clergy*, i. 51.

[5] Nicolson, *English Hist. Library*, second ed. p. 127.

[6] On the fly-leaf of the register of that parish we find the following memorandum in a neat bold hand: 'Cumberland, Roecliffe, at Easter, 1679. John Litle and Jeff. Urwin being ch[urch]wardens. This register book was bought at ye instigation of Mr. Tho. Stalker, Mr. A. Coll. Reg. Oxon., curate yn of this ch. of Roecliffe, lectʳ. of St. Cuthberts, Carlile, and minor canon of ye cathedˡˡ. ch. in yᵗ citty. There was not one yr before for many yeates, being taken away, with other utensills of ye church, by Scotts armyes, and last of all by Ld. Duke Hamilton's in ye year 1648.'

followed the military triumph of puritanism, the leading clergy of the diocese, as well as the dean and chapter, were ejected from their livings. If there was any tendency on the part of those with royalist proclivities to hold on, the committee of 'tryers' accepted the most flimsy charges wherewith to oust them from their parishes.

There can be no doubt that many of the clergy, specially those in the poorer and more secluded parishes, bent their necks to the puritan yoke and stood their ground. It is difficult to estimate the motives of those who accepted the directory and swore to maintain the covenant, but there is evidence that if some did so from conviction, others acted from policy.[1] Against these may be placed the example of Timothy Tullie, rector of Cliburn, who became 'the bright, particular star' of presbyterianism while the Commonwealth lasted, but who altered his orbit without dimming his lustre by becoming a canon of York [2] on the restoration of the church and crown. The committee of 'tryers,' notwithstanding the supposed leniency with which they exercised their unpleasant vocation, were quite unable to find substitutes of their own way of thinking for the vacant benefices. For fourteen years the precincts of the cathedral lay in ruins, and the floor of the cathedral itself was common ground at the disposal of all the sects. The principal churches of the diocese were supplied either by resident or itinerant ministers of the presbyterian, independent or baptist persuasion, but the presbyterians predominated in number and influence. If pluralism could be alleged with truth as a defect of the old order of church government, it was repeated in an aggravated form, though perhaps from necessity, when the sequestrators had finished their work, for it was no uncommon thing for one minister under the new regime to be the peripatetic pastor of three parishes. Some of the churches were shut up, and most of the preachers admitted by the commissioners were not ministers at all,[3] not even according to the religious conceptions of the period.

For some time after the fall of episcopacy there was no ecclesiastical or religious organization among the ministers and no cohesion among the parishes. The vacant churches had been allotted to members of various sects as each sect in turn had gained the mastery of the local committees. In any group of parishes it was possible to find the ministers in charge belonging to opposing denominations. The presbyterians endeavoured to form some sort of church discipline, but every attempt at combination created jealousy among the rest and led to controversy and strife. The first effort to form an alliance between the presbyterians and independents was begun in 1653, 'but it took not' among the brethren of 'congregational judgment.' It is a singular coincidence

---

[1] Thomas Denton, writing in 1687-8, stated that 'the Common Prayer was read in the church of Sebergham in all ye late times of trouble, and we never had a phanatick in the parish, neither then nor since' (Perambulation of Cumb. in 1687-8, MS. f. 85).

[2] Hardy, Le Neve, iii. 190. Timothy Tullie was collated to Cliburn by Bishop Potter on 19 June 1639 (Carl. Epis. Reg. Potter, MS. f. 301).

[3] Burton, Life of Sir Philip Musgrave (Carlisle Tracts), p. 34; Walker, Sufferings of the Clergy, i. 97; George Fox's Journal, Leeds edition, i. 223.

that it was in this year that George Fox commenced his mission in the county. There was a cloud upon the horizon, at this time no bigger than a man's hand, which soon grew to such stupendous proportions that the two principal denominations were forced to combine in order to preserve themselves from extinction. Fox made a progress from parish to parish through the western portion of the county. At Brigham he converted John Wilkinson, ' who was preacher of that parish and of two other parishes in Cumberland,' in which neighbourhood ' many hundreds were convinced.'[1] Consternation is scarcely the word to describe the state of feeling which filled the hearts of the religious leaders in that portion of the county at the missionary success of Fox. In the records of the independents of Cockermouth for the year 1654 we are told that ' the 16th day of the 4th month the churches met at Bride-kirk, where they solemnly made confession of their Faith, and renewed their covenant with God, begging of the Lord His grace and strength, that they might stand against that deluge of errors that had overflown the country, and had shattered to pieces the other congregations about Broughton ; only some few friends of the people had since come to land and kept together in communion.'[2] The religious instincts of the people, so far as they were represented by the preachers who had supplanted the old order of clergy, began to gravitate towards Fox, who, in a few years, was almost universally accepted as the sovereign pontiff of Cumberland. The puritan teachers were so utterly forsaken that the churches in some parishes stood empty.[3]

It can be readily imagined that the external pressure of Fox's preaching contributed in no small measure to ' the agreement of the associated ministers and churches of the counties of Cumberland and Westmorland,' which was brought to a successful issue in 1656. Those who take the trouble to read the Articles of Association and reflect on the application of the rules of discipline and government will see nothing extravagant in the epigram of Milton, that ' new Presbyter is but old Priest writ large.' Even ' the power of the keys,' which was claimed to be latent in presbyterianism, was accepted in a modified form by the independents. The formulary of excommunication obtained a wider range and descended to more minute detail than was ever known in the strictest days of the English church. For the better carrying out of the agreement, the county was divided into three districts or associations, Carlisle, Penrith, and Cockermouth, which should meet monthly, more or less, as occasion required, or as the greater part of the association thought fit. The ministers of Westmorland gave their consent to the Agreement so far as the general propositions were concerned, but made their own arrangements about places of meeting. An eirenicon was

<hr>

[1] *George Fox's Journal*, Leeds edition, i. 220–6.

[2] Lewis, *Hist. of the Congregational Church of Cockermouth*, pp. 17–8.

[3] *George Fox's Journal*, i. 226–30, 441. This statement by Fox cannot be regarded as an exaggeration ; it is fully borne out by the records of congregationalism at Cockermouth (*Hist. of the Congregational Church*, pp. 14–25). The weapon of excommunication, which the ministers used against the seceders, had no effect on the general apostasy.

addressed ' to all that profess the Name of the Lord Jesus in the counties of Cumberland and Westmerland, both magistrates and people ' in explanation of the Articles and with an exhortation to obedience. All scandalous persons, such as episcopalians, papists and quakers, were rigidly excluded from the Association till they had publicly recanted their errors.[1]

The moving spirit of this great effort for unity among the sects was Richard Gilpin, pastor of Greystoke, a minister of refined and scholarly attainments, who exercised a well-deserved influence over the presbyterian section of the community. His soul had been vexed at the profaneness which he saw thriving around him for want of˙ discipline in the churches, and at the divisions and jealousies fomented among brethren of the same household of faith. In order to help in rebuilding the spiritual Sion, he laboured day and night to bring about reconciliation. On 19 May 1658 he preached his famous 'acceptable sermon ' on the ' Temple Rebuilt,' at Keswick, before a general meeting of the associated ministers of the county, which was printed at the unanimous request of those who heard it. Notwithstanding Gilpin's eloquent pleading for peace, it is to be feared that his labours for unity were only partially successful. There can be little doubt that the presbyterian body looked up to him as their counsellor and guide, but it is questionable whether the leaders of independency were in full sympathy with the Association movement. At least we find the discipline of the congregational connexion exercised independently of the Association at Bridekirk in 1656, the delinquent being the incumbent of Plumbland. However much the fusion of the sects fell short of Gilpin's ideal, one cannot help admiring the zeal of the ministers in guarding the ordinances of religion from profanation and their self-denying courage in making a stand for godliness at a time when faith and hope and love had almost deserted the mass of the Cumbrian population.

When the church and monarchy were restored in 1660 the diocese of Carlisle was in a pitiable condition of desolation. The west end of the cathedral lay in ruins ; the deanery and prebendal houses were uninhabitable ; Rose Castle, the historic seat of the bishops, had been mutilated during the Civil War and patched up for the residence of a Cromwellian general. Several of the benefices were vacant or held in plurality. All the old members of the capitular body had died before the Restoration with the exception of Lewis West, canon of the third stall. When Richard Sterne, who had acted as chaplain to Archbishop Laud on the scaffold, was consecrated on 2 December 1660, his task in the reorganization of the diocese was by no means easy or agreeable. The dean and chapter had to be constituted ; questions of disputed patronage made the appointment of incumbents to vacant parishes irk-

---

[1] The quarto pamphlet, from which this account is taken, is entitled, ' The Agreement of the Associated Ministers and Churches of the Counties of Cumberland and Westmerland, with something for Explication and Exhortation annexed.' It was printed in London in 1656 and sold 'by Richard Scott, bookseller in Carlisle.'

some and difficult. Though the new bishop met with many obstacles, something was done during his short episcopate to bring order out of chaos and to equip his diocese with the necessary agencies. Much of his attention at the outset was engrossed with the arrangement of the revenues and temporal concerns of the see ; but it cannot be said that the spiritual wants of the people were overlooked. The bulk of the incumbents returned to their episcopal allegiance, but those who had been made ministers according to the rites which obtained during the Commonwealth were objects of sympathy and concern. Few of these ministers awaited the passing of the Bartholomew Act in 1662 to be driven from their parishes. The tide of adversity had set in, and nobly bowing to the inevitable they retired without compulsion. Dr. Gilpin quietly relinquished the cure of Greystoke to William Morland, the former rector, who had been ejected in 1650. Some of the leaders among the presbyterians and independents followed his example. When Bishop Sterne put the Act of Uniformity into force he found a general inclination to accept it. As the organization and visitation of the diocese proceeded the bishop introduced a moderate system of ecclesiastical discipline ; he pressed the obligation of the festivals and fasts of the church on the observance of the faithful[1] ; and he took steps 'to afford the rite and benefit of Confirmation by prayer and imposition of hands upon all such people as shall come duely prepared for the receiving of the same.' It may be said that while Bishop Sterne ruled the diocese of Carlisle, he gave no indications of possessing those untoward qualities of popery, sourness, and ill-temper with which Burnet[2] has loaded his memory.

The attention of Bishop Rainbow, during the early years of his episcopate, was directed to the supply of spiritual ministrations and the lawful performance of divine service in the parish churches. The diocese had not yet recovered from the devastation of the Cromwellian period. In many parishes little provision was made for the due celebration of the sacraments. To remedy these defects he bent all his energies. Visiting the dean and chapter on 6 September 1666, he found the cathedral staff to consist of thirty-six persons—a dean, four prebendaries, six minor canons, a master of choristers, six choristers, six lay singing men, a verger (*virgifer*), a subsacrist, six almsmen, a gate-keeper, a butler, a cook (who seems to have been considered a person of some consequence in the community), and an assistant cook. It then transpired that the necessary instruments for the performance of divine service had been provided with the exception of ornaments such as copes, etc., which were promised in a short time. The chapter also reported to the bishop that 'some of the church utensils were imbezilled in the late times of usurpation, as the brazen eagle upon which ye chapters were read.'[3] For the purpose of meeting the wants of the parish

---

[1] Carl. Epis. Reg. Sterne, ff. 199, 257–8.
[2] *Hist. of His Own Time*, Oxford, 1823, ii. 427.
[3] Carl. Epis. Reg. Rainbow, ff. 410–1 ; Chapter Minute Books, MS. viii. 468.

churches, commissions were issued in the four deaneries of Carlisle, Cumberland, 'Alndale,' and Westmorland, to make inquiries. The commission for the deanery of Carlisle was delivered on 7 December 1668 ; those for the other deaneries on 14 September 1669. Bishop Rainbow stated that as it belonged to his pastoral office to see the service of God duly performed, His churches repaired and beautified, and all things therein done in decency and order, it was his duty to take notice of what had happened during the long discontinuance of church government in these late times of war and rebellion. 'The churches of this our diocese of Carlisle are become very ruinous, the Communion plate and linnen plundered and stollen away, and many disòrders committed to ye great dishonour of Almighty God, the scandall and offence of all good Christian people and the breach of the ancient lawes of this land.' The commissioners in the respective deaneries were empowered to call before them churchwardens and parishioners, and to inform themselves 'of all the decayes, defects, ruines and incroachments wᶜʰ are in any of the roofs, leads, windowes, walls, steeples, floores, pavements, pulpitts, reading desks, seats and stalls in any of the said churches, chappells or in any of their churchyards, houses, edifices, buildings and grounds.' It was the duty of the commissioners also ' to see that the said churches be provided of plate, pewter, linnen, and other things necessary for the Communion Table, as likewise of bookes, cushions and other things required for the pulpit and reading desk and other uses.' In addition, inquiry was made about the temporal concerns of the benefice, glebe lands, mansions, buildings, church stocks, augmentations, legacies and other charitable uses.[1] To these episcopal acts in 1668–9 must be ascribed the supply of the ornaments in many parish churches and the recovery of much church property lost or embezzled during the Commonwealth.

While Bishop Rainbow was making strenuous efforts to build up the church in his diocese, he was not unmindful of those who had rejected him as chief pastor. It is well known that he was a conciliatory prelate who did everything in his power to soften the asperities of the penal code. But it was beyond his power to save nonconformists from the consequences of resistance to the law ; it was the civil magistrate who dealt with those who dissented from the national religion. For this reason it is to the court of Quarter Sessions, and not to the ecclesiastical courts, that we turn for a record of the troubles of the various religious denominations at this period. The followers of George Fox were the first to feel the rigour of the law. The quakers were the only people who ostentatiously defied the new enactments. In their ill-regulated enthusiasm they entered the parish churches and denounced the lives and doctrines of the parish clergy in the presence of their congregations. It was no rare thing for churchwardens to have half a dozen quakers before the justices at Quarter

---

[1] Carl. Epis. Reg. Rainbow, ff. 460–1.

Sessions 'for disturbing the minister in tyme of preaching.' At the Summer Sessions in 1670 Sir Philip Musgrave paid into court the sum of £7 as the king's moiety 'due upon a conviction of several seditious persons,' which sum was paid over to the sheriff. Sir Philip Musgrave was a notorious opponent of all sectaries. His spies were sent in all directions with strict orders to watch the 'bad people,' as he roughly called them, and many meetings were captured by these agents. John Lamplugh did not hesitate to levy a fine of £10 on the overseers of the poor of the parish of Dean, 'for negligence in their office in not making information to the next justice of the peace of a conventicle at Pardsay Cragg.' Moreover, the quakers carried on a stout resistance to the payment of tithes, 'steeplehouse rates and clerk's wages,' which added not a little to their other troubles. When Charles II. granted his temporary indulgence in 1672, very few of the quakers took advantage of it. Almost all the licences for preaching houses in Cumberland were taken out by persons of the presbyterian or congregational persuasion.[1] Several of those who were licensed to preach are well known in the annals of Cumberland nonconformity.

It is a matter of general history that the King was forced by the Cavalier party to revoke his declaration of indulgence, and that the law known as the Test Act of 1673 was passed to which he reluctantly gave his consent. There is a long entry in the records of Quarter Sessions explanatory of the new Act. It is singular that though the Act affected all kinds of dissenters, it is designated in the preamble as 'an Act for preventing danger which may happen from Popish Recusants.' The justices seemed very impartial in carrying out these penal enactments, as they affected both protestant and papist. At the Easter Sessions, 1674, above a hundred persons were summoned 'for not repayreing to church within 6 months after ye 6th of July last.' Neither degree nor sex was considered. No part of the county was overlooked. The non-churchgoers were indicted from places so wide apart as Alston and St. Bees, Kirklinton and Bootle. Knights and squires as well as yeomen and rustics, were fined the Sunday shilling. Members of fourteen different families were fined out of the parish of Kirklinton. There was a goodly contingent from Wetheral, and among them Francis Howard of Corby and Anne his wife. The yeomen of Leath Ward were conspicuous. We may name also Sir Francis Salkeld of Whitehall ; Henry Curwen, with five of the same name from Camerton ; Katherine Curwen of Workington Hall ; Skeltons of Branthwaite, and Porters of Bolton. We hear no more of church neglect till the October Sessions, 1680, when Sir George Fletcher was high sheriff. The majority of the offenders this time were evidently papists, and of the squirearchy ; whereas the lists of 1674 were principally quakers and of the yeomen and humbler classes.

---

[1] *Dioc. Hist. of Carl.* (S.P.C.K.), pp. 152–3. The list of Northumberland licences has been printed in *Arch. Æliana*, xiii. 63. Both lists will be found in 'Domestic Entry Books of Charles II.' at the Record Office.

The Toleration Act of 1689 was welcomed by the dissenting communities of the county. Whatever they suffered in past years was now happily at an end. Though the provisions of the Act were meagre enough, they were sufficient to ease dissenters of harassing disabilities, and give them scope for the free exercise of their religion. The Act required them only to take out licences for their meeting houses, and the justices had no alternative but to grant them.[1] Some of the dissenting ministers, however, disregarded the obligations of the Toleration Act and refused to take out licences. Daniel Jackson was not content with ministering to his Stanwix congregation, but intruded into the parish of Burgh, where he held conventicles at night in wilful defiance of the law. With eight of the principal inhabitants of that place he was brought before the Christmas Sessions, 1692, 'ffor an unlawfull assemblie under pretence of religious worshipp.' It is stated in the indictment that to the number of forty persons they had assembled in the night at the house of Jannet Hodgeson of Westend, widow, for that purpose. Nicholson of Kirkoswald was charged at Michaelmas, 1694, for a conventicle, probably at Penrith, as the others with whom he was indicted belonged to the immediate neighbourhood. At the same sessions Anthony Sleigh of Penruddock, clerk; George Nicholson of Kirkoswald, clerk; and Thomas Dawes, of the same place, clerk, were similarly indicted with sundry of their co-religionists. It is a matter of no surprise that the law should be put in force against these dissenting ministers who were foolish enough to disregard it.

Towards the close of the seventeenth century public attention was directed to the alarming increase of coarseness and immorality throughout the kingdom. It soon became the subject of a royal proclamation, which was ultimately embodied in an Act of Parliament. But the friends of the 'Society for the Reformation of Manners' were destined to meet with considerable opposition in Cumberland. The dissenting element went cautiously to work in order to entrap the leaders of the church party into blessing the enterprise. One great mistake the originators seem to have made, when they called the movement a covenant, a league, or association. There was something in a name to the churchmen of this period, and it is manifest they did not relish a novelty on English ground which came to them wearing a presbyterian aspect and dressed in the Genevan garb. The bishop of Carlisle was surprised into giving his patronage, and matters looked like peace. But that hope was doomed to sudden disappointment. Few outside those versed in church matters can well understand the position of Archdeacon Nicolson in his attitude to the movement. His action was not prompted by expediency or bigotry, but by conscience and duty. Though he admitted the evil needed the efforts of all Christian people, he yet maintained that the 'Established Church' was the responsible

[1] The licences issued by the justices in Quarter Sessions to the nonconforming communities of the county are very numerous and extend over a long period. Many of them will be noticed in the parish history.

agent which should of itself provide the remedy. He took his stand on the canons, which, he alleged, were binding on his conscience, and denounced those clergy who ignored them by joining in 'conventicles' with dissenting ministers, under cover of furthering the interests of morals, while in reality they were causing schism and breaking the law. The clergy, as a whole, were willing enough to follow their archdeacon's advice, till Chancellor Tullie ranged himself on the other side, and went in strongly for the amalgamation of church and dissent. Under his ægis Cockburn, the vicar, aided by a few of the neighbouring clergy, set up the covenant at Brampton, which soon brought down the archdeacon's thunders on his honest head. Archdeacon and chancellor were summoned to Rose Castle to answer to their aged diocesan for the strife they were causing in his diocese. Little came of it. The bishop was too old and too infirm to curb the zeal of his subordinates. An appeal was made to the archbishop of York, but he shelved the question ; the bishop of Chester was inclined to side with the chancellor, so Nicolson was forced to struggle on alone.[1]

The episcopates of Bishops Rainbow and Smith, which covered the period between 1664 and 1702, were devoted chiefly to the discharge of their functions within the diocese. It was their endeavour to set a good example to their clergy and to urge them to follow it. An attractive picture of the private life of Bishop Rainbow has been drawn by the hand of one who knew him. 'Four times a day was God publickly called upon by prayers in that family : twice in the chappel, which part his lordship's chaplains performed : and twice in the dining room, the latter of these at six in the morning and nine at night was the usual task of our right reverend worthy prelate himself, if not disabled by sickness.'[2] His enforcement of discipline among some of the clergy 'who had been sufficiently criminal and neglectful in the discharge of their function' was attended with unpleasantness and often provoked opposition. But his personal example in devotion to duty acted as a stimulus to the diocese, and cleared him of all suspicion of favouritism or private grudge. The life of Bishop Smith, who had been dean of Carlisle before his consecration, was fashioned on the same model. The policy of both prelates was to raise the tone of the clergy, and increase the reverence and regularity of their public ministrations. The dangers of the episcopate, to which the bishops of Carlisle after the Reformation had succumbed, were happily avoided by their successors after the Restoration. It has been pointed out that the Elizabethan bishops were mainly concerned with the suppression of heresy and the enforcement of conformity, a policy negative in its aims as it was disastrous in its results. The bishops of Carlisle, who came immediately after 1660, set themselves the task of rebuilding the church as a spiritual edifice, and meddled as little as possible with the demolishing of the religious shelters which the mistaken policy of their predecessors had

[1] *Letters of Wm. Nicolson*, pp. 109, 145–58, 161–72, etc.
[2] *Life of Bishop Rainbow* (London, 1688), pp. 68–9.

forced earnest men to erect for themselves. When they came in contact with nonconformity, their attitude was that of conciliation ; but they spared no pains, as Jonathan Banks said of Bishop Rainbow, to urge the clergy 'in the diligent preaching of God's word : in the due administration of the Holy Sacraments, in catechising of youth, and in admonishing and reclaiming the more loose from their immoralities.'[1] It is to this policy of positive teaching that one must ascribe whatever measure of success the churchmen of that period attained in rebuilding 'the city of their fathers' sepulchres.' The munificence of Bishop Smith in the distribution of his private fortune is still bearing fruit in some of the schools, churches and parsonages of the diocese.

The pastoral care exercised by the bishops, and the condition of the parish churches at this time, may be gathered from the articles of inquiry and the replies sent in by the churchwardens at visitation. The earnestness of the bishops cannot be doubted, but if we judge the clergy and people according to modern standards, the verdict cannot be given that they were filled with sentiments of decency and order in the care of the churches and the performance of divine service. From a study of the parish churches it is pleasant to turn to the mother church of the diocese, of which we get a contemporary account from the pen of one who had little sympathy with ecclesiastical observance. Thomas Story states that about 1687 he went diligently to the public worship, especially to the cathedral at Carlisle, where in time of public prayer they used all, male and female, so soon as that creed called the Apostles' Creed began to be said, to turn their faces towards the east ; and when the word JESUS was mentioned, they all as one bowed and kneeled towards the altar-table, as it was called, where stood a couple of Common Prayer Books in folios, one at each side of the table, and over them painted upon the wall I.H.S., signifying *Jesus Hominum Salvator.*[2]

William Nicolson, archdeacon of Carlisle, an ecclesiastic of a different type to his immediate predecessors, succeeded to the see on the death of Bishop Smith in 1702. This prelate was a scholar of considerable repute, a strong politician, a laborious and tireless worker, whose fame was not confined to the district in which he lived. In his letters, diaries, controversies and visitations, apart from his solid contribution to the scholarship of his day, there is embodied a local literature of which we have no parallel in the history of the diocese.[3] In his primary visitation in 1703–4 he has left an account of the condition of the churches and the character of the clergy under his spiritual rule, invaluable indeed as a record of many things which have long since passed away, but so highly coloured that it is difficult to accept it as a faithful delineation of the ecclesiastical life of the period. His views of men and things not up to his own standard appear, like those of all

[1] *Life of Bishop Rainbow* (London, 1688), pp. 63–4.
[2] *Journal of the Life of Thomas Story* (ed. 1747), pp. 3–4.
[3] *Letters of William Nicolson* (ed. J. Nicols, London, 1809) ; *Diaries of Bishop Nicolson* (ed. Bishop of Barrow-in-Furness) in the *Cumb. and Westmor. Arch. Soc. Trans.* new series, vols. i. ii. iii. iv. ; *Miscel. Accounts of the Diocese of Carlisle*, 1877.

Effigies Reverendi admodum Viri
Thoma Smith Episcop Carliolensis
Anno Christi 1701.   Ætatis Suæ 87.

THOMAS SMITH, BISHOP OF CARLISLE.

earnest reformers, to err on the side of pessimism. It is very painful to read that the Bibles were torn or wanted binding, or were of the old translation ; the altars were rotten or crazy, or placed irregularly ; the seats were mean, or too high, or scurvily low ; the fonts were ill-placed, broken, or shallow and lumpish ; the parsons were bad managers, lazy, non-resident, melancholic, a little loose, pluralists, irregular, or read too fast. Such are some of the musings of a supercilious young prelate who had been a canon of the cathedral at the age of twenty-six, archdeacon of Carlisle at twenty-seven, and bishop of the diocese at forty-seven. If the church was in the deplorable condition described in the journal of his visitation tour, it must have been in some measure due to his own negligence during the twenty years of his archidiaconate. On the other hand, when we think of the conditions under which parish priests exercised their vocation, it is little wonder that the internal fittings and arrangement of the parish churches and mountain chapels were not up to the canonical standard. In very many places the church was the parish school, and the incumbent or curate was the schoolmaster. These clergymen, so severely handled by their young diocesan, were the pioneers of modern education, and if for no other reason we may look with sympathy rather than condemnation on the methods they were forced to employ. What was lost in the sacrifice of external ceremonial and orderly service was gained in the systematic religious instruction of the young. Perhaps it was only in the diocese of Carlisle where Wordsworth[1] could find in a parish register the memorable entry ' that a youth who had quitted the valley (of Borrowdale), and died in one of the towns on the coast of Cumberland, had requested that his body should be brought and interred at the foot of the pillar by which he had been accustomed to sit while a schoolboy.' The bishop has given it as his own experience, while rector of Great Salkeld, that it was not till he had built a school and removed the children thereto that anything like the decencies of public worship could be maintained in that church.

But the condition of the church in Cumberland should not be estimated solely from the hasty judgments formed by Bishop Nicolson on his first perambulation of the diocese. We have from his own pen a more trustworthy test by which a more accurate opinion can be formed of the church's supremacy over the agricultural population. The order of confirmation is a distinctive rite which differentiates the doctrinal observance of the church from every class of protestant nonconformity. Neglect of this rite is a sure sign of leakage or paralysis. What do we find ? When the bishop ' ended ye work of Confirmation ' on his first circuit of visitation in 1702, he had conferred the gift on 5,537 persons, a number which throws into the shade, when population and area are considered, the best efforts of any of his successors in our own day. On 28 August at Kirkbystephen he ' confirmed 799 without a pause and singly,' the throng being so great that one of the candidates was ' almost killed,' and at Penrith on 30 August, ' 889 in ye forenoon and 102 in

---

[1] *Description of the Scenery of the Lakes* (London, 1823), p. 54.

afternoon, in all 991, whereof about 300 were parishioners of Penrith,'[1] feats of human endurance characteristic of this extraordinary prelate, as well as incontestable evidence of the influence and zeal of the parochial clergy.

The political troubles which preceded the Hanoverian accession were a source of much embarrassment to a small section of the community which was suspected of disaffection to the government. As early as 1706 parliament had acquainted the Queen 'with several circumstances of the very great' boldness and presumption of the Romish priests and papists in this Kingdom,' and the privy council notified to the bishops 'that a distinct and particular account should be taken of all papists and reputed papists with their respective qualities, estates and places of abode.'[2] The Acts of 1708 were put in force without delay in Cumberland. At the Midsummer Sessions of that year eighteen reputed papists were summoned to appear and conform to the law. In the following August Bishop Nicolson informed the primate that 'popery has advanced by very long strides of late years in this country and too many of our magistrates love to have it so. At the very time that the French were on our coasts and our people daily expected the news of their being landed, the wealthier of our papists, instead of being seized, were cringed to with all possible tenders of honour and respect, and those very gentlemen, who were entrusted with the taking of them into custody, seemed rather inclined to list themselves in their services.'[3] The rigour of the law was sorely felt by the papists during the period of the abortive insurrection of 1715. While the panic lasted stringent measures were adopted for the security of the county. The bishop issued a circular letter to his clergy on 15 October, in which he stated that 'there being now a most unnatural and dangerous rebellion raised in the neighbourhood of this diocese by several papists and other wicked enemies to our happy establishment in church and state, I cannot but think it a necessary duty on this pressing occasion to exhort you and the rest of my brethren to animate and encourage your respective parishioners in defence of their religion, laws and liberties against all such traitorous attempts towards the destruction of his majesty's royal person and the subversion of his most gracious government.'[4] The civil authorities had not been backward in preparing for emergencies. At the Hilary Sessions, 1714–5, the high constables handed in lists of papists or persons so reputed in their respective wards who had been summoned to appear. As the vigilance of the justices increased, a greater number of papists was discovered. At the Sessions of January, 1715–6, no fewer than fifty persons, esquires and yeomen, rich and poor, were summoned to take the oath of allegiance, 'being persons by us suspected to be dangerous or disaffected to his majesty or his government.'

---

[1] *Trans. Cumb. and Westmor. Arch. Soc.* new series, ii. 177–9, 181 ; *Miscellany Accounts of Dio. of Carl.* pp. 133, 147.
[2] *Letters of Wm. Nicolson,* pp. 330–2.   [3] Add MS. 6116.
[4] *Letters of Wm. Nicolson,* p. 432.

ECCLESIASTICAL HISTORY

When the scare of the Pretender's invasion had faded away, the Roman Catholic body in Cumberland suffered little inconvenience from the penal laws except during the rebellion of 1745, when they were disarmed and the sleeping laws were revived and put in force till the danger was passed. Roman Catholicism never took deep root in Cumberland. Except in a few families of distinction like the Howards, Curwens and Radcliffes, with their tenants and servants, this form of religious belief had almost died out before the Irish immigration at the beginning of the nineteenth century. Bishop Leyburne, who visited the northern counties in 1687, when papists were much favoured in high quarters, reported that he had confirmed 22 persons at Greystoke, 127 at Corby, and 426 at Brampton. But from the statistics sent to the Propaganda by Bishop Petre on 8 September 1773, it may be gathered that 'few Catholics' were found. In Bishop Smith's account of his vicariate on 14 October 1830, there were only four stations or meeting places for Roman Catholics in the county. The number of stations was increased to six in 1839 during the vicariate of Bishop Briggs.[1]

An unfortunate broil among the members of the capitular body about the administration of their domestic affairs disturbed the peace of the diocese for some time during Bishop Nicolson's episcopate. The appointment of Dr. Francis Atterbury to the deanery of Carlisle in 1704 was warmly resented by the bishop,[2] and it was soon evident that the old jealousies which existed between them as scholars and antiquaries would be imported into their public concerns. It is not necessary to follow step by step the unseemly wrangles between bishop and dean. Another member of the chapter, Hugh Todd, also an antiquary, had old scores to wipe out, and he lost no time in taking sides against his diocesan. Occasions soon arose to fan the smouldering embers into flame. A small matter of discipline among the minor canons, who had behaved themselves indecorously in the vestry of the cathedral, and the nomination of an incumbent to one of the benefices in the patronage of the chapter were the pretexts on which Atterbury and Todd set the city of Carlisle in an uproar and involved the heads of the diocese in an altercation, the sounds of which had reached to every corner of the kingdom. The quarrel was mainly concerned with the position of the dean in the capitular body, about which there was some doubt owing to an apparent discrepancy between the authority of the statutes and the endowment charter. Denying the validity of the statutes as not having received the sanction of the Crown and parliament, Dean Atterbury claimed it as his sole right 'to take cognisance of and punish offences and disorders' in the church, and as the majority of the chapter ignored his claims, he went further and formally objected to everything that was done by the other members, in which resistance he was supported by Dr. Todd. The dean withheld the key of the box in which the chapter seal was kept and refused his consent

1 Brady, *Engl. Catholic Hierarchy*, pp. 143–4, 263, 276–7, 280.
2 *Trans. Cumb. and Westmor. Arch. Soc.* new series, ii. 197.

to chapter acts. As the position had become intolerable, Bishop Nicolson interposed and urged the members of the church to compose their differences, but as the admonition was without effect he determined to visit and enforce obedience. The scene in the chapter house between the bishop and Dr. Todd, the dean's proxy, was not edifying. Formal objection was taken to the visitation on the ground that the Queen alone was the legal visitor. Compromise was now impossible. The bishop excommunicated Dr. Todd. A war of pamphlets ensued. The quarrel was carried to the civil courts and to the House of Commons. At length an Act of Parliament (6 Anne, c. 21) was passed confirming the validity of the statutes[1] ; the doctor was released from the ban of excommunication, and the trouble was at an end.[2]

The preaching of John Wesley in Cumberland was not attended with the enthusiasm and wholesale conversions which marked the progress of George Fox a century before. The mass of the population, though they listened with respect, remained unmoved ; the gentry as a rule stood aloof. When the great preacher visited the county, he was not recognized by the bishop of the diocese, and had neither sympathy nor support from the clergy. In a private house or at the market cross or in some public building like a town hall, Wesley exercised the gifts of his vocation as he journeyed from place to place. On 11 April 1753 he found that the love of many of the society in Whitehaven had ' waxed cold,' though ' a considerable number appeared to be growing in grace.' On the following Sunday ' he preached in the afternoon at Cockermouth to well nigh all the inhabitants of the town.' At Branthwaite in 1757 ' many of the congregation came from far ' to hear him ; ' the word had free course ' at Cockermouth, ' even the gentry seemed desirous' of accepting his doctrine. On his return to Cumberland in 1761 it can scarcely be said that he was otherwise than disappointed with the fruits of his previous labours. The whole congregation at Workington behaved well, but he could not perceive that the greater part understood anything of the matter. Wesley's experience of the people of Wigton had a depressing effect upon him. ' The congregation when I began,' he says, ' consisted of one woman, two boys, and three or four little girls, but in a quarter of an hour we had most of the town. I was a good deal moved at the exquisite self-sufficiency, which was visible in the countenance, air, and whole deportment of a considerable part of them.' When he reached Carlisle in 1770 he found that ' it was here a day of small things, the society consisting but of fifteen members.' On a further visit to the

---

[1] A full account of this squabble may be gathered from the numerous documents collected by Nichols and printed in his *Letters of Wm. Nicolson*, and the bishop's private sentiments may be seen in *Bishop Nicolson's Diaries*, now in course of publication by the Bishop of Barrow-in-Furness in the new series of the *Cumb. and Westmor. Arch. Soc. Trans.* The legal aspect of the case has been treated exhaustively by Burn, *Eccl. Law* (ed. Phillimore, 1842), ii. 94–104, and by Phillimore, *Eccl. Law* (ed. 1873), i. 173–84.

[2] Another dispute arose in 1752 on the interpretation of the statutes in relation to the dean's negative power in the conferring of benefices. Compare Phillimore, *Eccles. Law*, i. 192–4, with Carl. Epis. Reg. Osbaldiston, ff. 175–7, 235–7. The peace of the capitular body was again disturbed in 1858 by the interference of Dean Close with the duties of the precentor.

city in 1772 little progress seems to have been made ; he was received
by ' a small company of plain loving people.' It is evident that Carlisle
did not at first take to methodism. Wesley had but a poor opinion
of his prospects in the cathedral city. When he preached at the town
hall there in 1780, it was to the poor only, as the rich could not rise
in time to hear him. From the number and seriousness of his hearers
at a later meeting, he 'conceived a little hope that even here some good
will be done.'[1] The same opinion was expressed in 1797 by a churchman who described the people of Carlisle as 'very ignorant in religion :
they wander as sheep without a shepherd. They seem, however, open
to conviction, they have conscience. There are here some methodist
and dissenting interests, but feeble and of little weight, nor is there
a dissenter here of any popularity, or as it should seem of any
religious zeal.'[2] Of all the scenes of Wesley's personal ministrations
in Cumberland, his hopes of Whitehaven, where he often preached,
were the brightest. Of this town he wrote in 1784 that there was a
fairer prospect than there had been for many years. The society was
united in love, not conformed to the world, but labouring to experience
the full image of God, wherein they were created. His meetings had
been attended by all the church ministers and most of the gentry of the
town, but they behaved with as much decency as if they had been
colliers.[3]

There can be little doubt that methodism made slight impression
on the people of Cumberland before the secession of 1791–1836. It
was only after it had become an integral portion of nonconformity that
its influence began to be felt in towns or country villages. The process
of separation went on gradually for almost fifty years, and it is only now
and again that we get glimpses of it as an organized religious community.
As soon as its members determined to create charitable trusts and to
accept gifts of real property for the support of their distinctive tenets,
it may be said that its independent existence was assured. One of the
earliest establishments in the county was made at Brampton in 1789
during the lifetime of Wesley. No other charitable trust had been
registered on behalf of the methodists during the eighteenth century.
But very soon after, the endowment of the society went on apace. In
1802 and 1817 gifts of real property were registered for their use at
Carlisle, in 1806 at Maryport, in 1811 at Alston, in 1814 at Keswick,
in 1826 at Workington, in 1827 at Whitehaven, and in 1828 at
Wigton.[4] In all these places there was no rapid cleavage between the
church and methodism. It is quite true that chapels sprang up and
congregations to some extent came together, but among those early
methodists there was a lingering love for the sacramental ministrations
of the parish clergy. Attendance on the services of the church was not
wholly relinquished. The parish priest was often called in to baptize

1 *Journal of John Wesley* (London, 1829), pp. 359, 412, 490, 640, 666, 720, 766–7.
2 *Life of Dean Milner*, p. 130.   3 *Journal of John Wesley*, p. 808.
4 *Trans. Cumb. and Westmor. Arch. Soc.* new series, ii. 348–79.

infants[1] and to bury the dead, while not a few availed themselves of the Holy Eucharist at Easter and on other great festivals. Traces of this respect for the ordinances of the church are still visible in many country villages. It is only in our own day that the general body of methodists has drifted completely into separation.

The pecuniary assistance given to the chapelries and poor benefices by Queen Anne's Bounty had a considerable effect in raising the tone and increasing the efficiency of the clergy of the diocese. In Cumberland there was much need of it. To meet the requirements of the large and scattered parishes in the mountainous districts, chapels of ease arose with stipendiary curates dependent for their salaries on parochial incumbents, the impropriators, or the free will offerings of the inhabitants. Several of these chapelries were served by a reader and schoolmaster not in holy orders. By statute 1 Geo. I. st. 2, c. 10, a new ecclesiastical status was created, and protection was afforded to those curacies which had received an augmentation of revenue from the Bounty. It was this Act that practically abolished the lay reader in the Cumberland dales. From this date the chapelries which received augmentation became perpetual cures and benefices. In returning a schedule of the forty-eight perpetual curacies in the diocese on 26 January 1739, Bishop Fleming declared that all the chapelries he had named were entirely distinct from their respective mother churches, and the parishes were so very large, and many of them situated in such inconvenient parts, that there was the greatest occasion to have distinct curates settled in them all, as there were in most of them constantly, except Newlands, Thornthwaite, Wythburn, Borrowdale and Nicholforest, though their situation was such that none could require it more if the salaries had been sufficient for their maintenance. The rectors or vicars of the mother churches had no advantage from these chapelries except the right of nomination to some of them, the nomination to many being with the inhabitants.[2]

No trustworthy evidence has been produced to show that the church in Cumberland had lapsed into a state of lethargy in the eighteenth century. The facts are all on the other side. The bishops of Carlisle were prelates of distinguished ability who devoted their time and energy to episcopal work, and not a few of them were men of saintly life. The names of Nicolson, Lyttelton, Law and Douglas shed a lustre on the episcopate of the eighteenth century for learning and literary culture. Bishop Fleming, the head of a great house in Westmorland, has left a name behind him for the possession of Christian virtues[3] which

---

[1] The practice of keeping a register of births and baptisms is a sure sign of final separation from the church. For the Wesleyan Methodists these registers begin in 1814 for Fisher Street, Carlisle; in 1824 for George Street, Wigton; in 1806 for Michael Street, Whitehaven (chapel formed in 1747); in 1814 for Sandgate Chapel, Penrith; in 1810 for Alston; in 1811 for Garrigill; and in 1827 for Nenthead. Primitive Methodism was established in Alston in 1823, their registers commencing in 1825 (*Com. Rep. on Nonconformist Registers* [1838], pp. 89, 119).

[2] Carl. Epis. Reg., Fleming, ff. 67-73.

[3] In the obituary notice of this prelate which appeared in the *Gentleman's Magazine* (xvii. 324-6) of 1747, it is stated that he punctually joined with his family 'four times a day in the publick devotions

Painted by G. Romney

Engraved by W. Dickinson

Edmundus Law, L.L.D. Episcopus Carliolensis.

EDMUND LAW, BISHOP OF CARLISLE.

reminds us of the character of Bishop Rainbow. The parochial activity of the century is written in the ecclesiastical architecture of the diocese. It was a time for the rebuilding and enlargement of churches. The Georgian or 'churchwarden' type of church is too well known : a large rectangular building with sash-windows, overhanging galleries, and 'three-decker' pulpits, providing accommodation for the increasing population, may still be seen in many parishes. The episcopal registers contain many licences for restorations and rededications, as well as the consecrations of new edifices to meet the wants of the growing industries on the western coast. The inhabitants of Cumberland were a church-going people, and traditions are still handed down to tell us of the vast numbers that came from far and near in extensive parishes for the Sunday service and the Easter sacrament. In the churchwardens' accounts of many parishes we read of the amount of wine used at the Easter or one of the quarterly sacraments with as much astonishment as we view the uncomfortable, high-backed pews. The parish church may have been more of 'a preaching house' than 'a place of worship,' but nobody can deny that the Cumbrian looked upon it as his spiritual home. There were few organs in the churches of the eighteenth century. Instrumental accompaniments to divine service were of a different character : surpliced choirs were unknown except in the cathedral. The musical portion of the service in the larger churches was rendered by a medley of men, women and school children perched in a gallery at the west end, with the assistance of the pitch-pipe or 'loud bassoon.' The parish clerk was precentor, and the pitch-pipe was the badge of his office. In most of the country parishes of Cumberland this instrument of music is preserved to remind us of an extinct custom in divine service. Men still live who were acquainted with no other church music in their earlier years.[1]

The first symptom of the evangelical revival reached the diocese through the agency of Dr. Isaac Milner, a distinguished mathematician, the senior wrangler *incomparabilis* of his year, who became dean of Carlisle in 1792. The sermons of the new dean took the people of Carlisle by storm. 'When the dean of Carlisle preaches,' wrote Dr. Paley, 'you may walk on the heads of the people. All the meetings attend to hear him. He is indeed a powerful preacher.'[2] The orator was untrammelled by considerations of formulary or creed : the nonconformist was captivated by his eloquence as well as the churchman. During Milner's decanate (1792-1820) a transformation of ecclesiastical feeling was made in Carlisle and the immediate neighbourhood. The spirit of church party, soon to result in divided counsels, had been intro-

---

of the church,' and that by his death society had lost one of its most valuable members, and the Church of England one of its chiefest ornaments.

[1] In answer to Bishop Goodwin's articles of inquiry in 1872 'whether any and what instrument is used in each church,' the churchwardens made replies which the bishop tabulated thus :—'organ in 93 churches; harmonium in 171 ; barrel organ in 3 ; and no instrument in 15 ' (*Primary Visitation Charge*, p. 16).

[2] E. Paley, *Life of Dr. Paley*, p. clxxxvi.; M. Milner, *Life of Dean Milner*, pp. 116, 272.

duced. The diocese as a whole had been devoted to the support of the Society for Promoting Christian Knowledge, as representing the work of the church at home, and to the Society for the Propagation of the Gospel, which embodied the corporate action of the church in the mission field. It was customary for churchwardens to make a house to house collection every year in their several parishes for these societies. As the dean was a great favourite with nonconformists, the agents of the British and Foreign Bible Society prevailed upon him to establish an auxiliary branch in the cathedral city. This was done in 1813 to the delight of 'all the meetings,' and Lord Morpeth was appointed the first president.[1] The introduction of the Church Missionary Society was a task of greater delicacy. Bishop Goodenough remained aloof; in the capitular body the dean stood alone; few persons of rank or station among the laity enrolled themselves among the supporters of the scheme. But Dean Milner was not to be thwarted, for he accepted the presidency of the Carlisle association in February 1818. Nor did he confine his sympathies to missionary agencies within the church: he was a warm advocate of Moravian and Methodist missions and a liberal subscriber to their funds.[2] Nowhere can the bent of his mind be better gauged than by his action with regard to the management of the central or diocesan school which the bishop had founded in Carlisle in 1812. The dean was for the admission of the children of dissenters with certain privileges by way of 'a conscience clause.' The bishop's firmness may be gathered from his rejoinder to these proposals: 'I have no idea of refusing the benefit of education upon account of his or her parents' religious principles. Any child will be allowed to enter, provided he will conform to the rules of the school. The principal of those rules will be that they learn the Catechism of the Church of England, be instructed in our Liturgy, and give their regular attendance on the Sundays at our church. These are indispensable conditions, if I have anything to do with the conduct of the school.'[3] But the seed sown by this eminent man took root downward and bore fruit upward. The principles of which Dean Milner was the champion are stamped broad and visible on the ecclesiastical life of the nineteenth century in the diocese of Carlisle.

The spread of nonconformity in country villages was largely due to the system of pluralities which prevailed to such an alarming extent during the period immediately before the accession of Queen Victoria. When the heads of the church like bishops, deans, and prebendaries held more than one dignity, it was impossible to deny the parish priests a participation in the same system. In 1835 about one-half of the benefices of the diocese were filled in plurality.[4] To one of these the incumbent as a rule gave his attention, but the other was delivered over

[1] *Life of Dean Milner*, pp. 565, 577-8.
[2] Ibid. pp. 608, 610, 672.   [3] Ibid. pp. 486-9, etc., 574.
[4] *Rep. of the Commissioners on Eccl. Revenues* (1835), pp. 214-22. Of the bishops of Carlisle, Dr. Percy was the last pluralist. At this date he held the chancellorship of Salisbury Cathedral and a prebend in St. Paul's (ibid. p. 3).

to a stipendiary curate, often ill-paid and poorly equipped for the cure of souls. This custom was not observed only in small parishes with little endowment, where there might have been a difficulty in obtaining the services of an incumbent. Fortunate clergymen, commanding private or ecclesiastical patronage, were in possession of most of the valuable benefices. The total amount expended on the employment of assistant curates in the ancient diocese was £3,684, nearly the whole of which was found by the pluralists for the provision of substitutes in the parishes which they held but could not serve.[1] When extensive tracts of country were deprived of the religious ministrations and pastoral oversight of resident incumbents, it cannot be wondered at that in a period of political ferment and constitutional change there should be a shrinkage of the church's influence and that the sects should occupy the lost ground. To Cumberland people, imbued with the idea that priests work at their trade for wages like other men,[2] the disinterested services of the methodists appealed with such irresistible force that chapels of this religious persuasion were established in every considerable village of the county before 1840.

But reform was in the air : a new era was at hand. The commissioners appointed to consider the state of 'the established church' with reference to ecclesiastical duties and revenues made their third report in 1836 in which it was recommended 'that the sees of Carlisle and Sodor and Man be united, and that the diocese consist of the present diocese of Carlisle, of those parts of Cumberland and Westmorland which are now in the diocese of Chester, of the deanery of Furnes and Cartmel in the county of Lancaster, of the parish of Aldeston now in the diocese of Durham, and of the Isle of Man.'[3] By subsequent legislation (6 and 7 Will. IV. c. 77, and 1 Vict. c. 30) the diocese was extended to its present limits : the ecclesiastical annexation of the diocese of Sodor and Man did not take place, and the parish of Alston, though in Cumberland, was allowed to remain as aforetime in the diocese of Durham. Under the authority of these Acts, the deanery of Coupland in Cumberland and the deaneries of Furness and Cartmel, which included the whole of Lancashire north of the Sands together with the portions of the deaneries of Kirkby Lonsdale and Kendal within the county of Westmorland, that is, the old barony of Kendal, were severed from the diocese of Chester and archdeaconry of Richmond and annexed to the diocese of Carlisle, the whole addition having been formed into a new

---

[1] To the non-residence of the incumbent must be ascribed the decay of so many parsonage houses in the diocese at this time. The commissioners returned fourteen parsonages as unfit for habitation, and thirty-one benefices in which there was no parsonage at all.

[2] This feature of the Cumberland character struck John Wesley as he passed through Bowness on Solway in 1753, and caused him to make a note of it. 'Our landlord, as he was guiding us over the Frith, very innocently asked, "How much a year we got by preaching thus ?" This gave me an opportunity of explaining that kind of gain which he seemed utterly a stranger to. He appeared to be quite amazed and spake not one word, good or bad, till he took his leave ' (*Journal*, pp. 359–60).

[3] *Third Report of the Church Com.* (1836), pp. 9, 11, 23. On the map of the proposed diocese attached to the report, the archdeaconry of Carlisle is divided into only three deaneries, viz. Carlisle, Alderbie or Allerdale or Alnedale, and Westmorland.

archdeaconry, which, for lack of a better territorial name, was called the archdeaconry of Westmorland. This final arrangement was made by Order in Council, dated 10 August 1847, but did not come into force till the death of Bishop Percy in 1856. After a history of 723 years the diocese of Carlisle entered on a new epoch. Its enlargement marks the turn over of a fresh page. The period of organization and activity had come. The railway was discovered to be a useful agency in diocesan work, and bishops of Carlisle were not slow in taking advantage of it.

The whole of the nineteenth century, and specially the latter portion of it, is distinguished for the ceaselessness of its manifold activities and the variety of its diocesan and parochial organizations. It is true that at all times the diocese of Carlisle was administered on plans suited to its geographical situation and spiritual necessities, but when we reach the Victorian period the church became more plastic and adaptable to the requirements of increasing population and advancing education. The history of the episcopate is embodied in 'the daily round and common task' of diocesan movement. Under the new conditions the bishop became the most indefatigable worker in his diocese. Bishop Villiers lost no time in carrying out the legislation of 1836 for the enlargement of his charge. One of his first acts after consecration was the nomination of an archdeacon of Westmorland on 9 May 1856, and so bent was he on diocesan organization that the long obsolete machinery of ruridecanal action was revived on 1 January 1858 by the subdivision of the diocese into eighteen rural deaneries and the appointment of a beneficed clergyman in each district with a nominal oversight.[1] Very soon the actual condition of things began to dawn on the chief pastor of the flock. The rural deans brought back a report of the nakedness of the land. Populous and extensive parishes needed subdivision : new churches, new parsonages, increased incomes—this was the mournful tale. Bishop Waldegrave lamented in 1861 that of the 267 incumbencies in the diocese, 58 had no glebe houses at all, and to these should be added nine places in which the residences were unfit for habitation. In six parishes the income did not attain to £50 a year ; in eight it did not exceed £70 ; in three it barely reached £80 ; while but few exceeded 120.[2] While this undesirable state of things was being remedied by the action of the Church Extension Society, founded by himself in 1862, the supply of the right sort of clergy became the pressing problem of his episcopate. It troubled Bishop Waldegrave as it had troubled many of his predecessors. Apprehension was expressed that the bishop was lowering the status of the clergy by admitting men of inferior educational equipment to holy orders. The charge brought a spirited defence at the diocesan visitation of 1864. Of the sixty candidates ordained during the four years of his episcopate, twenty-two were of academic rank, twenty-six had been trained in theological colleges, and only twelve were literates, men

[1] Carl. Epis. Reg. Villiers, ff. 81, 145-50.
[2] *Charge at his Primary Visitation* (1861), p. 16.

qualified by service as nonconformist ministers, Scripture readers or lay assistants. 'If these figures,' he said, 'be compared with those of the four years immediately preceding the enlargement of the diocese in 1856, it will be found that, while the number of candidates ordained have been multiplied rather more than threefold since that date, that of University men has been exactly doubled.' He further stated that a comparison of his own episcopate with that of Bishop Villiers would show to a slight extent a more favourable result. Bishop Waldegrave was fully alive to the gravity of the problem, and was making earnest efforts to grapple with it. 'Forty-seven churchless villages still cry out for sanctuaries ; fifty-one pastors still have no home to call their own ; ninety-six benefices still fall short of £100 per annum ; sixty-four of them exceed that sum, but do not; attain to £150.' The supply of a good class of clergy depended on adequate provision for their mainten_ance. While life lasted, he would· devote himself to this work. Be it said to the credit of this amiable prelate that he kept his word.[1]

At no previous period in the nineteenth century had the church in Cumberland made such rapid progress in its various spiritual and philanthropic aspects than during the long and remarkable episcopate of Bishop Harvey Goodwin, 1869–91. His fame as a mathematician and man of science, his power as a preacher, his methodical habits and almost exhaustless capacity for work, all combined to stamp the iron energy of his will and character upon the diocese of which he was the revered and honoured chief for over twenty years. The history of his episcopate has been written by the bishop himself, and no description by another pen can approach in completeness the narrative which he has left behind him in his annual pastoral letters and triennial charges. His efforts to improve the material condition of the clergy, to pro_vide new districts with churches, to attract men of ability into his diocese, and to raise the tone and stimulate the zeal of those already at work, were but a small portion of his policy. The character and frequency of parochial ministrations were never lost sight of. It was his endeavour by counsel and encouragement to raise the religious organization of every parish to a high standard. In 1872 the Holy Eucharist was celebrated at least monthly in 158 churches ; in 1887 the number of churches had increased to 255, and in 1890 to 271. His aim was to promote a celebration of the divine office in every parish church on Sundays and holy days. In the same manner the observance of Ascension Day, which had become almost obsolete in Cumberland, the frequent advocacy of missionary enterprise in foreign lands, the preparation of young people for confirmation and systematic teaching in the parish schools were constantly urged upon the clergy.

Cumberland has been singularly free from scandals among the clergy either in their private lives or public ministrations. No instance of ritual aberration has disturbed the ecclesiastical harmony of the

---

[1] Bishop Waldegrave, *Charge at his Second Episcopal Visitation* (1864), pp. 23, 25–9.

county. When Bishop Goodwin had occasion to refer to methods of church ministration, ritual defects rather than ritual excesses were the subject of his allocution. Sounds of conflict in the ecclesiastical courts over the colour of vestments or the posture of priests in divine service have not been heard. The full tide of the Oxford Movement was spent before it reached our shores. Clergymen of forty or fifty years' standing speak in admiration of the change which has passed over the county during their ministerial life in the matter of restored churches, bright and orderly services, and reverent behaviour. Here and there an incumbent vests his choir-men and boys in cassock and surplice, takes 'the eastward position,' lights two candles, and perhaps puts on a special vestment for the celebration of the weekly sacrament. But in most of the churches there is no attempt at outward ceremony ; a plain brass cross with two vases for flowers is the only ornament of the altar, and the cassock, surplice, stole and academic hood are the only vestments of the priest. The Public Worship Regulation Act has been a dead letter in Cumberland.[1] During the writer's experience the only rag of ritualism he has ever seen in the county was the black or academic gown for use in the pulpit. In 1872 this strange vestment was reckoned among the 'ornaments' of 118 churches.[2] The black gown now takes its place with the pitch-pipe and the barrel organ as the relic of an extinct ritual.

Not a little uneasiness in ecclesiastical circles was caused by the extreme line taken up by Dean Close on the ritual controversies of his time, 1856–81. He was a masterful figure in the religious life of Carlisle, and belonged to the straitest sect of militant protestantism. For his earnest eloquence as a preacher and his unwearying advocacy of church extension, temperance, foreign missions and other philanthropic agencies, he deserves a grateful recognition. But he was an uncompromising opponent of Trac-tarianism, which he regarded as ecclesiastical reaction. The vehemence of his denunciation served to propagate the principles he condemned. In 1873 proposals to establish a religious community in Caldewgate, a poor and populous district of the cathedral city beneath the windows of the deanery, were carried to completion. It was indiscreetly called 'an oratory,' and had the patronage of a notorious ritualist of a southern diocese. At the same time the incumbent of a neighbouring parish made some alterations in his method of conducting service after the restoration and beautifying of his church, which were interpreted as an advance to Romish practices. In addition to this, the bishop made a state-ment in the cathedral pulpit of what he ' conceived to be sober Church

---

[1] Under the eighth section of this Act, only one representation was made in the diocese of Carlisle between 1874 and 1898, and the bishop refused to allow proceedings to be taken. It was the case of the vicar of St. George's, Barrow-in-Furness, in 1878 (*Public Worship Regulation and Church Discipline*, parl. paper, pp. 36–40). The ritual practices complained of were harmless enough, and most of them are now common in the diocese and excite no suspicion. In 1899 Bishop Bardsley testified ' that there is not one instance of a confessional box put up in a church in the diocese of Carlisle ' (*Church of England Confessional Boxes*, parl. paper, pp. 8–9).

[2] Bp. Goodwin, *Primary Charge*, p. 23.

of England views on the subject' ot sacramental confession. The indignation of the dean of Carlisle found vent in a series of comminations which are read with astonishment at the present day. It was a passing excitement and soon cooled down. When a pastoral staff was presented to Bishop Goodwin in 1884, on the occasion of the visit of the Church Congress to Carlisle, 'in grateful recognition of his faithful and unwearied efforts during the past fourteen years in tending the flock of God committed to his charge,' the memories of past controversies had been forgotten, and the unanimity among clergy and laity in selecting this form of gift marked the arrival of a new and better state of things.

APPENDIX I

THE DIOCESE OF CARLISLE

AS the diocese of Carlisle was founded nearly half a century before the counties of Cumberland and Westmorland took their present shape, the boundaries of these civil divisions had no effect in determining its extent. The district or land of Carlisle from which Dolfin was expelled by William Rufus was a strip of territory between the rivers Esk and Derwent, extending eastward from the Solway to the Reycross on Stanemore on the borders of Yorkshire, and cut off from Northumberland and Durham by the Pennine range of hills. It embraced the whole of Cumberland as it now is, with the exception of the south-western angle between the Derwent and the Duddon, known as the county or barony of Coupland, and the eastern portion of Westmorland, known as the county or barony of Appleby. The present county of Westmorland was thus divided into two parts, the barony of Appleby, which was included in the land of Carlisle, and the barony of Kendal, which at the date of the creation of the bishopric was a part of the great county of York. Some time after the conquest in 1092, the new district was placed under the rule of Ranulf Meschin as the vassal of the English crown, and its ecclesiastical supervision passed at once to the jurisdiction of the archbishop of York. In order to set at rest the rival claims of the bishops of Glasgow and Durham, who from certain historical associations were contending for its oversight, and to assist more directly its ecclesiastical development, Henry I. created the new province into a bishopric with the seat of the bishop in the priory church which he had founded in Carlisle. Except in the cases of three parishes on the northern and eastern bounds of modern Cumberland with very peculiar histories, the extent of the diocese of Carlisle had undergone no alteration from the date of its formation in 1133 till its enlargement in 1856.

The parish of Alston on the eastern border has the peculiar distinction of being in the county of Cumberland and diocese of Durham. It is quite certain that this district formed no part of Ranulf Meschin's fief, and that the church there was never within the jurisdiction of the bishop of Carlisle. The parish, cut off from the land of Carlisle by the natural barriers of hills and wastes, was part of the liberty of Hexham or Tyndal, and lay without the county of Cumberland after its formation as a fiscal area about 1174.[1] On the other hand, the small parish of Over Denton in the same neighbourhood, consisting only of a thousand acres, though in the county of Cumberland, remained in the diocese of Durham till the beginning of the eighteenth century.[2] Both of these churches were in the deanery of Corbridge and archdeaconry of Northumberland, and were valued as such in the taxation of Pope Nicholas IV. on 20 December 1291; though Over Denton is not noticed in the valuation of Henry VIII. in 1535, it is included, with the parish of Alston, in the deanery of Corbridge on the appended map of the diocese of Durham.[3] How this singular arrangement came about will be more conveniently explained when the history of individual parishes and advowsons of churches

---

[1] The early history of the advowson of Alston is stated on the pleadings in *Quo Warranto* (Rec. Com.), p. 120. Its subsequent history may be seen in Raine, *Priory of Hexham* (Surtees Soc.), ii. pp. ix. 119, and the references there given. In the Nonæ Rolls of Northumberland for 1340 the commissioner reported that he did not answer for Alston ' quia est infra libertatem de Hextildesham ubi nullum breve regis currit ' (Hodgson, *Hist. of Northumberland*, iii. pt. iii. p. xxxvii.)

[2] The advowson of Over Denton was given to the priory of Lanercost by Buethbarn in the twelfth century (Reg. of Lanercost, MS. iii. 1, 2, xii. 26, i. 4, 5). It is stated in the Nonæ Rolls that Denton in Gyldesland formed part of the deanery of Corbridge, but was not in the county of Northumberland (Hodgson, *Hist.* iii. pt. iii. p. xxxvii.) For the final transference of the church of Denton from the diocese of Durham to that of Carlisle in 1703, and for its history as far as it could be gathered at that date from the episcopal registers of Durham, see Bishop Nicolson, *Miscellany Accounts* (Cumbld. and Westmorld. Archæol. Soc.), p. 4.

[3] Compare *Taxatio Eccl.* (Rec. Com.), p. 316, with *Valor Eccl.* (Rec. Com.), v. 328. The distinction between Nether Denton and Over Denton in both valuations is clearly discernible.

comes under review. The present parish of Kirkandrews-on-Esk was formed out of the Debatable Land on the Scottish frontier by letters patent of Charles I. in 1631.[1] There can be no doubt that there was a church of Kirkandrews near the present site in the early part of the twelfth century,[2] when the land of Carlisle extended into Scotland further than the international boundary finally agreed upon by the commissioners of Edward VI. But so far as the history of the diocese is concerned, the parish of Kirkandrews had no separate ecclesiastical existence till the date named.

The enlargement of the diocese in 1856, so as to include the whole of Cumberland with the exception of the parish of Alston, the whole of Westmorland, and Lancashire north of the Sands, has been already noticed. It consists of 297 ecclesiastical parishes, of which 169 are in Cumberland.

APPENDIX II

THE ARCHDEACONRIES

THERE is little doubt that the archdeaconry of Carlisle was not only conterminous with the diocese, but was also coeval with its formation in 1133. At a very early period the benefices of the diocese were taxed to maintain the dignity of the archdeacon as well as that of the bishop. When Adelulf, the first bishop, confirmed the appropriation of certain churches to the priory of Wetheral, he imposed on the monks the obligation of paying the synodals and archidiaconals due from these churches. In subsequent confirmations to this house, the reservation of archidiaconal dues was made a feature of the bishop's sanction.[3] Previous to the extension of the diocese in 1856, there was but one archdeaconry, the archdeaconry of Carlisle.

During the long vacancy of the see which followed the death of the first bishop, the archdeacon was the local head of the diocese, having an official of his own in the diocesan court,[4] and employing chaplains in quasi-episcopal fashion for the maintenance of his dignity.[5] Sometimes the archdeacon was entrusted with the custody of the bishopric,[6] and sometimes with the duties of official. One of them administered the affairs of the diocese throughout the greater portion of the reign of Henry II., and another held Carlisle for a short time with the archdeaconry of Durham. During the prolonged vacancy of the bishopric, appointments to the archdeaconry were made by the Crown.[7]

It is not certainly known what provision was made for the maintenance of the office during the twelfth century. The archdeacon probably had a share of the endowments of the church of Carlisle, out of which the bishopric and priory were supported in common.[8] In the thirteenth century, when the succession of bishops became regular, two benefices appear to have been burdened one after the other for the maintenance of the archdeacon. When

---

1 Carl. Epis. Reg. Smith, MS. ff. 325-6.

2 *National MSS. of Scotland* (Rec. Com.), i. No. 38.

3 *Reg. of Wetheral* (Cumbld. and Westmorld. Archæol. Soc.), pp. 44, 54, 58, 211, 213, 216.

4 Archdeacon Geoffrey de Lascy had an official in the time of Bishop Bernard (*Reg. of Wetheral*, p. 72). Thomas de Morland was archdeacon's official in the time of Bishop Walter (Reg. of Fountains, f. 324b). Thomas de Foveis filled a like post in 1264 (*Whitby Chartul.* i. 230, 285). The official of the archdeacon of Carlisle was recognized by the diocesan synod in the fourteenth century (Carl. Epis. Reg. Welton, ff. 134-5).

5 Reg. of Lanercost, MS. viii. 2; · *Reg. of Wetheral*, p. 101.

6 Each of the archdeacons in turn was *custos* of the see during the long vacancy in the twelfth century. Archdeacon Robert was probably *custos*, for he had power of institution to benefices (*Whitby Chartul.* i. 42). Peter de Ross was certainly *custos* as well as archdeacon (*Reg. of Wetheral*, pp. 216, 219); so also was Americ Thebert (Reg. of Lanercost, MS. viii. 2).

7 Hoveden, *Chron.* (Rolls Series), iv. 14; *Rot. Litt. Pat.* (Rec. Com.), i. 35b.

8 This appears from Bishop Adelulf's address to Elyas, the archdeacon, and the chapter of St. Mary, as if he were a member of that body (*Whitby Chartul.* i. 38). While there was no bishop, if the archdeacon performed the administrative work of the diocese, he would claim a rightful share of the emoluments.

Americ Thebert, rector of Dalston, was promoted to the archdeaconry in 1196, the revenues of that church became contributory to the support of the office. By ordination of Bishop Irton in 1285, a third portion of the fruits of Dalston was annexed to the archdeaconry *propter evidentem ipsius exilitatem*, the amount in 1292 being as much as £15.[1] For some years the pension continued to be paid, but it appears to have ceased after the church was appropriated to the bishop's table in 1307.[2] It is not known at what time the rectory of Great Salkeld, granted to Bishop Walter on 27 September, 1237,[3] became annexed to the archdeaconry, but there is no doubt that it had been enjoyed by the archdeacons of Carlisle from the close of the thirteenth century till 1855, when a canonry in the cathedral was substituted by Order in Council.[4]

Another source of revenue arose from the procurations paid by parish churches to meet the expenses of the archdeacon's visitation. These parochial dues were of prescriptive obligation. The payment was a natural sequence of archidiaconal visitation. When the church of Newton Arlosh was founded in 1304, Bishop Halton made it clear in the deed of consecration that the incumbent should pay the archdeacon forty pence by way of procuration.[5] The archdeacon of Carlisle was invested with a nominal or inquisitorial jurisdiction as 'the eye of the bishop' for the purpose of visiting churches and clergy and reporting to his diocesan what he had seen and heard. His visitations came under the administrative surveillance of the diocesan synod, which, as occasion required, laid down rules for his guidance. By a constitution of the Carlisle synod in the fourteenth century, it was declared that procurations were due to the archdeacon on the principle that 'the labourer was worthy of his hire,' but the clergy insisted on the application of another maxim when that officer did not visit, namely, that no procurations should be paid, 'for if a man did not work, he should not eat.' This synod enacted that procurations in all cases should be moderate for man and beast, and that the archdeacon's retinue should not exceed what was allowed by the constitutions of the church.[6] The necessity for synodical supervision is evident from the proceedings of Archdeacon Richard called 'de Lyth,' who was punished in 1291 for exacting immoderate procurations from the rectors of the diocese, inasmuch as the number of persons who attended him consumed more victuals than the amount of the legal dues.[7]

The collection of procurations was a constant source of trouble to the archdeacons of Carlisle. Again and again did the bishop instruct his rural deans to exhort the clergy to an immediate discharge of their obligations.[8] In some cases when they were too backward, the archdeacon was authorized to proceed against them by the weapons of ecclesiastical censure, suspension, excommunication, and interdict in the diocesan court.[9] But it should not be forgotten that all these things took place by the exercise of the bishop's authority alone. It was the bishop who sent out his rural deans to warn the clergy of the archdeacon's visitation, and it was he who dealt with them for the non-payment of their archidiaconal obligations. Bishop Halton complained in 1318 that the archdeacon's procurations could not be recovered because the churches were burnt and travelling was so perilous that no visitations could be undertaken.[10] But a time came when there was an archdeacon who could visit, and who caused a commotion in the diocese by claiming co-ordinate jurisdiction with the bishop. In many respects the vagaries of Archdeacon William de Kendale are most interesting in diocesan history. Provoked by the execution of a papal writ *in negocio provisario* without authority, Bishop Kirkby wisely grappled with the situation by issuing a commission to review the ecclesiastical status of his subordinate, including his title to hold the church of Great Salkeld and to

---

[1] Reg. Abp. Romanus of York, MS. f. 131 ; *Taxatio Eccl.* (Rec. Com.), p. 318.

[2] Archdeacon Appleby, in a return of the emoluments of his benefice in 1366, reported to the bishop that 'the portion of the archdeacon in the church of Dalston was taxed at £15, of which he had never received anything, nor any of his predecessors, for forty years as he had heard' (Carl. Epis. Reg. Appleby, MS. f. 152).

[3] Chart. R. 21 Hen. III. No. 31, m. 2. In 1262 the patronage was in dispute between the bishop of Carlisle and the King of Scotland (Close, 46 Hen. III. m. 12d ; Rymer, *Fœdera* (ed. 1816), i. 417). The bishop maintained his right to the patronage in 1292, when Richard de Whitby was *persona impersonata* of Salkeld and archdeacon of Carlisle (*Quo Warranto* [Rec. Com.], p. 116). From the latter date at least the rectory was annexed to the archdeaconry.

[4] Carl. Epis. Reg. Villiers, MS. ff. 64–6.

[5] Harl. MSS. (Reg. of Holmcultram), 3911, ff. 7–8, 3891, ff. 20–1.

[6] Carl. Epis. Reg. Welton, ff. 135–6.

[7] *Cal. of Papal Letters*, i. 538.   [8] Carl. Epis. Reg. Welton, f. 18.

[9] Ibid. ff. 25, 35.   [10] Ibid. Halton, ff. 209–10.

receive 'the third penny' as the perquisites of chapters and synods.[1] The gravamen of the indictment was not so much that he held two benefices with cures of souls, but, as the bishop told the Archbishop of York, that he wished to find out by what right the archdeacon usurped and meddled with his episcopal jurisdiction contrary to universal custom.[2] The suit lasted over three years and ended disastrously for the archdeacon, for he was deprived in 1340 for persistent contumacy in the bishop's court and diocesan synod.[3] The right of the archdeacon to the church of Salkeld could not have been seriously questioned, but his claim to exercise a concurrent jurisdiction within the archdeaconry, which was conterminous with the diocese, provoked the bishop to action.

When the ecclesiastical atmosphere had cleared after the storm raised by the contentions of William de Kendale, the bishop adopted a more conciliatory attitude towards his archdeacon and drew up an agreement which marked a new era in the history of the office. By this scheme the tenure of the archdeaconry was made more agreeable to its occupant, and all occasion of friction was for ever done away. As the terms of the deed, which is dated 2 May 1360, while William de Rothbury was archdeacon, are in many respects remarkable, its chief provisions may be noticed. In the first place the bishop conceded to his subordinate the right to have a proctor in the chapters, celebrated by the official, to help him in making corrections, and to keep a counter-roll of the corrections so made ; also to summon by his letters the clergy to his visitation and to proceed by ecclesiastical censure against those who did not appear. Moreover power was given him to distrain for his procurations. And, lastly, it was allowed that when the rural deans rendered their accounts, the archdeacon was to receive the third penny of all corrections and synodals, or he may proceed against the said deans to recover his dues.[4] It should be borne in mind that no concessions were made of a judicial or coercive jurisdiction, and no power was delegated in contravention of the bishop's ordinary right of visitation. The archdeacon resided at his country rectory situated almost in the centre of the diocese, from which he made periodical circuits of diocesan inspection. As the procurations were understood to be a reward for his exertions they were not paid when the visitation was omitted. The third penny continued to be advanced by the rural deans out of the capitular fees. In the bishops' accounts, which are still extant for several years between 1402 and 1509, it is invariably noted by the deans in the schedule of receipts that the *tercia pars* of corrections and synodals, always of course a varying sum, belonged of right and had been paid to the archdeacon.[5]

The history of the archdeaconry from the Reformation to the extension of the diocese in 1856 possesses few incidents of ecclesiastical interest. The archdeacons had fallen to the level of country parsons, and exercised no special functions except the induction of clergymen to benefices after they had been instituted by the bishop, the presentation of candidates for ordination, which they were bound to do by the rubric of the Ordinal, and the personal visitation of churches which they frequently omitted. During the religious unsettlement of the Tudor period, the office came to be looked upon as a sinecure. The archdeacon of Carlisle was usually non-resident. If not employed elsewhere, the cure of the parish of Great Salkeld claimed his attention. The importance of the office of diocesan chancellor, which is but a modified form of the offices of official principal and vicar general, rose out of the ashes of the archidiaconate. Owing to the lethargy of archdeacons, the chancellors pushed them on

---

1 Carl. Epis. Reg. Kirkby, ff. 358-9. Kendale claimed the third penny of synods and chapters by right of his institution to the archdeaconry as his predecessors had received it before him by ancient custom (ibid. f. 362).
2 Ibid. f. 367.   3 Ibid. MS. ff. 407-8.
4 Ibid. Welton, ff. 67, 74.
5 For the history of archidiaconal jurisdiction and the archidiaconal court see the excellent account by Bishop Stubbs in *Eccl. Courts Com. Rep.* (1883), i. pp. xviii. xix. 21-51. In the diocese of Carlisle the archdeacon's court seems to have been suppressed about 1270, except for the adjudication of trifling causes, and his vested interests in the issues were compounded. By this composition the *tercius denarius* was allowed out of all fines and impositions levied in the diocesan courts. When Bishop Halton collated Peter de Insula in 1302, he made it clear that the new archdeacon should not meddle with matters requiring judicial investigation contrary to the custom observed in that diocese for thirty years or more (Carl. Epis. Reg. Halton, f. 62). By a constitution of the diocesan synod, the archdeacon or his official was forbidden to exercise coercive power (ibid. Welton, ff. 129-40). From the date of the composition, above referred to, the archdeacon of Carlisle lost all title to a disciplinary jurisdiction, and as long as the office was reckoned a constitutional department of diocesan administration, the bishops never relinquished control of the courts to which their clergy owed allegiance.

one side and gradually usurped all their prescriptive rights in the visitation of the clergy. But in the diocese of Carlisle the archdeacons had a poor chance in the competition. The chancellors, as the delegated officers of the bishops, held correctional courts in various centres for the transaction of the legal business of the diocese. These courts were held not only when the bishop visited, but when they did not visit. For two centuries after the Reformation, the clergy were not much troubled with episcopal visitation. Matters were worse in the case of the archdeacons. We have not noticed a single record of archidiaconal visitation from the Submission of the Clergy in 1534 until the new departure of recent years. Throughout the long period of three hundred and fifty years, the visitorial power of the archidiaconate had been suspended.

After the Restoration in 1660, when the bishops began to hold their triennial visitations with more frequency, their chancellors followed their example in holding chapters for the hearing of causes. As time rolled on, the chapters held by the chancellors came to be regarded in the nature of a visitation. In due course they utilized those occasions,in the years when the bishops did not visit, for the delivery of homilies to the clergy and churchwardens. Dr. Paley, who had been appointed archdeacon in 1782 and chancellor in 1785, at once detected the incongruity of visitorial charges as delivered by the bishop's legal adviser. In speaking of ' the discourses ' usually delivered at a chancellor's visitation, he remarked, ' I embrace the only opportunity afforded me of submitting to you that species of counsel and exhortation, which, with more propriety perhaps, you would have received from me in the character of your archdeacon, if the functions of that office had remained entire.' [1] Still the custom went on. When a new archdeaconry was added to the diocese in 1856, the chancellor, relying on his letters patent, undertook its oversight. Bishop Goodwin, however, on the death of Chancellor Burton, made a new arrangement whereby he appointed a layman to the chancellorship and invested his archdeacons with as much authority in visitation as the law of the land and the custom of the diocese allowed them. Dr. Prescott now unites in his own person the offices of archdeacon of Carlisle [2] and chancellor of the diocese. When the diocese was extended, the new portion, consisting of the barony of Coupland or Egremont in Cumberland, the barony of Kendal in Westmorland, and Lancashire north of the Sands, was constituted into the archdeaconry of Westmorland by Order in Council, dated 10 August 1847, which order was to come into force with consent of Bishop Percy or on the next avoidance of the see. As the bishop withheld his consent, the new archdeaconry did not come into being till after his death in 1856, when his successor, Bishop Villiers, appointed the first archdeacon of Westmorland in that year.[3]

The formation of the archdeaconry of Furness in 1884 occasioned some difference of opinion. Bishop Goodwin explained his action in these words : ' Great changes have taken place in this diocese in the course of the last thirty years in consequence of the development of industries connected with our rich possessions of iron ore. Large towns have sprung up where small villages alone existed, or perhaps not even villages ; and the whole of the western side of the diocese has a new and immensely multiplied population.' This consideration, however, did not cause the bishop to apply to the Ecclesiastical Commissioners for the purpose of creating a new archdeaconry till the Duke of Devonshire and the Duke of Buccleuch offered to provide £200 a year for its endowment.[4] The archdeaconry of Furness was constituted to consist of the rural deaneries of Gosforth in Cumberland, and of Cartmel, Dalton, and Ulverston in Lancashire, by Order in Council dated 19 May 1884, and the first archdeacon was appointed on 29 May following.[5]

In order to carry out the new scheme no regard was paid to historic boundaries, and the ancient landmarks were obliterated. Twelve parishes in the south-east of Cumberland were dissevered from the archdeaconry of Carlisle and added to that of Westmorland ; the ancient deanery of Coupland was split in two and divided between Westmorland and Furness. After an unbroken continuity of seven and a half centuries the archdeaconry of Carlisle was muti-

---

[1] *Works of William Paley* (ed. E. Paley, 1830), vi. 61.
[2] The first ' charge, delivered to the clergy and churchwardens of the archdeaconry of Carlisle ' by Archdeacon Prescott, took place ' at his ordinary visitation in May, 1888,' the subject being ' Visitations in the ancient diocese of Carlisle.' The charge, which has been printed, contains a scholarly survey of past visitations. It is the first of its kind on record.
[3] Carl. Epis. Reg. Villiers, f. 81.
[4] Bishop Goodwin, *Charge* (1884), pp. 22–3.
[5] Carl. Epis. Reg. Goodwin, ff. 391–2.

lated, and its boundaries, which lay at the very roots of northern history and were in existence before the formation of the counties of Cumberland and Westmorland, were uprooted and changed. The name of the deanery of Coupland, which had a separate history dating at least from the early years of the fourteenth century [1] as an outlying portion of the great and famous archdeaconry of Richmond, was expunged from local nomenclature. The three archdeacon-ries, into which the present diocese of Carlisle is divided, have neither ecclesiastical associ-ations nor historical significance.

Each of the archdeacons of the diocese holds what he calls ' a general chapter and ordinary visitation ' in various centres of his archdeaconry in the years when the bishop does not visit, to which he summons ' all rectors, vicars, and curates as also churchwardens and chapelwardens, both old and new, the old to make true presentments of all defaults and offences of ecclesiastical cognizance, with the names and places of abode of the several delinquents, and those newly elected or re-elected, to be admitted to their office.'

APPENDIX III

THE RURAL DEANERIES

THE division of the diocese of Carlisle into four districts [2] had undergone no modification while rural deaneries remained an effective part of church organization, the deaneries of the twelfth being of the same extent as those of the sixteenth century. When we find the deans describing themselves in early documents, say from 1160 to 1190, their decanal areas were set out in the four divisions of Carlisle, Cumberland, Allerdale, and Westmorland,[3] the identical divisions which were in use till the office became extinct. It is true that deans some-times changed their territorial titles, but it is certain that the decanal divisions underwent no alteration to justify the practice. On comparing the parishes comprised within each of the four divisions in 1292, the date of the valuation of Pope Nicholas IV., with the divisions recognized at various periods up to 1560, when the office was in a state of decay, we find no shifting of decanal boundaries. In the meantime, of course, new parishes had been formed and old parishes had been absorbed into other parishes, but the territorial extent of each of the four deaneries had remained stationary. As the deanery of Westmorland lay without the limits of Cumberland as we now know it, we are not concerned with its place in the dio-cesan scheme. The remaining portion of the county, not included in the old diocese, was constituted into the deanery of Coupland, a partition of the archdeaconry of Richmond and diocese of York. It was conterminous with the barony of Egremont, the great fief granted by Henry I. to William Meschin, and often went by that name. This deanery was included in the diocese of Chester, created in 1541, and remained under the jurisdiction of the bishop of that see till 1856, when the diocese of Carlisle was enlarged to its present dimensions. The historic division of the county into four deaneries may be thus tabulated : (1) Deanery of Carlisle, comprising thirty-five parishes, namely, St. Cuthbert's and St. Mary's, Carlisle, Bowness, Aikton, Cumwhitton, Irthington, Wetheral, Warwick, Farlam, Burgh by Sands, Stanwix, Crosby on Eden, Beaumont, Kirkandrews on Eden, Dalston, Carlaton, Thursby, Brampton, Stapilton, Eston, Cambok, Athuret, Kirklinton, Bewcastle, Castle Carrock, Orton, Kirkbampton, Rocliffe, Cumrew, Hayton, Scaleby, Grinsdale, Nether Denton, Walton, and Sebergham. (2) Deanery of Allerdale, eighteen parishes : Aspatria, Wigton, Kirkbride, Bromfield, Bolton, Ireby, Uldale, Crosthwaite, Caldbeck, Isell, Bassenthwaite (Beghokirk), Torpenhow, Plumbland, Gilcrux, Bridekirk, Crosscanonby, Dearham and Camerton. (3) Deanery of Cumberland, seventeen parishes : Greystoke, Castlesowerby, Skelton, Dacre, Hutton, Penrith, Edenhall, Great Salkeld, Lazonby, Kirkland, Ousby, Melmerby, Kirkoswald,

---

[1] Gale, *Reg. Honor. de Richmond*, App. pp. 63-4, 76.

[2] For the antiquity of rural deaneries in England and their formation on the basis of the civil divi-sions, see the arguments and the authorities quoted by Gibson, *Codex Iuris Eccl. Ang.* (ed. 1713), ii. 1010-2 ; Kennett, *Parochial Antiquities* (ed. 1818), ii. 337-45 ; Dansey, *Horæ Decan. Rurales* (ed. 1844), ii. 22-110.

[3] It is stated by Bartholomew de Cotton that the bishopric of Carlisle had four deaneries : ' 1. Cum-berland, 2. Westmerland, 3. Karlesle, 4. Alredale ' (*Hist. Anglicana* [Rolls Ser.], p. 417).

Ainstable, Renwick, Addingham and Croglin.[1] (4) Deanery of Coupland. The boundaries of Coupland are so well defined by nature that there is no need to name the parishes of which it was composed. In 1292 it included the whole of the south-west angle of Cumberland between the Derwent and the Duddon, together with Lancashire north of the Sands. At some date before the valuation of 1535 the Lancashire portion was dissevered from it and constituted into the deanery of Furness and Cartmel.[2]

While the institution remained a factor in diocesan administration, it does not appear to have been of much consequence in the constitutional history of the church. In whatever way the office was at first filled, whether by election of the clergy of the deanery or by appointment of the bishop or archdeacon, it may be taken that in its later history the bishop of Carlisle nominated his rural deans. As so little is known of the method of appointment, we may reasonably infer that it was not a patent office with delegated powers like that of the official or vicar-general, nor yet a benefice with a territorial jurisdiction like that of the archdeacon. In the fourteenth century, while we have a very full record of the acts of five successive bishops, no evidence has been preserved of the form of commission entrusted by them to the rural deans of the diocese. The appointments of these officers were not considered suitable for or worthy of record. But there is one entry[3] in the register of Bishop Welton, perhaps unique in the registers of the English episcopate, which shows conclusively that the method of appointment was by oral declaration or nomination without any writ or designation in writing. It is a memorandum to the effect that on 10 October 1355, Bishop Welton gave authority to John, vicar of Penrith, to be his dean of Cumberland. It is satisfactory to have this solitary nomination, for it is sufficient to prove, so far as the diocese of Carlisle is concerned, that rural deans, like chaplains, apparitors and bailiffs, were the personal officers of the bishop, who engaged or dismissed them at his pleasure, and that their duties were regulated by local custom and the will of their employers. It has been thought that it was the delivery of the decanal seal[4] which constituted the office, but as the canons of the church are very explicit on the use of the seal by rural deans, no claim to jurisdiction can be constructed on this basis. The absence of record shows the precarious nature of the tenure by which the office was held.

If we turn to the recorded acts of rural deans and inquire into the use the bishops made of them, as it suited their convenience, we shall not be left in doubt of the nature of the office. We find no trace of the exercise of jurisdiction over the benefices within the deanery. The deans invariably acted under mandate from the bishop. It was ' by the tenor of these presents ' that ' power was conceded ' to them to transact his business. In these circumstances it may be expected that their duties were multifarious. They carried the bishop's summons to every parsonage warning the clergy of his visitation. When a subsidy was granted in synod, the deans were instructed to collect it. From several of the benefices pensions were due to the bishop, and the deans annually accounted for their collection. When parsons were amerced for non-appearance at synod, it was the duty of the deans to recover the fines. We might enumerate a long list of decanal duties, but all of them have the same complexion. The rural deans were the messengers, summoners, process servers, and tax gatherers of the diocese.

From what has been stated it may be easily inferred that the decanal office was closely associated with the diocesan registry. Year by year the deans presented their accounts to the registrar. Several of these accounts are still extant at various dates between 1402 and 1509. They are all of the same character, each consisting of a schedule of moneys received and paid on the bishop's behalf, the balance going to the registrar, who in turn rendered account

---

[1] The order of parishes in these deaneries has been taken from the schedules in Carl. Epis. Reg. Halton, ff. 501-2, and Ibid. Appleby, MS. f. 340. Though the benefices were the same in 1292, the order was different (*Taxatio Eccl.* [Rec. Com.], pp. 318-20). The same rule holds for the valuation of 1535 (*Valor Eccl.* [Rec. Com.], v. 278-92).

[2] Compare *Taxatio Eccl.* p. 328 with *Valor Eccl.* v. 265-7, and the map of the diocese of Chester attached thereto.

[3] 'Prefeccio vicarii de Penreth in decanum Cumbrie. Memorandum quod decimo die Octobris anno domini millesimo ccc^mo lv^to venerabilis pater, G(ilbertus), dei gracia Karliolensis episcopus, prefecit dominum Johannem vicarium de Penreth in decanum suum Cumbrie' (Carl. Epis. Reg. Welton, f. 22). Lyndwood says that rural deans were yearly elected and sworn in the diocesan synod (*Provinciale* [Oxford, 1679], p. 85).

[4] No impression of a decanal seal has come down to us in this diocese. But we know that the deans used a ' seal of office ' for certifying the receipt and delivery of mandates, inquisitions *de jure patronatus* and such matters (Carl. Epis. Reg. Appleby, ff. 166-7, 184-5).

to the bishop. One feature of these schedules is always present, that is, the salary of the dean. The bishop employed him to collect the spiritualities arising within his deanery from synodals, corrections and testamentary causes, and awarded him his annual allowance for the service rendered.

There are two questions, not without interest at the present day, about the ancient position of rural deans in the scheme of diocesan administration, that deserve a passing notice, namely, their relation to the archdeacon and to the rural chapter. It does not appear that the archdeacon had any power over them at the date when the diocesan registers begin to give us guidance. They were the officers of the bishop alone. When the archdeacon ' disposed himself ' to make his visitation in 1356, it was the bishop who sent out instructions to the rural deans for the citation of abbots, priors, rectors, vicars and others to appear on the days and at the places appointed. It was not the duty of the deans to drudge for the archdeacon. When the clergy were slack in their payment of archidiaconal dues, some of the bishops used the deans to urge the clergy into an early discharge of their liability. Bishop Welton had an arrangement with his archdeacon whereby the rural deans collected them for him.[1] In the rural chapters we might have expected the deans to have had pre-eminence, but that was not the case. The holding of chapters in the diocese of Carlisle was regulated by a constitution of the diocesan synod. By this enactment it was the archdeacon or the official who was required to celebrate rural chapters at places most convenient to the clergy, and not oftener than once a month.[2] When arduous business was brought before this consultative body, the official or the dean was commissioned to summon the clergy by mandate of the bishop. The presidency of rural chapters was not vested in the dean. It was *coram officiali* that the business was transacted.

During the progress of the Reformation the usefulness of rural deans declined in this diocese. Bishop Best found the old order in existence when he succeeded to the charge in 1561. The diocese, as he reported to the privy council in 1563, was divided into five ' regiments,' one deanery of the cathedral church, and the four rural deaneries of Carlisle, Allerdale, Cumberland, and Westmorland. He also supplied the names of the deans, the parishes within each deanery, and the number of households within each parish.[3] This is the last mention of rural deans that has been met with in the diocese. Though they ceased apparently to be nominated, the ecclesiastical divisions were continued for various purposes up to the close of the eighteenth century. In 1618 the diocese was assessed according to the above-named deaneries ' for horse and armour ' by Bishop Snowden,[4] on the strength of ' letters from the lords of his Majesty's most honourable privy council to him directed.' It was by the same divisions that Bishop Rainbow made inquiries in 1668–9 about the condition of church plate and church furniture after ' the long discontinuance of church government in those late times of war and rebellion.' [5] The same bishop held his visitation in 1682 at the four principal towns in these deaneries, at the cathedral for the deanery of Carlisle, at Wigton for Allerdale, at Penrith for Cumberland, and at Appleby for Westmorland.[6] In 1752 Bishop Osbaldiston collected his procurations and synodals by the same ecclesiastical divisions.[7] In later years these rural deaneries came to be known by the names of their four principal towns, Carlisle, Wigton, Penrith, and Appleby.[8] The tradition of the former existence of rural deaneries had died out in the diocese in the time of Bishop Percy. That prelate was unable to trace them in his diocesan registers ; writing on 28 September 1843 he said definitely that ' there are no rural deans in the diocese of Carlisle ' [9] It may be taken that for almost three centuries the office was extinct in the northern diocese.

It is to the credit of Bishop Villiers that it was he who revived the institution in our own time. On 1 January 1858, by the stroke of his pen, he subdivided the diocese into eighteen rural districts and nominated a beneficed clergyman in each district to be his dean. The

1 Carl. Epis. Reg. Welton, ff. 25, 28, 67.
2 Ibid. Appleby, f. 136
3 Harl. MS. 594, f. 9.
4 Carl. Epis. Reg. Snowden, f. 249.
5 Ibid. Rainbow, ff. 460–1.
6 Browne Willis gives the names of the deaneries as Allerdale, Carlisle, Penrith, and Westmorland (*A Survey of Cathedrals*, i. 284).
7 Manuscript schedule in Diocesan Registry.
8 Nicolson and Burn, *Hist. of Cumberland*, ii. 6.
9 Dansey, *Horæ Decan. Rurales*, ii. 371.

same bishop re-arranged the deaneries and re-appointed the deans on 1 January 1862.[1] Again, on 27 January 1870 Bishop Goodwin altered the boundaries and increased the number of deaneries, making twenty for the whole diocese.[2] Another shuffle was announced in the *London Gazette*, which contained an Order in Council, dated 10 March 1882, ratifying the new scheme of deaneries prepared by the Ecclesiastical Commissioners and sanctioned by Bishop Goodwin.[3] At the present time (1904) the archdeaconry of Carlisle contains eight rural deaneries and 146 benefices; the archdeaconry of Westmorland, 6 deaneries and 91 benefices; the archdeaconry of Furness, 4 deaneries and 60 benefices. These divisions now follow no recognized boundaries and have no historical significance. The decanal areas were fortuitously chosen as convenience dictated; they vary in extent from 12 to 22 benefices. In announcing the rearrangement of 1882 Bishop Goodwin very truly remarked: ' I can scarcely believe that even after all the trouble that has been taken the scheme will give absolutely universal satisfaction in every one of its details.' But there was the assurance that further change would be made, if thought desirable.[4]

When Bishop Villiers revived the office, he appears to have been satisfied with the nomination of the deans. The entry in his register simply records the fact that he had divided his diocese into deaneries and appointed deans. In later years the institution has been elevated into a patent office with a commission *in scriptis*. Bishop Goodwin commissioned his deans (1) ' to inquire into and duly report to us all such things within the said deanery, as it is meet for the honour of God and for the welfare of the flock of which we are overseers that we should know,' (2) ' to co-operate with the archdeacon of your archdeaconry in making inquiry into the state and condition of the churches, chancels, and churchyards, and all things thereunto belonging, and also into the state and condition of the glebe houses and glebe lands and all things thereunto belonging, within your said deanery rural,' and (3) to inspect ' the schools existent within your deanery, if the trustees and managers thereof shall permit you so to do.' This form of commission has varied little or nothing since 1865, according to a book of forms preserved in the diocesan registry. In making a record of appointments, the present registrar follows the style of his predecessors. On every avoidance of the see, the office of dean lapses, but it is customary for the new bishop to reappoint all the old deans who are willing to serve.

APPENDIX IV

DIVISION OF THE PROPERTY OF THE CHURCH OF CARLISLE BETWEEN THE PRIORY AND THE BISHOPRIC [5]

I. OMNIBUS sancte Matris ecclesie filiis presentem cartam inspecturis, B. humilis Prior Karliolensis et ejusdem loci Conventus, salutem in Domino. Ad universitatis vestre noticiam volumus pervenire, quod cum a domino G. tituli Sancti Martini presbitero Cardinali quondam legato in Anglia, secundum mandatum apostolicum prout in literis apostolicis sibi destinatis continetur, ordinacio facta fuisset ecclesie Karliolensis, et secundum formam ejusdem mandati per eundem legatum distribucio fieri debuisset, inter venerabilem patrem Hugonem Episcopum nostrum et nos, omnium bonorum, possessionum, ac reddituum ejusdem ecclesie, equali porcione ipsi et nobis assignanda, ut perpetuo nos medietatem optineremus omnium ad eandem ecclesiam pertinencium mobilium et inmobilium, que tunc temporis eadem ecclesia nostra possederat vel possidere debuerat; et similiter idem dominus Episcopus et successores ejus reliquam medietatem. Tandem, cum propter repentinum recessum ejusdem legati ab Anglia, predicta perfici non potuissent; de iterato mandato apostolico dominus P. Norwycensis electus domini pape Camerarius, post ipsum apostolice sedis in Anglia legatus, que minus in eadem ordinacione vel distribucione facta fuerant sicut receperat in mandatis apostolicis per viros venerabiles Abbatem de Holomo et

---

[1] Carl. Epis. Reg. Villiers, ff. 145–50, 274–9.   [2] Ibid. Goodwin, ff. 646–53.
[3] These deaneries are set out in full detail for each of the three archdeaconries in the *Carlisle Diocesan Calendars* from 1885 to 1904. When the archdeaconry of Furness was created by Order in Council, dated 19 May 1884, the rural deaneries in each archdeaconry were again named and sanctioned. For the modern statutes affecting rural deaneries and rural deans, see Phillimore, *Eccles. Law*, i. 258.
[4] *Pastoral Letter* (1882), p. 19.   [5] Taken from Charter Roll 18 Edw. I. No. 26.

Priorem de Exsthildésh[am] fecit completi. Ita tamen, quod cum quedam inter ipsum Episcopum et nos remansissent pro indiviso ; pro eo quod tunc nequibant prefati viri plenius hiis vacare. Postmodum placuit eidem Episcopo et nobis ut compromitteremus in quosdam bonos viros, qui juramento prestito reliqua, que remanserant indivisa, fideliter dividerent, et in omnibus medietate partibus assignata omnia terminarent. Omnibus igitur per eos rite peractis ; in pleno sinodo Karliolensi tam prima quam secunda distribucio a predicto Episcopo sunt approbate, et ab ipso et nobis recepte et acceptate, sicut in originali inde confecto in eodem sinodo recitato et quamplurium Abbatum et aliorum magnorum virorum sigillis munito, plenius continetur. Sane cum idem dominus Episcopus et nos, per literas apostolicas prefato domino P. legato delegatas, Magistrum Michaelem Belet super medietate ecclesie de Corbrigg, et S. de Heind' super ecclesia de Werkewrth coram eodem legato traxissemus in causam, quas ecclesias dicebamus ad nos et ad ecclesiam nostram pertinere de jure, et in proprios usus possidere debere. Post litem super hiis legittime contestatam, cum jam fere perventum fuisset ad extremum examen, tandem predicti viri Magistri M. Belet et S. de Heind' in presencia ejusdem domini legati, jus ecclesie Karliolensis super eisdem ecclesiis sponte per se recognoscentes, eas in manu domini H. Episcopi nostri resignarent. Unde predictus dominus legatus Priori de Tinemue et Priori Augustald' dedit in mandatis, ut predictas ecclesias cum omnibus ad eas pertinentibus domino Episcopo et nobis assignarent, et in earundem inducerent corporalem possessionem, et a quibuslibet contradictoribus auctoritate legacionis sue seu delegacionis tuerentur inductos. Post traditam vero ecclesiarum possessionem, cum sepedictus Episcopus posuisset in opcione nostra, ut eligerimus, quod de duobus nobis magis placeret, videlicet, ut eidem Episcopo et successoribus ejus nos septuaginta marcas assignaremus in annuis reddituibus in partibus Karliolensibus, et totaliter ecclesiam de Werkewrth cum omnibus pertinenciis perpetuo possideremus, aut ipse sexaginta marcas assignaret nobis in eisdem partibus, et eandem ecclesiam ipse et successores sui perpetuo totaliter possiderent, et omnia sustinerent onera ad eandem ecclesiam pertinencia, videlicet, de vicario instituendo, de solvenda porcione quadraginta marcarum domino Dunolmensi, secundum quod contingere deberet ecclesiam de Werkewrth de ipsis quadraginta marcis, quas pro omnibus ecclesiis, quas ecclesia Karliolensis habet in Northumbria, idem Episcopus Dunolmensis percipere debet sicut continetur in carta Hugonis Episcopi Dunolmensis, archidiaconalia nichilominus exhibendo, et si qua alia contigerint emergenda. Nos de communi consensu, libera et spontanea voluntate, previa deliberacione elegimus, quod dominus Episcopus in partibus Karliolensibus, secundum quod dictum est, assignaret nobis redditum sexaginta marcarum in recompensacione medietatis ejusdem ecclesie de Werkewrth, et nos eandem ecclesiam cum omnibus pertinenciis suis quietam clamaremus, et perpetuo possidendam concederemus, nec aliquando ei vel successoribus suis super hiis questionem moveremus. Ipse autem Episcopus, acceptans electionem nostram et concessionem, ad consideracionem trium bonorum virorum ex parte ipsius, et trium ex parte nostra, de ipsis sexaginta marcis plenius satisfecit. Ipsi vero in quos compromisimus, prestito juramento, quod in neutram declinarent partem, set bona fide cuncta perfectius ordinarent, universa plenius perfecerunt, et ea que subscripta sunt de redditibus Episcopi nobis assignaverunt, videlicet, medietatem alteragii ecclesie sancte Marie, que erat in manu ejus pro viginti marcis, quinque skeppis farine et siliginis, de Haiton in Gilleland pro sexdecim solidis, viij denariis. De terra Rogeri fratris Prioris, xl. denarios. De rusticis et firmariis de Karleton propter servicium quod Johannes de Crofton debet, xxxj. solidos. De Nicholao de Askerton et Waltero de Brunskayt et Maria de Staynton et Johanne Musee de Scal', xvj. solidos. De terra Marthepet' j. skeppam de farina pro xl. denariis. De pensione de Kirkeland, x. solidos. De Uckemanby, ij. solidos, vj. denarios. De Camberton, ij. marcas. De Ulnesby, dimidiam marcam. De terra de Ireby, ij. solidos, vj. denarios. De Timpaur' et Neubigging, xxiij. solidos. De minutis redditibus infra Karliolum et circa, prout continetur in magno rotulo de prima distribucione, C. et iiij. solidos. De vastis infra Karliolum et circa, xv. solidos, viij. denarios. De porcione Episcopi de pensione de Ireby, xx. solidos. De Blencarn', iiij. solidos. De Buthecaster, xl. denarios. De Hoton in foresta, xij. denarios. De Radulpho de Caldecot, xij. denarios. Totam decimam de Birkscagh preter scalam Hospitalis sancti Sepulcri pro xliiij. solidis. Decimam de Hubbricteby pro iiij. libris xvj. denariis. Decimam de Neuby pro xl. denariis. Decimam de Morton pro vj. solidis. Decimam de Kunelholm pro xl. denariis. Totam partem Episcopi de Neubigging preter communam foreste et pasture, que sunt xij. bovate terre, duabus acris minus. Totam partem Episcopi de Birkscagh, preter unam carucatam terre, quam tenet Odardus clericus de eo et successoribus ejus. De Adam de Milneburn, vj. denarios. De Talkan in Gilleland, xij. denarios. De Bramton in Westmorlanda, vj. denarios. De Caber, vj. denarios. De Louth, ij. marcas. De Camboc, ij. solidos. De Cnochubert, ij. solidos. De vico Bochardi, xl. solidos. Faciunt autem omnes hii redditus summam lx. marcarum, exceptis ij. solidis, quos remisimus domino Episcopo pro expensis suis, quas fecit circa adquisicionem ecclesie de Werkwrth. Sciendum autem, quod dominus Episcopus et successores ejus retinent in manu sua jus patronatus omnium predictarum ecclesiarum ; nec recipimus pensiones ex eis nomine pensionis set in recompensacione summe lx. marcarum suprascriptarum. Ut vero omnia supramemorata eidem domino Episcopo et successoribus ejus firma sint imperpetuum et inconcussa, presentem cartam nostram eis contulimus sigillo nostro munitam. Hiis testibus Magistro A. tunc Officiali Karliolensi, A. de Espatric tunc decano Karliolensi, Magistro Th[oma] de Denton, Odardo clerico, L. monacho de Holmo, W. monacho Belli Loci tunc capellano domini Episcopi, Fratre G. et fratre W. conversis Episcopi, Johanne de Crofton cive Karlioli, et multis aliis.

II. ˙Universis Christi fidelibus ad quos presens scriptum pervenerit, Johannes Francus, Canonicus Lichefeldensis, Magister W. de Glovernia, Canonicus Cicestrensis, et Magister P. Legat, Officialis domini Karliolensis, salutem in Domino. Noveritis, quod cum contencio esset inter venerabilem patrem nostrum, S., Dei gracia Karliolensem Episcopum, ex parte una, et R. Priorem et Conventum Karliolensem, ex altera, super medietate ecclesie de Corbrigg, ecclesia et terra de Ireby, et quibusdam aliis ecclesiis et possessionibus, quas Prior et Conventus Karliolensis possident contra distribucionem factam inter predecessores predicti Episcopi, Prioris et conventus, et super ecclesia de Penred et molendinis de Hornecaster et quibusdam aliis possessionibus et rebus quas idem Episcopus possidet contra distribucionem predictam, et super libertatibus Priori et Conventui per felicis recordacionis W. quondam Karliolensem Episcopum concessis, et super obedienciariis in Prioratu Karliolensi instituendis ac destituendis et rebus aliis. Tandem iidem Episcopus, Prior et Conventus ordinacioni nostre super omnibus premissis totaliter se supposuerunt sicut plenius liquet per literas utriusque partis patentes. Nos autem tenore distribucionis predicte plenius inspecto et intellecto, et utriusque partis jure considerato, paci et tranquillitati eorundem providere volentes et Deum pre oculis habentes, unanimi assensu or dinavimus quod ecclesie de Penred et molendina de Hornecastre, ecclesia de Meleburn cum capella de Chelardeston, et manerium de Batwe, advocacio ecclesie de Rowbirie, advocacio ecclesie Novi Castri, advocacio ecclesie de Caldebeck, salvo jure predictorum Prioris et Conventus in decem et octo marcis annuis in quibus vendicant se jus habere in eadem ecclesia post decessum vel cessionem Rectoris, qui nunc preest eidem, imperpetuum remaneant predicto Episcopo et successoribus suis quieta et soluta a predictis Priore et Conventu et successoribus eorundem. Et medietas ecclesie de Corbrigg et ecclesia de Ireby cum terra, et ecclesia de Camberton, et ecclesia de Cumrew, et eciam de Hayton, et Prioratus Hib[ernensis], advocaciones ecclesiarum de Hoton ˙et de Camboc et de Edenhal, et medietatis ecclesie de Wytingham, et terra de Soureby quieta de multura, et decime de dicta terra provenientes, imperpetuum remaneant predictis Priori et Conventui et eorum successoribus quieta et soluta de predicto Episcopo et successoribus suis, salvo jure ordinario. Et sciendum, quod idem dominus Episcopus confirmabit predictis Priori et Conventui libertates per predecessorem suum[1] eisdem concessas. Et quocienscunque Supprior vel Celerarius in Prioratu Karliolensi fuerit preficiendus, predicti Prior et Conventus eligent duos vel tres ad illa officia idoneores, quos presentabunt domino Episcopo si fuerit in diocesi, sin autem, infra mensem postquam eorum electio ad ejus pervenerit noticiam committet alicui vices suas in hac parte, ita quod illa officia per ejus defectum non vacent ultra tempus predictum, et erit in opcione ejusdem domini Episcopi quem voluerit de illis tribus Electis admittere et eidem assensum suum prebere. Preterea ordinamus, quod omnia in utraque distribucione contenta, de quibus in hac ordinacione nulla fit mencio, in suo robore permaneant imperpetuum secundum tenorem utriusque distribucionis. Ita tamen, quod idem dominus Episcopus alias donaciones factas eisdem Priori et Canonicis, de quibus hic nulla fit mencio, confirmabit eisdem. Et ut omnia premissa perpetuum robur firmitatis optineant, predictus Episcopus uni parti hujus scripti, et predicti Prior et Conventus alteri parti una cum sigillis nostris, sigilla sua apposuerunt. Acta in ecclesia sancti Laurencii de Appleby in crastino sancti Egidii anno gracie M.CC. quadragesimo nono.

---

[1] This concession of liberties by Bishop Walter to. the Prior and Convent of Carlisle is recited by *inspeximus* in Chart. R. 6 Edw. III. pt. i. No. 30.

ECCLESIASTICAL MAP

OF

CUMBERLAND

Showing ancient Rural Deaneries and the Religious Houses.

Scale.

MILES 5 · 0 · 5 · 10 · 15 MILES

William Stanford & Company, Ltd.

BEWCASTLE
15

LANERCOST
2

CARLISLE

CARLISLE
1,9,10,12,13.   DIOCESE OF
WETHERAL
6

HOLMCULTRAM
3

CARLISLE

WICTON
14

ARMATHWAITE
7

PART OF
DEANERY OF
CORBRIDGE

ALLERDALE
DIOCESE OF CARLISLE

KIRKOSWALD
19

DIOCESE OF
DURHAM

CALDBECK
16

GREYSTOKE
18

CUMBERLAND

OF   CARLISLE

PENRITH
11

DIOCESE

ST JOHN IN THE
VALE
17

ST BEES
5

COUPLAND

CALDER *DIOCESE OF*
4   *CHESTER*

SETON
8

FRIARS.

9. Carlisle.Dominicans.
10. Carlisle, Franciscans.
11. Penrith,Austin.

HOSPITALS.

12. Carlisle, St.Nicholas.
13. Carlisle. St.Sepulchre.
14. Wigton, St.Leonard.
15. Bewcastle.
16. Caldbeck.
17. St. John in the Vale.

COLLEGES.

18. Greystoke.
19. Kirkoswald.

RELIGIOUS HOUSES.

AUSTIN CANONS.

1. Carlisle Priory.
2. Lanercost Priory.

CISTERCIAN MONKS.

3. Holmcultram Abbey.
4. Calder Abbey.

BENEDICTINE MONKS.

5. St Bees Priory.
6. Wetheral Priory.

BENEDICTINE NUNS.

7. Armathwaite Priory.
8. Seton Priory.

THE RELIGIOUS HOUSES
OF CUMBERLAND

INTRODUCTION

The religious houses of Cumberland, though not individually of great fame and importance, played no inconspicuous part in the moral well-being of a district unfortunately situated for the cultivation of the arts of peace and civilization. Within a comparatively small area six monastic foundations carried on their work with varying success for almost four centuries. Four of these houses were close to the border, and suffered much during the long period of hostility between the two kingdoms. The priories of Carlisle and Lanercost, separated only by 10 or 11 miles, were of the Augustinian order ; the abbeys of Holmcultram and Calder, between which there seems to have been little communication, were of the Cistercian ; and the priories of Wetheral and St. Bees were cells of the great Benedictine abbey of St. Mary, York. The houses of Calder and St. Bees were in the archdeaconry of Richmond and diocese of York, but the rest were in the old diocese of Carlisle. With the exception of Holmcultram, which owed its origin to the Scottish occupation, the foundation of all the Cumbrian houses may be ascribed to Norman influence. We are indebted to the great period of religious revival under Henry I. for the foundation of Carlisle, Wetheral, St. Bees and Calder. Four of the houses were undoubtedly founded by subjects. Carlisle was of royal foundation. It is difficult to tell whether Holmcultram, which was an offspring of Melrose, was founded by Alan son of Waldeve, in whose fee the lordship was situated, or by Henry son of King David, who at the time ruled Cumberland.

The priory of Carlisle stood apart from the rest of the religious houses by reason of its peculiar association with the ecclesiastical life of the district. At the creation of the diocese in 1133 the church of the priory became the cathedral of the bishop, and the canons were constituted his chapter. In the fourteenth century the capitular body consisted of a prior and twelve canons, which number may be taken as the normal strength of the chapter. At the same period only four canons and a prior were reckoned on the foundation of Lanercost, and though Wetheral was founded as a community of twelve monks its numbers had dropped at the date in question to a prior and three monks. Holmcultram was the largest and most important house in the county, and its abbot was for a time a lord of parliament.[1] The number of monks varied according to the political state of the country. In 1379 the abbot and fourteen monks contributed to the royal subsidy, but at the time of the dissolution the surrender of the abbey was signed by the abbot and twenty-four brethren. All the houses on the border were subject to vicissitude. In times of special distress, when the Scots were successful in frequent raids, the revenues were found incapable of supporting the inmates, and orders had to be issued to houses in more peaceable parts of the kingdom to admit brethren of the northern monasteries to hospitality till the pressure was relaxed.

It is a peculiar feature of monastic history on the border that the heads of religious houses were not exempt from the international custom of trial by battle which prevailed in the twelfth and thirteenth centuries. In spite of condemnation by the highest authorities,[2] the duel was observed among clerics as well as laymen. In 1216 Pope Innocent III. issued his famous bull *contra duellum religiosi* to all the faithful throughout the province of York and realm of Scotland, describing 'the pestiferous custom' then in fashion between the two kingdoms as quite contrary to the law and honesty of the church. 'Even to this day its observance is so far abused,' he said, 'that if a bishop, abbot or any cleric happened to be prosecuted for an offence for which the duel was wont to be fought between laymen, the religious man was compelled to undergo the duel in person.'[3] Some years later, in 1237, the clergy of England presented a list of grievances which they wished Henry III. to redress. In one of the articles it is declared that by the command of the kings of England and Scotland not simply clerics but also abbots and priors in the diocese of Carlisle were forced to fight with lances and swords the duel which was called *Acra* on the marches of the realms. An abbot or prior, whatever his dignity or order, was obliged to sustain the combat in person or to provide a champion. If the champion succumbed, he was slain, and the abbot or prior, who was a prisoner on the scene of battle, was likewise beheaded.[4] Though the clergy petitioned that so detestable an abuse should be no longer allowed with respect to ecclesiastical persons, churchmen remained subject to the duel in the border laws promulgated in 1249.[5] As late as 1279 we have an instance of preparation for a duel at Appleby before the justices itinerant between the champions of the abbot of Furness[6] and Roger son of Ralf

[1] *Parl. Writs* (Rec. Com.), i. 1, 25, 72; ii. 37; *Lords' Report on the Dignity of a Peer* (Index Summonitionum).
[2] The ordeal by hot or cold water or hot iron was condemned by the Lateran Council of 1215 (Landon, *Manual of Councils*, i. 331). Henry III. instructed the justices itinerant in Cumberland and Westmorland in 1219 to discontinue the custom 'cum prohibitum sit per ecclesiam Romanam judicium Ignis et Aquæ' (Pat. 3 Hen. III. m. 5).
[3] *Reg. Epis. Glasguensis* (Bannatyne Club), i. 94. In 1176 a letter was obtained from Henry II. in which he declared 'that no cleric should be forced to fight the duel' (Ralph de Diceto, *Opera* [Rolls Ser.], i. 410).
[4] *Ann. Mon.* (Rolls Ser.), i. 256–7.
[5] Nicolson, *Leges Marchiarum*, 8.
[6] For some churchmen's champions see Neilson's *Trial by Combat*, 50–3, which is considered the standard authority on this subject.

de Hestholm in a plea of common pasture at Meles in Kirksanton in Cumberland. Roger had disputed the right of the abbot to the common, and as an agreement could not be arrived at, one of the parties appealed the other in wager of battle that God might defend the right. The justices sat *in area duelli* attended by members of the county court, and as the combat proceeded the affair was abruptly ended in the abbot's favour by Roger renouncing his claim to the property and withdrawing his champion.[1]

It will be readily admitted that a county on the Scottish frontier was ill adapted to the multiplication of nunneries. In fact, one marvels that a religious society of women could exist during the periods of barbaric strife which broke out from time to time between the two kingdoms in the fourteenth and fifteenth centuries. The few nuns at Armathwaite in the valley of the Eden, nine miles to the south of Carlisle, were often plundered and impoverished, but managed to hold together till the dissolution. The nunnery of Seton, though far removed from the scene of frequent forays, did not increase in wealth or influence. The glimpses we get of it betoken its miserable condition of poverty. Both institutions were entitled in the name of Our Lady and constituted under the Benedictine rule.

All the monastic bodies in the portion of Cumberland within the ancient diocese of Carlisle were subject to episcopal visitation and correction except the Cistercian abbey of Holmcultram. The value of the bishop's periodic inspection was proved on several occasions of dispute or mismanagement. Monks, canons and nuns were alike amenable to his pastoral advice. In the early centuries of diocesan history the Bishop of Carlisle was not a popular figure with the regular clergy. Whether the hostility took its rise from his differences with the priory of Carlisle about the distribution of the property of his church, or on account of his zeal in keeping cloistered life up to the requisite standard, there can be no doubt that the monasteries smarted under his supervision. In cases of dispute between neighbouring houses the bishop was the natural referee for the readjustment of friendly relations. From some instances on record we see that he did not spare the litigating parties ; his award was often drawn up in language of sternness, not to say of asperity. But as time went on more amicable relations prevailed. The monks found the bishop a useful ally in promoting their interests, and they were too worldly wise not to grapple with the situation by making him their friend. Holmcultram was a papal peculiar over which the bishop of

---

[1] Beck, *Ann. Furnesienses*, 224–5. The deed of quitclaim which followed was witnessed by William son of Thomas de Craystok, Roger de Loncastria, Thomas de Muletona, Roger de Lasceles, Ranulf de Daker, Thomas de Musegrave, Alan de Orretona, and Robert de Mulcastre. On the back of the deed there is the following endorsement : 'Die et anno contentis in hoc scripto Inrotulata fuit tota sententia scripti istius cum divisis eo contentis in rotulis Justiciariorum hoc scripto nominatorum. Ipsis Justiciariis sedentibus in area duelli in parte percussi, et retractis utrimque campionibus pacificati ad instanciam Rogeri de Estholme ibidem presentis et tam Inrotulamentum predictum quam presentis scripti tenorem gratis concedentis et approbantis.' A somewhat similar duel was fought in Yorkshire in 1239, when an abbot was intimidated by armed force to withdraw his champion and renounce his right (*Cal. of Papal Letters*, i. 179–80).

the diocese had no visitorial jurisdiction. Like the priories of Carlisle and Lanercost, the monks had the right of electing their own superior, but that election would be void unless it took place under the presidency of the abbot of Melrose. In this respect the abbot of the mother house stood in much the same relation to Holmcultram as the bishop did to Carlisle and Lanercost, for in these houses the bishop's licence was the necessary prelude to every election as his confirmation was indispensable for its completion. By virtue of a series of papal bulls Holmcultram was freed from episcopal control. An unwarrantable exercise of papal privilege brought the monks into conflict with the secular clergy in 1401, when proctors were employed in the deaneries of Carlisle and Allerdale, where the influence of Holmcultram was predominant, 'to labour *pro clero* against the Cistercians' in the matter perhaps of the refusal of that house to contribute to a subsidy due to the Bishop of Carlisle.[1] It is worthy of note that it was only in this house that undoubted evidence of anarchy and disorder was discovered during the great agitation which preceded the final overthrow of the monasteries in the county.

The coming of the friars to Carlisle at so early a date as 1233 seems to have been due to the ecclesiastical sympathies of Bishop Walter. At all events in that year the Dominicans or Black Friars and the Franciscans or Grey Friars were introduced into that city. Soon after the Augustinians gained a footing in Penrith. The Carmelites or White Friars settled at Appleby, and, though not in Cumberland, they were reckoned among the four mendicant orders which exercised their vocation in the diocese of Carlisle. All the friars were under episcopal control. The houses in Carlisle and Penrith were furnished with churches and churchyards.

It is claimed that hospitals should rank as religious houses among eleemosynary institutions. Little is known of the nature or origin of those which at one time must have been numerous in Cumberland. No other hospital in the county, of which record has been discovered, attained to the importance of St. Nicholas, Carlisle. It was of royal foundation and originally a house for lepers only, but in process of time, as it increased in wealth, it became an asylum for the sick and needy.

The foundation of colleges seems to have been attended with considerable difficulty in Cumberland. The first attempt, undertaken at Melmerby in 1342, utterly failed, and it was only after prolonged negotiation that the project for converting the parish church of Greystoke into a college was carried to a successful issue. The college of Kirkoswald was founded a few years before the dissolution.

---

[1] In the accounts (*compoti*) of the deans of Allerdale and Carlisle for the financial year 1401-2 certain sums were allowed to the accountants for 'procuratoribus laborantibus pro clero contra ordinem Cisterciensem.' These entries can only be explained in their relation to the monks of Holmcultram. Compare statute 2 Hen. IV. cap. 4 and *Chron. mon. de Melsa* (Rolls. Ser.), iii. 271-2, 279.

SEAL OF THE PRIORY OF CARLISLE.

DEAN AND CHAPTER OF CARLISLE (1660).

ARCHDEACON WILLIAM
BYRBANKE.

SEDE VACANTE (LATE 14TH
CENTURY), WRONGLY USED BY
ARCHDEACON OF CARLISLE.

VICAR GENERAL OF CARLISLE
(15TH CENTURY).

CHANCELLOR OF BISHOP
BARNES.

ABBEY OF HOLMCULTRAM

PRIORY OF ST. BEES

PRIORY OF LANERCOST

RELIGIOUS HOUSES

HOUSES OF AUSTIN CANONS

1. THE PRIORY OF CARLISLE

We naturally look to Carlisle for the earliest evidence of ecclesiastical life and movement in the new province which had been added to the English kingdom in 1092. It has been pointed out that very early in his reign, most probably in 1102, Henry I. granted a site within the city for the purpose of founding a religious establishment.[1] For various reasons already stated, little else seems to have been done till after the political changes of 1120-2, when Ranulf Meschin, the civil ruler, left the district and the king took it into his own hand. From this date onward a vigorous policy was carried on for its ecclesiastical development. How much progress had been made with the building of the church or the religious organization of the city during Ranulf's consulate we cannot tell. The happy turn of its fortunes may be ascribed to the pious instincts of Walter the priest, who, on taking the religious habit and becoming an inmate of the house, endowed the institution with all his churches and lands.[2] The king, at whose instigation the step was taken, granted the reversion of four churches in Northumberland which he had previously given for life to Richard D'Orival (de Aurea Valle),[3] his chaplain, and added to the gift two other churches in the same county. But the landowners of the neighbourhood were slow to emulate these great examples. It is true that Waldeve son of Gospatric, who had succeeded to the barony of Allerdale, was one of the first patrons of the royal foundation; the churches of Aspatria and Crosscanonby; the chapel of St. Nicholas, Flimby; and a house near the church of St. Cuthbert, Carlisle, were of his gift.[4] In the earlier stages of its history the priory does not appear to have created much enthusiasm. Its possessions consisted chiefly of spiritualities, with the notable exception of the manors of Linstock and Carleton bestowed by Walter the priest. But the king was pursuing a steady policy. In 1130 the canons were busy in completing their church.[5] The time was ripe for a fresh development.

The foundation of the bishopric in 1133, with the seat of the bishop in the new priory church of St. Mary,[6] gave unity and force to the ecclesiastical life of the district, and was chiefly instrumental in bringing in endowments to support the organizations which followed. Little is known of the constitution of the priory before it was raised to the dignity of a cathedral chapter. It was probably a house of secular canons. But it seems satisfactorily proved, if we trust the evidence of the chronicles, that it was Adelulf the first bishop, soon after his consecration in 1133, who changed the constitution of the priory by the introduction of regular canons of St. Augustine.[7] To this circumstance, there can be little doubt, we owe the unique position which the priory of Carlisle held as the only cathedral chapter of regular canons in England. Adelulf had been prior of the Augustinian house of Nostell near Pontefract, and was a well known patron of his order before he was raised to the episcopal dignity.[8] When we take into consideration the late creation of the bishopric and the antecedents of the first bishop, the singularity of the constitution of the cathedral church appears to need no further explanation. The bishop was not only master of his church, but he also enjoyed a participation in its endowments. The church of Carlisle was one ecclesiastical corporation with the bishop at its head. It is a curious fact in illustration of the bishop's predominance in his cathedral that the monastic order, to which the canons of his chapter belonged, could not make statutes or ordinances for the enlargement or modification of the rule under which they lived without his sanction. In 1302, many years after the endowments of the priory and bishopric had been separated, when the heads of Augustinian houses were assembled at Drax in Yorkshire, Bishop Halton sent a mandate forbidding them to enact anything to the prejudice of his church of Carlisle without his pontifical consent and authority, inasmuch as his chapter was composed of regular canons of their order, and those, making new ordinances and statutes, should be guided by moderation that the bond of love between subjects and rulers (inter subditos et parentes) might be strengthened. This mandate was carried to the conclave at Drax by Brother William, a canon of the house, nominated for that purpose by the prior and chapter.[9]

[1] Assize Roll (Cumberland), No. 132, m. 32; Scotichronicon, i. 289, ed. Goodall.
[2] Charter R. 35 Edw. I. No. 100.
[3] Dugdale, Mon. vi. (1), 144. [4] Ibid.
[5] Cal. of Doc. Scot. (Scot. Rec. Pub.), i. 26.

[6] Sym. of Dur. (Rolls Ser.), ii. 285.
[7] Marth. Paris, Chron. Mag. (Rolls Ser.), ii. 158; Dugdale, Mon. vi. (1), 91. [8] Ibid.
[9] Carl. Epis. Reg., Halton, f. 64.

The bishop's supremacy over his cathedral church cannot be questioned. It has been already pointed out that the bishop and his chapter formed one ecclesiastical corporation and held the lands and spiritual possessions of the church of Carlisle in common. When a division of the property was made and the see became an institution in some measure separate from the priory, care was taken to define the relationship of the head of the diocese to the corporate body occupying the church which represented the unity of his diocese and contained the seat of his jurisdiction. There is little doubt that at the outset the appointment of the prior was in the patronage of the bishop, and perhaps of the king when the bishopric was void. When the terms of the arrangement for the separate endowment of the see were complete, this privilege seems to have been relinquished to the chapter in compensation for the redistribution of emoluments. At all events it was not until 1248 that the canons had the liberty of electing their own superior. On 25 November in that year, Pope Innocent IV. granted protection and confirmation of possessions to the prior and convent, and especially the chapelry of the church of Carlisle, with all offerings, tithes, and parish rights belonging to the said church, except the offering at Whitsuntide, all the land formerly belonging to Walter the priest, which King Henry gave and confirmed by his charter, and other possessions. The pope also granted to the canons the right of electing the prior and prohibited the bishop from disposing of their emoluments without their consent.[1]

The bishop however did not give up altogether his control of the internal affairs of the priory when the property was divided. It was part of the bargain that he should have a voice in the selection of the sub-prior and cellarer, the two principal officers of the house. By virtue of an ordination made on 2 September 1249, between Bishop Silvester on the one part, and R(obert), the prior, and convent on the other, it was stipulated that as often as the office of sub-prior or cellarer fell vacant, the prior and convent should nominate two or three fit persons and present them to the bishop that he might select one for the vacant post ; if the bishop was absent from the diocese at the time, he was required to issue a commission within a month after the presentation had been brought to his notice, that the offices might not remain vacant beyond the aforesaid period ; and that it should be at the option of the bishop when

present, or of his commissioned deputy when absent, to select one of those candidates nominated by the priory and to admit him to the office.[2] This ordination remained in force throughout the history of the priory, and sometimes the canons were not backward in keeping the bishops up to the letter of the original agreement.

A vacancy occurring in the office of cellarer in 1331, while Bishop Ross was residing at his church of Melbourne in Derbyshire, the canons nominated two of their number, Brothers Geoffrey de Goverton and Ralf Gray, and requested the bishop by special messenger to select one of them for the post or issue a commission for that purpose. The letter of nomination was dated 25 July, and the latest time allowed to the bishop for signifying his choice was 8 September. 'Although we are not compelled by law,' so the letter runs, ' to write to you while you are out of the diocese (in remotis), yet for the sake of peace and under protest, lest it be quoted hereafter as a precedent against us, we are directing these presents for this turn.' It is evident that the canons were trying to impress their bishop with a sense of their magnanimity by pretending to confer a favour upon him, whereas in reality it was no favour at all, as they were obliged by law to do what was done. In response the bishop appointed the prior of Lanercost and the official of the diocese to

[2] An abstract of this ordination, recited by *inspeximus* in Charter Roll, 18 Edw. I. (83), No. 26, may be given to illustrate this important point : ' Universis Christi fidelibus ad quos presens scriptum pervenerit, Johannes Francus, canonicus Lichefeldensis, magister W. de Glovernia, canonicus Cicestrensis, et magister P(eter) Legat, officialis domini Karliolensis, salutem in Domino. Noveritis quod cum contencio esset inter venerabilem patrem nostrum S(ilvestrem), Dei gracia, Karliolensem Episcopum, ex parte una, et R(obertum) Priorem et Conventum Karliolensem, ex altera, super . . . Et quocienscunque Supprior vel Celerarius in Prioratu Karliolensi fuerit preficiendus, predicti Prior et Conventus eligent duos vel tres ad illa officia idoniores, quos presentabunt domino episcopo si fuerit in diocesi, sin autem, infra mensem postquam eorum electio ad ejus pervenerit noticiam, committet alicui vices suas in hac parte, ita quod illa officia per ejus defectum non vacent ultra tempus predictum, et erit in opcione ejusdem domini Episcopi, quem voluerit de illis tribus Electis admittere et eidem assensum suum prebere. Preterea ordinamus . . . Et ut omnia premissa perpetuum robur firmitatis optineant, predictus Episcopus uni parti hujus scripti, et predicti Prior et Conventus alteri parti, una cum sigillis nostris, sigilla sua apposuerunt. Acta in ecclesia sancti Laurencii de Appleby in crastino sancti Egidii anno gracie M°CC° quadragesimo nono.'

[1] *Cal. of Papal Letters,* i. 250.

choose the ablest and fittest of the candidates and induct him to the office.[1] A similar custom was observed in 1338–9, when Bishop John de Kirkby was residing at Horncastle, with respect to the vacant office of sub-prior. The official of the diocese was commissioned to select the fitter of two canons, R. Paule and T. de Stanlaw, submitted to him for the post.[2] In 1379 the tenure of the office of cellarer came before Bishop Appleby for his decision. For some reasons not stated, Prior John de Penreth removed Robert de Clifton from his office without the consent of the majority of the chapter, which caused dissension and discord in the house. Both parties submitted the dispute to the bishop, who ordered the restoration of the cellarer to his office as he had been irregularly deposed.[3]

In no instance have we met with the deprivation of a prior of Carlisle,[4] though Bishop Halton was obliged to deliver stern injunctions to Prior Adam de Warthwyk, and Bishops Ross and Appleby were reduced to the extremity of excommunicating Priors John de Kirkby and William de Dalston respectively. Many examples of resignation are on record. Pensions were allowed to the retiring priors and suitable provision was made in accordance with their exalted station for the rest of their lives. These pensions were voted by the canons as a charge upon their revenues and approved by the bishop. In cases, of course, where the voidance arose from preferment, no pension was assigned.

The bishops of Carlisle possessed an undisputed power of visitation of the convent, which they exercised as occasion called. Individual bishops as a rule took an early opportunity after their appointment to make a general visitation of the diocese, in which not unfrequently the priory of Carlisle was included. At other times they visited when a cause of dispute or some irregularity in the house was brought to their notice. The results of some of these visitations are not devoid of interest. In 1301, after Bishop Halton had visited by his ordinary authority the convent as well in head as in members at the request of Adam de Warthwyk the prior, and inspected the state of the institution within and without, he delivered a series of injunctions to the prior

which show us how indispensable was the episcopal oversight to the internal discipline of the capitular body. By the depositions of certain canons of the said monastery examined according to custom, a copy of which was sent to Prior Warthwyk, the following charges were preferred against him : negligence and remissness in the discipline of his house contrary to the statutes of the order ; his household was much too expensive in those days (*familia vestra est nimis honerosa hiis diebus*) ; in preferring and removing obedientiaries and in other matters affecting the house, he consulted only with Brothers Robert Karlile, William de Hautwysil, and William de Melburne, the advice of the rest of the chapter having been wholly omitted and despised contrary to the decrees of the holy fathers ; incompetency to rule the priory, inasmuch as, owing to his failings, order was not preserved among the brethren, the business of the house was not transacted, and its goods were wasted beyond measure by his expensive entourage ; by appropriating the perquisites of his court he had received the gressoms and profits of the green seal (*gressummas et appruyamenta viridis cere*), had held in his own hand for three years and more the grange of Newbiggin, whereof he received the issues and spent it at his own free will without consulting the majority of the convent, had returned no account contrary to the statute of the Legate ' de ratiociniis reddendis,' and worst of all he had converted the proceeds to his own private uses contrary to the vow of his profession ; misappropriation of the profits of the trade in wine and other merchandise which Brother W. de Melburne carried on with his connivance without rendering any account ; holding back money due from the tenants of the monastery and converting it to his own use, till the treasurer and barons of the Exchequer made a levy on the common goods of the house to its great damage and loss ; the employment for a long time of W. the clerk, as a sower of discord between the brethren in his own interest ; improvident concession of a corrody to Stephen, rector of Castle Carrock, for £4 without converting the money to the use of the house ; letting to farm the houses and courts of his manors of Corbridge and Wyden without the knowledge or consent of the convent to its great detriment ; failure to account for 100 marks paid to him by Master W. de Lowther in the name of the monastery, and £200 of old money and 40 marks of new money left in the treasury by Robert the late prior ; appropriation to his own use of the profits of a ship made at the costs of the house ; by reason of his negli-

---

[1] Carl. Epis. Reg., Ross, f. 265.
[2] Ibid. Kirkby, f. 390.
[3] Ibid. Appleby, ff. 319–20.
[4] Bishop Nicolson stated in his ' Case of the Bishop of Carlisle ' that his predecessors had ' corrected and sometimes deprived the priors for misapplication of the common revenues' (*Letters of Bp. Nicolson*, pp. 341–2), but we have been unable to verify the statement.

gence and the bumptiousness (*elacionem*) of Robert de Warthwyk his steward, the house had an evil reputation in the neighbourhood; want of sympathy with his sick brethren; and making known the proceedings of the daily chapter when the secrets of the order were discussed, and scoffing at them in his own chamber in the presence of the laity. Unless these charges were forthwith remedied and a reformation made without delay, the bishop informed the prior that he should be obliged to proceed against him according to the insistance of the canons and to decree against him what was just.[1]

A scandal of great magnitude convulsed the diocese in 1385 when the patience of Bishop Appleby was exhausted by the refusal of Prior William de Dalston to accept his judicial decision in some matters of debate between the canons or to give him canonical obedience. At last the bishop brought matters to a crisis by excommunicating the prior and ordering the parish priests of St. Mary's and St. Cuthbert's to publish the sentence at the celebration of mass. The city of Carlisle was in an uproar. Many of its leading citizens and clergy, espousing the cause of the prior, entered the cathedral as well as the parish churches at the head of an armed mob, and snatching the bishop's letters from the hands of the officiating priests carried them forcibly away. The bishop threatened to put the whole of the city under an interdict with the exception of the castle and its chapel. Charges of adultery against the prior were raised in the controversy. The majority of the canons implored the bishop to visit the house; the archbishop cited the prior and his abettors for their disobedience; the king wrote deploring the scandal and asking for particulars. The upshot of the unpleasant business was that Prior Dalston was induced to give obedience to the bishop's judgment and to resign his office.[2] Perhaps no period of equal length in the whole history of the priory of Carlisle witnessed more exciting scenes than the months of August and September 1385, while Bishop Appleby stood up so resolutely for the maintenance of discipline and order in his cathedral chapter in spite of the threats and opposition of the rulers and the mob of his cathedral city.[3]

Though we have notice of the resignation of several of the priors of Carlisle, only in one instance have we found particulars of a pension allotted to any of them out of the revenues of the church. The exception occurs in the case of Adam de Warthwyk, who showed such incompetence in administering the affairs of the house. In 1304, three years after the bishop's onslaught on his mismanagement, the prior resigned of his own free will. The reasons he alleged for taking this step do him credit. He confessed that, broken with old age and weakened in bodily senses, he was quite unable to rule the priory any longer. Bishop Halton, on his part, in assigning him a pension, was not backward in complimentary appreciation of the prior's long service to the church. For forty years he had lived as a canon regular under the rule (*doctrina*) of St. Augustine in the venerable assembly of the convent of his cathedral church, and for twenty-one years and more he filled the laborious office of prior in times of war and troubles, and now, as he had stated, he was so burdened with cares and stricken with age that he was no longer able to remain. In these circumstances the bishop determined, with the unanimous vote of the chapter, to make suitable provision for his comfort as long as he lived. Among the particulars of his pension may be mentioned the new chamber which the prior had built for himself and those who ministered to him daily; rations equal to three times those of an ordinary canon according to the custom of the priory; the tithe sheaves of Langwathby towards the expenses of his household, for as he was the scion of a noble family in the diocese, a provision in proportion to his station and the hospitalities expected of him should be made; an allowance of twenty marks yearly for his clothing; one servant and a boy to wait upon him; and when he went outside the precincts of the monastery for a change of air (*ob æris intemperiem*), or for recreation, or to visit the granges or manors of the priory, or any of his friends within the diocese, or for any lawful reason, the prior and convent for the time being, under their debt of obedience, were obliged to provide him and his household with suitable means of travelling.[4]

The traditional relationship of the cathedral as the chief temple of the diocese to the

---

[1] Carl. Epis. Reg., Halton, f. 43.

[2] Ibid. Appleby, ff. 348–54, 357.

[3] The declaration of obedience made by Prior Dalston a fortnight before his resignation was as follows: 'In Dei nomine amen. Ego, frater Willelmus de Dalston, prior prioratus Karlioli, ordinis sancti Augustini, ero fidelis et obediens vobis, venerabili in Christo patri et domino meo, domino Thome, Dei gracia, Karliolensi episcopo, et successoribus vestris canonice intrantibus, officialibus et ministris, in canonicis et licitis mandatis. Sic Deus me adiuvet et hec sancta Evangelia' (ibid. f. 353).

[4] Carl. Epis. Reg., Halton, f. 80.

parish churches was preserved and perpetuated by an annual homage made by the parish priests during the week after Pentecost. Though the practice was not confined to the church of Carlisle, it is interesting to notice how jealously the bishops of that see insisted on its observance. In 1372 Bishop Appleby, on the complaint of the prior and sacrist that some of the rectors and vicars failed to put in an appearance, issued a mandate to the official of the diocese to proceed against the truants. The clergy were bound, the mandate continued, to visit the cathedral church once a year and to join in the procession in their surplices with the cross carried before them (*processionaliter in superpelliciis crucem ante se deferri facientes*), and to do other things requisite to show the reverence due from them to the bishop's seat. This custom which had been observed *ab antiquo* should on no account be allowed to fall into disuse. It was one of the most beautiful and instructive phases of medieval ritual in its assertion of the corporate life and work of the church. From a subsequent mandate in 1386 we learn that the procession wended its way up to the high altar when the clergy made their oblations due to God as a sign of their subjection to the cathedral church.[1] In this way annually, on some appointed day in Whitsun week, the clergy paid the *cathedraticum* due from every benefice in token of subjection to the bishop's jurisdiction and of allegiance to the church which represented the unity of the diocese.

Processions of various descriptions were not of unfrequent occurrence at the cathedral, inasmuch as it usually led the way in all matters affecting the welfare of the district. It was to the prior and official of Carlisle that the bishop addressed himself in 1365, when he instituted special processions with the solemn chanting of the seven penitential psalms, the litany and other suitable prayers to be undertaken in the cathedral and all churches collegiate and non-collegiate throughout the diocese, for good weather. The autumn of that year was remarkable for violent storms of wind and rain and the crops were much injured by the rains and floods.[2] Much the same procedure took place when processions were ordered as propitiatory ceremonies for the averting of a threatened pestilence or for success of the English arms against the Scots.[3] Another great day in the Christian year at Carlisle was Ash Wednesday, when penitents flocked from places far and near to receive

the sacrament of reconciliation in the mother church of the diocese. It was the privilege of the bishop to attend personally on these occasions, but in his absence the duty was assigned to the prior. It was by the bishop's licence or commission that the prior was able to introduce penitents into the cathedral and reconcile them to the church *ut est moris*.[4]

A peculiar privilege was enjoyed by the prior and convent on very high authority. Pope Alexander IV. granted them an indult in 1258 to wear birettas or caps in the choir on account of the cold, provided they were removed at the Gospel and the elevation in time of mass.[5] At a subsequent period, when the utilitarian convenience of the privilege was forgotten, the canons of Carlisle were collated to their prebends by the delivery of a biretta (*per byretti nostri traditionem*) from the bishop, perhaps, like the verge or rod in civil life, as a symbol of seisin. This custom was in force at Carlisle throughout the reign of Elizabeth.[6]

From an early period the enclosure of the priory or monastic precinct at Carlisle has been called 'The Abbey,' though the church had never an abbot distinct from the bishop. Freeman[7] has pointed out that the same peculiarity existed at Bath and Durham.[8]

[1] Carl. Epis. Reg., Appleby, ff. 250, 361.
[2] Ibid. ff. 144, 203.
[3] Ibid. Kirkby, f. 371.
[4] Ibid. Welton, ff. 16, 25.
[5] *Cal. of Papal Letters* (Rolls Ser.), i. 361.
[6] Carl. Epis. Reg., Barnes, ff. 35, 61, 84, 93, etc. ; *Letters of Bp. Nicolson* (ed. J. Nichols), 335–6.
[7] *William Rufus*, i. 139.
[8] As the antiquity of the usage at Carlisle has been called in question, it may be convenient to trace it back far enough to show that it is not of modern introduction. At the time of the ecclesiastical survey in 1535, *via abbathie* was the name of the street whith connected the north-west gate of the precincts with the Caldew gate of the city (*Valor Eccl.* [Rec. Com.], v. 277). In 1488 the bishop was said to be *in abbathia* (Diocesan MS. 3 and 4 Hen. VII.). In 1388 the priory is described as St. Mary's Abbey (*Cal. of Doc. Scot.* iv. 75) ; and in 1299 it is again referred to as the abbey (ibid. ii. 285). Hemingburgh, describing the destruction of Carlisle by fire in 1292, particularly noted that the city *cum tota abbatia* was burnt and consumed (*Chron.* [Engl. Hist. Soc.], ii. 40). It is generally supposed that the name had originated from the peculiar position which the bishop is alleged to have occupied as the abbot of his cathedral. The bishop's seat on the south side of the choir, as distinct from his throne, is pointed out as an evidence of the immemorial usage. But no good authority in support of the statement has been found. Local custom gives the bishop the seat of dignity on the south side as the head of the church, and to the dean, as successor of the prior, the corresponding seat on the north side as head of the chapter. By charter of William the Con-

It was customary for the bishops at their first visitation to demand an inspection of the title deeds of all holders of ecclesiastical preferment or spiritual endowments within the diocese. When these were produced, letters of dimission were issued confirming the holders in possession. Numerous deeds of this nature are on record with respect to the spiritualities of religious houses to which churches within the bishop's jurisdiction were appropriated. From one of these records of dimission we may take a schedule of the spiritual possessions of the priory of Carlisle in 1355, in which the ecclesiastical status of each of the churches is declared as they existed at that date : the parish churches of the blessed Mary and St. Cuthbert, Carlisle, with the chapel of Sebergham, the churches of Hayton with its chapels, Cumrew and Cumwhitton (Comquityngton), the churches of Crosscanonby (Crossebye in Allerdale), Camerton, Ireby, Bassenthwaite (Beghokirk), Castle Sowerby (Soureby), Rocliffe (Routhecliff), Edenhall with the chapel of Langwathby, and Addingham with the chapel of Little Salkeld (Salkeld), all of which were held *in proprios usus*. In the churches of St. Mary and St. Cuthbert, Carlisle, Hayton, Rocliffe, Ireby, Crosscanonby, Camerton and Bassenthwaite vicars were never instituted, nor were the vicarages ever taxed or 'ordained,' but all of them were served by stipendiary chaplains (*per capellanos conducticios*). The prior and convent also possessed the following pensions from churches, viz. 26s. 8d. from Lowther, 26s. from Kirkland, 6s. 8d. from Ousby (Ulnesby), 2s. from Hutton in the Forest (Hoton), 2s. from Castle Carrock, 2s. from Cambok, 6s. 8d. from Bewcastle (Bothecastre), 2s. 6d. from Allhallows (Ukmanby), and £6 from the abbot and convent of Holmcultram.[1] If this schedule be compared with the ecclesiastical surveys of 1535 and 1540,[2] it will be seen that the only addition of consequence which was made in the spiritualities of the priory, during the intervening period, was the rectory and patronage of the parish church of St. Andrew, Thursby, which Sir Robert Ogle, lord of Ogle and Thursby, and Isabel his wife gave to the prior and canons

queror in 1084, which was confirmed by King John in 1204, the priors of Durham obtained all the liberties, customs, dignities and honours of an abbot and had the seat of the abbot *in choro sinistro* and all the privileges of the deans of York (Cart. Antiq. B. No. 4 ; *Rot. Chart.* [Rec. Com.], i. 118; Rymer, *Fœdera* [new ed.], i. [i.], 3).

[1] Carl. Epis. Reg., Welton, f. 19.

[2] *Valor Eccl.* (Rec. Com.), v. 274 ; Dugdale, *Monasticon*, vi. 145.

in 1468, with permission to appropriate the said church and serve it by a canon of their cathedral or any other suitable chaplain, without endowment of a vicarage in the church or compulsion to distribute a yearly sum of money to the poor of the parish.[3] The churches belonging to the priory in the diocese of Durham were not included in Bishop Welton's dimission as they were not within his jurisdiction.

The cathedral served as the parish church of St. Mary, Carlisle, from the date of its foundation, as the priory church of Lanercost had done for that parish. It can scarcely be denied that the churches with which Walter the priest endowed the priory, when he took the religious habit on becoming an inmate thereof, were those of St. Mary and St. Cuthbert, Carlisle, and Stanwix. The rectory of the latter church was equally divided between the bishop and the convent in the great award of the papal legates, but the rectories of the two Carlisle churches were wholly appropriated to the canons. The church of St. Cuthbert may be numbered among the earliest ecclesiastical institutions in the diocese of Carlisle, of which authentic record has come down to us. A house near it was given to the priory by Waldeve son of Gospatric, one of its first benefactors. We have found no trace of a church of St. Mary apart from the cathedral and no vicarial jurisdiction over the parish of that name, except what was exercised by the prior as the impropriator of the revenues. An attempt was made in 1342 to raise it from its position as a chapelry to the dignity of a vicarage, and the provincial court of York was moved by the parishioners for that purpose. In the appeal to the metropolitan it was stated that the church of the Blessed Mary from its foundation had been and was at that time a parish church with an independent cure (*per se curata*), having people separate from the parishioners of other churches and a wide and extensive parish with limits and bounds of its own, insomuch that its own parish church had abounded in times past and did then abound with powers, issues, fruits and revenues sufficient to maintain a perpetual vicar of its own and to support all ecclesiastical claims upon it. Furthermore the parishioners complained that the sacrist of the priory, to whom the issues of the parish were committed, had neglected the cure of souls and that insufficient ministrations were supplied to the people. Notwithstanding the espousal of the cause of the appellants by the provincial court, the Bishop of Carlisle gave judgment in favour of

[3] Pat. 8 Edw. IV. pt. i. m. 23.

the priory, because we have found, he said, after due examination of the evidences, that the prior and chapter are well able to serve the church through their own chaplains under the care and direction of the prior for the time being, no other vicar having been ever instituted in the same.[1] The parish of St. Mary was not unfrequently called the parish of Carlisle cathedral,[2] and the church-yard or burial ground around the church was known as the churchyard of St. Mary's or the churchyard of the canons of St. Mary's, Car-lisle.[3] The parish church remained within the cathedral, probably in the nave, *ab antiquo* as it was within living memory, till 1869, when the present church of St. Mary was built within the abbey.

The ownership of the tithes arising from assart lands in the forest of Inglewood was a constant source of irritation and dispute be-tween the bishop and the priory. It has been already mentioned that these tithes were granted by Henry I. to the church of Carlisle and confirmed by Henry II. In the division of the church property by the papal legates, the ownership of the tithes of lands to be assarted in the future was not clearly laid down. Edward I. however acknowledged in 1280 the claim of the priory to the tithe of venison in the forest.[4] The whole matter was reviewed in the king's court in 1290, when claims were separately set up by the bishop, prior and parson of Thursby for the tithes of two places, Linthwaite and Kirk-thwaite, newly assarted in Inglewood, the king intervening as owner of the forest. Bishop Ralf stated that the places in question were within the limits of his church of

Aspatria : Henry de Burton claimed that they were situated in his parish of Thursby ; the prior of Carlisle produced a certain horn of ivory (*quoddam cornu eburneum*), by means of which, he said, Henry the old king enfeoffed the canons of Carlisle with the said tithes.[5] Ultimately judgment was given in favour of the king's claim, but in 1293 that claim was relinquished and the tithes were re-granted to the canons.[6] From time to time the right of the canons was after-wards disputed by the king's foresters or by the bishop's, but the position of the canons on inquiry remained unshaken. It was found, after inquisition in 1330, that the prior and his predecessors were seised of the tenth penny arising from all extra-parochial agist-ments within the forest of Inglewood in the times of all keepers of that forest by the hands of the receiver of the issues thereof, from the time of the foundation of the priory by grant of Henry son of the empress (*im-peratoris*), until Henry le Scrop, the late keeper, detained the said tenth penny. The king confirmed them in their possession.[7] It was at this date that a long dispute raged between Bishop Ross and Prior John de Kirkby about the tithes, resulting in the excommunication of the prior and the death of the bishop.[8] The revival of litigation was the means of procuring a confirma-tion from the Crown, in the shape of a notification of the record of a cause between Edward I. and Adam, then prior, tried at Carlisle before the justices itinerant, on the morrow of All Souls, 1285, on a writ of *quo warranto* touching the following liberties in Inglewood Forest : common of pasture in right of their church for themselves and their tenants within the metes of the forest : tithes of venison and of hay, pannage, after-pan-nage, agistment of foals, calves, lambs, swine, goats and other animals, also of fish taken in the lake of Tarnwadling, called 'layke-brait,' the hides of all beasts found dead by the foresters, the right to hunt the hare and fox with their hounds without the covert, and that their hounds be quit of expeditation ; the right to a charcoal burner to make charcoal from all dead wood in the grass and to such

[1] Carl. Epis. Reg., Kirkby, ff. 448-9, 452, 454-5. The conflict between the diocesan and provincial courts is very interesting. Bishop Kirkby showed the people at York that he was master of his own diocese. He not only rejected the vicar that the provincial court sought to obtrude into the parish, but added a sentence to his judgment which is worthy of attention : 'prefatos priorem et capitulum ab impeticione dictorum parochianorum et officii nostri in hac parte absol-vimus, et per decretum absolutos dimittimus in hiis scriptis' (ibid. f. 452), thus summarily dis-missing the appeal without hope of a future revival and ignoring altogether the intervention of the metropolitan court.

[2] In 1506 Henry, Earl of Cumberland, ac-counted to the king for the enclosures made by him in the parish of Carlisle cathedral within the bounds of the forest of Inglewood (Inq. p.m. 21 Hen. VII. Nos. 19-39).

[3] *Testamenta Karleolensia* (Cumb. and Westmld. Arch. Soc.), 11, 114-5, 118.

[4] Close, 8 Edw. I. m. 2.

[5] *Rot. Parl.* (Rec. Com.), i. 37-8 ; ii. 44-5 ; Ryley, *Plac. Parl.* (ed. 1661), 49-51.

[6] Pat. 22 Edw. I. m. 27.

[7] Close, 4 Edw. III. m. 31. There is a curious confusion of Henry I. and Henry II. in this roll, arising no doubt from the fact, as pre-viously stated, that Henry II. inspected and con-firmed the charter of the forest given by Henry I. to the church of Carlisle.

[8] Carl. Epis. Reg., Ross, ff. 263, 266.

oaks thrown down by the wind as they and their servants can, before others, mark with an axe stroke to the core : all which the canons claimed by immemorial usage, producing a horn which they said was given with the liberties by Henry I. the founder of their house. Edward III. also confirmed a writ, dated 7 February 1286, whereby these liberties were permitted to the canons with the exception of trees blown down by the wind.[1] It is probable that the horn of ivory above mentioned was seen by Tonge[2] in his heraldic visitation of the northern counties in 1530, when he described it as a 'great horne of venery, havyng certeyn bondes of sylver and gold and the versus folowyng graven upon, " Henricus primus nuster foundator opimus ac dedit in teste carte pro jure foreste." ' The dean and chapter of Carlisle still possess certain objects catalogued in the inventories of the cathedral furniture as ' one horn of the altar in two parts' or 'two horns of the altar,' which have given rise to much antiquarian discussion.[3]

The property of the priory, scattered in small parcels over the border and central districts of the county, was frequently wasted and destroyed by the inroads of the Scots. Again and again the canons petitioned for redress or alms on account of their poverty and sufferings. The documentary evidences of the fourteenth century are burdened with appeals and complaints from Carlisle and the other religious houses describing the woes and wrongs perpetrated by the hereditary enemy.[4] It would serve no useful purpose to recount the numerous licences and gifts made in response to such appeals. The strong walls of Carlisle were insufficient to protect their church and cloisters from fire and damage. In 1316, when the Scots were particularly aggressive, the canons petitioned for a grant of timber to renovate their burnt cathedral,[5]

and complained against the conduct of Sir Andrew de Harcla, sheriff of the county, who made a ' fosse' through the prior's ground under the wall of the city and set fire to all the priory houses outside the walls, which could not be replaced for £100. As the damage had been done for the safety of the priory as well as the town, owing to the rigorous necessities of the siege, the brethren were requested to wait for peace and the king would not forget their interests.[6] So heavily lay the destroying hand on the priory at this period, that Edward II. sent writs to the abbots of Leicester and Thornton on Humber, and to the priors of Thurgarton, Bridlington, Worksop and Kirkham, each to receive into their houses one of the canons of Carlisle to be nominated by the prior's letters patent and to maintain him as one of their own canons until the priory of Carlisle was relieved from its present state, as its goods were so robbed and wasted by the Scottish rebels that they were insufficient for the maintenance of the canons of the house.[7] It was a privilege of the Crown to exact a corrody from all the religious houses of royal foundation, and in times of prosperity the king was accustomed to demand it from the priory of Carlisle. In 1331 Richard Champion, in consideration of his good service to Edward I. and Edward II., was sent to the convent to receive such maintenance as Peter de Kirkoswald, deceased, had in that house at the request of the former king.[8] But the time came when the kings were obliged to relinquish the privilege. In 1386 Richard II., in consideration of the great losses and destruction by the Scots, remitted to the prior and convent and their successors for ever the right of corrody or maintenance, which his progenitors were accustomed to give therein and which the king in his time had given to John Hobcrone.[9] At that time their losses were exceptionally severe. As late as the reign of Queen Mary it could be said that the Scots 'are verey cruell at present.'[10] The kings must have stayed several times at the priory on their various visits to Carlisle. Edward I. was certainly a guest there in August 1306, for on the tenth of that month he requested James de Dalilegh, his agent in Cumberland, to put the houses of the priory in readiness for his reception as he intended

[1] Pat. 5 Edw. III. pt. i. m. 8.

[2] *Visitation of the Northern Counties,* 1530 (Surtees Soc.), 102.

[3] *Arch.* iii. 22–3, v. 340–5, where the horns so called are figured ; *Trans. Cumb. and Westmld. Arch. Soc.* ii. 337–47 ; *Cat. of the Arch. Mus. formed at Carlisle in* 1859, p. 16.

[4] It was little wonder that the name of Robert Bruce, the cause of many of their misfortunes, was held in detestation on the English side of the Border. When Cardinal Peter of Spain, the papal legate, came to Carlisle, he preached in the cathedral and 'revested himselfe and the other bishops which were present, and then with candels light and causing the bels to be roong, they accursed in terrible wise Robert Bruce the usurper of the crowne of Scotland with all his partakers, aiders and maintenders' (Holinshed, ii. 523).

[5] Anct. Petitions, No. 4897.

[6] *Cal. of Doc. Scot.* (Scot. Rec. Pub.) iii. 100–1.

[7] Close, 10 Edw. II. m. 29d.

[8] Ibid. 5 Edw. III. pt. i. m. 5d.

[9] Pat. 10 Ric. II. pt. i. m. 18, 35.

[10] Hist. MSS. Com. Rep. xii. App. vii. 9 (Rydal Hall MSS.)

to occupy them immediately.[1] The cloisters were sometimes utilized as a storehouse for the provisions of the army. It was one of the complaints against Sir Andrew de Harcla in 1319 that his brother John broke through the wall of the 'lunge celer' in the priory and the doors of others, and took out twenty tuns of the 'élite' of the king's wine.[2]

The statue of the Blessed Virgin Mary was a conspicuous figure among the 'ornaments' of the cathedral, as we should expect in a church entitled in her name. If we consider the ecclesiastical relation of the cathedral to the diocese we can in a measure understand the meaning of Bishop Welton's phrase when he spoke of the people under his jurisdiction as 'the subjects of God and the glorious Virgin Mary, His mother, in whose honour the said church was erected.'[3] The cult of the Virgin was a devotional instinct of considerable power in the religious life of the city and diocese of Carlisle. In 1363 Bishop Appleby obtained from the pope indulgences extending over ten years for penitents who visited the cathedral (which had been burned) on the five feasts of the Blessed Virgin, or who lent a helping hand to the fabric.[4] When the Scots were assaulting Carlisle in the time of Richard II., a woman appeared to them and announced the near approach of the king's army, but that woman, said Henry of Knighton,[5] was believed to be the glorious Virgin Mary, the patroness of Carlisle, who had often appeared to the inhabitants of that city. In 1380 Joan, wife of John de Dundrawe, bequeathed a girdle wrought in silver for the image of the Blessed Mary in the cathedral.[6] The prior and convent, inflamed with the energy of pious devotion, made application to Bishop Close and Archbishop Kempe in 1451 for an indulgence to aid them in procuring a richly decorated statue of the Virgin for the cathedral of Carlisle. Nothing would satisfy them short of an image or statue covered with plates of silver and overlaid with gold, gems, precious stones, and many other costly ornaments, for the praise of God, the increase of the veneration and honour of the most glorious Virgin and for provoking the devotion of Christ's faithful people daily flocking there on pilgrimage.[7] In 1469 John Knoblow, parson

of Lamplugh, gave a legacy to the prior and convent that five candles might be lighted in honour of the five joys of the Blessed Virgin in front of her image in the conventual church every night after compline when the antiphon, *Salve Regina*, was sung.[8] This fervid devotion to sumptuous imagery was general throughout the diocese in the fourteenth and fifteenth centuries.[9]

Though it was a special veneration for the Blessed Virgin which was the chief cause of making Carlisle a place of pilgrimage, its possession of some relics of the saints contributed not a little to its fame. According to a statement of J. Denton,[10] Waldeve son of Earl Gospatric brought from Jerusalem and Constantinople a bone of St. Paul, and another of St. John the Baptist, two stones of Christ's sepulchre, and part of the Holy Cross, which he gave to the priory. There can be no doubt that Alan son of the said Waldeve gave the Holy Rood which was in their possession as late as the fourteenth century. But it is not stated whether or not it was part of the real cross of our Lord.[11] Waldeve and Alan were great benefactors of the church of Carlisle in various other ways. As Hugh de Morvill, one of the assassins of Archbishop Becket, had a family connection with the diocese, it is not to be wondered at that some relics of the martyr should find their way to Carlisle. In the early years of the thirteenth century, when John de Courcy founded an establishment of regular canons at Toberglorie in the suburb of Downpatrick (Dun) in Ulster, and made it a cell of Carlisle, the new institution was entitled in the honour of St. Thomas the martyr out of respect to the canons of the mother house.[12] At that date

[8] *Richmondshire Wills* (Surtees Soc.), 7.
[9] When Bishop Bell rebuilt the chapel at Rose Castle in 1489 he purchased three images at York for its decoration (Compotus W. Skelton, MS.). In 1359 John Lowry made a bequest in his will for painting the image of the Holy Rood in the church of Arthuret, and in 1362 Robert de Whyterigg expressed a wish to be buried in the choir of Caldbeck before the image of St. Mary Magdalene (Carl. Epis. Reg., Welton, ff. 60, 103). Richard de Aslacby, vicar of St. Michael's, Appleby, desired his body to be buried *coram Cruce* in his own church, and Nicholas de Motherby bequeathed the modest sum of 12*d*. in 1362 for the use of the Holy Rood in the church of Soureby (ibid. ff. 102, 178).
[10] *Cumberland*, 99.
[11] Dugdale, *Mon.* iii. 584–5 ; *Cal. of Doc. Scot.* (Scot. Rec. Pub.), ii. 16.
[12] Pat. 12 Edw. II. pt. i. m. 19 ; Dugdale, *Mon.* vi. 145. Edward II. confirmed to the canons of Carlisle all those donations 'quas Johannes de

[1] *Cal. of Doc. Scot.* (Scot. Rec. Pub.), ii. 488.
[2] Ibid. iii. 127.
[3] Carl. Epis. Reg., Welton, f. 109.
[4] *Cal. of Papal Petitions*, i. 437.
[5] Twysden, *Decem Scriptores*, col. 2675.
[6] Carl. Epis. Reg., Appleby, f. 327.
[7] *The Priory of Hexham* (Surtees Soc.), i. pp. xcvii.–xcviii.

it is evident that St. Thomas must have been held in high esteem in the church of Carlisle. At a later period we learn the cause. It was in the cathedral in presence of Bishop Halton that Robert Bruce in 1297 swore on the holy mysteries and on the sword of St. Thomas to be faithful and vigilant in the cause of King Edward.[1] It must have been the possession of this relic that made so great an impression on that king, for on several of his visits to the city he paid special veneration to the memory of the saint. In 1300 the king made his oblations at the altar in the church of the priory in honour of St. Thomas the martyr.[2] At a later visit in 1307, a few weeks before his death, the old warrior endowed the canons with the advowson of the church of Castle Sowerby for the devotion he bore to the glorious Virgin Mary and the relics of the blessed Thomas the martyr and other saints which they had.[3] In 1536, before the dissolution of the religious houses, the royal commissioners reported that the priory had a portion of the Holy Cross, the sword with which Thomas of Canterbury was martyred,[4] and the girdle of St. Bridget the virgin.

The only relics of the ancient ritual of the priory which have survived to our day are two copes, one of which has been ascribed to the fifteenth century and the other to the sixteenth. The older vestment has richly embroidered orfrays with representations of the saints, and the other is of cloth of gold. In a seventeenth century inventory of 'things to be provided, corrected, ordered and done in the cathedral church of Carlisle and about its revenues,' it was directed ' that the two copes be mended and worn by the Epistler and Gospeller.' The date of the inventory appears to be 1685–6. How long after they continued to be worn at Carlisle is not known.[5]

The revenues of the priory varied greatly from time to time according to the peaceful or disturbed state of the border. The value of the temporalities in 1291, which may be taken as a normal period, was assessed by the commissioners of Pope Nicholas IV. at £96 19s.; whereas in 1319, after the devastations of the Scottish wars, the value had fallen to £20.[6] The spiritualities, consisting chiefly of tithes and pensions, would fluctuate in a corresponding proportion. The prior contributed £4 to the subsidy granted by the clergy of Carlisle to Richard H. in 1379, the value of his benefice having been assessed at £200 ; each of the eleven canons contributed 3s. 4d.[7] In the valuation of 1535 the gross value of the spiritualities was set down at £332 5s. 10d., and the temporalities at £150 2s. 3d., which made a total of £482 8s. 1d. The necessary outgoings in Crown and manorial rents, pensions, ecclesiastical payments, alms, and fees to civil officials, amounted to £64 4s. 8d., leaving a net revenue of £418 3s. 4d.[8] The alms exacted of the canons by ordination or foundation are of the greatest interest. The schedule enumerates[9] stated sums by ordination

Curceio fecit Deo et canonicis regularibus ecclesie predicte de loco quem fundavit in honore St. Thome martyris ad honorem ipsorum canonicorum juxta fontem que vocatur Toberglorie in suburbio de Dun, inter duas vias, quarum una tendit ad Crems, alia ad grangiam de Saballo.' No vestige of the site now remains. Robert son of Troite forfeited his land in Cumberland because he went into Ireland with John de Courcy, but he regained possession in 1207 (Pipe R. 9 John). There is at least one church in the diocese of Carlisle, that of Farlam in Gillesland, which is entitled in the name of St. Thomas of Canterbury. At an early period Walter de Wyndesoure granted some land to the church of St. Thomas the martyr in Farlam, *et sanctis ibidem adoratis,* a gift which was afterwards confirmed by Ranulf de Vaux, lord of the fee (Reg. of Lanercost, MS. i. 20).

[1] Hemingburgh, *Chron.* (Engl. Hist. Soc.), ii. 129.

[2] *Liber Quot. Contrar. Garderobæ* (Soc. Antiq.), 43.

[3] Pat. 35 Edw. I. m. 17.

[4] *L. and P. Hen. VIII.* x. 364. Denton, who died in 1617, said that ' the sword that killed St. Thomas was at Ishall in my father's time and since remaineth with the house of Arundel ' (*Cumberland*, 68). It was probably brought from the priory at the time of the dissolution to Isell by Dr. Legh, the royal commissioner for the viewing of religious houses, who was a cousin of John Legh of that place (ibid. v. 1447, vi. 1346).

[5] These copes were described in detail by Chancellor Ferguson in 1885 (*Trans. Cumb. and Westmld. Arch. Soc.* viii. 233–6). The manuscript book belonging to the dean and chapter of Carlisle, in which the inventory is recorded, is entitled, ' A perfect Rental of all Rents due and payable to the dean and chapter of Carlisle, A.D. 1685–6.' Henry Lord Scrope and Bishop Barnes were commissioned in 1572 to search the diocese of Carlisle for vestments, copes, etc., which had been concealed (*S.P. Dom. Elizabeth,* Add. xxi. 65). The copes shown at Durham Cathedral were regularly worn during the communion service by prebendaries and minor canons until the time of Warburton (Raine, *North Durham,* 94 ; *Quart. Rev.* xxxii. 273). Accounts agree that the copes ceased to be used at Durham about 1780.

[6] *Pope Nich. Tax.* (Rec. Com.), 320b, 333b.

[7] Exch. Cler. Sub. Dioc. of Carl. bdle. 60, No. 1.

[8] *Valor Eccl.* (Rec. Com.), v. 275–6.

[9] Bishop Walter's gift of Old Salkeld in 1230 is omitted from this enumeration. For the health

of Henry I., the founder of the priory, and Maud his queen, for the souls of themselves and their successors : by ordination of William Strickland, Bishop of Carlisle, for the celebration of a solemn obit for himself annually and for priests celebrating for his soul : by ordination of Bishop Marmaduke Lumley, for a wax candle to be continually burning before the most venerable sacrament of the Eucharist in their church for ever : by ordination of Bishop Gilbert Welton for a solemn obit celebrated for him and for priests celebrating annually : by ordination of Edward IV. given to three bedells annually : by ordination of the same king to priests celebrating for the souls of himself, Elizabeth his consort, and all his successors[1] : and by ordination of Sir Gilbert Ogle, lord of Ogle,[2] for an annual obit. Of the monastic houses in the county, the priory of Carlisle ranked after the abbey of Holmcultram in point of revenues. These two houses, having incomes of more than £200 a year, were reckoned among the greater monasteries, and thus escaped the first dissolution.

After the canons had obtained the privilege of electing their own superiors, they usually made choice of one of their body to fill the office. Almost all the priors of Carlisle were north-country men ; several of them, like Adam de Warthwyk, William de Dalston, Thomas de Hoton, Simon Senhouse, and Lancelot Salkeld, are known to have belonged to families of distinction in Cumberland. As the election of the bishop was vested in the chapter, the way was open for a canon of Carlisle to obtain the highest ecclesiastical position. Perhaps it is to this consideration that we owe the social status of the families from which the priors of Carlisle were re-

cruited. In the neighbouring priory of Lanet-cost, a house of the same religious order, no such family distinction is observable. It is scarcely necessary to suggest that some of the bishops, like Halton, Kirkby and Appleby, had been previously members of the cathedral chapter. Had the choice of the canons been always unfettered and had their elections been uncontrolled by the political necessities of the Crown or the growing arrogance of the papacy, the number of bishops of Carlisle trained in their own house would have been much greater. It amounted almost to a scandal that Prior John de Horncastle, who had been elected bishop by the chapter in 1352 and confirmed by the king, should have been ousted from the bishopric by a papal intrigue before his consecration. In other ways also preferment was open to the canons. In 1273 Geoffrey de Stok, canon of Carlisle, was appointed abbot of St. Patrick's, Saul, on the nomination of the Bishop of Down, with the counsel and consent of the king's lieutenant in Ireland.[3]

The priors of Carlisle were frequently employed in secular affairs as the occasions of state demanded. In the great controversy about the hereditary claims of the royal line of Scotland over the northern counties, the prior was appointed one of the king's assessors in 1242, for the purpose of assigning 60 librates of land in Cumberland to King Alexander towards a settlement, with instructions to return the 'extent' in writing under his seal that the king might know of what the allotments consisted.[4] It is not necessary to pass in review the various posts of trust they were called upon to fulfil from time to time in the civil administration of the district. The prior of Carlisle was found a convenient coadjutor or substitute for the sheriff, either as paymaster or overseer of the various repairs and alterations required in maintaining the fortifications of an important frontier town.[5] In 1524 a commission was issued to Thomas Lord Dacre, the prior of Carlisle, Sir Christopher Moresby and Richard Salkeld to settle disputes which had arisen between the subjects of the two kingdoms relative to the fishgarths of the river Esk.[6] Up to the very last the priors of Carlisle were found useful agents in forwarding the civil and philanthropic interests of the community.

of the soul of King John and W., father of the bishop, he gave to the priory all his holding in 'Old Salkhil,' in free alms, for the support of two regular canons, one to celebrate mass for the soul of Henry III. and the other to do likewise for the said bishop and his successors (Chart. R. 14 Hen. III. pt. ii. m. 7).

[1] The revenues of the hospital of St. Nicholas by Carlisle were granted to the priory and convent in 1477 by Edward IV., on the condition that they should find a canon priest, to be called the king's chaplain, to celebrate masses and other divine services in the monastery for the good estate of the king, and his consort Elizabeth, and their children, and for their souls after death (Pat. 17 Edw. IV. pt. i. m. 16).

[2] Sir Robert Ogle and Isabel his wife gave land in Thursby with the advowson and patronage of the church to the prior and canons regular of Carlisle in 1468 (Pat. 8 Edw. IV. pt. i. m. 23).

[3] Pat. 1 Edw. I. m. 4.
[4] Ibid. 26 Hen. III. m. 7d.
[5] Close, 10 Edw. II. m. 25 ; 7 Edw. III. pt. i. m. 11 ; 12 Edw. III. pt. ii. m. 19 ; Pat. 2 Ric. II. pt. ii. m. 8 ; 4 Ric. II. pt. i. m. 26.
[6] B.M. Cott. MS. Caligula, B. v. 69.

Adelulf is reputed by a venerable tradition to have been prior of Carlisle when the bishopric was founded in 1133. The statement was accepted as early as the fourteenth century. On 17 September 1343 a return was made by the prior and chapter of Carlisle of the succession of the bishops of the see, as far as it could be ascertained from the chronicles and ancient books in their possession, at the request of the prior and convent of Conishead, with the view of settling some dispute about the church of Orton in Westmorland which had been appropriated to the latter house. In that return it was stated on the evidence then at their disposal that Adelulf, prior of Carlisle, was consecrated Bishop of Carlisle in the year 1133.[1] If that be the case, he is the first prior on record, but we have not discovered his name in any contemporary document.

Walter, prior of Carlisle, was a prominent figure in some notable functions of great interest in the ecclesiastical history of the district. With Bishop Adelulf he witnessed the foundation charter of the abbey of Holmcultram on 1 January 1150, and was also present at the courts of David I. and Malcolm IV. when the said charter was confirmed.[2] When Robert de Vaux founded the priory of Lanercost about the year 1169, Prior Walter of Carlisle witnessed the charter.[3] These two events are of considerable importance in fixing the exact period in which this prior lived. Walter witnessed two charters of Alan son of Waldeve, by which he granted land in 'Scadebuas' and 'Goseford' to the monks of St. Bees.[4] He must have lived for some time after 1169, for he witnessed several subsequent charters to the priory of Lanercost granted by Robert de Vaux and others of that neighbourhood.[5] His name is also found in connection with several deeds in the monastic registers of Wetheral and Whitby.[6] It is usually maintained that Prior Walter is the same person as Walter the priest who endowed the priory of Carlisle with all his possessions before he took the religious habit in that house, but no such supposition can be entertained without violence to chronology.

Gilbert, prior of Carlisle, made a composition with Robert de Vaux in the presence of Robert, Archdeacon of Carlisle, renouncing the right which his convent claimed in the churches of Irthington and Brampton. He also witnessed a charter of David son of Terry and Robert son of Asketill to the priory of Lanercost on the church of Denton and the hermitage which Leising held.[7]

John appears to have been prior of Carlisle for a considerable period, as his name is often found in local evidences of the reigns of Richard I. and John. In the monastic registers of Holmcultram, Lanercost and Wetheral there are recorded several deeds to which he is mentioned either as a party or a witness.[8] John was prior when the convent of Carlisle leased 'Waytecroft' to Thomas son of Gospatric, and quit-claimed the tithes of Scotby to the priory of Wetheral. With a number of Cumberland men, he was present at Winchester in 1194 when King Richard granted Old Salkeld to Adam, cook of Queen Eleanor, for his good services.[9] In 1196 Prior John had come to an agreement with Henry de Wichenton about the third part of the church of Lowther, and a similar agreement was arrived at between him and Ralf de Bray in 1204 with respect to the church of Rocliffe.[10]

[1] Duchy of Lanc. Chart. Box A, No. 416. The deed which has been printed in the *Reg. of Wetheral* (Cumb. and Westmld. Arch. Soc.), pp. 417–8, goes on to state that to Bishop Adelulf succeeded immediately afterwards (*postea immediate*) Bernard and then Hugh, who died in 1233, in whose time Bartholomew, prior of Carlisle, with the consent of his chapter, confirmed the church of 'Overton in Westmeria' to the prior and convent of 'Coningeshevid.' The errors and misstatements in this portion of the return are manifest, for Bishop Bernard did not succeed immediately after Bishop Adelulf, inasmuch as the see was vacant for nearly fifty years between the two episcopates, and Bishop Hugh died in 1223, not in 1233. The appropriation of the church of Orton to the priory of Conishead by licence of Bishop Hugh is still on record. The witnesses of the deed were B(artholomew), prior of Carlisle ; Thomas son of John, then sheriff of Cumberland ; Hugh de Plessiz, constable of Carlisle ; William de Yrebi ; Master A(dam) de Kirkebi, official of Carlisle ; Adam de Aspatric, dean and Alan de Caldebec, dean of Allerdale (Duchy of Lanc. Chart. Box A. No. 412).

[2] Reg. of Holmcultram, MS. ff. 221–3 ; Dugdale, *Mon.* v. 594 ; *Chron. of Melrose*, in ann. 1150 ; Hoveden, *Chron.* i. 211 (Rolls Ser.)

[3] Reg. of Lanercost, MS. i. 1.

[4] Reg. of St. Bees, MS. ff. 31b, 132 (Harl. MS. 434).

[5] Reg. of Lanercost, MS. i. 9, 14 ; ii. 18 ; v. 3 ; viii. 5.

[6] *Reg. of Wetheral* (Cumb. and Westmld. Arch. Soc.), 63, 80, 86, 100–1, 110 ; *Whitby Chartul.* (Surtees Soc.), i. 38.

[7] Reg. of Lanercost, MS. viii. 5 ; iii. 13.

[8] Reg. of Holmcultram, MS. f. 35 ; Reg. of Lanercost, MS. ii. 12 ; v. 4 ; viii. 2–4 ; *Reg. of Wetheral* (Cumb. and Westmld. Arch. Soc.), 69, 176, 212, 218.

[9] Cart. Antiq. F. 14 ; Rymer, *Fœdera*, i. 63.

[10] *Pedes Finium* (Pipe R. Soc.), 7 & 8 Ric. I. No. 128 ; ibid. (Rec. Com.), Cumberland, pp. 7–8.

RELIGIOUS HOUSES

The priory was vacant on 6 May 1214, when the king bestowed the latter church on Odo de Ledreda his clerk.[1]

In the summer of 1214 four canons of Carlisle were deputed to carry the record of the election of a new prior for the confirmation of King John.[2] On 25 August in that year the king informed the archdeacon of Carlisle by letters close that Brother Henry, canon of Merton, was canonically and with his assent elected to the priory of Carlisle and had done homage : he was to be admitted without delay to the office.[3] The Chronicle of Lanercost, which gives his name as Henry de Mareis, adds that the appointment received papal confirmation in November 1214.[4] After the death of Bishop Bernard, Prior Henry confirmed the appropriation of the church of Crosby Ravensworth made by that bishop to the abbey of Whitby,[5] and did a similar service to the priory of Lanercost in respect of certain of their churches.[6]

Bartholomew was prior during some portions of the episcopate of Bishops Hugh and Walter. He was not only a witness to the charter whereby the former bishop confirmed the spiritual possessions of the priory of Lanercost, but also granted a charter to the same effect on behalf of the convent of Carlisle.[7] This prior did a similar service to the abbey of Whitby[8] in respect of the church of Crosby Ravensworth in Westmorland. He witnessed a charter which Bishop Hugh granted to the priory of Wetheral, confirming to the monks the churches of St. Michael and St. Laurence, Appleby;[9] and in company with Bishop Walter and Archdeacon Gervase he was a witness to the charter of Ivo de Vipont, granting lands in Alston to the priory of Hexham.[10] He also confirmed a charter of Bishop Hugh to the abbey of Newminster,[11] and witnessed the licence given by the same bishop to the priory of Conishead to appropriate the church of Orton in Westmorland.[12] Prior Bartholomew died in 1231.[13]

Ralf Barri, nephew of Bishop Walter, succeeded Bartholomew in 1231 and ruled the priory till his death on 9 February 1247.[14] When Bishop Walter confirmed the church of Burgh-by-Sands to the abbey of Holmcultram on 12 April 1234 Prior Ralf and Archdeacon Gervase were witnesses to the charter. The same prior afterwards issued a charter to the same effect on behalf of the convent of Carlisle.[15] With Bishop Walter and William, prior of Wetheral, he witnessed the charter whereby Roland de Vaux granted certain land of his fee in Treverman to the canons of Lanercost for the soul of Robert de Vaux his brother.[16] In 1235-6 Ralf de Duffeld and Emma his wife brought a suit in the king's court against Bishop Walter and Prior Ralf for an unjust ejectment from their free tenement in Sebergham, which had been previously bestowed on Prior Ralf by William Wasthose, father of the said Emma.[17] About the same period the dispute between this prior and the abbey of Holmcultram about the tithe of fish caught in the river Eden was submitted to the adjudication of Walter, Bishop of Carlisle.[18] Prior Ralf was a party to several deeds and leases belonging to the priory of Wetheral.[19]

When Robert succeeded in 1247 the custody of the lands of John de Vipont was delivered to him on the same condition as Ralf his predecessor had held it, the lands having been taken into the king's hand by reason of the death of the said Ralf, prior of Carlisle.[20] On 22 October 1248

[1] *Rot. Chart.* (Rec. Com.), i. 206b. There can be little doubt that the year of the vacancy was 1214.
[2] *Rot. Litt. Claus.* (Rec. Com.), 16 John, i. p. 207b.
[3] Ibid. 211, 211b.
[4] *Chron. de Lanercost*, 14. It is probable that Prior Henry was a brother or relative of Richard de Mareis, the notorious chancellor of King John, afterwards Bishop of Durham. Richard had been Archdeacon of Richmond and Northumberland in 1213, when the king conferred on him a canonry of York (*Rot. Litt. Pat. John* [Rec. Com.] 105). The same person is also found acting as official of Carlisle in Bishop Bernard's time (Reg. of Lanercost, MS. viii. 3, 4). Merton was an Augustinian priory in Surrey.
[5] Hist. MSS. Com., Rep. xii. App. vii. 322 (Rydal Hall MSS.) ; *Chart. of Whitby* (Surtees Soc.), i. 43. In the latter reference Canon Atkinson has called him Prior Hugh in error.
[6] Reg. of Lanercost, MS. viii. 4.
[7] Ibid. viii. 7, 8.
[8] *Whitby Chart.* (Surtees Soc.), i. 45-6, 262.
[9] *Reg. of Wetherhal*, 53-5, 67-8, 118, etc.

[10] *Priory of Hexham* (Surtees Soc.), ii. 120-1.
[11] *Newminster Cartul.* (Surtees Soc.), 216-7.
[12] Duchy of Lanc. Chart. Box A, No. 412.
[13] *Chron. de Lanercost* (Maitland Club), 41.
[14] Ibid. 41, 53.
[15] Reg. of Holmcultram, MS. ff. 17, 18.
[16] Reg. of Lanercost, MS. ii. 21 ; v. 2 ; vii. 18.
[17] *Bracton's Note Book* (ed. F. W. Maitland), No. 1153 ; *Plac. de Quo Warr.* (Rec. Com.), 125.
[18] Reg. of Holmcultram, MS. ff. 20-1 ; Harl. MS. 3891, f. 29b.
[19] *Reg. of Wetherhal*, 182, 200, 205-6, etc.
[20] *Rot. Orig.* (Rec. Com.), i. 10. This prior is called Robert de Morvill by some writers, but no contemporary authority for the surname has been found.

143

Bishop Silvester of Carlisle and Robert, prior of the same, gave a bond to the prior and convent of Durham that they should be held free of cost and expense if they would confirm the appropriation of the churches of Newcastle, Newburn, Warkworth, Corbridge and a moiety of Whittingham, which Bishop Nicholas of Durham had made to the church of Carlisle on the ordination of Masters William de Kilkenny, Archdeacon of Coventry; Thomas de Wymundeham, precentor of Lichfield; Odo de Kilkenny and Walter de Merton, clerks.[1] Robert was prior on 2 September 1249, when the ordination already referred to was made between Bishop Silvester and the priory about the final redistribution of the property of the church of Carlisle.

Robert had ceased to be prior about 1258. On 17 December 1258 Pope Alexander IV. issued a mandate to the priors of Hexham, Lanercost and Wetheral, on the petition of the prior and convent of Carlisle, to inquire about the conduct of Robert, a canon, then prior, who, submitting to the bishop's visitation, and thinking that on account of his excesses he was about to be removed, resigned ; on which the bishop ordered him to reside in the church of Corbridge in Northumberland with one canon at least, and to pay from its proceeds 40 marks a year to the prior and chapter, keeping the rest, which was estimated to amount to 90 marks, for their sustentation. The Bishop of Durham admitted Robert to the said church by order of the Bishop of Carlisle on the petition of the convent whose church it was. But the new vicar of Corbridge broke out into dissolute living, and was likely to perish, placed as he was outside all discipline. The pope ordered the priors, if the facts were found as stated, to cause Robert to return to his cloister and to remain there under his prior's obedience.[2]

The names of Adam de Felton and Alan are usually introduced after Robert de Morville in lists of the priors of Carlisle, but no reasons

have been given for their adoption. As Nicolson and Burn[3] have apparently followed the list of Hugh Todd,[4] these priors should be received with the greatest suspicion till some evidence is put forward to establish their titles.

John, prior, and the convent of Carlisle, confirmed, on 15 May 1263, an ordination made by Bishop Robert de Chause between Isabel, prioress of Marrick, and Ralf de Kirkandres, chaplain, with respect to the church of Kirkandrews on Eden.[5]

Robert was prior of Carlisle on 27 December 1278, when the convent elected Ralf, prior of Gisburne, to be Bishop of Carlisle.[6] On 16 July 1282 Bishop Ralf de Ireton confirmed the appropriation of the church of Addingham with its chapel of Salkeld to him and the convent, the advowson of which had been granted by Christiane, widow of Robert de Brus. The prior and canons had petitioned for the licence on the ground of the extraordinary burdens the cathedral church had to bear by reason of its geographical position and the frequent concourse of clergy and people *in confinio duarum regionum.*[7] On 24 April 1283 Prior Robert confirmed a pension to Adam de Coupland, clerk, by grant of the same bishop. At a subsequent period it was stated that Robert had vacated the priory by resignation at a time when the house was in a good financial condition.[8]

The next prior was named Adam, against whom Edward I. in 1285 issued a writ of *quo warranto* touching certain liberties which the priory claimed in Inglewood Forest.[9] The full name of the prior afterwards appears as Adam de Warthwyk. In 1287 this prior confirmed the taxation of Walton vicarage ordained by Bishop Ralf de Ireton for the

---

[1] By the kindness of Canon Greenwell this deed, now in possession of the dean and chapter of Durham, has been perused by the writer. The seals of the bishop and priory are in a fair state of preservation. The legend on the bishop's seal : + SILVESTER DEI GRA KA . . . LEOLENSIS EPISCOPVS. The counterseal : + TE ROGO VIRGO REGI SIS VIGIL ERGO GREGI. The legend on the seal of the priory is very much mutilated : + . . . LESIE SANCTE MARI . . . EOLI. The deed is endorsed : 'Obligacio Episcopi et Prioris Karln' de indempnitate confirmacionis ecclesiarum eorundem in proprios usus.'

[2] *Cal. of Papal Letters,* i. 361–2.

[3] *Hist. of Cumb.* ii. 301.
[4] *Notitia Eccl. Cathed. Carl.* (ed. R. S. Ferguson), 4.
[5] *Coll. Topog. et Gen.* v. 235–6, where four most interesting deeds are set out at length. In Todd's list the names of John de Halton, Bishop of Carlisle, and John de Kendal are mentioned among the priors about this date (*Notitia Eccl. Cathed. Carl.* 4) ; but Todd's list is intolerable.
[6] Chan. Eccl. Pet. for Elections, 24 June 1278, file 6 ; *Dep. Keeper's Rep.* vi. App. p. 94.
[7] Carl. Epis. Reg., Halton, ff. 181–2 ; *Letters from the Northern Reg.* (Rolls Ser.), 251–2.
[8] Carl. Epis. Reg., Halton, ff. 14, 43. With Nicholas de Lewelin, Archdeacon of Carlisle, he witnessed a grant of Maud de Vaux in her widowhood to the priory of Lanercost (Reg. of Lanercost, MS. x. 7).
[9] *Cal. of Pat.* 1330–4, pp. 111–2.

priory of Lanercost,[1] and in 1303 did a similar service to the abbey of St. Mary, York, by confirming the appropriation of the church of Bromfield to that monastery.[2] His name is inscribed on the famous Ragman Roll[3] of 1296 as Adam 'prior de Cardoyl del counte de Are,' a county in which the priory probably had some property. At the bishop's visitation in 1300 he heard some grievous complaints against the prior's negligent administration of the house, and delivered a code of drastic injunctions[4] for a speedy reformation. These injunctions have been already referred to. Adam de Warthwyk resigned the priory of his own free will and accord on 18 September 1304, when a very liberal pension and ample privileges were conceded to him, because he was a cadet of a noble family in the diocese (*quia a magnatibus et personis nobilibus nostre diocesis procreatus et oriundus*). He had been forty years a canon and twenty years and more prior of the house. The pension was decreed by Bishop Halton with the unanimous consent of the chapter.[5]

William de Hautewysil was prior for only four years, as he resigned on 28 September 1308. On the same day licence was obtained by Robert the sub-prior for the canons to elect a successor.[6]

On the cession of the last prior, Robert de Helpeston was canonically elected, and the Bishop of Carlisle, having examined the record of the election and found that it had been conducted according to the decrees of the holy fathers, confirmed him in the priory on 1 October 1308.[7] On the same day a mandate was sent to the official of the diocese to induct and install him. In 1320 Prior Robert demised to Robert de la Ferte a messuage, 13 acres of land and 2 acres of meadow in Salkeld, lands which were afterwards forfeited by the adherence of Robert de la Ferte to the Scots and delivered back to the priory.[8]

Simon de Hautwysell succeeded, but died after a short incumbency. On 13 July 1325, Roger, the sub-prior, and the chapter of Carlisle petitioned the bishop for his licence to elect a successor, William de Hurworth, a

canon of the house, being the bearer of the petition. As Bishop Ross had just been consecrated, the canons had previously sent him a laudatory letter informing him that the receipt of the papal bulls announcing his appointment to the see of Carlisle had filled their breasts with ineffable joy.[9]

It is said that William de Hurworth was the next prior, but we have not succeeded in finding any good authority for the statement. In fact the evidences are against it, inasmuch as his name is found as a canon of the house for many years during subsequent priorates.[10] On 8 February 1329 Thomas Peytefyn, chaplain, was presented to the vicarage of Edenhall, which was in the king's gift by reason of the priory of Carlisle being in his hand.[11] We know for certain that John de Kirkby was prior in 1330, and that Bishop Ross issued an excommunication against him on 3 January 1330-1 for failing to pay the papal tenth granted to John XXII. by the clergy of Carlisle.[12] About this time there was a long and bitter dispute between the bishop and the priory as to the tithe of assart lands in the forest of Inglewood which was ultimately referred to the secular courts.[13] The controversy was brought to a sudden termination by the death of Bishop Ross and the elevation of Prior Kirkby to fill his place. When William de Hurworth and

[9] Carl. Epis. Reg. Ross, ff. 268-9.
[10] Hugh Todd appears to have been the first to suggest that William de Hurworth was prior (*Notitia Eccl. Cathed. Carl.* p. 5). The lists of priors of Carlisle given by Browne Willis and Dugdale were founded on that of Todd. As the Episcopal Registers have been quoted as the authority, it is evident that Todd had not read carefully the record of the petition to elect a prior in the room of Simon de Hautwysell, deceased, which William de Hurworth was directed to convey to the bishop, 'dilectum nobis in Christo fratrem Willelmum de Hurword, canonicum nostrum, latorem presencium, vobis dirigimus, vestre paternitati reverende humiliter supplicantes quatinus ad eiusdem ecclesie prioratus regimen nobis licenciam priorem elegendi ut est magis liberaliter concedatis' (Carl. Epis. Reg., Ross, ff. 268-9). It is clearly stated in the record that he was the proctor of the convent seeking for power to elect and not its nominee to the priorate. William de Hurworth, canon of Carlisle, was employed in various capacities, as bishop's proctor, diocesan penitentiary and such like during the episcopate of Bishop Kirkby. He was commissioned to transact diocesan business as late as 1342 (ibid. Kirkby, ff. 300, 307-8, 363, 454).
[11] Pat. 3 Edw. III. pt. i. m. 36.
[12] Carl. Epis. Reg., Ross, f. 263.
[13] Ibid. f. 262; Close, 5 Edw. III. pt. i. m. 16d.

[1] Reg. of Lanercost, MS. xi. 3.
[2] Add. Chart. 17155, 17156.
[3] *Cal. of Doc. Scot.* (Scot. Rec. Pub.), ii. 208.
[4] Carl. Epis. Reg., Halton, f. 43. In the same year he confirmed a pension of £40 granted by Bishop Halton to John de Drokensford, king's clerk, from the issues of the manor of Horncastle (ibid. f. 49).
[5] Ibid. f. 80. [6] Ibid. f. 113. [7] Ibid. f. 114.
[8] *Cal. of Close*, 1330-3, p. 357.

Richard de Whytrigg, canons of Carlisle, brought the news of the bishop's death to the king, letters patent were sent to the convent authorizing the election of a bishop to the vacant pastorate who should faithfully serve his church, king and country.[1] On 8 May 1332 the king signified to the Archbishop of York his assent to the election of John de Kirkby, prior of Carlisle, to be Bishop of Carlisle.[2] By a similar writ the temporalities of the bishopric were restored to him in the following July.[3] By an order in 1334 the prior of Carlisle was respited for rendering his account to the king for the time when the late prior (John de Kirkby), his predecessor, was receiver of the money for the victuals of the king and his father, sold in Cumberland.[4] From this it would appear in the absence of direct proof that John de Kirkby was the prior that succeeded Simon de Hautwysell, or at least that he was prior for some time during the reign of Edward II.

Geoffrey was the next prior, for on 8 March 1333-4, Bishop John de Kirkby acknowledged that he owed him £400, which was to be levied, in default of payment, on his lands and chattels in Cumberland.[5]

It is said that John de Horncastle was prior in 1352 when he was elected to fill the see of Carlisle. As the elect and confirmed but not the consecrated Bishop of Carlisle, he performed certain diocesan acts which are on record.[6] In 1363 a plenary remission at the hour of death was granted by the pope to 'John de Horncastell,' prior of Carlisle.[7] Bishop Appleby cited the prior and convent to undergo his visitation in 1366, to which citation the prior expressed his readiness, and conveyed to the bishop the names of the capitular body. It is interesting to note their names: John de Horncastell, prior; John de St. Neots, sub-prior; Thomas de Warthole; Thomas de Colby; Richard Bully; William de Dalston; Thomas de Penreth; Adam del Gille; John de Overton; Thomas Orfeor; William Colt; Robert del Parke and Robert de Edenhale, that is, a prior and twelve canons. It was intimated that Thomas de Penreth was absent for purposes of study, which was held to be a valid excuse. John de Horncastle signified his intention to the

bishop in November, 1376, of retiring from the priorate on account of old age and bad health, and the Archdeacon of Carlisle was commissioned to receive his resignation and to absolve him from his duties.[8]

In obedience to the bishop's licence to elect a successor, the choice of the canons fell on John de Penreth. This prior had a dispute with Robert de Clifton, the cellarer, in 1379, with the result that the cellarer was removed from his office. The whole case was ultimately submitted to the arbitration of the bishop.[9] Prior John de Penreth was associated with Robert de Rawebankes, abbot of Holmcultram, and Lambert de Morland, abbot of Shap, in 1379, as collectors of a subsidy granted by the clergy of the diocese of Carlisle to Richard II. in the second year of his reign.[10] In the return of the collectors the benefice of the prior of Carlisle was assessed at £200, the amount of his contribution being equal to that of the bishop, viz. £4. The following canons were named in the assessment at the rate of 3s. 4d. each: Thomas de Warthehole, Thomas de Colby, John Cole, Robert Bury, Robert de Clyfton, John de Overton, Richard Herwyk, Richard Bellerby, Richard Brumley, Thomas Dalston and Hugh Thoresby,[11] a prior and eleven canons. For certain lawful causes the priory was resigned by John de Penreth on 9 August 1381.[12]

The Bishop of Carlisle, having learnt by proclamation that there was no opposition to the election of William de Dalston, a canon of the house, decreed that he should be installed in the vacant priorate. That was in August 1381. The choice of the canons was the source of a great scandal in the diocese of Carlisle. The prior had refused to make the declaration of canonical obedience to the bishop which led to his excommunication. He was ultimately persuaded to resign on 28 September 1385, after he had made the requisite declaration.[13] This prior had been employed under the Crown in January, 1384-5, as surveyor of the works for the repair of the castle of Carlisle.[14]

After the cession of Prior Dalston,[15] great

[1] Carl. Epis. Reg., Ross, ff. 249-50.
[2] Pat. 6 Edw. III. pt. ii. m. 33.
[3] Ibid. 6 Edw. III. pt. ii. m. 25 ; Carl. Epis. Reg., Kirkby, ff. 251-2.
[4] Cal. of Close, 1333-7, p. 306.
[5] Close, 8 Edw. III. m. 33d.
[6] Registrum Domini Johannis de Horncastro, electi et confirmati anno domini mccclij.
[7] Cal. of Papal Petitions (Rolls Ser.), i. 437.

[8] Carl. Epis. Reg., Appleby, ff. 165, 289.
[9] Ibid. ff. 319-20.
[10] Ibid. ff. 314-5.
[11] Exch. Cler. Sub. Dioc. of Carl. bdle. 60, No. 1.
[12] Carl. Epis. Reg., Appleby, f. 387.
[13] Ibid. ff. 337-8, 348-52.
[14] Cal. of Doc. Scot. (Scot. Rec. Pub.), iv. 73.
[15] It would appear that Dalston, on his return to a subordinate position in the priory, became a troublesome inmate of the house. In 1390 he was cited with two other canons, Robert Clifton

circumspection was exercised by the bishop before he admitted a successor. The official of the diocese was commissioned to see that the election was conducted according to law, and to certify the formalities to the bishop. Having satisfied himself that Robert de Edenhall was the choice of the canons, and that there was no opposition, he directed his letters to the Archdeacon of Carlisle on 10 October 1385, to give the said Robert corporal possession of the prior's stall in the choir and his place in the chapter house.[1]

It is difficult to distinguish the priors during the fifteenth century, inasmuch as all those that have been met with bear the same Christian name. In the old lists no fewer than five priors of the name of Thomas have been mentioned. John Denton has given the order of succession as Thomas Hoton, Thomas Barnby, Thomas Huthwaite and Thomas Gudybour.[2] In their revised list, Nicolson and Burn have placed between Hoton and Barnby the name of 'Thomas Elye who built the grange of New Lathes near the city (of Carlisle) on the walls of which his name is legible.' From the latter source we learn that 'Thomas de Haythwaite erected the bishop's throne in the quire on the back part whereof his name was inscribed.'[3] Neither of these inscriptions is now to be found.

A few dates may help to ascertain the chronological order with more certainty. By letters patent, dated 4 January 1413-4, William, Bishop of Carlisle, appointed Thomas de Hoton, prior of the cathedral church of Carlisle, to collect the subsidy granted to the Crown by the convocation of York on 27 July 1413.[4] It was certified by Thomas, prior, and the convent of Carlisle, on 20 September 1423, that Joan, wife of John de Gaytford in the county of Nottingham, formerly wife of Elias de Thoresby, deceased, and daughter of Master John de Welton, was legitimate and born of the said Master John and Alice his wife in holy wedlock.[5] Thomas

Barnby, prior of Carlisle, was returned in a list of gentry of the county of Cumberland by certain local commissioners, one of whom was Marmaduke Lumley, Bishop of Carlisle, in the twelfth year of the reign of Henry VI. 1433-4.[6] In the muniment room of Lowther Castle there is an original lease of a tenement in Cardew, dated at Rose on 11 August 1457, and given by William, Bishop of Carlisle. The lease was confirmed by Thomas de 'Huthuayte,' prior of Carlisle, on behalf of the convent. Damaged impressions of the seals of the bishop and prior still remain.

During an inquisition for proving the age of Hugh, son and heir of Hugh Lowther, late of Lowther, taken on 8 November, 1482, it was deposed that he was born at Lowther on the Feast of the Assumption in 1461 and baptized in the church of that vill, the godfathers being Richard Wherton, rector of the said church, and Thomas, prior of Carlisle, and the godmother, Elizabeth Moresby.[7]

In the statute of 13 Edward IV., 1473, it was provided—

that this Acte of Resumption, or any other made or to be made in this present Parlement, extend not nor in any wise be prejudiciall, disavauntage, derogation or hurt to Edward Bishop of Carlill, nor to his predecessours nor successours, nor to Thomas Priour of Carlill, and Covent of the Monestery or Priorie of Carlill, nor to their predecessours nor successours, nor to any of theym, nor to any yefte or yeftes, graunte or grauntes, licence or licences, ratifications, releases, assignations or confirmations to theym, or to their predecessours, or to any of theym, made, graunted or had, by what name or names the Bishop or Priour and Covent of the seid Monestere or Priorie, or their predecessours be or were named or called in the same.[8]

It is not known precisely at what date the priorate of Thomas Gudybour began or ended. It is certain that he was prior of Carlisle in 1476, for in the early part of that year he was present at Hexham when William Bywell was elected head of that house.[9] It is probable that he was in office for a considerable period. During his time the cathedral church had been renovated,[10] the legends of the saints

and Richard Everwyk, for disobedience. On their deliverance from custody, they gathered some soldiers of the town and castle and took forcible possession of the priory, denying an entry to the bishop and the prior (Pat. 13 Ric. II. pt. ii. m. 2d).

[1] Carl. Epis. Reg., Appleby, ff. 353–4.
[2] Cumberland (ed. R. S. Ferguson), 98.
[3] Hist. of Cumb. ii. 303.
[4] Exch. Cler. Sub. Dioc. of Carl. bdle. 60, No. 8a.
[5] B.M. Add. Chart. No. 15770. The seal of the priory attached to this deed is very much broken and the legend indistinct.

[6] Fuller, Worthies of England (ed. J. Nichols), i. 240–1.
[7] Inq. p.m. 22 Edw. IV. No. 58.
[8] Rot. Parl. (Rec. Com.), vi. 76.
[9] Priory of Hexham, i. App. No. xc. Thomas Godebowre was parson of the parish church of Dacre in the diocese of Carlisle on 23 February 1462 (Pat. 1 Edw. IV. pt. iv. m. 9).
[10] The renovation of the cathedral while Thomas Gudybour was prior is well authenticated.

stencilled on the back of the choir stalls, and the tithe-barn near St. Cuthbert's church built. His initials in monogram, T(homas) G(udybour) P(rior), have been found in various parts of the cathedral and monastic buildings, and it was stated in an inscription on the door of an old cupboard in the sacristy that the house flourished under his rule (*domus hec floruit Gudebowr sub tegmine Thome*). In 1484 King Richard III. granted to Thomas, the prior, and the canons of the cathedral church, a great part of the possessions of which had been destroyed by the Scots, two tuns of red wine of Gascony yearly in the port of Kingston on Hull for use in their church, that they might pray for the good estate of the king and his consort Anne, Queen of England, and for their souls after death and the souls of the king's progenitors.[1] Among the muniments of the city of Carlisle there is an 'indenture made at Karlell' on 1 March 1484–5 'betwixt the right worshipfull ffather in God, Thomas Gudybour, priour, and his brethre the convent of the cathedrall kirke of Karlell,' on the one part, and the mayor and citizens of Carlisle on the other, about 'the teynde multure of the mylnes belongyng to the said Citee.' To this deed the seal of the priory is attached, together with a counter-seal of singular design.[2]

Simon Senus, Senose, or Senhouse, is said to have been chosen prior of Carlisle in 1507, but there must be an error of some years in the date. On 10 December 1505 Thomas, Lord Dacre, and Sir Edward Musgrave entered into a recognizance of 1,000 marks for the finding of four sureties before Simon, prior of Carlisle, and Cuthbert Conyers, clerk, for the payment of 540 marks due to the king. The money was paid and the debt cancelled on 12 July 1509.[3] By a

Richard III. sent the following letter 'to o' welbeloved servant John Crakenthorp, receyvor of our landes within our countie of Cumberland. We woll and charge you y' of such money as is now in yo handes or next and furst shall come unto y' same by vertue of yo' office, ye contente and pay (*among other disbursements*) unto o' trusty and welbeloved in God y' priour of oure monastery of Carlile the some of v' which we have geven towardes ye making of a glasse windowe within y' same o' monastery. And thise o' lettres shalbe yo' warraunt and discharge in y behalve. Yiven etc. at Gaynesburgh the xth day of Octobre the first yere of o' teigne' (Harl. MS. 433, f. 120a).

[1] Pat. 1 Ric. III. pt. ii. m. 20.
[2] *Trans. Cumb. and Westmld. Arch. Soc.* vii. 330–4; *Cat. of the Arch. Mus. formed at Carlisle in 1859*, p. 24; Nicolson and Burn, *Hist. of Cumb.* ii. 303.
[3] *L. and P. Hen. VIII.* i. 296.

deed 'geven att Karlisle the xiii. day of June the viiith yere of the reign of our most naturall Soverayn lord king Henry the VIIIth' (1516), Simon Senhouse, prior of Carlisle, joined Thomas Lord Dacre, the lord warden of the Marches, Sir Christopher Dacre, Robert Coldale, 'maire of the citie of Karlell,' and other gentlemen, aldermen and bailiffs of the city in an appeal for funds for 'the reedifyeng and bulding of a new brige of xxi jowelles adionyng the wallis of the forsaid Citie standing over the river of Eden now beyng decayed, and a perte of the same fallen down.'[4] On 15 July 1518 a grant in frankalmoin was made by the Crown to Simon, prior, and the canons of Carlisle, of the fishery of Carlisle at the annual rent of one mark, and of one tun of red wine annually at the port of Newcastle for sacrament.[5] While Senhouse was prior, his chamber or residence was rebuilt or renovated, for in a room, now the drawing-room, of the deanery, there remains a curiously decorated ceiling with quaint couplets inscribed on the crossbeams. A drawing of one of these verses by Miss Close, daughter of the Dean of Carlisle, was exhibited at the meeting of the Archæological Institute held at Carlisle in 1859,[6] the record of which is as follows :

Symon Senus Prior sette yis roofe and scalope here,
To the intent wythin thys place they shall have prayers every daye in the yere.
Lofe God and thy prynce and you nedis not dreid thy enimys.

Among the painted ornaments on the ceiling are roses, birds, the escallop shell, the ragged staff, and escutcheons of arms. Other verses have been recorded by Hutchinson,[7] but they have no particular interest. The whole of the ornamentation of the chamber is now very faint. The altar-tomb in the north transept of the cathedral, in front of the consistorial court, is reputed to commemorate this prior, but the inlaid brass plates, now to be found there, are no parts of the original structure.

Christopher Slee must have been prior for some time before 1528, for in that year the north-western gate of the precincts of the abbey was built. Around the elliptical arch on the inside, facing 'the Fratry,' there is an inscription now very much worn by the

[4] Hist. MSS. Com. Rep. xii. App. vii. 6 (Rydal Hall MSS.)
[5] Pat. 10 Hen. VIII. pt. ii. m. 6; *L. and P. Hen. VIII.* ii. 4323.
[6] *Cat. of the Arch. Mus. formed at Carlisle in 1859*, p. 26.
[7] *Hist. of Cumb.* ii. 602.

148

weather, but still legible : 'Orate pro anima Christoferi Slee prioris qui primus hoc opus fieri incepit A.D. 1528.' Christopher, prior of Carlisle, was joined in a commission on 22 September 1529, with Sir William Pennington, Sir John Ratclyf and Richard Irton to survey the castle of Carlisle, and to deliver the ordnance found in it to Sir Thomas Clifford and the castle to William Lord Dacre.[1] In 1534 'Christofer prior of the cathedrall churche of Karliol' was one of the signatories of the inventory taken on 9 May, 26 Henry VIII., of the 'moveables' of Lord Dacre remaining at his house of Naworth by the Earls of Westmorland and Cumberland.[2] He was returned in the ecclesiastical valuation of 1535 as prior of Carlisle and vicar of Castle Sowerby, a church appropriated to the priory.[3] In the discredited report of the royal commissioners on the condition of the religious houses, ascribed to the year 1536, Prior 'Slye' was charged with incontinency.[4] Soon after this date Prior Slee was deposed, but for what reason we have not ascertained. In an undated letter addressed 'to the ryght worshupffull Master cecretorie to y⁰ kynges grace be this letter delyvered,' Robert Cokett thus informed Cromwell of the event :—

Right worshupffull S'. I (thowgh unable) have me recomendyt unto yo' discreitnes, besechynge you of yo' grett goodnes to have me excusyd of my rude and symple letter. Pleasyth it yow to know that y⁰ Prior of Carelell is deposed and put downe, wherapone yf it pleas yow of yowt goodnes to be so good unto one kynsmane of myne called S' Will Florens, chanon of y⁰ foresaid howsse, as make hyme Prior yerof, for of a trewth he is most able reportynge me unto y⁰ kynges grace vicitours, and both he and I shalbe bownd unto yow to pay unto y⁰ kynges grace all suche thynges as it shall pleas yow to require, and yow to have for yowt payn takynge an hundreth markes. Besekynge yow of yowt answere by y⁰ beret hereof. Yo' bedman, Robert Cokett.[5]

Lancelot Salkeld, a canon defamed in the report of the royal visitation, was made prior of the house for the purpose of its surrender. From an entry in Cromwell's accounts[6] under date 17 February 1538-9, 'prior of Carlyle by Dr. Bellysys, 40 marks,' we may gather that he had not been long appointed,[7] as the

receipt suggests the amount for which the post was purchased. Sir Thomas Wharton was not a welcome visitor to the priory when he took up his abode there in December 1539, in anticipation of the coming of the commissioners for the suppression. He complained to Cromwell that he was 'straitly lodged,' and, while pleading for better accommodation, he urged his preferential claim to what was sold or let for the king's use.[8] The priory was surrendered with all its possessions by Lancelot Salkeld, prior, and the convent on 9 January 1540, and acknowledged the same day before Richard Layton, one of the clerks of Chancery.[9] Pensions were assigned on the day following to those canons who had retired, viz. a pension of £6 13s. 4d. to John Birkebek, and £5 6s. 8d. each to Richard Throp and William Lowther.[10] By letters patent, dated 2 May 1541, the king reconstructed the late monastery of St. Mary, Carlisle, as a cathedral of one dean and four prebendaries to be the see of Robert Aldridge, Bishop of Carlisle, and his successors, the new establishment to consist of Lancelot Salkelde, dean, William Florence, first prebendary ; Edward Loshe, second ; Barnaby Kyrkbryd, third ; and Richard Brandeling, fourth.[11] A few days later, on 6 May, by royal charter, the new institution, henceforth to be known as the Dean and Chapter of the Cathedral Church of the Holy and Undivided Trinity of Carlisle, was endowed with the revenues of the dissolved priory of St. Mary, and with most of the revenues of the dissolved priory of Wetheral.[12] Lancelot Salkeld, the last prior of the old institution, became the first dean of the new, thus perpetuating the succession.

The canons of the priory submitted to the new state of things with a bad grace. The name of the institution had changed but that was all : the old leaven was still there. It took time to reconcile the canons to the liturgical changes in the public service of the cathedral. Master 'Hew' Sewell, M.A., one of the most notorious of the local clergy of the Tudor period, lodged an information with the civil authorities against their non-compliance with recent ecclesiastical legislation.

of St. Nicholas, Newcastle, as appears by a copy on record in the Dean and Chapter Registers (ii. 37).
[8] *L. and P. Hen. VIII.* xiv. pt. ii. 734.
[9] Close, 31 Hen. VIII. pt. iv. No. 17 ; Rymer, *Fœdera* (old ed.), xiv. 668.
[10] *L. and P. Hen. VIII.* xv. 44.
[11] Pat. 33 Hen. VIII. pt. ix. m. 28. The charter was enrolled and issued to the new body on 8 May 1541.
[12] Ibid. 33 Hen. VIII. pt. 9, m. 11-5 ; *L. and P. Hen. VIII.* xvi. 878.

---

[1] *L. and P. Hen. VIII.* iv. 5952.
[2] Ibid. vii. 676.
[3] *Valor Eccl.* (Rec. Com.), v. 274-88.
[4] *L. and P. Hen. VIII.* x. 364.
[5] Ibid. vii. 1632. This letter has been calendared under the year 1534, but it must be ascribed to a later date, perhaps 1536.
[6] Ibid. xiv. pt. ii. 782, p. 325.
[7] He must have been appointed before 1 August 1537, for on that date he issued a lease of the tithes

He brought to the justices of the peace 'one book called a legend' which, he said, was daily 'occupied' in the church of the late monastery of Carlisle, and in which, contrary to the Acts of Parliament, the service of Thomas Becket and the usurped name 'papa' of the Bishop of Rome were unerased. Lancelot Salkeld, late prior, and at that time (1 May 1540) guardian of the monastery, demanded the return of the book, and offered sureties for it; but the justices, John Lowther, Edward Aglionby, Thomas Dalston and Lancelot Salkeld, thinking the matter too high for their determination, sent it to the king together with the depositions of the sub-chanter and another brother. The effect of the depositions was that Lancelot Robynson, one of the deponents, would have rased out the service of Thomas Becket, but William Florence, chief chanter of the monastery, took the book from him, gave it to the clerk of the choir, and bade him keep it secret, for he would correct it. Before they rose in the morning of 2 May, Florence had disappeared. Salkeld, the guardian, informed the constable of the castle that the absent canon would return by noon on that Sunday 'or else he to be hanged.' Sewell added that John Austane, a brother of the monastery, exclaimed when the book was taken, 'Tush, it is but for a book, it will be despatched well enough for money.'[1] But matters soon settled down. William Florence remained a canon of the new capitular body till his death in 1547, when he was succeeded by Sewell.[2] Austane was one of the eight minor canons of the foundation. Salkeld died Dean of Carlisle on 3 September 1560,[3] leaving behind him a name for piety, rectitude and consistency second to none in the history of the diocese.

PRIORS OF CARLISLE

Adelulf,[4] ? circa 1133

Walter,[5] occurs 1150 and 1169
Gilbert[6]
John,[7] occurs 1194 and 1204
Henry de Mareis,[8] elected 1214
Bartholomew,[9] occurs circa 1224, died in 1231
Ralf Barri,[10] elected 1231, died 9 February 1247
Robert[11] de Morville (?), elected 1247, resigned circa 1258
Adam de Felton[12] (?)
Alan[12] (?)
John,[13] occurs 1263
Robert,[14] occurs 1278 and 1283, resigned circa 1284
Adam de Warthwyk,[15] elected circa 1284, resigned 18 September 1304
William de Hautewysil,[16] elected 1304, resigned 28 September 1308
Robert de Helpeston,[17] elected 1308, occurs 1320
Simon de Hautwysell,[18] died before 13 July 1325
John de Kirkby,[19] occurs 1330, elected Bishop of Carlisle 1332
Geoffrey[20] occurs 8 March 1333–4
John de Horncastle,[21] occurs 1352, 1363, resigned 1376

---

[1] L. and P. Hen. VIII. xv. 619, 633
[2] Rymer, Fœdera (old ed.), xv. 190.
[3] Exch. Cert. of Bishop's Inst. Carlisle, No. 1.
[4] Adelulf is said to have been prior when the bishopric of Carlisle was founded in 1133 (Duchy of Lanc. Chart. box A, No. 416); there is no contemporary evidence on the point however, and the statement is somewhat doubtful, since he is said by Matthew of Paris to have been prior of Nostell near Pontefract (Chron. Maj. [Rolls Ser.], ii. 158). On the other hand Adelulf held the priory of Nostell with the bishopric, for in 1140 he was prior of that house when Augustinian canons were brought to the priory of St. Andrew from St. Oswald's through his instrumentality—'ecclesiam Sancti Oswaldi cui ipse episcopus jure prioris præerat' (Skene, Chron. of Picts and Scots, 191–2).

[5] Reg. of Holmcultram, MS. ff. 221–3; Dugdale, Mon. v. 594; Chron. of Melrose in anno 1150; Roger Hovedon (Rolls Ser.), i. 211; Reg. of Lanercost, MS. i. 1, 9, 14; ii. 18; v. 3; viii. 5.
[6] Ibid. viii. 5; iii. 13.
[7] Cart. Antiq. F. 14; Rymer, Fœdera, i. 63; Pedes Finium (Pipe R. Soc.), 7 and 8 Ric. I. No. 128; ibid. (Rec. Com.), Cumberland, pp. 7–8.
[8] Rot. Litt. Claus. (Rec. Com.), 16 John, i. 207b; Chron. de Lanercost, 14.
[9] He was contemporary with Bishops Hugh and Walter Mauclerc (Reg. of Lanercost, MS. viii. 7, 8). Reg. of Wetherhal, 53–5, 67–8, 118, etc.; Chron. de Lanercost (Maitland Club), 41.
[10] Chron. de Lanercost (Maitland Club), 41, 53.
[11] Rot. Orig. (Rec. Com.), i. 10; Cal. of Papal Letters, i. 361–2.
[12] The names of these priors are given by Nicolson and Burn in Hist. of Cumb. ii. 301, but no evidence is given to establish their claim, and the statement should be received with suspicion.
[13] Coll. Topog. et Gen. v. 235–6.
[14] Chan. Eccl. Pet. for Elections, 24 June 1278, file 6; Dep. Keeper's Rep. vi. App. p. 94; Carl. Epis. Reg., Halton, ff. 14, 43.
[15] Cal. of Pat. 1330–4, pp. 111–2; Carl. Epis. Reg., Halton, f. 43.
[16] Carl. Epis. Reg., Halton, f. 113.
[17] Ibid. f. 114; Cal. of Close, 1330–3, p. 357.
[18] Carl. Epis. Reg., Ross, ff. 268–9.
[19] Ibid. f. 263; Pat. 6 Edw. III. pt. 2, m. 33.
[20] Close, 8 Edw. III. m. 33d.
[21] He was said to be prior of Carlisle when he

John de Penreth,[1] elected 1376, resigned 9 August 1381

William de Dalston,[2] elected 1381, resigned 28 September 1385

Robert de Edenhall,[3] elected 1385

Thomas de Hoton,[4] occurs 1413 and 1423

Thomas Elye.[5]

Thomas Barnby,[6] occurs 1433–4

Thomas Huthwaite,[7] occurs 1457

Thomas Gudybour,[8] occurs 1476 and 1484–5

Simon Senus or Senhouse,[9] occurs 1505 and 1518

Christopher Slee,[10] occurs 1528 and 1535, deposed circa 1536

Lancelot Salkeld,[11] appointed before 1 August 1537, surrendered 9 January 1539–40

DEANS OF CARLISLE

Lancelot Salkeld, last prior and first dean, 1541 ; resigned in 1548

Sir Thomas Smith, knight, LL.D., 1548 ; resigned *quasi sponte* in 1554

Lancelot Salkeld, restored in 1554 ; died in 1560

Sir Thomas Smith, re-appointed in 1560 ; died in 1577

Sir John Wolley, knight, M.A., 1577–96

Sir Christopher Perkins, knight,1596–1622

Francis White, S.T.P., 1622–6

William Peterson, S.T.P., 1626–9

Thomas Comber, S.T.P., 1629–42

Guy Carleton, S.T.P., 1660–71

Thomas Smith, D.D., 1671–84

Thomas Musgrave, D.D., 1684–6

William Grahme, D.D., 1686–1704

Francis Atterbury, D.D., 1704–11

George Smalridge, D.D., 1711–3

Thomas Gibbon, D.D., 1713–6

Thomas Tullie, LL.D., 1716–27

George Fleming, LL.D., 1727–35

Robert Bolton, LL.D., 1735–63

Charles Tarrant, D.D., 1764

Thomas Wilson, D.D., 1764–78

Thomas Percy, D.D., 1778–82

Geoffrey Ekins, D.D., 1782–92

Isaac Milner, D.D., F.R.S., 1792–1820

Robert Hodgson, D.D., F.R.S., 1820–44

John Anthony Cramer, D.D., 1844–8

Samuel Hinds, D.D., 1848–9

Archibald Campbell Tait, D.C.L., 1849–56

Francis Close, D.D., 1856–81

John Oakley, D.D., 1881–3

William George Henderson, D.C.L., D.D., 1884

The seal of the priory of Carlisle[12] is round, representing the half length figures of the Virgin and Child upon a bridge, between two angels with outstretched wings censing. A Gothic building stands on each side of the bridge, which has two trefoiled arches, within which, on the left, is an ecclesiastic, probably a canon, and on the right a bishop with mitre and crosier. Between the arches is, in a small countersunk oval panel, a cross. At the base is an embattled wall. The legend is : SIGIL' . . . CCLESIE SANCTE MAR . . . EOLI. Two impressions of this seal[13] are at the British Museum attached to deeds about the appropriation of the church of Bromfield in 1303.

A counter seal,[14] perhaps that of Adam de Warthwyk, the prior, is the impression of an antique gem representing a winged Fortune or Minerva with inscription in field : DIVS F . . . . . . In the metal setting at the points between the gem and the legend are two shields of arms : top three bars base fretty.

The seal of the dean and chapter[15] is a pointed oval showing the Virgin kneeling before an altar on which is an open book. Behind is a classical niche with a round headed arch, and below is the shield of arms of the chapter. The legend runs : SIGIL · DECANI · ET · CAP · ECCL · CATH · B · MARIE · VIRG · CARLIOL · 1660.

was elected to the see in 1352. *Cal. of Papal Petitions,* i. 437 ; Carl. Epis. Reg., Appleby, ff. 165, 289.

[1] Carl. Epis. Reg., Appleby, ff. 319–20, 387.
[2] Ibid. 337–8, 348–52.
[3] Ibid. ff. 353–4.
[4] Exch. Cler. Subs., Dioc. of Carl., bdle. 60, No. 8a ; B.M. Add. Chart. No. 15770.
[5] Nicolson and Burn, *Hist. of Cumb.* ii. 303.
[6] Fuller, *Worthies of England* (ed. J. Nichols), i. 240–1.
[7] He confirmed a lease, dated 11 August 1457, of a tenement in Cardew (original in muniment room of Lowther Castle).
[8] *Priory of Hexham,* i. App. No. xc.
[9] *L. and P. Hen. VIII.* i. 296 ; Pat. 10 Hen. VIII. pt. 2, m. 6.
[10] From an inscription on the arch of the north-western gate of the precincts of the abbey. *Valor Eccl.* (Rec. Com.), v. 274–88 ; *L. and P. Hen. VIII.* vii. 1632.
[11] Carl. D. and C. Reg. ii. 37 ; Close, 31 Hen. VIII. pt. 4, No. 17 ; Rymer, *Fœdera* (old ed.), xiv. 668.

[12] The seal reproduced here is from a deed in the possession of the dean and chapter of Durham, but see also B.M. Seals, 2412–7.
[13] Add. Chart. 17155, 17156.
[14] B.M. Seals, 2412.
[15] See Mrs. Henry Ware's article 'On the Seals of the Bishops of Carlisle, and other Seals belonging to that Diocese,' in *Transactions of Cumb. and Westmld. Arch. Soc.* xii. 226.

2. THE PRIORY OF LANERCOST

On the banks of the Irthing close to the Roman wall, in the country which we now associate with the genius of Sir Walter Scott, Robert de Vaux son of Hubert de Vaux, lord of Gillesland, founded the priory of Lanercost for regular canons of the Order of St. Augustine. Tradition places the foundation in 1169, which agrees with the evidence of the earliest charter of the house.[1] The church was entitled in the name of St. Mary Magdalene, a dedication of singular rarity in Cumberland and Westmorland. Early in the seventeenth century John Denton mentioned, but seems to have rejected, the legend which ascribed the foundation to the remorse felt by the noble founder for having slain Gille son of Boet who owned the fief before it was given to Hubert his father. The story, however, has found its way into some of the editions of Camden, and been often repeated on his authority. Denton rightly appealed to Robert's charter of foundation, which states that the benefaction was made for the sake of Henry II., who had enfeoffed his father with the barony and confirmed it to himself, and for the health of the souls of his father Hubert and his mother Grace.

Before Robert de Vaux granted the charter, the scheme must have reached almost to the verge of completion, so full and comprehensive are its terms and references and differing so conspicuously from the successive charters which marked the various stages in the foundation of Wetheral and St. Bees. The grantor assigned to God and St. Mary Magdalene of Lanercost and to the regular canons there the lawn (landa) of Lanercost between the ancient wall and the Irthing and between Burth and Poltros, the vill of Walton by stated bounds, the church of that vill with the chapel of 'Treverman,' the churches of Irthington, Brampton, Carlaton and Farlam, certain lawns by bounds as 'Gille son of Bueth' held them, besides numerous immunities and privileges throughout the whole barony. The tenor of the charter[2] betokens

a generous disposition and a liberal hand in the multiplication of gifts for the start of the new institution, and the concourse of witnesses, who assembled to subscribe their names to the deed of endowment, is a striking evidence that the occasion was regarded as one of unusual dignity and importance. In addition to many tenants and clergy of Gillesland, the foundation charter was witnessed by Christian, Bishop of Whithern in Galloway, suffragan to York during the vacancy at Carlisle, Walter prior of Carlisle, and Robert archdeacon of the same place, as representative of the ecclesiastical authority at that date. The marginal note in the register of the house which states that the church was dedicated by Bernard, Bishop of Carlisle, in 1169, the sixteenth year of Henry II. and the twelfth of his pontificate, is not worthy of credit, for though the year of foundation must be approximately correct, it is not true that Bernard was Bishop of Carlisle in 1169. The note belongs to a class of legends about Bishop Bernard that arose at an early period.

The liberality of the founder was not confined to the endowments granted in the first charter. The register of the priory contains many other deeds of gift and confirmation extending over his long tenure of the barony. In several of these charters, when he had occasion to refer to his territorial title, he reverted to the old phrase[3] employed by Henry II. in the original enfeoffment of his family and repeated by himself in his foundation charter, 'infra baronian quam dominus rex Henricus dedit patri meo et mihi in terra que fuit Gille filii Bueth.' Few of the religious houses founded by subjects in the northern counties can point to a patron more distinguished in personal qualities than Lanercost, for Robert de Vaux, immortalized by Jordan Fantosme,[4] his contemporary, was a valiant soldier, a great judge, a prudent statesman, and a munificent benefactor of his church and country. The example

necessary to call attention to the distinction between the Register or Chartulary of Lanercost and the Chronicon de Lanercost or Chronicle of Lanercost. The Register is a collection of deeds of the usual character belonging to a religious house and still remains in manuscript, a copy of which is in the custody of the dean and chapter of Carlisle. The Chronicon belongs to the class of medieval chronicles and has been printed by the Maitland and Bannatyne Clubs.

[3] Ibid. i. 13, viii. 17.

[4] *Chron. of the War between the English and the Scots in 1173 and 1174* (Surtees Soc. No. 11), 1370-1460, etc.

---

[1] Reg. of Lanercost, MS. i. 1. In 1761 George Story, vicar of Lanercost, erected a stone tablet in the church to the memory of Robert de Vaux, founder of the priory, and of his wife Ada Engaine, on which he inscribed 1116 as the year of foundation. The vicar evidently took his date from a note in the register of the priory on the foundations of the religious houses in the diocese of Carlisle (ibid. f. 267). Story's error has been often repeated.

[2] Reg. of Lanercost, MS. i. 1. It is scarcely

he set was infectious, for his family, kindred and descendants rank foremost among those who contributed to the prosperity and welfare of the priory. It would carry us beyond the limits of this notice to refer to all the benefactors who assisted in its endowment, members of the families of Morville, Engayne, Windsor, Denton, Castelcayroc, Neuton, le Sor, Tilliol, de la Ferte, Ireby and others. In common with the other religious houses of the county, the small proprietors were as forward in making bequests according to their station as the great magnates.

The priory was rich in the possession of churches, for over and above the five churches probably all that were at that time in the barony granted by the founder, the church of Grinesdale was given by Richard de Neuton and Robert le Sor, that of Lazonby was brought into relations with the priory by Ada Engayne and afterwards bestowed by her son Hugh de Morvill, and that of Denton by Buethbarn, the lord of the place. Ada Engayne granted an annuity of three marks out of the revenues of the churches of Burgh-by-Sands and Lazonby for the souls of William Engayne her father and Eustachia her mother, and for the soul of Simon de Morvill her late husband, to which Christian, Bishop of Whithern, and Robert, Archdeacon of Carlisle, were parties.[1] This pension was afterwards the occasion of scandal to the canons of Lanercost, involving them in a contest with the monks of Holmcultram about the church of Burgh,[2] as the pension out of Lazonby led to an estrangement with the abbey of Kelso.[3] The policy of appropriation was pursued with as much vigour at Lanercost as elsewhere. The Bishop of Whithern confirmed to the canons

the churches Robert de Vaux gave them at the foundation of the priory. Americ, Archdeacon of Carlisle, issued a licence at a later period for their appropriation, including those of later donation on the death or resignation of the incumbents in possession, the canons undertaking to discharge all diocesan obligations. The bishops, when the succession was restored, carried on the tradition. Bishop Hugh was the first Bishop of Carlisle who espoused the interest of the parishioners in the matter of appropriations and made it a principle of diocesan administration, a policy which brought him into disrepute with the religious corporations. He made it the usual condition of his assent that fit vicars should be presented to the bishop for the service of the churches and that a competent portion should be set aside out of the revenues for their maintenance. Subsequent prelates imitated his example, and as the power of the episcopate began to strengthen after the prolonged vacancy, the vicarages of appropriated churches were taxed, that is, the sources of the incumbent's income were set out with legal exactness in the deed of episcopal confirmation. The canons of Lanercost obtained ecclesiastical recognition in customary form for the appropriation of all their churches.

In this recognition of course there was included the papal sanction, an opportunity rarely neglected for advancing the papal influence. The confirmation of Alexander III. in 1181 is an interesting document. With alacrity the pope took the church of Lanercost under the protection of the blessed Peter and decreed that the rule of St. Augustine should be observed inviolate therein for ever. After reciting and confirming the grants to the priory, licence was given to receive clerks and laymen flying from the world and to retain them in the religious life. No brother after profession was allowed to depart without leave of the prior. For their appropriated churches the canons were authorized to select suitable priests and present them to the bishop of the diocese for institution to the cure of souls, the priests answering to the bishop in spiritual matters and to the canons in temporal. In times of general interdict, it should be lawful to celebrate divine offices in the priory with low voice and closed doors and without the ringing of bells. The right of burial to all those who desired it was granted to the church,[4] except for those under

---

[1] Reg. of Lanercost, MS. v. 4–6 ; ii. 15–6 ; iii. 1–2 ; xii. 26.

[2] Reg. of Holmcultram, MS. ff. 12–3. It is rarely that we meet with a bishop using such emphatic language as Bishop Hugh of Carlisle employed on that occasion. He stated that danger was likely to accrue to his diocese by reason of the collusion between the brethren of the two houses. In gross and reckless ignorance of the canons of the church they had made compositions and meddled with matters with which they had no concern and over which they had no power. The bishop pronounced the whole transaction unlawful, and forced John, prior of Lanetcost, to renounce on behalf of his house the claim to an annual pension from the church of Burgh. Having heard all the arguments and seen all the evidences, he also awarded the patronage to the abbey of Holmcultram.

[3] Reg. of Lanercost, MS. xiii. 25–6; *Liber de Calchou* (Bannatyne Club), ii. 351.

[4] Robert de Vaux son of Ralf de Vaux bequeathed his body to the canons of Lanercost, 'ubicunque et quandocumque ex hac vita migraverim' (Register of Lanercost, MS. ii. 4).

excommunication or interdict, with due respect to the rights of other churches. The liberty of free election of the prior, conceded by the founder, was also recognized and confirmed. Later popes laid down strict rules for the regulation of the priory in its relations to the diocese. It was stipulated by Honorius III. in 1224 that the chrism, holy oils and ordination of clerks should be procured from the diocesan bishop if he be a catholic and in communion with the holy Roman See, and no one should be allowed to erect a new chapel or oratory within the bounds of any of their churches without the bishop's licence, saving only the privilege of the Roman pontiffs.[1]

Notwithstanding the privileges of the Holy See, the priory of Lanercost was an integral portion of the diocese of Carlisle, and the bishop's ordinary power of visitation was effective and unimpaired. Again and again was it exercised by successive bishops for the correction of abuses and the maintenance of discipline. The author of the *Chronicle of Lanercost* describes the first visitation of Bishop Ralf Ireton on 22 March 1281, the year after his consecration. The canons vested in their copes met the new prelate at the gates of the priory, as they had met King Edward and Queen Eleanor a few months before. Having given his benediction, the bishop received them to the kiss of peace, kissing first their hands and then their lips. In the chapter house he preached from the text, 'Lo, I myself will require'; the preaching being ended, the bishop proceeded with his visitation, 'during which,' says the chronicler, 'we were compelled to accept new constitutions.'[2]

There are several monitions on record in the episcopal archives by which intimations were given of visitations by various bishops. Bishop Kirkby gave notice on 1 February 1344-5 that he intended to visit the priory, in head and members, in their chapter house

on a stated day.[3] The like was done by Bishop Welton in 1356 and 1358,[4] and by Bishop Appleby in 1368 and 1373.[5]

In many ways the bishop of the diocese exercised a pastoral oversight of the house other than by the function of visitation. It was his office to confirm the election of the canons when the priory was vacant, to institute the new prior and to lay down rules, if need be, for his future guidance. According to custom he required the nominee of the canons to be in priest's orders, of canonical age and legitimate birth. Having been satisfied in these matters, the bishop administered the oath of canonical obedience and then issued his letters to the Archdeacon of Carlisle or some diocesan official like a rural dean to induct the new prior into the temporal possessions and to assign him his stall in the choir and his place in the chapter. The form of the oath of obedience to the diocesan is of some interest: 'In the name of God, Amen. I, Brother Thomas of Hexham, prior of the priory of Lanercost of the Order of St. Augustine, of the diocese of Carlisle, will be faithful and obedient to you my venerable father in Christ and lord, the Lord Gilbert, by the grace of God, Bishop of Carlisle, and to your successors canonically appointed, your officials and ministers, in canonical and lawful demands. So help me God and these holy Gospels of God, and this I subscribe with my own hand.'[6] Sometimes the bishop dismissed the new prior with the injunction to promote amity among the brethren and exercise mildness, as his station required, in the internal administration of the convent.

According to the idiosyncracies of the bishop or the necessities of the occasion, more stringent obligations had to be undertaken by a new prior before his institution. Bishop Welton exacted a formidable list of promises in 1354 from Prior Thomas of Hexham

---

[1] The whole of these ecclesiastical confirmations will be found in the eighth part of the Register of the priory of Lanercost, where they form an interesting series.

[2] 'Finita prædicatione, visitationem suam prosecutus est in qua coacti sumus novellas constitutiones recipere' (*Chron. de Lanercost* [Maitland Club], p. 106). This passage is fatal to Stevenson's contention that the *Chronicon de Lanercost* was written by a Minorite of Carlisle and not by an inmate of Lanercost. The visitation referred to was clearly that of the priory and not of the diocese. He has mistaken the meaning of the passage altogether. The new constitutions were issued 'finita prædicatione,' when his sermon, not his visitation, was ended (*Chron.* pp. vii. viii.).

[3] Carl. Epis. Reg., Kirkeby, f. 477.

[4] Ibid. Welton, ff. 26, 44.

[5] Ibid. Appleby, ff. 197, 254.

[6] Ibid. Welton, f. 12. The form of obedience subscribed by Prior Richard de Ridale in 1355 is as follows: 'In Dei nomine amen. Ego frater Ricardus de Ridale, ordinis sancti Augustini, in Priorem Prioratus de Lanercost, Karliolensis dioceseos, postulatus, et in eiusdem loci Priorem canonice confirmatus, ero fidelis et obediens vobis venerabili in Christo patri et domino meo, domino Gilberto, Dei gracia, Karliolensi episcopo, vestrisque successoribus canonice intrantibus, officialibus et ministris, in canonicis et licitis mandatis. Sic Deus me adiuvet, et hec sancta Dei evangelia, et hoc propria manu mea subscribo' (ibid. f. 20).

(Hextildesham) in addition to the cherishing of goodwill among the brethren and the practice of gentleness in his government of the house. Some of these conditions may be mentioned : that he should not by any means transact important business without the consent of the convent : that the common seal should be faithfully kept in the custody of three canons or two at the least : that he should keep only a few dogs (*canes nisi paucos*): that he should not frequent or mix himself up with common sports (*communibus venationibus*): that no religious or secular man of the priory should keep dogs of any sort : and that, as a pension had been allotted to his predecessor, he should abide by the award the bishop had made.[1] The peculiar provisions in restraint of the sporting proclivities of the canons can be easily understood in a country which abounded in game. The priory was not always at peace with the lords of Gillesland about the rights of hunting in the barony. In 1256 a final concord was accepted by Thomas son of Thomas de Multon before the justices itinerant at Lancaster whereby the litigating parties came to an understanding about the hunting of their respective demesnes.[2] By this agreement, which contains many interesting features of forest law, the convent was entitled to enclose with a ditch and low hedge their part of Warth-colman and to maintain a deer-leap (*saltorium*) therein for the purpose of enabling the big game to enter the enclosure and of preventing them coming out again : and besides to keep a pack of hounds consisting of four harriers *cleporarios*) and four swift brachs (*brachettos* (*urrentes*) to take, as often as they wished, foxes, hares and all other animals known as 'clobest.' It was natural that the canons, as large landowners, should regard with jealousy any encroachments on the sporting rights of their estates, game being an important article of food, but there was just a possibility that the ways of the world might invade the quiet seclusion of the cloister. Bishop Welton was apparently of opinion that things were going too far at Lanercost, for on his coming to the see in 1353 he took the first opportunity that presented itself to curb the sporting propensities of the brethren and to keep the ruling passion within the line of moderation.

It is pleasing to note that at Lanercost as well as at Carlisle the head of the house, when feeble in health or broken down with age, was able to retire from the cares of office and to pass the evening of his life in comfort within the precincts of the priory. The procedure on the resignation of a prior was no doubt regulated by the rule of the Augustinian Order. It was customary at Lanercost for the convent to name the pension and submit it to the Bishop of Carlisle for his approval, or at least the matter was arranged between the bishop and the canons. In 1283 Prior John retired on a pension confirmed by Bishop Ralf Ireton.[3] The nature of the retiring allowance which John de (Bothecastre) Bewcastle received in 1354 throws a much needed light on the simple habits of cloistered life in the fourteenth century. It was ordained by Bishop Welton that Brother John, broken with old age and burdened with weakness of body, should have for the term of his life a fit place to dwell within the confines (*septa*) of the priory : two canonical allowances (*libratas*) daily of meal and drink, two pairs of new boots and two pairs of new socks at such times of the year when these articles of apparel were usually delivered, a sufficient supply of fire and light, and 46s. 8d. in lieu of clothing and other necessaries payable at three terms of the year, viz. at Christmas, 13s. 4d. ; at Pentecost, 20s. ; and at Michaelmas, 13s. 4d. The bishop also, out of respect to his former station, required the convent to make him an allowance for a valet (*minister*) with a suitable livery (*roba*) or half a mark in lieu thereof.[4]

When a vacancy occurred by the death or resignation of the prior, jurisdiction over the house at once passed to the sub-prior till the office was filled by the free election of the canons. At times the bishops did not fail to impress this on all concerned. When Prior Thomas of Hexham died in 1355, Bishop Welton sent the vicars of Irthington and Brampton to inform the canons that the care of the convent was entrusted to the sub-prior 'as well of right and custom as by our authority it is known to belong.' If disputes arose over an election, the bishop was the sole referee, by whose kindly mediation an amicable arrangement was made. When Richard de Ridale, a canon of Carlisle, and John de Nonyngton, a canon of Lanercost, were postulated to the priory in 1355 by two parties in the house, the bishop cited them to Rose Castle, where he gave judgment in favour of the former candidate and confirmed him in the office.[5]

Soon after the foundation of the house,

---

[1] Carl. Epis. Reg., Welton, f. 12.
[2] *Pedes Finium* (Cumberland), case 35, file 2, No. 68 ; Reg. of Lanercost, MS. ix. 4.

[3] *Chron. de Lanercost*, 113.
[4] Carl. Epis. Reg., Welton, f. 13.
[5] Ibid. ff. 20-1.

Robert de Vaux, the founder, granted to the canons the right of free election, so that when the lord prior died the person on whom the choice of the canons or the greater part of them fell should be elected in his place. To this concession Robert, archdeacon of Carlisle, Walter, prior (of Carlisle), and others were witnesses.[1] It was not always that the patron of the house acted with such consideration to the canons. At later periods the lords of Gillesland betrayed an interest in the internal affairs of the priory which was, to say the least, not a little embarrassing to the inmates. In 1261 the Bishop of Carlisle was obliged to invoke the power of the Crown to eject Sir Thomas de Multon, who had held the priory for a year or more by lay force to the exclusion of the bishop and his officers and to the detriment of the discipline of the house. It is curious to find at this period the phrase *laicalis insolentia* used to denominate lay interference in ecclesiastical affairs.[2] The same practical interest in the affairs of the priory was again manifest in 1524, when, at a time of great monastic activity, Lord Dacre reprimanded the prior for occupying himself so much in building and outward works that he

[1] Reg. of Lanercost, MS. i. 14. This privilege was afterwards confirmed by Pope Alexander III. in 1181 (ibid. viii. 17) and by Robert de Vaux, son of Ranulf (ibid. i. 22).

[2] As the letter of Bishop Robert de Chause has many points of interest and seems to be little known locally, it may be useful to give the full text : 'Serenissimo principi et domino reverendo H(enrico). Dei gratia, regi Anglorum illustri, devotus suus R(obertus), permissione divina Karleolensis ecclesiæ minister humilis, salutem et promptum ad obsequia famulatum, cum omni reverentia pariter et honore. Cum dominus Thomas de Multon prioratum de Lanercost jam per annum et amplius per vim laicalem tenuerit occupatum, ita quod nec nobis aut officialibus nostris ad ea exercendum quæ officio nostro incumbunt, nec priori ejusdem, quem ibidem præfecimus, ad corrigendum canonicorum suorum excessus, seu ad disponendum de utilitatibus ejusdem prioratus aliquo modo patere potest ingressus, vestræ majestati regiæ omni qua possumus devotione humiliter supplicamus, quatenus vicecomiti Cumberlandiæ vestris velitis dare literis in mandatis, ut vim laicalem a prioratu predicto auctoritate regia studeat amovere : ne locus ille divino cultui dedicatus per laicalem insolentiam ulterius profanetur. Valeat et vigeat excellentia vestra regia per tempora longiora. Datum apud Bellum Locum, sexto idus Martii, anno Domini millesimo ducentesimo sexagesimo primo et pontificatus nostri anno quinto. Domino regi Angliæ illustri' (*Royal and Hist. Letters*, Hen. III. (Rolls Ser.), ii. 167). Sir Francis Palgrave gave an abstract of this letter in 1843 (*Dep. Keeper's Rep.* iv. 142).

was apt to neglect the more serious duties of his vocation. The following 'copie of a lettre to the prior of Lanrecost' throws a welcome light on monastic institutions at this date :—

Maistar Prior of Lanrecost and convent of the same, I recōmende me to youe, and at my being last wᵗ youe I shulde have spokin wᵗ youe and shewed youe my mynde and opynyoñ in diverse mattiers most proufitable and beneficiall to youe and yoʳ monastery, whiche for lak as well of leaser, the bushop being ther, as also for the mattiers of importaunce concernyng the Kinge busines in hand to be fulfilled, that I couthe not have tyme and space so to doo. Albeit a parte of my mynde is that forasmiche as youe, Maister Prior, being soo often occupied aswell in outward warkes and businesses as buylding, oversight of warkmen, quartiours, maisons, wrightes, wallers as others nedefull to be sene to for the cōmon weale of youe all, yoʳ monastery, servante and store, cannot have tymes convenient and space to see to the inwarde parte of yoʳ chirche as to take hede and see the service of God contynuallymaignteyned, the order of Religion wᵗ the Cerymoneys of the same wᵗin the Chirche, Closter, Dortoʳ and frater observed and kept so weale as nedefull it were. Therfore expedient it is that ye have eas and help of a parte of yoʳ said charge to be taken of youe, bereason that two persounes may the better take hede to the execution of many businesses than one person. And in as muche as I am yoʳ Foundoʳ and bounde in consciens to see for yoʳ weales and geve unto youe my most fruytfull counseill, woll therfore and hertely prey youe that wᵗ convenient diligence after the recept herof, ye woll assemble youe to gidders in yoʳ chapitoʳ Hous and ther lovingly condescend aggre youe and elect ooñ of yoʳ selfe to be yoʳ supprior, siche as ye in yoʳ consciences most assuredly truste may and shalbe most beneficiall aswell to the maynten*nce of Godde service wᵗin yoʳ monastery, conversacion in his owne person, as prouffitable to yoʳ said monastery yerely and frome tyme to tyme herafter. So as the same person so choseñ may have the charge of the service of the churche and ordoʳ of his bretherñ undre youe, maister Prior, trusting therby that persounes now highe mynded, wolfull and obstacle there, may and woll fro thensfurthe knaw their selfe the better, And use the vowe of obedience according to profession. And youe, maister Prior, to reasorte to the charge of the churche, chapitoʳ Hous, and frater at all tymes that ye conveniently may. And not wᵗstanding the obstinacie som tyme used by Sʳ Richard Halton aftre his profession conrʳry thordoʳ of Religion, whiche he all utterly has refused, and be the help of the holy goost is vertuously reduced of his owne good mynde to my singular pleaser, comforth, and consolacion above any temperall man, seing the good qualities in hym and his inward goodness and mynde to yoʳ House and me knowen, faithfully professed in his hert to God, Mary Magdalen, and that Hous. In Myn opynyon, upon my feith and conscience, I think unfeynedly that

RELIGIOUS HOUSES

the said Sr Richard Halton is most dyscrete, sufficient, and able to be yor supprior. And for my parte, as far as in me is, being yor foundo^r, I assent to his election, trusting ye woll all or the most parte of youe assent to the same, yor most prouffet and weales perfitely remembred, notw^{t}standing he having a vicary, whiche makes him more able to occupie the same Rowme. And upon a parte of yo more towardly, humbly, and obedient demeanors to be used hereafter then has bene of late, may and shall have me to be yor better good lord and com to promotion upon yor good demerette, w^{t}out whose help I see not as y^t shall cum therunto. Wherefore I counseill youe all thus to be contented and elect hym w^{t}out any obstinacie or grudge as ye intende to pleas me. At Morpath the penult day of February Anno xv^0 H. VIII.[1]

From these evidences it will appear that the advowson of the priory, which passed from one lord of Gillesland to another as a piece of real property,[2] existed in reality as well as in name, and was a potential force in the regulation of the house.

From its geographical position the priory was exposed to constant dangers from the attacks of Scottish marauders. Its unprotected condition so close to the frontier served as an invitation to the Border clans to harass it in retaliation for the depredations of their English enemies. After the outbreak of the War of Independence its real troubles began. In 1296, the year of the rupture with Balliol, the Scottish army encamped at Lanercost after burning the priory of Hexham and the nunnery of Lambley, and laying waste the valley of the Tyne.[3] By a timely alarm, no doubt created by the artifice of the canons, the Scots retreated through Nicolforest with their plunder, having burnt only certain houses of the monastery but not the church.[4] No words were too strong on the lips of English writers to describe the cruelties and impieties practised by the enemy on that occasion. The poet historian of Bridlington[5] narrates that

Corbrigge is a toun, the brent it whan thei cam :
Tuo bous of religioun, Leynercoste and Hexham,
Thei chaced the chanons out, ther godes bare away,
And robbed alle about : the bestis tok to pray.

The devastation, added the chronicler of Lanercost, cannot be imputed to the bravery of warriors, but to the cowardice of robbers, who invaded a thinly-populated country where they were sure to find no resistance.[6] The bold initiative taken by the Scots in this and in the following year under Wallace caused a sensation throughout the northern counties. Their savage deeds provoked loud calls for reprisals on the part of the English. One writer declared that as the house of Lanercost had suffered innumerable evils, inexorable vengeance should be enacted in return. Fordun, the Scottish historian, regarding the whole thing with complacency, remarked that Wallace returned safe and sound to his own country after a successful expedition.[7]

Several visits of Edward I. to the priory in the latter part of his reign are on record. A few days were spent there with Queen Eleanor in the autumn of 1280 on his way to Newcastle, when the convent met him at the gate in their copes and the king graciously made a votive offering of silk cloth to the church. It was reported that during his short stay he took 200 stags and hinds while hunting in his own domain of Inglewood. Again, soon after midsummer 1300, as he passed through Carlisle with the nobles and magnates of his kingdom on his way to the siege of Carlaverock, he turned aside and made a short stay at Lanercost. On his last fateful visit to the north in 1306, he came to the priory with Queen Margaret at Michaelmas and continued there till the following Easter, the journey having been completed by easy stages in a horse litter owing to age and infirmity. It was while he sojourned at Lanercost that the brothers of Robert de Brus and other Scottish captives were sent to Carlisle for execution, the stern old warrior having with his own mouth sentenced Thomas de Brus to be dragged at the tails of horses from Lanercost to Carlisle before the dread sentence of hanging and beheading was carried out. The heads were suspended on the three gates of Carlisle, except the head of Thomas de Brus, which was reserved to decorate the keep of the castle.[8]

---

[1] B.M. Add. MS. 24,965, f. 218.
[2] The advowsons of religious houses founded by subjects descended to their heirs, unless alienated or forfeited, as the houses of royal foundation remained with the Crown. For instance, the advowson of Lanercost was reckoned in the 'extent' of the Dacre possessions in 1340 and 1485 (Inq. p.m. 13 Edw. III. 1st Nos. 35 ; Cal. of Inq. p.m. Hen. VII. i. 157). Similarly the advowsons of St. Bees and Calder descended among the lords of Egremont (Inq. p.m. 15 Edw. II. No. 45 ; 39 Edw. III. 1st. Nos. 17). These examples might be easily multiplied.
[3] Chron. de Melsa (Rolls Ser.), ii. 261.
[4] Heminburgh, Chron. (Engl. Hist. Soc.), ii. 102.
[5] Quoted by J. Raine as the lines of Peter Langtoft in The Priory of Hexham (Surtees Soc.), i. p. lxxxii.

[6] Chron. de Lanercost, 174, 193.
[7] Scotichronicon (ed. W. Goodall), ii. 172.
[8] Chron. de Lanercost, 105, 194, 205–6. On the last day of June 1300, Edward I. sent an oblation by the hand of Henry de Burgo, canon

157

If the king was too unmindful of the trouble and expense his prolonged stay had caused the priory, the canons were not slow in refreshing his memory. They begged him, having regard to the reduced state of their house and the damages they suffered by him and his attendants, which a great sum would not suffice to restore, that by way of recompense he would grant them the church of 'Hautwyselle,' worth about 100 marks a year, but as the abbot of Aberbrothok, to whom the church belonged, indignantly refused to accept an allowance in exchange, the proposal fell through.[1] Before his departure however the king granted his licence for the appropriation of the churches of Mitford in Northumberland and Carlatton in Cumberland, for the relief of their necessities. In his letter to the pope the king alleged, as reasons for his liberality, the special devotion he felt to St. Mary Magdalene in whose honour the convent was founded, the long stay he was forced to make on account of illness, the burning of their houses and the robbery of their goods by the Scots, insomuch that the priory was much impoverished and depressed.[2] The same motives were repeated in his letters patent.[3] In confirming the appropriations, the bishops of Durham and Carlisle told the same mournful tale of the distressed condition of Lanercost.[4] It seemed as if, at that time, burnt houses and an exhausted treasury were the distinguishing characteristics of this once flourishing foundation.

The fate of Lanercost henceforward depended on the political relations of the two kingdoms. In times of truce the house was at rest and employed the breathing space for the repair of its waste places ; when hostilities broke out, it was the objective of raid and robbery. In August, 1311, Robert Bruce, King of Scotland, came to the monastery with a great army and made it his headquarters for'

three days, imprisoning several (*plures*) of the canons and committing infinite evils. At length however he set the canons at liberty.[5] In fulfilment of the treaty between the same king and Edward III. in 1328, a mutual interchange of good offices was effected between the priory of Lanercost and the abbey of Kelso in respect of their common revenues out of the church of Lazonby.[6] One of the worst trials experienced by the house occurred in 1346, when David II. ransacked the conventual buildings and desecrated the church. Fresh from the overthrow of the fortalice of Liddel and the unchivalrous slaughter of Walter of Selby, its gallant defender, the Scots, with illustration manifestations of joy, David *cum diabolo* being their leader, marched to the priory of Lanercost, where the canons, men venerable and devoted to the Lord, dwelt. They entered the holy place with haughtiness, threw out the vessels of the temple, stole the treasures, broke the doors, took the jewels, and destroyed everything they could lay hands on.[7] One of the priors was taken prisoner by the Scots in 1386, and set at ransom at a fixed sum of money and four score quarters of corn of divers kinds. There was a difficulty in conveying the corn to Scotland, which added somewhat to the prior's misery and the prolongarion of his imprisonment.[8]

An effort was made in 1409 to retrieve the fallen fortunes of the house by an appeal to the Archbishop of York for letters of quest [9] throughout the northern province.

[5] *Chron. de Lanercost*, 218.

[6] Close, 2 Edw. III. m. 16 ; *Cal. of Doc. Scot.* (Scot. Rec. Pub.), iii. 173–4.

[7] *Chron. de Lanercost*, 345–6. This reference to Lanercost has been omitted from Stevenson's argument on the authorship of the Chronicle. It is certainly the description of an eye-witness.

[8] *Rot. Scotiæ* (Rec. Com.), ii. 86.

[9] Abstracts of many of these letters of quest, referring to institutions at home and abroad, have been recorded in the fourteenth century registers of the Bishops of Carlisle. One of these, taken at random, may be given here as an illustration : 'Memorandum quod septimo die Novembris, anno M'CCC'LIX°, apud manerium de Rosa, renovate fuerint littere pro questoribus fabrice ecclesie collegiate beati Johannis Beverlacensis sub sigillo domini Karliolensis episcopi, durature per unum annum extunc immediate sequentem, ad prosecucionem Thome de Coketon, procuratorem dicte ecclesie Beverlacensis' (Carl. Epis. Reg., Welton, f. 60). As the practice often led to great abuses, it needed the constant vigilance of the bishops. In 1342 Bishop Kirkby issued a warning to the clergy of his diocese to beware of false and fraudulent questors (Carl. Epis. Reg., Kirkby, f. 446). A noble was the usual fee to the diocesan registrar

of the priory, to be offered on the great altar of the church of Lanercost (*Liber Quot. Garderobæ* [Soc. of Antiq.], p. 40).

[1] *Cal. of Doc. Scot.* ii. 503.

[2] Rymer, *Fœdera* (new ed.), i. 1012.

[3] Pat. 35 Edw. I. m. 25.

[4] Carl. Epis. Reg., Halton, f. 140. This appropriation involved the canons of Lanercost in a dispute with the priory of Durham on the issue whether the church of Meldon was a chapel dependent on Mitford or a parish church separate from it. In 1310 an amicable arrangement was made at Lanercost whereby Prior Henry on behalf of his house acknowledged the independence of Meldon. The deeds of this acknowledgment still exist at Durham, and have been printed by Hodgson, *History of Northumberland*, ii. pt. iii. 54–6.

In response Archbishop Bowet sent a monition to his suffragans, inviting them to give facilities to the proctors of the priory for making the requisite collection ; the bishops were also enjoined to see that the object of the alms should be properly explained by the parish priests in the churches, and that the money collected should be delivered without diminution to the questors. The causes which reduced the canons to such straits were recounted to the archbishop in doleful tones by the prior ; the monastery with its principal buildings were threatening ruin ; their possessions were in a state of dilapidation or consumed with fire by the frequent incursions of the Scots ; their lands, especially those near the confines of Scotland, were lying uncultivated and practically useless. With these and other burdens and expenses, the canons had sunk to such a condition of poverty and want that they were unable to live and serve God according to the profession of their order without the help of other Christians. An indulgence of forty days was granted to all persons who contributed of their goods to the repair of the monastery or to the maintenance of the poor canons.[1]

The priory was in comparatively affluent circumstances before the outbreak of the war between the two kingdoms in 1296. The annual revenue of the house was returned at £74 12s. 6d. in the valuation of Pope Nicholas IV. in 1291, whereas at the time of the new taxation in 1318 the valuation of the temporalities had fallen to nothing, like that of several parish churches on the frontier, inasmuch as their goods were utterly wasted and destroyed by Scottish incursions.[2] It has been already stated that the prior's benefice was assessed at £20 for the royal subsidy in 1379–80. The gross revenues of the house in 1535 amounted for spiritualities and temporalities to £79 19s., which, after deducting such necessary outgoings as synodals, fees and salaries, left a net annual revenue of

£77 11s. 11d.[3] It is quite evident that the value of the priory fluctuated from time to time according to the peaceful or disturbed state of the Borders.

From the records of the great Scrope and Grosvenor controversy, which lasted from 1385 to 1390, we get a curious glimpse into the conventual buildings under the guidance of the prior. Among the superiors of the religious houses in the north of England, who gave evidence relative to the antiquity of the arms of Scrope from windows, seals, monuments and embroidered vestments, William, prior of Lanercost, was called. His depositions are of great local interest. William, prior of the house, stated that he was thirty-four years of age, and that on a window in the west end of his church were the arms of Scrope within a *bordure or*, and the same arms were placed in the refectory between those of Vaux and Multon, their founders ; and that in the refectory and west window of their church were the old arms of the King of England, the arms of France, the arms of Scotland, and the arms of Scrope, *azure a bend or*, the which arms had been in the said window since the building of their church in the time of Henry II., and by common report throughout the country they were the arms of Scrope ; that there remained banners used at the funerals of great lords and embroidered with their arms, amongst which were those of Scrope. He also deposed that the arms of Scrope were entire in an old chapel at Kirkoswald, and that they had at Lanercost the said arms embroidered on the morse of a cope with a white label for difference, and that the same had been in the priory from beyond the time of memory. Being asked how he knew that the said arms belonged to Sir Richard Scrope, the prior said that such had always been the tradition in their house, and that he had heard his predecessor, who was an old man, say that he had heard from ancient lords, knights and esquires that the Scropes were come of a noble race and high blood from the time of the Conqueror, as appeared by evidences, and the prior who preceded him also said that they were cousins to one Gant who came over with the Conqueror, and that their arms were descended in right line to Sir Richard Scrope, as was known by common report in all parts of the north. As to Sir Robert Grosvenor, the prior deposed on oath that he had never heard of him or his ancestors until the day of his examination. The suit, which commenced at Newcastle on 20 August 1385,

---

for the bishop's licence or its renewal to make the collection. For instance, Master Robert Whelpedale, Bishop Bell's registrar, returned the following sum in his diocesan accounts in 1480 : 'Fines Questorum. Set respondet de xxxiiis. iiijd. receptis de finibus questorum sanctorum Thome Rome, vis. viiid. Antonii vis. viiid., sancti Roberti iuxta Knaresburgh, vis. viiid., et sancti Johannis Beverlaci, vis. viiid., et sancti Lazari, vis. viiid., pro licencia questandi per unum annum integrum, etc. Summa, xxxiiis. iiiid.' (Accounts of Bp. Bell, MS.).

[1] *The Priory of Hexham* (Surtees Soc.), i. p. xcv.–xcvi.

[2] *Pope Nich. Tax.* (Rec. Com.), 320.

[3] *Valor Ecc.* (Rec. Com.), v. 277.

was finally closed in 1390 when the 'coat' was awarded to Scrope by the king in person in his palace of Westminster.[1]

Amid the sorrows and confusion attending the fall of the religious houses, John Robinson, the last prior of Lanercost, managed to keep his name unsullied from the aspersions of the royal visitors which blackened the characters of so many of his contemporaries and to steer a clear course through the political troubles which followed the dissolution. In 1534 Prior John was deputed with other gentlemen of the county to make an inventory of the 'moveables' of Sir Christopher Dacre when he was in disgrace.[2] As 'Leonardecoste' was one of the northern houses suspected of complicity in the insurrection of 1537 it is to be feared that hard fate awaited some of the canons. The king writing to the Duke of Norfolk in that year said—

Forasmoche as all thise troubles have ensued by the sollicitation and traitorous conspiracyes of the monkes and chanons of those parties, we desire and pray you, at your repaire to Salleye, Hexam, Newminster, Leonerdecoste, Saincte Agathe, and all suche other places as have made any maner of resistence, or in any wise conspired, or kept their houses with any force, sithens th' appointement at Dancastre, you shall, without pitie or circumstance, now that our baner is displayed, cause all the monkes and chanons, that be in anywise faultie, to be tyed uppe, without further delaye or ceremony, to the terrible exemple of others, wherin we thinke you shall doo unto us highe service.[3]

There was no charge made against the prior in this wrathful missive. When the priory of Lanercost was brought to an end, John Robinson its last head was awarded in 1539 a retiring allowance of £8 a year.[4]

Some difficulty was experienced by the authorities in the gift of the possessions of the dissolved priory. At first they were demised or leased to Sir William Penison, a court favourite, a proceeding which was hotly resented by the Dacres, who considered that their family claims were pre-eminent.[5] A lively correspondence ensued. Sir William complained that—

my lorde Dacre, contrarie to my will and pleasure or any promise to him therof made, dothe usurpe the ferme of Lanercoste demaynes and benefice therto appropriat, taking all thinges as his owne, puttyng out and in tennantes and prestes, so that by his maintenances the hole convent do confeder and flok to gither there in their chanons cotes very unsemely.

Lord William Dacre, replying to the charges made against him—

by the relacion of maister Penison being the Kinges maiesties fermour of Lanercoste,

assured Cromwell that he had not exceeded the commands of the king's commissioners—

and as unto the flocking of any chanons ther or empeching to be made to his deputies by me or any oder for me in the receipte of the revenues or any oder prouffettes ther, I did never nor no one for me medled therwithal.[6]

The priory was subsequently granted to Thomas Dacre of Lanercost, the king's servant, by letters patent dated 22 November 1542. It was a grant in tail male of the house and site of the dissolved priory of Lanercost with the water mill there, the 'tannehowse,' gardens, closes, messuages and all the demesne lands of the said late priory, all which lie in Lanercost parish and belonged to the said priory; except the church and churchyard of Lanercost and the mansion called the Utter Yate House there for the dwelling of the curate or vicar, to be held of the king by the service of one twentieth of a knight's fee rendering for the same 9s. yearly.[7]

PRIORS OF LANERCOST

Symon, circa 1181-4 [8]
John, 1220 [9]

---

[1] The depositions of William, prior of Lanetcost, were considered of sufficient interest to entitle them to special mention by the able writer who reviewed Sir Harris Nicholas' edition of 'The Controversy between Sir Richard Scrope and Sir Robert Grosvenor in the Court of Chivalry, A.D. MCCCLXXXV–MCCCXC, folio, London, 1832,' in the *Quar. Rev.* (April, 1836), lvi. 24–5.

[2] *L. and P. Hen. VIII.* vii. 646. The only charge made in the Black Book against the inmates of Lanercost was one of personal uncleanness against Edward Ulwalde and Thomas Rideley, two of the canons. The girdle of St. Mary Magdalene was stated to be amongst the relics of the house.

[3] Ibid. xii. (i.) 479; *Priory of Hexham* (Surtees Soc.), App. No. ci.

[4] *L. and P. Hen. VIII.* xiv. (i.) 596.

[5] Ibid. xiii. (i.) 588; xiv. (i.) 604.

[6] Ibid. xiii. (i.) 304, 522.

[7] Pat. 34 Hen. VIII. iii. m. 23; *L. and P. Hen. VIII.* xvii. 1154 (76).

[8] Reg. of Lanercost, viii. 9, 14, 17, 18. Symon was probably the first prior, for it was to him that Bishop Christian of Whithern confirmed the churches given by Robert de Vaux at the foundation of the house.

[9] Reg. of Holmcultram, MS. ff. 14–6. The award of Bishop Hugh of Carlisle between John, prior of Lanercost, and the monks of Holmcultram is dated in 1230 by a clerical error in the copy of the register with the dean and chapter of Carlisle. The correct date of 1220 is given in the Harleian copy (3891).

Walter, 1256 [1]

John of Galloway (de Galwythia), circa 1271, resigned with a pension in 1283, died in 1289 [2]

Symon de Driffeld, elected 16 August 1283 [3]

Henry (de Burgo), circa 1310, died 9 December 1315 [4]

Robert de Meburne, elected in December 1315 [5]

William de Suthayk, died in 1337

John de Bowethby, elected in 1337, died in 1338 [6]

John de Bewcastle (Bothecastre), elected in 1338, resigned with a pension in 1354 [7]

Thomas de Hexham (Hextildesham), elected 2 December 1354, died in July 1355 [8]

Richard de Ridale, elected in 1355, custody of the priory delivered to Martin de Brampton, canon of the house, in 1360, during Prior Richard's absence [9]

Peter Froste, circa 1379 [10]

John, 1380 [11]

William, circa 1385–90

Alexander Walton, 1434 [12]

John Werke, installed in 1465 [13]

Richard Cokke, received benediction in 1492–3

John Robinson, circa 1534–9

The seal of Lanercost [14] is of the usual monastic pattern, pointed oval with the figure of Mary Magdalene on a platform holding a palm branch in her right hand and a covered unguent pot in her left. In the field on each side a wavy branch of flowers and foliage, above which is on the left a crescent and on the right a star. The legend is S : CAPIT'LI : SCE : MARIE : MAGDALENE : DE : LANRECOST.

[1] Reg. of Lanercost, vii. 21, ix. 4.

[2] Ibid. ix. 14, xii. 13, xiii. 9 ; *Chron. de Lanercost*, 113, 133.

[3] Symon appears to have ruled the house for a long period, as a prior of that name exemplified a papal dispensation in 1306 to a canon of Lanercost (Carl. Epis. Reg., Halton, f. 101).

[4] *Chron. de Lanercost*, 232. There is good reason to believe that this prior was the same person as Brother Henry de Burgo, or Brother H. as he was oftener called in the Chronicle of Lanercost, who was the poet of the house for some time before his election to the priorate, and whose muse supplies a perpetual source of diversion to the readers of the Chronicle. The verses between 1280 and 1290 may be regarded as his best, notably his ironical effusion on the subsidy exacted by Bishop Ireton from the clergy in 1280 and the accounts he wrote of his detention in prison for three days at Durham in 1282. The versification introduced after 1290 was anonymous, and contributions of this sort ceased altogether after 1315, the year of Prior Henry's death.

[5] Carl. Epis. Reg., Halton, f. 180.

[6] Ibid. Kirkby, ff. 356–7.

[7] Ibid. ff. 379–80 ; Pat. 32 Edw. I. m. 10.

[8] Ibid. Welton, ff. 12, 20, 21.

[9] Ibid. ff. 20, 21, 73. Bishop Welton stated in his commission that Prior Richard had forsaken his post and withdrawn himself to some remote and distant place, and as the bishop wished to provide for the house during his absence, he committed the priory to Brother Martin with the injunction that he should give the bishop, while the prior was absent, or to the prior when he was present, a faithful account of his administration.

[10] Exch. *Cler. Subs.* bdle. 60, No. 1, dioc. of Carl. The value of the prior's benefice was set down at £20, the amount of his assessment being 10s. The canons of the house were Thomas Prest, Richard Felton, John Forth and Robert Estwake, who paid 12d. each to the subsidy.

[11] Ibid. No. 22. Prior John of Lanercost and Abbot Robert of Shap were commissioned by Bishop Appleby to collect the sixteenth granted by the clergy of Carlisle to Richard II. in the third year of his reign.

[12] Jefferson, *Leath Ward*, 495.

[13] In the *compotus* of William Raa, registrar of the diocese, from the morrow of Michaelmas, 4 Edw. IV. to the vigil of Easter, 5 Edw. IV., that is for a year and a half, we find this entry : 'Et de xl s. receptis de Johanne Werke (Clerk *cancelled*) canonico pro installacione sua in prioratum de Lanercoste, etc.' In a similar *compotus* of Robert Fisher, registrar, from 6 March, 7 Henry VII. to 11 March, 8 Henry VII., there is recorded this item of episcopal revenue : 'Benedictiones abbatum et priorum. Et de xl s. receptis pro benedictionibus Ricardi Cokke, prioris de Lanercost hoc anno.'

[14] Attached to deeds dated 1310 respecting an arrangement made between the canons of Lanercost and the priory of Durham, which are now in the possession of the Dean and Chapter of Durham. See also B.M. Seals 3395. Hodgson in his *History of Northumberland*, ii. pt. iii. 54–6, has reproduced a poor impression of this seal.

HOUSES OF CISTERCIAN MONKS

3. THE ABBEY OF HOLMCUL-TRAM[1]

The abbey of Holmcultram, situated in the low-lying district between Carlisle and the Solway, was founded as an affiliation of the great Cistercian house of Melrose by Prince Henry, son of David, King of Scotland, in the year 1150,[2] while he was ruler of the province ceded to Scotland by King Stephen and afterwards known as the county of Cumberland. In this great work he was assisted by Alan son of Waldeve, the lord of Allerdale, who relinquished to the new foundation the tract of territory which Henry had given him for a sporting domain. The act of the prince of Scotland and his vassal was confirmed by King David. It is difficult to account for the statements of the chronicles which mention the name of the founder. Scottish writers, in exuberant admiration of his benevolence, have ascribed the foundation to David himself.[3] Of these perhaps Fordun is the most positive, for he states that Earl

Henry, on the suggestion of Waltheve, abbot of Melrose, enriched with ample possessions the illustrious abbey of Holmcultram which his father had founded, and brought the work to a successful issue by applying to the Scottish house for its first superior.[4] Leland on the English side, with the foundation charter before him, recognized Alan son of Waldeve as the originator of the scheme, and credited Earl Henry only with its completion.[5] In after years when the district was recovered from Scotland, and Henry II. had taken the abbey under his protection and confirmed it in his possessions, the King of England was reputed as its legal founder.[6]

There is much to be said in favour of the theory that Alan son of Waldeve was the real originator of the institution. In the charter of foundation which gave the scheme practical shape Earl Henry declared that he had given in perpetual alms to the abbot and monks the two parts of Holmcultram (Holme Coltria), which he had caused to be marked with bounds at the time he had granted the third part to Alan as a hunting ground. 'But besides I have confirmed,' the charter proceeds, 'the donation of the said Alan, son of Waldeve his son, that is, the third part of Holmcultram which I had given Alan for his hunting and which he in the presence of my father, myself, and my barons gave and confirmed by his charter at Carlisle to the abbot and monks of the said place.' It is clear that Alan son of Waldeve was a participator in the foundation, though Earl Henry, his superior lord, has properly

---

[1] By indulgence of the Cumberland and Westmorland Antiquarian Society access has been had to its fine transcript of the Register or Chartulary of Holmcultram, which has been collated with all the copies known to be extant. These are (*a*) the Register in the custody of the dean and chapter of Carlisle, of date about 1250–1300 with later additions, which came into their possession in 1777 by will of Joseph Nicolson of Hawkesdale; (*b*) Harleian MS. 3911, date about 1300 with later additions; (*c*) Harleian MS. 3891, date about 1350 with some later additions; (*d*) Harleian MS. 1881, an untrustworthy copy as stated in the *Catalogue of the Harleian MSS.*, said to have been made at the expense of Hugh Todd, canon of Carlisle. *a* contains a number of entries not found in *b* or *c*, but on the other hand *b* and *c* contain many entries not found in *a*. *b* has some entries which are not in *c*, while *c* has many entries which are not in *b*. When the Register of Holmcultram is quoted *a* is the copy referred to unless where otherwise stated. In Bishop Nicolson's opinion the copy in the possession of the dean and chapter 'is not the same Reg[r] book which was in my Lord William Howard's custody.' It may be mentioned that the Harleian MS. 294, ff. 203b–6, contains extracts made by Roger Dodsworth in 1638 from a Register of Holmcultram then in the possession of Lord William Howard of Naworth. That MS. is referred to in Dugdale's *Monasticon*.

[2] *Chron. of Melrose*, in ann. 1150; Roger de Hoveden, *Chron.* (Rolls Ser.), i. 211; *Scotichronicon*, i. 296 (ed. Goodall), ii. 539.

[3] Wyntoun, *Orygynale Cronykil*, ii. 181; (ed. Laing) iii. 333.

[4] *Scotichronicon*, i. 347.

[5] *Collectanea* (ed. Hearne, 1774), i. 33. Hearne quotes *Camden* (p. 773, ed. Holland), who ascribed the foundation to David, for 'hoc tempore Scotus præfuit Cumbris.' Camden referred to the place as 'the abbey de Ulmo or Holme Cultraine.'

[6] In official documents the foundation is invariably ascribed to 'our royal progenitors,' the confirmation of Henry II. having been viewed as the source of the title of the monastery to its lands. In 1278–9 the jurors at the Carlisle Assize stated that the Isle of Holmcultram was the demesne of King Henry the elder (although this is the usual style of Henry I., Henry II. of course is meant, and the jurors may have been making a comparison between Henry II. and Henry III.), who founded that abbey. The abbot proffered the king's charter to that effect. He had also confirmations from Richard I., John and Henry III. (*Cal. of Doc. Scot.* [Scot. Rec. Pub.] ii. 146, p.36). The acts of the Scottish rulers in Cumberland were not recognized in English law.

got all the credit, inasmuch as it was he who granted the foundation charter, by which the whole of the lordship was assigned to the monks. In addition, the founder granted materials from his forest of Inglewood (Engleswoda) for the purpose of constructing the buildings of the new monastery, and within the bounds of Holmcultram he established all the liberties and privileges which his father had conferred on the abbeys of Melrose and Newbottle. The deed was witnessed by 'Adulf,' Bishop of Carlisle, and Walter, prior of the same, together with several Scottish and Cumbrian dignitaries.[1]

Of the numerous royal confirmations of its possessions which the house obtained it is not necessary to notice more than those of the early kings to whom allegiance was due. David I. confirmed his son's donation of Holmcultram 'and also that third part of Holm(cultram) which Alan son of Waldeve had given to the monks for the health of his soul.' The charter of Malcolm IV. dealt more at length with the separate gifts, and confirmed them 'as the charter of my father and the charter of Alan himself testify.' Malcolm also sanctioned ' the confirmation of David, King of Scotland, my predecessor.' Both of these confirmations are short and have the same witnesses, Adelulf, Bishop of Carlisle, and Walter, prior of the same, who had been parties a few years before to the foundation charter of Prince Henry. The English king, Henry II., ignoring all previous charters, took into his custody and protection the abbey and all its belongings, and gave and confirmed to the monks the island of Holmcultram with its appurtenances, Raby with its boundaries, the right to take wood in his forest for the building of their houses, pasture for their swine without pannage and the bark of fallen trees. By the charters of succeeding kings, notably those of Richard I. and John, the house was endowed with many valuable privileges and immunities.[2]

This great abbey, which overshadowed in riches and influence the rest of the religious houses in Cumberland and Westmorland, had many friends and benefactors on both sides of the Border before the rupture with Scotland in 1296. Endowments were freely lavished upon it by landowners, large and small, in various parts of the two counties. It would not be easy to single out a family of distinction within its sphere of influence which had not sooner or later some dealings with its monks. Though districts of the county like Penrith and Coupland may be regarded as the special preserves of the priories of Carlisle and St. Bees and the abbey of Calder, it was not unknown that the monks of Holme trespassed on their brethren and secured firm footholds in these places. Into the barony of Gillesland, specially devoted to the interests of the priory of Lanercost, they do not seem to have penetrated ; but in the great lordship of Allerdale, the fief of Alan son of Waldeve, they obtained many possessions outside their own extensive franchise of Holmcultram. The house kept up friendly relations, as long as it was politically prudent, with the kings and magnates of Scotland, and procured from them lands and liberties of considerable value to the community. The Scottish possessions were chiefly in Annandale, the fief of the Brus or Bruce family, and in Galloway, the principality of Fergus. Free trade with Scotland was conceded by William the Lion and free passage through the Vale of Annan by Robert de Brus. The kings of Man allowed the ships of the monks to visit the ports of the island and to buy and sell free of toll.[3] Some idea of the rapid rise to wealth of this house, in comparison with other houses in the county, may be gathered from the fact that before 1175, or about thirty years from its foundation, the monks had established no fewer than seven granges within their lordship, viz. the old grange and the granges of ' Ternis,' Mayburgh, Skinburness (Schineburgh), ' Sevehille,' Raby and Newton Arlosh (Arlosk), possessions which Pope Lucius thought of sufficient importance to be placed in the forefront of his charter of confirmation.[4]

It cannot be said that Holmcultram was ever wealthy in spiritual endowments. The

---

[1] Reg. of Holmcultram, MS. ff. 221-2 ; Dugdale, *Mon.* v. 594 ; *Reg. of Wetherhal*, 421-2. The part that Alan son of Waldeve took in the foundation was considered by his successors of sufficient moment whereon to build a claim to the advowson of the abbey. In 1219 the abbot and convent complained to the king and council that although their house was founded by his ancestors, Kings of England, and they had, among others, a charter of King John of a certain hermitage and stud (*haracium*) in the forest of Inglewood, the Earl of Albemarle, claiming the advowson of the abbey, vexed them unjustly (Close, 3 Hen. III. pt. ii. m. 1).

[2] Reg. of Holmcultram, MS. ff. 157-63, 221-3 ; Dugdale, *Mon.* v. 594-5, 602-6.

[3] Reg. of Holmcultram, MS. ff. 77, 99-101, 113, 234-6 and passim.

[4] Harl. MS. 3911, f. 138 ; 3891, ff. 110-2. In Dugdale's edition of this charter the granges of Mayburgh and Skinburness have been omitted (*Mon.* v. 598). The granges in 1535 were at Silloth (Selaythe), Calvo (Calfehou), ' Sanderhous' and Raby (*Valor Eccl.* v. 282).

neighbouring church of Burgh-by-Sands was bestowed by Hugh de Morvill for the purpose of finding lights, wine and all things necessary for the adornment of the abbey church, the ministers of the altar and the sacraments of Christ. In sanctioning the appropriation Bishop Hugh provided that the monks should appoint a fit vicar to have the cure of souls and pay episcopal dues, and assign him a competent maintenance.[1] Burgh-by-Sands was the only church in England that the monks possessed till 1332, when the Lady Margaret de Wigton gave them the church of Wigton in consideration of their great losses by the perpetual forays of the Scots. For this grant the house was under obligation to find four monks of the Order to celebrate divine offices daily in the abbey church and to found a chantry of two secular chaplains to do the same at Wigton.[2] The relations of the abbey with the Scottish church of Kirkwynny were often disturbed by political or ecclesiastical contingencies. In a roll dated 17 June 1391, presented to the anti-pope Clement VII., it was stated that this church, which used to be served by one of the monks of Holme, had been for some time neglected and committed to laymen ; it was therefore petitioned that the monastery of Glenluce might serve it.[3] This church was committed to Holmcultram free of synodals and all episcopal burdens by Joceline and other Bishops of Glasgow.[4]

Though the papal bulls are lengthy and numerous, there is little of special or local interest in the privileges which the monks of this house enjoyed. By these bulls[5] the bishop in whose *parochia* the abbey was founded was prohibited to call the abbot or monks to synods or outside conferences ; nor should he presume to visit the monastery for the purpose of celebrating orders, trying causes, or calling public assemblies ; nor should he meddle with the election, institution, or removal of an abbot contrary to the statutes of the Order. But the bishop should be requested with becoming respect to give benediction to new abbots, and on these occasions the abbots were instructed not to go beyond the form of profession allowed by the Cistercian institutes. In the matter of

the consecration of altars, churches and holy oil, the ordination of monks, or of any other ecclesiastical sacrament, the diocesan bishop would bestow all these things upon them. In 1357 Hugh Pelegrini, the papal nuncio, requested Bishop Welton to search his registers carefully and make a report on the number of churches, monasteries and other places in his diocese exempt from episcopal jurisdiction and immediately subject to the Holy See. The bishop replied that there were no such places in his diocese except the monastery of Holmcultram of the Cistercian Order and the monastery of Shap of the Premonstratensian Order.[6] Notwithstanding this immunity it was usual for the abbot to attend at Carlisle soon after his election and make his profession of canonical obedience.[7] In the ordination lists of the diocese of Carlisle the monks of this house are found in comparatively large numbers.

The abbey of Melrose was brought into intimate relations with Holmcultram, and often exercised an effective jurisdiction over the affairs of the monastery. Its influence in the choice of an abbot must have been considerable, inasmuch as no election could be canonically conducted without the presence of the abbot of the mother house. When Abbot Robert died in 1318 the convent petitioned the king for a safe conduct for the abbot of Melrose to attend the election of his successor, as the abbey, being *domus filialis domûs de Meuros in Scocia*, could not otherwise fill the vacant post.[8] In various ways we see the subjection of Holmcultram to the Scottish house. In 1326-7 the abbot obtained licence from Edward III. to visit Scotland during the truce on the ground that he wished to survey his grange in Galloway and

[1] Reg. of Holmcultram, MS. ff. 13-7.

[2] Pat. 6 Edw. III. pt. 1, m. 12 ; Carl. Epis. Reg., Kirkby, ff. 245-9, 280-1 ; Dugdale, *Mon.* v. 599.

[3] *Cal. of Papal Petitions*, i. 576.

[4] Reg. of Holmcultram, MS. ff. 108-10.

[5] Ibid. ff. 239 et seq. ; Dugdale, *Monasticon*, v. 599-603.

[6] Carl. Epis. Reg., Welton, f. 33. The house of Shap belonged to the Order of White Canons, who lived after the reformed rule of St. Austin and wore a white habit. The Order took its territorial name from Prémonstré in the diocese of Laon in Picardy, where the rule was first used.

[7] As the abbey of Holmcultram was a papal peculiar, the form of canonical profession to the Bishop of Carlisle is interesting : ' Obediencia abbatis de Holmo facta xxiiij die Augusti, anno etc. (m°ccc°) lxv°. Ego, frater Robertus Rawbankes, abbas de Holmcultram, Cisterciensis ordinis, subiectionem, reverenciam, et obedienciam a sanctis patribus constitutam secundum regulam Sancti Benedicti tibi, pater Episcope, tuisque successoribus canonice substituendis, et ecclesie tue Karliolensi, ac sacrosancte sedi apostolice, salvo ordine meo, perpetuo me exhibiturum promitto' (Carl. Epis. Reg., Appleby, f. 144).

[8] Pat. 12 Edw. II. pt. 1, m. 28 ; Rymer, *Fœdera* (new ed.), ii. 370.

treat with the abbot of Melrose, his superior, about the rule of his house.[1] During a vacancy at Holmcultram Abbot Richard of Melrose, when visiting the house by virtue of his ordinary jurisdiction and presiding at the election of a new pastor by virtue of the same jurisdiction, delivered to the monks a code of injunctions, which he caused to be read in the chapter house of the monastery in presence of them all on the last day of November 1472. The injunctions were concerned with the internal rule of the house in the regulation of the services of the church and the discipline of the monks. It was ordered that the daily and nightly offices of the Blessed Virgin and the Canonical Hours should be skilfully and devoutly celebrated, and that the form delivered to them by their father Bernard should be observed in the reading, intoning, chanting and other ceremonies. The priests of the monastery were expected to receive the Eucharist four times a week (*quater septimana*) unless hindered by some sufficient impediment, and those who were not priests twice at least within the space of fifteen days (*bis saltem infra quindenam*). As the cloister would be a tomb without learning—'quia claustrum sine literatura vivi hominis est sepultura '—the study of the Holy Scriptures should be indefatigably pursued, for in them they had, as Bernard taught, the surest refuge in all their troubles. The abbot was recommended to observe the greatest circumspection that no monk should visit persons or places beyond the monastic bounds, unless he was attended by a companion of honest conversation, and that no woman should be allowed to pass through or make a stay within the precincts lest the good name of the house should be blackened to the detriment of religion. In addition to strict rules for the regulation of diet, fasting and discipline, the abbot was ordered to procure a man learned in grammar for the instruction of the younger brethren in the Holy Scriptures, to rebuild the infirmary (*cellam pro fratribus egrotantibus*) as quickly as possible and to refit it with the necessary utensils, and also to supply the inner doors of the monastery with locks to keep out unwelcome visitors. Furthermore, as monks by the traditions of the sacred canons and the monastic rule were dead to the world and forbidden to mix themselves up with secular affairs, no one professed within that monastery should be allowed to exercise the office of bailiff or forester, which savoured of irregularity ; and as complaints were made about the occupations of Brother John Ribtoun, the abbot was desired to withdraw him from secular business till the next visitation, unless some other order was signified to him in the meantime.[2]

The fame of the abbey as a religious institution may be gathered in some measure from the frequency with which men of position and influence bequeathed their bodies to be buried within its precincts. Of the notable personages who were buried there, we may give the most distinguished place to Christian, Bishop of Candida Casa or Whithern, and to the father of Robert Bruce, King of Scotland. The bishop was held in such high esteem by the monks that the charter, in which he declared that he had given his allegiance to the Cistercian Order and become an inmate of that house, where he willed his body to be buried, was rubricated as the ' confirmation of St. Christian the bishop.' His interest in the affairs of the abbey may be judged by the vigorous language of excommunication with which he invoked *eterni incendii penas* on all who presumed to damage the monks or their possessions.[3] The historian of Lanercost was shocked at the impiety of Bruce, because in his devastating expedition of 1322 he spoiled the monastery though the body of his father had been buried there.[4] It might be expected that Hugh de Morvill, the lord of Burgh, who had been in such close association with the house, should

[1] Pat. 1 Edw. III. pt. 1, m. 29.

[2] *Liber S. Marie de Melros* (Bannatyne Club), ii. 596–9. With reference to the educational equipment of the monks, it may be mentioned that the abbot of Holmcultram and the prior of Carlisle alone of all the religious houses in the county were required to search their chronicles and archives for historical matter relating to King Edward's dispute with Scotland, and to transmit the same by the best informed member of each monastery to the Parliament at Lincoln on 20 January 1301 (Rymer, *Fœdera*, i. 923 ; *Parl. Writs* [Rec. Com.], i. 92). The valuable report from Carlisle has been printed in Palgrave's *Documents and Records* (Rec. Com.), 68–76, and is known as the *Cronica de Karleolo*, and also in the *Calendar of Documents relating to Scotland* (Scot. Rec. Pub.), ii. 115–7). Some of the books and MSS. which belonged to Holmcultram have found their way to the British Museum. A ' bestiary' inscribed with the words, ' liber sancte Marie de Holmcultram,' will be found among the Cotton MSS. Nero A. v. 1–3. An early manuscript, written in a hand of the twelfth century, containing an account of the miracles of St. John of Beverley, which once belonged to Holmcultram, is catalogued in the same collection as Faustina B. iv. 8, and has been printed by Raine (*Historians of the Church of York* [Rolls Ser.], i. 261).

[3] Reg. of Holmcultram, MS. ff. 112–3.

[4] *Chron. de Lanercost* (Maitland Club), 246.

select it as his burial place. The monks cannot have been averse to a custom which gave them a claim upon the benevolence of the deceased man's descendants. Thomas son of Andrew de Kirkconnell, at the request of Robert, abbot of Holmcultram, where the body of his father was entombed, made a grant to the abbey for his father's soul.[1] In all such cases the rights of parish churches were invariably recognized by the payment of parochial dues. When Adam de Bastenthwayt, whose will was proved at Rose in January, 1358-9, bequeathed his body to be buried in the cloister of the monastery near to his father and mother, if the consent of the convent could be obtained, he stipulated that the mortuary due to the parish church of St. Bees, 'Bastenthwayt,' should be delivered.[2] These examples will be considered sufficient to illustrate the custom.

This abbey was one of the Cumbrian houses at which Edward I. stayed from time to time while on his expeditions against Scotland. It was to Holmcultram that Robert Wisheart, Bishop of Glasgow, came of his own free will to meet the king in October 1300, and to renew his broken vow of allegiance. For the fourth time the bishop took the oath upon the consecrated Host, upon the Gospels, upon the Cross of St. Neot, and upon the Black Rood of Scotland, in the presence of Bishop Halton of Carlisle, the abbot of Holmcultram, and many of the great lords of England and the envoys of France.[3] It is not easy to account for the king's presence at Burgh-by-Sands, where he died on 7 July 1307, as it was impossible that he should propose to lead his army into Scotland by that route. It is probable that as the host was encamped at Carlisle, the king was on his way thither from Holmcultram[4] when he was seized with the fatal sickness.

The position of the abbey on the southern shore of the Solway jeopardized its safety at every outbreak of hostilities between the two kingdoms. The story of its losses and sufferings would necessitate a detailed narrative of Border feuds. The fact that the house was of Scottish foundation did not save it from attack or in any way mitigate its hardships. As early as 1216 the Scots, in revenge for

King John's invasion, broke into Cumberland by way of the Solway and pillaged the abbey of Holmcultram in spite of the orders of Alexander II. who had extended his peace to religious houses. The chronicles of Melrose and Lanercost describe the mischief done in almost the same words. It was a wholesale spoliation. The Scots took everything they could lay hands on, the holy books, vestments, chalices, horses and cattle, utensils and garments, going to the extremity of stripping a monk who was lying at his last gasp in the infirmary. But their impiety did not pass unpunished. On their return homewards with the spoils, nearly two thousand Scots were drowned in the tide as they forded the river Eden.[5] At a later date the sufferings of the monks were more protracted owing to continuous warfare.[6] In addition to the forfeiture of their Scottish possessions, the house was impoverished by losses at home. In 1315-6 they petitioned the king for the advowson of the church of Kirkby Thore in Westmorland, as the abbey was plundered, their houses burned, their lands wasted, and their cattle, horses and oxen were driven away.[7] The strain was so great at this period that the resources of the house were unable to support the community as aforetime. In 1319 some of the monks were dispersed in different abbeys of their own order until Holmcultram was relieved of its oppressions.[8] On one occasion, in 1385, the monks paid £200 to the Earl of Douglas as an indemnity for the ransom of their church and lands from destruction.[9] In fact, up to the very time of the dissolution, the abbey was in danger of spoliation. As late as 1527 the monks petitioned parliament that they might be discharged from the office of collectors of tenths, aids, loans and other exactions, and from the payment of taxes and tallages, as their house was situated on the frontier and often in great danger from the Scots.[10]

It must not be taken that the abbey was in a perpetual state of siege and never enjoyed

---

[1] Reg. of Holmcultram, MS. ff. 21, 121-2.

[2] Carl. Epis. Reg., Welton, f. 30.

[3] Rymer, Fœdera, i. 924; Palgrave, Doc. and Rec. (Rec. Com.), clxxviii. 344.

[4] This supposition is consistent with the official memorandum of the king's death (Rymer, Fœdera, i. 1018). Letters patent were issued from Holmcultram on the day before and the day after the fatal event (Cal. of Pat. 1301-7, pp. 535-6).

[5] Chron. of Melrose, in ann. 1216; Chron. de Lanercost, 18.

[6] Even in times of peace the abbey was situated in a dangerous locality. In 1235 the king, having heard that the monks had suffered great damage from malefactors in the places where their granges were, granted them liberty to have, outside the forest, their servants armed with bows and arrows to protect their goods (Pat. 19 Hen. III. m. 5).

[7] Parl. Petitions, No. 3946.

[8] Close, 13 Edw. II. m. 18d.

[9] Parl. Petitions, No. 4165; Pat. 9 Ric. II. pt. i. m. 5; Cal. of Doc. Scot. (Scot. Rec. Pub.), iv. 78.

[10] L. and P. Hen. VIII. iv. 3053 (iv.)

RELIGIOUS HOUSES

periods of repose. Like the rest of the country on the immediate frontier, its prosperity depended on international relations. At one time the ships of the convent traversed the Irish Sea and carried on a brisk trade with Ireland and the Isle of Man. In 1224 leave was given that the abbot might send his ship where he pleased with a cargo of wool.[1] On the patent rolls of the thirteenth and fourteenth centuries numerous licences are on record to permit the buying of victuals in Ireland, Gascony and elsewhere. The monks had a good port at Skinburness within their own franchise, which was used as a naval base for the supply of provisions and stores during the wars with Scotland,[2] and so great was its use on these occasions that Edward I. gave the monks the liberty to have a free borough and a fair and market there in 1300, with an allowance for wool seized to the king's use.[3] The monks like other practical men looked after the affairs of their house and were not afraid to assert their rights when occasion demanded. In 1263 the abbot impleaded the Archbishop of York for hindering the free passage of his carts and carriages beyond the bridge of Hexham which his predecessors had always obtained when needful.[4] Before the justices itinerant in 1292 the convent successfully maintained its title to all the lands and privileges which were claimed as belonging to the house.[5] There was no fear that a powerful personage like the abbot of Holmcultram should tamely submit to unjust treatment from the secular magnates of the land. In 1300 a commission of oyer and terminer was appointed to try a cause on his complaint that William de Mulecastre, lately while he was sheriff, and others at divers times, took some of the abbot's carts, laden with victuals and other goods, on the high road in the middle of the city of Carlisle and town of Torpenhow, with the oxen drawing them, and refused to let them be replevied, so that a great number died, sold a palfrey the abbot had lent him, broke his grange at Ellenborough (Alneburgh) and carried away his oats, took away a boat with its gear at Skinburness, led away some of his beasts and sheep at Holm-

cultram, distrained his men and tenants of Ellenborough by their carts and draught cattle and detained them till they extorted ransom.[6]

The disturbed state of the Border did not divert attention from the need of monastic discipline. We read of John de Foriton forsaking his habit in 1352 and William de Levyngton escaping from the monastery by night in 1354, but these refractory monks were not permitted to return until they had received a papal dispensation to be reconciled. When John de Monte took it into his head to visit the Roman Court without the leave of his superior, the abbot of Holmcultram was instructed to carry out the ordinances against apostates as the monk wished to be reconciled to his Order. It is pleasing to find that some of the monks like Richard Gray, who was made a papal chaplain in 1402, had attained to ecclesiastical distinction.[7]

The exercise of the king's right to grant corrodies for good service was often a burden to the religious houses. An instance of one of these may be given to illustrate the custom. Edward II. informed the abbot and convent in 1309 that he had caused Thomas de Ardern, who served the king and his father, to be sent to them, and requested them to admit him to their house and to find him and a yeoman and two grooms serving him, food and clothing according to their stations, and to provide reasonable sustenance for his two horses. Letters patent for his lifetime to this effect were to be given him under their chapter seal and a speedy report made to the king on what they had done therein.[8] A royal pensioner of this sort could not have been a welcome visitor at Holmcultram in the crippled condition of their finances at that period.

<hr/>

[6] *Cal. of Pat.* 1292–1301, p. 554.

[7] *Cal. of Papal Letters*, iii. 470, 522, 572–3, iv. 316. No inmate has attained to the fame of Michael Scott, wizard and necromancer, celebrated alike by Dante (*Inferno*, c. xx. ll. 115–7), Boccaccio (*Decameron*) and Sir Walter Scott (*Lay of the Last Minstrel*), who is said to have passed some time in the monastery. Camden was told on his visit to Cumberland that in Wolsty Castle near Holmcultram, built by the monks for a treasury and place of safety to lay up their books, charters and evidences against sudden invasion of the Scots, the secret works of Michael the Scot lay in conflict with moths, 'which Michael, professing here a religious life, was so fully possessed with the study of mathematickes and other abstruse arts, about the yeere of our Lord 1290, that beeing taken of the common people for a necromancer, there went a name of him (such was their credulity) that he wrought divers wonders and miracles' (*Brit.* [ed. Holland] 773).

[9] Close, 3 Edw. II. m. 26d.

[1] Pat. 8 Hen. III. m. 5.

[2] *Cal. of Pat.* 1292–1301, pp. 389, 488, 554, 585.

[3] Harl. MS. 3891, ff. 21–3, 108.

[4] *Cal. of Doc. Scot.* (Scot. Rec. Pub.), i. 462. The house had a charter of quittance from toll pontage, passage, and all custom in England or Ireland from King Richard (*Fine R.* 2 John [Rec. Com.], 117–8 ; *Chancellor's R.* 3 John [Rec. Com.], 68–9).

[5] *Plac. de Quo Warranto* (Rec. Com.), 130.

167

Some idea of the hardships that houses so near the frontier had endured may be gathered from a comparison of the valuations of the temporalities of the monastery in 1291, just before the outbreak of the Scottish wars, and in 1319, the palmy days of Robert Bruce after the battle of Bannockburn. At the former period the annual revenue was returned at £206 5s. 10d., and at the later date it amounted only to £40.[1] This abbey was the wealthiest house in the counties of Cumberland and Westmorland, and owing to its exposed situation it sustained greater losses than any of the others, with the exception perhaps of Lanercost. In 1535[2] the gross valuation of the temporalities amounted to £370 17s. 0d. and the total revenues of the house to £535 3s. 7d. After the deduction of necessary outgoings, the clear net value was taxed at £477 19s. 3d.

The abbots of Holmcultram were employed in general affairs and went about the world more than any of the heads of the local religious houses. In the great dispute between the bishop and the priory about the division of the revenues of the church of Carlisle in 1221–3, the abbot of that date was associated with the prior of Hexham as papal assessor.[3] When differences arose between the Archbishop of York and the Bishop of Durham in 1329–30 touching the question of jurisdiction and the cognizance of causes, the pope appointed the abbot of Holmcultram, the prior of the friar preachers of Carlisle, and the archdeacon of the same place to act as mediators, but they petitioned to be excused as there were no lawyers thereabouts to consult, the people were ill-disposed, and Carlisle was so far from the diocese of York.[4] In 1340 and 1341 the king appointed the abbots of Holme and Calder and three laymen as collectors of the ninth of lambs, fleeces and sheaves in Cumberland.[5] During the vacancy of the see in 1352, while John de Horncastle was the elect and confirmed but not the consecrated Bishop of Carlisle, the abbot of Holme acted as vicar-general of the diocese and was re-appointed on the accession of Bishop Welton.[6] Again and again safe conducts were issued to the abbot when he wished to attend the chapter general of his order at Citeaux, and the keeper of Dover

was instructed to allow him to embark at that port.[7] The daughter house of Grey Abbey and a small property in Ireland brought the abbot from time to time to that country,[8] and the fealty he owed to Melrose as well as his oversight of the grange in Galloway[9] necessitated occasional visits to Scotland in time of truce. Though the house is not reckoned among the mitred abbeys of the kingdom, the abbot was summoned to parliament and to the great Councils of State between 1294 and 1312.[10] In days of national mourning the house was selected among the greater monasteries to celebrate the obsequies of the deceased. The abbot was requested to pray for the soul of Edmund, Earl of Cornwall, in 1296, for Joan, Queen of France, in 1305, and for Philip the Fair in 1314.[11] From these circumstances we may conclude that Holmcultram occupied a pre-eminent position among the religious institutions of the county.

Some of the superiors of this monastery attained individual distinction or notoriety from various causes. Everard, the first abbot, ruled the house for the long period of forty-two years from the date of its foundation in 1150 till his death in 1192. His name is often found in the records of that time. It was probably at Holmcultram that Huctred son of Fergus executed the deed whereby he gave a carucate of land in Crevequer to the hospital of St. Peter, York, several of the witnesses being local men, such as Everard the abbot, Robert the prior, and William the cellarer of Holmcultram, Robert archdeacon of Carlisle, Ralf clerk of the same place, Robert son of Trute sheriff of the same, Richard his brother, Hubert de Vaux, Peter del Teillos, Christian, Bishop of Whithern, who often visited the house, besides others from Galloway near to the English border.[12]

[7] Rymer, *Fœdera*, ii. 78 ; Close, 15 Edw. II. m. 30d, and passim.
[8] Pat. 5 Edw. II. pt. i. m. 24 ; Reg. of Holmcultram, MS. ff. 241, 245.
[9] Pat. 1 Edw. III. pt. i. m. 29.
[10] *Parl. Writs* (Rec. Com.), i. 26, and passim.
[11] Rymer, *Fœdera* (new ed.), i. 842, 922, 971 ; ii. 258.
[12] *Cal. of Doc. Scot.* ii. 422. The date of Everard's promotion to Holmcultram has been doubted. Bishop Stubbs dated his tenure from 1175 to 1192, but his error apparently arose from identifying the *abbacia de Holme*, one of the twelve vacant houses in 1175, with Holme in Cumberland (*Benedict Abbas*, i. 92, ii. 80). It is clear from the deed of Uctred son of Fergus that it was passed before 1164, the year in which Hubert de Vaux, one of the witnesses, died. The Chronicle of Melrose mentions Everard in connection with the foundation in 1150.

[1] *Pope Nich. Tax.* (Rec. Com.), 320, 333.
[2] *Valor Eccl.* (Rec. Com.), v. 282–3.
[3] *Cal. of Papal Letters*, i. 81, 91 ; ii. 112, 256.
[4] Ibid. ii. 320 ; *Letters from the Northern Registers* (Rolls Ser.), p. 359.
[5] Pat. 14 Edw. III. pt. ii. m. 45 ; 15 Edw. III. pt. i. m. 31.
[6] Carl. Epis. Reg., Welton, MS. f. 1.

Robert de Brus and Eufemia his wife (*mulier*) gave a fishery in Torduff to Everard and the brothers of Holme which was afterwards confirmed by Robert their son.[1] Abbot Everard perambulated the boundaries of his land of Kirkwinny in company with Christian, Bishop of Whithern, and Huctred son of Fergus,[2] and was present at Peebles when William the Lion granted the great charter to the abbey of Jedburgh.[3] The greatest function in which he ever took part was the coronation of King Richard,[4] which he attended on 3 September 1189. It was to Abbot Everard in 1185 that Pope Lucius confirmed all the possessions of the house.[5] Fordun has left us a beautiful picture of his saintly life from childhood to old age,[6] and tradition has supplemented it by ascribing to him many scholarly accomplishments. It is said that he wrote the life of St. Adamnan, of St. Cumen, and of St. Waltheve, the latter being his old superior at Melrose, but the manuscript of none of these biographies is known to be extant.[7] In 1192 he entered into rest in a good old age, full of days and virtues.[8]

Adam de Kendal has been made famous in a Scottish chronicle as the unfortunate abbot of Holmcultram. The new abbot, who succeeded about 1215, seeing the Bishop of Carlisle crippled with age and infirmity and at the gates of death, conceived the lofty ambition of gaining the episcopate at an early period. By secret intrigue and public bribery he squandered the revenues of the monastery in order to make friends of those who might be able to influence the election. Intelligence of his methods in due time reached the ears of the superior-general of the Cistercian order, who caused inquiries to be made which ended in the deposition of the abbot. Throwing himself on the mercy of the chapter, he was permitted to take up his abode at Hildekirk in the forest of Inglewood, a hermitage belonging to the abbey. When the Bishop of Carlisle died and the day for the election of his successor arrived, the deposed abbot sent a secret messenger to learn the result. But the name of Adam de Kendal was not mentioned. The disappointment so preyed on his spirits that he became insane and died in great misery at Holmcultram as a terrible warning to the ambitious.[9] The Chronicle of Melrose is silent on Adam's faults, mentioning only his resignation (*suo cessit officio*) in 1223. While he was abbot he made a grant of ten measures of salt annually at Martinmas to the priory of Lanercost.[10]

Another abbot of Holmcultram, deserving a special notice, was Robert Chamber, who flourished during the religious revival which preceded the dissolution of the monasteries. He was a local man of the family of Chamber of Raby Cote in that lordship and is commemorated by many fragmentary memorials scattered in various parts of that neighbourhood, either built into farm houses or still existing about the abbey church. Over the arch of the present porch of the church there is inscribed—'Robertus Chamber fecit fieri hoc opus A° D^{ni} M.D.VII.' Upon the pedestal of a statue of the Virgin may be seen the 'chained-bear,' the well-known rebus of his name with the legend beneath, 'Lady deyr save Robert Chamber.' The inscription 'orate pro anima Roberti Chamber abbatis,' which Bishop Nicolson observed in the church at his visit in 1703, has disappeared.[11] In almost every considerable house of the parish some remnant of Abbot Chamber's work may be seen, bearing his name, initials, or some enigmatical conceit about him. In the bitter disputes which followed the suppression of the monastery, the great days of Abbot Chamber were often referred to by witnesses and their recollections recorded on the depositions. But inferences about the dates of his tenure of office are very conflicting, and no reliance can be placed on such evidences. On 12 March 1512 he was joined in a commission with the Bishop of Carlisle and William Bewlay to inquire into the possessions of

---

[1] Reg. of Holmcultram, MS. ff. 66–7.

[2] Harl. MS. 3891, f. 87b.

[3] National MSS. of Scotland, 1, 38; *Monastic Annals of Teviotdale*, 57–9.

[4] Bened. of Peterborough, *Gesta Hen. II. et Ric. I.* (Rolls Ser.), ii. 80.

[5] Harl. MS. 3911, ff. 137b–141b; Dugdale, *Mon.* v. 598.

[6] *Scotichronicon* (ed. Goodall), i. 347.

[7] *Descriptive Cat. of Materials* (Rolls Ser.), ii. 225–6. The editor of *Camden* had views of his own (ed. Gibson, ii. 1059). John Denton, who wrote about 1610, must have seen some manuscript ascribed to Abbot Everard, for he said that 'Everardus some time abbot of Holm Cultram, who lived in the days of Henry II., hath registered to posterity that the Danes had a house or temple of sacrifice or a publick place at Thursby where the pagans offered up the blood of captives to a God whom in that sort they honoured' (*Hist. of Cumb.* 93).

[8] *Chron. of Melrose*, in ann. 1192. On two occasions we find him witnessing charters of Richard de Morevill, constable of the King of Scotland (*Liber S. Marie de Melrose*, i. 82, 98).

[9] Fordun, *Scotichronicon* (ed. Goodall), ii. 12–6.

[10] Harl. MS. 3891, f. 33b.

[11] *Miscellany Accounts*, 24–5.

George Kyrkebryde, deceased.[1] He established an alms in the abbey church for priests singing yearly masses at the altar of our Holy Saviour Jesus for the souls of Henry II. and Henry VIII. and for his own soul.[2] Robert Chamber is said to have 'rygned' as abbot of Holmcultram for thirty years.

As soon as the destruction of the religious houses became a subject of agitation in the country, it was almost impossible to preserve discipline in large communities. In Holmcultram a discreditable state of anarchy was disclosed. During the seven years before the surrender no fewer than four abbots ruled the monastery. Dan Matthew Dyves or Deveys, a monk of the house, became abbot in 1531 through the instrumentality of Robert Cokett of Bolton Percy in Yorkshire, an honour which cost the new abbot £100 in fine to the Crown. His death took place in the following year under suspicious circumstances. Sir John Lamplugh, in a letter bearing date 16 September 1532, told Cromwell that Gawyn Borradale, one of the brethren, was suspected of being implicated in the death of the abbot of Holme. The monk was arrested and imprisoned in the abbey of Furness, where he remained for about half a year. The depositions of the religious and temporal men connected with the abbey of Holmcultram have been preserved, from which it may be gathered that Borradale was suspected of poisoning Abbot Deveys in a fit of jealousy or disappointment after the election. Borradale had powerful friends and eventually attained the object of his desires. It was he who afterwards surrendered the house to the king's commissioners.[3]

The surname of the next abbot of Holmcultram was variously written as Yerbye, Jerbye and Irebye, but he probably belonged to the Cumberland family of Ireby or originated from the parish of that name. Thomas Ireby succeeded soon after the death of Abbot Deveys and gave promise of ruling the house 'according to right and conscience,' as John Lord Husey expressed it to Cromwell on 19 November 1532. The new abbot had restitution of the temporalities on 11 March 1533, for which he paid a fine of £50. The discipline of the monks was a great concern to him, and something was done during his term of office to restore confidence and promote charity after the disaster to his predecessor. Thomas Graham, a refractory brother, who held a proctorship in the church of Wigton, was called to account for neglect of his duty and his seal was revoked. Some of his letters are preserved at the Record Office, and his signature may still be read with that of Christopher Slee, prior of Carlisle, in attestation of an inventory of the 'moveables' of Lord William Dacre, seized in 1534 by the Earls of Westmorland and Cumberland and Sir Thomas Clifford, the king's commissioners. It 'pleased Gode almyghtt to call unto his mercy Thomas Irebye, our discreitt father and laitt abbot of our monasterye, whiche dyde depart from this present lyffe the x[t] day of August (1536), whosse sowlle Gode pardon, leivyng' the monks of Holmcultram a 'powre floke without heide or governore.'[4]

On 11 August 1536, the day following the death of Abbot Ireby, the whole monastery consisting of the sub-prior and twenty-one monks signed a petition to Cromwell 'to suffer us to have our free and liberall election accordyng to the statutes and rewlles of our holly religion to elect one of the brethern of owre monastery to be heide and governore of the same,' alleging as an excuse for haste their nearness to the Scottish border and the fear 'leist the ravyschyng wolffe doo enter into the floke,' in the event of any delay in the appointment of their head.[5] Intrigues were on foot. Sir Thomas Wharton recommended Graham, the monk already referred to, who offered to give 400 marks to the king's highness for the office besides his first fruits, but other arrangements were made. Thomas Carter, who was apparently not a member of the chapter of Holmcultram, was placed over the house.[6] His name appears loaded with infamy, a few months after his appointment, in that 'cleane' but unreliable 'booke of compertes' which the royal visitors presented to Parliament. In the insurrections of 1537 Abbot Carter was a prominent figure, urging his tenants to join the commons,

[1] Pat. 3 Hen. VIII. pt. ii. m. 14d; L. and P. Hen. VIII. i. 3075.

[2] Valor Ecc. (Rec. Com.), v. 282.

[3] L. and P. Hen. VIII. v. 277, 657, 1317. The following documents have been copied by the writer from the originals at the Record Office and printed by the Carlisle Scientific and Literary Society: Dr. Legh's defence of the accused monk (ibid. vi. 985); petition from Furness protesting his innocence and claiming a fair trial (ibid. vi. 986); John, abbot of Byland's letter of intercession to Cromwell on behalf of the monk (ibid. vi. 987); depositions of monks and others before Abbot Ireby concerning the death of the late abbot (ibid. vi. 988); letter of Roger, abbot of Furness, on the character of Borradale and his abettors (ibid. vi. 1557).

[4] Ibid. v. 1556; vi. 228 (i.), 781, 988, 1205; vii. 676; xi. 276.

[5] Ibid. xi. 276.　　[6] Ibid. xi. 319.

organizing processions in his church as a supplication for their success, and going in person as an envoy on their behalf to demand the surrender of Carlisle.[1] Thomas Graham, the monk who was foiled in his ambition to become the head of the monastery at the last vacancy, was employed by the civil power as a spy on the doings of the new abbot.[2] Out of the many charges made against the abbot, Graham's depositions only may be selected:—

At the furst Insurreccon agan the Abbott.

Item, y^t the abbot sent to W. Alanbe y^t he schuld scend to James Hounter to warn all abowt hym to be at Waytlynghow upon payn of hayngynge too meet ye comanes there.

Item, the abbot was mayde comyssyon^r to Carlell ffrom ye comanes and rode towert Carlell as nere as he durst and send to them y^t was wthin ye cetee and askytt delyver of ye town to ye comones,

Item, the abbot rod to Pereth to ye comanes y^t rod to Yorke, and ther the said abbatt gayve them ample to ther expensys.

Item, the said abbot spake with one Hew Will'mson at the last Insurreccon, the day afor the comanes lade siege to Carlell, and askytt hym 'qwhat newys' and the said Hew answer^d & said to hym agayn, 'ther was never sayke agatheryng to ye brodfeld as ther was y^t day afore': and the abbot answerytt & sayde, 'All myghty god prossper them, for yffe they sped not this abbe ys lost:' and upon the sayng he sent for ys subprior and comandyt hym to cawse the brether to goo daly w^t processcon to speed ye comones jorney.

The Articles of brakyng of ye Kynges graces Iniunccons as her after folloys :

Item, y^t the abbot hays broght dyvers woman in the inwart partes of o^r monistry to dyn and suppe agans o^r Iniunccons.

Item, y^t the said abbott hays sold, wthoute ony lycens of ye kynges grace or hys vicittores, as myche platt as com to houndreth poundes & more.

Item, the said Abbat hays gyffyng o^r covent seyll agayns iij or iiij of ye bred^{rs} myndes agayns o^r monist^y profett,

Item, the said abbatt gayffe too ye abbott of Byland, ffor helpyng hym too ys promocon, a salt of gold & sylver to valoo of xx^{ts} markes & more.

Item, y^t the abbot haithe sold o^r joelles of o^r kyrke.

Item, the said abbot hays lattyng o^r demaynes agans ye kynges grace Iniunccon.

Item, the abbot, sens the kynges graces pardon was gyffyng, cawsytt hys tennands a gayns ther wyll to must^r afor hym in the kyrke, & therby wold hayve them to ryddyng to ye brodfell to the comanes, & ye denyett hym & said they wold not go, excepe he went wth them hys selffe : and befor them all the said abbot comandytt Cudbert Musgrave, of ye comones nayme, to take the tennandes

& go to the brod fell, & so bothe Cudbert & all tenands denyett ye abbot comandment & wold not go : & y^{ts} aforsaid I will refere me to tennandes qwether it was so or nay : & this comandment & mettyng was the day befor the comanes laid sieges to Carlell.

Item, all the sterryng of ye tennandes w^{t}hin the Holme lordscheppe was euer be ye commandment of ye abbot, bothe at the furst insurreccon & also at ye last, qwhen he caws^t them to com to ye abbey.

At ye last Insurreccon qwhen he comandytt them to ryde too ye brod feld wth Cudbert Musgrave.

per Tho. Graym, monicum.

(*Endorsed.*) The Abbot of Holm to incite his Tenants to come wth the Rebells at the broadfeild.[3]

It is probable that the life of Abbot Carter was forfeited by his complicity in the insurrection, for before the year 1537 was ended another abbot reigned in his stead.

Gawen Borudale or Borradale, the monk previously suspected of poisoning Abbot Deveys, was appointed a few months before the dissolution of the monastery. In a letter to Cromwell, dated 23 January 1538, Sir Thomas Wharton stated he had seen in the abbot of Holme 'ryght honest procedynges and a good borderer in ye kynges graces affayres.' On 6 March following, the house was surrendered to Thomas Leigh, LL.D., in the presence of John Leigh, William Blithman, James Rookesby, William Leigh, Thomas Dalston and others. The deed of surrender was signed by the abbot and twenty-four monks and sealed with the seal of the convent. Within a fortnight after the surrender, 18 March, the community was turned adrift, or in the words of Dr. Leigh, the monastery was 'withe moche quyetnes and contentacion of the cuntry dissolvyd and the monckis in secular apparell, having honest rewardis in ther purses, be disparsyd abrode.' The late abbot continued in spiritual charge of the lordship of Holmcultram and had 'for his logyng,' with which he was 'ryght well contentyd, the chambre that he was in before he was abbot, then called the selleras chambre, and the chambre at the stayr hed adjoynyng to the same.' The brethren received pensions in varying sums from 40s. to £6 and returned to secular life.[4] On the earnest supplication of the inhabitants of Holme the abbey church was not destroyed. It was not only to them their parish church, they pleaded, 'and little

---

[1] *L. and P. Hen. VIII.* xii. pt. i. 687.

[2] Ibid. xii. pt. i. 1259 ; Cott. MS. Caligula B, iii. 286.

[3] Cott. MS. Caligula B, iii. 285.

[4] *L. and P. Hen. VIII.* vol. xiii. (i.) 128, 434, 436, 547, and passim.

ynoughe to receyve all us your poore orators, but also a grete ayde, socor, and defence for us ayenst our neighbors the Scotts, withe out the whiche few or none of your lordshipps supplyants are able to do the king is saide hieghnes our bounden duetye and service.'[1] Since that date the church has been shorn of many of its glories and suffered many misfortunes.

ABBOTS OF HOLMCULTRAM

Everard, 1150–92 [2]
Gregory, 1192 [3]
William de Curcy, translated to Melrose in 1215,[4] thence to Rievaulx in 1216
Adam de Kendal, 1215–23 [5]
Ralf, 1223 [6]
William, resigned in 1233 [7]
Gilbert, 1233–7 [8]
John, 1237–55 [9]

[1] Cott. MS. Caligula E, iv. 243 ; Ellis, *Original Letters*, ser. 1, ii. 90.

[2] The authorities for these dates may be seen ante, p. 168 *et seq.*

[3] *Chron. of Melrose*, in anno 1192. During his time Affreca, daughter of Godred, King of Man, wife of John de Curcy, founded the house of Grey Abbey (Jugum Dei) in Ulster, which was colonized from Holmcultram and became affiliated thereto (*Chron. Manniæ*, in anno 1204). When the floors of the Irish house were cleared of rubbish about 1840, a leaden seal of Bishop Ralf de Ireton of Carlisle was found. It bore the following legend : RADULPHUS DEI GRACIA KARLEOLENSIS EPISCHOP (Reeves, *Antiq. of Down*, 92).

[4] *Chron. of Melrose*, in anno 1215. Fordun is very enigmatical on this abbot's tenure of Holmcultram (*Scotichronicon* [ed. Goodall], ii. 12). Abbot William is often found in association with Bishop Bernard of Carlisle (*Cuisbro' Chart.* [Surtees Soc.], ii. 319 ; Duchy of Lanc. Chart. Box B, No. 164 ; Reg. of Holmcultram, MS. ff. 18, 19). He also witnessed a charter of Melrose in company with Ralf, Bishop of Down, and Warin, abbot of Rievaulx (*Liber S. Mariæ de Melrose* [Bannatyne Club], i. 53, 54).

[5] See ante, p. 169.

[6] *Chron. of Melrose*, in anno 1223 ; Reg. of Holmcultram, MS. ff. 23, 24. He had been formerly abbot of Grey Abbey in Ireland.

[7] *Chron. of Melrose*, in anno 1233.

[8] Ibid. in annis 1233, 1237 ; Harl. MS. 3891, f. 19b ; Feet of F. (Cumb.), 19 Hen. III. No. 22. He had been previously master of the 'converts' in Holmcultram and died at Canterbury on his way home from the general chapter of his order.

[9] *Chron. of Melrose*, in annis 1237, 1255. This abbot made an agreement with the prior of St. Bees 'pro mina nostra suam terram suam apud Whithofthaven reponenda' (Reg. of St. Bees, MS. x. 7). See also *Cal. of Doc. Scot.* (Scot. Rec. Pub.), i. 509.

Henry, 1255,[10] 1262,[11] 1267 [12]
Gervase, 1274,[13] 1279 [14]
Robert de Keldesik, 1289,[15] 1292,[16] 1296,[17] 1318 [18]
Thomas de Talkane, 1331,[19] 1336 [20]
Robert de Sitthayk or Sothayk, 1351,[21] 1359 [22]

[10] *Chron. of Melrose*, in anno 1255. He had been a monk of the house.

[11] Several of his transactions about property in Carlisle and Newcastle are on record about this date (Reg. of Holmcultram, MS. ff. 70, 151–2 ; Harl. MS. 3891 ff. 78–9, 81–2).

[12] The *Chron. of Melrose*, in anno 1267, states that Abbot Henry was deposed from Holmcultram by Adam de Maxstun, abbot of Melrose, but was restored to his former seat by the Cistercian chapter.

[13] *Newminster Chartul.* (Surtees Soc.), 238.

[14] Reg. of Holmcultram, MS. ff. 40–1, 212.

[15] Ibid. ff. 216–7.

[16] Harl. MS. 3911, f. 63b. In reply to a letter from the king's chancellor, requesting him to send a horse in 1291 to carry the rolls of chancery, Abbot Robert pleaded for delay, 'as God knows' he was at that time unprovided with one fit for the work (*Royal Letters*, No. 1140 ; *Cal. of Doc. Scot.* [Scot. Rec. Pub.], ii. 138). See also Reg. of Holmcultram, MS. A, 201–2 ; Harl. MS. 3891, f. 76b.

[17] His name appears on the famous Ragman Roll for the reason no doubt that his house held lands in Scotland (Stevenson, *Documents*, ii. 68–9 ; *Cal. of Doc. Scot.* [Scot. Rec. Pub.], ii. 196). In 1297 he recovered a rent in Blencreyk against William de Bretteby (*Orig. R.* [Rec. Com.], i. 102).

[18] He must have died in that year, for on 12 August 1318, a letter of safe conduct was issued to the abbot of Melrose that he might come to Holmcultram to preside at the election of a successor (Rymer, *Fædera*, ii. 370). In 1319 William, prior of the house, was sent into Scotland to treat for the liberation of the men of the Bishop of Ely lately captured in the battle of Miton near York (*Rot. Scotiæ*, i. 204, 205).

[19] Harl. MS. 3891, f. 142b. He cannot have been abbot for many years before, for in 1327 he was described as a monk of Holmcultram (*Close Roll*, 1 Edw. III. pt. i. m. 18). He carried out the negotiations with Lady Margaret de Wigton for the transfer and appropriation of the church of Wigton to his house in 1331–2 (Carl. Epis. Reg., Kirkby, ff. 245–9, 280–1).

[20] In this year he made presentation to the church of Dronnok, diocese of Glasgow, the advowson of which had been given to Holmcultram by Edward, King of Scotland (*Glasg. Epis. Reg.* [Bannatyne Club], i. 249–51), and to the church of Wigton, diocese of Carlisle (Carl. Epis. Reg., Kirkby, ff. 333–4).

[21] *Cal. of Papal Petitions*, i. 215 ; *Cal. of Papal Letters*, iii. 453, 461 ; *Chron. Mon. de Melsa*, iii. 108.

[22] Carl. Epis. Reg., Welton, ff. 57, 103. In 1362 he had a dispute with William, perpetual vicar of Wigton, about the will of William de Bromfeld.

Robert de Rawbankes or Rabankes, 1365, 1379[1]

(?) Gregory,[2] temp. Richard II.

(?) Robert Pym, ascribed to the fifteenth century[3]

William Reddekar, circa 1434[4]

Thomas York, circa 1458–65.[5] Vacancy in 1472[6]; again in 1480[7]

Robert Chamber, 1507, 1512,[8] 1518[9]

John Nicolson[10]

Matthew Dyves or Deveys, 1531[11]

Thomas Ireby, Yerbye, or Jerbye, 1533, 1536

Thomas Carter, 1537

Gawen Borudale (Borrodale), last abbot, 1538

The seal of the convent attached to the deed of surrender[12] bears a full length figure of the Blessed Virgin with the Child on her left arm and the inscription slightly mutilated : SI : COMUNE : ABBATIS : ET : CONVENTUS : DE : HOLM : COLTRAM.

In the British Museum there is the cast of a seal, injured in places by pressure, and ascribed to the thirteenth century,[13] which may have belonged to Abbot Gervase (1274, 1279), or to either of his predecessors, Gregory or Gilbert. It is a pointed oval. The Virgin with a crown holds the Child on the left arm and stands on a shield of the arms of England under a trefoiled canopy supported on slender shafts. At the base of the shield are two busts with hands supporting it. On each side is a small niche containing, on the left a saint with crown and sceptre, on the right a bishop or abbot. In the base is a lion dormant. The legend has been mutilated : S. C . . . . BATIS ET CONVENTVS DE HOLMCOLTRAM.

A counter-seal of the thirteenth century[14] bore a right hand vested, holding a pastoral staff, embowered with foliage, with the words : CONTRA SIGILLUM DE HOLMO[15]

There is in the British Museum the cast of a seal ascribed to Abbot Thomas,[16] of date about 1350. The abbot is standing under a canopy supported on slender shafts with a pastoral staff in his right hand and a book in his left. In the base is a lion's face and outside the shafts on each side is a wavy sprig of foliage. This legend is imperfect : SIGILLUM ABBA . . . HOLMCOLTRAM.

---

[1] Carl. Epis. Reg., Appleby, ff. 144, 314; Exch. Cler. Subs. bdle. 61, No. 1, diocese of Carl. See also Cal. of Doc. Scot. (Scot. Rec. Pub.), iv. 47. In the porch of the abbey church there still exists a fragment of his tomb with the lettering '. . . DE RAWBANKYS ABBAS . . .'

[2] Reference to Abbot Gregory is made in a case for the opinion of counsel about 1720, that in the time of Richard II. he demanded tithe from the copyholders of Holmcultram.

[3] In the British Museum a cast of a signet bears the legend : 'ROB'TI PYM ABB'TIS DE HOLME' (Cat. of Seals, i. 586). These two abbots are received into the list with much hesitation.

[4] Fuller, Worthies of England, (ed. Nichols), i. 240–1. The gravestone of this abbot, dug up in 1867, shows beneath a rich canopy a pastoral crook with a shield on either side bearing a cross moline and lion rampant, the arms of the monastery. Around the edge runs the inscription : 'HIC IACET WILLM̄S RY(DE)KAR ABBAS XXI (?) DE HOLME COLTRAN CVIVS AIE PROPICIETUR DEUS, AMEN.'

[5] Arch. Æliana (old ser.), ii. 399. He was selected in 1458 to act as one of the English commissioners for the preservation of truces with the Scots (Rot. Scotiæ, ii. 387–8). One of the bells of Holmcultram is inscribed with the legend in black letter : ' + IHS : THOMAS : YORK : ABBAS : DE : HOLM : CŪ : DOMINIO : ANNO : DNI : MILLº : CCCC : LXV.' There is also a fragment at one of the farm houses in the parish which carries a shield with his initials supported by monks.

[6] Liber S. Marie de Melros (Bannatyne Club), i. 596–9.

[7] In the accounts of the diocesan registrar of Carlisle for 20 Edw. IV. the following payment is on record : 'Et soluti iiij clericis Karlioli existentibus apud Rosam ad benedictionem abbatis de Holme, ijs.'

[8] For the date of this abbot see ante, pp. 169–70.

[9] In this year, 10 Hen. VIII., he appointed Thomas Lord Dacre and William his son as stewards of all the abbey lands (Nicolson MS. iii. 107).

[10] The only notice of Abbot John Nekalson or Nicolson that has been found is in a memorandum among the family papers of Chambers of Raby, dated in 1591, now in the parish chest of Holmcultram, and submitted to the writer for inspection by Mr. F. Grainger. It is as follows : 'Lord Robt. Chambers rygned the abbet of Holem lordshep 30 yeates, and after him rygned John Nekalson 5 yeares, and after him rygned Thomas Jerbie fower yeates and moor, and after him rygned on(e) Gaven Borradell tow yeares and moor wᶜʰ waes the last of all the lords (abbits cancelled in the MS.). Abbet Chambers died threscore year and towell (twelve) yeares senc, 1591.' He is also mentioned in another list of abbots who succeeded Chamber (Nicolson MS. iii. 100).

[11] For this abbot and his successors, see ante, p. 170.

[12] Aug. Off. Deed of Surrender.

[13] B. M. Seals 3288.

[14] Ibid. 3289.

[15] Cal. of Doc. Scot. ii. 542.

[16] B. M. Seals 3290. There is also the signet of Abbot Robert Pym used as a counterseal. It shows a pastoral staff (ibid. 3291).

4. THE ABBEY OF CALDER

The abbey of Calder is situated in a wooded recess nearly a mile from the village of Calderbridge, on the high road midway between Egremont and Gosforth, in the south-west of the county, not far from the priory of St. Bees. It was an affiliation of the neighbouring monastery of Furness and at first of the order of Savigny which in 1148 was united to the Cistercian Order.[1] As no chartulary of the house is known to exist, we are dependent for its history on incidental notices gathered from various sources.

From a trustworthy narrative of the founding of the abbey of Byland in Yorkshire[2] by Philip the third abbot of that monastery, we derive almost all we know of the early history of Calder with great fulness of detail. As Abbot Philip obtained his information from Roger his predecessor, one of the original monks of Calder, and as his story fits in well with the local events of the period and contradicts no ascertained historical facts, it may be taken that his narrative is worthy of credit. Other evidences of undoubted authority seem to support his statements.

This abbey is the third house in the county which owes its origin to the great and famous family of Ranulf Meschin, the first Norman lord of Cumberland. The priory of Wetheral was founded by him in the early years of the reign of Henry I., and the priory of St. Bees was founded by his brother, William Meschin, soon after 1120, both as cells of the Benedictine abbey of St. Mary, York. It may be admitted that Ranulf, the son of William, took an interest in St. Bees, which lies within the fee of Coupland, and was a great benefactor of his father's foundation. The time came, perhaps after his father's death, when this Ranulf founded another house at Calder[3]

a few miles from his baronial seat at Egremont. The abbey was founded on 10 January 1134, when Ranulf gave the land of Calder (Kaldra) with its appurtenances for that purpose. It was at a later date probably that he added 'Bemertone' and 'Holegate,' a burgage in Egremont, two saltpans at Whitehaven, fisheries in the Derwent and Egre, pasture for the cattle of the monks in his forest, and materials for building their houses. A colony of twelve monks with Gerold as their abbot went out from Furness and occupied the new foundation. Abbot Philip of Byland has left their names on record, viz. Robert de Insula, Tocka de Loncastre, John de Kynstan, Theodoric de Dalton, Orm de Dalton, Roger the sub-cellarer, Alan de Wrcewyk, Guy de Bolton, William de Bolton, Peter de Pictaviis, Ulf de Ricomonte and Bertram de London. These monks remained in community at Calder for four years, living in great hardship and privation under the constitutions of the order of Savigny in Normandy, to which at that time the abbey of Furness belonged.

The political troubles which followed the death of Henry I. were disastrous to the new institution at Calder. David, King of Scots, while he was laying siege to the castle of Norham, sent William son of Duncan, his nephew, into Yorkshire, who wasted the province of Craven and obtained possession of Furness. The atrocities committed during that expedition by the Picts and Galwegians of the Scottish army are well known.[4] Philip of Bywell tells us that the abbey of Calder was one of the victims of the raid. Thirsting for the blood of the English, 'the barbarian Scots' came unexpectedly with great fury on the newly founded (nuper inceptam) abbey and took away all they could lay hold of, entirely spoiling the house. The desolate monks sought refuge at the gate of Furness, but they were refused admittance. It was said in excuse for the cruelty of the convent that as Abbot Gerold was unwilling to resign his office and absolve his monks from their profession to him, it would have been inconvenient to have had two abbots with

---

[1] Though the abbey of Calder, like all Cistercian churches, was entitled in the name of the Blessed Virgin, we have on record an indulgence, granted by Thomas, Bishop of Whithern, and dated at Furness on 26 July 1314, for the soul of Richard Carpenter, who formerly lived in the vill of 'Goderthwayt' and was buried in the churchyard of St. Andrew within the monastery of Calder (Duchy of Lanc. Chart. Box A, No. 121).

[2] Dugdale, Mon. v. 349–53.

[3] Pope Eugenius III. (1145–53) said in a letter that William son of Duncan gave Calder to the monks of Furness, but further on he qualified the statement by saying that 'Ranulf Mustin' was the real founder (Dugdale, Mon. v. 249–50). At the time of the suppression, the tradition was that the abbey 'was founded by Lord Raynalld Meschynne, lord of Copland, in 1134' (Harl. MS. 604, f. 122).

[4] The Priory of Hexham, i. 82. Canon Raine has pointed out the singularity of King David's injunction to his nephew William son of Duncan that he should devastate the district of which he was feudal chief. The only explanation seems to be that an effort was made in 1138 to keep William out of his inheritance. John of Hexham tells us that the seignory of Skipton was restored to him in 1151 by King David. It is almost certain that Ranulf Meschin was dead at the time of the raid.

their communities dwelling in the same abbey. Others have assigned a more sordid motive to the monks of Furness. We need not follow the wanderings of the monks of Calder till, under the protection of Archbishop Thurstin and by his mediation, they were established at Byland. One cart drawn by a team of eight oxen was sufficient to convey all their books and household stuff as they set out from Calder never to return. As soon as Abbot Gerold had found a resting place and begun to increase in this world's goods, fearing lest the abbot of Furness would exercise a patronal jurisdiction over him, he set out to Normandy and laid the whole truth of his departure from Calder before Serle, abbot of Savigny. On the feast of St. John the Baptist, 1142, a chapter general of the Order was held and he was released from his allegiance to Furness. Returning to England in haste, he repaired to York, where he died on 24 February following. Roger, who had come from Furness with him and was sub-cellarer at Calder, was chosen abbot in his place. When the news of these proceedings was noised abroad, the abbot and convent of Furness, perceiving that they had been outwitted by the deceased Gerold, and that the monks who were driven from their gates had submitted themselves and their successors to the church of Savigny and were settled elsewhere with no intention of returning, ordained Hardred, one of their monks, and sent him out, in or about 1143, at the head of another community to occupy the deserted house of Calder. Thus was the succession resumed and the original foundation revived.

, The confusion arising from disputed jurisdiction did not end with Gerold's renunciation of Furness. Abbot Hardred of Calder set up a claim to jurisdiction over Byland on the ground of affiliation, as the monks had departed from his house and the church of Savigny had unjustly obtained their allegiance. Roger, then abbot of Byland, answered with becoming dignity that no such claim could be entertained, and reminded Hardred of their rebuff from the gates of Furness. Ultimately a friendly arrangement was made and the claims of Calder were abandoned. On the other hand the convent of Furness challenged jurisdiction over Byland by similar arguments, but at a general chapter in the presence of many abbots and priors of the northern counties, with the famous Ælred of Rievaulx as referee, the claims of Furness were disallowed.

It is needless to say that the successors of Ranulf Meschin in the barony of Coupland, including William son of Duncan, his

brother-in-law, who had previously ravaged the district, continued to befriend the abbey and augment its possessions. Cecily, Countess of Albemarle and lady of Coupland, confirmed the monks in all their lands, for the souls of her father and mother and of King Henry, to which Master Robert the constable, Isaac de Scheftling, Simon de Scheftling, William Chirtelig, William de Scheftling and Thomas, chaplain of the countess, were witnesses. The example of the founder's successors was followed by the landowners of the vicinity. William de Esseby and Hectred his wife, benefactors of St. Bees, gave Beckermet and the mill of that place in memory of William, Earl of Albemarle, and Cecily the countess, and of Ingelram the earl's brother, as the donor had received it from the earl. The witnesses of this deed were Richard, prior of St. Bees, Robert priest (*presbiter*) of Ponsonby, Roger priest of Egremont, Jurdan parson of Goseford, Richard son of Osbert of St. Brigid, Richard vicar of the same church, and Ketel son of Ulf. Beatrice de Molle bestowed on the monks 5 oxgangs of land in Little Gilcrux (Gillecruch) and the fourth part of the mill in Great Gilcrux. The land had been previously confirmed to Beatrice by Adam son of Uhtred, her uncle, as the gift of William, his nephew, as the charter of the said William son of Liolf de Molle testified. Richard de Boisville gave 10 acres of land in his part of Culdreton with common of pasture pertaining thereto.

The lords of Millom were also benefactors of Calder. By a charter given at 'Milnam' in the month of April, 1287, John de Hudleston bestowed on the abbey pasture for six cows, four horses and forty sheep with their following on the common of Millom, saving to the monks the other privileges granted by his ancestors. At a later date in 1291, John son of John de 'Hideleston' gave William son of Richard de Loftscales his 'native' and all his belongings, quit of all villenage as far as the donor was concerned.[1] The abbot paid a fine in 1300 for the alienation in mortmain to his convent by John de Hudleston of 8½ acres of land, 1 acre of meadow

---

[1] The six charters, of which a summary is given above, were copied by the Rev. John Hodgson in 1830 'from the originals in possession of W. J. Charlton of Hesleyside, Esq., which came into his family in 1680 by the marriage of his great-great-grandfather with Mary, daughter of Francis Salkeld of Whitehall, in the parish of All-hallows, Cumberland,' and were printed in full by him in *Arch. Æliana*, ii. 387–90. S. Jefferson has given a good account of these charters in *Allerdale Ward*, 314–7.

in Bootle, and a place in Millom called 'Barkerhals' containing 9¾ acres of land and 1½ acres of meadow.[1]

The abbey had also been endowed by John son of Adam and Matthew his brother with the whole land of 'Stavenerge'; by Robert Bonekill, with a carucate in Little Gilcrux (Gillecruz) which Ralf the clerk of Carlisle occupied, 12 acres and 1 perch in Little Gilcrux, 1 acre of meadow between these two places and pasture for twenty oxen, twelve cows and six horses with their following of one year; by Roger son of William with land in 'Ikelinton' and 'Brachamton' and part of the mill in the latter place; by Richard de Lucy, with a moiety of the mill in Ikelinton[2]; by Thomas son of Gospatric, with a toft in Workington, an annual gift of twenty salmon, and a net in the Derwent between the bridge and the sea; and by Thomas de Multon, with a moiety of the vill of 'Dereham in Alredale' with the advowson of the church of the same vill. These donations were confirmed to the monks in 1231 by charter[3] of Henry III.

The convent was called upon from time to time to defend its title to its possessions. Adam son of Gilbert de Comwyntyn impleaded the abbot in 1279 in respect of a messuage in Cockermouth as the right of Emma his wife.[4] Certain manorial privileges of the abbey lands were questioned by the Crown in 1292, when it was stated that the monks had enjoyed them since the reign of Richard I. From this suit at law we gather that the house possessed 3 carucates of land in Gilcrux, a carucate in Dearham, an oxgang in Millom, 10 acres in Irton and 2 oxgangs in Bootle.[5]

The abbey was not rich in appropriated churches. At the time of the dissolution, the monks only possessed the rectories of Cleator, Gilcrux, and of St. John and St.

Bridgid, Beckermet.[6] An attempt was made by Thomas de Multon to transfer the advowson of Dearham from the priory of Gisburn, to which Alice de Romelly had given it, but the attempt failed, and the church continued in the appropriation of the Yorkshire house to the last.[7] In 1262 the Archdeacon of Richmond prevailed on the abbey to bestow upon him the church of Arlecdon (Arlokedene), as he had no convenient retreat in Coupland wherein he could lodge for the exercise of the duties of his vocation.[8] That powerful official had only a poor opinion of the natural features or the climate of Cumberland. It needed the attraction of the church of Arlecdon to induce him to cross the sands of Duddon and to brave the swollen rivers and uncertain weather of that outlying portion of his spiritual charge.[9] An arrangement was made apparently to the advantage of the abbot as well as the archdeacon. The church of Arlecdon had been a trouble to the abbey, inasmuch as the abbot had paid a fine of 40s. in 1255 for having an assize of last presentation against Richard son of John le Fleming.[10] The church of St. John lay near to Calder and to the parish church of St. Bridgid which already belonged to the monks. By judgment of the Archbishop of York, St. John's was appropriated to the abbey in consideration for the abbot's consent to the appropriation of Arlecdon to the archdeaconry of Richmond. It is stated by J. Denton[11] that John le Fleming had given the patronage of the rectory of Arlecdon to Jollan, abbot of Calder, in 1242. The abbot and convent proved their title to the church of Gilcrux in 1357 before Bishop Welton of Carlisle.[12]

Little on record has been found about the history of the abbey church or precincts.   J.

---

[1] Pat. 28 Edw. I. m. 13; Inq. p.m. 20 Edw. I. No. 172.

[2] Roger de Lucy held 15 librates of land in Ickleton (Ikelington) in the hundred of Whittlesford, Cambridgeshire, late of the Honor of Boulogne, and Richard de Lucy held a knight's fee there in 1212 (The Red Book of the Exch. [Rolls Ser.], ii. 529, 582; Testa de Nevill [Rec. Com.], 274b). In 1302–3 the abbot of Calder was assessed at 10s. to the royal aid for the fourth part of a knight's fee held of Thomas de Multon as of the Honour of Boulogne (Feud. Aids, i. 144, 161, 175, 180).

[3] Chart. R. 15 Hen. III. m. 9; Dugdale, Mon. v. 340–1.

[4] Three Early Assize R. of Northumb. (Surtees Soc.), p. 297.

[5] Plac. de Quo. Warr. (Rec. Com.), 116–7.

[6] Valor Eccl. (Rec. Com.), v. 264.

[7] Dugdale, Mon. v. 340–1, No. i.; vi. 271, No. xv.

[8] Ibid. v. 341, Nos. ii. and iii.

[9] By all accounts the climate of Cumberland was considered a distressing experience by outsiders. In this year, 1262, a justice itinerant prayed to be excused going on circuit, 'in partes Cumberlandiæ . . . tum propter loci distantiam, tum propter distemperantiam æris meæ complexioni valde discordantem' (Royal and Hist. Letters, [ed. Shirley], ii. 222).

[10] Fine R. 39 Hen. III. m. 10 (Excerpta E. Rot. Fin. [Rec. Com.], ii. 203).

[11] Cumberland, 27. Denton must have had in mind the plea between the parties in 1241 when the right of Calder was confirmed and the benefits of the prayers of the monastery were granted to John le Fleming (Feet of F. Cumberland, case 35, file 3, No. 26a).

[12] Carl. Epis. Reg., Welton, f. 51.

Denton was of opinion that the abbey 'was not perfected till Thomas de Multon finished the works and established a greater convent of monks there.' In 1361 Bishop Welton issued a licence with indulgence to a monk of that house to collect alms in his diocese for the fabric of the monastery.[1]

It cannot be said that Calder was ever a rich house. In 1292 its temporalities were valued at £32 a year,[2] and in 1535 the gross revenues of the abbey amounted only to £64 3s. 9d., which, after deducting certain outgoings, was reduced to the clear annual income of £50 9s. 3d.[3]

The abbots of Calder do not often appear in the public life of the country. They occasionally come into notice when applying for royal protection to go beyond the sea on the business of their house or to attend the general chapters of the Cistercian Order.[4] In the fourteenth century they were sometimes employed in the collection of ecclesiastical subsidies.[5]

The abbey was visited by the king's commissioners[6] in 1535 and an unfavourable report was made in the Black Book. Five monks, Robert Maneste, William Car, John Gisburne, Matthew Ponsonby, and Richard Preston were accused of uncleanness ; William Thornton and Richard Preston of incontinency ; and John Gisburne and Richard Preston were said to desire freedom from their conventual vows. The only relic of superstition found in the monastery was a girdle of the Blessed Virgin supposed to be efficacious to women in child-bed.[7]

The monastery seems to have been surrendered to the commissioners and dissolved on 4 February 1536, Richard Ponsonby, the abbot, receiving a pension of £12 a year which was to date from the Feast of the Annunciation following. William Blithman was the actual agent in its overthrow. The rectories of St. Bridgid, St. John, St. Leonard, and Gilcrux were leased to William Leigh, but the house and site of the abbey and the adjoining lands were granted to Thomas Leigh, LL.D., the notorious commissioner for the northern suppression. To Dr. Leigh were also given a right of common on Coupland Fells and the fishery called Monkegarth on the sea sands near Ravenglass.[8] The clear annual value of the doctor's grant was £13 10s. 4d., and the rent of 27s. 1d. due to the Crown continued to be paid by the owners of Calder Abbey till its late owner redeemed it.

ABBOTS OF CALDER

Gerold, 1134, afterwards abbot of Byland, Yorks

Hardred (Hardreus), circa 1143 [9]

Adam, towards the close of the twelfth century [10]

David, circa 1200 [11]

John, circa 1211 [12]

G., circa 1218 [13]

Ralf [14]

Jollan, 1241–6 [15]

John, 1246 [16]

Nicholas, circa 1250 [17]

Walter, circa 1256 [18]

William, circa 1262 [19]

Warin, circa 1286 [20]

---

[1] Carl. Epis. Reg., Welton, f. 81.

[2] *Pope Nich. Tax.* (Rec. Com.), 329 b.

[3] *Valor Eccl.* (Rec. Com.), v. 264.

[4] Pat. 16 Edw. I. m. 6 ; 20 Edw. I. m. 7.

[5] Ibid. 14 Edw. III. pt. ii. m. 45 ; 15 Edw. III. pt. i. m. 32 ; Close, 6 Edw. III. m. 16 d.

[6] Harl. MS. 604, f. 122.

[7] The *Compendium Compertorium* or 'Cleane Booke of Compertes,' as arranged by John ap Rice, otherwise called the 'Black Book,' is well known. Fragments of it will be found in L. *and P. Hen. VIII.* x. 364 ; Cott. MS. Cleop., E, iv. 147 ; Lansd. MS. 988, f. 1.

[8] L. *and P. Hen. VIII.* vol. xii. (i.), 1025 ; vol. xiii. (i.), 577, 588. The grant to Dr. Leigh has been enrolled on Pat. 30 Hen. VIII. pt. vi. m. 20, of which an abstract has been made in the L. *and P. Hen. VIII.* vol. xiii. (i.), 1519 (71).

[9] Duchy of Lanc. Chart. Box B, No. 262.

[10] He was contemporary with Prior Robert of St. Bees and witnessed Richard de Lucy's charter of incorporation to the borough of Egremont (*Trans. Cumb. and Westmld. Arch. Soc.* i. 282–4).

[11] Duchy of Lanc. Chart. Box B, No. 80, printed in Farrer's *Lanc. Pipe R. and Early Chart.* 362. He was a witness to this charter.

[12] An unnamed abbot of Calder received benediction from Ralf, Bishop of Down, in 1211 (*Chron. of Melrose*, in anno ; *Chron. de Lanercost*, 2), and about the same time John, abbot of Calder, witnessed several charters (Duchy of Lanc. Chart. Box B, Nos. 164, 260 ; Reg. of Fountains abbey [Cott. MS. Tib. C, xii.], ff. 104–11).

[13] With Augustin, prior of Conishead, he witnessed a deed in the Reg. of St. Bees (Harl. MS. 434), vij. 5.

[14] Dugdale, *Mon.* v. 340. Professed obedience to Archbishop Walter Gray (1216–55).

[15] Between these dates he was engaged in suits at law with John le Fleming, Alexander de Ponsonby, and John, prior of Conishead, about the property of the abbey (Feet of F. Cumberland, case 35, file 3, Nos. 26a, 34, 54b).

[16] J. Denton, *Cumberland*, 23.

[17] Duchy of Lanc. Chart. Box B, No. 187.

[18] Reg. of St. Bees, MS. xii. 1 ; Denton, *Cumberland*, 23.

[19] Dugdale, *Mon.* v. 341.

[20] *Trans. Cumb. and Westmld. Arch. Soc.* ix. 232.

Elias, 1298 [1]
Richard, 1322,[2] 1334 [3]
Nicholas de Bretteby (Birkby), 1367 [4]
Richard, circa 1432 [5]
Robert de Wilughby [6]
John, 1462 [7]
John Whalley, 1464
John Bethom, 1501

Lawrence Marre, 1503–13
John Parke, 1516
John Clapeham, 1521
Richard Ponsonby, 1525–36

Only one impression of the seal of this house is known.[8] It is a pointed oval, showing an abbot in vestments. The legend is much mutilated : + . . . TIS DE CALDRA.

HOUSES OF BENEDICTINE MONKS

5. THE PRIORY OF ST. BEES [9]

The Benedictine priory of St. Bees occupies a favourable position on the western coast at the opening of a valley sheltered by a great berg or hill, which projects into the sea like a vast irregular bastion, and is known as St. Bees Head. It is said that the valley which connects the promontory with the mainland was once traversed by the tide. But there is no warrant for assuming that any appreciable change has taken place in the physical configuration of the neighbourhood within the historic period. As the site of the priory marks the level of the valley beneath the south-eastern spur of the headland, the sea must have receded long before its foundation.

The priory took its name from a previous religious establishment, of which nothing seems to have survived till the twelfth century except the tradition of its former existence. From the legendary life of Bees or Bega, written in all probability by a monk of the priory at a late date,[10] we learn that she was the daughter of an Irish king, who reigned as a Christian monarch in the seventh century. For good reasons she fled from her father's court, and taking ship, landed after a prosperous voyage 'in a certain province of England called Coupland.' Bega found the place covered with a thick forest, and admirably adapted for a solitary life. Wishing to dedicate her life to God, she built for herself a virgin cell in a grove near the seashore, where she remained for many years in strict seclusion and devout contemplation. In the course of time the district began to be frequented by pirates. The good saint however dreaded not death, nor mutilation, nor the loss of temporal goods, of which she was destitute except her bracelet (*armilla*), but she feared the loss of her virginity, the most precious treasure with which heaven can endow her sex. By divine command Bega hastened her departure from the place, but she was induced to leave her bracelet behind her, that miracles in ages to come might be performed in that neighbourhood in testimony of her holy life.

At this time Oswald was the king of Northumbria, and the holy Aidan was the chief bishop of Lindisfarne. To the bishop, Bega directed her steps and disclosed the secret of her heart. The man of God, struck by her story, admitted her to sacred vows, putting upon her head a veil for a royal diadem and a black garment for a purple robe, for before that date, as Bede testified, the kingdom of Northumbria was without nuns. By the

[1] Dugdale, *Mon.* v. 340.   [2] Ibid.
[3] Close, 7 Edw. III. pt. ii. m. 4d.
[4] Dugdale, *Mon.* v. 340 ; *Dur. Obit. R.* (Surtees Soc.), p. 58.
[5] *Testamenta Eboracensia* (Surtees Soc.), iii. 327. Quotation from Register of the Archdeacon of Richmond in Harl. MS. 6978, f. 25b.
[6] A monumental inscription still preserved among the ruins of the abbey, records the name of this abbot whose place in the list is not known, but entered here as being its probable position. The inscription may be thus read : HIC IACET DOMPNVS ROBERTVS DE WILVGHBY ABBAS DE CALDRA CVIVS ANIME PROPICIETVR DEVS.
[7] For this and the subsequent abbots see Dugdale, *Mon.* v. 340 : Torre MS. (York) f. 1408, compiled from the archiepiscopal registers.
[8] *Anct. D.*, L 478.
[9] The source from which the materials for this account of St. Bees has been taken, is, unless otherwise stated, the chartulary of the priory, Harleian MS. 434.
[10] The story of the life and miracles of St. Bega is written on a small folio of vellum among the Cotton MSS. Faustina B. iv. ff. 122–31. It was printed at Carlisle in 1842 by Samuel Jefferson,

with a translation, introduction and notes by G. C. Tomlinson. The author's name is unknown. All historical notice of the saint appears to have been lost from the time of her death, except the incidental allusion to her connection with St. Hilda by the venerable Bede (*Historia Eccles.* iv. 23), but the writer of her life determined to collect all that had survived by tradition. Sir Thomas Hardy ascribed the compilation to the end of the twelfth century (*Descriptive Catalogue of Materials*, Rolls Ser. i. 224–5). From the internal evidence in the account of the saint's miracles the writer is inclined to put the date at a much later period.

influence of St. Aidan she prevailed on King Oswald to grant her a place fit for religious uses, by name 'Hereteseia,' which by interpretation is called Hartlepool. Here she built a beautiful monastery to which many maidens flocked for the service of religion. Thus the pious Bega was the first to establish a nunnery in Northumbria.

Several centuries have elapsed since the historian gathered up the traditions of the priory, and wove them into a connected story. We have little to say about the life or miracles of the saint except as they bear on the district with which her name is connected. Leland mentions that 'Bega at first built a humble little monastery in Coupland not far from Carlisle in the extreme limits of England where there are now so many monks of St. Mary's, York, commonly called Sainct Beges,'[1] but the venerable Bede is silent on the saint's residence in Cumberland. The legendary life gives no support to the belief that a nunnery was continued at St. Bees after Bega had taken her departure. If such were the case, all trace of it must have been lost during those dark centuries in northern history which preceded the Norman Conquest.

There can be little doubt that the influence of Bega was a power in the south-western portion of the county in the early years of the twelfth century. The district had borne her name, and a parish church was entitled in her honour before the Norman lord of that place determined to found a religious house within a few miles of his baronial seat at Egremont. The date of the foundation of the priory by William Meschin, the first Norman owner of Coupland, can only be approximately given. His first charter was, as one might say, only declaratory of his intention to proceed with the undertaking. It was also an invitation to his own knights and to the proprietors of neighbouring fiefs to aid him in the work. The new institution was to be founded as a cell or subordinate house of the great abbey of St. Mary near the walls of York, to which his family apparently owed some obligation. In the first instance he made it known that he had given to God, St. Mary and the holy virgin Bega, six carucates of land in Kirkby (Cherchebi), as well as the manor which William the Bowman (balistarius) had in addition, and moreover that he would confirm similar gifts for the same purpose by any of his knights from their own lands. Most of those who witnessed this deed, Waldeve, Reiner, Godard, Ketel, William the chaplain, Coremac and Gillebecoc, were

afterwards the foremost in forwarding the scheme. When the project had taken practical form, Thurstin, Archbishop of York, in whose diocese the barony of Coupland was included, was called in to advise on the character of the institution about to be established. It is evident that the great archbishop was the moving spirit of the whole scheme. The large landowners of the neighbourhood associated themselves with the founder, and contributed their share to its first endowment. Waldeve, lord of Allerdale below Derwent, who had received his barony from Henry I., granted the manor of Stainburn ; Ketel gave Preston ; Reiner, two oxgangs of land in Rottington with the native who dwelt there. As a supplement to his former gift, William Meschin added the church of Kirkby and its parish, the bounds of which were defined by trustworthy men as from Whitehaven to the river Keekle (Chechel), and as the Keekle falls into the Egre, and as the Egre flows to the sea. He also gave the chapel of Egremont within the said bounds and the tithes of his domain and of all his men, as well as the tithes of his fisheries and the skins of his venison. One of the most interesting grants in the early endowment of the priory was that of Godard, lord of Millom, who gave the churches of Whicham (Witingam) and Bootle (Bothle), with two manses (mansuræ), and their whole parishes and tithes. The gift was made by the advice and assent of William the founder, his liege lord, in the presence of Archbishop Thurstin on the day of the dedication of the church of St. Bees for the special purpose of finding lights for divine service. These churches and estates were demised to the Benedictine abbey of St. Mary, York, with the view of founding a monastic establishment in the church of St. Bees consisting of a prior and six monks of their obedience. The pious work was done for the health of King Henry and Archbishop Thurstin, for the souls of Queen Maud and William the Atheling, and for the relief (pro remedio) of his ancestors and successors. From these deeds it may be inferred that the foundation of the priory could not have taken place before 1120.[2]

William Meschin the founder paid a graceful tribute to the co-operation of his wife

---

[1] Collectanea (ed. Hearne, 1774), v. 39.

[2] The good Queen Maud died in 1118 and was buried at Westminster (Hoveden, Chron. [Rolls Ser.] i. 172). Thurstin was not consecrated Archbishop of York till 19 October, 1119 (Symeon of Durham, Opera et Coll. [Surtees Soc.], p. 110). William the son of Henry I. was lost at sea in the wreck of the White Ship in 1120.

Cecily and his son Ranulf in his efforts to establish the institution. His children and descendants in after years were foremost among its benefactors. To the memory of his father and by the advice of Fulk, his uncle, Ranulf gave the monks the manor of Ennerdale (Avenderdale), and endowed them with many liberties in his woods and forests. Alice de Romilly, when she became owner of the barony on the death of Ranulf her brother, was a munificent patron of her father's foundation. There can be no truth in the story that Ranulf Meschin was jealous of the possessions of the priory, and sought to diminish the boundaries of their franchise. It is said that men, envious of the monastic life, had instilled into that nobleman's ear that the monks had encroached upon his lands. In the suits at law which ensued the cause was defended, and ample evidences were produced on behalf of the priory, but no agreement could be arrived at. On the day appointed for measuring the landmarks and setting the bounds, the dispute was settled by divine intervention, for the whole of the surface of the adjacent country was covered with a deep snow, but within the bounds that the monks had attached to the church of St. Bees not the vestige of a single flake appeared.

It would be tedious to enumerate the gifts of lands, churches and rents made to the monks at various periods. Numerous deeds of endowment have been preserved in the fine chartulary of the priory. Landowners, great and small, distinguished and obscure, had contributed a share to its possessions. But there is one noticeable feature of the endowments worthy of special mention. It is very remarkable how the traditions of a family were carried on in connection with a single religious house. It is not only true that the descendants of William Meschin in the barony of Coupland were generous to his foundation, but the descendants of Waldeve, Ketel, Godard and Reiner, who were associated with him in its first establishment, were liberal in their benefactions. In fact it might be said that the priory owed whatever measure of prosperity it possessed to the munificence of these families, the Romillys, Albemarles, Lucys, Multons, Curwens, Milloms, Hudlestons, Rotingtons and others.

Though most of the property of the priory was confined to that portion of the county bordering on St. Bees, where the magnates in question lived, the monks kept up a frequent communication with the Isle of Man, where they enjoyed some manors. It is said that the prior of St. Bees had a seat in the little parliament of that kingdom. It is very probable.

Guthred, King of the Isles, gave the priory the land called 'Eschedale' and 'Asmundertofts' quit of all service, *tam de pecunia quam de aconeux,* in exchange for the church of St. Olave and the little vill of 'Evastad.' King Ragdnald bequeathed the land of 'Ormeshau' which lay towards the sea at the port of 'Corna,' while King Olave granted licence to buy and sell in the island. The abbot and convent of Rushen were consenting parties to some of these charters. In later years, when Thomas Ranulf, earl of Moray, and Anthony Bec, Bishop of Durham, ruled the island, the grants of the former kings were recognized and confirmed. The priory also owned some property in the south-west of Scotland, chiefly of the gift of the families of Curwen and Brus.

In comparison with the other monastic houses in the county St. Bees was wealthy, ranking in the matter of revenues after Holmcultram and Carlisle. In 1291 the cell was valued at £66 13s. 4d., and in 1535 the gross annual income was assessed for taxation at £149 19s. 6d. or £143 16s. 2d. after the deduction of reprises.[1] In 1545 a sum of £280 2s. was returned to the Augmentation Office as the total issues of the late priory with arrearages.[2]

In 1178 the church of Neddrum, now called Island Magee in Strangford Lough, was remodelled into a monastic establishment by Sir John de Courcy, the conqueror of Ulster, and affiliated to St. Bees, as a cell of St. Mary of York. The island was a portion of the ancient possessions of the see of Down, but as Malachi, the bishop, was a prisoner in the hands of Sir John, his consent to the alienation was easily obtained. In the bishop's confirmation of the grant it is stated that, when he gave and confirmed to the monks of St. Bees the church and two-thirds of all the lands and benefices belonging to it, he was acting of his own free will out of devotion to God, and not under any compulsion. Courcy's gift was also confirmed by Thomas and Eugene, archbishops of Armagh. The monks of St. Bees do not seem to have taken kindly to their Irish relation, for no memorandum of the transaction was made in the register of their house. The only connection that we have noticed between the two institutions is that one of the early priors of St. Bees was transferred to the priory of Neddrum. Its conventual existence seems to have been of short duration, for at the date of the taxation of Pope Nicholas it is mentioned simply as the church of Neddrum, and was

---

[1] *Pope Nich. Tax.* (Rec. Com.), 308 ; *Valor Eccl.* (Rec. Com.), v. 11.
[2] Dugdale, *Mon.* iii. 580.

valued at the small sum of seven marks.[1] The chief relic to which the monks of St. Bees paid veneration was the bracelet above mentioned, which St. Bega left behind her on her flight from Cumberland. In the legendary life of the saint several stories are told of the power of this talisman. It had been the means of convincing Walter Espec, the great Yorkshire baron, that he was claiming wrongfully some possessions of the abbey of St. Mary, York ; and it brought destruction on Adam, son of Ailsi, who had forsworn himself in favour of the lord of Coupland on the subject of the Noutgeld to the detriment of the people of that district. On one occasion, when the holy bracelet was exhibited in public on account of its great sanctity, a certain perverse creature sacrilegiously stole the precious cloth in which it had been wrapped and hid it in his boot. By the vengeance of St. Bega the leg of the thief became paralysed, and thus was his sin discovered. Having been carried to the priory church, he confessed his guilt, and his leg was restored to its original soundness by the goodness of the most merciful Virgin, who is wont to pity those who are truly penitent. There can be no doubt that the bracelet of St. Bega was a powerful institution in Coupland. The monks used it to give special sanction to their agreements. Obligations were rendered pre-eminently binding and sacred when they were made on the bracelet. For instance, John de Hale, for the greater security of faithfully observing his obligation, bound himself and his heirs on his corporal oath by touching the holy relics *et super armillam sancte Bege*. The touching of the relics was the usual mode of taking an oath, but in matters of high importance the bargain was made upon the bracelet as the means of giving it the greatest sanction.

The priory appears to have had little dealings with the ecclesiastical world in its papal or diocesan aspect. There are few papal documents in the register. Far removed from the centre of the great diocese of York, it pursued the even tenor of its way in solitude. It is true there are some deeds of the mother house of St. Mary and some commissions from the archbishop with the mention here and there of an archdeacon of Richmond, but they are comparatively few in number. Unlike the religious houses or the county within the bounds of the see of Carlisle, episcopal authority was seldom invoked for the purpose of discipline or for the confirmation of the acts of the convent. At some date between 1154 and 1181 Archbishop Roger of Pont l'Evêque confirmed to the priory all their churches, chapels and tithes in Coupland, with the lands belonging to them, viz. the churches of Workington, Gosforth, Corney, Bootle, Whitbeck and Whicham ; the chapels of Harrington, Clifton, Loweswater, and the chapel and tithes of Weddicar. He also freed the church of St. Bees for ever from attendance on synods, and from all aids to archbishop or archdeacon, at the same time granting the priory disciplinary powers to deal with the clergy of their appropriate churches. Except for the short period during the reign of Stephen, when David, King of Scots, exercised sovereignty over Cumberland as far south as the river Duddon, the kings claimed no royal prerogative in confirming the charters of this house.

The priors of St. Bees did not take a prominent part in the public affairs of church or state. Some of them, like Alan de Nesse, Roger Kirkeby and Edmund Thornton, rose to high dignity on becoming abbots of York; but few of the others were known outside their immediate surroundings. In 1219 Pope Honorius III. appointed the priors of St. Bees, Lancaster and Cartmel to determine a dispute between the abbot of Furness and the vicars of Dalton and Urswick about the right of burial in the chapelry of Hawkshead ; they delivered judgment in favour of the monastery, and ordered the chapel yard to be consecrated for sepulture. At a later date Gregory IX. delegated plenary authority to the priors of the same houses as a sort of ecclesiastical syndicate to dissolve sentences of excommunication and interdict against the Cistercian monasteries of the province of York.[2] It will be seen from the list of priors that we have been able to collect how few of them had attained to anything like distinction in the general history of the county. Perhaps the geographical isolation of the district had a depressing effect on the chances to promotion of its leading ecclesiastical magnates.

John Matthew, who was prior while the clouds were beginning to gather around the monastic houses, was not a favourite with his superior, William, abbot of York. In a letter ascribed to the year 1533, the abbot

---

[1] Nine deeds connected with this transaction have been printed in a summary by Dugdale (Dugdale, *Mon.* iii. 575–6) from the Cotton MS., but they have been given more at length by Reeves (*Eccl. Antiq. of Down*, 187–97). The Cotton Roll is much mutilated, but Dr. Reeves has deciphered the material parts of the charters.

[2] Beck, *Ann. Furnesienses*, 43, 181, 185.

told Cromwell that 'this man, in whos favor ye writ to me of, hayth beyn prior at Lincoln and at seynt Martin's, parcell of our monasterie, who alwey hayth beyn of such ordre, condicions and liberalte that he thereby brought our house to great dettes and other cherges and vexacions.' On representations from Cromwell, Matthew was transferred to the priory of St. Martin near Richmond. Sir George Lawson, in support of the abbot's action, told the secretary that the prior was 'a verey yll husband as hath bene well proved at Lincoln, Saynt Martyn's and Seynt Bees where he hathe bene prior. And now of late gret complayntes cumyng of extorcion and other gret urgent wronges done at Saynt Bees to the tenauntes and inhabitantes ther. Wherapon on Saynt Calixt daye last, at the generall chapitor yerely holden at Saynt Mary abbey, as the usuall custume is, when all the priors of the celles and other hede officers of the said Monasterie dothe assemble to see and aview the state and accomptes of the same, knowing the demeanor and yll husbandrye of the said Dan John, exchanged and revoked hym from Saynt Bees. And yete when he shuld have bene a conventuall, for your sake and favour of your former letter, named hym to be prior of Saynt Martynes, a propir Celle nye unto Richemond and a reasonable good liffing, whiche he cold never obtayne but in your favour. And now it is reported unto you that he shuld be otherwise entreated, whiche of a suretie is not so, but my lord abbott dothe and woll do at your complentacion all that reasonably is to be done. And yete his brethren and covent is sore sett against the said dan John Mathew for his mysdemeanour many wayes.' Sir George urged Cromwell 'to give no credens to any person that shall make suite or labour agaynst my said lord abbott, for it hath not bene sene that any perpetuite hath bene graunted undir covent seale to such like person' as 'Dan John Mathew, late prior of Saynt Bees, without a special and urgent cause and a man proved of good demeanour and husbandrye for the well of his house.' Robert Cokett, a kinsman of the deposed prior, denied all the charges made against him, and appealed 'to ye gentyllmen and yomen in ye cowntre with all ye honest men yerin' in proof of John Matthew's honesty and good behaviour.[1] At

the dissolution of the religious houses John Matthew was a cloister monk of St. Mary's, York, and received a pension of £6 13s. 4d.[2] It is evident that Prior Matthew was permanently deposed, for John Poule was incumbent of St. Bees in 1535 when the ecclesiastical survey was made.[3]

The clouds had burst over the religious houses and the end was drawing near. Priors were made or unmade as it suited the royal will. The last prior of St. Bees was Robert Paddy, who caused a memorandum to be entered on the flyleaf of the chartulary of his house that he had agreed with Christopher Lyster for all manner of labour, debts, payments, wages and covenants from the beginning of the world till Michaelmas Day 1538, and that the said Christopher had undertaken to pay at the following Martinmas his yearly rent with all fines due to the said Prior Robert from his entry or coming to the priory. The prior of St. Bees was suspected of complicity with the 'Pilgrimage of Grace.' William, Abbot of York, wrote to Cromwell early in 1537 that he had sent Dan Robert Paddy 'to his room,' but was afraid of what might befall him on the journey. 'I sent him thither,' he said, 'and as it is surmised he should be lettyd by ye commons in these parts in his riding thither un knowledge or writing of me.'[4]

The king's agents in 1536 were unable to find cause of complaint against the prior, and though efforts were made to connect him with the northern rebellion, nothing seems to have come of it. The only evil report made by the commissioners was that two of the monks, John Clyffton and John Fullscroft, were accused of personal depravity. When the priory was surrendered Robert Paddy, the last prior, received an annual pension[5] of £40, the warrant being dated 3 June, 1538. In his survey of the monastery at the time of the dissolution James Rokeby, auditor of the Court of Augmentations, thus described[6] the priory precincts : 'The scite of the late house, with a towre koveryd wt lead called the Yatehouse, and other edificez with garthings lienge within the utter walls, contenyng one acre and di. (a half) and is worth by the yere over and above the reparacons, wt one dufe cote wt in the same scite, vs.'

On 21 November, 1541, Thomas Leighe was granted a lease[7] for twenty-one years of

<hr>

[1] These three letters from the *L. and P. Hen. VIII.* vi. 746, 1359, vii. 295, have been printed as an appendix to a lecture given by the writer before the Carlisle Literary and Scientific Society in March, 1898, and will be found in the Society's *Transactions.*

[2] Dugdale, *Mon.* iii. 569.
[3] *Valor Eccl.* (Rec. Com.), v. 11.
[4] *L. and P. Hen. VIII.* xii. (i.) 132, 133, 640.
[5] Ibid. xiv. (i.) 601.
[6] Dugdale, *Mon.* iii. 578-9.
[7] *L. and P. Hen. VIII.* xvi. 728.

'St. Bege monastery, with the rectory of Kyrkeby Beycoke and chapels of Lowse-water, Ennerdale, Eshedale and Wasedale.'

PRIORS OF ST. BEES

Robert [1]
Deodatus,[2] late twelfth century
Richard [3]
Waleran,[4] circa 1197
Robert,[5] 1202
John,[6] circa 1207
Daniel,[7] circa 1210
Ralf, circa 1220
Guy,[8] circa 1235
John de Lestingham, circa 1254
William de Rothewel, circa 1256
Nicholas de Langeton,[9] circa 1258–82
Benedict, circa 1282–6
Absalon,[10] circa 1287
William de Dereby, circa 1288–94
Hugh de Cumpton, circa 1301
Alan de Nesse,[11] 1313, transferred to St. Mary's, York

William de Seynesbury,[12] 1360
Thomas de Brignol, circa 1370
Thomas de Cotingham,[13] circa 1379
Nicholas de Warthill, circa 1387
Roger Kirkeby,[14] 1434–6
Dr. Stanlaw,[15] circa 1465
John Warde, circa 1474
Roger Armyn, circa 1485
Edmund Smyth or Thornton,[16] circa 1496
Edmund (Whalley ?),[17] circa 1516
Robert Alanby,[18] circa 1523
John Matthew, 1533
John Poule, 1535
Robert Paddy, 1536–8

There is an indistinct cast of a seal [19] at the British Museum, showing what appears to be an ornamented cross, the legend of which is defaced.

An impression of the seal of Prior Absalon, circa 1287, exists.[20] It is a pointed oval, and shows the Lamb of God. The legend is SIGILL' FRIS' ÆSALON' PRIORIS DE BIGEE.

[1] Leland, *Collectanea*, i. 25.
[2] He was prior when Abbot C[lement] of York conferred the chapel of Clifton on Waltheof son of Thomas, clerk of Dene. Among his co-witnesses was William, prior of Wetheral.
[3] He was the first witness to the grant of Beckermet by William de Esseby and Hectreda his wife to the abbey of Calder. The gift was made for the souls of William, Earl of Albemarle, and of his wife Cecily and of Ingelram, the earl's brother (*Arch. Æliana* [old ser.], ii. 388).
[4] He was afterwards prior of Neddrum in Strangford Lough, an affiliation of St. Bees, while Thomas O'Conor and Eugene MacGillivider filled the primacy of Ireland, that is, for the latter part of the period between 1185 and 1216 (Dugdale, *Mon.* iii. 574 ; Reeves, *Antiq. of Down*, 192–3).
[5] He was prior when Richard de Lucy founded the borough of Egremont. The charter has been printed in facsimile in the *Cumb. and Westmld. Arch. Soc. Trans.* i. 281–5 (see ante, i. 329). He was also engaged in a plea with Richard, son of Peter, in 1202, about land in Whitehaven (*Feet of F., Cumb.* 1195-1214 [Rec. Com.] 5). His name occurs often in the chartulary about this date.
[6] Walter of Coventry (Rolls Ser.), ii. 199, with chartulary.
[7] Compare *Itin. of K. John* (Rec. Com.) with chartulary.
[8] He was a contemporary with Ralf, prior of Carlisle, and William Rundel, prior of Wetheral (*Reg. of Wetheral* [Cumb. and Westmld. Arch. Soc.], 345.
[9] Many of his acts have been registered in the chartulary of the priory at various dates between 1258 and 1282.
[10] Anct. D., L. 282.

[11] Dugdale, *Mon.* iii. 538 ; Pat. 7 Edw. II. pt. 1, mm. 20, 15.
[12] *Cal. of Papal Petitions*, i. 315–6, 357–8.
[13] The name of this prior is found often in leases of that date. His grave-cover is still in existence, though in a sadly mutilated condition. It is a fine example of an incised stone bearing the figure of a monk. Around the edge of the slab runs the legend : HIC JACET [BONE MEMO] RIE FRATER THOMAS DE COTYNGHAM QUONDAM PRIOR HUJUS ECCLESIE QUI OBIIT ANNO DNI M°CCC....... CUJUS AĪE PPI' DE'.
[14] Jefferson, *Leath Ward*, p. 495 ; Dugdale, *Mon.* iii. 539.
[15] Hist. MSS. Com. Rep. x. App. pt. iv. 227 (Lord Muncaster's MSS.)
[16] In 1496 William Senhouse, Bishop of Carlisle, was called in to settle a dispute between the prior of the cell of St. Bees and Christopher Sandes about falcons on St. Bees Head (*pro falconibus in lez berghe*). The priory was vacant or the prior was absent in 1498, for in that year William son of Christopher Sandes entered into an agreement with Thomas Barwyke, *custos* of the cell of St. Bees, about the bounds of the land of Rottington.
[17] *L. and P. Hen. VIII.* iv. 2216 ; Dugdale, *Mon.* iii. 539. As Edmund Whalley succeeded Edmund Thornton as abbot of St. Mary's, York, in 1521, it is probable that both of them had been previously priors of St. Bees.
[18] He was late prior of Wetheral and St. Mary's, York. During his priorate, in 1523, there was a threatened invasion by the Duke of Albany, and there are interesting letters between the prior and Lord Dacre, Warden of the Marches, in Add. MS. 24,965, ff. 96, 99.
[19] B.M. Seals, 3953. [20] Anct. D., L. 282.

6. THE PRIORY OF WETHERAL [1]

The priory of Wetheral, of the Benedictine order, was founded in the beautiful valley of the Eden a few miles above Carlisle by Ranulf Meschin, the first Norman lord of Cumberland, at a date not later than 1112 and perhaps in 1106. Ranulf conveyed the manor of 'Wetherhala' and all the land belonging thereto, which no doubt included the churches of Wetheral and Warwick, to Stephen, abbot of St. Mary's, York, in perpetual alms, and when the priory was brought into being as a cell of that great Benedictine house, he supplemented his former gift by the concession of a salmon weir and a water mill in the Eden close to the site of the new institution. The munificent founder soon afterwards gave to the priory the two churches of St. Michael and St. Lawrence in his *castellum* or fortified town of Appleby, and two parts of the tithe of his domain on both sides of the Eden, and two parts of the tithe of Meaburn and Salkeld. From these charters [2] we are not able to gather the size of the institution Ranulf founded, but we afterwards learn that the priory was constituted with twelve monks [3] at the outset, though that number was not maintained at a subsequent date. In the formalities attending the foundation of this house some of the leading men of the district appear for the first time. In one or other of the four charters granted by the founder, such well-known persons as Waldeve son of Earl Gospatric, Forn son of Sigulf, Ketel son of Eldred, Odard, Hildred the knight, Wescubrict, and Godard, are mentioned at this early period. We know little of other local magnates associated with the scheme, such as Richer, sheriff of Carlisle, to whom Ranulf addressed the foundation charter, (unless indeed he be identified with

Richard the knight of subsequent fame,) Hervey son of Morin and Eliphe de Penrith. Of his own relations William Meschin and Richard, his brothers, as well as his wife Lucy, took part in the foundation as witnesses to his charters. The priory was entitled in the name of St. Constantine, but the dedication was afterwards changed to the Holy Trinity and St. Constantine, perhaps an amalgamation of the original dedication with that of the parish church of Wetheral.

The priory had many influential patrons, not only amongst the kings but among the great landowners of the district. Henry I. was of course the first royal patron [4] who confirmed the acts of his subordinate and added to his foundation grants of all the pasture between the Eden and the highway called the 'Hee-strette' running parallel to the river and leading from Carlisle to Appleby, and also the privilege of feeding swine in the king's forest, free of pannage. Other privileges were bestowed by succeeding kings with the exception of Stephen, who had yielded up the land of Carlisle to David, King of Scots, as a preliminary to his attainment of the Crown. The lords of Corby on the opposite side of the Eden were good and generous neighbours to the monks, though at times the fishing rights in the river were the occasion of disputes, but to the credit of both parties be it said that they soon made up their differences and settled their disputes. Some of the greatest families of the district as well as some of the humblest are numbered among the benefactors of the house.

In its ecclesiastical aspect the priory of Wetheral differed very widely from that of St. Bees, though both were cells of the same abbey, arising no doubt from their geographical situation, the one being in the diocese of Carlisle and in close proximity to the cathedral city, and the other being in the vast diocese of York far removed from the centre of diocesan life. The bishops of Carlisle exercised an immediate supervision over the affairs of Wetheral, but no evidence has been traced whereby it may be assumed that a similar oversight was extended to St. Bees either by the archbishops of York or by the arch-

---

[1] The authority for the statements in this article will be found in the *Register of Wetherhal*, edited for the Cumb. and Westmld. Arch. Soc. by J. E. Prescott, D.D., Archdeacon of Carlisle. Reference has been made to the deeds and charters according to their numbers in the printed book, and also to the illustrative documents when taken from original sources. The inferences or historical conclusions, drawn from the documents in notes and appendices, have not always been followed. It should be mentioned that the *Register of Wetherhal* has been printed from late seventeenth century copies of the original, and in consequence there are some manifest corruptions in the text of the charters. A more authoritative text, ascribed to the fourteenth century, has recently been recovered and lodged in the custody of the dean and chapter of Carlisle.

[2] *Reg. of Wetherhal*, Nos. 1-4.

[3] Ibid., Illust. Doc. No. lii.

[4] It is worthy of note that it was Henry I. and not any earlier king who survived in tradition as the royal associate of Ranulf Meschin, while he held Carlisle. Pope Lucius, writing in 1185 to Everard, abbot of Holmcultram, in confirmation of the possessions of that house, spoke of the island of Holmcultram 'Sicut fuit foresta (sive forestata) tempore Henrici Regis senioris et Radulphi comitis Cestrie' (Reg. of Holmcultram, M.S. ff. 137b-141b, Harl. MS. 3911).

deacons of Richmond. At one time the bishops of Carlisle claimed the custody of the priory of Wetheral during a vacancy, as well as the right of institution and deprivation of the priors. These episcopal privileges were contested in 1256 while Robert de Chause was bishop of Carlisle. The dispute was settled in a manner agreeable to the litigants. The bishop consented to relinquish his right to the custody, and to institute the nominee of the abbey of York in consideration of the grant of 2½ marks which the monks were accustomed to receive out of the church of Nether Denton since the episcopate of Bishop Walter.[1] The bishops of Carlisle exercised their ordinary power of visitation when they thought fit, and never gave up the right of benediction and institution of the priors to the very last.

The bishops also kept a firm hand on the churches and spiritual revenues in the diocese which belonged to the priory. Adelulf, the first bishop of the see, confirmed to the monks of St. Mary's, York, the churches they were known to possess in his diocese, viz. the cell of Wetheral with the parish of Warwick, all the tithes of Scotby, the churches of St. Michael and St. Lawrence in Appleby, the churches of Kirkby Stephen, Ormside, Morland, Clibburn, Bromfield, Croglin, and the hermitage of St. Andrew in the parish of Kirkland, with the only condition that the monks should make decent provision for the maintenance of a priest in each of these churches, and pay their episcopal dues which included of course synodals and archidiaconals.[2] As a rule the monks thought it desirable to obtain similar confirmation from successive bishops, thereby differing materially from the priory of St. Bees, in whose register very few of these confirmations from the archbishops have been recorded. It must not be assumed that all these churches continued in the patronage of the priory. As all the religious houses in Cumberland had been founded and for the most part endowed before the diocese of Carlisle enjoyed a regular succession of bishops, many of the churches in the county were in some way connected with these institutions. In after years the bishops were not reluctant to obtain possession of some of these churches where it was possible. It was ever the policy of the see to gain a supremacy within its own jurisdiction. Nor were the heads of houses loth to conciliate the bishops

by an occasional indulgence of this kind, for in many ways the good offices of the bishops of Carlisle were of the greatest moment to the monks.

In 1248 Bishop Silvester obtained from the abbey of York the right of patronage of the churches of Ormside, Musgrave and Clibburn, and also of the churches of Burgh-under-Stanemore and St. Michael in Appleby,[3] all of which remain to the present day in the hand of the Bishop of Carlisle, except the church of Clibburn, which passed into lay patronage in 1874.[4] The laity were not backward in protecting the interest of parishioners in case the appropriate churches of the monks were insufficiently served. In 1366 Sir John de Warthewyk complained in forcible terms to the Archbishop of York that the priory had been dealing unjustly with the churches of Wetheral and Warwick in not supplying proper ministrations.[5]

Papal interference with the affairs of this priory was not always successful. In 1165, when the see of Carlisle was void, Alexander III. granted an indult to the abbey of St. Mary, York, which applied to Wetheral, permitting chaplains to serve in the churches where there were no vicars.[6] Gregory IX., relying on the confirmation of previous bishops, allowed the priory to enter on the appropriation of St. Michael's, Appleby, notwithstanding the opposition of Bishop Walter.[7] But the papal court had not always its own way. In 1309 Clement V. provided a prior for the house in the person of Robert de Gisburne, though the convent of St. Mary's, York, the lawful patrons, had a prior of its own presentation already in possession. The Crown intervened and prohibited the induction of the papal nominee until the letters of collation were examined in regard to any encroachment on the royal prerogative.[8] It is known that at this time Bishop Halton was a prelate of pronounced anti-papal proclivities.[9] By a natural process the controversy with Bishop Kirkby in 1338 about the advowsons of Wetheral and Warwick was referred to Rome, when the English ecclesiastical courts

---

[1] *Reg. of Wetherhal*, No. 34. A record of this convention has been made in Bishop Sterne's Register (Carl. Epis. Reg., Sterne, ff. 251–2), 'Ex Registro Prioratus de Wederhal, ff. 20, 21.

[2] *Reg. of Wetherhal*, Nos. 15, 16.

[3] This deed was extracted in 1664 'ex Registro Prioratus de Wederhal, fo. 21,' and put on record in Bishop Sterne's Register (Carl. Epis. Reg., Sterne, f. 253. See also ibid. Halton, f. 67).

[4] By an Order in Council dated 20 October 1874, Bishop Harvey Goodwin exchanged the rectory of Clibburn with the Earl of Lonsdale for the churches of Embleton and Lorton.

[5] Carl. Epis. Reg., Appleby, f. 148.

[6] *Reg. of Wetherhal*, No. 33.

[7] Ibid. No. 25.

[8] Pat. 3 Edw. II. m. 34.

[9] *Rot. Parl.* (Rec Com.), i. 178–9.

A HISTORY OF CUMBERLAND

failed to grant redress to one or other of the contending parties.

One of the most interesting features in the history of Wetheral is the right of sanctuary or freedom from arrest which it afforded to criminals for offences committed outside its bounds. This privilege was conferred on the priory by Henry I. when he endowed it with all the customs and liberties enjoyed by the churches of St. Peter in York and St. John in Beverley.[1] It was also confirmed by later kings. The bounds of the sanctuary were not conterminous with those of the manor, but were marked by six crosses, viz. the cross on the bank of the Eden opposite Corby, the cross near St. Oswald's chapel, the cross by the lodge (*juxta le loge*) on the bank of the river, the cross by the hedge at Warwick on the boundary of the manor, called the Wetheral 'gryth crosse,' the cross between the vill of Scotby and the prior's grange there, and the cross on the bank of the burn at Cumwhinton.[2] It is a curious fact that no refuge was allowed to those whose offence was committed within the liberty. When the felon reached the desired asylum, he was obliged to toll a bell in the church and swear before the bailiff of the manor that he would henceforth behave himself as a law-abiding subject.

The right of sanctuary was a conspicuous privilege involving such far-reaching consequences to the community to which it appertained, that claims to the exercise of this liberty were regarded by the law with a jealous eye. It may be taken, we suppose, that the church which enjoyed this privilege was called upon at some time or another to prove its title. There are few places of sanctuary that have not figured in the law courts. The sanctuary of Wetheral was not singular in this respect. Three cases of considerable interest came before the justices itinerant at Alston in 1292, whereby the title of the priory to the liberty was established. Andrew, son of Thomas of Warwick, having slain a man by a blow on the head with a stick, fled to Wetheral and obtained 'the peace' according to ancient custom. As it was not known by what warrant the priory exercised such a privilege, the abbot of St. Mary's, York, was summoned to prove the title. It was maintained that from time immemorial the liberty of receiving felons within its jurisdiction (*infra banlucam*) was possessed by the priory of Wetheral, an oath having been first taken by such felons that they should conduct them-

selves well and not depart beyond the bounds. The verdict of the jurors was given in favour of the right of sanctuary. In two other cases of manslaughter at the same assize, the felons sought refuge at Wetheral, and the jurors found to the same effect.[3] From the fact that Edward III. offered pardon in 1342 to all the 'grithmen' or criminals who had obtained the 'grith' or peace at Wetheral, Beverley, Ripon and Tynemouth, on the condition that they should go out and fight in Scotland, it may be inferred that the liberty of sanctuary was largely used in the northern counties at that date.[4]

During the wars of Scottish independence the resources of the religious houses[5] on the Border were put to a severe strain by the entertainment of royalties and magnates on their way to Scotland. The English side was of course the basis of military operations. The depredations of the Scots or the expenses incurred by hospitality were the principal excuses alleged for the appropriation of churches to meet the increased outlay. Edward I. had stayed at the priories of Carlisle and Lanercost and the abbey of Holmcultram, as well as with the bishop of the diocese at Rose Castle. It is not surprising therefore that the Prince of Wales should have sojourned at Wetheral about the same period. He was there, presumably, as the guest of the monks, on 20 October, 1301, and again early in the year 1307, a few months before he came to the throne. It was on the latter occasion that Dungall Macdowill, a Galwegian captain, brought to the prince's court at Wetheral Sir Thomas de Brus and Alexander his brother, brothers of Robert de Brus, King of Scots, and Reynold de Crauford, whom he had wounded and taken in battle, together with the heads of certain Irish and Cantire men decapitated by him and his army during the war. The Chronicle of Lanercost gives a grim account of the subsequent execution of the prisoners at Carlisle, the head of Thomas de Brus having been placed on the keep of the castle.[6]

Several of the priors of Wetheral were advanced to the distinction of being abbots of the mother church of St. Mary, York, and one of them was appointed to the great

[1] *Reg. of Wetherhal,* No. 5.
[2] Ibid. Illust. Doc. No. xxx.

[3] *Reg. of Wetherhal,* Illust. Doc. No. xxix.
[4] Ibid. No. xxviii.
[5] At this time garrisons were sometimes kept in religious houses when their walls were strong enough for fortification. In 1300 Edward I. placed garrisons in divers abbeys of Scotland (*Liber Quot. Contrar. Garderobæ,* 180).
[6] *Reg. of Wetherhal,* Illust. Doc. No. viii.

186

priory of Durham. William Rundel rose to be abbot of York in 1239, John de Gilling in 1303, William de Brudford in 1382, Thomas Pigott in 1399, Thomas Bothe in 1464, and William Thornton in 1530, the latter being the last abbot of St. Mary's.[1] William de Tanfeld was 'provided' to the priory of Durham by Clement V. in 1308, and the monks of Wetheral were not sorry at his promotion. It is said that he paid for the appointment 3,000 marks to the pope and 1,000 marks to the cardinals, the enormous sum having been extorted from the priory of Wetheral to the impoverishment of the house. Robert de Graystanes, an official of Durham at the time and one of its historians, described the new prior as tall in stature, handsome in countenance, pleasing in manners, and liberal in spending money, but ignorant of the way to get it, inasmuch as he increased rather than diminished the debts of the house.[2]

In 1536 the royal commissioners made their report on this house, when, strange to say, they had only an accusation of personal depravity to make against two of the monks, Nicolas Barneston and Robert Goodon. At that time the priory was reputed to have possessed as relics a portion of the Holy Cross and some of the Blessed Virgin's milk.[3] It is probable that Ralf Hartley, the last prior, was put in by Cromwell's influence for the purpose of the dissolution. The deed of surrender was executed on 20 October 1538, and authenticated, not with the official seal of the house, but with a seal bearing the prior's initials. The document has only two signatures: 'per me Radulphum Hartley priorem Monasterij sive prioratus de Wederhall: per me Johannem Clyfton monachum ibidem.'[4] The surrender was enrolled on 28 January following before Thomas Legh, one of the clerks of the Chancery.[5] By a warrant dated 20 November 1539, a pension of £20 was allotted to the late prior, and smaller sums to Thomas Hartley, John Wytfeld alias Batson, John Clyfton, and John Gale, brethren of the house. On 31 January 1539-40, Ralf Hartley's pension was revised and fixed at £12 with the addition of his interest in the rectory of Wetheral and Warwick and the annexed chapels of St. Anthony and St. Severin.[6] In

1555 only two of the pensioners of Wetheral were alive, viz. Ralf Hartley, who was still drawing his pension of £12, and one Edward Walles who was enjoying his annuity of 40s.[7]

The demesne lands and churches of this house were granted to the dean and chapter of Carlisle by their charter of endowment, with the exception of the churches of Wetheral and Warwick, which were afterwards bestowed by letters patent, dated 15 January 1547, on the petition of that body.[8] The work of dismantling the priory was soon commenced. Account was rendered by Sir Thomas Wharton and James Rokebie, the commissioners of surrender, on 31 December 1538, of the sale of divers church utensils, tables of alabaster, brass candlesticks, various wooden images, choir stalls, vestments, censers, altar linen, and a lectern, not to mention the domestic furniture and farming stock, implements and produce belonging to the monks, the more costly articles like chalices, vases and jewels having been delivered to William Grene, the king's receiver.[9] In 1555 Lancelot Salkeld, dean of Carlisle, reported 'that one bell of the thre bells perteyning to the layte sell of Wetherell came to Carlysle, whiche bell was hanged upon the walle called Springall Tower in Carlyle to call the workmen to worke at the making of the new cytydall in Carlyle and mending of the castell ther.' The other two bells, he said, remained in a house at Wetheral unbroken awaiting removal.[10] The priory buildings soon went to decay and were never repaired. Thomas Denton, writing in 1687, stated that only the gatehouse remained entire and in good repair in his time. Its survival may probably be accounted for by the fact that it then 'served the minister for a vicarage-house.'[11] As for the dormitories and cloisters, iam seges ubi Troja fuit.

[1] Dugdale, Mon. iii. 538–9.

[2] Hist. Dunelm. Scriptores Tres. (Surtees Soc.), 85–9 ; Anglia Sacra, i. 753.

[3] L. and P. Hen. VIII. x. 364.

[4] Ibid. xiii. (ii.) 657 ; Dep. Keeper's Rep. viii. App. ii. 48.

[5] Close, 30 Hen. VIII. pt. ii. m. 62.

[6] L. and P. Hen. VIII. xiv. (i.) 599, 602, 609.

[7] Trans. Cumb. and Westmld. Arch. Soc. xiii. 382. Edward Walles was the bailiff of Wetheral and had a vested interest in the priory (Valor Eccl. [Rec. Com.], v. 10).

[8] Reg. of Wetherhal, Illust. Doc. xl. xli.

[9] Ibid. No. xlii.

[10] Trans. Cumb. and Westmld. Arch. Soc. ix. 264.

[11] Peramb. of Cumb. f. 96. The story imposed upon Hutchinson (Hist. of Cumb. i. 156) that ' what was left of this edifice by the zealots of Henry VIII.'s days was demolished, except the gateway or lodge, with a fine elliptic arch (which is now converted into a hayloft), by the dean and chapter of Carlisle, who built a prebendal house, etc., in Carlisle with the materials' is evidently a fabrication. It is also false that 'when this was in agitation Mr. Howard, the late beautifier of Corby, offered a sufficient compensation if they would suffer the building to stand, but his proposition was rejected.' The state-

PRIORS OF WETHERAL

Richard de Reme, early twelfth century [1]
Ralf, circa 1130
William, late twelfth century [2]
Thomas, circa 1203–14 [3]
Suffred, circa 1218–23 [4]
William Rundel, circa 1225–39 [5]
Thomas, circa 1241
Richard de Rouen, circa 1251
Henry de Tutbury (Tutesbiri), circa 1257
Thomas de Wymundham, circa 1270–90
William de Tanfield, 1292, [6] prior of Durham in 1308
John de Gilling, resigned on becoming abbot of York in 1303 [7]
John de Thorp, appointed on 16 November, 1303 [8]
Robert de Gisburn, circa 1309, [9] excommunicated in 1313 [10]
Gilbert de Botill, instituted in 1313, [11] prior of St. Mary, York, in 1313–9

Adam de Dalton, 1319, [12] 1330, [13] 1341 [14]
William de Tanfield, 1341, [15] 1366 [16]
William de Brudford, admitted in 1373, [17] abbot of York in 1382 [18]
Robert Grace, circa 1379 [19]
Richard de Appilton, circa 1382 [20]
Thomas Pigott, admitted in 1386, [21] abbot of York in 1399
John de Stutton, 1399 [22]
Thomas Stanley, 1434 [23]
Robert Hertford, 1444, 1446 [24]
Thomas Bothe, 1456, abbot of York in 1464 [25]
Robert Esyngwalde, 1490

[12] Ibid. f. 214.
[13] Reg. of St. Bees, MS. ff. 96, 96b. Two deeds of this date were given 'apud Wedirhale in presencia fratris Ad. de Dalton tunc prioris eiusdem loci.'
[14] In this year he was in trouble with the chapter of York for which he was probably obliged to retire. The record of the dispute occupies three folio pages (Carl. Epis. Reg., Kirkby, ff. 420–2).
[15] Ibid. f. 428, but see ibid. Welton, f. 6.
[16] Archbishop Thoresby described him in 1366 as *modernus prior*, and Sir John Warwick had already spoken of him to the archbishop as a busybody (*satageus*) in local matters (Carl. Epis. Reg., Appleby, f. 148).
[17] Ibid. f. 258.
[18] Pat. 6 Ric. II. pt. i. m. 27. In the royal assent to his election, he is described as a monk of St. Mary's and a doctor of theology.
[19] Exch. Cler. Subs. dioc. of Carl. bdle. 60, No. 1. Contributed to the *malum subsidium* granted to Richard II. by the Parliament of his second year. The writ to Bishop Appleby, ordering the collection, is dated 8 July 1379 (Carl. Epis. Reg., Appleby, f. 314). Three monks of the house, Simon West, William Faxton and John Estone, also contributed.
[20] Carl. Epis. Reg., Appleby, f. 342. The record of admission is undated, but it appears among entries of that year.
[21] Engaged at York in 1392 as proctor of the abbey of St. Mary in a great dispute about liability to repair the chancel of Bromfield church (ibid. ff. 362, 365–7).
[22] One of the collectors of a tenth granted on 12 May 1399 to the king by the clergy of Carlisle, deputed for that purpose by letters patent of W., Bishop of Carlisle, as appears by a memorandum of 4 Henry IV. *inter Recorda* in the Michaelmas term. By a similar memorandum of the sixth year, we learn that John Soureby acted as proctor for the collectors (Exch. Cler. Subs. dioc. of Carl. bdle. 60, No. 2b).
[23] Fuller, *Worthies of England*, ed. J. Nichols, i. 240–1.
[24] *Trans. Cumb. and Westmld. Arch. Soc.* viii. 424.
[25] In the royal assent to his election, he is described as a monk of St. Mary's, York (Pat. 4 Edw. IV. pt. i. m. 11). He resigned the abbey in 1485 (ibid. 2 Ric. III. pt. iii. m. 2).

ment of Thomas Denton, who wrote more than a century before Hutchinson, is conclusive. The dean and chapter made an effort in 1703 'to build a good house for our curate' at Wetheral, but the curate at that time had other ideas (Carl. Epis. Reg., Nicolson, f. 56).
[1] Leland, *Collectanea*, i. 25. Todd, evidently copying Leland, added that Richard presided over the priory in the time of William Rufus (*Notitia Eccl. Cathed. Carl.* 34). Both statements lack confirmation.
[2] William was prior when Clement was abbot of York, and Deodatus was prior of St. Bees (Reg. of St. Bees, MS. ff. 54b, 55 ; Harl. MS. 434).
[3] He was a contemporary of Bernard, Bishop of Carlisle (Reg. of Holmcultram, MS. f. 14).
[4] Contemporary with Bishop Hugh of Carlisle (Reg. of Lanercost, MS. viii. 7, 8 ; *Whitby Chart.* [Surtees Soc.], i. 45).
[5] It must have been this prior who received twenty-four oaks in the forest of Carlisle *ad fabricam ecclesie sue de Wetherhal* of the gift of Henry III. in 1229 (Close, 14 Hen. III. m. 19).
[6] The sequence of priors about this date is very confused owing to papal interference and conflicting evidence. Compare *Cal. of Papal Letters* (Rolls Ser.), ii. 40, Palgrave, *Parl. Writs*, i. 186, and *Rot. Parl.* i. 191 with Carl. Epis. Reg., Halton, f. 76.
[7] Pat. 31 Edw. I. m. 17.
[8] Vacancy caused by his predecessor's election to York—'per creationem nostram in abbatem dicti monasterii' (Carl. Epis. Reg., Halton, f. 73). Papal attempt to supersede him in 1309, but resisted by the Crown (Pat. 2 Edw. II. pt. i. m. 8, and 3 Edw. II. m. 34 ; Carl. Epis. Reg., Halton, ff. 125, 131).
[9] Called prior in a papal licence of that year (*Cal. of Papal Letters*, ii. 53, 94).
[10] Carl. Epis. Reg., Halton, ff. 168, 214.
[11] Ibid.

Robert Alanby, 1497, afterwards prior of St. Mary's, York,[1] and St. Bees
William Thornton, made abbot of York in 1530[2]
Richard Wederhall, 1535[3]
Ralf Hartley, last prior, 1539

The only known seal referring to this monastery is that attached to the deed of surrender,[6] which is Prior Ralf Hartley's signet. It is shield-shaped and bears his initials united by a knot looped and tasselled.

HOUSES OF BENEDICTINE NUNS

7. THE NUNNERY OF ARMATHWAITE

The nunnery of Armathwaite was situated in a lovely glen near the junction of the river Croglin with the Eden in the southern angle of the parish of Ainstable, a few miles from the vill of Armathwaite on the other side of the river Eden in the forest of Inglewood. At an early period it was known as the nunnery of Ainstable from the name of the parish. It was said to have been founded by William Rufus on 6 January 1089 for black nuns of the Order of St. Benedict in the honour of Jesus Christ and the Blessed Virgin Mary, but no one at the present time credits the extraordinary charter upon which the allegation was made. Freeman stated that the charter was 'spurious on the face of it,'[4] and the editors of the Calendars of Patent Rolls have pronounced it 'a forgery.'[5] The genuineness of the document was accepted without question by the older writers, no doubt for the reason that it was confirmed in 1480 by Letters Patent of Edward IV. It is very difficult to conceive how a document so full of anachronisms could have imposed on anybody. By this so-called charter William Rufus, King of the English and Duke of the Normans, was supposed to give the nuns the 2 acres of land upon which the house was built, and in addition the 3 carucates of land and 10 acres of meadow lying next the nunnery, 216 acres in the forest of Inglewood on the north of a certain water called Tarnwadelyn, common of pasture throughout the same forest for themselves and their tenants, sufficient wood for their

buildings by delivery of his foresters, an annual rent of 40s. from the king's tenements in Carlisle to be paid by the keeper of the city at the feasts of Pentecost and St. Martin, and freedom from toll throughout the whole of England. Besides it was claimed in this charter that Rufus had granted to the nuns, within their house and their lands adjoining, all the liberties which he had conceded to the monastery of Westminster without molestation of any of the king's sheriffs, escheators, bailiffs or lieges. All these privileges were to be had and enjoyed from the king and his heirs in pure alms of his free will and concession 'as hert may it thynk or ygh may it se.'[7] It cannot be said that the nuns were too modest in their desire for special privileges.

---

[6] Aug. Off. Deeds ot Surrender and B.M. Seals 4325. Hutchinson has given an illustration of Prior William de Tanfield's seal (Hist. of Cumb. i. 348).

[7] The charter has been printed in full by Dugdale (Mon. iii. 271) from the Inspeximus in Pat. 20 Edw. IV. pt. i. m. 4. The confirmation is dated at Westminster, 20 June, 1480, when the nuns paid half a mark in the hanaper. The adroit allusion by the nuns to the alleged charters of King Athelstan to St. John of Beverley—'Swa mikel fredom give I ye, Swa hert may think or egbe see' (Mon. ii. 129–30)—and to St. Wilfrid of Ripon— 'I will at thai alkyn freedom have : and in al thinges be als free as hert may thynke or eygh may se' (Thorpe, Diplom. Angl. 182)—need not be pointed out. The phrase in the Armathwaite charter must have been considered of great consequence at this period, for it is quoted in Letters Patent of Henry V. as the conspicuous privilege of Beverley and Ripon (Mon. vi. 1312). This allusion alone is enough to condemn the document as a forgery without the more visible evidence that Cumberland did not belong to the King of England in 1089, and that Rufus never used the title of 'Duke of the Normans.' In the paper survey of the nunnery at the time of the dissolution it is stated that the 'yerely rent going out of the lands of o' Sov'ane lord the king in Karlell, to be paid by the hands of the keeper of the towne of Karlisle, by the yere xl'.' was 'ex concessione Willelmi Regis Conquestoris' (Mon. iii. 273), a blunder worthy of comparison with the statements of the Rufus charter.

---

[1] B.M. Add. MS. 24,965, f. 99.

[2] Dugdale, Mon. iii. 539. Over the south chancel window of Wetheral church is the inscription : 'Orate pro anima Willelmi Thornton abbatis.'

[3] Valor Eccl. (Rec. Com.), v. 10. Over the chancel door of Wetheral church is the inscription : 'Orate pro anima Richardi Wedderhall.' From these inscriptions it would appear that the chancel was rebuilt about the time of the surrender of the priory.

[4] William Rufus, ii. 506.

[5] Cal. of Pat. 1476–85, p. 208.

On the strength of the forged charter a claim to the liberty of sanctuary was put forward, for we are probably justified in ascribing to this date the erection of the square pillar about 3 yards high, inscribed with a cross and the words 'Sanctuarium 1088,' which was placed on rising ground above the nunnery, and by which the nuns bolstered up their claim to exercise the rights in this respect enjoyed by the abbey of Westminster. This sanctuary stone [1] has been the delight and puzzle of antiquaries for many generations.

Very few authentic references to this house which may be said to possess the element of interest have been found.[2] The earliest notice of its existence that has been met with may be dated about 1200. It occurs in a charter of Roger de Beauchamp to the priory of St. Bees, wherein it is stated that the land he gave to that monastery was near the land of the nuns of 'Ainstapillith' in 'Leseschalis' or Seascale on the western coast.[3] Like the rest of the religious houses the nuns of 'Ermithwait' suffered heavy losses during the Scottish wars. Edward II. compassionating the state of the poor nuns of 'Ermynthwait' who had been totally ruined by the Scots, granted them pasture for their cattle in Inglewood Forest during pleasure.[4] In 1331 they were excused the payment of £10 due to the Crown for victuals bought by them in the previous reign, for the reason that their lands and rents were greatly destroyed by the wars with Scotland.[5]

It is fortunate that we have at least one undoubted record which throws a good light on the internal constitution of the nunnery and its relation to the diocese of Carlisle. From this we learn that the nuns had the liberty of free election of a prioress, and that with the bishop, to whom she made obedience, rested the confirmation and institution of the person elected. There is little doubt that the bishop exercised a jurisdiction in the visitation of the house.[6] In their petition to Bishop Welton in 1362 the nuns stated, through Cecily Dryng the sub-prioress, that the convent, wishing to provide a prioress in the room of Dame Isabel deceased, assembled in the chapter house on the Thursday next after the Feast of St. Bartholomew for the purpose of consultation, and unanimously elected Dame Katherine de Lancaster, their fellow-nun, to the vacant post. A record of the election was sent to the bishop under the seal of the house, whereupon he confirmed it and committed to Dame Katherine the cure and administration in spiritualities and temporalities of the said priory, due profession of obedience having been first made. On 2 September the bishop issued his mandate to

---

[1] A drawing of the 'sanctuary stone or pillar at Nunnery,' as the place is now called, will be found in B.M. Add. MS. 9642, ff. 91, 170. A dissertation with a picture of the stone was written by Mr. S. Pegge in the *Gentleman's Magazine* of 1755, pp. 440, 451. The same author writing in 1785 on the 'History of the Asylum or Sanctuary' stated that the sanctuary stone built into the pillar must have been the *fridstoll*. This however was very wonderful, as the stone, if it were the *fridstoll*, ought in all reason to have been within the nunnery. It could not well be taken thence and included within the pillar since the Reformation, because, to judge from the form of the letters in the inscription, the pillar appeared to be as old as the foundation of the nunnery. The matter deserved to be further inquired into ; this however might be determined in the meantime that the privilege of sanctuary at this place extended to that pillar (*Arch.* viii. 28). The nuns made it clear in their charter that they wanted the liberty to extend to the lands adjacent to the house and not to the house alone. For this reason they were consistent in placing the 'sanctuary stone' on the boundary.

[2] Fordun mentions as a report current in his time that David I. founded a monastery of nuns of St. Bartholomew near Carlisle, but no institution of this name has been found (*Scotichronicon* [ed. Goodall], i. 301).

[3] Similar references, though of somewhat later date, will be found in the *Reg. of Wetherhal*, 267, 269, 272, 276.

[4] Pat. 11 Edw. II. pt. i. m. 25.

[5] Pat. 5 Edw. III. pt. ii. m. 5 ; Dugdale, *Mon.* iii. 271. The petition of the 'poutes Nonaynes, la Prioresse et le Covent de Ermythwait en Comberland, que sount si nettement destruitz par les enemys descoce qeles nount unquote dount viure' is still on record. The victuals had been purchased from Sir John Lowther and his companions in the late reign. They prayed the king for the soul of his father and of his ancestors, and in the name of charity to pardon the debt 'a les dites dames' (Anc. Petitions, No. 2230). Bishop Nicolson refers to 'Ermithwaite' as the ancient spelling of Armathwaite in his etymology of the place-name : 'In this neighbourhood there is also the site of a nunnery founded (or re-established) by William Rufus : one of the territories whereof is still called Armethwait (antiently Ermit-thwait) and another Nunclose,' thus deriving it from 'Eremit' or 'hermitage,' the place of a recluse, a solitary recess (*Letters* [ed. J. Nichols], 404-6).

[6] The bishop's right of visitation is clear from the fact that the nunnery paid 7s. 6d. triennially in lieu of procurations at his visitation (*Valor Eccl.* [Rec. Com.], v. 292). In a later survey it is stated that a yearly pension of 2s. 6d. was due to the bishop out of the church of 'Aneslaplith' (Dugdale, *Mon.* iii. 273).

the Archdeacon of Carlisle to assign to the said prioress her stall in the choir and place in the chapter.[1]

When we come to the period when the foundation charter was forged we get some hint to account for its fabrication, and to explain why it was that the nuns were able to impose on the authorities. From letters patent of Edward IV., dated 9 April 1473, we learn that it was represented to the king by the prioress and convent of the house or priory of 'Armywayte,' situated near the marches of Scotland, which was of the foundation of his progenitors and of his patronage, that the houses, enclosures and other buildings of the said priory had been destroyed by the Scots, and that the house had been despoiled of its goods, relics, ornaments, books and jewels, and the charters and other muniments burnt or carried off, and in these circumstances the king confirmed the nuns' estate in the priory and all its possessions, and especially in an ancient close called 'the Noune close,'[2] that they might pray for his good estate and the good estate of Elizabeth his consort and of Edward his son, and for their souls after death.[3] Seven years after this date, that is on 20 June 1480, Isabel the prioress and nuns, bereft of charters and title-deeds, presented their compilation, which they ascribed to William Rufus, and had it inspected and confirmed as already mentioned.

From the fourteenth century wills on record in the diocesan registers, we learn that this nunnery had some friends and received bequests as well as the other religious institutions in the county. In 1356 Dame Agnes, the consort of Sir Richard de Denton, bequeathed 10s. and in 1358 John de Salkeld 40s. to the prioress and her sisters of 'Hermythwayt.' Richard de Ulnesby, rector of Ousby or Ulnesby, was good enough in 1362 to bequeath them a cow which he had in that parish, while a citizen of Carlisle, William de London, in 1376, and a country gentleman, Roger de Salkeld, in 1379, made them bequests of money.[4]

In the valuation of 1291 the temporalities of the prioress of 'Ermithwayt' were assessed at £10, but in 1318 they were not taxed as they were totally destroyed[5] by the Scots. The value of the priory in 1535[6] amounted to the sum of £19 2s. 2d., which included £6 from the rectory of the church of 'Aynstablie,' of which the prioress was patron. The annual outgoings, amounting to 110s. 2d., were composed of a pension of 12d. to the priory of Wetheral, 2s. 6d. for procurations to the bishop, and 106s. 8d. for the stipend of the chaplain of the nunnery. There is no evidence to show by whom or at what date the rectory of Ainstable was appropriated to the nunnery, and, strange to say, there is no record of any institution to the benefice in the mediæval registers of the see of Carlisle. The real property of the house at the time of the dissolution was scattered in small parcels so far apart as Ainstable, Kirkoswald, Cumwhitton, Blencarn, Kirkland, Glassonby, Crofton and Carlisle. The most extensive estate they possessed in one place was 'the Nouneclose,' consisting of 216 acres, and split up into several tenements. The 40s. rent in Carlisle said to have been 'given by William the Conqueror' was worth nothing.[7]

The house seems to have been dissolved soon after 31 July 1537, when the inventory of its possessions was made. It consisted of a prioress and three nuns, against none of whom did the commissioners bring an accusation in their notorious Black Book. Anne Derwentwater received a pension of 53s. 4d. a year, and was still in receipt thereof in 1555.[8] The priory and rectory of Ainstable were leased to Leonard Barowe of Armathwaite on 20 July 1538,[9] but the manor was afterwards sold by Edward VI.

In the neighbourhood of this house many reminiscences of the nuns still survive to tell of their former occupation. The site of the priory has been called Nunnery from the dissolution to the present time, and the name of Nunclose in the forest of Inglewood near Armathwaite has not changed. When Mr. Samuel Jefferson wrote in 1840, part of the wall of the

---

[1] Carl. Epis. Reg., Welton, ff. 98–9.

[2] It is very odd that in 1348 Edward III. should have granted to Thomas le Eawer and Robert de Meurose for their good service a certain close near Ternwatheland called 'la Nouneclose' within the king's forest of Inglewode (*Rot. Orig.* [Rec. Com.], ii. 193). From the name of the place it must have had some previous connection with the nunnery.

[3] Pat. 13 Edw. IV. pt. i. m. 13 ; Dugdale, *Mon.* iii. 271–2.

[4] Dioc. Reg. of Carl. MS. ii. ff. 29, 49, 86, 292, 304.

[5] *Pope Nich. Tax.* (Rec. Com.), 320b, 333b.

[6] *Valor Eccl.* (Rec. Com.), v. 291–2.

[7] Dugdale, *Mon.* iii. 272–4.

[8] Q. R. Misc. Bks. xxxii. f. 71. The list of the pensioners in Cumberland and Westmorland, with the amount of their pensions, has been extracted by the present writer from this record and printed in the *Trans. Cumb. and Westmld. Arch. Soc.* xiii. 375–83.

[9] *L. and P. Hen. VIII.* xiv. (i.) 606.

monastic buildings was standing on the west side of the dwelling house.[1] The field in which the sanctuary pillar was erected is still called ' Cross Close ' to the north-east of the site. At a short distance was the burial ground, a small square of land surrounded by lofty trees. At this place was found a monk's head with a cowl very rudely cut in stone. When the old nunnery was taken down, as it is said, in 1715, a small painting on copper of a Benedictine nun, with a rosary, cross, a book in her hand and a veil on her head, was found in a niche in the wall. In the north-west end of the present house a stone from the old buildings was inserted bearing the following couplet :—

Though veiled Benedictines are remov'd hence,
Think of their poverty, chastity, faith, obedience.

Near the site of the old house there is a spring still called the Chapel Well. Nicolson and Burn,[2] writing in 1777, printed a facsimile of an old inscription on a bed-head at Nunnery, then called the nun's bed, which may be read, ' Mark the end and yow shal naver doow amis.' Hutchinson,[3] a few years later, could not trace the inscription or find anybody who had ever seen it.

PRIORESSES OF ARMATHWAITE

Isabel,[4] died 1362
Katherine de Lancaster,[5] elected 1362
Isabel,[6] occurs 1480
Isabel Otteley,[7] died 1507
Agnes or Annis Elvyngton,[8] died 1507
Agnes or Anne Derwentwater,[9] occurs 1535, 1537

8. THE NUNNERY OF SETON OR LEKELEY

The nunnery of Seton occupied a picturesque position on the northern boundary of the parish of Bootle beneath the rising grounds of Corney. It was originally called the nunnery of Lekeley from the name of the land in the vill of Seton on which it was built. No fewer than four religious houses owned land in this vill. The abbey of Holmcultram had the whole of Lekeley with the exception

of the land granted to the nunnery,[10] and the priory of St. Bees had a grant of land in Seton from Henry son of Thomas, which Thomas was at one time parson of Bootle.[11] Before 1190 the abbey of Cockersand was in possession of 6 acres in Seton in Coupland with a share of the pasture of the vill.[12]

The nunnery was founded at Lekeley by Henry son of Arthur son of Godard, lord of Millom, towards the close of the twelfth century. Though the foundation charter is not forthcoming, we have authentic evidence of the grant. When Henry son of Arthur, with the consent of Godit, his wife, gave Lekeley in free marriage to Henry son of William with his daughter Gunnild, he excepted the land there which he had already bestowed on the nuns (excepta terra in Lekeleya quam dedi sanctimonialibus servientibus Deo et sancte Marie in Lekeleya).[13] As Henry Kirkby was reputed to have been the founder at the time of the dissolution,[14] it must have been Henry son of Arthur, lord of that district, to whom reference was made. The nunnery was entitled in the name of the Blessed Virgin and its inmates observed the Benedictine rule.[15]

Religious associations of women did not flourish in Cumberland. The rough life and continual warfare of a border county did not tend to promote institutions more adapted to settled and peaceful districts. Though the

[1] Leath Ward, 239–41.
[2] Hist. of Cumb. ii. 431.
[3] Hist. of Cumb. i. 192.
[4] Carl. Epis. Reg., Welton, ff. 98, 99.
[5] Ibid.
[6] Cal. of Pat. 1476–85, p. 208.
[7] Dugdale, Mon. iii. 272–4. She is perhaps the same person as the previous Isabel.
[8] Ibid. 270.   [9] Ibid. 272.

[10] Reg. of Holmcultram, MS. ff. 60–2.
[11] Reg. of St. Bees, MS. xiii. 8–9.
[12] Cockersand Chart. (Chetham Soc.), i. 4.
[13] Reg. of Holmcultram, MS. f. 60. Henry son of Arthur appears to have succeeded to the lordship of Millom in 1185 (Pipe R. 30 and 31 Hen. II.). The grant to the nuns was made before his daughter's marriage. As Dugdale printed an irrelevant charter under the title of this house from the Register of Holmcultram in the Harleian collection, the usual accounts of the priory of Seton are misleading. J. Denton, who had seen the copy of the register now in the custody of the Dean and Chapter of Carlisle, has not been misinformed (Cumberland, pp. 13–4). It was Henry son of Arthur who gave a portion of Lekeley to the nuns. The rest of Lekeley, afterwards bestowed on his daughter Gunnild in marriage, was granted in her widowhood to the monks of Holmcultram and confirmed by other members of her family.
[14] L. and P. Hen. VIII. x. 364.
[15] ' Monasterium Beate Marie de Ceton in Coplandia, Ordinis sancti Benedicti Dioc. Ebor' (Durham Obit. R. [Surtees Soc.], 19, 54). Tanner was in error when he said that the nunnery was ' dedicated to St. Leonard,' thus confusing the real dedication with that of the hospital of Lancaster which belonged to the nuns (Notitia Monastica, 77).

nunnery of Lekeley was far removed from the Scottish frontier, in a secluded position on the south-western seaboard, it was always in a crippled state of finances. On 13 November, 1227, Archbishop Walter Gray granted, with the assent of William, archdeacon of Richmond, the appropriation of the church of St. Michael of Irton to the prioress and convent of Lekeley in consideration of their poverty.[1] At a later date the condition of the institution was even more deplorable. On 1 April, 1357, Henry, Duke of Lancaster, in the sixth year of his palatinate, learning on undoubted authority that the priory of Seton was so poor (*ita exilis*) that there was not a sufficiency to support the prioress and nuns, granted the appropriation of the hospital of St. Leonard, Lancaster, which was at that time vacant and of his patronage, with all its lands and possessions, as a help to the sustentation of the house. The duke also gave to the prioress and nuns the advowson of the chantry of one chaplain in the hospital, and enjoined the burgesses of Lancaster to assent to the gift and to bestow the alms and duties on the said hospital which were incumbent on them from time immemorial.[2] The abbey of Holmcultram seems to have been considerate to the poor nuns of Seton. On 18 October, 1459, Thomas York, abbot of that house, leased all the lands the abbey possessed between Esk and Duddon, called Lekeley, to Elizabeth Croft, prioress, for twelve years at an annual rent of twenty shillings.[3]

A fragment of what appears to have been the monumental slab of a prioress is built into the wall of a barn at High Hyton not far from the nunnery towards the sea. It has occupied this position from a time beyond memory. One end of the slab has been broken off and lost. The inscription cut on either side of a pastoral crook reads : + HIC IACET . . . DENTONA AN . . . The fragment measures 34 inches in length and 22 inches in width. From the charges made in 1536 by Layton and Legh in their infamous ' book of compertes' we learn that Joan Copland was the prioress at that date and that Susanna Rybton was an inmate of the house. In the previous year, when the ecclesiastical survey

was made, Joan Seton is named as the prioress, but she was probably the same person under another surname.

The total revenue of the nunnery in 1535 was returned at £13 17s. 4d., and after deducting reprises, £12 12s.[4] This sum was made up of the following items : value of the site of the priory, 30s. ; rents and farms in ' Whitebyke ' and tenements in ' Furdes ' and ' Bolle,' 14s. 4d. ; rents in the vill of Lancaster, £6 0s. 4d. ; spiritualities of the church of Irton, £5 12s. 8d. By the valuation of James Rokeby on 24 June, 1536, the demesne lands in the occupation of the priory were worth £3 6s. 8d., and the gross issues of the rectory of Irton were £13 6s. 8d. The value of the demesne lands when granted to Hugh Ascue of the king's household in 1542 was set down at £4 11s. 4d. In the following year the rectory of Irton was leased to the same person for twenty-one years.[5]

A tradition about the manner of granting Seton Priory, which survived till late in the seventeenth century, is of curious interest. Edmund Sandford, writing about the year 1675, has left us this version of it. ' The religious house was gott,' he said, ' by one Sir Hugo Askew, yeoman of the seller unto Queen Catherin, in Henry the Eights time, and borne in this conrry. And when that Queen was deforced from her husband, this yeoman was destitute, and he aplied himself for help to Lo(rd) Chamberlain for some place or other in the king's service. The Lord Steward knew him well because he had helpt him to a cup wine the best, but told him he had no place for him, but a charcole carrier. Well, quoth this Mons[r.] Askew, help me with one foot and let me gett in the other as I can. And upon a great holiday, the king looking out at some sports, Askew got a cortier, a frinde of his, to stand before the king, and then he got on his vellet cassock and his gold chine and baskett of chercols on his back, and marched in the king's sight with it. O, saith the king, now I like yonder fellow well that disdains not to doe his dirty office in his dainty clothes—what is he ? Says his frinde that stood by on purpose, It is Mr. Askew that was yeoman o'th celler to the late Queen's Ma[tie] and now glad of this poore place to keep him in y[r] Ma[ties] service, which he will not forsake for all the world. The kinge says, I had the best wine when he was i'th

[1] *Reg. of Abp. Walter Cray* (Surtees Soc.), 18.

[2] Dugdale printed this deed from an imperfect autograph in the Office of Arms (*Mon.* iv. 227). Sir Thomas Hardy has supplied the date and witnesses from the Rolls of the Chancery of the County Palatine of Lancaster, Class xxv. A. 3a, No. 19 (*Dep. Keeper's Rep.* xxxii. App. i. 335).

[3] A copy of the original indenture has been printed by J. Hodgson in *Arch. Æliana* (old ser.), ii. 399.

[4] *Valor Eccl.* (Rec. Com.), v. 265 ; *Mon.* iv. 227-9.

[5] Pat. 33 Hen. VIII. pt. 1, m. 41 ; *L. and P. Hen. VIII.*, xiii. (i.), 585, xvii. 220 (56), xviii. (i.), 549. The priory seems to have been granted to Ascue on lease in the first instance.

celler; he is a gallant wine taster, let him have his place againe and afterwards knighted him.'[1]

After Askew got his lease of the priory lands in 1537, he was not allowed to have peaceable possession, for an attempt was made, when the commonalty of the northern counties rose in rebellion, to oust him and restore the nuns to their old home. By a petition in 1540 'to the Righte Worshipfull Sor Richarde Riche, Knighte, Chauncellor of the Kynge's Courte of Augmentacons in (of) the Revenues of his Crowne, moste humblye sheweth, and complaynethe unto your good maystershippe, your dailye oratour, Hughe Ascue, officer in the kynges graces sellar, that where your seide oratour bathe of the kinges grace's dymyse by indenture undre his grace's grete seale of his Courte of Augmentacons of the revenues of his Crowne, the house and scite of the late pryorye or house of nunes of Seyton in the countie of Cumberland w[t] all and singuler the appurtenances, by auctorytie of parlyamente suppresside and dissolvyde, into whiche saide house or pryorye by vertue of his seide lease yo[r] saide oratour dyd entre and was therof peassablye possesside and the same did furnyshe w[t] suche goodes and catalls as he then hadd. So y[t] is that one Thomas Skelton beynge accompanyde w[t] diverse other rebellyous and mysdemenyde persons at the tyme of the commocon in the Northe, ryoutouslye entryde into the seyde late

pryorye then beinge in your oratour's hande, as ys aforesaide, and there put in the late pryores of the same late pryorye, whoe remanede ther afterwarde by the space of a quarter of a yere and more w[t] here hole retinue at the onlye coste and charge of your oratour, and the goodes and catalls of your seid oratour dyd waste, dystroye, and carye awaye to the value of xxiii[l]. Wherfore it maye please your good maistershipe the premises tenderlye consideryde to graunte the kynges graces lettres of pryvye seale to be directide unto the saide Thomas Skelton, commaundynge him by the same, other to restore unto your said oratour his saide goodes and catalls so by him so dystraynede and caryede awaye, or agrewithe your seide oratour that he be and personallye appere before your maistershippe in the Kinges Courte of Augmentacons of the revenues of his crowne at a certayne daye and undre a certeyne payne by your good maistershippe to be lymittede, then and ther to aunswere to the premisses and further to abyde suche ordre and dyrectyon in the premisses as shall seme to your good maistershippe to stonde w[t] equite and good consceyence, and your seide oratour shall daylye praye to God, etc.'[3]

PRIORESSES OF SETON

Elizabeth Croft,[4] occurs 1459
Joan Seaton,[5] occurs 1535
Joan Copland,[6] occurs 1536

THE FOUR HOUSES OF FRIARS

9. THE DOMINICAN FRIARS OF CARLISLE
10. THE FRANCISCAN FRIARS OF CARLISLE
11. THE AUSTIN FRIARS OF PENRITH
THE CARMELITE FRIARS OF APPLEBY

The four orders of mendicant friars had obtained settlements in the diocese of Carlisle before the close of the thirteenth century. The same year witnessed the coming of the friars preachers, black friars or Dominicans, and the friars minors, minorites, grey friars, or Franciscans, to Carlisle while Walter was bishop of the diocese. In 1233, says the Chronicle of Lanercost,[2] the order of friars

minors came to the city of Carlisle about the Feast of the Assumption, 15 August, and received a house (mansionem) within the walls of the city; and the order of friars preachers about the feast of St. Michael, 29 September, without the walls. It is said that the friars of St. Mary of Mount Carmel, Carmelites, or white friars, were established in Appleby by the Lords Vesey, Percy and Clifford in 1281,[7] and it is known as a certainty that the friars eremites of the order of St. Augustine, Augustinians, or Austin friars, were carrying on their mission in Penrith before 1300.[8] These religious communities occupied a prominent ecclesiastical position in the district, and

[1] A Cursory Relation of all the Antiquities and Familyes in Cumberland (Cumb. and Westmld. Arch. Soc. 1890), p. 6.
[2] Chron. de Lanercost (Maitland Club), 42.

[3] Dugdale, Mon. iv. 228–9.
[4] Arch. Æliana (old ser.), ii. 399.
[5] Valor. Eccl. (Rec. Com.), v. 265.
[6] L. and P. Hen. VIII., x. 364.
[7] Dugdale, Mon. vi. 1581.
[8] Liber Quot. Contrar. Garderobæ (Soc. Antiq.), 40, 43.

though the black friars and grey friars exercised the greater influence, they were all usually associated in the minds of the people as the four orders of friars.

The friars minors, having obtained a settlement on the south-east side of the city of Carlisle, were not long in starting to erect their chapel and buildings. In July 1235 Thomas de Multon, keeper of the forest of Carlisle, was instructed to supply them with twenty oaks as the king's gift for the construction of their church, and in the following November the king made them another present of twenty pieces of timber (*fuste*) for the building of their houses.[1]

The friars preachers met with greater obstacles to a final settlement when they chose an habitation without the walls. There can be no doubt that the statement of the Chronicle of Lanercost is correct upon this point. Soon after their arrival, viz. on 12 March 1233-4, it was stated that the friars preachers of Carlisle had petitioned the king for a place (*placia*) in the public highway (*strata publica*) which lay between their chapel on the one side and their land on the other, and as the king had learned by inquisition that it would be no injury to the city or loss of any one if he should grant their request, the sheriff of Cumberland was ordered to give them seisin of the said 'place' for the enlargement of their houses and buildings.[2] But in June 1237 they were obliged to remove the house they had erected in the public highway without the city (*extra civitatem*) on the ground that it was a nuisance.[3] At this time they must have gained a footing within the walls, for in 1237, both before and after the injunction to pull down the house outside, they obtained leave to perforate the city wall,[4] or make an excavation beneath it for the purpose of carrying the water conduit of their chambers *extra civitatem*.[5] Their church was not completed

for several years after this date, for in 1239 and 1244 they had gifts of timber in Inglewood Forest for the purpose of its construction.[6]

After the establishment of the houses we have only occasional notices of their existence for a long time, except as the recipients of alms from public sources or of gifts of land for the enlargement of their premises. In 1278 the king, hearing that Bishop Robert de Chause before his death left a deposit in the custody of the friars minors within the city of Carlisle, ordered Thomas de Normanville, his steward, to repair thither in person, and take it to the king's use in satisfaction of the late bishop's debts to him. Two years afterwards King Edward gave to the same friars six oaks fit for timber out of his forest.[7] The Augustinians 'of Penrith were active in enlarging their borders early in the fourteenth century. In 1318 John de Penrith granted them a piece of land for the extension of their habitation,[8] and in 1331 and 1333 John de Crumbewell made them gifts of tenements and land for a similar purpose.[9] In like manner it was found by inquisition taken at Carlisle on 4 February 1333-4 that Thomas le Spencer, chaplain, might alienate to the friars preachers there a piece of land 240 feet in length and 7 feet in breadth to form a road straight from the street to their dwelling-place. The land was held in chief by house-gavel, and was worth 40d. a year in all issues.[10] No licence for the transfer has been recorded on the patent rolls.

The houses of friars in Carlisle had a share in all the vicissitudes which go to make up the chequered history of that city. From their situation close to the walls, the preachers on the west and the minorites on the south-east, their buildings occupied dangerous positions in times of siege and assault. In the great fire of 1292, when the whole city including the abbey and the houses of the friars minors were reduced to ashes, the preachers alone, says the historian, were saved with the

---

[1] Close, 19 Hen. III. pt. i. m. 7 ; 20 Hen. III. m. 24.

[2] Ibid. 18 Hen. III. m. 28.

[3] Ibid. 21 Hen. III. m. 9.

[4] Ibid. 22 Hen. III. m. 14 ; 22 Hen. III. m. 2.

[5] Some rectification of the city boundaries or alteration of the walls must have taken place at this period to cause the displacement of the friars preachers. In 1232 the citizens had obtained from the Crown a licence to levy tolls on merchandize for two years to help them to inclose the city (*ad villam suam claudendam*) for its security and defence (Pat. 16 Hen. III. m. 4 ; Rymer, *Fœdera*, i. 205). Their position within the city was not changed after 1237. In 1315, when Bruce besieged Carlisle, their buildings are mentioned with those of the Austin canons as being

near the walls on the west side, as the friars minors were located on the east (*Chron. de Lanercost*, 231). Leland found 'withyn the walles ii howses of freres, blake and gray' (*Itinerary* [ed. Hearne, 1711], vii. 48).

[6] Close, 24 Hen. III. m. 19 ; Liberate R. 28 Hen. III. m. 5 ; Pipe R. (Cumb.), 29 Hen. III.

[7] Ibid. 6 Edw. I. m. 3 ; ibid. 8 Edw. I. m. 2.

[8] Inq. a.q.d. 12 Edw. II. No. 57; Pat. 12 Edw. II. pt. i. m. 19.

[9] Inq. p.m. 5 Edw. III. pt. ii, No. 109 ; 7 Edw. III. pt. ii. No. 36 ; Pat. 7 Edw. III. pt. ii. m. 20 ; Dugdale, *Mon.* vi. 1591.

[10] Inq. a.q.d. 7 Edw. III. No. 12.

greatest difficulty.[1] Another chronicler, lamenting in verse over the unspeakable calamity, has told us that amid all the ruins of ' the renowned vill ' only the Jacobins, the French name for the friars preachers, survived the catastrophe.[2] During the panic occasioned by the fire two thieves escaped out of prison, one of whom took sanctuary in the cathedral church and the other in the church of the friars minors. In consequence the citizens were amerced in a fine of £16 to the Exchequer, but the king pardoned them on condition that .they should recognize that they were bound to the safe custody of felons flying for sanctuary to churches within their city.[3]

During the progresses of the king or members of the royal family through the country, the religious houses on the route, at which they called or stayed, were the recipients of royal bounties in consideration of the outlay made by the religious men on their behalf, or as gifts in alms to meet their immediate wants. When the kings were in the north on their various military expeditions against Scotland, the local houses were often called upon to provide accommodation for them in person or for members of the court. In 1300 Edward I. stayed occasionally with the friars preachers and friars minors in Carlisle, and made complimentary gifts to them by way of acknowledgment of their hospitality. Sometimes he gave them alms for their food, or for the performance of some religious act like the celebration of mass for the soul of the Count of Holland or the Earl of Cornwall. Similar oblations were offered to the friars of St. Augustine of Penrith and the friars of Mount Carmel of Appleby, with the former of whom he stopped two days and with the latter one day on his journey south. The wardrobe accounts of the first three Edwards contain many items of gifts and offerings made to the four houses of friars in the diocese of Carlisle by these kings or by members of their households on their journeys through the district.[4] In other ways also the kings were benevolent in dealing with these institutions. In 1334 the friars minors of Carlisle purchased victuals to the value of £8 from Robert de Barton, the king's receiver, for their maintenance, but the king ordered the debt to be discharged

and the brethren acquitted in the following year as an act· of grace.[5] Edward III. must have had pleasant memories of the happy Christmas he spent with the minorites of Carlisle in 1332, when the commonalty of the city and neighbourhood displayed in a marked degree evidences of loyalty and affection.[6]

Few things betoken the popularity of the friars among the laity of every grade more than their success with 'the dead hand' in the matter of testamentary bequests. There was no attempt to gain possession of real property in lands or houses, like the monks and nuns, beyond what was necessary for their habitations and chapels or immediate convenience, their vows of poverty forbidding them to hold such possessions. But gifts of money or in kind kept flowing in at their solicitation. It is a striking feature of medieval wills that the four orders of friars as a class or one of the orders in particular usually figured as a beneficiary in testamentary dispositions. It would be difficult to decide whether the Dominicans or Franciscans were most popular with the dying man. The churchyards in Carlisle seem to have been often used as places of burial by people in the neighbourhood. When it is remembered that the secular priest of the parish in which the testator lived invariably claimed the mortuary due to him wherever the body of his parishioner was laid, it will be seen that burial in the churchyards of the mendicant orders involved a double burden to the deceased man's estate. But financial considerations did not prove a barrier to the persuasion of the friars. In 1356 Matthew de Redman, dating his will at Carlisle, bequeathed his body to be buried in the churchyard of the friars preachers of Carlisle with his best beast as a mortuary to his parish church ; to the friars preachers he left 20s. ; and a like sum to the friars minors ; also 6s. 8d. to Brother Robert Deyncourt. A great local dignitary like Sir Robert Tilliol of Scaleby desired his body to be laid among the friars preachers of Carlisle in 1367, as Robert del Shelde, a humble citizen, had done ten years before among the friars minors. Secular priests often came under the same spell. In the same year, 1362, two incumbents in distant parts of the diocese disposed of their bodies in this fashion : John de Seburgham, vicar of Walton, desiring to be buried in the church of the friars minors, and Richard de Ulnesby, rector of Ulnesby or Ousby, in the church of the

[1] Chron. W. de Hemingburgh (Engl. Hist. Soc.), ii. 40.

[2] Chron. de Lanercost (Maitland Club), 147.

[3] Lysons, Brit. Cumb. Mag., 73, quoting Close Roll, 21 Edw. I.

[4] Liber Quot. Contrar. Garderobæ (Soc. Antiq.), 42–3, etc. ; Trans. Cumb. and Westmld. Arch. Soc. vi. 140–2.

[5] Close, 8 Edw. III. m. 4d ; 9 Edw. III. m. 33.

[6] Chron. de Lanercost, 271.

friars preachers ; John de Dundrawe of Carlisle, in bequeathing his body to be laid among the friars minors in 1380, made arrangements for the payment of 15 marks to two chaplains for one year, or to one chaplain for two years, to celebrate for his soul at Our Lady's altar in their church, adding a jug and a mazer bowl as a personal gift.[1] These benefactions were not confined to testators in the immediate vicinity of Carlisle. The friars had a wider field of missionary enterprise which knew no frontier of county or diocese. Sir Brian de Stapilton was not forgetful of the friars of Carlisle in 1394, and Sir Richard le Scrop, lord of Bolton, bequeathed 20s. in 1400 to every house of friars in Carlisle, Penrith and Appleby,[2] whereas John Knublow, rector of Lamplugh, in the archdeaconry of Richmond, singled out the friars preachers and friars minors of Carlisle as the objects of his generosity when he was making his will in 1469.[3] The friars were not backward in looking after their own interests, in cases where executors neglected to pay the amounts left to them by will. A curious case arose in the diocesan court of Carlisle in 1340, in which the Dominican prior was complainant and Agnes widow of William Hare of Derham was the defendant. After much litigation the bishop decided that the friars were entitled to the benefaction of five marks sterling bequeathed by the deceased, and ordered Agnes the executrix to pay that sum within six days together with 20s. 1d. as costs.[4]

The relationship of the friars to the corporate life of the church should not be misunderstood. It was the bishop who conferred holy orders on the inmates of their houses, and it was under his licence that they exercised their vocation in his diocese. In the ordination lists on record in the diocesan registers, the names of friars admitted to successive degrees will be found. To William de Eyncourt, a friar preacher, Bishop Ross committed in 1330 the faculty to preach throughout his whole diocese, to hear the confessions of all who were willing to confess to him, to give absolution, and to enjoin salutary penance except in cases reserved by the canons to the bishop himself.[5] The same

licence was given to Brother Thomas de Skirwyth in 1356 on the recommendation of Robert de Deyncourt, a friar preacher of Carlisle.[6] On 24 February 1354–5, Brother William de Croft of the order of the Blessed Mary of Mount Carmel in Appleby, having been presented by the prior provincial *iuxta capitulum super cathedram*, was admitted by Bishop Welton to the office of preaching and the hearing of confessions in the place of John de Haytefeld of the same order.[7] In the licences, the cases reserved to the bishop were often set out by name. When William de Dacre, *lector* of the convent of friars minors in Carlisle, in whose integrity of conscience the bishop of the diocese was fully confident, was admitted to exercise his office *in foro penitencie*,[8] cases of the violators of nuns, perjurers in assizes or indictments, matrimonial causes, divorces and crimes involving the loss of life or limb were specially excepted. In the faculty which Thomas de Thornton of the Augustinian Order in Penrith received in 1365 for one year, Bishop Appleby added to the reservations the practice of usury and breaking and entering his parks of Rose or Beaulieu to take anything away.[9] It is evident that the Bishops of Carlisle exercised an effective jurisdiction over the acts of the mendicant orders within the diocese.

It is not to be expected that the friars, established in the three different centres of the diocese, would be popular with the parochial clergy if we have regard to the nature of their vocation and method of life. At every turn they were apt to intrude on the office and tread on the toes of the secular priest. They had a roving commission to enter parishes, to preach, hear confessions, solicit alms, and to perform various ecclesiastical functions which in many instances must have brought them into conflict with the country clergy. As a matter of fact, much unpleasantness had arisen and complaints were numerous about the intrusion of the friars. The privileges of the parochial clergy were violated to such an extent that they

---

[1] *Testamenta Karleolensia* (ed. R. S. Ferguson), 10, 16, 40, 82, 135–7. William de Laton of Newbiggin bequeathed his body in 1369 to be buried in the church of the Augustinian friars of Penrith (ibid. 90).

[2] *Testamenta Eboracensia* (Surtees Soc.), i. 198, 274.

[3] *Richmondshire Wills* (Surtees Soc.), 8.

[4] Carl. Epis. Reg., Kirkby, f. 414.

[5] Ibid. Ross, f. 261. Bishop Kirkby, having

formerly granted to Symon, prior of the Carmelites of Appleby, licence ' penitenciarie nostre curam gerere,' recalled the licence and revoked the prior's commission in 1341. The same bishop made J. de Levyngton, a minorite, the penitentiary of Cumberland in 1346 (ibid. Kirkby, ff. 442, 488). In 1355 Brothers Richard de Swynesheved, warden (*gardianus*) of the convent of friars minors of Carlisle, William de Kirkby and Adam de Waldyngfeld of the same convent were admitted to preach in place of Robert de Shirewode, Thomas Faunell and John de Dalton removed (ibid. Welton, f. 117).

[6] Ibid. f. 118.   [7] Ibid. f. 115.

[8] Ibid. f. 118.   [9] Ibid. Appleby, f. 146.

appealed to the pope for redress in 1300. The bull of Boniface VIII. *contra Fratres* is on record.[1] It was not by any means entirely in favour of the secular clergy, though regulations were laid down to restrain the friars in their aggressions on the parochial office. The pope prescribed the cases in which they might preach and hear confessions, and at the same time recommended the parish priests to receive them kindly for the sake of the apostolic see. In 1352 the clergy of Carlisle moved Bishop Welton for relief. It was represented to him that the mendicant orders, not content with their own bounds, were in the habit of betaking themselves frequently to divers churches and chapels, not for the sake of preaching the word of God, but in the same churches and chapels on Sundays and Festivals during the solemnity of mass, when a great multitude of people were present, to the impediment of divine culture and the stirring up of tumult, with vain and heedless displays of excessive indulgences and plenary remission, sought quest of money and not gain of souls with open books in their hands like questors, contrary to canonical sanctions and the rules of their orders and the customs anciently observed, for which reason uproars among the people and injurious reports were almost of daily occurrence. The bishop, wishing to remedy these abuses, sent his mandate to all deans, rectors, vicars and parish chaplains, forbidding them under pain of the greater excommunication to permit any friar of the mendicant orders, even when licensed by him in the form of the constitution, to exercise a quest of any sort in their churches or chapels, and specially in time of divine service, unless on production of special letters.[2]

The Augustinians of Penrith had recourse to various devices for the maintenance of the house. It appears that the voluntary alms of the people of that district were not sufficient. Bishop Welton assisted them in some measure by appointing the prior in 1360 during pleasure to the church of Newton Reigny, which had been vacant for some time, and allowing him to discharge the cure of souls by some fit brother of the community.[3] The same consideration was shown by Bishop Appleby in 1365, when R. the sacrist of the house was appointed to the same charge for four years.[4] The brothers contrived a new expedient in 1360, from which they expected a substantial addition to their encumbered finances. In that year they started and intended to continue a light at mass in the conventual church at Penrith in honour of the Nativity of the Saviour and the blessed Mary, so that when the divine office was sung the light should burn on the feast of the Nativity every year. But they were unable to continue this without the alms of the faithful. In order to promote such a praiseworthy devotion, the bishop issued a firm indulgence for forty days to all in his diocese who went to the conventual church in a contrite and penitent spirit for the purpose of hearing mass on that day or who contributed of their goods for the keeping up of the said light.[5]

It may be regarded as a testimony of the estimation in which the prior of the friars preachers was held that he was sometimes employed in important and delicate negotiations or he was present at great functions. The prior of the Carlisle preachers was a witness to the award made in 1289 for the settlement of a dispute between the Augustinian priory of Pontefract and the Cluniac house of Monk Bretton.[6] In 1329 he was appointed in a commission with the abbot of Holmcultram and the archdeacon of Carlisle by Pope John XXII. to hear a cause between the Bishop of Durham and the Archbishop of York, but they refused to undertake the task owing to the scarcity of lawyers in the district and their distance from York.[7] Dr. Saunderson was one of the last wardens of the grey friars in Carlisle, having been in possession of that dignity in 1523.[8] When the end of the religious houses was drawing nigh, the king made what use he could of the preaching capacities of the friars in upholding the authority of a general council[9] and belittling the power of the pope, but no allegiance to the national policy could avert their fall. In 1534 was begun the royal visitation with a view to their extinction. George Browne, prior of the Augustinian hermits in London, was appointed by the Crown to the office of provincial prior to the whole order of friars hermits in England, and John Hilsey received

---

[1] Carl. Epis. Reg., Halton, ff. 44–5 ; Hist. MSS. Com. Rep. ix. (i.), 180.

[2] Ibid. Welton, f. 43.

[3] Ibid. f. 69. The church cannot have been vacant very long, for in June 1357 John de Bramwra was appointed on the resignation of Gilbert Raket (ibid. ff. 33–4).

[4] Ibid. Appleby, f. 146.

[5] Ibid. Welton, f. 73.

[6] Dugdale, *Mon.* v. 123–4. In vol. vi. 1485, the date is given as 1269 by an oversight.

[7] *Letters from the Northern Registers* (Rolls Ser.), 359–60.

[8] B.M. Add. MS. 24, 965, ff. 115–6.

[9] B.M. Cott. MS. Cleopatra E, vi. f. 312; *L. and P. Hen. VIII.* vi. 1487.

a similar commission over the whole order of friars preachers for the purpose of visiting the houses of all friars of whatever order throughout the kingdom, viz. the friars minors of the order of St. Francis, the friars preachers of the order of St. Dominic, the friars hermits of the order of St. Augustine, the Carmelite friars of the order of St. Mary, and the crossed friars, and making inquiry concerning their lives, morals and fealty to the king. If needful, they were authorized to instruct them how to conduct themselves with safety, to reduce them to uniformity, calling in the aid of the secular arm as occasion required.[1] This visitation was the precursor of their destruction.

In the spring of 1539, the task of suppressing the northern houses of friars was entrusted to the capable hands of Richard, Bishop of Dover. Writing from Lincoln on the first Sunday in Lent, he conveyed to Cromwell the sentence of their impending doom in these words : ' I trosteyd to a made an ende of the vesytacyon : but I am certefyyd that yet ther be stondeyng in the north parte above xx placeys of freyrs, as in Grantham, in Newarke, in Grymsseby, in Hull, in Beverley, in Scharborow, in Carlehyll, in Lancaster, and in dyverse placeys more, for the which bowseys I well serge so that I trost to leve but fewe in Ynglond before Ester, and I thyngke yt woll be ner Ester or that I can make an ende, besecheyng yower lordschyp to be good lorde

for the pore ffreyrs capacytes : they be very pore and can have lytyll serves withowtt ther capacytes. The byschoyppys and curettes be very hard to them, withowtt they have ther capacytes.'[3] Pursuing his way northward and finding nothing but ' povertye and lytyll lefte scarce to pay the dettes, so that in these houses the king's Grace shall have butt the lede,' he arrived at Grimsby, from which he intimated to the Lord Privy Seal on 'thys xxix day off February ' (1 March) that he was riding ' to Hull, and so to Beverlaye and to Skarborrowe and Karlehyll, and to Lancaster, and other houses as I shall here off by the waye.'[4] Before the close of 1539, the four houses of friars were swept away and their sites leased or sold, with the exception of the buildings of the black friars in Carlisle, which were retained in the king's hand, enclosed with a paling, and converted into a council chamber, magazine and storehouse for the convenience of the garrison. Nothing now remains but the name to tell of their former occupation. Blackfriars Street on the west walls preserves the name and indicates the site of the friars preachers, as Friars Court behind Devonshire Street marks the locality of the minorites or grey friars in Carlisle. In Penrith the Augustinians are commemorated in a house called the Friary and a street known as Friars Gate. The name and the site of the Carmelites in Appleby have altogether disappeared.

HOSPITALS

12. THE HOSPITAL OF ST. NICHOLAS, CARLISLE

The vicissitudes of the hospital of St. Nicholas, Carlisle, the best known house in the county, display many features of great interest in the history of eleemosynary institutions. It was of royal foundation at some period before the reign of King John, but the name of the founder or the date of the foundation has not been preserved. Hugh Todd, a former canon of Carlisle, ascribed the foundation to William Rufus,[2] the most unlikely of all the kings. As its records and muniments perished after the outbreak of the wars of Edward I. with Scotland, when the hospital was plundered and burnt, its early history must remain in comparative obscurity. Only two deeds of endowment, which are of any

value, are known to exist, and these are on record in the register of Bishop Kirkby.

The first reference to the hospital that has as yet come to light is a letter of protection from King John sent in 1201 to the lepers of Carlisle.[5] About the same date we have a charter from Hugh de Morvill endowing the hospital of St. Nicholas outside the city of Carlisle with a ploughland of his demesne in the village of Hoff near Appleby, the land and goods of Richard the smith of Burgh, his villein, 40s. of land in Thurstonfeld, and other lands and rents elsewhere on the condition of finding one chaplain to celebrate divine offices for the souls of the faithful, and maintaining, with the consent of the master and brethren, three infirm brothers

[1] Pat. 25 Hen. VIII. pt. ii. m. 6 d ; L. and P. Hen. VIII. vii. 587 (18).

[2] Notitia Eccl. Cath. Carl. (Cumb. and Westmld. Arch. Soc.), 35.

[3] B.M. Cott. MS. Cleopatra E, iv. f. 212 ; Wright, Suppression of the Monasteries (Camden Soc.), 191-3.

[4] L. and P. Hen. VIII. xiv. (i.), 413 ; Ellis, Original Letters, ser. 3, iii. 179-81.

[5] Rot. Chart. 2 John (Rec. Com.), 101b.

(*tres fratres infirmos*) on his presentation and on that of his heirs for ever.[1] At a later period perhaps, while Bernard was bishop and Geoffrey his archdeacon, Adam son of Robert, the true patron of a moiety of the church of Bampton near Carlisle, gave to the hospital and the sick people (*infirmis*) there serving God a moiety of the tithe sheaves of Little Bampton, with the proviso that two sick persons should be maintained on the nomination of himself and his successors. If these nominations were not made, five skeps of meal should be distributed to the poor on the Feast of St. Nicholas. In any other eventuality, the bishops of Carlisle were authorized to dispose of the tithe as they thought best for the good of the donor's soul.[2] It is evident from the tenor of these charters that the advantages of the institution were not exclusively confined to lepers at the opening of the thirteenth century, for though it had been originally founded as a leper-house, the qualifications for admittance must have been modified to some extent by the conditions attached to successive endowments. That such was the case we shall presently see.

The early history of the hospital was the subject of an inquest before a royal commission in 1341, when all the available evidences were brought under review and a verdict was returned on the oath of the jurors.[3] It was ascertained by this commission that the institution was founded by some king of England, long before the time of memory, for the sustenance of thirteen lepers, men and women, a master in Holy Orders who should be resident and sing mass at his will, and a chaplain who should sing mass daily for the benefactors of the hospital. This king, whose name the jurors knew not, endowed the institution with great possessions of lands for the perpetual support of the master and lepers as well as the brethren and sisters, appointed for them a chapter and a common seal which should remain in the custody of the master and of two or three or four of the lepers, and ordained that the lepers should always be clad in clothes of russet and live under the rules of the hospital for ever. It was also appointed at the foundation that the master as well as the brethren and sisters should have commons together within the precincts, saving this, that the master might appoint a temporary substitute if he had to attend to the business of the hospital elsewhere.

The original constitutions of the hospital were observed until by lapse of time the greater part of the lepers died,[4] when by common consent of the master, brethren and sisters, their places were filled by poor, weak and impotent folk (*pauperes, debiles et impotentes*), which led to a modification of the existing rules. We have already noticed how the bequests of Hugh de Morvill and Adam son of Robert contributed to this change. Other donations followed with similar conditions. The commonalty of the city of Carlisle granted to the hospital on every Sunday for ever a pottle (*potellum*) of ale from each brewhouse of the city, and a loaf of bread from each baker exposing bread for sale on Saturday, in return for which the master should receive into the hospital, on the presentation of the mayor and commonalty, all the lepers in the city. By virtue of these grants, the donors and their successors possessed the right to present lepers and other poor persons for maintenance in the institution.

In 1292 a dispute arose about the patronage of the hospital.[5] The Bishop of Carlisle claimed the right of instituting the master on the presentation of the brethren who made choice of a fit person for that purpose. The Crown denied the right of the inmates to elect a master from their own body, and challenged the jurisdiction of the bishop over the hospital for any purpose whatever. When the matter was referred to the judges of assize, the jury found that the patronage was in the king's hand, for though Bishop Ireton made the last appointment, the king's ancestors always conferred it till the time of Henry III. Besides, the brethren were never in the habit of electing any one. The gross value of the hospital was returned at that time at £35 13s. 4d., out of which twelve sick persons (*languidi*) were maintained with a master and a chaplain to celebrate divine offices, which chaplain had the assistance of a clerk.

[4] The disease of leprosy was not extinct in Cumberland in the fourteenth century. In 1357 the Bishop of Carlisle had learned with sorrow that Adam, rector of 'Castelkayrok,' was besprinkled with the spot of leprosy (*lepre macula est respersus*), insomuch that by reason of the horror and loathsomeness of the disease (*morbi deformitatem et horrorem*) he was unable to minister the sacraments and sacramentals to his parishioners. The rector was cited to appear personally in the bishop's presence at Rose and show cause why a coadjutor should not be appointed to assist him (Carl. Epis. Reg., Welton, f. 43).

[1] Carl. Epis. Reg., Kirkby, f. 303.
[2] Ibid. f. 482. J. Denton says that Gilbert son of Gilbert de Dundraw gave the hospital a portion of Crofton called Gillmartinridden (*Cumberland*, 83).
[3] Pat. 15 Edw. III. pt. i. m. 49, 48.
[5] *Plac. de Quo. Warr.* (Rec. Com.), 122.

The verdict of the jury, by which the Crown recovered the patronage, had a momentous effect on the internal observances of the hospital. The master nominated by the bishop resigned or was dispossessed. Hugh de Cressingham, a justice in eyre and 'an insatiable pluralist,' according to Prynne, before whom the case was decided, was appointed in his place. The new master drew up a code of rules, formed no doubt on the old model, for the government of the house.[1] These constitutions are of considerable interest and may be summarized as follows : All the brethren and sisters on their first entry should take an oath of obedience and fealty to the master and to live chastely and honestly within the cloister and without when sent on business of the hospital ; that they should rise in the morning at the ringing of the bell and come in person to the church or chapel to pray for the faithful departed, all the benefactors of the hospital, and specially for the royal family ; that they should have a cloister, the gates of which should be closed with iron bars both day and night, and specially by night ; that a general porter should be specially appointed and sworn to guard the gates according to rule, whose business also it would be to keep the well (*fontem*) and the court within and without the cloister clean from all defilement ; that the brethren should sleep in one house and likewise the sisters in another by themselves ; that none of the brethren or sisters should go out of the cloister wandering about the country or city without special leave of the master; that the brethren should work as long as they could for the common benefit of the hospital ; that no brother or sister should go out of the cloister under penalty by night by the walls or the gate, or by day from the ringing of the bell in the hall until the ringing of the bell in the church ; that the brethren and sisters should be obedient to the precepts of the master or his deputy in all things lawful and honest, and any brother or sister found refractory or disobedient, for the first offence should lose his or her livery and be admonished, for the second should lose the two next liveries and be admonished to amend, otherwise on the third offence he or she should be expelled from the cloister and be entirely deprived of his or her corrody without hope of return ; that the master should not permit any married man or woman staying within the cloister to pass the night with wife or husband, brother or sister, within the cloister, to commit fornication or other offence on pain of expulsion ;

that a brother or sister making a quarrel or charge unjustly, whereby public or private scandal should arise, should suffer similar penalties ; and that none should usurp any office or power within the hospital without the assent of the master and the more discreet part of the chapter.

When the war broke out in 1296 between the two kingdoms, the hospital from its position without the walls of Carlisle was open to attack and soon became impoverished and almost ruined. It was found next to impossible to observe the rules laid down a few years before. Whereupon Richard Oriell, the custos during the absence of Hugh de Cressingham the master, managed as best he could in the altered state of political affairs. It was arranged by him that each of the brethren and sisters should receive yearly from the hospital by the hands of the master for sustenance two skeps of barley, two skeps of oats, two skeps of flour, three strikes of wheat, if there was wheat enough from the wainage of the hospital, two cart and two wagon loads of wood, a portion of the bread and ale received from the commonalty of Carlisle, and 4*s.* out of the rents of the hospital for clothing and other necessaries till the house was relieved.[2]

The procedure introduced by Oriell and followed by some of his successors was a great benefit to the house, whereby it was much enriched, and many poor persons other than foundationers were participators in its alms. When Edward II. bestowed the custody on Thomas de Wederhale, the good governance of the hospital began to decline. The new master was not a chaplain and did not observe the rules of the foundation or the constitutions made by his predecessors. He wasted the goods in many ways and kept the common seal in his own possession, and charged the hospital with corrodies to divers people without the assent of the brethren and sisters. The chapter of the hospital soon ceased to exist under his methods. When an inmate of the hospital died, no other was admitted to residence according to the rules of the foundation, those being non-resident who were admitted on the presentation of benefactors like the heirs of Hugh de Morvill and the commonalty of Carlisle. During the mastership of Wederhale the number of lepers and other poor persons was curtailed, and divine worship and works of piety were wholly withdrawn, except that he retained a chaplain to sing mass daily and eight poor persons who dwelt elsewhere and lived on the goods of the hospital. The affairs of the house went from

---

[1] Pat. 15 Edw. III. pt. i. m. 49.

[2] Ibid.

bad to worse. Each succeeding master was no better than the last. The hospital became the perquisite of the master and was farmed for his own profit.[1] Nor did that official cease to forward his own interests. In 1336 the royal tax gatherers were forbidden to assess the goods of the hospital, as it had been founded by the king's progenitors, and was so slenderly endowed that there was scarcely a sufficiency for the maintenance of the master and brethren and other poor persons who resorted there.[2]

The condition of the hospital became a public scandal, and reports on its dilapidation and mismanagement were laid before the Bishop of Carlisle and the Crown. The king prohibited the bishop from visitation, no doubt on the representation of Thomas de Goldyngton, the master, as irregular and inconvenient in institutions of royal foundation or patronage.[3] Commissions of inquiry into the misrule of the hospital became the order of the day. In 1335 an inquisition *ad quod damnum* found that the rules had not been observed as they ought to have been for thirty-six years and more, because the said place was burned and totally destroyed, first by the Earl of Buchan's war and afterwards several times by the Scots, so that the constitution had not been and as yet could not be observed.[4] Matters dragged on till the summer of 1340, when a visitation of the hospital was made by a commission consisting of the bishop and prior of Carlisle, Robert Parvyng, and Robert de Eglesfeld, parson of Burgh under Stainmore. The whole history and management of the institution was probed to the bottom and a sweeping report on its condition, as already detailed, was made. The master was ordered to appear before the king in his chancery at Westminster, the common seal was taken from him, and the corrody holders were delivered to the custody of the prior of Carlisle.[5]

The internal condition of the hospital was again an anxiety to the authorities in 1380. It was the duty of Simon, Archbishop of Canterbury, to visit it, but as he was unable through urgent business to do so personally, he commissioned the prior of Wetheral, Hugh de Westbrook, and Adam, parson of Bolton, to undertake the inquiry. The terms of reference extended to divers defects in respect of its houses, books, vestments and other ornaments, the diminution of its chaplains, the alienation and waste of its lands, and quarrels among its ministers.[6] As a new master was appointed a few months afterwards, it may be taken that a reformation had been effected by the visitation. The hospital lingered on as an independent institution till 1477, when Edward IV. transferred it with all its lands, tenements, rights, liberties, franchises, commodities, and emoluments, to the priory of Carlisle, the grant to take effect on the death or cession of the master. For this concession the priory was obliged to find a canon who was a priest, to be called the king's chaplain, to celebrate masses and other divine services in the monastery for the good estate of the king and his consort Elizabeth, Queen of England, and their children, and for their souls after death.[7] It should be remembered that the change in the constitution of the hospital did not impair the right of those who had a legal interest in its endowments. The Dacres continued to exercise the privilege of presentation of poor men to corrodies as the lords of Burgh had done since the days of Hugh de Morvill. On the death of Humphrey Lord Dacre in 1484, the nomination to a corrody in the hospital of St. Nicholas, Carlisle, at that time worth 13s. 4d. a year, was reckoned among the Dacre possessions in right of the barony of Burgh-by-Sands.[8]

One feature of the endowments of the hospital deserves a special mention inasmuch as it appears to have been a common appurtenance of leper houses, that is, a thrave of corn was due from time immemorial from every ploughland in the county of Cumberland. In 1358 a jury reported a long list of defaulters in various parishes who had detained their contributions for the past eight years. These dues ought to have been delivered in the autumn of each year to the bailiff of the hospital.[9] Bishop Appleby was obliged to denounce the practice in 1371. The

[1] Pat. 15 Edw. III. pt. i. m. 49.
[2] Close, 10 Edw. III. m. 14.
[3] Carl. Epis. Reg., Kirkby, f. 329.
[4] Inq. a.q.d. 9 Edw. III. No. 6; Pat. 9 Edw. III. pt. ii. m. 14d. The hospital was burnt in 1337 by the Scots (*Chron. de Lanercost*, 292).
[5] Pat. 15 Edw. III. pt. i. mm. 49, 48. To the researches made in 1340 and to the exemplification of the results of the inquiry on this patent roll we are indebted for much of what we know of the history of this hospital. The roll has been printed in full by Dr. Henry Barnes of Carlisle (*Trans. Cumb. and Westmld. Arch. Soc.* x. 114–23), and an excellent summary has been given in the Calendar prepared by Mr. R. F. Isaacson of the Public Record Office. To this inquiry, no

doubt, we owe the record of the two ancient deeds in the register of Bishop Kirkby.
[6] Pat. 3 Ric. II. pt. ii. m. 20d.
[7] Ibid. 17 Edw. IV. pt. i. m. 16.
[8] *Cal. of Inq. p.m. Henry VII.* i. 157.
[9] Inq. p.m. 31 Edw. III. pt. ii. No. 53.

sheaves were called 'thraves of St. Nicholas,' and were due, in the bishop's opinion, by grant of the kings of England.[1]

In 1541 the possessions of the hospital were included in the endowment charter of the dean and chapter of Carlisle,[2] whose estates were charged under the letters patent to maintain a chaplain to celebrate divine offices in the hospital in presence of three 'bedells' and the lepers therein, with a pension for the said poor 'bedells.' There is now no trace of the buildings of the hospital in existence; nothing is left of the institution but the name of the district of St. Nicholas in Botchergate to the south of the city. From the parliamentary survey of 1650 we learn that the hospital was altogether destroyed during the siege of Carlisle in 1645, and that the churchyard belonging to it abutted on the highway on the south and east. Evidences of burial have been found in that district during the last century. The whole site is now covered with streets and modern dwellings.

MASTERS OF THE HOSPITAL OF ST. NICHOLAS, CARLISLE

William, chaplain, circa 1200[3]
Robert son of Ralf, temp. John[4]
William, rector, circa 1240[5]
John, rector, circa 1245[6]
Symon, master, 1270[7]
Hugh de Cressingham, 1293–7[8]
Richard de Oriell, custos, 1300[9]
Henry de Craystok, master, appointed in 1303[10]

John de Crosseby, 1309–27[11]
Thomas de Wederhale, temp. Edw. II. confirmed in 1327[12]
Ralf Chevaler, 1328[13]
William de Northwell, 1332[14]
Thomas de Goldyngton, 1334[15]
John de Appleby, 1369[16]
William de Cotyngham, 1380,[17] resigned in 1388
Nicholas de Lodal, warden, 1388,[18] resigned in 1389
John de Grysedale, warden, 1389[19]
William Hayton, clerk, resigned in 1423
John Canonby, 1423[20]
John de Thorpe, last independent master, circa 1477[21]

13. THE HOSPITAL OF ST. SEPULCHRE, CARLISLE

This hospital appears to have been a vigorous institution in the thirteenth century,[22] but very little is known of its later history. At a date between 1309 and 1327 John de Crosseby, 'mestre del Hospital de Seynt Nicolas dehors Kardoil,' sent a petition to the king in council on behalf of John de la More and John de Boulton, brothers of the hospitals of St. Nicholas and St. Sepulchre, about certain arrearages due to the Crown from the demesne lands in the suburb of Carlisle leased to them by Henry III.[23]

[1] Carl. Epis. Reg., Appleby, f. 212. It is said that King Athelstan endowed in 936 the hospital of St. Leonard, York, with a thrave of corn, called Petercorne, from every plough in the bishopric of York (Dugdale, *Mon.* vi. 608–9). Certainly Bishop Appleby issued a monition in 1378 to his subjects of Carlisle not to neglect the payment of the *blada sancti Petri* to the same establishment (Carl. Epis. Reg., Appleby, f. 306). A similar mandate had been issued by Edward III. in 1333 to the sheriffs of Cumberland and Westmorland to aid the proctors and bailiffs of the hospital of St. Leonard, York, in levying one thrave of corn for every plough in these counties taken by virtue of charters granted by former kings (Pat. 7 Edw. III. pt. i. m. 11).
[2] Ibid. 33 Henry VIII. pt. ix. mm. 11–5; *L. and P. Hen. VIII.* xvi. 878 (11).
[3] *Reg. of Wetherhal* (Cumb. and Westmld. Arch. Soc.), 114.
[4] *Plac. de Quo Warr.* (Rec. Com.), 122.
[5] *Reg. of Wetherhal* (Cumb. and Westmld. Arch. Soc.), 276.
[6] Ibid. 176–9.   [7] Ibid. 180–1.
[8] Pat. 21 Edw. I. m. 13.
[9] Carl. Epis. Reg., Halton, f. 46.
[10] Pat. 31 Edw. I. m. 17. It is stated in the

letters patent that the office was vacant through the death of Cressingham, an event which took place in 1297.
[11] Ibid. 2 Edw. II. pt. i. m. 17. This master was instrumental in the rebuilding (*refeccione*) of the chapel of the hospital in 1319 (Close, 13 Edw. II. m. 21), and caused John de Culgayth, rector of a moiety of Bampton, to be arrested in 1310 for the non-payment of his dues (Carl. Epis. Reg., Halton, f. 138).
[12] Pat. 1 Edw. III. pt. ii. m. 22.
[13] Ibid. 2 Edw. III. pt. ii. m. 4; 3 Edw. III. pt. i. m. 37.
[14] Ibid. 6 Edw. III. pt. ii. m. 18.
[15] Ibid. 7 Edw. III. pt. ii. m. 3. In 1342 it is said that he, described as *medicus*, passed into Scotland with Johan le Spicer of Carlisle to give medical aid to the king's enemies (Pat. 16 Edw. III. pt. ii. m. 28d).
[16] Dugdale, *Mon.* vi. 757.
[17] Pat. 4 Ric. II. pt. i. m. 26.
[18] Ibid. 11 Ric. II. pt. ii. m. 20.
[19] Ibid. 12 Ric. II. pt. ii. m. 4.
[20] Ibid. 1 Hen. VI. pt. ii. m. 4.
[21] Ibid. 17 Edw. IV. pt. i. m. 16.
[22] Inq. p.m. 31 Hen. III. No. 25; 34 Hen. III. No. 46.
[23] Anct. Petitions, No. 1949.

14. THE HOSPITAL OF ST. LEONARD, WIGTON[1]

This house had property in Waverton at an early date, for it is mentioned in a charter of Lambert son of Gillestephen of Waverton that the land of the hospital was situated on the east side of the vill.[2] When the chantries were dissolved in 1546, George Lancaster was incumbent of the hospital of St. Leonard, Wigton.[3]

15. THE HOSPITAL OF LENNH', BEWCASTLE

The collectors of the tenth, given by the clergy of the diocese of Carlisle in 1294 to Edward I. for the Holy Land, refer to this house and reported that the hospital of Lennh' in Bewcastle (*Hospitale de Lennh'* in Bothe-

caster) was unable to pay the assessment as the land belonging to it lay uncultivated.[5]

16. THE HOSPITAL HOUSE OF CALDBECK

Gospatric son of Orm gave this hospital (*hospitalem domum de Caldebech*) with the church of that place to the priory of Carlisle[6] some time before 1170.

17. THE HOUSE OF ST. JOHN, KESWICK

The house of St. John (*domus sancti Johannis*) existed either as a hospital or hermitage in the early years of the thirteenth century[7] and has bequeathed its name to the vale of St. John near Keswick.

COLLEGES

18. THE COLLEGE OF GREY-STOKE

The district served by the collegiate church of Greystoke ranks third in the list of the extensive parishes in Cumberland, the civil parishes of St. Bees and Crosthwaite being considerably larger. The church occupies a picturesque corner of Greystoke Park near to the gates of the castle on the eastern side of the parish, close to the boundary of the parish of Dacre. It contains two ancient chapelries, Threlkeld on the west side of the parish and Watermillock on the south towards the lake of Ulleswater. The area of the whole district is over 48,000 acres. In 1291 the church of Greystoke, valued at £120,[4] was the richest parochial institution in the diocese of Carlisle.

When the fashion of founding collegiate churches was introduced into Cumberland, a start was not made with the church of Grey-

stoke. The credit of the first attempt was due to Sir Robert Parvyng, the well known chancellor of Edward III., who owned considerable property in the county. Though his foundation at Melmerby was never completed, mention may be made of the preliminary steps taken with that intent, inasmuch as they furnish us with some very interesting features of collegiate institutions at an early period of their history. In 1342 Sir Robert entered into negotiations with the ecclesiastical authorities for the purpose of transforming the parish church of Melmerby into a college of eight priests, one of whom, Richard de Caldecote, was designated the *custos* or master. The fragmentary record[8] of the proposed

[5] Reg. of Holmcultram, MS. f. 278.
[6] Dugdale, *Mon.* vi. 144.
[7] Reg. of Fountains Abbey (Cott. MS. Tib. C, xii.), f. 78b.
[8] Carl. Epis. Reg., Kirkby, MS. f. 459. The deed, as recorded in the episcopal register, ends abruptly without apparent cause, but it is undoubtedly authentic, for on 4 May 1342 Robert Parvyng had licence from the king for the alienation in mortmain of the advowson of Melmerby to certain chaplains to celebrate divine offices in that church and for its appropriation by the chaplains (Pat. 16 Edw. III. pt. i. m. 7). It may be taken that the scheme was abortive owing to the death of Sir Robert in the following year and the division of his property among grandchildren (Inq. p.m. 17 Edw. III. ser. i. No. 48). The proposed institution was described as a college or chantry, but there is no doubt that the former was intended : a chaplaincy in a collegiate church was frequently described as a chantry.

[1] At one time hospitals such as this and those following must have been numerous in Cumberland, for near to many villages the name of Spittal, the usual term in the vernacular for hospital, still survives to remind us that some such institution once occupied that site though all record of it has been lost. Nothing has been discovered to show the nature of these institutions, but it may be taken that in them some provision was made to isolate cases of endemic disease or to supply the wants of the poor or to afford shelter to the destitute.
[2] Reg. of Holmcultram, MS. f. 73.
[3] Aug. Off. Chant. Cert. No. 12.
[4] *Pope Nich. Tax.* (Rec. Com.), 320.

foundation supplies us with the particulars of the institution in contemplation. One messuage and an oxgang of land in Melmerby together with the advowsons of the rectories of Melmerby and Skelton were assigned for the support of the college. In the former parish the master was to be responsible for the cure of souls, but in the latter a vicar was to be appointed. No member of the college could be removed by the Bishop of Carlisle except for reasonable cause, and all chaplains were subject to the master. The founder strictly reserved to himself and his heirs the rights of patronage. It was arranged that the master and chaplains should repair daily in the morning (*aurora*) or at sunrise to the church of Melmerby, vested in surplice, amice, and black cope, and sing the Canonical Hours devoutly and distinctly, viz. matins and prime according to the use of Sarum ; which done, immediately without pause, the mass of the Blessed Virgin should be celebrated *cum nota* by one of the chaplains ; then two chaplains by the direction of the master should celebrate two masses at the altar of St. Nicholas, one a mass of St. Nicholas, and the other a mass of St. Margaret. In this abortive attempt to found the college, licences were sought from the king, the bishop and chapter of Carlisle, and Thomas de Blith, rector of Melmerby, but there is no evidence to show why the foundation was not completed, except that Sir Robert Parvyng died in 1343, the year after the proposal was made.

A similar incident attended the next attempt to found a collegiate church in Cumberland, though the scheme was ultimately successful. In 1358 Lord William de Greystoke proposed to change the rectory of Greystoke into a college with a master or *custos* and chaplains, and obtained a licence from the Crown to bestow the advowson of the church and certain lands and tenements in Newbiggin on the new foundation.[1] Bishop Welton of Carlisle gave his sanction and confirmed the appointment of the rector, Richard de Hoton Roof, to be the master, and Andrew de Briscoe, Richard de Brampton, William de Wanthwaite, Robert de Threlkeld and William de Hill, to be the chaplains.[2] The scheme, however, was carried no further at that time owing to the death of Lord Greystoke in July 1359, and the minority of the heir.[3]

Soon after Ralf, Lord Greystoke, came of age, the scheme for founding the college was revived. In 1374 the licence granted to Lord William, his father, was renewed to him[4] by Edward III., but many difficulties had to be surmounted before the foundation was brought to a successful issue. Lord Greystoke appealed to Bishop Appleby of Carlisle in January 1377–8, alleging that the church of which he was patron was wealthy ; that in the absence of the rector the church was badly served and the sick were not properly visited ; and that in consequence the parishioners were not as devout as they should be. The bishop issued a commission, composed almost equally of clerics and laymen, which made a report on the local conditions. It was found after inquiry that the church was valued at £100, or £80 after taking away all deductions ; that it was served by one parochial chaplain and his parish clerk (*clericum aquebajulum*) in the parish church, and by another chaplain and his clerk in the chapel of Watermillock (Wethirmelok), three miles distant from the mother church, and by another chaplain and his clerk in Threlkeld, four miles distant ; and that the parish of Greystoke, though it was extensive, being seven miles long and four miles broad, was thus served from time immemorial.[5] The report was apparently not satisfactory to the bishop, for in April 1379 he issued another commission with substantially the same reference. After the second inquiry it was reported that the church was rich, though not so rich as of old ; the revenues were on the decrease rather than the increase ; that the value was £100, though it was once £120 ; that the said church used to be ruled by three chaplains and three clerks, and that it was at that time so served ; and that it could not be on account of the size of the parish or the fewness of the ministers that the parishioners were spiritually neglected, as the

he had the king's pardon for acquiring lands and tenements in Greystoke without licence (Orig. R. 35 Edw. III. m. 49). His nuncupative will was proved on 22 January 1365–6, by which he bequeathed his body to be buried in the churchyard of Greystoke, and made certain dispositions by way of settlement with his successor for dilapidations in the choir of the church and houses of the rectory (Carl. Epis. Reg., Appleby, f. 145).
[4] Orig. R. 48 Edw. III. m. 33. The licence was again renewed by Richard II. on 6 December 1377, in which the two former licences were confirmed. The decease of William, Lord Greystoke, is stated to have been the cause of delay in the first instance as the alienation was incomplete when he died (Pat. 1 Ric. II. pt. ii. m. 10).
[5] Carl. Epis. Reg., Appleby, ff. 306–7.

[1] Orig. R. 32 Edw. III. m. 25.
[2] Nicolson and Burn, *Hist. of Cumb.* ii. 362.
[3] Inq. p.m. 33 Edw. III. ser. i. No. 43. That the scheme was not completed at the death of Lord Greystoke is certain, for Richard de Hoton was rector, and not master or *custos*, in 1361 when

parish and the ministry were constituted then as of old ; yet it would be to the greater glory of God if the number of ministering clergy was increased ; and that the revenues were able to sustain a provost and five chaplains at the parish church as well as the chaplains at Watermillock and Threlkeld.[1] Notwithstanding all these negotiations, nothing more appears to have been done for two or three years.[2]

The bishop and the patron were not turned from their purpose by the continued opposition to the scheme, for the college was formally founded in 1382. When all the preliminaries were arranged Bishop Appleby sent a mandate to the parochial chaplain of Greystoke and to the chaplains of Threlkeld and Watermillock, calling their attention to the great defects in the nave of the parish church, its stone walls, wood work, fittings, and glass windows, and to the ruinous condition of the tower (campanile eiusdem totaliter ruit ad terram), and setting them a time for their repair. He had heard also at his recent visitation that certain of the parishioners were frequenting the chapels of Threlkeld and Watermillock for divine offices, and were refusing to pay their portions to the maintenance of the mother church. It was intimated to them that all the inhabitants were obliged to contribute or incur the usual penalty.[3] On the petition of Ralf, Lord Greystoke, setting forth the urgent need of the new foundation, Pope Urban issued the necessary faculties in May 1382 for the erection of a college of seven perpetual chaplains, and Archbishop Nevill of York, his legate, completed the work. Gilbert Bowet was constituted the first master or keeper of the perpetual college of Greystoke, and to the six chantries other appointments were made : John Lake, of the diocese of Lichfield, to the chantry of the altar of St. Andrew ; Thomas Chambirleyne, of the diocese of Norwich, to the chantry of St. Mary the Virgin ; John Alve, of the diocese of York, to the chantry of St. John the Baptist ; Richard Barwell, of the diocese of

Lincoln, to the chantry of St. Katharine the Virgin ; Robert de Newton, of the diocese of Lichfield, to the chantry of St. Thomas the Martyr ; and John de Hare, of the diocese of York, to the chantry of the Apostles, St. Peter and St. Paul.[4] The master and chantry priests were bound in canonical obedience to the Bishop of Carlisle. Not one of the first collegiate staff was drawn from the diocese, except Gilbert Bowet, the master, who had been chaplain there from 1365 till the foundation of the college.[5] The patronage of the new establishment in head and members was retained in the house of Greystoke.[6]

The relationship of the college to the chapelry of Threlkeld was the subject of an ordination or award (laudum) made by Bishop Lumley of Carlisle in 1431. As discord had arisen between the rector or master and chaplains, fellows (consocios) or chantry priests (cantaristas) of the collegiate or parochial church of Greystoke on the one part and Sir Henry Threlkeld and the tenants of the vill or lordship of Threlkeld on the other, about the appointment of a chaplain or chaplains successively in the church or chapel of Threlkeld, which is dependent on the said church of Greystoke, and about the manner of tithing corn and hay and other fruits within the vill of Threlkeld, the whole dispute was placed in the bishop's hands at his personal visitation of the diocese in the collegiate church of Greystoke on 26 September 1431, and both parties undertook to abide by his award. It was decided by the bishop that Sir Henry Threlkeld and his heirs after him, with the consent of their tenants, should nominate the chaplain, within one month after the time of vacation, to the rector or master and chaplains of the college, and if they found him fit and able to celebrate divine offices and to minister the sacraments and sacramentals, they should admit him within six days to the chaplaincy ; but if they considered him unfit or unable they should send him to the bishop or his official for fuller examination. If the bishop found the nominee unfit, it should be lawful for the master, with the consent of the chaplains or chantry priests, for this one turn to nominate a fit person to the bishop within ten days from the rejection of the former candidate ; otherwise the nomination for that

---

[1] On 12 February 1379–80, the rector, John de Claston, had leave to absent himself for two years and to farm the cure during that period (Carl. Epis. Reg., Appleby, f. 321). It seems that William Eston acted as his substitute, for he was returned as the rector of Greystoke for the clerical subsidy granted to Richard II. in the second year of his reign, the value of the benefice having been returned at £40 and the tax at £1 (Clerical Subsidies, $\frac{5}{12}$, dioc. of Carlisle).

[2] Carl. Epis. Reg., Appleby, f. 342.

[3] Ibid. ff. 309–10.

[4] Ibid. f. 343.

[5] Ibid. ff. 145–6 ; Clerical Subsidies, Ψ, dioc. of Carlisle.

[6] Cal. of Inq. p.m. Hen. VII. i. 109 ; Inq. p.m. 9 Hen. VIII. Nos. 32–8.

turn only should pertain to the bishop, future nominations remaining with Sir Henry Threlkeld and his heirs. It was also ordained that the college of Greystoke should receive all the tithes of Threlkeld except tithes of corn and hay together with the oblations due and accustomed ; that the inhabitants should pay to the chaplain celebrating in the chapel £3 17*s.* *in diem denariis* at the feast of St. Peter ad vincula and Michaelmas in lieu of the tithes of corn and hay, whether the land was cultivated or not ; and that the college should allow the chaplain a yearly stipend of 12*s.* sterling over and above the sum contributed by the inhabitants.[1]

When the ecclesiastical survey was taken in 1535, the total value of the rectory and college was set down as £82 14*s.*, out of which the master was obliged to pay £42 6*s.* 8*d.* in pensions, synodals and procurations to the Bishop of Carlisle, and in stipends of the chaplains. Each chantry priest received an annual allowance of £3 6*s.* 8*d.* for victuals, and a like sum in money for private use, at the hands of the master of the college.[2]

In pursuance of the Act of Parliament (1 Edw. VI. cap. 14) for the dissolution of chantries, the king issued a commission, dated at Westminster on 14 February 1547–8, 'for thenquyrie, survey and examynacon of all colleges, chauntries, frechappelles, fraternyteis, guyldes, stipendaries, priestes, and other spirituall promocons' within the county of Cumberland 'whiche are geven and oughte to come unto his highnes.' From the survey we learn that there were 3,000 'howslinge people' in the parish of Greystoke, and that the 'colledge in the parish churche there' was 'off the foundacon of one Urbane, bishoppe of Rome, at the peticon of one Rafe, baron of Graystocke, auncestor to the lorde Dacre that nowe is.' John Dacre, clerk, of the age of forty years, was the master, and had for his annual salary £40 'over and besides £61 in other places.'[3] It is also

stated that 'James Beamont, of th'age of 80 yeates, George Atkinson of th'age of 56 yeres, Anthony Garnett and Lancelot Levyns of th'age of 40 yeres, Edwarde Elwood of th'age of 50 yeres, and John Dawson of th'age of 58 yeres,[4] have every of them yerely for his salarie, over and besides £26 wch James Beamont hath in other places, £3 6*s.* 8*d.* besides their borde wch is in the hole £20.' The lands and tenements belonging to the college were valued at £84 19*s.* 8*d.*, from which £2 17*s.* 10*d.* should be deducted for reprises, 'and so remayneth clere by yere £82 1*s.* 10*d.*' The goods and chattels were valued at £16 17*s.* 8*d.* As a postscript to the survey the commissioners noted that 'the said John Dacre, master there, is also parson and hath no vycare indowed, but serveth the cure hymselfe.'[5]

When the king's agents had seized the chantries, the valuation of the college of Greystoke was returned at £78 14*s.* From the notes added to the new survey we may gather that there was some doubt in the minds of the commissioners about the legality of their proceedings in seizing the property of this college. To the schedule of pensions, in which the annual sum of £19 was assigned to the master, that is, somewhat less than half of his stipend, and £5 to each of the chaplains, the following memorandum was appended : 'Forasmuch as the title of this colleage is supposed doubtefull, respeit the pencions untill it be examyned in the court.' It is odd that it was to the college of Greystoke, and not as an appendix to the whole survey, that the commissioners affixed this observation : 'In all whych colleges, chauntryes, frechappelles, guyldes, fraternytyes, stypendaryes, ther ys no precher founde,. grammar scole taught, nor pore people relevyd, as yn ther severall certyfycates yt doth appere.' It

bility may be identified with the 'parson Dakers of St. Nicholas Hostell,' Cambridge, who 'hurt Christopher, Mr. Secretary's servant,' in 1530. When the vice-chancellor committed him to ward he escaped from the beadle, 'and that night there was such a jetting in Cambridge as ye never heard of, with such boyng and crying, even against our college, that all Cambridge might perceive it was in despite' of the vice-chancellor. It must have been a 'town and gown' row, for the vice-chancellor complained that it was 'made a country matter and greatly labored' (ibid. iv. 6325).

[4] It may be mentioned that the three chaplains, first named in this list, held respectively the chantries of St. Katharine, St. Peter and St. Mary the Virgin, in 1535 (*Valor Eccl.* [Rec. Com.], v. 287).

[5] Chant. Cert. No. 11, Cumberland.

---

[1] Carl. Epis. Reg., Smith, ff. 364–9. A notarial copy of this deed was entered in Bishop Smith's register on 27 July 1698, by desire of Archdeacon Nicolson, from the original in possession of Lord Lonsdale.

[2] *Valor Eccl.* (Rec. Com.), v. 287.

[3] In July 1526 the churches of Folkton, in the diocese of York, and Wemme, in the diocese of Coventry and Lichfield, were united during the incumbency of John Dacre, LL.B., of noble birth (*L. and P. Hen. VIII.* iv. 2360). Dacre can have been only about nineteen years of age at that time. Perhaps this young sprig of no-

was also reported that 'ij chaples are belonging to this colleage caulled Watermelike and Threlkett, thone distant vii myles and thother vi myles from the parish churche.'[1] When the legality of seizing the rectory and its profits on the king's behalf came to be reviewed in court, it was argued by the incumbent that he was possessed by presentation, admission, institution and induction ; that the church was indeed made collegiate, but it was by the pope's authority only ; that they had no common seal, and therefore were not a legal corporation. As judgment was given against the king, the church continued rectorial and parochial. In reporting the case Judge Dyer laid stress upon the want of a common seal, but Lord Coke was of opinion that the king's title failed owing to the fact that the church was made collegiate by the pope's authority only without the royal assent.[2] The argument of the appellant and the remarks of Lord Coke seem strange in the light of the letters patent of Edward III. and Richard II., by which the proposal to found the college of Greystoke received the royal sanction.

Masters of Greystoke

Gilbert Bowet, first master, 1382

Richard Lascy, 1412[3]

Adam de Aglionby, 1420[4]

Richard Wryght[5]

Thomas Eglisfelde[6]

[1] Chant. Cert. No. 12, Cumberland.

[2] Nicolson and Burn, *Hist. of Cumb.* ii. 363, quoting *Dyer's Reports*, f. 81, and *Coke's Reports*, iv. 107. See also Tanner, *Notitia* (ed. 1744), p. 77.

[3] Named in a commission with John de Burgham, rector of Melmerby, and Robert de Bampton, vicar of Crosby by Eden, to collect a tenth given to Henry IV. by the clergy of Carlisle, 20 Jan. 1411–2 (Clerical Subsidies, 9/9, dioc. of Carlisle).

[4] Sued in that year by William Rebanks and his wife for lands in Raughton (Nicolson and Burn, *Hist. of Cumb.* ii. 363). Aglionby was appointed priest of the chantry of St. Mary in 1386 on the death of Thomas Chamberlayne (Carl. Epis. Reg., Appleby, fo. 359).

[5] In 1704 Bishop Nicolson copied the following inscription in a window over the south door of the choir : 'Orate pro anima Ricardi Wryht quondam magistri Collegii de Graystok' (*Miscellany Accounts*, ed. Ferguson, pp. 129–30). As no date has been found, the name is placed here for convenience.

[6] Commemorated with Walter Readman on a sepulchral brass in the choir, the inscription on which was copied by the Rev. T. Lees about 1860 : 'Hic jacent corpora magistri Thome Eglisfelde et Walteri Readman veritatis professoris quondam huius collegii prepositorum. Qui Walterus obiit iiij° die Novembris Anno domini

Walter Readman, S.T.P. 1507,[7] died in 1509[8]

William Husband, 1509,[9] 1518[10]

John Whelpdale, died in 1526[11]

John Dacre, last master, 1535,[12] 1547[13]

19. THE COLLEGE OF KIRK-OSWALD

The collegiate church of Kirkoswald, situated in the Eden valley about fourteen miles to the south of Carlisle, was of late foundation and only existed for about twenty-five years before it was dissolved. It served

M° cccc° ix°. Quorum animabus propicietur Deus.' Browne Willis set down the date of Eglisfelde's mastership about 1440 (Tanner, *Notitia*, app. of edition, 1744), but from his association with Readman on the brass the date must be considerably later. He seems to have been Readman's immediate predecessor.

[7] One of the executors of Roger Leyburn, Bishop of Carlisle, under his will, dated 17 July 1507 ; appointed by the dean and chapter of York to collect the bishop's goods (*Test. Ebor.* Surtees Soc. iv. 262–3).

[8] Memorial brass given above.

[9] For the term, Michaelmas 1509–10, the registrar of the diocese of Carlisle accounted to the bishop for 13*s.* 4*d.* 'de institutione domini Wilhelmi Husbande ad ecclesiam collegiatam de Graistok' (MS. in diocesan registry).

[10] Jefferson, *Leath Ward*, p. 360. If Jefferson's date is correct, this was the master of Greystoke sent by Thomas, Lord Dacre, into Scotland on 8 Aug. 1516, to levy the queen's feoffment (Ellis, *Orig. Letters*, first ser. i. 133 ; *L. and P. Hen. VIII.* ii. 2293).

[11] On the floor in the south transept there is a memorial brass plate containing a half length figure of a doctor of laws, clad in gown and fur tippet with the arms of Whelpdale—three greyhounds current in pale and collared—on either side of the inscription : 'Orate pro anima Johannis Whelpdall, legum doctoris, magistri Collegii de Graystok et rectoris de Caldebek qui obiit viij° Julii anno domini 1526.' Around the head of the east window of Caldbeck church there runs a Latin legend that John Whelpdale 'hoc opus fieri fecit.' Care should be taken to discriminate between two rectors of Caldbeck of that name. The younger succeeded the elder in that church in 1488.

[12] *Valor Eccl.* (Rec. Com.), v. 287.

[13] Chant. Cert. (Cumb.), Nos. 11, 12. In the church there is a through-stone bearing the inscription : 'J.D.P.G. anno domini 1557.' The initials seem to mean 'John Dacre, provost of Greystoke,' as if he had resumed his old title in Queen Mary's reign. He conformed to all the ritual changes during the first years of Queen Elizabeth and died in 1567 (Carl. Epis. Reg., Best, fo. 22).

as the parish church for an area of 11,000 acres. Though the instrument of ordination cannot be traced, there is evidence enough to show that the institution was founded by Thomas, Lord Dacre, who died in 1525. The value of the benefice before the church was made collegiate was taxed at £48 1s. 5d. in 1291,[1] and at £5 in 1318,[2] owing to the devastation of the Scottish wars. In 1486,[3] on the death of Lord Dacre, the advowson was declared to be appurtenant to the manor and to belong to Thomas, his son and heir, at that time eighteen years of age.

In the ecclesiastical survey of 1535 the college is called 'the rectory and college of Kyrkowswald and Dacre,' and the superior is styled 'the master or provost of the collegiate church of St. Oswald of Kyrkoswald and Dacre.' The college was endowed with the advowsons and fruits of the associated churches of Kirkoswald and Dacre, both of which were in the patronage of the Dacre family. The foundation consisted of a master or provost and five chaplains, together with two perpetual vicars for the pastoral oversight of the parishes.[4] The total value was assessed at £78 16s. 6d., out of which several payments were due in rents, stipends and pensions. The perpetual vicars of Kirkoswald and Dacre received individually a stipend of £8 a year, and each of the five chaplains £6 13s. 4d. After all outgoings were deducted, there remained £27 17s. for the stipend of the master, £4 of which was in dispute between the college and the Bishop of Carlisle. The names of the collegiate staff were John Hering, LL.D., master or provost ; Thomas Moyses, perpetual vicar of the church of Kirkoswald ; Thomas Langrig, perpetual vicar of Dacre, and John Scailes, Roland Dawson, John Blencarne, Peter Levyns, and William Lowthyan, perpetual chaplains of the college.[5] The patronage of the college in head and members belonged to Lord Dacre.

The advisers of Edward VI. were a little too precipitate in their attempt to dissolve this college under the authority of the Act of 37 Henry VIII. cap. 4. On 19 April 1547 they despatched letters to Rowland Threlkeld (Thirkeld), the provost, intimating the altera-

tion of the college to another use and promising pensions of reasonable sort to the members. On the following day, when the commissioners arrived at Kirkoswald and took possession, it seems that the provost refused to surrender the house and offered resistance. There are no signatures to the deed of surrender,[6] and as the impression of the seal is broken and very much obliterated, it is impossible to say whether the official seal of the college, if one existed, was used for that purpose. Later on, 8 June, it was intimated that the privy council had once resolved to have punished the disobedience to the king's commissioners and make an example for the terror of others, but as the members of the college were now grown more manageable and were bent on compliance, and seemed sorry for their former stubbornness, it was thought fit to continue them on the premises till further orders should be taken for their pensions and for the disposal of the college. For the present only an inventory of the goods should be taken.[7] In this way a virtue was made of a necessity and the commissioners retired with as much dignity as they could under the circumstances.

Under the Act of 1 Edward VI. cap. 14 the privy council was on surer ground. The surveyors of chantries and colleges, appointed on 14 February 1547–8 by the powers given under the above Act, stated that the parish of 'Kirkeswolde' contained 500 'howseling people,' and that the 'colledge in the parishe churche there' was 'off the foundacon of Thomas late lorde Dacres,[8] father of the lorde Dacres that nowe is.' The lands and tenements belonging to the college were valued at £89 10s. 9d., and 'Rowlande Threlkelde, clerke, provoste there, of th'age of 68 yeres, hathe yerely for his salarye, over and besides £52 in other places, £20.[9]

Some of the particulars of the dissolution of the college are not devoid of interest. It transpired that 'one thowsand howseling people,' no doubt including the inhabitants of the parish of Dacre, were dependent on the college, and that there were 'too vycars indewyd in the sayd colledge, viz. John Scoles, vycar ther, and Rowlande Dawson, serving in the churche of Dacre appropriate to the

---

[1] *Pope Nich. Tax.* (Rec. Com.), 320.
[2] Ibid. 333.
[3] *Cal. Inq. p.m. Hen. VII.* i. 157.
[4] The editors of Dugdale's *Monasticon*, vi. 1450, were misled by Tanner (*Notitia*, p. 78) and Nicolson and Burn (*Hist. of Cumb.* ii. 426) in supposing that Kirkoswald was a college of twelve secular priests founded by Robert Threlkeld.
[5] *Valor Eccl.* (Rec. Com.), v. 290–1.

[6] *Dep. Keeper's Rep.* viii. App. ii. 25.
[7] Collier, *Eccl. Hist.* v. 231, ed. Lathbury ; *Acts of P.C.* 1547–50, p. 504.
[8] In 1536, when Drs. Layton and Legh compiled their celebrated *Black Book* or *Compendium Compertorum*, they reported that 'Dominus Dakres' was founder of the college and that its revenues were worth £71 (*L. and P. Hen. VIII.* x. 364).
[9] *Chant. Cert.* (Cumberland), No. 11.

II   209   27

same colledge, eyther of theym having £8 yerely.' The total revenue of the house was set down at £79 19s. 6d., and 'so remayneth clere' £71 19s. 6d., after deducting £8 'for the wages' of the vicar of Dacre. The net stipends 'whych the sayd incumbents yerelye recevid for ther lyvynges' were as follow: 'Roland Threlkeld, master of the sayd colledge, for his pencion and fyndynge of the howse, £35 19s. 6d. ; John Scalles, £7 6s. 8d. ; Robert Thomson, John Blenkerne, Robert Redshawe, William Lauthean and William Hayre, £6 each.' The incumbents of the two parishes were allowed to remain in spiritual charge, but the master and five chaplains were ejected, the former receiving an annual pension of £17 10s., and each of the latter £5.[1]

As the last master of the college was in many respects a remarkable man, the account of him written in 1677 by Richard Singleton may be given here. In describing the church of Melmerby, of which Roland Threlkeld had been rector, he says :—

The window at the east end of the quire hath 3 lights, proportionable to the rest of the building, wherin formerly hath been store of curious painted glasse. In the midlemost of which lights towards the top ther is yet to be seen a coat of the Threlkelds in its colours, a maunch gules in a ffield argent : and in the midst of the uppermost part of the maunche there is, I take it, a trefoil. In the light between the said midle light and the vestry hath been set up or painted in his gown and cassoke I conceive (not much unlike to ours at this day) one Rol[and] Thr[elkeld] which is yet to be seen entire from his midle to his feet, and his right arme is yet extant, with this inscription underneath at the bottom, in black letters : '𝕺𝖗𝖆𝖙𝖊 𝖕𝖗𝖔 𝖆𝖓𝖎𝖒𝖆 𝕽𝖔𝖑𝖆𝖓𝖉𝖎 . . . . . (under that these words) 𝕯𝖚𝖋𝖙𝖔𝖓.' I suppose this inscription hath gon all along the bottom of the three lights and sett out all his titles, ffor report tells us, he was rector of Dufton and vicar of Lazonby as well as rector of Melmorby : he was rector also of Haughton in the Spring neer Duresme and prebendary of Carlisle and master of Kirkoswald Colledge. 'Twas he that built a bridge at Force mill for his

own convenience to passe between Melmoreby (wher he most resided) and Lazonby. He was not married, nor did he admitt any womane to manage about his house, but kept (as I have heard by some) a dozen men, by another, sixteen men to wait on him, and for every man he usually kild a hiefe at Martinmasse time (pluralities sure were not scrupled then since a man might have enjoyed *tot quot*).

From the same narrative[2] we learn that while master of Kirkoswald he made considerable additions to the church of Melmerby.

Masters of Kirkoswald

John Hering, LL.D. 1523,[3] 1535[4]
Roland Threlkeld, last master, 1539, 1543,[5] 1548.

[1] Chant. Cert. (Cumberland), No. 12.

[1] The MS., entitled 'The Present State of the Parish and Man' of Melmerby in Cumberland from Mr. Singleton, Rector there, and sent to me 19 of June, 1677. T[homas] M[achel],' is bound up in vol. vi. of the Machel collection in the custody of the dean and chapter of Carlisle. As Singleton's information was only traditional, his facts should be accepted with great caution.

[2] On 5 December 1523, Thomas Lord Dacre, the founder of the college, appointed Thomas Moyses, one of the five perpetual chaplains in the said college, John Hering being at that time 'provost of the church of St. Oswald, Kirkoswald' (Add. MS. 24965, f. 123b ; L. and P. Hen. VIII. iii. 3606). The college cannot have been founded long before this date.

[3] Valor Eccl. (Rec. Com.), v. 290.

[4] Mentioned in the First Fruits Composition Books under 1539 and 1543 in connection with the college of Kirkoswald ; rector of Halton in Lancashire in 1542 (Jackson, Papers and Pedigrees, ii. 295). Singleton confounded Halton with 'Houghton in the Spring near Duresme' as aforesaid. At the time of his death in 1565, Threlkeld was rector of Melmerby and Dufton (Carl. Epis. Reg., Best, f. 21). By his will proved at Carlisle on 3 October 1565, he made certain bequests to poor people in the parishes of Melmerby, Dufton, Halton, Kirkoswald and Lazonby ; his body 'to be buryed within the quere of the parish church of Melmerby.' In his will the ancient phraseology was maintained (Jackson, Papers and Pedigrees, ii. 306–12).

MONUMENTAL
EFFIGIES

THE county of Cumberland is fairly rich in ancient monumental effigies. Forty-one are still to be found in twenty-four churches in the county. All are described in detail in this article. It will be seen that in some instances there are as many as two or more independent figures, while in six churches the effigies of man and wife are lying side by side. Images of warriors in mail armour, perhaps of the thirteenth century, are to be seen at Calder Abbey, Dacre, Lanercost and Ousby. Fourteenth century effigies exist at Cumrew, Croglin, Greystoke, Kirkland, Kirkoswald, Great Salkeld. Of fifteenth century date we find specimens at Ainstable, Crosthwaite, Greystoke, Millom and Workington. At Camerton we have 'Black Tom' Curwen, who is supposed to have died in 1510. Others of the sixteenth century are Sir Richard Salkeld and Dame Jane his wife at Wetheral, and Bishop Barrow (possibly) in the cathedral at Carlisle. At Great Salkeld A. Hutton and his wife, 1637, lie on altar tombs in the churchyard, and a mural tablet to the memory of Thomas and Margaret Bertram (1609) adorns the east wall of the church of Kirkoswald.

The only ecclesiastics are two bishops in the cathedral, and an archdeacon at Great Salkeld. Civilians with their wives remain at Crosthwaite and Great Salkeld, while knights with their wives are at Ainstable, Millom, Wetheral and Workington. Female effigies alone are seven in number, viz. at Cumrew, Croglin, Kirkoswald, Milburn, Stanwix, Torpenhow and Whitbeck. Only two wooden effigies are in existence, viz. at Ousby and Millom. The small figures at Holme Cultram and Bowness-on-Solway are clearly fragments of altar tombs. Perhaps the most curious is the small figure at Ainstable, which is so far a puzzle to antiquaries.

AINSTABLE

I. An effigy of red sandstone of a man in plate armour with shirt of mail showing at the neck. Length, 5 feet 6 inches. The head is bare, with a band round the forehead, and rests on a tilting helmet with crest-wreath, but without crest. The face has beard and moustachios. A tight fitting surcoat with escalloped lower edge covers the body. This is charged with the armorial bearings of the Aglionby family, viz. argent, two bars, and in chief three martlets sable. A bawdric of panels of quatrefoils supports a dagger on the right side. The arm defences consist of plain pauldrons, brassards, elbow cops, and vambraces of several plates. The gauntlets are very large (probably of leather faced with steel) and perfect, the thumbs and joints of

211

the fingers being seen distinctly. The thighs are covered with plain plates and the knees have knee cops, also small and plain. The armour is of early fifteenth century date. Built into the wall, close by this effigy, is the crest of the Aglionbys (a demi-eagle displayed, gold).

II. A lady with horned head-dress resting on a pillow. The features are well marked and strong. The upper bodice is plain; the waist is encircled by a girdle with buckle. The under garment is shown at the wrists buttoned up the arms as far as seen. The hands are placed in an attitude of prayer; the ends of the fingers are gone, but the thumbs are visible. The feet are broken off. Around the tomb is this inscription : ORATE PRO ANIMA KATARINE DENTON QUE OBIIT A DNI M CCCCXXVIII.

These effigies, representing John Aglionby and Katherine Denton his wife, were originally in St. Cuthbert's Church, Carlisle, but are supposed to have been removed when it was rebuilt in 1778. Bishop Nicolson, in his *Miscellany Accounts* (p. 101), writing of St. Cuthbert's Church, Carlisle, says : 'In the north isle, over against the middle window (in which are the Aglionbys' arms in cross), lies a man in armour with his wife by his side, and over her, Orate, etc. (as above).'

III. A small red sandstone effigy 3 feet long, now in the chancel of Ainstable Church. The figure is clad in a loose robe or surcoat, and the feet rest on a dog. The head, which has been covered with a mitre or cap, possibly a bascinet, is much broken. On the breast, suspended by a band round the neck, is a heater-shaped shield [1] charged with a fret, probably for Salkeld.

BOWNESS-ON-SOLWAY

Built into the wall of the rector's stable is a red sandstone headless trunk of an ecclesiastic wearing a chasuble and holding a book. The portion which remains of the original effigy is 2 feet long by 1 foot 6 inches broad.

CARLISLE CATHEDRAL

I. The effigy, which is of Purbeck marble, is now in an arch in the north aisle on the floor. It was placed in this arch in 1856, at the time of the restoration of the cathedral, and it only goes into it owing to the fact that the feet have been broken off. The follow-

ing is a description by Mr. Bloxam, F.S.A. : 'The effigy of a bishop of the thirteenth century. He is represented bearded, with the *mitra pretiosa* on his head, the amice about his neck, and in the alb, tunic, and dalmatic, over which is worn the chesible, which is long, with the rationale in front of the breast. The right hand, now gone, was in the act of benediction. The pastoral staff is on the left of the body. Above the head is an Early English canopy, now much mutilated. This is said to be Bishop de Everdon, who died in 1254 or 1255.'[2]

Chancellor Ferguson considered that this effigy might be that of Bishop Ireton,[3] who died in 1292. There is no evidence that de Everdon had a monument in the cathedral. The canopy has an angel with clasped hands on either side.

II. In the south aisle is a recumbent effigy of a bishop in red sandstone. Mr. Bloxam describes this figure thus : 'His face is closely shaven; on his head is worn the *mitra pretiosa* with pendent infulæ behind. The amice is worn about the neck. On the body appear, first the skirts of the alb, then the extremities of the stole, then the tunic, over that the dalmatic, over all the chesible, with the rationale in front of the breast. The maniple hangs down from the left arm ; the right hand is gone, but was upheld in the act of benediction. The pastoral staff, enveloped in a veil, appears on the left side, but the crook is gone ; the left hand is also gone. The shoes or sandals are pointed, and the feet rest against a sculptured bracket. The head reposes on a square cushion. Above is a canopy partly destroyed. The effigy appears to be of the middle of the fifteenth century, *circa* 1469.'[4] This effigy reclines on an altar tomb between the south aisle and St. Katherine's Chapel. The panels on the south side are of original work. Those visible on the north side are modern, having been carved when the wooden screen separating the aisle from the chapel was moved from the north to the south side of the monument. In the centre of the groining of the canopy is a rose. On each side of the mitre are three roses of the same pattern as the rationale and the designs at the ends of the stole and maniple.

---

[1] Mr. Mill Stephenson, F.S.A., says : 'I think the shield shows that this is a warrior in his ordinary attire. The shield proves this. With regard to the size, my own opinion on these little figures is that they are placed over heart burials.'

[2] *Arch. Jour.*, xxxix. 449.

[3] It is more probably the monument of Bishop Robert de Chause or Chalix (1258–78). See the account of the fire of 1292 at Lanercost : 'ita ut mausoleum improbi exactoris [i.e. Bishop Ireton] fiamma voraret, sed termini predecessoris sui, Roberti de Chalix, ex omni parte intacti perseverent' (*Chron. de Lanercost*, Maitland Club, 1839, p. 145).

[4] *Arch. Jour.*, xxxix. 449.

The drapery and feet are beautiful. The shoes show the toes. The bracket at the feet has, to the left, an animal with long ears, and on the right a small lion with curly mane. Chancellor Ferguson concluded that it was the effigy of Bishop Barrow, who died in 1429.

CALDER ABBEY

I. This figure is clothed in a complete suit of chain mail. The right hand is broken off; it has evidently been holding the large cross-hilted sword which is hung in front. The head rests on an oblong pillow. The features of the face are bold. A sleeveless surcoat of linen or cloth is worn over the armour and confined at the waist by a cord. On the left arm is a heater-shaped shield emblazoned with the arms of Layburne, or Layburn,[1] of Cunswick in Westmorland. There is also a label for an eldest son.

II. Another figure of the same period as No. I. In this one the top of the coif of chain mail is round, in the last it is flat. The hands are joined in prayer. The head rests on two cushions, the top one being round, the other oblong. The mittens of chain mail are perfect, being continued from the sleeves of the hauberk and undivided for the fingers. This figure carries a heater-shaped shield, suspended by a guige or strap passing over the right shoulder, and emblazoned with the arms of the Flemings.

III. Another man in armour very similar to No. I. though slightly larger. The device on the shield is obliterated. The right hand rests on the hilt of the sword. There is no clue as to whom this effigy represents.

IV. Two arms in chain armour. A large slab carved with a very mutilated head in a coif of chain mail, with a rich crocketted canopy of thirteenth century work above. It is very much worn with the weather, yet upon it we can trace angels as supporters, and very clearly, a five pointed star in one panel of the top or back of the canopy, and a moon with a crescent on it.

All the four effigies are of red sandstone.

[1] Dr. Parker of Gosforth wrote to me on 26 September, 1901, as follows : 'We have been excavating the chancel at Calder Abbey, and have found what appears to be the missing end of the effigy of De Layburne. The bevelled slab and the pattern of chain mail correspond with the effigy ; the legs have been crossed, the foot is inclosed in a stocking of chain mail, and the feet have rested on an animal which seems to be a double-headed lion, or two lions conjoined. There is also part of the life-sized head of an ecclesiastic which was found two or three years back, and a right hand grasping a staff.'

CAMERTON

Thomas Curwen, ' Black Tom of the North.' A red sandstone effigy, painted black.

The head, bare with long hair, rests on a tilting helmet, surmounted by the crest of the Curwens, a unicorn's head erased. The horn however is broken off. A shirt of mail is visible under the tuilles and possibly at the neck. On the breastplate is a spear rest. The arms are protected by pauldrons (the left as usual being larger than the right), brassards, scalloped elbow cops and vambraces. Gauntlets cover the hands and wrists. To a skirt of four taces are suspended, by straps, three large invected tuilles. The leg armour consists of cuissards or thigh pieces, knee cops, and jambes, and on the feet are broad-toed sabbatons. The rowel spurs are fastened with broad straps. At the feet is a sheep or lamb. A gypciere is beside the dagger. The long sword with ornamental hilt is perfect, and is held in its place by a strong belt with large buckle with elaborate pendant. At the last restoration in 1890, this effigy was replaced on its original altar tomb in the south transept.

The writer has received the following communication from Lord Dillon : ' Mr. Mill Stephenson to-day showed me the photograph of Black Tom Curwen's effigy in Camerton Church. It appears to be a very interesting one, especially for some details. The "arming points " or laces for attaching portions of the armour (in this case the shoulder and elbow pieces), are found in some effigies elsewhere, e.g. the Harcourt (see Hollis) and the Crosby and Hungerford effigies (see Stothard), but the points for fastening the arming shoes to the sollerets are uncommon. . . . In the National Gallery in a picture of St. William, and in one of the Archangel Michael, by Simone Papa, at Naples, this detail is well shown. In actual suits of armour the two holes in the sollerets for the *points* are too often ignorantly filled up with false rivets. A photo showing this point of the Camerton effigy would be very interesting. The single central *tuille* and the pendent sword belt are also noteworthy.' On the sides of this altar tomb are shields, some bearing various curious devices, others coats of arms.

CROSTHWAITE

Effigies of a civilian and lady in limestone. The male figure wears the costume of a merchant of the fifteenth century. A long loose tunic reaches from the neck to the feet, with wide sleeves which grow tight round the wrist. It is secured round the waist by a belt from which hangs a gypciere or purse. The head is bare and the hair is parted in the middle. A collar showing traces of colour encircles the neck. A long mantle is secured by a cordon crossing from shoulder to shoulder and the hands enclose a heart. The feet rest on a dog and the head on a cushion with tassels.

The lady is habited in a close fitting kirtle with tight sleeves, encircled round the waist with a broad girdle and fastened across the hips by other bands. Over this is worn the sideless côte-hardi. The head is covered with a peculiar kind of crown or cap with a small rosette at the top and rests on two cushions. Beneath the cap a veil falls gracefully on the shoulders. Round the neck is an ornamental collar and a necklace from which a pendent jewel rests on the bosom, while from the girdle hangs a cord whose broken ends fall nearly to the feet. A mantle also falls from the shoulders and is held by a band across the bosom, fastened by brooches. The hands hold a heart.[1]

The effigies are on the south side of the altar rails. Over them, resting on stout pillars, is a heavy slab of marble in which is embedded the brass of Sir John Ratcliffe and Dame Alice his wife. There is very little detail in the dress to help in the identification of these effigies, but they are generally believed to be those of Sir John de Derwentwater and his lady, who lived in the reigns of Henry VI. and the three preceding sovereigns.

CUMREW

Effigy of a lady. A massive sepulchral red sandstone monument found under the floor of the old church near where the chancel arch should have been. It is that of a lady whose head reclines on a cushion, behind which is a small dog with pendulous ears and smooth hair, not unlike a dachshund. A similar but larger and much broken dog is at the feet. The lady wears a wimple; a coverchief is on her head and falls gracefully on the shoulders. The hair is concealed. The rest of the costume consists of supertunic and kirtle. The former envelopes the entire person. It has no waist cincture and its sleeves are loose and long hanging. Of the kirtle nothing is visible but the tight sleeves. The feet are large, in clumsy pointed shoes. The hands, showing the

thumbs, are in the attitude of prayer. This effigy is now in the vestry.

CROGLIN

The much mutilated effigy of a lady, very similar in size, about 6 feet, and in almost exactly the same dress as the effigy at Cumrew. The lady's feet are visible and rest on an animal. The face and head-dress are destroyed. It rests in the churchyard on the south side of the church and is nearly overgrown with grass. The lady is said to be a member of the Wharton family.

Cumrew and Croglin are adjoining parishes, and the same sculptor probably worked both effigies from the same model.

DACRE

A red sandstone effigy of a man in banded mail armour. The belts for shield and sword are ornamented with crosses. The mail mittens hang from the wrists; as far as can be seen, the left leg is crossed over the right. This effigy is now on the floor of the north side of the chancel. It is said to be the monument of one of the Dacre family of the time of Henry III.

GREYSTOKE

Jefferson in his *History of Leath Ward*, p. 364, says : 'On the north side of the choir is a fine alabaster altar tomb on which recline two knights. . . . The front is enriched with angels in compartments, bearing shields emblazoned with the arms of Greystoke in proper colours. On the end towards the nave are two shields with the arms of Greystoke (ancient) and Grymethorpe.' The front of one tomb is still in the church. As the knights are of quite different sizes, it is certain they were not originally on the same tomb. Now they lie side by side on the pavement in the west end of the south aisle.

I. The larger figure, broken off at the knees, is clad in the plate armour of the early part of the fifteenth century. The head is bare, and rests on a huge tilting helmet. The pauldrons are massive and fluted, the left one being larger than the right. The elbow cops are ornamented as well as the knee cops. He wears a collar of SS. Attached to the skirt of taces are tuilles. The straps and buckles of the armour generally are well preserved. The large bawdric has a pattern of quatrefoils. Another band is passed over the right hip, but the sword which it supported has disappeared. Traces of colour are still visible. Mrs. Hudleston says : 'This figure represents a Baron of Greystoke of about

[1] *History of Crosthwaite Church*, p. 60, published by J. B. Nichols & Sons, London, 1853, where is an illustration.

1440, the date of a very similar effigy of Sir Robert Grashill in Haversham Church, Notts. It is perhaps John, the 16th Baron Greystoke, who married Elizabeth, daughter and heiress of Robert, Baron Ferrers of Wemme. By his will dated 10 July, 1436, he ordered his body to be buried in the collegiate church of Greystoke and bequeathed to that church his best horse as a mortuary, and all his habiliments of war, consisting of coat armour, pennon, gyron, etc.'

II. The smaller figure, Mrs. Hudleston suggests, is that of the founder of the college, or collegiate church of Greystoke, William le Bon Baron, who died 1359. He lies below a canopy which bears many shields, formerly charged with painted armorial devices, now too defaced to be made out. Portions of angels are discernible. He wears a plain, acutely pointed steel bascinet to which the camail or tippet of mail is laced. The hands, in gauntlets, are in attitude of prayer. The surcoat with fringe border covers the body. The arms and legs are protected with the usual plate armour. The feet rest on a lion with a long tail reaching almost to the surcoat. A dagger hangs from the bawdric. The head, supported by two draped angels, rests on a cushion. On each side of the ankles is a shield without device.[1]

HOLME CULTRAM ABBEY CHURCH

The figure of an abbot is on the front of a dismembered altar tomb, now in the porch. The abbot is seated on a throne. His head is mitred : he wears a chasuble with rationale on his breast. The alb with apparel is seen distinctly under the chasuble. The feet project from below the robes. He holds his staff over his left shoulder. Three monks pray on each side of him. There are two other portions of the same tomb in the porch. The whole is clearly the monument of Robert Chambers, for at one end is a shield with the chained bear and R.C. so familiar to every local antiquary and so common in the Abbey holme. He was Abbot from 1507-1518.

KIRKOSWALD

I. The effigy of a lady in red sandstone. The mutilated head, from which flows a veil, showing a curl on either side, rests on a

[1] Mr. Mill Stephenson says : 'This is interesting as an early example of the bascinet and camail. The high pointed bascinet is significant. There is an effigy of Sir John de Herteshull at Ashton, Northamptonshire, who died 1365 (circa), very like it.'

cushion. Her dress, without girdle, is plain and reaches to the feet, which are large for the size of the figure. On each of the shoulders is a small decorated band something like an epaulette, not visible in the sketch. The simplicity of the gown, and the tresses of hair on each side of the face, lead to the belief that the effigy is of the fourteenth century. It lies on the north side of the sanctuary.

II. An alabaster monument put up to the memory of Margaret Bertram, who died in the year 1609, by Thomas Bertram, her husband. The picture speaks for itself. Thomas Bertram and Margaret his wife are kneeling on opposite sides of a prayer desk, the two sons kneel behind the father and a daughter is seen behind the mother. The tablet containing the inscription has suspended at one end of it a censer and at the other a book. The hour-glass and skull remind the reader of death. The dresses are those of the late sixteenth or seventeenth century. Bishop Nicolson gives the inscription, which he calls tedious and blundering. Margaret Bertram was one of the sisters and co-heirs of Thomas Brougham of Brougham, and wife of Thomas Bertram.

KIRKLAND

An effigy of white chalk stone, of the middle of the fourteenth century. The figure is clad in a surcoat of remarkable length, and has a large sword hanging in front. There is no trace of mail armour now, although the head seems as if it had a close-fitting helmet, from the sides of which tufts of hair project. The hands hold a heart. This is said to be the effigy of a Fleming. It now rests on the floor on the north side of the chancel.

LANERCOST

I. Two fragments of an armed figure in red sandstone of the latter part of the fourteenth century. The body is clothed in hauberk of chain mail with surcoat embroidered with the armorial bearings of Vaux of Triermain. The thigh has a cuissard of plate. The bawdric is very richly ornamented. The other fragment gives the left foot in a solleret of plate, resting on a recumbent lion, from whose mouth depends a scroll.

II. A recumbent effigy of a layman 6 feet 3 inches long by 1 foot 7 inches. The figure is clothed in a tunic without belt, reaching a little below the knee. The legs appear to be covered with tight-fitting hose. The feet without shoes rest on a dog. The hands are palm to palm on the breast. The head rests on a cushion, and on it there appear to have been three angels, one at the crown of the head, the other two at the sides of the face. The hair is long and curly. The date is late fourteenth or early fifteenth century. This effigy now rests on a Dacre altar tomb, and is said to have been brought from the church-yard. A modern inscription in cursive letters has been cut across the lower part of the figure, as follows : John Crow of Longlands died March 23rd, 1708, aged 25 years.

Tradition says he was a workman at the building of the abbey, who fell from the clerestory and broke his neck, but Pennant says he broke his neck by a fall he had in climbing round the ruins of the church on 23 March, 1708.

III. The headless bust of a figure, assumed to be that of a deacon, is in an aumbry of the transept.

MILBURN

Resting against the south wall of the church on the outside is the recumbent effigy of a lady in white stone, very much worn from exposure. She is clad in a robe with girdle. The head, hands and feet are all missing. Length of the fragment 4 feet.

MILLOM

I. On a very handsome altar tomb of ala-baster are the effigies of a gentleman and his lady, undoubtedly of the Hudleston family ; but there is nothing to show which members they are. The man is on the sinister side of the slab, and is bareheaded with long flow-ing hair. The head rests on a tilting helmet of which the crest is gone, but the mantling on the sinister side remains. The crest in most cases is found on the dexter side of the head. Chain mail is seen at the neck. The pauldrons are large and plain. A skirt of invected taces with dependent tuilles covers the lower part of the body. A collar of roses and stars hangs from the neck. The date is the middle or end of the fifteenth century.

The lady's costume is of a similar date to that of her husband. Her head-dress appears to be knitted, she wears an elaborate collar with a sexfoil ornament—the pendants of both hers and her husband's are defaced. A sideless côte-hardi conceals part of the belt which encircles the plain kirtle. A long mantle is seen hanging at the side of the dress, but the cord on the breast and the folded hands have been entirely destroyed.

The tomb on which the effigies rest is in the south-east corner of the aisle, one side and end being against the walls. The other side

and end contain seven cusped pinnacled and crocketted niches, each containing a figure of an angel bearing a plain shield. Six of these are attended by one small kneeling figure and the other by two. A date is given to the whole monument because these small figures are those of females, wearing the butterfly head-dress which was in fashion between the reign of Edward IV., 1461, and the early years of Henry VII., 1485.

II. A grotesque looking fragment of the effigy of a man in oak. The figure is very much worn, but plate armour is seen at the knees. The feet rest on a lion. It is of late fourteenth or early fifteenth century date.

OUSBY

An effigy (7 feet long) in oak of a man in chain mail of the thirteenth century, very similar to the stone ones of the same period previously described. Figure in chain mail with plate knee cops, camail, and long sleeveless surcoat, cut up the middle. Under it a 'hawberk of mail over a haqueton. Apparently banded mail on legs and ringed elsewhere. The spur straps are left, but spurs gone. Narrow guige over right shoulder, but shield and part of left side of effigy gone. Narrow waist belt but broader sword belt with long ends hanging down. The hilt and blade of sword gone. Legs crossed at knee. Feet on a dog.

Bishop Nicolson has stated that ' the tradi-tion is that he was an outlaw who lived at Cruegarth in this parish, and that he was killed, as he was hunting, at a certain place on the neighbouring mountain, which (from that accident) keeps the name of *Baron-Syde* to this day. For all great men were anciently call'd *Barons* in this country.' [1] The figure is now in the chancel ; formerly it was in a recess on the south side of the nave.

ST. BEES

Two fragments of male effigies. The older one (thirteenth century) has traces of surcoat, hood, waistbelt, and shield tolerably perfect, having the armorial bearings of the Ireby family (a shield fretty).

The second figure is also that of a knight, but of the fourteenth century, probably about 1370. Slight traces of the pauldrons, camail, surcoat, bawdric, etc.[2]

---

[1] *Miscellany Accounts*, p. 66.

[2] Gough states on the authority of Nicolson and Burn's *History* that there is a wooden effigy at St. Bees, but Lysons could not find it, and it cer-tainly is not there now. It is said to be that of Anthony Lord Lucy, 41 Edw. III.

MONUMENTAL EFFIGIES

GREAT SALKELD

I. ANTHONY HUTTON and ELIZABETH BURDETT his wife. The effigies and the slab on which they lie have been carved out of one block of stone. Mr. Watson says it is tufa, a rock formed by springs depositing magnesian limestone. The slab is now split down between the effigies into two pieces. 'The effigy to the dexter side, that of a man, wears a legal costume, a gown with long hanging sleeves, richly laced over the upper part of the arm, the "crackling" as it would be called at Cambridge. His right arm is extended along his side and the hand grasps his long hanging sleeve near its end. His left arm is doubled on the chest, and the hand holds a folded paper. The gown reaches to the ground and has a deep round falling collar, probably of lawn : the sleeves close-fitting from elbow to wrists, with plain cuffs of lawn or linen. The lady's attitude is similar to that of her husband, except that her left arm is extended at her side and her right doubled upon her chest. She has a ruff round her neck, a flowing veil over her head, and full sleeves : her gown is gathered in at the waist by a knot of ribbons.' [1]

Anthony Hutton died at Penrith in 1637, and was buried in the quire of St. Andrew's Church. His wife, Elizabeth Burdett, who survived him for thirty-six years, placed these effigies in Penrith parish church.

It is a difficult matter to explain how these monuments ever came to be brought to Great Salkeld. It is supposed that at the pulling down of the old Penrith parish church in 1720 they were removed for safety to Hutton Hall, in Penrith, until perhaps a place might be found for them in the new building. In the course of time Mr. Watson says they were claimed by 'Mr. William Richardson, doctor of physic, of Town Head, Penrith, and afterwards of Nunwick Hall,' then called Low House, in Great Salkeld parish. He had married a daughter of Mr. Richard Hutton of Gale, a manor in Melmerby, and of Penrith, on the strength of which connection with the Huttons Mr. Watson thinks that he 'assumed the Hutton arms, cast the Hutton crest upon the leaden heading of his water spouts, and carried off the Hutton effigies.'

Bishop Nicolson gives a long account of this monument and the inscription on it.[2]

Mrs. Elizabeth Hutton did not die till 1673, so that she must have lived thirty-six years after her own monument was erected,

[1] *Trans. of Cumb. and Westm. Antiq. Soc.*, xii. 65.
[2] *Miscellany Accounts*, pp. 151, 152.

and all those years have worshipped beside her own recumbent effigy in her parish church.

II. THOMAS DE CALDEBECK, Archdeacon of Carlisle, died 1320. The archdeacon is clad in amice, alb, chasuble and maniple. His head (on which is the tonsure) rests on a pillow, while at the feet is the figure of a small lion. His hands are clasped in the attitude of prayer. The following inscription runs along the chamfered margin of the slab under the figure · HIC : JACET : MAGISTER : THOMAS : DE : CALDEBEC : ARCHIDIAC : KAR(L).

STANWIX

A much worn effigy of a female in red sandstone lies in the churchyard south of the church, buried in the grass. There is little to give any clue to the date except the shape of the head, which seems to be without cap, but with a curl on each side. This leads us to believe the effigy to be of the fifteenth century. The arms are very straight and are partly covered with large sleeves, which are seen below the elbows. The feet rest on a greyhound. The effigy is 5 feet 5½ inches long. The Rev. J. R. Wood, the present vicar, says that sixty years ago the figure had the letters G.H.S. cut legibly on the breast, no doubt a modern usurpation, like that of John Crow at Lanercost. This he learnt from a caretaker, who remembered, as a child, often playing upon the monument.

TORPENHOW

A very much worn recumbent figure of a lady now standing vertically in the churchyard near the gate.

WETHERAL

I. SIR RICHARD SALKELD and DAME JANE his wife, only child and heir of Roland Vaux of Triermain, about 1500.

Two figures of alabaster, showing traces of colour, gold and vermilion especially. Sir Richard is in plate armour with shirt of mail appearing at the throat and below the taces. The head bare, with hair cut short in front and left long behind, rests on a tilting helmet, much broken, but the crest wreath remains. At the back of the helmet is a shield with the arms of Salkeld (vert a fret silver). On the shoulders are pauldrons, and, as usual in the fifteenth century, the right one is of lighter construction than the left in order to give more freedom to the sword arm. Around his neck is a collar of roses and SS. The arms are broken off, but the hands are seen to have been clasped in prayer on the breast. A paunce covers the lower part of the breastplate and is scalloped at the edges, running to a point and buckling to the breastplate below the chin. There are three taces with dependent fluted tuilles covering the thighs. The legs are covered with cuissards, knee cops and greaves. Part of one leg is gone, but the other is fairly perfect. The foot, showing the strap of the spur, rests on a lion, whose head is gone, but whose long tail is clearly seen. The sword has disappeared, but traces of the hilt are visible. The sword-belt is narrow and transverse, covered with small quatrefoils. The outline of the dagger is discernible on the right side of the slab.

The armour is of a slightly earlier date than 1500, but the monument may easily have been executed before Sir Richard's death, and then placed in its position under the inscription, which was clearly drawn up by Dame Jane, as there is no mention of her decease.

Dame Jane's head rests on two cushions. At the back of these is a shield with arms of Salkeld impaling those of Vaux of Triermain (a red and gold chequered band across a silver shield). On her head she wears a cap something like a biretta, as at Crosthwaite, with a button in the centre of the top. Under it is a coverchief, and under that her long hair hanging down. She wears a collar of SS and roses, with a jewel pendant, like her husband. The lady's kirtle is seen at the waist, where it is held in its place by a narrow belt, tied at the right side with a long end hanging down. A rosary is tucked through the belt; above the kirtle is the sideless côte-hardi. Over all is a mantle, open, but fastened by a strap across the breast. The feet are hidden by the skirt.

In the heraldic collection of monumental records in the Lansdowne MSS. of the British Museum is a description of the tomb and copy of the epitaph made in the reign of Queen Elizabeth, when no doubt the tomb and inscription would be perfect.

Here lyes Sir Richard Salkeld, rgt Knyth
Who sometyme in this land was mekill of myth
The Captain and kep of Carlisle was he,
And also the lord of Korbe.
And now lyes under this stayne.
And his lady and wiff dayme Jayne,
In ye year of our Lord God a Thousand
And Five Hundreth, as I understand
The aighteen of Feweryere
That gentill Knyth was berit here
I pray you all that this doys see
Pra for ther saulys for charite
For as yay yr so mon we be.

Bishop Nicolson, in 1703, says the inscription was 'over the arch betwixt the Quire and ye North Isle, and under it an old monument whereon are laid two alabaster bodies (male and female).' [1] After this the effigies were moved within the altar rails, where they remained until the restoration in 1882. They were then moved into the Howard mausoleum, but Sir Henry Howard (Mr. Philip Howard's second brother), our ambassador at The Hague, objected because he considered they spoiled the Nollekens statue and endangered the vault beneath. The tomb was then placed in its present position, and the rector thinks it is the original one, as the Corby pew formerly stood here.

WHITBECK

Effigy of a lady in red sandstone, which has been sometime painted. Local tradition calls her the Lady of Annaside. The head rests on a pillow. A wimple is drawn over her chin, and a veil covers her head and falls on her shoulders. A large mantle covers her dress and is tucked up under her left arm. Her feet rest on a dog. The date of the effigy is about 1300. Possibly the lady may be one of the Hudlestons of Anneys. The effigy used to be in the churchyard, where it was much worn by heedless feet; now it is carefully preserved in the church.

WORKINGTON, ST. MICHAEL'S

SIR CHRISTOPHER CURWEN and his wife ELIZABETH DE HUDLESTON, 1450. Two effigies of grey limestone on an altar tomb, 7 feet 4 inches long, having on the west side five niches with cinquefoil heads, each bearing a shield. The arms at the head of the dexter side are those of Curwen impaling lozengy for Croft, being the arms of Christopher's father and mother; the next are those of Curwen and Hudleston, his own and those of his wife; the third coat Curwen only; the fourth Curwen impaling six annulets gold, for Lowther, their son's arms and those of his wife; and the last Curwen impaling the eldest son of a Pennington who predeceased his father; which last were the arms of Christopher, the grandson of the entombed pair, and those of his wife.

The head of the effigy of the knight has round its brow an embroidered band or cap, and rests on a cushion with a tilting helmet behind, bearing the crest of the Curwen family, a unicorn's head erased silver, armed gold. A large collar of plate protects the upper

[1] *Miscellany Accounts*, pp. 49-50.

pierced hand and arm for   the lady's face—one is biting the end of her
ı pointed-toed sollerets rest   mantle.

,d has a peculiar head-dress,   The monument was formerly under the
  to the one at Hawkshead,   tower, but is now in the north-east corner
o cushions, one above the   of the north aisle.   This inscription runs
on either side looks on her.   round the top edge of the tomb : 'Orate pro
k is a collar with pendent   animabz Xtoferi Curwen militis et Elizabethe
                             uxoris ejus.'

POLITICAL HISTORY

THE geographical position of the modern county of Cumberland has had an important influence in determining its formation as a political unit of the English commonwealth. On every side, with insignificant exceptions, the boundaries are well marked by river, mountain or sea. The district is wedged in between the Pennine range and the Solway Firth, and is almost cut off from Scotland by a long arm of the sea which runs inland for such a distance that only a few miles of outlet are left towards the north. The approach from the south is blocked by great mountain masses, through which there are few passes except towards Yorkshire through the valley of the Eden. The whole district occupies such a peculiar position that its delimitation as a political area must have been determined to some extent by its natural boundaries. The Roman general who chose the Solway as the termination of the Great Wall would seem almost instinctively to have traced a frontier on the western side which was to be the boundary between contending tribes and nations. The wall as a whole was the real limit of the effective power of Rome, beyond which she never permanently established her authority. Occasionally indeed her dominion extended as far as the more northern barrier between the Clyde and the Forth, but in that region it had scarcely passed the stage of military occupation and was held only by an intermittent and precarious tenure. The wall of Hadrian remained the true frontier. Nowhere therefore more than on its western side, owing to the isolation of the district from the rest of the country, was the momentous change felt which took place when the emperor Honorius sent letters to the cities of Britain, announcing the withdrawal of the legionaries and bidding them to provide in future for their own safety. Thus at the opening of the fifth century was terminated that Roman occupation which had endured for more than three hundred years, and which must have in many ways influenced the fortunes and affected the characters of the inhabitants.

For a long period after the withdrawal of the Roman forces the district south of the Solway has little or no history. There is nothing but darkness, unrelieved by a single gleam of light, during the centuries which elapsed between the departure of the Roman and the coming of the Teuton. Of documentary record there is none. It is true that we read much in the pages of Gildas and Bede of what the Britons suffered from internal dissensions and the constant inroads of hostile races like the Picts, Scots and Angles, but we cannot justify the exclusive application of the narratives to the political conditions of any special locality. The memories of their struggles for independence have been handed down in the legendary poetry of the race. At an early date the immortal name of Arthur was known and his exploits were celebrated in this district. It is needless to inquire whether or not he was a local personage. The pertinacity of the tradition which has covered the modern county with Arthurian sites[1] may not be set aside as altogether valueless. It is possible that we have in Arthur the eponymous hero who represents in himself the vicissitudes of the British race, the ideal and never-to-be-forgotten champion in whose deeds the struggles of the nation for liberty and independence have been personified, an early type of all that was high and noble which was to stir men's hearts for ages yet to come. From another class of legend with more claim to be considered historical we derive a circumstantial account of the political triumph of the Christian faith and the establishment of a British kingdom of which our district formed a part. If the general features of the narrative be genuine, the victory of Rederech over the forces of paganism in the great battle of Ardderyd in 573 forms an important landmark in local history. On one side were the Britons, who had remained steadfast to the faith of their Christian teachers, and on the other were those who had apostatized and wished to adhere to the old religion of their race. The struggle ' to break the heathen and uphold the Christ' was eventually successful. After the battle, the site of which has been identified with Arthuret, a parish about eight miles to the north of Carlisle, it is said that Rederech, the Christian leader, became king of the Britons and consolidated the mixed tribes of the western coast into a kingdom which stretched from the Clyde to the Mersey. The capital was fixed at Alcluyd or Dumbarton, and the kingdom was called Strathclyde.[2]

Whatever value may be ascribed to these traditions it is quite certain that the kingdom of Strathclyde did not survive in its entirety for many years, for we know that in the seventh century the district south of the Solway was an integral portion of the English kingdom of Northumbria. The district at that time had no distinctive name and perhaps no separate political existence. All we know is that it was subject to English[3] rule. But there is one circumstance from which, in the ab-

---

[1] The legend of King Arthur has been a fruitful subject of controversy which cannot be noticed here. The Arthurian sites in Cumberland have been discussed by writers of ability like Dr. Skene (*Celtic Scotland*, i. 152–8). See also his *Four Ancient Books*, and his ' Notice of the site of the Battle of Arderyth ' in *Proceedings of the Soc. of Antiq. of Scotland* (1867), vi. 95. Mr. Stuart Glennie has gone minutely into the Cumberland section of Arthurian Scotland (*Arthurian Localities*, pp. 68–76). Apart from the statements of writers like Gildas and Nennius, the earliest reference that we have found of Arthur's connection with the district is contained in the confirmation charter of Henry II., dated about 1175, in which some land in Carlisle is described as being ' circa Burum Arthuri in Kaerlelol iuxta mansionem Canonicorum ' (*Trans. of Cumb. and West. Archæol. Soc.* iii. 248, new ser.). Welsh traditions were very prevalent among the antiquaries of Cumberland in the twelfth century. What is meant by the ' burum Arthuri' may be considered a subject of debate.

[2] The battle of Ardderyd, the centre of a group of Welsh traditions, has been fully described by Dr. Skene in *Celtic Scotland*, i. 157–9, where he has collected the most valuable of the authorities.

[3] On the use of the word ' English' to designate the inhabitants of Britain before the Norman Conquest as distinguished from ' Saxon ' or ' Anglo-Saxon,' the interesting and learned note of Mr. Freeman should be consulted (*Norman Conquest*, i. 528–41).

sence of direct evidence, certain deductions may be drawn. The Roman city of Luguvallum, or Luguvallium as it is called on the itinerary of Antonine, now known as Carlisle,[1] never lost its identity amid all the changes and chances of tribal wars. One of the political legacies that Rome left behind in Britain was the organization of cities as the centres of local authority for the surrounding territory. There is every reason to believe that Luguvallum, which was close to Hadrian's wall in a situation with great natural advantages for defence and or easy access from the Romanized district to the south, formed the centre of a territorial rule which was not obliterated by the departure of the legions, but which was carried on by the native population and may have had something to do indirectly with the ultimate evolution of the modern county. Of all the Roman sites in this corner of the empire, Luguvallum is the only political organism of importance that has survived. The district in the neighbourhood had no distinctive designation except what it received from its territorial association with the city. The Roman name continued, though the language of the inhabitants had changed. When the light of genuine history falls on the district, the city of Lugubalia is revealed as a place of strength and a centre of settled government. It is not known at what date or by what king the English conquest was pushed to the western sea, but at some time in the seventh century, earlier or later, the western districts from the Solway to the Mersey had passed under English dominion. The Northumbrian supremacy was a very real thing at that period. Lands in Lancashire between the Ribble and the Cocker[2] were bestowed on Wilfrid about 666–9, and the see of Lindisfarne was endowed by King Ecgfrith in 685[3] with the city of Lugubalia, then called Luel, and a circuit of fifteen miles around it. Bede gave no name to the land in which the city was situated, but he speaks as if it were the centre of a flourishing English community in which the ecclesiastical organizations had reached a high standard under the patronage of Cuthbert, Bishop of Lindisfarne, and the royal family of Northumbria. From Bede's pen we have a pleasant picture of Lugubalia and its neighbourhood. From the city Cuthbert went forth on his episcopal errands to ordain ministers or to dedicate a church, and

[1] Carlisle appears in the list of British cities given by Nennius (cap. 67) under the name of Caer-Luadiit, Caer-Ligualid, or Cair-Lualid, which has been identified by Usher as Lugubalia (*Mon. Hist. Brit.* p. 77). Henry of Huntingdon, probably with the list of Nennius before him, mentions 'Kair-Lion quam vocamus Carleuil' (*Historia Anglorum*, p. 7), but he is apparently mistaken in that identification, for the 'Cair-Legion' of Nennius has the alternative reading of 'Cair-Legion guar Usic,' that is, Caerleon on Usk. The statement of Geoffrey of Monmouth (bk. ii. 9) that Leil son of Brute, a lover of peace and justice, succeeded his father and built a city in the north part of Britain and called it Kaerliel after his own name, may be accepted as pure romance.

[2] This grant marks an important event in local history. Eddi (*Vita Wilfridi*, cap. 17) says that Gaedyne, perhaps Castle or Little Eden, was given to Wilfrid with Caetlevum and other places. Caetlevum is probably the ancient name of Cartmell in Furness. The anonymous author of the *Historia de S. Cuthberto*, erroneously ascribed to Symeon of Durham, mentions that 'dedit ei (S. Cuthberto) rex Ecgfridus terram quae vocatur Cartmel, et omnes Britannos cum eo, et villam illam quae vocatur Suthged-luit, et quicquid ad eam perrinet' (*Symeon of Durham* [Surtees Soc.], i. 141 ; [Rolls Ser.] i. 200). The date of this tract has been ascribed by Mr. Hodgson Hinde to the tenth century.

[3] Symeon, *Hist. de S. Cuthbert.* (Rolls Ser.), i. 199 ; Haddan and Stubbs, *Councils and Eccles. Doc.* ii. pt. i. 6.

to the city Herebert came from his lonely retreat in Derwentwater twenty-five miles away to consult with his revered diocesan.[1] There was a nunnery in the city, graced by a superior of noble birth, and there was a school founded by the saint himself. The citizens pointed with pride to the ancient walls and conducted St. Cuthbert to see a fountain built with marvellous skill by the Romans.[2] Every notice of the city at this date bespeaks a long occupation by the Teutonic conqueror. In English mouths the Latin name had taken an English form, for we are told by Bede that Lugubalia was corrupted by the English into Luel. It was the capital of an extensive district, wider than the area which Ecgfrith had added to the temporal possessions of Lindisfarne. For more than eight centuries after the legions were withdrawn from Lugubalia, its Roman name clung to the city as if to proclaim its continuous existence.[3] Though successive masters changed or corrupted it at pleasure, the city as an institution remained the political centre of the district. No other designation has appeared above the surface of history to indicate the region south of the Solway as a political state. As the district was nameless when it was won by the Norman, the land of Carlisle or the county of Carlisle was utilized to describe it for nearly a hundred years.

There is every reason to believe that the district of Carlisle continued a portion of the Northumbrian realm till the whole of northern England was thrown into confusion and anarchy by the Danish invasion. The overthrow of Ecgfrith by the Picts in the disastrous battle of Nechtansmere[4] in 685 does not appear to have disturbed the political allegiance of its inhabitants. It is true that Northumbrian power was weakened by Ecgfrith's defeat, and that some of the Britons, presumably those in the valley of the Clyde, had regained their independence in consequence, but the region south of the Roman wall on the Solway shore remained faithful to English dominion. In 854 Bishop Eardulf of Lindisfarne, according to Symeon of Durham,[5] claimed that Luel, or Carleol, as the city was called in Symeon's day, had belonged to his bishopric since the time of King Ecgfrith, and when the same bishop took flight from the pagan Danes in 875, and entered on his seven years' pilgrimage with the relics of St. Cuthbert, it was through this district, not apparently as through a hostile region, that he made his way to the mouth of the Derwent for the purpose of embarking to Ireland.[6] In all probability the political relations of the district with Northumbria remained un-

---

[1] Bede, *Hist. Eccles.* iv. 29.   [2] Bede, *Vita S. Cuthberti*, cap. 27.

[3] Lugubalia as the ancient name of Carlisle survived in authentic documents till a late period. When Pope Honorius III. confirmed Bishop Hugh in the bishopric of Carlisle in 1223, he spoke of it as 'the episcopal see in St. Mary's church, Carlisle, called of old "Lugubalia," in which are to be observed all the customs of other bishoprics in England' (*Cal. of Papal Letters*, i. 91, ed. Bliss). It is used by Walsingham in relation to the bishop and the bishopric of Carlisle in 1345 and 1400 : Bishop Kirkby is described as 'episcopus Lugubaliæ,' and the bishopric, to which William Strikeland succeeded, as 'pontificatum Lugubaliæ' (*Hist. Angl.* [Rolls Ser.], i. 266-7, ii. 247).

[4] Symeon, *Hist. Dunelm. Eccles.* (Rolls Ser.), i. 32, ed. Arnold.

[5] Ibid. 53 ; Symeon, *Hist. Regum*, (Rolls Series), ii. 101, ed. Arnold.

[6] Symeon, *Hist. Dunelm. Eccles.* (Surtees Soc.), i. 146, 163, ed. Hinde ; Geoff. of Monmouth, *Mon. Hist. Brit.* i. 681.

changed for the remaining portion of the ninth century. After the death of Halfdene, Bishop Eardulf returned to Northumberland, but not to his ruined cathedral of Lindisfarne ; and his companion, Abbot Eadred, surnamed Lulisc from Luel, the place of his habitation, had returned to Luercestre or Luelcestre, as Carlisle was then called, from their sacred odyssey with the saint's body.[1] It was at the monastery of Carlisle, which had apparently escaped destruction during the first outburst of heathen invasion, that St. Cuthbert appeared in a vision to Abbot Eadred, and from which he sent him to proclaim to the Danes that Guthred son of Hardacnute should be their king.[2] Though there is a discrepancy in the date when this mission took place, one authority fixing it in 883 and another in 890, it is of small consequence. The fact of interest to be remembered is that the monastery of Carlisle remained intact till the death of Halfdene. It is a point of great importance in the history of the district if additional probability can be given to the statements in the tracts ascribed to the authorship of Symeon that Abbot Eadred returned to the monastery of Carlisle after his seven years' pilgrimage.[3] The total destruction of the city by the Danes rests on the sole authority of Florence of Worcester. In describing the conquest of William Rufus in 1092 Florence advanced on the account given in the Anglo-Saxon Chronicle by stating that the city, like some others in these parts, had been destroyed by the pagan Danes two hundred years before, and had remained deserted up to that time. This statement was accepted by Symeon, and embodied in his history of the kings.[4] But the destruction has not been noticed by either of the chroniclers in the ordinary sequence of events during the Danish invasion, and no special weight can be attached to the authority of Symeon in support of this remarkable statement, inasmuch as he was but the faithful copyist of Florence for the events of the period. There is much reason to believe that the monastery of Dacore or Dacre, about 20 miles to the south of Carlisle, at which miraculous cures are said to have been wrought in 728 by the agency of St. Cuthbert's relics,[5] was untouched by the ravages of the Danes. It was at this place, as it would seem, that Athelstan received the homage of the kings in 926.[6] From the latter date, every

---

[1] Symeon, *Hist. Regum*, ii. 114, ed. Arnold ; i. 73, ed. Hinde.

[2] The *Historia de S. Cuthberto* calls Eadred the abbot of Luercestre, but it must be a scribal error for Luelcestre (*Symeon of Durham*, i. 143, 231, ed. Hinde). Mr. Freeman has suggested a similar confusion between the letters *l* and *r* in *Guillermus* for *Guillelmus* (*Trans. of Cumb. and West. Archæol. Soc.* vi. 244).

[3] It may be pointed out that Mr. Freeman at first stated that Lugubalia was part of the lands lost to Northumbria by the fall of Ecgfrith (*William Rufus*, ii. 545), but he afterwards revised this opinion, as he 'had not given heed enough to the story of Eadred, which clearly fixes the loss of the country, as well as the destruction of the city, to the Danish invasion of 875' (*Trans. of Cumb. and West. Archæol. Soc.* vi. 258). This paper on 'The Place of Carlisle in English History,' read at the joint meeting of the Royal Archæological Institute and the Cumberland and Westmorland Archæological Society held at Carlisle in 1882, deserves careful study.

[4] *Hist. Regum*, ii. 220, ed. Arnold. 'Haec enim civitas, ut illis in partibus aliae nonnullae, a Danis paganis ante cc annos diruta, et usque ad tempus id mansit deserta.'

[5] Bede, *Hist. Eccl.* bk. iv. c. 32.

[6] The *Anglo-Saxon Chronicle* (i. 199) states that the submission was made 'on thaere stowe the genemned is aet Eamotum,' which Mr. Thorpe understood to be Emmet, but he has not indicated

place name within the limits of the modern county disappears from history for a century and a half. The city of Carlisle ceased to be so far as recorded history is concerned. The memorials of the district south of the Solway perished. It is just possible that Florence, full of the ruthless ravages of the Danes in the north, and finding no materials for the history of the north-western district, jumped to the conclusion that Carlisle shared the fate of many cities in the rest of Northumbria. Subsequent events may help to throw doubt on the alleged destruction of Carlisle and the desertion of its site.

After the Danish conquest of Northumbria all is dark or indistinct in the region south of the Solway. We lose the guidance of Carlisle in our efforts to disentangle the obscure allusions which may possibly refer to the district. In the tenth century the chroniclers make incidental mention of tribes and peoples inhabiting the western shores, but it is very difficult to say with certainty that our district was included. As yet the territory between the Solway and the Duddon had no political existence as a separate state, and we know not whether it had been dissevered from Northumbria when that kingdom began to decline. There is no evidence that Strathclyde extended south of Hadrian's wall at any time subsequent to the English conquest. The territorial name is a warrant that it comprised only the valley of the Clyde, and can have extended little beyond what is now known as Clydesdale. In that case allusions to the Straecled-Walas, Streatcledwali, Stratcluttenses, or Welsh of Strathclyde, need present no difficulties. But it is different with the Cumbri, a race which has given its name to the modern county, and of which we have no mention before 875. Ethelwerd is the first of the chroniclers who uses the word,[1] but he gives no indication of the terri-

---

where that locality is (ii. 85). Florence of Worcester (*Mon. Hist. Brit.* p. 573) almost used the same phrase, 'in loco qui dicitur Eamotum,' in which he is followed by Symeon of Durham (*Hist. Regum,* ii. 124). Mr. Arnold, the editor of Symeon, suggests that Etton in the east riding of Yorkshire is meant. The importance of 'Dacore' in Bede's day furnishes a strong probability that the 'Eamotum' of the *Chronicle* and Florence may be identified with Eamont, formerly Eamot, in Cumberland, which is close to Dacre. But we have the positive testimony of William of Malmsbury that the Scots submitted to Athelstan, 'ad locum qui Dacor vocatur,' which is sufficient to settle the identity of 'Eamotum' (*Gesta Regum Anglorum,* i. 147, ed. Stubbs). There is a tradition that the conference was held in a room of Dacre Castle, still pointed out as 'the kings' chamber.' E. W. Robertson denies the truth of the whole story of the submission of the kings to Athelstan, and suggests that the account in the Cottonian MS. of the Anglo-Saxon Chronicle is an interpolation ; he also says that Malmsbury's authority for the statement was an old poem (*Early Kings,* ii. 397–8).

[1] It may be taken that 'Cumbri' and 'Cumbria,' as the designation of the people and their territories, did not come into use before the eleventh century, but it is an open question whether Ethelwerd was the first to employ the terms. In the tractate on the *Life of St. Cadroë* it is stated that King Donald conducted the saint to the city of Leeds, which was the boundary between the northmen and the Cumbrians, 'conduxit usque Loidam Civitatem quae est confinium Normannorum atque Cumbrorum' (Skene, *Chron. of the Picts and Scots,* p. 116). As Cadroë died about 976, and as the author of the *Life* states that he had his information from the saint's disciples, Dr. Skene has dated the tract in the eleventh century. Ethelwerd certainly lived and wrote in the same century (Hardy, *Descriptive Catalogue,* i. 571–4 ; ii. 65). The people of this region were called Britons by Gildas, Nennius and Bede, and their kings were spoken of by Adamnan and the Ulster Annals as reigning in Petra Cloithe or Alocluaithe, but no mention is made of Cumbri. Strathclyde was introduced by later writers as the name of the kingdom over which the kings ruled. In the matter of territorial titles Sir Henry Maine's remarks on the history of tribe sovereignty (*Ancient Law,* pp. 103–9) and Mr. Freeman's notes on early geographical nomenclature are of great value (*Norman Conquest,* i. 584–6, 597–605).

tory they occupied. As a matter of fact he employs the designation as if it were synonymous with the people of Strathclyde. When Halfdene had subdued the valley of the Tyne in 875, we are told by the Anglo-Saxon Chronicle, Asser and Florence,[1] that he often made war on the Picts and Strathclyde Welsh, whereas Ethelwerd[2] in describing the same exploit calls the native tribes by the names of Picts and Cumbri. In describing later events the chroniclers are still more indefinite. Florence relates that in 901 Edward the Elder received the submission of the kings of the Scots, Cumbrians, Strathclyde Welsh and all the west Britons;[3] and in 921 the same authority states that the king of Scots with his whole nation, Reinald king of the Danes, with all the Angles and Danes that dwell in Northumbria, and also the king of the Strathclyde Welsh, accepted King Edward as their father and lord, and made a firm treaty with him.[4] Symeon of Durham and Geoffrey Gaimar follow in the same strain. In his description of the battle of Brunanburh in 937, Symeon says that Athelstan put to flight Onlaf, the Danish king of Northumbria, Constantine, King of Scots, and the king of the Cumbri, with their whole host; but Gaimar differentiates the people taking part in the battle as Scots, Cumbri, Galwegians and Picts.[5] Again and again we meet with 'the king of the Cumbri,' without any hint of the region over which he ruled. It is curious that no English equivalent of the word was admitted into the pages of the Anglo-Saxon Chronicle till a late date. In the account of the famous cession by King Eadmund in 945 we get the first glimpse of the tribe in the name of Cumbraland or Cumberland, the territory which he had harried and delivered to Malcolm, King of Scots, on condition that he should be his ally on sea and on land. Florence translates the 'Cumbraland' of the Chronicle into the Latin form of 'the land of the Cumbri,' though the Welsh annalists, referring to the incursion, identify the region as Strat Clut or Ystrat Clut, that is Strathclyde.[6] From these scattered notices of the inhabitants it would be hazardous to suggest that the region south of the Solway was a separate territorial unit belonging to the Cumbri, or to draw any positive conclusions on its political affinities to the neighbouring states. It is possible that the Cymric race, breaking away from Northumbrian rule, made common cause with their kinsfolk of Strathclyde, and attained some measure of national independence during the declining period of the Northumbrian kingdom. The rise of the racial name of Cumbri[7]

---

[1] *Mon. Hist. Brit.* pp. 355, 478, 558.   [2] Ibid. p. 515.   [3] Ibid. p. 568.
[4] Ibid. p. 572.   [5] Ibid. pp. 686, 808.   [6] Ibid. pp. 388, 574, 837, 847.
[7] There does not appear to be any doubt of the origin of the word Cumbti or Cumbria. It is from the Welsh Cymru, meaning exclusively the Principality, and pronounced as if spelled Kumry or Kumri (Rhys, *Celtic Britain*, p. 142). Geoffrey of Monmouth had no compunction in deriving the name from Kamber, one of the sons of King Brute, as he accounted for the origin of Alban, the name of Celtic Scotland, from Albanach, and Lloegr, the Welsh name for England, from Locrinus, members of the same family (*Hist. Britonum*, p. 23, ed. Giles). Jocelyn of Furness, who wrote in the twelfth century, has adopted the forms Cambria, Cambrensis and Cambrinus, in connection with the north-western district (*Life of St. Kentigern*, pp. 54, 58, 87, etc.; *Hist. of Scotland*, v.) Cambria and Cumbria were at first used indiscriminately for the same region. It is curious that St. Petroc, who was a native of Wales, is called a Cumber or a Cimber in one old life (*Celtic Britain*, p. 141). Cumbria seems the more correct

as distinctive of the people appears almost to warrant the existence of some sort of political autonomy on the western seaboard. But two events are clearly discernible amid all the confusion of the tenth century. The submission of the western tribes to Edward the Elder in 924,[1] and the grant of the district to Malcolm, King of Scots, by King Eadmund in 945,[2] are noteworthy incidents with which the future history of the country was intimately concerned. It is with the latter event only that we need to trouble ourselves here.

It is not without significance that the introduction of Cumberland as a geographical term synchronized with the so-called cession of the district to the Scottish crown. There can be little doubt that at this period the name embraced a definite territory which extended north and south of the Solway from the Firth of Clyde to the river Duddon. Its southern boundary has been described by a fairly respectable Scottish authority as the Rerecross on Stainmore, a pillar standing on the confines of Yorkshire and Westmorland, which still in part remains.[3] The canons of Carlisle, however, when they made their report on the history of the district to Edward I. in 1291, appear to have had no knowledge of this grant to Malcolm and offered no opinion on the territorial extent of Cumbria as it existed after the cession of 945.[4] But if the statement of the Scottish Chronicle on the southern boundary be accepted as conclusive, it may be taken that the territory south of Solway had been withdrawn from Northumbrian influence and that the previous independence to which it had attained was completely destroyed. In the course of its history the land had been British, Roman, English, perhaps British again, and now for a time it was to be subject to Scottish rule.

Considerable diversity of opinion exists on the precise nature of the grant made to Malcolm by King Eadmund in 945. Mr. Freeman interpreted the records of the transaction as indicating a permanent

form, as it has been admitted into the Anglo-Saxon Chronicle : Cumberland, Cumbraland, or Cumerland—the land of the *Cumbras*, Cumbri or Kymry. There was a notable personage of the name of Cumbra in the south of England in the eighth century. The Anglo-Saxon Chronicle calls him 'Aldorman Cumbra,' unjustly slain in 755 by Sigebryht and the West Saxon witan (i. 82, ed. Thorpe). The same person is referred to by Ethelwerd as 'Dux Cumbran,' by Florence of Worcester as 'Dux Cumbranus,' and by Geoffrey Gaimar as 'Combran,' 'Cumbrat,' or 'Enconbrand' (*Mon. Hist. Brit.* pp. 507–8, 543, 787). Henry of Huntingdon alludes to him as 'Cumbra consul ejus nobilissimus' (*Hist. Anglorum*, p. 122, ed. Arnold). But there is no evidence that he exercised any sway in the Welsh region of Britain.

[1] Florence of Worcester gives the year of submission as 924, but the Anglo-Saxon Chronicle places it in 921.

[2] Some of the Scottish chronicles insist on a grant of Cumberland to Scotland by King Eadmund before 945. In the *Chronicles of the Picts and Scots* (ed. Skene, p. 204) it is said that the country as far as 'Reir Croiz de Staynmore' was given to Donald mac Dunstan, King of Scotland, and in the *Life of St. Cadrol* it is suggested that Donald was king of the Cumbri when the saint visited that people (ibid. p. 116).

[3] Skene, *Chron. of Picts and Scots*, p. 204. For the erection of this stone by Marius or Meuric, King of the Britons, to celebrate his victory over Roderic, King of the Picts, and for the legends about the origin of Westmorland, Westymar, Westmering or Gwysmeuruc, by reason of that monument, see the Welsh 'Bruts' in Skene, *Chron. of Picts and Scots*, pp. 122, 156–7. Some antiquaries think that the pillar is the fragment of a Roman milestone.

[4] Palgrave, *Documents and Records*, 68–76. It should be remembered that the extent of Cumbria described by the canons of Carlisle can be applied only to 1069 and to no previous date. To make the statement retrospective violates the whole purport of the return.

feudal benefice lasting till the Norman conquest of the district in 1092, for which the kings of Scotland or their heirs did homage or military service as occasion required. It was probably, he said, the earliest instance in Britain of a fief in the strictest sense as opposed to a case of commendation.[1] It is difficult to reconcile the events of subsequent history with this view. Without attaching too much weight to the gradual introduction of feudal ideas by the later chroniclers into the earliest account of the grant,[2] it may be pointed out that a permanent cession to Scotland was neither maintained nor recognized by those who had the closest interest in the original agreement. It appears improbable that King Ethelred regarded the grant by his predecessor as permanent when he plundered Cumberland in 1000,[3] or that Symeon of Durham should have stated that the district was under the dominion of Malcolm III. in 1070, not possessed by right but subjugated by force,[4] had he been aware of the compact. Scottish writers have put forward sundry explanations to account for the non-admission of their national claims upon the territory. Fordun[5] ascribed the raid of King Ethelred to the refusal of the Prince of Cumbria to contribute to the Danegeld, alleging that the Cumbrians owed no other tax than to be ready at the king's command to defend their liberties with the sword. An earlier Scottish writer better informed than Fordun, unable to close his eyes to the facts of history, confessed that the province had not remained in the uninterrupted possession of Scotland, for King Eadmund's donation had been often conquered and abandoned for the sake of peace between the two kingdoms.[6] In view of this admission it is

---

[1] *Norman Conquest*, i. 62, 124, 571–3.

[2] According to the statement of the Anglo-Saxon Chronicle under 945, 'Her Eadmund cyning oferhergode eal Cumbraland and hit let eal to Malculme Scotta cyninge on thaet gerad thaet he waere his midwyrhta aegther ge on sae ge on lande.' The compact is not noticed by Ethelwerd, but Florence (*Mon. Hist. Brit.* p. 574) and *Symeon of Durham* (ii. 126, ed. Arnold) render 'midwyrhta' as 'fidelis,' thus importing into the word the feudal ideas of a later age. Henry of Huntingdon is more literal in his translation : 'commendavit eam Malculmo Regi Scotiae hoc pacto, quod in auxilio sibi foret terra et mari.' Subsequent chroniclers have transformed the agreement into a permanent feudal transaction. On the death of Eadmund in 946, the same compact was renewed with his successor Eadred after he had reduced all Northumberland under his power—'and Scottas him athas sealdan thaet hie woldan eal thaet he wolde.' But we hear nothing more of the renewal of oaths on a succession to the English Crown, nor do we read of the Scottish kings fighting often on the English side, as they were bound to do by their oath of fealty, had this cession of Cumberland been a permanent agreement. In E. W. Robertson's opinion Cumberland south of the Solway, 'when it was not under the authority of the Northumbrian earls in whose province it was included, may be said to have remained in a state of anarchy till the conquest' of 1092 (*Scotland under Early Kings*, i. 72).

[3] *Anglo-Saxon Chronicle* (Rolls Series), i. 249; *Mon. Hist. Brit.* (Florence of Worcester), p. 583.

[4] 'Erat enim eo tempore Cumbreland sub regis Malcolmi dominio, non jure possessa sed violenter subjugata' (*Hist. Regum*, ii. 191, ed. Arnold).

[5] Unde rex Etheldredus, regulo Cumbrie supradicto Malcolmo scribens, per nuncium mandavit, quod suos Cumbrenses tributa solvere cogeret, sicut ceteri faciunt provinciales. Quod ille protinus contradicens rescripsit, suos aliud nullatenus debere vectigal, preterquam ad edictum regium, quandocunque sibi placuerit, cum ceteris semper fore paratos ad bellandum. Nam pulchrius esse, dicebat, ac multo praestantius, viriliter cum gladio, quam auro defendere libertatem (*Chronica Gentis Scotorum*, iv. c. 35 ; *Historians of Scotland*, i.)

[6] Donald Mac Dunstan ij. aunz. Edmound, freir Athelstan, duna a cesti Donald, roy Descoce, tout Combirland, pur quoi lez Escoces ount fait clayme, tanque al Reir croiz de Staynmore : mais cel doune ad este souent conquys puscedy et relesse en maint peise fesaunt (Skene, *Chron. of Picts and Scots*, p. 204). The date of the chronicle from which the above extract is taken has been ascribed to 1280.

difficult to defend the old theory of the effective sovereignty of Scotland over the district south of the Solway from the date of King Eadmund's grant till the conquest of Carlisle in 1092. It would appear that the compact lasted only for the lifetime of the contracting parties, for Kenneth son of Malcolm soon after his accession in 971 plundered part of the district of Strathclyde and the whole of Northumbria as far as Stainmore.[1] In these circumstances it must be concluded that Scottish claims to the sovereignty of Cumberland, founded on King Eadmund's grant, must have been put forward at a later date.

Early authorities like the Anglo-Saxon Chronicle and Florence of Worcester are content with the bare statement of King Ethelred's invasion of Cumberland in 1000. Henry of Huntingdon[2] however enlarges on the older narratives and supplies a reasonable account of the object of the expedition. King Ethelred, he says, assembled a powerful host and went into Cumberland, which was at that time a stronghold of the Danes, and he conquered the Danes in a great battle and laid waste and pillaged nearly the whole of Cumberland. In this statement we have a more likely pretext for the invasion than that supplied by Fordun, to which attention has been called, and it possesses the additional recommendation that it seems to harmonize with the general sequence of events in the northern districts. It is noteworthy how much the Danish colonization is mixed up with the political vicissitudes of Cumberland, whether that geographical term be taken in its limited or enlarged sense, and how often these vicissitudes resulted from, or were associated with, the history of Northumbria. It was an unjustifiable exercise of Danish power in that kingdom which drew the attention of King Eadmund to northern affairs and caused the expulsion of the two kings in 944,[3] and it was probably some insubordination on the part of the people of Cumberland, if we can trust Huntingdon's description of their character, that led in the following year to the cession of this treacherous and lawless race to the dominion of the Scottish king.[4] Both acts seem to have been parts of one plan, the annexation of Northumbria to his own kingdom of Wessex and the cession of Cumberland to Scotland, as he was himself, owing to its turbulence and isolation, unable to keep it under effective control. If it be admitted that the evidence is insufficient to predicate a permanent grant of Cumberland to Scotland in 945, it cannot be denied that the district

---

[1] Statim (Cinadius filius Maelcolaim) predavit Britanniam ex parte. Scotti predaverunt Saxoniam ad Stanmoir, et ad Cluiam, et ad Stangna Dera'm (Skene, *Chron. of Picts and Scots,* p. 10). Skene interpreted the *Britannia* of the 'Pictish Chronicle' as the land of the Strathclyde Britons, and *Saxonia* as 'the northern part of Northumbria as far as Stanmore, Cleveland, and the pools of Deira, that is, the part of Northumbria which had been placed as a separate earldom under Eadulf' (*Celtic Scotland,* i. 369). E. W. Robertson understood *Britannia* to refer to Cumberland (*Early Kings,* i. 72). As Kenneth II. began to reign in 971, the expedition against Strathclyde must have taken place soon after (*statim*) his accession.

[2] *Historia Anglorum,* p. 170, ed. Arnold. There is no mention of Scottish sovereignty in this account ; the Danes were in possession of the district called Cumberland at this time.

[3] *Anglo-Saxon Chronicle,* i. 89–90.   [4] *Historia Anglorum,* p. 162, ed. Arnold.

had attained some measure of independence or had reverted to the dominion of Northumberland, with which it had been politically connected before the government of that kingdom had been thrown into confusion by the Danish inroads.

Of the Danish predominance in the district south of the Solway there can be no doubt. It has been pointed out by Mr. Freeman[1] that no proof was needed to show that Cumberland and Westmorland were largely Scandinavian to this day, but there was no record how they had become so. In Northumberland, he says, we know when the Danes settled, and we know something of the dynasties which they founded. But the Scandinavian settlement of Cumberland—Norwegian no doubt rather than Danish—we know only by its results. We have no statement as to its date, and we know that no Scandinavian dynasty was founded there. The clue to the great puzzle of Cumbrian ethnology might not have been so difficult to find, had attention been given to the political association of the western district with Northumberland. There was no occasion for a Scandinavian dynasty, and no need for a separate record of the Scandinavian settlement on the understanding that Cumberland continued subject to Northumbrian dominion, except at rare intervals, during the Danish ascendency. There is documentary proof, however, the value of which cannot be exaggerated, that the territory in the neighbourhood of Carlisle was politically connected with Northumberland for some period during the eleventh century, subject to Northumbrian law, and ruled by Northumbrian earls. As this evidence is new to history, it calls for special examination.

The document in question, of which a thirteenth century copy written on vellum and wonderfully well preserved exists in the muniment room at Lowther Castle, is a writ or grant of Gospatric bestowing certain privileges on his freemen and dependants in the neighbourhood of Carlisle. The deed, which is in English and of unrivalled interest, throws a welcome light on the political and territorial history of Cumberland, and adds much to our knowledge of the district before it was conquered by William Rufus in 1092. As the contents display so many evidences of genuineness, both philological and topographical, there is no hazard in regarding the document as of unquestionable authority. By its means we can compel the darkness in some measure to yield up its secret, and we are enabled to set back the domain of ascertained knowledge, imperfect though it be, for a period of at least half a century. Before Gospatric's writ was made public, we could not get behind the statement in the Anglo-Saxon Chronicle that Dolfin was ruler of Carlisle in 1092, and we possessed no trustworthy evidence about the tenure or tenants of the district, except what might be gathered from the great Inquest of Fees in 1212, a feudal transaction which we were compelled to accept, in the absence of the Domesday Survey, as the foundation of the territorial history of Cumberland. The date of the grant is very difficult to fix with any approach to exactness, but it may be assigned to some period

_____
[1] *Norman Conquest*, i. 634.

before the Conquest by William Rufus. It can scarcely be earlier than 1067 when Gospatric purchased the earldom of Northumberland from William the Conqueror, though it may have been issued after 1072 when King Malcolm of Scotland gave him Dunbar and the adjacent lands in Lothian.

Before deductions are made from this new evidence on the political condition of the district, it is desirable that the writ[1] should be printed in full.

> Gospatrik greot[2] ealle mine wassenas[3] & hyylkun mann, freo & ðrenge, þeo woonnan on eallun þam landann þeo weoron Combres & eallun mine kynling[4] freond‑lycc ; & ic cyðe eoy þ̄ myne mynna is & full leof þ̄ Thorfynn Mac Thore beo swa freo on eallan ðynges þeo beo myne on Alnerdall swa ænyg mann beo, oðer ic oðer ænyg myne wassenas, on weald, on freyð, on heyninga & æt ællun ðyngan, þeo bȳ eorðe bænand & ðeoronðer, to Shauk, to Wafyr, to poll Waðœn, to bek Troyte & þeo weald æt Caldebek ; & ic wille þ̄ þeo mann bydann mið Thorfynn æt Carðeu & Combeðeyfoch beo swa freals myð hem swa Melmor & Thore & Sygoolf weoron on Eadread dagan, & ne beo neann mann swa ðeorif, þehat mið þ̄ ic heobbe gegyfen to hem, ne ghar brech seo gyrth ðyylc Eorl Syward & ic hebbe getyðet hem cefrelycc swa ænyg mann leofand þeo welkynn ðeoronðer ; & loc hyylkun bȳ þar byðann geyld freo beo swa ic bȳ, & swa willann Wallðeof & Wygande & Wyberth & Gamell & Kūyth & eallun mine kynling & wassenas ; & ic wille þ̄ Thorfynn heobbe soc & sac, toll & theam, ofer eallun þam landan on Carðeu & on Combeðeyfoch þ̄ weoron gyfene Thore on Moryn dagan freols myd bode & wytnesmann on þyylk stow.

> Gospatrik greets all my dependants and each man, free and dreng, that dwell in all the lands of the Cumbrians, and all my kindred friendlily; and I make known to you that my mind and full leave is that Thorfynn[5] Mac[6] Thore be as free in all things that are mine in Alnerdall[7] as any man is, whether I or any of my dependants, in wood, in heath, in enclosures, and as to all things that are existing on the earth and

[1] This document, the existence of which has been well known to Lord Lonsdale, was submitted to Chancellor Burn when he was examining the muniments at Lowther for the *History of Westmorland and Cumberland*, published in 1777, and bears an endorsement in his handwriting, but he appatently did not fully recognize its importance. The present writer's attention was called to it by Canon Greenwell, at whose suggestion he examined it at Lowther and contributed an article thereon to the *Scottish Historical Review*, October, 1903. The deed has been the subject of an article in the *Ancestor*, October, 1903, by the Rev. F. W. Ragg, who saw it and procured a photograph of it in 1902. It has been also printed by Canon Greenwell in *A History of Northumberland*, vii. 25-6, and with facsimile by Professor Liebermann in *Archiv für das Studium der neueren Sprachen und Literaturen*, cxi. pt. 3-4, 275-8.

[2] The rapid transition from the third person to the first in Gospatric's mode of address is common and idiomatic. Compare the letter of Ælfthryth to Ælfric, Archbishop of Canterbury, and that of Wulfstan, Archbishop of York, to King Cnut, for the identical phraseology of our charter (Thorpe, *Diplomatarium*, pp. 295, 313).

[3] This is a rare word and is used thrice in the writ. It cannot be Norman for vassals, for 'vassal' was not adopted into English at this date. It is apparently British, a form of the Welsh 'gwassan,' a dependant or retainer, but it is from the same Celtic root as the Frankish 'vassallus.' For the use of *vassalus* before the Conquest, see Maitland, *Domesday Book and Beyond*, p. 293.

[4] For the use of this word, which is of very rare occurrence, the reader may be referred to the alleged charter of Edward the Confessor printed by Kemble (*Codex Diplomaticus*, iv. 236).

[5] A personal name not uncommon in Cumberland in the twelfth century. In the Chartulary of St. Bees, 'Thorfinsacre' is named as a plot of land. The parish of Torpenhow is written 'Thorphin-how' in some early deeds. The hill overlooking the village of Thursby is still known as 'Torkin' probably from this person.

[6] This word for 'son' is extremely rare in local evidences. We have Gospatric Mapbennoc, that is, 'Mac Bennoc,' in the Pipe Roll of Cumberland of 1158 : his name appears in the Roll of 1163 as 'Gospatric fil. Beloc.'

[7] The great district of Allerdale situated on the western seaboard between the Wampool and the Derwent, so called perhaps because it was traversed by the river Alne or Ellen. Near its mouth is the vill of Alneburg or Ellenborough.

under it, at Shauk and at Wafyr and at Pollwathoen [1] and at bek Troyte [2] and the wood at Caldebek [3]; and I desire that the men abiding with Thorfynn at Cartheu and Combetheyfoch [4] be as free with him as Melmor [5] and Thore [6] and Sygulf were in Eadread's days, and that (there) be no man so bold that he—with what I have given to him—cause to break the peace such as Earl Syward and I have granted to them for ever as any man living under the sky; and whosoever is there abiding, let him be geld free as I am and in like manner as Walltheof and Wygande [7] and Wyberth [8] and Gamell [9] and Kunyth [10] and all my kindred and dependants; and I will that Thorfynn have soc and sac, toll and theam over all the lands of Cartheu and Combetheyfoch that were given to Thore in Moryn's [11] days free, with bode and witnessman [12] in the same place.

It may be inferred from the general tenor of the document that Gospatric held a high position in the district, for it is most improbable that he should have used such a style of address to the men of Cumbria had he been only the lord of Allerdale. Subsequent events, such as the position of his son Dolfin at Carlisle in 1092 and the succession of Waldeve to the paternal estates in Allerdale, appear to warrant the belief that Gospatric ruled the district south of the Solway. As no allusion is made to Scottish sovereignty, and as Gospatric appeals to the laws which Earl Siward and he had established in Cumberland, there can be little doubt of the political subjection of the district to Northumberland at the period to which the grant refers.

It is interesting to inquire how northern events during Siward's tenure of the earldom (1041–55) [13] will suit this Northumbrian overlordship. It

[1] Shauk, Waver and Wampool, three streams well known as boundaries of Allerdale on the north and north-east. The Wampool is usually found in early evidences as Wathunpol, which is much the same form as that in this charter.

[2] Troutbeck is the common name for a small stream in northern England.

[3] Caldbeck, a parish forming the eastern limit of Allerdale.

[4] Cardew and Cumdivock, two vills in the parish of Dalston, separated from Allerdale by the water of Shauk and lying over against Thursby.

[5] Probably the owner from whom the parish of Melmerby in the east of Cumberland took its name.

[6] Apparently the same person as the father of Thorfynn above mentioned, who gave his name to Thursby or Thoresby, as the parish was called in the twelfth century.

[7] Probably the owner of Wiggonby, a vill to the north-west of Thursby in the parish of Aikton near the Wampool.

[8] Not identified unless he was the owner of Waberthwaite, formerly Wyberthwaite, a small parish in the lordship of Millom, which was within the portion of ancient Cumbria surveyed under Yorkshire in Domesday as part of the possessions of Earl Tostig.

[9] Perhaps the owner of Gamelsby, a vill on the Wampool in the parish of Aikton. It is almost certain that another Gamel, the son of Bern, who lived somewhat later, bequeathed his name to Gamelsby in Leath Ward. It is very striking that we should have the names of Thore, Wygande, and Gamell embodied in a group of places close to the Wampool.

[10] The reading of the script here is somewhat doubtful owing to the condition of the ink. The name may be intended for some form of the uncertain Celtic or Pictish name Kenneth, which appears in Symeon of Durham under 774 as 'Cynoht.'

[11] The owner of the district of Dalston, of which Cardew and Cumdivock are parcels. Dalston was afterwards forfeited by Hervey son of Morin; was an escheat in the hand of Henry II.; and was granted to the See of Carlisle by Henry III.

[12] The services of 'bode and wytnesmann' were well known institutions in the early history or Cumberland. In 1292 John de Hodelston excused the monks of Furness of suit at his court of Millom, of pannage and puture, and of 'bode and wyttenesman' for ever, which services were formerly claimed from them in respect of their land of Brotherulkill in Coupland (*Duchy of Lancaster Charter*, Box B, No. 155). Opinions differ on the exact nature of these institutions.

[13] *Symeon* (i. 91, ii. 198, ed. Arnold) says that Earl Eadulf was slain by Siward in 1041, and Florence (*Mon. Hist. Brit.* p. 600) calls Siward earl of the Northumbrians in the same year. He was certainly in possession of the earldom in 1043 according to *Symeon* (ii. 163) and died at York in 1055 as stated by the Anglo-Saxon Chronicle..

is possible that Siward had seized Carlisle after his successful expedition into Scotland against Macbeth in 1054,[1] and that the *gyrth* spoken of in Gospatric's writ may have been extended to the Cumbrians as a result of the war. In this connection we should not pass over the statement of Gaimar, not found elsewhere, that 'Earl Syward made an agreement with the King of Scotland when he went ; but Macbeth destroyed the peace and ceased not to carry on war.'[2] There is little need to accept every statement in the mythical history of Siward[3] or to press unduly the testimony of Bromton[4] in support of Gospatric's writ, but the story, common to both of these authorities, that Siward was made Earl of Westmorland, Cumberland and Northumberland, and was the means of effectually tranquillizing (*potenter pacificavit*) these territories cannot be rejected without some show of reason. The Norse names borne by the potentates of the district seem to lend probability to the conclusion that the Danish earl found sympathetic associates in establishing his peace in the western province of his charge.

In the statement of Gospatric's deed that the magnates of Cumberland held their lands free of geld we may find some explanation of Earl Siward's success as a legislator. To what does this tribute refer ? As it cannot be suggested that no territorial service was exacted from the chief tenants of the district, we are compelled to assume that some extraordinary or exceptional burden on the land is referred to. It is possible that Fordun used the exemption of Cumberland from the Danegeld as the pretext whereon to build his argument that it was the refusal of the inhabitants, as subjects of the Prince of Scotland, to contribute to the tax which stirred up the energies of King Ethelred in 1000 and brought about the invasion. However that may be, the fact of the freedom from geld is incontestable, and there seems to be no good ground for rejecting its identity with the Danegeld.[5] The district comprised a strong Scandinavian settlement ; while Siward held the reins of power, it was ruled by a Danish earl ; the people were reduced to order by Northumbrian legislation. Everything appears to suggest the influence and protection of Northumberland at this period.

[1] Siward's expedition into Scotland in 1054 is mentioned by most of the chronicles, but the *Annals of Ulster* (i. 595, ed. Hennessy) add the interesting fact that 'three thousand of the men of Alban were slain, and fifteen hundred of the men of Saxonia with (*im*) Dolfinn mac Finntuir (Thorfinn).'

[2] *Mon. Hist. Brit.* p. 825. 'Li quens Syward donc s'accordat al rei d'Escoce, u il alat ; mais Macheden defuit la pes : de guerreier ne fist releis.'

[3] The tract 'Origo et gesta Siwardi Dani' has been often printed, but see it in Langebech, *Scriptores Rerum Danicarum*, iii. 287 : also 'Vita et Passio Waldevi Comitis' in *Original Lives of Anglo-Saxons before the Conquest* (Caxton Soc.), 8, 22–3. Mr. Freeman has rejected the whole story with the exception of 'the one bit of history which lurks in all this,' viz. 'the fact of the union of the earldoms of Northumberland and Huntingdon in the person of Siward' (*Norman Conquest*, i. 768–9).

[4] Twysden, *Decem Scriptores*, col. 946.

[5] It is thought that Danegeld was a popular name of dislike for the tax originally applied to payments made to buy off the Danes and afterwards transferred to these other payments made to Danish and other mercenary forces (Freeman, *Norman Conquest*, ii. 124, 574–5). In that case it was unlikely that the nickname should be used by Gospatric in his declaration of its remission to one of his vassals. The earliest occurrence of the word seems to be in Domesday (336*b*), but instances of its payment during the reign of Ethelred are often alluded to by later writers. Though the Danegeld was remitted by the Confessor, its payment was revived at an early period by the Conqueror. It had afterwards become subject to numerous exemptions (Ellis, *Introduction to Domesday*, i. 350–1).

There is no doubt that during the confusion which followed the Norman invasion in 1066 King Malcolm seized Cumberland and became sovereign of the district between the Solway and the Duddon. The statement of the 'Cronica de Karleolo' cannot be gainsaid that Cumbria in 1069 embraced the southern province to its furthest limit.[1] But how long the Scottish sovereignty lasted is another question. It is difficult to discuss Gospatric's relation to Cumberland apart from the general history of Northumbria, though it is clear enough from the evidence of the writ above mentioned that he was not only a great landowner in the district like Earl Tostig, his predecessor,[2] but that he was its ruler and overlord. If the date of the grant could be settled with certainty,[3] a more trustworthy deduction might be made about the part Gospatric played to preserve the integrity of the Northumbrian earldom against Scottish and Norman intrigue. He was a personage of great prestige in the northern province. A scion of the illustrious house of Bamborough, allied in blood on his father's side with the reigning family of Scotland, and the grandson of Ethelred, the English king,[4] Gospatric exercised a predominant influence in Northumberland when William the Conqueror landed at Pevensey. On no other assumption than that he attempted at the outset to revive the independence of the ancient kingdom, or at least to maintain an independence comparable to it, can the statements of the chronicles be explained or reconciled. It was his policy to play the Scot against the Norman and to hold the balance of power between them. He courted the protection of Malcolm or William as it suited his purpose. In 1067 he secured from King William a recognition of his title to Northumberland as an earldom,[5] upon which he had manifest claims in right of his mother, Aldgitha, daughter of Earl

---

[1] The 'Cronica de Karleolo' was drawn up in 1291 by the prior and convent of Carlisle, after a diligent examination of the chronicles and writings in their possession, and transmitted to Edward I. by the hand of Alan de Frysington, precentor of the church, when that king was seeking historical information concerning Scotland. The entry relating to the extent of Cumbria in 1069 is as follows :—
'1069. Cumbria dicebatur quantum modo est Episcopatus Karleolensis et Episcopatus Glasguensis et Episcopatus Candidecase et insuper ab Episcopatu Karleolensi usque ad flumen Dunde ' (Palgrave, *Documents and Records*, p. 70). This statement is often regarded as retrospective, but if so, why should the canons have been so particular in recording the date at which Cumbria attained such dimensions ? It is quite clear that its territorial extent had undergone some alteration in 1069.

[2] *Domesday Book*, i. 301b.

[3] It is not known in what year Gospatric died, though Roger of Hoveden (i. 59, ed. Stubbs) has recorded the place and manner of his death. When the grantor speaks in the writ of the peace which Earl Syward and he had bestowed on their vassals, he appears to be referring back to a period when he had been Earl of Northumberland. He would scarcely have used such a phrase had he been the earl in possession. In that case the date must have been after 1072, when he was deprived of the earldom (*Symeon*, ii. 196, ed. Arnold ; *Hoveden*, i. 126, ed. Stubbs). There is nothing in the writing to suggest whether Gospatric ruled the district as an independent sovereign or as a subject of the Scottish crown. If the date be taken after 1072, there can be no question of his dependence on Scotland notwithstanding the absence of any mention of Scottish sovereignty. On the assumption that the grant was made while he was Earl of Northumberland, 1067–72, his independence of Scotland is unassailable.

[4] *Symeon*, i. 216, ii. 199, 383 ; *Chronicle of Melrose*, in ann. 950.

[5] There is little doubt that Gospatric succeeded to the earldom in 1067, though the date of his appointment is often placed in 1068 or 1069. If we compare the statements in the Anglo-Saxon Chronicle under 1067 that ' Gospatric eorl and tha betstan menn foron into Scotland ' and under 1068 that ' Gospatric eorl mid Nordhymbrum and ealle tha landleoden ' took part in the destruction of York, we can form no other conclusion.

Uhctred, and in 1068 he fled to Scotland[1] after the rebellion of Edwin and Morcar, in which he was probably implicated. It can scarcely be disputed that the appointment of Robert Cumen[2] was an attempt to supersede Gospatric in the earldom. Malcolm seized the occasion of Gospatric's disgrace and took possession of Cumberland. But his name was still a power in the land. As a counter-move in the game Gospatric submitted to King William in 1070,[3] and immediately turned his wrath on King Malcolm for the betrayal of his interests by harrying Cumberland in turn,[4] and no doubt recovering its possession. Events proved however that the Conqueror was aware of the political situation in the north, for on his return after the invasion of Scotland in 1072 he deprived Gospatric of his earldom on charges which he had hitherto overlooked.[5] The exiled earl again sought refuge in Scotland and made common cause with the Scottish people against Norman power. Malcolm gave him Dunbar and the adjacent land in Lothian till better days dawned and Gospatric recovered his lost possessions.[6] At this date the curtain falls on Cumbrian affairs, and is not again uplifted till the conquest by William Rufus in 1092.

The time was at hand when political affairs in the north-western district were destined to take a fresh turn and the limits of the Scottish kingdom to be settled beyond dispute. Hitherto the northern nation had shown a tendency to advance rather than to recede. The Scots were restless in their efforts to obtain an enlargement of their territories towards the south. But William Rufus was determined to check their aggressions and to secure a natural frontier between the two nations. With this view, there can be little doubt, as we read in the *Anglo-Saxon Chronicle*, King William went north to Carlisle with a large force in 1092, restored the town and built the castle ; and drove out Dolfin who

[1] Symeon, *Hist. Regum*, ii. 186 ; Hoveden, *Chronica*, i. 117. Gospatric with other Northumbrian nobles accompanied Edgar the Ætheling, Agatha his mother, and Margaret and Christine, his sisters, in their flight to Scotland.

[2] This happened in 1069 when Earl Gospatric with the whole host of Northumbria joined the Danes in resisting the advance of the Normans. Robert Cumen was slain before the gates of Durham (*Symeon*, ii. 187, ed. Arnold).

[3] 'Reconciliati sunt Guallevus presens, et Caius-Patricius absens, sacramento per legatos exhibito' (*Orderic Vitalis*, bk. iv. c. 5). It is significant that Gospatric did not commit himself to the king's power by personal attendance : he made his submission by deputy. In 1071, the following year, he was deputed by order of King William to meet Bishop Walcher at York and conduct him to Durham (*Symeon*, ii. 195 ; *Hoveden*, i. 126).

[4] *Symeon*, ii. 191–2 ; *Hoveden*, i. 121–2. Symeon states that Gospatric, having wasted Cumberland 'atroci depopulatione,' retired with much plunder 'in munitionem Babbenburch firmissimam,' from which he harassed the forces of the enemy by frequent forays, for Cumberland was at that time under the dominion of Malcolm, not possessed of right but subjugated by force. Mr. Hodgson Hinde, in view of his belief in the effectiveness of Scottish sovereignty over Cumberland from 945, has rejected the authority of Symeon's text on the mutual reprisals of Malcolm and Gospatric (*Symeon of Durham*, xxviii–xxx. 86–8). If the present text is corrupt and untrustworthy, it has not altered to any appreciable extent since 1291, for the canons of Carlisle told the same story to Edward I. (Palgrave, *Documents and Records*, p. 70). The atrocities committed on both sides may be incredible on Mr. Hinde's hypothesis, but the incredibleness disappears when the political necessities of Gospatric's position are recognized.

[5] *Symeon*, ii. 196 ; *Hoveden*, i. 126. Gospatric was charged with aiding and abetting the murder of Robert Cumen and his men at Durham, though he had not been present in person, and that he had been on the side of the enemy when the Normans were slain at York.

[6] *Symeon*, ii. 199 ; *Hoveden*, i. 59.

had previously ruled the land there ; and garrisoned the castle with his own men and then returned to the south ; and sent very many country folk with their wives and cattle to dwell there and to till the land.[1] We are not told whose vassal Dolfin was, but from the previous connection of Earl Gospatric, his father, with the Scots, it is probable that he owed allegiance to the Scottish king. If the region south of the Solway had been held by Dolfin on behalf of Scotland, the sovereignty of that kingdom had been definitely annulled by the expedition of 1092.

It is noteworthy that no name came into use for the district from which Dolfin had been expelled except what had been taken from its vicinity to Carlisle. In documents of the early portion of the twelfth century it was known as the Power (*potestas*) or Honor of Carlisle,[2] a designation which was continued till the formation of the counties of Cumberland and Westmorland as fiscal areas in 1177. This point is very significant and needs not to be stated at great length. The expedition of 1092 is described in the Anglo-Saxon Chronicle as an expedition to Carlisle. Florence of Worcester regarded Carlisle, to which Rufus marched his host, as being in Northumbria, an opinion adopted by Symeon of Durham without protest.[3] When Henry of Huntingdon enumerated the shires of England, he had no name to give the new district except ' that region in which is the new bishopric of Carluil.'[4] As the northern boundary of the land of Carlisle was, roughly speaking, the Solway, there must have been some recognized frontier to Dolfin's province which Rufus accepted, and up to which he claimed as the right of his crown. A fortuitous delimitation of Cumbria in 1092 is almost inconceivable if under that name we understand the state, homogeneous and indivisible, which is said to have reached from the Clyde to the Duddon and to have been held by the Scottish king under the treaty of 945. The records of the conquest undoubtedly assume that the district of Carlisle was a political state of itself, and that it was governed by usurped authority. There is no question that the Solway was a settled boundary and was accepted as such by both nations. When King David established Robert de Brus in Annandale, the fief was described as extending ' to the bounds of Ranulf Meschin,' the first Norman lord of Carlisle of whom there is mention. The Scottish king ordained that his vassal should enjoy ' all

---

[1] The history condensed in this entry of the Chronicle is of the utmost interest : 'On thisum geare se cyng W. mid mycelre fyrde ferde nord to Cardeol and tha burh geaedstathelede, and thone castel arerde, and Dolfin ut adraf, the aeror thaer thes landes weold, and thone castel mid his mannan gesette, and syddan hider sud gewaende, and mycele maenige cyrlisces folces mid wifan and mid orfe thyder saende thaer to wunigenne that land to tilianne.' Florence of Worcester, who closed his history in 1117 (Hardy, *Descriptive Catalogue*, ii. 133), has incorporated the statement in these words : ' Rex in Northimbriam profectus, civitatem quae Brytannice Cairleu, Latine Lugubalia, vocatur, restauravit et in ea castellum aedificavit.' For a critical examination of the technical words in the account given by the Anglo-Saxon Chronicle, which deserve close attention, the paper by Mr. Geo. Neilson in *Notes and Queries* (8th ser. viii. 321-3) should not be overlooked.

[2] *Reg. of Wetherhal*, pp. 2, 25, ed. J. E. Prescott.

[3] *Hist. Regum*, ii. 220, ed. Arnold. Symeon has incorporated in his history the exact words used by Florence.

[4] ' Illa regio in qua est novus episcopatus Carluil' (*Hist. Anglorum*, p. 10, ed. Arnold).

the customs which Ranulf Meschin ever had in Carlisle and in all his land of Cumberland.'[1] The land of Cumberland, as the name for the district south of the Solway, is a singular admission to be found in a Scottish document of that date. At a later period, when David was sovereign of Carlisle, there is nothing remarkable in his address to his faithful sheriffs and justices of all Cumberland (*totius Cumberlandie*) or in the gift to the see of Glasgow of certain royal perquisites of his courts throughout Cumbria (*per totam Cumbriam*).[2] That the Scots claimed the province as far south as Stainmore everybody admits. The wise men who made the famous Inquest of David[3] about 1120 entered a feeble protest that the prince of Cumbria was not the ruler at that time of the whole of the Cumbrian region, though they were unable to point to a single bit of property south of the Solway ever possessed by the see of Glasgow, in the diocese of which the land was said to have been.

There is no mistaking the English appropriation of Cumberland as a territorial designation. The name came into informal use at an early period after the conquest of 1092. When Henry I. endowed the canons of Carlisle with the churches and lands of Walter the priest he directed his writ to all his barons of 'Cumbreland and Westmarialand.'[4] The same division was recognized in the Pipe Roll of 1130 under the titles of 'Chaerleolium' and 'Westmarieland.'[5] These names had been floating about from time immemorial as indicative of territorial areas. Gaimar relates that the Picts baptized by Ninian were 'Westmaringiens,'[6] and the Anglo-Saxon Chronicle has recorded under 966 the wasting of 'Westmoringa-land' by Earl Thored,[7] or 'Westmereland' as Gaimar called it in his account of the foray. But a long period elapsed after 1092 before the names of Cumberland and Westmorland were adopted by the English Exchequer as definite fiscal areas. Throughout the reign of Henry I. there had been a county of Carlisle[8] which at first

---

[1] *Nat. MSS. of Scotland*, i. No. xix. Rec. Com.   [2] *Reg. Epis. Glasg.* i. 12, Bannatyne Club.

[3] This famous document, entitled 'Inquisicio per David, Principem Cumbrensem, de terris ecclesie Glasguensi pertinentibus facta,' was dated in 1116 by Mr. Cosmo Innes, but it is probably later, in 1120 or 1122. In it we have Cumbria described as 'regio quedam inter Angliam et Scotiam sita'; David as 'Cumbrensis regionis principem (non vero toti Cumbrensi regioni dominabatur)'; and the diocese of Glasgow as 'Cumbrensis parochia.' The inquest was made and witnessed by some well known magnates on both sides of the frontier. It is printed in facsimile in *Reg. Epis. Glasg.* i. 3–7, Bannatyne Club.

[4] This charter has been printed under the section of 'Ecclesiastical History.'

[5] *Pipe Roll*, 31 Hen. I. pp. 140–3, ed. J. Hunter.

[6] 'Ninan aveit alnz baptizé les altres Pictes del regné; ces sunt les Westmaringiens ki donc esteient Pictiens' (*Mon. Hist. Brit.* p. 776).

[7] 'Her Thored Gunneres sunu forhergode Westmoringaland.' This Thored is described in the Chronicle under 992 as 'Thored Eorl.' It was conjectured by Mr. E. W. Robertson that he was Earl of Deira or Yorkshire (*Scot. under Early Kings*, ii. 441–2), to which Mr. Freeman gives his assent (*Norm. Conq.* i. 646). Gaimar noted the event: 'Fors sul Torel, ki revelat: Westmereland sur lui preiad' (*Mon. Hist. Brit.* p. 808).

[8] The foundation charter of the priory of Wetheral, one of the earliest documents relating to the district in existence, was addressed by Ranulf Meschin to 'Richerio vicecomiti Karlioli et omnibus hominibus suis, Francis et Anglis, qui in potestate Karlioli habitant' (*Reg. of Wetherhal*, pp. 1–2). Archdeacon Prescott has dated the deed between 1092 and 1112, but the witnesses seemed to agree better with the later date. Though there can scarcely have been a fully equipped county at so early a date, the mention of a sheriff of Carlisle is very significant. On the relation of a sheriff to a county, see Pollock and Maitland, *Hist. of Engl. Law before Edw. I.* (2nd ed.), i. 533–4.

was probably conterminous with the fief of Ranulf Meschin, that is, the district which was formed into a diocese in 1133. It is well known that Ranulf was ruler of a portion of the present county of Westmorland ; he built a castle at Appleby and made various grants of churches and lands in that neighbourhood to St. Mary's Abbey at York.[1] Though we meet with a sheriff of Carlisle about 1106, there is no mention of a sheriff of Westmorland till 1130,[2] ten years after Ranulf had resigned his fief into the king's hand. It is probable that it was between 1120 and 1130, while Henry I. administered the affairs of the district,[3] the fiscal reconstruction took place, for in the latter year Westmorland was a definite area under the jurisdiction of a separate sheriff. The local administration of Carlisle (*Chaerleolium*) and Westmorland (*Westmarieland*) was thrown into confusion after the death of Henry I., when the whole district was wrested from Stephen by the Scots during the anarchy. On the recovery of the province in 1157 by Henry II. the old territorial arrangement was revived and continued till the Scottish invasion in 1174. For a few years the sheriff of Carlisle was unable to make returns for the county by reason of the war. Meanwhile a reconstruction of the fiscal areas must have taken place at the Exchequer, for in 1177 the Pipe Rolls are resumed with the name of Cumberland substituted for that of Carlisle as the official designation of the county.[3] The great barony of Coupland, reaching from the Derwent to the Duddon, which lay outside the fief of Ranulf Meschin and the Honor of Carlisle, must have been incorporated with the county of Carlisle soon after the recovery of the district in 1157. Though it retained for many years the name of the county of Coupland, and was reckoned a separate area in the rota of itinerant justices in 1176,[4] its revenues were accounted for by the sheriff as early as 1162, and pleas in Coupland became one of the sub-titles in the rolls of the sheriff of Cumberland in 1178. In these circumstances it can scarcely be doubted that the formation of the county of Cumberland, as we now know it, must be assigned to the year 1177. The final application of the name to a definite area presents one of those curious vagaries in territorial nomenclature often difficult to explain. The chief difficulty in this case arises from the early method of geographical description in naming territories after their inhabitants. The varying fortunes of the Cymric race subjected the land of their habitation to a continual state of change. After many vicissitudes of contraction and expansion, the geographical term which had undergone a slow process of formation was at last crystallized and adopted by the Norman conqueror as the name of a fiscal area in the heart of ancient Cumbria.[5]

---

[1] *Reg. of Wetherhal*, pp. 10–14, ed. J. E. Prescott.

[2] *Pipe Roll*, 31 Hen. I. pp. 26, 133, 142, ed. J. Hunter.

[3] All this may be clearly seen from a study of the Pipe Rolls under the years named.

[4] *Benedict. Abbas*, i. 108, ed. Stubbs. For a more detailed account of the formation of the counties of Cumberland and Westmorland, see ante, i. 309–11.

[5] Mr. Freeman has pointed out a similar phenomenon in the formation of the county of Northumberland, inasmuch as 'that part of old Northumberland, which is quite away from the Humber, has kept the name of Northumberland to this day,' though the usage certainly began as

The statement in the Anglo-Saxon Chronicle [1] about the expedition of 1092 may be regarded as a summary of the work of William Rufus in reclaiming the land of Carlisle and incorporating it into the English kingdom. The Solway was accepted as the international boundary. The remaining portion of the reign was employed in rebuilding the city and colonizing the district in its neighbourhood. The king never visited the north again. It rested with his successor, Henry I., to secure the permanence of the work by the appointment of Ranulf Meschin,[2] a Norman nobleman, to the lordship of the recovered province with ample powers of jurisdiction and defence. The new ruler fixed his residence at Appleby [3] in the valley of the Eden, where his castle commanded the passes into Yorkshire. For the defence of his charge on the north Ranulf created two baronies which stretched almost the whole length of the frontier, that of Burgh by Sands on the southern banks of the estuary of the Eden as it falls into the Solway, and that of Liddel on Esk, a strip of territory which lay athwart the outlet into Scotland, and committed them to the care of trusty men, the former to Robert de Trivers and the latter to Turgis Brundas. As a supplement to the gift of Burgh by Sands, the custody of the forest of Cumberland was added to the benefice of Robert de Trivers at an annual rent of ten marks. These are the only acts of infeudation ascribed to Ranulf Meschin, while he was lord of Cumberland, in the great Inquest of Fees of 1212.[4] There appears to have been no displacement of the original territorial owners, except perhaps in those instances when it was necessary at the outset for defensive purposes. It is probable that Dolfin, who was expelled by William Rufus in 1092, had opposed that king's policy of annexation ; but taking the district as a whole there

early as the eleventh century (*Norm. Conq.* i. 644–5). He attributes the allocation of the names for the present area to the predominance of the English settlement between Tyne and Tweed, which had been undisturbed by Danish power. If we accept this explanation, it will afford a strong reason for the adoption of Cumberland on the western coast as the name of a region which had continued subject to the English traditions of Northumbrian rule (E. W. Robertson, *Early Kings*, ii. 436–7).

[1] *Anglo-Saxon Chron.* (Rolls Ser.), i. 359.

[2] The date of Ranulf Meschin's appointment to the lordship of Cumberland is not known, but it must have been early in the reign of Henry I. His foundation charter of the priory of Wetheral cannot have been granted later than 1112, when Stephen, Abbot of St. Mary's York, died, to whom the manor of Wetheral was conveyed for the endowment of the new institution (Dugdale, *Mon.* iii. 529, 538, 583). It was Henry I., and not an earlier king, who confirmed this donation (*Reg. of Wetherhal*, 14–19). Ranulf is frequently associated with Henry I. when his tenure of Carlisle is referred to. For instance, in 1175 Pope Alexander speaks of the Island of Holmcultram, 'sicut fuit foresta tempore Henrici Regis et Radulphi comitis Cestrie' (Reg. of Holmcultram MS. f. 245), and Pope Lucius repeated the same phrase in 1185 (Harl. MS. 3911, f. 138). For the disputed passage in the foundation charter of Wetheral in which the name of William has been substituted for that of Henry, thus antedating the issue of the charter to the reign of Rufus, see *V.C.H. Cumb.* i. 301–2.

[3] Ranulf gave to St. Mary's, York, for the endowment of Wetheral, ' ecclesiam sancti Michaelis et ecclesiam sancti Laurentii castelli mei de Appelby cum omnibus quae ad eas pertinent sicut Radulphus capellanus meus tenuit quietas et liberas ab omni terreno servicio ' (*Reg. of Wetherhal*, 10–12). The word *castellum* in this charter must be understood in its archaic sense of a fortified town or enclosure, whether surrounded by walls or earthworks, as it included the two ancient parish churches which remain to this day. For the distinction between ' tower and castle ' in early documents, see Round, *Geoffrey de Mandeville*, 328–46. In 1130 the ' castellum de Aplebi ' was in the king's hand (*Pipe R.* 31 Hen. I. p. 143, Rec. Com.)

[4] Exch. K. R. Knights' Fees, ⅓, m. 2 ; *V.C.H. Cumb.* i. 421.

can be little doubt that the great body of local magnates quietly acquiesced in the new state of things.[1] Though the recorded acts of the Norman ruler are few and unimportant they may be taken as emblematic of the future history of the territory under his charge. It was a frontier state, exposed to continual incursion and attack, always on the defensive, the barrier against a hostile kingdom.

The political status of the new district was scarcely completed before Ranulf Meschin's connection with it was severed by his succession to the earldom of Chester after the wreck of the 'White Ship' in 1120, in which his cousin Earl Richard perished with William the Aetheling and several of the Norman nobility. The change of government occasioned by Ranulf's withdrawal was fraught with consequences to the northern province. King Henry appointed no vassal in his place, but took the lordship into his own hand, and lost no time in visiting it in person. In 1122, on the occasion of a visit to Northumberland, we are told on good authority that he turned aside towards the western sea with the view of taking into consideration the condition of the city of Carlisle, which he ordered to be fortified with a castle and towers, and left money for that purpose.[2] The strategic importance of the city of Carlisle as a bulwark against the Scot was recognized by King Henry as it had been recognized by Rufus thirty years before. Occupying the crest of a bold headland, protected in the front by the deep and swiftly flowing Eden, to the west by the Caldew and to the east by the Petteril, the ancient city which had played no inconspicuous part in the conquests of Roman, Englishman and Dane was withdrawn from the oblivion in which it had lain for two hundred years, and was rebuilt and garrisoned to defend the district from northern attack. If it be admitted that the settlement of England's frontier against Scotland and the fortification of Carlisle were the most important deeds of the Red

---

[1] The writ of Gospatric, printed above, throws a new light on the Inquest of Service of 1212, in which Henry I. is described as the original source of enfeoffment of several of the knights of Cumberland in their fees. If we were compelled to accept the literal interpretation of the verdict of the jurors, there could be no dispute that many of the great territorial owners were displaced by Henry I. to make way for the Norman immigration. Gospatric's writ, however, in which he is described as the owner of Allerdale, makes it quite clear that the infeudation was not originated by King Henry, but that the jurors of 1212 ignored all previous possession by Gospatric the father, and looked upon the king's confirmation of Waldeve the son, in the fee of Allerdale, as the source of the title. The same interpretation may be applied to the tenure of the barony of Greystoke. The jurors stated that it was Henry who gave it to Forne, the son of Siolf or Sigulf, but from the mention of the name of Sigulf as one of the magnates of Cumberland 'in Eadread's days,' it may be assumed that he was the owner of Greystoke before he was succeeded by his son Forne, to whom Henry I. in after years confirmed the barony. There is no inconsistency in the evidence of the two documents, for the jurors were following a well-established law in regarding the king's confirmation as the source of title. The displacement of Dolfin by William Rufus in 1092 may be accounted for by his resistance to the annexation, for we are told that his brother Waldeve, who succeeded to Allerdale, was retained ' as an ally on account of the war between the Scots and England, as he was a Scotsman' (Tower Misc. Roll, $\frac{1}{6}\frac{5}{4}$).

[2] 'Hoc anno (1122) Henricus post festum Sancti Michaelis Northymbranas intrans regiones ab Eboraco divertit versus mare occidentale, consideraturus civitatem antiquam quae lingua Brittonum Cairleil dicitur, quae nunc Carleol Anglice, Latine vero Lugubalia appellatur, quam data pecunia castello et turribus praecepit muniti' (Symeon, *Hist. Regum*, ii. 267). King Henry's attention to the fortification of Carlisle was evident at a later date, as may be gathered from the money he expended in 1130 ' in operibus Civitatis de Caerleolio, videlicet, in Muro circa Civitatem faciendo,' and in the maintenance of a garrison of knights and serjeants for its defence (*Pipe R*. 31 Hen. I. pp. 140–1).

King's life,[1] the credit of recognizing the value of the work done by his predecessor, and of developing and defending the policy he had initiated, must be ascribed to King Henry. The military measures taken by the vassal contrast strangely with the defensive precautions of the sovereigns while the district remained in their hands. Ranulf Meschin was content with entrenching himself forty miles away from the frontier and leaving its protection to his sub-feudatories, but as soon as King Henry relieved him of his charge he revived the policy of King William by making Carlisle the key of the military situation as well as the political centre of the district. The wisdom of the Norman kings was amply justified by subsequent history. The castle of Carlisle continued for five centuries the true defence of England on the western border.

The political allegiance of Cumberland was diverted into a new channel after the death of Henry I., when the district was ceded to Scotland in 1136 as the price of Stephen's usurpation.[2] The change of government, though not regarded with repugnance by the inhabitants, was the occasion of unrest and insecurity while it lasted. King David took up his residence in Carlisle with the view perhaps of making it ultimately the southern capital of his dominion, and for the purpose of adding to its defences he built the mighty keep (*fortissimam arcem*) of the castle and heightened the walls of the city.[3] The Cumberland men fought by David's side at the battle of the Standard in 1138, and it was to Carlisle the army retreated after its defeat.[4] On this occasion a memorable attempt was made to mitigate the horrors of warfare. It was arranged by the terms of the peace established between David and Stephen that all women taken prisoners by the Scots should be brought to Carlisle and set at liberty, churches should thenceforth be secure from attack, and children and women, the sick and aged, should be spared.[5] Though the Scottish king had little to fear from the distrust in which he was held by Stephen, his title to the sovereignty of Cumberland was menaced on more than one occasion by Ranulf, Earl of Chester, a fickle and restless nobleman, who claimed the territory by right of inheritance.

---

[1] Freeman, *William Rufus*, i. 313 ; *Norm. Conquest*, v. 117-8.

[2] *Chron. Steph. Hen. II. Ric. I.* (Rolls Series), iii. 146.

[3] Mr. George Neilson was the first to throw doubt on the accepted view that the keep of Carlisle was built by William Rufus in 1092. After a critical examination of the evidences, he has come to the conclusion that it was the work of King David about 1139. The argument is based on the positive statement in the 'Cronica Beate Marie Huntingdon' (Palgrave, *Documents and Records*, 103), a statement repeated by Bower (*Scotichronicon*, i. 294, ed. Goodall), that David built the *fortissimam arcem* of Carlisle (*Notes and Queries*, 8th series, viii. No. 200). If that be the case it is curious that Jordan Fantosme should speak of it in 1174 as 'the great old tower' (*la grant tur antive*) from which William the Lion threatened to throw Robert de Vaux unless he surrendered the city (*Chronicle* [Surtees Soc.], ll. 614-5).

[4] Prior Richard of Hexham distinguishes between the Picts, Cumbrians and the men of Carlisle and the adjoining district who were summoned to join David's army on his invasion of the territory of St. Cuthbert (*Priory of Hexham* [Surtees Soc.], i. 85). Aelred relates that the Cumbrians were under the command of Henry, Prince of Scotland, at the battle of the Standard, and that he behaved with valour and skill throughout the fight (Twysden, *Decem Scriptores*, 342). The Continuator of Florence (*in anno*, 1138) says that the prince reached Carlisle on foot attended by a single knight. The chronicles generally agree that the defeat of the Scottish army was disastrous, many having been slain *in segetibus et silvis* in the rout which followed the battle (*Henry of Huntingdon* [Rolls], 264 ; *Hemingburgh* [Eng. Hist. Soc.], i. 61-2). To the numbers of the slain the Cumbrians contributed their share (*Priory of Hexham*, i. 93).

[5] *Richard of Hexham* (Rolls Series), 170-1 ; *Priory of Hexham* (Surtees Soc.), i. 99-100.

In 1140, when Henry, Prince of Scotland, set out for Stephen's court, we are told by John of Hexham that Ranulf stirred up strife against him on account of Carlisle and Cumberland, which he demanded for himself by right of patrimony, and wished to take him by armed force on his return. But Stephen, urged by the entreaty of the queen, saved him from the meditated peril, and thus provoked the bitter enmity of his powerful vassal.[1] Ranulf had recourse to diplomacy to attain his ends. Impressed by the political significance of the visit of Henry of Anjou to Carlisle in 1149, and of the magnificent reception given to him by King David, he renewed his claims on Carlisle. It was one of the most remarkable gatherings that ever took place in the northern city, and boded nothing but ill to the English king. Stephen came to York to watch the proceedings.[2] For the present negotiations were successful. Henry of Anjou undertook, when he became King of England, to restore Newcastle and the whole of Northumberland to David, and Earl Ranulf, remitting his indignation for the loss of Carlisle, obtained the Honor of Lancaster in satisfaction.[3] The political entanglements of the Scottish occupation were not confined to the pressure of external enemies. David had foes in his own household. For some reason not recorded an estrangement existed between the king and William fitz Duncan, his nephew, who in right of his wife, Alice de Rumelli, was entitled to the barony of Coupland in south-west Cumberland as well as the Honor of Skipton in Craven. It was probably his inability to obtain this inheritance that caused him to overrun the district with relentless barbarity in 1138, and to destroy the monastery of Calder.[4] At all events it was not till 1151 that he was restored to his fief by David.[5] Death wrought a wonderful change in the political

---

[1] *The Priory of Hexham* (Surtees Soc.), i. 131–2, 134. There can be little doubt that Ranulf Meschin did not voluntarily resign Carlisle to Henry I. when he succeeded to the earldom of Chester. The claims of Ranulf, his son, at this period seem to suggest compulsion. Orderic Vitalis (bk. xii. cap. 28) states that 'Ranulf of Bayeux obtained the earldom of Chester, with all the patrimony of Earl Richard, being the next heir as nephew of Matilda, Earl Hugh's sister,' but Dugdale says that he ' left the earldom of Cumberland on condition that those whom he had enfeoffed there should hold their lands of the king *in capite*, and settled himself at Chester ' (*Baronage*, i. 37).

[2] Twysden, *Decem Scriptores* (Gervase of Dover), 1366.

[3] *Priory of Hexham* (Surtees Soc.), i. 159–61.

[4] Prior Richard's description of the atrocities committed by the Picts under William fitz Duncan in 1138 is appalling. Bursting into Yorkshire,' propter peccata populi, victoriam optinentes, possessiones cujusdam nobilis coenobii, quod in Fuththernessa situm est, et provinciam quae Crafna dicitur, ex magna parte, ferro et flamma destruxerunt. Igitur nulli gradui, nulli aetati, nulli sexui, nulli conditioni parcentes : liberos et cognatos in conspectu parentum suorum, et dominos in conspectu servorum suorum, et e converso, et maritos ante oculos uxorum suarum, quanto miserabilius poterant, prius trucidaverunt ; deinde, proh dolor ! solas nobiels matronas, et castas virgines, mixtim cum aliis feminis, et cum praeda pariter, abduxerunt. Nudatas quoque, et turmatim resticulis et corrigiis colligatas et copulatas, lanceis et telis suis compungentes, ante se illas abegerunt. Hoc idem in aliis bellis, sed in hoc copiosius fecerunt (*Priory of Hexham*, i. 82–3). Canon Raine remarks on the singularity that any injunction should induce William fitz Duncan to devastate the district of which he was the feudal chief. The only reason that can be alleged to account for his ferocity is that he was kept out of his inheritance by force. The area of devastation was extended to Coupland in Cumberland when the monastery of Calder was destroyed (Dugdale *Mon.* v. 349). There is no doubt that the family of William's wife had been expelled from Coupland during the anarchy in 1136–9, for about that time William of Lancaster had possession of the fief by gift of King Stephen. See the charter of Stephen to the abbey of Furness, printed by Mr. Farrer from the Coucher Book of Furness in *Pipe Rolls of Lancashire*, 304–5.

[5] *Priory of Hexham*, i. 163.

aspect of Cumberland in a few years by removing King David and Henry his' son, King Stephen, and Ranulf, Earl of Chester.[1] Stephen died in 1154, the year after David, and was succeeded by Henry II., the son of Maud, whose claims he had displaced. The Scottish succession had fallen into the hands or Malcolm, a mere boy, from whose feeble grasp Henry wrested the territory which the necessities of Stephen had driven him to resign.

For almost a century after the retrocession by Malcolm the Maiden in 1157,[2] the Scots continued to press their national claims to the district south of the Solway, and on every opportune occasion demanded some equivalent in compensation. It may be said that England's difficulty was Scotland's opportunity for reviving her demands. The administration of Cumberland during the reign of Henry II. was a delicate task in view of its Scottish sympathies and associations, requiring all the resources of tact and skill to complete its incorporation as a portion of the English commonwealth. The king took a personal interest in the recovered province and visited Carlisle from time to time as the public affairs of the district called for his immediate attention.[3] He came north in 1158 and held a conference with King Malcolm in that city, but the kings separated mutually displeased, in consequence of which the King of Scots was not knighted at that time.[4] It was on this visit that King Henry committed to Hubert de Vaux the barony of Gillesland, a wide tract abutting the frontier on the east which had been previously held by Gille son of Boet, a local chieftain who appears to have acknowledged no feudal superior.[5] The presence of a Scottish element among the territorial owners, which the King of Scotland was not backward in utilizing as it suited his purpose, was a constant danger

---

[1] Prince Henry died on 12 June 1152 (*Anglia Sacra*, i, 161 ; *Chron. of Melrose*, in anno) ; David died at Carlisle on 24 May 1153 (*Priory of Hexham*, i. 168) ; Earl Ranulf died on 16 December 1153, having been poisoned as was thought by William Peverel (Twysden, *Decem Scriptores*, 1374). King Stephen died in 1154.

[2] *Anglia Sacra* (Chron. of Holyrood), i. 161 ; *Decem Scriptores* (Ralf de Diceto), 531

[3] The king was certainly in Carlisle in 1158 and 1186 : possibly also in 1163. Compare the outline itinerary of Henry II. prepared by Bishop Stubbs (Benedict Abbas, *Gesta Hen. II. Ric. I*. [Rolls Series], ii. app. i. to Preface) with Eyton's *Itinerary of Henry II*. 32–3, 39, 62, 269. The visit in 1186 was of great political and ecclesiastical importance. The king came north with a powerful army to assist William, King of Scotland, in punishing Roland son of Uctred son of Fergus, lord of Galloway, for his evil conduct to his kinsman, Duncan son of Gilbert son of Fergus. Messengers were sent to summon Roland to the king's presence in Carlisle. Under safe conduct Roland came and made his submission, giving hostages for the performance of his pledges (*Benedict Abbas*, i. 348–9 ; *Hoveden* [Rolls Series], ii. 309). It was on this occasion that Henry made an effort to fill the vacant see of Carlisle by the nomination of Paulinus de Ledes, master of the Hospital of St. Leonard, York ; but Paulinus refused the bishopric, though the king offered to endow it with a rental of the value of 300 marks issuing from the churches of Bamborough and Scarborough, the chapelry of Tickhill, and two royal manors near Carlisle (*Hoveden*, ii. 309 ; *Benedict Abbas*, i. 349).

[4] *Hoveden*, i. 216 ; *Chron. de Mailros* (Bannatyne Club), 76.

[5] The charter of enfeoffment has been printed in facsimile from the record in the *Cartae Antiquae* in a previous volume (i. 320). Though witnessed at Newcastle-on-Tyne, there can be little doubt that it was the outcome of the king's visit to Carlisle. In the Pipe Roll of 1158 (4 Hen. II.) the sheriff of Carlisle accounts for £11 3s. given to Hubert de Vaux by the king's writ as a corrody in preparation of his visit. For the tenure of Gillesland by Gille son of Boet, see *V.C.H. Cumb.* i. 310, and an article by the present writer in the *Scottish Antiquary*, xvii. 105–11.

to the peace of the district.[1] Taking advantage of complications in England, William the Lion made a desperate attempt in 1174 to regain the lost possessions of his crown. By a sudden and well-directed inroad, he succeeded in taking the castle of Liddel, which belonged to Nicholas de Stuteville, and the king's castles of Appleby and Brough under Stainmore which had been in the custody of Robert de Stuteville, but the castle of Carlisle, garrisoned by the baronage of the county, resisted his repeated assaults during a prolonged siege.[2] For the gallant defence of Carlisle Jordan Fantosme has ascribed the credit to Robert de Vaux, whose heroic conduct and unsullied honour he has immortalized in his metrical ' Chronicle of the War.'[3] The capture of King William at Alnwick brought hostilities to a close, and the land had rest from Scottish incursions for a considerable time. Though the attempt to regain the county failed, the attendant devastations were not without effect on its economic condition and fiscal administration.[4]

King Richard began his reign with a magnanimous act of restitution to Scotland by which he restored to ' his dearest cousin ' William the Lion the castles of Roxburgh and Berwick with the Honor of Huntingdon, and released him from the humiliating conditions extorted by Henry II. after his capture at Alnwick.[5] The Scottish chieftains in their turn gave security that they should not pass the border during Richard's absence on the Crusade.[6] But the understanding did not last long. In 1194 the Scottish claims were again renewed and diplomatic negotiations followed with the inevitable result that Richard retained his sovereignty over the northern counties and William departed *dolens et confusus* from the English court. At this time Richard made a most interesting proposal to the Scottish king with the view, no doubt, of establishing a friendly alliance between the two kingdoms. There was to be a marriage between Otho son of Henry, Duke of Saxony, nephew of Richard, and Margaret daughter of King William, with the stipulation that the King of Scotland should dower his daughter with the whole of Lothian and the King of England should give Otho and Margaret the whole of Northumberland and the county of Carlisle. The proposed agreement, however, was declined by King William, and the settlement of the Scottish claims was in consequence postponed.[7]

The unprecedented nature of King John's taxation created so much discontent in Cumberland and produced so serious a strain on the loyalty of the people that the safety of the county was in jeopardy towards the close of his reign. Immediately after his accession precautions had been

---

[1] See the list of Scottish landowners ' qui morabantur in regno Scotiae, habentes terras et tenementa infra ballivam meam Cumbrie,' which the sheriff took into the king's hand in 1296 on the outbreak of the war (*Doc. of Hist. of Scot.* [Scot. Rec. Pub.], ii. 41–3).

[2] Benedict Abbas, *Gesta Hen. II. Ric. I.* (Rolls Series), i. 64–70 ; *Walter of Coventry* (Rolls Series), i. 225 ; *Hoveden* (Rolls Series), ii. 60.

[3] Published in the Rolls Series of Chronicles and Memorials, and also by the Surtees Society.

[4] *V.C.H. Cumb.* i. 309–11.

[5] Rymer, *Fœdera*, i. 50 ; *Nat. MSS. of Scotland,* i. No. 46.

[6] *Chron. Ric. Divis.* (Eng. Hist. Soc.), 9.

[7] *Hoveden* (Rolls Series), iii. 243, 250, 308 ; *Walter of Coventry* (Rolls Series), ii. 95–6.

taken to resist the Scottish claims, but as time went on more was to be feared from the exasperation of the inhabitants than from any external enemy. The wave of constitutional movement, which reached its highest water mark in the signing of the Great Charter in 1215, had swept the kingdom to its northern limits and awakened the baronage of Cumberland to the historic character of their tenemental services. Not scared by the arbitrary nature of the Inquest of 1212 the jurors boldly appended the significant clause to their return of knights' fees that the tenants by cornage, the prevailing tenure of the county, were obliged at the king's precept to occupy the post of danger in the royal army to Scotland, in going in the vanguard and in returning in the rearguard, thus declaring that their obligations exempted them from service abroad in consideration of their extraordinary services in the protection of the frontier at home.[1] The men of Carlisle were urged by the baronage of England to make common cause with them for the assertion of their ancient liberties.[2] Alexander the young King of Scotland favoured the constitutional movement in the hope of regaining the northern counties. Crossing the border he laid siege to Carlisle and eventually took both the city and the castle.[3] It is undoubted that the sympathies of the people of Cumberland were at this crisis favourable to Alexander and alienated from their own sovereign. The canons of Carlisle were on the baronial side and voluntarily submitted themselves to the King of Scotland. Despite the interdict of the pope they elected a Scotsman to the vacant bishopric and celebrated divine offices with excommunicated persons.[4] During the anarchy a portion of the Scottish

---

[1] A translation of the Inquest of 1212 for Cumberland has been printed (*V.C.H. Cumb.* i. 421–2). Mr. J. H. Round has pointed out the historical interest of this remarkable survey. Politically, he says, it illustrates John's exactions by its effort to revive rights of the Crown alleged to have lapsed, a grave and alarming feature selected for mention by the annalist of Waverley. Institutionally, it is of great interest, not only as an instance of 'the sworn inquest' employed on a vast scale, but also for its contrast to the inquest of knights in 1166 and its points of resemblance to the Domesday inquest of 1086. Of far wider compass than that of 1166, it was carried out on a different principle. Instead of each tenant-in-chief making his own return of his fees and sending it in separately, the sheriff conducted the inquiry Hundred by Hundred for the county; and out of these returns the feudal lists had to be subsequently constructed by the officials (*Commune of London, etc.*, 274–5).

[2] In the 'Catalogus Munimentorum' delivered to Edward I. at Berwick in 1291 we have suggestive abstracts of the lost Scottish evidences which are relevant to the troubles of this period. Some of these may be quoted : 1. Charta baronum Angliae probis hominibus de Karleol' contra Johannem regem Angliae de civitate Karl' reddendo regi Scotiae. 2. Charta baronum Angliae missa tenentibus Northumbriam, Cumbriam, Westmerlandiam contra Johannem regem Angliae' (Ayloffe, *Cal. of Ancient Charters*, 327–8). This catalogue has been often printed : see it in the *Acts of the Parliament of Scotland*, vol. i., appendix to Preface, No 1. Edward I. has been accused by the Scottish historians, Hector Boece and Buchanan, of having burned the original charters, but for the disappearance of those early Records of Scotland, the temperate judgment of Mr. Bain may be referred to (*Cal. of Scot. Documents*, i. pref. v.–ix.)

[3] It is stated in the Chronicle of Melrose (*in anno*, 1216) that Alexander did not obtain possession of the castle of Carlisle at that time, a statement adopted without demur by the chronicler of Lanercost— 'castellum tamen illa vice non oppugnavit' (*Chron. de Lanercost* [Bannatyne Club], 18). There is evidence, however, to show that the castle was in the hands of the Scots. On 23 September 1217 Alexander was ordered to restore to Robert de Vipont the castle of Carlisle and all the lands he had seized and all the prisoners taken by him during King John's troubles with his barons (Pat. 1 Hen. III. m. 3).

[4] *Cal. of Papal Letters*, i. 48, 57. The king's complaint to the pope against these rebellious churchmen was couched in emphatic terms. He informed him that the canons of Carlisle were favourers and adherents of the King of Scotland, the enemies of pope and king, and despisers of the legate's authority;

army, devils rather than soldiers as the Chronicle of Melrose calls them,[1] contrary to the command of the king who had taken men of religion under his protection, savagely attacked the monastery of Holmcultram, pillaged the whole district, and spread terror and confusion among its peaceful inhabitants. Retribution quickly followed, for on their retreat across the estuary of the Eden, the ' dainty Cumbrian queen' of Drayton, they were enveloped in its swiftly rising tide, and it is said that 1,900 Scots perished in one brief hour.[2] The death of King John brought this tumultuous period to a close ; peace was established between the two kingdoms, and the people of the county returned to their allegiance.[3]

The Scottish claims on the northern counties, handed on as a *damnosa hereditas* from one English sovereign to another, were at length settled by papal intervention. Pope Gregory made strenuous efforts to compose the estrangement between the two kingdoms arising from this dispute. The matter was now taken up in earnest and carried to a successful issue. Writing to the parties in 1236 the pope described himself as specially bound by ties of affection to Henry III. and as sincerely loving the King of Scotland, and urges them to come to an agreement, believing that from peace great benefits would accrue to either kingdom.[4] In 1237 King Henry issued his letters patent, embodying the terms agreed upon in presence of the legate's clerk and envoy at York, for the ' extension ' of his demesnes in Cumberland and Northumberland, where there were no castles, up to £200 of land annually, excepting his manor of Penrith and forest of Cumberland, it not being the king's intention that the said manor or forest should be ' extended.'[5] After much disputing between the assessors deputed to select the lands, an agreement was ultimately arrived at in 1242, when King Henry handed over the manors of Langwathby, Salkeld, Scotby,

---

they irreverently and contumaciously celebrated divine offices in forbidden places in the presence of excommunicated persons ; they became the subjects of the King of Scotland who was in hostile possession of the city, received him as their patron and lord, and did fealty to him ; and, worse than all, in prejudice of the king's right and that of the Church of York, they elected at the instance of the King of Scots an excommunicated clerk as their bishop and pastor (Pat. 1 Hen. III. m. 3d ; Rymer, *Fœdera*, i. 147). The chronicler of Lanercost endeavours to rehabilitate the reputation of the canons by saying that they were compelled by fear of death to celebrate divine offices with the excommunicated King of Scots (*Chron. de Lanercost*, 27).

[1] *Chron. de Mailros* (Bann. Club), 122–3.

[2] *Chron. de Lanercost*, 18.

[3] Eodem anno (1217) omnes vero barones Angliae fecerunt homagium Henrico filio Johannis : et rex Scottorum Alexander, antequam absolvi mereretur, Carliolum voluntati regalium Angliae tradidit (*Chron. de Lanercost*, 25). See the list of knights who returned to their allegiance on the accession of Henry III. in *Close Rolls* (Rec. Com.), i. 373–5.

[4] The pope's letters, dated 4 January 1235–6, one to the Archbishop of York and the Bishop of Carlisle, and another to the King of Scotland, have been printed by Rymer (*Fœdera*, i. 214–5). A summary of another letter to the King of Scotland, dated 26 April 1236, has been given by Bain (*Cal. of Scot. Doc.* i. 232–3).

[5] Pat. 21 Hen. III. m. 1 ; Pipe, 22 Hen. III. m. 4 ; Pat. 22 Hen. III. m. 8. See also Pat. 22 Hen. III. mm. 5d, 6. Fordun says that on the day of St. Maurice (21 September) in the year 1237, Alexander, King of Scots, and Henry, King of England, with their queens and the lords of either kingdom, met at York ; where, for fifteen days, they talked over the entangled affairs of the kingdoms in the presence of Cardinal Otho, the papal legate. When the negotiations were over, the King of Scotland went home again in safety (*Chronica* [ed. Skene], i. 291).

Soureby (Castlesowerby) and Carlatton, and £60 of land in the manor of Penrith with all liberties and free customs as contained in the chirograph made in the presence of Cardinal Otho at York, the said lands to be held by the render of a sore goshawk yearly at Michaelmas at Carlisle. It was stipulated that the advowsons of the churches with a certain lime-kiln (*rogo*) in Castlesowerby should remain to the King of England.[1] Thus was the long controversy between the two kingdoms brought to a happy close. The King of Scotland, in compensation for the surrender of his hereditary rights to the northern counties and some other claims, received £200 of land in Cumberland, for which he did homage and fealty, and paid an annual acknowledgment.[2] Perhaps no better evidence can be adduced to show how the good understanding affected the peace of the county than the condition of Carlisle Castle as it existed in 1255. The keep was in decay, the walls in a 'bad state, and the joists and planking broken and rotten. Maunsell's turret, and the turret of William de Ireby, as well as the turret beyond the inner gate, which were levelled in the war in the time of King John, were never after restored or repaired ; a great part of the paling (*paliciarum*) within and without the castle was likewise burned and destroyed.[3] There was no pressure from without to necessitate elaborate defences ; the county had entered on an era of almost unbroken peace and of steady progress and prosperity.

There can be little doubt that the agreement between the monarchs in 1242 cleared the way for the settlement of many outstanding differences between their subjects on both sides of the frontier. A specific complaint in 1248,[4] that the ancient laws and customs of the marches of the two kingdoms were not so well observed as formerly, was made the occasion of an inquiry for ascertaining what these laws and customs were, and for enforcing their observance. As a sequel to this preliminary investigation a convention was held on 14 April 1249, and a jury of twenty-four knights, after formal and exhaustive inquiry, framed and adopted the famous Border code called the *Leges Marchiarum* or

---

[1] *Chart*, 26 Hen. III. m. 5. The advowson of the church of Salkeld was in dispute between the Bishop of Carlisle and the King of Scotland in 1262 (Close, 46 Hen. III. m. 12d ; Rymer, *Fœdera*, i. 417).

[2] Alexander II. was not regular in his payment of a hawk annually to the king for his Cumberland manors according to the agreement, for he was five years in arrear in 1248 (Close, 32 Hen. III. m. 6). The manor of Castlesowerby, lying within the forest of Inglewood, was assigned in 1257 by Alexander III. to his consort Queen Margaret for her chamber (*ad cameram suam*), with liberty to improve and assart the wastes thereof (Pat. 41 Hen. III. m. 10 ; Close, 41 Hen. III. m. 5 ; Pat. 47 Hen. III. m. 15).

[3] This very interesting report on the condition of Carlisle Castle about 1257 has been printed in *Royal and Hist. Letters* (Rolls Series), ii. 124–5. The names of the knights of the county who made the inspection were Thomas de Lascelis, William de Derewentewater, Robert de Castelkayrok, and Alan de Orreton.

[4] The complaint was made by the King of Scotland by reason of injustice done to Nicholas de Sules against the laws of the March. Under authority of a writ of Henry III., inquiry was made on the March by twelve knights, six from either side, according to ancient March law and custom, who said that Nicholas de Sules had been injured by being impleaded elsewhere than at the March, although he held land in England ; for no one of either kingdom, although holding lands in both, was liable by March law to be impleaded anywhere but at the March for any deed by his men dwelling in England done in Scotland, or for any deed by his men dwelling in Scotland done in England (Inq. p.m. 33 Hen. III. No. 65). The inquest has been printed by Mr. Bain in *Cal. Scot. Documents*, i. 559–60. See also Inq. p.m. 8 Edw. I. No. 81.

Laws of the Marches,[1] that regulated the intercourse of the inhabitants of the Border shires of the two kingdoms. It should be remembered that these laws were not formulated at random or enacted to meet the requirements of the Border as they existed at that period. It was the task of the jurors to find out the customs that had prevailed *ab antiquo*, and to codify them into a system. This great statute, which eventually became the basis of international law for the people on both sides of the frontier, had its roots in the distant past, and played an important part in the regulation of the political and civil life of Cumberland for several centuries.

Everything seemed to promise a continuance of the happy relations between the two kingdoms when Edward I. ascended the throne. King Alexander attended his coronation and did homage for the estates he held in England.[2] Edward's first visit to Cumberland after his accession was made in September 1280, when he stayed at Carlisle, visited the priory of Lanercost in company with Queen Eleanor, and hunted in Inglewood Forest.[3] In 1283 the castle of Carlisle was placed in the custody of Robert de Brus, afterwards called the Competitor, who was at the same time made sheriff of the county, both of which positions his father filled under Henry III.[4] International jealousies were to a large extent allayed, and magnates owning lands in both kingdoms were able to take part in local government and perform the civil functions due to their positions without straining their allegiance. But the intervention of Edward in the disputes about the succession to the throne of Scotland after the death of the Maid of Norway ruptured the good relations between the two countries and eventually led to the War of Independence, the full weight of which was to fall on the Border counties. The real troubles began in 1296 when the Earl of Buchan broke into Cumberland and ravaged the county with savage ferocity. In this raid the Scottish army is said to have behaved with unwonted cruelty; for not being able to seize upon the strong, the soldiers wreaked their vengeance on the weak, the decrepit and the young; children of two or three years old they impaled upon lances and threw into the air; consecrated churches they burned; women dedicated to God they ravished and slew.[5] But when they advanced on Carlisle they were repulsed by the citizens with much bravery. There is no need to recite in detail the story of carnage and bloodshed which disgraced the civilization of this gloomy period. Raid followed raid and reprisal provoked reprisal. In 1297 William Wallace, the famous Scottish patriot, after defeating the Earl of Warenne at Stirling, harried Cumberland, leaving burnt home-

---

[1] The *Leges Marchiarum* will be found in *Acts of the Parliaments of Scotland* (Rec. Com.), i. 413–6. Bishop Nicolson of Carlisle printed them in 1705 from an imperfect text (*Leges Marchiarum*, 1–9). Ridpath compiled a summary from Nicolson's book (*Border History*, 138–42).

[2] Close, 2 Edw. I. m. 5; Pipe, 2 Edw. I. m. 18d; Liberate, 3 Edw. I. m. 12.

[3] *Chron. de Lanercost* (Bann. Club), 105–6; *Cal. of Close Rolls* (1279–88), 61–2; *Cal. of Pat. Rolls* (1272–81), 396–7.

[4] Q. R. Memoranda, 11 Edw. I. m. 2d; Orig. R. 11 Edw. I. m. 8; Pat. 39 Hen. III. m. 3.

[5] *Chron. de Lanercost* (Bann. Club), 174; *Hemingburgh* (Engl. Hist. Soc.), ii. 94–6.

steads and a wasted country to mark his route.[1] Carlisle became the rendezvous of the English army and the basis of military operations on the western coast. Skinburness was the chief port on the Solway for the collection of stores shipped from Ireland and elsewhere.[2] The king was in the north on several occasions conducting operations and ordering levies. In 1300 there were gathered together to meet him the flower and glory of the English nation, and seldom, if ever, has Carlisle seen such an assemblage within its walls. His son Edward, Prince of Wales, was with him, and among other illustrious names may be mentioned those of Mortimer, Valence, Vere, Bigod, Bohun, and Beauchamp. After the fall of Caerlaverock the king returned to Cumberland in September and divided his time between Holmcultram, Rose Castle and Carlisle, till urgent affairs called him to Yorkshire. In 1306 Robert Bruce killed the Red Comyn in the church of the Grey Friars at Dumfries and stepped at once into the place of national hero left vacant by the execution of Wallace in the previous year.[3]

King Edward at once saw the gravity of the crisis and nerved himself for a final effort. His army was summoned to assemble at Carlisle in July, but seized with dysentery he turned aside to Lanercost where the winter of 1306–7 was spent in extreme bad health.[4] In March he was removed to Linstock,[5] a seat of the Bishop of Carlisle, for the purpose no doubt of attending the sitting of parliament in Carlisle at which was passed the well-known statute directed against papal encroachments.[6] But Edward's days were drawing to a close, and the grim struggle on which he had entered was to be left to other hands. Having offered up the litter, in which he travelled, in the cathedral, the indomitable old man set forth from Caldcotes to Burgh by Sands, where he expired on 7 July 1307, 'non relinquens sibi similem in sapientia et audacia inter principes Christianos.'[7] The effect of the international struggle in Cumberland, which lay so near the theatre of military operations, may well be imagined. Nowhere perhaps can be found a more doleful picture of the ravages of the war than in the plaintive letter of the Bishop of Carlisle, written in 1301, in which he described the devas-

---

[1] *Chron. de Lanercost* (Bann. Club.), 190–1 ; *Wyntoun*, bk. viii. ll. 2189–90.

[2] *Cal. of Pat. Rolls* (1292–1301), 389, 488, 585 ; *Liber Quot. Gard.* (Soc. of Antiq.), 83, 123, 274.

[3] *Chron. de Lanercost*, 203 ; *Nich. Trivet* (Engl. Hist. Soc.), 407.

[4] The chronicles seem to agree that Edward treated his Scottish prisoners with unaccustomed severity immediately before his death. In February 1307 Dougall Machduel, a Galwegian potentate, having taken prisoners the brothers of Robert de Brus and Sir Reginald de Crauforde while on a foray into Galloway, brought them first to the Prince of Wales at Wetheral and afterwards to the king at Lanercost. Though the prisoners were wounded with lances and arrows the stern monarch sentenced with his own mouth Thomas de Brus to be drawn at the tails of horses from Lanercost to Carlisle, and there to be hanged and beheaded. The other brother Alexander, dean of Glasgow, and Crauforde were sentenced to be hanged and beheaded. The head of Thomas de Brus was placed on the keep of the castle, and the heads of the other two, with the heads of other chieftains, brought by Machduel, were suspended on the three gates of Carlisle. Nigel de Brus, another brother of Robert, was hanged at Newcastle after condemnation by the king's justices (*Chron. de Lanercost*, 205–6 ; *Nich. Trivet*, 410 ; *Cal. of Scot. Doc.* [Scot. Rec. Ser.], iv. 489).

[5] *Cal. of Pat. Rolls* (1301–7), 479–502.

[6] Commonly called the Statute of Carlisle and the first of our anti-papal statutes. See the petitions on which it was founded in *Rotuli Parl.* (Rec. Com.), i. 219–20.

[7] *Chron. de Lanercost* (Bann. Club.), 207.

tation of the county since the hostilities began. The treacherous Scottish race, he complained, by repeated incursions during the past four years, had destroyed and burned the greater part of his diocese with its inhabitants, so that the monasteries were pillaged and the religious men dispersed ; some of the churches with their parishes were reduced to ashes and their incumbents forced to beg alms for their sustenance ; and taxation was out of the question, for in many places there was nothing for the tax-gatherer to find.[1]

The war with Scotland was the means of reviving the old subject of the military immunity of the Cumberland and Westmorland men from service beyond their own frontiers. In their conflict with King John, the knights of Cumberland maintained that their obligation consisted in the safe convoy of the army on its passage through the two counties to and from Scotland. As soon as war was declared in 1297 they reasserted their constitutional rights and made agreement with the king's northern officers that if they joined the expedition their action must be regarded as voluntary service. It was stipulated that the expedition (*ceste chevauchee*) they were about to undertake of their own free will should not be turned as a service to them or their heirs ; nor should the king nor his heirs be able to challenge any service as of right from them nor their heirs by reason of that expedition. The required guarantee was given to the lieges of the two counties by the king's officers,[2] and afterwards ratified in 1300 by letters patent in which King Edward acknowledged that the said expedition (*equitatus*) should not be to their prejudice, and should not be drawn into a precedent, and that neither he nor his heirs should claim any service by reason thereof.[3] In the tumultuous days which followed, the people of Cumberland and Westmorland asserted their right to the enjoyment of these exceptional privileges, maintaining that their service to the king and his ancestors in war consisted in meeting the army on its march to

---

[1] Carl. Epis. Reg., Halton MS. f. 59 ; *Letters from the Northern Registers* (Rec. Com.), 151.

[2] Mr. Stevenson has printed this important deed from the Privy Seals, 25 Edw. I., in the Public Record Office. As it is of undoubted interest in the political history of Cumberland, it may be reproduced here : ' Henry de Percy e Robert de Clifford a touz les loiaus e feus nostre seigneur le roi du cunte de Cumberlaund, saluz. Cum vous nous eies grantez greablement de chivaucher ad tout vostre pouer sur les enemyes nostre segneur le rei en Escoce, en aide du dist nostre seigneur le rei e de nous, qe a coe fere sumes ordynez par ses lettres patentes, aleganz pur vous qe coe ne deves fere de drait, e priaunz qe coe a vous ne a vos heirs ne soit tourne en servage : nous eantz regars a vostre bone volentee, vous grauntoms, e par cestes noz lettres patentes obligoms de fere vous aver les lettres patentes nostre seigneur le rei seeles de sun seel, entre le jour de cestes lettres fetes e la feste Saint Michel prochain suaunt, qe ceste chevauchee qe vous de vostre bone volentee ove nous enpernes, ne sait tourne en servage a vous ne a vos heirs : ne qe le dist nostre segneur le reys ne ses hers vers vous ne vers vos heirs nul servis de drait par ceste chevauchee peuse chalanger. En tesmogne de queu chose, a cestez nos lettres patentes avous mys nos selz. Escrites a Kardoil, le jour de Saint Johan le Batist en le an du dist nostre segnur le rei Edwarde vint e quynt ' (*Doc. illustrative of Hist. of Scot.* ii. 186–7). In the same collection of Privy Seals occurs a document in similar terms for the satisfaction of the men of Westmorland.

[3] Pat. 28 Edw. I. m. 6. The letters patent, after a recital of the terms of the agreement between the men of Cumberland and Westmorland and Henry de Percy and Robert de Clifford, ' nuper custodes municionis nostre in partibus Cumbr' et Westmerl',' end thus : ' Nos concessionem et obligacionem predictas acceptantes volumus et concedimus pro nobis et heredibus nostris quod dictus equitatus, quem prefati homines comitatuum predictorum in Comitiva dictorum Henrici et Roberti fecerunt, sicut predictum est, non cedat eis vel eorum heredibus in prejudicium vel trahatur in consequenciam in futurum.' This document has been printed by Palgrave in *Parl. Writs*, i. 345.

Scotland, 'a la Rerecroiz sus Estaynmor,' and going in the vanguard as far as 'la Marche de Solewathe,' and on the return from Scotland they should take the 'reeregarde' from Solway to the 'Rerecroiz.' It was further alleged that if it happened for the defence of the realm that the king required their services within it, he should pay their wages in their own country before they started. In addition it was pleaded that they should be allowed to be at war or truce with the Scots, as they considered most for the king's honour or their own profit, by the advice of his officers on the frontier, without hindrance or challenge.[1] It is evident that the men of Cumberland and Westmorland were inspired with the belief that the military burden on the two counties was confined to the protection of the frontier, and there can be little doubt that the idea of local sovereignty to which they had so often asserted their claim was handed down from a period when Cumbria was mistress of her own destinies.[2]

In the thirteenth century the first steps towards parliamentary representation were taken in the reigns of Henry III. and Edward I. Cumberland no doubt was represented in the assemblies which Henry summoned in 1254 and 1261, while Carlisle also in 1283 was invited to send 'two of its wiser and more experienced citizens' to the national council which Edward brought together at Shrewsbury for the trial of David brother of the Welsh prince Llewelin. On this occasion, in contradistinction to the usual practice, the writ was addressed to the mayor and citizens.[3] In his later parliaments Edward treated the town

---

[1] Tower Miscell. Roll, No. 459; *Cal. of Scot. Doc.* (Scot. Rec. Ser.), iii. 135. Mr. Bain has dated this petition between 1315–20, but there is a strong presumption that it belongs to the period 1297–1300, when the lieges were disputing with Percy and Clifford about their obligations to service in the Scottish wars. For a discussion of the early history of these claims to immunity from service beyond the frontier, see *V.C.H. Cumb.* i. 321–8.

[2] It may be, as Professor Maitland has said, that Northumbrian tenures were extremely puzzling to the lawyers at Westminster (*Engl. Hist. Rev.* v. 630), but the tenants of Cumberland and Westmorland succeeded at this time in establishing their historic claims to what are not unlike the military privileges of a palatine state. The exemption of the two counties from service beyond their own borders, by reason of the exceptional burden of defence thrown upon them owing to their geographical position, may be illustrated by reference to the privileges enjoyed by the people of Chester on the frontier of Wales. Among the privileges confirmed to the barons of that shire by Earl Ranulf (Blundevil) late in the twelfth century occur the following: 'that by reason of the heavy service which the barons discharged in Cestreshyre none of them shall do service to the Earl without the border (*extra lymam*) except of his own free will and at the Earl's cost: and if the Earl's knights of England, who owe ward to the Earl at Chester, be summoned to perform their ward, and there be no army of the Earl's enemies present, and no need for the barons, the barons may return to their homes and rest; and if an army of the Earl's enemies be in readiness to come into his land of Cestreshyre, or if the castle be besieged, the said barons with their army and view (*et visu suo*) shall come forthwith at the Earl's summons to remove that army to the best of their power, and when that army has retired from the Earl's land, the said barons may return to their own lands and rest while the knights of England perform their ward, and the said barons are not needed, saving to the Earl the services which are due from them' (Pat. 28 Edw. I. m. 22, by *inspeximus*). There is much reason to believe that these palatine claims may be accounted for by the previous incorporation of Cumbria in the old kingdom of Northumberland. It is a striking feature of northern history how palatinates, regalities, and liberties, like Durham, Hexham, Tyndale, Sedbergh, and Lancaster, sprang up on its ruins. For a full discussion of this important subject, see Mr. Page's article on 'Northumbrian Palatinates and Regalities' in *Archæologia*, li. 1–12, and Dr. Lapsley's argument in *The County Palatine of Durham*, 16–21, 109. There was no opportunity for the district of Cumberland and Westmorland to grow into a fully equipped palatinate like its northern neighbours, as it devolved to the administration of the Crown so early as 1120.

[3] *Parl. Writs* (Rec. Com.), i. 16.

communities as parts of the shire and his summons was issued through the sheriffs. To these early writs, however, we have no returns, and we do not know the names of those who were elected. The first original writ on record, endorsed with the names of the knights returned, is for the parliament held at Westminster in 1290, when Walter de Mulcaster, Hubert de Multon and William de Boyvill were elected to serve as representatives of the county.[1] In 1295 representatives of the cities and boroughs were permanently added ; and to the parliament of that year the city of Carlisle and the boroughs of Cockermouth and Egremont were invited to send members, two for the county, two for the city, and two for each of the boroughs. The names of these eight representatives are known.[2] No further summons appears to have been issued to the boroughs till 1640, when the privilege of representation was restored to Cockermouth.[3] From that date it continued to return two members till 1867, when the number was reduced to one. It was finally disfranchised under the Act of 1885. It is unquestionable that boroughs such as Egremont looked upon the privilege of returning members in the light of a serious burden by reason of the salaries connected with it. These were fixed at 4s. a day for a knight of the shire and usually 2s. for a borough member, and were due for the whole time of his service, his journey to and from and his stay in parliament. We can easily understand, therefore, the plea made on behalf of some of the smaller communities asking to be relieved of the burden which had been maliciously, as they conceived, placed upon them.[4]

The representation of the clergy in the early parliaments is worthy of observation. From a writ, dated 30 September 1295, we learn that the prior and archdeacon of Carlisle, one proctor for the chapter and two proctors for the clergy of the diocese were summoned to the parliament at Westminster in that year.[5] In the parliament of Carlisle in 1307 a great number of ecclesiastics were permitted to appear by proxy, probably on account of the remote distance of the place of meeting. At this parliament Bishop Halton of Carlisle and the abbot of Holm-cultram were present ; and the clergy of the diocese were represented by John de Boghes, William de Goseford, Robert de Suthayke, and

---

[1] *Parl. Writs* (Rec. Com.), i. 21.

[2] Ibid. i. 35.

[3] The subject of representation was much discussed in the parliament of 1640. It does not appear upon what principle a precept should have been sent to Cockermouth when Egremont was omitted, as both boroughs had been represented in the parliament of 1295 (*Lords' Report on the Dignity of a Peer*, i. 375–8).

[4] The first writ on record for the expenses of the knights for the shire of Cumberland appears to be that dated 20 March 1300, wherein the sheriff was directed to pay to them ' racionabiles expensas suas in veniendo ad nos, ibidem morando, et inde ad propria redeundo ' according to custom (Close, 28 Edw. I. m. 12d ; *Parl. Writs* [Rec. Com.], i. 85–6). In 1328 we have a writ to the mayor and bailiffs of the city of Carlisle to pay John de Harrington and Simon de Sandford, their burgesses, the sum of £7 12s. for thirty-eight days' service in parliament, that is, at the rate of 2s. a day (Close, 2 Edw. III. m. 9d ; *Rot. Parliam.* [Rec. Com.], ii. 441). By Act 35 Henry VIII. cap. 11, the wages of a knight of the shire were fixed at 4s. a day, and of a burgess of a town at 2s. a day, according to ancient custom. There is much on the wages of parliamentary representatives in the *Lords' Reports on the Dignity of a Peer*, i. 325, 336, 369 and passim.

[5] Carl. Epis. Reg., Halton, ff. 21–2.

Adam de Appleby.[1] Among the names of the knights of the shire to be found in the earlier returns are those of Mulcaster, Boyvill, Harrington, Multon, Cleter, Whitrig, Wigton, Tilliol, Joneby, Moresby, Lucy, and Bampton. The name of Lowther first appears in 1324 in the person of Hugh de Lowther, though a scion of that great family represented the county of Westmorland in 1305.[2] Carlisle in early days was most frequently represented hy the Grenesdales, two persons of that name, Robert and Alan, being the burgesses in 1305. In these parliaments the owners of the great baronies of Egremont, Greystoke, Gillesland and Liddel sat amongst their peers.

Before the outbreak of hostilities in 1296 none of the castles except the castle of Carlisle played an important rôle in the political history of Cumberland. The absence of great fortresses may be to some extent accounted for by the geographical position of the county and the peculiar dangers to which it was exposed. Protected on three sides by natural defences, the outlet towards Scotland, its only vulnerable side by land, was guarded by the castle of Carlisle, which watched over the safety of the district with 'the outlook of a sentinel.' It was the county castle, under control of the sheriff, the rallying point of the *posse comitatus*, and the key of the military strength of the western border. None of the other castles, of which there were comparatively few, came into political prominence before the death of Edward I. It is true that some of the great baronies like Allerdale, Coupland and Liddel had fortresses of one kind or another in the twelfth and thirteenth centuries, but with the exception of the castle or peel of Liddel on the actual frontier, the district depended little on them for its safety. The castles of Cockermouth and Egremont were too far removed from the zone or danger to be of much service in keeping the Scots in check. The international troubles which arose at the close of the thirteenth century had a tendency to undermine feudal methods of defence by driving the large landowners to shift for their own protection, thus weakening the old obligation of ward in the county castle. The safety of the county was taken out of the hand of the sheriff and committed to the custody of another royal officer, first called the captain and then the warden of the western march, at whose call the tenants were obliged to muster for the repelling of an inroad or the arrangement of a truce.[3] It was an exceptional expedient created to

---

[1] *Rot. Parliam.* (Rec. Com.), i. 188–91. In this roll the names of those who appeared by proxy are recorded. In 1309 Bishop Halton sent Adam de Appelby to represent him at Westminster, having had leave of absence 'propter distanciam, temporis brevitatem, timorem invasionis Scottorum, necnon corporis infirmitatem qua affligimur' (Carl. Epis. Reg., Halton, f. 120).

[2] *Parliaments of England* (Blue Book), i. 20, 69.

[3] Though the origin of the warden of the march is involved in some obscurity, there can be little doubt that it took its rise as an institution or was reconstituted soon after the outbreak of the war with Scotland in 1296. On 12 July 1297, Robert de Clifford was appointed ' capitaneus municionis Regis in partibus Cumbrie ' against the Scots till further orders, and a writ of aid in favour of the said Robert was directed to the sheriff, bailiffs, and other ministers of the county (Pat. 25 Edw. I. pt. ii. m. 1 ; Parl. Writs [Rec. Com.], i. 294–5). In 1298 he was appointed captain in the counties of Cumberland, Westmorland, Lancaster, Annandale and the Marches as far as the county of Roxburgh ; all persons having lands in the said counties and liberties were to assemble at ' Cardoyl ' within eight days from receipt of notice (Pat. 27 Edw. I. m. 41). In 1299 Clifford was called captain of the defence (*municionis*) in the parts of Carlisle

meet the political necessities of the situation. With this revolution in military policy, there sprang up a number of inferior defences, castles, towers, peels and fortified houses, posted here and there on the chief estates, where their owners might be secure from sudden incursions.[1] Noteworthy evidence of the political change may be gathered from the prompt action of some of the local dignitaries as soon as the protecting presence of the great Edward was withdrawn. On the same day of the month following his death, 24 August 1307, three licences to crenellate and enclose with a stone wall were granted for the security of the Cumberland march ; to Robert de Tilliol for his house of Scaleby ·on the north of the Eden, to Richard le Brun for Drumburgh (Drombogh) on the southern shore of the upper reach of the Solway, and to William de Dacre for Dunmalloght at some distance from the Border.[2] The licences on record do not represent the activity which prevailed in the fourteenth century in the progress of self-defence. Though the castle of Carlisle was still regarded as the bulwark of the county's safety, every considerable landowner took measures to protect himself and his dependants with leave or without it. The commune of Cumberland was not always satisfied with the military protection afforded them by the new devices of the central authority. In 1322 the most famous of Border captains was declared to be of little use, and a petition was sent up that he might be superseded.[3] Again and again representations were made that the castle and city of Carlisle were in perilous state and too little attention was given to the defence of the northern frontier.[4] The neglect of the central government threw the district on its own resources. During the reign of Edward II. we have John de Denum showing that he had kept his fortress called the Tower of Melmerby at his own expense with a garrison of twelve men, ' always well defended by the grace of God against the Scots to the great damage and loss of their men ' ; he now petitioned that his lands were so wasted that he could not support a garrison in the Tower, and it would be a serious inconvenience to the county if ' she ' was taken.[5] Individual efforts like

and the king's lieutenant there (Pat. 27 Edw. I. m. 28). The chronicler of Lanercost writes under the years 1309 and 1311 as if the office had not been long created : ' Nec potuerunt custodes, quos rex Angliae posuerat in Marchia, resistere tantae multitudini Scottorum quos (Robertus de Bruse) adduxerat ' (*Chron. de Lanercost*, 213, 217). For the obligation of the tenants of Cumberland to attend the Border meeting, called Endemot, in the twelfth century, and its character as an institution, see *V.C.H. Cumb.* i. 324–6.

[1] When the custody of the March changed hands in February 1323, the castles and peels delivered to the charge of the new warden were Carlisle, Naworth, Cockermouth, Egremont and Highhead in Cumberland, and the castles of Appleby, Brougham and Mallerstang in Westmorland, with small permanent garrisons (Excheq. Accts. bundle 16, nos. 9, 13). The garrison of Carlisle consisted of five knights, thirty-four men-at-arms, forty hobelars and forty foot. The men maintained in the other castles were very few in comparison. The feudal levy of Cumberland, returned by the sheriff in 1323–4, was made up of twelve knights and forty-eight men-at-arms (*hominum ad arma*), whose names are given by Palgrave (*Parl. Writs*, ii. [ii.], 650).

[2] Pat. 1 Edw. II. pt. i. mm. 15, 16, 18.

[3] This complaint was made against Sir Andrew de Harcla in 1322 (Royal Letter, No. 4342). The document has been printed by Mr. Stevenson in *Chron. de Lanercost* (Maitland Club), 537–8.

[4] See specially the petition of the commune of Cumberland about 1355 in *Cal. of Scot. Doc.* (Scot. Rec. Pub.), iii. 290.

[5] Ancient Petition, No. 5208 ; see also ibid. No. 5206.

this were not always thrown on the side of established government. In 1349 the constable of Carlisle and the sheriff of the county were commanded to arrest William de Stapleton and commit him to Carlisle castle for seizing certain Scotsmen who came to Carlisle under safe conduct and carrying them off to his fortress on the water of Eamont (Amote) and refusing to deliver them up to the king's officers.[1]

From this period resistance to Scottish inroads was distributed over the whole county ; licences to crenellate became more frequent ;[2] castles like Cockermouth were supplied with keepers and permanent garrisons answerable to the Crown ;[3] the whole frontier was studded with defences. Though the rectangular peels, still so plentiful in the county and so characteristic of it, were mainly the product of a later date,[4] the

[1] Pat. 24 Edw. III. pt. ii. m. 21d.

[2] In addition to the licences already noticed the following may be mentioned : to Hugh Lowther for his dwelling-place (mansum) of Wythope in Derwentfells on 12 July 1318 (Pat. 12 Edw. II. m. 31) ; to Ranulf de Dacre for Naworth (Naward) on 27 July 1335 (ibid. 9 Edw. III. pt. ii. m. 20) ; to John de Hodleston for Millum on 24 August 1335, to enclose with a dyke and crenellate (ibid. 9 Edw. III. pt. ii. m. 20) ; to John (Kirkby), Bishop of Carlisle, for his mansum of La Rose on 9 April 1336 (ibid. 10 Edw. III. pt. i. m. 27) ; to Bishop Gilbert (Welton) for same (ibid. 29 Edw. III.) ; to William Lengleys, the king's yeoman (dilectus vallettus noster), for his manerium of Highhead (Heyheved) on 6 October 1342 (ibid. 16 Edw. III. pt. ii. m. 1) ; to the abbot of Holmcultram for his manerium of Wolsty within the bounds of Holmcultram (ibid. 22 Edw. III.) ; to the men of the vill of Penrith for the vill of Penrith on 10 April 1346 (ibid. 20 Edw. III. pt. i. m. 18) ; to William Lord Greystoke, 'quod ipse mansum suum de Graystok muro de petra et calce firmare et kernellare et mansum illud sic firmatum et kernellatum tenere possit sibi et heredibus suis imperpetuum,' on 5 October 1353 (B. M. Lansdowne Chart. No. 122) ; to Gilbert de Culwen, knight, for the house that he had built at his manor of Workington (Wirkyngton) in the March of Scotland, on 4 March 1380 (Pat.3 Ric. II. pt. ii. m. 15) ; to William de Stirkeland, clerk, for his chamber (camera) in the vill of Penrith in the March of Scotland on 12 February 1397 (ibid. 20 Ric. II. pt. ii. m. 22) ; to same, 'unum mantelettum de petra et calce facere et camerae predictae conjungere et mantelettum predictum kernellare,' on 2 April 1399 (ibid. 22 Ric. II. pt. iii. m. 37). It may be noted here that the above William Strickland, afterwards Bishop of Carlisle, was a considerable landowner in that district and a benefactor of the town of Penrith.

[3] On 26 November 1309 the king commanded Gilbert de Culewenne, keeper of the castle of Cockermouth, to pay David, Earl of Athol, 50 marks in aid of his expenses in the March of Scotland (Close, 3 Edw. II. m. 14). In 1314 Sir Thomas de Richmond held the castle as warden with Richard de Richmond his brother, and 19 vallets, 10 crossbowmen, and 80 archers (Cal. of Scot. Doc. [Scot. Rec. Pub.], iii. 77). The 'Piel of Ledel' was also in the custody of a warden in 1310-1 (ibid. iii. 45), and surrendered in 1316 (ibid. iii. 128).

[4] Mr. George Neilson, in his Peel : its Meaning and Derivation (Glasgow, 1893), has traced the historical evolution of the Border peel from its first conception as a palisaded or stockaded enclosure to its latest development as a rectangular tower of stone surrounded with a barmekan. One of the earliest examples of this institution in Cumberland is the peel of Liddel, which may be taken as an illustration of this class of stronghold. The castellum or fortified close of Liddel was taken by William the Lion in 1174 (Benedict. Abbas, Gesta Hen. II. Ric. I. [Rolls Series], i. 65) ; in 1282 it is described as the site of a castle with hall of wood, a chapel, etc. (Inq. p.m. 10 Edw. I. No. 26) ; arrangements were made on 10 November 1300 for ' repairing the mote and the fosses around : strengthening and redressing the same, and the pele and the palisades, and making lodges within the mote if necessary for the safety of the men-at-arms of the garrison ' (Cal. of Scot. Doc. [Scot. Rec. Pub.], ii. 299). Some of the titles by which it was designated are interesting. In 1310 it was referred to as the 'Piel of Ledel,' and in 1319 as the 'Pele of Lidell ' (ibid. iii. 45, 128) ; as the 'fortalitium de Lidelle' in 1346 (Chron. de Lanercost [Maitland Club], 345 ; Hist. Dunelm. Script. Tres [Surtees Soc.], ccccxxxiv.) ; the ' municipium de Lidallis quod apud Marchias erat ' (Scotichronicon [Goodall], ii. 340) ; as ' quoddam manerium dominae de Wake vocatum Ludedew ' (Galf. le Baker [Giles], 170) ; best known as ' Liddel Moat,' or ' Liddel Strength,' the latter of which has been adopted by the Ordnance Survey. The great ditches, which still remain, show that it was a hill-fort surrounded by a moated palisade. It is quite certain that many of the peels constructed by Edward I. as military expedients were made of wood. In 1300 money was paid to ' carpentariis facientibus pelum in foresta de Ingelwode assidendum circa castrum de Dunfres ' (Liber Quot. Contrar. Garder [Soc. Antiq.], 165) ; similar payments were made to carpenters and sawyers in 1298-9, ' ad sarranda ligna pro constructione peli ' at the castle of Lochmaban (Doc. of Hist. of Scot. [Scot. Rec. Pub.], ii. 360-1). When rectangular towers of stone were erected in the sixteenth century to cope with the unceasing spoliations of the Border land,

fourteenth century witnessed the rise of many strongholds throughout the land. The building of embattled churches, 'half church of God, half fortress 'gainst the Scot,' to which the parishioners flocked in time of danger, is a curious feature of this movement. Close to the estuary of the Eden, two of these churches remain intact to the present day. Shortly after 1303 the monks of Holmcultram erected one of these fortified churches at Newton Arlosh for the protection of their tenants,[1] and at a subsequent date the strong tower of the church of Burgh by Sands was rebuilt[2] with walls 6 or 7 feet thick, two notable examples of the medieval fortress with arched chambers, loop-holes and embrasures capable of resisting a siege. The rector of Bowness on Solway dwelt in a fortalice close to the churchyard wall, the vestiges of which were only recently demolished.[3] Places of defence erected by the voluntary efforts of the community were afterwards utilized by the Crown. In 1380 the king commanded all laymen holding 100 marks or more of land or rent to reside constantly on their estates for the defence of the March, and to see that all castles and fortalices within 3 or 4 leagues of the frontier were well fortified and provided with men and stores to resist the Scots ; similar instructions were given to all captains, lords, wardens of castles, mayors and other officers to obey the king's lieutenant in charge of the March.[4] This distribution of responsibility, occasioned by the necessity of the time, was not without effect on the military position of the

the old word 'peel' was used to describe them, the name by which they are known to the present day. Almost every old house of considerable size in Cumberland includes one of these square towers or peels, though it is often difficult to find them except by the thickness of the walls. In many places they stand alone by farm houses, once the seats of country squires.

[1] The bishop's licence for the building of the church of Newton Arlosh is dated 11 April 1304, and runs thus : ' considerantes insuper statum vestrum per hostiles invasiones et depredaciones Scottorum adeo depauperatum quod terras vestras more solito ad commodum vestrum excolere non potestis . . . concedimus . . . ut liceat vobis in territorio vestro de Arlosk infra fines vestros predictos unam capellam seu ecclesiam de novo construere pro vestris inquilinis et inhabitantibus infra fines vestros de Holm morantibus . . . Quam capellam seu ecclesiam, cum constructa fuerit, iuxta decenciam, etc. (Harleian MS. 3911 [Reg. of Holmcultram], ff. 7–8). Ground plans, elevations and sections of this church, as it existed at the beginning of the nineteenth century, have been given by Messrs. Lysons (*Hist. of Cumberland*, pp. cxc.–cxci.).

[2] The erection of the present tower of the church of Burgh by Sands is often ascribed to the reign of Edward I., but that date is much too early. In a commission for inquiring ' super prostracione quorundam arcuum in ecclesia de Burgo super Sabulones,' dated 15 July 1360, Bishop Welton speaks of 'quemdam arcum operi novi campanilis adherentem in dicta ecclesia ' (Carl. Epis. Reg., Welton, f. 68). From this statement it may be concluded that the tower was not at that time an ancient structure.

[3] In 1464 William Raa, registrar of the diocese of Carlisle, made this entry in the bishop's accounts of that year : ' De fine rectoris de Bowness pro una litera questandi pro reparacione unius domus defensionis ibidem non respondet hic quia conceditur per dominum gratis ' (Diocesan MS.). Leland says that ' Bolnes ys at the Poynt or Playne of the Ryver of Edon whet ys a lytle poore Steple as a Fortelet for a brunt, and yt ys on hyther syde of the Ryver of Edon, abowt a viii. myles from Cair Luel ' (*Itinerary*, vii. 52 [ed. Hearne], 1744). In a survey of Border fortresses made by Christopher Dacre in 1580, the condition of ' Bownes Towre ' is thus described : ' This house or towre doth belonge to y⁰ parsonage theire, standing about 4 miles west and by north from ye said house of Drumburghe adioyning to the sea criek w⁰ͪ devideth ye English and Scotesche borders and the furthest parte towardes y⁰ west, y⁰ y⁰ Scotts may enter otherwise then by botinge, and about a mile and a half over the same criek to Scotland at a full sea, a place of small receipt and yet very necessairy for defence of y⁰ parte of the Border, partly decayed, the charges of w⁰ͪ reparacon with a plattforme for ordinance w⁰ͪ were necessarie to be made upon y⁰ same towre is esteamed to £40 and without the platforme to £10 ' (S. P. Dom. Eliz. Add. xxvii. 44 [3]). A wall of this tower was standing close to the rectory in 1856.

[4] Pat. 3 Ric. II. pt. ii. m. 5.

county castle of Carlisle. Defiantly it still stood out from its steep sandstone bluff towards the north, but the change of tactics adopted by Scotland from the occasional invasion of a regular army to a perpetual and exasperating system of guerilla warfare needed a more extended line of defence at every strategical point. Except in times of special emergency, the ward of the town and castle was relegated to the citizens aided by a small permanent garrison, and its defences were neglected and fell into decay. The historic service of castleguard as an obligation on the whole county had become obsolete. The change in the political importance of the county castle was well summed up about 1385 by the mayor and citizens of Carlisle, who complained to the Crown that their walls were in part fallen, their fosses were filled up, and their gates could not be shut without much difficulty; they had neither 'pount leve, portcolys, barmecan, bretage, bareres, ne garetts'; their inhabitants were so few that they could not resist the Scottish attacks; and the seigneurs of the county around, who used to repair to the city in war time, had raised castles of their own on account of its weakness, and many knights, esquires and others no longer came to the city for the same reason.[1] Local strongholds were appraised at such a high value in the defence of the Border that their number became the subject of international agreement in 1388 when it was stipulated that no fortress should be built anew or repaired in the counties of Cumberland or Northumberland, or of Berwick, Roxburgh or Dumfries, except those in progress at that date.[2]

The wars of Edward I. with Scotland brought into prominence the political divisions of the county as units for the raising of military levies. It has been already pointed out that these divisions must have had their origin at a very early period in connection with the great baronies, each of the divisions being, as most likely, an administrative area or constabulary dependent on a royal or baronial castle.[3] About a century after its fiscal formation, the county appears divided into five parcels, Carlisle or Cumberland, Lyth or Leath, Eskdale, Allerdale or Allerdale below Derwent, and Coupland or Allerdale above Derwent, the names of which are in use at the present day. These were the civil areas under the name of bailiwicks which supplied the juries and made presentments at the Assizes of Carlisle in 1278 and 1292.[4] Before the death of Edward I. these divisions were used for military purposes. When commissions of array were issued, letters dated at Carlisle on 19 March 1307 were directed to John de Castre for the levy of 200 footmen in 'the parts' of Eskdale and Gillesland; to Richard le Brun for a like number in 'the county' of Cumberland; to Richard de Cletere for the same in 'the parts' of Coupland and Cockermouth; to Richard de Kirkbride for the same in 'the parts' of Allerdale; and to Roger de

---

[1] Ancient Petition, No. 5950: *Cal. of Scot. Doc.* (Scot. Rec. Pub.), iv. 78.
[2] Tower Miscell. Roll, No. 459; *Cal. Scot. Doc.* (Scot. Rec. Pub.), iv. 85.
[3] *V.C.H. Cumb.* i. 327–9.
[4] Assize Rolls (Cumberland), 6 Edw. I. No. 132, m. 32d; 20 Edw. I. No. 135, m. 10, 17d; *Three Early Assize Rolls of Northumb.* (Surtees Soc.), 266; *Doc. of Hist. of Scot.* (Scot. Rec. Pub.), i. 358.

Laton for 100 footmen in 'the bailiwick' of Lyth.[1] In a previous
commission, dated at Lanercost on 20 February 1307, the separate
liberties or franchises of Penrith, Cockermouth, Egremont, the bishopric of Carlisle, and the priory of Carlisle were named with 'the bailiwicks' of Cumberland, Allerdale, Eskdale and Gillesland, and Lyth and
Alstonmore, for the contribution of quotas of footmen, varying from
20 to 200, according to the extent or capacity of the area.[2] It is
singular that the name of ward, the equivalent in Cumberland for the
hundred or wapentake of other counties, has not been found as a designation of these political divisions till we reach the muster rolls of the
sixteenth century.[3] The bailiwicks of the forest of Cumberland were
known as wards throughout the fourteenth century,[4] and probably at a
much earlier date.

The frontier position of Cumberland continued to mould its
political history for several centuries. Though the county was called
upon from time to time to withstand invasion by the organized forces
of Scotland, its chief embarrassment was caused by a system of predatory incursions which rendered life and property insecure. The
long continuance of Border feuds had a demoralizing effect on the inhabitants of both sides. Civilization had made little advance. The
history of the county for the three centuries before the union of the two
kingdoms is written in blood. The occasional intervals of truce serve
only as a background to throw out the principal lineaments of slaughter
and devastation which dominate the picture. Mutual reprisal was reduced to a science. The dangers with which the district was menaced
bred a rough and sturdy race of independent men whose duty to fight
coincided with the safety of themselves and their families.[5] The
stern necessities engendered by such conditions of warfare were instrumental in training the great territorial families in habits of continual
watchfulness, and supplying some of the best commanders for the defence of the county. Families like the Tilliols of Scaleby, the Lucies
of Cockermouth, the Greystokes of Greystoke, the Dacres of Naworth,
and others became conspicuous as fighting families, and displayed qualities
which one would expect from the nature of their position and the employments on which they were engaged. The records of the fourteenth

---

[1] Pat. 35 Edw. I. m. 23; Parl. Writs (Rec. Com.), i. 380.   [2] Pat. 35 Edw. I. m. 32.

[3] Border Papers (Scot. Rec. Pub.), i. 37–62. In the records of Quarter Sessions for the seventeenth
and eighteenth centuries each of the five wards of the county is found in the administration of a chief
constable.

[4] In 1307 the forest of Inglewood was composed of the three 'wards' of Penrith, Allerdale and
Gatesgill (Gaytescales), each of the two former wards having four foresters, and the latter two (Pat.
35 Edw. I. m. 15). The ward of Penrith was an important division of the forest (Cal. of Pat. Rolls,
1399–1401, pp. 34, 200; Cal. Rot. Pat. [Rec. Com.], 166, 172, 173b, 210). In 1371 we have the 'warda
de Gateshales infra forestam de Inglewood' (Pat. 45 Edw. III. pt. i. m. 38) The present parish of
Westward took its name from 'le Westwarde in Allerdale,' as it was called in 1383 (Cal. of Pat. Rolls,
1381–5, p. 392).

[5] For a description of the state of the Border at this period see Vrayes Chroniques (ed. Palain), i.
47–8. Jehan le Bel gained his information about the methods of Border inroads either from personal
observation or by the report of Sir John of Hainault, whose friend he was. Froissart acknowledges his
indebtedness to this chronicle, as well he might, for several of his chapters are wholly or in part
appropriated from it (Anct. Chronicles [ed. Berners], i. 63–4).

century teem with deeds of incursion and reprisal. In 1357 Sir Robert Tilliol, called Tuylliyoll by the Scots, accomplished some very successful expeditions, or 'drives' as we should call them according to the nomenclature of modern warfare. In company with Sir Thomas de Lucy he forayed the lands of William, lord of Douglas in Eskdale, with a great force raised in Cumberland and Westmorland, and robbed the people there in open day of 1,000 oxen, cows, and other young beasts, 1,000 sheep and horses, and plundered all the houses. It was complained that Lucy lay in ambush and seized the people who attempted to rescue their goods. The crime, as it was alleged, was bad enough when committed in time of war, but the raiders, starting from Lochmaban Castle, which was nothing but a den of thieves, ravaged the land in open day with banners displayed in time of truce, and had set to ransom many of the people to their damage of £5,000 sterling.[1] Some of the Bishops of Carlisle were military personages, captains of Carlisle Castle and strenuous leaders in the field. John de Kirkby was a martial prelate, on whom the mantle of his predecessor, John de Halton, had fallen ; on more than one occasion he proved himself a valiant fighter. In 1345 he was nearly captured by the Scots ; he was unhorsed but regained his saddle, rallied his forces and defeated the foe.[2] The chronicler of Lanercost says that the Scots held him in the greatest detestation (*summo odio habuerunt*) because he often went against them in battle.[3]

But there are few military figures to compare with Andrew de Hartcla for the distinguished part he played on the stage of Border history in the earlier period of the international struggle. Fighting in Scotland, defending Carlisle, resisting invasion, quelling insurrection, wise in council, brave in battle, sheriff of Cumberland, knight of the shire, captain of Carlisle, warden of the March, lieutenant of the northern counties,[4] Andrew de Hartcla rose in his sovereign's favour with astonishing rapidity, till he was created Earl of Carlisle on 25 March 1322, with the grant of 1,000 marks and other revenues for the main-

---

[1] *Cal. Doc. Scot.* (Scot. Rec. Pat.), iii. 306-7.

[2] Walsingham, *Hist. Anglie* (Rolls Ser.), i. 266-7. On this occasion the Scots, under Sir William Douglas, had burnt several villages between Carlisle and Penrith. Bishop Kirkby and Sir Thomas de Lucy, a very brave knight, surrounded them on every side in the night, and made such a noise with horns and trumpets that the Scots were unable to take food or sleep.

[3] *Chron. de Lanercost* (Maitland Club), 291-2.

[4] Michael de Hartcla had been sheriff of Cumberland from 1285 to 1298 (Pat. 13 Edw. I. m. 9 ; Q. R. Memoranda, 27 Edw. I. m. 4d). Monsire Andrew de Hartcla was on the king's service in Scotland in 1310 (*Cal. Doc. Scot.* [Scot. Rec. Pub.], iii. 32) ; sheriff of Cumberland in 1311 (Pat. 5 Edw. II. pt. ii. m. 11) ; knight of the shire in 1312 (*Parl. Writs* [Rec. Com.], ii. [ii.], 77) ; held Carlisle against the Scots, who might have been harassed oftener in the March if he had a more numerous garrison, and defeated them near 'le Redecros' on Stainmore in 1314 (*Cal. Doc. Scot.* iii. 70, 76-7) ; successfully defended Carlisle in 1315 against Bruce, who, flushed with his victory at Bannockburn, made a formidable attack upon it (Hemingburgh, *Chron.* [Eng. Hist. Soc.], ii. 294 ; *Chron. de Lanercost* [Maitland Club], 230-2), in the same year received 1,000 marks as 'geredoun' for making prisoners certain Scotsmen of note (*Cal. Doc. Scot.* iii. 86) ; taken prisoner by the Scots in 1316 (Barbour, *The Brus*, 327) and redeemed at a heavy ransom (*Cal. Doc. Scot.* iii. 98, 132) ; at the siege of Berwick in 1319 at the head of 980 foot, and 360 hobelars (ibid. iii. 125-6) ; complaints by the commonalty of Carlisle in 1319 about his trafficking with the Scots, releasing prisoners, and interfering with justice on the March (ibid. iii. 127-8) ; chief warden of the whole Border, and sovereign arrayer of the men-at-arms on foot of these Marches in 1322 (ibid. iii. 144) ; summoned to undertake various expeditions and to perform special duties between 1309 and 1322 (*Parl. Writs* [Rec. Com.], ii. [iii.], 971-2).

tenance of his dignity. This distinction was conferred upon him, as stated in the patent, for his signal victory at Boroughbridge and his delivery of Thomas, Earl of Lancaster, into the king's hand.[1] Hartcla became the most powerful personage in the north. But his fall was no less rapid than his rise. His degradation within a year of the conferring of the earldom is one of the most striking and dramatic episodes in Cumbrian history. It is very doubtful that, in the action which he had taken in concluding a peace with the Scots, Hartcla was really a traitor to the best interests of his country. He had already been appointed a commissioner to deal with Bruce,[2] and subsequent events may have increased his conviction of the wisdom of such a step. The position of the county was full of gloom, and no one better than he could gauge the hopelessness of the unequal contest between a tried warrior like Robert Bruce and a man like his own king, infirm of purpose and animated only by a vague desire to revenge himself on his enemies. In 1322 a petition had been sent to King Edward from the dwellers on the Marches, telling how dreadful were their sufferings and that they had nothing but their naked bodies to give to his service, at the same time imploring him to come to their relief.[3] But Hartcla knew by experience the futility of such a course, and he was aware how little could be expected from the king. It would seem that, actuated by such impressions, he responded to the advances made by Bruce, whom he met at the castle of Lochmaban on 3 January 1323.[4] On his return to Carlisle, the earl reported the terms of the peace to an assembly of the principal men of the county (*omnes majores comitatus ejusdem, quam regulares quam etiam seculares*) by whom they were accepted, more from fear than of their own wish. The news was received with different feelings by the commonalty (*pauperes et mediocres et agricultores*), who made no secret of their pleasure that the King of Scotland should be allowed to hold his own kingdom on condition that they should live in peace.[5] King Edward, however, looked at the matter from another standpoint, though he seemed not to have been clear in the first place how far Hartcla was in the wrong. He ordered an inquiry into the rolls of Chancery for the exact terms of the earl's commission to treat with the Scots, but it is doubtful that he waited for a reply. On 1 February the king and his council issued a commission to Sir Anthony de Lucy to arrest the earl, which was carried out in the castle of Carlisle. Intelligence of the event reached the king at Knaresborough on 28 February, and so .

---

[1] Rymer, *Fœdera*, ii. (i.), 481; Pat. 15 Edw. II. pt. ii. m. 22; *Lords' Report on the Dignity of a Peer*, iii. 175. Leland states that Lancaster tried to corrupt Hartcla at Boroughbridge by offering him one of the counties he had in his possession if he would favour his cause. ' But Herkeley refusid his offre. Then Thomas prophetied that he wold sore repent and that shortely so fair, and that he should dy a shameful deth, that is to say, to be hangid, drawen and quartered (*Collectanea*, i. 464).

[2] Pat. 15 Edw. II. pt. ii. m. 29.

[3] Royal Letters, No. 4342; *Cal. Doc. Scot.* (Scot. Rec. Pub.), iii. 148. This petition has been printed by Mr. Stevenson in *Chron. de Lanercost*, 537–8.

[4] The indenture made between them has been printed in a summary by Bain with remarks on the character of the peace (*Cal. Doc. Scot.* iii. pp. xxx., xxxi. 148–9).

[5] *Chron. de Lanercost* (Maitland Club), 248–50.

overjoyed was he that he gave a free pardon to the messenger of all his offences.[1] Judgment was pronounced against the earl on 3 March by Geoffrey le Scrope, the king's justiciar, and on the same day the sword of the county was wrested from his hand and the golden spurs of knighthood were torn from his heels. He was then dragged to the gallows at Harraby and hanged, drawn and quartered, his head being sent to London, and his quarters to Carlisle, Newcastle, York, and Shrewsbury. To the last he professed he had acted only in the best interests of the kingdom.[2] It may well have been so, for two months after his disgrace, Edward himself was obliged to come to terms, and made a truce with the Scottish king to last for thirteen years.[3] At a subsequent date, during the regency which governed in the time of the minority of Edward III., the English claims on the northern kingdom were abandoned and a fresh truce[4] was concluded on terms very similar

---

[1] *Cal. Doc. Scot.* (Scot. Rec. Pub.), iii. 149.

[2] On 8 January 1322-3 the king sent a mandate to the inhabitants of Cumberland and Westmorland, forbidding them to enter into any truce with the Scots, and on the same day he requested the earl to inform him personally of the reported truce that he had made (Pat. 16 Edw. II. pt. i. m. 8 ; Close, 16 Edw. II. m. 16d ; Rymer, *Fœdera*, ii [i.], 502). On 13 January he ordered a search for the terms of the earl's commission to treat with the Scots and its endurance (*Cal. Doc. Scot.* iii. 148), and on 19 January a transcript of the articles of the agreement between Hartcla and Bruce was sent to the council at York, with the remark that in the king's opinion the truce was fraught with great danger (ibid. iii. 148-9). The arrest took place on 25 February by Lucy, with the assistance of Sir Hugh de Lowther, Sir Richard de Denton and Sir Hugh de Moriceby, who entered the great hall of the castle for that purpose without arousing suspicion (*Chron. de Lanercost*, 249-50). The king ordered his condemnation and degradation on 27 February, and the sentence was pronounced and carried into execution on 3 March (*Parl. Writs* [Rec. Com.], ii. [ii.], 262-3 ; *Abbrev. Placit.* [Rec. Com.], 351). In the record of the judgment, the destination of portions of the earl's body was ordered as above, but the author of the *Chronicle of Lanercost* (Maitland Club, 251) has substituted Dover and Bristol for York and Shrewsbury. There seems to be an error in both authorities, for on 10 August 1328 Sir Andrew's sister Sarah, widow of Roger de Leyburn, obtained royal licence to gather his bones and commit them to ecclesiastical sepulture, orders to that effect having been issued to the keeper of Carlisle castle, the mayor and sheriffs of London, the mayor and bailiffs of Newcastle and Bristol, and the bailiffs of Shrewsbury (Close, 2 Edw. III. m. 20d). Opinions differ whether the earl was actuated by patriotic or treacherous motives in concluding the peace with Bruce. The *Chronicle of Lanercost* (pp. 250-1) states that his confessors after his capture 'justificabant et excusabant ab intentione et nota proditionis et vitam suam priorem notabiliter commendabant.' His unsuspicious conduct in allowing himself to be captured so easily is a strong point in his favour. In 1327 Henry, his nephew and heir, petitioned Edward III. for a restoration of his lands on the ground that he had never been regularly convicted of treason, he and his forefathers having served the king and his ancestors since the Conquest (Anct. Pet. No. 2500). The Scots, who were impressed with the renown of his 'beaux faites d'armes,' attributed his fall, when Earl of Carlisle, to pride (*Scala Cronica*, 149). In the wardrobe accounts of Edward III., under the year 1338, a notice appears of thirteen silver dishes marked on the border with the arms of Hartcla, valued at £16 (*Cal. Doc. Scot.* iii. 234). According to Sir Harris Nicolas in *A Roll of Arms of the Reign of Edward the Second*, compiled between 1308 and 1314, the arms of the Hartcla family were, 'Sire Michel de Herteclaue de argent a une crois de goules : Sire Andrew de Herteclaue meisme les armes e un merelot de sable.' The initial letter of a charter of Edward II. to the city of Carlisle, dated 12 May 1316, is embroidered with a well-executed vignette, representing the siege of a walled town and showing two groups of figures outside the frame of the letter. The chief of the defenders is a knightly figure in complete armour, in his right hand a lance in the act of striking, and on his left a shield bearing the arms of Hartcla ; the scene, no doubt, was intended to depict the gallant defence of the city by Sir Andrew de Hartcla against the Scots in 1315 (*Trans. Cumb. and Westmld. Arch. Soc.* vi. 319 ; *Royal Charters of Carlisle*, 13).

[3] Close, 16 Edw. II. m. 5d ; Rymer, *Fœdera*, ii. 521-2.

[4] Pat. 1 Edw. III. pt. i. m. 19 ; *Fœdera*, ii. (ii.), 696. There is a very interesting account of this treaty in *Chron. de Lanercost* (Maitland Club), 261, where it is stated that the policy of Edward I. was reversed, and the claim to the sovereignty of Scotland was abandoned. 'Reddidit etiam eis partem crucis Christi, quam vocant Scotti Blakerode, et similiter unum instrumentum sive carta msubjectionis et homagii faciendi regibus Angliæ, cui appensa erant sigilla omnium magnatum Scotiæ, quam fecerant avo regis, et a Scottis, propter multa sigilla dependentia, Ragman vocabatur.'

REPRESENTATION OF THE DEFENCE OF CARLISLE BY SIR ANDREW DE HARCLA
AGAINST THE SCOTS IN 1315, ON A CHARTER OF EDWARD II.
TO THE CITY OF CARLISLE.

to those which had been arranged only four years before at Lochmaban and for the acceptance of which Hartcla had died a martyr.

During the occasional periods of truce which occurred intermittently in the reign of Richard II., cordial relations sprang up and ways were opened for more frequent intercourse between the two kingdoms. The English king was fond of the tilt and tournament, and his tastes in that direction brought about an international rapprochement which diplomacy had failed to effect. The court of chivalry had become an established institution under his patronage. Though appeal to arms had been from an early period a conspicuous feature of Border law,[1] the internecine wars of the fourteenth century had a tendency to hasten the decay of the personal duel. The reviving interest in chivalry brought in a new type of combat which combined the old idea of judicial award with the more modern instinct of sport and the exhibition of individual skill. By special provision in the patent of the warden of the March it was enjoined that in every case when the duel was challenged between combatants, the acceptance, offer or wager should be reserved to the king or his lieutenant.[2] With such regulations in force, the adjudication of points of honour or dispute became a matter of public interest, and distinguished men of both countries were brought face to face under guarantees of safe conduct to settle their differences by feats of arms. On 6 June 1390 Sir William Douglas, knight, had licence to come to England with a retinue of forty horsemen, knights, squires and valets, and armour for his own person only, and prosecute a plea in the court of chivalry before the marshal of England which he had with Sir Thomas de Clifford, chivaler, lord of Westmorland.[3] A more famous joust in war (*de guerra hastiludium*) took place in the city of Carlisle from 21 to 27 June 1393, when Sir Richard de Redemane encountered William de Halyborton and three other Scotsmen in the presence of Sir Henry de Percy, who was ordered to be present as the king's lieutenant.[4] These instances of international tilting bespeak a lull in the hostile relations of the two kingdoms, and though peace was liable to interruption at any moment, the custom may be regarded as an evidence of a good understanding, which was scarcely possible at any time since the outbreak of the War of Independence at the close of the thirteenth century.

Amid the vicissitudes of Scottish warfare a new mode of military enterprise was introduced about the year 1382, which was destined in time to revolutionize the whole system of frontier defence. Guns and gunpowder, cannon and calivers were brought into use as engines of destruction.[5] But it cannot be said that the shield, lance and bow-

---

[1] *Leges Marchiarum* (ed. Nicolson), 6. Neilson's *Trial by Combat* (London 1890), should be consulted for the history of duel by law.

[2] *Rot. Scotiæ* (Rec. Com.), ii. 49–50.   [3] Chancery Files, bundle No. 416.

[4] Pat. 16 Ric. II. pt. iii. m. 16; Tower Privy Seals, 16 Ric. II. file 5; *Cal. Rot. Pat.* (Rec. Com.), 226b.

[5] John Prior of Drax accounted for provision of 'gun-poudre' and 'artelar' among lists of other victuals for the castles of Berwick and Roxburgh between 1382 and 1384, and in the accounts of the sheriff of Cumberland for 1384–5 there are several entries which show that the new power had been called into play for the defence of Carlisle. Two great 'gunnes' were placed on the keep of the castle

string were abandoned at this period ; the new engine seems to have been confined at first to purposes of defence. The archer had his usefulness as well as the artillery, for at the above date fifty men-at-arms and a hundred mounted archers were maintained at Carlisle as a permanent garrison, and in 1488 hobelars and archers, 'bumbards' and artillery were reckoned as the munitions necessary for the fortification of Carlisle and Bewcastle.[1]

One of the causes of exasperation between the two peoples was a small strip of territory on the frontier, variously called the Threapland, Batable or Debatable land, sometimes the Batail land, which had never been properly determined by bounds nor acknowledged as belonging to either kingdom. In the fifteenth century several attempts were made by means of friendly negotiations to bring this thorny controversy to a close. By a convention at Durham in 1449 between English and Scottish commissioners it was agreed ' that all the claymers and chalongours of the landez called Batable landez or Threpe landez in the West Marchez' should have free entry and use of the district in dispute without prejudice of the right of the King of Scotland.[2] At subsequent dates between 1451 and 1457 this international understanding was renewed.[3] A new element of strife, however, was introduced in 1474 when a fishgarth or dam was constructed by the inhabitants of Cumberland in the lower waters of the Esk, whereby salmon were prevented ascending the river to the detriment of the fishing industry in the upper or Scottish waters. The fishgarth was complained of as a nuisance, and as often as it was removed, it was replaced by the Cumberland men. In the heat of the crisis a commission was appointed ' to visite and see the place and by inquisition and recorde taken of the eldest and feithfullest persoones of the Marches there' to inform themselves of the truth and how 'the said fishgaert hath been kepte,' and thus to finish and determine the quarrel, safe conducts to the envoys having been guaranteed by both sovereigns.[4] English subjects maintained that they had the right by law and custom to erect and hold the fishgarth, while the Scots asserted the contrary. The fishing of the Esk, being but a part of the greater dispute about the international boundary, continued to be a burning question of debate for many generations. The larger issue was the subject of inquiry during a truce in 1493 when Thomas Lord Dacre, Sir Richard Salkeld, and Sir John Musgrave were appointed to meet the delegates of the King of Scots for the purpose of settling the disputes which had arisen afresh in the West Marches, both as to the fishings of the Esk, the bounds of the Debatable Land, and the site, limits

and a lesser gun in the angle of the outer bailey, mounted on wooden frames (*bochez de fuistez*) and bound with iron 'ligatures.' Richard Potter was paid for casting three brass cannon in the city, for which Robert Delmane, probably a German, supplied the iron hoops. Purchases of ' poweder de salt-petre' and 'live' sulphur were made at York, and a mason was employed for five weeks polishing (*scapulanti*) 120 stones for the guns. These munitions of war were handed over to John de Thirlwalle, deputy warden of the castle, by indenture dated 4 December 1384 (*Cal. Scot. Doc.* [Scot. Rec. Pub.], iv. 71, 74–6).

[1] Chancery Signed Bills, 3 Henry VII. No. 35.   [2] Rymer, *Fœdera*, xi. 244.
[3] Ibid. xi. 288, 336, 399.   [4] Chancery Signed Bills, 5 Hen. VII. No. 27.

and bounds of the monastery of Canonby ; also for perambulating and surveying the same and placing new metes and bounds if necessary.[1] But there was no finality in these negotiations ; the dispute was handed on to embitter international feuds. At a later date the controversy raged specially around the question whether the lands of Canonby were debatable ground. It was claimed by the English in 1531 that 'the boundes of Cannonby is inverouned of thre partis withe the Debatable grounde, that is to saye, of the este, weste and northe : and of the southe syde adjoynethe upon Englonde : soo that noo parte therof adjoynethe upon Scotlande, and bathe bene alwayes used as a hous of prayers and newtre betuixt bothe the realmes.'[2] In 1537 we learn from a description of the Debatable Land that it contained the ' grownde callede Canabye, thatt sayme beyng in lenghtt bye estymatione two myllys est annde west, annde in brede two myllys.'[3] For some time longer the territory in dispute was to be occupied as it had been heretofore by 'byt of mouth alanerlie,'[4] an arrangement under which rights of pasture were enjoyed during the daytime only by the inhabitants of both countries,[5] the Threaplands having been treated as international common. At length a compromise was arrived at by commissioners representing both kingdoms and a partition of the land in dispute was made. In the award, dated 24 September 1552, it was set forth that as the inhabitants of the western part inclined more to be subjects of England, and the inhabitants of the eastern part inclined more to be subjects of Scotland, the partition should be guided by local feeling. An earthen barrier was thrown up between the Esk and Sark, and its terminations marked by square pillars with the arms of England on the west sides thereof and the arms of Scotland on the east sides. Lest the pillars should be destroyed by length of time or removed by evil counsel, the sites where the stones were to be placed were described as the bend of the Esk at the western side of a field called Dimmisdaill, where a syke of that name joins the river, and a bank on Scottish ground by the red cliff in Kirkrigg where the Sark in turn makes a curve in its course.[6]

[1] Chan. Signed Bills, 9 Hen. VII. No. 31. [2] Armstrong, *Liddesdale*, App. No. 25.
[3] Cotton MS. Calig. B. iii. 83. [4] *Hamilton Papers* (Scot. Rec. Pub.), i. 54.
[5] Cott. MS. Caligula, B. vi. ff. 167–8.

[6] Rymer, *Fœdera*, xv. 315–9. In this important international document the disputed territory is described as ' dictus ager nunc variabilis, nunc litigiosus, nunc terra contentiosa vocari solitus, communi vero utriusque gentis vocabulo nuncupatus *the Debatable Land,* quasi quis dicat terram de cujus jure tam Angli quam Scoti decertare ac contended sint soliti, forma oblonga atque inæquali protendatur ab occidente in orientem ' ; and the partition is set out ' ut in ipso utriusque partis discrimine, trames linearis rectus transversim ab Esk ad Sark fluvium ducatur, fossa vel sulco vestigium ipsius denotante ; ac præterea, singulæ piramides lapide quadrato singulis ipsorum Esk et Sark fluviorum ripis interius imponantur, in ipsis potissimum (quoad ejus fieri potest) locorum punctis construendæ ac collocandæ, ubi linea seu trames ille transversus hac illac extendetur. Quosquidem locos, quo planius dinoscantur, ut si quo vetustatis aut doli mali vitio piramides corruerint, nihilo secus locorum vestigia ad ipsarum reparationem innotescant, in hunc modum hinc describendos putavimus : locus igitur piramidi Esk fluvii tipæ imponendæ is esto, ubi fluvii ipsius cursus sinuose incurvatus est, ad campi cujusdam (vulgari sermone vocati Dimmisdaill) latus occidentale, qua torrens seu rivulus quidam vicinus (vernacule nuncupatus Dimmisdaill syke) in fluvium jam dictum præcipitat. Similiter, piramidi Sark fluvii quæ imponetur ripæ is esto locus, qui clivo rubro situs est, e regione loci vocati Kirkrigg in Scotia paulum supra le Eatgyw', ubi vicissim Sark fluvii alveolus in sinus incurvatur.' For the identification of the pillars it was ordered ' uti arma seu principum prædictorum insignia insculpantur ; ita scilicet, ut quod latus

It is worthy of mention that during the struggles of political factions about the succession to the crown in the reigns of Richard II. and Henry VI. the people of Cumberland were ranged on the side of the reigning house. Far removed from the intrigues of the central government and inured to the hardships of frontier defence, the constitutional subtleties which divided the nation had little attraction for them. Perhaps it was the famous stand said to have been made by Bishop Merks of Carlisle,[1] that influenced the people of his diocese to uphold the cause of King Richard. At all events, in 1401–2, it was reported to Henry IV. that certain churchmen, exempt and not exempt, and laymen as well, within the diocese were telling the people that the late king was still alive and dwelling in Scotland, and that he was about to invade England with the aid of the Scots enemy. Repressive measures were taken to stop the reports in Cumberland and Westmorland, and orders were issued to arrest and imprison all persons who maintained that King Richard was alive in Scotland.[2] In like manner, during the Wars of the Roses, the county, so far as it took part in the constitutional struggle, was largely Lancastrian in sympathy, though the city of Carlisle was held in the Yorkist interest notwithstanding a close siege by the Scots, who had crossed the Border to assist Queen Margaret.[3] Several of the great families espoused the Lancastrian cause and brought disaster on themselves and their estates. Thomas, lord of Egremont, was slain at Northampton in 1460[4]; Ralf, Lord Dacre, fell on the field of Towton in March 1461 and was buried in Saxton churchyard under 'a meane tumbe.'[5] After the battle of Wakefield, Ralf, Lord Greystoke, was suspected of treachery and thereby suffered many indignities, but he succeeded in clearing himself and swore allegiance to Queen Margaret and her son.[6] When accounts came to be reckoned with the vanquished Lancastrians in the first Parliament of Edward IV. the act of attainder included the names of several Cumberland and Westmorland men.[7] The estates of the late Lord Dacre were confiscated, and his castle of Naworth (Neuwarde) was delivered to the custody of Lord

---

utriusque piramidis quod occidentem spectat, dicti serenissimi Angliæ regis insigniatur armis, quodque orientem respicit præfatæ illustrissimæ reginæ Scotiæ armis condecoretur.' This earthen barrier is now known as the Scotch Dyke.

[1] See his speech in the Parliament of 1399 on behalf of King Richard, which has occasioned such a lively controversy (*Chron. de la Traison et Mort.* [Eng. Hist. Soc.], 70–1).

[2] Anct. Pet. No. 5945 ; Pat. 3 Hen. IV. ; *Chron. de la Traison et Mort* (Eng. Hist. Soc.), p. lxx.

[3] One of the acts of treason alleged against certain of the Lancastrians was that they procured the Scots to enter the realm, ' bringyng the same Scotts and ennemyes to his Cite of Carlile, besegyng and environyng it, brennyng the Subarbes therof, destroiyng the Howses, Habitacions and Landes of his Subgetts nygh therunto in manere of Conquest : purposyng ayenst their feith and Liegeaunce to have delyvered the seid Cite, the key of the Westmarches of Englond into the possession and obeysaunce of the seid Kyng of Scotts, and to have spoiled the Coroune of Englond therof ' (*Rot. Parl.* [Rec. Com.], v. 478). In compensation for the immoderate violence and cruelty of this siege Edward IV. granted the city of Carlisle a charter reducing the fee farm rent of the city from £80 to £40, and bestowing other privileges (*Royal Charters of Carlisle* [Cumb. and Westmld. Antiq. Soc.], 53–5).

[4] William of Worcester, *Annales* (Liber Niger), ii. 481.

[5] Leland, *Itinerary*, vi. 11, ed. Hearne, 1711.

[6] William of Worcester, ii. 486.

[7] *Rot. Parl.* (Rec. Com.), v. 476–88.

Montague,[1] but at a later date both his title and much of his property were restored to Humfrey his brother, who had succeeded in winning the king's favour.[2] A similar policy of clemency was pursued towards the other victims of the struggle, for before the close of 1461 we find Lord Greystoke and other Lancastrians named in a commission for Cumberland and Westmorland to array all the good men of these counties for defence against the king's enemies of Scotland, and Henry VI. and Margaret his wife and their adherents.[3] The work of pacification was completed through the instrumentality of the Earl of Warwick, who came to Carlisle in 1462 for that purpose.[4]

The aim of the new dynasty was to come to an understanding with the Scottish people and to promote peace on the Border. The young king of Scotland sent ambassadors to Edward IV. in April 1461, and a truce between the two countries was concluded in 1463.[5] After the death of the Earl of Warwick at the battle of Barnet, the Duke of Gloucester, the king's brother, afterwards Richard III., was appointed to influential offices in the northern counties and became for several years closely identified with the north-western district. In 1471 he had a grant of the lordship and castle of Penrith[6]; in 1474 he is found acting as warden of the Western Marches[7]; and in 1475 he was made sheriff for life of the county,[8] offices which he retained till his accession to the throne. There was peace in Cumberland while Gloucester was at the head of its military affairs.[9] So successful was his administration that the parliament of 1482, in consideration of his services, made special provision that the wardenship of the West Marches should descend to his heirs male with the possession of Carlisle and various lands in Cumberland and such adjoining parts of Scotland that

---

1 William of Worcester, ii. 493.

2 *Rot. Parl.* (Rec. Com.), vi. 43; *Lords' Reports on the Dignity of a Peer*, iii. 214-5; Dugdale, *Bar.* ii. 23-4.

3 Pat. 1 Edw. IV. pt. ii. m. 12d.

4 There is a curious entry in the minister's accounts of Bishop Kingscote, dated 30 September 1462, which shows that the Kingmaker had taken up his residence at Rose Castle during the summer of that year, and that the horses of his army had spoiled the meadows of the demesne lands there. John Yong, the receiver-general, thus accounted for the issues of Rose Park: ' Et de decremento firme alterius prati dominicalis ibidem vocati le Brademedewe superius onerati ad xxs. per annum eo quod dimittitur hoc anno nisi pro viiis. pro eo quod maxima pars eiusdem per equos hominum exercitu Comitis Warwicensis. tempore estivali infra clausum huius compoti depasta fuit et consumpta ' (MS. in diocesan registry). The earl's stay at Rose Castle occurred during the vacancy of the see between the death of Bishop Percy and the consecration of Bishop Kingscote. He was afterwards appointed keeper of the temporalities on 12 December 1463, on the death of the latter bishop (Pat. 3 Edw. IV. pt. ii. m. 11). His appointment as captain of Carlisle Castle and warden of the West Marches dated from the king's accession on 4 March 1461, and was renewed for twenty years on 5 April 1462, the yearly wages being £2,500 in time of war, and £1,250 in time of truce or peace at the hands of the treasurer of England and the chamberlains of the Exchequer (Pat. 5 Edw. IV. pt. i. m. 25).

6 *Cal. Doc. Scot.* (Scot. Rec. Pub.), iv. 267, 272.

6 Pat. 11 Edw. IV. pt. i. m. 18.

7 Ibid. 14 Edw. IV. pt. i. m. 22.   8 Ibid. pt. ii. m. 4.

9 In 1482 he had licence to buy 2,000 quarters of wheat and 1,000 quarters of barley, rye, oats, meslin, beans and peas in any places of the realm, Wales or Ireland, for the support of the additional garrison maintained on the Border (Pat. 21 Edw. IV. pt. i. m. 10). At that time there was a daily increasing scarcity of provisions, especially corn, on the West Marches on account of the great number of soldiers the king had been ' occasioned ' to send there to resist the ' manyfold assaults and continuel wertes ' of the Scots (Tower Privy Seals, 21 Edw. IV. file 1).

they might be able to subdue.[1]   He is said to have occasionally resided at Carlisle Castle, where there is a tower, bearing his name, on the southern face of which is sculptured the figure of a boar, which was his badge.

Cumberland enjoyed a period of comparative rest during the closing years of Henry VII., but with the advent of the strong will and quick temper of Henry VIII. matters soon assumed a different aspect.   His foreign policy, directed as it was at first against France, the old ally of Scotland, brought him into dangerous collision with his brother-in-law, James IV.   Lord Dacre was employed as an intermediary to compose the points of difference and to confirm the existing peace.   Nothing however would satisfy James short of Henry's desisting from his designs on France and his active participation in the league against that country.   In 1513, while Henry was still abroad, he crossed the Border at the head of a large army and took Norham Castle, but was subsequently encountered by the Earl of Surrey at Flodden and defeated and slain with many of his greatest nobles.   On the English side Lord Dacre commanded the levies of Gillesland, and his intervention at a critical moment was a powerful factor in the victory that was won.[2]   The battle of Flodden was the prelude to a fresh outbreak of sanguinary feuds in which Dacre played a principal part.   His letters to the privy council respecting his work as warden of the March are little more than reiterated accounts of the destruction he was engaged to carry out.   One of these, dated 17 May 1514, in which he defends the vigilance and success of his administration, may be selected as an indication of what was taking place at this period.   'For oone cattell taken by the Scotts,' he reported, 'we haue takyn, won and brought awey out of Scotland c[th] : and for oone shepe, cc[th] of a surity.   And has for the townships and housis burnt in any of the said Est, Middill and West Marches within my reull, fro the begynnyng of this warr unto this daye, as well when as the late King of Scotts laye in the same Est Marches as at all other times, I assure your lordships for truthe that I haue and hes caused to be burnt and distroyed sex tymes moo townys and howsys within the West and Middill Marches of Scotland in the same season then is done to us, as I may be trusted and as

---

[1] *Rot. Parl.* (Rec. Com.), vi. 204-5.   In the preamble of the Act it is stated ' that the seid Duc, beyng Wardeyn of the seid Westmarches, late by his manyfold and diligent labours and devoirs, hath subdued grete part of the Westbordures of Scotlande, adjoynyng to Englond, by the space of xxx miles and more, therby at this tyme not enhabite with Scotts, and hath gete and acheved diverse parcelles therof to be under the obeissaunce of oure said Soverayne Lorde, not oonly to the grete rest and ease of th' enhabitauntes of the seid Westmerches, but also to the grete suerty and ease of the North parties of Englond, and moche more therof he entendith, and with Goddis grace is like to gete and subdue herafter : and the seid Westmerches the more suerly to be defended and kept ayenst the Scotts, if the seid appoyntements and agrements be perfourmed and accomplished.'

[2] In the official account of the battle it is said that the Scots charged ' in good order after the Almayns manner without speking a word.'   Edmund Howard was on the right wing of Lord Howard with 1,000 Cheshire and 500 Lancashire men, who were defeated by Alexander Lord Hume, lord chamberlain of Scotland.   Mr. Gray and Sir Humphrey Lyle were taken prisoners ; Sir Wynchard Harbottle and Maurice Barkley were slain ; Edmund Howard was thrice ' feled,' when Dacre came to his relief and routed the Scots (*L. & P. of Henry VIII.* i. 4441).

I shall evidently prove.' As Dacre went on to describe his destructive progress, he boasted that for twelve miles along the water of the Liddel, where there were an hundred ploughs, and along the Ewes for eight miles, where there were an hundred and forty ploughs, every inch of the country lay desolate and no corn was sown on the grounds. He had burnt and destroyed the township of Annan and thirty-three other places in that region, all of which he named. Whereas, he concluded, there were over four hundred ploughs in these places in time past, they were all clearly wasted and no man dwelt in any of them, save only in the towers of Annan steeple and Woolhope.[1] Such was the contribution to the progress of agriculture that the lord warden of the Western Marches could make four hundred years ago !

The disaster of Flodden left Scotland with a widowed queen, sister of Henry VIII., and an infant son. The Duke of Albany, who had been brought up in France and was naturally devoted to the interest of his adopted country, was made regent, and kept the county of Cumberland for a time in a state of panic by reports of intended invasion. By a letter, ' scriblyed in hast at Sainct Bees upon Sainct Luke daye thevangelist,' 1523, dan Robert Alanby, the prior of that house, informed Lord Dacre that a great number of ships were seen upon the coast : they were supposed to be a portion of the fleet of the Duke of Albany and likely to land in Coupland and destroy them utterly. The prior urged the lord warden to command Christopher Curwen of Workington, John Lamplugh, lieutenant of Cockermouth Castle, and Richard Skelton of Branthwaite, to come with all their power to their assistance and to defend that district ' with the grace of God and the prayer of his holy sainctes.' Dacre reported the occurrence to the Earl of Surrey and added particulars about the number of the ships and the places where they had been seen, at the same time assuring him that his neighbours of Annandale had never moved or stirred, but remained still at home in their habitations.[2] Nothing came out of this naval demonstration : there was distrust on both sides ; but Lord Dacre, by working on the fears of Albany, adroitly succeeded in obtaining a truce.

The lawless condition of the Scottish clans in the vicinity of the Debatable Land became at this time a serious danger, and engaged the attention of the rulers of both kingdoms. In defiance of law and truce they wasted the English frontier and extended their depredations to their own country as circumstances favoured their prospects of plunder. Their allegiance was claimed by both sovereigns, but rendered to neither. It soon became manifest that united action between the two governments was necessary to deal effectively with the anarchy on the Western Marches. Complaints were made in 1526 and satisfaction demanded for the ' offences doon within Englound by the surenamez of Armestrongs, Elwolds, Croosyers and Nixsonnes dwellyng' on the

1 Cotton MS. Calig. B. ii. f. 190; L. & P. of Henry VIII. i. 5090.
2 Add. MS. 24,965, ff. 96, 99 (now ff. 188, 190).

opposite side,[1] but the answer came back to the Earl of Cumberland, the English warden, that if he wished to meddle 'with suche as Armestronggs ar and other like wilde and mysguyded men,' he would be obliged to use craft and espial as well as the power of the sword.[2] Repeated complaints from the English warden and the indiscriminate slaughter of his own subjects at length stirred up King James to attempt redress, and for this purpose he entered into an agreement with Wolsey for combined action against the outlawry on the Border. These negotiations had little practical effect. The Armstrongs continued to 'run day forays, robbed, spoiled, burned and murdered' within England. Again it was proposed to take from them all their goods and possessions, burn and destroy their houses, corn, hay and fuel, and take all their wives and bairns and bring them to ports of the sea, and send them away in ships to be put on land in Ireland or other far parts, from which they may never return home again,[3] but the Armstrongs replied to the threat by seizing on the Debatable Land, and in spite of truces and Border law built divers houses and edifices, probably peels or towers, for their protection.[4] William, Lord Dacre, incensed by their audacity, collected a force of 2,000 men and marched secretly upon them in the hope of taking them by surprise, but the Armstrongs had timely warning of the intended raid and succeeded in defeating the English warden and scattering his host. Failures like this roused the Border clans to acts of retaliation. The history of this period is a tale of atrocious robberies and devastation. In 1528 Henry, Earl of Northumberland, estimated the power of the Armstrongs with their adherents at above 3,000 horsemen, and stated that any undertaking on behalf of the Scottish king to subdue them was 'but a braigg and no thing likely to take any effect.'[5] The opinion however was not well founded, for James was determined to try conclusions with those unruly subjects who owned not his authority. In 1530 the king approached the Border and hanged a number of the Armstrongs, including their famous leader, Johnie of Gilnochie, who had been betrayed into his hand. The merciless execution of the chieftain and 'threty sax o' his cumpanie' produced a deep impression on the minds of the commonalty of the district, and became a fruitful subject for celebration in the ballad and dramatic poetry of the sixteenth century.[6]

The people of Cumberland joined in the resistance of the northern counties to the ecclesiastical policy of Henry VIII. when he had entered on the suppression of the monasteries. Disaffection was imported from Yorkshire, and the agents of Robert Aske and Lord Darcy, the northern leaders, were busy in fomenting discontent and urging the commonalty to strike a blow on behalf of the ejected monks. The local symptoms

---

[1] Cotton MS. Calig. B. vi. f. 409. [3] Ibid. iii. f. 115.
[2] Ibid. i. f. 296. [4] Ibid. vii. f. 212.
[5] L. & P. of Henry VIII. iv. 5055.
[6] Mr. Bruce Armstrong has collected much information about this notorious freebooter from Scottish chronicles and Border ballads, as little about his capture and execution can be gleaned from the public records (Hist. of Liddesdale, 273-80).

of insurrection were first observable in Westmorland, when the parishioners of Kirkbystephen and Brough under Stainmore mustered on Sanford Moor on 16 October 1536 in response to the rising in Richmondshire and Durham. The commons, as the insurgents were called, chose as their leaders Robert Pullayn, Nicholas Musgrave, Christopher Blenkinsopp and Robert Hilton, who undertook the task of swearing the people to be true to God, the church, the king and the commonwealth. Dividing themselves into two bands, Musgrave at the head of one party marched down one side of the Eden towards Penrith, and Pullayn with his company went down the other. In vain did they search for the gentry dwelling on either side. Sir Thomas Wharton, Mr. Warcop of Lammerside Hall, and Sir John Lowther had fled; but they succeeded in catching Mr. Dudley and others at Eamont Bridge. In a few days the insurrection was general. Penrith became the rallying point for the rebellious commons of the eastern part of the county. After a tumultuous meeting on Penrith Fell, the captains of that place, Anthony Hutton, John Beck, Gilbert Whelpdale and Thomas Birbeck, who received the names of Charity, Faith, Poverty and Pity, sent messengers to Edenhall and compelled Sir Edward Musgrave to take the oath. Parties were scattered in all directions to fan the flame of rebellion. The commons of Caldbeck rose on 23 October and brought Chancellor Towneley, their rector, with them to a meeting at Cartloganthorne, where they were joined by the commons of Greystoke, Skelton, Castlesowerby, and the townships beyond Eden. Robert Thomson, vicar of Brough under Stainmore, who was regarded as a prophet by the insurgents, took novel measures to overcome the unwillingness of the parochial clergy to espouse his cause. At the assemblage on Kylwatlynhow, he ordered the crier to proclaim that if Parsons Towneley and Threlkeld and others refused to join the commons ' they shuld stryke off owr heydes and set my heyd (Towneley's) on the heyst playce within the diocese.' It was necessary, he argued, that the commons should be supplied with a staff of able chaplains to instruct them in the faith. At the daily mass in Penrith church, where the four captains followed him in procession through the aisles with drawn swords, this singular man expounded one by one the ten commandments and declared ' that the brekyng of these comaundementes was the cause of all that grete troble.' In the western division of the county the centre of the insurrection was at Cockermouth, to which Thomson and twenty followers repaired for a meeting to be held on Moota Hill. Thither came the abbot of Holmcultram with the tenants of his lordship. Repeated messages were sent to Carlisle, but that city remained loyal to the king under the guardianship of Sir Thomas Clifford, bastard son of the Earl of Cumberland. Great anxiety was felt for its safety when the insurgents to the number of 15,000 men assembled on 3 November at Burford Oak on Broadfield, about seven miles from the city, but by the intervention of Sir Christopher Dacre they were dissuaded from besieging it. There were rumours that the king desired to conciliate the people, and that proclamation to that effect had been made on the previous day. In the proclamation it was stated that all offences committed before 1 November 1536 should be forgiven on condition that the rebels gave up their leaders, returned to their homes, and made submission before the Duke of Norfolk, whom the king intended to send into these parts as his lieutenant-general. In the absence of the vicar of Brough, some or the leaders joined with Dacre in advising the commons 'to recule and go home every man to his howsse and to rest ther without any fforder insurrection untill siche tyme as the kynges plesure wer forder knowen.' Sir Christopher Dacre undertook to act as mediator between them and the mayor and captain of Carlisle, and gave them pledges that 'no man shuld be stopyd from Carlill to sell ther stuff in the merkett,' and that 'the sawgers of the lorde Clifforthe shuld not ride on the commens.[1] The notable feature of the first insurrection in Cumberland was the entire absence of men of position from the movement. The rabble had no capable leaders. Even the parish clergy held aloof. It was but a feeble performance from first to last. As the people returned to their homes sullen and discontented, the Border men of Esk and Line and 'the black quarters' offered to harry the two counties in revenge, but they were restrained by Sir Thomas Clifford.[2]

Though the suppression of the monasteries was the ostensible cause of the rebellion, motives of a more selfish nature were at the bottom of the political unrest in Cumberland. It cannot be denied that agrarian grievances contributed much to the exasperation of the people against their rulers. When the people had dispersed to their homes they pulled down enclosures, took possession of tithe-barns, broke the heads of bailiffs and threatened the landlords with penalties unless their demands were granted. The Earl of Cumberland told the king on 12 January 1537 that the people were so wild there was danger of a further rebellion.[3] On Saturday, 13 January, Robert Wetlay and Parson Wodall, agents of Dr. Leigh, one of the commissioners for the suppression, were taken at Muncaster and brought to Egremont and afterwards to Cockermouth, barely escaping with their lives. A few days later the commons spoiled all the tithe barns on the west side of the Derwent.[4] The fire of a second insurrection was smouldering, and needed only a spark to burst into flame. A pretext was not long delayed. On Monday, 12 February, Sir Thomas Clifford went to Kirkbystephen to arrest two of the ringleaders of the first insurrection, who had taken refuge in the

---

[1] The details of the progress of the first insurrection are fully stated by Chancellor Towneley and the vicar of Brough in their examinations before Tregonwell, Layton and Leigh 'in the Towre of London' on 20 March 1537 (*L. & P. of Henry VIII.* xii. [i.], 687 [1–2]). These depositions with other documents of this period have been printed by the present writer in *The Monasteries of Cumberland and Westmorland* (Carl. Scient. Soc.), 25–94.

[2] *L. & P. of Henry VIII.* xi. 993.

[3] Ibid. xii. (1), 18, 71. In the opinion of the Duke of Norfolk, expressed to Cromwell on 21 February, 1537, agrarian grievances were the chief cause of the rebellion in Cumberland and Westmorland (ibid. xii [1], 478).

[4] Ibid. 185.

steeple of the church. His horsemen, composed in great part of 'strong thieves of the Westlands,' that is, of Esk and Line, began to spoil the town and roused the inhabitants to resistance. A skirmish ensued, and Sir Thomas was defeated and forced to retire to Brougham Castle.[1] The rout of the king's forces was the signal for a general rising. Under the command of Nicholas Musgrave and Thomas Tibbee, the heroes of Kirkbystephen steeple, a force of 4,000 or 5,000 men marched to Penrith and Greystoke, where they were joined by other contingents, and 'mayd a sawtt at Carlill the fryday next afor the fryst sowndey of Lent,' 16 February 1537. The 'a sawtt' of Carlisle was vigorously repulsed by Sir Christopher Dacre, who fell upon the rebels, scattered them, and took 700 or 800 prisoners. Sir Thomas Clifford atoned for his imprudence at Kirkbystephen by bursting out of the city and following the chase at least twelve miles. The Duke of Norfolk was hastening to the relief of Carlisle, but when he arrived on 19 February nothing was left for him to do but to execute the prisoners.[2]

When the news of the overthrow of the rebels reached the king, he was profuse in his thanks to Dacre and Clifford for their acceptable services. The day had come for exacting retribution on those misguided men who had dared to question his proceedings. To the Duke of Norfolk he sent the following merciless instructions, which show the fury into which he was thrown by the rebellion :—

> We doo ryght well approve and allowe your procedinges in the displayng of our baner : and forasmoche as the same is now spredde and displayed, by reason wherof, tyll the same shalbe closed again, the cours of our lawes must geve place to th'ordenaunces and estatutes marciall : our pleasure is, that, before you shall close upp our said baner again, you shal in any wise cause suche dredfull execution to be doon upon a good nombre of th' inhabitauntes of every towne, village and hamlet, that have offended in this rebellion as well by the hanging of them uppe in trees, as by the quartering of them, and the setting of their heddes and quarters in every towne, greate and small, and in al suche other places, as they may be a ferefull spectacle to all other herafter, that wold practise any like mater : whiche we requyre you to doo, without pitie or respect according to our former letters.'[3]

In obedience to the terms of this commission the work of execution began. Out of 6,000 prisoners seventy-four were chosen as principal offenders and judged to suffer death, the king's banner being displayed. Had the duke attempted trial by jury, not a fifth man of them, he thought, would have suffered. As iron was marvellously scarce in Cumberland, it was necessary that some of the prisoners should be despatched by ropes only ; twelve however would be hanged in chains in Carlisle, and as many more as chains could be made for in their native villages.[4] Chancellor Towneley and the vicar of

---

[1] *L. & P. of Hen. VIII.* xii. (i.), 419, 439. [2] Ibid. xii. (i.), 448, 468.

[3] Ibid. xii. (i.), 479 ; *Priory of Hexham* (Surtees Soc.), i. pp. cl.–cliii.

[4] Of the seventy-four victims executed, twenty-one were Cumberland men from the districts of Penrith and Cockermouth, the value of their forfeited goods being estimated by Sir Thomas Wharton at only 100 marks, and the goods of the Westmorland men at 300 marks (*L. & P. of Hen. VIII.* xii. [i.], 498, 641). The bodies were left to hang in their respective villages in the sight of their families and friends, no one being allowed to take them down. The wives and daughters of some of the rebels took the bodies

Brough were sent to London for examination, as Norfolk was doubtful about their guilt.

The results of these insurrections had a tendency to aggravate the differences that existed between Henry VIII. and James V. Many of the 'rebellis and brokin men,' 'grey freris, uther doctouris, and religious men' took refuge beyond the Border and were there 'resett wythin the reaulme of Scotland,' to the great indignation of the English king.[1] The death of his sister, Queen Margaret, in 1541 removed an influence that served to maintain peaceful relations between the two kings. James was unable to approve of his uncle's attacks on the church, and the two countries gradually drifted into a renewal of war. In the autumn of 1542 the Duke of Norfolk was commissioned to enter Scotland from the eastern side. King James proceeded at once to organize a counter attack against the West March, the main brunt of which was to fall on Carlisle. The Scottish army of about 14,000 men left Lochmaban on 24 November, but without a responsible leader, James himself coming no nearer to the scene of conflict than ' a hill caulid Burnswarke,' whose square-topped height overlooks the district from Burdoswald to the Solway, from whence he witnessed the complete overthrow of his forces. As the army crossed the Esk, the smoke of the burning houses of the Grahams[2] soon made the presence of the invaders known and roused the garrison of Carlisle who had been already forewarned. Rapidly gathering together what gentlemen and borderers he could find, Sir Thomas Wharton, captain of the castle, despatched them across the Line under the leadership of Sir Thomas Dacre, a natural son of Lord Thomas and founder of the Dacres of Lanercost, and Jack Musgrave, the captain of Bewcastle. The Scottish troops, retiring upon 'Arthureth tower,' were quickly dislodged and forced across the Esk 'at a strate ford which is called Sandyforde.' Beyond this was the Solway Moss, from which the disastrous day was to take its name, lying between the Esk and Sark, in the bogs of which those who had escaped drowning or capture soon lay at the mercy of their pursuers. Never before had there been a more pitiful defeat. Fourteen

and buried them in churchyards by night or in ditches, the priests refusing burial. In order to pacify the king's wrath at this new offence, inquiries were held at Carlisle, Penrith and Cockermouth, to ascertain the names of the culprits and the circumstances of the crime. The depositions of these wretched wives, mothers and daughters who cut down or gathered up the decaying remains and buried them in secret, in some cases ' with the chynes about them,' furnish one of the most gruesome episodes on record. One instance may be given. Richard Cragg's wife deposed ' that she knowyth not of hys lowsyng furthe of the chyne, but she sayth that she brought hym home upon a carre and had with hyr Jenet Harres, wedow, and Jenet Newcom of Egyllsfelde, and the prest wolde not suffer hym to be bureyd, and so in the nyght she bureyd hym in a dyke as she says ; she further stated 'yt a cosyn of hys afterward died of the corruption of hyr husband and takyn hym down' (ibid. xii. [i.], 1214, 1246).

[1] *Hamilton Papers* (Scot. Rec. Pub.), i. 41, 84.

[2] The Grahams of Esk supported the king against the rebellious commons in 1536-7. The Duke of Norfolk wrote on 16 May 1537, that the ' fowre bretherne of the Greymes ' were ' the furst that did set uppon the Kinges highnes rebelles at th'assault of Carliell ' and ' the furst that ever brake spere uppon any of the commons after th'assault ' (*L. & P. of Hen. VIII.* xii. [i.], 1215). In a curious petition to the king from Arthur Graham and his brethren for reward, their valiant deeds are picturesquely described, the most notable of which was that they had taken seven score prisoners during the rout of the rebels in 1537, ' and I the forsaid Arthur Grame toke one of the chief capteyns named Thomas Tebold,' the notorious leader of the Westmorland insurgents (ibid. xii. [i.], 1217 [1]).

thousand men were completely vanquished by less than three thousand. It was a rout rather than a battle. Two earls, five barons, and some thousands of men were taken prisoners, and the fugitives who escaped had to face the tender mercies of the men of Liddesdale, 'who spoyled them of all their arrayment and because they shuld the more spedely flye, they toke also their botes from them.'[1] There was great jubilation in London at the entry of some of the prisoners on 19 December, for which occasion it was ' provided that every off the sayde Scottisshe prisoners sholde have att theyre entre, for a knowlege, a redde Saynt Androwes crosse.'[2]

The victory of Solway Moss, followed so soon by the death of James V., roused Henry VIII. to pursue a vigorous policy on the Border. The wardens of the marches were urged to harass the enemy on every opportunity.[3] The king was assured that it was within his power to lay hands ' on as much of Scotland as is on this side the Firth on the east side, and as much as is on this side Dumbarton on the west side,' and that there would be no peace ' untill your highness hath set your marches to the limits aforesaid.' ' Oh,' the letter continued, 'what a godly act should it be to bring such a sort of people to the knowledge of God's laws, the country so necessary to your dominions, by reason of which so many souls should live in quietness.'[4] The released prisoners from Solway Moss returned to Scotland bound by pledges to further English interests in that country. There was a general forward movement. The wild spirits on the Border, inured to fray and foray, plunged into the struggle with such zest that the record of their depredations in the shire of Dumfries and the adjacent districts forms a dreadful catalogue of burning and pillage which has few equals in the annals of predatory war. In 1547, when Edward VI. succeeded his father, English rule prevailed throughout the greater part of Dumfriesshire. The conflict was continued with unabated vigour by William, Lord Dacre, who had succeeded Lord Wharton in the wardeny. But the long struggle, carried on with such barbarity, was fast bringing the belligerents to a state of exhaustion. On the fall of the Protector Somerset new counsels prevailed

---

[1] *Hamilton Papers* (Scot. Rec. Pub.), i. pp. lxxxiii.-lxxxvi., 307-8, 317-9. The number of Scots routed at Solway Moss has been variously estimated by those who took part in the battle. Sir Thomas Wharton, fresh from the conflict and eager to magnify his victory, estimated the Scots at 14,000, though some said 20,000. After diligent inquiry Lord Lisle reported to King Henry that there were 17,000 at least. The English forces were variously estimated from 2,000 to 3,000. It was said that 5,000 horses were captured, as the Scots fled towards the moss through which horses could not pass. The Scottish army ' had fowre fawconnettes of brasse, twolfe bases two upon every carte, and three half bases uppon one carte, havyng aboue thirtye standertis besides flaggis.' The battle was decided between ' Akeshaw-hill ' and ' Howpsikehill,' in the region in which Longtown is now situated. ' Ten men was drawyn with fisher nettes furthe of Heske thre daies after.'

[2] *Acts of P.C.* (new ser.), i. 63. The prisoners were lodged in the Tower for a short time, from whence they were brought to the Star Chamber, ' by two and two together in new gowns of black damask and other apparell sutable' at the king's cost, to be admonished for their offences by the Lord Chancellor before their liberation (Herbert, *Life of Hen. VIII.* pp. 485-6). Twenty of the Solway prisoners were selected to be sent to London (*Hamilton Papers* [Scot. Rec. Pub.], i. 326).

[3] As early as 1532, Henry instructed Lord Dacre to tamper with the men of Liddesdale and that region in order to ' annoye the King of Scottis ' (*Hamilton Papers* [Scot. Rec. Pub.], i. 6).

[4] Ibid. i. 331.

under the influence of Dudley, who worked for peace between the two countries. A truce was arranged on 20 March 1549–50 in the church of Norham, which formed the basis of an international settlement,[1] and subsequently led to the division of the Debatable Land. The stringency of the regulations re-established[2] in 1552 for watch and ward on the northern frontier of Cumberland, and the number of men employed by day and night in carrying out this territorial system of self-defence, show the insecurity which prevailed in the county at this period. Each township had its own organization of watchers who perambulated in assigned places, and the principal men of the district acted as overseers to set the watch and report on its regularity. Every man was obliged to rise and follow the fray upon the sound of horn, shout or outcry upon pain of death.[3] Under this police system a great advance was made for the pacification and government of the Border district.

The turn in Scottish affairs, which sent Mary, the ill-fated daughter of James V., across the Solway after her disastrous defeat at Langside, was full of evil consequences to Cumberland. Landing at Workington on 16 May 1568, she was met next day by Richard Lowther, deputy warden of the march, and conveyed to Carlisle Castle. The Earl of Northumberland, on the plea that she had landed within his liberty of Cockermouth, endeavoured without success to remove her from Lowther's hands.[4] The weeks the Queen of Scots spent at Carlisle were some of the most anxious that her troubled life had seen. She had appealed to Elizabeth, but knew not what would be the answer. Friends crowded round her, and she was soon the centre of a little court. From the walls of her prison she could see the blue hills of her native land. It would be easy to signal to her friends and not difficult to escape in the course of some of the excursions she was at first allowed to make. Sir Francis Knollys, writing on 15 June, says :—

> Yesterday her Grace went out at a postern to walk on a playing-green towards Scotland : and we with twenty-four halberders of master Read's band, with divers gentlemen and other servants, waited on her. Where about twenty of her retinue played at football before her the space of two hours very strongly, nimbly and skilfully, without any foul play offered, the smallness of their balls occasioning their fairplay. And before yesterday since our coming she went but twice out of the town : once to

[1] *Leges Marchitarum,* 77–98.
[2] It is a mistake to suppose that the system of watch and ward originated in 1552. In the Court Rolls of the manor of Dalston for 1496–7 provision is made for the watching of the manor on the lines adopted in 1552. One clause of the regulations then in force will serve as an illustration : 'Hawksdale ; Willim Nicson [and] Willim Holme schall begyn the wach with dayly light att evyn and schall come to Thomas Louthre house thare to tak ye wach ; so to remayne to light of the morne and thare gif over thare wach at thare departyn : and they schall kepe wach from the said Thomas house on to the entend beyonde Will Nicson hous : and the said Th : Louthre schall presentt every defaltt onwith upon the morne to the bailyay of the Roos ; and the said Th : schall hire a wachman and gif hym iiij[d] when so ever eny defalt is mad att evyn in takyng of eny manner wach. Ric. Thomlynson [and] Th : Bullok schall begyn thar wach for the tothar parte of the said town and take itt and kepe itt as is afore said in every parte.' The tenants were obliged to watch in couples nightly.
[3] These very interesting regulations, with the names of watches, divisions of districts, and other matters explanatory of the whole system of defence, have been embodied by Bp. Nicolson in *Leges Marchiarum,* 206–28.
[4] *Cal. of State Papers relating to Scotland,* 1509–1603, ii. 853–5, 873.

MAP OF CASTLES AND FORTRESSES

Victoria History of Cumberland.

Bewcastle

LIDDEL
Askerton

Towers of
the Grahams
Tryermain

Rocliffe   Scaleby
Over Denton

Bowness
Burgh by Sands
Naworth

Drumburgh
Linstock

Arlosh
CARLISLE

Rose

Wolsty
Highhead

Harby

Kirkoswald
Melmerby

Edenhall

COCKERMOUTH
Greystoke
Penrith

Wythop
Dacre

Workington
Dunmalloght

Hayes

EGREMONT

Millom

REFERENCE

● Castles in the 12th. Century

■ Castles, Peels, Fortified Houses,
and Churches, in the 14th. Century.

▲ Castles, Peels, Fortified Houses
and Churches, in the 16th. Century.

SCALE OF MILES
10   5   0   10

William Stanford & Co. Ltd.,   Oxford

the light play of football in the same place: and once rode a-hunting the hare, she galoping as fast upon every occasion and her whole retinue being so well horsed, that we upon experience thereof, doubting that upon a set course some of her friends out of Scotland might invade and assault us upon the sudden to rescue and take her from us, we mean hereafter, if any Scottish riding pastimes be required that way, so much to fear the endangering of her person by some sudden invasion of her enemies that she must hold us excused in that behalf.[1]

The dangers surrounding her presence at Carlisle were obvious.[2] On 13 July she was removed to Bolton Castle, the residence of Lord Scrope, the warden of the Western March. The intrigues which gathered round her were dangerous to the peace of the county. The Earl of Northumberland, who soon raised the standard of rebellion, had a vast territorial influence in the district, and many of the country gentlemen sympathized with his plans on behalf of the exiled queen. Though there were few acts of treason committed in Cumberland in connection with the rebellion of the earls in 1569, public feeling was in a heated condition and a source of anxiety.[3] When the danger passed, a fresh trouble arose in which one of the most powerful families in the county was to play a principal part.

Thomas, Lord Dacre, at his death in 1566 had left an infant son George, who was killed in 1569 by a fall from his vaulting-horse at Thetford. The estates passed to his three sisters as co-heiresses. But Leonard Dacre, their uncle, who was next heir male, 'stomached it much,' as Camden said, 'that so goodly an inheritance descended by law to his nieces.'[4] Their mother, after Thomas, Lord Dacre's death, had married the Duke of Norfolk, who eventually became guardian of her daughters;[5] and Leonard Dacre proceeded to attempt by intrigue what he was likely to lose at law. It was a dangerous game, but he played it with the art of a master. He plunged headlong into the proposal for the marriage of the Scottish queen with the duke. Whilst courting the patronage of Elizabeth, he was deeply implicated in the treasonable schemes against her. He encouraged the Earls of Northumberland and Westmorland to rebellion, and at the same time offered his services for its suppression.[6] After the flight of the earls, he fortified Naworth and held it with a force of 3,000 men on the pretence of an expected invasion from Scotland.

1 Cotton MS. Calig. B. ix. 291.
2 S.P. Dom. Eliz. Add. xiv. 17. It was suspected that the affray in Carlisle Cathedral in August 1568 was connected with her cause (ibid. xiv. 22 [1–9]).
3 Lord Scrope informed Sir William Cecil, on 30 November 1569, that Cumberland stood in great peril for a few days, and very likely would have entered into rebellion, by means of some tenants and agents of the Earl of Northumberland, had not great care been exercised on his part to prevent it (S.P. Dom. Eliz. Add. xv. 56). The earl's tenants in the lordship of Cockermouth were capable of mustering a force of 1,200 men (ibid. xv. 76 [i.]). The Bishop of Carlisle made a long declaration about a conspiracy to kill him and take Carlisle Castle, of which he had charge during the temporary absence of Lord Scrope (ibid. xv. 89–90).
4 Hist. of Elizabeth, p. 136.
5 For the story of the litigation over the Dacre estates, see the account written by Lord William Howard, one of the duke's sons, who married Lady Elizabeth Dacre, one of the co-heiresses (Household Books of Lord W. Howard [Surtees Soc.], 365–93). On Leonard's title to the barony of Dacre, the note of objections and answers in S.P. Dom. Eliz. Add. xviii. 11 (v.) may be consulted.
6 Ibid. xiv. 104.

But the English queen was not deceived by his political manœuvres. Peremptory orders were sent to Lord Hunsdon, her lieutenant in the north, to arrest ' that cankred suttill traitor, Leonard Dacres,' as she afterwards called him.[1] He was summoned to Carlisle on the plea of holding a consultation on the state of the country. With skilful diplomacy he pleaded the state of his health as an excuse, and in turn asked Lord Scrope to dine with him in his chamber.[2] Lord Hunsdon, disregarding the warning of Scrope as to the popularity of the Dacres and the impossibility of getting Cumberland men to act against any of them,[3] determined to advance with what troops he could collect. After a night march from Hexham, he came before Naworth at daybreak on the morning of 20 February 1570 ; the beacons had been burning all night and every hill was full of horse and foot, crying and shouting as if they had been mad. As the castle was well furnished with ordnance, men and munition, Lord Hunsdon thought it more prudent to evade an encounter till he joined forces with Lord Scrope at Carlisle. Dacre, however, had no intention of allowing him to escape. He pursued him for four miles, and fell upon him with vigour in a heath as he was preparing to cross the river Gelt, not far from the cliff on which are found the letters which

the vexillary

Hath left crag carven o'er the streaming Gelt.

The onslaught of Dacre's tenants on the royal forces was terrific. In his report of the skirmish[4] Hunsdon told the queen that ' hys footmen gave the prowdyst charge on my shott that I ever saw.' Leaving Sir John Forster with 500 horse to protect his rear, Lord Hunsdon charged with the rest of his cavalry, slew between 300 and 400, and took between 200 and 300 prisoners. On the following day Dacre was proclaimed a traitor,[5] his castles of Naworth, Rocliffe, Greystoke and Kirkoswald were seized, and a great part of his force, who had been induced to rebel in defence of what they conceived to be the rights of their feudal superior, surrendered and submitted themselves to the queen's mercy.[6]

Scottish affairs continued to dominate the political fortunes of Cumberland. To meet any emergency that might arise on the western frontier, steps were taken to inquire into the military levies of the county and the condition of its defences. The names of the well-

---

[1] *S.P. Dom. Eliz. Add.* xvii. 112.

[2] His letter has been printed by Sharpe (*Mem. of Rebellion*, etc., 217).

[3] *S.P. Dom. Eliz. Add.* xvii. 56, 67 (i.).

[4] Sir John Forster gave a graphic description of the encounter to Sir William Cecil (Cotton MS. Calig. C. 1, 384), which has been printed by Sharpe (*Memorials of the Rebellion*, 221–2).

[5] In the proclamation of Lord Scrope, Dacre was accused of levying the queen's subjects in Gillesland by firing and burning the beacons on pretence of an invasion by the Scots, and other enormities. To avoid deception in future, the lieges were ordered, upon the burning of the beacons, to repair to none save to the beacon of the castle of Carlisle (*S.P. Dom. Eliz. Add.* xvii. 108 [i.]).

[6] Leonard Dacre fled to Scotland and afterwards to Flanders, where he died on 12 August 1573 as a pensioner of the King of Spain. One of the English spies reported in 1575 that he was buried in the church of St. Nicolas, Brussels, with an epitaph representing him as exiled for the sake of his religion (*S.P. Dom. Eliz.* cv. 10 ; *Douay Diaries*, i. 298–9).

affected gentlemen were carefully tabulated and distinguished from those in whom confidence could not be placed. Special attention was given to the musters of horse and foot with the view of ascertaining the force that could be put in the field. When preparations like these were taken in hand in 1580 by Lord Scrope as warden of the West March, it was found that there were 520 light horsemen within his wardenry besides gentlemen and their household servants to the number of 200. The musters of footmen were taken according to the division of the county into wards, the total in 1581 for the wards of Eskdale, Leath, Allerdale-below-Derwent and Cumberland being estimated at over 6,000 men, in which returns ' is sett downe everie man as furnyshede at his daye.' The equipment consisted of jacks, steel caps, spears, lances or bows, but it cannot be said that there was a plentiful supply of such weapons. In a few instances there is a gun ; while one adventurous man, Richard Atkinson of Cumwhitton, whose name may be handed down, was prepared to do battle ' with a piche forke.'[1] The survey of the fortresses made by Christopher Dacre in 1580, showing the condition of their armaments and recommending repairs, is of the greatest interest. The frontier was studded with a chain of castles besides peels and strongholds of lesser note.[2] Some thought these strongholds insufficient to guard the western frontier, and at the height of the panic a proposal was made to call into use the crumbling ruins of the Roman wall. It might either be restored, or a similar barrier erected, at a cost, it was reckoned, of some thirty thousand pounds.[3] The preparations to resist invasion were not altogether valueless after the scare had passed away. There was much to test the ability of the local authorities in protecting life and property on the Border. Petty acts of wrong-doing were on the increase ; no man's dwelling was secure from attack ; the days of moss-trooping as an organized system of robbery had begun. Pictures of forays at this period through 'Solway Sands, through Tarras Moss,' so familiar to the readers of Sir Walter Scott,[4]

[1] *Border Papers* (Scot. Rec. Pub.), i. 37–62.

[2] Bewcastle, three miles from Scotland, a place of great strength ; Askerton Tower, two miles south by west from Bewcastle and six miles from Scotland ; Rocliffe Castle, two miles from Scotland and three miles from Carlisle ; Carlisle Castle, a place of great respect : the Citadel of Carlisle, a fortress or bulwark for the defence of the city, about a quarter of a mile to the south of the castle ; Drumburgh, neither castle nor tower, but a house of convenient strength and defence, about six miles west and by north from Carlisle Castle and two miles from Scotland, a very fit place of defence for that part of the Border ; Bowness Tower, belonging to the parsonage, four miles west and by north from Drumburgh, adjoining a sea creek which divides the English and Scottish borders, very necessary for defence, partly decayed, a new platform for ordnance required ; Wolsty Castle, about seven miles west and by south from Bowness Tower and a quarter of a mile from the sea creek, ' and about 4 houres boting over the said crick to Scotland ' ; the castles of Cockermouth, Greystoke, Penrith, Kirkoswald, Naworth and Triermain. It was recommended that two new fortresses should be built on the ring of the Border, between Wolsty and Rocliffe (ibid. i. 32 ; *S.P. Dom. Eliz. Add.* xxvii. 44 [i.–iii.], xxxii. 70 [ii.]. The rough outline of the defences of the West Border in the Cotton Manuscript [Calig. B. viii. 239] probably belongs to this period. The date must be subsequent to the division of the Debatable Land in 1552, for the Scotch Dyke is traced on the 'Plott.' On the English portion of the district between Esk and Sark, south of the dyke, there are five towers, and between Line and Esk nine towers : with the remark that 'all these little stone houses or towers ar betwene Serk and Eske and betwene Eske and Leven and belong the Greyms.'

[3] *Border Papers* (Scot. Rec. Pub.), i. 300–2.

[4] For instance, see *Lay of the Last Minstrel*, i. 21.

are not overdrawn. In spite of all the efforts of statesmen, the inhabitants of these districts were known as ' the bad Borderers.'

It is to the period under review that the famous episode of Kinmont Willie belongs. This noted freebooter, whose name is so familiar in the complaints presented to the march courts, had been arrested by the Musgraves in 1596 while in attendance at the court of Kershope, and handed over to Mr. Salkeld, who immured him in the castle of Carlisle. The legality of his arrest seems doubtful, and the explanations of his captors read a little like accusations against themselves. In the opinion of Lord Scrope there could be no question of the legality if the attestation of the witnesses was true. Other reasons for detaining him were his notorious enmity to the warden's office and the many outrages lately done by his followers.[1] In a later despatch he added that men of experience in Border causes regarded him as a lawful prisoner, if a Scotsman ' in time of peace' may be so.[2] The bold Buccleuch, however, took the law into his own hands and made his ' proude attempt' against her Majesty's castle of Carlisle, ' the chiefest fortresse in these partes.' On 14 April 1596 the Scots, with ' 500 horsemen of Buclughes and Kinmontes frendes, did come armed and appointed with gavlockes and crowes of iron, handpeckes, axes and skailinge lathers, unto an owtewarde corner of the base courte of this castell, and to the posterne dore of the same : which they undermyned speedily and quietlye and made themselves possessores of the base courte, brake into the chamber where Will of Kinmont was, carried him awaye, and in their discoverie by the watch lefte for deade two of the watchmen, hurte a servante of myne, one of Kynmontes keperes, and were issued againe oute of the posterne before they were descried by the watche of the innerwarde, and ere resistance coulde be made.' The guard, Scrope continued, by reason of the stormy night, were either asleep or had taken shelter from the violence of the weather, by which means the Scots achieved the enterprise with little difficulty.[3] Great was the rejoicing of the deliverers and deep was the annoyance of Lord Scrope. Queen Elizabeth was not less incensed at the outrage offered to her representative. Sir William Bowes, her agent at the court of James, was instructed to bring the matter before the king, and to declare that peace could be no longer maintained unless Buccleuch was handed over to answer for his offence. In the end, after long negotiations, he was induced to surrender himself in October 1597 to the queen's commissioner at Berwick,[4] where he remained until the beginning of the following year. He was then released, leaving his son, a lad of ten years, to answer for the pledges he had given of good behaviour.[5] In 1599 the queen gave him leave to reside abroad, and it was probably on this occasion that she used the words so often quoted that ' with ten thousand of

---

[1] *Border Papers* (Scot. Rec. Pub.), ii. 114-5. The attestation of the Musgraves will be found in *Cal. of Salisbury MSS.* (Hist. MSS. Com.), vi. 84-5.
[2] *Border Papers* (Scot. Rec. Pub.), ii. 171. [3] Ibid. ii. 120-2.
[4] Ibid. ii. 416-9. [5] Ibid. ii. 516-7.

such men our brother of Scotland might shake the firmest throne in Europe.' Buccleuch always asserted, and in this he was supported by Scrope, that he was, assisted in his exploit by the Grahams, and that he could have done nothing without their co-operation,[1] naming more especially Francis Graham of Canonby and Walter of Netherby, the chief leaders of that clan. The Grahams at that time were a constant thorn in the side of Lord Scrope. In 1596 he proposed that a 'straight' letter should be addressed to him by the Privy Council, commanding him to send up some of them, whose names he specified, without letting them know the cause beforehand, and on their appearance to commit them to prison. He added that he would amply justify the step, and that it would greatly contribute to the common benefit and peace of the district.[2] But the family was too powerful and its position too assured to be thus summarily dealt with. Scrope's language about them was vigorous ; he called them ' caterpillars,' ' a viperous generation,' ' malignant humours,' and such like terms.[3] The northern authorities seem to have been of Lord Scrope's opinion, for in 1600 the gentlemen of the county presented a petition to the Council, in which they affirmed that the Grahams, their clan and children, were the chief causes of the decay of the country,[4] and in 1606 the English commissioners informed the Earl of Salisbury that the people of Cumberland abhorred and feared the name of Graham.[5] There was wisdom in the advice tendered to Cecil that they ought not to be lost if they could be kept on reasonable terms. Elizabeth, who took a personal interest in the affairs of the Border, refused her sanction to extreme measures, to Lord Scrope's great annoyance.

Carlisle was at this time the meeting place of a commission appointed to consider the grievances under which the Border suffered and to suggest a remedy. It was composed of delegates, representative of both countries, who drew up an agreement called the Treaty of Carlisle. The principal recommendations were that good ministers should be planted in every Border church, to inform the lawless people of their duty and to watch over their manners ; no warden or keeper should ride in hostile manner in the opposite realm without special command under royal hand and seal ; no borderer should keep about him idle persons such as remain in village alehouses ; Border councils should be appointed to enrol all notorious thieves and to put them to death after the first conviction.[6] The Bishop of Durham, who was chairman of the commission, told Burghley on 2 June 1597, in justification of the severity of some of the articles of the treaty, that ' I have found by experience many years in these parts that levity does little good and severity no harm, and that however it prevailed elsewhere, fearful proceeding is no policy here.'[7] One of the chief grievances, the

[1] *Border Papers* (Scot. Rec. Pub.), ii. 367–8. [2] Ibid. ii. 120.
[3] Ibid. ii. 160, 486, etc. [4] Ibid. ii. 690–1.
[5] *Hist. MSS. Com. Rep.* (Muncaster MSS.), x. App. iv. 248.
[6] Nicolson, *Leges Marchiarum*, 149–69 ; *Border Papers* (Scot. Rec. Pub.), ii. 316–7.
[7] Ibid. ii. 332–4.

levying of blackmail, was dealt with by the Act of 43 Elizabeth, cap. 13. It recited that many persons residing in Cumberland, Northumberland, Westmorland and Durham were taken from their houses and carried away as prisoners and kept till they were redeemed with great ransoms; and that of late there had been many incursions, raids and spoiling of towns, villages and houses within the said counties, so that many had been forced to pay a certain rate of money, corn or cattle, commonly called blackmail,[1] to divers persons inhabiting near the borders. By this Act, which was not repealed till 7 and 8 George IV., the takers of blackmail were judged to be felons and punished with death without benefit of clergy. King James proceeded to the Border to consult for the due enforcement of the international agreements, and was met at Newby near Annan by Mr. Leigh, the deputy warden, and Mr. Aglionby, the mayor of Carlisle. The main object of James during the closing years of the century was to secure his accession to the English throne, and no doubt his interest in Border affairs was quickened by his desire ultimately to unite the two kingdoms and carry to a successful conclusion the policy at which Edward I. and Henry VIII. in earlier days had aimed.

The union of the two kingdoms under one monarch, though not accompanied by the union of the nations, prepared men's minds for that most desirable event. At the very outset of his reign King James was confronted with the old difficulties of the Border land, for while he was at Berwick on his way to London intelligence was brought of a destructive foray into Cumberland which reached as far as Penrith. Sir William Selby was at once despatched to the rescue at the head of a strong escort. Though the raiders fled in terror at his approach, some of them were captured and hanged, and many of their habitations were blown up and burnt.[2] For the speedy suppression of offenders and the restoration of law and order, the middle shires, as the borders were now called, were placed under the jurisdiction of a royal commission and governed as a Crown colony. The first meeting of the commissioners was held in Carlisle on 9 April 1605, when certain articles for their guidance were agreed upon, and Sir Wilfrid Lawson was elected convener. All persons living within the bounds of the commission or in certain other specified districts were forbidden the use of armour, weapons, and horses, 'savinge meane naggs for their tillage,' and the troublesome inhabitants should be removed to some other place 'where the change of aire will make in them an exchange of their manners.' The Grahams of Esk were the first to feel the inconvenience of the new regime. The commissioners were determined to root them out. Sir Wilfrid Lawson stated in 1605

---

[1] The local definition of blackmail is very curious. The Grahams defined it in 1596 as 'a protection money or a reward *pro clientela*'; it was called 'a defence' by those who received and 'a black maile' by those who paid it (*Border Papers*, ii. 143-4, 156, 163-4).

[2] Ridpath, *Border Hist.* p. 703, quoting Stowe, *Chron.* p. 819. The raid was made by the Grahams to the number of eighty, headed by Walter Graham of Netherby, who were persuaded that until James was a crowned king in England, the laws of the kingdom ceased and were of no force, and that all offences done in the meantime were not punishable (*Hist. MSS. Com. Rep.* [Muncaster MSS.], x. App. iv. 244).

that 'if the Grahams were not, these parts would be as free from blood and theft as Yorkshire.' No time was lost in arranging for their removal. One hundred and fifty of them were selected as 'fytt for his Majestee's service,' and transported to the cautionary towns of Flushing and Brill, the cost of their journey to Newcastle having been defrayed by the Exchequer. But the members of the clan who submitted voluntarily to expatriation were not contented in their new sphere. True to their traditions of lawlessness, they returned for the most part without leave ; some by desertion and others by passport, at which the king was highly offended and ordered their arrest and imprisonment till his pleasure was known. It was easier to give the order than to carry it out. The Grahams rode about in small companies with pistols and lances, and succeeded for a considerable time in eluding their pursuers. Sir Henry Leigh, provost marshal of Carlisle, was sent to reside at Netherby with fifteen horsemen, and Sir William Cranston with a like number at the Hollows Tower. Friction, however, arose between the commissioners, and Cranston was accused by Sir Wilfrid Lawson of showing undue leniency to the Grahams. The king wrote in February 1606 and demanded an explanation of the delay in proceeding against the 'runagates' from the cautionary towns. As soon as a resolute course was taken, the Grahams, not wishing to hazard their lives, submitted to transportation to Ireland. The commissioners were able to report to the Earl of Salisbury, on 13 September 1606, that the chief Grahams were sent to Workington[1] under the escort of the sheriff and John Musgrave's horsemen ; there were not then left between Line and Sark more than three Grahams of ability, of whom two were more than eighty years of age. All the notorious offenders, whose manner terrified peaceable men, had gone away : some of their wives, who could not go then, would follow in the spring. Although Esk, Sark and Line were purged of evil men, there remained others in Bewcastle and Gillesland fit to follow. The contributions made by the gentry and freeholders of the county towards the expenses of the transplantation did not meet with the approval of the central government. Though the contributions in Cumberland and Westmorland, varying in sums from £5 to 2s. 6d. amounted to over £400, a balance of £200 was still needed, and the council censured the backwardness of the northern gentry in offering money to make it up, and especially the conduct of Sir John Dalston, who refused on the bench in open court to contribute anything.

The expatriation of the Grahams did not reduce the district to peaceable government. There was 'that bloodie and theevish clanne of Armstrongs of Whithaughe in Liddesdale by whom and their allies many horrible spoils and cruell murthers have been committed,' and much dissatisfaction was expressed at the inertness of the commissioners. From the end of 1606 Lord William Howard of Naworth took

---

[1] They were conveyed to Dublin in six ships and sent to Connaught, the company consisting of 114 Grahams and 45 horses.

an active part in civilizing the late border, and seems to have regarded the employment as a pleasant pastime. Writing to Lawson on 9 January 1607 he says:

> I would have been very glad to have seen you in my poor house, but sorry that you should lose so much labour in this cold weather, and in such foul ways. I was away fishing, and I took as many as I could get. I was in hopes to have taken Anton's Edward himself, but, for want of a better, was glad to take his son Thomas Gifford, and Jock Sowlugs,[1] the last but not the least in villainy. I desire you to keep him for a jewel of high price. Pray cause the records to be searched. If you find matter sufficient to hang the other two, hould up your finger and they shall be delivered. I confess myself a southern novice.[2]

For a novice, however, he was successful in his expeditions, and it was in a great measure due to his efforts that the pacification of the district was carried out. In his advice to the king in 1615, he recommended firm government rather than transplantation as the best cure for the troubles of the middle shires. Lord William was a radical reformer of the best type: he suggested as a first step a change of governors. Of the commissioners Sir William Selby dwelt in Kent and Sir John Fenwick was a gentleman that aimed more at private life than public employment; Sir Wilfrid Lawson, who dwelt in the inmost part of Cumberland and was nearly eighty years of age, and Sir William Hutton, who was in poor health, were both learned and sufficient men, but altogether unable to serve in the field; John Musgrave, the provost marshal, had been a serving man, was of mean condition and weak estate, and in alliance and kinship with many surnames that had been heinous offenders, 'and some of them as yett no saintes.' Among his recommendations he gave prominence to the keeping and training of ' slue doggs ' for the purpose of hunting thieves and outlaws through the mosses and waste lands of the marches as the king formerly commanded.[3] In a short time this recommendation was put into practice. On 29 September 1616 the commissioners revived the old institution of setting watches in the dangerous districts and made provision for the keeping of ' slough dogs ' at the charge of the inhabitants.[4]

---

[1] The real name of this villain was John Armstrong, who was accused of divers murders, and especially of inhuman barbarity to a woman in the presence of Anton's Edward or Edward Armstrong, another villain, guilty of twelve murders. Almost everybody in Cumberland at this period had ' to-names ' or nicknames, from some peculiarity of person, dress, or belongings, some of them being reproachful or offensive, like Jock Sowlugs. The custom was inevitable among clans where many persons of the same name dwelt in one place. In the parish registers of the county the nicknames are often recorded in order to distinguish the marriage or burial of the right person.

[2] The above account of the pacification of Cumberland after the union of the Crowns is founded, unless otherwise stated, on the records of the northern commission in possession of Lord Muncaster and the Earl of Crawford and Balcarres, as reported in *Hist. MSS. Com. Rep.* x. App. iv. 229–73, and *Rep.* ii. App. pp. 181–2. The volume at Muncaster is supposed to have been written by Joseph Pennington, a member of the commission, and that at Dunecht appears to be the official record kept by Sir Wilfrid Lawson, as ' liber Wilf. Lawson ' is inscribed on the first page.

[3] *Household Books of Lord W. Howard* (Surtees Soc.), 417–20.

[4] These blood hounds, whose game was man, were disposed as follows : ' Imprimis, beyond Eske, by the inhabitants there to be kept above the foot of Sarke, one dogge : item, by the inhabitants the inside of Eske to Richmont's Clugh, to be kept at the Moate, one dogge : item, by the inhabitants of the parish of Arthered, above Richmont's Clugh, with the Bayliffe and Black quarter, to be kept at the Bayliehead, one dogge : item, Newcastle parish, besides the Baylie and Black quarters, to be kept at Tinkerhill, one

Lord William Howard had a difficult part to play, inasmuch as he was a recusant and could hold no official post under the Crown, but King James refused to notice the charge of recusancy [1] and employed his great local influence on the side of good government. As a successful hunter of moss troopers he has won undying renown. Speaking of those marauders, Fuller said : ' they had two great enemies, the laws of the land and the Lord William Howard of Naworth.' [2] His manifold activities spread such terror among the wrongdoers that it became a common belief in the county, which his enemies tried to use to his detriment, that ' ther is mercie with God but no mercie with my Lord Willyam.' [3] There is no need to accept the fanciful picture which Sir Walter Scott has left us of this famous chieftain. Stripped of all poetic glamour and judged by the dry light of authentic records, Lord William Howard stands out as the greatest figure of his time in the civilization of the marches, and though he sent many moss-troopers ' to that place where the officer always doth his work by daylight,' the regeneration of the county was effected by legal process without recourse to those summary methods which tradition has connected with his name. [4]

The union of the Crowns revived once more the old controversy on the nature of Border service. The tenants of Cumberland and Westmorland during the long period of Border warfare had held their lands on the condition of rendering military service when summoned by the warden of the Western Marches. The necessity of this obligation ceased with the Union. As this main incident of the tenure was no longer to be enforced, the baronial owners assumed that the rights of the tenants were also terminated and that the lands had reverted to themselves. It was a distressing period for the cornage tenants. Fortunately in the case of Lord William Howard, one of the most extensive landowners in the county, the dispute was amicably settled at an early period by the grant of long leases. [5]

The visit of King James to Carlisle in 1617 on his return from Scotland seems to have had little political significance. Bishop Snowden reminded him that the city was in great ruin and extreme poverty, and that in the country at large, many of the meaner sort lived dispersedly in cottages or little farms, scarcely sufficient for their necessary maintenance, whereby idleness, theft and robberies were

dogge : item, the parish of Stapylton, one dogge : item, the parish of Irdington, one dogge : item, the parishes of Lanercost and Walton, one dogge : item, Kirklington, Skaleby, Houghton, and Richarby, one dogge : item, Westlinton, Roucliff, Etterby, Stainton, Stanwix, and Cargo, to be kept at Roucliff, one dogge' (Nicolson and Burn, *Hist. of Cumb.* i. pp. cxxx.–cxxxi. ; *Hist. MSS. Com. Rep.* iii. App. p. 39).

[1] *Hist. MSS. Com. Rep.* (Rydal MSS.), xii. App. vii. 15.

[2] *Worthies of England* (ed. Jefferson), p. 5.

[3] S.P. Dom. James I. xl. 11, lxxxvi. 34. It was said in 1617 that Lord William Howard had gotten the greatest footing in the northern counties that ever any subject had, and that he could command a greater following there than the king himself (ibid. xcii. 17).

[4] It is scarcely necessary to direct attention to the Surtees Society edition (No. 68) of *Selections from the Household Books of Lord William Howard of Naworth Castle*, where Mr. Ornsby has collected many documents relating to the life and time of this remarkable nobleman.

[5] *Household Books of Lord W. Howard* (Surtees Soc.), 413, 425-7. On the early history of tenure by Border service, see *V.C.H. Cumb.* i. 321-7.

occasioned.[1] The citizens were more definite in their 'demand of his Majestic at hys being at Carlisle,' for they petitioned to have a nobleman to reside in Carlisle Castle as some compensation for the reduction of the garrison after the Union, to have one of the three sittings of York kept at Carlisle once in the year, no doubt to indulge their litigious propensities of which Bishop Snowden warned the king, and that he should be pleased for the honour of his name and posterity to create an university in that poor city.[2] After hearing a sermon from the bishop and taking leave of the civic dignitaries, James departed, and nothing further was heard of the requests of the citizens.[3]

The first symptom of the struggle which was to occupy the whole of the reign of Charles I. may be assigned to the king's letter to the Earl of Cumberland, on 17 September 1625, asking for the levy of a loan on privy seal. The justices of the peace made the common excuse of inability to pay, owing to the poverty of the county, and sent up a list of contributions, amounting to £320, which it was hoped would meet immediate necessities.[4] The aid of Lord William Howard was called in on account of the influence he was known to wield, as the earlier appeal had met with such scant response. In spite of the disinclination of the gentry of Cumberland to lend the king money, the county as a whole stood firm in its allegiance. The development of the disputes between him and his subjects and the resistance offered by Scotland to his policy in that country soon brought Carlisle into a position of the first importance.[5] For several years before the crisis came, there were signs of military activity everywhere : the trainbands of the county were mustered and drilled ; the magazines were replenished with gunpowder ; munitions of war were collected and stored ; the equipment of an army was in preparation, from the supply of field-pieces and pistols to the music to be beaten by the drummers.[6] The nobility and gentry were ordered in 1638 to be in readiness to repel the impending invasion of the Scots, and Sir Philip Musgrave was appointed colonel of the musters of the two counties with instructions to secure Carlisle.[7] Having left Carlisle in charge of Sir Francis Willoughby, Sir Philip took up his quarters at Scaleby Castle with 100 men of his own company and sent a like number to hold Bewcastle. Wentworth urged the king in May 1639 to increase the garrison of Carlisle by 1,500 men : ' 500 men being too

[1] A copy of the bishop's loyal address to the king, found among the papers of the first Duke of Buckingham, has been printed by Chancellor Ferguson in *Dioc. Hist. of Carlisle* (S.P.C.K.), 131-3.
[2] *Some Municip. Rec. of Carlisle* (Cumbld. and Westmld. Archæol. Soc.), 95.
[3] In the register of the guilds there is the following interesting entry : ' The King's most excellent Majestye, James I., was here at Carliol, the 4th daye of August, 1617, where the Maiore of the city, Mr. Adam Robinson, with Thomas Carleton, recorder, and the brethern presentyd hym firste with a speech, then wyth a cup of golde, valued at £30, and a purse of sylke with 40 jacobuses or pieces of the same' (Jefferson, *Hist. of Carlisle*, 46-7).
[4] *Hist. MSS. Com. Rep.* iii. App. p. 39 ; Rushworth, *Hist. Coll.* i. 422.
[5] *Hist. MSS. Com. Rep.* iii. App. p. 79 ; iv. App. p. 55.
[6] Ibid. (Muncaster MSS.), x. App. iv. 273-4.
[7] Burton, *Life of Sir P. Musgrave* (Carlisle Tracts), p. 6.

small a number to make it good against an enemy ; however, not to
divide those 500 at least, as lately they were, one hundred of them
being taken forth of the town to defend Beucastle, and another hundred to the guarding of another castle, being places of no strength or
consequence, and which an enemy would scarcely ever think upon,
unless incited thereunto out of hope to have execution of these two
companies, so separated from the rest of the regiment.'[1]   In July 1640
Sir Nicholas Byron was appointed military governor of the castle and
city of Carlisle with extensive powers.[2] When Leslie crossed the Border
and took Newcastle, the idea became generally prevalent that the victory
would be followed by an advance on Carlisle.   Information was
despatched throughout the county by Sir William Howard, Sir George
Dalston and Sir Thomas Dacre that the Scots were preparing to invade
Cumberland and to deal with it as they had done with Northumberland
and the Bishopric of Durham.   Orders were issued for a general muster
of the military strength of the county, including trainbands and 'dra-
gooners,' at Carlisle on 3 October 1640.   The deputy lieutenants and
justices of the peace gave instructions ' that one able man out of every
five be chosen to defend the country, and that the four who stay at
home shall provide arms and allowances ; that all freeholders shall come
themselves or send an able man with arms and allowance, except the
trainbands of horse and foot, in regard of their more immediate service ;
that the country in general shall contribute towards the charges of
making such works as shall be thought necessary by the lieutenant
governor for the defence of the city ; and that upon the firing of the
beacons all the chosen men shall repair to Carlisle with seven days provision upon pain of death.'   It was also ordered that every soldier
should bring with him, besides his arms, a spade, shovel or pickaxe to
Carlisle, from whence they should be carried in carts to the places where
they should be used.[3]   For the moment however the danger passed from
Carlisle, and under the provisions of the treaty with the Scots its
garrison was disbanded and the two counties were obliged to contribute to the maintenance of the Scottish army while the truce
lasted.   The county had no opportunity of showing its military
prowess in defence of the king, but the lord lieutenant was probably
right when he stated ' that it was not possible to keep the counties of
Cumberland and Westmorland out of the Scottish power, whensoever
they should endeavour to take them in.'[4]

When the royal cause began to decline in the northern counties
after the defeat of Marston Moor, Carlisle alone remained faithful to the

---

[1] Rushworth, *Hist. Coll.* ii. 929.
[2] Rymer, *Fœdera,* xx. 427-8. In the same month the king sent three troops of horse under Sir
Thomas Lucas for the defence of the Border. Sir Thomas Lucas's troop of 100 men was quartered in
the Abbey holme ; another troop at Arthuret and Howend ; and a third of some 60 soldiers at Bewcastle
(*Hist. MSS. Com. Rep.* vi. App. p. 329).
[3] Ibid. (Muncaster MSS.), x. App. iv. 274-5 ; ibid. (Devonshire MSS.), iii. App. p. 40.
[4] Rushworth, *Hist. Coll.* ii. 1309.

cavaliers.[1] An attempt had been made in 1643 to take it in the interest
of the parliament by ' a Rascall rout,' as it was called at the time, under
the leadership of Sir Wilfrid Lawson and others, but it was defeated.
To Carlisle fled in the spring of 1644 the famous Marquis of Montrose,
and there found shelter, and it was from Carlisle that he set forth in
August, disguised as a groom with only two companions, on his
desperate plunge into Scotland. But a more formidable attempt was
now to be made on the city. David Leslie was sent after the taking of
York to operate against it. Sir Thomas Glenham, general of the
northern counties, retreated with some broken troops into Cumberland
and shut himself up in Carlisle. In his pursuit of Glenham, Leslie
encountered Sir Philip Musgrave and Sir Henry Fletcher, who retired
before him ; he crossed the Eden near Great Salkeld, and arriving before
Carlisle surveyed the approaches to the city from Harraby Hill, where
the gallows stood ;—' a place,' says Isaac Tullie, the historian of the siege,
' more proper for them he could not have chosen.' Then commenced
the famous siege of 1644–5, the surrounding forces being stationed at
Newtown, Stanwix and Harraby. The headquarters of Leslie were at
Dalston Hall. The garrison was reduced to great straits, which are
forcibly depicted in the pages of the diary of Isaac Tullie, a lad of
eighteen years, who has left a history of the siege.[2] On 10 May 1645
a fat horse taken from the enemy was sold for ten shillings a quarter.
Captain Blenkinsop came in with the news on 30 May, ' yt the king
was come into Westermerland and yt Leslie had warned ye countries
carts to fetch away his badgige ; which caused the joyfull garrison to
eat that day three days provision, and repent with a cup of cold water
for three dayes after. At this time three shillings peeces were coined
out of the cyttysens plate.' In June hempseed, dogs and rats were eaten,
and the ' gentlemen and others [were] so shrunk that they could not
chuse but laugh one at another to see their close hang as upon men on
gibbets, for one might have put theire head and fists between the
doublet and the shirts of many of them.' But the end was drawing
nigh. On 23 June ' the townsmen humbly petitioned Sir Thos Glenham
yt their horse flesh might not be taken from them as formerly and
informed him yt they were not able to endure ye famine any longer ; to
wch he gave no answer nor redresse in four dayes space ; at which time
a few woomen of ye scolds and scum of the citty mett at ye Cross,
braling against Sr Henry Stradling there present who first threatned to
fire upon them ; and when they replyed they would take it as a favor,

[1] Sir Richard Graham, writing in 1644, said that the prime gentlemen of the county had lately
certified Sir Thomas Glenham of the ill-doings of Leonard Dykes, the sheriff, and desired his removal.
He recommended Edward Musgrave to be appointed sheriff of Cumberland and Philip Musgrave sheriff
of Westmorland ; ' these two men are the most powerful to serve the king in their counties and with the
assistance he would give them would carry both the counties for the king ' (*Hist. MSS. Com. Rep.* vi.
App. p. 335).
[2] In 1840 Mr. Samuel Jefferson printed Tullie's *Narrative of the Siege of Carlisle in 1644 and 1645*,
from Harl. MS. 6798, with an introduction and some useful notes. It forms one of a series known as the
' Carlisle Tracts,' published by Jefferson.

he left them wth tears in his eyes, but could not mend their commons.'
But no relief was coming for Carlisle ; and after the defeat of the king
at Naseby on 24 June 1645, Sir Thomas Glenham, whom Clarendon[1]
calls ' an officer of very good esteem in the king's armies and of courage
and integrity unquestionable,' felt that nothing was left for him but to
capitulate, which he did on 25 June ' upon as honourable conditions as
any that were given in any surrenders.' The garrison marched out with
all the honours of war, ' with their arms, flying colours, drums beating,
matches lighted at both ends, bullets in their mouths, with all their bag
and baggage, and twelve charges of powder a piece.' Provision too was
made in the articles of surrender for the protection of the lives and
property of the citizens. Carlisle had once more covered itself with
glory.[2] It was, said Tullie, ' little in circuite but great and memorable
for loyalty.' As an instance of the changes and chances that happened
to men in this stirring period, it may be mentioned that the next time
David Leslie saw the city he had besieged and taken, he was in command of the army which Charles II. was leading on its way to ' the
crowning mercy' of Worcester.

Though Carlisle was surrendered, the principal men of the county
did not think at the time of making peace with the parliament.
With Sir Thomas Glenham they marched southwards and joined the
remnant of the Naseby army at Cardiff, where they requested the
king that they might serve him in one troop under the command of
Sir Philip Musgrave. The battle of Rowton Heath, which soon
followed, was fatal to the Cumberland contingent of the royal forces.
Sir Henry Fletcher and Mr. Philip Howard were slain, and Sir Philip
Musgrave and Sir Thomas Dacre were wounded and taken prisoners,
as were many of Sir Philip's troop.[3] Meanwhile an unsuccessful
attempt was made to retake Carlisle in October 1645 by the royalists
under Lord Digby and Sir Marmaduke Langdale, but they were
defeated in an engagement on Carlisle Sands.[4] In the following year
the growing estrangement between the Scottish and parliamentary forces
resulted in the dismissal of the former in December 1646, but the Scots
appear to have delayed their departure from Carlisle. When the commissioners, sent down to inspect the condition of the city, made their
report in February 1647, they stated that they had commenced the
work of slighting (dismantling) the fortifications on 26 January last, and
had found the town a model of misery and desolation as the sword,
famine and plague had left it. The garrison was ' yet in town,' and
recommended them an engineer to take down the ordnance from the
castle, citadel and walls, and remount them on carriages which were so

[1] *Hist. of Rebellion* (Oxford, 1826), iii. 185.
[2] The articles of surrender will be found in Todd's *Account of the Citty of Carlile* (Cumbld. and
Westmld. Archæol. Soc.), pp. 23–6. On 8 October 1644, Sir William Armyne informed Lenthall that the
castles of Scaleby, Naworth and Millom were holding out against the parliamentary forces as obstinately
as Carlisle (*Hist. MSS. Com. Rep.* [Portland MSS.], xiii. App. i. 185–6).
[3] Burton, *Life of Musgrave* (Carlisle Tracts), pp. 9–10.
[4] Baker, *Chron. of the Kings of England*, p. 544.

decayed and deprived of their irons as to be unserviceable for those weighty burdens.[1]

The struggle, renewed afresh in 1648, was due to the difficulties that arose in reconciling the conflicting interests that the previous hostilities had brought into existence. Sir Philip Musgrave, again at large, hurried from Edinburgh, where he was making arrangements for a Scottish invasion, and by a bold stroke on the night of 29 April surprised Carlisle, many gentlemen of the neighbourhood being in and about the town, so that the citizens were thrown into confusion and made little resistance.[2] The capture of Carlisle raised the hopes of the royalists of the county, and though many of the leading men had already compounded for their estates, yet they entered again so actively into the king's service that upon the last day of May there appeared in the field 5,000 foot well armed and 800 horse, raised in Cumberland and Westmorland.[3] On the departure of Sir Philip Musgrave, who went to Edinburgh to urge the Duke of Hamilton to advance with the Scottish army, General Lambert, the leader of the parliamentary forces in the northern counties, marched from Yorkshire, took Rose Castle by storm,[4] and besieged Scaleby Castle, which surrendered without firing a shot. On the approach of Hamilton, the parliamentary forces retreated, leaving a garrison in Appleby Castle. By order of Sir Marmaduke Langdale, the castle and city of Carlisle were put at the disposal of the duke, who placed in them a Scottish garrison and left Sir William Livingstone as governor. When Appleby Castle was recovered and the Scottish and English forces marched into Lancashire, Sir Philip Musgrave was appointed to remain behind for the protection of the two counties. Few men were left with him, but in a short time he collected together a force of 800 horse and 1,200 foot, which he considered sufficient for his immediate necessity. The defeat of the Duke of Hamilton at Preston by Cromwell and Lambert, who had joined forces, was felt to be a decisive blow to the royal cause in the two counties. Cromwell now demanded the surrender of Carlisle. Writing in September, he said : ' If you deny me herein, I must make an appeal to God,' that is, he would resort to sterner measures.[5] Musgrave urged the governor of Carlisle to join forces with him and hold the city for the king. Amid jealousies and divided counsels between the Scottish and English troops, nothing was left but to treat with the enemy and obtain the best terms for surrender.[6] After the delivery of the castles of Carlisle and Appleby the royal cause was completely shattered in Cumberland and Westmorland.

[1] *Hist. MSS. Com. Rep.* (House of Lords MSS.), vi. App. p. 158. Some sixteen pieces of ordnance were sent to Cockermouth. The commissioners asked whether they should remove ' the two murderers' which had ' of old time continued upon ground within the castle.'

[2] Clarendon, *Hist. of Rebellion*, vi. 52–4. Burton states that by Sir Philip's order sixteen men, the chief of whom were George Denton and John Aglionby, entered the city and made themselves master of it. ' This was done ye 29th of April in ye fatall year '48 ' (*Life of Sir P. Musgrave*, p. 12).

[3] *Hist. MSS. Com. Rep.* (Rydal MSS.), xii. App. vii. 19–20.

[4] Ibid. (Hamilton MSS.), xi. App. vi. 125.

[5] Carlyle, *Letters of Cromwell*, Nos. lxxii.–lxxvi.   [6] *Life of Sir P. Musgrave*, pp. 13–5.

After the execution of Charles I., Cumberland was the first English county to welcome his successor. Charles II. having made terms with his Scottish subjects and become their covenanted king was crowned at Scone on New Year's day, 1651. He determined to invade England, and started in July accompanied by Leslie. Their spirits rose as they crossed into Cumberland. 'As soon as we came into England, his Majesty was by an Englishman, whom he made king-at-arms for that day, proclaimed king at the head of the army with great acclamation and shooting of cannon.' Passing from Dalston, they were greeted at Hutton by the rector of that place and the widow of Sir Henry Fletcher, who had been slain at Rowton Heath. At Penrith the king was again proclaimed and 'will be in all the market towns where we march.' But so broken was the spirit of the county, few joined his ranks. People saw his army pass, but there was no flocking to his standard. The young king, we are told, as he came through Hutton, looked pale and pensive, seated in a coach with some of the Scottish nobility.[1] His depressed feelings were but the premonition of coming disaster, for his cause was lost for the time on the field of Worcester, and England, Scotland and Ireland lay at Cromwell's feet.

During the Commonwealth, Cumberland was placed under the government of Sir Arthur Haselrig and left to settle down after its troubles as best it might. Many of the county families had suffered in lives and property for their devotion to the king. In 1651, for instance, Sir Timothy Fetherstonhaugh, whose two sons had been slain at Worcester, was named among the nine persons who were adjudged by the Council of State as 'fit to be brought to trial and made examples of justice.' Three only appear to have been brought to execution, of whom Sir Timothy was one. Before his execution at Chester in October 1651, he stated in a farewell letter to his 'unparalleled wife' that, 'though his death be fatal, and some would make it scandalous, yet posterity, truth and other generations might not call it so, nor would our age have called it so ten years since. God knows he had nothing.'[2] His losses amounted to £10,000, and the only recompense his family received at the Restoration was a pageship for his son and a portrait of Charles I. Sir Patrick Curwen was fined £2,000; Charles Howard, the great-grandson of Lord William Howard, was cleared of his delinquency for having borne arms against the parliament by the payment of £4,000. The towns were equally in distress. The state of the whole county is described as lamentable, and no less than 30,000 families are said to have been without seed or bread, corn or money. Parliament ordered a collection to be made for them, but the amount raised was quite inadequate to meet their needs.

In the Long Parliament, as it is termed, which assembled in 1640, and the 'rump' of which was not dissolved until the memorable 20

---

[1] Jefferson, *Leath Ward*, pp. 23, 425–6, quoting Dr. Todd's MS. history of the diocese of Carlisle, which cannot now be traced.

[2] *Hist. MSS. Com. Rep.* (Rydal MSS.), xii. App. vii. 20.

April 1653, Cumberland was at first represented by Sir Patrick Curwen and Sir George Dalston, the former of whom had been first elected in 1625, and the latter had been member since 1620.[1] They were both ardent royalists, and were excluded as such under the disabling order of 1645, their places being taken by William Ermyn and Richard Tolson ; the latter was probably one of the Tolsons of Bridekirk near Cockermouth, which was a stronghold of the Puritan party. Only one of the members for Carlisle was rejected, as Richard Barwise was already known as a supporter of the revolutionary movement. The next parliament to be summoned was that which lived in history under the name of the Barebones Parliament. It was a nominated assembly called together on the authority of Cromwell alone.[2] For the purpose of this parliament, the four northern counties were grouped together, and four members were allotted to them. One of these was Colonel Charles Howard, who has been already named as having purged his delinquencies by the payment of a fine. Since that time, however, he had fought at Worcester on the parliamentary side and done very gallant service, ' though at his personal smarts.' He would seem now to have enjoyed the entire confidence of the Protector, for he was also made a member of the new Council of State.[3] Before this he had been appointed governor of Carlisle. In the parliament of 1654 two members were once more assigned to Cumberland, and Colonel Howard and Mr. William Brisco were elected, as they were again in that of 1656. When Cromwell determined in 1657 to form a second or upper house, Howard was called to it as Baron Gillesland and Lord Morpeth, one of the few peerages that Cromwell bestowed. He is marked as being in attendance when the Houses met in 1658.[4] After the Protector's death Howard remained one of the close advisers of his son Richard, the county being represented by Sir Wilfrid Lawson and Mr. Brisco. In the Convention of 1660 Colonel Howard resumed his place as member for Cumberland with Sir Wilfrid as his colleague. It was this assembly that decreed the restoration of Charles II. To the new parliament of 1661 the county sent its old representatives, Sir Patrick Curwen and Sir George Fletcher. Sir Patrick's former colleague, Sir George Dalston, who had represented Cumberland for more than thirty years, did not live to see the king's return. He died in 1657 respected by parliament and loved by kings, a leading man, prevailing by his great reputation of justice and integrity.[5]

The legislation of the early parliaments of Charles II. produced some notable changes in the political obligations of the inhabitants of Cumberland, and almost brought them into line with the rest of the

[1] *Parliaments of England* (Blue Book), i. 450, 463, 487.
[2] Masson, *Life of Milton*, iv. 501.
[3] Gardiner *Commonwealth and Protectorate*, ii. 259.
[4] Masson, *Life of Milton*, v. 323.
[5] Bishop Jeremy Taylor preached his funeral sermon on 28 September 1657, which was printed in 1658 under the title of ' A Sermon preached at the Funerall of that worthy Knight Sʳ George Dalston of Dalston in Cumberland.'

country. The last shred of feudal tenure was abolished ; the levies of the county received parliamentary recognition ; a new system of military service was begun. The necessity of providing for their own safety, which was a burden on the frontier counties, had ceased since the union of the Crowns, and though the old customs were temporarily revived during the civil war, they fell into abeyance during the Protectorate. By the enactments of 1662 the county was absorbed into the military organization of the nation as a whole, and subjected to the burden of contributing its quota to the national forces. The exceptional position of the frontier counties, however, was not yet at an end. An additional obligation was thrown upon them of dealing with a state of society which had been fostered by their past history and associations. The attention of parliament in 1662 was directed to the condition of the northern borders, and an Act[1] was passed for the declared purpose of putting down disorderly and lawless persons, commonly called moss-troopers, who had for many years frequented the counties of Northumberland and Cumberland, and who had increased ‘since the time of the late unhappy distractions.’ The justices of the peace in Quarter Sessions were now constituted in the place of the special commissioners of James I., who had in turn succeeded the lord wardens of the marches. In Cumberland the new authority was empowered to levy a yearly tax not exceeding £200 for the defence of the county. A crude police system was established, consisting of an officer, called the country keeper, and twelve men, for the purpose of hunting the thieves and bringing them to the gallows.[2] Book-keepers were appointed in all the market towns of the county, where the country people were at liberty to register their cattle. The office of country keeper[3] was a sort of insurance agency responsible to the owner for the value of all booked cattle stolen or lost. The records of Quarter Sessions for about a century after the system was instituted teem with evidence of the working of this new machinery. It should be mentioned that the Act was permissive and had to be revived, as occasion called, at the expense of the county.[4] The office of country keeper was a yearly appointment, and it often happened that the same person was re-appointed for several years in succession. The allowance varied from year to year according to the state of the country, but it could not exceed £200 as allowed by the Act.

The application of the Border service for the protection of property may be illustrated by an entry in the sessional records :—

[1] 13 & 14 Charles II. c. 22, entitled ‘An Act for preventing of theft and rapine upon the Northern Borders of England.’ It was amended by the subsequent Acts 18 Charles II. c. 3, and 29 & 30 Charles II. c. 2. Compare this legislation with 43 Elizabeth c. 13, and 13 Geo. III. c. 31. The reputation of the county for thieving was noticed by George Fox on his visit to Gillesland in 1653 (*Journal* [Leeds, 1836], i. 241).

[2] By the Act 18 Charles II. c. 3, great and notorious thieves and spoil takers in the counties of Northumberland and Cumberland shall suffer death as felons without benefit of clergy, or may be transported for life by order of the judges of assize.

[3] It was customary to select one of the justices for the office of country keeper. Bonds of the country keepers continued to be registered with the clerk of the peace, Carlisle, till 1756, about which time, probably, the justices ceased to have the Act renewed.

[4] In the proceedings of the sessions there are frequent orders for this purpose.

> Whereas it appears upon oathe that James Bell of Corby, upon ye 11th of May last, had two oxen stolen from Snowdon's Close, price £8, and ye same was lawfully booked [1] by Matthew Whitfield, book-keeper there, Ordered that Thomas Warwick, Esq., treasurer for ye money collected for ye Border service, doe pay ye said James Bell ye sume of six poundes for ye s^d oxen (Easter, 1668).

It will be seen from the working of the new institution that moss-trooping was not what it used to be, that is, exclusively confined to Scots who made sallies into the county and retreated with their booty across the Border. It had degenerated into a sneaking system of brigandage and outlawry,[2] when bands of thieves concealed themselves in the wild moorlands of Bewcastle or among the hills of Borrowdale, where the agents of the law found a difficult entry. Not the Debatable Land alone, but every inch of the county had to be watched and guarded, book-keepers having been stationed in Carlisle, Wigton, Penrith, Kirkoswald, Brampton, Longtown, Cockermouth, Keswick, Bootle, Ravenglass, Egremont, Whitehaven, Workington, Ireby, Holmcultram, and Alston Moor. Judging from the entries in the order books of Quarter Sessions, the Border service was instrumental in destroying this long-standing species of crime. It is said by Gray[3] that the practice lingered on among the dalesmen of Borrowdale till the accession of George III.

The statutes which provided machinery ' for ordering the forces in the several counties of this kingdom ' present no special features in their application to Cumberland. In times of scare or political unrest, the forces of the county were put in array to meet the emergency. When the news of the fire in London of 1666, supposed to have been caused by the French and Dutch, reached the north, Lord Carlisle called out the trained bands and stationed Major Lowther's and Mr. Fleming's companies at Kendal, Sir George Fletcher's at Appleby, Sir William Carleton's at Penrith, Sir Francis Salkeld's and Captain Hudleston's at Cockermouth, Sir Thomas Dacre's at Brampton, and the light horse at Penrith. Again when troubles broke out in Scotland, in the summer of 1679, there was a general muster of the two counties at Carlisle, and Sir Daniel Fleming was obliged to inform Lord Morpeth that there were many defects and gaps to be supplied in his contingent, as it had not been called out since June 1676.[4] The militia played no part in the affairs of Cumberland during the Revolution of 1688. After the flight of King James, however, a bold initiative was taken by the local leaders to hold the county for King William. On 10 December 1688, when an alarm was raised of an Irish and Scottish invasion, Sir John Lowther of Lowther issued warrants for a muster of militia at Penrith on 19

---

[1] It was ordered at the Midsummer Sessions 1704 ' that only one shilling be taken for booking stollen goods and nothing for a copy or certificate of the bookinge.'

[2] Lord Thanet, writing on 3 April 1685, told Lord Dartmouth that Cumberland was in no little disorder, and if a militia were anywhere needed it was certainly there, where they were ' often alarrummed by the Borderers whose trade was and ever will be fighting and stealing for their daily bread ' (*Hist. MSS. Com. Rep.* [Dartmouth MSS.], xi. App. v. 124).

[3] *Journal of a Tour in the Lakes*, 3 October 1769.

[4] *Hist. MSS. Com. Rep.* (Rydal MSS.), xii. App. vii. 42–3, 159.

December, but they were disbanded when it was found that the report was false. On that occasion Sir Christopher Musgrave and Sir George Fletcher found themselves at the head of 3,000 men.[1] In any case, the Cumberland levies could have been of little value as a fighting force, for they had not been mustered during the lieutenancy of Lord Preston, and their arms were taken from them in the late king's time.[2]

The parliament elected in 1661 sat for eighteen sessions and was in reality the Long Parliament, though that title has been accorded to the last parliament of Charles I. Cumberland was represented in it from January 1665 by Sir John Lowther of Whitehaven, and Westmorland had for one of its members from 1677 his cousin, Sir John Lowther of Lowther.[3] These two members of the Lowther family continued to represent their respective counties for a long period : Sir John of Whitehaven, in every parliament down to 1700, and Sir John of Lowther, with a brief interval in 1679, down to 1696, when he was called to the upper house as Viscount Lonsdale. They were of great business capacity and commanding influence, and their long tenure of the representation, almost unbroken, marks the growing position of the house of Lowther in the political affairs of the two northern counties. Thus Sir John Lowther of Whitehaven could write to Sir Daniel Fleming of Rydal on the eve of the election in 1679 : 'I and Lord Morpeth stand for Cumberland, Sir Richard Graham for Cockermouth, Sir Philip Howard and Sir Christopher Musgrave for Carlisle, all agreed.'[4] It was an influence deserved by high character and good service. They belonged to the moderate country party and acted with the Whigs in resistance to the reactionary policy of Charles II., and in the attempt to exclude his brother James from the throne.[5]

When James II. attempted to pack the parliament with his own supporters, the Lowthers stood firm for the constitutional party. No effort, however unscrupulous, was spared on the king's part. The lords lieutenants were sent down to their counties with instructions to issue interrogatories to the justices of the peace to ascertain how they would vote at the next election. Many refused to discharge the odious service and were dismissed. The Earl of Thanet was deprived of his lieutenancy, and Viscount Preston, the third baronet of the family of Graham of Netherby, was appointed in his stead.[6] He came down, but he returned with ' cold news from Cumberland and Westmorland,'[7]

---

1 *Hist. MSS. Com. Rep.* (Rydal MSS.), xii. App. vii. 227, 231.   2 Ibid. 267, 331.
3 *Parliaments of England* (Blue Book), i. 521, 530.
4 *Hist. MSS. Com. Rep.* (Rydal MSS.), xii. App. vii. 155.
5 Lord Lonsdale, *Memoir of James II.* pp. ix.–x.
6 The commission of lieutenancy of Westmorland and Cumberland to Thomas, Earl of Thanet, is dated 3 March 1685 (Pat. 1 James II. pt. i. No. 14), and to Richard, Viscount Preston, revoking that to the Earl of Thanet, is dated 29 August 1687 (Pat. 3 James II. pt. 8, No. 4d). See *Dep. Keeper's Rep.* xlii. App. p. 728.
7 Macaulay, *Hist. of England* (ed. 1858), iii. 63. The king's instructions to the lord lieutenant of Cumberland and Westmorland will be found in *Memoirs of Great Britain* (ed. 1771-3), iii. 129–30, printed by Sir John Dalrymple from Lord Preston's despatch book at Netherby. By the last article Preston was required to inform the king ' what catholicks and what dissenters are fit to be added either to the list of the deputy lieutenants or to the commission of the peace throughout the said lieutenancy.'

counties in which the king had great confidence. Justices had been disjusticed wholesale to no purpose. The corporation of Carlisle had indeed proved more subservient. The charter of that municipality had been withdrawn by Charles II. and replaced by one which made its chief officers removable at the king's discretion.[1] James II. exercised the power that had been so conferred. The corporation, packed with nominees, yielded to his wish, and promised 'to elect such members as shall concur with your majesty,' and at the same time expressed the hope that there might be no want of his issue 'to sway the sceptre as long as the sun and moon endure.'[2] But very different was the issue in the county. Every effort was made to win the Lowthers to the king's side. Sir Daniel Fleming wrote to Sir John of Lowther on 2 December 1687 informing him of the report that he had been 'closeted,' and had become an affirmative man, affirmative, that is, to the questions that had been issued.[3] But it was not so. There is, indeed, every reason to believe that the answers of the chief men in the two counties, which are said to have been framed with admirable skill, were the result of concerted action throughout the country.[4] The famous meeting to which the justices had been summoned took place at Penrith on 24 January 1688. Lord Preston was very active beforehand in persuading the justices to accede to the royal will. Sir John of Lowther came to Penrith ' in his coach with six horses,' attended by a few of the justices, while Sir Daniel Fleming and others accompanied the lord lieutenant on horseback from Hutton, where he had been staying. The place of meeting was the George Inn, where the gentlemen ' took their seats around a long table.' Lord Preston made a short speech, declaring his Majesty's commands, and intimating that if they preferred to give oral answers he would call in his secretary to write them down. After a considerable pause Sir John of Lowther proposed that the answers should be given in their own handwriting, and for this purpose those who wished should be allowed to withdraw from the council chamber for the space of an hour. The proposal was at once agreed to, and ' the protestant gentlemen did go into one room and the papists into another.' After the deliberation Sir George Fletcher stood up and read aloud his answers, announcing his determination to stand for parliament and leave the king's questions to the judgment of the House of Commons. Sir William Pennington, who followed, was more prudent, expressing his readiness to help the king in all things reasonable, and to vote for the abolition of the penal laws, if the safety of the Church of England were guaranteed. Sir Richard Musgrave of Hayton did not disguise his attachment to the Protestant religion, and promised to support those only who, in his opinion, would best promote the public good. Then

---

[1] *Hist. MSS. Com. Rep.* (Carlisle Corporation MSS.), ix. App. i. 199–200.

[2] Rapin states that the servile address of the corporation of Carlisle was ' supposed to be drawn up by a Jesuit ' (*Hist. of England* [ed. Tindal, 1731], xv. 141–2).

[3] *Hist. MSS. Com. Rep.* [Rydal MSS.], xii. App. vii. 207.

[4] Macaulay, *Hist. of England* (ed. 1856), iii. 61. He says too that the form of answer to the king's questions was circulated all over the kingdom and generally adopted.

SIR JOHN LOWTHER, BART.

came the answers of Sir John of Lowther, who deferred his opinion on the first question till he heard the debates of the House, and in reply to the second, he would support those who were loyal and well affected to the king and the established government. The same answers were given by the majority of the justices present, disagreeing with the king on the first two issues, but all of them expressed the desire to satisfy his third question by striving to live in love and charity with their brother Christians of every persuasion. Of the thirty-one justices who attended the meeting, only eleven ranged themselves on the king's side, and these were mostly papists and men of little influence. At the conclusion of the business Lord Preston 'treated all the gentlemen very kindly and nobly with wine, ale, and a good dinner.' Though the outcome of the Penrith meeting was disappointing to the king and his advisers, a more decided opposition was given by those who, for some reason or other, were absent. Sir Wilfrid Lawson of Isell was the only absentee who gave unqualified adhesion to the proposals, except, perhaps, John Fisher of Stainebankgreen, who, with inconsistent hesitation, suspended his opinion on the first question and assented to the second. Of the others who answered by letter, all were apparently for the maintenance of the penal laws, some answering evasively, a few with firmness. In a few months all the old justices of Cumberland were disjusticed ' excepting eight whose names here follow : Sir Wilfrid Lawson, Sir William Pennington, Mr. Charles Orfeur, Lawyer Aglionby, Mr. Warwick, Squire Dacre, Mr. Thomas Dalston, and Mr. William Christian,'[1] who had declared themselves in favour of the king's plans.[2]

Cumberland had its share in the confusion and excitement of the Revolution. Shortly before the landing of the Prince of Orange, the justices retained in the commission of the peace drew up an address of sympathy with the king, in which they told him that at that juncture they thought it their duty to offer their lives and fortunes to his Majesty's service, not doubting but a happy success would attend his Majesty's arms ; and if he thought fit to display the royal standard they faithfully promised to repair to it with their persons and interest.[3] But it was too late, the Revolution had begun. In a fit of panic the ejected

---

[1] *Hist. MSS. Com. Rep.* (Rydal MSS.), xii. App. vii. 212.

[2] The authorities for the above narrative on the events of 1687–8, unless where otherwise stated, are the collection of original documents in the Bodleian, printed by Sir George Duckett in *Penal Laws and Test Act in* 1688, and in *Transactions of Cumbld. and Westmorld. Archæol. Soc.* iv. 346–71, and the letters and papers at Rydal Hall, printed by Nicolson and Burn, *Hist. of Westmorld. and Cumbld.* i. 165–71.

[3] Chambers, *Book of Days* (1883), ii. 550. This was no idle boast on the part of the papist justices, for Mr. Howard and his son, Mr. Curwen, and Mr. Salkeld joined the army of King James as volunteers in November 1688 (*Hist. MSS. Com. Rep.* [Rydal MSS.], xii. App. vii. 220). Scottish troops to the number of 2,000 passed through Carlisle on 10 October 1688 on their way south, and threw the county into consternation. The *posse comitatus* was called out and marched to Kirkby Lonsdale, where, as it was reported, a skirmish took place and the Irish and Scotch were routed (ibid. 215, 227, 229). There was not much bloodshed, if we are to believe a popular ballad which satirized the courage of the local militia in the encounter :—

> In '88 was Kirkby feight
> When ne'er a man was slain :
> They ate their meat and drank their drink,
> And so went yham again.

justices were reinstated,[1] and an order was issued on 17 October 1688 to restore ' all the corporations of England to their ancient privileges, the displacing all officers whatever in them that claimed their places by anie grant made by the Crown since 1679, and the reinstating all those turned out since then.'[2] Events moved fast in Cumberland. After failing to induce the justices to call out the militia, Sir John Lowther of Lowther summoned a meeting at Penrith on 1 December, and issued a declaration in favour of a free parliament. At the same time an order was sent to the constables to keep watch and ward, and fire the beacons in case of invasion or insurrection.[3] Sir Christopher Musgrave and Sir George Fletcher took possession of the corporations of Carlisle and Appleby, 'entering into the ffirst,' says Sir John of Lowther, ' in a kind of cavalcade and ostentation of meritt, when in realitie they had so far complied with those times as to deliver up the charters of Carlisle, Kendal, &c., which was the illegal action now redressed.' On the seizure of Carlisle, the popish garrison fled.[4] Before the end of the year the county was held for King William. It was a bold venture on the part of the local leaders, and though personal and political differences prevented concerted action in promoting the Revolution, they were all united in settled determination to stand up for institutions untainted by corruption, and the right of free election untrammelled by arbitrary power.[5]

One of the features of county government during the reign of William III. was the persecution of those who were opposed to the political settlement which followed the Revolution. Affairs in Cumberland reached a climax in May 1692, when Sir John Lowther, in company with the deputy lieutenants, held a court at Penrith for the purpose of settling accounts with ' the popish recusants or such as are soe reputed.' It was here that many of the Protestant Jacobites returned to their allegiance and took the oath of fidelity, but the great body of the papists remained true to their traditions : they ' were all summoned but none of them appeared.' William Fletcher was ' a prisoner in Carlisle.' Dr. Bradley, ' a phisitian of Whitehaven,' had fled to Ireland ; William Cragg was ' convicted ' ; John Skelton appeared, refused the first time, and paid a fine of £1 ; Richard Skelton, John Warwick, and Francis Howard appeared, refused a second time, and each paid a fine of £5 ; Henry Dacre had bolted ; ' John Story of the Know, but his name being George, he avoyded appeareing upon the misnomer ' ; William

¹ *Hist. MSS. Com. Rep.* (Rydal MSS.), xii. App. vii. 212-3, 215.
² Lord Lonsdale, *Memoir of the Reign of James II.* p. 52.
³ *Hist. MSS. Com. Rep.* (Rydal MSS.), xii. App. vii. 223, 225-6; ibid. (Lonsdale MSS.), xiii. App. vii. 97-8.
⁴ *Memoir of the Reign of James II.* p. 52 ; *Hist. MSS. Com. Rep.* (Lonsdale MSS.), xiii. App. vii. 99-100.
⁵ The clergy of the diocese were piloted through the dangers of the Revolution by Bishop Smith and Archdeacon Nicolson. The bishop was in close touch with the leaders of public opinion in the county, and his advice was often sought (*Hist. MSS. Com. Rep.* [Rydal MSS.], xii. App. vii. 203, 209-11). When the political crisis was past, Archdeacon Nicolson issued an able and forcible letter to the clergy, dated 15 May 1689, urging ' that a firm allegiance is due to their present Majesties, King William and Queen Mary ' (*Letters of William Nicolson*, 6-12).

Howard was 'sicke and not able to appeare' ; Thomas Brewer of Penrith ' refused to sweare, and was fined 40s., and did afterwards take the oathes.' The Jacobites of Cumberland appear to have suffered little further inconvenience till the suspicion of the privy council was aroused by the reports of plots in France on behalf of the exiled king. On 25 February 1696 the local authorities were instructed by Lord Carlisle to have the two counties in readiness, and to secure the horses, arms and persons of all persons disaffected to the government. 'You must be careful,' he said, ' to leive no armes or horses that may be serviceable to them upon such an occasion as this in any Roman Catholicks' hands, and you will also be careful to return theme their horses againe when this matter is over.' Warrants were issued in accordance with these instructions, but little came of them. Papists and nonjurors were so few and inconsiderable that they were not considered dangerous. Moreover the mob was so averse to popery that there would be twenty to one against the Jacobites.[1] It must be said that unless danger was actually imminent, or the justices were forced by imperative orders, the penal laws were put in force in Cumberland with as much leniency and consideration as possible.

The first effect of the legislative union with Scotland in 1707 was to stir up a feeling in favour of the Stuarts, which the friends of the pretender were careful to keep alive by promises of immediate invasion. Parliament took precautionary measures by passing an Act for the better security of her Majesty's person and government, and for the apprehension of those who were suspected of conspiring against them. At the Easter Sessions 1708 the deputy lieutenants and justices of Cumberland arranged for a special meeting at the Moothall, Carlisle, on 28 April following, ' in order to put ye said Act in execucon by tendring ye oath of abjuration to all papists, nonjurors and such others as may be suspected to be dangerous or disaffected to her Majesty or her government.' In pursuance of this order, the high constables were directed to summon 'the severall persons whose names were underwritt' to appear accordingly. The report made to the privy council on the loyalty of the county did not indicate that the pretender had a large following of sympathizers. The persons who refused the oath of abjuration numbered about eighteen in all, and included such names as Thomas Fletcher of Moresby, Joseph Porter of Wearyhall, John Porter of Flimby, Joseph Curwen of Seton, John Warwick of Warwickhall, Thomas Howard of Corby, William Tonstall of Wetheral, James Dacre of Lanercost, Richard Skelton of Armathwaite, and Marcus Fletcher of Hutton. Bishop Nicolson took an active part in enforcing the law, and held individual conference with papists for the purpose of persuasion. Writing to Mr. Salkeld of Whitehall on 24 July 1708, he explained that the hazard of invasion was not quite blown over, and that he was more than ever apprehensive of danger from the great numbers of those

[1] *Hist. MSS. Com. Rep.* (Rydal MSS.), xii. App. vii. 339–43.

who refused the oath.[1] In a short time the scare passed away and the rigour of the penal laws was relaxed.

The accession of George I. was the signal for a renewal of plots on behalf of the pretender and a revival of the law. In obedience to the king's proclamation the justices of the county at the Hilary Sessions 1715 issued warrants to the high constables to summon certain 'papists or soe reputed or soe suspected to be, and all others as they shall know or suspect to be papists or nonjurors' to appear at the Town Hall, Cockermouth, on 1 February, that they may be dealt with according to law. The activity of the justices in holding adjourned courts in various parts of the county for the purpose of putting the penal laws in force betokens their anxiety to prepare for the coming danger. The first note of warning that the pretender was meditating an invasion of the kingdom was conveyed to Lord Carlisle, the lord lieutenant of Cumberland, on 20 July 1715, when he was commanded to enforce the law against suspects, to take from them their horses and arms, and to confine them to their usual habitations.[2] It is no exaggeration to say that the news of the rising in Scotland threw the local authorities of Cumberland into a panic, and found them unprepared to withstand an invasion. On 16 September orders came down from the privy council for the embodiment of the militia, and in a few days after for the seizing of the persons and horses of papists and nonjurors. The confusion and dismay which had taken possession of the local gentry may be gathered from Lord Lonsdale's letter, dated 8 October, to the Earl of Carlisle. The deputy lieutenants had given instructions for seizing the persons and arms of papists, but did not meddle with the horses, for it would be doing a great hardship to several papist gentlemen who kept running horses for their diversion which were fit for no other service whatever ; and it would be as much security to the country, for when their persons and arms were secured, such horses as they had could be of no danger to the government. In the matter of the militia orders were given for a muster, but there was a difficulty about the officers' commissions. For a like reason the raising of the light horse was postponed. One thing at least the justices and deputy lieutenants agreed upon doing, and that was to seize the papists and immure them in Carlisle.[3] The bishop seems to have been the only person in authority who had his wits about him, for on 15 October he sent a circular letter[4] to his clergy, informing them of a most unnatural and dangerous rebellion raised in the neighbourhood of this diocese by several papists and other wicked enemies to our happy establishment in church and state, and urging them to animate and encourage their respective parishioners in defence of their religion, laws and liberties against all such traitorous attempts towards the destruction of his Majesty's royal person and

[1] *Letters of Bishop Nicolson*, pp. 380–7
[2] *Hist. MSS. Com. Rep.* (Lord Carlisle's MSS.), xv. App. vi. 14.
[3] Ibid. pp. 15–7.
[4] *Letters of Bishop Nicolson*, p. 432.

the subversion of his most gracious government. The sheriff was induced to raise the *posse comitatus*, which was posted on Penrith Fell a day or two before the arrival of the rebels. On the last day of October a small body of troops reached Longtown. Avoiding Carlisle they advanced by Brampton, where James VIII. was duly proclaimed. It was calculated that the invaders numbered a thousand or twelve hundred foot and six hundred horse. Robert Patten, vicar of Allendale and formerly curate of Penrith, who was with the Northumberland contingent, states that as the rebels drew near Penrith they had notice that the sheriff had got together the posse of the county to the number of 14,000 men commanded by Lord Lonsdale and the Bishop of Carlisle, for the purpose of opposing their march into England. But they gave the rebel army no occasion to try whether they would stand or no ; for, as soon as a party of scouts had reported on the advance, the rustic soldiery broke up their camp in the utmost confusion, shifting every one for himself as best they could, as is generally the case with an armed but undisciplined multitude.[1] To Patten was assigned the task of cutting off the retreat of the bishop, but Forster afterwards countermanded the order. Having proclaimed King James and stayed the night at Penrith, the insurgents set out next day for Appleby. No damage was done to the town, and no one received hurt but one man, who was shot through the arm.[2]

The conduct of the local levies at Penrith has been a fruitful subject of controversy, and various reasons have been alleged for its ineffectiveness. The most unlikely of all is that which ascribes it to secret sympathy with the objects of the insurrection.[3] It is better to listen to the testimony of those who were on the field and most capable of forming a correct judgment. Lord Lonsdale and Bishop Nicolson appear to lay the blame on the want of arms. The former told Lord Carlisle on the eve of the invasion that the militia was almost throughout ill-armed, and that orders had been issued to the men before the muster to put the arms they had in the best condition possible, and to throw away their pikes and get firelocks in their place.[4] With shame and humiliation the bishop informed his friend, Ralph Thoresby, that the county had been ' in a great pother on the dry visit that was lately made us by the united rebels of Scotland and Northumberland. The posse of our county was drawn up against them, and our men were at least four to one : but having no arms, they modestly gave way, and I was an eyewitness of the enemy's vanguards marching peaceably into Penrith.' They had been told that General Carpenter was on the heels of the rebels and would assuredly be up with them before they reached Cumberland : ' and that we should have nothing more to do than to pick up some of the shattered fragments into which he would chop

---

[1] Patten, *History of the Late Rebellion* (ed. 1717), pp. 82–3.   [2] Ibid. pp 84–5.
[3] G. G. Mounsey, *Carlisle in 1745*, pp. 97–100. Most of the local writers, jealous of the reputation of their countrymen for bravery in battle, have adopted Mr. Mounsey's views.
[4] *Hist. MSS. Com. Rep.* (Lord Carlisle's MSS.), xv. App. vi. 18.

301

them : for such a service we were well enough equipped.'[1] It should be remembered that the militia made up only a small portion of the posse of the county, though perhaps that body was little better armed or trained than the general concourse which assembled at the sheriff's summons. None of these men had ever faced an enemy before. Two-thirds of them, as one of them afterwards related, were armed with scythes, bill-hooks and pitchforks : the remainder with rusty spears, swords and muskets which had laid peaceably in the chimney since the fighting days of Oliver Cromwell.[2] Bishop Nicolson, who had every opportunity of gauging the political sympathies of the' two counties, has cleared them of leanings to the cause of the pretender. Writing to Archbishop Wake on 16 September 1716, he said that along the Western Marches they pretended to an universal fealty and allegiance to King George. In speaking of the Scottish prisoners sent to Carlisle for trial after the battle of Sheriffmuir, it did not concern him to know why they had been sent to Cumberland, but he was willing to believe that it was the unsullied reputation of the county which had brought that burdensome honour upon it.[3] Nobody of consequence joined the rebels as they advanced through the two counties. Dacre of Lanercost, who had promised to raise forty men, had been 'taken with a fortunate fever,' which hindered his purpose and saved his estates. It is possible that some of the servants of the papists in prison at Carlisle had marched to Preston, but the number was insignificant.[4] The great mass of the people appears to have been apathetic ; to the last an invasion was not anticipated ; for many years the training of the militia had been neglected ; the men who assembled at Penrith had no military experience, no arms, no discipline.

The disgraceful flight of the county forces at Penrith was not sufficient to open the eyes of the central government to the inefficiency of the militia and *posse comitatus* as a line of national defence. There is no evidence that special attention was given to the training and arming of the rural soldiery after the rebellion was quelled and the immediate danger over. The old system was allowed to continue, and the country soon settled down in a sense of security as if nothing had occurred. But in the next generation there was to be a rude awakening: once again history would repeat itself. The rebellion of 1715 brought little credit to the bravery and manly qualities of the people of Cumberland, nor was the county destined to retrieve its sullied reputation in the subsequent events of 1745. The government, alarmed by the defeat of Sir John Cope at Preston Pans, despatched Colonel

---

[1] *Letters to Ralph Thoresby*, ii. 319–20.

[2] *Literary Remains of Thomas Sanderson*, pp. 9–22. The poet claims that the events of the day were related to him ' by one who had a share in its glory.'

[3] Ellis, *Original Letters*, first series, iii. 364–5. Twenty-one letters from the bishop to the primate have been printed in this series. Several of them are of considerable interest on the trial of the Scottish prisoners in 1716 and their treatment during their imprisonment in Carlisle Castle. Among the records of the corporation there are some interesting entries on the same subject.

[4] Patten, *History of the Late Rebellion*, pp. 84–5.

Durand to undertake the defence of Carlisle. Arriving on 11 October, the new governor found the city in a weak and defenceless condition. The castle had no ditch, no outworks of any kind, no covered way. The garrison consisted of two companies of invalids, making about eighty men, very old and infirm ; two companies of militia, about one hundred and fifty men ; a troop of light horse, about seventy, and the town guard, said to consist of nine companies of thirty men each. Five companies of the militia, which had been posted in the open villages of the county, were brought in as a reinforcement of the garrison, and ten pieces of ship cannon, which Captain Gilpin, one of the officers of the invalids, had sent from Whitehaven, were mounted on the ramparts. The outposts of the army of Prince Charles Edward appeared on Stanwix Bank on 9 November, which was Martinmas term day, when the city was thronged with people from the surrounding country, and the investment was begun on the following day. Two days after, however, the prince, hearing that Marshal Wade was approaching from Newcastle, withdrew his force and retired in the direction of Brampton. The deputy mayor, with all the self-assertion of a municipal busybody, immediately forwarded a jubilant despatch to the government, stating that he had routed the rebels, and claiming ' that the town of Carlisle had done his Majesty more service than the great city of Edinburgh or than all Scotland together.' ' The king,' says Walpole in one of his letters, ' spoke of him at his levee with great encomiums. Lord Stair said, ' Yes, sir, Mr. Patterson has behaved very bravely.' The Duke of Bedford interrupted him : ' My lord, his name is not Paterson, that is a Scotch name ; his name is Patinson.' But the deputy mayor had made his boast too soon. On 13 November the Duke of Perth returned, and two days after the castle and city were surrendered to the rebels. The part played by the doughty Pattinson was treated with great ridicule by the ballad-mongers of the period. Walpole only expressed the universal contempt for the blustering and pompous burgher when he said you may spell his name any way you like.[1]

The extraordinary conduct of the militia of the two counties, to which the early surrender of the town was chiefly due, is indefensible, and can only be explained by their want of moral and discipline. The military governor was thwarted at every turn by their mutinous attitude and by the intermeddling of the municipal authorities. A few days after the militia arrived, the statutory month of service having expired,[2] they were with difficulty persuaded to remain on a promise of advance of pay. ' In this manner,' said Chancellor Waugh, ' some of the militia officers were in some sort compelled to stay, though much against their inclinations or real intentions ; others of them were ready and willing to do their best service for the defence of the place ; the

---

[1] *Letters of H. Walpole to H. Mann* (ed. Lord Dover), ii. 156–9.
[2] The order in council for raising the militia is dated 5 September 1745 ; Lord Lonsdale's letter to the deputy lieutenants of the two counties to call a meeting for a muster is dated 9 September ; the muster roll was taken on 28 September.

former were always complaining of ill usage ; and all of them thought they were not treated as they ought to be by the corporation ; and that Pattinson was only seeking his own gain, which indeed was very plain, and his insolence to be dispensed with by nothing but real and hearty zeal for the publick and for · his Majesty's service, which made it necessary to avoid all disputes at this time.' As soon as the news spread that Marshal Wade was unable to come to their relief, the militia threw down their arms and deserted their posts. In spite of the remonstrance of Colonel Durand, the officers, amid ' such a general distraction and confusion as no tongue can describe,' drew up a statement on 14 November, the fifth day of the siege, that ' the militia of the countys of Cumberland and Westmoreland, having come voluntarily into the city of Carlisle, for the defence of the said citty, and having for six days and six nights successively been upon duty, in expectation of relief from his Majesty's forces, but it appearing y^t no such relief is now to be had, and ourselves not able to do duty or hold out any longer, are determined to capitulate, and do certify that Colonel Durand, Captain Gilpin, and the rest of the officers have well and faithfully done their duty.' The inhabitants of the town soon followed the example of the militia. The officers of the permanent garrison, deserted on all sides, had nobody on whom to rely but two companies of invalids, many of whom were extremely infirm and unable to man the walls or work the guns. In this desperate predicament they determined to hold the castle alone. Meanwhile the mayor and militia officers sent messengers to treat with the rebels, but the capitulation of the city was refused unless the castle was also surrendered. Protesting against such an infamous and dishonourable capitulation, as Colonel Durand described it, the little garrison of the castle was forced to bow to the inevitable or turn their guns on the inhabitants of the town. The mayor and corporation went to Brampton, and on bended knees delivered the keys to the prince, apparently oblivious that but a month before they had presented an effusive address of loyalty to George II., expressing their indignation that an abjured and popish pretender should be fomenting a rebellion in Scotland.[1]

It is idle with the documents before us to plead that it was discontent with the reigning dynasty that led to the mutiny of the militia and the lukewarmness of the citizens. Political sympathy with the Stuarts does not appear to have influenced the conduct of anybody. When the preparations for the defence were in progress, the militia and citizens were valiant and confident, but in a few days, when the city was encircled with the enemy, the proud boasts of the defenders were no longer heard. The capitulation of the city before a single battery was raised against it filled the county with shame and dismay. There can

---

[1] It is pleasant to chronicle what is known of the conduct of the Highlanders while they sojourned in Cumberland. ' I must do the rebels the justice to say,' wrote George Smith, ' that they never used so much as a single woman in the whole country with the least indecency, notwithstanding the crimes of that nature laid to their charge. 'Tis said that the Prince had given strict orders to the contrary, and declared that every officer should suffer as the criminal for actions of that nature committed by any of the ruffians under him ; whether true or not I cannot say ' (*Gentleman's Magazine* [1746], xvi. 233-4).

be little doubt that George Smith, a local antiquary of some distinction, was right when he wrote to a friend that—

> we are yet in doubt whether that ignominious surrender was caused by cowardice or treachery or both ; I think it most probable that it was lost through a presumption that it would never be attacked and for want of a regular discipline among the men. The Pretender's son was proclaimed at the Cross, the keys of the city being carryed to him at Brampton by the mayor and attendants. It should seem a necessary question how the keys of a garrison town, the custody of which was always till then committed to the governor, nominal or residential, came to be delivered into the mayor's hands for such a use at such a time.[1]

As it was in 1715, so it was in 1745. Neither officers nor men of the militia, foot and horse, had training or discipline. When the light horse were mobilized in September there were no officers to take the command ; the foot came to Carlisle with pouches full of bullets which would not fit the bores of their muskets. The fighting qualities of the men of Cumberland were atrophied by neglect. The military ardour of the eighteenth century was not the ardour of the men who so gallantly faced Lord Hunsdon's 'shott' at Gelt Bridge in 1570, and routed the nobility of Scotland at Solway Moss in 1542 ; nor was it the ardour of those who held Carlisle against William the Lion in 1174, flouted William Wallace in the zenith of his power in 1297, Robert Bruce in 1315, and marched out with all the honours of war after the long siege of 1645. The uselessness of the county forces was entirely responsible for the surrender. After the rebellion was quenched, Colonel Durand was tried by court-martial and acquitted of all blame ; the mayor and town clerk were ordered into custody for a time[2] ; but the militia officers were treated with contempt and no notice was taken of their conduct.

When the Highlanders marched southwards, strengthened with the prestige attaching to the capture of Carlisle, they left behind them a garrison under Captain Hamilton, who experienced much difficulty in preserving order in the city and neighbourhood. Symptoms of anarchy were observable throughout the county, though no overt act of pillage took place. The citizens of Carlisle, exasperated by the tyranny of Highland government, began to rouse themselves, necessity inspiring them with courage ; secret associations were formed, and a scheme was laid to storm the castle and destroy the rebel garrison. Chimerical as the project appeared, it terrified the governor to invite the mayor and aldermen to an entertainment in the castle, where they were secured, though soon after released on parole. Others were confined on suspicion, and every village in the surrounding district was searched for arms and ammunition. Frequent skirmishes happened between the citizens and the rebels, in which it appears that the townsmen held their

---

[1] *Gentleman's Magazine* (May 1746), xvi. 234. William Gilpin stated that the British militia in 1745 was neither trained nor exercised. Every soldier pretended to be as wise as his officer : and in fact he was as wise, for in the two regiments of Cumberland and Westmorland there was not an officer who knew how to draw up a platoon (*Memoirs of the Gilpin Family*, p. 67).

[2] *Gentleman's Magazine* (1746), xvi. 41.

own. The governor endeavoured to check the lawlessness against his authority by seizing the parents of the offenders, as if the punishment of the fathers would atone for the faults of their sons. As the hostility of the inhabitants began to be more clearly displayed, Hamilton resorted to menaces by threatening martial law. This was the state of affairs in the middle of December, when the governor was informed of the retreat of the pretender's forces towards Carlisle. He then seized on the market and fixed his own price on the commodities, ransacking the country people and impressing beds for the use of the garrison.[1] Notwithstanding many complaints it was maintained by impartial observers that the rebel forces were under excellent discipline and did less mischief than had been feared.[2] Some of the clergy of Carlisle became so friendly with the Highland officers that they came under the suspicions of the Duke of Cumberland, and were but coldly received by the bishop when the trouble was over.

The retreat of the pretender's army threw the county into consternation, as it was feared that 'a mob of exasperated ruffians, disappointed of their grand project and in want of all things,' would devote itself to plunder. The Duke of Cumberland, who was in close pursuit, sent expresses, warning the inhabitants to arm and intercept the flight or to cut off straggling parties before they regained Carlisle. Penrith beacon was fired as a signal of distress, and the whole county flocked to its relief, but as the rebels kept in a compact body an attempt to engage them was considered impracticable. The rearguard action at Clifton in Westmorland, in which Lord George Murray checked the advance of his pursuers and secured the safe retreat of his army, was fought on 19 December, and on the following day the whole force reached Carlisle. Little time was spent in the city. Prince Charles, before taking his leave, left a garrison of some four hundred men to hold the city with the view of retarding the pursuit. The Highlanders crossed the flooded Esk at Longtown, nothing being seen of them but their heads and shoulders as they crossed. On reaching the opposite side it is said that the pipers at once struck up and the men danced to the music till their clothes were dry. On the same day the Duke of Cumberland arrived before Carlisle and commenced the siege. He took up his quarters at Blackhall in the same house in which the pretender's son had stayed about a month before. Six guns from Whitehaven were brought to Rocliffe and conveyed to the batteries erected on Primrose Bank.[3] Dispositions of the royal troops were so made that it was impossible for any of the garrison to escape. Colonel Townley, the governor of the city, was determined to defend it to the last extremity, resolving that 'it was better to die by the sword than fall into the hands of those damned Hanoverians.' Gallant attempts had been made to repair the breaches of the castle walls against which

---

[1] *Gentleman's Magazine* (1746), xvi. 234–5, 302.
[2] Gilpin, *Memoirs of the Gilpin Family* (ed. W. Jackson), p. 69.
[3] *Gentleman's Magazine* (1746), xvi. 301–2.

the batteries were directed. After an investiture of ten days the garrison displayed the white flag, and the duke carried out his threat that he would soon bring down about the rebels' ears 'the old hencoop,' as he is reported to have called the castle when he first viewed it. The only terms of surrender allowed were that the rebels should not be put to the sword, but be reserved for the king's pleasure.[1] The duke took up his residence at Mr. Highmore's house in English Street, where the prince had lodged, and the garrison was imprisoned in the cathedral. Carlisle was handed over to the care of Colonel Charles Howard, one of the burgesses, a somewhat unusual duty for a member of parliament to discharge. The quartering of the retaining force on the citizens was a constant grievance. The clergy were loud in their protests against the desecration of their church. On 10 January 1745–6 the prisoners were sent off to Lancaster and Chester. It was a melancholy procession as it filed through the English gate. The officers were pinioned, with their legs tied beneath the bellies of their horses ; the footmen marched two abreast, the ranks connected by a rope. Though the people of Carlisle received little glory by the events of 1745, it retains the distinction of being the last of English cities to stand a siege, as Cumberland was the last English county that was trodden by the foot of an invader.

After the decisive battle of Culloden, the machinery of the law was set in motion to avenge the rebellion. Carlisle was one of the places selected for the trial of prisoners. Thither were sent no less than 382, including some who had been taken at the surrender of the city, but most of them were Scots captured at Culloden. The commission of assize was opened on 12 August 1746 by Chief Baron Parker and other judges. As the trial of such a large number was beyond the power of judges and juries, it was proposed as an act of extrajudicial grace to the common prisoners, said to have been about 370, that they should draw lots for one in every twenty to be tried and the rest to be transported. Some of the prisoners agreed to these terms, and in this way the number of those who were indicted was reduced to 127, all of whom with the exception of two were thrust into the dungeons of the castle. True bills were found by the grand jury, of which Sir George Dalston of Dalston Hall was the foreman. That time might be allowed the prisoners for the preparation of a defence, the court was adjourned till 9 September. On the return of the judges the assize sermon was preached in the cathedral by Erasmus Head, one of the prebendaries, who had been absent from his stall during the troublous period. The wrathful ecclesiastic, hearing the 'clamorous blood' of

---

[1] A medal was struck in commemoration of the reception of the city by the Duke of Cumberland, a specimen of which may be seen in the museum of that city. It shows a bust of the duke in profile with the legend : 'WILL : DUKE : CUMB. : BRITISH HERO : born 15th April, 1721.' On the reverse there is depicted a representation of the rebellion—a figure in armour destroying a monster : round the edge is the motto : 'For my Father and Country,' and beneath, 'Carlisle reduced and Rebels flew, December 1745.' An illustration of the medal has been reproduced by Mr. J. A. Wheatley in his little monograph on *Bonnie Prince Charlie in Cumberland*, p. 48.

murdered Englishmen 'loudly calling amidst the piteous cries of the widow and the fatherless for a legal vengeance,' condemned the wretched rebels in frenzied rhetoric and committed them to divine mercy, with the profane assurance 'that they may penitently suffer in this, as not to suffer infinitely more in the next world.'[1] Little need be said of the individual indictments. The trial of Thomas Cappock, commonly called the mock bishop of Carlisle, lasted six hours, while the culprit, who appeared at the bar in gown and cassock, skilfully pleaded for his life.[2] Pleading was of little avail, for very few were acquitted. When the prisoners were brought up for sentence it is said that Cappock endeavoured to cheer his fellows by bidding them to be of good courage, for 'they should not be tried by a Cumberland jury in the next world.' Of those sent to trial, ninety-one were sentenced to death. At the conclusion of the assize the judges released 'the gentlemen of Carlisle who were confined there without any questions asked them,'[3] those no doubt who had been arrested by the Duke of Cumberland on the recapture of the city. The work of execution was not long delayed; nine, including 'Thomas Cappock the Pretender's bishop,' suffered at Carlisle on Saturday, 18 October; nine at Brampton on the following Tuesday; and on the same day nine at Penrith.[4] By way of commemorating the surrender of Carlisle to the rebel forces on 15 November, eleven more victims, including Sir Archibald Primrose of Dunipace, were selected to grace the first anniversary. All those unfortunate men are said to have behaved on the scaffold with great firmness. The last act of this bloody drama is summed up in an order of Quarter Sessions, when the justices of the peace voted a fee to 'Henry Holstead, sexton of St. Mary's, for sixteen graves for the Rebells who dyed at Carlisle.'[5]

Among the more enduring results of the rebellion was the military road, as it is commonly called, which was now projected between Carlisle and Newcastle-upon-Tyne. It is said that General Wade, who had found difficulty in 1745 in moving his troops from one side of the country to the other, had recommended an improvement of the communication between the two towns as soon as the nation had settled down. A petition was sent to the House of Commons from the districts most interested that the road should be made at the public expense.[6] Power to carry out the scheme was ultimately given to certain local commissioners by the Act 24 George II. The new road, made in 1751–8, followed to a large extent the course of the old Roman

[1] This amazing sermon was printed in 1747 under the title of 'Loyalty recommended on proper principles.' The sentiments of the audience may be judged from those of the pulpit. The sermon at York on 21 August, to which the judges had just listened, was of a similar character.
[2] *Gentleman's Magazine* (1746), xvi. 494–5. It is stated here that Cappock 'left a good benefice to follow the rebels, and was made by the young Pretender Bishop of Carlisle.'
[3] Ibid. 555.
[4] Ibid. 557, 610. The accounts of the numbers executed at these places often differ.
[5] The above account of the rebellion in 1745 is founded, unless otherwise stated, on the letters and papers collected by Mr. G. G. Mounsey in his *Authentic Account of the Occupation of Carlisle in 1745 by Prince Charles Edward Stuart*, published in 1846.
[6] *Hist. MSS. Com. Rep.* (Lord Carlisle's MSS.), xv. App. vi. 204. Lord Lonsdale's letter is dated 19 July 1750.

military way on the north side of the river Eden. Before the making of the military road, cómmunication between Carlisle and Newcastle was by a road crossing ·the Eden at Warwick Bridge, which was by all accounts of difficult transit. The grand jury of the county, at the Quarter Sessions held at Carlisle in July 1691, requested ' that a bridge at Botcherby be built and a new way purchased there ; the whole river of Petterill having broken into the old way, by which means neither the Judges nor any other persons can safely passe, unlesse they goe through the corne fieldes; and if the river be high noe person can passe that way ; and the present bridge at Botcherby hath twice beene repaired by the county of late yeares.' The new road to the eastern districts was the beginning of an era of road making in Cumberland. From this time forward, under a settled government, and with the blessing of continuing peace, so long denied to the Border counties, dates that steady growth of trade and agriculture which has taken place.

The failure of the territorial levies to check the inroad of the rebel forces directed men's minds to national defence. But as time went on the enthusiasm of the military reformers cooled down, and little was done for the improvement of the county forces till 1756–7, when the Act 30 George II. brought into existence what is known as the new militia. In 1761–2 it was thought necessary to repeal the old militia laws and reduce their substance into one act of parliament. By this statute (2 Geo. III. cap. 20, sec. 41) the contribution of Cumberland to the national forces was fixed at the quota of 320 men. A scheme was adopted in 1782 by which every English regiment, not bearing the title of royal, was attached to a county and granted the county title in order to cultivate a local connection for the popularization of each unit of the army and the furtherance of recruiting. For some reason not known the 34th Regiment, first raised in 1702, was allotted to Cumberland, and the 55th, first raised in 1756, to Westmorland. It must be admitted that the attempt at localization had failed, as no real connection between the regiments and the counties was ever attained. Under the army localization scheme of 1871 the two regiments were linked together in the second sub-district or Cumberland and Westmorland brigade, with the headquarters or depôt at Carlisle Castle. When Colonel Newdigate assumed the command in 1873 sanguine hopes were expressed that the ranks of these two regiments would soon be filled with Cumberland and Westmorland men. To celebrate the formation of the regimental district, two sets of shot-torn and weather-beaten colours of the 34th Regiment were deposited with much solemnity over the regimental tablet in Carlisle Cathedral on 9 October 1873, and on 18 July 1874 a Chinese standard captured by a lieutenant of the 55th Regiment at the battle of Tinghai in 1841 was laid up in Kendal church amongst the old colours placed there in 1851.[1] By another military device the Cumberland

---

[1] Much information about the services of these two regiments will be found in Noakes's *Historical Account of the 34th and 55th Regiments* (Carlisle, 1875).

and Westmorland regiments were more closely allied on 1 July 1881, under the name of the Border Regiment, which is now composed of the old corps, the 34th and 55th, the former being styled the first battalion, and the latter the second battalion, together with the militia and volunteer battalions of the two counties. Up to the present time the localization of the regiments has not borne much fruit in the encouragement of recruiting from these districts. It is stated on good authority that the young men of Cumberland and Westmorland show little disposition to adopt soldiering as a profession.

The early years of the reign of George III. witnessed the rise of a powerful force in local politics, which, for ambition and daring, has been seldom equalled and never surpassed in the north-western counties. The conspicuous part that Sir James Lowther played in parliamentary constituencies for almost a generation may be regarded as a great era in the political history of Cumberland. Sir James had succeeded not only to the Lowther property, but also to the accumulated wealth of the Whitehaven branch of the family. He had been returned for Cumberland in 1757, and for Cumberland and Westmorland in 1761, but decided to serve for the latter county. In this year he married a daughter of the Earl of Bute, and though originally a Whig he was soon drawn into closer alliance with the Tories. In 1762, on the death of Sir Wilfrid Lawson, fearing that a Whig might be elected in his stead, Sir James resigned his seat for Westmorland, and was returned again for Cumberland. The Duke of Portland, who was strongly opposed to Lord Bute, was Lowther's rival in territorial influence in the north. The duke was fourth in succession to the Bentinck who had come over with William III., and had received from him in 1694 a grant of the Honor of Penrith and of land in the parishes of Great Salkeld, Langwathby, Gamelsby, Scotby, and Castlesowerby, called the Queen's Hames, the property in fact which had been given to the Scottish king in 1242, in compensation for the abandonment of his claims, and which had subsequently reverted to the English crown. The grant was held to include the forest of Inglewood, with the lordship of Carlisle Castle and the socage manor thereof, and successive dukes had always acted on that assumption. In the course of an action which the duke had brought against Sir James in relation to some interference with a fishery at Carlisle, the legal advisers of the latter discovered that in the original grant to the first Earl of Portland by King William, the forest and manor of Carlisle had been expressly excluded. As rights of ownership had been exercised by the Bentincks for more than sixty years, that period constituted a valid title to possession which no one could impugn but the Crown. According to a legal maxim, however, *nullum tempus occurit regi*, no lapse of time could prejudice the right of the sovereign; and Sir James Lowther, in order to put himself into a position to test the claim of the Portlands to the property, applied to the government for a lease of it to himself. The lease was granted and notice given to the tenants on the estates to pay no further rents to the Portland agents.

The first step taken to defend the interest of the titles was the introduction into the House of Commons of the Nullum Tempus Bill, as it was called, which proposed to take away the privilege of the Crown. After a stormy debate it was rejected by a majority of twenty. Parliament was immediately dissolved, and the election of 1768 was naturally fought in Cumberland under conditions of great excitement. Money was freely spent on either side, and the costs of the two parties are said to have been not less than £130,000. After a severe contest, the poll being open for nineteen days, the candidates returned were Henry Curwen and Sir James Lowther. It was a drawn battle, a representative of each interest having been elected. On petition, however, Sir James was unseated, and Henry Fletcher, the other Portland nominee, was elected in his room. The Nullum Tempus Bill was again introduced and passed, with a clause inserted saving the rights of Sir James if he prosecuted them within a year. This he undertook to do at once, serving more than three hundred notices of ejectment on the tenants. The trial came on in 1771, when Sir James was non-suited on the ground that the rents reserved to the Crown under his lease were not sufficient to comply with the provisions of the Civil List Act of Queen Anne. The real claim of the Duke of Portland was therefore never decided. The estates continued in his possession till they were ultimately sold to the Duke of Devonshire in 1787.[1]

After the political uproar of 1768, a concordat was agreed to by the contending factions, under which each party was to return a member for the county, both sides being apparently exhausted. This local compromise was observed by the Whig and Tory leaders till so late a date as 1831. In the art of unscrupulous electioneering, Sir James Lowther seems to have had few equals, and to him was due the notorious stratagem by which in 1784 no fewer than 1,195 freemen were added to the electors of Carlisle, 500 of them being his own colliers. The artifice resulted in the return of his cousin, John Lowther, for the constituency in 1786, but he was unseated on petition. The committee appointed by the House of Commons reported in 1791 that the right of election for the city of Carlisle was in the freemen of the said city, duly admitted and sworn freemen, having been previously admitted brethren of one of the eight guilds or occupations of the said city, and deriving their title to such freedom by being sons of freemen, or by seven years of apprenticeship to a freeman, residing

---

[1] The literature of this great contest is somewhat voluminous. In the present writer's possession are three contemporary pamphlets : (1) *The Case of His Grace the Duke of Portland respecting two leases lately granted by the Lords of the Treasury to Sir James Lowther, Bart., with observations on the motion for a Remedial Bill for quieting the possession of the subject.* (2) *An Answer to the Duke of Portland's Case.* (3) *A Reply to a pamphlet entitled 'The Case of the Duke of Portland respecting two leases granted by the Lords of the Treasury to Sir James Lowther, Bart.'* The three pamphlets were printed in 1768. A full account of the political uproar of this period will be found in Mr. Richard S. Ferguson's *Cumberland and Westmorland M.P.'s*, pp. 126–67. See also the account of the debate in parliament in the *Annual Register for 1768*, pp. 78–82, and Walpole's *Memoirs of the Reign of George III.* (ed. Le Marchant), iii. 143–6, 161–3, 290–2.

during such apprenticeship within the said city and in no others.[1] The unseating of John Lowther prevented Carlisle from becoming a pocket borough in the hands of Sir James, who was created Lord Lonsdale in 1784, but an arrangement was subsequently made by which he controlled one seat and the Howards the other. By the exercise of his powerful influence and his great wealth he could usually return, in addition to the two seats for Cumberland and Carlisle, two members each for Westmorland and Cockermouth, and one for Appleby. These, with the two he nominated for the pocket borough of Haslemere, which he purchased, constituted the political clique known as 'Lord Lonsdale's Ninepins,' who were obliged to vote in parliament according to his directions. This remarkable politician is thus satirized in a contemporary ballad :—

> Even by the elements his power confessed :
> Of mines and boroughs Lonsdale stands possessed,
> And the sad servitude alike denotes
> The slave who labours, and the slave who votes.

To his credit, however, it must be put down that he returned Pitt for his borough of Appleby, and opposed the American war.

The leader of the Carlisle Whigs in the election of 1786 was John Christian of Workington Hall, who subsequently adopted the name of Curwen, and who represented either the city or the county with a short interval till his death in 1829. During this long period there is no man who better deserves to have his name recorded, whether he be viewed as a parliamentary representative or a country gentleman devoted to the progress of agriculture. Though he never attained the first rank as a parliamentarian, his public services were considered so great, that he is said to have been offered a peerage by two prime ministers, which, however, on each occasion he declined. It was at Mr. Curwen's feet that young Sir James Graham of Netherby drank in that political wisdom which was to bear such splendid fruit in after years. Carlisle was Graham's first constituency in Cumberland, which he represented from 1826 to 1829. On the death of J. C. Curwen in the latter year, he resigned Carlisle and was returned for the county, where he remained till his defeat in 1837. After serving other constituencies outside the home counties from 1837 to 1852, he was recalled to Carlisle, which he represented till his death in 1861. The political career of Sir J. R. G. Graham is more of a national than a local possession.[2] He was, perhaps, the most illustrious parliamentary figure the county of Cumberland has ever produced, illustrious beyond others in the senate and the state, and no less useful to those among whom he was born and died. When Mr. Gladstone, who had been for twenty years in the habit of seeking his advice, heard of 'the sad and unexpected news from Netherby,' he wrote to the Duchess of Sutherland that he had lost a friend whom he seemed

---

[1] R. S. Ferguson, *Cumbld. and Westmorld. M.P.'s*, p. 208.
[2] A Life of Sir James R. G. Graham has been written in two volumes (London, 1863) by Mr. McCullagh Torrens, and another by Dr. Lonsdale in his series of *Cumberland Worthies* (1868).

John Christian Curwen Esq.

Published by R. Smirke N.º 15 Charlotte street Rathbone Place June 1ˢᵗ 1796.

JOHN CHRISTIAN CURWEN, ESQ.

to appreciate the more because the world appreciated him so inadequately; his intellectual force could not be denied, but he had never known a person who had such signal virtues that were so little understood.[1]

The Reform Act of 1832 made considerable changes in local constituencies. Carlisle and Cockermouth returned their two members, but Whitehaven was made a parliamentary borough with a single member; while Cumberland was divided into two divisions, east and west, each with two representatives. The last election under the old conditions was that of 1831, and old electors have often told the tale how on that occasion they walked to Cockermouth, where the polling was held, from the most distant parts of the county, to vote for 'the bill, the whole bill, and nothing but the bill.' Still further changes followed under the Representation Act of 1884. Cockermouth, which had lost one member in 1867, was now disfranchised altogether; Carlisle lost one of its seats; and Cumberland was parcelled out into four single member constituencies, called respectively the Eskdale, Penrith, Cockermouth and Egremont divisions.

---

[1] Morley, *Life of W. E. Gladstone*, ii. 88.

LIST OF SHERIFFS OF CARLISLE OR CUMBERLAND [1]

Before 1112 [2]	.	Richer [3]
Mich. 1129 or earlier		Hildret
„ 1157	. .	Robert, son of Troite
„ 1165	. .	Robert Troite
„ 1172	. ..	Adam his son
„ 1173	. .	Adam son of Robert Troite
„ 1174	. .	Robert de Vaux

CUMBERLAND

Mich. 1175	. .	Robert de Vaux or Vallibus
„ 1179	. .	Roger de Legecestria
„ 1180	. .	Robert de Vaux, in person
East. 1185	. .	Hugh de Morewich
Mich. 1186	. .	Nicholas his brother
„ 1187	. .	Nicholas de Morewich
„ 1188	. .	William son of Aldelm
„ 1197	. .	Robert de Tateshale
„ 1198	. .	William de Stuteville
„ „		John le Aleman
East. 1199	. .	Hugh Bardulf
Mich. 1200	. .	William de Stuteville [4]
„ „		John le Aleman
„ 1201	. .	Philip Escrop
East. 1203	. .	Robert de Curtenai
„ „		Alan de Caudebec
1 Dec. 1204	. .	Roger de Lasci, constable of Chester
Mich. „	. .	Walter Marescallus
„ 1209	. .	Hugh de Neville
30 Jan. 1213	. .	Robert de Ros
Mich. „	. .	Alan de Caudebec [5]
7 Jan. 1216	. .	Robert de Vipont
11 Feb. 1222	. .	William de Rughedon and
„ „	. .	Walter Mauclerc
17 Mar. „	. .	Walter Mauclerc [6]
Mich. 1222	. .	Alan de Caudebec
„ 1223	. .	Walter, Bishop of Carlisle
„ 1224	. .	Robert, son of William de Hampton
„ 1225	. .	Walter, Bishop of Carlisle
„ „		Robert, son of William de Hampton, or Robert de Hamton
„ 1230	. .	Thomas, son of John
27 Jan. 1233	. .	Thomas de Muletone [7]

5 Feb. 1236	.	Charles de Garderoba [8]
30 May „	.	William de Acra, or de Dacre, and
East. „	.	John de Mora [9]
Mich. „	.	William de Acra or de Dacre
29 Apr. 1248	.	John de Bayll or Bailol
22 Aug. 1255	.	Robert de Brus [10]
28 Oct. „	.	William, Earl of Albemarle
Mich. „	.	Remy de Poclinton
„ 1259	.	William, Earl of Albemarle, in person
24–26 May 1260		Robert de Mulecastre [11]
9 July 1261	.	Eustace de Bailliol
Mich. „	.	Matthew de Eboraco
20 Sept. 1265	.	Roger de Leyburne
		Walter de Morton, his clerk
24 Oct. 1268	.	Ranulf de Dacre
26 Oct. 1270	.	Robert, Bishop of Carlisle
Mich. „	.	Ralph de Pokelinton
„ 1271	.	Matthew Cardoil, and
„ „	.	Roger de Poklinton
8 May 1272	.	Richard de Crepping
17 Oct. 1274	.	Robert de Hamtone
27 Oct. 1277	.	John de Swynburn
Mich. „	.	Michael de Newbigging
25 Oct. 1278	.	Gilbert de Corwen [12]
14 Apr. 1282	.	William de Boyvill [13]
3 May 1283	.	William de Boyvill, knt. [14]
East. „	.	Robert de Brus
Mids. 1285	.	Michael de Harcla
14 June 1298	.	William de Mulecastre
3 Dec. 1303	.	John de Lucy
7 Oct. 1304	.	William de Mulecastre
26 Mar. 1307	.	Alexander de Bastengthwaite
18 Nov. 1308	.	Gilbert de Colewenn
4 Oct. 1309	.	Alexander de Bastengthweyt.
10 Apr. 1310	.	John de Castre [15]
15 Oct. 1311	.	Andrew de Hartcla [16]
15 Dec. „	.	John de Castre
25 Jan. 1312	.	Andrew de Hartcla [17]
5 Feb. 1316	.	John de Castre [18]
8 June 1318	.	Andrew de Hartcla [19]
20 July 1318	.	Anthony de Lucy [20]
8 Apr. 1319	.	Andrew de Harcla

---

[1] This list has been compiled, unless where otherwise stated, from the List of Sheriffs, published by the Master of the Rolls.
[2] The dates here given are those of appointment or of commencement of account.
[3] Reg. of Wetherhal, p. 1.
[4] Robert de Nuers occurs as sheriff in the beginning of the 13th century (Reg. of Wetheral, pp. 96, 240, 255).
[5] Served till Mich. 1214.
[6] Account in his name begins Mich. 1222.
[7] Accounted from Mich. 1232 to East. 1236.

[8] Did not account.
[9] Accounted from Easter 1236.
[10] Did not account.
[11] Accounted till Mich. 1261.
[12] Accounted to East. 1283, though ordered to be removed from office, 6 Dec. 1282.
[13] Did not account.
[14] Did not account : elected in county court.
[15] Accounted till East. 1312.
[16] Did not account.
[17] Accounted from East. 1312.
[18] Accounted from Mich. 1315.
[19] Did not account.
[20] Accounted from East. 1318.

11 Feb. 1323	.	Anthony de Lucy
23 July „	.	Henry de Malton
24 Mar. 1325	.	Hugh de Louthre
13 Apr. „	.	Robert Brun or le Brun
4 Feb. 1327	.	Peter de Tilliol [1]
5 Dec. 1330	.	Ranulf or Ralph de Dacre
27 Jan. 1336	.	Richard de Denton [2]
8 Feb. 1338	.	Rowland de Vaux
12 May „	.	Anthony de Lucy
19 Nov. 1341	.	Hugh de Moriceby
5 Nov. 1345	.	Thomas de Lucy
16 Apr. 1350	.	Richard de Denton
3 Nov. 1351	.	Hugh de Louthre
4 Mar. 1354	.	William de Lye
15 „ „	.	Hugh de Louthre
16 Jan. 1355	.	William de Threlkeld
10 Nov. 1356	.	Robert Tilliol
3 Nov. 1358	.	William de Lancastre
1 Oct. 1359	.	Matthew de Redman [3]
24 Mar. 1360	.	Christopher de Moriceby [4]
10 Dec. 1361	.	Robert Tilliol
20 Nov. 1362	.	Christopher de Moriceby
16 Nov. 1366	.	Robert Tilliol [5]
20 May, 1367	.	William de Wyndesore [6]
27 Nov. 1368	.	Adam Parvyng
5 Nov. 1371	.	John de Denton
12 Dec. 1372	.	Robert Moubray, knt.
7 Nov. 1373	.	John Derwentwater, knt.
12 Dec. 1374	.	John de Denton
4 Oct. 1375	.	John Derwentwater, knt.
26 Oct. 1376	.	John Bruyne
9 Mar. 1377	.	Roger de Clifford
26 Nov. „	.	John Derwentwater
25 Nov. 1378	.	William Stapelton
5 Nov. 1379	.	Gilbert Culwen, knt.
18 Oct. 1380	.	John Derwentwater, knt.
1 Nov. 1381	.	Amand Mounceux
24 „ 1382	.	Robert Parvynges, knt.
1 „ 1383	.	Amand Mounceux
11 Dec. 1384	.	John Thirllewall the younger
20 Oct. 1385	.	Amand Mounceux
18 Nov. 1386	.	John Thrillewall
18 „ 1387	.	Peter Tilliol, knt.
1 Dec. 1388	.	John Irby, knt.
15 Nov. 1389	.	Richard Redeman
7 „ 1390	.	Christopher Moriceby, knt.
21 Oct. 1391	.	John de Irby, knt.
18 „ 1392	.	Thomas Musgrave, knt.
17 Nov. 1393	.	Richard Redeman, knt.
1 „ 1394	.	Peter Tilliol, knt.
9 „ 1395	.	John de Ireby, knt.
1 Dec. 1396	.	Richard de Redeman, knt.
3 Nov. 1397	.	William Culwen, knt.
17 „ 1398	.	Richard Redeman, knt.
30 Sept. 1399	.	William Legh or Lee, knt.
24 Nov. 1400	.	William Lowther
8 „ 1401	.	Richard Redeman, knt.
29 „ 1402	.	William Osmunderlowe, knt.
5 „ 1403	.	Peter Tilliol or Tyliolf
22 Oct. 1404	.	John Skelton, knt.
22 Oct. 1405	.	Richard Skelton
5 Nov. 1406	.	William Lowther
23 „ 1407	.	Robert Louther, knt.
15 „ 1408	.	John Skelton, knt.
4 „ 1409	.	John de Lamore
29 „ 1410	.	Robert Rodyngton
10 Dec. 1411	.	Richard Redeman, knt.
3 Nov. 1412	.	William Lye or de Legh, knt.
6 „ 1413	.	James Haryngton
10 „ 1414	.	William Stapelton
1 Dec. 1415	.	Christopher Culwen, knt.
30 Nov. 1416	.	John Lancastre, knt.
10 „ 1417	.	William Osmunderlowe, knt.
4 „ 1418	.	Robert Louther, knt.
24 „ 1419	.	John Lamplogh, knt.
16 „ 1420	.	William Stapulton the elder
1 May 1422	.	Nicholas Radclif, knt.
14 Feb. 1423	.	William Legh, knt.
13 Nov. 1423	.	Christopher Culwen, knt.
6 „ 1424	.	Christopher Moriceby, knt.
15 Jan. 1426	.	Nicholas Ratclyf, knt.
12 „ 1427	.	John Penyngton, knt.
7 Nov. 1427	.	Christopher Culwen or Curwen knt.
4 „ 1428	.	Thomas Moresby, knt. [7]
10 Feb. 1430	.	Thomas de la More
5 Nov. 1430	.	John Penyngton, knt.
26 „ 1431	.	John Skelton, knt.
5 „ 1432	.	John Lamplogh, knt.
5 „ 1433	.	Christopher Culwen or Curwen knt.
3 „ 1434	.	John Penyngton, knt.
7 „ 1435	.	John Broghton
8 „ 1436	.	Henry Fenwyk
7 „ 1437	.	Christopher Curwen, knt.
3 „ 1438	.	Christopher Moresby, knt.
5 „ 1439	.	Hugh Louther
4 „ 1440	.	John Skelton
4 „ 1441	.	William Stapilton
6 „ 1442	.	Thomas Beauchamp
4 „ 1443	.	Thomas de la More
6 „ 1444	.	Christopher Curwen
4 „ 1445	.	John Skelton
4 „ 1446	.	John Broghton
9 „ 1447	.	Thomas de la More
9 „ 1448	.	Thomas Crakenthorp
20 Dec. 1449	.	Thomas Curwen, knt.
3 „ 1450	.	John Skelton
3 Nov. 1451	.	Roland Vaux
8 „ 1452	.	Thomas de la More
Mich. 1453	.	No sheriff [8]
4 Nov. 1454	.	John Hodylston
4 „ 1455	.	Hugh Louther
17 „ 1456	.	Thomas Curwen, knt.
7 „ 1457	.	Richard Salkeld
7 „ 1458	.	Henry Fenwick, knt. [9]
7 „ 1459	.	John Penyngton, knt.
7 „ 1460	.	Christopher Moresby [10]
6 Mar. 1461	.	Richard Salkeld [11]
7 Nov. 1461	.	Rowland Vaux

[1] Accounted from Mich. 1326.
[2] Accounted from Mich. 1335.
[3] Did not account.
[4] Accounted from Mich. 1359.
[5] Did not account.
[6] Accounted from Mich. 1366.

[7] Christopher Moresby, knt., accounted.
[8] Hugh Lowther afterwards collected what he could for the King. See Pipe Roll.
[9] Account rendered by his executor.
[10] Did not account.
[11] Accounted from Mich. 1460.

5 Nov.	1463	. John Hodilston, knt.
5 ,,	1464	. Thomas Lamplough, knt.
5 ,,	1465	. Richard Salkeld
5 ,,	1466	. Rowland Vaux
Mich.	1467	. No sheriff.[1]
5 Nov.	1468	. John Hodilstone, knt.
5 ,,	1469	. William Legh, knt.
6 ,,	1470	. Richard Salkeld.[2]
10 June	1471	. Christopher Moresby, knt.[3]
9 Nov.	1471	. William Par, knt.
9 ,,	1472	. John Hudilleston, knt.
5 ,,	1473	. William Legh, knt.
7 ,,	1474	. Richard Curweyn, knt.[4]
18 Feb.	1475	. Richard, Duke of Gloucester [5]
Mich.	1474	. John Hudleston, knt.
,,	1477	. John Crakenthorp, knt.
6 Nov.	1483	. Richard Salkeld [6]
12 Sept.	1485	.. Christopher Moresby, knt.
5 Nov.	1486	. Richard Kirkeby [7]
4 ,,	1487	. Christopher Moresby, knt.[8]
4 ,,	1488	. Thomas Beauchamp
5 ,,	1489	. John Musgrave, knt.[9]
5 ,,	1490	. Henry Denton [10]
5 ,,	1491	. Launcelot Thirkeld
26 ,,	1492	. Edward Redmayn
7 ,,	1493	. John Musgrave, knt.
5 ,,	1494	. Richard Salkeld, knt.
5 ,,	1495	. Christopher Moresby, knt.[11]
12 Feb.	1497	. Thomas Beauchamp [12]
5 Nov.	1497	. Christopher Dacre
1 Dec.	1505	. John Huddelston, knt.
27 Nov.	1506	. Hugh Hoton or Hutton
3 Dec.	1507	. John Ratclyff
15 ,,	1508	. Hugh Hoton or Hutton
14 Nov.	1509	. Thomas Curwen, knt.
9 ,,	1510	. John Penyngton, knt.
8 ,,	1511	. John Skelton of Armathwayt
7 ,,	1512	. John Crakenthorp
14 Apr.	1514	. Edward Musgrave, knt.
7 Nov.	1514	. John Radclyf, knt.
26 Apr.	1516	. John Louther, knt.[13]
10 Nov.	1516	. Thomas Curweyn, knt.
9 ,,	1517	. Gawin Eglesfeld
8 ,,	1518	. John Ratcliff, knt.
8 ,,	1519	. Edward Musgrave, knt.
6 ,,	1520	. Thomas Fayrefax
3 Feb.	1522	. Christopher Dakres, knt.[14]
12 Nov.	1522	. John Penington
13 ,,	1523	. John Ratclyf, knt.
10 ,,	1524	. Christopher Curwen
27 Jan.	1526	. Christopher Dakres, knt.

7 Nov.	1526	. John Ratclyff, knt.
16 ,,	1527	. Edward Musgrave, knt.
7 ,,	1528	. William Penyngton, knt.
9 ,,	1529	. Thomas Wharton
11 ,,	1530	. Richard Irton
9 ,,	1531	. Christopher Dacre, knt.
20 ,,	1532	. William Musgrave, knt.
17 ,,	1533	. Christopher Curwen, knt.
14 ,,	1534	. Cuthbert Hutton
22 ,,	1535	. Thomas Wharton, knt.
27 ,,	1536	. Thomas Curwen, knt.
14 ,,	1537	. John Lamplewe, knt.
15 ,,	1538	. John Thwaites
17 ,,	1539	. Thomas Wharton, knt.
17 ,,	1540	. Thomas Dawston or Dalston
27 ,,	1541	. William Musgrave, knt.
22 ,,	1542	. John Loder or Lowther, knt.
23 ,,	1543	. Thomas Salkeld
16 ,,	1544	. Edward Aglondby or Aglyonby
22 ,,	1545	. Robert Lamplugh
23 ,,	1546	. Thomas Sandeford
27 ,,	1547	. Thomas Wharton, knt.
3 Dec.	1548	. John Leigh or a Lee
12 Nov.	1549	. John Lamplugh
11 ,,	1550	. John Lother, knt.
11 ,,	1551	. Richard Eglesfeld
10 ,,	1552	. William Penyngton
8 ,,	1553	. Thomas Leigh of St. Bees
14 ,,	1554	. Richard Musgrave, knt.
14 ,,	1555	. Thomas Sainford or Sandford
13 ,,	1556	. Richard Eglysfeld [15]
12 Apr.	1557	. Robert Lampleugh [16]
16 Nov.	,,	. John Legh
23 ,,	1558	. William Penyngton
9 ,,	1559	. Thomas Dacre of Lannercost, or Thomas Dacres the elder
12 ,,	1560	. John Lamplugh
8 ,,	1561	. Hugh Ascue, knt.[17]
20 Mar.	1562	. Henry Curwen [18]
19 Nov.	1562	. William Musgrave
8 ,,	1563	. Anthony Hodleston
9 ,,	1564	. Thomas Dacre, knt.
17 July	1565	. Christopher Dacres [19]
16 Nov.	1565	. William Pennyngton
18 ,,	1566	. Richard Lowther
18 ,,	1567	. John Dalston
18 ,,	1568	. Cuthbert Musgrave
12 ,,	1569	. Simon Musgrave
13 ,,	1570	. Henry Curwen, knt.
14 ,,	1571	. George Lampleighe
13 ,,	1572	. John Lamplughe
10 ,,	1573	. William Musgrave
15 ,,	1574	. Anthony Hudleston
15 ,,	1575	. Henry Tolson or Towelson
13 ,,	1576	. John Dalston
27 ,,	1577	. George Salkeld of Corbridge
17 ,,	1578	. Francis Lampleugh
23 ,,	1579	. John Lamplugh
21 ,,	1580	. Henry Curwen, knt.
27 ,,	1581	. Christopher Dacre
5 Dec.	1582	. Wilfrid Lawson

[1] J. de Appilby, receiver, was exempted by pardon from accounting for any issues.
[2] Did not account.
[3] Accounted from Mich. 1470.
[4] Did not account.
[5] Pat. 14 Edw. iv. pt. ii. m. 4.
[6] Accounted from East. 1483.
[7] Did not account.
[8] Accounted from Mich. 1486.
[9] Accounted to Mich. 1491.
[10] Did not account.
[11] He made the proffer at Easter 1496, and was amerced for non-attendance at Mich. following, but, according to Pipe Roll, Richard Salkeld was sheriff.
[12] Accounted from Mich. 1496.
[13] Accounted from Mich. 1515.
[14] Accounted from Mich. 1521.

[15] Did not account.
[16] Accounted for whole year.
[17] Did not account.
[18] Accounted from Mich. 1561.
[19] On death of Sir Thomas Dacre.

25 Nov.	1583	. John Dalston
19 ,,	1584	. John Middelton
22 ,,	1585	. George Salkeld [1]
14 ,,	1586	. John Daulston [2]
Mich.	1587	. George Salkeld
25 Nov.	1588	. Richard Lowther
24 ,,	1589	. Henry Curwyn, knt.
24 ,,	1590	. Christopher Pykeringe
25 ,,	1591	. John Southwicke
16 ,,	1592	. William Musgrave
20 ,,	1593	. Gerard Lowther
21 ,,	1594	. John Dalston
27 ,,	1595	. Launcelot Salkeld
22 ,,	1596	. Christopher Dalston
25 ,,	1597	. Wilfrid Lawson
28 ,,	1598	. Thomas Salkeld
2 Dec.	1599	. Joseph Pennyngton
24 Nov.	1600	. Nicholas Curwen
2 Dec.	1601	. William Orfeur
7 ,,	1602	. Edmund Dudley
1 ,,	1603	. William Hutton
5 Nov.	1604	. John Dalston, knt.
2 Feb.	1606	. Christopher Pickeringe
17 Nov.	1606	. Wilfrid Lawson, knt.
9 ,,	1607	. Christopher Pickeringe, knt.
12 ,,	1608	. Henry Blencoe or Blinko
,,	1609	. William Hutton, knt.
6 Nov.	1610	. Joseph Pennington
,,	1611	. Christopher Pickeringe, knt.
,,	1612	. Wilfrid Lawson, knt.
,,	1613	. Thomas Lamplugh
,,	1614	. Edward Musgrave, knt.
,,	1615	. Richard Fletcher
11 Nov.	1616	. William Musgrave of Holme
6 ,,	1617	. William Huddleston of Milham
9 ,,	1618	. George Dalston, knt.
,,	1619	. Henry Curwen, knt.
6 Nov.	1620	. John Lamplughe of the Fells
,,	1621	. Henry Fetherstonhaughe
7 ,,	1622	. Thomas Dudley
11 May	1623	. Edmund Dudley
16 July	1623	. Thomas Lamplughe, knt.
,,	1623	. Richard Sanforde, knt.
,,	1624	. Richard Fletcher, knt.
,,	1625	. Henry Blincowe, knt.
,,	1626	. Peter Senhouse
4 Nov.	1627	. Christopher Dalston
,,	1628	. William Layton
,,	1629	. William Musgrave, knt.
7 Nov.	1630	. Christopher Richmond
,,	1631	. Leonard Dykes
,,	1632	. John Skelton
10 Nov.	1633	. William Orfeut
5 ,,	1634	. Richard Barwis
,,	1635	. William Lawson
3 Oct.	1636	. Patrick Curwen, bart.
30 Sept.	1637	. Thomas Dacres or Darcye, knt.
4 Nov.	1638	. Timothy Fetherstonhaugh, knt.
,,	1639	. William Penington
,,	1640	. Christopher Lowther
,,	1641	. Henry Fletcher, bart.
,,	1645	. Wilfrid Lawson
6 Feb.	1647	. William Orfeut

1 Accounted till Mich. 1588.
2 Did not account.

13 Feb.	1647	. Henry Tolson
17 ,,	1647	. John Barwis
7 Nov.	1649	. Charles Howard of Naward
21 ,,	1650	. William Briscoe
4 ,,	1651	. John Barwis
12 ,,	1652	. Miles Halton
24 Mar.	1653	. Wilfrid Lawson, knt.
,,	1657	. George Fletcher, bart.
,,	1658	. William Pennington
5 Nov.	1660	. Daniel Fleminge
,,	1661	. John Lowther, bart.
,,	1662	. Francis Salkeld, knt.
,,	1663	. John Lamplough
,,	1664	. Edward Musgrave, knt.
12 Nov.	1665	. William Dalston, knt.
7 ,,	1666	. Richard Tolson
6 ,,	1667	. William Layton
6 ,,	1668	. Miles Penington
11 ,,	1669	. Thomas Curwen
4 ,,	1670	. Anthony Bouch
9 ,,	1671	. Richard Patrickson
11 ,,	1672	. Barnard Kirkbride
,,	1674	. William Orfeur
10 Nov.	1676	. William Blenerhassett
14 ,,	1678	. Wilfrid Lawson
13 ,,	1679	. George Fletcher, bart.
4 ,,	1680	. Leonard Dykes or Dikes
13 ,,	1682	. Edward Hasell or Hassell
12 ,,	1683	. Andrew Huddleston
20 ,,	1684	. Richard Musgrave of Haton Castle, bart.
,,	1685	. William Pennington, bart.
25 Nov.	1686	. John Dalston, bart.
5 Dec.	1687	. Henry Curwen
8 Nov.	1688	. Edward Stanley
18 ,,	1689	. Wilfrid Lawson, bart.
27 ,,	1690	. Richard Lamplugh
14 Dec.	1691	. Christopher Richmond
17 Nov.	1692	. Joseph Huddlestone
16 ,,	1693	. Henry Brougham
19 Dec.	1694	. John Ballantine, knt.
5 ,,	1695	. John Ponsonby
3 ,,	1696	. John Latus
23 ,,	1697	. Timothy Fetherstonhaugh
22 ,,	1698	. Thomas Dawes
20 Nov.	1699	. Robert Carleton
28 ,,	1700	. Thomas Lamplugh
1 Jan.	1702	. Christopher Crakenthorp
19 ,,	1702	. Richard Crakenthorpe
3 Dec.	1702	. John Dalston
2 Dec.	1703	. John Senhouse
21 ,,	1704	. John Brisco
3 ,,	1705	. Christopher Curwen
14 Nov.	1706	. Robert Pennington
20 ,,	1707	. Richard Lamplugh
29 ,,	1708	. Richard Hutton
1 Dec.	1709	. William Ballentine
16 July,	1710	. Henry Fairclough
26 Sept.	1710	. Robert Blacklock
13 Dec.	1711	. John Fisher
11 ,,	1712	. Charles Dalston, bart.
30 Nov.	1713	. Thomas Pattinson
16 ,,	1714	. Humphrey Senhouse
5 Dec.	1715	. Thomas Brougham of Scales
25 June	1716	. John Nicholson
12 Nov.	1716	. Henry Blencow

21 Dec. 1717	.	Robert Lamplugh of Dovenby
21 „ 1718	.	Thomas Fletcher of Hutton
6 Jan. 1719	.	John Ponsonby
3 Dec. 1719	.	John Stanley
3 Jan. 1721	.	Joshua Laithes
14 Dec. 1721	.	Charles Highmore of Armathwaite
„ 1722	.	Peter Brougham
7 Jan. 1724	.	Joseph Dacre Appleby
10 Dec. 1724	.	John Fletcher of Cleahay
13 Jan. 1726	.	Thomas Lutwidge of Whitehaven
29 Nov. 1726	.	John Ballantine
16 Dec. 1727	.	Edward Hasell of Dalmaine
18 „ 1728	.	Gustavus Thompson
18 „ 1729	.	Eldred Curwen
14 „ 1730	.	Richard Musgrave, bart.
9 „ 1731	.	Augustine Erle
23 „ 1731	.	Edward Stanley of Ponsonby
14 „ 1732	.	Henry Aglionby
20 „ 1733	.	John Benn
„ 1734	.	Fletcher Partis
18 „ 1735	.	John Dalston of Milrigg
19 Jan. 1737	.	William Hicks of Whitehaven
12 „ 1738	.	John Gaskarth of Hiltop
21 Dec. 1738	.	Joseph Dacre Appleby
27 „ 1739	.	Richard Cooke of Cammarton
24 „ 1740	.	Montague Farrer
31 „ 1741	.	Henry Fletcher of Hutton
16 „ 1742	.	Humphrey Senhouse of Netherhall
5 Jan. 1744	.	Jerome Tullie of Carlisle
10 „ 1745	.	Joshua Lucock of Cockermouth
16 „ 1746	.	Christopher Pattenson of Penrith
15 „ 1747	.	Thomas Whitefield of Clargill
14 „ 1748	.	Walter Lutwidge of Whitehaven
11 „ 1749	.	Henry Richmond Brougham of Highead [1]
28 June 1749	.	John Ponsonby of Hale
17 Jan. 1750	.	Richard Hilton of Hilton Castle, bart.
6 Dec. 1750	.	George Irton of Irton
14 Jan. 1752	.	George Dalston of Dalston, bart.
7 Feb. 1753	.	Henry Curwen of Workington
31 Jan. 1754	.	William Fleming of Skirwith, bart.
29 „ 1755	.	Timothy Fetherstonhaugh of Kirkoswald
27 „ 1756	.	Wilfrid Lawson of Brayton, bart.
4 Feb. 1757	.	Edward Stephenson of Keswick
27 Jan. 1758	.	John Senhouse of Calder Abbey
2 Feb. 1759	.	James Spedding of Whitehaven
23 Apr. 1759	.	John Gale of Cleator
1 Feb. 1760	.	William Dalston of Milrigge
28 Jan. 1761	.	John Langton
15 Feb. 1762	.	John Richardson of Penrith
4 „ 1763	.	Henry Aglionby of Nunnery
10 „ 1764	.	Henry Ellison of Whitehaven
1 „ 1765	.	Samuel Irton of Irton
17 „ 1766	.	John Christian of Unerigg

13 Feb. 1767	.	Thomas Lutwidge of Whitehaven
15 Jan. 1768	.	Wilfrid Lawson, of Brayton, bart.
27 „ 1769	.	John Robinson of Watermillock
9 Feb. 1770	.	Michael le Fleming of Skirwith
6 „ 1771	.	John Spedding of Armathwaite
17 „ 1772	.	William Hicks of Papcastle
8 „ 1773	.	John Dixon of Whitehaven
7 „ 1774	.	George Edward Stanley of Ponsonby
6 „ 1775	.	Anthony Benn of Hensingham
5 „ 1776	.	Roger Williamson of Snettlegarth
31 Jan. 1777	.	Robert Walters of Whitehaven
28 „ 1778	.	John Brisco of Crofton
1 Feb. 1779	.	Williams Hasell of Dalemain
2 „ 1780	.	Henry or Christopher Aglionby of Nunnery
5 „ 1781	.	Thomas Storey of Mirehouse
1 „ 1782	.	William Dacre of Kirklinton
10 „ 1783	.	John Orfeut Yates of Skerwith Abbey
9 „ 1784	.	John Christian of Unerig
7 „ 1785	.	Edward Knubley of Wigton
13 „ 1786	.	James Graham of Netherby, bart.
28 June 1786	.	William Wilson of Brakenbar
12 Feb. 1787	.	Thomas Whelpdale of Skirsgill Hall
8 „ 1788	.	Frank Vane of Hutton, bart.
26 May 1789	.	Thomas Denton of Warnell Hall
29 Jan. 1790	.	William Browne of Tallentire
4 Feb. 1791	.	Edmund Lamplugh Irton of Irton
3 „ 1792	.	Edward Hasell of Dalemain
6 „ 1793	.	Thomas Pattenson of Melmerby
5 „ 1794	.	William Henry Milbourne of Armathwaite Castle
11 „ 1795	.	James Graham of Netherby, bart.
5 „ 1796	.	James Graham of Barrock Lodge
1 „ 1797	.	Hugh Parkin of Skirsgill
7 „ 1798	.	Richard Hodgson of Carlisle, knt.
1 „ 1799	.	John Hamilton of Whitehaven
21 „ 1800	.	John Charden Musgrave of Edenhall, bart.
4 June 1801	.	Wilfrid Lawson of Brayton Hall, bart.
3 Feb. 1802	.	Edward Lawson of Dalemain
3 „ 1803	.	Robert Warwick of Warwick Hall
1 „ 1804	.	John de Whelpdale of Penrith
6 „ 1805	.	Charles Smallwood Featherstonhaugh of Kirkoswald
1 „ 1806	.	Joseph Dykes Ballantine Dykes of Dovenby
4 „ 1807	.	John Tomlinson of Briscoe Hill
3 „ 1808	.	Thomas Irwin or Irvin of Justice Town
6 „ 1809	.	Miles Ponsonby of Hail Hall
Jan. 1810	.	Henry Fletcher of Clea Hall bart.
8 Feb. 1811	.	John Losh, of Woodside
24 Jan. 1812	.	Thomas Hartley of Linethwaite

[1] Died in office.

10 Feb.	1813	. Wastell Brisco of Crofton Place, bart.
4 ,,	1814	. Thomas Benson of Wreay Hall
13 ,,	1815	. William Ponsonby Johnson of Walton House
12 ,,	1816	. William Brown of Tallantire Hall
12 ,,	1817	. Philip Musgrave of Edenhall, bart.
24 Jan.	1818	. Milham Hartley of Rosehill
10 Feb.	1819	. Thomas Salkeld of Carlisle
12 ,,	1820	. Wilfrid Lawson of Brayton House
6 ,,	1821	. John Marshall of Hallstead
4 ,,	1822	. William Crackenthorpe of Bank Hall
31 Jan.	1823	. Edward Stanley of Ponsonby Hall
31 ,,	1824	. Thomas Henry Graham of Edmund Castle
2 Feb.	1825	. Matthew Atkinson of Staingills
30 Jan.	1826	. Humphrey Senhouse of Netherhall
5 Feb.	1827	. William James of Barrock Park
13 ,,	1828	. Thomas Parker of Warwick Hall
28 Apr.	1828	. William Blamire of Thackwood Nook
11 Feb.	1829	. Edward Williams Hasell of Dalemain
2 ,,	1830	. Christopher Parker, Petterill Green
31 Jan.	1831	. John Taylor, Dockray
6 Feb.	1832	. Henry Howard, Corby Castle
, ,,	1833	. Henry Curwen, Workington
3 ,,	1834	. Henry Howard,[1] Greystoke
7 ,,	1835	. Richard Ferguson, Harker Lodge
8 ,,	1836	. Thomas Irwin, Calder Abbey
2 ,,	1837	. Sir Francis Fletcher Vane, bart., Armathwaite
6 ,,	1838	. John Dixon, Knells
11 ,,	1839	. Thomas Hartley, Gillfoot
1 ,,	1840	. Sir George Musgrave, bart., Edenhall
5 ,,	1841	. James Robertson Walker, Gilgarron
5 ,,	1842	. Fretchvill Lawson Ballantyne Dykes, Dovenby Hall
4 ,,	1843	. Robert Hodgson, Salkeld Hall
3 ,,	1844	. George Harrison, Linethwaite
6 ,,	1845	. Timothy Fetherstonhaugh, Kirkoswald
2 ,,	1846	. Joseph Pocklington Senhouse, Netherhall
4 ,,	1847	. Gilfrid William Hartley, Rosehill
11 ,,	1848	. Henry Dundas Maclean, Lazonby Hall
13 ,,	1849	. Andrew Fleming Hudleston, Hutton John
5 ,,	1850	. Thomas Salkeld, Holm Hill
11 ,,	1851	. George Head Head, Rickerby
2 ,,	1852	. George Henry Oliphant, Broadfield

7 Feb.	1853	. Francis Baring Atkinson, Rampbeck
30 Jan.	1854	. Thomas Alison Hoskins, Higham
8 Feb.	1855	. Thomas Story Spedding, Mirehouse
30 Jan.	1856	. Sir Henry Ralph Vane, bart., Hutton Hall
2 Feb.	1857	. Charles Fetherstonhaugh, Staffield Hall
3 ,,	1858	. Anthony Benn Steward, Chapel House
3 ,,	1859	. Gamel Augustus, Lord Muncaster
23 Jan.	1860	. Philip Henry Howard, Corby Castle
4 Feb.	1861	. Thomas Ainsworth, The Flosh
5 ,,	1862	. Samuel Lindow, Cleator
3 ,,	1863	. William Nicholson Hodgson, Newby Grange
3 ,,	1864	. Thomas Brocklebank, Greenlands
4 ,,	1865	. William Postlethwaite, The Oaks, Millom
3 ,,	1866	. Sir Frederick Ulric Graham, bart., Netherby
2 ,,	1867	. William Edward James, Barrock Park
30 Jan.	1868	. Sir Robert Brisco, Crofton Hall
4 Feb.	1869	. John Ewart, Kingfield House
5 ,,	1870	. Timothy Fetherstonhaugh, Kirkoswald
8 ,,	1871	. William Banks, Highmoor
5 ,,	1872	. George Moore, Whitehall
5 ,,	1873	. Thomas Holme Parker, Warwick Hall
2 ,,	1874	. John Lindow, Ehen Hall
4 ,,	1875	. John Porter Foster, Kilhow
12 ,,	1876	. George John Johnson, Castlesteads
7 ,,	1877	. Jonas Lindow Burns Lindow, Irton Hall
22 ,,	1878	. Frederic John Reed, Hassness
22 ,,	1879	. Henry Charles Howard, Greystoke Castle
26 ,,	1880	. James Lumb, Homewood
2 Mar.	1881	. Samuel Porter Foster, Kilhow
27 Feb.	1882	. George Routledge, Stonehouse
3 Mar.	1883	. Jonas Lindow, Ehen Hall
4 ,,	1884	. Henry Anthony Spedding, Mirehouse
5 ,,	1885	. Lamplugh Fretchvill Ballantine Dykes, Dovenby Hall
8 ,,	1886	. Henry Pearson Banks, Highmoor
7 ,,	1887	. Thomas Hartley, Armathwaite Hall
17 ,,	1888	. Henry Fraser Curwen, Workington
6 Apr.	1889	. Edwin Hodge Banks, Highmoor
21 Mar.	1890	. Henry Jefferson, Springfield
20 ,,	1891	. John Stirling Ainsworth, Harecroft
16 ,,	1892	. Humphrey Pocklington Senhouse, Netherhall
15 ,,	1893	. George William Mounsey Heysham, Castletown

1 The names of the sheriffs from 1834 to 1904 have been taken from the official record kept by the Clerk of the Peace of Cumberland.

10 Mar. 1894	. Sir Richard James Graham, bart., Netherby	
8 „ 1895	. Joseph Harris, Calthwaite	
6 „ 1896	. Louis Carruthers Salkeld, Holm Hill	
26 Feb. 1897	. Colonel Thomas Angelo Irwin, Lynehow	
7 Mar. 1898	. George Graham Kirklinton, Kirklinton Hall	

7 Mar. 1899	. William Parkin Moore, Whitehall	
3 „ 1900	. Charles Lacy Thompson, Milton Hall	
9 „ 1901	. Hamlet Riley, Ennim	
6 „ 1902	. Captain William Percy Standish, Breckonhill Tower	
12 „ 1903	. Thomas Dixon, Rheda	
7 „ 1904	. Richard Heywood Thompson, Nunwick Hall	

APPENDIX No II

KNIGHTS OF THE SHIRE ELECTED FOR CUMBERLAND [1]

1290 . . Walter de Mulcaster
Hubert de Multon
William de Boyvill
1295 . . Robert de Haveryngton
Hubert de Multon
1297 . . William de Boyvill
Robert de Wytering
1298 . . No returns found
1299–1300 Richard de Cleter
Robert de Witerige
1300–1301 John de Wyggeton
Robert de Tilliol
1302 . . Robert de Joneby
Nicholas de Moresby
1304–5 . John de Wygeton
1306 . . John de Lucy
Walter de Bampton
1306–7 . [John de Denton [2]
William de Langrigg]
1307 . . Richard le Brun
Alexander de Bastenthueit
1309 . . William de Mulcastre
Alexander de Bastenthuit
1311 . . Robert de Leyburn
Walter de Bampton
1311 . . William de Mulcastre
Henry de Malton
1312 . . Andrew de Hartcla
Alan de Grensdale or Grynnesdale
1312–13 . No returns found
1313 . . No returns found
1313 . . John de Wygeton
Robert de Layburne
1314 . . No returns found
1314–15 . Robert de Tilliol
Henry de Malton
1315–16 . No returns found
1316 . . Alexander de Bastenthwayt
Walter de Kirkbrid
1316 . . Robert le Brune

1316 . . John de Skelton
1318 . . John de Boyvill
Adam de Skelton
1319 . . Robert de Laybourn
Alexander de Bastenthwayt
1320 . . Alexander de Bastenthweyt
Robert le Broun
1321 . . Robert de Leybourn
William de Aykeheved
1322 . . Peter Tyliol
1322 . . Henry de Malton
No returns found
1323–4 . Hugh de Louthre
John de Orreton
1324 . . Richard de Denton
John de Skelton
1325 . . Robert de Mulcastre, knt.
Robert Parvynk
1326–7 . Robert le Brun
John de Orreton
1327 . . John de Orreton
Robert Parvynk or Parvyng
1327–8 . Peter de Tilliol
Robert Parvyng
1328 . . Robert de Eglefeld
Richard de Salkeld
1328 . . Peter de Tilliol
John de Skelton
1328–9 . No return found
1329–30 . John de Orreton
Thomas de Hardegill
1330 . . Peter de Tilliol
John de Orreton
1331 . . Richard de Denton
Robert Parvyng
1331–2 . Richard de Denton
Robert Parvyng
1332 . . Richard de Denton
John de Haveryngton
1332 . . Peter de Tilliol
Richard de Denton
1333–4 . Richard de Denton
John de Haveryngton
1334 . . Hugh de Moriceby
William Lengleys, nepos, or Lenglis le Cosyn
1335 . . Peter de Tilliol

[1] The following lists of knights and burgesses before 1880 have been compiled from the *Parliaments of England*, printed by order of the House of Commons ; those of later date have been collected from various sources.
[2] These two names are found in the Writ de Expensis without reference to any county, but there is little doubt that they belong to Cumberland.

1335 . .	Richard de Denton
1335-6 .	John de Orreton
	Henry de Manton
1336 . .	No returns found
1336-7 .	Peter de Tilliol
	Richard de Denton
1337 . .	Richard de Denton
	Hugh de Moriceby
1337-8 .	John de Orreton
	Thomas de Skelton
1338 . .	Thomas de Hardegill
	Richard de Bery
1338-9 .	Peter de Tilliol
	John de Haveryngton
1339 . .	John de Orreton
	John de Haveryngton
1339-40 .	John de Orreton
	John de Haveryngton
1340 . .	Peter de Tilliol
	John de Orreton
1341 . .	Peter de Tilliol
	Hugh de Louthre
1343 . .	Richard de Denton
	John de Orreton
1344 . .	Hugh de Louthre
	Henry de Malton
1346 . .	No returns found
1347-8 .	Peter de Tilliol
	John de Orton
1348 . .	John de Orreton
	Thomas de Hardgill
1350-1 .	Richard de Denton
	John de Orreton
1351-2 .	Richard de Denton
	Robert de Tillioll
1352 . .	Henry de Malton
1353 . .	Richard de Denton
1354 . .	Thomas de Rokeby le Cosyn
	Thomas de Hardegill
1355 . .	Richard de Denton
	John de Orreton
1357 . .	John de Orreton
	Robert de Tillioll
1357-8 .	Robert de Tillioll
	Adam Parvyng
1360 . .	John de Orreton, knt.
	Christopher de Moriceby
1360-1 .	Henry de Malton
	Robert de Tillioll
1362 . .	Robert de Tillioll, knt.
	William Lengleys or Lenglish, knt.
1363 . .	William Lengleys, chivaler
	Christopher de Moriceby
1364-5 .	Robert de Tillioll, knt.
	William Engleys, knt.
1366 . .	Christopher de Moriceby
	William de Stapilton
1368 . .	James de Pykeryng, knt.
	John de Denton
1369 . .	William Lengleys, chivaler
	Robert Moubray, chivaler
1370-1 .	Robert Culwenne
	William de Stapilton
1371 . .	Gilbert Culwenne [1]

1372 . .	Robert Moubray, knt.
	John de Denton
1373 . .	Gilbert de Culwen, chivaler
	Adam Parvyng, chivaler
1375-6 .	Gilbert de Culwenn, chivaler
	William Stapelton
1376-7 .	John de Denton
	Amand Monceux
1377 . .	Robert Moubray, chivaler
	Richard del Sandes
1378 . .	Peter Tillioll
	Clement de Skelton
1379 . .	John Derwentwatre
	Thomas de Whitrigg
1379-80 .	Robert de Moubray, chivaler
	William de Culwen, chivaler
1380 . .	Peter Tillioll
	William de Huton in the Forest
1381 . .	Gilbert de Culwen
	John de Denton
1382 . .	Richard de Salkeld
	John Dalmore
1382 . .	Clement de Skelton
	Thomas Bowet
1382-3 .	Clement de Skelton, chivaler
	John de Dalston
1383 . .	Thomas de Blenkansop
	Amand Mounceux
1384 . .	John de Corkeby
	John de Brouham
1384 . .	John de Ireby, chivaler
	Thomas de Lamplogh, chivaler
1385 . .	Peter de Tillioll, chivaler
	Richard de Beuleu
1386 . .	Amand Mounceux
	John de Thirlwall, jun.
1387-8 .	John de Derwentwatre, chivaler
	John de Ireby, chivaler
1388 . .	Robert de Mulcastre, chivaler
	Amand Mounceux
1389-90 .	William de Threlkeld, knt.
	Amand Mounceux, knt.
1390 . .	William de Stapilton
	Thomas del Sandes
1391 . .	Peter Tillioll
	Robert de Louther [2]
1392-3 .	Geoffrey Tilliol, knt.
	William de Louthre, knt.
1393-4 .	Clement de Skelton
	Robert de Louther
1394-5 .	William Stapilton
	Thomas del Sandys
1396-7 .	John de Ireby, chivaler
	Clement de Skelton, chivaler
1397-8 .	Peter Tillioll
	William de Osmundrelawe
1399 . .	William de Leegh, chivaler
	Rolland Vaux
1400-1 .	Robert de Louther
	William de Stapilton
1402 . .	William de Legh
	John de Skelton
1403 . .	Robert de Louther, chivaler
	William de Louther, chivaler

[1] Curwenne in the enrolment of the Writ de Expensis.   [2] Loweyer in the enrolment of the Writ de Expensis.

1404 . . John de la More, chivaler
William de Bewelieu, chivaler
1405–6 . Robert de Louther, chivaler
John de Skelton, chivaler
1407 . . William Stapilton
William Dalmore
1411 . . No returns found
1413 . . Peter Tillioll, knt.
William de Beaulieu
1413–14 . Robert de Louthre, chivaler
William del Legh, chivaler
1414 . . Christopher de Culwen, knt.
John de Eglesfeld
1415 . . No returns found
1415–16 . John de Lancastre, chivaler
William de Stapilton, sen.
1417 . . Peter Tillioll, knt.
Robert de Louthre, knt.
1419 . . William Legh, knt.
Richard Restwold
1420 . . Peter Tillioll, chivaler
Thomas Delamore
1421 . . John de Lamplough, knt.
Richard Restwold, jun.
1421 . . Peter Tillioll, chivaler
Nicholas Redclyff, chivaler
1422 . . Peter Tillioll, chivaler
John Skelton, chivaler
1423 . . Christopher Culwen, knt.
William del Legh, jun., knt.
1425 . . Peter Tillioll
Christopher Culwen
1425–6 . Peter Tillioll, chivaler
Hugh de Louthre, esq.
1427 . . Christopher Curwen, chivaler
Nicholas Radcliffe, chivaler
1429 . . Thomas Parr
Thomas de la More
1430–1 . Christophet Curwen, chivaler
Hugh Louther
1432 . . Christopher Curwen, chivaler
John Penyngton, chivaler
1433 . . William Leigh, chivaler
William Laton, esq.
1435 . . Thomas Curwen, esq.
William Dikes
1436–7 . William Stapilton
John Broughton
1441–2 . Ralf de Dacre, esq.
Thomas Curwen, esq.
1446–7 . John Penyngton, esq.
William Martyndale, esq.
1448–9 . Thomas Curwen
Hugh Louther
1449 . . John Skelton
Richard Belyngham
1450 . . Thomas Crakanthorp, esq.
Thomas Dalamore or Delamore, esq.
1452–3 . John Skelton, esq.
Roland Vaux, esq.
1455 . . Thomas Colt, esq.
Thomas Delamere, esq.
1459 . . Thomas Curwen, knt.
William Legh, esq.
1460 . . No returns found
1467 . . John Huddilston, knt.

1467 . . Richard Salkeld, esq.
1472 . . John Parr, knt.
Richard Salkeld.
1477–8 . William Par, knt.
James Moresby
1529 . . Christopher Dacre
John Leigh
1541–2 . Thomas [Wh]arton
1545 . . Thomas Wharton, son and heir of
Thomas Lord Wharton
Cuthbert Huton, esq.
1547 . . Thomas Warton, knt.
Richard Musgrave, esq.
1552–3 . Richard Musgrave, knt.
Henry Curwen, esq.
1553 . . Thomas Wharton, knt.
Thomas Dacres, jun., knt.
1554 . . John Leigh, esq.
Robert Penruddock, esq.
1554 . . . . esq.[1]
Robert Penruddok, esq.
1555 . . Thomas . . . [1]
Henry Curwen, esq.
1557–8 . Leonard Dacres, esq.
John Dalstone, esq.
1558–9 . No returns found
1562–3 . Leonard Dacres, esq.
Henry Curwen, esq.
1572 . . Simon Musgrave, knt.
Edward Scroope, esq.
1584 . . No returns found
1586 . . Robert Bowes, esq., treasurer of Berwick
Henry Leighe, esq.
1588–9 . Thomas Scroope, knt.
Robert Bowes, esq.
1592–3 . Nicholas Curwen, esq.
Wilfrid Lawson, esq.
1597 . . Joseph Pennington
Christopher Pickerringe
1601 . . William Huddleston, esq.
Gerard Lowther, esq.
1603–4 . Wilfrid Lawson, esq.
Edward Musgrave, esq.
1614 . . William Lawson, knt.
Thomas Penruddock, knt.
1620–1 . George Dalston, knt.
Henry Curwen knt.
1623–4 . George Dalston, knt., of Dalston
Ferdinand Hudleston, esq., of Millome
1625 . . George Dalston, knt., of Dalston
Patrick Curwen, esq., of Workington
1625–6 . George Dalston, knt.
Patrick Curwen, esq.
1627–8 . George Dalston, knt.
Patrick Curwen, bart.
1640 . . George Dalston, knt.
Patrick Curwen, bart.
1640 . . George Dalston, knt.
(Long Par- Patrick Curwen, bart.
liament)
1646 . . William Ermyn, esq., and Richard
Tolson, esq., *vice* George Dalston,
knt., and Patrick Curwen, bart., disabled to sit

[1] Returns defaced.

1654 . .	Charles Howard, esq.
	William . . . . [1]
1656 . .	No return found
1658-9 .	No return found
1660 . .	Col. Lord Charles Howard
	Wilfrid Lawson, knt.
1661 . .	Patrick Curwen, bart.
	George Fletcher, bart.
1664-5 .	John Lowther, bart., of Whitehaven
	vice Patrick Curwen, bart., deceased
1678-9 .	John Lowther, bart., of Whitehaven
	Richard Lamplugh, esq.
1679 . .	Edward Lord Morpeth
	John Lowther, bart., of Whitehaven
1680-1 .	George Fletcher, bart.
	John Lowther, bart., of Whitehaven
1685 . .	Richard Viscount Preston
	John Lowther, bart., of Whitehaven
1688-9 .	George Fletcher, bart., of Hutton
	John Lowther, bart., of Whitehaven
1689-90 .	George Fletcher, bart.
	John Lowther, bart., of Whitehaven
1695 . .	George Fletcher, bart.
	John Lowther, bart., of Whitehaven
1698 . .	George Fletcher, bart.
	John Lowther, bart.
1700-1 .	Richard Musgrave, esq.
	Wilfrid Lawson, esq.
1701 . .	Edward Hasell, knt.
	George Fletcher, esq.
1702 . .	Richard Musgrave, esq.
	Wilfrid Lawson, esq.
1705 . .	George Fletcher, esq.
	Richard Musgrave, esq.
1708 . .	James Lowther, esq.
	Wilfrid Lawson, esq.
1710 . .	James Lowther, esq., of Whitehaven
	Wilfrid Lawson, esq., of Brayton
1713 . .	James Lowther, esq.
	Wilfrid Lawson, esq.
1714-15 .	James Lowther, esq.
	Wilfrid Lawson, esq.
1722 . .	Christopher Musgrave, bart.
	Wilfrid Lawson, esq.
1727 . .	James Lowther, esq.
	Wilfrid Lawson, esq.
1734 . .	James Lowther, bart.
	Joseph Pennington, bart.
1741 . .	James Lowther, bart., of Whitehaven
	Joseph Pennington, bart., of Muncaster.
1744-5 .	John Pennington, bart., *vice* Sir Joseph Pennington, deceased
1747 . .	James Lowther, bart.
	John Pennington, bart.
1754 . .	James Lowther, bart.
	John Pennington, bart.
1755 . .	William Lowther, bart., of Whitehaven, *vice* Sir James Lowther, deceased
1756 . .	William Fleming, bart., *vice* Sir William Lowther, deceased
1757 . .	James Lowther, bart., *vice* Sir William Fleming, deceased

[1] Return torn.

1761 . .	John Pennington, bart.
	James Lowther, bart.
	Wilfrid Lawson, bart., *vice* Sir James Lowther, who elected to sit for Westmorland
1762 . .	James Lowther, bart., *vice* Sir Lawson, deceased
1768 . .	Henry Fletcher, esq.[2]
	Henry Curwen, esq.
1774 . .	James Lowther, bart.
	Henry Fletcher, esq.
1780 . .	James Lowther, bart.
	Henry Fletcher, esq.
1784 . .	Henry Fletcher, bart.
	William Lowther, esq.
1790 . .	Henry Fletcher, bart., of Clea
	Humphrey Senhouse, esq., of Netherhall
1796 . .	Henry Fletcher, bart., of Clea
	John Lowther, esq., of Swillington, Yorks.
1802 . .	Henry Fletcher, bart.
	John Lowther, esq.
1806 . .	John Lowther, esq., of Swillington, Yorks.
	George Howard, commonly called Lord Viscount Morpeth
1807 . .	John Lowther, esq., of Swillington
	George Howard, called Lord Morpeth
1812 . .	John Lowther, esq., of Swillington
	George Howard, esq., of Naworth Castle, commonly called Viscount Morpeth
1818 . .	John Lowther, esq., of Swillington
	George Howard, Lord Morpeth
1820 . .	John Lowther, esq., of Swillington
	John Christian Curwen, esq., of Workington Hall
1826 . .	John Lowther, bart.
	John Christian Curwen, esq.
1829 . .	James Robert George Graham, bart., of Netherby, *vice* John Christian Curwen, deceased
1830 . .	John Lowther, bart.
	James Robert George Graham, bart.
	James Robert George Graham, bart., re-elected after appointment
1831 . .	James Robert George Graham, bart.
	William Blamire, esq., of Thackwood

EASTERN DIVISION

1833 . .	James Robert George Graham, bart., of Netherby
	William Blamire, esq., of Thackwood

WESTERN DIVISION

William Viscount Lowther, of Whitehaven

Edward Stanley, esq., of Ponsonby Hall

Samuel Irton, esq., of Irton Hall, *vice* William Viscount Lowther, who elected to serve for Westmorland

[2] Return amended by order of the House, dated 16 Dec. 1768, by erasing the name of Sir James Lowther and substituting the name of Henry Fletcher.

EASTERN DIVISION

1835 . . James Robert George Graham, bart., of Netherby
William Blamite, esq., of Thackwood

1836 . . William James, esq., of Barrock Lodge, *vice* William Blamire, appointed Chief Commissioner of Tithes

WESTERN DIVISION

1835 . . Edward Stanley, esq., of Ponsonby Hall
Samuel Irton, esq., of Irton Hall

EASTERN DIVISION

1837 . . Francis Aglionby, esq., of Nunnery
William James, esq., of Barrock Lodge

1840 . . Charles Wentworth George Howard, esq., Naworth Castle, *vice* Francis Aglionby, deceased

WESTERN DIVISION

1837 . . Edward Stanley, esq., of Ponsonby Hall
Samuel Irton, esq., of Irton Hall

EASTERN DIVISION

1841 . . Charles Wentworth George Howard, esq.
William James, esq.

WESTERN DIVISION

Edward Stanley, esq.
Samuel Irton, esq.

EASTERN DIVISION

1847 . . Charles Wentworth George Howard, esq.
William Marshall, esq.

WESTERN DIVISION

Edward Stanley, esq.
Henry Lowther, esq.

EASTERN DIVISION

1852 . . Charles Wentworth George Howard, esq.
William Marshall, esq.

WESTERN DIVISION

Henry Lowther, esq., of Whitehaven Castle
Samuel Irton, esq., of Irton Hall

EASTERN DIVISION

1857 . . Charles Wentworth George Howard, esq.
William Marshall, esq., of Patterdale Hall

WESTERN DIVISION

Henry Wyndham, esq., of Cockermouth Castle
Henry Lowther, esq., of Lowther Castle

EASTERN DIVISION

1859 . . Charles Wentworth George Howard, esq., of Castle Howard
William Marshall, esq., of Patterdale Hall

WESTERN DIVISION

Henry Lowther, esq., of Whitehaven Castle
Henry Wyndham, esq., of Cockermouth Castle

1860 . . Percy Wyndham, esq., *vice* Sir Henry Wyndham, K.C.B., deceased

EASTERN DIVISION

1865 . . Charles Wentworth George Howard, esq.
William Marshall, esq.

WESTERN DIVISION

Henry Lowther, esq.
Percy Scawen Wyndham, esq.

EASTERN DIVISION

1868 . . William Nicholson Hodgson, esq.
Charles Wentworth George Howard, esq.

WESTERN DIVISION

Henry Lowther, esq.
Percy Scawen Wyndham, esq.

1872 . . Lord Muncaster, *vice* Henry Lowther, esq., called to the Upper House as Earl of Lonsdale

EASTERN DIVISION

1874 . . Charles Wentworth George Howard, esq.
William Nicholson Hodgson, esq.

1876 . . Edward Stafford Howard, esq., *vice* W. N. Hodgson, deceased

1879 . . George James Howard, esq., *vice* Charles W. G. Howard, esq., deceased

WESTERN DIVISION

1874 . . Percy Scawen Wyndham, esq.
Lord Muncaster

EASTERN DIVISION

1880 . . Sir R. C. Musgrave, bart.
Edward Stafford Howard, esq.

1881 . . George James Howard, esq., *vice* Sir R. C. Musgrave, deceased

WESTERN DIVISION

1880 . . David Ainsworth, esq.
Hon. Percy Scawen Wyndham

COCKERMOUTH DIVISION

1885 . . Charles James Valentine, esq.
1886 . . Sir Wilfrid Lawson, bart.
1892 . . Sir Wilfrid Lawson, bart.
1895 . . Sir Wilfrid Lawson, bart.
1900 . . John Scurrah Randles, esq.

ESKDALE DIVISION

1885 . . Robert Andrew Allison, esq.
1886 . . Robert Andrew Allison, esq.
1892 . . Robert Andrew Allison, esq,
1895 . . Robert Andrew Allison, esq.
1900 . . Claude William Henry Lowther, esq.

EGREMONT DIVISION

1885 . . Lord Muncaster
1886 . . Lord Muncaster
1892 . . David Ainsworth, esq.
1895 . . Hon. H. V. Duncombe
1900 . . James Robert Bain, esq.

PENRITH DIVISION

1885 . . Henry Charles Howard, esq.
1886 . . James William Lowther, esq.
1892 . . James William Lowther, esq.
1895 . . James William Lowther, esq.
1900 . . James William Lowther, esq.

CARLISLE
BURGESSES

1295 . . Robert de Grenesdal
     Andrew le Seler
1302 . . Henry le Espicer
     Andrew le Serjaunt
1304-5 . Robert de Grynnesdale
     Alan de Grynnesdale
1306 . . Alan de Grinesdale
1307 . . Andrew le Serjaunt, of Carlisle (*de Karliolo*)
     Richard de Hubrychby
1309 . . William, son of Ives
     Robert de Grinnesdale
1311 . . John de Crofton
     William, son of Henry, son of Ives [1]
1311 . . Alan de Grinnesdal
     William le Taylour or Taillour
1312 . . John de Ireland (Hibern')
     Thomas de Wraton
1313 . . Robert de Grinnesdal
     John de Wynton [2]
1314-15 . Robert de Grinnesdal
     Bernard Lacatour
1318 . . Robert de Grinnesdal
     William, son of Ives
1319 . . Robert de Grinesdale
     Bernard Pulter
1320 . . William, son of Henry
     Henry le Spicer
1321 . . John de Capella
1321 . . John de Ba . . .
1322 . . John de Wylton
     Thomas de Colston
1323-4 . John de la Chapele
     Gilbert de la Chapele
1325 . . Bernard le Poleter
     John de la Chapele
1326-7 . John Flemyng
     Nicholas le Despenser [3]
1327 . . John de la Chapell

[1] The enrolment of the Writ de Expensis gives Alan de Grenesdale and Andrew son of Peter of Carlisle.
[2] The enrolment of the Writ de Expensis gives Andrew le Serjaunt and William son of Henry.
[3] The enrolment of the Writ de Expensis gives John Flemyng and Robert de Grenesdale.

1327 . . Thomas Caskell
1327-8 . Alan de Grynnesdall
     John de Capella
1328 . . Robert de Grynnesdall
     Alan de Grynnesdall
1328-9 . John de Haveryngton
     Simon de Sandford
1329-30 . John de Haverington
     Richard de Skelton
1330 . . John de Haveryngton
     Robert de Gryndon
1331-2 . John de Haveryngton
     Simon de Sandford
1332 . . John Flemyng
     Adam de Crofton
1333-4 . John Flemyng
     Adam de Crofton
1334 . . John de Pikeryng
1334 . . Henry Pepir
1335 . . John de Eslington
     Thomas Worthschypp
1335-6 . Thomas de Hardgill
     Thomas de Frisington
1337 . . John de Denton
     Adam de Broghton
1337-8 . Thomas de Pardishowe
     Giles de Orreton
1338 . . William Broun
     Thomas de Fresington
1338-9 . John de Exlyngton
     Thomas de Hardegill
1340 . . John Flemyng
     Adam de Crofton
1341 . . Thomas de Hardegill, jun.
     John Flemyng, jun.
1344 . . Thomas de Hardegill, jun.
     Thomas de Grynnesdale
1347-8 . Adam de Crofton
     Robert de Tybay
1348 . . Adam de Crofton
     Thomas de Appelby
1350-1 . Robert de Tebay
     John de Raghton
1353 . . No return found
1355 . . William de Artureth
     Thomas de Alaynby
1357 . . Thomas de Alaynby
     John de Thorneton
1357-8 . Thomas de Alaynby
     William le Spenser
1360 . . Thomas de Alaynby
     William Spenser
1360-1 . John de Thornton
1360-1 . Adam de Agillounby
1362 . . William Artureth
     William Spenser
1363 . . Adam Halden
     William Spenser
1364-5 . William de Artureth
     Richard de London
1366 . . Richard Orfevre
     William de Clyfton
1368 . . Adam de Agylounby
     William de Clifton
1369 . . William de Artureth

1369 . . John de Waverton
1371 . . John de Whitlawe
1372 . . William de Raghton
William de Carlisle (*Karliolo*)
1373 . . Richard de Denton
Thomas Taillour
1376–7 . Richard de Denton
John de Burgh
1378 . . Robert de Karlelee
John de Levyngton
1379–80 . Robert de Karlellee
William del Park
1381 . . Robert de Karlelee
John de Blenerhayset
1382–3 . William de Osmounderlawe
John de Skelton
1383 . . Richard de London
John de Appelby
1384 . . Stephen de Karlell
Thomas de Bolton
Richard de Lundon
John de Blenerhayset
1385 . . William de Agliounby
John de Blencowe
1386 . . Adam de Denton
Robert de Briscowe, jun.
1387–8 . Robert de Karliolo
William de Aglionby
1388 . . John de Corkeby
Nicholas Leveson
1389–90 . John Mounceux
Alan de Kirkebrig
1391 . . John Mounceux
Robert de Bryscowe
1392–3 . John de Redesdale
John de Werk
1394–5 . John Brugham
John Mounceux
1396–7 . John de Helton
John de Burgham
1397–8 . Robert de Briscowe
John de Briscowe
1399 . . John Helton
Robert de Briscowe
1402 . . John de Sourby
William Boweson
1413 . . Robert de Karlell, jun.
Ralf de Blenerhaisset
1414 . . Robert de Karlell, jun.
William Cardoile
1415–16 . Robert de Lancastre
William Bell
1417 . . Robert de Karlell, jun.
William Cardoile
1419 . . Robert Karlell
Thomas Manyngham
1420 . . Thomas de Derley
Richard de Mulcastre
1421 . . Robert de Karlell, jun.
Thomas Pety
1421 . . William de Manchestre
John Thomson
1422 . . Robert Karlell, jun.
Richard Draxe
1423 . . Richard Briscowe
William Whiteheved

1425 . . Thomas Petyt
Robert Maderer
1425–6 . Richard Mulcastre
Nicholas Toppy
1427 . . John de Helton
William Camberton
1429 . . Thomas Derwent
Adam Heveryngton
1430–1 . Averard Berwyk
Robert Clerk
1432 . . John Sharpp
Thomas Cuthbertson
1433 . . Richard Briscowe or Briskowe
Richard Beaulieu
1435 . . William Morthyng
Nicholas Thomson
1436–7 . Robert Mabsen
Thomas Mareschall
1441–2 . John Blenerhassett
William Butler
1446–7 . Thomas Stanlawe
George Walton
1448–9 . Robert Karlill, jun.
Richard Alanson
1449 . . Thomas Colt
John Bere
1450 . . Richard Alanson
Alvered Mauleverere
1452–3 . Richard Alanson
Thomas Derwent
1455 . . John Bere
Thomas Derwent
1459 . . Richard Bewley
Thomas Rukyn
1467 . . Henry Denton
Richard George
1472 . . Robert Skelton
John Coldale
1477–8 . Edward Redemayn
John Appilby
1529 . . Edward Aglyonby
John Coldeale
1541–2 . William Stapilton
. . . .
1545 . . Hugh Aglionby
Robert Smyth
1547 . . Edward Eglonby, esq.
Thomas Dalston, esq.
1552–3 . Edward Aglionby, jun.
John Dudley
1553 . . John Aglionbie
Simon Briscoe
1554 . . Robert Whitley
Richard Mynsho
1554 . . Robert Whitley
Richard Mynsho
1555 . . William Middilton
William Warde
1557–8 . Richard Asshton, esq.
Robert Dalton, esq.
1562–3 . Richard Assheton, gent.
William Mulcaster, gent.
1572 . . Thomas Pattenson, gent.
Robert Mulcaster, gent.
Thomas Tallentyer, gent., *vice* Robert
Mulcaster, deceased

1586	. .	Henry Mackwilliams, esq.
		Thomas Blenerhassett
1588–9	.	Henry Scroope, esq.
		John Dalston, esq.
1592–3	.	Henry Scroope, esq.
		Edward Aglionbye or Eglionby, esq.
1597	. .	Henry Scrope, esq.
		Thomas Samford, jun., esq.
1601	. .	Henry Scroope, esq.
		John Dudleye, esq.
1603–4	.	Thomas Blenerhassett, esq.
		William Barwicke, esq.
1614	. .	George Buttler, esq.
		Nathaniel Tomkins, esq.
1620–1	.	Henry Fayne, knt.
		George Butler, esq.
1623–4	.	Henry Fayne, knt.
		Edward Aglionbye, esq.
1625	. .	Henry Fayne, knt.
		Edward Aglionby, esq.
1625–6	.	Henry Fane, knt.
		Richard Grame, esq.
1627–8	.	[Richard] Barwise, esq.[1]
		Richard Graime, esq.
1640	. .	William Dalston, esq.
		Richard Barwis, esq.
1640	. .	William Dalston, esq.
(Long Par-		Richard Barwis, esq.
liament)		Thomas Cholmley, esq.[2]
1654	. .	. . . .[3]
1656	. .	Mr. Downing [4]
1660	. .	William Brisco, esq.
		Jeremiah Tolhurst, esq.
1661	. .	Philip Howard, knt.
		Christopher Musgrave, esq.
1678–9	.	Philip Howard, knt.
		Christopher Musgrave, knt.
1679	. .	Philip Howard, knt.
		Christopher Musgrave, knt.
1680–1	.	Edward Lord Morpeth
		Christopher Musgrave, knt.
1685	. .	Christopher Musgrave, knt.
		James Graham, esq.
1688–9	.	Christopher Musgrave, knt. and bart.
		Jeremiah Bubb, esq.
1689–90	.	Jeremiah Bubb, esq.
		Christopher Musgrave, esq.
1692	. .	William Lowther, esq., son of John Lowther, esq., late of Hackthorp, *vice* Jeremiah Bubb, deceased
1694	. .	James Lowther, esq., *vice* William Lowther, deceased
1695	. .	William Howard, esq.
		James Lowther, esq.
1698	. .	William Howard, esq.
		James Lowther, esq.
1700–1	.	Philip Howard, esq.
		James Lowther, esq.
1701	. .	Philip Howard, esq.
		James Lowther, esq.
1702	. .	Christopher Musgrave, esq.

1702	. .	Thomas Stanwix, esq.
1705	. .	Thomas Stanwix, esq.
		James Mountague, knt.
1708	. .	James Montague, knt.
		Thomas Stanwix, esq.
		James Montague, knt. (re-elected on becoming Attorney General)
1710	. .	Thomas Stanwix, esq.
		James Mountague, knt.
1710–11	.	Brigadier Thomas Stanwix re-elected after appointment to an office of profit by the Crown
1713	. .	Christopher Musgrave, bart.
		Thomas Stanwix, esq.
1714–15	.	Thomas Stanwix, esq.
		William Strickland, esq.
1721	. .	Henry Aglionby, esq., *vice* Thomas Stanwix, appointed to an office of profit by the Crown
1722	. .	Henry Aglionby, esq.
		James Bateman, esq.
1727	. .	Charles Howard, esq.
		John Hylton, esq.
1734	. .	Charles Howard, esq.
		John Hylton, esq.
1741	. .	Charles Howard, esq.
		John Hylton, esq.[5]
1746	. .	John Stanwix, esq., *vice* John Hylton, deceased
1747	. .	John Stanwix, esq.
		Charles Howard, esq.
1754	. .	Charles Howard, knt.
		John Stanwix, esq.
1761	. .	Raby Vane, esq.
		Henry Curwen, esq.
1768	. .	Edward Charles Cavendish Bentinck, esq.
		George Musgrave, esq.
1774	. .	Fletcher Norton, esq.
		Anthony Storer, esq.
1775	. .	Walter Stanhope, esq., *vice* Fletcher Norton, who accepted the stewardship of the manor of East Hendred
1780	. .	Charles Howard, commonly called Earl of Surrey
		William Lowther, esq.
1783	. .	Charles Howard, Earl of Surrey, re-elected after appointment as one of the Lords Commissioners of the Treasury
1784	. .	Charles Howard, Earl of Surrey
		Edward Norton, esq.
1786	. .	John Christian, esq., *vice* Edward Norton, deceased [6]
		Rowland Stephenson, esq., *vice* Charles Howard, called to the Upper House.[7]
1790	. .	John Christian Curwen, esq.

[1] Return defaced.
[2] Elected *vice* Sir William Dalston, bart., disabled to sit (*Commons Journals*, 25 Sept. 1645).
[3] Return torn.
[4] Returned also for Peebles, but elected to sit for Carlisle.

[5] Return amended by order of the House, dated 26 January, 1741–2, by erasing the name of John Stanwix and substituting that of John Hylton.
[6] Return amended by order of the House, dated 31 May 1786, by erasing the name of John Lowther and substituting that of John Christian.
[7] Return amended by order of the House, dated 26 Feb. 1787, by erasing the name of Edward Knubley and substituting that of Rowland Stephenson.

1790 . . Wilson Braddyll, esq.[1]
1796 . . John Christian Curwen, esq.
Frederick Fletcher Vane, bart.
1802 . . John Christian Curwen, esq.
Walter Spencer Stanhope, esq.
1806 . . John Christian Curwen, esq.
Walter Spencer Stanhope, esq.
1807 . . John Christian Curwen, esq.
Walter Spencer Stanhope, esq.
1812 . . James Graham, bart., of Edmund
Castle
Henry Fawcett, esq.
1816 . . John Christian Curwen, esq., vice
Henry Fawcett, deceased
1818 . . John Christian Curwen, esq.
James Graham, bart., of Edmund
Castle
1820 . . James Graham, bart., of Edmund
Castle
John Christian Curwen, esq.
William James, esq., vice John Chris-
tian Curwen, esq., who elected to
serve for Cumberland.
1825 . . Philip Musgrave, bart., vice Sir James
Graham, deceased
1826 . . James Robert George Graham, bart.
Philip Musgrave, bart.
1827 . . James Law Lushington, esq., vice Sir
Philip Musgrave, deceased
1829 . . William Scott, bart., vice Sir James
Robert George Graham, who ac-
cepted the stewardship of the Chiltern Hundreds
1830 . . James Law Lushington, esq.
Philip Henry Howard, esq.
1831 . . William James, esq.
Philip Henry Howard, esq.
1833 . . Philip Henry Howard, esq.
William James, esq.
1835 . . Philip Henry Howard, esq., of Corby
Castle
William Marshall, esq., of Patterdale
Hall
1837 . . Philip Henry Howard, esq.
William Marshall, esq.
1841 . . Philip Henry Howard, esq.
William Marshall, esq.
1847 . . John Dixon, esq.
William Nicholson Hodgson, esq.
1848 . . William Nicholson Hodgson, esq.,
vice
John Dixon, whose election was declared void
Philip Henry Howard, esq., vice William Nicholson Hodgson, whose
election was declared void
1852 . . James Robert George Graham, bart.
Joseph Ferguson, esq.
1853 . . James Robert George Graham, bart.
re-elected after appointment
1857 . . William Nicholson Hodgson, esq.
James Robert George Graham, bart.

1859 . . James Robert George Graham, bart.
Wilfrid Lawson, esq.
1861 . . Edmund Potter, esq., vice Sir James
R. G. Graham, deceased
1865 . . William Nicholson Hodgson, esq.
Edmund Potter, esq.
1868 . . Wilfrid Lawson, bart.
Edmund Potter, esq.
1874 . . Robert Ferguson, esq.
Wilfrid Lawson, bart.
1880 . . Robert Ferguson, esq.
Wilfrid Lawson, bart.
1885 . . Robert Ferguson, esq.
1886 . . William Court Gully, esq.
1892 . . William Court Gully, esq.
1895 . . William Court Gully, esq.
1900 . . William Court Gully, esq.

COCKERMOUTH

BURGESSES

1295 . . William Bully
Peter de Hale
1640 . . John Fenwicke, bart.
(Long Par- John Hippesley, knt.
liament)
1642 . . Francis Allen [2] vice Sir John Fenwicke,
bart., who elected to serve for
Northumberland
1660 . . Richard Tolson, esq.
Wilfrid Lawson, esq.
1661 . . Hugh Potter, esq.
Wilfrid Lawson, knt.
1661–2 . Robert Scawen, esq., vice Hugh Potter,
deceased
1670 . . John Clarke, esq., vice Robert Scawen,
deceased
1675 . . Richard Graham, bart., vice John
Clarke, deceased
1678–9 . Richard Graham, bart.
Orlando Gee, esq.
1679 . . Richard Graham, bart.
Orlando Gee, esq.
1680–1 . Richard Graham, bart.
Orlando Gee, esq.
1685 . . Orlando Gee, knt.
Daniel Fleming, knt.
1688–9 . Henry Capel, knt.
Henry Fletcher, esq., of Hutton
1689–90 . Orlando Gee, knt.
Wilfrid Lawson, bart.
1695 . . Charles Gerard, bart.
Goodwin Wharton, esq.
1698 . . William Seymour, esq.
1698 . . George Fletcher, esq.
1700–1 . William Seymour, esq.
George Fletcher, esq.
1701 . . Goodwin Wharton, esq.
William Seymour, esq.
1701–2 . Thomas Lamplugh, esq., of Lamplugh, vice Goodwin Wharton, who
elected to serve for Bucks.

[1] Return amended by order of the House, dated 3 March
1791, by erasing the names of James Clarke Satterthwaite
and Edward Knubley, and substituting those of John Christian Curwen and Wilson Braddyll.

[2] Another indenture returning Sir Thomas Sandford, bart.
was taken off the file by order of the House, 3 Dec. 1645
(Commons Journals).

1702 . . James Stanhope, esq.
Thomas Lamplugh, esq.
1705 . . James Stanhope, esq.
Thomas Lamplugh, esq.
1708 . . James Stanhope, esq.
Albermarle Bertie, esq.
1710 . . Nicholas Lechmere, esq
James Stanhope, esq.
1711 . . James Stanhope re-elected, his election
having been declared void
1713 . . Joseph Musgrave, esq.
Nicholas Lechmere, esq.
1714–15 . James Stanhope, esq.
Nicholas Letchmere, esq.
1717 . . Thomas Pengelly, serjeant-at-law, *vice*
James Stanhope, appointed to an
office of profit by the Crown
1717 . . Percy Seymour, esq., commonly called
Lord Percy Seymour, *vice* Nicholas
Letchmere, appointed to an office of
profit by the Crown [1]
1721 . . Anthony Lowther, esq., *vice* Lord
Percy Seymour, deceased
1722 . . Thomas Pengelly, knt.
Wilfrid Lawson, bart.
1726–7 . William Finch, esq., *vice* Sir Thomas
Pengelly, appointed to an office of
profit by the Crown
1727 . . William Finch, esq.
Wilfrid Lawson, bart.
1734 . . William Finch, esq.
Wilfrid Lawson, bart.
1737–8 . Eldred Curwen, esq., *vice* Sir Wilfrid
Lawson, deceased
1741 . . William Finch, esq.
John Mordaunt, esq., of Freefolk,
Hants.
1742 . . William Finch, re-elected after appointment as vice chamberlain of
the Household
1747 . . Charles Wyndham, bart., of Westminster
John Mordaunt, esq., of Freefolk
William Finch, esq., *vice* Sir Charles
Wyndham, who elected to serve for
Taunton
1754 . . Percy Wyndham O'Brien, esq., of
Short Grove, Essex
John Mordaunt, knt., of Freefolk,
Southamptonshire
1755 . . Percy Wyndham O'Brien, re-elected
after appointment as one of the
Lords Commissioners of the Treasury
1757 . . Percy, Earl of Thomond, Ireland, re-
elected after appointment as treasurer of the Household
1761 . . John Mordaunt, knt.
Charles Jenkinson, esq.
1762 . . Charles Jenkinson, esq., re-elected
after appointment as treasurer and
paymaster of the Ordnance

1767 . . John Elliot, esq., *vice* Charles Jenkin-
son, appointed one of the Lords
Commissioners of the Admiralty
1768 . . George Macartney, knt.
Charles Jenkinson, esq.
George Johnstone, esq., *vice* Charles
Jenkinson, who elected to serve for
Appleby
1769 . . James Lowther, bart., *vice* Sir George
Macartney, who accepted the stew-
ardship of the Chiltern Hundreds
1774 . . George Johnstone, esq.
Fletcher Norton, esq.
1775 . . Ralph Gowland, esq., *vice* George
Johnstone, who elected to serve for
Appleby
James Adair, esq., *vice* Fletcher Norton, who elected to serve for Carlisle
1780 . . John Lowther, esq.
John Baynes Garforth, esq.
1784 . . John Lowther, esq.
James Clarke Satterthwaite, esq.
1786 . . Humphrey Senhouse, esq., *vice* John
Lowther, who accepted the stewardship of the Chiltern Hundreds
1790 . . John Anstruther, esq., of Lincoln's Inn
John Baynes Garforth, esq., of Steeton,
Yorks.
1793 . . John Anstruther, esq., re-elected after
appointment
1796 . . John Baynes Garforth, esq.
Edward Burrow, esq.
1800 . . Walter Spencer Stanhope, esq., *vice*
Edward Burrow, deceased
1802 . . Robert Ward, esq.
James Graham, esq.
1805 . . George Steward, esq., commonly called
Viscount Garlies, *vice* James Graham, who accepted the stewardship
of the manor of East Hendred, Berks.
1806 . . John Lowther, esq.
James Graham, esq.
1807 . . Thomas Hamilton, commonly called
Lord Binning, *vice* John Lowther,
esq., who elected to serve for Cumberland
1807 . . John Lowther, esq., of Swillington
James Graham, esq., of Edmond Castle
John Osborn, esq., of Chicksands
Priory, Beds., *vice* John Lowther,
who elected to serve for Cumberland
1808 . . William Lowther, esq., commonly
called Viscount Lowther, *vice* John
Osborn, who accepted the stewardship of the Chiltern Hundreds
1810 . . William Lowther, Viscount Lowther,
re-elected after appointment
1812 . . William Viscount Lowther
John Lowther, esq., of Swillington
Augustus John Foster, esq., of Killar-
ney, Ireland, *vice* John Lowther, esq.,
who elected to serve for Cumberland
1816 . . John Henry Lowther, esq., of Swillington, *vice* Augustus John Foster, esq.,
who accepted the stewardship of the
Chiltern Hundreds

[1] Double return, dated 18 Jan. 1717–18; the indenture
by which Sir Wilfrid Lawson was returned was taken off
the file by order of the House.

1813 . . Thomas Wallace, esq., of Carlton Hall, *vice* Viscount Lowther, appointed one of the Lords Commissioners of the Treasury

1818 . . Thomas Wallace, esq., re-elected after appointment

1818 . . John Henry Lowther, esq., of Swillington
John Beckett, esq., of Somerby Park, Linc.

1820 . . John Beckett, esq.
John Henry Lowther, esq.

1821 . . William Wilson Carus Wilson, esq., Casterton Hall, *vice* John Beckett, who accepted the stewardship of the Chiltern Hundreds

1826 . . Randolph Stewart, Viscount Garlies

1826 . . William Wilson Carus Wilson, esq.

1827 . . Lawrence Peel, esq., *vice* William Wilson Carus Wilson, who accepted the stewardship of the manor of East Hendred, Berks

1830 . . Randolf Stewart, Viscount Garlies
Philip Pleydell Bouverie, esq.

1831 . . John Henry Lowther, esq.
James Scarlett, knt.

1833 . . Fretcheville Lawson Ballantine Dykes, esq., of Dovenby Hall
Henry Aglionby Aglionby, esq., of Newbiggin Hall

1835 . . Henry Aglionby Aglionby, esq., of Newbiggin Hall.
Fretcheville Lawson Ballantine Dykes, esq., of Dovenby Hall

1836 . . Edward Horsman, esq., of Edinburgh, *vice* Fretcheville Lawson Ballantine Dykes, who accepted the stewardship of the Chiltern Hundreds

1837 . . Henry Aglionby Aglionby, esq., of Newbiggin Hall
Edward Horsman, esq.

1840 . . Edward Horsman, esq., re-elected after appointment

1841 . . Henry Aglionby Aglionby, esq., of Nunnery
Edward Horsman, esq.

1847 . . Henry Aglionby Aglionby, esq.
Edward Horsman, esq.

1852 . . Henry Wyndham, esq., of Cockermouth Castle
Henry Aglionby Aglionby, esq., of Nunnery

1854 . . John Steel, esq., of Derwent Bank, *vice* Henry Aglionby Aglionby, esq., deceased

1857 . . John Steel, esq., of Derwent Bank
Richard Southwell Bourke, Lord Naas

1858 . . Richard Southwell Bourke, Lord Naas, re-elected after appointment

1859 . . John Steel, esq., of Derwent Bank
Richard Southwell Bourke, Lord Naas

1865 . . John Steel, esq.
Richard Southwell Bourke, Lord Naas

1866 . . Lord Naas re-elected

1868 . . Andrew Green Thompson, esq., *vice* John Steel, deceased

1868 . . Isaac Fletcher, esq., of Tarnbank

1874 . . Isaac Fletcher, esq.

1879 . . William Fletcher, esq., Brigham Hill, *vice* Isaac Fletcher, deceased

1880 . . Edward Waugh, esq.

WHITEHAVEN

BURGESSES

1833 . . Matthias Attwood, esq., of London

1835 . . Matthias Attwood, esq.

1837 . . Matthias Attwood, esq.

1841 . . Matthias Attwood, esq.

1847 . . Robert Charles Hildyard, esq.

1852 . . Robert Charles Hildyard, esq.

1857 . . Robert Charles Hildyard, esq.
George Lyall, esq., *vice* Robert C. Hildyard, deceased

1859 . . George Lyall, esq.

1865 . . George Cavendish Bentinck, esq.

1868 . . George Augustus Cavendish Bentinck, esq.

1874 . . George Augustus Cavendish Bentinck, esq.

1875 . . George A. C. Bentinck, esq., re-elected

1880 . . George A. F. C. Bentinck, esq.

1885 . . George A. F. C. Bentinck, esq.

1886 . . George A. F. C. Bentinck, esq.

1891 . . Sir James Bain

1892 . . Thomas Shepherd Little, esq.

1895 . . Augustus Helder, esq.

1900 . . Augustus Helder, esq.

EGREMONT

BURGESSES

1295 . . William de Gylling
Alexander, son of Richard

INDUSTRIES

THE principal industries of Cumberland, which may be regarded as characteristic of the county from a remote date, are in a large measure determined by its maritime position and natural features. The coast line of an inland sea, forming numerous bays and estuaries and extending from north to south throughout its whole length, is so admirably adapted to fish production and specially to the breeding of salmon, that the district has attained a well-deserved distinction for this industry. Owing to the nature of its geological formation, the upper strata of the greater part of its surface have been stored with rich veins of mineral wealth, such as iron ore, coal, lead, silver, copper, plumbago and other metals, a great laboratory which has contributed to the material prosperity of the county and afforded employment to large numbers of the population. The working of certain of those minerals ranks in point of antiquity, as far as ascertained knowledge is concerned, with the salmon industry. Though the coal measures are now one of the most valuable and important assets in Cumberland industries, the production of coal by means of mining dates back but a very short period. Few of the minor industries are sufficiently characteristic of the county to call for special treatment in this place.

As salmon is victual, and nothing is more precious than victual, according to the proverbial saying of lord Coke, it may be expected that the salmon industry should take precedence in a district so peculiarly adapted by nature to its pursuit. It is not suggested that the fisheries are the most lucrative source of wealth in Cumberland, but there can be no dispute that they constitute an historic industry for which the county has been famous from the earliest period of which there is authentic record. Few counties of the kingdom are so favourably situated for the development of this industry. The coast line is included in the arm of the Irish Sea known as the Solway Firth, and embraces a fishing area shaped in the form of a cone. At its narrow end it is little more than a sandy estuary, which at low water dwindles into a contracted channel fordable in some places at low tide. At the base of the cone towards the west the Solway broadens out into a wide expanse of open sea, so that the Scottish shore is only distinctly visible in clear weather. Within this area all the salmon producing rivers of the county are situated. The seaboard starts with a crescent sweep from south to north from the estuary of the Duddon, its natural termination and the natural boundary between Cumberland and the detached portion of Lancashire called Lancashire north of the Sands. During its progress in a northwesterly direction it is pierced at Ravenglass by an estuary formed by the mouth of three rivers, the Esk, Mite and Irt, which take their rise in the mountainous district of that neighbourhood. From this place the coast line bends seaward, forming a bold headland at St. Bees, the most westerly point of the county, and then sweeps north-east to Workington, where it is again pierced by the outlet of the Derwent close to that town. To the north of Workington the Ellen forms a small estuary at Maryport, where the coast curves gradually inland to form Allonby Bay, and then proceeds in a northerly direction to Skinburness Point in the upper reaches of the firth. From Skinburness to the Scottish border the coast is irregular and broken by the mouths of several rivers which discharge themselves into the narrow portion of the Solway. The southern shore, indented by a wide basin into which, at its opposite extremities, flow the waters of the Waver and Wampool, takes an easterly direction at Bowness Point and sweeps inland to its termination, where it is pierced by the estuary of the Eden, the largest river in the county, and a little further north, beyond Rocliffe Marsh, by the estuaries of the Esk and Sark, both of which are for the greater part Scottish rivers.[1]

From the natural features of the county, bounded by the Pennine range, which forms

[1] The *Spectator* (Supplement), 12 March 1870 : *Report of the Royal Commissions on the Solway Fisheries*, 1881 and 1896.

331

the watershed on its eastern side, and comprising some of the greatest mountain masses in England in its central and southern districts, it may be assumed that its rivers, though not attaining to any dimensions in length or volume of water, are well adapted to the breeding of salmon. With the exception of the Eden, which rises on the borders of Yorkshire and flows through Westmorland and Cumberland, the other rivers can scarcely be dignified by that name owing to the shortness of their course. Wordsworth was of opinion that the streams of the county were more of the nature of large brooks than rivers, especially while they flowed through the mountain and lake country. But if not of great dimensions all the rivers possess the general feature that their water is remarkably clear and flows with considerable swiftness and often at a good depth over gravelly and rocky channels. At Appleby the Eden is considerably above the sea level, and its average fall is said to be about 28 feet per mile. The Derwent, which flows through two lakes, Derwentwater and Bassenthwaite, receives the Cocker at Cockermouth, so called from the confluence of the streams, and runs into the sea at Workington, forming many pools and sheltered beds in its course. The southern Esk, rising on the side of Great End, enters the sea at Ravenglass, where it mixes on the sands with the Mite and the Irt. The beauty of river scenery in Cumberland is proverbial, and if we take the Eden, Derwent, and southern Esk as the chief examples, few streams in any county can rival them, either for their waterbreaks and wooded banks or for the picturesque valleys through which they pass. When we consider the migratory habits of the salmon and the laws by which the species is maintained, the spawning on the upper or shallow beds of inland streams, and their mature existence spent in passing to and fro between salt and fresh water, it will be seen how suitable the rivers of the county are to their production and how well adapted is the sheltered condition of the Solway shore to their growth and nurture.

In these circumstances it is not surprising that the salmon fisheries should be found among the earliest industries of the county. As soon as we touch the record evidence of the district, clauses about fisheries or fish pools or liberty to fish are embodied in the earliest charters granted to local magnates or religious establishments. Henry I. endowed the priory of Carlisle with a fishery in the Eden.[1] By a special charter Ranulf Meschin made a grant of a sluice and pool for a fishery

in the same river to the monks of Wetheral at a date before 1120.[2] Alice de Rumelli, daughter of William Meschin, gave to the priory of St. Bees about 1140 the sole liberty of making fisheries in the port of Whitehaven, in all places in the sea, and in other waters within their bounds.[3] Henry III. confirmed in 1231 to the abbey of Calder fisheries in the Derwent and 'Egre,' which had been the gift of Ranulf Meschin almost a century before.[4] In 1227 Thomas de Multon paid the king a fine of five marks for licence to make a fishery in the forest of Inglewood at a place called Forst' on the bank of the Eden, the condition of grant being that the said fishery should not injure the neighbouring fisheries and especially the fishery which belonged to the city of Carlisle.[5] These examples will be sufficient to show that at the very dawn of documentary history the creation of private rights in fishing was in full operation.

In addition to the grant of fisheries, it was the habit of territorial owners at an early period to make annual grants of salmon from their own waters to the religious houses. Thus Alice de Rumelli, the great lady of Allerdale, daughter of William fitz Duncan, confirmed the grant of fourteen salmon every Lent to St. Bees, which had previously been bestowed by Alan son of Waldeve, and six more on her own behalf.[6] Thomas son of Gospatric gave to the abbey of Calder out of his own fisheries twenty salmon yearly at the feast of St. John the Baptist, together with a net in the Derwent between the bridge and the sea.[7] In 1250 Patric son of the foregoing Thomas bound himself and his heirs to give to St. Bees fourteen salmon annually, viz. six in Lent before Palm Sunday and eight at the feast of St. Peter ad vincula, at his house in Workington.[8] These gifts should not be confounded with the tithe of fish owned by the church. For example, when William Meschin founded the priory of St. Bees, he endowed it with the tithes of his fisheries in Coupland.[9] In a dispute between

---

[1] Dugdale, *Mon.* vi. 144.
[2] *Reg. of Wetherhal* (Cumb. and Westmld. Arch. Soc.) 6–9.
[3] Reg. of St. Bees, Harl. MS. 434, lib. i. 6.
[4] Chart. R. 15 Hen. III. m. 9.
[5] Ibid. 11 Hen. III. pt. i. m. 24 ; Fine R. 11 Hen. III. m. 9. In 1485 a fishery in the Eden under 'Baronwod' in the manor of Lazonby was reckoned among the possessions of the Dacres of Gillesland (*Cal. of Inq. p.m.* 1 *Hen. VII.* i. 70).
[6] Reg. of St. Bees, Harl. MS. 434, lib. i. 7.
[7] Chart. R. 15 Hen. III. m. 9.
[8] Reg. of St. Bees, Harl. MS. 434, lib. v. 15.
[9] Ibid. i. 2.

the abbey of Holmcultram and Gilbert de Feritate, rector of Bowness, an amicable agreement was arrived at whereby the rector conceded to the abbot the tithe of fish of a standing net (*retis stantivi*) and all kinds of fishing practised in the Eden by the people of Burgh-by-Sands, and the abbot in turn yielded to the rector the fish tithes of Bowness and Drumburgh, except the fishing of the river reaches at Polleburgh.[1] In a similar dispute which the same abbey had with the priory of Carlisle, bishop Walter acted as mediator. The bishop awarded that the tithe of fish caught in the Eden at Fleminghalse, Vaerhalse, Depedraif, and at other places within the parish of Rocliffe, and drawn to land in that parish, should belong to the canons of the priory as rectors of the church, but that for the sake of peace the canons should pay the monks an acknowledgment of two shillings a year.[2]

Disputes about fishing rights and fish tithes were not confined to the religious houses at this early period. The fisheries of lay proprietors were also guarded with jealous care. In 1208 an action was decided in the king's court at Carlisle before the justices itinerant between Alan de Pennington and others, complainants, and Richard de Lucy, lord of Allerdale, deforciant, in which the fisheries of Ravenglass formed a conspicuous feature. At that time fishing rights on the Mite (Mighet) and Esk were considered worth a suit at law.[3] Other instances might be given to show that fishery disputes were not confined to recent centuries.

A singular reservation of the eighth fish, which appears to have been a feudal rent, is mentioned in several charters in connection with the fisheries in Eden belonging to the monks of Wetheral.[4] William son of Odard of Corby reserved the eighth fish from the coup of the monks as his own perquisite of the fishery granted to them by his ancestors. This tribute reminds us of the practice of the bishop of Glasgow, who claimed the eighth of the royal profits issuing out of the civil courts of that diocese.[5]

It is unfortunate that the earliest record

evidence is so silent about the tenure of fisheries and methods of fishing. In the upper parts of rivers the tenure is simple enough. Though the running water in common law belonged to no one, riparian ownership excluded the public as trespassers on the lands adjoining the rivers. In 1393, when the famous fishing statute of 17 Richard II. cap. 9 was passed, it was found on inquisition that the owner of the Honor of Cockermouth had the oversight of the Derwent from source to sea with power to punish trespassers and to burn nets and unlawful engines. In the barony of Burgh-by-Sands there appears to have been a common right in the fishing of the Eden, which forms its northern boundary. Like right of pasture on common land, the tenants possessed a certain interest in the fishing in proportion to the value of their tenements. Hugh de Morvill granted to the monks of Holmcultram an entire net at Polleburgh and in all other places on the Eden in common with the men of the vill of Burgh, together with a booth and a fit place to dry their net.[6] At a later date, about 1240, in an agreement between Thomas de Multon and the same abbey about a net in the Eden, which was appurtenant to the tenancy, it was stated that a carucate of land in the barony carried with it the right of fishing with two nets.[7] In a similar manner the tenants of Workington were associated with the lord in the fishing of Derwent. Patric son of Thomas son of Gospatric conceded to Holmcultram the whole of his fishery of Seton and one free net in Derwent wherever his free men drew the river.[8] The manorial aspect of fishing rights is very interesting at this early period.

The earliest methods of fishing of which there is documentary evidence do not seem to have differed from those now in use. Angling with a hook and fishing with a net obtained in the twelfth century as they do to-day. In the concession of William son of Odard to the monks of Wetheral about 1175 the exclusive right of fishing was granted in a portion of the Eden near the priory, so that neither he nor his heirs could fish with hook or net or in any other way between Munchewat and the mill pool.[9] Fish coops, coffins or baskets were employed in the upper reaches of the Cumberland rivers. The monks above named obtained from the owner of Corby, a

---

[1] Reg. of Holmcultram (Harl. MS. 3891), f. 31*b*.

[2] Ibid. ff. 20–1 ; Dugdale, *Mon.* v. 598.

[3] *Fines* (Rec. Com.), 10, 11.

[4] *Reg. of Wetheral* (Cumb. and Westmld. Arch. Soc.), 84, 93 ; Dugdale, *Mon.* iii. 588–9 ; Neilson, *Annals of the Solway*, 53.

[5] *Reg. Epis. Glasguensis* (Bannatyne Club), i. 12, 22. It should be noticed that this perquisite was granted by David, king of Scotland, and was applicable *per totam Cumbriam*

[6] Reg. of Holmcultram, Carl. Cath. Lib. ff. 5, 6.

[7] Ibid. ff. 19–20.

[8] Reg. of Holmcultram, Harl. MS. 3891, 54–5.

[9] *Reg. of Wetheral* (Cumb. and Westmld. Arch. Soc.), 84.

manor on the opposite side of the river, not only the right to fix their weir in the bank but the whole of the bank on that side and the fishery in the Eden belonging to the vill.[1] A charter to Holmcultram mentions both sea and sand fisheries in the mouth of the Wampool.[2] It is scarcely open to question that the sand fishings were practised by means of some contrivance fixed by stakes in the sand. Concessions of fishing from boats were of ordinary occurrence. William son of Simon de Skefteling granted a fishery in the sea at the mouth of the Ellen (Alne) and one fishing boat (*naviculam pischatoriam*) and a toft on the beach whereon to dry the nets, with free passage over his land to the fishery.[3] Alan son of Waldeve ordered that as often as the ship (*navis*) of the monks of St. Bees should fish at 'Scaddebuas' no rent or exaction should be claimed from the men who manned the fishing craft.[4] The owners of fishing rights on the Scottish side of the Solway were not always careful to tie down their grantees to any special method. William de Brus, in his grant of fisheries to Melrose and Holmcultram, gave the monks liberty to exercise the art in any way they chose.[5]

In many of the early grants of fisheries the sturgeon and a fish called the great fish or *le graspes*, which is usually but doubtfully identified as the whale, were reserved to the grantor. It is supposed that these great fishes were the right of the Crown, and that it lay outside the power of the manorial owner to deal with them. The same custom was common to England and Scotland. In the Brus charters to Melrose cited above the sturgeon only is reserved, but in the charters to the English abbey sturgeon and *le graspeis* are named as the perquisites of the lord of Annandale. In this connection it may be interesting to observe that Thomas de Multon had licence in 1281 to take sturgeon[6] in the king's fishery of Carlisle during his life at the yearly rent of 13*s.* 4*d.* This fish cannot have been very plentiful in Scottish waters, for we find 'ferdekyns' of sturgeon[7] purchased in the London market in 1424 for James I. In the survey of the barony of Burgh taken by royal com-

mission in 1589 on the attainder of Leonard Dacre the jury was of opinion 'that the lord of the said manner ought to have all the royall and principall fysshes, viz. : whales, sturgeons, porposes, thirlepolles, sealles, turbettes and such like' caught on the English side from Skinburness to back of Garth Head, being about ten miles from Carlisle. It was customary for the lord of the manor at that time to allow the tenants for a sturgeon 3*s.* 4*d.*, for a thirlepolle 20*d.*, for a turbot 12*d.*, but the other fishes were wont to be distributed among the lord's officers and tenants there. In the subsequent history of that barony the same reservation of royal fishes was made in the leases of fisheries in the Eden.[8]

That the rivers of Cumberland were famous for the production of salmon we have every reason to believe. It was the only article of food particularly specified by king John in 1215, when he sent messengers to procure merchandise from the citizens of Carlisle.[9] From the instructions of Henry III. to the various sheriffs and bailiffs of the northern counties on the occasion of the marriage of the princess Margaret at York in 1251 the same peculiarity may be noted. The provision of salmon was ordered only from the sheriff of Cumberland and the bailiff of Newcastle-on-Tyne, the former having to send fifty 'calivered' salmon put 'in pane.'[10] About this time public opinion was taking practical shape for the regulation of fisheries, and a formal presentment was made at the Assizes of Newcastle in 1269 about the destruction of salmon and their fry in the northern rivers.[11] In consequence the justices made an order which afterwards received recognition as possessing statutory force. The same judgment of assize was made at Carlisle in 1278 on the presentment of a Cumberland jury.

[8] The survey of the barony of Burgh-by-Sands on the attainder of Leonard Dacre has been printed among the documentary evidences used in an exchequer action between the citizens of Carlisle and the earl of Lonsdale in 1867. Many interesting facts about the history of the Eden fisheries are included in that collection. Mr. Geo. Neilson's note on the 'guhail' in its relation to Scots law should be consulted (*Annals of the Solway*, 54). The tongue of the fish called 'le graspes' or 'craspeis' was reserved to William the Conqueror according to custom (*Harl. Chart.* 83 A, 12 ; Rymer, *Fœdera,* i. 4). See *Cal. of Doc. France* (P.R.O.), 81, for the reservation of the sturgeon in 1107, and also Madox, *History of the Exchequer,* 349–81, ed. 1711.

[9] *Close R. John* (Rec. Com.) i. 191*b.*

[10] Ibid. 35 Hen. III. m. 1.

[11] *Three Early Assize Rolls of Northumberland* (Surtees Soc.), 208-9.

[1] *Reg. of Wetherhal* (op. cit.), 78–82.
[2] Dugdale, *Mon.* v. 604.
[3] Reg. of Holmcultram, Carl. Cath. Lib. ff. 44-5.
[4] Reg. of St. Bees, Harl. MS. 434, i. ii.
[5] Reg. of Holmcultram, Carl. Cath. Lib. f. 67 ; Harl. MS. 3911, ff. 102*b,* 104-6; *Liber de Melrose,* (Bannatyne Club), 668 ; Neilson, *Annals of the Solway,* 52.
[6] Pat. 10 Edw. 1. m. 22.
[7] *Cal. of Doc. Scot.* (Scot. Rec. Pub.) iv. 197-8.

It is very interesting for the light it throws on the common law and ancient custom of fishing in the rivers of the county.[1]

It will be expedient to refer to the proceedings of the assize in 1278 at some length, for here we touch upon what may be termed the foundation of legal enactments in connection with fishing customs in Cumberland. The records of the court may be construed as follows: The jurors of Lythe and Eskdale and of Cumberland and Allerdale made a presentment regarding the great destruction of salmon coming up to spawn and of the fry going down to sea in the waters of Eden and Esk and other rivers of the county. Therefore the whole county, knights and freeholders, unanimously determined that from Michaelmas to St. Andrew's Day no net should be drawn or placed at weirs, pools or mills, or mill pools, and that none should fish in any waters of the county with nets, 'sterkilds' or other engine, or without engine, within the said close time. Also that from the feasts of the Apostles Philip and James till the nativity of St. John the Baptist no net or 'wile' or 'borache' should be placed at pools or mills or mill pools, nor any net placed at weirs, save by the conservators of rivers, and that the meshes should be wide enough to let the salmon fry through, viz. of four thumbs' length. It was provided also that so often as any fisher or miller or other person infringed this provision and was convicted he should be sent to the king's prison and not repledged, unless by consent of the conservators. The jurors likewise attested that Thomas de Multon of Gillesland, as his ancestors had done before him, took fines from all illegal nets in the Eden at a place called Polleburgh by view of knights and others appointed to the custody of the waters; but if the king's bailiffs had arrived, then the judgments pertained to the king for that turn.

It was also provided that all 'boraches' at mills should henceforth be removed under forfeiture of forty shillings for each conviction, and that there should be no more than three small nets in the Eden by custom, the meshes whereof with a knot should be of three thumbs' length for catching lampreys; and none should fish with these except from the feast of St. Andrew till the quinzaine next before the feast of St. John Baptist. The king for his castle of Carlisle should have one; the citizens of Carlisle another in their pool at the garden leased to the city for £15, in which none should fish without leave of the citizens; and if more nets were found they might be put down by the conservators. The jury presented and the whole county complained that the prior of St. Bees had two engines called coops (cupe) for catching salmon in his pool of Stainburn, where in times past he had but one; and the other was set up six years before without warrant and after the last circuit of the judges, on which account he was amerced. The sheriff was instructed to remove the second coop at the prior's expense. It was enjoined moreover that in each pool of the Eden, Esk and Derwent and other waters where salmon might be taken, in midstream by ancient custom there ought to be a pass wide enough for a sow with her five little pigs; and as the following were unduly narrowed, viz. at Cockermouth, Camerton, Stainburn and Workington, these openings ought to be so enlarged at the costs of those who contracted them. The judges then named as conservators twelve persons chosen by consent of the whole county, who were obliged to make oath in court for the faithful discharge of their office. It was also provided that all nets and engines found on the waters contrary to law and custom should be burned in the presence of the conservators. This enactment was to endure for ever to the good of the whole county and others adjacent.[2]

The width of the fish-gap or free passage in midstream, 'according to old custom wide enough for a sow with her five little pigs,' is a subject of curious interest in the history of Cumberland fisheries. The same measurement was in use several years later. In 1293 a plea was heard at Newcastle before the itinerant justices against the monks of Wetheral for raising the fish pool and contracting the fish pass in the Eden contrary to ancient custom, by which the gap was to be wide enough for a sow with her five little pigs to pass through.[3] It would be difficult to determine in feet and inches the exact width of

---

[1] Fisheries in Cumberland were not altogether confined to salmon. The herring was a staple article of food at an early date. Waldeve son of Gospatric and William Engaine, two magnates who owned land on the western seaboard, gave to the priory of Carlisle the tithes of their herring fisheries, which grants were confirmed by Henry II. about 1175 (Dugdale, *Mon.* vi. 144). Waldeve and Alan his son bestowed a manse and a herring fishery in Eltadala or Allerdale on the canons of Hexham (*The Priory of Hexham* [Surtees Soc.] i. 59). A fishery for lampreys in the Eden near Cumwhitton belonged to the Dacres in 1485 (*Cal. of Inq. p.m. Hen. VII.* i. 69).

[2] *Cal. of Doc. Scot.* (Scot. Rec. Pub.) ii. 38–9.

[3] Assize R. (Northumb.), No. 651, 21 Edw. I. rot. 36; *Reg. of Wetherhal* (op. cit.), 400–1.

the passage necessary for a sow and her litter. Turning to Scots law we find an analagous measurement in use at an earlier period. It was laid down in a statute made at Perth in 1177 that according to the king's assize the midstream was always to be free to the extent that a swine of three years old, well-fed, could not touch either side with its head or its tail. Between 1293 and 1372 this unique method of measurement appears to have been dropped in Cumberland, for in the latter year the aperture was expressed in feet in a judgment between the lord of Cockermouth and John de Camerton about a fishing dispute in the Derwent. The earl of Angus, the complainant, brought an action for injury to his part of the river by John de Camerton's weir. It was alleged that the complainant had from time immemorial an aperture of the breadth of 24 feet, commonly called the free water, which aperture ought always to be in the deeper part of the river and in all mill pools and demesnes from that weir to the sea. The cause of the action was that John had filled up the aperture with stones to divert the water to his mill, whereby only four salmon were taken then for the forty that were taken before. It was decided that 8 feet of the handiwork of stones was a nuisance, and it was ordered to be abated at John's expense.[1] When the measure became a matter of statute law the legislature left it to the discretion of the justices, who were empowered to survey and search all weirs that they should not be too narrow so as to lead to the destruction of salmon fry, but with 'a reasonable opening' according to ancient custom (17 Ric. II. c. 9).

The citizens of Carlisle have possessed a fishery in the Eden from an early date. It was found by inquisition in 1221 that a fishery in that river was included in the 'farm' of the city which they held of the king.[2] At

an assize in Carlisle in 1292 they claimed that, when Henry II. demised the city to them at a certain rent, the fishery was an appurtenant of the 'farm,' though a jury of country gentlemen returned the verdict that it was without the borough and in the jurisdiction of the county.[3] Whatever doubt may have existed at this time about their right to the fishery, which according to the record was located at 'Beumund' or Beaumont, it was set at rest by a charter of Edward II. in 1316, who granted a fishery to the citizens 'for the betterment of our city of Carlisle.' Another gift was made by Edward IV. in 1461. Not only did that king confirm 'the king's fishery in the Eden water,' but also 'out of his more abundant grace' he granted 'the custody of our fishery of Carlisle otherwise called the sheriff's net or fishery of frithnet in Eden water in the county of Cumberland to have to themselves, their heirs, and successors for ever without yielding anything therefor.' Regulations for the good ordering of these fisheries were made from time to time and recorded among the bye-laws of the city. In the Dormont Book, the earliest official record of the Corporation, it was directed in 1561 that the farmers of the King Garth and Free Net should yearly present the market of Carlisle 'with the half part of all such fyshe as thei shall gyt at the same (fisheries) for the better furnishment and releef of all the inhabitantes of the same city upon paine and forfitor of 6s. 8d. for everie default.' A century later the King Garth fishery could not have been so productive as to allow the lessees to give half their yield of fish by way of rent, for in 1680 the Corporation granted them a substantial abatement. In former times there must have been good years and bad years for the taking of salmon in the Eden as the rent of the fisheries fluctuated from one year to another. In 1597 the rent of the Free Net was £14 and of the King Garth £32, whereas in the following year the former was only £11 10s. and the latter £20 3s. 4d. In 1600 the value of the Free Net had risen to £13 6s. 8d., while the rent of King Garth remained as it had been two years before. In 1648 the rent of King Garth was only £10; in 1652 both fisheries were let to one farmer for £10, the Free Net now assuming the name of 'Freebote,' but in the following year the rent of 'the fishgarthe with ye free boate' was demised at £38. The annual letting of the fisheries was stopped by order of the Corporation in 1673, when it was provided that

[1] Assize R. 45 Edw. III. summarized in the report of the Special Commission on *Lord Lonsdale's Salmon Hall Fishery* in 1868. In the same report there is reference to another document, being an Elizabethan survey on the death of the earl of Northumberland, dated 1577, in which it is stated that for twenty-four years past the river Derwent was a free water and kept open in all places without coop, fish-garth, or any other let from the sea or foot of the said river unto an old coop or fish-garth then decayed, which stood about Cockermouth Castle. But the river had been then (1577) stopped and shut up with a fish-garth made of late years by Sir Henry Curwen to the prejudice of the said earl and to the great damage and loss of his tenants and farmers.

[2] Fine R. 5 Hen. III. m. 2 ; *Royal Charters of Carlisle* (Cumb. and Westmld. Arch. Soc.), 1–3.

[3] *Plac. de Quo Warr.* (Rec. Com.), 118b ; *Royal Charters of Carlisle*, 4–6.

they should be let to farm for terms of seven years, the farmer doing all repairs. George Sowerby was then the lessee under a lease of seven years at an annual rent of £24.[1] Owing to the change in the bed of the Eden at King Garth, the citizens of Carlisle had some trouble in maintaining their full right of fishing there. A 'new goyt' or 'gote,' commonly called 'the goat,' a dam course, gut or sluice, was made about 1597, through which the Eden afterwards broke its way, forsaking its old channel and soon converting 'the goat' into the main stream. The fishing of the new channel was the subject of negotiation in 1683 and 1684 with the lord of the barony of Burgh upon whose property the river had encroached.[2] In 1693 the dispute was settled by an agreement with Sir John Lowther whereby the right of fishing in the new bed was demised to the Corporation for an annual acknowledgment. By the action of the owner of Burgh the agreement was terminated in 1670 and the fishing of 'the goat' was the occasion of a suit at law. Since that date the citizens have had other lawsuits in defence of their fishing rights.[3] In later years King Garth has kept up many associations with municipal life unconnected with fishing broils. In 1733 need was felt for a house there for the use of the lessees of the fishery, and the mayor was empowered to contract for the purchase of a piece of ground whereon to erect the desired building. This house became the rendezvous of the mayor and commonalty, and high revel was held from year to year when the common councilmen treated his worship to a good dinner and an inspection of the fishing grounds. The last dinner to the mayor held at this place was celebrated under canvas in 1892.

As the northern Esk, from its junction with the Liddel to the Solway, practically formed the international boundary between England and Scotland, the right of fishing in its waters was the occasion of many disputes between the Borderers, and the subject of many conferences and arbitrations between the envoys of both kingdoms. The inhabitants of Cumberland constructed a dam, known as a fishgarth, on the river by which they intercepted the fish on their way to the upper pools, thus depriving the Scottish fishermen of their rightful share. The Scotsmen, denying the English right to stop the fish, removed the obstruction. The dispute which arose in consequence of its removal lasted for about a century and caused much ill-feeling between the inhabitants in the neighbourhood of the river. For the purpose of doing justice between the parties it was agreed at Westminster in 1474, touching the matter in dispute, that,—

certaine lordes, not borderers, of both parties, shall be auctorized by their princes to visite and see the place and by inquisition and recorde taken of the eldest and feithfullest persoones of the Marches there, aswele of the one partie as of the othir, and by alle othir convenient and reasonable weyes and moyens, they shall enfourme thaym of the truth, and hough in old tyme the said fishgaert hath been kepte, and thereuppon put thaym in thair devoir to fynyssh and determe that debate and querelle. The lordes of both sides shall mete in the Westmarche for this matier the tenth day of Marche nex to come. Both princes shall wright and gefe straitly in charge to thir subgiettes of either side, that during the said inquisition noon of thaym be so hardy to make any rode, dispoille, brennyng or werre upon the othir, by occasion of setting upp or taking downe of the said fishgaert, nor for noon othir matier nor cause : but that the trewes be observed and kept, and that they that fyndeth themselves wronged or grieved sue for redress to their superiors as reason requireth.[4]

But the dispute did not end with the appointment of this commission. Again and again in subsequent years the English asserted their right to erect and hold on the river Esk a hedge or enclosure, commonly called a fishgarth, where the fish might be more easily caught by them, and they maintained that such right belonged to the king of England and his subjects by law and custom, while the subjects of the king of Scotland as stoutly maintained the contrary. In true border fashion the fish-garth was destroyed by the Scots as often as it was erected by the English.[5] Questions about the bounds of the debatable land were imported into the controversy which did not tend to simplify matters. After many abortive attempts to settle the dispute, it was finally decided in 1493 that damage to the fish-garth should not be considered a violation of the peace. Later on, in 1498, Thomas lord Dacre had a grant from king James of 'al and hale oure fisching of the water of Esk for the space and termez of thre yeris,' with power to put in 'garth or

---

[1] *Some Municipal Records of the City of Carlisle* (Cumb. and Westmld. Arch. Soc.), 62, 307.

[2] Ibid. 273, 311, 318, 321.

[3] *Plea of the Corporation of Carlisle against Lord Lonsdale,* printed in 1868, where the evidences are embodied.

[4] Rymer, *Fœdera,* vol. v. pt. iii. p. 53, old ed. ; Bruce Armstrong, *History of Liddesdale,* 172.

[5] *Rot. Scotiæ* (Rec. Com.), ii. 450, 452, 478, 490, 493, 498 ; *Cal. of Doc. Scot.* (Scot. Rec. Pub.), iv. 317, 324.

garthis for the dew lauboring and occupying of the said fisching' for the annual rent of 'four seme of salmond fisch, ilk seme contenand xiij fisch salmand' payable ' to our capitan constable, and keparis of our castell of Lochmabane.' It does not appear how this agreement was brought about, though possibly it was reckoned at the time the most feasible way to overcome the difficulty. But it did not last long, for at various periods from 1502 up to the time of the Union the fish-garth on the Esk was the subject of negotiation between the people of both realms.[1] Taken as a whole the fisheries occupy a prominent place among the industries of the county and supply an interesting aspect of its history.[2]

The mineral wealth of the county was known at the earliest period of which there is trustworthy record. The first Norman settlers soon made themselves acquainted with the numerous veins of metalliferous ores which run through the upper strata, and have been one of the chief sources of Cumberland industries. The silver mines of Carlisle may be said to occupy the place of pre-eminence, as they have supplied the first distinctive industry on record, and their fame has been great in the history of the district. When one of the chroniclers stated that a vein of

silver had been discovered at Carlisle in 1133 [3] he must have been in error about the date, for these mines were worked by the citizens of Carlisle and other lessees several years before. As a matter of course much is known of them,[4] as they were retained in possession of the Crown, and from them metal was obtained for the royal mint at Carlisle. They occupy a prominent place in the sheriff's annual returns of the revenues of the county. By a curious fiscal arrangement, the mines were recorded at the Exchequer as the mines of Carlisle though they were situated at Alston,[5] a parish on the border of Northumberland nearly thirty miles away. It is strange that they should be called silver mines, for they are really lead mines with a small impregnation of the more precious metal.

From the Pipe Rolls may be gathered many interesting particulars about the lessees and rents of the mine of Carlisle during the twelfth and thirteenth centuries. In 1158 the rent paid by William son of Erembald [6]

---

[1] The authorities and references in Bruce Armstrong's *History of Liddesdale*, 172–4, should be consulted.

[2] Much information about the later history of this industry, as carried on in the Eden and northern Esk, may be gathered from a curious pamphlet entitled *The Fisherman's Defence* (8vo, pp. vii. 79), published in 1807 by Charles Waugh, a fisherman of Bowness on Solway. Its sub-title will be sufficient to indicate its character and contents : 'A few remarks and observations on some sections of "An Act of Parliament" made and passed in the Forty-fourth year of the reign of His Majesty King George the Third intituled " An Act for the better regulating and improving the Fisheries in the Arm of the Sea between the county of Cumberland and the counties of Dumfries and Wigton and the Stewartry of Kirkcudbright : and also the Fisheries in the several streams and waters which run into or communicate with the said arm of the sea." Also, a description of several sorts of nets used in the arm of the sea, showing the strength of twine used in making, and the manner of knitting, rigging, setting, cleaning and using the said nets. Also, a short description of several sorts of fish taken in the arm of the sea, which are not prohibited by the Act to be taken in close time, showing the time of their spawning being in full perfection &c. To which is annexed the substance of a letter sent to the committee appointed by owners, farmers, or occupiers of fisheries in the rivers Eden, Esk, &c. to carry the Act into execution.'

[3] *Eulogium Historiarum* (Rolls Ser.), iii. 64; *Pipe R.* (Rec. Com.) 31 Hen. I. p. 142.

[4] The mine of Carlisle was not the only lead mine in Cumberland in the king's hand. In 1331 Robert de la Forde and Richard Campion were appointed to search for a mine of silver and lead reported to exist in Minerdale and Silverbeck in Cumberland and Harcla in Westmorland, by view of Robert de Barton whom the king nominated keeper of the mine (Pat. 5 Edw. III. pt. 2, m. 13).

[5] A jury declared in 1414–5 'quod mineatores minere de Aldeston que currit in Scaccario domini Regis per nomen minere Karlioli tempore quo minera predicta fuit in manu domini Edwardi, nuper Regis Anglie, proavi domini Regis nunc, etc., semper habuerunt quasdam libertates' (Inq. a. q. d. 3 Hen. V. No. 7). It is evident that reference is made here to letters close of 1356, in which the mine of ' Cardoil,' as understood at the Exchequer, is identified with the mine of ' Aldeneston' (Rymer, *Fœdera*, vol. iii. pt. 1, p. 330). The same view is expressed in letters patent of 1414 when William de Stapleton was lessee of the mines (Pat. 2 Hen. V. pt. 2, m. 13).

[6] Hodgson has suggested with much probability that William son of Erembald or Erkenbald may have been an unfortunate German speculator, as the name has a German sound (*Hist. of Northumb.* vol. iii. pt. 2, p. 45). Germans and Dutch, it will be seen hereafter, have been associated with mining in Cumberland from an early period. In 1359 Tilman of Cologne, of whose nationality there can be no doubt, was the lessee of the mines of silver, copper and lead in ' Aldeston More,' in which year he obtained letters of protection for himself and his workmen so that they might carry on their mining without molestation (Rymer, *Fœdera*, vol. iii. pt. 1, p. 422).

was 100 marks, though the rent returned by him in 1159 was 100 pounds, a sum paid by his successor, William son of Holdegar, for some years. In 1165 the management of the mine reverted to William son of Erembald. This lessee began to show signs of insolvency in 1172, and the arrears continued to accumulate till they were over £2,000 in 1179. Soon after the mine passed to other hands, but the debt was carried on from year to year, according to a well known custom at the Exchequer, in the sheriffs' rolls of Cumberland and Northumberland for over a century. Consignments of lead were despatched from this mine by the king's writ to various places; to Windsor in 1167 for the king's house; fifty-five cartloads in 1168 for the sheriff of Northumberland for transport to Caen; to Grandmont in 1176 for the use of the abbey; and 100 cartloads in 1179 for the building of the church of Clairvaux. Gifts of this sort from the royal mine might be multiplied to any extent. The king gave orders for the supply of silver or lead as occasion required. He had his mint and exchequer at Carlisle, and transacted his business through his local officers.[1]

The importance of the mine of Alston may be estimated in some measure by the letters of protection issued at various times for the protection of the miners and the liberties conferred upon them as a community. In 1222 the king's miners of Cumberland had letters of protection till Henry III. came of age, and in the following year a similar favour was bestowed on the miners of Yorkshire and Northumberland who were regarded as within the bailiwick of the county of Cumberland.[2]

Several letters of a similar character were issued during the reign of Henry III. In 1234 and 1235 royal mandates signified that the miners of Alston should enjoy the privileges and immunities which the miners in times past were accustomed to have, and be allowed to dig and mine without molestation; merchants were also obliged to repair to the mine with victuals for the sustentation of the miners.[3]

Among the presentments made in 1278–9 before the justices itinerant at their special session in 'Aldenestone,' it was stated that the king should receive each ninth 'disc' dug up by the miners, and each 'disc' should contain as much ore as a man could lift from the ground. As to the remaining eight 'discs' the king should have the fifteenth penny of all the ore sold, but that the king should find at his own expense for the miners a certain man called a 'drivere,' who knew how to separate silver from lead. The jury on being asked the value of the mine replied that it depended on the nature of the ore they found, good or bad, but that there was ore enough of one sort and another to last till the end of time.[4] The justices of the same assize found that very many evil-doers from Cumberland and elsewhere were harboured by the miners. By all accounts the little community at Alston was composed of a troublesome class of people. As early as 1170 the men of William the moneyer were amerced for a misdemeanor.[5]

The first designation of the liberties enjoyed by the miners of Alston that we have met with is contained in the well known record of 1290 quoted by Coke[6] from the Plea Rolls. From this it would appear that the miners had the privilege of cutting down wood, to whomsoever it belonged, nearest and most convenient to the silver vein they happened to find, and to take as much of such wood as they pleased for the roasting and smelting of the ore. The further liberty was claimed of preventing the owners from cutting wood till the needs of the mines were satisfied. In fact the miners did as they pleased with the woods in the vicinity of Alston on the

---

[1] In 1164 William the moneyer rendered account of £200 for the mines of Carlisle (Pipe R. Cumb. 10 Hen. II). In quittance of the rent of a house at Carlisle which the justices delivered to Nicholas the assayer for the carrying on of his business (*pro labore suo*) 3s. (ibid. 33 Hen. II). The king ordered bishop Walter in 1231 that he should cause to be made out of the money (*de denariis*) in his custody *viii scutellas argenteas*, each dish of four marks weight, and *viii salsaria argentea*, each of one mark weight, and have them forwarded to York (Close 15 Hen. III. m. 2). For the constitution of the mint of Carlisle and the names of the officers in 1242, see *Red Book of the Exchequer* (Rolls Ser.), iii. 1078.

[2] Pat. 6 Hen. III. m. 2; ibid. 7 Hen. III. m. 5. There is no doubt that the original mine was in Cumberland. In 1163 William son of Holdegar rendered account for the mine of Carlisle and the mine of Yorkshire (Pipe R. 9 Hen. II.), and in 1166 two mines are scheduled under the title of the mine of Carlisle (ibid. 12 Hen. II.). It is probable that all the royal mines in the northern

counties at this date were reckoned as within the bailiwick of Cumberland.

[3] Pat. 18 Hen. III. m. 7; ibid. 20 Hen. III. m. 13; ibid. 21 Hen. III. m. 10. These three rolls have been printed in full by Hodgson (*Hist. of Northumb.* vol. iii. pt. 2, p. 46–7).

[4] *Cal. of Doc. Scot.* (Scot. Rec. Pub.), ii. 41, quoting the Assize R. of 6–20 Edw. I.

[5] Pipe R. (Cumb.) 16 Hen. II.

[6] *Institutes*, ii. 578; Nicolson and Burn, *Hist. of Westmld. and Cumb.* ii. 440; Hodgson, *Hist. of Northumb.* vol. iii. pt. 2, pp. 47–8.

assumption of immemorial usage. In 1356 Edward III. caused an inquiry to be made by a jury at Penrith for the purpose of finding out the immunities which justly belonged to the miners. The verdict was to the effect that they dwelt together in shiels (*in shelis suis*) and enjoyed the liberty of choosing from among themselves one coroner and one bailiff called a 'kynges sergeant'; the coroner had cognizance of all pleas of felonies and trespasses, debts and other matters, arising among themselves; the king's bailiff made executions among them respecting themselves and their servants. When the miners were dispersed, one or two in a place, the liberties ceased to be exercised by those separated from the rest, but while they dwelt together and followed their mining occupations it was customary for them and their predecessors to exercise these privileges from time immemorial, rendering to the king ten marks at the Exchequer of Carlisle.'[1] The claims of the miners to traditional liberties were not always accepted without challenge. In 1292 they were summoned to answer the king by what warrant they claimed that the justices itinerant in Cumberland should come to Arneshowe in Alston to hold pleas of the Crown[2] touching the mine there without the licence of the king and his progenitors. The miners pleaded that from the time that the justices began to itinerate in these parts they and all the miners that preceded them always used such liberty without interruption, but at the same time petitioned that the matter should be inquired into by the country. It would appear from the record that the claim was not sustained as the miners had totally lost the liberty to hold pleas of the Crown.

The Stapletons, while they were lords of the manor in the fifteenth century, were lessees of the mine and seem to have been actively interested in mining. In 1414

William de Stapleton complained that from time beyond memory he and his predecessors, lords of the manor of Alston, had been paying an annual rent of ten marks for the mine, notwithstanding that the said mine for the past fifty years and more had been profitless, to their manifest expense and impoverishment. Several concessions were made to the lessees at this period for the development of the industry,[3] but it is evident that the product of the mine was inconsiderable and of little value to the Crown. When new arrangements were made by Edward IV. for the working of royal mines in the north, the mine at Alston More called 'the Fletcheroos,' now called 'the Fletchers,' a little over a mile to the north-east of Garrigill, was demised in 1475 with the mines of Keswick in Cumberland, Richmond in Yorkshire and Blanchland in Northumberland, to Richard, duke of Gloucester, and others for fifteen years.[4] From this date the rise of mining companies comes into full view, with the consequent extension of the mining industries throughout Cumberland. The mineral resources of the Alston district have contributed largely to the wealth of the northern counties.

The iron mines rank among the earliest industries, and their working appears to have been confined at first to the great barony of Coupland in the south-western portion of the county. It is not necessary to inquire which of the local mines may claim the precedence in order of time, for soon after the Norman settlement, as soon as we touch on charter evidence, liberty to work iron mines and the grant of forges or of wood for the making of charcoal for furnaces were subjects of frequent concession by the lords of that barony to the neighbouring religious houses. The mines about the town of Egremont, justly famous as an industrial centre, have been continuously worked since the early years of the twelfth century. William son of Duncan, who succeeded to the fief of William Meschin, granted to the monks of St. Bees an iron mine (*minam ferri*) in his land at 'Chirnaby,' sometimes called 'Achirnaby,' near Egremont, to make iron (*ad ferrum faciendum*) for ever.[5] The mining of iron ore (*mynera ad ferrum*) was carried on at 'Thyrneby' by

---

[1] Inq. p. m. 30 Edw. III. (2nd Nos.), No. 70. The verdict of the jury was afterwards confirmed by letters patent (Pat. 30 Edw. III. pt. 3, m. 23). In the same year the king forbad the bailiff of Tynedale on any account to cause the miners to appear beyond the county of Cumberland to answer for the payment of any contribution charged upon them for their mines in prejudice of their ancient rent of ten marks (Close 30 Edw. III. m. 16).

[2] *Plac. de Quo. Warr.* (Rec. Com.), p. 117. Pleas were held at Alston on 16 January, 1278–9, before Hugh de Multon and Robert de Wardewyk sent there by John de Vaux and the other justices itinerant at Carlisle. The causes heard were wholly concerned with the conduct of the miners and the working of the mines (*Cal. of Doc. Scot.* [Scot. Rec. Pub.], ii. 40).

[3] Pat. 2 Hen. V. pt. 2, m. 13. It may be mentioned that Pat. 4 Hen. V. m. 8 recites by *Inspeximus* several instruments previously referred to about the liberties of the miners, the greater part of which has been printed by Hodgson (*Hist. of Northumb.* vol. iii. pt. 2, pp. 52–3).

[4] Pat. 15 Edw. IV. pt. 1, mm. 15, 22.

[5] Reg. of St. Bees, Harl. MS. 434, i. 39; viii. 8.

the lords of Egremont in the fourteenth century.[1] It was stipulated in 1338 when the lands of John de Multon were parcelled among his three co-heiresses that the iron mines of 'Thernby' and 'Grabergh' and the forges in the market-place of Egremont and opposite the rector's wall should be held in common.[2] Another mine at Egremont was given to the monks of Holmcultram by William, Earl of Albemarle.[3]

The lords of Coupland were most generous to Holmcultram in the matter of mines and forges within their fee. In addition to the above mentioned mine at Egremont the same earl granted a forge at Winfel, and as much green and dead wood as was necessary to make charcoal (carbonem) for its maintenance. In the confirmation of the grant by Cicely his wife, the location of the forge is described as being in her forest of 'Wynfell,' and the liberty of cutting wood was confined to the district between the Ehen (Eigne) and Cocker (Koker).[4] This monastery carried on an extensive industry in the manufacture of iron. Lambert de Multon gave twenty-four measures of his iron ore (xxiiij duodenas mine ferri) in Coupland annually to sustain one forge, whenever he and his men worked the mine, with free access through his land on condition that the monks should not smelt the said ore within the barony of Coupland. The same privilege was afterwards accorded by his heirs with further provisions about the digging of the mine and carrying away the ore. The monks had furnaces within their own lordship of Holmcultram and rented land at Whitehaven from their brethren at St. Bees for the purpose of smelting. John, abbot of Holmcultram (temp. Henry III.), acknowledged himself bound to the prior of St. Bees for the payment of six pence of silver yearly for setting up their furnace at Whitehaven, but the prior was at liberty to remove it at any time.[5] In the grants of wood for the maintenance of the abbey the lords of Coupland forbad the monks to make charcoal for their forges in the lordship of Holmcultram[6] without his special licence.

Another historic industry contingent on the geographical position of the county was the manufacture of salt, which for several centuries was plied on the seaboard from the mouth of the northern Esk to the sands of Duddon. In various districts the low-lying marshes bordering the principal estuaries, with extensive peat mosses to landward, were well adapted for the furtherance of this industry. Though no saltpans have been worked in Cumberland for more than a century, evidence that it was once a flourishing business is still visible almost everywhere along the coast. Survivals of the hollow basins formed by embankment with convenient access to the sea in which the brine was stored for the purpose of evaporation may still be traced in many places. But perhaps a stronger proof of its prevalence and antiquity may be gathered from the number of place-names which still carry a reminiscence of its former existence. The names on the ordnance map could be multiplied to any extent from ancient documents. The northern boundary of the manor of Rocliffe in 1589 was 'Salt Coote Hylles on the syde of the ryver of Eske.' Then again Salcotes near Newton Arlosh was so named as early as the reign of Edward I.[7] In fact the marshes about the common estuary of the Wampool and Waver were celebrated for their saltpans from an early period.[8] As we proceed further south we meet successively with Salta and Salta Moss north of Allonby; Saltern, with its extensive ruins, the name of the place north of Parton; Saltom Bay between Whitehaven and St. Bees Head; Saltcoats beside Ravenglass, and Salthouse on the sands of Duddon near Millom. But saltworks were not confined to those places which retain the name, for in numberless other localities along the shore we know that the industry was carried on without having bequeathed the name to the ordnance survey.

The importance of the industry may be reckoned in some measure from the nature of the concessions made to religious houses by local magnates who owned land on the coast. The priory of Carlisle received from William Engaine a grant of four saltpans (salinas) between Burgh and Drumburgh[9] on the banks of the Eden where the waters are tidal. Two saltpans in the same district were given to the priory of Wetheral, one by Ralf Engaine and the other by William his son aforenamed, both of which gifts were afterwards confirmed by Simon de Morville,[10] who succeeded to the barony of Burgh in 1157. The same house

---

[1] Inq. p.m. 15 Edw. II. No. 45.
[2] Pat. 12 Edw. III. pt. 1, m. 10.
[3] Reg. of Holmcultram, Harl. MS. 3911, f. 50b; Dugdale, Mon. v. 597.
[4] Reg. of Holmcultram, Harl. MS. 3911, ff. 50, 51, 52.
[5] Reg. of St. Bees, Harl. MS. 434, x. 7.
[6] Reg. of Holmcultram, Harl. MS. 3891, ff. 15, 16.

[7] Cal. of Doc. Scot. (Scot. Rec. Pub.), iv. 392-3.
[8] Liber Quot. Garderobæ (Soc. Antiq.), 123.
[9] Dugdale, Mon. vi. 144.
[10] Reg. of Wetheral, 187-8.

was endowed by Maurice de Man with a place in the territory of Ayringthwait close to Whitehaven, whereon they might construct a saltpan, with free access by the same road that he had granted to saltpans in the same place belonging to the monks of St. Bees.[1] The two priories were at liberty to take their estovers and easements as well in land as in water as they thought most convenient. In addition to several saltpans in Galloway and Dumfries the priory of St. Bees had one on the sands of Duddon[2] of the gift of Adam son of Henry, lord of Millom, known before 1247 as 'Salthus in Coupland,' beside which the monks of Furness possessed a grange.[3] On the principle that *sal sapit omnia* we may be sure that convenience for the manufacture of salt was regarded as a valuable perquisite by the religious communities. At all events by their frequent mention in local chartularies, it may be taken that concessions of saltpans were eagerly sought after and carefully protected by them.

The profits arising from the manufacture of salt were not an inconsiderable portion of the revenues of lay proprietors as well as of religious houses. At the time of the dissolution of the monasteries the annual rent of saltpans belonging to the abbey of Holmcultram was estimated at £13 11s. 8d.[4] After this date the industry in the lordship of Holmcultram fell into decay, though the 'pannes' continued to be farmed by the Chamber family for almost a century. In one of the rentals of Henry VIII., now among the parish papers, it is stated that there were within that lordship certain saltpans, the most part of which were utterly decayed, and the rest were likely to decay unless they were demised to tenants for a term of years.[5] In 1589 in the survey of the manor of Bowness on Solway after the attainder of Leonard Dacre, 'the profit to be aunswered for makinge of salte yerely,' together with the turbary set apart for that purpose, was valued at £5 16s. according to the rate of the market. The rent varied according to the quantity produced and the price in the market. In that year 'the said salte came but to a xiiij lodde that is in busshels lviij,' the price of a bushel ranging from twenty pence to two shillings.

The saltpans on the coast in the parish of Crosscanonby, presumably the property of the dean and chapter of Carlisle, were worth £40 a year in 1684 without coal,[6] and those 'under the hill called Lowkey' near Workington were of the same value.[7] From the evidences it would appear that pitcoal was substituted for peat as the fuel used in this industry during the latter period of its history. In the eighteenth century, when salt became subject to excise duty, we learn from the records of the quarter sessions that badgers and sellers of salt were often in trouble with the magistrates for evading the law. The fair of Rosley enjoyed a considerable reputation at that time for the sale of such merchandise.

The great industry of coal mining, for which Cumberland has a well-merited distinction, cannot be traced back to a very early period. Though we have frequent mention of the use of coal we have not found any record of coal mines being worked in Cumberland before the fifteenth century. It is true that the monks of St. Bees[8] were acquainted with the coalfields near Whitehaven as early as the reign of Henry III., but it is doubtful whether the value of coal was sufficiently recognized at that period to encourage them to work it as an industry. It is at a much later date that digging for coals became an organized institution. The Dacres of Naworth worked the coal mines of 'Tynyelfell' or Tindal Fell[9] in the eastern part of the county till they were forced to desist by the inroads of the Scots. In 1485 the mines were valueless for that reason. In the sixteenth century the uses of pitcoal became generally recognized in the county, and coal mining sprang up into one of the most extensive industries in the north.

The copper mines of Newlands near Keswick were selected by Camden to disprove the assertion of Cæsar that 'the Britons had ore of copper brought unto them beyond the sea,' and as these mines contained veins of gold and silver the great antiquary showed the groundlessness of Cicero's statement that there was not a particle of silver in the island.[10] The Keswick mines appear to have been worked at intervals since the reign of Henry III.[11] This is very probable, for in 1318 Edward II. appointed two engineers to search

[1] *Reg. of Wetherhal* (op. cit.), 233 ; Reg. of St. Bees, MS. v. 4. Ayringthwait is given on Greenwood's map of 1830 as Harrathwaite.
[2] Reg. of St. Bees, Harl. MS. 434, i. 23–5.
[3] *Coucher Book of Furness* (Chetham Soc.), iii. 604 ; Beck, *Ann. Furnesienses*, 208.
[4] Dugdale, *Mon.* v. 619.
[5] *Trans. Cumb. and Westmld. Arch. Soc.* (new ser.), i. 199.

[6] Ibid. i. 11.
[7] Thomas Denton, *Perambulation of Cumb.* in 1687-8, MS. f. 31.
[8] Reg. of St. Bees, Harl. MS. 434, lib. v. 5.
[9] *Cal. of Inq. p.m. Hen. VII.* i. 157.
[10] *Brit.* (ed. Holland), 767.
[11] Camden quotes a Close Roll for this statement, but we have not succeeded in finding the reference.

INDUSTRIES

and examine the mines of copper and silver at Caldbeck and the parts adjacent in the presence of the sheriff of Cumberland, and to make a report of what they had found there.[1] In the fifteenth century there can be no question that they were known to the officers of the Crown. In 1468 Richard, earl of Warwick, and John, earl of Northumberland, had a lease for forty years of all the mines of gold and silver, and all the mines of lead containing gold and silver found north of the Trent, with power to dig and search freely after agreement with the owners of the soil.[2] George Willarby, the prospecting engineer, reported in 1474 that he had found three notable mines in the north of England, one of which yielded 27 lb. of silver to the fodder of lead. One of these was the mine of 'Fletcheroos' in Alstonmoor, and another was the mine of Keswick in Cumberland. In 1475 Walter Barsonhowson was appointed master refiner of ' les ewres ' of the king's four mines in the north,[3] and in 1478 the old lease was surrendered and all the mines of gold, silver, copper and lead in Northumberland, Cumberland and Westmorland were granted to a colony of Dutch and German miners for ten years, on condition that they paid to the king a fifteenth part of the ore and to the lord of the soil and curate of the parish an amount to be agreed upon, with power to appoint a steward born in the realm to hold a court in the king's name in the mines and to determine all pleas except those of land, life and members.[4]

The foreign miners must have continued working at Keswick with more or less success till the great revival of mining operations at that place in the beginning of the reign of queen Elizabeth. As early as 1516 'the Hugstettyrs and Belzers' were in the service of Henry VIII.[5] Joachim 'Hœgstre' was the principal surveyor and master of all the mines in England and Ireland in 1528, in which year he proposed the employment of six experienced Germans and 1,000 men for the development of this industry,[6] but it was not till 1565 that the Keswick mines jumped into prominence as the most lucrative veins of copper in the kingdom. The influx of foreign

workmen at that time soon became a danger to the peace of the community, and the warfare between the miners and the inhabitants was often attended with disastrous results. It was suspected that the attacks on the miners were connived at by lady Ratcliffe,[7] who resented the intrusion of the foreigners into her neighbourhood. In 1566 a commission was issued to lord Scrope and the local magistracy to repress the assaults, murders and outrages on the Almain miners, who had lately come to Keswick for the purpose of searching for and working minerals.[8]

But another opponent of the industry arose when the earl of Northumberland had ascertained in 1567 that the minerals dug up at Newlands belonged without doubt to him only, and that the workers were trespassers on his land. A suit at law followed, but as the mines yielded a proportion of gold and silver they were adjudged to the Crown.[9] The principal overseer was Daniel 'Hechstetter,' no doubt a scion of the house of Joachim above mentioned, who had brought with him 400 men in 1565.[10] Operations were carried on in Newlands and Borrowdale, and six smelting furnaces were at work daily in Keswick and elsewhere. A piece of ground was purchased in 1568 from Mr. Curwen at Workington with the view of building a wharf for the export of the ore.[11] Though coal[12] and wood were sometimes used, peat was recognized as the staple fuel for the supply of the furnaces. In 1597 Marcus Stainbergus, Richard Ledes, and Emanuel 'Hechstetter' complained to Cecil, governor of the royal mines, that there was a great lack of peat owing to the wet summer at Keswick, which hindered mining, and in consequence the men had only poor wages.[13] But there was a suspicion that the strangers were not dealing fairly with the authorities, some thinking that the Dutchmen were only seeking their own profit. Inasmuch as the mines were becoming less productive and presumably going to decay, lord Scrope was instructed in 1599 to pay a surprise visit to Keswick and take the opinion of the local gentry on the state of affairs. If the mines were worn out as the Germans pretended, some course

[1] Orig. R. 12 Edw. II. m. 7.
[2] Pat. 8 Edw. IV. pt. iii. m. 14.
[3] Ibid. 14 Edw. IV. pt. i. m. 7d ; 15 Edw. IV. pt. i. m. 22 ; 15 Edw. IV. pt. i. m. 12.
[4] Ibid. 18 Edw. IV. pt. ii. m. 30.
[5] Cott. MS. Vitellius, B. xix. 234 ; L. and P. Hen. VIII. ii. 2310.
[6] Pat. 20 Hen. VIII. pt. i. m. 37d ; Cott. MS. Titus, iv. 147 ; L. and P. Hen. VIII. iv. 5110.

[7] Cal. S. P. Dom. Eliz. xl. 81.
[8] Ibid. xl. 87.
[9] Ibid. xlii. 31, 35 ; Camden, Brit. (ed. Holland), 767.
[10] Cal. S. P. Dom. Eliz. xxxvi. 59.
[11] Ibid. xlvii. 52.
[12] There was a great difficulty of procuring coals for the Keswick mines in 1568 (ibid. xlviii. 13).
[13] Ibid. cclxiv. 30.

should be taken for the maintenance of the workmen.[1]

Robinson of Ousby, who saw the books of the German miners in 1702, says that when queen Elizabeth won the suit against the earl of Northumberland, her officers seized a hundred tons of ore in her name.[2] Operations continued till 1642, when the smelting houses were destroyed and most of the miners were slain during the Civil War.[3] An attempt was made by the duke of Somerset to re-open the mines at the beginning of the eighteenth century, but the project was abandoned after a great outlay, because the operator, not understanding the nature of the ore, burnt and destroyed fifty tons of the best goldscope ore without the production of one pound of fine copper.[4] Various attempts to work the Keswick mines had been made by private companies in the nineteenth century, but they met with scanty encouragement, and were finally abandoned in 1864.[5]

The black lead mine of Keswick was of sufficient interest to attract the notice of Camden who described the mineral product as a 'kind of earth or hardened glittering stone which painters use to draw their lines and make pictures of one colour in their first draughts.'[6] The mine was situated on the eastern side of Seatoller Fell near the hamlet of Seathwaite in the manor of Borrowdale about 9 miles from Keswick. The mineral otherwise known as plumbago, or wad in the vernacular of the district, is reputed to be of remarkable purity. It drew from Robinson of Ousby a curious panegyric setting forth the uses to which it was put in the latter half of the seventeenth century. 'The most remarkable mundick vein upon these mountains,' he said, 'is that we call wadd or black lead. This was found upon Borrowdale mountains near Keswick, and there is not any other of the same kind in England nor perhaps in Europe, at least that I have heard of. Its composition is a black, pinguid and shining earth, impregnated with lead and antimony. This ore is of more value than either copper, lead, or iron. It was bought up by the apothecaries and physicians of the day and used medicinally for various sorts of ills with good success. At the first discovering of it, the neighbourhood made no other use of it, but for marking of sheep; but it is now (1709) made use of to glazen and harden crucibles, and other vessels made of earth or clay that are to endure the hottest fire. It was also used by dyers of cloth to make their "blues" to stand unalterable and for the polishing of fire-arms. The vein was but opened once in seven years, as the quantities obtained were sufficient to serve the country. The mineral was bought up at great prices by the Hollanders.'[7]

This industry was protected by a special Act of Parliament (25 Geo. II. c. 10), in which it is stated that the mineral was necessary for 'divers useful purposes, and more particularly in the casting of bomb-shells, round-shot, and canon-balls,' and by which it is made a felony 'to enter unlawfully any mine, or wad-hole of wad, or black-cawke, commonly called black-lead, or unlawfully taking or carrying away any wad therefrom, or buying or receiving the same, knowing it to be unlawfully taken.' In 1800 it is said that a house was built over the mouth of the principal mine, and armed men were kept on guard there during the night. As a further precaution the miners were stripped and carefully searched on leaving their work, and

---

[1] S. P. Dom. Eliz. cclxxi. 40. It may be remarked that the State Papers of this period contain numerous references to the progress of mining at Keswick from the incorporation of the company in 1561 (ibid. xviii. 18) till the end of the reign.

[2] Robinson, *Essay towards a Nat. Hist. of Cumb. and Westmld.* (ed. 1709) 61-4. When Robinson stated that the copper works at Keswick in queen Elizabeth's time were the most famous in England and perhaps in Europe, he was probably right; certainly they were the most famous in Cumberland for 'the mynes royale' there were the only mines marked by Speed on his map of 1610. Bishop Nicolson noted in his diary, under date 25 July 1702, that 'Mr. Robinson of Ousby, giving an account of the Copper works at Keswick, saies the Account Book of the old German miners, very fairly written, is in ye hand of old Mrs. Hechstetter in that parish: and that, by one of them, it appears that they refined their metal with ye hoofs and pairings of horses.' In the same diary it is stated in 1705 that the account books relating to the mines were in possession of the duke of Somerset's agent (*Trans. Cumb. and Westmld. Arch. Soc.* [new ser.], ii. 173-4; iii. 34).

[3] Thomas Denton, Perambulation of Cumb. in 1687-8, MS. ff. 38, 40, 41. Our author was of opinion that it would have taken £4,000 to begin work at these mines in his day. Remains of the smelting houses may still be seen at the east end of Keswick: notably the mill race by the side of the Greta, part of which has been cut through the solid rock.

[4] Robinson, *Essay towards a Nat. Hist.* 63-4.

[5] For a description of these mines and of the modern attempts to re-open them, the reader may be referred to Postlethwaite, *Mines and Mining in the Lake District,* 19-32.

[6] *Brit.* (ed. Holland), 767.

[7] *Nat. Hist. of Cumb. and Westmld.* 74-6 (published 1709).

when the plumbago was sent to London an armed escort accompanied it as far as Kendal.[1]

The deposits of plumbago are not found in veins, like other minerals, but in pipes or sops of varying sizes at some distance from them. In 1778 one of these yielded 417 casks, each cask containing 70 lb. of the best plumbago. Another deposit found in 1803 produced over 31 tons. As the current price of the ore was about 30s. a pound, plumbago mining in the eighteenth century was regarded as a very lucrative industry. Since 1833 the mine has been worked at intervals, but no deposit of value has been found.[2] Though the ore is scarce, Keswick still retains its ancient reputation for the manufacture of lead pencils, as an inferior species of foreign plumbago, when compressed, can be utilized for that purpose. There is a tradition that plumbago was first discovered by the uprooting of an ash tree in a storm.

Cumberland retains its position as one of the most flourishing and important centres of the tanning trade in the United Kingdom. The large tanneries in Maryport and Whitehaven are still regarded by those engaged in this industry as examples of modern enterprise and effective management. But like other minor industries the manufacture of leather has undergone many changes and fluctuations in recent years. Half a century ago there were thirty-three tanneries in the county with the yearly output of 60,800 tanned hides; at the present time, though the number has been reduced to ten, the yearly output has increased to 215,200 hides. In the eighteenth century almost every considerable village had a tannery; some of them had more; but the introduction of steam power and the employment of chemicals instead of oak bark had a tendency to crush out the small tanneries and to concentrate capital in the more convenient centres for trade. Within living memory there were seven tanneries in operation at Cockermouth, four at Egremont, and one each at Brampton, Harrington and Parton, but they have all disappeared. In other places the declension is also observable. The tanneries in Carlisle have been reduced from five to one, at Wigton and Whitehaven from three to one, at Penrith from two to one. The number has remained stationary at Maryport, Scotby, Workington and Thurstonfield, with an enormous increase in the output of tanned hides.[3]

It is natural that a mountainous county like Cumberland should be prolific in the production of stone and slate for building purposes. The Honister slate and Lazonby flag hold a high reputation for durability in the northern counties. From an early period the lessees of the bishops of Carlisle worked the red sandstone quarries of Shauk and Unthank in their lordship of Dalston, from the former of which, judging by the inscription which once existed on the face of the rock there, it is almost certain the Romans took some of their stone for the construction of the Great Wall. The quarries in various localities on mountain side and undulating uplands may be classed among the minor but important industries.

At the opening of the nineteenth century Cumberland enjoyed some reputation for the manufacture of textile fabrics. Hand-loom weavers plied their calling in every village. Numerous small mills had sprung up. The manufacture of coarse linen cloth had been established in Carlisle as early as 1750, and was followed in a few years by the introduction of calico stamperies, which gave employment to a large number of people and caused a considerable influx of Irish and Scotch into the city. Machinery for the carding and spinning of cotton was erected in various parts of the district, and manufactories thrived beyond the expectation of the promoters. But it may be said now that the day of country mills and small industries has passed away. In most country districts the old industries, on which a section of the population depended for subsistence, are fast becoming extinct. The segregation of the industrial classes in large centres and the concentration of capital for the promotion of limited companies have sounded the death knell of the smaller industries of the county.

There can be little doubt that improved methods of communication had an important influence in bringing about this industrial revolution. Much had been done in Cumberland between 1750 and 1770 to facilitate transit by means of turnpike roads. Before this period the roads of the county were for the most part narrow lanes fitted only for transport by pack horses. When the local acts were obtained for their widening and improvement, the exaction of tolls gave rise to considerable popular discontent, and it was a long time before the inhabitants were reconciled to the innovation. But experience eventually proved that the amount of tolls

---

[1] Postlethwaite, *Mines and Mining in the Lake District*, 33–5.

[2] Ibid. 34–5.

[3] We are indebted to Mr. Alfred Sutton of Scotby for the statistics of the tanning industry of the county.

levied for the formation and repair of the roads was more than counterbalanced by the advantages of the new means of transit. In addition to these facilities for commerce between neighbouring districts, an artificial canal from Maryport by Carlisle to Newcastle-on-Tyne, thus connecting the Solway with the North Sea, was proposed in 1794. Application was made to Parliament in 1797 for the necessary powers, but owing to disputes in Northumberland, whether the canal should be constructed on the north or south side of the Tyne, the project was abandoned. At a later period a more moderate scheme for connecting the city of Carlisle with its port on the Solway was revived and successfully carried out. In 1819 a ship canal nearly twelve miles in length with eight locks or sluices was commenced, and in 1823 it was opened with great ceremony and amid much rejoicing. It commenced at Port Carlisle and terminated in Caldewgate, near the Cumberland Infirmary, where a capacious basin and a large warehouse were constructed. Vessels of 100 tons were able to discharge their freights on the outskirts of the city within half a mile of the Market Cross, and communication was facilitated with the ports along the western coast as far as Liverpool. The canal was the means of stimulating the trade of Carlisle and the surrounding district. In a short time after it was opened the price of coal fell from 6½d. to 3½d. per Carlisle peck. The canal was abandoned in favour of the railway after having been of immense benefit to the inhabitants of Carlisle for about thirty years.

The old project of connecting the eastern and western seas by means of a canal, which was dropped in 1797, was revived in another form in 1829, when an Act was obtained to construct a railway from Carlisle to Newcastle through the Tyne valley, a distance of about 60 miles. The work was commenced in 1830, and the line was opened for traffic throughout its entire length in 1838. One of the engineering features of this line in its passage through Cumberland is the magnificent bridge over the Eden at Wetheral, consisting of five semicircular arches of 80 feet span each, with an elevation of 100 feet above the water level. With the help of the ship canal from Carlisle to the Solway, the new railway afforded a cheap and expeditious transit to the Liverpool and Irish merchants for the carriage of goods and merchandise to and from Hamburg and Holland. The Newcastle and Carlisle railway, amalgamated in 1862 with the North-Eastern, is the oldest railway line in Cumberland, and takes rank with the oldest railways of the kingdom.

This experiment in railway enterprise was soon followed in other places in Cumberland, and for thirty years the construction of lines in various parts of the county was pursued with vigour. The act of incorporation[1] for the Maryport and Carlisle Railway Company was obtained in 1837, and sections of the line were opened between Maryport and Arkleby in July 1840, between Arkleby and Aspatria in December 1841, between Carlisle and Wigton in May 1843, and the line was ready for traffic throughout its whole length of twenty-eight miles on 10 February 1845. The line was extended through the towns of Workington and Harrington to Whitehaven in 1847 by the Whitehaven Junction Company (incorporated in 1844), a distance of twelve miles, thus connecting the four important ports on the western coast and providing direct communication between the great industrial centres of that region. The Furness Railway Company, incorporated in 1845 by Act of 8 & 9 Victoria, cap. 100, opened their line between Whitehaven and Ravenglass, a distance of nearly 17 miles in 1849, and from Ravenglass to Millom, about the same distance, in the following year. Thus a great thoroughfare was laid from the extreme south of the county along the coast to Maryport where the line turned inland to Carlisle. Offshoots were sent out in the course of time to connect country towns and local industries with the main line. The company which laid the line from Cockermouth to Workington was incorporated in 1845 by Act of 8 & 9 Victoria, cap. 120, and the line was opened throughout in 1847. The Cleator and Workington Junction railway with a distance of about thirty miles, was opened for mineral traffic on 1 July 1878, and for passengers on 18 October 1879, the general offices being at the central station, Workington. From Ravenglass the Furness Company made a line with a 3-feet gauge through the Eskdale valley as far as Boot, a distance of 7¼ miles. This little railway, much utilized during the tourist season, was opened for goods traffic on 24 May 1875, and for passengers on 20 November 1876. The portion of the Lancaster and Carlisle railway, which enters Cumberland near Penrith, was opened for traffic in 1846, the company having been incorporated in 1844 by Act of 7 & 8 Victoria, cap. 37. The line was leased in 1859 for a period of 900 years to the London and North-Western

[1] Act 1 Vic. cap. 3.

Company and became an integral part of the great trunk line from London to Glasgow and Edinburgh. The locomotive and iron road have penetrated into the heart of the Lake District and connected Keswick, its capital, with Penrith on the east and Cockermouth on the west. The south of Scotland was brought into immediate relations with the coal district of West Cumberland by the construction of the Solway Junction railway, remarkable for its great viaduct which spans an arm of the Solway between Annan and Bowness. It now forms a part of the Caledonian system. The Whitehaven, Cleator and Egremont Company was incorporated in 1854 by Act of 17 & 18 Victoria, cap. 64, and the line was opened for the conveyance of passengers in 1857, having been previously used for mineral traffic for about eighteen months.

A new development of railway extension took place in 1853 when an Act[1] was obtained to convert the ship canal from Carlisle to the Solway into a railway. From a financial point of view the canal was never a success to the shareholders owing to the shifting nature of the channel in the neighbourhood of the port. A little lower down the firth a natural haven was recognized in Silloth Bay, and powers were procured in 1885 to construct docks at this place and to extend the new railway to that termination. The railway which follows the track of the canal for some distance, has been incorporated with the North British system. The Midland Railway was long excluded from the county and the Scottish traffic beyond it. The shareholders were alarmed at the engineering difficulties in the way of extension of the line from Settle in Yorkshire to Carlisle, and the bill for the necessary powers of construction

[1] Act 17 Vic. cap. 119.

was opposed by the landowners on the route. Eventually all obstacles were surmounted and the line was opened for goods in August 1875, and for passengers in May 1876.

For a maritime county, so peculiarly situated as Cumberland, with great mountain masses forming its southern boundaries and severed from Northumberland and Durham by the Pennine range of hills, its whole area may be said to be well supplied with railway communication. The Citadel station, which forms the terminus for eight important railways running into Carlisle, viz., Midland, London and North-Western, North-Eastern, Caledonian, North-British, Glasgow and South-Western, Maryport and Carlisle, and Carlisle and Silloth lines, is built of white stone in the Elizabethan style with a fine entrance to the city through Court Square. It is under the joint management of the Caledonian and London and North-Western companies. The station was extended under the powers of an Act of 1873, and greater accommodation was provided for the enormous traffic, occasioned by the completion of the Midland line. It is now reckoned one of the finest railway stations in England. The glass in the roof alone is said to cover an area of 7 acres. The present staff consists of one superintendent, one secretary, one night stationmaster, seven inspectors, seven foremen, twenty signalmen, eighteen ticket examiners, four luggage-room attendants, four lavatory attendants, eight ladies' room attendants, eleven shunters, six shacklers, seven policemen, thirty-six porters, four lampmen, two engine-men, ten platelayers, eight painters, joiners, plumbers, etc., one chief booking clerk, nine booking clerks, one chief parcels clerk, and sixteen parcels clerks, making a total of 182 persons in the employment of the railway authorities at Carlisle station.

A HISTORY OF CUMBERLAND

COAL MINING

The supreme importance of the West Cumberland coalfield, exposed to view along the sea-board from Barrowmouth near Whitehaven to Maryport, and thence inland to Bolton Low Houses, is apt to cause other and minor tracts of coal in Cumberland to be overlooked. There are, however, in the eastern part of the county, the true Coal Measures, forming the western extremity of the Newcastle coalfield, at Midgeholme; the seams of coal found in the Carboniferous Limestone, along its escarpment at the great Pennine fault, and also in the Alston district; and the seams of coal occurring in the tract of Carboniferous Limestone lying between the eastern extremity of the West Cumberland coalfield and the Permian sandstone near Penrith.

WEST CUMBERLAND COALFIELD

Area.—According to the Geological Survey of England and Wales, the West Cumberland coalfield apparently terminates to the north at the Aspatria fault which puts in the Permian sandstone; but, as a matter of fact, workings have been driven a considerable distance beyond it in the Yard Band from Brayton No. 4 Pit. Similarly to the south, judging from the same Survey, it might seem that the coalfield ends at the Permian sandstone of St. Bees Head, whereas the Croft Pit workings, Whitehaven Colliery, extend, in the Main Band, a long way under the Permian sandstone; and the Gutterfoot borehole conclusively proved the continuity of the principal coal seams as far south as the village of St. Bees.

The eastern boundary, formed by the Carboniferous Limestone, is the only one that can at present be defined with any precision.

Westward the Coal Measures dip to the sea, but their extent in that direction can only be surmised.

The exposed coalfield may be described generally as a belt of Coal Measures, reposing either on the Millstone Grit or on the Yoredale rocks of the Carboniferous Limestone series, along the north-west base of the Cumberland hills.

From Barrowmouth, the exposed coalfield measures about 16 miles to Crosby Colliery. Throughout that distance it has an average width of about 4½ miles. Near Crosby Colliery the coalfield trends to the east, and is there only three-quarters of a mile wide. The eastern extremity of the uncovered coalfield is about 12 miles from Crosby Colliery, and

has an average width of about 1½ miles. Thus the total area of the coalfield, as shown by the Geological Survey, is about 90 square miles. To this must be added the area of coalfield already proved under the Permians, say 6 square miles, and the known area under the sea, say 12 square miles, making the total extent of coalfield known up to the present time to be about 108 square miles.

Thickness.—The Coal Measures of West Cumberland consist of two unconformable divisions, viz.:—

1. The Upper or Whitehaven Sandstone series.

2. The Lower or Productive Measures.

The upper beds of the Whitehaven Sandstone series were first recognized by Mr. W. Brockbank[1] in 1891, in the section of the borehole put down at Frizington Hall, a few miles east of Whitehaven, where they were found, 418 feet thick, immediately underneath the Permian *breccia*, to contain two thin beds of *Spirorbis* limestone, and three thin coal seams.

The sandstone forming the cliffs at Whitehaven, where it is about 170 feet thick, and covering the Lower Coal Measures there and at Cleator Moor, Ellenborough, Crosby, Oughterside and Bolton, belongs to the lower part of the Upper Coal Measures.

Mr. Newell Arber[2] considers the Whitehaven sandstone series to be at least 600 feet thick; but probably its maximum thickness is 778 feet in the Bolton district.

Mr. J. D. Kendall has estimated[3] that the Lower Coal Measures are the thickest at Workington, viz. 1300 feet, but 'there is some doubt as to the vertical extent of the series since the base has not so far been definitely determined.'

The aggregate thickness of the West Cumberland Coal Measures may therefore be taken to be 2,078 feet.

The Whitehaven Sandstone Series.—This series consists chiefly of purple sandstones and shales; but the lower part also comprises light and dark coloured shales resembling those of the Lower Coal Measures, and several workable seams of coal. At the Bolton, Crummock and Weary Hall collieries two of these seams, viz. the Crow Coal and Master Band,

[1] *Mem. & Pro. Lit. & Phil. Soc. Man.* sec. 4, iv. 418.
[2] *Quart. Journ. Geol. Soc.* lix. 2.
[3] *Trans. North of Eng. Inst. Mining Engineers,* xxxii. 347.

348

ST HELENS COLLIERY

High Water Mark

All Hallows Rd

EAST

Iron Man Houses

Erickson Pit

Belton Wood Lione

High Water Mark

GERMAN

have been worked extensively. The Crow Coal, 2 ft. 6 in. thick, is about 5 fathoms above the Master Band, which is 4 ft. 9 in. thick, and 30 fathoms above the 'Main Band,' as the Yard Band is termed in that locality.

. At Aspatria Bank End Pit these two seams were called the 'Crow Band' and the 'Ten Quarters' seam. At Ellenborough, Ewanrigg and Flimby Collieries only the upper of these two seams has been worked, and was there known by three different names—the Yard Band, the Whitecroft Seam and the Senhouse High Band.

Lower Coal Measures.—These may be designated the productive measures, because they are by far the more prolific in coal.

The following sections give a list of the principal seams proved in the various parts of the coalfield :—

WHITEHAVEN.

Seam	Thickness of coal ft. in.		Depth at Wellington Pit faths.
1. Metal	3	6	48
2. Preston Isle Yard .	2	6	53
3. Bannock . . .	6	0	74
4. Main	9	0	96
5. Yard	3	0	109
6. Little Main . .	2	0	127
7. Six Quarters . .	6	0	139
8. Four Feet . . .	2	3	187

CLEATOR MOOR

Seam	Thickness of coal ft. in.		Depth at Lindow Pit faths.
1. Six Feet . . .	3	10	51
2. Four Feet . . .	4	7	56
3. Five Feet . . .	4	5	65
4. Bannock . . .	5	0	78
5. Main	9	0	95
6. Yard	2	8	104
7. Little Main . .	2	3	120
8. Low Bottom . .	3	2	133

HARRINGTON

Seam	Thickness of coal ft. in.		Depth at John Pit faths.
1. Metal	2	0	20
2. Two Feet . . .	2	0	35
3. Three Feet . .	3	0	52
4. Four Feet . . .	3	6	90
5. Udale	3	0	118

WORKINGTON [1]

Seam	Thickness of coal ft. in.		Depth faths.
1. Brassey	3	0	28
2. Cannel	1	10	40
3. Metal	1	7	48
4. Fiery	1	6	55
5. Moorbanks . .	2	6	60
6. Little Main (No. 1)	1	6	64

[1] Compiled from the sections of several pits.

Seam	Thickness of coal ft. in.		Depth faths.
7. Main	10	0	98
8. Yard	2	0	113
9. Little Main (No. 2)	2	8	134
10. Hamilton or Four Feet . . .	4	6	150
11. Udale	3	0	174

ST. HELENS

Seam	Thickness of coal ft. in.		Depth faths.	
1. Brassey . . .	2	10	16	
2. Upper White Metal . .	3	0	23	At No. 2 Pit.
3. Lower White Metal . .	2	8	32	
4. Slaty	2	4	43	
5. Ten Quarters .	4	6	49	
6. Rattler . . .	3	0	53	
7. Cannel and Metal : Metal 3 ft. } Cannel 5 „ }	8	0	84	
8. Yard Band . .	1	6	97	
9. Little Main . .	2	0	117	
10. Lick Bank . .	2	4	136	

FLIMBY, ELLENBOROUGH AND EWANRIGG [2]

Seam	Thickness of coal ft. in.		Depth faths.
1. Hamilton . . .	4		52
2. White Metal . .	3		61
3. Top Yard . . .	2		64
4. Slaty	5	8	70
5. Ten Quarters . .	7	9	83
6. Rattler	3	8	90
7. Brick	1	5	93
8. Crow	3	0	110
9. Cannel and Metal : Metal . . .	3	4	111
Cannel . . .	5	0	115
10. Yard	2	0	127
11. Little Main . .	2	0	146
12. Lick Bank . . .	2	0	157

CROSBY, DEARHAM AND GILCRUX

Seam	Thickness of coal ft. in.		Depth at Lonsdale Pit, Dearham faths.
1. White Metal . .	2	2	30
2. Ten Quarters . .	7	4	59
3. Rattler	2	10	72
4. Brick	2	0	74
5. Crow	2	6	83
6. Cannel and Metal : Metal . . .	3	0	} 85
Cannel . . .	5	0	
7. Yard	2	0	96
8. Brassey	2	6	108
9. Little Main . .	2	0	113
10. Lick Bank . . .	2	0	131

[2] Compiled from sections of Watergate Pit (down to the Cannel and Metal Band) and Robin Hood Pit (below that seam).

In the dip north drift, driven from No. 1 Pit, Crosby Colliery, the following seams were passed through below the Lick Bank Seam, viz. :—

	Thickness of coal ft. in.	Depth from Lick Bank Seam faths.
11. Coal Seam . .	2 3	. . 21
12. ,, ,, . .	2 0	. . 27
13. ,, ,, . .	2 2	. . 37

OUGHTERSIDE AND ASPATRIA [1]

Seam	Thickness of coal ft. in.	Depth faths.
1. Yard	4 9	. . 89
2. Little Main . .	2 2	. . 108
3. Lick Bank . .	1 0	. . 123

BROUGHTON, RIBTON, CLIFTON AND GREYSOUTHEN [2]

Seam	Thickness of coal ft. in.	Depth faths.
1. White Metal . .	3 0	. . 17
2. Slaty	1 6	. . 24
3. Ten Quarters . .	5 6	. . 31
4. Rattler . . .	1 2	. . 37
5. Crow	2 0	. . 58
6. Cannel and Metal .	7 0	. . 60
7. Yard	2 0	. . 73
8. Little Main . .	2 0	. . 93
9. Lick Bank . . .	2 0	. . 99

The base of the Lower Coal Measures cannot at present be defined because the Millstone Grit has not been identified in any shaft or borehole ; but the Yoredale rocks or Carboniferous Limestone have been proved, in several parts of the coalfield, through the Coal Measures. The Limestone was reached in two boreholes, put down near Fitz, Aspatria, in the strata below the Yard Band, at the depth of 70 fathoms from the surface ; at Crosby Colliery, in the dip north drift, at 43 fathoms below the Lick Bank Seam ; at John Pit, Harrington, at 33 fathoms below the Udale Seam ; and lastly, at Ladysmith Pit, Whitehaven, at 54½ fathoms below the Main Band.

Correlation of the Seams.—Until the publication of Mr. J. D. Kendall's paper, in 1883, on the ' Structure of the Cumberland Coalfield,' the correlation of the seams met with in the different districts of the coalfield had not been thoroughly undertaken. It may now be summed up as follows :—

(1) The Five Feet Coal at Cleator Moor corresponds to the Moorbanks Seam at Workington and the Ten Quarters Seam at Greysouthen, Ellenborough, Bullgill, Dearham, Flimby and Broughton Moor.

[1] Compiled from the sections of No. 3 Pit, and the bore-hole at No. 1 Pit, Aspatria.

[2] Compiled from the sections of William and Lowther Pits, Clifton.

(2) The Bannock Band at Cleator Moor and Whitehaven corresponds to the Little Main Band at Workington and the Rattler Band at Ellenborough.

(3) The Main Band at Whitehaven, Cleator Moor and Workington is one and the same seam, and corresponds to the Cannel and Metal Band, together with the Crow Coal, in the Maryport district.

(4) The Yard Band (known as the Main Band in the Bolton Colliery) is continuous throughout the coalfield.

(5) The Lick Bank seam of Greysouthen is the Hamilton Band at Workington, the Three Feet Seam at Harrington, the Six Quarter Seam at Whitehaven, and the Low Bottom Seam at Cleator Moor.

The Coal Seams : Thickness, character and mode of working.—The sections given above furnish the number and names of the seams, with the approximate average thickness of coal in each.

The thickness of the coal and the bands of ' metal' almost invariably found intercalated with the coal in all the seams differ so much, even in the same colliery, that it would be tedious and confusing to give numerous and detailed sections to show the different phases in which each seam is found all over the coalfield.

But the Main Band, the most important of all the seams, deserves more than a passing notice. At Whitehaven, Cleator Moor, Montreal, Asby, Walkmill, Oatlands, and Clifton it may be said to form one seam, though divided by thin layers of ' metal.' North of Workington these ' metal' bands develop in thickness, dividing the coal into three separate and distinct seams, known respectively by the names of the Crow Coal, the Metal Band, and the Cannel Band.

The following section, taken in the Delaval district, William Pit, Whitehaven, will give some idea of the character of the Main Band where it forms one seam, in the greatest perfection :—

	ft. in.	ft. in.	ft. in.
Little Top coal . .	0 6	. —	
Metal	—	. 0 2	
Bearing Top coal .	2 0	. —	
Main Top coal . .	2 4	. —	
Metal	—	. 0 5	
Undergrowth coal .	1 6	. —	
Metal	—	. 0 1	
Coal (' four-inch') .	0 7	. —	
Metal	—	. 0 2	
Spar coal . . .	1 4	. —	
Benk coal . . .	3 6	. —	
Metal	—	. 0 2	
Mother coal . . .	0 5	. —	
	12 2	+ 1 0	= 13 2

Although the Main Band in other parts of the coalfield may be said to be divided into three seams, it is generally known in those localities by the names of two of its members, viz. the ' Cannel and Metal Band,' the highest being little worked.

An illustration of this triple division may be taken from the shaft at Watergate Pit, Flimby Colliery, where the section is :—

	ft.	in.	ft.	in.	ft.	in.
Crow coal—						
Coal	2	9	.	—		
Metal	—		.	2	6	
Coal	0	8	.	—		
	3	5		2	6	
						5 11
Metal						5 11
Metal Band—						
Coal	1	8	.	—		
Metal	—		.	1	0	
Coal	1	8	.	—		
	3	4		1	0	
						4 4
Metal . .						
Cannel Band—						
Top coal . .	1	2	.	—		
Metal	—		.	0	1¼	
Coal . . .	0	7	.	—		
'Tom' . . .	—		.	0	2	
Spar coal . .	1	5	.	—		
Cannel . . .	—		.	0	8	
Stone	—		.	0	3	
Bottom coal . .	1	6	.	—		
'Scram' . . .	—		.	0	3	
Dirt	—		.	0	3¼	
	4 8	+	1	9	=	6 5

The Main or Cannel and Metal Band has of all the seams been worked to the greatest extent, both under land and sea ; and next to the Main Band the Bannock Band of Whitehaven and the Ten Quarters Seam of other districts have received the most attention.

Since the introduction of the long-wall system of mining within recent times into the West Cumberland coalfield, the thin seams below the Main Band—the Yard, Little Main, and Lick Bank—have been worked at St. Helens, Clifton, Flimby, Broughton Moor, and Dearham Collieries to a considerable but much less extent than the superior and thicker seams throughout the coalfield.

Generally the produce of the West Cumberland coal seams may be described as house, gas and coking coals. The cannel found in the Cannel Band is of a stony nature, and most of it is left underground. About the middle of the eighteenth century, when the smelting of iron in blast furnaces with coke

had become an assured success, furnaces of that kind were built within the West Cumberland coalfield at Little Clifton, Maryport, Seaton and Frizington.

' About 1750, or possibly a little earlier, Messrs. Cookson & Co., who worked coal mines at Clifton and Greysouthen, erected a blast furnace at Little Clifton, on the banks of the Marron.'[1]

In 1765 M. Jars visited the Clifton furnace and described the primitive mode in which coal was then converted into coke.[2] Large coals were stacked so as to allow circulation of air amongst them, in conical heaps, from 10 to 12 feet in diameter at the base, and about 5 feet high. These heaps were lighted from the top, after which they were covered all over with a thin layer of clay and coaldust, and care was taken to stop up any openings that might be formed in this covering, on the windward side, in order to prevent the destruction of the coke when formed.

Except at Seaton little success seems to have attended the iron furnaces built *circa* 1750 in West Cumberland ; and with their abandonment, after a brief career, any particular demand for coke would cease. Little appears to have been done in the district in the manufacture of coke from those early days, until the introduction of railways and the establishment of the iron and steel works along the west coast led to a demand for a local supply of coke to supplement that derived from the east coast, although, in the interim, ' cinders ' (as coke was often styled) were made on a limited scale at several collieries.

A great drawback to the use of West Cumberland coke was at one time due to the impurities contained in the coal from which it was made ; but that difficulty has in a great measure been overcome by the adoption of the improved pulverising and coal-washing machinery now in use.

All the ovens, until 1894, were of the beehive pattern, about 11 feet diameter by 9 feet in height ; and at most of the existing ovens the gases, formerly wasted, are utilized for raising steam, thus effecting a great saving in colliery consumption. But nowhere in the district are the bye-products recovered.

In 1894 a great innovation was made in coke-making, in West Cumberland, by the erection of 24 Coppée coke ovens at No. 3, St. Helens Colliery. Each of these ovens is 30 ft. long, 6 ft. 6 in. high, and 2 ft. wide, and produces about 4 tons of coke

[1] *Archæology of West Cumberland Iron Trade*, by Mr. H. A. Fletcher.
[2] *Voyages Métallurgiques*, tome i. 236.

every 48 hours, the coking process occupying nearly one half the time taken by the bee-hive oven.

All coal used for coking is now washed by means of special machinery for that purpose, the Sheppard and the Coppée washers being chiefly used. In 1890 a Luhrig washing plant was erected at Ellenborough Colliery at a cost of upwards of £4,000, exclusive of the buildings, but it was removed in 1892 when the owners of the colliery went into liquidation.

Mode of Working.—Until the introduction of the 'long-wall' system within recent times, when the thin seams came to be worked, the method of working the coal was exclusively by 'bord and pillar.'

In the early days of coal mining, when the coal was worked near the outcrops or at very shallow depths, the coal pillars were left very small, in some cases only 4 or 5 yards square, and in others 15 yards long by 2 yards wide; but as seams were worked at greater depths the sizes of the pillars were increased. At Whitehaven at the present day the pillars of coal left in the first working, under the sea, are 25 yards square, and the workings are generally 6 yards wide. Thus 35 per cent of coal is obtained in the first working and 65 per cent of coal is left in the pillars.

Before the beginning of the nineteenth century none of these pillars were removed, and it may be said without exaggeration that in some of the old collieries fully half of the coal has been left and may never be recovered. On the other hand, at many of the old pits at Whitehaven the pillars have been left suffi-ciently large and will undoubtedly be worked at some future day when a scarcity of coal arises.

Underneath the sea at Whitehaven some of the pillars have been removed [1] where the cover was 100 fathoms or more; but during the continuance of the Crown lease, from 1860 to 1880, the pillars were only allowed to 'split' in the second working, and thus in most of the districts where the pillars were 'robbed' probably 30 per cent of the coal has been irretrievably lost.

Since 1890 a system of working in panels underneath the sea has been adopted, and enables the coal to be almost entirely got.

Under the sea, at Harrington, the Main Band has been worked 'bord and pillar' at 21 fathoms, the pillars having been left in; and the Six Quarters seam is being worked long-

wall at 45 fathoms. At St. Helens, the Ten Quarters seam at 70 fathoms, and the Cannel and Metal Band at 105 fathoms, are being worked long-wall under the sea.

A method resembling long-wall is said to have been introduced probably about the middle of the eighteenth century at Warnell Fell, Sebergham, where a seam of coal 16 in. thick was worked; but long-wall, on any extended scale, was not adopted till about 1870, when it was applied in the Rattler Band, No. 2 Pit, St. Helens.

Long-wall means the extraction of all coal in one operation, the full length of a long 'face,' the roof settling down behind as the 'face' advances. There are many modifica-tions of long-wall, but what is generally fol-lowed in West Cumberland may be thus de-scribed. The coal is worked against the line of 'cleat,' and brought out by 'gateways' made 12 yards apart through the goaf, and supported on each side by pack-walls a few yards wide, built either of stone 'brushed' from the roof, or of 'metal' out of the seam, or of 'bottom' that has been lifted in the 'gateways.' It is only in the 'gateways' that height is made for the conveyance of the coal by ponies or hand-trailing.

Between the 'gateways' nothing but the coal is worked. These gateways are cut off by cross-gateways which are made every 60 yards so as to lessen the length of roadway to be maintained.

Since 1870 the thin coals, e.g. the Yard, Little Main and Lickbank seams, have been invariably worked by long-wall; but at Buck-hill Pit, Clifton, in the first instance, and afterwards, in 1895, at No. 3 Pit, St. Helens, that method has been successfully applied to getting the Cannel and Metal Band where that seam is divided by a stratum of 'metal' several feet thick. The Cannel Band (the lower portion of the seam) is worked long-wall first, the 'metal' dividing the seam, and the Metal Band being left up in the first working. The Metal Band is afterwards worked long-wall.

Pumping, Winding, Haulage and Ventilation.—Inasmuch as coal was first worked in this county to the rise, or along the level from 'day-holes' made from the outcrops or where the seams were exposed on the surface, no machinery was requisite, even if it had been known, in those early times. The water naturally flowed from the workings; and the coal was probably borne out, in the earliest days, in baskets carried by women and girls on their backs. The places still known as 'bearmouths' at Whitehaven were the en-trances to the roads (made from the outcrops

---

[1] Evidence of Mr. G. B. Forster, *Report of Coal Commission,* 1871, vol. ii.; also *Trans. North of Eng. Inst. of Mining Engineers,* xiii. 97.

Ancient Corves or Baskets used at Whitehaven Colliery.

of the seams) along which the coal was thus borne out from the mines.

The second development of coal-mining in West Cumberland would probably take place *circa* 1650, when, to win new tracts of coal, pits were sunk and drifts were cut horizontally through the strata from the lower grounds to drain the workings. That arrangement was called the 'pit and adit system.' At the pit the coal was raised originally by jack-rolls and subsequently by horse gins, whilst the adit served the purpose for draining the rise coal. The pit also caused a natural ventilation sufficient for the limited extent of workings in those early days.

It was probably about 1675 that corves were introduced in West Cumberland for the conveyance of coals from the workings, for they are mentioned in the pay-sheets of the Greenbank Colliery, Whitehaven, in that year. The corf was a circular basket made of hazel rods, provided with an iron bow for attachment to the hook at the end of the winding-rope. The first corves carried $2\frac{1}{2}$ cwt. of coal each; but the size of the corf increased as larger pits were sunk, and when the horse-gins were superseded by steam winding-engines. In fact, the corves or baskets, used in some of the Main Band pits, in latter days carried as much as 12 cwt. of coal each. Although the tub, cage and guide-rod system was introduced into the Newcastle coalfield about the year 1834, corves continued to be used in West Cumberland until a much later date. And at William Pit, Whitehaven, large baskets made of hazel rods, carrying 12 cwt. of coal each, were used up to the year 1875, when they were superseded by steel tubs.

The accompanying illustration of the old William Pit top, Whitehaven, shows the last of the corves or baskets and the ingenious contrivance of William Golightly, the overman, in 1839, for landing the baskets on to the trams at the top and bottom of the shaft.

The corves were undoubtedly in the earliest days placed on ashen runners, resembling a sledge, and conveyed along the corf-way, constructed of two parallel lines of wooden rails. These old wooden roads were continued to be used for the conveyance of coals underground until the end of the eighteenth century, when cast iron tram rails (of the angle-iron pattern) and edge rails were adopted.

After the introduction of tram plates the corves were placed upon low trams fitted with small plain wheels without flanges, and conveyed to the sidings at the rolley roads which were laid with edge rails. At these sidings there were hand cranes which were used for lifting the full corves off the small trams on to larger trams with flanged wheels, which were drawn by horses along the rolley-roads to the shaft bottom.

After the use of cranes was abandoned in the Main Band collieries at Whitehaven and Workington, light wooden bogies, also fitted with small plain wheels, were used on tramplate roads for bringing the rise coals down from the workings to 'stears,' which were tips erected at the sidings, and at which the bogies were emptied into the corves or baskets for conveyance to the shaft. These baskets were made up into trains or 'rollies' which were drawn by horses to the pit bottom; and where the rolley-road was long there were stages at which there were sidings or pass-byes.

As the main underground roads were extended to the dip and the horse work became correspondingly heavier, it became imperative to contrive some other means for traction underground. Accordingly the steam-engine, which had proved so useful for pumping and winding in shafts was applied for drawing trains of tubs along those roads by means of hemp ropes in the first instance and afterwards by wire ropes.

It is difficult to say when mechanical haulage was first introduced for underground haulage in the Cumberland coalfield, but probably it was in the year 1818, when a high-pressure engine was erected underground in William Pit, Whitehaven.

Since that time several systems of underground mechanical haulage have been adopted in the West Cumberland collieries. The 'main-and-tail rope' would probably be the first method tried. Then, where there was a dip road into the workings, a single rope was used, the 'empty set' of tubs taking the rope inbye and the engine drawing the 'full set' outbye. In some cases the engine is placed near the shaft bottom, and in others on the surface. The system now generally in use in the West Cumberland coalfield is that known as the 'endless rope.' It may be described as an endless steel wire rope driven by a steam-engine at bank. At the engine the rope is lapped several times round the drum in order to give the engine the necessary grip; and, inbye, the rope passes round a terminal pulley. The rope is kept taut upon the drum by a balance-weight attached to a sliding pulley (near the engine) round which the rope on the 'empty' side is made to pass; and in the case of a long and undulating engine plane a similar tightening arrangement is also placed at the far end.

There are two lines of rails, one being used for the full sets coming out and the other for the empty sets going in. The sets of tubs are attached to the rope by means of clutches or clips, of which there are many varieties.

The third era in West Cumberland coal-mining may be said to commence at the time when it became necessary to win the coal to the dip of the adit-levels. This involved the use of pumping machinery, and therefore un-til the invention of the steam engine nothing very great in this direction could be under-taken.

The first steam pumping engine, or 'fire engine,' in Cumberland was erected for Mr., afterwards Sir James, Lowther, at Stone Pit, Ginns, Whitehaven. A 'Licence from the Committee of Proprietors in the Fire-Engine to Mr. James Lowther,' dated 22 February, 1726, recites that Thomas Newcomen, iron-monger, of Dartmouth, Devon, and others, by articles of agreement dated 10 November, 1715, covenanted with Mr. Lowther to set up a 'fire-engine,' with a steam barrel of at least 16 inches diameter within and 8 feet in length, at his Stone Pit situate between Whitehaven and a place adjoining called Howgill, and that such engine had accordingly been erected and 'since continued to be wrought there.'

This engine was hired from the proprietors by Mr. Lowther for £182 per annum, under the agreement dated 10 November, 1715. On the surrender of that agreement, and in consideration of the payment of £350, the in-denture, dated 22 February, 1726, was made between several London gentlemen, who were then the committee appointed 'by the Pro-prietors of the Invention for raising water by fire,' and Mr. Lowther, by which he, his heirs and assigns were licensed to use the engine and to erect in its stead another of the same kind, the cylinder of which should not exceed 22 inches in diameter and 9 feet in length, at his or their collieries in the manor of St. Bees, at a peppercorn rent. A schedule and valuation of this historic engine was made by Mr. Lowther's agents, the Spedding brothers (John and Carlisle); and in 1726 Mr. Lowther bought the engine at the Ginns Pit for £100, above and beyond the amount agreed to be paid for the licence to use the patent.

Although there are no drawings of the Ginns 'fire-engine,' some idea of it may be gained from the particulars given in Speddings' schedule and from existing drawings of other of Newcomen's early fire-engines.

The foundation of the engine was a copper boiler, built in the form of a haystack, probably 10 or 12 feet in diameter. On the top of the boiler was fixed the cylinder, 17 inches diameter and 8 feet long, closed at the bottom

and open at the top. The piston, inside the cylinder, was 6 inches thick and made steam-tight with hemp packing. The piston-rod was attached by a chain to one end of a beam of wood, 20 feet long, at the other end of which, attached in a like manner, was the rod which worked the pumps in the pit. The pumps, then called 'pump trees,' because in fact they were trees bored out to form pipes, were 7 inches diameter; and the whole set was 18 fathoms long.

The pressure of steam used was only 1 or 2 lb. per square inch more than that of the atmosphere. The action of the engine has been described by the late Mr. Isaac Fletcher, M.P.,[1] as follows:—

The engineman opened a valve communicating with the boiler and admitted steam into the cylin-der, and another valve or tap from the cylinder to the atmosphere being opened for a few moments, all the air was expelled from it and its place sup-plied with steam. A valve was then opened ad-mitting a jet of cold water into the cylinder, which condensed the steam and created an in-stantaneous vacuum. The pressure of the atmo-sphere on the top of the piston (14 lb. on the square inch) then caused the piston to descend, and at the same time lifted the column of water by the other end of the beam. This completed the first stroke of the engine, and a repetition of the process by the engineman kept the engine going at the rate of five or six strokes per minute.

Mr. Fletcher further adds:—

The engine was afterwards made self-acting, and many improvements were made by the celebrated Smeaton and others in its details, but in its main features it remained as left by its inventor, and was the only pumping-engine used for draining mines for a period of fifty or sixty years; and indeed with the addition of a separate condenser and air-pump invented by Watt, there are to this day many examples of the 'atmospheric engine' at work, notably the very fine one at William Pit, White-haven Colliery.[2]

A second 'fire-engine' was afterwards erected at the Ginns, and was in continual use till about 1780. It had a copper boiler about 10 feet in diameter with a lead top, a brass cylinder 28 inches diameter, and wooden pumps 8 inches diameter, with a brass work-ing-barrel.

The success of the Ginns 'fire-engine' led to a still larger one, on the Newcomen atmo-spheric principle, being erected at Saltom Pit, in 1731, which had then been sunk close to the shore to the Main Band—a depth of 76 fathoms. The boiler was 12 ft., the cylinder 40 in., and the pumps (in four lifts) were 7 in. diameter.

[1] *Archæology of the West Cumb. Coal Trade.*
[2] Ceased working 1899.

This engine, being found inadequate to deal with the quantity of water, was supplemented by a duplicate engine. In 1782 both these engines were replaced by an engine that was, at that day, regarded as a great mechanical wonder. It was an atmospheric engine with a cylinder 70 in. diameter and 6 ft. stroke. It had an air pump 3 ft. in diameter and 3 ft. stroke. The beam was oak, 24 ft. long, 21 in. deep and 19 in. broad. There were four lifts of pumps, the two top sets 11 in. and the two bottom sets 11⅝ in. diameter; and three malleable iron boilers, each 13 ft. 6 in. diameter, 9 ft. 4 in. high, with hemispherical tops. This engine continued at work until 1866, when the pit was abandoned.

Prior to the abandonment of the Clifton Collieries in 1781, Sir James Lowther had erected two large atmospheric engines, viz. one near the Marron at Little Clifton, and the other at Reelfitz Pit, sunk in 1780, near the Marron, a quarter of a mile from the Derwent. The latter was very powerful, having a cylinder cast in two lengths, 60 in. diameter, with 8 ft. stroke, working two 12 in. pumps, each lifting from the Main Band 35 fathoms.

In 1794 Mr. John Christian Curwen sunk Lady Pit, near the shore at Workington, where he erected both large pumping and winding engines of the best designs in those days.

Although William Pit, Whitehaven, had been sunk to the Main Band a depth of 95 fathoms in 1805, the permanent pumping engine thereat was not erected until 1810. The cylinder, open-topped, was 80 in. diameter, with 9 ft. stroke. There were four haystack boilers, 13 ft. diameter, which supplied steam at 5 lb. pressure per square inch. The original wood beam was afterwards replaced by a cast-iron one with parallel motion at each end. The pumps, 12 in. diameter, were four bucket-lifts.

At Isabella Pit, Workington, sunk by Mr. Curwen, 1812–18, there was a pumping-engine said to have been the most powerful that had been erected in Cumberland up to that time. It had a cylinder 66 in. diameter, 9 ft. stroke ; worked six sets of pumps, four of them being 16 in. diameter, down to a depth of 130 fathoms; and was on Boulton and Watt's principle.

Since the beginning of the nineteenth century there have been many improvements made in pumping-engines, but it is not proposed to deal any further here with their evolution than by describing two of the best engines now at work in the coalfields.

The pumping-engine at Wellington Pit,

Whitehaven, is the most powerful in the district. It is a high pressure, single-acting inverted Cornish engine, erected for the Earl of Lonsdale in 1866. The steam cylinder is vertical, 90 in. diameter with 10 ft. stroke, and it has three double-beat equilibrium valves. The beam, placed underneath the cylinder, is formed of two wrought iron parallel plates, of girder section, each 30 ft. in length by 7 ft. deep in the centre, tapering to 3 ft. at each end. The steam acts on the top side of the piston only, the piston rod forcing one end of the beam, which is cushioned, down 10 ft., while the pump rods and lower column are raised 10 ft. at the other end of the beam, also cushioned. In the up-stroke of the piston the steam is in equilibrium, and the surplus weight of rods forces up the two upper columns of water.

The water is pumped from a depth of 140 fathoms in three lifts, the top and middle sets having 20 in. rams, and the bottom set a 20½ in. bucket.

At William Pit, Whitehaven, is a pumping-engine of quite a different type. It superseded in 1899 the old atmospheric engine described above. It is placed 8 fathoms below the Main Band, and forces the water through a main 10 in. diameter, to the surface, and was constructed for the Whitehaven Colliery Company. It may be described as a horizontal high-pressure, duplex ram-pumping engine with suction condenser. The cylinders are 30 in. diameter with 18 in. stroke, and the rams are 10 in. diameter.

It is remarkable that the steam-engine should have been seventy years in use for pumping before any attempt was made to apply it to winding in pits. Perhaps the reason was that the early engineers did not know that rectilinear could be converted into rotary motion by means of the crank, and how the engine could be reversed.

The first recorded departure from winding by horse-gins was made at George Pit, Whitehaven, in 1787, where, on the same shaft as the rope-rolls, was an overshot water-wheel driven by the water pumped by the 'fire-engine.'

The first winding-engine, or 'rotative machine' in West Cumberland, was probably that erected at Davy Pit, Whitehaven, in 1791, by Messrs. Heslop & Millward, Seaton Iron Works, Workington. It had two open-topped cylinders, one on each side of the main centre of the beam (which was made of wood), called respectively the hot cylinder and the cold cylinder. The steam, on being admitted under the piston in the larger or hot cylinder, raised it ; the return stroke was then made by the momentum of the fly-wheel assisted by the weight of the connecting rod and the action of the cold cylinder. The exhaust steam from the hot cylinder passed to the smaller or cold cylinder by means of the connecting pipe, which being constantly immersed in cold water acted as a condenser, producing sufficient condensation to reduce it to atmospheric pressure as it entered and filled the cold cylinder. The cold piston having arrived at the top of its stroke, and its cylinder being thus filled with steam, the injection valve was opened, thus admitting a jet of water which condensed the steam so that the unbalanced atmospheric pressure assisted in the down stroke.

This form of engine came into general use ; and an engine of this kind, in use at Wreah Pit, Hensingham, up to 1878, may be seen in the South Kensington Museum.

Since the days of the Heslop engine many improvements have been made in winding and pumping machinery. Firstly, with the inventions of Watt and others—the closing in the top of the cylinder, the parallel motion, and making the steam act on both sides of the piston—came the vertical and beam engines made on the Boulton and Watt principle. These, in their turn, have been replaced by horizontal high pressure engines, which are now generally used for winding in West Cumberland.

The present winding engine at Henry Pit, Whitehaven, is an example of one of the best modern engines of that class in the coalfield. It was erected in 1871 ; has two horizontal cylinders, 36 in. diameter with 6 ft. stroke, and Cornish valves ; and a drum 18 ft. 4 in. diameter, fitted with a powerful steam brake. Round steel wire ropes, 5¼ in. circumference, are used for winding. The engine raises four steel tubs (on two decks in each cage), each tub carrying about 14 cwt. of coal. The conductors are flat-bottomed steel rails, 50 lb. per yard.

There were no guides or conductors for the baskets in their journeys through the shafts, William Pit, Whitehaven, being the sole exception ; and it was therefore not surprising that the ascending and descending baskets, swinging at the end of the ropes, should collide at 'meetings,' and sometimes precipitate their freight—occasionally workpeople going to or coming from their work—to the bottom.

The general adoption of cages with guides, the regulations of the Mines Acts, and the use of detaching hooks at most of the pits in the district, have reduced the hazards in raising and lowering persons in shafts to a minimum. When coals were drawn by horse-gins, round

hemp ropes were used, but when the steam engine came to be applied to winding, flat hemp ropes were adopted because the varying diameter of the rope roll, due to the coiling and uncoiling of the rope, tended to counterbalance the engine. Lastly, the flat hemp ropes were succeeded by flat wire ropes, and these, again, by round wire ropes now invariably used for winding.

In the earliest days of coal-mining, the only ventilation which circulated in the limited area of workings was that resulting from natural causes. But when the workings became more extensive, and it became imperative to deal more effectually with the firedamp that was given off in larger quantities as new fields of coal were opened out, the underground furnace was the means generally adopted to create artificial ventilation, and was continued in use for that purpose at all of the collieries in the county until about 1870, when mechanical ventilation came into vogue.

The furnace was, in some cases, placed on the surface in connection with a tall chimney or air-tube, but its usual situation was at the bottom of the upcast shaft, where better results were obtained.

The furnace was a huge open fire, placed on a grate 10 or 12 ft. wide by 8 or 9 feet long, a short distance from the shaft foot in a brick archway ; and all the return air from the workings passed over it. In other coalfields 'dumb' drifts were used to carry the return air into the upcast shaft without passing over the furnace, which was fed with a 'split' of fresh air ; but this practice did not obtain in Cumberland.

At Duke Pit, Whitehaven, in 1806, firedamp was piped to the bottom of the shaft, and burned there to produce a ventilating current ; but this practice did not last very long. A velocity of four miles an hour was obtained, whereas common furnaces seldom produced more than three miles an hour.[1]

Notwithstanding all the care that could be used, the open furnace, especially without a dumb drift, was a constant source of danger. In 1814, Mr. Swinburn, agent for Mr. Curwen, invented a mechanical ventilator, which was tried at Union Pit, Workington ; but it did not prove to be a success.

In 1840, Mr. James Reed, engineer at Whitehaven Colliery, constructed a 'fanning machine,' which was tried at Duke Pit, Whitehaven, but after running a few years was discontinued.

It was not until 1870 that mechanical ventilation, as it is now understood, was intro-

[1] *Monthly Magazine*, xxiii. 499.

duced into West Cumberland. In that year a Guibal fan, 36 ft. diameter by 12 ft. wide, was erected for the Earl of Lonsdale, at Duke Pit, Whitehaven. This ventilator is still at work. It is driven by two duplicate horizontal engines working alternately. Each engine has a cylinder, 30 in. diameter by 30 in. stroke, and works direct on to the fan shaft, at 60 revolutions per minute. The quantity of air produced is 70,000 c. ft. per minute with 2½ in. of water gauge.

Since then Guibal fans of various sizes have been erected at other collieries in Cumberland.

At Watergate Pit, Flimby, there is a Waddle fan (erected in 1880) at work. It is 30 ft. diameter by 2 ft. wide. It is driven by a single engine with a cylinder 24 in. diameter by 4 ft. stroke at the rate of 60 revolutions per minute, and produces about 40,000 c. ft. of air per minute with a water gauge of 1½ in. The air is received at the centre on one side of the fan, and is expelled at the periphery.

The most recently erected fan in West Cumberland is at William Pit, Whitehaven, and was made for the Whitehaven Colliery Company in 1899, and is styled 'Walker's Indestructible Fan.' It is 22 ft. diameter by 7 ft. wide. It is driven by an engine with a single cylinder, 36 in. diameter by 42 in. stroke. The driving pulley on the crank shaft is 18 ft. diameter by 2 ft. 2¼ in. wide, grooved for ten 1¾ in. cotton ropes ; the pulley on the fan shaft is 7 ft. diameter, 2 ft. 2¼ in. wide, and similarly grooved. With the fan running at 120 revolutions per minute, 120,000 c. ft. of air are produced with a water gauge of 6 in.

Perhaps in no other coalfield was the danger of working with naked lights in coal mines sooner or more thoroughly appreciated than in this county. In the earliest Whitehaven Colliery pay-sheets there are frequent entries relating to 'burnt' men.

Probably about 1730, Mr. Carlisle Spedding, Sir James Lowther's colliery viewer, invented the famous steel mill for the production of a light by which miners could work with some degree of safety in an atmosphere where, by reason of its being so highly charged with firedamp, the use of candles was dangerous. In an account of the firedamp at Saltom Pit, Whitehaven,[1] which Sir James Lowther contributed to the Royal Society in 1733, allusion is made to the use of flints and steel for the purpose of affording a light to miners in places abounding with firedamp.

[1] *Philosophical Transactions* (1733), vol. xxxviii.

The use of the steel mill, which began in the Whitehaven pits, extended to other coalfields. About 1760 it was introduced into the collieries on the Tyne and Wear, and was used there, in dangerous places, up to 1813.

The steel mill was a small steel disc made to revolve rapidly by means of a cogwheel and pinion, against a piece of flint, the stream of sparks thereby emitted affording a glimmering light which enabled the collier to perform his task.

Steel mills were only used in workings where a dangerous quantity of gas was given off, candles being generally used by miners until the invention of the miner's safety-lamp by Sir Humphrey Davy superseded both them and the steel mill which had been proved to be quite unsafe.

The improved system of ventilating mines, known as 'coursing the air,' was invented about 1760 by Mr. James Spedding, son of Mr. Carlisle Spedding. 'Coursing the air' consisted of threading the current of air up certain workings and down others until it ventilated the whole waste. That system, which involved numerous doors and the air travelling round the workings long distances in one current, was superseded by the 'split air' system, carried out first at Wallsend Colliery in 1810 by Mr. Buddle.

Soon after its invention, Sir Humphrey Davy's safety lamp was tried and adopted at Whitehaven Colliery. 'On the 28th of March, 1816, the safety lamp of Sir H. Davy was put to the severest test possible in the workings of William Pit, Whitehaven, the most dangerous in the kingdom.'[2] As in the case of the steel mill, the use of the safety lamp was not made compulsory in all parts of the mine, and candles were still used where little or no gas was to be seen. It was also a common practice to use the lamps with the tops off unless too much gas was present.

When so much was left to the discretion of the officials and the work-people in that respect, it was not surprising that explosions did not cease with the advent of the safety lamp, and that it soon became necessary to adopt stringent regulations to enforce the exclusive use of locked safety lamps beyond stations fixed by the management.

After the introduction of the Davy lamp other forms of safety lamps, particularly the Stephenson and Clanny, were also used ; but since the issue of the report of the Royal Commission on Accidents in Mines in 1886, and the passing of the Coal Mines Regulation Act, 1887, the use of those three types of

[2] *Newcastle Courant*, April 13, 1816.

lamps was prohibited, because the Davy lamp passed the flame in a current with a velocity of 400 ft., the Clanny lamp at 600 ft., and the Stephenson lamp at 800 ft. per minute.

The safety lamp now usually adopted in this district is of the Marsant type. It has a thick glass cylinder surrounding the flame, like the Clanny lamp, and above the glass cylinder are two and sometimes three conical gauze caps which fit close together at their lower extremity on to the top of the glass, and gradually diverge from each other in proceeding upwards. The gauze caps are protected by a bonnet of sheet iron screwed on to a flange above the glass. The air is admitted by a number of holes round the base of the bonnet, and after descending on to the wick, ascends and escapes through a series of large holes round the top of the bonnet.

Lamps of this description can be used with safety in currents having a velocity of 3,000 ft. per minute.

Dip.—From Whitehaven to Maryport the general dip of the Coal Measures is to the west, towards the sea. Between the William Pit workings of the Whitehaven Colliery and Parton there is an anticlinal towards which the strata rise from the Micklam fault westward, and over which they again have the normal dip to the west. The Main Band outcrops at low water mark near the mouth of Lowca Beck, but occurs again over the summit of the anticlinal. From Maryport to the eastern extremity of the coalfield the dip is to the north-west.

Faults and Nips.—Numerous faults, the majority of which have a north-west and south-east direction, divide the coalfield into narrow strips, and in some cases throw off the upper measures altogether, thus bringing the lower seams nearer to the surface, and more easily rendering them accessible. The principal faults are :—

(1) The James Pit Fault, which runs from near James Pit, Whitehaven, to Bigrigg, is a downthrow fault to the north-east.

(2) The Micklam Fault, which runs from Micklam Pit, Harrington, to near Rheda, Frizington, is an upthrow fault to the north-east of about 120 fathoms.

(3) The Distington Fault, which runs from near Harrington towards Distington, throws in the Carboniferous Limestone, at the Barf Quarries to the north-east.

(4) The Flimby Fault, which runs from near Rischow, towards Camerton Colliery, is an upthrow fault to the west, throwing off the Cannel and Metal Band.

(5) The Dearham Fault, which runs from near Birkby towards Dovenby, is a downthrow fault to the north-east.

(6) The fault separating the Nos. 1 and 2 Pits from the No. 3 Pit, Brayton Domain Colliery, is 90 fathoms down to the north-east.

(7) The large downthrow fault to the north-east which separates the No. 3 Pit, Brayton Domain Colliery, from Allhallows Colliery.

(8) The downthrow fault to the north-east near Crummock Old Colliery, about 80 or 90 fathoms.

(9) A large downthrow fault to the north-east, between Crummock Old Colliery and Bolton Colliery.

(10) Terminal Fault, near Bolton Wood Lane, which throws in the Permian sandstone.

Other faults run north-east and south-west. Of these the principal are :—

(1) The Montreal Fault, which is estimated to be about 200 fathoms.

(2) The fault, south of Crosby Colliery, which is an upthrow to the south of about 170 fathoms. It throws up the Carboniferous Limestone which forms the southern boundary of the eastern division of the coalfield.

(3) The Aspatria Fault, a downthrow fault to the north, which runs from Maryport to near Aspatria to near Bolton Low Houses, and was considered to be the northern boundary of the coalfield.

'Nips' are narrow tracts resembling silted-up river beds in the coal seam, where the coal has been replaced by deposits of sandstone, or shale. Cumberland miners term these barren tracts 'geld' ground. 'Nips' in West Cumberland vary in width from a few yards to hundreds of yards, and extend sometimes considerable distances. Perhaps the most notable 'nip' in West Cumberland is that on which the Isabella Pit, Workington, was sunk. In 1814 that pit had been sunk by Mr. John Christian Curwen to the Moorbanks Seam, which was found in its normal thickness at a depth of 90 fathoms from the surface. Mr. Curwen then continued the pit to a depth of 128 fathoms, reached in 1818, where the Main Band should have been found, but the seam was proved to be 'nipped' out. This was a bitter disappointment after the expenditure of £50,000. The Main Band was, however, ultimately proved, through the 'nip,' by a drift 400 yards long.

HISTORY

The existence of coal in Cumberland may have been known from an early period ; but little of it was worked before the middle of the sixteenth century. In 1560, Sir Thomas Chaloner, lord of the manor of St. Bees, in granting certain leases of lands within that manor, reserved to himself the right to dig for coals, at the same time granting his lessees liberty to take coals from the lord's coalpits for their own use on condition that they paid therefor and laboured from time to time therein according to the custom of the manor.[1]

In 1586 he granted the governors of St. Bees Grammar School liberty to take forty loads of coals at his coal pits, in the parish of St. Bees, for the use of the school.

In the St. Bees Grammar School leases of 1608 the tenants covenanted to permit the governors and their successors to get coals in the demised premises; but there is no record of any advantage having been taken of the covenant until 1650, when the governors demised their pit or bearmouth within the closes called Stephen Ridding,[2] in the parish of St. Bees, with liberty to dig for coal therein, for the term of four years at the yearly rent of £3. In 1664 the governors demised to other lessees Stephen Ridding Pit, to hold the same from the first day that 20 tons of coals should be there gotten for the term of seven years, at the yearly rent of £3. The colliery was surrendered in 1679.

The copper works at Keswick, built in 1567, used coal which was supplied from Bolton Colliery;[3] and according to the 'State Papers' the owners of those works were complaining in 1568 about the great difficulty in procuring coal.

Whitehaven.—Whitehaven must occupy by far the most prominent place in any account of the Cumberland coal trade, because of the extent and importance of its collieries, which owe their great development to the Lowther family.

After the dissolution of the monasteries the manor of St. Bees remained in the possession of the Crown till 1553, when King Edward VI. granted the priory of St. Bees, with the manor and rectory, to Sir Thomas Chaloner. It was sold by his son to Thomas Wybergh, who mortgaged it, in 1600, to the Lowthers, into whose hands it eventually came.

Sir Christopher Lowther, the founder of the Whitehaven branch, died in 1644, and was succeeded in the estates and baronetcy by his infant son Sir John, who on his attainment of manhood began to develop the coal mines at Whitehaven with great energy and enterprise. His efforts were directed in the first place to acquiring as much land as he possibly could in the immediate neighbourhood of his inheritance, in order to form an area sufficiently large for his mining projects; and afterwards to the improvement of the harbour

of Whitehaven, so as to facilitate the export of coal.

On 24 March, 1669 (21 Chas. II.), he obtained from the king a grant of 150 acres of land between high and low water marks near Whitehaven.[4] In 1678 (30 Chas. II.) Sir John Lowther obtained from the Crown a further grant of land between high and low water marks near Whitehaven,[5] after a rival but unsuccessful claim had been set up thereto by the Earl of Carlingford and others.

The first coal worked by Sir John Lowther was from the outcrops of the Yard, Burnt, and Prior Bands, along the western side of the St. Bees valley, in the locality called Howgill, between Greenbank and Ginns.

The Yard Band was a seam lying above the Bannock Band. Burnt Band was the original name of the Bannock Band, and the Prior Band was the original name of the Main Band.

The first workings from the outcrops of the seams would naturally be much impeded by surface water; and to overcome this difficulty at Howgill Colliery would be Sir John Lowther's object in driving a level or watercourse from Pow Beck. This level was, about 1663, commenced near the old Copperas Works, Ginns, and driven due west until it intersected the Burnt or Bannock Band, in which it was continued along the level course of that seam in a southerly direction, to the east of Monkwray. It was afterwards extended to Knockmurton Pit, near the southern boundary of the cemetery—a total distance of about 1,800 yards. It is still known as the Bannock Band surface water level, and is used for draining the outcrop water into Pow Beck.

North of Whitehaven harbour, Mr. Robert Bigland had worked, prior to 1668, coal under the Duke of Somerset's Bransty estate; and from that year to 1696, Sir John Lowther worked the Bransty Colliery for the supply of coals to Bransty salt-pans. The band of coal worked there was 22 in. thick.

The only existing details of Sir John Lowther's first collieries south of Whitehaven are contained in two wages books relating to the Greenbank Colliery and Three Quarters Band Collieries for 1675. According to an account of wages and disbursements for the week ended 14 April, 1675, it appears that five haggers were employed at Greenbank at a fixed wage of 8½d. a day, and that the darg was 21 burthens, of which eight were

[1] *Report of Commissioners on Cumberland Charities,* 1819–37.
[2] Two-and-a-half miles from Hensingham.
[3] Robinson's *Nat. Hist. of Cumb. & Westmorland.*

[4] *History and Laws of the Foreshore and Seashore,* by Stuart A. Moore, barrister-at-law, p. 415.
[5] Ibid. p. 418.

equivalent to a 'ton.' Four 'bearers' conveyed the coals to the bearmouth at a fixed rate of 7½d. a day each. There the coals were turned into a bank, whence they were either carted or taken by pack-horses to the harbour at a cost of 1s. a ton.

The Greenbank corf contained about 2½ cwt. of coal. In addition, ten other men were employed underground, so that the whole crew of this seventeenth century pit, including a bankman above-ground, numbered 20.

The selling prices of coal then were : To ships, 3s. per ton (including leading) ; country, 2s. per ton ; and tenants, 1s. 4d. per ton.

At the 'Three Quarters Band Colliery,' undoubtedly one of the earliest pits at Howgill, there were four haggers paid at a fixed wage of 8½d. a day each, three trailers at 7½d. a day each, and two winders and one bankman who received 3s. 2d. a day amongst them.

Up to 1679 several pits had been sunk at the Howgill Colliery. In that year the Woodagreen Pit was sunk near the Ginns.

At this time the coals were carted from the pits to the harbour, and copper tokens were issued to the carters as a method of checking. The tokens used at Whingill in 1679 have been described by the late Chancellor Ferguson.[1]

In 1680 Mr. Christian appears to have been one of the principal workers of coal in the neighbourhood of Whitehaven. He held leases of Mr. Anthony Benn's coal in Hensingham, Mr. Thomas Skelton's coal at Corkickle, Mr. Fletcher's Whingill Colliery, and other royalties in Moresby and Distington.

In 1680, coal was shipped at Whitehaven from the Howgill, Greenbank, Whingill, Wray, and Scalegill pits.

It had then become the practice to staith the coals near the harbour when the ships could not or would not take them.

Sir John Lowther's object in staithing may be gathered from the following letter written by him from London on 28 August, 1680, to Mr. Tickell, his agent at Whitehaven :—

As to staithing my intentions are not to staith a coal when yͤ ships doe take, but my single design is yᵗ Dublin may not complain of dearness of coales in winter or spring as they did last year, for wᵗ betwixt yͤ imployment of ships in yͤ cattle trade, and a stop ther was of Moresby coales, they were 30s. yͤ tun at Dublin.

The coals from Moresby were shipped at Parton and entered into keen competition with the Whitehaven coals in the Dublin market. Whilst Sir John Lowther, in 1680,

was improving Whitehaven harbour, Mr. Fletcher conceived the idea of doing likewise at Parton. He attempted to build a pier and harbour there, near low water mark, upon the land that had been granted to Sir John Lowther by Charles II., whereupon Sir John exhibited a bill in the Court of Exchequer against Mr. Fletcher and others

setting forth the ill consequences of such an attempt to the Revenue, to trade, to the Rights of Sir John Lowther, and of persons who have settled in Whitehaven, and to the interest and benefit of the county in general, and after the defendants' answers, upon a full hearing of the matter, the Court prohibited the said Mr. Fletcher by a perpetual Injunction.[2]

In 1682 a violent explosion occurred at Mr. Christian's colliery at Priestgill near Hensingham, by which one man was killed and six injured. The flame and smoke from it could be seen half a mile off.

Hitherto the coals appear to have been conveyed from the Whitehaven pits to the harbour in sacks, carried on the backs of horses, and there emptied into the ships. During 1682 Mr. Gale advocated the construction of a 'coalway' to the Woodagreen Pit to enable 'carts and wains' to be drawn with greater facility and to obviate the use of sacks in loading the vessels in the harbour. This intended road was described as a 'causeway' bounded on each side with wood balks on which the cart-wheels would run. Such a cartway was constructed during the following year and proved to be a great improvement on the old mode of transport, which however was still continued from the more distant pits.

During 1685 Sir John Lowther introduced at his Whitehaven pits an engine, the 'cog and rung gin,'[3] and the 'wind engine' for raising water from the mines. The latter was a windmill with six sails, working one or more chain pumps which were not uncommon in the north of England at that time.

In 1685 Mr. Christian found a 'Three Quarter' coal in Corkickle, adjoining Sir John's Flatt property, and sank two pits close to the boundary. The seam was 24 in. thick. The coal therefrom was got by Mr. Christian's four Newcastle haggers at a cost of 12d. a ton, and could be led to the harbour at a further charge of 7d. a ton. The output of coal was 10 tons per day.

Denton, in his MS. 'Perambulation of Cumberland and Westmorland, 1687-8,' thus refers to Whitehaven : 'The vessels there are

[1] *Cumb. and Westm. Antiq. and Arch. Soc. Trans.* xv. 392-416.

[2] Broad sheet preserved in Lincoln's Inn.
[3] *Annals of Coal Mining*, by R. L. Galloway, p. 168.

fraught with coal from Hensingham and Moresby Pitts.' Further on he mentions : 'Stokehow is a little Manor of Mr. Thomas Patricksons, his demesne, tenements and colliery being per ann. £150.'[1] The colliery referred to in this quotation was undoubtedly that at Scalegill near Whitehaven, which then was the property of Mr. Patrickson of Stockhow.

In 1692 Sir John Lowther was working the Prior Band at Howgill and Greenbank, Whitehaven, and Lattera Colliery, Moresby ; and was actively engaged in negotiations for the purchase of neighbouring coal properties.

The output of coal from Sir John Lowther's collieries during 1695 was : Howgill, 15,196 tons ; Greenbank, 2,321 tons ; Lattera, 1,387 tons ; total, 18,904 tons.

In 1695 Mr. Lamplugh began the erection of a pier upon the foundations of Mr. Fletcher's venture against which the injunction had been obtained by Sir John Lowther in 1680. Sir John again interfered because it was a trespass on the land granted to him by Charles II. ; and the Court of Exchequer, at his instance, prohibited Mr. Lamplugh by perpetual injunction from building the projected new pier. The baronet did not, however, oppose the repairing of an old pier.

During 1697 Mr. Gilpin (Sir John Lowther's agent) suggested the establishment of the Copperas Works, which were eventually erected at Ginns, Whitehaven. There, green vitriol (ferrous sulphate) was made from the iron pyrites, or 'marchasites' as they were called by Mr. Gilpin, which were picked out of the coals.

At this time an iron forge was in operation at Cleator, and ironstone obtained from a band, 3 in. thick, at Hensingham Colliery, was smelted thereat, without mixture with other ore.

During 1699 a commencement was made with a level from Pow Beck near Thicket, to drain the coal between that point and Greenbank. This watercourse, at a distance of 400 yards from its mouth, cut the Prior Band, in which it was continued until it reached the Greenbank dyke, a distance altogether of about 1,400 yards.

During 1700 the new Ginns Pit and the Stone Pit were sunk near Ginns to the Prior Band, and were ultimately connected to the 'end gills' of the various pits to the south in the same seam, thereby forming one continuous watercourse as far as Fish Pit, a distance of 1,400 yards. There the level passes through a fault into the Bannock Band,

in which it pursues its way past Gameriggs to Fox Pit, finally to the level end in Wilson Pit Bannock Band. This level is now known as Gameriggs surface water-level, and is still used.

The first steam pumping engine, then called 'a fire-engine,' was set up at Stone Pit in 1715. Up to that time twelve pits had been sunk in the Howgill Colliery near the outcrops of the Burnt and Prior Bands besides those mentioned.

The output of coal from Sir John Lowther's pits for the year 1700 was :—

		Tons
Howgill, Prior Band	. . . .	4,817
„ New Gin	. . . .	13,837
„ Knockmurton	. . .	3,713
„ Yard Band	. . . .	3,336
Lattera (Moresby)	. . . .	1,584
		27,287

In 1705 an Act of Parliament was passed, at the instance of Mr. Fletcher, Moresby Hall, and the inhabitants of Parton, for enlarging the pier and harbour there, notwithstanding the opposition of Sir John Lowther, in the interests of Whitehaven.

Sir John Lowther died in 1705, after a life of unceasing effort to develop the trade of Whitehaven. He left his estates to his second son, Mr. James Lowther (who succeeded to the title in 1731), who followed up his father's schemes for the development of Whitehaven with such success that at the time of his death it was second in importance only to two or three other ports in the kingdom.

In all his colliery undertakings Mr. (afterwards Sir James) Lowther had the assistance of the two brothers, John and Carlisle Spedding. But it was the latter who had the practical direction of the collieries, which under his management prospered exceedingly.

After the introduction of the steam pumping or 'fire' engine at Howgill Colliery in 1715, Mr. Lowther proceeded to open out the Whingill Colliery. The first Whingill pits which Mr. Lowther sank were near the outcrop of the Prior Band on the top of Harras Moor, about 450 ft. above the level of the sea. In 1716 the output from them was about 200 tons a week. Mr. Lowther conceived the idea of draining the coal under Harras Moor by means of a level watercourse, which he commenced from Bransty Beck near Whitehaven. This level in course of time was driven as far as the Bateman Pit, a distance of about 1½ miles. It drained eventually all the Whingill Colliery in the Bannock and Main Bands except the workings in George, Lady and James Pits, which are below its level. The water from the George and Lady Pits

[1] fol. 30.

was pumped at the George Pit up to a level which discharged into Bransty Beck, near to Lonsdale Place. The James Pit Main Band was drained to the Saltom Pit through the single stone drift, driven in 1796 underneath Whitehaven, which, until a connection was made many years afterwards seawards, was the only communication underground between the Howgill and Whingill Collieries.

The success that had attended the introduction of the steam engine for pumping, at Ginns Pit, the water from the workings bordering upon the outcrops of the seams in the St. Bees valley undoubtedly led Mr. Carlisle Spedding to propose to Mr. Lowther the bold project of sinking a pit close to the seashore, as near to the dip as possible, for the purpose of winning and working not only the land coal which lay between the coast line and the workings to the rise, but also the coal under the sea.

The site selected for this great undertaking was close to high water mark, and a commencement was made there in 1729 with the sinking of the pit which was afterwards named Saltom. It was completed to Main Band in 1731.

The coals at Saltom Pit were drawn to bank at the shore level by gins, conveyed by a short drift to the bottom of the Ravenhill Pit and there drawn to the top of the cliffs, a height of 27 fathoms, again by gins. Thence the coals were taken by waggons to the staith at the south side of the harbour. It is generally believed that the first waggon-way was made to Parker Pit; but it is not unlikely that the first railway of that kind was made either to Ravenhill Pit or to Saltom Pit. The Parker Pit waggon-way is shown in the 'Bird's-eye view of Whitehaven,' engraved by Richard Parr from a painting by Mr. Matthias Read, executed in 1738 (*vide* illustration). The waggons, carrying 44 cwt. of coals, were mounted on cast iron wheels and ran on wooden rails. At Howgill, these railways were laid from the pits to a large staith, capable of holding 3,000 waggons of coals, that was constructed close to the quay at the south harbour. The coals could either be shipped from the five spouts which were erected there, or stored in the staith, which was for the greater part covered in.[1] All the waggon-ways had a descent to the harbour. The full waggons were braked down by means of a 'convoy' fixed to the side of the waggon, and the empties were taken back to the pits by horses. The coals

from the Whingill pits were conveyed at this time in a similar manner to a large staith situate on the site of the present cab stables, and thence they were carted to the shipping. To dispense with this dilatory and costly mode of shipment it was decided to carry the waggon-way direct to the shipping berths on the north wall across Tangier Street. Bransty Arch was built with this object, and the incline over it was opened with great *éclat* on 9 August, 1803.

In 1737 a violent explosion occurred at Corporal Pit, Arrowthwaite, by which twenty-one men, one woman and three horses were killed; and in 1740 an explosion at Hinde Pit killed two persons, did a lot of damage, and stopped the pit for several weeks.

In addition to Saltom Pit, Mr. Carlisle Spedding sank Thwaite, King, Duke, Kells, Fish, Newtown, Country, Moss and Hinde Pits, on the Howgill side; and sank Carr, Pearson, Pedlar, Taylor, Fox, Daniel, Jackson, Hunter, Watson, Harras, Green and other pits on the Whingill side.

In 1740 the output of Howgill Colliery was 88,801 tons, derived from the Prior and Bannock Bands at Watson, Banks, Hinde, Fish, Saltom, Thwaite, Parker, Gameriggs and Howgill Heads Pits. The output at the Whingill Colliery was only 8,419 tons, raised from the Prior Band at Hunter, Furnace, Tate, and Gibson Pits. During the same year the Parton and Scalegill Collieries, producing small outputs, were being worked in connection with the Whitehaven pits.

In 1742 the Governors of St. Bees Grammar School leased to Sir James Lowther all their coal mines in the manor of St. Bees, at the yearly rent of £3 10s. No coal seems to have been worked under the school lands from 1680 until that year. In 1819 this lease formed the subject of an inquiry by the Charity Commissioners; and in 1821 the Attorney-General, in accordance with their Report instituted proceedings in Chancery with a view of setting aside the lease, on the plea that Sir James Lowther and his steward, Mr. John Spedding, being governors of the school when the lease was granted, the same was therefore void. In 1827 Lord Chancellor Lyndhurst gave judgment. The lease was annulled, and the Earl of Lonsdale, the successor of the original lessee, was ordered to pay the governors £13,280, out of which the expenses of the suit had to be defrayed.

In 1765 M. Jars visited the Whitehaven pits and described them in *Les Voyages Métallurgiques*, from which it appears that the Saltom Pit workings were then two-thirds of a mile under the sea.

[1] Dr. Joshua Dixon, in his *Life of Brownrigg*, p. 112, states that the covered part of the staith held 5,244 waggons of coals and the uncovered part 2,352 waggons, in the year 1801.

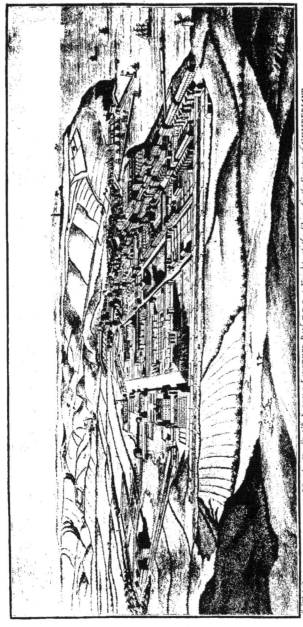

TOWN AND HARBOUR OF WHITEHAVEN.

In 1765 the output of coal at Whitehaven during the week ending 6 November was :—

Howgill Colliery, 2,253 tons, derived from the Prior Band at Duke, Kells, King, Fox, Wilson, Hinde and Saltom Pits ; from the Bannock Band at Kells, King, and Fish Pits ; and from the Yard Band at Thwaite Pit.

Whingill Colliery, 1,094 „ derived from the Prior Band at Jackson, Pearson, Fox, Hunter, Pedlar and Scott Pits.

Total . . 3,347 tons

The shipping price was then 3*s*. 4*d*. a ton.

The chief winning during Mr. James Spedding's stewardship was the sinking of Croft Pit. It was drawing coals from the Prior Band in 1774, and has worked continuously ever since until the present day.

On the Whingill side, Wolfe, Davy, Lady, Bateman, George, North, and Howe Pits were sunk to the Main Band, and Scott Pit to the Six Quarters Seam, during the agency of Mr. James Spedding, who retired in 1781, and was succeeded by Mr. John Bateman.

In 1781 Lady, George, Davy, North, Jackson, Pearson, Bateman were working at Whingill Colliery, and turning out 1,732 tons of coal per week.

At Howgill Colliery in 1781 the following pits were at work, and capable of producing weekly :—

	Tons
Duke Pit, Prior Band	216
King Pit „	360
„ Bannock Band	180
Kells Pit, Prior Band	180
„ Bannock Band	180
Croft Pit, Prior Band	648
„ Bannock Band	360
Total	2,124

In January, 1791, the Main Band was being worked underneath the town of Whitehaven, and the workings had reached the neighbourhood of Duke Street, where, on 31 January, a holing was made into an old waste, and liberated a large quantity of water, drowning two men, one woman, and five horses in the workings. The ground suddenly shrank in the garden behind Somerset House (then the residence of Mr. H. Littledale), which, together with a number of other houses in Scotch Street and George Street, were cracked and otherwise damaged.

At Carlisle Assizes in the following August Mr. Littledale brought an action against the Earl of Lonsdale for the damage caused to his house. The case was tried before Justice Thompson and a special jury, who found for the plaintiff. In great wrath the earl shut up all his collieries and works at Whitehaven rather than run the risk of having other actions brought against him. This closing of the pits thoroughly alarmed the town, and a petition, signed by 2,500 people, was forwarded to the earl, praying him to continue the working of the mines, and promising in that case to indemnify him against all actions in the future. A reply acceding to the prayer of the petition was sent from Lowther on 21 September; and great was the joy of the populace.

After the subsidence of the houses in Whitehaven in 1791 Mr. Bateman left the service of the Earl of Lonsdale, and was succeeded by Mr. Thomas Wyley and others, under whose management the Whitehaven Collieries so suffered that Mr. Bateman was reinstated in 1802.

In 1792 a great subsidence of the surface took place at Scalegill Colliery where Stanley Pond now is.

An excellent description of the Whitehaven Collieries in 1793 was contributed at the time to the *Transactions of the Royal Irish Academy* by Dr. Fisher, M.D.,[1] who asserted that in Great Britain the Howgill Colliery, which covered an area of 2,400 acres, was then the most extensive colliery, and that King Pit, in that colliery, which had been sunk 160 fathoms to the Six Quarters Seam, was the deepest pit. He also said the Whitehaven Colliery had produced for a few years last past from 100,000 to 120,000 tons of coal, Dublin measure, yearly. The Whitehaven waggon contained 2 Dublin tons, weighing 21 or 22 cwt. each.

In 1797 Sir Wilfred Lawson was the owner of the Low Hall Colliery near Ingwell, Hensingham, where the Six Quarters Seam was worked.[2]

In 1800 James Pit, Whingill Colliery, was sunk.

Mr. Bateman's greatest undertaking was the sinking of the William Pit on the shore near Bransty. It was begun in 1804, and completed in 1812. The first coal shipped therefrom was on 10 March, 1806.

In 1810 William Pit fired when a party consisting of Messrs. John Peile and Caleb Hetherington, viewers, and four workmen were making some change in the ventilation. Two of the workmen were killed. The others were severely burned, particularly

[1] *Annual Register*, 1794, xxxvi. 326.
[2] *Cumb. and West. Antiq. and Arch. Soc. Trans.* xv. 402.

Mr. Peile, who subsequently became Lord Lonsdale's chief colliery agent.

In 1811 Mr. Bateman was succeeded in the management of the Whitehaven Collieries by Mr. John Peile.

At that time the pits drawing coals at the Howgill Colliery were Kells, Croft, and Wilson; and at the Whingill Colliery, William, North and James.

In 1812 Mr. Taylor Swainson, engineer at the Whitehaven Collieries, tried his invention of the 'iron horse,' or locomotive engine, on the Croft Pit waggon-way. The engine answered admirably, but the track was not strong enough to bear the weight.

The output for 1814 was :—

	Waggons	Waggons
Howgill Colliery—		
Kells Pit . .	10,694	
Croft Pit . .	25,031	
Wilson Pit . .	22,836	
		58,561
Whingill Colliery—		
William Pit . .	34,151	
North Pit . .	9,835	
James Pit . .	14,072	
		58,058
		116,619

A waggon of coals weighed 42 cwt.

On 27 February, 1819, three successive explosions occurred in Kells Pit, Main Band, Howgill Colliery, by which twenty persons were killed. Candles as well as Davy lamps were in use; and it was thought that the gas had fired at a candle.

In 1821 there was an explosion of firedamp in the Main Band workings, William Pit, which caused the death of five haggers and seven boys and girls. The explosion was attributed to a sudden great outburst of gas that had ignited at an open light. Although a Davy safety-lamp was supplied to each hagger, its use with the top on was 'more honoured in the breach than the observance.'

William Pit was the scene of a still more dire calamity in 1823, when a violent explosion of firedamp in the Main Band workings resulted in the death of 15 men, 15 boys, and 2 girls. Seventeen horses also perished. It was the general opinion that the explosion had been occasioned by some one having had the top of a safety-lamp off.

In 1826 nine men were suffocated in William Pit by the smoke from a fire which had originated in an underground engine-room. In explosions at Croft Pit 6 lives were lost in 1828 and 23 lives in 1831. Both disasters were caused, it was thought, by the men working with their lamp-tops off, as they did unless

ordered to the contrary by the officials. In 1839 23 men and boys were killed by an explosion of fire-damp in the Main Band workings, William Pit, about a mile and a half from the shaft. The gas had fired at the open light of a boy who was accompanying the deputy on his rounds.

The undertaking with which Mr. Peile's name will always be identified is the sinking of the Wellington Pits, Whitehaven, which was begun in 1840. The Main Band was reached in 1843, and the Six Quarters Seam in 1845. Thence level stone-drifts were driven seaward and intersected the Main Band at a distance of 900 yards. Peile's design was to sink the pits a further depth of 160 fathoms —a total depth of 300 fathoms from the surface. The last 100 fathoms, it was assumed, would be in the Carboniferous Limestone. At the increased depth he proposed to drive a pair of level drifts westward until they intersected the Six Quarters Seam, then the Main Band, and finally the Bannock Band at a total distance of 4,500 yards from the shafts.

Messrs. George Stephenson (the celebrated engineer) and Frank Forster, who were consulted about this scheme by Lord Lonsdale, reported against it.

In 1844 a violent explosion of firedamp in the Six Quarters Seam workings, Duke Pit, killed 11 men and 11 horses. The coroner in summing up the evidence at the inquest said that if the tops had been on the lamps the accident would no doubt have been prevented.

In 1847, Wilson Pit ceased drawing coals; 4 coal-hewers were killed by an explosion of gas in the Main Band workings of Croft Pit; and Mr. John Peile retired from the office of principal colliery agent to Lord Lonsdale, being succeeded by Mr. Peter Bourne, with Mr. William Anderson, South Shields, as consulting viewer.

The output of the Whitehaven Collieries in 1847 was :—

	Waggons	Waggons
Howgill Colliery—		
Saltom Pit . .	12,384	
Croft Pit . .	7,577	
Wilson Pit . .	8,861	
Wellington Pit .	34,630	
		63,452
Whingill Colliery—		
William Pit . .	24,846	
North Pit . . .	3,597	
Wreah Pit . .	1,849	
		30,292
		93,744

The waggon contained 48 cwt. of coals.

In 1847 the selling price of screened coals was 21*s.* per waggon of 48 cwt.

In 1855 an explosion of firedamp occurred in the Bannock Band workings of Croft Pit, about a mile from the shaft, whereby 4 men were killed.

In 1862 the Main Band was proved in the St. Bees Grammar School royalty, over the large downthrow fault which had stopped the workings in Croft and Wilson Pits to the south, and which was supposed to form the southern boundary of the West Cumberland coalfield. This fault has since been crossed seawards by the main dip haulage road, in Croft Pit, and the Bannock and Main Bands have been won therefrom, the workings in the latter seam being now about 2,300 yards west of the St. Bees fault, underneath the Permian sandstone.

In 1863 an underground fire broke out in the workings in the Six Quarters Seam, Wellington Pit. The fire originated in this underground flue and spread to such an extent that it was determined to exclude all the air from the fire by hermetically sealing Duke Pit and flooding the entrance to the workings in the Six Quarters Seam at the Wellington shaft-foot, admitting the sea down one of the Wellington Pits by means of a drift, fitted with sluices, driven from the shore between high and low water marks. It was not until 1866 that the fire was completely extinguished.

After the death of Mr. Anderson, in 1862, Messrs. T. E. and G. B. Forster and T. G. Hurst were appointed Lord Lonsdale's consulting viewers.

In 1866 the total output of the Whitehaven Colliery was 255,505 tons, derived from William, Croft, Wellington, and Wreah Pits.

Henry Pit (alongside William Pit) was sunk, 1870–2, to a depth of 155 fathoms, whence drifts were set away and won over faults, the Six Quarters Seam, a considerable area of which, both under land and sea, was worked up to 1891, when the workings were abandoned.

An important bore-hole was put down with the diamond rock-drill, 1873–4, at Gutterfoot, St. Bees, with the view of proving the Coal Measures under the Permian rocks. In this it was entirely successful, for at a depth of 1,438 ft. it passed through the Main Band.

In 1874 Mr. R. F. Martin became viewer for the Earl of Lonsdale's collieries. During his three years in office, he thoroughly modernized the plant, abolished the use of baskets, and introduced compressed air haulage on the main roads in William Pit. He erected a Guibal fan at William Pit, and also at Kells Pit, and abolished the last of the under-ground furnaces. Both above-ground and under-ground he made many improvements.

In 1877 Mr. G. H. Liddell, from Burnhope Colliery, Durham, was appointed colliery agent.

The output of coal at the Whitehaven Pits for the year 1876 was 281,968 tons.

At William, Wellington, and Croft Pits the Main Band was worked. A little of the Bannock Band was worked at Wellington Pit ; and the Six Quarters Seam was worked at Henry and Wreah Pits.

In 1878 Wreah Pit, Hensingham, was abandoned. In 1878 Lord Lonsdale bought from the Crown the coalfield ten miles under the sea from Lowca Beck to the River Calder.[1]

In 1881 the coke industry was revived at Whitehaven by the building of coke-ovens on the foreshore near William Pit.

In 1882 an explosion of firedamp took place in the Countess district Main Band, William Pit, by which four men were killed.

The greatest output of the Whitehaven Collieries whilst the Earl of Lonsdale worked them was attained in the year 1886, when 417,039 tons of coal were produced from William, Henry, Croft and Wellington Pits.

On 11 August, 1888, the Whitehaven Collieries, worked without interruption by the Lowther family since the middle of the seventeenth century, were leased to Sir James Bain ; his sons, Messrs. J. R. and J. D. Bain ; and Mr. J. S. Simpson, who assumed the title of the Whitehaven Colliery Company. The new company made many changes and introduced the endless rope haulage.

In 1900 the output of the Whitehaven Collieries was :—

	Tons
William Pit	246,850
Wellington Pit . . .	113,094
Croft Pit	176,549
	536,493

At the present time the workings of the Whitehaven Collieries are solely in the Main Band, and with the exception of those in the St. Bees Grammar School royalty are all under the sea.

The Whitehaven Collieries now extend to a greater distance underneath the sea than any others in the world. The furthest workings have been made from William Pit in the Main Band, where a distance of nearly 4 miles from high water mark has been reached. The cover at that extreme point is about 200 fathoms.

[1] 43 & 44 Vict. c. 3.

365

Cleator Moor.—The first collieries at Cleator Moor were Litt's Pit at Bowthorn, and Mr. Dean's at Keekle Grove; at work in 1802 in the Five Feet Seam.

In 1839 Messrs. Barker and Harrison sank the Whinny Hill Pit 114 fathoms to the Main Band, from which, and from the Five Feet Seam, coals were raised in 1843; and in 1847 this Whinny Hill or Wyndham Colliery was taken over by the Whitehaven Hæmatite Iron Company, who afterwards sank No. 2 Pit to the south-east.

In 1848 a terrible explosion took place in the Five Feet Seam workings in Whinny Hill Pit, causing the death of 30 persons.

In 1849 the Threapthwaite Coal Company put down at Threapthwaite two shafts, whence the Bannock and Main Bands were worked until 1872.

In 1861 the Whitehaven Hæmatite Iron Company completed Hope Pit to the Main Band, a depth of 120 fathoms, and continued No. 2 Pit to the Low Bottom or Six Quarters Seam.

In 1863 three men and a boy lost their lives in No. 2 Pit. They had walked into a body of gas that had accumulated in consequence of a fall of roof.

Wyndham Colliery (No. 2 and Hope Pits) was closed in 1871. The Five Feet, Bannock, Main, Yard and Low Bottom Seams had been worked there.

In 1869 the Whitehaven Hæmatite Iron Company sank the Lindow Pits and worked the Main, Five Feet, Bannock and Yard Bands there between Wyndham and Threapthwaite Collieries. In 1891 the Lindow Pits were put down to the Six Quarters Seam, and in 1897 the colliery was laid in.

Mr. Stirling's Montreal Colliery, Moor Row, is the only one now working in the Cleator Moor coalfield. It was sunk in 1867 to the Main Band, a depth of 81 fathoms, and there the Five Feet, Bannock and Main Bands have been worked. At this colliery may be witnessed the unique sight of coal and iron ore being drawn at the same shaft, a rich deposit of hæmatite having been won from the Main Band, through the large upthrow fault that throws up the Carboniferous Limestone.

Workington, Harrington, Distington, Moresby, Arlecdon and Dean.—The Curwens are said to have worked and exported coal at Workington before 1650;[1] but in an account of the mines in the manor of Workington in 1673 no mention of any colliery

is made, and Sandford, whose MS. is in the library of the dean and chapter at Carlisle, describing Workington in 1676, says: 'The haven was not then frequented with ships and the colliery was decayed.'

Denton in his MS. 'Perambulation of Cumberland and Westmorland, 1687-8,'[2] observes that the colliery within Mr. Curwen's demesne at Workington was worth £200 a year.

Coal mining appears to have been conducted on a small scale until the invention of the steam engine enabled the Curwens, about 1730 or 1740, to sink Union, Moorbanks, Hunday[3] and Schoolhouse Pits, which were at work in 1750.

M. Jars visited the Workington coal mines in 1765, and described them in his *Voyages Metallurgiques.* According to his account six workable seams of coal had been proved, the lowest bed, 4 feet thick, occurring at the depth of 60 fathoms at the Engine Pit. Firedamp abounded in the mines, and explosions, notwithstanding the use of steel mills, were frequent. Indeed, during M. Jar's visit two men were killed and many burned.

In 1771 the output of coal raised at the Workington Colliery was 1,701 tons, and in 1772, 10,742 tons. In 1774 the quantity had increased to 23,600 tons, and in 1780 to 33,350 tons.

Up to 1794 all the coal had been obtained from pits in the Banklands or eastern division of the Workington Colliery. In that year Mr. John Christian Curwen had, under the advice of Mr. John Grieve, engineer, Edinburgh, completed the sinking of Lady Pit on the shore to the Main Band, which was found to be in great perfection at a depth of 84 fathoms. This was the commencement of the Chapel Bank or western division of Workington Colliery.

At that date Mr. Curwen's colliery comprised 9 pits; but there was another colliery, comprising 5 pits, worked by Mr. Walker for the trustees of Anthony Bacon, Esq., M.P., London. The daily shipment of coals from Mr. Curwen's pits was 100 waggons, and from the other pits 50 waggons[4] of three English tons each.

The sinking of Union Pit, Chapel Bank Colliery, was begun in 1795, and finished to the Main Band, 58 fathoms, in 1798.

An action was brought in 1800 by the Earl of Lonsdale against Mr. Curwen for a trespass alleged to have been made from John Pit, Banklands Colliery, into his lordship's

---

[1] *Archæology of West Cumberland Coal Trade,* by Isaac Fletcher, M.P.

[2] f. 33.   [3] Winscales.

[4] Hutchinson, *History of Cumberland,* ii. 140.

royalty, under the Cloffocks, in the Moorbanks Seam. The trespass was clearly proved, and the action was compromised by the payment of a goodly sum to the earl.

In 1799 the output of the Chapel Bank Colliery was :—

	Tons
Lady Pit, Main Band . .	21,059
Union Pit ,, . .	11,089
	32,148

In 1800 the output of Banklands Colliery was :—

	Tons
John Pit, Moorbanks Seam .	2,276
Elizabeth Pit ,, ,, .	6,135
Hope Pit, Main Band . .	6,473
Henry Pit ,, . .	2,578
Old Engine Pit, Main Band .	2,978
Crosthwaite Pit, Yard Band .	6,134
Bowness or Well Pit, Four Feet Seam	5,015
	31,589

In 1808 Mr. Curwen began the sinking of Isabella Pit, which reached in 1814 the Moorbanks Seam, found in perfection at 90 fathoms.

In 1816 the sinking of Isabella Pit was resumed, and in 1818 the pit had been sunk 128 fathoms to the position of the Main Band, which was discovered to be 'nipped-out.' However the lower part of the Main Band was subsequently proved through the 'nip,' by a stone-drift 400 yards long, driven to the west; and, eventually, 100 yards further south, the seam was found, in its normal thickness, in 1822.

The output of the Workington Collieries during 1816 was :—

Chapel Bank Colliery—	Tons
Lady Pit, Main Band .	8,846
Union Pit ,, .	12,834
Isabella Pit, Moorbanks Seam	9,634
	31,314
Banklands Colliery—	
Church Pit, Main Band . .	9,393
	40,707

The 'nip' prevented the Main Band being worked east of Isabella Pit ; but that seam was worked therefrom to a considerable extent under the land towards Union and Lady Pits, and to the south-west, under the sea, to the dip of Lady Pit.

When Chapel Bank Colliery became to be thoroughly developed, Banklands Colliery was laid in and all the shafts were filled up. Church Pit, the last to be closed, was abandoned in 1820, when the removal of some of the Main Band pillars on the east side of the 'Sand-wash' (separating the Chapel Bank and Banklands Collieries) had liberated the 'sand feed' which overcame the pumping engine.

Buddle Pit had then been sunk 27 fathoms to the Hamilton Seam, and from that pit a small area of Main Band that had been left in Church Pit was worked from a drift made, at a subsequent date, over a down east fault of 40 fathoms.

The output of Workington Colliery (then limited to Chapel Bank) in 1829 was :—

	Tons
Isabella Pit, Moorbanks Seam	6,541
,, Main Band . .	17,665
	24,206
Lady Pit, Main Band . . .	15,464
	39,670

Workington Colliery until 1837 had been free from any very serious catastrophe. On the 28th of July in that year a disaster took place, causing the deaths of 27 persons and 28 horses and the loss of the Chapel Bank Colliery. On that date the sea broke into the Main Band workings at the rise of Camperdown district in Lady Pit, and speedily filled every working in Lady, Union, and Isabella Pits. Fortunately, access to the district, being confined to two drifts, so limited the passage of the sea into the other parts of the colliery that time was afforded for 30 persons to escape by the bearmouth, near Union Pit. The fall, by which the sea effected its entrance into the mine, was about 80 yards in diameter, and occurred $1\frac{1}{2}$ miles south of Lady Pit, and about 50 yards below low water mark, opposite Salter Beck.

The Camperdown district was worked to the rise of the main south road, leading direct from Lady Pit towards the land. The workings had reached within 20 fathoms of the bed of the sea and were nearly up to the line of the 'Sand-wash,' which divides Chapel Bank and Banklands Collieries. The coal in this area had been cut up into pillars, 15 yards by 10 yards, which the manager had begun to remove. Heavy falls of roof, accompanied with sea-water, ensued; but regardless of these warnings the manager persisted in working the pillars until the fall of roof took place which let the sea into the colliery.

After the abandonment of Banklands and Chapel Bank steps were taken to open out Buddle and Moorbanks Engine Pits. The latter was again abandoned in 1840, the Main Band, supposed to have been left, having been found to have been worked.

From 1837 to 1845 the output of coal at Workington Colliery was from Buddle Pit, where a small area of Main Band, left to the dip of Church Pit, was worked.

The sinking of Jane Pit near Buddle Pit was commenced in 1843, and the Hamilton Seam was won in 1846, at 73 fathoms.

In 1851 the output of coal from the Yard and Hamilton Seams at Jane Pit, and the Main Band at Buddle Pit, was 20,000 tons.

The Jane and Buddle Pits worked until 1853, when Buddle Pit was abandoned, the gravel feed liberated by pillar workings proving to be too much for the old engine and pumps.

In 1854, Hope Pit, Ellerbeck, was sunk to the Four Feet Seam, a depth of 30 fathoms to the rise of Banklands Colliery. The pit turned out to be unprofitable and was abandoned in 1858.

A small output of coal was kept up at Jane Pit until 1864 from the Yard and Hamilton Bands.

In 1864 Mr. Curwen leased the Workington royalty at Jane Pit to Mr. William Irving, who afterwards sank Annie Pit 72 fathoms to the Hamilton Seam, which he worked until his death in 1872, whereupon Mr. H. K. Spark, Darlington, took a lease of the colliery. In 1875 coal work ceased at Annie Pit and pumping was discontinued at Jane Pit.

In 1875 the Workington Collieries Company acquired Mr. Spark's interest, but after pumping the water out of the pits the company collapsed.

Later Mr. W. A. Wooler, Darlington, became the lessee of Workington Colliery; but he did nothing in the way of development. The lease was surrendered in 1893.

In the manor of Harrington, in 1673, the two coal pits, one of which supplied the salt pans with fuel, were valued at £100 per annum.

For nearly 100 years afterwards there is no information respecting coal mining at Harrington, though it may be taken for granted that coal was worked in a small way during that time for use at the salt-pans of Parton and Harrington.

Near Lowca, the Bannock and Main Bands outcrop along the shore and were worked a little before 1750.

In 1770 and long afterwards, ironstone was worked by Mr. Curwen along the shore and sent to Seaton, Clifton, Backbarrow and Netherhall Furnaces.

Coal on the upthrow side of Micklam fault was worked from the Three Feet, Four Feet, and Udale Seams, from a dozen or more pits, between 1750 and 1790; and was conveyed along wooden railways to Harrington Harbour. These pits were drained by the 'Snout Brow level,' which extended from the sea to Hodgson Pit.

In 1796 coals were drawn at Bella, Udale, Old Basket, Fox, Natty, Laybourne, Henry, and John Pits, on the upthrow side of the Micklam fault.

From John Pit a long drift, set over several faults, won the Udale Seam, which was worked towards the Micklam fault; and from Bella and Hodgson Pits the Four Feet Seam was worked close up to that fault.

In 1804 Harrington Colliery consisted of Udale, Tarn, Jane, Bella and Henry Pits, where 41,420 tons of coal were raised and about 70 hewers employed. Hodgson Pit was sunk during that year.

About 1825 Mr. Curwen began the sinking of Micklam Pit to win the upper seams west of Micklam fault. The pit was sunk on the upthrow side of the fault, through the Three Feet, Four Feet, and Udale Seams to a depth of 90 fathoms, at which level the Main Band was cut by a short drift over the fault in 1830, and a large feed of water liberated. Nothing further was done until 1865.

In 1838 John Pit was the scene of the most terrible explosion of firedamp that has ever been chronicled in the annals of Cumberland coal mining, by which no less than 40 men and boys were killed.

Mr. Curwen worked John and Hodgson Pits until 1864, when Messrs. Bain, Blair, and Paterson (the predecessors of the present firm of Messrs. James Bain & Co.) entered upon the Harrington Ironworks and Harrington Coal royalty.

The lessees re-opened Micklam Pit and worked a little coal from the lower seams on the east side of the Micklam fault. But the chief use to which Micklam Pit was ultimately put was for draining the unwrought field of coal on the west side of the fault. For that purpose, in 1867, a pumping engine was established there.

At this time No. 3 Pit was sunk north of Micklam Pit, and there the coal remaining in the Three Feet and Four Feet Seams, between Mr. Curwen's old workings and high water mark, was worked till 1879.

In 1871 No. 4 Pit was sunk to the Four Feet Seam, a depth of 49 fathoms, and from it the coal remaining in that seam between the old Hodgson Pit workings and Lowca Beck on the east side of the Micklam fault was worked up to 1879.

About the same time No. 6 Pit was sunk near Lowca Point, on the west side of the Micklam fault, to the Bannock and Main Bands. It was discontinued in 1874.

West of No. 6 Pit, No. 8 Pit was sunk on the foreshore, to win the Main Band which outcrops near low water mark. The pit, which was 11 fathoms to the Main Band, continued at work till 1874, when an influx of water stopped operations. The Bannock and Main Bands on the west side of Micklam fault was principally worked from No. 7 Pit from 1874 to 1901. The workings in the Main Band extended to the north, underneath the sea, to a distance of about a mile from low water mark, beyond which limit it was deemed imprudent to go by reason of the thinness of the cover.

The output from Harrington Colliery is now altogether from No. 9 Pit, which was sunk near No. 7 Pit in 1880, to the Six Quarters Seam, which has been worked alongside the Micklam fault both under the land and the sea.

The earliest recorded coal mining at Clifton was on the Curwen property about 1673. The Lowthers and the Cooksons of Newcastle were amongst the first to work coal in Clifton. Reelfit Colliery was at work in 1735. The Lowthers began to work coal in Clifton on an extensive scale before 1750, Sir James Lowther having constructed a wooden railway from Workington to a staith at Great Clifton, to which the coal was carted. Some of these pits were drained by adits into the Marron and Lostrigg, others by a water-wheel at Bridgefoot, and the rest by two atmospheric pumping engines.

In 1771 Sir James Lowther closed all his collieries at Clifton, Flimby, and Seaton, at short notice, on becoming aware of the existence of a clause in the lease of the Beerpot Ironworks, Workington, which he had granted in 1763 to Messrs. Hicks, Spedding & Co., whereby he was bound, so long as he worked any pits within a distance of four miles, to supply the ironworks with coals from those pits at the shipping price.

In 1781 the Clifton coals were sold to the country at 2s. 3d. and to the shipping at Workington at 3s. 4d. a ton.

When Sir James Lowther stopped his Clifton pits, Mr. Cookson's pits in Greysouthen and Clifton became flooded out.

From 1781 there was no coal-mining of any consequence at Clifton until 1803, when the Earl of Lonsdale began opening out a colliery on Clifton Moor near Quarry Hill, on the west side of Lostrigg Beck, in two little seams lying above the Main Band, the lower one being 10 fathoms deep at John Pit. The workings were drained by a level into Lostrigg Beck. This colliery was worked by the Earl of Lonsdale up to 1815.

From 1815 to 1822 Mr. John Johnson leased the Clifton Moor pits ; and Mr. John Fletcher had them from 1815 until 1829, when they were abandoned.

In 1827 Mr. Thomas Westray sank the Westray or Clifton Pit to the Cannel and Metal Band (a depth of 55 fathoms) in Mr. Isaac Cookson's royalty at Great Clifton.

In 1842 the Earl of Lonsdale, having acquired Mr. Cookson's royalty and Mr. Westray's interest therein, proceeded to work the colliery, and continued to do so until 1856.

In 1852 Messrs. Isaac and William Fletcher became lessees of Mr. Curwen's royalty in Little Clifton, and sank a pit (40 fathoms to the Main Band) near Crossbarrow. In 1854 the same firm sank Harry Gill Pit on Mr. John Cookson's royalty to the same seam. The success of their efforts induced Lord Lonsdale to sink Lowther Pit, half a mile to the westward, which reached the Main Band in 1855 at a depth of only 30 fathoms. About this time disputes arose as to the Earl of Lonsdale's title to the royalty under certain lands in Great and Little Clifton, but those differences were settled by his lordship purchasing the estates, and thus becoming the owner of nearly all the land in both townships. In 1856 Lord Lonsdale granted a lease of all his royalty in Great and Little Clifton to Messrs. Fletcher, who completed the Lowther Pit.

In 1860 Lowther Pit was sunk 30 fathoms deeper, and from that depth a short drift won the Cannel and Metal Band to the west over a downthrow fault of 30 fathoms. Besides the Ten Quarters Seam and the Cannel and Metal Band, the Little Main Seam, won in 1873, and Lickbank Seam, won in 1878, were also worked to a large extent by Messrs. I. and W. Fletcher on the east side of the same fault. In 1861 William Pit, Great Clifton (still at work), was sunk by the same firm, and from it has been worked the Main Band on the west side of the large downthrow west fault, which bounds the workings in Lowther, Clifton and the old pits to the south as far as the outcrop of the Main Band near the Marron. The William Pit Main Band workings to the south are now beyond Lostrigg Beck and eastward have reached the outcrop in Stainburn.

In 1873 the West Cumberland Iron and Steel Co., Ltd., became the sub-lessees of the Clifton Collieries, and continued to work them until 1887, when the Allerdale Coal Co., Ltd., took them over.

In 1875 Westray Pit was laid in.

In 1885 Lowther Pit was abandoned.

The Cooksons of Newcastle were working

coal in the township of Greysouthen anterior to 1750.

Since then many pits have been sunk by various persons, and a large area of coal has been worked, more particularly in the Cannel and Metal Band, south-eastward to the outcrop. The most southerly workings are those that have been made from Allan Pit near to Dean parish boundary, upwards of 2 miles from the confluence of the Marron and Derwent. The most northerly workings in the Cannel and Metal Band have been made from Melgramfitz and other pits up to an upcast east fault of 40 fathoms that runs underneath the village of Greysouthen.

In 1761 Sir James Lowther was working the Cannel and Metal Band, in Greysouthen, at the depth of 34 fathoms at Reelfitz Pit, east of the Marron.

In 1766 two small pits, 20 fathoms deep, were being worked, presumably by Mr. John Cookson near the Marron, about half a mile south of Bridgefoot, for the supply of coal to the Clifton furnace.

In 1783 Mr. Cookson was working Windy Hill or Linefitz Colliery, on the east side of the Marron, in the Cannel and Metal Band.

In 1787 Messrs. William Walker & Co. leased the coal under a considerable portion of the township, and carried on an extensive and profitable business for a period of eighty years.

In 1800 Messrs. John Wilson & Co., in which Mr. J. W. Fletcher was a partner, opened a new colliery in Greysouthen. They obtained, in 1807, at an Assize trial at Carlisle, £16,000 damages from Messrs. William Walker & Co., who, it was proved, had worked a large quantity of coal belonging to Messrs. Wilson & Co., whose colliery they had also damaged by throwing water upon it.

Messrs. Walker & Co. were then working Agill, Walker and Moss Pits, and Messrs. Wilson & Co. were working Wilson Pit.

In 1816 Messrs. Lysons include amongst the list of collieries 'Greysouthen, belonging to Messrs. Walker, Harris & Co., supposed to have a sale of about 10,000 waggon-loads annually.'[1]

In 1829 there were two collieries belonging to Messrs. Birbeck and Fletcher and Messrs. Harris & Co.[2]

In 1831 Messrs. Birbeck and Fletcher were working George and Hope Pits, in the Cannel and Metal Band, in the Earl of Egremont's royalty, south of Mayfield, near the boundary of the parish of Dean.

In 1837 Messrs. Joseph Harris & Co. were working the Cannel and Metal Band at Nepgill, and in 1838 at John Pit, both of which were comprised in the Millbanks Colliery.

In 1842 Mr. Harris was still carrying on Millbanks Colliery near Bridgefoot, in Greysouthen, whilst Messrs. Fletcher & Co. were raising coal a little to the south at Mary Pit. The Millbanks Colliery produced about 130 waggons, and Mary Pit, 100 waggons per week.

From 1855 to 1863 Messrs. Fletcher did not work any coal in Greysouthen, but Messrs. Harris & Co. did. In 1860 the latter had one colliery in the Cannel Band, 42 fathoms deep, where 70 persons were employed.[3]

In 1863 Messrs. Isaac and William Fletcher completed Melgramfitz Pit, from which the Ten Quarters Seam and the Cannel and Metal Band were extensively worked until 1886, when the pit was closed.

Mr. Harris continued working coal at Nepgill Pit until 1874. At this pit, which was sunk to the Cannel and Metal Band, a considerable area of Lickbank Seam was worked to the south through an upthrow fault.

In 1877 New Banks Pit near Nepgill Pit had been opened out by Messrs. Kenyon and Campbell. It was sunk to the Rattler Band, a depth of 25 fathoms from the surface, and continued at work till 1884.

Since the closing of Melgramfitz Pit in 1886 no coal has been worked in Greysouthen.

In the township of Winscales, the Curwens worked coal from 1783 to 1806. Coal was again worked in 1873, when the Rev. A. F. Curwen and Messrs. Were and Blair took a lease of the Curwen royalty, and sank a pit at Wythemoor, 10½ fathoms to the Yard Band. After 1875 Mr. Blair, and after 1880 Dr. Richmond, Greenock, carried on the colliery, which was closed in 1886.

Coal had been found in the parish of Distington early in the seventeenth century. In 1614 Mr. John Fearon demised his coal mines at Great Gunnerdine to Mr. George Fletcher, Tallentire; and in 1615 the court-roll refers to the coals under certain tenements.

The Christians, Fletchers and Lamplughs were the earliest workers of coal in Distington.

In 1675 Sir John Lowther acquired the lease of the Fearon coal mines from Mr.

[1] *Magna Britannica*, iv. p. cxxiv.
[2] *History, etc. Cumb. and Westm.* 1829, Parson and White, p. 188.

[3] Whellan, *History of Cumberland*, p. 298.

Henry Fletcher, Tallentire; and in 1709 his son, Mr. James Lowther, purchased the reversion.

From that time the Lowthers bought coal property in Distington whenever opportunity offered; and in 1737 Mr. John Brougham of Scales, who purchased the manor when it was sold in 1720, under a decree of Chancery, on the Fletcher family becoming extinct, conveyed it to Sir James Lowther.

In 1694 Mr. Lamplugh was working a colliery at Stubscales. North of Boonwood fault, Gunnerdine Level, driven from Stubsgill to Moss Pit, West Croft, drained the old Main Band pits, sunk on the outcrop; and south of the fault Rugard's or Castlerigg level, made from the hillside, near Bottom Bank, to Rugard's or Castlerigg Pit, served a similar purpose.

Although the records are scanty, coal was worked continuously during the eighteenth century at Distington. In 1768 a colliery was working at Boonwood, Distington, at which there was a cinder oven. In 1781 Mr. Crosthwaite worked the Three Feet or Six Quarters Seam at Moss and High Pits, on his own property, at Gunnerdine near Boonwood; and Sir James Lowther was working the Metal Band (12 fathoms under the Main Band) at Moor Gate and Moss Pits, also known as Gunnerdine Colliery. The Main Band at those pits and the adjacent Glaister Pit had been exhausted at that date, up to the outcrop. Mr. Walker had then a pit, 19 fathoms to the Yard Band, north of Mr. Crosthwaite's Moss Pit. In 1805 Jackson Pit was at work in Mr. Crosthwaite's royalty. In 1806 the output of Moss and Moor Gate Pits, Gunnerdine, still worked by Lord Lonsdale, was 6,581 tons. In 1812 Lord Lonsdale's Gunnerdine Colliery consisted of Moss and Rugard's Pits, with an output of 3,258 tons. In 1813 Mrs. Martin was working two thin seams of coal from two 'bearmouths' at Fisher Beck near Prospect House. Coal was drawn at Gunnerdine Colliery until 1815, when Bottom Bank Colliery superseded it. In that year Stubscales or Dyan Pit was sunk to the Main Band, 36 fathoms. In 1820 there were three 'cinder' ovens at Castlerigg Pit, which was worked in connection with Bottom Bank Colliery. In 1831 Jane Pit, Boonwood, belonging to Mr. Allinson Crosthwaite, was drawing coals from the Bannock and Four Feet Seams. In 1845 Bottom Bank Colliery was abandoned. The Main Band and the seams underneath, viz. the Metal, Two Feet and Three Feet Bands, had been worked from Boonwood fault to the line of Parton drifts.

From 1845 to 1851 the Dyan Pit was

the only colliery worked by Lord Lonsdale in Distington.

In 1859 Mr. Ralph Tate worked a colliery at Commonside. In 1863 he took a lease of Haycastle Colliery, Distington, where he worked the Yard Band until 1872.

In Gilgarran Captain Robertson Walker began mining coal about 1830. He had three pits from which the Yard Band was worked at depths varying from 10 to 20 fathoms. He had also six 'cinder' ovens.

In 1843 Mr. Ralph Tate worked the Gilgarran Pits sunk by Captain Walker. Lack of capital compelled him to desist in 1854.

The next coal-mining at Gilgarran was in 1872, by a company in which Messrs. Mackenzie and Main were interested. After reopening the old Yard Band Pits, the company abandoned active operations in 1875.

In 1866 Mr. James Rankin put down Greyhound Pit at Studfold near the Dean boundary. He worked an upper seam, 2 ft. 6 in. thick, at 25 fathoms, and the China Band, 4 ft. thick, at 35 fathoms; but the workings in both seams were very limited.

After the closing of the Gilgarran and Haycastle Pits no coal was worked in Distington until 1880, when the Moresby Coal Co., Ltd., completed their Oatlands Pit to a depth of 108 fathoms, whence the Main Band was won by a short drift. Since that date the Main Band has been worked over a large area to the south-west, and to the west up to the great 'nip' lying immediately to the dip of the Old Gunnerdine Colliery. At the same pit the Bannock Band has been and is being worked extensively in conjunction with the Main Band; and the China Band has been worked to a less extent.

Records of coal-mining in the parish of Moresby date back to 1680, when Mr. Thomas Addison was working Howgate Colliery, and Mr. Thomas Tickell (Sir John Lowther's agent) had a colliery at Goosegreen.

In 1693 Howgate Colliery was still at work, whilst Mr. Richard Sanderson and Mr. Henry Birkett were working adjacent pits in Moresby; and Sir John Lowther began the working of Lattera Colliery, which drained into a level made from the ghyll, descending to Lowca Beck, near Moresby House.

The output from Lattera Colliery in 1695 was 1,387 tons, derived from the Little Main and Yard Bands.

In 1697 the owners of the copper mines in Dunnerdale, Millom, erected works in Moresby for the smelting of their ore with coal.

In 1706 at Lattera Colliery, the Main Band and 'Square Coal' were worked at Towerson Pit; the 'Square Coal' at White Close Pit; and the Yard Band at Punfulldale Pit, the total output of coal being 3,789 tons.

By the Act of Parliament obtained in 1705 by Mr. Thomas Fletcher, lord of the manors of Moresby and Distington, Mr. Thomas Lamplugh and others, 4d. a ton was charged upon coal exported at Parton for 11 years to raise £1,600 for the improvement of the harbour there.

That Act was intended to benefit Parton; but a print published *circa* 1717, entitled *The Miserable Case of the Poor Inhabitants of Parton*, etc., alleged that Mr. Lamplugh had taken advantage of the Act for his own private gain.

It appears from that document that the trustees under the Act, most of whom owed their appointment to the influence of Mr. Lamplugh, left the management of the harbour to him, and, in 1707, entered into a contract with him whereby he covenanted to make a harbour sufficient for 'fifty sail of ships for £1,210.'

Mr. Lamplugh, so *The Miserable Case* states, failed to complete his contract, although he received the payment agreed upon, and had sold his collieries.

The inhabitants of Parton, foreseeing the impending ruin of the harbour, and knowing that they had no power over Mr. Lamplugh or the trustees, were willing that the harbour duties should be continued for a further term in order that the harbour might be kept up.

In 1724 the duties, which had lapsed in 1716, were re-enacted for a further term of 15 years.

The passing of the Parton Harbour Act, 1705, was strenuously opposed by Sir John Lowther, but the application for the Act of 1724 received the support of his successor, Mr. James Lowther. Both had in the interim acquired large interests at Parton.

In 1713 Mr. Lowther purchased Mr. Lamplugh's collieries at Parton.

In 1731 Lattera Colliery consisted of Fisher and Lister Pits, in the Main Band, and Punfulldale Pit in the Yard Band.

In 1738 Sir James Lowther's collieries in Moresby comprised the Hall and Lattera Collieries. At the Hall Colliery, Hutton Pit was the only one at work, but in that year a commencement was made with working coal at Long Bransty Barugh. At the Lattera Colliery coal work was still going on in Lister and Fisher Pits.

No coal was raised at the Hall Colliery after 1739, but pumping went on at Hutton Pit till 1743.

Lattera Colliery at this time was worked intermittently. Lister and Fisher Pits were stopped in 1741, and coal work was not resumed at Lattera until 1742, when Lamb Hills Pit was opened out and the Metal Band worked until 1750.

In 1751 at Lattera Colliery, Blearbank Pit, afterwards known as White Pit, was sunk. In 1776 this pit was working the Main Band towards the High farmhouse but was soon discontinued.

The next coal working in Moresby took place from Parton Drift and Countess Pit, begun in 1827 and 1832 respectively. The Parton Drift had reached, when abandoned in 1863, the Distington parish boundary— 1½ miles from Parton; and at its extremity a small district of Main Band was wrought in Moresby parish. The Parton Drift was the outlet for coal produced at Countess and Moresby New Pits.

At these pits, coals from the Bannock, Main, and Six Quarters Seams were raised to the level of the Parton Drift, and thence conveyed to Parton Pit, 10 fathoms deep, where they were drawn to bank.

Countess Pit was sunk a total depth of 91 fathoms, but coals were only drawn up to the level of the Parton Drift, which was there 25 fathoms from the surface. The Main Band and Six Quarters Seam were worked thereat until 1863, when the pit was stopped.

Moresby New Pit was sunk in 1849, east of Millgrove, 52 fathoms to the Main Band, 14 fathoms below the level of Parton Drift, and was abandoned in 1850.

The Main Band was worked south-east of the pit towards Gillhead and Canada; and through an upthrow fault the Six Quarters Seam was worked to the north.

From 1863 no coal was worked in the parish of Moresby until 1879, when Walkmill Pit was sunk by the Moresby Coal Co., Ltd., 25 fathoms to the Main Band, which has been and is being worked on the rise side of the Micklam dyke from Parton drifts on the north, to Dub Beck in Weddiker on the south, and to the east under Weddiker Rigg.

Coal and ironstone (from the Coal Measures) were worked in the parish of Dean in early times. In 1777 Nicolson and Burn stated that there were coal pits at the Edge, Branthwaite, where catscalp (ironstone) used at the Clifton and Seaton furnaces was obtained up to 1813, when the manufacture of iron at Seaton ceased.

From this time until 1824 Mr. J. C.

Curwen, Workington Hall, was working coal at Branthwaite.

In 1815 George O'Brien, Earl of Egremont, lord of the manor of Dean, granted a lease of his coal mines in Whillimoor to Anthony Wild, Kidburngill, Arlecdon, coal miner, and Henry James Johnson, Whitehaven, grocer ; and in 1834 the lease was renewed to Anthony Wild's widow and Johnson.

Wild's pits were situated near Dean Cross, and were drained by a level into Thief Gill.

Dean Moor Colliery was worked from 1856 to 1859 by General Wyndham, and in 1860 by Mr. Percival.

Subsequently it was taken by Mr. George Grierson, who sank the present shafts 34 fathoms deep to the Yard Seam. It passed through the 'Anthony Wiley' Seam 30 in. thick at 27 fathoms.

In 1880 Mr. William Summerson, Cockfield, Durham, became lessee of the colliery, which is now being worked by the Dean Moor Colliery Co., Ltd.

Adjoining Dean Moor Colliery Messrs. W. Baird & Co., Gartsherrie, worked the Moorside royalty in Whillimoor from 1874 to 1880. A seam 3 ft. thick was worked by that company at No. 1 Pit at a depth of 14 fathoms. Afterwards Mr. A. Johnston worked Moorside Colliery until 1899.

In the parish of Lamplugh Messrs. Sherwen, Moore, Brown and Burnyeat, sank in 1872, near Whitekeld, a pit from which were worked a seam 3 ft. thick, at 15 fathoms, and a seam 5 ft. 2 in. thick, considered to be the Main Band at 26 fathoms. The colliery was abandoned in 1879.

In the parish of Arlecdon Messrs. Brady & Co. sank a pit near the Mosses about 1819, but their efforts were unsuccessful. Little coal mining was done until Mr. William Irving, Workington, took a lease of Lord Lonsdale's royalty in 1860 and put down the present Asby Colliery 53 fathoms to the Main Band which was found in great perfection. The Irving family along with other partners carried on Asby Colliery until 1899, when Messrs. Johnson and Peile, the present lessees, took it.

Coal was worked anterior to 1700 in the township of Whillimoor. Since that date coal has been worked in a small way at intervals.

The colliery at which most coal has been worked in Whillimoor was Venture Pit, sunk near Greenspot in 1852, by Mr. Thomas Hinde, sailmaker, of Whitehaven. It was let to Mr. Joseph Ward, Cleator Moor, and others in 1860 ; and was discontinued in 1865.

At Venture Pit the upper seam, 2 ft. 6 in. thick, at 14 fathoms, and the lower seam, said to be the China Band, 3 ft. thick at 26 fathoms, were worked.

Coal was first worked in the parish of Frizington about 1718. Mr. John Wood in 1728 worked coal in Howth Gill, where he had established furnaces for the manufacture of ' pit-coal iron.' In 1730 Mr. Wood's pit-coal iron was proved to be worthless at a public test that took place at Whitehaven. From 1783 to 1789 Sir James Lowther worked the Howth Gill Colliery, the output from which was only 10 tons a day. The last coal mining in Frizington was undertaken in 1861 by Messrs. Gibson, Cook and Musgrave, who sank the pit known as ' Boghole,' on Frizington Moor, 48 fathoms to the ' Top Seam,' 5 feet thick, which was worked until the colliery was closed in 1878.

Seaton, Camerton, Flimby, Ellenborough, Broughton, Dearham, Dovenby, Crosby, Gilcrux.—Two miners named Gorton from Swailedale, Yorkshire, played a prominent part in the early development of the coal mines within the manor of Seaton.

In 1722 they obtained from Mr. Henry Curwen, Workington, lord of the manor, a lease of the Seaton colliery for a term of thirty-eight years.

A map of Seaton coal works in 1722 shows several pits, 16 fathoms deep, in Moorhouse Guards, sunk on a level discharging into Eagle Gill ; other pits near Seaton Town Head ; and a level, driven in ' Pearson Wood,' to the Yard coal in a pit near St. Helens No. 2 Colliery.

The manor passed by bequest from the Curwens to Mr. Charles Pelham, Brocklesby, Lincolnshire, from whom it was purchased by the Earl of Lonsdale.

In 1727 the Gortons took from Mr. Pelham a lease of his coal mines in Seaton on terms identical with those in Mr. Curwen's lease.

In 1728 Captain Walter Lutwidge and Mr. John Spedding, Whitehaven, bought the Gortons' interest in the leases from Mr. Pelham and Mr. Curwen. Thereupon Seaton Colliery was carried on by Captain Lutwidge, John Spedding and Thomas Benn, Whitehaven.

In 1729 the output of coal at Seaton Colliery was 8,290 tons from Smithy, Murra Gards and Aygill Pits.

In 1732 Sir James Lowther had bought out Messrs. Spedding and Benn, and from that date until the end of the lease in 1760, in conjunction with Captain Lutwidge, carried on the colliery. In 1740 they had waggon-ways to all their pits. The length of the main waggon-way from Workington harbour to Goodly Croft Pit, in Muncaster Close, was nearly 3 miles, and there were branches to the other pits. Goodly Croft Pit, the terminus of the waggon-way, was in Seaton Banks near Kirklands.

Seaton Colliery consisted of two groups of pits, one at St. Helens and Moorhouse Guards; and the other, in Seaton Banks, on the north bank of the Derwent. To the pits at St. Helens a waggon-way proceeded from the north side of Workington harbour through Fullock Meadow. A branch up Hazell Gill brought the coals from High Seaton pits down to the harbour.

In 1741 the output of coal at Seaton Colliery from Muncaster, Holden, Cragg Close, Pearson Close, Wales, Murra Gards, and Loaning Head Pits was 34,566 tons; in 1748, from Stephen, High, Low, Falcon, Well, Crag and Pattinson Pits, 32,188 tons; and in 1753, from Hill, Pearson, Muncaster and Moor Pits, 39,328 tons.

The seams worked were called the Murra Gards, Smithy and Crow Bands.

After 1760 Sir James Lowther carried on Seaton Colliery alone.

In 1781 Robinson Pit, in Seaton Banks, produced daily 18 tons of coal from a 5 ft. seam at 24 fathoms; and two pits in Kirklands, 28 tons from a 26 in. seam. In 1781 Sir James Lowther stopped his pits at Seaton for reasons already given. In 1800 Lord Lonsdale was again working two pits in Kirklands and supplying coal to Seaton Iron Works. Since then little has been done in Kirklands until Dr. Mutch began operations in 1883.

About 1825 Mr. John Fletcher, Seaton Green, became lessee of Mr. Ralph Cook's Camerton Colliery and sank Greengill Pits, completed to the Ten Quarters Seam, 30 fathoms, in 1829. His tenancy lasted until 1840.

Mr. William Thornburn, Papcastle, then took Camerton Colliery, being succeeded in 1857 by Messrs. Cook & Co.

In 1873 Mr. Joshua Mulcaster became lessee. Since 1876 Dr. Mutch has carried on the colliery, which consists of two pits and a drift in Israel Gill, where the Little Main, Potash and Lickbank Seams have been worked.

From 1840 coal and fireclay have been worked continuously at Moorhouse Guards, Seaton, from seams above the Ten Quarters, by successive lessees, the present being the Seaton Firebrick Co.

About 1850 Messrs. Buckham, Mulcaster, Nicholson and Harris sank Mary or Buckham Pit, No. 1, Seaton Moor Colliery, in the eastern part of Seaton to the Ten Quarters Seam, 32 fathoms. This pit was abandoned in 1869.

In 1861 Messrs. Mulcaster, Nicholson, Cook, Bell and Westray reopened and enlarged two of Sir James Lowther's old pits at St. Helens and continued them to the Cannel and Metal Band. These pits were called Nos. 1 and 2, St. Helens Colliery; and there the Rattler, Ten Quarters, and Cannel and Metal Bands were worked until the colliery was stopped in 1887.

In 1870 Messrs. Mulcaster and Bell became the lessees of St. Helens Colliery, and in 1877 began the sinking of No. 3 Colliery, Siddick, which was completed by their successors, the St. Helens Colliery and Brick Works Co., Ltd., to the Ten Quarters Seam in 1880, and to the Cannel and Metal Band, a depth of 119 fathoms, in 1882. In 1889 the shafts were put down to the Lickbank Seam, a depth of 170 fathoms.

The Ten Quarters, Cannel and Metal, Little Main and Lickbank Seams have been worked extensively from this colliery under the land, and the workings in the two upper seams have now entered the under-sea area.

In 1888 an explosion of firedamp occurred in the Cannel Band workings in No. 3 Colliery, causing the loss of 30 lives.

In 1901 Nos. 1 and 2 shafts at St. Helens were reopened, enlarged and deepened to win the coal over the faults that had stopped the former lessees. The Carboniferous Limestone was reached, but, owing to faults, its position below any known seam of coal could not be determined.

Coal mining in the parish of Flimby began at Flimby Park or Woodside Colliery, which was worked by Sir James Lowther in 1781. At that time it must have been an old colliery, because a level had then been driven from the Ellenborough boundary for a distance of 1,200 yards to the south for the drainage of the rise coal, in which had been sunk seventeen pits, of which Wren Pit, the most important, was 58 fathoms to the Cannel Band. The Colliery was stopped in 1781.

In 1802 Mr. John Walker entered upon the Flimby Park Colliery and worked it until 1825. In 1802 it had a daily output of 70 tons, and gave employment to 23 men.

From 1839 to 1842 Mr. John Fletcher worked the Cannel and Metal Band at a pit, near Risehow. About 1850 Messrs. John Harris, Darlington, and Robert Wilson sank John and Risehow Pits. The Cannel Band under the foreshore was worked at the latter until 1858, when it was closed.

In 1855 they sank Robin Hood Pit, also in Mr. Curwen's property.

In 1854 Messrs. Harris, Nicholson and Mulcaster took Lord Lonsdale's Seaton Moor royalty, and opened Nos. 2 and 3 in Flimby in the Cannel Band. These pits were stopped in 1869.

In 1855 Messrs. Isaac Bass and Robert Wilson became the lessees of Lord Lonsdale's Flimby royalties. Subsequently Flimby Collieries were worked by Mr. Wilson and his sons until 1893, when the concern was formed into the Flimby and Broughton Moor Coal and Firebrick Co., Ltd. The pits now drawing coals at Flimby are Watergate Pit, sunk in 1866 ; Robin Hood Pit ; and Moor Pit, sunk in 1873 ; from which most of the seams occurring in the coalfield have been worked over a large area. Mr. Wilson took over the Seaton Moor Collieries in 1870.

The only other colliery in Flimby is at Gillhead, where the Gillhead Coal and Firebrick Co. have been working coal, fireclay and ganister from the Little Main and Lickbank Seams since 1897. Mr. John Scurr had a pit at Gillhead in 1832, but the present shaft was sunk by Messrs. Lucock and Carlton in 1867. In 1875 Mr. Henry Graves, Aspatria, took the colliery, and was in 1881 succeeded by his son, Mr. Richard Graves, who carried it on until 1897.

In the manor of Ellenborough Mr. Senhouse of Netherhall began to work coal in a small way about 1740. In 1767 he let his colliery at Ellenborough to Messrs. Monkhouse and Laws, who required coal for their glass works. The colliery having been surrendered, Mr. Senhouse resumed working it in 1772.

In 1772 Ellenborough Colliery or Mally Pit produced 60 tons of coal per week, and in 1786 the output had risen to 500 tons a week.

Soon afterwards Mr. Senhouse engaged Mr. George Wrightson of Byker, Newcastle-on-Tyne, to be his viewer. In 1790 he erected a 'fire-engine' made by the Carron Company at the new winning, Great Pit, Ellenborough. It had a 36 in. cylinder, and the pumps were 9 in. diameter. In 1792 it was removed to a more advantageous position at Engine Pit in Ellenborough Gill.

From 1786 to 1790 Morrison, Ashley, Common, Martin, Gavel and Meadow Pits were sunk. In 1790 the output was about 250 tons a week.

After 1790 Gill, Kirkborough, Beck Moor, Brick and Ann Pits were sunk.

Mr. Senhouse continued working Ellenborough Colliery until 1808. None of the Ellenborough Pits had yet been sunk below the Senhouse High Band, then called the Orfeur Seam.

It will be convenient to refer here to the adjacent Ewanrigg estate belonging to Mr. Christian, because after 1849 Mr. Joseph Harris carried on both Ewanrigg and Ellenborough Collieries. Prior to 1755 Mr. John Christian had sunk pits in his manor of Ewanrigg. He and his son, Mr. John Christian Curwen, sank John or Dog Kennel, Henry, William, Thompson, Cass, Rough Ground, Mall Scott, Middle Tarn and High Pits to the Cannel Band.

Ewanrigg and Broughton Collieries were from an early period worked together; and at the latter coal was worked from numerous shallow pits.

In 1755 Messrs. Humphrey Senhouse, Netherhall ; John Christian, Ewanrigg ; Thomas Hartley, John Gale, Edmund Gibson, Whitehaven ; and James Postlethwaite, Maryport, entered upon Broughton Colliery. They worked the 'Main' and 'Little' Bands at the Three Quarters, East and West Saw Pits, at the rate of 200 tons a week.

During 1773 Mr. Christian bought out the other partners in Broughton Colliery, which he, and afterwards his son, Mr. John Christian Curwen, carried on in connection with the Ewanrigg Colliery.

During twenty-six years ended 1781, 765,530 tons, of 36 Winchester bushels each, were raised from Broughton pits.

In 1802 Mr. J. C. Curwen took a lease of Broughton Colliery from the Earl of Egremont, who stipulated that Ewanrigg level should be extended to No. 35 Pit in Broughton Moor. This water-level had been made from the low ground, near Ewanrigg Hall, to the Cannel Band in Broughton, and on its extension measured, with its branches, nearly 2 miles. Mr. Christian also constructed a wooden waggon-way from Broughton pits to the Arches near Ewanrigg Hall, whence the coals were carted to Maryport. In 1812 18,498 tons of coal were raised at Mr. Curwen's Broughton Colliery, chiefly from the Cannel Band.

The area mined in Broughton Moor is divided into six distinct strips by north and south faults. In the most westerly of these divisions next to Flimby, Seaton, and Ribton, Mr. Curwen sank Middle Tarn, High Tarn, Brough and Country Pits, and Messrs. Ross, Fletcher & Co., Wyndham Pit. In the next or second division to the east, separated from the first by an upthrow west fault of 20 fathoms, were Old Level, Fiery, Low Tarn, and Standing-stone Pits, sunk by Mr. Curwen. Buckhill Pit is in this tract. The third tract, separated from the second by an up east fault of 30 fathoms, is studded with numerous old pits, including Philip Pit, sunk by Mr. Curwen, at the north, and old Ruston Pit at the south. In the fourth tract, separated from the third by an upthrow west fault of 18 fathoms, were numerous old pits (sunk along the outcrop near a down east fault of 30 fathoms which divides the fourth and fifth tracts), and Bertha Pit from which coal was worked to the south as far as Bradmoor Pits. In the fifth tract, the chief pits were the Henry or Nelson (closed in 1862), and Mary Pits. In the sixth tract, furthest to the east, separated from the fifth by an upthrow east fault of 12 fathoms coal was worked from the fault to the outcrop by scores of old pits, extending to Little Broughton.

In recent years a piece of Cannel Band, in the northern part of the sixth tract, was wrought from Road End Pit up to the outcrop.

From 1837 to 1856 Messrs. Ross, Fletcher & Co. worked Wyndham, Standing-stone, Nelson, Mary and Road End Pits.

In 1860 Mr. John Harris, Darlington, sank the first Bertha Pit, and worked it until 1872, when Mr. Robert Wilson took the northern portion of Broughton Moor, upon which the new Bertha Pit is sunk, and Messrs. I. and W. Fletcher took the remainder of Lord Leconfield's Broughton royalty on which Buckhill Pit is sunk.

At Bertha Pit, 72 fathoms to the Lickbank Seam, the seams below the Cannel Band are now being worked by the Flimby and Broughton Moor Coal and Firebrick Co., Ltd., Mr. Wilson's successors.

At Buckhill Pit 66 fathoms deep to the Little Main Seam, the Main, Yard, and Little Main Seams are being worked by the Allerdale Coal Co., Ltd., who succeeded Messrs. Fletcher.

Near Dearham boundary, in the township of Little Broughton, the Ten Quarters Seam was worked to Lonsdale Pit, Dearham, until its abandonment in 1894.

In 1898 Messrs. Williamson and Walton sank Alice Pit, Outfields, in Little Broughton, to the Ten Quarters Seam.

To revert to Ewanrigg and Ellenborough Collieries. Ewanrigg Colliery was worked by the Christian family up to 1836, when it was taken by Mr. A. W. Hillary, son of Sir William Hillary, who worked the colliery up to 1840, when Mr. Joseph Harris took it. He abandoned the old pits and began a new winning, at Risehow, which was unsuccessful.

On entering upon Ellenborough Colliery, Mr. Joseph Harris began the sinking of No. 2 shaft which was completed to the Ten Quarters Seam, 100 fathoms, in 1851.

The Maryport Hæmatite Iron and Steel Co., Ltd., were lessees of the colliery from 1878 until 1891, when they went into liquidation.

From the shafts now open, the Rattler, Ten Quarters and Cannel and Metal Seams have been worked to the north up to the fault which throws in the Permian Sandstone, at Maryport.

In 1892 Ellenborough Colliery was closed.

In 1895 the present lessees, the Ellenborough Colliery Co., Ltd., took the colliery, and began working the Senhouse High Band.

In the parish of Dearham, Sir James Lowther, Whitehaven, was amongst the first to work coal. From 1723 to 1758 he worked the Dearham Crosa or Crosey Pits.

In 1728 Crosa Colliery, comprising Hazel, Gill and Wilson Pits, at which there were only 6 hewers, was under the supervision of Mr. Carlisle Spedding, Whitehaven.

From 1732 to 1736 Troughear, Bell, Reavel and Bowerham Pits, and from 1736 to 1750, Tolson, Fortune, Winder, Shilton, Grindall, Simond, Armstrong, Jacob, Fletcher, Gardner, Cason and Birkby Pits were sunk at Crosa.

In 1750 the output of coal at Crosa Pits was 100 tons a week.

In 1752 Hazel Gill and Wren, and in 1755 Cason Bell, Orfeur and Wilson Pits were producing a total output of 150 tons a week.

In 1758 Sir James Lowther was working Little and Sim Pits at Crosa, probably the last which he worked in Dearham.

Since then others have worked coal further up Row Beck towards Townhead.

In 1803 Mr. James Penn worked the Rattler Band from a pit 13 fathoms deep, near Dearham Hall ; and the pillars in the Ten Quarters Seam were being brought back from day-holes in the east bank at Row Beck.

In 1808 Dearham Row Colliery, on the opposite side of Row Beck, was at work.

About 1820 Mr. John Walker, Flimby Park Colliery, became lessee of the Earl of Lonsdale's Dearham royalty, and worked the Ten Quarters Seam at Hope, William and Bell Pits.

After his day his sons (Messrs. John and Thomas Walker), and after them Messrs. John Mackintosh and Thomas Walker (sons of Mr. Thomas Walker) further developed Dearham Colliery in the Ten Quarters and

Cannel and Metal Bands. They sank Scott, George, Croft and Victoria Pits, but their principal pits were Lowther and Lonsdale.

Lonsdale Pit was sunk in Dearham Out-gang about 1830. Several years afterwards, the pumping plant proving to be inadequate, the workings became flooded. The pumping engine was then removed to the new winning (completed in 1840), named Lowther Pit, in Garlic Gill; and Lonsdale Pit stood till 1852, when more powerful machinery was erected and enabled it to be re-opened.

In 1877 Messrs. J. M. and T. Walker sold Dearham Colliery to Mr. John Osmaston, Derby. The colliery was not successful during his tenancy, and was taken over by the Cumberland Union Banking Co., who carried on Lonsdale Pit, until 1894, when the lease was surrendered and the colliery abandoned.

Others besides the Walker family worked coal in Dearham after the Lowthers, but none to the like extent. In 1820 Mr. Ephraim Barker had a pit near Bell Pit, from which he worked the Ten Quarters Seam, at 14 fathoms; and in 1823 he was working a pit, 5 fathoms deep to the Cannel Band, at High Crosshow.

In 1840, Messrs. Ostle and Duglinson were working the Cannel Band, 30 fathoms deep, at a pit on the east bank of Row Beck, near Townhead. In its vicinity Messrs. Wood and Steel worked the Cannel and Metal Band at John Pit from 1846 to 1850. The same firm also sank, about 1842, Orchard Pit, near Dearham Hall, which was afterwards sunk by Mr. John Steel, M.P., to the Little Main Seam.

In 1842 waggon roads were made from the Dearham pits to the Maryport and Carlisle Railway.

In 1860 Orchard Pit, still worked by Mr. Steel, found employment for 80 persons, and produced about 11,000 tons of coal.

Messrs. W. Tickle & Sons were getting coal and fireclay, between 1866 and 1877, in Dearham, from the thin seams below the Yard Band out of adits on the east bank of the Ellen. From 1894 to 1901 Messrs. Steele and Beveridge were working coal and fireclay in the same locality.

After the abandonment of Lonsdale Pit, a company of working men re-opened a pit, worked by Mr. John Paitson in 1823, at Townhead, and began working the Cannel and Yard Bands between Lonsdale Pit workings, and Row Beck. The company went into liquidation in 1903.

At the same time the Dearham Colliery Co., Ltd., composed largely of working men,

was formed. They reopened the old shafts at Crosshow, and worked the 18 in. Little Main and Lickbank Seams until 1903, when the company went into liquidation.

In the parish of Dovenby the principal coal workings have been made in recent times near the outcrop of the Cannel Band, near Sepulchre Beck.

From 1830 to 1838 Messrs. Henry Tickle & Son worked the Cannel and Metal Band from a pit sunk south of Row Beck Mill.

About 1853 Messrs. Steel and Miller sunk a pit 25 fathoms deep near Dovenby Close and worked the Cannel and Metal, Yard and Little Main Seams until 1860.

The next venture was by Messrs. Harris and Carlton, who sank in 1872 a pit near the south-east corner of Dearham parish, and worked the Cannel and Metal, Yard, Little Main, and Brassey seams. Messrs. Harris & Son, Derwent Thread Mills, and afterwards Messrs. James and William Wood, Glasgow, continued the colliery until 1895, when it was laid in. Since then no coal has been worked in Dovenby.

The collieries that have been worked in Gilcrux parish lie between the Ellen and the fault which throws up the Carboniferous Limestone near the village. The first coal mining was by the Dykes family, Dovenby Hall, in 1740. In 1784 Miss Dykes, lady of the manor, and Mr. Sealby had each two pits at work in Gilcrux.

In 1807 the original Gilcrux Colliery, covering an area of 40 acres in the Metal and Ten Quarters Seams, which had been drained by the water mill at the 'Bob' Pit near the Ellen, was standing full of water. The actual working part of the colliery was so much troubled in 1807 that Mr. Grieve, Edinburgh, who was consulted, advised its removal from the vicinity of the springs at Gilcrux village and that a new winning be made west of the old Water Mill Pit.

In 1808 Mr. Grieve surveyed the route of a projected waggon road from Gilcrux Colliery to the sea at Blue Dial. At the same time he suggested the alternative scheme of an underground level from the sea at Blue Dial to Gilcrux Colliery, similar to the Bridge-water Canal, inasmuch as it could be used not only for the conveyance of coal but also for the drainage of the colliery.

Mr. Dykes did not live to carry out either of these proposals, and in 1831 his widow decided to lease the colliery. At that time the field of coal won by Jane Pit, the sole one then at work, was nearly exhausted.

In 1831 the colliery was leased to Messrs. William Quayle and Williamson Peile, colliery viewers, Whitehaven, and after their deaths carried on by their widows until the expiration of the lease in 1852.

Mr. Edward Bowes Steel then became the lessee of Gilcrux Colliery and continued to work Jane Pit. In 1854 Eliza Pit, or Ellenside Colliery, was sunk about a mile east of Jane Pit.

In 1860, when Messrs. John Steel, M.P., Cockermouth, and William Miller, Whitehaven, became the sub-lessees of the colliery, coal was worked at Jane and Eliza Pits. Jane Pit had then been sunk to the Yard Band, a depth of 76 fathoms, whence the upper and principal seams were gained by drifts through downthrow faults ; and, at Eliza Pit, the Ten Quarters Seam was worked. The total output at both pits was 250 tons a day.

In 1859 the sinking of Ellen Pit near Bullgill Station was commenced, and in 1862 was finished to the Lickbank Seam, a depth of 101 fathoms.

In 1866 Mr. Dykes granted a lease of the colliery to the Gilcrux Colliery Co., Ltd., who sublet it in 1868 to the Crosby Colliery Co., in which Mr. William Mulcaster, Flimby, was the managing partner ; and they worked it in conjunction with Crosby Colliery, comprising No. 1 and Rosegill Pits.

The sinking of No. 1 Crosby Pit was begun in 1854 and the Ten Quarters Seam was reached in 1856.

Rosegill Pit was completed to the Ten Quarters Seam in 1863, and subsequently the lower coal seams down to the Yard Band were won by a dip drift.

In 1867 No. 1 Crosby Pit was continued to the Little Main Seam, which however was only worked for a few years. The shaft was afterwards the upcast for the other two pits until 1893, when it was abandoned.

Crosby and Gilcrux Collieries were transferred to the Lonsdale Hæmatite Iron and Steel Co., Ltd., Whitehaven, in 1883, and in 1885, at No. 1 Crosby Pit, the dip drift which proved the Carboniferous Limestone, 60 fathoms below the Little Main Seam, was begun from that seam.

In 1896 the Bullgill Colliery Co., Ltd., took Crosby and Gilcrux Collieries, and Rosegill Pit was closed.

In 1901 the Bullgill Coal Co., Ltd., took over the Gilcrux, or Bullgill Colliery, and are now raising coal at Ellen Pit from the Crow Coal and Metal Band.

The manor of Birkby with that of Broughton was purchased in 1738 from the Duke of Wharton's trustees by Charles, Duke of Somerset, from whom it has descended to Lord Leconfield.

In 1781 Mr. John Christian, Ewanrigg, took a lease of Birkby Colliery from the Earl of Egremont.

In 1796 the vend of coal had increased to 6,430 tons.

The colliery was untenanted from 1802 to 1832, when Messrs. Tickle and Thompson leased it from the Earl of Egremont. They gave it up in 1836. Birkby royalty was let, from 1837 to 1856, to Messrs Ross, Fletcher and Thompson, who however did not work any coal there.

About 1860 Mr. W. Tickle established Birkby Brickworks and began to work from adits in both banks of the Ellen the thin seams of coal and fireclay below the Little Main.

From 1879 to 1883 Messrs. Croudace and Watson were tenants of Birkby works, which were then sold to a company promoted by Mr. David Burns, Carlisle. Mother Pit was then sunk to the Little Main Seam, 12 fathoms, and in 1893 a further depth of 10 fathoms to No. 2 Seam. Shortly afterwards the pit was abandoned, and thus ended all coal mining in Birkby.

The earliest reference to coal mining at Oughterside is in the will of William Orfeur, High Close, dated 1681, by which he bequeathed the gear belonging to his colliery at Oughterside to his son. An old map shows that in 1700 the Duke of Somerset had two pits north of Mr. Orfeur's colliery near the Ellen. Nicolson and Burn in 1777 recorded that there was then a good colliery at Oughterside. Coal mining in Oughterside was only on a small scale until 1830, when Mr. Kirkhaugh sank a pit at Westmoor to the Yard Band, a depth of 48 fathoms. The seams of coal in Oughterside are the Ten Quarters, 30 in., and Yard Bands. The two first are in the Whitehaven Sandstone, and are absent at Westmoor Pit; but were wrought at numerous old pits and by Mr. Fletcher at the Bank End Pit, abandoned in 1858.

Before the construction of the Maryport and Carlisle Railway, Oughterside coals were carted to staiths at Allonby for shipment. Mr. Kirkhaugh continued working his colliery until 1850, when he was succeeded by the Aspatria Coal Co. (Messrs. Westray, Fletcher and Bragg).

In 1857 the Yard Band was exhausted, and a trial of the 30 in. seam, 30 fathoms above, proved it to be unsatisfactory.

About the same time as Mr. Kirkhaugh began operations, Mr. Joseph Harris, Greysouthen, was engaged at old Domain Colliery, Oughterside, at Nos. 1, 3, and Hall Pits, where the Yard and 30 in. seam were extensively worked.

The old Domain Colliery was stopped in 1861.

In the Aspatria district, the Yard Band is found, in great perfection, upwards of 4 feet thick.

Mr. Joseph Harris, Greysouthen, embarked in coal-mining there in 1822, when he sank a pit in Plumbland, and worked the Yard Band up to the outcrop.

In 1826 Messrs. Drewry & Co., and in 1836 Mr. Thornthwaite, were working the Yard Band from pits at Arkleby.

In 1850 Mr. Harris, son of the lessee of the Plumbland and Oughterside Collieries, sank Nos. 1 and 2 Pits, Brayton Domain Colliery, from which the Yard Band was worked, until 1870, when the coal was exhausted up to the outcrop and to faults.

In 1869 Mr. Harris's trustees sank No. 3 Brayton Domain Pit, over a large downthrow fault, which puts in the Yard Band again to the east.

At No. 3 Pit, closed in 1902, a large tract of Yard Band has been worked eastward to the outcrop at Blennerhasset and Baggrow, and northwards to the Permian fault.

No. 4 Brayton Domain Pit was sunk near Brayton Junction, 1888–92, by Mr. Joseph Harris, Calthwaite Hall, 92 fathoms to the Yard Band, 5 ft. thick, beyond the fault, which was regarded, at one time, to be the northern limit of the coalfield.

East of No. 3 Pit is Allhallows Colliery, sunk near Mealsgate Station, by Messrs. I. and W. Fletcher, in 1874, to the Yard Band, 5 ft. thick, a depth of 105 fathoms. The Allerdale Coal Co., Ltd., who now have the colliery—the only one now at work in the eastern part of the coalfield, sank the Brayton Knowe Pit to the same seam in 1902.

East of Allhallows lie the old disused Priestcroft, Weary Hall, Crummock, and Bolton Collieries at the eastern termination of the coalfield where the Crow, Master and Yard Bands were worked. Coal in this region had been worked in 1567, but not very largely until the middle of the eighteenth century.

In 1782 two 'fire-engines,' one with a 42 in. and the other with a 30 in. cylinder, were advertised to be sold at Weary Hall Colliery.

In 1809 Messrs. Fawcett, Crosthwaite & Co. held a lease of Low Bolton and Weary Hall Collieries from the Earl of Egremont. The aggregate output for the year was 28,000 tons of coal.

Crummock Colliery lay to the east of Weary Hall Colliery. In 1830 the Crow and Master Bands were approaching exhaustion in that pit. A nip which occurs in those seams there was described by Mr. Williamson Peile in 1831.[1]

In 1858 Messrs. Thomas Addison & Co. had Bolton, Weary Hall and Crummock Collieries, and Messrs. Drewry & Co., Priestcroft Colliery near Mealsgate. In 1863 Priestcroft Colliery, and in 1865 Weary Hall Colliery, ceased work. Bolton Colliery, held by Messrs. Addison & Co., remained open till 1869. Coal was last worked in Bolton in 1874 by the Maryport Iron Company.

MID-CUMBERLAND COALFIELD

This title may be given to that part of the belt of Carboniferous Limestone strata, ranging from the eastern extremity of the western coalfield towards Penrith, in which several thin beds of coal have been worked, notably in Caldbeck and Warnell Fells.

According to Hutchinson, writing in 1794, Mr. Joseph Dobson, manager of Warnell Fell Colliery, had stated there was evidence to prove that coals had been dug there 300 years before that time. The Rev. Thomas Robinson, rector of Ousby, writing in 1709, said the seam of coal worked at Warnell was 18 in. thick, and that the colliery, which was very ancient, had 'served the neighbouring towns for some ages.'[2]

In 1738 Charles, Duke of Somerset, purchased from the trustees of the Duke of Wharton the manor of Caldbeck, including a colliery. Caldbeck Colliery down to 1750 was held under the Duke of Somerset; but it was leased by the Earl of Egremont to various tenants from that date to 1822, since when it has been unlet. In 1774 Sir James Lowther bought the manor of Warnell. Coal had then been worked in the manor at Holmes Colliery, where there were three powerful water 'bob' engines, and also at Stockdale Gill level driven into the high ground northeast of the Hall.

These collieries were standing in 1775, but Broadmoor Colliery near Shauk Beck, in the parish of Westward, was then at work. At Stockdale Gill Colliery the seam had been worked long-wall.

About 1780 the Rev. J. Watson, Cumrew, recorded that a few coals were got in Scalefield, Greystoke.

In 1794, according to Hutchinson, Warnell Colliery was a considerable undertaking, carried on by the Duke of Norfolk, who held it under the Duke of Portland ; but, owing

[1] *Trans. Nat. Hist. Soc. of Northumberland and Durham*, ii. 178–80.
[2] *An Essay towards a Nat. Hist. of Cumberland and Westmorland.*

to untoward circumstances, coal had not been worked for 40 years in Warnell Denton.

Jefferson, in 1840, alluded to unsuccessful trials for coal at Motherby and Hutton John, and remarked upon the poor quality of the coal got at Hewer Hill.

In 1839 Warnell Colliery, which had for years been standing, was restarted, under a lease from Lord Lonsdale, by Messrs. Taylor & Co., who sank two pits, 26 fathoms deep, in 1843, to the seam of coal, 20 inches thick, worked to the rise in the old colliery.

In 1851 nine hewers were getting coal there.

EAST CUMBERLAND COALFIELD

Until 1893 the coal produced in east Cumberland was obtained from two sources—the true Coal Measures and the Carboniferous Limestone series; but since then exclusively from the latter.

The Coal Measures in East Cumberland are at the western extremity of the Newcastle Coalfield, and extend along 'the 90 fathoms Dyke' for about one mile westward from Midgeholme (near the Northumberland boundary) and have an average width of half a mile.

The following coal seams, in this area, were passed through in the Midgeholme Pit :—

Seam	Thickness feet	Depth from surface fathoms
Five Quarters, or High Crag Nook . . .	4	38
Low Crag Nook . .	4	39
Three Quarters . .	2¼	48
Wellsyke	5	66
Slag, or Midgeholme .	5	80

A seam named the Low Main, 2 ft. 6 in. thick, 5 fathoms below the Midgeholme Seam, was proved through an upthrow fault met with in the workings. The coal measures dip 1 in 4 to the 'dyke.'

The Carboniferous Limestone series is thrown up to the surface in East Cumberland by the enormous dislocation called the 'Pennine fault,' which commences in Dumfriesshire and passes through Talkin Tarn, Renwick, Melmerby, Milburn, Dufton and Hilton to Brough in Westmorland.

Coal has been worked in the Carboniferous Limestone series, along the escarpment on the east side of the Pennine fault, chiefly from three seams found in the Yoredale or Upper Limestone division above the 'Whin Sill,' a bed of basaltic trap which varies in thickness from 24 ft. in some localities to 120 ft. in Alston Moor. In the Scar or Lower Limestone division, beneath the 'Whin Sill,' there

is one thin seam of coal which was worked formerly at Renwick.

In the Upper Limestone division the seams are the Top Coal, 4 in. to 6 ft. 2 in. thick; the Tindale coal, 3 ft. 3 in. to 5 ft. 2 in. thick; and the Hynam Coal, 2 ft. 3 in. thick,[1] from which coal has been mined at Ousby, Hartside, Alston, Croglin, Oakshaw, and other places, but to the greatest extent on the Earl of Carlisle's property at Tindale Fell and Talkin.

HISTORY

The record of an early attempt to prove coal in East Cumberland is in the books of the Newcastle Corporation, wherein it is stated that in 1522 coal was bored for on Greenside Rigg, in the parish of Farlam.[2]

In a household book of Lord William Howard there are entries, beginning in 1618, relating to coal exploration. In 1628 the sum which he paid for sinking a pit is recorded; and a little later on, it is stated that he sold, in one year, coal worth £61. The Crag Nook Seam was then being worked from the outcrop at Midgeholme, and boring for coal on Tindale Fell was in progress. During the next 100 years doubtlessly coal was worked on a small scale, but there are no records for that period.

Rev. T. Robinson, rector of Ousby, in 1709,[3] said the Coal Fell[4] Colliery was very ancient, and was then leased to Mr. Mowbray. In 1735 Charles, Earl of Carlisle, granted a lease of Coal Fell and other collieries in the barony of Gillesland to Mr. Thomas Howard.

In 1736 Crag Nook and Pryor Dyke Pits were at work, in the Coal Measures, between Roachburn and Midgeholme. The output, 400 loads per week, was all sold at the banks.

In 1739 the Earl of Carlisle was getting from 100 to 450 loads of coal per week at Midgeholme Pit.

In 1747 Lord Carlisle's Talkin Colliery comprised Caroline, Moss, and Wyatt 'Pits,' in reality adits, from which the Limestone coal seam was worked.

In 1769 the Earl of Carlisle was carrying on Tarnhouse or Tindale Fell Colliery, besides the Talkin and Midgeholme Collieries.

In 1775 the first railway to Tindale Fell Colliery was made on which cast-iron fish-bellied rails were used. This railway was made between Tindale Fell and Brampton, and the coals were conveyed along it in chaldron waggons drawn by horses. The waggon road

[1] Geol. Sur. Sheet, 106, S.W.
[2] *Carlisle Patriot*, 9 August, 1889.
[3] *Natural History of Cumberland and Westmorland.*
[4] Near Greenside.

did not take the same route exactly, nor was it so long as the existing railway which begins at Brampton and terminates at the Alston branch of the North Eastern Railway.

In 1808 wrought-iron rails were introduced on the Tindale Fell railway.

In 1818 Mr. R. Stevenson, Edinburgh, first called attention to Lord Carlisle's Colliery waggon way of malleable iron rails.

In 1824 Tindale Fell Colliery railway improvements came to be better known when the relative merits of a canal and a railway from Newcastle to Carlisle were under discussion, and doubts were cast on the permanency of the malleable iron rails. The *Newcastle Courant*, 7 December, 1824, quoted a letter by Mr. James Thompson, Kirkhouse, in which he stated that rails of this description, laid sixteen years previously, were then in use at Tindale Fell and presented no appearance of lamination.

In 1801 Tarnhouse, or Tindale Fell, and Talkin Collieries comprised Shop, Venture, Fox, Caroline and Chance drifts, and produced 197,015 loads of coal. The output rose to 278,615 loads in 1810, and the drifts then at work were William, Morpeth, Fox, George and Henry.

In 1819 the output had fallen to 198,859 loads of coal.[1] In that year the Earl of Carlisle appointed Mr. James Thompson to be his colliery agent. Mr. Thompson began the sinking of Blacksike Pit, Talkin, in 1819, and King Pit, Midgeholme, in 1821.

In the early part of Mr. Thompson's management Tarnhouse and Talkin Collieries consisted of Henry, Morpeth, West, George, Blacksike, Moss and Catch Pits or drifts.

In 1825 the Earl of Carlisle became the lessee of Croglin Colliery, belonging to the Earl of Egremont.

In 1829 Tarnhouse, Talkin and Midgeholme Collieries produced 34,795 chaldrons of coal, and Croglin Colliery 3,772 chaldrons. The pits drawing coals at the former were Henry, Blacksike and George.

In 1835, under Mr. Thompson's management, the output of Lord Carlisle's collieries, which comprised Howgill, Blacksike, King and George Pits, had risen to 76,002 chaldrons.

Mr. Thompson was a man of progressive ideas, as may be judged by the many improvements he effected on the Tindale Fell railway. But the greatest innovation which he introduced there was the adoption of the locomotive steam engine.

[1] A load was 3, and a chaldron, 36 imperial bushels.

In 1837 he purchased from the Liverpool and Manchester Railway Co. Stephenson's famous locomotive engine the 'Rocket,' and placed it upon the Earl of Carlisle's railway.

The 'Rocket' worked on the railway to Midgeholme from 1837 to 1844, and in 1862 Messrs. James Thompson & Sons presented it to the South Kensington Museum, where it may still be seen.

On 8 August, 1837, on the occasion of the polling for a member of Parliament in East Cumberland, the Alston returns were brought by conveyance to Midgeholme, where the 'Rocket' was in waiting and conveyed them to Kirkhouse, accomplishing the distance of four miles, it is said, in four and a half minutes.

In 1839 the Earl of Carlisle leased his collieries to Mr. James Thompson, who continued to develop the collieries with the same energy and ability that had characterized his administration of them for his lordship. Furthermore, he took practical steps to ameliorate the social condition of his workpeople by building improved dwellings, by carrying on a farm to supply their wants, and by initiating an allotment system by which each workman was allowed an acre of land upon which to graze a cow.

At the beginning of Mr. Thompson's lease coal was drawn from seams in the Coal Measures at King Pit, Midgeholme Colliery, and from the Limestone Seam at Howgill Pit, Tindale Fell, Blacksike Pit, Talkin and at Guide Pit, Croglin.

Midgeholme Colliery was just sunk within Cumberland, east of Tindale Fell.

Howgill 'Pit' was an adit near Howgill Burn, from which the coal under Tindale Fell was worked. The Limestone Seam had also been wrought at Morpeth, Henry, Stagg, Fox, Hazard and Colliery Thorn drifts, which, with Howgill drift, constituted Tarn House, or Tindale Fell Colliery, carried on with Clowsgill Lime Works.

Talkin Colliery, or Blacksike Pit, lay a mile to the west of Tindale Fell Colliery. It was a shaft 30½ fathoms deep to the Limestone Coal, 3 ft. 2 in. thick, which had also been worked from Caroline, Duke, Dove, Wyatt, Venture, Shop, West and William day-levels.

Geltsdale Colliery, situated about two miles south of Talkin Colliery, comprised Moss and George drifts where the Limestone Coal, 4 ft. thick, was worked.

Guide Pit, Croglin Colliery, was about three miles south-west of Geltsdale Colliery, on Croglin Fell. A seam 1 ft. 4 in. thick, in the Limestone Series, was worked there for lime burning.

No account of Mr. James Thompson, the first lessee of the Naworth Collieries, would be complete without reference to the 'dandies' or carriages which he put on to the colliery railway for the convenience of his workpeople who lived at Midgeholme, Howgill and Forest Head, going to Brampton on market days. The first 'dandies' were drawn by horses. Mr. James Thompson died in 1851, having 'laid the foundation of that large, prosperous, and self-supporting colony of miners that now exists along the sides of Tindale, Haltonlea and other neighbouring Fells.'[1]

He was succeeded by his son, Mr. Thomas Charles Thompson, who continued the good work initiated by his father, and on his death the Blenkinsop and Naworth collieries, which in 1820 only gave occupation to 180 men, afforded work for nearly 1,000 hands. Mr. T. C. Thompson died in 1888 and was followed in the control of the collieries by his sons, Mr. Charles Lacy Thompson and Mr. James Thompson.

Howard Pit was sunk in 1875 near old Coalfell Colliery and abandoned in 1896.

At the present day the Roachburn Colliery, situated between Brampton Junction and Lambley, and Bishop Hill drift near Tindal Tarn, from both of which the Limestone Coal is worked, are the only places where coal is being raised, in Cumberland, at Naworth Collieries.

In addition, Messrs. Thompson & Sons are working, from Blenkinsopp Colliery, Greenhead, Northumberland, coal from the Little Limestone Seam within the parish of Midgeholme in Cumberland. At Blenkinsopp the Little Limestone Seam is reached from the hillside by a stone drift about one mile long, and thence there is a haulage road in that seam into the Midgeholme coal for a further distance of three miles.

The quantity of Little Limestone Coal wrought in Cumberland, but brought to bank at Blenkinsopp, about 40,000 tons a year, is included in the Government returns for Northumberland.

Coal has been worked from early times at other places from the Carboniferous Limestone Series along the Pennine range, mainly for lime-burning.

The most important of such mining was at Croglin.

The manor of Croglin was purchased in 1738 by Charles, Duke of Somerset, from the trustees of the Duke of Wharton, and included a colliery which was worked continuously from that date until 1864, when all operations ceased. From 1759 it was held under the Earl of Egremont by various lessees, the most important of whom were the Earl of Carlisle, who worked the colliery from 1825 to 1839, and Messrs. James Thompson & Sons, who had it from 1839 to 1852. It remained unlet till 1854, when Mr. Joseph Watson took it and carried it on up to its finish in 1864.

The coal workings at Hartside and Renwick were as early as any in the Crossfell range.

Singleton's 'Account of Melmerby,' a MS. in the library of the Dean and Chapter at Carlisle, dated 1677, refers to coal mining at Hartside and Renwick.

The Rector of Ousby, in 1709, also referred to the collieries on Hartside and Renwick Fells, where a seam of coal 18 in. thick was worked.

In 1777, according to Nicolson and Burn, and in 1794, according to Hutchinson, Renwick Colliery was let at £33 a year.

In 1888 boreholes, put down at Rayson Hall, Ousby, in the Upper Limestone Series, proved several seams of coal, varying in thickness from a few inches to 4 feet; and in 1892 Mr. T. Kirkbride, Arlecdon, was reported to have struck a promising seam of coal on the same property.

M. Jars, in 1765, described the Crow Coal, in the mountains of Alston Moor, as being unfit for the forge, but excellent for burning lime.

At the present time Messrs. Benson & Co. at Alston drift; the Veille Montagne Zinc Co. at Dowgang and Guttergill, Nenthead; and the Alston and Nentforce Quarry Co., are the only producers of coal at Alston, and, in the aggregate, do not employ more than 40 persons underground. The three firms are all working the 'Little Limestone Coal,' which, in the Alston district, is found in two distinct seams, lying 20 feet apart, the upper being about 20 in. and the lower 12 in. thick.

Several thin seams of coal have been worked in the Carboniferous Limestone Series, in the parish of Bewcastle, and at Penton, near the Liddle. At the latter place a shaft was sunk in 1836, 19 fathoms, and proved several seams of coal.

In Bewcastle the last coal mining was at Oakshaw, on Black Line river, where a small quantity of coal was worked from a seam 18 in. thick, from 1898 to 1900.

STATISTICS

Output.—Prior to 1854, no reliable record of

---

[1] *Carlisle Journal*, 13 March, 1888.

the production of coal from Cumberland mines had been kept. In that year the publication of mineral statistics by Mr. Robert Hunt, of the Mining Record Office, was commenced.

Since 1872 the Home Office has issued annual Blue Books, which give more reliable statistics than Mr. Hunt's figures, which were little better than approximations compiled from voluntary returns and estimates.

In 1854 the output of coal for Cumberland was 887,000 tons. In 1873 it had risen to 1,747,064 tons, but dropped to 1,102,267 tons the following year. In 1877 it had recovered to 1,515,783 tons, but fell away the ensuing year to 1,388,283 tons. Then it advanced, with slight relapses in 1882 and 1884, up to 1,796,594 tons in 1887. After then the output declined until 1892, when it was only 1,424,749 tons. Next year saw a marked improvement, and in 1894 the production reached 2,058,867 tons, which was the 'record' quantity until 1898, when 2,061,878 tons were produced. In 1901, 2,108,360 tons were raised.

Employees.—In 1854 the number was 3,579; in 1884, 6,480; in 1899, 7,897; and in 1901, 8,884.

Exports.—Before 1836 coals were sold by measure—sometimes by chaldron but generally by waggon. Over measure was prevented by a 'streaker,' placed at a certain height above the railway. Originally the waggon contained 2 tons, but the contents were increased, as time went on, to 42, 44, 45 and eventually to 50 cwt. On account of the uncertain size of the waggon, the measure in which up to 1836 the exports was invariably expressed, there is considerable difficulty in determining the weights at different periods and places.

In 1765 M. Jars said that it was alleged that the collieries at Whitehaven, Workington, Harrington and Maryport produced each day 1,000 tons of 14 cwt. each.

Assuming that such a rate of export was maintained for 250 days throughout the year, the total quantity of coal shipped at the four ports must have been 175,000 tons.

Hutchinson gives the exports for 12 years, 1781 to 1792, in waggons. Assuming the waggons to have each contained 2 tons of coal, the quantities exported in 1781, 1788 and 1792 were :—

	1781 Tons	1788 Tons	1792 Tons
Whitehaven . .	111,200	158,124	111,944
Workington, Maryport and Harrington .	110,256	150,966	157,480
	221,456	309,090	269,424

From 1792 no complete account can be given of the coal shipments at each of the Cumberland ports, excepting Whitehaven.

During Mr. Bateman's absence from the management of the Whitehaven Collieries the Whitehaven exports had dwindled to 90,628 tons in 1802 ; but, on his return in 1803, they at once bounded up to 153,728 tons. They kept to about that figure until 1808, when 201,766 tons were shipped, and after several fluctuations reached 220,386 tons in 1814. Between 1814 and 1831 the Whitehaven coal shipments never exceeded 200,000 tons per annum.

In 1831 and 1839 the coals shipped were :

	1831 Tons	1839 Tons
Whitehaven . .	204,543	230,287
Maryport . .	66,298	99,382
Workington . .	78,080	61,741
Harrington . .	14,233	47,692
	363,154	439,102

In 1855 and 1865 the coal exports (Harrington not given) were :—

	1855 Tons	1865 Tons
Whitehaven .	212,665	148,043
Maryport . .	286,106	466,701
Workington .	112,426	146,506
	611,197	761,250

In 1867, 476,162 tons of coal were exported from Maryport, the largest quantity that has ever been shipped in one year from any port in Cumberland.

In 1873 the Whitehaven shipments, owing to a strike, sank to 89,434 tons—the lowest quantity recorded since 1781.

The following figures, taken from mineral statistics issued by the Home Office, show the fluctuations in Cumberland coal exports up to 1901 :—

	Whitehaven Tons	Maryport Tons	Workington & Harrington Tons	Total Tons
1885 .	183,599	191,796	82,824	458,219
1897 .	300,442 [1]	169,190	106,141	575,773
1901 .	253,401	236,167	114,127	603,695

---

[1] The greatest shipment of coal at Whitehaven.

LIST OF COLLIERIES (43) IN THE YEAR 1900

Colliery	Situation	Owner	Persons employed
Allhallows	Mealsgate . .	Allerdale Coal Co.	316
Alston Drift	Alston . . .	Wm. Benson	15 [1]
Asby	Asby . . .	Asby Coll. Co.	50
Birkby Drift	Birkby . .	Steele & Co.	24
Bishop Hill	Brampton . .	Thompson & Sons	7 [1]
Branthwaite Drift . .	Branthwaite .	Branthwaite Coll. Co.	5
Brayton Domain, No. 3 Pit	Aspatria . .	Jos. Harris	227
„ „ No.4 „	Brayton . .	„	488
Broughton Moor . . .	Broughton . .	Flimby & Broughton Moor Coal etc. Co. .	364
Buckhill	Broughton . .	Allerdale Coal Co.	350
Bullgill	Bullgill . . .	Bullgill Coal Co.	239
Camerton	Camerton . .	Camerton Coll. etc. Co.	151
Clifton	Clifton . . .	Allerdale Coal Co.	436
Crosshow	Dearham . .	Dearham Coal Co.	142
Dean Moor	Dean Moor .	Dean Moor Coll. Co.	67
Dowgang	Nenthead . .	Veille Montagne Co.	7 [1]
Ellenborough	Maryport . .	Ellenborough Coll. Co.	252
Gillhead	Flimby . . .	Gillhead Coal etc. Co.	41
Greengill	Camerton . .	Camerton Coll. etc. Co.	17
Guttergill	Alston . . .	Veille Montagne Co.	7 [1]
Harrington, No. 5 Pit .	Harrington . .	James Bain & Co.	20
„ No. 7 „ .	„ . .	„	72
„ No. 9 „ .	„ . .	„	319
Marron Drift	Clifton . . .	Allerdale Coal Co.	9
Montreal	Moor Row . .	John Stirling	81
Moorhouse Guards . .	Seaton . . .	Seaton Firebrick Co.	38
Oakshaw	Bewcastle . .	Richard Mitchell	5 [1]
Oatlands	Distington . .	Moresby Coal Co.	207
Outfields	Broughton . .	Outfields Coll. Co.	85
Renwick	Renwick . .	Robert Watson	2 [1]
Roachburn	Brampton . .	Thompson & Sons	278 [1]
Robin Hood	Flimby . . .	Flimby & Broughton Moor Coal etc. Co. .	384
Rock Hill	Alston . . .	Alston & Nentforce Limestone Quarry Co.	6 [1]
Seaton Moor	Seaton Moor .	Flimby & Broughton Moor Coal etc. Co. .	67
St. Helens, Nos.1 & 2 Pits	Flimby . . .	St. Helens Coll. etc. Co. Ltd.	97
„ No. 3 Pit . .	Siddick	„ „ „	771
Townhead	Dearham . .	Townhead Coll. Co.	22
Walkmill	Moresby . .	Moresby Coal Co.	354
Watergate	Flimby . . .	Flimby & Broughton Moor Coal etc. Co. Ltd.	402
Whitehaven, Croft Pit .	Sandwith . .	Whitehaven Coll. Co.	626
„ Wellington Pit	Whitehaven .	„ „	500
„ William „	„ . .	„ „	1,055
Wood Drift	Camerton . .	Camerton Colliery etc. Co.	41
			8,646

[1] Working coal in the Carboniferous Limestone Series.

HÆMATITE MINING

A history of hæmatite mining in Cumberland would be incomplete without some reference to the subject in its earliest infancy. Unfortunately, very few trustworthy records are obtainable prior to the dawn of the Victorian era, and this precludes the possibility of any connected account being given of the early working of this important mineral. Judging however from the slag heaps that are found scattered over the mountains and dales of many parts of the Cumberland lake district, where small veins of hæmatite are known to exist in the syenite and other older rocks, it may be safely asserted that as far back as the time of the Romans iron ore was worked and smelted by the primitive methods then in use.

In Mr. J. D. Kendall's recent work, entitled *The Iron Ores of Great Britain and Ireland*, mention is made of an iron ore mine in the parish of Egremont near Whitehaven, as far back as the twelfth century, and the same author also refers to iron ore having been worked intermittently at Yeathouse in the parish of Arlecdon during the seventeenth century. These doubtless were merely surface scratchings. Hutchinson states that there was 'at Crowgarth (in Cleator parish) the most singular mine of iron ore supposed to be in Great Britain,' and that 'in 1790, and 1791, the annual exportation from this source to the Carron foundry in Scotland, amounted to over 20,000 tons.' The same author also says that 'in the parish of Arlochden (Arlecdon) freestone, iron ore, coal and limestone are found and worked.'[1]

It was not until about the year 1825 that the value of the Whitehaven district as an important mining field began to be appreciated, and that any regular and systematic working of hæmatite was attempted. The early pioneers in the discovery and opening up of the great mineral wealth, which was destined to play so important a part in the iron industry of the country during the reign of Queen Victoria, were Mr. Anthony Hill of the Plymouth Iron Works, South Wales, Mr. R. Barker and Messrs. Fitzsimmons & Co., who under leases from the Earl of Egremont began to work the outcrop ore at Bigrigg in the parish of Egremont, and that near the surface at Crowgarth in Cleator parish. No certain record of the output

[1] *History of Cumberland*, ii. 30, 89 (published 1794).

raised at this time seems to be obtainable, but that the lessees mentioned were fairly successful is evidenced by the fact of other mining adventurers shortly afterwards commencing operations. In Mr. Kendall's work already referred to, two instances are given of the finding of old oak spades about this time, one at Langhorne in Egremont parish, and the other at Yeathouse in Arlecdon parish. Another instance of the relics of ancient mining came under the writer's own observation when working (about the year 1872) a shallow deposit of ore on the Crossfield estate near Cleator Moor, and within a short distance of the Crowgarth mine mentioned by Hutchinson. At about 5 or 6 fathoms from the surface, several rounded pieces of old oak were found, which had the appearance of having been parts of old mining implements, showing that workings had been carried on here also at a very early date.

The first records of the quantity of iron ore raised in Cumberland are given by Mr. Richard Meade, assistant keeper of mining records, in his work entitled *The Coal and Iron Industries of the United Kingdom*. He gives the output and the number of mines at work in the year 1849 as follows :—

Position of mine	Number of pits	Name of owner or firm	Output
Cleator .	2	Messrs. Ainsworth & Co.	30,000
Bigrigg .	4	Messrs. Hill & Co. .	20,000
Gutterby	3	Mr. John Lindow .	20,000
Yeathouse	2	Messrs. Tulk & Ley	15,000
Woodend	2	Messrs. Attwood & Co.	15,000
	13		100,000

Between the years 1849 and 1855 there does not appear to have been any complete record of output kept, but from the latter year onwards, the total annual quantity raised is given in the Board of Trade mining returns. The outputs from the individual mines are not shown until the year 1872, when the first metalliferous Mines Act came into operation. Tables containing these outputs will be given and made use of hereafter. The output of iron ore for the year 1855 was 200,000 tons, showing an increase of 100,788 tons over that of 1849. This increase of production clearly proves that

A HISTORY OF CUMBERLAND

between these periods hæmatite mining in the Whitehaven district had received an impetus, and that the district, as an important mineral field, was being more fully recognized and was attracting greater attention and larger capital to its development.

Prior to the year 1856 only five blast furnaces had been erected. These were as follows:—

Name of ironworks	Owners	Furnaces built	Furnaces in blast
Cleator Moor	Whitehaven Hæmatite Iron Co.	4	3
Harrington .	C. H. Plevins . .	1	0
		5	3

Ironworks at Seaton (Messrs. Smith & Co.) were put in blast in 1857. In 1856, 259,167 tons of hæmatite were raised in the Whitehaven district, of which 152,875 tons were carried by rail, and 39,617 tons were smelted at the local ironworks. The destinations of this ore, as well as that raised in 1857, when the production reached 323,812 tons, were as follows:—

Destination	Quantities 1856	1857
South Wales	124,630	163,354
Staffordshire	26,768	36,758
Newcastle	51,470	44,489
Scotland	15,865	22,377
France	817	323
	219,550	267,301
District Ironworks . .	39,617	56,511
Total	259,167	323,812

A large proportion of this ore was carted from the mines to Whitehaven harbour, the principal port of Cumberland, and shipped to the various smelting centres in England, Scotland and Wales; only a small quantity (as will be seen from the above table) was consumed locally. The high railway rates for east coast coke at this time appear to have deterred capitalists from building local furnaces, as, with the exception of an extension of the Harrington ironworks in 1857, and the erection of the Workington ironworks in 1858, it was not until 1863, when the West Cumberland Iron and Steel Co. began opera-

tions, that any additions were made to the ironworks already mentioned.

The following is a list of the ironworks and the year of their erection from 1857:—

Year of erection	Name of ironworks	Place of erection
1857	Harrington . .	Harrington
1858	Workington . .	Workington
1863	West Cumberland	Workington
1870	Maryport . . .	Maryport
1870	Solway	Maryport
1870	Millom . . .	Millom
1872	Moss Bay . . .	Workington
1872	Lonsdale . . .	Whitehaven
1873	Parton	Parton
1874	Derwent . . .	Workington
1876	Lowther . . .	Workington
1879	Distington . . .	Distington

The Whitehaven Hæmatite Ironworks at Cleator Moor, of which special mention has been made, were erected in the year 1841.

The important discovery of the Bessemer process about the year 1856 caused an increasing demand for Cumberland hæmatite, and hence the ore was year by year more largely exported into the other iron smelting centres of the kingdom, where, being mixed with the ores of these districts, it greatly improved the quality of the manufactured iron and steel.

A great impetus was given to the development of hæmatite mining in the Whitehaven district by the opening of the Whitehaven, Cleator and Egremont railway (now worked by the London and North Western and Furness joint railways) to Egremont and Frizington, in 1857. This railway was opened for passenger traffic on June 1 of that year, although a portion of the mineral traffic had been conveyed to Whitehaven for a short time prior to that date. It was extended to Rowrah in 1863, and finally to Marron in 1865, forming there a junction with the Cockermouth and Penrith railway. A connection with the Furness railway was also effected by an extension southwards from Egremont to Sellafield. The phenomenal advance of the district as an important mining centre very soon made this railway one of the best dividend paying concerns in the kingdom. Before the opening of the Whitehaven, Cleator and Egremont railway, all the ore raised in the Whitehaven district, with the exception of that consumed at the local ironworks, was carted to Whitehaven (a distance of from three to five miles), where, in the

386

event of there being no vessel in readiness in the harbour, the ore was deposited in the depôts situated in different parts of the town. Mr. Thos. Ainsworth, Messrs. Attwood & Son, and Messrs. Tulk & Ley each owned one of these depôts.

The following mines were at work in the neighbourhood of Whitehaven in the year 1858, when the output of hæmatite was 331,544 tons, of which quantity the Parkside mines alone raised 96,107 tons.

Parishes	Names of mines	Names of owners
Egremont	Bigrigg Moor, etc.	S. & J. Lindow
	Bigrigg . .	Anthony Hill
	Bigrigg . .	Wilson, Peile & Co.
	Langhorne .	Lord Lonsdale
	Woodend . .	Henry Attwood & Son
Cleator .	Cleator . .	Thos. Ainsworth
	Crowgarth .	Anthony Hill
	Jacktrees . .	S. & J. Lindow
	Todholes . .	John Stirling
Arlecdon.	Birks . . .	H. Attwood & Son
	Frizington Parks	D. & J. H. Robinson & Co.
	High House .	S. W. Smith & Co.
	Parkside . .	Fisher, Dees, Fletcher & Co.
	Yeathouse. .	Fletcher, Miller & Co.
Salter and	Salter . . .	Nicholson & Co.
Eskett	Eskett . . .	D. & J. H. Robinson & Co.
Lamplugh	Knockmurton	Thos. Carmichal
	Agnes . . .	Fletcher, Miller & Co.

This list is taken from the *Mineral Statistics of Great Britain and Ireland*, by Robert Hunt, F.R.S., Keeper of Mining Records, but each mine is here arranged under its respective parish.

Before proceeding further with the historical part of the subject, it is desirable that a brief general outline should be given of the districts, geological position, and modes of occurrence of the hæmatite of Cumberland.

DISTRICTS.—(1) That known as the 'Whitehaven district,' lying to the north-east and south-east of Whitehaven, and extending from Knockmurton in the parish of Lamplugh in the north to the town of Egremont in the south, covering a distance of between seven and eight miles. This district has hitherto been the source from which the largest portion of the hæmatite raised in the county has been obtained. The iron ore bearing area embraces the parishes of Lamplugh, Salter and Eskett, Arlecdon, Cleator and Egremont. As it may be of advantage in localizing the

individual mines, these will be afterwards dealt with and classified under their respective parishes.

(2) The district around Millom, known as the 'Millom district,' forming the extreme south-eastern portion of Cumberland, and embracing the extensive mines of Hodbarrow in Millom parish, and Whicham and Silecroft in the parish of Whicham.

(3) The Eskdale valley, near Boot, in the parish of St. Bees, occupying a central position between the Whitehaven and Millom districts.

(4) The Alston Moor or Weardale district, in the north-eastern part of the county.

GEOLOGICAL POSITION. *Districts 1 and 2.* The hæmatite deposits in the first two districts mentioned occur principally in the carboniferous or mountain limestone, which rests immediately (as in the Whitehaven district) on the Skiddaw slate of the lower Silurian system, and in the Millom district, on the Borrowdale or Coniston series of rocks. The greatest aggregate thickness of the beds comprising this limestone formation has been found to be over 900 feet.

The carboniferous limestone series is divided into seven distinct beds, as follows :—

> First, or top limestone.
> Second   „
> Third   „
> Fourth, or clints „
> Fifth   „
> Sixth   „
> Seventh   „

The largest and best deposits of hæmatite are most commonly found in the first and second beds, although good payable bodies of ore have been discovered and worked in the whole series. A large number of 'faults' traverse the limestone, running for the most part north-west and south-east, at angles varying from 5° to 25° from the magnetic meridian. These are termed 'north and south' faults. A smaller number of 'east and west' faults also occur, some of them of considerable importance. It is along the line of these 'faults,' or in close proximity thereto, that the best deposits of hæmatite are found. There are three forms of hæmatite occurrence, viz. vein-like, bed-like, and irregular and patchy masses, the latter locally termed 'pockets,' 'sops' and 'guts,' the. gut-like deposits continuing longitudinally for considerable distances and frequently running parallel to the 'faults' which are found near them. Veins of hæmatite also occur in the Skiddaw slate at Kelton Fell and Knockmurton, and, as will be seen later on, these have been worked largely and profitably during the last thirty years.

District 3. The veins or hæmatite most largely worked in the Eskdale valley, near Boot, occur in the granite, and for some time attracted considerable attention. Veins of ore also occur, as has been already said, in the syenite and other igneous rocks throughout the more mountainous parts of the county, but these have rarely been found of sufficient size to be profitably worked.

District 4. The brown hæmatite of Alston Moor is found in the limestone at Kilhope Fell. It is associated with the important and rich lead veins of the district, but owing to its uncertain quantity and variable quality, the ore has not been worked on a large scale.

The first of the following two analyses is an average of a number of samples of first class hæmatite from Salter and Eskett parish in the Whitehaven district, and the second is from a sample of similar ore from Cleator parish in the same district. The average yield of metallic iron from ores of the Whitehaven district has however been materially reduced of late years, and reasons are afterwards given explanatory of this fact.

ANALYSES OF HÆMATITE FROM THE WHITEHAVEN DISTRICT

	No. 1	No. 2
Ferric oxide	82·285	85·461
Manganous oxide. . .	·419	·055
Alumina	3·062	3·017
Magnesia	·180	
Lime		·904
Silica	10·525	7·400
Carbonic acid	·600	
Phosphoric acid . . .	·042	·022
Sulphur	·144	·074
Water	2·204	3·100
	99·461	100·033
Metallic iron	57·60	59·82

The yield of metallic iron from some of the richest samples of this district ranged from 60 to 65 per cent. Analyses of hæmatite from Millom (Hodbarrow) and Eskdale will be given later, when further dealing with these districts.

The total output of Cumberland hæmatite from the year 1855 to 1860 inclusive is shown in the following table :—

Year	Output of hæmatite, Whitehaven district	Alston Moor district	Total output of hæmatite	Value of output
1855 . . .	200,788		200,788	£110,433
1856 . . .	259,167	8,089	267,256	146,991
1857 . . .	323,812	10,113	333,925	183,659
1858 . . .	331,544	17,094	348,638	183,478
1859 . . .	400,306	1,871	402,177	201,088
1860 . . .	466,851	1,930	468,781	222,671
	1,982,468	39,097	2,021,565	£1,048,320

From 1858 the production of hæmatite increased at a very rapid rate, and mining operations which had hitherto been confined to the outcrop and shallower deposits were largely extended.

Boring (which was the principal method used for ascertaining the depth and position of the ore) was also vigorously carried on. A very prevalent idea was held by many of the older miners about this time that it was useless to bore or prove the ground below the first bed of limestone, and many instances of disappointment have occurred where, by the stoppage of boring operations too soon, large and valuable deposits of hæmatite remained undiscovered. These were found after the royalty had been given up by the first lessees and retaken by others possessing greater enterprise, and stimulated by discoveries at lower

depths in other parts of the district. Owing to the erratic deposition of hæmatite, a large amount of capital had necessarily to be spent in this way in prospecting the various royalties in the district, and even after mines had become productive in many royalties, boring was extensively carried on, as being the best means of maintaining and increasing the output. In one instance over 250 boreholes were put down in a royalty having an area of about 65 acres. In this case however the greater number of these were only to shallow depths, having been bored between the years 1865 and 1872. Many of the later borings in this royalty were put down over 100 fathoms to the slate rock. Percussion boring by means of the 'spring-pole,' worked by hand, was the method first adopted in the Whitehaven district. Afterwards the boring engine and 'tilt-pole' were brought into use, and later, during the year 1873, the diamond boring system was introduced by Mr. John Vivian, C.E., and largely carried on in Cumberland. This method of boring, although considerably more costly per fathom of ground bored, has decided compensating advantages both in saving of time and in securing solid cores of the various strata passed through. It is still most successfully carried on by Messrs. Vivians' Boring and Exploration Co. Ld. of Whitehaven; and Mr. Vivian, the managing director of the company, has devoted much time and attention to improve the system, with the result that its capabilities for producing a perfect cylindrical core from over 3,000 feet are unsurpassed. The apparatus consists of a crown head screwed on to a cylindrical core tube, which head is set on the face with diamonds (carbon or bort). This is caused to revolve and cuts an annular ring in the rock, leaving a solid core for withdrawal in the core tube; water is used for flushing away the debris from the crown face and keeping it cool. The Diamond Boring Co. have put down 165 boreholes in Cumberland, the total depth bored being 103,833 feet. The aggregate thickness of hæmatite passed through was 1,159½ feet.

In 1871 a remarkable upward movement in the iron trade of the country occurred, largely owing to the then increasing trade in iron with America. The 'boom' was at its height in 1873, when the highest prices obtained for hæmatite and hæmatite iron were 37s. 6d. and 195s. respectively. Capital was freely spent in extensive boring, sinking and drifting operations; in fact, the greatest activity known in the history of the industry prevailed in the various districts, and as a result, the total output of hæmatite was largely augmented. The culminating effect of this increased expenditure in development work was not however fully realized until 1880, when, for that and the following three years, the aggregate output of Cumberland hæmatite amounted to 6,309,605 tons, or an average of 1,577,401 tons per annum. The maximum total yearly output was reached in 1872, when 1,725,478 tons were raised.

The following table, giving the number of furnaces built and in blast in Cumberland, reflects the great activity in the iron trade during the early part of the 'seventies.' Up to the year 1869, seventeen furnaces had been built, of which only nine were in blast. During the following year (1870) ten more furnaces were erected, making a total of twenty-seven, of which twenty-four were in blast.

Year	Furnaces Built	Furnaces In blast	Pig-iron made
			Tons
1871	34	28¾	336,569
1872	37	33¼	440,575
1873	39	33½	456,877
1874	51	30½	390,840
1875	51	31¾	486,112
1876	47	25	436,887
1877	50	26¾	538,156
1878	51	27	542,904
1879	51	27½	531,638
1880	51	40	790,343
Average per annum	} 46·20	30·40	495,090·10

It will be seen from the foregoing schedule that the average yield per furnace in blast was 16,285·85 tons per annum.

For a few years at this time the competition for the acquirement of good hæmatite royalties in Cumberland was very keen. As an instance, it may be mentioned that when the Jacktrees royalty in Cleator parish was advertised to let, the tonnage royalties offered ranged from 7s. 6d. to 14s. per ton, and a lease of the royalty was actually taken and the ore worked at the latter figure. Prior to the year 1870, leases were obtained at royalty rates ranging from 1s. to 1s. 6d. per ton, while, after the 'boom' of the early 'seventies' had passed, one sixth of the selling price of hæmatite, with a minimum of from 1s. 6d. to 2s., was considered a fair average royalty. This rate, unfortunately for the welfare of the mining interests of the county, was not by any means universally adopted, as higher rates were in some cases exacted, and this fact has undoubtedly had an apathetic effect (especially during the prevailing low prices of the last decade) in the development of new districts along the belt of low-lying land between the seacoast and the more mountainous parts of the Lake District, extending from Egremont in the north to Millom in the south. The condition of the iron trade in 1872 and 1873 was such that confident predictions were made that the price of hæmatite would not fall below 20s. per ton for many years to come. A study however of the average selling prices given in tables Nos. II., III. and IV. will show the fallacy of such reasoning.

Previous to the introduction of dynamite in 1871, blasting powder was almost exclusively used in the working of hæmatite, but for many years past dynamite has been in great demand for this class of mining, and very little powder is now used. In the working of all deposits of Cumberland ore, explosives are required to a greater or less extent. The quantity used per ton of ore worked varies considerably according to the character of the ore in the different deposits. Some ores are so compact and hard that they can only be worked by jumper boring and blasting ; others are of a softer and more friable nature, and merely require an occasional ' shot' partially to loosen the ground, after which the ore can be easily worked with the pick. Dynamite proved highly advantageous in the working of many of the harder ores, especially where water was present, and the deposit was 'honey-combed' with 'loughs.' Owing to the high cost of working such ground with powder, many of the workings had to be abandoned. It was afterwards found however that the quicker action of dynamite, as well as its greater explosive power, produced results which admitted of the profitable working of these hard, wet, and 'loughy' ores, and, as a consequence, many of the abandoned workings were reopened.

In the year 1881 blasting gelatine, gelatine dynamite, and gelignite were introduced into Cumberland. They are respectively 50, 25 and 10 per cent. stronger than dynamite. The last named is now more extensively used than any other explosive.

The tables which will now be given in further dealing with the subject afford the best illustration of the progress made in the working of hæmatite in Cumberland during the last four decades of Queen Victoria's reign, each table showing the total output for one decade as obtained from the Government returns. The average yearly selling price at the mines has been fixed as nearly as possible for ore of good average quality, and the gross value of the total yearly output calculated therefrom. The selling price of hæmatite pig-iron for each year is also given, the figures having been supplied by Messrs. Rylands of Birmingham from their Iron Trade Circular.

TABLE No. I

Year	Total output of hæmatite ore	Average selling price at mines	Value of output	Prices of hæmatite pig-iron
	Tons		£	
1861	472,195	9/–	212,488	48/6
1862	533,940	10/–	266,970	55/–
1863	690,974	12/6	431,859	65/–
1864	863,667	13/–	561,383	83/–
1865	797,059	14/–	557,941	70/– to 85/–
1866	838,047	14/–	586,633	80/– „ 92/6
1867	890,566	14/–	623,396	77/6 „ 87/6
1868	926,628	13/6	625,474	75/– „ 80/–
1869	1,047,819	13/9	720,375	65/– „ 80/–
1870	1,190,435	16/6	982,109	72/6 „ 80/–
	8,251,330	13/5.97	£5,568,628	Mean 72/4·80

Ratio of average price of hæmatite ore and mean average price of hæmatite pig-iron for ten years ending 1870 : 1 to 5·36.

TABLE No. II

Year	Total output	Average selling price	Value of output	Prices of hæmatite pig-iron
1871	1,290,703	18/6	1,193,900	77/6 to 85/–
1872	1,168,276	28/–	1,635,586	105/– „ 170/–
1873	1,229,826	31/6	1,936,976	175/– „ 195/–
1874	1,119,662	24/–	1,343,594	90/– „ 195/–
1875	1,147,968	19/–	1,090,570	77/6 „ 95/–
1876	1,353,910	15/6	1,049,280	72/6 „ 80/–
1877	1,351,441	15/–	1,013,581	65/– „ 72/6
1878	1,357,886	14/6	984,467	58/6 „ 70/–
1879	1,227,006	13/–	797,554	47/– „ 56/–
1880	1,491,440	18/6	1,379,582	55/– „ 97/6
	12,738,118	19/6·10	£12,425,090	82/3·60 111/7·20 Mean 96/11·40

Ratio of average price of hæmatite ore, and mean average price of hæmatite pig-iron for ten years ending 1880 : 1 to 4·96. The highest price obtained for hæmatite during this decade was 37/6 in 1873.

Year	Total output of hæmatite ore	Average selling price at mines	Value of output	Prices of hæmatite pig-iron
	Tons		£	
1881	1,615,635	14/9	1,191,531	56/– to 62/–
1882	1,725,478	14/9	1,272,540	53/6 „ 60/–
1883	1,477,052	12/9	941,621	50/– „ 56/–
1884	1,357,206	10/9	729,498	44/6 „ 46/6
1885	1,227,550	10/3	629,119	42/6 „ 44/–
1886	1,260,588	10/–	630,294	40/– „ 43/3
1887	1,479,516	10/3	758,252	44/– „ 49/6
1888	1,573,043	10/–	786,521	42/6 „ 44/6
1889	1,593,890	12/9	1,016,105	44/6 „ 50/–
1890	1,431,159	14/–	1,001,811	52/3 „ 76/–
	14,741,117	12/1·84	£8,957,292	46/11·70 53/2·10 Mean 50/0·90

Ratio of average price of hæmatite ore, and mean average price of hæmatite pig-iron for ten years ending 1890 : 1 to 4·12.

TABLE No. IV

1891	1,417,860	10/9	762,100	51/– to 53/–
1892	1,355,007	10/6	711,379	47/– „ 49/6
1893	1,352,410	10/–	676,205	44/– „ 46/–
1894	1,286,590	10/–	643,295	44/– „ 45/6
1895	1,215,410	10/6	638,090	42/6 „ 45/–
1896	1,279,558	11/6	735,746	47/– „ —
1897	1,294,160	12/–	776,496	47/– „ 51/–
1898	1,251,764	12/9	797,999	49/– „ 51/–
1899	1,137,750	15/–	853,312	59/– „ 76/6
1900	1,103,430	16/9	924,122	75/6 „ 83/6
	12,693,939	11/10·15	£7,518,744	50/7·80 55/8·00 Mean 53/1·90

Ratio of average price of hæmatite, and mean average price of hæmatite pig-iron for ten years ending 1900 : 1 to 4·48.

TABLE No. V

Summary of foregoing tables showing total output, average price, value of output, and average price of hæmatite pig-iron.

No. of table	Total output for each decade	Average price at mines	Value of output	Average price of hæmatite pig-iron
	Tons		£	
1	8,251,330	13/5·97	5,568,628	72/4·80
2	12,738,118	19/6·10	12,425,090	96/11·40
3	14,741,117	12/1·84	8,957,292	50/0·90
4	12,693,939	11/10·15	7,518,744	53/1·90
	48,424,504	14/2·84	£34,469,754	68/1·75

Ratio of average price of hæmatite ore, and mean average price of hæmatite pig-iron for four decades ending 1900 : 1 to 4·78.

The object of the following table (No. VI.) has been to classify as nearly as possible, within parish areas, the output of hæmatite, as shown by the Board of Trade returns, from the individual mines of the ore bearing districts in Cumberland, during the decades ending 1880, 1890, and 1900 respectively. As, however, a few of the returns from mine owners raising ore from more than one parish are not shown separately, the classification here given is only approximate. At the same time these aggregate returns have been as fairly apportioned as possible, and the results are sufficiently accurate to secure the object in view, viz. that of showing the most productive areas in the different districts.

Complete individual mining returns are not obtainable prior to the year 1872, and therefore the output for 1871 is dealt with proportionately, and added to the parish totals of the subsequent nine years of the first decade.

TABLE No. VI

WHITEHAVEN DISTRICT

Parishes	1st decade 1871–80	2nd decade 1881–90	3rd decade 1891–1900	Parish totals	District totals	Per cent. of inc. or dec. between 1st and 3rd decade	
	Tons	Tons	Tons	Tons	Tons	Inc.	Dec.
Arlecdon . .	2,059,645	1,724,149	1,528,674	5,312,468			25·77
Cleator . . .	4,505,951	3,508,899	2,165,333	10,180,183			51·94
Egremont . .	1,273,702	3,151,387	3,136,632	7,561,721		146·26	
Ennerdale . .	700	540		1,240			
Hensingham .			1,136	1,136			
Lamplugh . .	535,261	769,456	606,363	1,911,080		13·28	
Salter and Eskett	1,704,844	924,112	374,003	3,002,959			78·06
St. John Beckermet . . .			4,946	4,946			
	10,080,103	10,078,543	7,817,087		27,975,733		22·45

MILLOM DISTRICT

Millom . . .	2,597,767	4,487,618	4,742,092	11,827,477		82·54	
Whicham . .	731	161,705	134,760	297,196			
	2,598,498	4,649,323	4,876,852		12,124,673	87·67	

ESKDALE DISTRICT

St. Bees . . .	49,217	13,049		62,266	62,266		

ALSTON DISTRICT

Alston . . .	10,300	202		10,502	10,502		
					40,173,174		

A description of the more important mines and mining operations in each parish area will now be given, with a view of showing the part these have played in the rise and fall of hæmatite mining in the various districts specified.

WHITEHAVEN DISTRICT

ARLECDON PARISH.—The largest producing mines here prior to the year 1880 were the old Parkside, High House and Crossgill mines. The first bedlike deposit of hæmatite worked at Parkside was one of the best and richest deposits in the Whitehaven district. Mr. Kendall,

in his description of this deposit, says : 'The length of the deposit on a north and south line is about 450 yards, and its breadth from east to west is about 370 yards. Its area is about 34 acres as far as worked, being larger in superficial extent than any other deposit in the district. It has also yielded the largest quantity of ore.' The Crossgill and the High House mines, which are contiguous royalties, have also worked portions of this extensive deposit. The greatest output from the Parkside mines since 1872, as shown by the Board of Trade returns, was 144,880 tons raised during the year 1874, that from the High House mines 120,036 tons in 1873, and from Crossgill 41,134 tons in 1873. A list of the hæmatite producing mines in this parish in the year 1900, with their respective outputs, is afterwards given in Table No. IX. Among the mines which have now ceased working, Birks and Yeathouse may be mentioned as being two of the oldest mines in the parish ; the others include Dyke-Nook, Goose Green and Rattenrow. Table No. VI. shows a gradual decrease in the production of hæmatite from this area during the three decades specified, the falling off in output between the first and third decade being 25·77 per cent. The Parkside and Crossgill mines still yield considerable quantities of ore, both royalties being now worked by the Parkside Mining Co.

CLEATOR PARISH.—As will be seen by reference to Table No. VI., this parish produced by far the largest quantity of hæmatite during the ten years ending 1880. The principal producing mines at that time were Montreal, worked by Mr. John Stirling ; Cleator, worked by the Cleator Iron Ore Co. (Messrs. Ainsworth) ; Crossfield, worked by the Crossfield Iron Ore Co. from 1865 until 1894, and now carried on by Mr. James Robertson Walker, the present owner of the property ; Crowgarth, worked by Lord Leconfield ; and Longlands and Rowfoot at the south end of the parish, worked by the Messrs. Lindow.

The largest deposit of hæmatite in this area has been that in the Montreal mines along the east and west 'fault' forming the junction of the coal and limestone measures. This 'fault' has a 'downthrow' to the north of over 200 fathoms. The extent of this rich deposit will be best understood by the fact that during the decade ending 1880, 2,008,748 tons of hæmatite were obtained from these mines. The ore, as is the case with most of the deposits in this parish, is of a very good quality, one of the analyses previously being given from a sample obtained from this part of the district. It is worthy of notice that for many years a considerable output of both iron ore and coal has been raised from the No. 4 pit in the Montreal royalty. This, so far as the writer is aware, forms a unique feature in the mining records of the United Kingdom. The maximum yearly output of hæmatite from the Montreal mines was attained in 1877, when 265,678 tons were raised. For the decade ending 1880, the production of hæmatite from the Crossfield mines was 928,526 tons, and from the Cleator Iron Ore mines, 583,742 tons ;

while the maximum outputs were 136,597 tons in 1876 from the former, and 88,640 tons in 1877 from the latter. Coal was also found in a portion of the Crossfield estate, but this was worked by Mr. Stirling and raised from his No. 4 pit. Large quantities of rich ore were also raised during this period from Lord Leconfield's Crowgarth and Messrs. Lindow's Longlands, and Rowfoot mines. In this parish the ore was worked 'open-cast' in several places.

Mr. John Stirling, who afterwards proved so successful in opening up large and valuable deposits in the Montreal royalty, first began his mining operations at 'Todholes,' a small property near Cleator Moor. The deposit here was worked 'open-cast,' and had been working for some time before the year 1860. Mention is made of this 'open-cast' by Whellan as follows : 'At a place called Todholes near Cleator an openwork has for some time been in operation ; the superficial covering of 15 to 20 feet in thickness which contains very numerous angular fragments of limestone being removed, the red iron ore was worked as a quarry. The floor of the deposit is a white and red mottled shale ; boreholes have been sunk in it to a depth of 30 or 40 feet without meeting with any other material.'[1] The bed of hæmatite overlying this shale is said to have been upwards of 30 feet in thickness. The next important 'open-cast' was opened up and worked by Mr. Thomas Ainsworth near Cleator. This was an 'outcrop' of hæmatite lying on a north and south 'fault,' having an 'upthrow' to the west of about 40 fathoms, and in its extension northwards running through the Crossfield and Montreal properties. It was worked on an extensive scale and at a comparatively early date. Later, during the decade ending 1880, the Crossfield Iron Ore Co. worked similar deposits of hæmatite by means of two 'open-casts,' and Mr. Stirling, by another, further to the north, all being on the same 'fault' as that at Cleator. The three last 'open-casts' were situated in the low lying ground close to the river Keekle. This stream is subject in wet weather to sudden and heavy floods from its extensive watershed, although in dry seasons it contains very little water. To avert the danger from flooding of these open workings, as well as to insure the safety of the adjacent mines, it was found necessary to construct a large wooden trough in the bed of the river. This troughing was formed of 4-inch pitch pine planks, resting on 12-inch square pitch pine

---

[1] *History of Cumberland*, p. 77 (published 1860)

soletrees, about 30 feet in length, and placed about 5 feet apart, the inside size of the troughing being as follows : width of bottom, 20 feet ; width across top, 29½ feet ; and vertical depth, 9 feet. The first section of troughing was built by the Crossfield Co. in the year 1878, when about 60 yards of the river bed were boxed over, and from time to time other sections of varying lengths were added by this company. Mr. Stirling also extensively troughed the river bed running through his royalty, until the combined length of troughing in the two properties was about 528 yards. Although the first outlay was considerable, a great saving was effected in the cost of pumping from the mines in the low-lying ground in each royalty, whilst the ore immediately under the river bed with that forming the adjacent parts of the deposit has been worked out. This large body of ore, representing probably over a million tons, would, without the protecting troughing, have had to be left unworked. At the south end of the parish a portion of the river had to be diverted near to the junction of the rivers Ehen and Keekle. This work was jointly carried out by the Messrs. Lindow and Messrs. Bain & Co., in order to admit of the working out of the 'rise' ore resting on the slate-rock and to ensure the safety of the Longlands and Woodend mines. As will be seen from Table No. VI., the output of hæmatite from the Cleator parish during the three decades ending 1900 shows a large falling off, the decrease between the first and last decades being 51·94 per cent. Occupying as it does a central position in the Whitehaven district, this area has been well proved, and although it may continue to produce ore for many years, future mining operations will in all likelihood still continue to show a very material declension.

EGREMONT PARISH.—Although it was in this parish that some of the earliest mining of hæmatite took place, we find from Table No. VI. that during the decade ending 1880 it only occupied the fourth place among the ore producing areas of the Whitehaven district, Cleator, Arlecdon and Salter and Eskett taking the lead in the order named. Prior to and during this period the most important mines in the parish were the old Bigrigg mines of Lord Leconfield, the Woodend, Gutterby, Ironriggs and Peile pits of Messrs. Lindow, the Woodend mines of Messrs. Bain & Co., the mines of the Ehen Mining Co., Robin Benn, Billy Frears and Fletcher pits on Postlethwaite's Moor Row estate, and the Moor Row mines. Up to the year 1880

very little had been done in the way of mining near the town of Egremont, but operations are now being conducted there on an extensive scale.

The Wyndham and Gillfoot Park mines, which have produced the highest outputs in the Whitehaven district during the last ten years, only began to raise ore in 1879. From the Gillfoot mines 7,807 tons were returned for that year ; this was followed by an output of 72,880 tons for the year 1880, and up to the present time good and regular outputs have been maintained, the maximum output of 121,742 tons being reached in 1889. The Wyndham Co., who started sinking within a short distance of the river Ehen, a little to the south of the Egremont railway station, had a large quantity of water to contend with, their progress for a few years being considerably retarded from this cause. In 1883 however 73,139 tons were raised, while the maximum output up to the present time was attained in 1898, when the output reached 112,501 tons. Some years ago this company had to make a deviation in the river Ehen, owing to a threatened inbreak from the original river bed. This work was satisfactorily completed, and has enabled the company to work out a much larger quantity of ore than they could otherwise have secured. These two mines, which are now worked by the Wyndham Mining Co., are specially mentioned, as it is owing to their large outputs that the Egremont parish has taken the premier position during the last decade, as the largest ore producing area in the Whitehaven district. The Wyndham Co. (who also work the Falcon Mines) are about to commence the sinking of a shaft about 200 fathoms in depth near Orgill in this parish.

Other mines of considerable importance have for some years past been in operation, of which may be mentioned the Moss Bay Hæmatite Iron and Steel Co.'s mines, and Messrs. Bain & Co.'s mines at Woodend, the Syke House, and Sir John Walsh mines of Messrs. S. & J. Lindow, the Pallaflat and Southam mines, the Parkhouse mines of Messrs. Charles Cammell & Co. Ld., Postle-thwaite's Moor Row mines, and the mines at Moor Row worked by the executors of the late Mr. T. H. Dalzell. The Town-head Mining Co. in Egremont and the Ullcoats Mining Co. in St. John Beckermet parish have quite recently been added to the list of ore producers, while the Millom & Ascham Hæmatite Iron Co. Ld. are sinking a shaft in a small royalty at Ullbank in Beckermet parish near Egremont.

LAMPLUGH PARISH.—This is the most northerly parish in the Whitehaven district where hæmatite is worked. It is worthy of special notice, inasmuch as it is the only part in Cumberland where hæmatite is found in workable quantities in the Skiddaw slate. The properties of Kelton Fell and Knockmurton within a short distance of Ennerdale Lake have been profitably worked for many years by Messrs. William Baird & Co. of Scotland. The ore occurs, as has already been observed, in veins in the Skiddaw slate, having for the most part a north-west and south-east direction. These veins have a considerable extension both longitudinally and vertically, and although the ore deposits are not continuous, they are sufficiently persistent to permit of the mines being profitably carried on. Some idea of the extent of the deposits may be formed from the fact that over a million tons of hæmatite have been raised from these mines, the maximum output being reached in 1883, in which year it amounted to 61,377 tons. A shaft about 80 fathoms in depth has recently been sunk which will open up a large extent of ore bearing ground and add greatly to the life of the mines. Previous to the Messrs. Baird commencing operations early in the 'seventies,' two attempts had been made to work ore in this locality, one by Mr. Thomas Carmichal, and the other by Mr. John Stirling of the Montreal mines, both ventures proving unsuccessful. .

The district lying to the north of Lamplugh parish has hitherto produced very little ore; this may probably be owing to the fact that the limestone in its extension northwards is intersected by a smaller number of important 'faults' than is the case in the rich ore bearing ground farther south. The ground here has however not been sufficiently proved, and future explorations may lead to further discoveries in this direction. Ore in considerable quantity was got at Murton in this parish, where mining for a time was extensively carried on, and later, about the year 1880, a vigorous attempt was made to open up mines at Whinnah, but without much success. This district is however still worth attention. Work has now been suspended at the Windergill mines at the south end of the parish. These mines have produced in the past a large quantity of ore. The other mines at work here are the Winder mines, worked by the Parkside Mining Co., and Margaret pit worked by Messrs. Ainsworth. At the latter a fine deposit of ore has been worked for some years past. The pit is over 130 fathoms in depth,

the ore lying at that level on a north and south 'fault,' which outcrops in the Yatehouse estate. This deposit is likely to continue to yield good outputs of ore for many years.

SALTER AND ESKETT PARISH.—Considering the small area of this parish, it has produced a large quantity of excellent hæmatite. The production of ore for the first of three decades is shown in Table No. VI. to have amounted to over a million and a half tons. Owing however to the limited workable area, the decrease during the following two decades has been more marked than in any of the other parish areas described. As shown on Table No. VI., the output for the last period of ten years shows a decline of 78·06 per cent compared with that of the first decade. The older and more important mines in this parish were the Eskett, Salter and Eskett, and Postlethwaite's Eskett mines, from all of which large quantities of ore have been raised. The Salter Hall and Eskett Park mines have also in the past added largely to the output of the district. The bulk of the ore obtained from the Salter Hall mines was worked from a large vein-like deposit lying on a north and south 'fault,' which in its extension northwards formed also the best producing deposit in Postlethwaite's Eskett royalty. Only three mines are at present working in this area. These will be found in Table No. IX.

ENNERDALE AND KINISIDE, HENSINGHAM AND ST. JOHN BECKERMET PARISHES.—Table No. VI. shows that small quantities of hæmatite have been obtained from each of these areas, but up to the present time these additions to the output of the district have been of little moment. As will be gathered however from the remarks already made about Beckermet and other areas immediately to the south of Egremont, these are likely to form a very important mining centre in this part of Cumberland in the near future. The output shown in the table as having been raised from Beckermet parish was worked by the Wyndham Mining Co. of Egremont, and that from Hensingham parish by Mr. Stirling from the Montreal mines.

Various attempts have been made from time to time to work the ore veins in the older rocks about the hills around the Ennerdale lake, but these have proved abortive, owing to the small size of the veins and the hard nature of the rocks encasing them. Messrs. Charles Cammell & Co., Ltd., some years ago ran a prospecting drift into the hillside near the lower end of the lake, on its south-western side. This drift was driven for a considerable distance, but no ore was found of any commercial value. In the neighbourhood of Gosforth also some prospecting work has been carried out, but although the ore indications are abundant, no sufficient workable quantity has yet been found. The total quantity of hæmatite raised from the various parishes in the Whitehaven district during the last thirty years has amounted to nearly 28,000,000 tons. The present output from the mines in each parish will be found in Table No. IX.

MILLOM DISTRICT

Millom Parish.—Although the ore bearing area of this part of the county, so far as proved, is much smaller than that of the Whitehaven district, the deposit of hæmatite at Hodbarrow worked by the Hodbarrow Mining Co. Ltd. far surpasses in size and richness any other area of the same extent in Cumberland or even in Great Britain. This deposit is not only of vast dimensions, but the ore is noted for its uniformly high yield of metallic iron. The following is an average analysis of the ore :—

		Dried at 212° Fah.
Ferric oxide	85·20	88·57
Alumina	1·35	1·40
Manganese oxide . . .	·08	·09
Carbonate of lime . .	2·07	2·15
„ „ magnesia .	·11	·12
Silica	7·23	7·50
Sulphuric acid (SO_3). .	·16	·17
Phosphoric acid (P_2O_5) .	trace	trace
Moisture	3·80	
	100·00	100·00
Metallic iron	59·64%	62·00%
Insol. silic. residue . .	8·18%	8·50%

The total output from the Hodbarrow mines from 1864 to 1900 inclusive has (as shown in Table No. VII.) amounted to 12,790,126 tons, and it will be seen from Table No. VIII. that this quantity represents more than one third of the total output from all other mines in Cumberland. The annual average number of persons employed at these mines is as under : Above ground, 350 ; under ground, 1,050 ; total, 1,400.

TABLE No. VII

Output of hæmatite from the Hodbarrow mines.

Year	Output in tons	Total output in decades	Year	Output in tons	Total output in decades
1861 . . .	—		1881 . . .	358,621	3,564,670
1862 . . .	—		1882 . . .	453,523	
1863 . . .	—		1883 . . .	473,374	
1864 . . .	78,993		1884 . . .	488,208	
1865 . . .	117,329		1885 . . .	427,951	
1866 . . .	131,542		1886 . . .	441,044	
1867 . . .	181,504		1887 . . .	468,994	
1868 . . .	201,380		1888 . . .	474,238	
1869 . . .	198,705		1889 . . .	492,265	
1870 . . .	174,943	1,084,396	1890 . . .	405,146	4,483,364
1871 . . .	207,146		1891 . . .	535,010	
1872 . . .	211,771		1892 . . .	523,973	
1873 . . .	203,791		1893 . . .	531,041	
1874 . . .	201,663		1894 . . .	474,667	
1875 . . .	202,817		1895 . . .	451,327	
1876 . . .	271,098		1896 . . .	471,164	
1877 . . .	270,195		1897 . . .	483,559	
1878 . . .	274,962		1898 . . .	420,336	
1879 . . .	293,637		1899 . . .	435,400	
1880 . . .	343,194	2,480,274	1900 . . .	415,615	4,742,092
		3,564,670			12,790,126

Decade ending	Output from Hodbarrow mines	Output from all other mines in Cumberland	Total output of Cumberland hæmatite	Percentage
1870	[1] 1,084,396	7,166,934	8,251,330	15·13
1880	2,480,274	10,257,844	12,738,118	24·18
1890	4,483,364	10,257,753	14,741,117	43·71
1900	4,742,092	7,951,847	12,693,939	59·64
	12,790,126	35,634,378	48,424,504	35·90

The great interest these celebrated mines have excited in the mining world is a sufficient reason for quoting largely from a paper by Mr. Cedric Vaughan, managing director of the Hodbarrow mines, and also from a joint paper by Mr. Vaughan and Mr. H. Shelford Bidwell, the resident engineer of Messrs. Coode, Son & Matthews, which firm is constructing the 'Outer Barrier' works now in progress. The former of these articles gives a succinct account of the discovery and working of this wonderful deposit of hæmatite, and the latter a description of the sea wall and embankment works, which were designed and are now being carried out by the above firm of engineers.

These papers appeared in the *Transactions of the Institution of Mechanical Engineers* for 1902 at their meeting held in Barrow, and the Council of the Institute as well as the writers of the articles and engineers have kindly granted their consent to the following accounts being given :—

HODBARROW IRON ORE MINES, MILLOM

These mines were first discovered about 1845 through the occurrence of veins of ore in the carboniferous limestone which forms the rocks on the shore at Hodbarrow Point. The late William Earl of Lonsdale worked one of these veins by means of an adit level from the shore ; but, meeting with little success, he gave up the venture, and granted a 'take note' to the founders of the Hodbarrow Mining Co. in 1855. A shaft was sunk on the same vein, and the shaft and engine house are still visible on the top of the hill at Hodbarrow Point. As the vein was followed it began to nip out, and boring was resorted to. The late Mr. William Barratt observed that the veins converged towards the west, and, putting down a bore-hole at the probable point of intersection, proved 100 feet of solid hæmatite ore, and so discovered the first deposit in 1856. This deposit yielded excellent ore, and while the company were working it they built workmen's houses on the adjoining mains without knowing what was beneath them. While sinking a well to supply these houses with water, another large deposit was found by means of a bore-hole put down at the bottom of the well with the view of increasing the water supply. This led to other borings in the vicinity, when it was found that a very large deposit of ore existed under the Hodbarrow mains.

The first discovered deposit was comparatively shallow, with not more than 60 feet of cover over it at any part, and in one place it came almost to the surface. Between this deposit and the larger one was an intermediate deposit of smaller area, which overlapped the large or main deposit, this last named lying much deeper and having a cover about 200 feet thick. The first and second deposits are practically worked out, and it is the larger or main deposit which is now being worked. The company's first lease of the minerals only extended to ordinary high-water mark on the south, and was proved to exist right up to this boundary. But inasmuch as the surface caved in when the ore was extracted it was necessary to leave a barrier of ore 360 feet wide to protect the mains from the sea, which otherwise would have filled the hollows on the surface, and eventually have flooded the mine as well. This barrier was ultimately found to contain over five million tons of ore, and to enable the company to win this a sea wall (figs. 1 and 2) was erected in 1890 to exclude the sea from the foreshore immediately in front of the mine. Sir John Coode was the engineer, and it was the last work he finished just before his death. It was a novel piece of engineering, being a combination of a sea wall and a water-tight dam.

The Earl of Lonsdale then gave the company rights to search for ore under the foreshore seawards ; and, after boring for some years under considerable difficulty, owing to the heavy seas which frequently washed away the stagings and gear, it was satisfactorily proved that the main deposit of ore extended, not only under the old high-water mark, but also under the sea wall, and to a distance of some 500 yards beyond it. The full extent of this ore ground has not however even yet been fully proved.

The second sea wall, or 'Outer Barrier' as it is officially termed, will enclose an area of 170 acres, and when completed it will enable the company to win the ore under the foreshore, which could

[1] The output given here is from the year 1864, when Government returns were first recorded.

not otherwise have been worked with safety. The mine, which is liable to inrushes of sand and water from the cover, is drained by three Cornish pumping engines, each having a cylinder 70 inches diameter by 9 feet stroke. One of these engines works a plunger 25 inches diameter by 10 feet stroke, the other two each work a pair of 18-inch plungers by 10 feet stroke, all from a depth of 50 fathoms, with bucket lifts from 60 fathoms up to the 50 fathom level. As a general rule one of these engines is sufficient to keep the mine drained, but when a run of sand occurs it takes two and sometimes all three of them to contend with it. The plungers lift sand and water with ease so long as the sand is kept in a fluid state, and this is effected by taking a jet of fresh water down from the surface and discharging it into the sump, which, acting under a head of 300 feet, keeps the sand in the sump in such a condition of fluidity that the plungers lift it without difficulty; and should the sand during a temporary stoppage settle in the pump column, the door of the top clack is removed, the jet is turned up the column, which quickly clears it of sand, the door is then replaced, the column is filled with fresh water from the top, and the engine goes to work again at once.

The winding engines are direct acting. The last new one was made by Messrs. Walker Brothers of Wigan, and has two cylinders, each 24 inches diameter by 4 feet 6 inches stroke, with 11 feet drums. In the year 1898 a bed of quicksand was tapped in the mine, which established a connection between the sea and the underground workings, a cavity being formed on the outer foreshore, and a heavy rush of tidal water into the mine took place, passing many fathoms below the foundations of the sea wall. This however was promptly checked by filling up the cavity on the shore with furze and clay, but not before the sea wall showed signs of distress through deflection, caused by the undercurrent of tidal water into the mine. The clay embankment behind the wall subsided about 5 feet, and this subsidence had the effect of shutting off the connection with the sea, and the influx of tidal water shortly after ceased. Mr. Matthews, of Messrs. Coode, Son & Matthews, having been called in, advised that the sea wall would stand, provided it were not exposed to heavy strokes from the sea, and he designed a wave breaker of pell-mell blocks of concrete (20 tons each), which was placed in front of the damaged wall, and which has effectively protected it from sea action. He also not only levelled up the subsided embankment, but added to it also both in height and width, so as to give additional weight, and thus aid in shutting off the leakage into the mine. This accident had the effect of hastening the negotiations for the erection of an outer barrier, the necessity for which had already become apparent through the discovery of the fact that the ore body extended a long way seaward of the existing sea wall. In view of previous experience, Mr. Matthews, in designing this new and larger structure, which like its predecessor had to be both water-tight and sea proof, provided for a flexible bank instead of a rigid wall, so as to pro-

vide for such contingencies hereafter as connection between the outer foreshore and the mine, should such again occur.

OUTER BARRIER (figs. 1 and 3)

The following description of this work has been written by Mr. H. Shelford Bidwell, the resident engineer under Messrs. Coode, Son & Matthews :—

The outer barrier consists of a bank of rubble limestone, protected on the seaward side for the greater portion of its length by an outer covering of 25 ton concrete blocks deposited pell-mell, an inner and smaller bank of slag, with a filling of clay between these two banks. Where concrete blocks are not used, the bank is protected by large lumps of limestone weighing from 8 to 15 tons. Under the centre of the clay bank, in order to form a cut-off preventing percolation of water beneath the barrier, tongued and grooved sheet piling is driven into the bottom, this being of pitch pine varying in length from 18 to 27 feet, or of steel 32 to 35 feet long, according to the nature of the foundation. Where the natural clay is near the surface the piling is dispensed with, and a puddle trench is substituted, the puddle being well keyed into the natural clay.

Over the piling or the puddle trench, as the case may be, a puddle wall is constructed in the heart of the clay bank to prevent percolation of water through the barrier, being brought up to a level of five feet above high water of ordinary spring tides. The surface of the clay filling is to be covered with a layer of slag, and provision is made for a parapet of concrete blocks if found necessary. There will be four sluice culverts through the barrier, constructed of concrete-in-mass, faced at the openings with granite masonry. The total length of the barrier is 6,870 feet, or rather more than a mile and a quarter. It has an extreme height of 40 feet, and its greatest width at the base is 210 feet. The area reclaimed by this barrier will be 170 acres. The contract for the work has been entrusted to Messrs. John Aird & Co. of Westminster, who, as already stated, were the contractors for the first sea wall.

WHICHAM PARISH.—The principal mining operations carried on here were those of the Whicham Mining Co., begun about the year 1877 and continued until the year 1895. During this time about 300,000 tons of hæmatite were raised. Owing however to the ore deposit not being sufficiently large to meet the heavy expenditure incurred by pumping, etc., it was found impracticable to carry on the mines profitably, and this ultimately led to their abandonment. The returns of ore from the Millom district during the last three decades will be found in Table No. VI.

ESKDALE DISTRICT

ST. BEES PARISH.—Several veins of ore have been worked at the head of Eskdale valley near Boot. These occurring in the Eskdale granite have produced the largest quantity of ore. From 1872 to 1883, 59,266 tons were worked from these mines, principally from the vein known as 'Nab Ghyll.' About the beginning of the decade ending 1880 considerable interest was excited by the glowing reports which were made as to the productiveness and extent of these deposits. One of these reports on the Eskdale district reckoned the probable yield of some of the veins by millions of tons, and asserted that a large portion of the upper part of the deposits could be worked and conveyed to the terminus of the Ravenglass and Eskdale railway at a cost of 2s. 6d. per ton. After working for the period above stated, the Eskdale Mining Co. proved conclusively that, although the veins here were richer than other known veins in the older rocks, they were too irregular and too much mixed up with foreign matter to admit of their being carried on profitably. No ore appears to have been worked from these mines since the year 1883.

ANALYSIS OF ORE FROM 'NAB GHYLL' VEIN

	No. 1. Dried at 212° Fah.	No. 2
Ferric oxide	27·43	92·57
Manganous oxide	·03	·02
Silica	2·15	2·05
Alumina	6·10	·88
Lime	23·18	·50
Magnesia	9·04	·08
Phosphoric acid	·04	·03
Sulphuric acid	·02	·01
Carbonic acid and water	32·00	3·70
	99·99	99·84
Metallic iron	19·20	64·80

The quality of the Eskdale ore was found to be very variable, as the foregoing analysis, given by Mr. Kendall in his work already referred to, clearly shows.

ALSTON DISTRICT

This district has long been famous for its production of lead ore, but, as already mentioned, brown hæmatite ore occurring in the limestone and associated with the lead veins has been worked from time to time. No large deposits of ore however have at any time been found, and owing to its low yield of metallic iron it has not proved of much value commercially. Since the rich deposits of the Whitehaven and Millom districts have been so largely worked, little attention has been given to the iron ores of Alston, the Board of Trade returns since 1872 only showing an output of 8,639 tons.

The following table (No. IX.) shows the output of hæmatite from each mine and the total production from each of the ore producing parishes in Cumberland for the year 1900. The Hodbarrow Mining Co. Ltd. has been the only company outside the Whitehaven district returning an output of ore for some years past, and for the year 1900 the output obtained from these mines, viz. 415,615 tons, represents 60·43 per cent of the total quantity raised in the Whitehaven district, which amounted to 687,815 tons.

The numbers placed before the names of the different mines have reference to the position of the latter as shown on plan No. 1.

TABLE No. IX

Showing the output of hæmatite from the individual mines, in the various parish areas in Cumberland already enumerated, for the year 1900.

WHITEHAVEN DISTRICT

Parish	Nos. on plan	Name of mine	Name of owner	Output of hæmatite	Parish totals
Arlecdon	1	Crossgill	Parkside Mining Co.	26,377	
	2	Parkside	,, ,,	30,179	
	3	Frizington Parks	Chas. Cammell & Co. Ltd.	16,133	
	4	High House	Isaac Fletcher	7,477	
	5	Holebeck	Dalmellington Iron Co.Ltd.	22,611	
	6	Lonsdale	Lonsdale Mining Co. Ltd.	17,573	
	7	New Parkside	New Parkside M. Co. Ltd.	3,492	
	8	Mowbray and Landshaw	Chas. Cammell & Co. Ltd.	16,600	
					140,442

Parish	Nos. on plan	Name of mine	Name of owner	Output of hæmatite	Parish totals
Cleator . .	9	Cleator. . . .	Cleator I. O. Co. . . .	23,572	
	10	Crossfield . . .	Jas. Robertson Walker .	13,374	
	11	Crowgarth. . .	Lord Leconfield . . .	11,382	
	12	Jacktrees . . .	Carron Co. Ltd. . . .	19,036	
	13	Longlands ⎫			
	14	Rowfoot ⎬ . .	S. & J. Lindow . . .	29,268	
	15	Glebe ⎭			
	16	Montreal . . .	John Stirling	39,806	
	Pit in Egremont Parish, No. 19	Moor Row . .	Exors. of T. H. Dalzell .	2,502	
	Do. do. No. 23	Postlethwaite's Moor Row	Exors. of M. Postlethwaite	2,354	
	Do. do. No. 28	Woodend . . .	Jas. Bain & Co. . . .	14,541	
					155,835
Egremont .	17	Bigrigg. . . .	Lord Leconfield . . .	26,057	
	18	Gillfoot Park . .	Gillfoot Park Mining Co.	62,951	
	19	Moor Row . .	Exors. of T. H. Dalzell .	5,919	
	20	Moss Bay . . .	Moss Bay H.I. & S. Co. Ltd.	26,549	
	21	Pallaflat . . .	Pallaflat Iron Ore Co. Ltd.	22,250	
	22	Park House . .	Chas. Cammell & Co. Ltd.	8,723	
	23	Postlethwaite's Moor Row	Exors. of Miles Postlethwaite	17,478	
	24	Sir John Walsh ⎫			
	25	Syke House ⎬ .	S. & J. Lindow . . .	26,485	
	26	Southam . . .	Southam H. Co. Ltd.. .	7,398	
	27	Townhead. . .	Townhead M. Co. . .	9,502	
	28	Woodend . . .	Jas. Bain & Co. . . .	18,170	
	29	Wyndham . . .	Wyndham M. Co. Ltd. .	63,473	
					294,955
Hensingham	Pit in Cleator Parish, No. 16	Montreal . . .	John Stirling	1,136	
					1,136
Lamplugh .	30	Kelton and Knockmurton	W. Baird & Co. Ltd. . .	14,440	
	31	Margaret . . .	Cleator I. O. Co. . . .	42,932	
	32	Winder . . .	Parkside Mining Co. . .	7,699	
					65,071
Salter and Eskett	33	Eskett	Cleator I. O. Co. . . .	9,208	
	34	Postlethwaite's Eskett	Postlethwaite's Eskett M. Co. Ltd.	5,365	
	35	Salter Hall. . .	Wyndham M. Co. Ltd. .	10,856	
					25,429
St. John Beckermet	Pit in Egremont Parish, No. 29	Wyndham. . .	,, ,, ,,	4,483	
	36	Ullcoats . . .	Ullcoats M. Co. Ltd. . .	464	
					4,947
			Total from Whitehaven district . .		687,815

MILLOM DISTRICT

Millom . .	—	Hodbarrow . .	The Hodbarrow M. Co. Ld.	415,615	415,615
			Total . . .		1,103,430

It will be found by comparing the output of the Whitehaven district in the foregoing table with the average annual output of the totals given in Table No. VI. that the production of hæmatite in this part of Cumberland is still on the decline. The first decade ending 1880 gives an average annual output of 1,008,010 tons; the second decade ending 1890 gives an average annual output of 1,007,854 tons; the third decade ending 1900 gives an average annual output of 781,708 tons; while the actual output for the year 1900 is only 687,815 tons.

The one favourable feature in this district, as shown by Table No. IX., is the maintenance of the output from the Egremont parish, which for the year dealt with has yielded 294,955 tons, or nearly 1100 per cent more than any other individual parish in the district. The Hodbarrow mines also, in Millom parish, which are the mainstay of the county, are still producing the splendid outputs which have been so long the characteristic feature of these wonderful mines.

The following is a list of blast furnaces in Cumberland taken from the *General Report and Statistics of Mines and Quarries* for the year 1900 :—

TABLE No. X

Name	Situation	Owners	Furnaces	
			Number	Average in blast during the year
Cleator Moor . .	Cleator Moor	Whitehaven Hem. I. and S. Co. Ltd. .	4	2
Derwent I. and S.[1]	Workington .	Chas. Cammell & Co. Ltd.	5	5
Distington . . .	Distington .	Distington Hem. I. Co. Ltd.	3	2
Harrington . .	Harrington .	James Bain & Co.	4	2
Lonsdale . . .	Whitehaven .	Lonsdale Hem. Smelting Co. Ltd. . .	3	2
Lowther . . .	Workington .	Lowther Hem. I. and S. Co. Ltd. . .	3	$1\frac{6}{12}$ [2]
Millom	Millom . .	Millom and Askham Hem. I. Co. Ltd. .	6	$3\frac{3}{12}$
Moss Bay . . .	Workington .	Moss Bay Hem. I. and S. Co. Ltd. . .	4	2
New Yard . . .	,,	Kirk Bros. & Co. Ltd.	1	$\frac{7}{12}$
North-Western .	,,	North-Western Hem. S. Co. Ltd. . .	5	$1\frac{6}{12}$
Solway	Maryport . .	Chas. Cammell & Co. Ltd.	3	2
Workington . .	Workington .	Workington Hem. I. and S. Co. Ltd. .	3	2
		Totals . . .	44	$25\frac{6}{12}$

Total make of pig-iron, 856,851 tons; total iron ore used, 1,643,421 tons; average yield per furnace in blast for the year 1900, 33,392·48 tons.

As will be seen from a former table giving the number of furnaces in blast and their production during the decade ending 1880, the yield per furnace was only 16,285·85 tons per annum. The above yield for 1900 therefore exhibits an increase in the producing power per furnace of 105·04 per cent.

The exportation of hæmatite from the Whitehaven harbour, which during the decade ending 1870 amounted to 2,633,579 tons, fell in the next decade to 1,014,359 tons (as shown in Table No. XI.) while for the succeeding two decades the exports were only 73,820 tons and 18,490 tons respectively. For 1899 and 1900 exportation had altogether ceased. In spite of this, Table No. X. shows that with only about 57 per cent of the total number of furnaces in blast the consumption of hæmatite for the year 1900 was 1,643,421 tons, or 539,991 tons more than the total production of Cumberland.

1 Messrs. Chas. Cammell & Co. Ltd., who transferred their works from Dronfield to Workington, commenced rolling operations during the year 1883. The introduction of these extensive works into Cumberland has added greatly to the prosperity of the town of Workington as well as that of Maryport, where, as will be seen from the foregoing table, the Solway Ironworks (built and worked for many years by the Solway Hæmatite Iron and Steel Co. Ltd.) are now under the control of this firm.

2 Fractions show the proportion of the year the furnaces were in blast.

TABLE No. XI

Tonnage of hæmatite exported from Whitehaven harbour during the four decades ending 1900.

Year	Tons	Decade totals	Year	Tons	Decade totals
1861 . . .	300,000	(Estimated)	1881 . . .	13,865	
1862 . . .	307,079		1882 . . .	5,802	
1863 . . .	336,174		1883 . . .	8,956	
1864 . . .	337,518		1884 . . .	7,444	
1865 . . .	250,667		1885 . . .	1,009	
1866 . . .	188,016		1886 . . .	4,428	
1867 . . .	203,540		1887 . . .	662	
1868 . . .	206,845		1888 . . .	16,691	
1869 . . .	252,216		1889 . . .	11,628	
1870 . . .	251,524	2,633,579	1890 . . .	3,335	73,820
1871 . . .	152,297		1891 . . .	2,418	
1872 . . .	125,232		1892 . . .	1,784	
1873 . . .	58,450		1893 . . .	2,393	
1874 . . .	101,916		1894 . . .	3,483	
1875 . . .	102,801		1895 . . .	154	
1876 . . .	148,349		1896 . . .	nil	
1877 . . .	131,138		1897 . . .	8,257	
1878 . . .	80,056		1898 . . .	811	
1879 . . .	63,688		1899 . . .	nil	
1880 . . .	50,432	1,014,359	1900 . . .	nil	19,300
Total for two decades		3,647,938	Total for two decades		93,120

Small cargoes of Spanish ore from the extensive deposits in the Bilbao district were first imported early in the 'seventies,' but the increase in this traffic of late years has been so large that Spain has now become a formidable rival in supplying the hæmatite requirements of Cumberland. Table No. XII. shows the importation of Spanish ore to Whitehaven harbour during the last two decades, that for the first decade being approximately 70,154 tons, and for the second, 242,511 tons; the imported ore for the last five years representing 86·49 per cent of the total tonnage for the last decade. These quantities, however, also include the Irish ore supplied from the county of Antrim.

Large importations of Spanish ore have also taken place to the other important ports on the west coast of Cumberland, particularly to Workington and Maryport, but the above figures from Whitehaven harbour, kindly supplied by the authorities there, clearly indicate the advancement made in this direction. In view of the foregoing facts, much interest centres in the favourable developments now in progress in the southern parts of the Whitehaven district.

A short description of the usual methods adopted for the working of hæmatite deposits in Cumberland will not be out of place in this article, and the author has obtained the permission of the Council of 'The Institution

of Mining Engineers' to give extracts from his own paper on the 'Working of Hæmatite in the Whitehaven District,' read before the North of England Institute of Mining and Mechanical Engineers at their annual meeting at Newcastle-upon-Tyne on 4 August 1894.

TABLE No. XII

Year		Tons	Decade totals
1881	Estimated	7,500	
1882	,,	7,500	
1883	,,	8,000	
1884	,,	8,000	
1885		7,188	
1886		6,679	
1887		5,839	
1888		11,042	
1889		4,746	
1890		3,660	70,154
1891		4,716	
1892		7,313	
1893		4,561	
1894		6,952	
1895		9,217	
1896		11,981	
1897		12,772	
1898		23,664	
1899		67,168	
1900		94,167	242,511
Total for 2 decades			312,665

The three forms of hæmatite already noticed are vein-like, bed-like, and irregular or patchy masses. The working of each is described in the above paper as follows :—

VEIN-LIKE DEPOSITS (figs. 1 and 2).— The usual method of working vein-like ore may be briefly described. Having sunk the shaft in a suitable position, levels are driven off at right angles to the 'fault' at distances from 120 to 180 feet apart vertically, the number of levels depending on the extension of the vein in that direction. After the ore has been intersected and its width proved, longitudinal workings are commenced right and left, 'rises' are put up on the footwall as the various workings advance, the pillars between each 'rise' being from 60 to 70 feet in length. Intermediate horizontal workings are then driven from the 'rises,' middlings of from 15 to 30 feet being usually left between, and thus the system of splitting up the vein goes on. The 'rises' form hoppers, shoots, or (as locally termed) 'hurries' for conveying the ore from the intermediate workings to the different levels communicating with the shaft. Until communication by means of the 'rises' has been effected with the different levels, the ventilation of the workings is obtained in the usual way, viz. by bratticing of brick or canvas or by wooden boxes.

In the case of a wide vein, say from 100 to 120 feet, two longitudinal workings may be driven right and left from the shaft-drift, care being taken in so doing to 'blind' the opposite workings, not only to strengthen the drift, but as a safeguard in carrying on blasting operations. Unless the hanging and footwalls are of a strong character, it is advisable not to drive the workings close to them, but to leave a portion of ore against them for support. The size of the workings varies from 8 to 20 feet wide and from 8 to 12 feet high. These dimensions are, however, altogether regulated by the nature of the ore : where that is very hard and free from joints or cleats, larger workings than those stated may be safely carried on, and in such cases little or no timbering may be necessary. This however is the exception, not the rule, as in most deposits the character of the ore is subject to frequent changes, and renders timbering necessary to a greater or less extent, even in the first series of workings.

BED-LIKE DEPOSITS (figs. 3 and 4).—The usual method of working this class of deposit is by the pillar and stall system. The pit is sunk in a convenient position in the royalty and as far as possible to the dip. When the ore bed has been reached, and adequate provision has been made either by sump or lodge for contending with the water, a level is driven at right angles to the dip of the strata, while at the same time a heading is carried on to the 'rise.' As the branch workings on the levels advance, stalls, bords, throughs or (as locally termed) 'thirls' are commenced, leaving pillars 24 to 45 feet in length. From the heading also other workings are branched off, with from 18 to 36 feet of solid ground between each. The pillars thus formed (when the 'thirls' from the various level workings are holed) measure from 430 to 1,620 square feet. Smaller pillars will suffice in the case of very hard and strong ore.

The width and height of the workings depend very much on the hardness and thickness of the ore and the nature of the roof. In the case of very hard ore with a good strong roof, and where the thickness of the bed will permit, the workings may safely and with advantage be made from 15 to 20 feet square, but where the ore is tender they are usually driven from 9 to 12 feet square, while timbering in the latter case is necessary, more especially if a shale-bed (as very often happens) overlies the deposit. No definite dimensions, however, can be fixed for regulating the size of the workings in these deposits, as can be done, for instance, in the working of the thicker coal seams, as the varying conditions met with render it impracticable. The engineers or managers of these mines require therefore to exercise their discrimination and bring practical experience to their aid in coming to a decision on this point, although the writer thinks that in many instances errors of judgment have sometimes been committed (especially in the earlier working of these deposits) in making the first workings both too high and too wide, and thus not only incurring considerable risk to life, but likewise causing great loss of mineral to the proprietors of the mines.

The main heading is frequently used as the trail-road for bringing the ore from the workings to the shaft, and so long as the gradient is light, 'skutches' or sprags are used in running the loaded bogies or tubs down to the level drift. It frequently happens, however, that the beds rise at so steep an angle as to necessitate the making of an incline, worked either by a wire rope or chain pulley, or by a drum furnished with an efficient brake. As the gradients of the beds are variable, sometimes running nearly flat and at other times at a steep angle, a series of inclines are frequently in use in working a deposit. The full bogies (one or two at a time) bring up the empty ones, and swinging platforms are used where the different workings connect with the inclines.

After the level workings have reached the extreme limit of the ore, either by being cut off by a fault or stone trouble, or by the boundary line, the work of taking out the pillars is begun. When the roof is of a strong character, the pillar-ore can be obtained at considerably less cost than when driving the thirls or stalls, the chief care necessary being to protect the line of workings either by pillars built of the stone that may be got in working the ore, or by pillars of wood or strong props. When wood is employed for this purpose, old railway sleepers and squared Norway timber are often used. Very little ore is lost under such circumstances, probably not more than 2 per cent, and where the ore is thin, the loss does not reach 1 per cent. More care is necessary and greater expense is incurred when the roof consists of a softer or less sound limestone or shale bed, as a much larger quantity of timber is required, and in spite of all possible care being exercised, the superincumbent weight may cause a collapse of the roof. In such cases some of the pillars may have to be approached through fallen ground. Then slice after slice is taken off until the ore is removed. In this way the working back of the pillars is carried on until that supporting the main heading is reached, which in the meantime is left undisturbed. The heading pillars are then worked back from the inside in a similar manner until the deposit is exhausted. Should the ore extend further to the dip, the shaft is deepened and drifts or 'eyes' are driven out at lower levels. The mode of procedure in working out pillar-ore is to commence at the 'rise' side of the pillar, taking about 6 or 8 feet of the ore as a working face and carrying it down to the dip side of the pillar. When this has been done, and the roof behind secured as indicated, another strip of ore is in like manner taken out. Sometimes stumps of ore are left at the two corners of the pillars as a means of strengthening the roof until the building of the wood or stone pillars is completed. These stumps can then usually be taken out with safety. Timber is set round the pillar in some cases to keep up the roof whilst the pillar is being removed.

Where the ore-bed has been of great thickness and two tiers of workings are rendered necessary, the pillars of the top tiers may sometimes have to be left as near as possible over the bottom pillars, with substantial middlings between the workings and strong arches of ore in the roof of the higher workings.

The upper pillars are then first worked out down to the sole of the top tier of workings. If the roof and ore are strong and hard, the working of the ore takes place from the inside outwards, but if the reverse conditions are present, then the working proceeds from the outside inwards, while the roof will require timbering. In the latter case, before proceeding with the work it may be necessary to support the roof of the lower workings or fill them with debris (as afterwards described) if this has not already been done. When the top pillars have been brought back so far, as much of the roof ore should be taken as can be got out with safety; round larch timber is then placed across the top of the middlings with the ends resting on the top of the bottom pillars, and these are overlaid with coverwood and débris above the coverwood to a depth of 3 or 4 feet. The middlings may be then worked out from the bottom upwards and the working of the bottom pillars afterwards commenced. Should a general collapse of the workings take place before all the ore has been extracted, drifts are driven through the fallen ground from the nearest available points and the ore worked out, as has already been described in speaking of robbery workings in vein-like deposits.

In certain conditions of the roof and ore it is often considered advisable, before commencing to remove the pillars, to pack with débris the waste area round them close up to the bottom of the middlings, access drifts to the bottom of the pillars and 'rises' to the middlings being left through the debris. In this way the ore in the lower tier of workings may be extracted with comparative safety, even should there be a collapse of the roof in the upper tier. In some mines instead of taking all the débris obtained from the various workings and development drifts in the mine and depositing it on the spoil-bank at the surface, a large portion is used for the above purpose. The bed-like deposits are subject to the same irregularities as those that occur in the vein-like deposits, viz. nips, vertical enlargements, and 'horses' or large blocks of stone intermixed with the ore. These disturbances of course increase the cost of working the ore, and render the above method of working liable to considerable alterations. The stone blocks are left as pillars, and they frequently deflect the workings from their intended course.

A good example of a bed-like deposit is that in Postlethwaite's Fletcher pit near Moor Row. The ore is of a hard nature but very rich in metallic iron, and has the advantage of a strong limestone roof. In consequence of this there is a very small percentage of loss in working out the pillars. The uniform extension of the deposit over a large area is also very marked. This deposit occurs in the second limestone.

IRREGULAR DEPOSITS (figs. 5, 6, 7, 8, 9, 10).—The third form of ore deposit is that of irregular and patchy masses in the limestone. These deposits also occur in the vicinity of 'faults.' They may be, and sometimes are, connected with vein-like and bed-like deposits. This kind of deposit cannot be worked in any very systematic manner. The method usually adopted is as follows: Assuming that the pit has been sunk and a level driven out to the ore, care must be taken not to drive the workings too large until the nature of the deposit is thoroughly understood. About 9 feet square is an average-sized working, but this of course is altogether dependent on the character of the ore. The first workings are driven in the same way as in the bed-like deposits, viz. by a series of working places and pillars, until the enclosing stone is reached on all sides and the horizontal extension of the ore at that level is known. If ore has been left in the roof, it is followed upwards either at the junction of the ore with the stone, or by plumb-rises in the ore at the most suitable points with the view of ascertaining the vertical extension in that direction; and if the height of the ore will permit, another tier of workings is driven horizontally, leaving a middling of sufficient thickness between the sole of the upper and the roof of the first working. If the full height of the pocket of ore has been reached by the higher tier of workings, any leads of ore into the surrounding stone are now followed up, and if the royalty is a rich one other pockets of ore may be opened out in this way.

It may be that the connecting ore lead is very small and not workable to profit; but in this kind of deposit better results are obtained by following these than by drifting through the solid stone, unless ore has been proved by boring to lie at a convenient level and at a short distance from some part of the working. In such a case, should there be no direct lead of ore, a stone drift is at once driven in the direction of the bore-hole, advantage being taken of the existence of any shale beds running in this direction, even although it may be necessary to go a little out of the direct course in doing so, the difference in cost in driving through limestone and shale being of material consideration.

The stone surrounding these irregular deposits is often of a very hard and siliceous character and full of loughs, rendering the operation of driving very slow and expensive. It may be here stated that the cost of driving a limestone drift varies greatly, and ranges from 13s. to 40s. per foot, while a shale drift may be driven at a cost of from 7s. to 16s. per foot. As the development of the mine goes on, the workings will consist of a number of ramifications through the limestone. Sometimes the connection between one large pocket of ore and another is by a gut of ore of considerable size. These guts are usually enclosed between two stone backs forming the sides and by an irregular roof and sole. If any ore is left in the bottom of the first workings a downward or dip working is made, and in the event of its continuance or further development the shaft is deepened and another level driven out. In this way it may be found necessary to drive a series of levels, one below the other, from the same shaft. In the event of the ore, cut by the first level, exhibiting a marked extension upwards and necessitating the use of a number of hoppers or hurries before it can be conveyed to the shaft, it is often found advisable to set off an upper level from the same shaft, or, should the distance be too great, to sink a new shaft from the surface.

Careful timbering is also required in the working of this class of ore, more especially if the pockets are of large dimensions. In the working of some of the smaller pockets, where the enclosing stone is of a hard nature, no timber may be required. Small guts in this kind of ground are worked as far as possible from the dip to the rise, and are subject to similar nips and enlargements as those accompanying other forms of deposits. The guts usually run parallel to the main faults nearest to them, and often continue for considerable distances. The workings are first carried to their farthest extension, and any ore left in the roofs, soles or sides is stripped off from the inside outwards. The taking out of pillars and middlings left in the mine after the ore-bearing area has been worked over, is carried on in a similar manner to that already described in dealing with bed-like deposits.

The irregular masses of ore in the old and new No. 1 pits and the No. 4 pit of the Montreal mines may be mentioned as one of the largest deposits of this kind in the district. An immense quantity of hæmatite of good quality has been raised from these mines during the last thirty years, and although the three forms of deposits are found in the royalty, by far the largest proportion has been obtained from the irregular deposit. Other deposits, such as High House and Crossfield

No. 2 pit, have also been of an extensive character.

The particulars shown in the following table of the number of persons employed underground in hæmatite mining throughout Cumberland, from 1893 to 1900 inclusive, are taken from the annual reports of Mr. J. L. Hedley, H.M. Inspector of Mines and Quarries for the county.

Table showing annual outputs, number of persons employed underground, and output per person underground :—

Year	Output	Persons under-ground	Output per person underground
1891	1,417,860	3,764	376
1892	1,355,007	3,960	342
1893	1,352,410	3,725	363
1894	1,286,590	3,599	357
1895	1,215,410	3,564	341
1896	1,279,558	3,698	346
1897	1,294,160	3,817	339
1898	1,251,764	3,741	334
1899	1,137,750	3,560	320
1900	1,103,430	3,524	313
Average	1,269,393·90	3,695·20	343·10

These figures indicate a gradual decrease in the producing power of the mines, while as a result the cost of raising the ore is proportionately increased. This however only applies to the Whitehaven district, as the large outputs from the Millom district are likely to be maintained for many years.

In the older mines of the first district the cost of production is also adversely affected by an increased cost for timber and the greater care that has to be exercised in keeping the ore free from impurities. Where the strata have been much crushed by collapses of the roof and pillars it is practically impossible to keep some of the shale and other impurities from mixing with the ore, the result being that the yield of metallic iron is lowered and that of silica increased.

The following table shows the average yield of metallic iron, etc., from the principal producing mines of the Whitehaven district during the years 1889, 1895, and 1900. These analyses were made by the Lonsdale Hæmatite Iron and Steel Co. Ld. and include samples from twelve different mines :—

No. of mines from which samples were taken	Year	Metallic iron	Insoluble residue	Water
14	1889	54·38	9·03	6·91
12	1895	52·69	10·53	6·48
12	1900	52·43	12·74	6·05

The result for 1900 may therefore be taken as the present average yield of the Whitehaven district.

The hæmatite miners of Cumberland are on the whole a steady and industrious class. 'Strikes' have been of rare occurrence in the various districts, and this has largely contributed to the welfare and better social position of the miners. Most of them are now members of the Cumberland Miners' Association, which has for some years (after several previous failures) established a footing in the county. Well organized centres of the St. John Ambulance Association exist in the Whitehaven and Millom districts, in which the workmen take a great interest. The success of this movement in the former district has been largely owing to the well directed efforts of Mr. J. L. Hedley and his assistant Mr. W. Leck, H.M. Inspectors of Mines for Cumberland, who have devoted much time and attention to the work, and in the latter to the energy and zeal displayed in this direction by the managers of the Hodbarrow mines.

The activity now prevailing in prospecting work to the south of Egremont in the Whitehaven district, and the encouraging results obtained, will, it is hoped, induce further search along the low lying belt of land stretching between Egremont and Millom; so that, by the opening up of new mines, the falling off in the output from the northern portion of the Whitehaven district may be counteracted and a future period of prosperity assured for hæmatite mining in Cumberland.

THE EDEN AND ESK FISHERIES

The salmon fisheries in the Eden are and have been from time immemorial of some little importance, whether regarded as a source of food supply or as a means of livelihood to a not inconsiderable number of the inhabitants of the district through which the river flows. An attempt to form even an approximate estimate of the number of fish caught is a difficult if not an impossible task, owing to the fact that for various reasons the net fishermen are most reticent as to the extent of their takes. It would, however, be quite safe to say that in an average year several thousands of salmon are taken in the river and estuary. In addition to these, there would be grilse which would probably outnumber the salmon, and trout which would outnumber salmon and grilse combined. It is much easier to estimate the number of men who make the principal part of their living by fishing, as we have reliable data to guide us in the number of licences issued.

In dealing with the salmon fisheries as an industry I propose to divide the river into sections, commencing at its mouth, and for this purpose I cannot do better than adopt the boundaries which are fixed by the Eden Fishery Board for the purpose of levying licence duties. That part of the river, which lies below or westward of Burgh Marsh Point is, for licensing purposes, looked upon as public or common water, though whether it is really public water is open to considerable doubt. This, however, does not come within the scope of this paper. The method of fishing, practised in this part of the river, is now exclusively that of the haaf net. Up to the year 1893 the whemmle or drift-net fishermen, who were chiefly Scotsmen, used to fish as far eastward as Burgh Marsh Point, but in that year the Eden Fishery Board, with the approval of the Board of Trade, prohibited whemmle or drift nets eastward of the Solway Viaduct, thus establishing what is called a playground in that portion of the estuary. Quite recently whemmle or drift nets have been declared to be illegal and now no licences are issued ; haaf nets, however, are still allowed. This mode of fishing probably gives employment to a greater number of men than any other. The number of licences issued, which varies according to the productiveness of the season, has risen as high as 150. The haaf net is of a very simple character and consists of a beam of wood about 16 feet long supported by three legs from 4 to 5 feet in height, to which framework is attached a net having a considerable amount of bag. The fisherman wades into the river to the necessary depth, sets up his net and holds it in position till he feels a fish strike the bag, when he tilts his net imprisoning the fish in the bag and brings it ashore. A licence duty of 30s. for each net has to be paid to the Eden Fishery Board. A great deal depends on getting a good stand, and to avoid disputes it is the custom with most of the fishermen to draw lots for choice of places. Thus the element of luck enters very largely, as indeed it does in all methods of fishing.

The next section for licensing purposes is that which lies between Burgh Marsh Point and the North British Railway Bridge near Carlisle. The draught net is practically the only one used in it. The number of boats employed varies from twelve to fourteen or fifteen, and as each boat requires four men, it will be seen that about fifty men find employment in this portion of the river. The licence duty to be paid for each draught net is £5. There only remains that stretch of the river situated above the North British Bridge which practically means between that place and Armathwaite, as there is very little fishing except angling practised above that point. In this portion the mode of fishing is more varied, consisting of draught net, hang net, coracle net and coops. At Warwick and Corby coops still exist, the only species of fixed engine to be found in the Eden fishery district. The fisheries in this part of the river are generally most productive in the earliest months of the season, the water at that time being well stocked with fish that have run up during the annual close season which ends on February 2, and it frequently happens that considerably more fish are killed in the upper or middle reaches of the river in February and March than are killed in the lower waters. After that time the lower waters begin to have the advantage, as the fish that are then taken are nearly all fish that are ascending from the sea or estuary. The hang net is probably the most successful net in the upper waters, but in the light of a recent decision in the High Courts there appears to be some doubt as to its legality, and it is not unlikely that its use may have to be discontinued. The fishermen in this portion of the river are like those in the stretch below, who fish for hire and are occasionally employed at other kinds of work. Probably there are not more than a dozen of them altogether, as the coops require very little attention and there are not more than four or five net licences issued. Thus we may gather that in a good season upwards of 200 fishermen make the greater part of their livelihood out of the river and estuary. Some of those in the lower waters about Port Carlisle and Bowness supplement this by fishing for white fish during the close time for salmon, but those higher up do not enjoy this opportunity and have to make the best shift they can to obtain employment from farmers and others. Many years ago, when agriculture was prosperous, there was no difficulty in finding work such as fencing, draining, etc.; but nowadays, as farmers cannot afford to employ much extra labour and landowners cannot afford to drain more than is absolutely necessary, the poor fishermen often fare badly.

With regard to the ownership of the fisheries, it may be explained that though the waters below Burgh Marsh Point are called public waters and can be fished by any one who takes out a licence, those above that point are undoubtedly private property. In a general way the landowners have the right of fishing opposite their land, but in the course of time some of these rights have been bought, sold and severed from the land, so that the rule does not always apply at the present day. The Earl of Lonsdale is by far the largest owner. The Corporation of Carlisle, by virtue of an ancient grant, owns what is called the 'free boat,' which has the right to fish in that part of the river which lies between King Garth and Etterby. The said 'free boat' may fish at any of the numerous fishing stations between these two points, and at any one of them may take every third draught, no matter how many other boats may be fishing at the same station at the time. At one time the fishing of the Corporation was of considerable value, but owing to a change in the course of the river and other circumstances, that value has been very much reduced. A house standing in a small field, called King's Garth or King Garth, is an appurtenant to the fishery, and here until quite recently the complimentary dinner to the Mayor was held. This dinner was a very ancient institution, and in former times it was the custom for the members of the Corporation to proceed down the river and see that the 'free boat' fished through all the water in which it had a right to fish, by way of maintaining those rights, finishing off at King Garth, where a feast was prepared for them, and spending the rest of the day in conviviality. The other owners of fisheries

are practically the owners of the adjoining land or those who have bought the rights from some such owner.

Much has been written in recent years and still continues to be written about the decadence of the salmon fisheries in general, and more than one Royal Commission has been appointed to inquire into the matter, but without any practical results as yet. It is doubtful indeed whether the fisheries are likely to be benefited by anything the Commissioners may recommend, as after all there is a limit to the productive powers of a river just as there is a limit to the capacity of land for carrying a herd of stock or of game. There is no doubt that there have been times when the fisheries in Eden were at a very much lower ebb than they are at present, bad as they are. Such a time occurred fifty years ago when, as is proved by information in the possession of the writer and from conversations with old fishermen, it was a common enough occurrence to fish for several weeks without seeing a single fish. There are, however, reasons which might partially account for this, to which I may refer later. After that time the fisheries began gradually to improve, and the next thirty years were more or less prosperous until the year 1878, when a disease, which up to that time was unknown, suddenly made its appearance and caused serious devastation. This disease, known as 'saprolegina ferox,' attacked fish of all species and at all stages of their growth, and very few that were attacked recovered. The few that did recover were migratory fish of the salmon tribe which by a natural instinct made their way down to the salt water as soon as they were attacked, and there is reason to think that these fish recovered. Those, however, that were in the higher reaches of the river succumbed before they were able to reach those healing waters, and large numbers were taken both by poachers and by the water bailiffs. The latter in the year 1882 took out and buried no fewer than 2,036 salmon. Since that time the numbers have steadily decreased, till in 1900 only twenty salmon were so accounted for. It is hoped that like many other epidemics it is becoming less virulent and that shortly it will have spent itself and the river will be again free from disease. To this disease a great deal of the late and present scarcity of salmon may be attributed. There are other contributory causes, and one of these is the increased pollution of the river, particularly in the lower reaches, where on account of the sewage from the town of Carlisle, which is discharged into the river, there is a considerable diminution of the number of fish. A laudable attempt is being made to deal with the difficulty, but at present, it is to be feared, without any very satisfactory results.

A word as to the watching of the river may not be out of place. In 1870 the Eden Fishery Board was formed, having jurisdiction over the greater part of the Eden and its tributaries, together with the English side of the Solway Firth. It is composed of ex-officio members, appointed by the County Councils of Cumberland and Westmorland, and members elected by the licence holders in the common waters of the Solway. This Board, which has a revenue from licences reaching in good seasons almost to £1,000, employs a staff of bailiffs and an inspector who look after the district. The number of bailiffs varies slightly according to the money at the Board's disposal, but usually consists of ten permanent men with additional help in the spawning season. These men are stationed at various points ranging from Port Carlisle to Kirkby Stephen. It will be seen that some of them have a large extent of water to watch. The most difficult portion of the river is naturally that in the neighbourhood of Carlisle, where there has been always a certain number of poachers who work in gangs and are very difficult to deal with. About 100 years ago an association of fishing proprietors was formed for the purpose of protecting the fisheries, watchers were employed, and no doubt a certain amount of useful work was done ; but for some reason or other the association was broken up, and from that date till 1870 any watching that was done was the result of private enterprise. At that time the worst and most destructive form of poaching was the taking of fish from the spawning beds by means of spears and torches, or as it was called ' blazing or burning the water.' The spawning beds above Wetheral at Brocklewath and Holm Wrangle were favourite places for this form of diversion, and it was usual for the proprietors of the lower reaches to proceed in a body to these haunts during the spawning season and lie in wait for the poachers. Many a desperate fight was the result till, on one occasion about the year 1861, a watcher, who was employed by some of the lower proprietors, was killed during an encounter with poachers at Brocklewath. The assailants were identified and two of them were sentenced to long terms of penal servitude. This appears to have sounded the death knell of organized poaching. Shortly afterwards the Fishery Board was formed, and now the risk of detection is so great that few care to take the chance of it.

It has been mentioned that there were certain reasons which might partly account for the scarcity of salmon fifty years ago. At that time and up to the year 1861, when a new Act was passed prohibiting the killing of herling, or as they are locally called ' whiting,' it was the usual practice to kill large numbers of these fish in the nets, and although there is still some difference of opinion as to their species, there can be little doubt that they are the young of salmon, and that their destruction in large numbers was bound to have a prejudicial effect on the salmon fisheries. It may also seem strange that as late as 1861 it was lawful after March 15 to kill salmon with the spear or ' leister,' after which time it was supposed that the majority of the fish had all finished their reproductive work and descended to the sea to recuperate, and that not much harm could be done. Such, of course, was the method of fishing in the days of ' Red Gauntlet.'

Nor can we say that this is the only reminiscence of those days in face of the grievances that still exist between the fishermen on the English and those on the Scottish shores of the Solway. At the present time the Englishman has decidedly the worst of it. The Act of 1861 declared that fixed engines were illegal, thus at one stroke abolishing all the stake nets on the English side of the Solway. On the Scottish side however the proprietors, taking advantage of an old statute which was passed at a time when the two countries were engaged in hostilities, and which exempted the waters of Solway from the prohibition against the use of fixed engines, established their claim to their stake nets, and thus were enabled to retain a method of fishing which was declared illegal and was discontinued on the English side. This is held by the English fishermen to be a great injustice. In addition to this, as the weekly close time on the English side extends to forty-two hours, while that on the Scottish side is six hours shorter, the English fishermen have the mortification of seeing their rivals fishing on the other side of the channel while they are compelled to stand idly by. Moreover, the fishermen on the Scottish shore may use a net whose mesh measures 7 inches, while the Englishmen's mesh must measure not less than 8 inches except for two months of the year. Thus it will be seen that the Englishmen have very good reason to complain of the laws governing the fisheries of the two countries. Several recommendations have been made by Royal Commissions and other bodies that the Solway should be placed under one law, and that it should be administered by a Joint Board ; but the difficulties in the way are so great that it is doubtful whether it will ever be accomplished. The Commission which is at present sitting will probably have something to say in the matter, as well as on the causes which have led to the existing scarcity of salmon ; but it is quite possible that before that report is issued an improvement in the fisheries may have taken place, when the matter will probably be shelved until we have another period of depression, seeing that an Act of Parliament, which will be necessary before any alteration is made, will scarcely meet with the approval of all parties concerned, and is sure to be strenuously opposed.

A word upon the different migrations of fish may not be out of place in these observations. At the beginning of the year if the weather is open, considerable numbers of what are called spring salmon usually make their way from the estuary to the river. These are young fish that have never spawned, and are of the finest quality, having a very good reputation in all the markets and commanding the highest price. The average weight of these fish is 8 or 9 lb. Later the average weight increases, until in the months of July and August it is quite common to catch fish of 20 or even 30 lb. weight. These later fish are probably making their way up to the spawning beds, and on them the future stocking of the river depends. The nets in the river are discontinued at the end of August, and after that time the only enemies the fish have to contend against are the anglers and of course poachers. The migration of grilse, which are undoubtedly the young of salmon, commences about the end of May or the beginning of June, and goes on until the autumn. When these fish first arrive their weight does not exceed 4 or 5 lb., but later 6 or 7 lb. may be taken as the average. The salmon trout commence to run in April and continue till probably August. The weight of salmon trout does not vary as does that of grilse, and 1½ lb. may be taken as the average weight. The minimum size of mesh which is allowed, viz. 7 inches, will not take a trout of less than 1 lb. or 1¼ lb., so that the smaller fish escape the net, and are either caught by the angler or are left to reproduce their species.

Much has been written about the relation which the different species of salmon, grilse, sea trout and herling bear to each other, and many experiments have been made with a view of determining the question ; but authorities are by no means yet agreed on the subject, and the writer, after thirty years intimate connection with the fisheries, has only learned that the more he sees the more he is convinced of his ignorance of fishing matters.

It may be of some interest to refer in conclusion to the destination of the fish that are caught. Before the advent of railways and of rapid transit we are told that, after a good run of fish, the price was so low that a good salmon might be bought for one shilling, and that servants who were making engagements used to stipulate that they were not to be fed on salmon more than once or at most twice a week. At that time the fish had to be consumed at or within a comparatively short distance from the place where it was caught; consequently when the supply was in excess of the demand prices fell very low. At the present day, owing to the use of ice and the splendid service of trains, fish can be sent to all parts of England and even to the continent. It is not at all unusual for Eden and Solway fish to be sent to Paris, and it frequently happens that salmon can be bought cheaper in London than in Carlisle.

It may be noticed in connection with the migration of salmon that the Eden is very much earlier than its sister river the Esk, which in turn is earlier than the Derwent. This is somewhat difficult to account for. It is usual to attribute it to the fact that the Eden waters are warmer than those of other rivers, but why this should be so one can scarcely understand, as the Eden is fed from some of the highest watersheds in the country, such as the west side of Crossfell, the north side of Skiddaw, Lake Ulleswater, and the highest reaches of the Irthing. Whatever may be the explanation, the fact remains that salmon ascend the Eden two months earlier than they ascend the Esk, and that in the Derwent it is not usual to see any considerable number of salmon before May or June.

Although the Esk may be called the sister river to the Eden, falling into the same estuary and having many of the same characteristics, it occupies a very different position from a commercial point of view. In Eden the greatest interest is netting, which, as we have seen, is rather an important one, and in which a good deal of capital is employed ; in Esk the greatest interest is angling, netting occupying but a subordinate position. Indeed for the last fifteen years there have been no nets in Esk.

Previous to the year 1886 nets were used in the lower waters, which principally belong to the Earl of Lonsdale. These waters extend from the sea upwards to the junction with the river Lyne. Above that point the Duke of Buccleuch and Sir Richard Graham of Netherby are practically the sole owners. In 1886 these two gentlemen, with a view to improving their fisheries in the upper waters for angling, rented the Earl of Lonsdale's fishery and took off the nets. Curiously enough this experiment had not the effect expected from it, for, instead of improving, the angling appears to have deteriorated, and now the old arrangement has been reverted to, and nets will again be used in the lower waters.

There is no doubt that the Esk is a very fine river for angling. Large numbers of sea trout and herling usually ascend in their season, and furnish excellent sport. It is also comparatively free from pollution, which in dry weather gives it a great advantage over the Eden. In Esk the water comes down in flood very rapidly and subsides just as rapidly. This is owing to the hilly nature of its watershed, its principal tributaries being the Lyne, Liddel, Tarras, Wauchope and the Ewes, all of which carry the drainage of a very mountainous district. There is no Fishery Board which has jurisdiction over the Esk, consequently there is no power to levy licence duties, and the protection has to be undertaken by the proprietors. For the same reason there is a slight difference as compared with Eden in the weekly close time ; Esk is governed by the statute, and has its close time commencing at twelve noon on Saturday and terminating at six a.m. on Monday, while Eden, by virtue of a bye-law of the Fishery Board, commences and terminates six hours earlier. By another bye-law the Eden Board extended the season for angling to November 15, while Esk ends on November 1.

Owing to the fact that Esk is partly an English and partly a Scottish river, it has occupied a somewhat anomalous position with regard to legislation, the laws of the two countries differing very materially. Previous to 1862, when a Scottish Fishery Act was passed, that portion of the Esk which is in Scotland was subject to Scottish law and the portion in England to English law. In 1865 an English Act placed the whole of Esk from its source to the sea under the English law as far as salmon are concerned, but while doing so omitted to repeal previous statutes, thus leaving the Scottish portion of the Esk under four different and partly contradictory Acts, which sometimes leads to confusion.

DERWENT FISHERIES

Some time after the Norman Conquest we get the first insight of the value of the Derwent fishery from old grants and charters. Whenever we find in the history of the past that some particular interest or industry has at any time been protected by charter or statute, it is safe to assume that that particular interest or industry was at the time of its protection considered to be of some importance.

In the middle of the twelfth century Gospatric son of Orm gave two parts of the fishery in Derwent to the abbey of Holmcultram, except Waytcroft, which he gave to the priory of Carlisle. Thomas confirmed the grant of Flimby made by his father Gospatric to the convent of Holmcultram, and gave to that house the whole fishings of Derwent.[1] In 1190 we find in the papal confirmation of grants to the abbey of Holmcultram amongst a long list the following : ' Ex dono Thomæ filii Cospatricii, unam rete in Derwent cum visneto, et unam piscariam in Derwent, unam mansuram in ripa ejusdem fluminis, sicut carta ejusdem testatur.'[2] This papal confirmation is by Clement III.

About forty years later we find that the abbot and monks of Calder were claiming the sole possession of these fisheries, and indeed through all this period the religious houses exacted and clung tenaciously to rights of fishery which were confirmed as occasion required by different sovereigns. The monks of Calder seem to have been successful in substantiating their claim, for Henry III. confirmed to them their claims to the fishery of Derwent and that of Egre in 1231. The grant runs as follows : ' Ex dono Ranulphi Meschin piscariam de Derewent et piscariam de Egre—Ex dono Thomæ filii Gospatricii, 20 Salmones annuatim ad festum Sancti Johannis Baptistæ ; et unum rete in Derewent, inter pontem et mare.'[3] From this document we gather that the grant to Calder Abbey was made by Thomas son of Gospatric, who made

patric gave 8 acres of land in Seton, adjoining to 32 acres of their own there and one net in Derwent, and one toft nigh the bank where they may abide and manage the fishery. And John son of Alan de Camberton released to them a pool which they had made or should make to turn the water of Derwent, or so much thereof as should be prejudicial to their fishery of Seton.

[1] *Reg. of Holmcultram*, MS. ff. 34–6.
[2] Dugdale, *Mon.* v. 600. Thomas son of Gos-
[3] Ibid. v. 341.

the former grants to Holmcultram. It is also very noticeable that the Derwent could supply 20 salmon on Midsummer day, a thing which is very certain it could not do now.

The monks seem to have been very aggressive in all matters connected with their possessions. The prior of St. Bees[1] was worsted at an assize held in Carlisle 1278–9, when the jurors presented and the whole county complained 'that the prior of St. Bega has two engines called "cupe" for catching salmon in his pool of Staynburn, where in time past he had but one, and the other was set up six years ago without warrant and after the last justice eyre. Therefore he is in amercement.' The sheriff is ordered to remove the second 'cupa' at sight of the jury at the prior's expense. This seems to be the first mention of coops at what is now Salmon Hall, where Lord Lonsdale's coops are still situated. All the fishing previous to this may have been lower down between the bridge and the sea, unless the word 'piscariam' refers to some engine, which is unlikely. In all probability the whole fishing was done by net until the coops at Stainburn were erected.

This assize is also especially interesting for the glimpse afforded of the practical working of fisheries in this county during the thirteenth century. On this occasion the jurors of the county made a presentment regarding the great destruction of salmon coming up to spawn, and likewise of the young fry going down to the sea. The whole county, knights and freeholders, unanimously decided that they should observe a close time, 'that from Michaelmas to St. Andrew's Day no net shall be drawn or placed at weirs, pools, or mills, or mill-ponds, and that none fish in the above or any other waters in the county with nets, stergilds, or other engine within said close time or without engine. Also that from the feast of the Apostles Philip and James until the Nativity of St. John Baptist no net or "wile" or "borache" shall be placed at pools or mills or mill-ponds in said waters.' Only approved nets were to be employed, and the meshes were required to be wide enough to let the salmon fry through, viz. of four thumbs length. Persons convicted of illegal practices were to be summarily disposed of by being sent to the king's prison.

The voluntary adoption of close time and regulations for fishing seems to prove that up to

[1] William de Fortibus, Earl of Albemarle, by his charter granted and confirmed to the church of St. Bees in Coupland, all his ancestors' grants, that is to say, the salmons which they had by the gift of Alan, son of Waltheof, and six salmons which they had by the gift of the Lady Alice de Romely.

this time there had been no legal close time. It also seems to point to the fact that all kinds of fishing had greatly increased, and that the nets and fixed engines were getting very destructive. We can well understand this if there were no regulations attached to their working. This presentment would also argue that fishing was now general on the river and not confined to the mouth as previously. The coops at Stainburn were probably a development of the fishery formerly carried on between the bridge and the sea, and not an older or separate fishery. It would be found easier and more profitable to have a coop than to use nets, or if nets were used there were in addition the coops, and the business qualities of the monks have been shown before. One of the enactments of this jury survived until the last century, viz. their order that illegal nets were to be burnt in public when seized. In 1827 a large and no doubt useful collection of fishing nets was publicly burnt in the market-place of Appleby. This part of the presentment lasted, therefore, throughout the intervening period.

To the reign of Edward I. we must refer for the first attempt to make statutable provision for a close time for salmon. 'It is provided,' reads the statute of Westminster the Second (1285), 'that the waters of Humber, Ouse, Trent, Don, Aire, Derwent, Nid, Yare, Severn, Tees and all other waters wherein salmons be taken in the realm shall be in defence for taking salmon from the Nativity of our Lady unto St. Martin's day.' Richard II. reincorporated these provisions in an Act of the 13th of Richard II. (1389) and further declared that 'no fisher or garthman nor any other of what estate or condicion that he be should put in the waters of . . . nor any other waters of the realm nets called stalkers, nor any other nets or engines whatsoever by the which the fry or the breed of the salmon, lampreys or any other fish might in anywise be taken or destroyed.' Four years later the justices of the peace of all the counties of England were appointed conservators of the above mentioned Acts of Edward I. and Richard II. for the preservation of salmon 'in the counties where they be justices.' This was in 1393. History does not state that these close times were carefully observed, and the feud between the upper and lower riparian owners would be as bitter then as it is to-day. The only mention of salmon about this period in the upper waters of the Derwent is that salmon are seen at 'spawning time.' Evidently they were very scarce except at that time.

Coming to a later period we get references

to the fishery in the Derwent from Pennant, Camden, Denton, Leland and others, one of whom describes ' Wyrekinton as oppidum piscatorium.' Camden [1] says : ' After these rivers are united, the Derwent falls into the sea at Workington, famous for the salmon fishing. It is now the seat of the family of the Curwens.' Leland's description [2] is : ' Also on the west syde of Darwent is a prety creke, wher as shyppes cum to, wher ys a lytle prety fyssher town cawled Wyrkenton, and ther is the chefe howse of Sir Thomas Curwyn.' Pennant says : ' The Derwent washes the skirts of the town and discharges itself into the sea about a mile west.' It may be mentioned here that no reference is ever made to the use of the haf or haaf net so common at the head of the Solway. Doubtless the mouth of the river has never lent itself to the use of this net any more than it does now. Striking the fish with leisters in the tideway was always a favourite method of fishing, and was in vogue in 1785 on the whole of the Solway coast. In 1755 the *Gentleman's Magazine* makes reference to the value of salmon, ' which,' observes this anonymous writer, ' at their markets sells from three halfpence to twopence a pound ; but the people have so little notion of dressing it to advantage that they throw away the livers, and eat the fish without having so much as a little melted butter for sauce. If any remain unsold after the market is over, they cut it in pieces and salt it, putting it up close in a pot or earthen vessel, to be eaten as winter provision with potatoes or parsnips.' This anonymous writer apparently did not know that the Workington men sent their fish ' up to London upon horses, which changing often, go night and day without intermission, and, as they say, out-go the post, for that the fish come very sweet and good to London, where the extraordinary price they yield, from 2s. 6d. to 4s. per pound, pays very well for the carriage. They do the same from Carlisle.' In view of the bad roads which had to be traversed this method of marketing fish implies that those engaged in the industry were men of enterprise.

Clarke stated in 1787 that salmon never entered Derwentwater, but as they were found in Borrowdale this must be a mistake, and probably arose from the difficulty of observing fish in the lake. Pennant writing of the Derwent says that salmon

come up the river from the sea about Michaelmas, and force their way through both lakes as far as

[1] *Britannia* (ed. Gibson) ii. 1008.
[2] *Itinerary* (ed. Hearne) vii. 49.

Borrowdale. They had lately been on their return, but the water near the (Ouze) bridge proving too shallow to permit them to proceed, they were taken by dozens, in very bad order, in the nets that were drawing for trout at the end of the lake.

The author of *Observations chiefly Lithological* wrote in 1804 :—

The lake of Derwentwater has no char in it ; only perch, or bass, as it is here called, eels, pike and trout ; and the salmon which pass through the lakes of Derwent and Bassanthwaite from the river Cocker to spawn in the winter season. In the month of May the salmon smelts, or fry, as they are called, are on their way to the ocean. They may then be very easily caught. They are esteemed a great delicacy.

Hutchinson speaking of Workington says:—

The salmon fishery on the river Derwent is considerable. Mr. Curwen's tenant has the draught from the High Pier and on the Quay ; Lord Lonsdale's tenant draws from the Merchants' Quay up to Cammerton, about four miles in length. The sea coast fishery is farmed of Mr. Curwen by Richard Graham, who gives us the following account of his method of taking salmon, which he calls salmon hunting : 'The salmon hunter is armed with a spear of three points barbed, having a shaft fifteen feet in length. When the fish is left by the tide, intercepted by shallows or sand banks, near the mouth of the river, or at any inlets on the shore, where the water remains from one foot to four feet in depth, or when their passage is obstructed by nets, they shew where they lie by the agitation of the pool ; when my horse is going at a swift trot or a moderate gallop, belly deep in the water, I make ready my spear with both hands, and at the same time hold the bridle ; when I overtake the salmon, I let go one hand, and with the other strike with the spear, and seldom miss my stroke, but kill my fish ; then with a turn of my hand I raise the salmon to the surface of the water, turn my horse's head the readiest way to shore, and so run the salmon on to dry land without dismounting. In the fishery I am establishing at Workington, in the proper season, by different modes, I can kill, one day with another, one hundred salmon a day ; methods of my own invention I intend to put in practice, which never were practised before in any part of the world ; I have tried them, and they answer, and when known, they may become a public good. I can take the fish up at sea in ten fathom water. A man in the ordinary way of salmon hunting, well mounted, may kill forty or fifty in a day ; ten salmon is not a despicable day's work for a man and a horse. My father was the first man I ever heard of who could kill salmon on horseback.'

Our correspondent then offers a wager of 100 guineas that at this time he will kill more salmon on horseback in one day than any three men in England. He adds :—

The most noted places for killing salmon on horseback are the rivers Eden and Esk ; from

Sandsfield to Bowness, and sometimes as far to the west at Skinburness. The seasons for killing salmon at Workington are in August, September, October and sometimes in February.[1]

No commercial value seems ever to have attached to salmon fishing by net at any place above Stainburn. There are many who have netted, and do net, but for sport only and not for profit, and at present there would be encouragement for such a practice. Hutchinson, in describing Cockermouth, says : 'The rivers abound with salmon, trout, brandling, pike, eels and other smaller fish.' Other references about the latter end of the eighteenth century are similar in character, and would point to that period as the high water mark in the history of the salmon. The artificial condition of rivers at the present time are prejudicial to fish ; there is a maximum of pollution, a minimum of food for fishes. Drainage has been the cause of the destruction of spawn in summer, when the small streams run absolutely dry and thousands of fry and yearlings are thereby destroyed, the majority falling a prey to birds and rats.

The coops at Stainburn, first mentioned in 1278, have probably been in continuous use ever since. They are now the property of Lord Lonsdale, and are let to a few gentlemen who sublet to the Derwent Fishery Board. These coops have now for a very considerable time been let either from year to year or by lease, and no record has been kept either by the owner or tenant of the number or weight of fish taken. The late tenants, Messrs. Dalzell, used to net from Salmon Hall, where the coops are, as far as the Cloffocks, but the present tenants have done very little netting, preferring that the fish should run up the river and afford sport for the rod fishers. There has also been no record taken of the salmon caught by rod, either previous to or since the Fishery Board came into being, but the last few seasons have been wretched, and there seems to be a very bad outlook for the salmon fishery.

The Derwent Fishery Board was formed on the 29 March 1880, with the late Mr. William Fletcher as chairman, and with the exception of the first two years there are records of the revenue obtained from rod, net, coop and general licences. These last however have more interest in the trout than in the salmon. Appended are lists giving all the information which is available by the clerk to the Derwent Fishery Board, Mr. T. C. Burn, with reference to

the sources of revenue obtained. These figures are an index roughly of the various good and bad seasons, but cannot be taken as an exact exposition of the state of the Derwent and its tributaries during each year. The pursuit of salmon fishing has grown so remarkably during the last thirty years that all rivers here, as well as in Norway, Sweden and Finland, are ransacked by rods, so that, though the spoil is less, there is a greater rush even to the mediocre waters of the Derwent, and a somewhat fictitious value may be given to the later years. It cannot but be a matter of great regret that a fine river like the Derwent should produce such a miserable salmon harvest, but the varied interests make any scheme well nigh impossible to carry out, and the number of small proprietors are always a great hindrance to any complete arrangement or improvement. It seems that at the present time the salmon fishery of the Derwent is of much less value than it was when the first records are to be found.

DERWENT FISHERY BOARD
Amount received for Salmon Licences for the following years, viz. :—

Year	Instrument licensed			Total		
	Rods	Nets and coop	General licence			
	£ s. d.	£ s. d.	£	£ s. d.		
1880 [1]	—	—	—	—		
1881 [1]	—	—	—	—		
1882	166 0 0	15 0 0	9	190 0 0		
1883	149 5 0	23 0 0	9	181 5 0		
1884	178 10 0	16 0 0	20	214 10 0		
1885	208 15 0	25 0 0	12	245 15 0		
1886	221 0 0	22 0 0	17	260 0 0		
1887	162 10 0	31 0 0	12	205 10 0		
1888	161 10 0	36 13 4	12	210 3 4		
1889	180 0 0	40 0 0	12	232 0 0		
1890	172 5 0	30 0 0	12	214 5 0		
1891	201 0 0	24 0 0	18	243 0 0		
1892	260 5 0	21 0 0	18	299 5 0		
1893	219 5 0	27 0 0	18	264 5 0		
1894	167 0 0	27 0 0	18	212 0 0		
1895	209 10 0	22 0 0	18	249 10 0		
1896	210 10 0	17 0 0	18	245 10 0		
1897	200 5 0	17 0 0	18	235 5 0		
1898	151 7 6	17 0 0	18	186 7 6		
1899	147 7 6	17 0 0	18	182 7 6		
1900	122 0 0	17 0 0	18	157 0 0		
1901	140 5 0	22 0 0	18	180 5 0		

The Secretary of State's certificate of formation of the Board is dated 29 March 1880.

[1] Information for these years is not available. Salmon and trout licences included in the accounts in one amount ; it is therefore impossible to define salmon.

[1] *Hist. of Cumb.* ii. 139–41.

THE RAVENGLASS FISHERIES

The estuary of Ravenglass is formed by the confluence of three rivers which discharge themselves into the sea at that place. The Irt, which flows from Wastwater, approaches the estuary from the north, its course having been deflected by banks of sand on the sea shore. The Esk, which rises on the shoulder of Crossfell, meeting with the same obstruction, makes a bend towards the north a little below Waberthwaite church. The Mite occupies a central position. The combined waters of the three rivers have forced an opening through the sand banks to the sea, thus forming a spacious harbour on which the town is situated. The projecting tongues of sandhills approaching each other from the north and south, known as Drigg Common and Esk Meals, unite to make a natural harbour within which there is anchorage for small vessels. At high tides the depth of the estuary could register at least 20 feet on the bar. At low water nothing is seen but a wide expanse of sand fringed by a massive line of sandhills in the distance, with a streak of fresh water running through it as the combined rivers flow to the open sea. In days gone by, the natural advantages for anchorage made Ravenglass a port of considerable trade and importance for that district, but for many years past—that is, since the opening of the Furness railway—it has been on the decline. The visit of a ship or trading boat is now an event of rare occurrence.

The fisheries in this estuary, owing chiefly to the smallness of the streams which discharge themselves into it, have never been comparatively of great importance. The following schedule will give some idea of their productiveness as well as the size of fish taken in these waters.

SEA TROUT AND SALMON TAKEN AT THE NET FISHERIES AT RAVENGLASS

Year	Sea Trout		Grilse and Salmon		Total Sea Trout, Grilse and Salmon	
	No. of fish	Weight	No. of fish	Weight	No.	Weight
		lb.		lb.		lb.
1875	228	546	125	1,081	353	1,627
1876	349	836	383	2,920	732	3,756
1883	345	854	293	2,301	638	3,155
1884	506	1,478	444	3,220	950	4,698
1885	287	707	361	2,957	648	3,664
1886	412	1,082	213	1,480	625	2,562
1887	712	1,823	206	1,374	918	3,197
1888	467	954	332	1,980	799	2,934
1889	1,949	4,081	389	2,541	2,338	6,622
Total . .	5,255	12,361	2,746	19,854	8,001	32,215

lb.
Average size of sea trout 2.35
„ „ grilse and salmon . . . 7.23

It is admitted by the netsmen that the fisheries at Ravenglass during the four seasons ending with 1901 have been on the decline when compared with prior seasons. This fact, together with a short study of the above table, may show that no progress has been made in fish production since the formation of the West Cumberland Fishery District in 1879.

Of the three rivers, the Irt, Esk and Mite, falling into the sea at Ravenglass, the Irt is the most important considered as to the number of sea trout and salmon ascending. Three draught nets are generally in use by the riparian owners on this river : one at Drigg by Mr. Hodgkin, another at Holmrook by Mr. C. R. F. Lutwidge, and a third by Sir Thomas Brocklebank of Greenlands. But their use is not regular, and during some seasons it is understood no netting takes place.

The river Esk, although many fine fish run up it, is inferior to the Irt as to numbers. No net was used on the Esk above Ravenglass during 1901. The river Mite being small has only a few sea trout, with an occasional grilse, that run up it. It is not netted. The number taken up the rivers by netting may be estimated at about one-eighth of the total yield at Ravenglass on the average.

A few fish commence to run in May, but the principal numbers run in June, July, August and September. The sea trout are the first to run, which they do in June and July, the grilse coming usually in July and August. The largest salmon are the last to ascend. A few salmon are generally taken each season exceeding 20 lb. in weight, but only one exceeding 30 lb. in weight has been recorded. That was taken on 10 September 1902 and weighed 36 lb.

There are three modes of taking sea trout and salmon at Ravenglass by nets. Two are used in connection with a fixed stake net placed in the river Esk at Ravenglass. The first is by a trap, or as it is locally called a 'fish-house,' which takes fish on the flood tide, and into which the fish once entering cannot easily return. The second is on the ebb tide by an ordinary fish garth, a 2-inch grating stopping the fishes' descent to the sea. The third mode of capture is by a long draught net, worked by two fishermen with the aid of a boat. By this means all likely pools in the estuary are drawn. The principal one near the harbour mouth, called Mungarth,[1] is constantly drawn at every ebb, while the fish are running, during the netting season which closes on September 14.

The Ravenglass fisheries are in the West Cumberland Fishery District, which extends from St. Bees North Head lighthouse on the north to Haverigg Point on the Duddon on the south. This district was formed in 1879. All fishery rights at Ravenglass are owned by Lord Muncaster of Muncaster Castle.

THE SOLWAY FISHERIES

So far as can be ascertained the value of the Solway Firth as a fishing ground was first discovered in the year 1853, when trawling was commenced in the northern part of the Firth by a fisherman named James Baxter hailing from Morecambe with a boat called *James*. When he began trawling he found that shrimps, soles, plaice, cod and skate were very plentiful, and on this news spreading additional boats commenced fishing year after year until at the present time there are about sixty boats engaged in fishing from Silloth northwards to Burgh Marsh Point, a distance of about eighteen miles, and at least 240 boats to the south of Silloth, making altogether a total of about 300 boats at work on the Cumberland coast, including trawl-boats, draft and drift-net boats, and also boats used in line-fishing.

Draft-net fishing for sparling (otherwise known as smelts) was next discovered and for a time proved a valuable industry, but owing to the absence of any close time during the breeding season, the fishermen captured them all the year round, in consequence of which the fish became so nearly extinct that the pursuit of them almost ceased.

Up to about the year 1865 fishermen used any kind of nets they wished, including such as trap-nets, poke-nets and stream-nets, these of course being 'fixed engines,' but about this year their use was by Act of Parliament declared illegal on the English side of the Firth. The law, however, did not prevent their use on the Scotch side, and they still continue to be used there to the present time. Line fishing for cod and skate was also followed.

In the year 1864 oyster dredging was commenced opposite Maryport by a boat hailing from Fleetwood in Lancashire, and as the industry was found to be productive, it attracted some thirty large boats from Fleetwood, Jersey, and other ports. This fishing continued productive for about three years, but then gradually fell away owing to the bed being overfished. As the fishermen were unable to make a livelihood it practically ceased to be pursued.

As might naturally be expected, owing to there being no close season for any of the different kinds of sea-fish and no restriction in the size of the mesh of nets which were used, fish of all kinds grew scarcer and scarcer until in fact the Firth became almost valueless as a fishing ground, and this state of things continued up to the year 1897, when the Cumberland Sea Fisheries bye-laws came into force. Since that time the fishing industry has increased by leaps and bounds. In their first annual report the committee thought it only right, before dealing with the principal objects of the report, to give a short *résumé* of the circumstances which had led to the formation of the Cumberland Sea Fisheries District. The facts were shortly these : In the month of November 1893 the Sea Fisheries Committee, which was then composed wholly of members of the County Council of Cumber-

1 Monkgarth, a fishery formerly belonging to the monks of Calder (Dugdale, *Mon.* v. 342).

land and which worked in combination with Lancashire, considered that the time had come when application might advantageously be made to the Board of Trade under the provisions contained in the Sea Fisheries Regulation Act, 1888, to constitute a Sea Fishery District for the county of Cumberland and its estuaries, extending to the mouth of the river Sark at Sarkfoot, near Gretna, as its extreme northern boundary. A scheme for the creation of the district was accordingly formulated and submitted to the County Council of Cumberland who, after full consideration, gave it their sanction, and the committee thereupon proceeded to submit it to the Fisheries and Harbour Department of the Board of Trade with a view of obtaining their sanction and approval.

Owing to the innumerable public notices which are required by the Board of Trade Regulations to be given to all persons and bodies likely to be affected by such a scheme, the question had to be fully and carefully considered, and in consequence did not make such rapid progress as some people wished for, and in the month of November 1894 the point which had been fixed as the southern boundary of the proposed district was altered in order to meet the wishes of the Sea Fisheries Committee which existed in Lancashire, and the boundary was then defined as ' a line drawn true south-west from the seaward extremity of Haverigg Point in the said county of Cumberland.'

All these preliminary points having been disposed of, the scheme was placed before the Board of Trade and was sanctioned by them. Whereupon after having had nearly a year's experience of the bye-laws, it was found that they were proving of much benefit to the fishermen of Cumberland, not only on account of the efficient system of watching which was maintained throughout the whole district by the officers appointed by the committee, thus enabling poachers to be captured and dealt with in such a way as would put a stop to their nefarious practices, but also from the fact that immature fish were protected from being captured. The result was that as only the best paying size of fish was placed on the market the price of fish on the coast had risen considerably. The committee has throughout endeavoured to carry out the Acts of Parliament and the bye-laws sanctioned by the Board of Trade in such a manner as would prove beneficial to the fishing industry, and yet not be likely to press hardly on those persons who are dependent on that trade for their means of livelihood.

When the bye-laws first came into operation orders were given to the officers of the committee that all offenders should be warned in the first instance to desist from illegal practices, and it was not until warnings were found ineffectual that the aid of the law was invoked.

In the year 1898 these bye-laws were working admirably and proving to be of great service to the fishermen of Cumberland. The season was a very good one both as regards the quantity and quality of different kinds of fish obtained, with the exception of herrings, which were very scarce. Trawling, which commenced in the month of August, was very good, and a large number of boats came to the Cumberland district from Lancashire, Isle of Man, and even from Grimsby and other places. This experience affords good evidence that the committee has a valuable fishery to protect.

In the year 1899 the fishing season, notwithstanding the rough weather which prevailed in the autumn, was on the whole exceedingly prolific, and much better than that of the preceding year. Fish were for the most part abundant and of good quality, and very large takes of nearly all kinds of fish, including haddock (which had not been known to be so plentiful for years), were made by the fishermen, and good prices were realized. Herring and mackerel, as was the case in the year 1898, were scarce, and the sparling fishermen also complained, but they attributed their want of success not to the scarcity of fish, as they were known to be still plentiful, but to the shifting channels.

An entirely new feature in the fishing industry of the coast commenced in June 1899, viz. that of prawn trawling, which during part of the season proved very successful, but the weather throughout the latter part of the year was very stormy and interfered greatly with this fishing. The prices realized were not particularly high, but in spite of this good returns were obtained on account of the great number of prawns caught, and it is quite evident, from the large quantities of these fish which have been taken, that the Solway, more particularly off Maryport, abounds in prawns. This new class of fishing has attracted between twenty and thirty boats to our fishing ground, many of them being from Morecambe Bay, which is a recognized prawn trawling district.

The quantity and value of fish landed during the year ending 31 December 1899 on the Cumberland coast was—including soles, lemon soles, plaice, white flounder, sparling, cod, gurnet, red gurnet, grey gurnet, turbot, brill, whiting, herring, skate, bluet, conger, shrimps, prawns, crayfish, lobsters, oysters, mussels, periwinkles, and cockles—total weight, 747 tons 19 cwt. 1¼ qrs.; value, £10,473 9s. 11½d.

In the year 1900 the first and second class fishing boats had some excellent takes of various kinds of fish throughout the district, including soles, haddocks, and plaice, and more especially on the south side of Silloth, where such an abundant supply has not been known to exist for many years. The fish were of good size and quality. The stake-net and draft-net fishermen also had a very profitable season among the plaice in the northern portion of the district. Skate and sparling have not been so plentiful for years, but herring and mackerel (as was the case during the past two seasons) and cod were very scarce indeed.

Long-line fishermen along the coast from Silloth northwards, however, were very successful among small cod, the Firth being literally alive with this class of fish, but during the quarter ending 31 December of that year the stormy weather which prevailed seriously interfered with the efforts of the fishermen who pursued this industry. Off the coast of Workington and Maryport there were again some excellent takes of 'prawns,' the fishing for which, as mentioned before, only commenced in June 1899, and good prices were realized. The prawn trawlers had also some very successful catches from Workington northwards among small soles and plaice, which were very abundant in that portion of the district. Lobsters, shrimps, mussels and cockles of good size and quality were also plentiful in different parts of the district, and the prices obtained were, it is understood, in all cases equal to those of the year 1899.

On comparing the weight of fish landed on the Cumberland coast during the year 1900 with that of the previous year, there is an increase of 56 tons odd. The total weight and value are as follows :—

	tons	cwt.	qrs.		£	s.	d.
1900 .	804	7	0½	value	12,049	13	7½
1899 .	747	19	1½	„	10,473	9	11½
Increase	56	7	3	weight „	1,576	3	8

There is a large number of sailing and steam trawlers hailing from Scotland, Lancashire, Isle of Man, and Grimsby that constantly fish in the Firth, but as their catches are invariably taken to other markets it is impossible to say what weight of fish is landed by them annually.

In the year 1897, when the Cumberland Sea Fisheries bye-laws came in force, there were only two trawl boats fishing out of Maryport harbour, and now there may be seen at times forty boats sailing from that port, twenty-four belonging to Maryport, and the remainder hailing from other places.

Herrings were very plentiful in the years 1888 and 1889, some of the boats (containing three men each) getting as much as 30,000 herrings in one night's fishing. These fish seem to frequent the coast intermittently, one year they may be very plentiful and the next year very scarce, but so far as can be ascertained no reason has been discovered for this strange condition of things. Crabs are also plentiful along the shores of the Firth. Oysters, which were almost extinct in the year 1867 owing to overfishing, are now very plentiful, the beds extending from opposite Maryport to Selker rocks, a distance of about twenty-six miles.

There are hundreds of acres of cockles, the main bed extending from opposite Silloth to West Scaur near Bowness, a distance of about six and a half miles, and there is also a very fine mussel bed at Ravenglass extending for a distance of about a mile long.

It is not easy to calculate with accuracy the number of persons who are dependent on this industry for their livelihood, but we shall not be rating it at too high a figure if we place it at about 450 men. At times during the year when the rough weather prevails and the small boats are unable to get out to fish, some of the men follow other employments. There are also about 200 men and boys who follow line-fishing for cod, skate, crab and lobster along the shores. So that taken together perhaps 650 people dwelling on the seaboard are more or less dependent on the fishing industry for their subsistence.

In conclusion there can be no doubt that the Solway Firth is one of the finest firths in Great Britain as a fishing ground, and is yearly proving of greater value ever since the adoption of the Cumberland Sea Fisheries bye-laws and, it would seem, entirely through the protection thereby afforded.

SPORT ANCIENT AND MODERN

'THE popular diversions,' wrote Hutchinson [1] of the people of Eskdale, 'are hunting and cockfighting.' What was true of part of the county a hundred years ago has been true ever since of the whole, especially of the wilder districts. The natives of Cumberland are essentially sportsmen, keen about hunting of every kind, about fishing and wrestling and hound-trailing, even yet in places about cockfighting. They have been fortunate in their opportunities (such as an unenclosed mountainous country to roam over, and many lakes and rivers not very strictly preserved to fish in), and the traditions of sport have been handed down to each succeeding generation by enthusiastic teachers, masters of their different crafts. Long after the middle of last century, to thousands of men engaged in farming, hunting, in one form or another, was the chief relaxation, and such sports as those mentioned above were almost the only other amusements. At the present time some beasts of the chase are practically extinct ; game is more generally preserved than it was even twenty years ago ; and railways, if they have not done much to interfere with hunting, have tempted people away from their homes, and opened out new interests to them of quite a different kind. So an interesting race of men, which is referred to later on, is fast disappearing, and their place is being taken by others, also of sporting instincts, but with fewer opportunities of indulging them, leading busier lives, and moving more about in the world.

Of the various field sports and pastimes of which an account is given in this section two or three date back for some hundreds of years ; and the origin of the others must be almost coeval with the history of the human race. It is impossible to imagine a period when men were so rude and undeveloped that they did not catch fish, and,

after some fashion or another, kill animals or birds. The pedigree of the chase comes to us in a fairly consecutive line from very remote periods. Flint arrow-heads, relics of the ancient hunters of the Stone Age, have been found in different parts of the county ; stags' horns in barrows enclosed by stone circles, and in Roman graves.[2] Then, by strange laws and many quaint records and accounts, it is brought down to our own days.

The welfare of the deer was an object of the deepest concern to our early kings. They made a science of hunting ; they kept, or laid waste, immense tracts of country, so that it might be carried on with the least possible interference, and they defended it and furthered its interests with an elaborate code of formidable laws ; they held the life and limb of a country clown to be of small account compared with the life or even the distress of a stag.

In the Pipe Rolls there is frequent mention of deer, or what concerns deer, 'in the forest.' We read there the everyday little details of small offences and punishments as they occurred seven hundred years ago ; how in 1158 Gillo the forester owed 5 marks for a plea, the next year 33s. 4d., and then how, in 1160, he and William de Essebi each paid that sum into the treasury, 'and are quit.' Here are recorded the payments for the carriage of the king's venison, fines for animals taken, 'pounded' in the forest, for swine so taken, for 'rent of the forest,' many payments for this, 'of pleas of the forest.' We can understand something of the anxiety with which 'Robert son of Simon de Salkil renders account of 100s. that his son may be quit of a certain fawn which he took in the forest.'[3]

The modern owner of a partially enclosed

[2] *V.C.H. Cumb.* i. 228, 245, 251. For all the information concerning deer and hunting from the various Registers and Pleas of the Forest and Pipe Rolls, and for the notes upon hawking, I am indebted to the Rev. James Wilson, the editor.

[3] Ibid. i. 340, 344-5, 361, 404.

[1] *History of Cumberland*, i. 579.

Scotch forest has been known to erect, on that part of his 'march' where the ground was suitable, a fence over which his neighbour's deer might easily jump, but once inside could not get back without going perhaps many miles round. Exactly the same thing used to be done six or seven hundred years ago in Cumberland; landowners near forests were accustomed to empark their estate and construct deer-leaps, or 'saltatoria,' contrivances to enable beasts of the forest to enter the park and prevent them coming out again. If a deer leap was too near a forest, the justices in eyre could cause it to be removed as a nuisance.[1]

In 1225 the abbot of Holmcultram paid a fine of 20 marks for asserting and cultivating 10 acres of the king's wood in Caldbeck, and for enclosing the same between the lawn of Warnell and the river Caldew. But the enclosure must be so constructed that on the side of the lawn of Warnell towards the forest they should make a low hedge, so that the deer may enter and go out, and on the other side next the Caldew they shall make a high hedge and a good one, so that the king's deer may not get out of his forest by that hedge.[2]

'Strakur' was a dog used in poaching; the name occurs frequently in the Cumberland Forest Eyre Rolls of 15 Edward I. From this it may be gathered that poaching was a common offence in the county as early

as 1287. In the fourteenth century the poachers did not spare even the bishop. In 1375 Bishop Appleby was obliged to excommunicate 'the sons of iniquity' who had broken into his park of Rose and 'totally destroyed' all the beasts of chase therein, as well with dogs as with nets and other engines.[3]

Those who are interested in the general subject of red deer in the county, and the complicated system of forests instituted by the Normans, the names of which are so familiar to us at the present day, should refer to a recent book published by the Selden Society called *Select Pleas of the Forest*. It is perhaps worth mentioning that the word 'forest,' which has been used in Cumberland for eight hundred years, never necessarily meant a country covered with wood, but always a district where there were, or had been, deer. The word has the same significance in Scotland at the present time.

From that dim period when 'the whole of Britain was a land of uncleared forest, and only the downs and hill-tops rose above the perpetual tracts of wood,'[4] down to nearly the end of the eighteenth century, red deer roamed wild over Cumberland. Mr. Macpherson has given reasons for believing that the dying out of the last herd—in Ennerdale—took place about 1780.[5] If Hutchinson is correct they were very scarce in that immediate neighbourhood considerably earlier, for, writing in 1794, he mentions that a red deer was chased into Wastwater and drowned, 'within the memory of several persons living.'[6]

If falconry was ever much practised in Cumberland we know little about it, though scattered references to the sport are met with in the old registers and rolls. It was the most aristocratic of all field sports, but unsuited to any densely-wooded country. In the register of Bishop Welton it is related that 'while Sir William Lenglis, knight, was hunting in the neighbourhood of Brunstock, in the autumn of 1360, he set his falcon to flight, but the bird disappeared from view and did not return. Evoking the power of the Church he caused the bishop to have notice given to all the churches of the district of his loss, with a declaration of the penalties to be inflicted on those who detained the said falcon.'[7] In 1486 Bishop William Senos

---

[1] In 1256 an agreement was concluded between Thomas son of Thomas de Muleton and the prior and convent of Lanercost whereby the canons might enclose with a ditch or hedge their part of Warthcolman, and have a 'salterium' therein (Reg. of Lanercost MS. ix. 4). At the Cumberland forest eyre of 1285 a presentment was made that Isabel de Clifford held a park wherein there were two deer-leaps, one being a league, and the other a league and a half, from it. 'For a long time they have been a nuisance to the King's forest' (*Pleas of the Forest*, pp. cxvii.–cxviii., Selden Society).

[2] In the Close Rolls there are frequent mention of 'mandates' or orders concerning deer in Cumberland. In 1205 King John ordered Sir Richard de Lucy to supply the Constable of Chester with thirty stags 'on this side of the water of Carlisle' (*Close Rolls, John*, Rec. Com. i. 45b). There is a mandate from the same king in 1207 to Richard de Egremont to permit the constable of Chester to take ten stags in the forest of Carlisle (*Close Rolls, John*, Rec. Com. i. 90b). Henry III. ordered Thomas de Muleton to permit the Earl of Albemarle to take two stags in 1223, and ten in 1225, in the same forest (*Close Rolls*, Hen. III. Rec. Com. i. 549, and ibid. ii. 50b).

[3] Fine Roll, 9 Hen. III. pt. 2, m. 4; Bain, *Calendar of Documents*, i. 908.

[3] Reg. of Bishop Appleby, MS. f. 262.
[4] *Origins of English History*, p. 222.
[5] *Fauna of Lakeland*, p. 61.
[6] *History of Cumberland*, i. 580.
[7] Reg. of Bishop Welton, MS. f. 73.

SPORT ANCIENT AND MODERN

was called in to arbitrate between Edmund
Thornton, prior of the cell of St. Bees, and
Christopher Sandes in a dispute about falcons
in *lez berghe*, a place near St. Bees noted for
its breed of falcons.[1] Raughton near Dalston
was a celebrated eyry in the twelfth century,
as St. Bees was in the sixteenth. In the
Testa de Nevill there are eight references to
hawks' eyries in Cumberland, and six of these
refer to Ratton, Rauton, or Rauftone. ' The
vill of Ratton is a serjeanty to keep the
hawks' eyries (*erias accipitrum*) of the lord
the King, and is worth 100*s*. a year.'[2]

Hunting in Cumberland, both of deer, fox
and hare, is of great antiquity; nearly 700
years ago (1215) King John wrote to Robert
de Ros commanding him to licence William
de Ireby to have dogs and greyhounds for
hunting the fox and the hare in the forest
of Carlisle.[3] Henry III. in 1231 granted
licence to the Bishop of Carlisle that he or
his men might follow beasts of the chase
from his forest of Dalston into the king's
forest, and kill them there if necessary, and
to return with the venison without any
molestation to his servants or his dogs from
the king's foresters.[4] In 1276 Edward I.
gave licence to Robert de Ros to hunt with
his own hounds the fox in the king's lands
of Holderness till Pentecost, but he was not
to take the king's larger game nor hunt in
other men's warrens.[5]

Ten or fifteen years ago, scattered over the
country side, were many 'hunters' of the old
school, mines of information about everything
connected with hounds and vermin; a good
many lived in the Whitehaven district, notable
amongst whom were old Joe Irwin and 'Dr'
Longmire; what these two and their like did
not know about foxes and otters and greyhounds, and especially about 'foumats,' was
hardly worth knowing; they were of a race
of mighty hunters, and there was something
heroic in the fashion in which they followed
the chase. Nothing but pure love of sport
made such men as these sportsmen; they had
no fine horses to ride, no audience before

whom to perform brave deeds; they went
where the hunt led them, their wet clothes,
reeking like kilns, dried on them at nights,
as with rum and tobacco and never-ending
'cracks' mainly about the particular creature
they had been pursuing, they sat by the
kitchen fire of that house which happened
to be nearest to them when darkness stopped
them; at the earliest sign of dawn they were
afoot again. The otter hunter was a fox
hunter, and a foumart hunter as well, when
opportunity served, and sometimes a cock-
fighter, but the last-named was often a cock-
fighter only; physical strength and complete
indifference to weather were not indispensable
to him, though—after the act came into force
which made his favourite pursuit an illegal
one—a knowledge of the country and the
ability to use his legs well were sometimes
useful accomplishments.

The palmy days of cockfighting have long
passed away; the law which allows infinitely
more cruel sports has laid a heavy hand on
that one 'sporting' occupation, which was
thoroughly enjoyed by all who took part in
it, both animal and bird. Yet still in some
parts of Cumberland, at the end of a solitary
occupation road leading nowhere, or in a
quiet corner of the fells, a man taking a walk
on a Sunday afternoon may come upon a
patch of turf where not many hours before
a small crowd had gathered, and see by certain
infallible signs how hard it is for a custom
which has been ingrained into people for
generations altogether to die out.

We do not know when puntshooting was
first introduced into Cumberland, or indeed
into England. Nicholas Cox, the fourth
edition of whose book was published in 1697,
mentions nothing larger than a 'fowling piece'
with a barrel five and a half or six feet long,
and ' an indifferent bore under Harquebus.'[6]

It is to Colonel Peter Hawker, who was
born in 1786 and died in 1853, that every
modern wildfowler owes a deep debt of gratitude, for he made a science of punt-shooting,
and his *Instructions to Young Sportsmen*[7] may
be read as a handbook now. No one can
write upon that subject and not draw upon
the famous book, and every gunner on our
coast is indebted to him for some detail in
his gun or its fittings or in the lines of his
punt. Colonel Hawker only once visited
Cumberland, but it is interesting to compare

[1] Reg. of St. Bees (Harl. MS. 434), ff. 88, 181b.
The abbot of St. Mary's, York, ordered that two
falcons and a tersel be sent from St. Bees to secretary Crumwell in 1534. As none could take
them 'braunchers,' he caused them to be taken
as nigh flying as possible. The best eyrie at St.
Bees at that time was on the land of Roger Sandes
(*Letters and Papers of Henry VIII.* vols. vii. 832,
xiii. pt. i. 1325).
[2] i. 420.
[3] *Close Rolls, John*, Rec. Com. i. 187.
[4] *Charter Roll*, 15 Hen. III.
[5] Close Roll, 4 Edw. I. m. 13.

[6] *The Gentleman's Recreation, in Four Parts*,
'Fowling' (London, 1697), p. 13. Out of some
450 pages, Cox devotes only three or four to the
gun.
[7] 1st ed. 1814; 11th, 1859.

421

his work with that of the modern gunner on the Solway. We see that a man may spend a long life in punting and make his chief bags of a bird. which others, on apparently similar waters, hardly ever come across. According to Mr. Nichol 'barnacle geese are the birds that offer the best night shooting upon the Solway Firth.' In fifty years Colonel Hawker only killed three of this species of geese.[1] Mr. Chapman, speaking of the Northumberland coast and the same bird, writes : 'I have never met with them ; though numerous on the Solway and west coast they are practically unknown on the east.'[2]

The Cumberland puntsman 'can only recall a single occasion when he met with a large flock of brent.' Hawker killed 1,327.[3]

In the Outer Hebrides, next to barnacle, grey lags are the most common of all the geese. During thirty years the Solway gunner has only once been afforded sport by the latter.[4]

On most coasts wigeon greatly outnumber mallard ; the comparative scarcity of the latter, which Mr. Nichol mentions, and the lack of brent are certainly due to the absence of the seaweed *Zostera marina*, the favourite food of both.[5]

There is a curious statement in Denton's account of Cumberland as to the derivation of the name 'Rotington,' a village near Whitehaven. '*Rotington villa ad prata Rotinge*, so called because it was usually haunted with barnacles, rotgeese and wildfowl, before it was inhabited.'[6] No doubt rotgeese is rootgeese, and refers to the habits of the brent.[7]

Mr. Nichol's bag of thirty-eight barnacle at a shot is probably a record for Great Britain for this species of geese ; forty were killed in 1890 on the coast of Holland ; fifty-two and ninety-six are the British records for brent and wigeon.[8]

Racing in Cumberland is now carried on after a less primitive fashion than used formerly to be the case. For many years there was flat racing on Harras Moor near Whitehaven, and also an annual steeplechase meeting. The old grand stand may still be seen on the moor. In 1852 it was even thought worth while to publish an elaborate coloured lithograph of the finish of a race opposite this stand. Later a company was formed to carry on the steeplechasing, and part of the course was enclosed, but for some reason its efforts were not successful, and racing in the west of the county has now altogether died out.

FOX HUNTING[9]

That Cumberland is essentially a sporting county I think few will deny. No doubt the casual observer who flies through the country in an express train, or who spends a fortnight among the mountains in the Lake District, will smile incredulously when we talk of hunting in Cumberland, and express serious doubts as to the practicability of it. But yet I venture to state that Cumberland has long held, and does still hold its own as regards hunting ; and few are aware that we have between the mountains and the Solway a large stretch of country which is a surprise to the stranger and a delight to those who ride across it—a grass country of which Cumbrians are justly proud.

As a matter of fact the foxes bred in the low country rarely take to the hills except at the end of a long run. It is sometimes the case that hounds come upon a travelling fox or a hill-bred fox, and then the result is generally a finish on the mountains with a disappointed field left at the bottom ; equally the fell hounds I have met running in the low country have brought their fox from the hills ; but these occurrences are rare.

Of regular fox hunting, as we would term it now, there is little record up to last century. There were hounds which hunted the fox, but not exclusively, and it was a common occurrence in the early days of hunting for each sportsman to come to the trysting-place with his own hound ; this curious medley joined, and together hunted what came first to scent ; but the records show us that the

[1] *The Diary of Colonel Peter Hawker*, with Introduction by Sir Ralf Payne-Gallwey, ii. 357 (London, 1893).

[2] *Bird Life on the Border*, by Abel Chapman (1889), p. 199.

[3] *Diary*, ii. 357.

[4] If islands or suitable shores are wanting, grey lag, feeding on grass and not on mud, can seldom be approached in a punt.

[5] *Fauna of Lakeland*, p. 244.

[6] *An accompt of the most considerable estates and families in the county of Cumberland*, etc., by John Denton of Cardew (Cumberland and Westmorland Antiquarian and Archæological Society, 1887), p. 25.

[7] *Fauna of Lakeland*, p. 245-6.

[8] *Encyclopædia of Sport*, ii. 167-8.

[9] Some of these notes I have, by the courtesy of the editor of the *Badminton Magazine*, been allowed to republish.

deer was the animal usually selected for the chase. At the end of the seventeenth century three hounds were sent from Keswick to Hertfordshire, but after the first run two of them were found to be missing, and were next heard of at Keswick. This proves that hunting was indulged in at that period on the west side of Cumberland.

In the eighteenth century "Squire" Hasell kept hounds at Dalemain which were fox-hounds by name, but which would in point of fact hunt the deer or the fox. At the commencement of the following century the last two stags in Winfell and Inglewood forests were captured; and although there were stags then in Martindale, as there still are to-day, it was practically the end of stag-hunting; hounds were amalgamated, and the first pack of Cumberland foxhounds was established. These hounds were taken by Major Colomb of Armathwaite, who was a painter as well as a sportsman; but as he kept no diary himself the newspapers of that time are the only records. The late Sir Henry Howard often related his experience with those hounds under Major Colomb when they hunted Dumfriesshire as well as Cumberland, often going, as he told us, into Dumfriesshire with the hounds for a fortnight at a time. There are some pictures now at Greystoke Castle painted by Major Colomb. On his retirement in 1831 Mr. Hasell (who had been hunting privately during the Major's master-ship) again took the hounds. And it was at this period that the name of 'Inglewood Fox-hounds' was substituted for 'Cumberland Foxhounds' and the Dumfriesshire country was given up.

Shortly after Mr. Hasell's retirement the Inglewood hounds disappeared; I think the year given is 1839. They were sold, it is said, at a low price. During this time several packs of harriers had been advertised to hunt in Cumberland; the principal pack was the Carlisle harriers which was kept near Carlisle for some time, and when the Inglewood Foxhounds ceased to exist, they were turned into foxhounds. Later they were taken by Captain Ferguson, who turned them again into staghounds, and in order to procure stags went off to Scotland and captured three stags and two hinds from Lord Galloway's forest. On Captain Ferguson's retirement these hounds were taken by Colonel Salkeld of Holm Hill, who kept them at his own expense. While under his mastership foxes were hunted during the first part of the season and stags during the latter, but on Colonel Salkeld's retirement in 1849 the hounds were given by him to Dumfriesshire. This brings us to John Peel, who had for some time pre-vious been hunting the western country.

I have talked with several people who hunted with this famous sportsman, although I believe it to be true that many still think John Peel had almost a pre-historic existence. As a matter of fact he died as lately as 1854,[1] having hunted in some form or another for over forty years. As I said before, there are now several men in Cumberland who followed him and his hounds. They have narrated to me their recollections of the familiar figure: the blue-grey coat with its brass buttons, the white beaver hat and choker tie, the knee breeches, which were joined by a pair of long stockings, and then, most curious of all, the fact that he always wore shoes, to one only of which a spur was attached. No truer sportsman ever lived; for over forty years John Peel hunted his hounds. He has been immortalized in verse and song, and the romance and halo with which his name is sur-rounded will last as long as hunting remains the national sport of this country. John Peel was a statesman (the northern definition of a yeoman) living in Caldbeck village, and from there he hunted the west of Cumberland, and, as Matthew Graves tells us, 'no wile of a fox or a hare could evade his scrutiny.'

In 1850 Mr. Lawson, the present Sir Wilfrid Lawson, joined John Peel, keeping a few hounds of his own, the hounds often hunting together; and in 1858, after the death of the old sportsman, Mr. Lawson became the possessor of the entire pack of hounds, and of these were formed the second and present pack of 'Cumberland Foxhounds,' although they were not formally named as such until 1859.

The first records I can find of the doings of this pack are in the hunting diaries, the first of which runs as follows: 'November 12, 1850. Found two or three foxes. Ran one to Vitey's house and lost him in the wood again.' Again, 'November 22. Along with Peel's hounds drew Isel blank, found at Mumberson's, and ran him to ground in the earth at Isel with only three couples of hounds. Grand scent.' These records of each day were kept with great regularity. In February 1856 Mr. Lawson recounts that 'as they arrived at Westward, Peel's hounds ran a fox which they had found in Denton Side into the lower wood.' It would appear

---

[1] The inscription on his headstone in Caldbeck churchyard is as follows: 'In memory of John Peel of Ruthwaite, who died Nov. 13, 1854, aged 78 years.' The symbols of his craft are duly emblazoned on the monument.

during this period at times that foxes were scarce, and there is an amusing tale told of Mr. Lawson when he went south to have a few days with Lord Fitzhardinge's hounds. On being asked how he could leave his hounds, his reply was, ' Well, you see, there are only two foxes left, one called Scutty and one called Snippy ; the hounds have killed Scutty and Snippy wants a rest ! '

There are records of great runs in this diary, and in the third volume there is the following summary of the sport during eleven seasons commencing in 1850 and ending in 1861 :—

hunted three days a week. This joint mastership lasted for a period of nine years, Mr. Howard and Colonel Wybergh acting as huntsmen on alternate days. During this time there were some record runs, but Mr. Howard asserts that thirty years ago, when he first hunted, the foxes were better than they are now, but the scent not so good, and that he remembers when for six weeks on end scent was bad.

One of the best runs during this time is recorded in the diary. It took place on November 16, 1877, when hounds ran from Redmayne through the Tarnities and Blind-

Seasons	Days out	Killed	Run to ground	Lost	Hunted	Blank days	Accounted for
1850–1	36	3	6	26	35	8	9
1851–2	44	6	6	30	42	9	12
1852–3	39	6	4	27	37	12	10
1853–4	20	0	2	14	16	9	2
1854–5	37	7	8	22	37	7	15
1855–6	53	11	6	32	49	14	17
1856–7	65	17	12	41	70	13	29
1857–8	63	19	11	50	80	6	30
1858–9	68	16	11	61	88	8	27
1859–60	65	12	16	65	93	7	28
1860–1	72	27	22	27	76	14	49
Total	562	124	104	395	623	107	228

During these years the Carlisle Harriers were given up, and Mr. Lawson gradually increasing his country undertook to hunt the whole county in 1857, removing the hounds from Brayton to Raughtonhead. In 1861 Mr. Milham Hartley took over the hounds and they were then named the Cumberland Hounds. Mr. Briscoe followed three years later, but he retired after a very short time on the score of ill health. The hounds were again taken on by Mr. Hartley who records the following in his diary at the end of his sixth season : ' So ends my six years' mastership, during which time the hounds have killed ninety foxes and had some long runs. There are still a few foxes in the county, and it is to be hoped that the gentlemen who succeed will show sport.'

After Mr. Hartley's retirement, a committee of management was formed for a period of three years when Sir Wilfrid Lawson again resumed the mastership and was joined in 1872 by Major Wybergh. Captain Sharp is mentioned in the diary as ' keeping the whole establishment.' On Captain Sharp's retirement in 1876 the duty was undertaken by Mr. Howard of Greystoke and Colonel Wybergh, the country to be

crake into Isel Wood. The hounds pushed him through and breaking at the east end ran to Threapland Gill, out of it on the north side as if for Brayton, but changing his mind the fox went to the right past Bothel Craggs to Snittlegarth ; from thence we ran past Ireby on to Intachre, and leaving Snow Hill on the left kept a straight line to Caldeck village, when the fox being headed turned nearly straight back for a short distance, managing thereby to puzzle the hounds. On hitting it off the scent was weak, and as horses and men had had quite enough we gave the gallant fox up. A splendid run, distance from point to point about fifteen miles—a great deal more the way the hounds ran. Pace fast, a short check just before getting to Snittlegarth, otherwise they must have killed him before he reached Caldbeck.

In 1885 Colonel Wybergh retired and Mr. Howard hunted the whole county until he was joined by Mr. Lawson in 1886, who undertook the western division for four seasons, at the end of which time Mr. Howard again took the whole county till 1895, when a new arrangement was made, the Cumberland hunt handing over half the county to Mr. Salkeld of Holm Hill, who established a pack of hounds of his own at Holm Hill, while the Cumberland foxhounds hunted the other half under the joint mastership of Mr. Howard and Mr. C. J. Parker, the latter acting as huntsman, and under this régime the country is at present hunted.

There are altogether six packs of hounds and six packs of harriers in Cumberland. Four of these hunt the hills almost exclusively and are generally followed on foot. The oldest of these packs would appear to be the one named at present 'the Blencathra Hounds.' And it is generally believed that the hounds mentioned in the earlier part of this article which were sent from Keswick to Hertfordshire, and on being let loose were not heard of again till they reappeared at Keswick, were the predecessors of Mr. Crozier's present pack. To that gentleman I owe the following extracts which he has kindly sent me gathered by the honorary secretary of the hunt.

'The story of the origin of the Blencathra hounds is similar to that of most of the mountain packs. The ancient books of the churchwardens in many of the Lake parishes contain numberless entries of payments made for the heads of foxes. As much as a guinea was paid for the head of a " greyhound fox " and 10s. 6d. for a cub ; but the hill farmers could not depend upon this method of capture, and therefore many of them kept a hound or two. These animals had no pretension to purity of breed, and would hunt the hare as an alternative to the fox. Gradually the dalesfolk as well as their neighbours on the hills began to organize hunts, especially in the spring when foxes became dangerous to lambs. Newspapers were scarce in those days and seldom seen in farm-houses. But a very effective method of advertising hunts was adopted. Immediately after service the parish clerk mounted a tombstone in the churchyard and announced to the assembled crowd the dates and plans for meets and sales by auction during the ensuing week. Mr. Crozier recollects perfectly being a witness of this, nor has he forgotten the Sunday fox hunts which were a highly popular institution, the farmers asserting that Sunday was the only day they could spare for hunting purposes. Over 100 years ago Mr. Crozier's father kept several couples of hounds, including some which belonged to the famous hunter of the western country, John Peel. His son, Mr. John Crozier, was born in the year 1822, and while still a boy his father handed over to him the mastership of the hounds which office he has now held over sixty years, the first thirty of which he maintained the hunt at his own expense. The longest run he remembers was an after-

noon run when a fox started on Skiddaw, and after attempting to elude his pursuers by travelling in a ring but finding it of no avail was forced to take a line through Portinscale, Borrowdale, over the mountains into Westmorland, and under cover of darkness got away towards Broughton-in-Furness in Lancashire. The dogs were found the next morning lying asleep near Coniston Crag. The distance they had travelled in a straight line being 35 miles, but at least another 15 would be added by the many deviations, thus making a run of 50 miles. Fell hunting has many dangers both for hounds and men, and Mr. Crozier remembers many occasions on which hounds, having jumped clear on rocks and found themselves ' binked,' have been unable to return and eventually have met their death by falling over precipices in a desperate effort to escape.'

In the breeding of hill hounds there are many difficulties in maintaining the qualities which are essential for hill-work, but by judicious crossing the breed at intervals with south country and neighbouring packs of hounds this has been most successful. Another of the fell packs is the Ulleswater pack of hounds, which hunts exclusively on the hills, being followed (with rare exceptions) on foot. I have hunted with them, and it is a wonderful sight to watch the huntsman making his way to them with extraordinary rapidity up the mountains, running often far into the night. It is a curious fact worth mentioning that fell hounds when they kill a fox will not break it up, a peculiarity which I believe I am right in stating is all their own.

The inhabitants of Cumberland are sportsmen from hereditary instincts. As I said before, squires and statesmen, hill farmers and dalesmen alike have combined to keep alive and encourage these sporting qualities during many generations. But as in all other parts so in Cumberland, bad trade, agricultural depression, the depreciation of land have as natural consequences, affected the hunting. Perhaps Cumberland has suffered less than some counties, and hunting may continue longer. The stranger element, so strong in the south, does not exist in Cumberland. Those who hunt here belong to the soil and therefore we have not to contend with the same amount of damage which is done by those who come out to gallop and jump regardless of injury to the farmers. But still it is to be regretted that wire has made its appearance in this county. Thirty years ago it was unknown, and now in some parts of the hunting country fence after fence in succession is wired. It is particularly disastrous in the more cramped parts of the country where the jumping is incessant. In some parts of Cumberland we have tracts of open country, the wild grass and moorland stretching for many a mile, a stone wall here and there breaking the monotony. Those who would follow hounds in Cumberland must make up their minds that no weather will be too bad, no day too long, no fence too rough. Of fences we have plenty. Rough banks with ditches are more often to be met with than any other fence, and if, as is often the case, a horse who is a stranger to the country attempts to fly them disaster is sure to follow. The Irish horse or the horse bred in Cumberland will jump on to the bank, either placing his fore-feet on the top or lightly dropping his hind legs on it, which gives the necessary impetus for clearing the ditch beyond and landing himself well into the next field. Then there are the stone walls ; more frequent perhaps in the west of the country than the east, they appear very formidable, but are easier to manipulate than they seem at first sight. There is very seldom a ditch on the other side, and a horse who understands them will sometimes even bank them, and it is always better to ride at them slowly. There are a certain amount of posts and rails in Cumberland, and in the extreme east of the county the obstacles are mostly in the form of small flying fences, and the country being cramped there is continuous jumping.

A Cumberland hunter must be prepared for all sorts and conditions of fences, and there is no doubt that the Cumberland Irish bred horses are the best suited to the country. The Cumberland horses for the most part are generally of the short thick kind, wonderfully clever, though perhaps a trifle slow ; they will gallop and jump all day, and if you leave them alone will extricate themselves from most difficulties. The coverts in Cumberland are of a varied nature ; there are some very big woodlands in the west of the county forming a good home for many a fox ; these woodlands are bad to get away from, and some of them situated on the side of a hill running along for a mile or two make a hard draw for hounds and huntsmen, but add greatly to the picturesqueness of the scene. There are a great many gorse coverts, a good deal of this being natural, forming in some places very thick hedgerows ; and it is very difficult for the hounds to push a fox out, and these gorse coverts often take a very long time to draw. The most typical covert in . Cumberland is the ghyll (the north country definition of a woody ravine) planted on both

sides, with a stream as a rule running through the bottom. These ghylls form a very snug shelter for a fox and nearly always hold one. In a run these ghylls are our most formidable obstacles and generally cause a great delay for the field, as there is probably only one practicable path through it, and a good many are often left behind.

That Cumberland is a good scenting country is a fact that will, I think, be admitted by all who have hunted there, and those who have been associated with hunting the hounds for the last thirty years maintain that scent has much improved of late. In some parts of the country the constant fences check the hounds a little, but on the whole the country carries a very good scent. The foxes have not of late been as good, it is said, as formerly, although I am told they are improving again now. The Cumberland fox is hardy and fast, more of the ' greyhound ' type than the terrier. In some parts of the county they are too numerous, while in others there is a scarcity ; but a blank day in Cumberland is almost an unknown occurrence.

There have been one or two noted foxes. There was one that lived in Greystoke Park for years, nicknamed by the inhabitants ' The Thornyland Pet.' He was a huge fox with a white neck. He never left Thornyland pasture. The hounds hunted him round Greystoke Park during the space of four hours and lost him, and it is a curious fact that he was never seen again. Another fox I remember was found over and over again by Mr. Salkeld's hounds in one of their coverts. He always took the same line of twelve miles from Dobs Cross to Greystoke. This occurred several times in one season, and sportsmen went out with great hopes to draw the covert secure in the knowledge that if ' Peter,' as the fox was named, was about, a run was assured.

A curious coincidence I recollect many years ago. Towards the end of a long run, when hounds were close on to their fox, he turned into the little churchyard of Caldbeck, and running over John Peel's grave with the pack in full cry he was pulled down in the open just over the churchyard wall, an unconscious tribute to the old sportsman.

As I sit writing many memories of bygone runs come crowding over me, runs never to be forgotten by those who took part in them. We are at the covert side in breathless silence. No sound but the huntsman's voice and the rustle of the dead leaves under the hounds' feet as they race through on a fresh line of a fox. A solitary whip at the far end lifts his cap, and that cry of 'Gone away' rings through the air. From out of the covert the hounds stream, close behind them rides the field, each one scrambling for a start. A big stone wall confronts us. Side by side we take it; a few refuse and are lost. We are landed in a rough grass field, rather heavy going for the riders but carrying a strong scent. Through a small wood they race, their heads down. Making our way through the fir-trees we follow, a bank with a blind ditch carries us out of it, and down the green fields we gallop taking two sets of rails as we go. But the pace is beginning to tell; already some are being left behind; a rough fence into the road, another out of it; on we go through plough which rides light to-day. A ghyll is in sight, the wary huntsman turns to the right, he knows the only practicable spot; several of the unwary plunge in and we see them no more. Following close upon the hounds we descend the ghyll, our hands shading our faces from the thorn bushes, which are so thick that one man is literally pulled from his horse. This delays those behind him, but a few of us who are fortunate enough to be in front reach the bottom; a small running brook meets our eyes, the hounds are already across. For a moment on the other side they hesitate, they throw up their heads. But before the huntsman can get to them they pick it up and ascend the hill in full cry. Treading on each other's heels, reckless of consequences, we scramble through the water, and breaking through the rails on the far side speed up the hill; a big fence, about the biggest fence in Cumberland, is before us, a copper beech hedge with rails run through. We ride at it; several refuse; the field is becoming more and more select. Now and then the cry of 'Seeds' sounds in our ears, and this means a circuitous round, as the Cumberland farmer on that point is firm. Whether hard or soft the seed field is sacred. We are on rising ground, anxious eyes are turned with the hopes of viewing a second horseman, but they have had no chance. Banks and stone walls follow in quick succession, the scent is tremendous. As we cross a road an old shepherd on his pony greets us, 'I seed t' fox, nobbut a laal un.' And then the excitement overcoming him, he turns his pony at a fence exclaiming, 'T' sheep and t' dog can tak' care o' thersels. I must hev' a hunt,' and he joins us. We are crossing the moorland in Greystoke Park; it is heavy going and the hounds are leaving us. Blen-

cathra, or Saddleback as it is commonly called, looms high above us, but we can't stop. Across the broad open space we follow, down into the grey valley of the Caldew, and then begin the ascent. Hounds are facing the hill in full cry. We are forced into a slow trot and at times to a walk. Skiddaw Forest is in front of us. We struggle on. The hounds' notes get fainter and fainter, and only the huntsman and whips pursue as they must. We drop off our exhausted horses. We have done our utmost; we have lived with the best of them; and we ride our tired horses home with that consciousness within us and the hope that such a good fox may escape and live to give us another such day.

Harrier hunting in Cumberland is much the same as in other counties. One important pack of harriers, the 'Eamont,' has disappeared during the last few years owing to the death of their master, Mr. Carleton Cowper. One or two packs of beagles have sprung into existence, but for the most part the same packs of fell-hounds that have hunted for many years are continuing to do so. Hares in some parts of Cumberland are extremely scarce and becoming more so, and in no part of the country are they very numerous, except perhaps in Lowther Park and its surroundings.

I would repeat again that the hunting instincts are still strong in Cumberland. There are no doubt a few who condemn it—there are some who have suffered by their land being overridden—there are always some who have no sympathy with hunting, and there are a few pessimists who tell us that hunting will not last; that bad times, want of money, the prevalence of wire ever increasing will all tend towards its disappearance. But I am an optimist, and I am confident that this, the national sport of England, has a deep-rooted existence in the hearts of the people, and I venture to prophesy that it will be a bad day for the country when hunting ceases to be; it is the keynote to all sport, and tends to promote and strengthen good feeling and friendship between all classes of men.

The following is a summary of the sport during the last two years, which gives a fair average and bring this article up to date:—

Seasons	Days out	Killed	Run to ground	Lost	Hunted	Blank
1900-1	56	32	17	41	90	0
1901-2	48	48	15	44	107	0

A HISTORY OF CUMBERLAND

SHOOTING

The materials for writing an account of shooting in the county of Cumberland are but scanty. No squire of old days seems to have thought it worth his while to keep such a diary as did Colonel Hawker or Lord Malmesbury, and these mines of interesting information available to the Hampshire historian are quite wanting here. No game book or rough jottings of sport of the eighteenth century, or even very early in the nineteenth, are to be met with ; one at Greystoke which dates from 1825 goes back the furthest of all. Though the amount of game killed in a day or a season a hundred or a hundred and fifty years ago would seem small to us, it would not be so to those who killed it. Records would be established then from time to time, and no doubt these records still exist, hidden away in journals and letters in old country houses; but they are inaccessible now and not to be found except by chance. The present business-like volumes kept by all men who shoot much were unknown. If the strong and comely John Osbaldistone, who 'has most of the gamekeeper' in Sir Hildebrand's old Northumberland hall, had, instead of muddling himself with brandy, spent some of his abundant spare time in jotting down at night what he and his wild brothers had killed or hunted during the day, how grateful would we be to him now. As we would be too if someone had cared enough for them to write on the backs of the pictures 'dimmed with smoke and March beer' which hang in many an old hall, some brief particulars of the sitter and the artist, both now long since forgotten and never to be known.

Field sports are seldom mentioned by English historians : Lord Macaulay has only two or three references, one of which concerns the Cumberland border. After speaking of the wild state of the country in 1685, he comes down to later times and quotes from Scott's life in what state the then Duke of Northumberland's father found the 'people in Keeldar when he went up to shoot there. The women had no other dress than a bed-gown and petticoat ; the men were savage, and could hardly be brought to rise from the heather either from sullenness or fear.'[1] And he goes on to speak of their wild dances and songs.

About the year 1803 Colonel Thornton made his well-known expedition into Scotland and the north of England. He pene-

[1] *The History of England*, i. 286 (ed. 1849–61).

trated—the word is not an ill-fitting one to use considering the dangers and difficulties he seems to have met with on the way—as far north as Inverness, and returned to Yorkshire through Cumberland. A sloop manned by three sailors was sent first to Forres with heavy goods, and then with two boats, two baggage waggons and a tandem gig, and many horses for riding and driving, with a valet, groom, waggoner and other servants, a falconer, an artist, and endless supplies of food and liquors, guns, nets, hawks and pointers—with a paraphernalia, as Sir Herbert Maxwell says, calculated on lines for exploring Labrador—the colonel set forth and shot and fished and netted and hawked his way northwards. He must have been a man of great energy and power of organization ; the directions to his servants are given after a military fashion which is sometimes very amusing. Pike fishing and snipe and woodcock shooting seem to have been his favourite pursuits. He gives long descriptions of the scenery he passed through, which impressed him, as it did all travellers of that period, more by its desolation and dangers than by its beauty ; he never came across a pretty girl without chronicling the fact, and he devotes a considerable part of his diary to detailing the elaborate dinners he and his friends partook of in the wilderness, and the abundant liquid with which they washed them down. Probably this history gives in the main a correct account of what really took place, though now and then our confidence in its absolute accuracy is a little shaken, as, for example, when he so set his 'bullet gun' as to be sure of hitting a card at 200 yards, or when, after making a long shot at an old 'moor game' cock, he measured the distance and was disappointed to find it was 'only a hundred and three yards.'

On October 23 he reached Carlisle and travelling by Wigton, Bassenthwaite—where he met and entered into conversation with 'one of the most beautiful and innocent country girls' he ever saw—Keswick, Grasmere, Rydal, Ponsonby and Muncaster, he passed into Lancashire by Coniston.

It is unfortunate for our special purpose that Colonel Thornton did not devote much space to the latter part of his tour ; possibly he was a little stale, a little tired of shooting and fishing and hawking by the time he got into Cumberland ; even the dinners, though the quality of them is mentioned, are not given in detail. He saw men hunting salmon—

SPORT ANCIENT AND MODERN

and catching them—with Newfoundland dogs in the low Esk; he tried a brace of pointers near Ouse Bridge, but did not approve of them, and after a day or two spent at Rydal Hall he rode over by Hard Knott to Ponsonby with Sir Michael le Fleming and his daughter. The next morning the company divided, some shooting, others coursing, but with only poor results—'a brace of hares.' Sir Michael's shooting, adds the diarist, 'was quite harmless.' The colonel also found fault with his friend's greyhounds as having too much of the lurcher in them. The day following Sir Michael went out shooting by himself, but came back empty handed 'which he attributed to his gun being crooked.' After a pleasant stay at Ponsonby, from the windows of which 'on a favourable day you may discern Flintshire,' the colonel journeyed on to Muncaster, and greatly admired the house and views and splendid oaks. 'I never saw any place more fortunately situated.' But though Lord Muncaster pressed him to stay a few days, assuring him that there were plenty of woodcocks about, the traveller resisted the temptation and hurried back to Rydal, where on the 28th day of October he killed five woodcock and a snipe and so finished his stay in Cumberland. He remarked that woodcocks were very plentiful during the season, and formerly sold in great numbers at Hawkeshead for sixpence each. 'But now the Flys from Kendal take them south, they are as much increased in value as other articles of luxury.' A gruesome likeness of a 'heath cock' is the last engraving in the charming old first edition, and we are glad to think it was copied from a bird shot in Scotland and not in Cumberland.[1]

There have been no ptarmigan in Cumberland for at least a hundred years. There are no capercailzie. Mr. Howard Saunders[2] mentions thirty-one varieties of duck as having been killed in the three kingdoms, and of these the Rev. H. A. Macpherson[3] names twenty-one which have been shot in the county. Of the remaining ten most of them are so rare that they have been noticed only six or seven times or even once or twice. The three wild swans have all been killed, and the three snipe,[4] and seven out of eleven

species of geese. Here again of the four wanting to Cumberland only two specimens of one have been seen in Britain, and four of another, and the other two are only known in a wild state from having been first domesticated.

In a preface to the Rev. H. A. Macpherson's *Fauna of Lakeland*, the late Chancellor Ferguson carefully defined the borders or marches of that district, including in it the whole of Cumberland and Westmorland and a small part of Lancashire. With the two latter counties this paper has nothing to do, but we may make use of his description so far as it applies to the former. With an insignificant exception the 'whole of the western border is waterwashed' by fresh water for a comparatively short way. So far as shooting is concerned the coast from somewhat south of Allonby to St. Bees Head is practically worthless, and from St. Bees till we come into the neighbourhood of Drigg it is of little value. The shores, either rocky or occupied by grey beaches of shingle or barren sands, have no attraction for duck. Along the coast line from Drigg to the boundary of the county, the river Duddon, are various estuaries and mud flats formed by the Irt, Mite and Esk, and in these places they are fairly abundant. But on the north-west seaboard—the estuaries of the Border Esk, the Eden, the Wampool and the Waver—are the chief resorts of the many kinds of wildfowl which are shot in Cumberland, for here are the flat waterwayed mosses along the Solway, the rich mud flats and oozes, and sheltered bays and creeks where punts can be worked.

Following the division boundary of the county with Scotland lie first the moors of Netherby. Where it runs south with Northumberland the great stretches of wild country belonging to Naworth come in, the Gillesland moors and, a little further south, Tindale Fell and Geltsdale. The famous moor of Knaresdale is just over the county march, as are also the chief Alston moors, but Rotherhope, belonging to Mr. Horrocks, is in Cumberland. Here in 1866 over 1,400 brace of grouse were killed—a bird to the acre—and this remarkable average would have been still better if 'driving' at that time had not been carried on in a somewhat primitive fashion, with no 'flankers' and few drivers. Rotherhope has been much damaged by netting, reference to which is made further on in this article.

Howard Saunders, in the second edition of his book, classes this bird among the sandpipers (*Manual of British Birds*, p. 621).

---

[1] *A Sporting Tour through the Northern Parts of England and great part of the Highlands of Scotland,* etc. pp. 106, 149, 277–80 et seq. ed. 1 (London: printed for Vernor and Hood, etc. 1804).
[2] *Manual of British Birds,* pp. 419–78 (ed. 1899).
[3] *V.C.H. Cumb.* i. 199 et seq.
[4] One specimen of the red-breasted snipe (*Macrorhamphus griseus*) has been killed; but Mr.

429

Southward lie the moors belonging to Eden-hall and Greystoke and the Marshalls, and then a wide range of hills stretch from Keswick, by Wastwater and Dalegarth and Muncaster, to the mouth of the Duddon.

Grouse are to be found in Cumberland almost wherever there is heather, but many of the fells are very green and give better feeding for sheep than game. They are also plentiful on many of the lower mosses or flows.[1]

Partridges, besides being more or less common wherever there is cultivation, wander in places up into the hills, and then are to be met with in the great stone walled 'seeve' or rush-covered enclosures often far away from any turnips or cornfields. These enclosures, before the new law made their lives a burden to them, were the homes of many strong-limbed lusty hares, and were desirable places for coursing. The writer of this article well remembers in the 'seventies' forty-six hares being counted in a 4-acre field belonging to his father, feeding on a May morning on the young oats, and he was present at a coursing meeting in the same parish of Moresby when more than sixty hares were turned out of the 'Priest Ground,' a 30-acre patch of rough unpreserved land lying at the foot of Whillimoor. There is still plenty of cover on the 'Priest Ground' though it has been drained and limed since then, but hares now are very few and far between. In those days what were called the 'preserves' on Lord Lonsdale's Whitehaven estate stretched far and wide ; a country into which the harriers were on no account to be allowed to wander. It is little wonder then that with ' its heathery grouse moors . . . saltings, bogs and mosses along the Solway and the Irish Sea, highly cultivated arable and pasture land in the plain of Cumberland, richly-wooded river valleys and sheltered combes, mountains, metes, tarns and fells,'[2] this county has always been famous for the varieties of its game and wildfowl. But though the variety is great it is not, with some few exceptions, one where very big bags are obtained. The properties and farms are not as a rule large, and where the acreage is wide, as in the fell country, the land is, as has been said, unproductive of game.

If the first week in September sees the harvest well started,[3] there will be few small properties through the length and breadth of the land which are not carefully shot over, and though the reward may often be a small one, yet everything is a question of degree, and a man who comes home with eight or ten brace, when he only expected to shoot three or four, will probably enjoy his day more than the owner of a big manor whose bag falls short by twenty brace of the hundred he was told he should get. It is pleasant to think of these small parties of sportsmen out in the autumn ; statesmen on their own grounds, tenant farmers renting the shooting on their holdings and perhaps that of a neighbour or two ; the bags will not be swelled by hares as they used to be ; in some places a pheasant is never seen, a stray snipe or hare or duck make up the variety. The little holiday, the day snatched from the routine of the farm, is good for the men, and we may be sure for the country also.

Shooting in Cumberland during the last century seems to have been carried on for the most part after a quiet reasonable fashion, and owing to the number of small properties was participated in by many people. Where a large head of game was kept up the landlords have dealt fairly with their tenants, and these are the reasons, with one other to be added, why not so much has been heard in this county of the various troubles which game preservers often meet with elsewhere, viz. poaching on a large scale, grumbles from farmers as to damage done to crops by hares and rabbits and pheasants, to turnips by walking across them, to sheep by continually shifting them when driving grouse. Probably the other reason is the sporting instinct which exists in a greater or less degree in most Cumberland people's breasts. No doubt this sporting instinct accounts for some poaching, but it accounts also, we feel sure, for the wish the average farmer feels, if he and his landlord 'get on' at all together, that the latter should find a reasonable amount of game on his land when he comes to look for it. In olden days, sixty or seventy years ago, when, except on the larger estates, gamekeepers and preserving were practically unknown, any sportsman, who was also in the widest sense of the word a gentleman, was welcome to wander anywhere with his gun, would meet

---

[1] A few years ago a pair of grouse found out a small patch of heather, about 3 acres in extent, at Froggo Tarn near St. Bees, and bred on it. This patch is about 3 miles from the nearest bit of real moor, viz. Dent, and is surrounded entirely by cultivated land. The late Mr. Jefferson of Spring-field shot some of the brood.

[2] *Fauna of Lakeland*, p. x.

[3] In the *Carlisle Journal* of September 1 and 12, 1810–12, are notices calling attention to the lateness of the season and strongly recommending sportsmen to abstain from shooting ' till the whole crop is severed from the ground.'

with the truest kind of hospitality, and have given him all the help the farmer could give, as to the best line to take and the best places to meet with whatever he might be in search of. Though a wanderer of this old world fashion would, of course, be an impracticable person now, the kindly feeling is still very common, and in most places a considerate landlord will find game and rabbits waiting for him in ample abundance, and a cheery tenant anxious to show them to him, and proud if the bag taken off his farm is a good one. It goes without saying that a greedy or a mean landlord's experience will be different, and a poor one, who is forced to get as much rent as he can and give as little as possible back, however personally amiable he may be, cannot expect in this utilitarian age to have kept for him what he can make no return for. There is little doubt that in the not far distant future good shooting will only be for those who can afford to farm their own land and are able to put up with the loss, be it small or great, which *must* fall upon the shoulders of either the man who owns, or the man who feeds, game ; high farming and game in any quantities, with perhaps the exception of partridges and grouse, are incompatible.

The sporting feelings of the Cumberland farmer are easily seen when the question is the preservation of hares in a coursing district. The tenant there extends a most kindly toleration towards them, and though he may fidget at the very considerable damage they do if the meetings are held late in the season, yet he will rarely hustle them unfairly himself, or allow any one else to do so if he can help it. There is naturally plenty of petty poaching, of snaring rabbits, a little netting of partridges in some districts, killing of pheasants where they are plentiful and not well looked after ; but the organized raids so common in some counties, the attacks on great preserves by desperate men careless of life, are almost unknown. Till the Ground Game Act was passed where the keepers were active, often abounded and flourished exceedingly in the closest neighbourhood of towns. Dent, separated merely by a shallow river from a thickly populated mining district, may be given as one example, and Rheda in the same district as another.

On some large estates hares are numerous still. At Netherby for example they are very plentiful, but on many small holdings they are practically extinct. After the Ground Game Act came into force a fierce attack was made on them generally throughout the land, and farms which used to give ten or twenty or more in a day knew them no more. But now something of a reaction has set in, and their prospect of survival is much better than it was. The farmer, for one thing, has recognized that by exterminating the animal he was depriving himself of a very desirable addition to his table, as well as of the interest of securing it.

In Cumberland, as in all parts of the kingdom, the character of shooting and the way it is carried on have, where it is followed on any scale, entirely changed during the latter part of the last century. On small properties hunting the turnips and rough fields with a pointer, and beating the hedgerows for a stray pheasant with a spaniel or two, subjects which have been so often picturesquely written about and illustrated, are still the way in which a small bag is made up and a great deal of enjoyment gained, all the more enjoyment perhaps since the sportsman is now clad in tweed knickerbokers and cap instead of tight breeches, top boots and a high hat. But dogs are seldom seen on heather now ; driving is not put off to the end of the season but begins on the 12th, systematically and scientifically carried out on large moors, on small ones with two or three beaters and peat hags and walls instead of butts. Partridges are either driven or more generally walked up, a long line of men, spaced with retrievers, taking the place of the bag-carrying gamekeeper and his lads, and hurrying breathless pointers and setters. And, wherever it can be managed, pheasants are forced as high as possible over the heads of men standing well out from the cover, each armed with two guns, and at times sorry they have not got three. The object in cover shooting not long ago was to kill as much game as possible ; now it is to kill as much in the most sporting possible way.

But cover shooting has now to a great extent become an artificial sport, and a large stock of pheasants is only a question of more or less suitable woods, and a willingness to pay a considerable sum yearly in wages and food. And it is evident that cover shooting will become more artificial still, for wild duck are reared now in some places, and even pigeons and guinea fowl and bantams ; the death rate amongst these birds is less than amongst pheasants, of which in many places the land is 'sick' and their food is cheaper. In suitable places hand reared ducks fly well, and give often high and sporting shots. It is a drawback that they cannot be treated quite naturally : if hundreds or thousands of birds were put up together and heavily fired at the greater number would escape. In places where the woods are adapted for them such varieties of real game as wild turkeys and capercailzie add to the interest of shooting, but bantams and guineafowl seem hardly worthy of good sportsmen.

It is unnecessary to do more than mention the effect that a higher class of farming has had on shooting. It was the scantiness of the cover which first forced men to drive and walk up partridges, for, especially where they were numerous, except in turnips, they soon ceased to lie to dogs. The sickle was used all over the country till the 'sixties'; now the reaping machine makes the stubbles almost as bare as a lawn. In many places the great wide straggling fences which were famous places for nesting in, and where birds sat well late on in the season, have been done away with, often wire has taken their place, and those that are left are kept much more carefully trimmed. Rooks must either have increased, or have educated themselves into bad habits, for it seems certain that they do more harm to eggs than they used to do, perhaps because of this want of cover.[1] And, especially near the coast, gulls also are much more destructive, and there are many complaints of the havoc they cause amongst very young partridges and pheasants. Sir Richard Graham in a note on Netherby refers to these detrimental causes.

Through the courtesy of their editors a careful search has been made through the early files of the oldest newspapers in the county, the *Cumberland Pacquet*, the *Carlisle Journal* and the *Carlisle Patriot*. A hundred and twenty years ago little public interest seems to have been taken in shooting. The *Pacquet* during the six years 1774–9 has not a single reference to it. After this date the notices became more numerous and paragraphs relating to big and early and curiously marked woodcocks, and solitary snipe, warnings about trespassers, arrivals of sportsmen and their bags on the first days of grouse and partridge shooting, frequently occur. There are long warnings to men inclined to poach; dire examples held out of the fate of those

[1] Mr. Hartley (of Armathwaite Hall) suggests that the increase dates from the introduction of the rook rifle. Owners of rookeries are now often inclined to reserve the shooting for themselves, since there is certainly more sport in killing the birds with a rifle than with a gun. But if owing to weather, or any other cause, the 'big' days have to be postponed, a great many rooks cease to be 'sitters' and escape the bullet. Formerly the 'crow shutting' was handed over to the tenants and neighbours who took good care to keep the numbers down.

breaking the law. Indeed he must have possessed a considerable amount of courage who went in unlawful pursuit of game at the beginning of last century by day, and especially by night. The penalty for killing game out of season was £5 for each bird. In 1803 the *Carlisle Journal* shows what was likely to befall any one caught night poaching; the hapless wight was to be deemed a rogue and a vagabond, whipped and imprisoned for the first offence, and transported for the second. An old friend of the writer once announced that he had taken a small bit of rough ground to shoot over, and on our asking why he gave good money for worthless land, he replied: 'There's nowte on't, I ken there's nowte on't; but I gang til't through Mr. P.'s moss and cum back fra't through Mr. L.'s, an' I'se nut dune sae badly, efter a'.' What would this worthy, a man respected by most of the neighbours who were not in any way concerned in the preservation of game, have said if justice such as this was meted out to himself?

In 1814 Dr. Heysham fined three young men in Carlisle £10 each for killing game without a certificate, and the next year that well-known naturalist mulcted a Brampton man in £20 for using a net; 'which it is hoped will act as a warning to poachers,' remarked the *Journal*. In 1819, in the same paper, is a long article on the iniquity of the game laws, the cause being the wounding of a poacher by one of Lord Lonsdale's keepers; not, as the editor carefully explained, because the keeper was attacked, but because the man ran away. Nothing seems to have been done to the former. And as a last specimen of old fashioned penalty, the *Journal* relates how in 1824 two women were sent to goal for three months because they were unable to pay a year's wages 'four and five pounds for breaking, the one four pheasant's, the other five partridge's eggs,' and how penalties amounting to £350 were in 1822 hanging over a man in Leicestershire who had killed seven pheasants a few days before the time allowed by the law.

Now and then a gleam of humour passes down through the old pages as when in 1804 the *Pacquet* inserted the following erratum: '*For* "Sir Gilfrid Lawson's gamekeeper killed 14 woodcocks in one shot," *read* "one woodcock in 14 shots."' We wonder if it is recorded in any Lowther game book about the year 1808 that a keeper there shot in the Eden 'with two barrels the extraordinary number of 86 fish, the smallest 7 inches in length.' There comes a wail from October of the same year—'The preservation of the game is become a very arduous business, as our volunteers have now nothing to vent their fury upon !'—and a further lament two years later, 'Is it not a curious fact that the right of shooting partridges and pheasants is favourably investigated in Parliament while the growing importance of this city (Carlisle) is coldly and cruelly neglected ?'

There are many instances of remarkable shots. In 1819 'Mr. Thomas Craig killed in Alston moor 40 grouse in 17 shots. Such a thing is never recorded to have been in that part of the country before.' 'In 1822 near Allonby a gentleman from Essex levelled at the bird,' and to the astonishment of himself and his companion knocked down nine partridges 'all falling quite dead.' The *Pacquet* of that week sarcastically notices the incident and asks 'if this prodigious sporting feat be true, when will miracles cease?' The Rev. Richard Burn of Kirkandrews-upon-Eden is said to have killed two greylags with snipe shot; but this hardly seems worth chronicling when compared with what was accomplished by Wm. Nixon of Sandsfield, aged 11 years. This infant prodigy shot five barnacle geese with one ball at the 'amazing distance of 600 yards.' We may here mention the well known curious inscription on a tombstone in Bewcastle churchyard : ' Jonathan Telford of Craggy Ford, who died April 25, 1866, aged 72. Deceased was one of the best moor game shooters in the north of England ; in the time of his shooting he bagged fifty-nine grouse in seven double shots.'

Netting grouse is a matter on which owners of moors have much to say at the present time. It seems to have been an old habit in Cumberland. The *Pacquet* relates that in September, 1828, the keeper of Mr. Marshall of Hallsteads seized 180 brace in a cart on Haresceugh Fell. 'We do not entertain the idea,' remarked the editor, 'that the Alston and Garagill poachers killed the game with the gun.' He added that 'our market (Carlisle) is supplied weekly with three hundred brace of moor game.'

We bring these early newspaper notes to an end with an ominous extract from the *Pacquet* of September, 1779, in which it is stated that strict orders had been given for the apprehension 'of all idle young fellows as well as 'prentices, lawyer's clerks, etc.,' who should be found trespassing ; 'and all persons giving notice to the nearest recruiting party in the neighbourhood of the names and places of abode of the offenders will be handsomely rewarded, and their names concealed.'

Netherby is the best sporting estate in Cumberland, both for the total amount of game killed in a season, for record years for different kinds of game, and for record days. The earliest game books date from 1848, and as they have been carefully kept ever since it is possible to trace the progress of shooting better here, and to give a fuller account of it, than of any other property in the county.

In 1849 the total bag was 2,132 head ; grouse 401, blackgame 80, partridges 381, pheasants 242, woodcock 123, snipe 54, wildfowl 13, hares 704, rabbits 134. The total for 1887, the record year, was : grouse 1,962, blackgame 25, partridges 6,100, pheasants 3,015, hares 3,939, rabbits 2,351, woodcock 166, snipe 106, duck 45, various 60 ; total 17,769 head. Large as this total is, it happens that, except for the number of pheasants, 3,015, this year of 1887 was not a record for any other kind of game, for in 1872 3,643 grouse were killed ; in 1869, 6,602 partridges, in the same year 516 blackgame ; in 1876, 5,715 hares ; in 1852, 220 woodcock ; in 1889, 123 snipe ; in 1899, 5501 wildfowl (these latter hand reared). The record day for brown hares was in December 1876, 739 by seven guns ; for walking partridges, October 1887, 531 six guns ; for driving partridges 404, for ducks 4 and 5 December, 1900, when seven guns killed 1,025 and 1,229. The soil is somewhat rich and stiff, and the best seasons for partridges are the driest ones.

Grouse driving was first started on this estate in 1863, and since then the use of dogs has gradually grown less and less, and now none are taken on to the moors. In 1848, on 14 August, four guns killed 95 birds. Sir Richard Graham says that here, as is indeed invariably the case, the stock of birds has been much improved by the new system. Partridges have been driven only since 1894, and he does not think that 'this has increased the stock appreciably. There are, however, other agencies at work to counterbalance any benefit resulting from driving. I think perhaps the chief one is that the farmers now keep the fences very much closer than they used to, enabling the rooks (whose numbers have increased very much) to find the nests with greater facility. In many instances fences have been grubbed up and two fields thrown into one for agricultural purposes, thereby curtailing the nesting ground. As to ground game I do not think that the Hares and Rabbits Act has affected this estate very much' ; though he adds : 'Of course farmers, owing to agricultural depression, look upon ground game with a more jealous eye than they used to.'

Rabbits were unknown at Netherby in the early part of last century. Indeed, Sir Richard's father remembered them being introduced 'somewhere about the year 1825,' and they must have been singularly scarce for long afterwards, for in 1848 only 134 were killed during the whole season, and on 28 November, 1849, four guns got a mixed bag of 137 head without a single rabbit in it. The number shot (2,351) in the record year 1887 bears a very small proportion to the 15,418 head of other kinds of game. Sir Richard Graham turned out a hundred brace of Hungarian partridges in 1895 with the result of a 'marked increase of stock in 1896.' In a good season there are 15 days cover shooting at Netherby without going over the same ground twice.

From none of the old places of Cumberland would a series of far-stretching backrecords of sport be of more interest than from Muncaster, for all kinds of game and wildfowl were plentiful there, and such a display as that under the eyes of the Bolton Abbey monks—in Landseer's well-known picture—must often have been made and could sometimes no doubt be made now, though the two varieties of deer would be park-fed and not hill-fed. To sportsmen and also to antiquaries who, though accounts of modern shooting may be distasteful, take a keen pleasure in investigating little details of domestic life of ancient days, the rough jottings of long ago as to the deer missed or killed, the place and the weapons used, would be of the deepest interest. The great oaks of Muncaster must many a time have looked down upon tired men coming back from the hill or wood, exultant or disappointed, full of trying some new weapon, some crossbow or harquebuse, which were to them just what express rifles and hammerless ejectors are to us. But there is no game book going back any length of time here, or at Ponsonby or Crofton or Brayton or Workington Hall or Hutton, and we fancy that the registers of shooting, carefully kept day by day, are a comparatively modern invention, very little more than a hundred years old. No doubt entries of this kind *were* made in diaries and journals so far back as when men went to the chase, and diaries and journals were kept, but such documents are not of much interest to succeeding generations, and are often considered mere lumber and treated as such.

Muncaster formed part of the great forest of Copeland which was under Percy Earl of Northumberland, who gave the game to Sir John Pennington, and Lord Muncaster has among his deeds one of the nineteenth year of King Henry VII. granting to this Sir John the master forestership of Eskdale and Wastdale. Here were to be had deer both red and fallow, and grouse and blackgame from the hill ; salmon from the Esk, the Irt, and the Mite ; oysters from the Ravenglass shore ; trout, perch, pike and eels, and charr and sea fish of all kinds ; woodcock from the sunny hillsides and coppices, and wildfowl in great abundance. There is an old decoy pond in the park, but the ducks, so sensitive to any change in their surroundings, seldom visit it now.

Some fifteen years ago the estate of Dalegarth, which now belongs to Lord Muncaster, used to be shot over with dogs and yielded an average of about a hundred brace of grouse in a season. Since then it has been systematically driven, and five years ago the hundred brace were killed in *one* day, a very good proof of how judicious driving will improve a moor. The result would be better still if this moor were not, for various reasons, a difficult one to manage.

Hutchinson[1] says 'some pheasants were introduced by Lord Muncaster' ; also that he had a large rabbit warren at Drigg. 'In the winter season there is so great plenty of woodcocks in Muncaster (which they catch in snares or springes) that the tenants are bound, by the custom of the manor, to sell them to the lord for pence apiece.'[2] Hutchinson copies this and adds, 'they are of late years become very scarce.'

The park of Greystoke is one of the largest in England ; as seen on the map its green circumference would take in any halfdozen others in the county. If its owner cared for shooting as much as he does for hunting and farming, it could be made a great preserve. Without going outside the main boundaries of this far stretching enclosure, one to be measured by thousands instead of hundreds of acres, almost every species of game may be found. Its rich pastures and sunny banks and woodlands rise gradually towards the fells, and then run into wilder, thinner woods, and great stretches of heather, where there are grouse and blackgame. In addition to the ordinary varieties of game, some especial ones may be mentioned. When driving grouse here in the autumn of 1898, Mr. Senhouse of Netherhall shot a whitefronted goose which flew across the line, and

---

[1] *History of Cumberland*, i. 570 (published 1794).
[2] Nicolson and Burn, *History of Cumberland*, ii. 21 (published 1777).

a year or two before Mr. Hartley of Armathwaite killed a roe and a rabbit, 'right and left.' Roe are occasionally found in the park, but this does not exhaust the list. Half a century ago, a Greystoke keeper made, with evident indifference, two entries in the game book which certainly none of his successors would care about making now: '1852, February 15th. I shoot a fox that come out of Dickson's planting, fine day.' The next entry is still more cold blooded: '1854, October 10th. 1 fox in Neb side, sitting, fine day.' We have got no entry out of any game book so interesting and suggestive as this; the eight words form a perfect photograph.[1]

Some three miles as the crow flies from Greystoke is Gowbarrow Park, one of the few places in England where red deer, though fenced in, live in a natural state, and have to be stalked just as in a highland forest. Here, in 1894, Mr. C. B. Balfour shot a stag weighing 24 st. 4 lb., and in September, 1899, the Right Hon. J. W. Lowther got one weighing 28 st. 3 lb., both clean. These are the two heaviest stags killed at Lyulph's Tower, and they probably owed their size to many outside visits to cornfields and potatoes in the low country.

The average deer of Gowbarrow and Martindale are probably heavier than those in most Scotch forests. The stags just mentioned as killed in the former park were exceptional beasts. No genuine Scottish *hill* stag of our own time ever brought down the pointer of the scale to 396 lb. Though these Gowbarrow deer are imparked 'they are,' writes Mr. Macpherson [2] 'the lineal descendants of the stags which populated the dales and hills of Cumberland in the days when the Auroch and the Beaver were living in Lakeland.' In 1612 a Greystoke keeper was paid five shillings for taking two fawns to Naworth.[3] The deer are both red and fallow, and are only fed in snow time.

The game book dates back to 1825; in that year 279 grouse, 272 partridges, 55 snipe, 72 hares, 143 woodcocks and *one* pheasant were killed. In 1827 two gentlemen must have been made uncomfortable by the following entry opposite their names:

'September 13th, 2 guns had forty shots and killed 2 partridges.' The best year for partridges was 472, and the best day 90. For woodcocks the best day 16.

'Grouse abounds,' writes Hntchinson about this place 'on the mountains and commons, partridges on the lower grounds. Upon Saddleback and in Graystoke Park many foxes are allowed to breed.' [4] He also mentions that the Duke of Norfolk kept nearly 1,000 head of deer 'fallow, red, and a few American.'

Owing to its favourable position and to the care which has long been bestowed upon it, the shooting at Edenhall has been of a very high class for many years. One is struck here as at Netherby by the small number of rabbits killed. A search through the many great calf-bound folios, business-like ledgers, more like those we associate with commercial houses than records of sport, shows how few these have been. Two years before the Ground Game Act was passed the late Sir Richard Musgrave gave all the tenants on his estate the right to kill rabbits with ferrets, nets and traps during the whole year. Hares, no doubt chiefly because of this scarcity of rabbits, have always been very numerous; during the best years from 1866 to 1879 bags of 300 to nearly 500 in a day were not at all uncommon, and the average for big days during this period works out at about 250 a day, 2,179 in eight days in 1870–71 being the best. Since 1890, hares have become scarcer, 550 were killed in the season of 1897. The best day for grouse was in August, 1872, when four guns got 210 birds on Ousby Moor, and that famous year also gave the largest total, 1810.

Partridges also flourish abundantly: 53 'big' days between 1865 and 1874 give an average of 81 birds; 102 brace were shot in one day in 1873, and on 6 September, 1869, the late Sir Richard Musgrave shot to his own gun 87½ brace. From 1896 to 1899 an average of 536 partridges was obtained. The best day's cover shooting was in 1873 when 1,237 head were killed, chiefly hares and pheasants. Mr. Raine, who was head keeper at Edenhall for thirty-four years and who has now retired on a pension, says that during his time both Hungarian [5] and a change of blood of English partridges were tried, and he found the last do best; but the former were imported birds, and the latter, introduced in

---

[1] Mr. Howard writes: 'Two or three solitary snipe have been killed, but I cannot find out when.'

[2] In a letter written six days before his death.

[3] *Selections from the Household Books of the Lord William Howard of Naworth Castle*, p. 29 (Surtees Society).

[4] *History of Cumberland*, i. 406.

[5] Very few attempts to introduce Hungarian partridges seem to have been made in Cumberland.

eggs, probably had the best chance. Raine went with the late Sir Richard Musgrave for eighteen consecutive years to shoot, at Mr. Hasell's invitation, a stag on Martindale ; the best stag they got during that time was a 'royal' weighing 24 st. clean.

Hutchinson, writing in 1794, said that ' 7 or 8 years ago, quails abounded here (Edenhall) but they were nearly destroyed by a severe winter ; they are now beginning to increase again.' [1] Quails seem very scarce in Cumberland now. Mr. Heywood Thompson of Nunwick Hall, who shot four in the parish of Great Salkeld in September, 1898, informs us that a neighbour had also shot them in Melmerby parish 'but not recently.' Mr. Macpherson speaks of this bird as 'an irregular summer visitant' and as having been shot on Foulmire Moss in 1871 and seen at Rampside in 1885, while he himself saw a clutch of eggs taken in Rockliffe Marsh about 1882. It seems to have been commoner at the beginning of last century.[2]

Naworth is another provoking instance of a fine sporting property without game books going back for any length of time. Lord Carlisle writes that when he began shooting forty-five years ago, there was far more heather on his moors than there is at present, but the conservatism of old keepers, who objected to its temporary loss when burnt, led to its dying out in many places, and now some beats, which used to be good, are entirely covered with bent and useless for grouse. There was no driving in those days, and the birds lay well for a month or more after the 'twelfth' ; while at the present time, after the first week, it is little use pursuing them with dogs, and so Lord Carlisle, somewhat against his will, has to take to driving. In 1872— which here as everywhere stands out as the best year for grouse ever known—he and three other 'guns' killed a hundred brace over dogs in a day, 372 brace in five days. After several bad seasons the north moors on the Naworth property, which have suffered much from disease, show signs of improvement, six 'guns' having shot there in 1900 140 brace in a day, while on Geltsdale, also belonging to Lord Carlisle, Mr. Lacy Thompson's party (7 guns) killed 177 brace on 13 August of that year.

At times grouse disease has worked great havoc in Cumberland ; it is probable that the more universal and systematic way in which driving is now carried on will, to a certain extent at any rate, lessen its ravages ; the

birds are so hustled about, and mixed up in the autumn that in-breeding is much less likely to occur here than on moors shot over with dogs, where often some broods have nothing taken out of them, and remain quietly on the same part of a hillside all the following spring.

There is good partridge shooting about Brampton ; no pheasants are reared at Naworth, but wild ones do well as is the case in all this district. Blackgame here, as in most places, seem to be dying out ; nearly everywhere, except in such well established haunts as Dumfriesshire and Argyllshire, there is the same tale to tell—'blackgame used to be plentiful.' Lord Carlisle blames the shooting of greyhens for their decrease, and no doubt this is the chief cause. But even where hens are spared young cocks are seldom given any law ; in some parts few of them live beyond harvest time, and this annual clearing off of young blood must tell hardly on the race.

In the well known *Household Book of Lord William Howard* [3] there is a list of the prices paid for game and wildfowl, etc., from 1612 to 1640. A gorcock (red grouse) was valued at 5d., blackcock 6d. to 10d., greyhen 4d. to 6d., hare 4d. to 8d., mallard 5½d. to 9d., partridge 3d. to 6d., heron 6d., lapwing 1½d., bittern 8d., curlew 2½d. to 6d., do (jack) or 'knave' as it is called 2d., moorfowl 3d. to 5d. (As grouse and blackgame are previously mentioned it is difficult to say what this last bird is). With the prices given here we may compare those in a list 'communicated' to Hutchinson from the Roll of Birkby Manor belonging to Lord Muncaster.

' 'We do order and put in pain that every the inhabitants within the Manor of Birkby who shall hereafter take or catch, kill or come by any wildfowl whatsoever, shall not sell them to any foreigner or stranger, but shall bring them to the lord, or his bailiff, for the time being, at the prices and rates hereafter specified, viz. for every mallard 4d.—Duck 3d.—Every long mallard or widgeon, 2d.— Woodcock or partridges, 1d.—feelfaws throstles, ousles, each four 1d.—Every curlew, 3d., for two teals, 1d.—Plover, 1d.—Lapwings one halfpenny, under pain and forfeiture of 3s. 4d. for every fowl, otherwise sold, as formerly accustomed.' Hutchinson gives no date to the Roll ; the editor, Mr. Wilson, fixes it as of the seventeenth century, probably between 1670 and 1700. The

[1] *History of Cumberland,* i. 271.
[2] *Fauna of Lakeland,* p. 338.
[3] *Selections from the Household Books of the Lord William Howard of Naworth Castle,* p. lxxvii. (Surtees Society).
[4] *History of Cumberland,* i. 578.

purchasing price of money, when Lord William Howard's account book was kept, was about twelve times what it is now, so that a hare at its cheapest was quite up to its present price, and most game and wildfowl very much dearer.

There are later accounts at Naworth dealing with game and sport. In 1733 the price of ferrets 'bought to hunt' in Brampton Warren was 7s. each; the cost of keeping them 3d. and 4d. a week. John Dobson got 8d. for a day's work 'riveing wood to dry rabbett skins.' These skins were sold for 3s. 6d. a dozen. In 1736 it cost 16s. to convey 320 couple of rabbits from Naworth to Carlisle. In 1740 there was a payment of 5s. 6d. to Jos. Smith for 'cutting hollies for dear.' In 1744 1s. 10d. to call 'notices at church about game.' In the same year 3s. for 'convictions against shooters of game.' In 1787 'expenses as to game that year' came to £84.[1]

Sir Henry Vane, writing to lament the absence of old game books at Hutton-in-the-Forest, has some interesting notes as to shooting there and at other places in the county. He was one of three guns, Sir R. Musgrave and Lord Brougham being the others, who in the 'seventies' killed for the first time over a hundred brace of partridges in a day at Edenhall, and a little later on, he was one of four guns who doubled that bag and established a record at Netherby. One of the party, Colonel Baring, had only one arm, and shot with two very light guns. The most curious shot he has seen in his long life was made by the Rev. C. Burton of Cliburn, who in Wythop killed with one barrel a woodcock and a partridge flying over his head. In these days of modern guns, it is interesting to hear that the old keeper at Hutton, Satterthwaite by name, who taught Sir Henry to shoot, would not allow him to cock his hammers till the bird had risen or the hare started; but this rule was relaxed after the boy in his excitement let one of the hammers slip, and shot dead his teacher's best dog which was pointing a pheasant. The best day at Hutton for partridges was 80 brace for three guns. In the 'fifties' rabbits were very scarce on the Hutton estate; they were only to be found at Chapel Wood, Wythop. Blackgame seem dying out, as they are in so many places, and woodcocks are fewer. 'I blame rabbits,' says Sir Henry, 'for their deserting me.'

A little vellum bound book headed *Routen Burn Grouse*, belonging to Mr. R. D. Marshall of Castlerigg Manor, is, save that at Greystoke, the earliest game book we have been able to refer to. This book dates from 1828 and is very carefully kept. Sport must sometimes have been very good at Melmerby and Gamblesby and Ouseby and Bullman Hills. In five days in 1828, five guns killed 314½ brace of grouse. Then there is a jump to 1835 when 254 brace were shot in nine days. 'Helm wind' is put opposite one entry to account for a small bag. In 1836, 383 brace were killed in six days, 142 on the twelfth; 360 was the total for 1837. There was never more than two weeks' shooting in any year. The book comes down to 1844 when the entries of the well-known Cumberland names, Marshalls, Wyberghs, Lawsons, Dykeses, Musgraves, Fetherstonhaughs end. Below each gun is his total for the day. We see that on 12 August, 1836, Mr. H. C. Marshall shot 36 brace, and Sir W. Lawson 12, and Mr. A. Marshall 1 bird on the 26th. This is an interesting little book, a model of a game record so far as it goes. There is a careful list of the grouse given away, and at the end another list of 'poachers at Cross House in 1839–41,' of whom one John Smith seems to have had a share in the compounding of a felony with some one, for 'he begged to be let off and paid one pound part fine.'

The Abbey Holme has always been an interesting district for a sportsman. Cox[2] says 'this part of the country (Holmcultram) was a large forest and stock'd with red deer at the Conquest, the Demesne of Allerdale.' At the beginning of the nineteenth century, its 24,000 acres were chiefly held by statesmen, and at the present time Mr. Francis Grainger says that the number of owners is scarcely less. Owing to this fact and to the farms being also small, 'averaging about a hundred acres,' there has been no game preserving on a large scale. In the Survey of 1538 it is stated 'there is a warren and coneys upon and about the Sea Banks which be worth by year to let to farm 13/4.' And there still stretches a warren for five miles along those sea banks, which is worth a good deal more now than the fraction of a pound at which it was in the market 363 years ago.

This is a good country, though not so good as it used to be, for any one who loves wild

---

[1] In 1745 there are two significant items: '17th Dec, taking my horses to Spadeadam when the rebels came 1/4.' 'Carrying light horses into Northumberland out of the way of rebels 5/-'

[2] *A Compleat History of Cumberland*, 1700, p. 376. It is only right to say that Thomas Cox is not usually looked upon as an authority in matters of this sort.

shooting and is willing to live laborious days and nights without expecting a great reward, and who would be prouder of six or eight mallard or wigeon, killed in the dusk of a stormy winter evening, than of a share in a thousand tame wild ducks let loose out of a cover. Bit by bit the wet places loved by duck and snipe get fewer. The process of drying them began long ago, and is ever going on, but there are great mosses here, one called Wedholm Flow, the largest in Cumberland, and fine feeding grounds on the Solway and in the estuary formed by the Wampool and Waver. In hard and stormy winters, geese, both barnacle and grey, are to be found here, and many wigeon and mallard, with now and then a rarity such as a tufted duck or pintail. Mr. Grainger, to whom we are indebted for most of our information about this very interesting country, says that, before the drainage scheme of the Waver and Crummock rivers about 1850, the mosses stretching from Abbey to Dubmill afforded splendid duck shooting.

A somewhat novel sport was once carried on in Holmcultram. In an old tithe suit of 1586 occurs the following : ' That the defendant Mandeville agreed with John Hending for 40/- to kill the doves in Holme Cultram church ; he ripped up the lead to go in and shoot at them, and did often shoot at them during divine service, and put the people to great fear.'

In an old news-sheet of the sixteenth century, there is mentioned what seems to be a claim on the part of the Crown to the game in Holmcultram. 'The statutes of King Henry VIII. doth give liberty to shoot to any dwelling within v. miles of the sea, or within xii. miles of the borders of Scotland, and that it shall be lawful for the sayd inhabitants to use exercyses, and have their gunns, etc.' In the minutes of Quarter Sessions held at Cockermouth in 1701, it is stated that complaints have been made that persons not qualified by law possessed ' in her maties manor of Holme Cultram gunns, greyhounds, and other doggs, ferretts, coney dogs, harepipes, snares and other engines for the taking and killing of coneys, haires, pheasants, partridge.' It was ordered that search be made for all these and that they be destroyed. So that the modern flight shooter in the Abbey Holme is carrying on his sport in a district where it has been from very ancient times a care to kings and great people and to the law.

Mention has already been made of the lack of old game books at places where shoot has been carried on for many years ; Lowther is in the same category, but most of Lowther is in Westmorland, and will no doubt be treated of under that county. The Whitehaven Castle estates are also barren of details, and Dovenby and Irton. At nearly all the places mentioned here and elsewhere there is good shooting of various kinds ; at Greysouthen, where Mr. Harris has killed 173 brace of partridges in two days, and Calthwaite where he got 92 brace, each time with four guns ; at Gilgarran ; at Castlesteads, where the kindly red soil in that country adjoining the Roman Wall encourages and keeps together wild pheasants ; at Armathwaite on Bassenthwaite,[1] where Mr. Hartley gets in good winters many wildfowl with, now and then, such a rarity as a white-fronted goose amongst them ; at Ennim, Dalemain, Skirwith and Barrock ; at Holm Hill and Castlerigg and Isel and Irton and Brayton, and these by no means exhaust the list. Twenty-four woodcocks have been killed in a day at Isel (January, 1885). A hundred acres of poor land near Ennerdale lake was planted by the late Mr. Ainsworth some thirty years ago, and the wood now stands out as a huge oasis in that sparsely timbered district, and holds a great many pheasants.

' Becking ' is a means of capturing grouse in what Mr. Macpherson, in his natural history of that bird,[2] calls 'a dubious but not necessarily illegal fashion.' Any one who has fired at grouse on the ground when he himself was perfectly concealed, especially in thick misty weather, knows that the first shot will not always put them up or the second or the third ; we have known as many as seven shots fired at a covey of twelve before one rose. This indeed was with a small rifle, but if they are in the right humour they will take no heed of the louder report of a gun. Such a way of killing grouse is of course not confined to Cumberland, and probably the ' becking ' itself may be carried on in other parts under another name ; we have never heard of it in Scotland. It consists of imitating the note of the hen bird and so calling the cocks within shot, and Mr. Macpherson gives an instance of a man calling ten birds to him and shooting them all, one by one, with an old muzzle-loader. The man who practises ' becking,' gets up early, goes to a part of the

---

[1] There are a great many goldeneye ducks on Bassenthwaite which do much harm to the salmon fishing on the Derwent. As many as five and twenty may sometimes be seen just above Ousebridge, diving for spawn.

[2] *The Grouse*, p. 65 (1894), ' Fur, Feather and Fin ' Series.

moor where he knows there are plenty of birds, hides himself as well as he can, and, when the cocks begin to crow round about at dawn, imitates as nearly as possible, either with some instrument or his unaided breath, the call of the hen. Dry frosty weather is the best for the business. We have very much ·condensed Mr. Macpherson's graphic description of this curious practice which he says, though not given up altogether ' has lately fallen into disuse.'

It goes without saying that a tenant anywhere can, if he so chooses, do a great deal of harm to his landlord from a sporting point of view. But there is an additional way by which a man with a very small bit of land indeed, can, in a grouse district, cause grievous annoyançe and loss to his neighbours. The cause of offence may only be a tiny strip, a sour pasture, heatherless, grouseless, perhaps not worth sixpence an acre for any purpose but one. But if this strip is in the right place (from its owner's point of view) and there is good grouse ground round it, it will act like the fly in the ointment ; like a grain of sand in the eye putting the whole body wrong. Its want of food and shelter may be so evident that birds seldom light on it, but they have to fly over it, and nets judiciously arranged and managed will in the course of a season capture a very large number of them, and do very great harm to the adjoining beats. It would be interesting to find out, the process would be a difficult one, how many grouse such a patch would give in a season. There is always a large demand for strong birds to turn out, and a satisfactory price to be got for them. If, as is the case sometimes, a man rents a moor avowedly for the purpose of netting, and limited in number by his agreement, get his birds in this way, he would not do more harm than one who shot the same number, though probably some parts of a moor might be too hardly worked while others were scarcely touched. This seems to be a fair way of supplying a legitimate want. But it is quite another matter when the ideal case we mentioned first, which is a very real case indeed to many owners of moors, comes into working. A wide district of great yearly value might conceivably be quite bared of birds, quite ruined, by judicious working of nets on a narrow strip of land in itself worth just nothing at all. There is some analogy between a fowler with a few acres of land spoiling a grouse moor, and a fisherman with a few yards of water ruining a salmon river, both working with a net, but the second pays often a big rent. And the law as it stands can help neither of them.

To some owners of moorland this question of netting is a most serious one ; the case is imaginable of a poor man depending for his income on the rental of a fine moor, and being practically ruined by the operations of netters round him. In the autumn of 1897, a somewhat acrimonious correspondence on this subject was carried on in the *Field*. It is, in spite of what was said in these letters, difficult to see how legislation can help those who are injured. Any bill to render it illegal for a man to catch wild birds, or let others catch them, on his own ground, would have very little chance of becoming law. Some hard words were used against those who bought live grouse for the purpose of ' turning down ' ; the number of people doing this must be very considerable, and probably the greater majority of them have not the smallest idea that they are doing any injury to any one by their purchases ; and in some cases neither are they, for if a moor is rented for the purpose and a fair amount of grouse taken off it by netting instead of shooting, no one has any right to complain. The point as to whether turning out grouse was beneficial to new districts was discussed in the *Field*, and one or two correspondents asserted it was not. For our part we have not the very slightest doubt on the matter, for we have several times seen the most marked improvement rapidly take place in a stock of grouse where healthy strange birds had been introduced. All question of painting or marking grouse in any way seems quite unreasonable and useless ; if the stock in the first or second season (supposing these are normal) does not speak for itself, the identification of individual birds is merely of academic interest. Attempts have been made to net against the netters, and so tire them out and drive them away, but this involves expense and trouble which very few would be willing to undertake. To buy up bits of ground which, worthless in themselves, are valuable for erecting nets on, would be an endless and costly and often impossible task.

If it were made perfectly plain to every one interested in grouse that serious injury was done in some districts by this practice of netting, and then, if those interested in stopping it, were to see whether they could not among themselves do something towards supplying a perfectly natural and legitimate want, viz. the introduction of fresh blood, a great advance would have been made towards putting an end to a system which, while it is of benefit to the public, is so harmful to individuals.

HORSE RACING

Horse racing as a department of British sport can be traced back in Cumberland to the reign of Queen Elizabeth. From that date there is evidence that the county was not backward in this form of amusement. At whatever date horse racing may have been recognized as an institution elsewhere, it must have been a popular pastime in Cumberland at the very earliest period of our sporting history, for during the latter portion of the sixteenth century there were two notable racecourses in the county—'Langanby' moor for the people of the country, and Kingmoor for the burghers of Carlisle.

The moor of Langwathby, or as it is traditionally known, 'Langanby,' in the valley of the Eden, is the oldest and most famous horse course of Cumberland and Westmorland, rivalling Garterly in Yorkshire as the historic racecourse of the northern counties.

If we believe the narrative of Edmund Sandford, the jovial, inquisitive, gossiping squire of Askham, a man who might have sat as model for Addison's Will Wimble, fond of field sports and acquainted with every stable and cellar of note in the two counties, we can put our finger on the date when racing at 'Langanby' had begun. The account is so curious and so full of interest that it must be given almost in his own language, specially as it was 'writt about the year 1675,' a period of ultra-sporting notoriety. Writing of this racecourse he says : 'The most famous horse course ther for a free plate on midsomer day yearly : and the first founder thereof, squire Richard Sandford, younger brother of Thomas Sandford of Askame in Westmorland, was bred up with the Earl of Northumberland as master of his horse and a brave horseman. He persuaded the Lord Wharton and the Chevileir Musgraves, who had a brave breed of horses, and many of the country gentry to contribute to a prize of plate of £20 yearly. And it was the famous horse course of England and Scotland. The quondam Duke of Buckingham's horse called "Conqueror," and the Earl of Morray's wily horse "Fox," ran here for £100, but the "Conqueror" conquered him and won the money. The night before there was the terriblest blast ever blown, churches, towers, trees, steeples and houses all feeling the fury of the furies thereof, for without peradventure the devil was astir whether of England or Scotland he could not tell, but the English horse got the prize.'[1]

'Langanby' was a famous horse course in the reign of Queen Elizabeth, and racing possessed the same peculiarity then as it is supposed to have now, that it outweighed every other attraction. It has been pointed out as a sign of the degeneracy of the time that the great antiquary, Ralph Thoresby, was unable to muster a quorum to transact the business of a charity committee on account of the absence of the neighbouring gentry at a horse race.[2] But even a century earlier, in 1585, we find in Cumberland a justice of the peace refusing to meet the queen's commissioners on public business on account of his engagements at 'Langanby.'[3]

The date of the races over this course varied from time to time. In 1585, Richard Dudley's horse ran in April ; on 30 April, 1593, Lord Scrope, warden of the marches, refused to give Bothwell an interview 'on Langerbie moor at the horserace';[4] in 1612 the date was Midsummer Day, when we know that 'Langomby race' was patronized by the young bloods of the Howard family ;[5] on 27 May, 1663, Daniel Fleming of Rydal spent 4s. 6d. at 'Langanby Moor horse race,' and in two days afterwards he 'paid 10s. unto Mr. Layton as his subscription money towards the plate.'[6]

But the racing annals of the county of Cumberland are enriched by the possession of relics in the shape of racing bells which are unequalled in point of interest by any

---

[1] Edmund Sandford, *A Cursory Relation of all the Antiquities and Familyes in Cumberland*, p. 43 : Kendal, 1890.
[2] *Diary of Ralph Thoresby*, i. 129, 169 ; ii. 9, ed. J. Hunter.
[3] Richard Dudley in a letter dated at Yanwith, 13 April, 1585, stated that he could not meet the commissioners from Yorkshire concerning Rothay Bridge on the 26th, for he had a horse to run in the race at Langanbye (*Rydall Hall MSS.* p. 11, Hist. MSS. Com. 12th Report, Appendix, part vii.).
[4] *Calendar of Border Papers*, i. 831, ed. J. Bain.
[5] *The Household Books of Lord William Howard of Naworth Castle*, pp. 49, 51, 52, Surtees Society.
[6] *Rydal Hall MSS.* p. 373, Hist. MSS. Commission.

other survival of the ancient history of the 'turf.' If 'Langanby' moor afforded scope for the exercise and amusement of the people living in the country, Kingmoor was the trysting place for the citizens of Carlisle. The moor, an ancient estate of the Corporation situated on the north side of the river Eden within easy distance of the city, has been associated with racing transactions from an early period. The chamberlains' accounts in the city records contain various items of money paid out for the purchase of prizes for these races. Later the prizes were given by the local members of Parliament, the guilds from time to time voting or withholding a plate when such a racing prize came into fashion. One extract may be given in order to indicate the favour in which horse races were held by the commonalty of Carlisle in the days of the first Stuart as well as the nature of the prizes which may now be said to be extinct. It is in the form of a request made on 21 April, 1619, 'that Mr. Maior and his breathren shall call for the silver broad arrowes and the stock and the horse and nage bells with all expedytion to be imployed for manteyning of a horse race for the cytties use upon the Kingesmoor at such tyme yearely as they shall thinke convenient and to article that the same cup shall be brought in yearley as they shall thinke ffittinge.'[1] These 'horse and nage bells,' still the property of the Corporation of Carlisle, were exhibited before the Archæological Institute which met at Carlisle in 1859, and were pronounced as 'possibly unique' in their catalogue to the museum of antiquities collected together for that occasion. They are globular in form with slits at the bottom usual in bells of that class. The largest, which is $2\frac{1}{4}$ inches in diameter, is of silver gilt, and bears on a band round its centre the inscription—

+ THE SWEFTES + HORSE + THES + BEL +

TO + TAK + FOR + MI + LADE + DAKER

+ SAKE [2]

The other bell, also of silver, is smaller in size and bears the legend '1599, H.B.M.C.,' being the initials of Henry Baines, mayor of

Carlisle, 1599. As racing bells they have called forth a large amount of controversy throughout the country, and various claims have been made by other places that they possessed sporting relics of greater rarity and value. But the Carlisle bells still hold the field as the oldest and most curious racing prizes in existence.[3] Kingmoor shared the honours with 'Langanby' as the chief centres where races were held in Cumberland for a long period.[4]

question, though it may possibly be much earlier. In 1585 Humfray Musgrave's horse 'Bay Sandforth' ran and won all the three bells at a horse-race at Liddesdale. Thomas Carlton came home from the races and next day 'ranne the bell of the Wainerigge' (Cal. of Border Papers, i. 309).

[3] These bells have achieved considerable fame since they were re-discovered in an old box in the town clerk's office in Castle Street, Carlisle, about twenty-five years ago. They were described by the late Mr. Llewellyn Jewitt as 'unique' in the Art Journal, xix. 122, new series (April, 1880). The executive committee of both the Sports and Arts Exhibition and of the Tudor Exhibition, held in London in 1890, applied to the Corporation of Carlisle for the loan of these bells, and the Sports and Arts being the first to apply got them. At that exhibition the bells were displayed in a case containing some huge pieces of racing plate, such as the York Plate of 1717, the Newmarket Gold Cup of 1705, the Newcastle Cups of 1819 and 1823 and others. At that time they attracted much attention, and were engraved in several London papers. In a short time a rival to 'the horse and nage bells' of Carlisle appeared in the shape of a bell said to have been presented by William the Lion to the borough of Lanark in 1160. But the experts soon detected on this bell the mark of a seventeenth century silversmith, Robert Dennistoun of Edinburgh, so that it is probably not much older than 1628. The bell was not an uncommon prize either in horse racing or cockfighting, and was held by the victor as challenge cups and shields are at the present day, from one year to another, or from one race to another. To win this bell was considered a mark of honour, and gave rise to the popular expression of 'to bear away the bell.' At York the racing prize in 1607 was a small golden bell, and the Corporation records of Chester about 1600 show that in that city a silver bell was given to be raced for on the Roodee, but it is not known whether these trophies are now in existence (Cripps, Old English Plate, pp. 143, 339, 4th ed. ; Art Journal, April, 1880 ; Strutt, Sports and Pastimes, pp. 41-2).

[4] In the eighteenth century racing on Kingmoor began to decline. In the early portion of the century the Corporation let large areas of the moor to various people on leases for lives, and their descendants at the close of the century claimed the right to enfranchise on easy terms. In pursuance of these claims the racecourse was enclosed. In

[1] Municipal Records of the City of Carlisle, pp. 277-8 et passim, ed. R. S. Ferguson and W. Nanson (1887).

[2] This Lady Dacre has been identified with Elizabeth, daughter of George Talbot, fourth Earl of Shrewsbury, and wife of William, Lord Dacre of Gillesland, who was governor of Carlisle early in the reign of Queen Elizabeth. But the identification is fanciful. The bell given by 'milade Daker' cannot be of later date than the period in

It has been generally supposed that 'the Swifts,' a wide and undulating meadow on the south bank of the Eden near to Carlisle bridges, was selected to supersede Kingmoor as the municipal racecourse about the middle of the eighteenth century, when the ownership of the latter course became the subject of litigation, and that it was recognized as the place for annual meetings a few years before the grant of the king's plate in 1763. But the Swifts was used as a racecourse long before that time.[1] The Duke of Devonshire possesses amongst the archives of Bolton Abbey a survey of all the Crown lands in the neighbourhood of Carlisle made in 1612 by Mr. Anthony Curwen, agent of the Crown property. In speaking of the Swifts he indulges in the singular reminiscence that 'many old men and women about Karliell did well knowe and remember that all the grounds were one contynuse ground, and when he was a scholler at Karliell there was no hinderance to the footeball play nor to the essayes of running of naggs, men and women leaping, dauncing, etc., upon every Shrove Tuesday.' On George Smith's map of Carlisle, published in 1746, we have a picture of 'The Swiftes or City Horse Course,' on which there are rude drawings of horses with docked tails and riders in jockey costume, one horse being flogged up for the final struggle. The starting and other posts and a judge's box are shown, being apparently permanent structures. In the eighteenth century horses running on the Swifts were expected to do a large amount of work, the length of the course and the weight to be carried varying according to the age of the horse. In 1752 three year olds were obliged to carry 9 stones and run in two mile heats; four year olds, 9 stones and three mile heats; and so on till mature horses were expected to carry 10 stones over a four mile course.[2] Racing on the Swifts is now (1901) about to be

abandoned, a new course having been selected on the rising ground above the Caldew near the hamlet of Blackhall two miles to the south of Carlisle.

After the Restoration of Charles II. racecourses multiplied and interest in sport became more general in the county. It would seem that Cumberland, like the rest of England, had gone into excess when 'the king had come into his own again.' It is true that many of the leading families had been either beggared or impoverished by the civil war, yet notwithstanding these disadvantages racing and field sports came into greater prominence and were more widely practised after the strictness of the Puritanical days of the Commonwealth, like a stream rushing with greater force after a temporary confinement. If we return to the pages of Sandford, we get frequent peeps into the stables of the country gentry, as well as a vivid picture of the state of society during his time. In that writer's experience almost every gentleman in the county who could afford it, and perhaps who could *not* afford it, was in the habit of keeping open house and dispensing hospitality as occasion offered, the information being usually appended that he was not without a running horse or two in his stables. Sir George Fletcher, a man of great local repute as well as a member of Parliament, is described as 'a very brave monsir, great housekeeper, hunter and horse courser, never without the best running horse or two, the best he can gett,' a portrait of Sir George which agrees with everything else we know of him. A like account is given of old Sir John Dalston and Sir George Dalston of Dalston Hall, 'two brave gentill gallants and justiciers, great gamesters never without two or three running horses, the best in England.' The members of the Dalston family were ever great patrons of 'the turf,' so much so indeed that traditions of their sporting celebrity still linger in the parish from which they took their name, though a century and a half has elapsed since the ancestral hall and estates passed to other hands. It is still said of one of the last scions of this ancient house that he possessed a pair of running horses which were such a match in swiftness that the weight of the stable key would be sufficient to decide the race. Facts go to show that Cumberland, however backward it may have been in other matters, was pre-eminent as a sporting county, exposed to all the abuses which had so early crept into horse racing and which have been inseparable from it ever since. It would appear that the history of the Cumberland 'turf' at this period affords sufficient justifi-

the nineteenth century some of the freemen of Carlisle broke down the fences and held the race, out of which arose the assize trial of Ismay *v.* Barnes held at Carlisle in 1865, when the freemen lost their case and the races on Kingmoor came to an end (*Municipal Records of the City of Carlisle*, pp. 94, 100, 118, 142, ed. Ferguson & Nanson).

[1] It has been thought that the place-name of Swifts was derived from the races which took place there, but it is scarcely probable. The name occurs as 'Swyft' among the demesne lands of Carlisle Castle as early as 1353 (*Abbrev. Rot. Origin.* ii. 230*b*, 252*b*, Record Commission).

[2] Heber, *List of Horse-matches run in 1752*, pp. 18–20.

SPORT ANCIENT AND MODERN

cation for the remarks of Burton[1] that 'horse races are the desports of great men, and good in themselves, though many gentlemen by such means gallop themselves out of their fortunes.' One brilliant exception to this reflection is furnished by the squire of Ewanrigg Hall, who, though he engaged in all kinds of gaming, was sharp enough not only to keep the lands he had inherited, but to make ample provision for his family and to depart this life without an enemy. Strange and piquant is the description Sandford gives of him : 'Mr. Joseph Thwaits in my time one of the wittiest brave monsirs for all gentill gallantry, hounds, hawkes, horse courses, bowles, bowes and arrowes, and all games whatsoever—play his £100 at cards, dice and shovelboord if you please, and had not above £200 a year : yet he left his children pretty porcions and dyed beloved of all parties.'[2]

Whatever may be said of the popularity of other kinds of amusement, the racecourse was an institution that flourished in Cumberland towards the close of the Stuart period. In a manuscript history of the county, now in possession of the Earl of Lonsdale, written by Thomas Denton in the years 1687–8, several racecourses, at that time in high favour, have been noted by him as existing in the various parishes of his perambulation. Besides those already mentioned, he states that the sandy plain near the town of Drigg was converted into a horse course by Sir William Pennington, and a plate of the value of £10 was run for yearly in May. Vestiges of this ancient course can still be traced in that locality. A little above the village of Whitrig to the west there stands a high round hill called Carmot, from which, he says, you can see all the country round, at the foot of which began a horse course which ended upon the top of Mootha, the ascent of which being so great a climb that they called that part of the hill 'Trotter,' in regard that few horses could gallop to the top of it, but were forced to trot ere they

come to the top. Denton has also noted racecourses on Harethwaite Common and Woodcock Hill, in the parish of Westward ; on the sands of Skinburness ; on Low Planes and Barrock Fell, in the parish of Hesket-in-the-Forest. At the latter place the course circled round the fell, and measured four and a quarter miles.[3] In addition to these, Machell, who was a contemporary of Denton, mentions 'a brave horse rase along the seaside at Parton,' near Whitehaven.

This catalogue of racecourses can scarcely be considered exhaustive, though it appears appalling enough when compared with our notions of sporting matters and the number of race meetings which occur in our day. As it only represents the customary centres where horse matches took place,[4] it may well be said that racing had reached its climax at this period. During the latter portion of the seventeenth century 'Langanby' held its own as the county racecourse, though courses at Workington[5] and Burgh-by-Sands were fast rivalling it in popularity. At this period we meet with a strange custom in connection with horse racing. It was not enough for the local sportsmen to patronize 'the turf' in their private capacities, but they did not deem it inappropriate to import racing into the concerns of their public life. In fact, arrangements for the next horse race became a recognized part of the business transacted by the justices in Quarter Sessions. As the records of the sessional proceedings are of undoubted interest, and appear to be unique in the annals of sport, the extracts may be reproduced from the manuscript volumes in the custody of the clerk of the peace of the county, with the dates and places of the

---

[1] *Anatomy of Melancholy*, pt. 2, sec. i, cap. iv. ed. 1660. Henry Curwen, who was sheriff in 1688, went by the name of 'Galloping Harry,' owing to his partiality to racing transactions. It is said that he wasted much of the property of his family in this way.

[2] *A Cursory Relation of all the Antiquities and Familyes in Cumberland*, circa 1675, p. 22. Compare the quatrain of Tom Durfey, a contemporary poet, usually but unjustly called ' the Moore of the Restoration '—

'Another makes racing a trade,
  And dreams of his prospects to come ;
And many a crimp match he made,
  By bubbing another man's groom.'

[3] Thomas Denton, 'A Perambulation of Cumberland and Westmorland, written in the years 1687 and 1688,' MS. ff. 20, 53, 59, 65, 99.

[4] At this period the popular appetite was not satisfied with regular meetings. There are on record various challenges for private trials of horseflesh, as ambition or envy prompted the 'turfites' of the day. Among the manuscripts of Mr. Geo. Browne of Troutbeck there is a very curious agreement, dated 30 May, 1692, between a Cumberland gentleman and a Westmorland yeoman as to a race to be run by their respective mares in the demesne of Calgarth for the sum of £20 (*Browne MSS.* vol. ii. f. 199).

[5] These races took place on a piece of extraparochial ground, near Workington, called 'The Cloffock,' which is still used for sports of a different kind. It is situated on the north side of the town, between the river Derwent and, a small rivulet, which completely surrounds it. Races were held in this course within living memory.

443

Sessions at which the racing business was transacted :

Cockermouth, January, 169⅞.

Ordered that the High Sheriffe of this County doe give twenty pounds to be divided into two Plates equally. The one to be run for at Workington, the last Wednesday in June. And the other to be run for at Langwathby Moore the first Thursday after Apleby Assizes and p'clamacon to be made a moneth before each Race.

Cockermouth, January, 1699–1700.

Agreed by the Justices of the peace with the consent of the high Sheriffe That the Sheriffe give fifteene pounds towards a Plate in Liew of Dinners for the future. And to make the Plate as much more as he pleaseth to be runn for at the usuall course at Workington and Brough Marsh, the money equally to be divided, viz., halfe of it to be run for at the Race att Workington upon Wednesday the twenty-sixth day of June. And the other halfe to be runn for at Brough Marsh upon Fryday the nineteenth day of July.

Cockermouth, January, 170⅔.

Ordered that the Sheriffe finde a plate what he pleaseth above the value of fifteen pounds to be all in one plate & to be runn for the last Wednesday in June, the foure miles course att Workington tenn stone weight the bridle and sadle included in the said weight, whosoever runns his horse to putt in fforty shillings saveing the Cum'b'lnd gentlemen who are only to putt in twenty shillings if theire owne horses. And the Justices putting in theire owne horses to pay nothing and the second horse to have the stakes.

Carlisle, Easter, 1701.

Whereas the Sheriffes of this county have for some yeares by past been excused from entertaineing his Maties Justices of the peace at the gen'all Quarter Sessions of the peace for this county by reason of their findeing a ffree plate to be yearely run for at some horse course w^thin the county which for sev'all reasons is now found inconvenient and p'ticularly for that the Justices at their said Sessions doe not usually meete & eate together whereby they want opportunity to conferr & consider about the business of the country. It is ordered & desired by the Justices at this present Sessions that after this p'sent yeare the succeedinge Sheriffes for this county will for the time to come expend the wages of the Justices at their gen'all Quarter Sessions in entertaineing of the Justices with a dinner that they may have the better opportunity to discourse & consult about the countryes business. And it is ordered that the said wages shall not be suspended or otherwise laid out in any wise whatsoever.

Cockermouth, January, 170¼.

Ordered by this Cort that the order of this time twelve month concerning the Justices haveing dinners be discharged and that in lieu thereof the Sheriffe doe pay fifteene pound for a plate to be run for the last Thursday in August upon Langwathby-moore. The course to be three heats fower miles each heate. And the course to be set forth by John Dalston Esqr high Sheriffe of the said county, each horse to carry ten stone weight besides bridle and sadle. And each horse that runns to be sold for thirty pounds after he hath runn, the Sheriffe to have the first offer and the Justices the next. And then who thinkes fitt. And e'vy horse that runns to be entered with the Sheriffe one weeke before he runns. And ev'y Justice of peace horse that runns to be free. Every gentleman in the county that putts in a horse to pay ten shillings. And ev'y stranger to putt in twenty shillings. And the second horse to have the stakes.[1]

There is no necessity to point out the significance of these extracts from the sessional records in illustration of the sporting proclivities of the county. One peculiarity in these transactions is very striking. The professional element is conspicuous by its absence. The races were practically confined to the people of Cumberland and Westmorland, and as far as we can infer the instinct of sport innate in Englishmen was the determining cause of these county meetings. But the interest of the justices was not confined to their corporate action in promoting races. On 14 May, 1672, William Fletcher of Cockermouth wrote to Daniel Fleming of Rydal, that he was just starting to meet his relative, Sir George, at Burgh Marsh, ' where we are to have a famous race for a plate which he and I have given to make sport among the jockeys.' In the same strain Henry Fletcher

[1] The names of the justices who took part in these sporting deliberations on the judicial bench are as follows : Sir William Pennington, Sir Richard Musgrave, Sir Wilfrid Lawson, Sir Edward Hasell, George Fletcher, Richard Patrickson, Leonard Dykes, Robert Carleton, John Aglionby, John Briscoe, William Gilpin, Thomas Brougham, Edward Stanley, Richard Lamplugh, Anthony Hudleston and James Nicholson. There was evidently a difference of opinion among them whether the sheriff should provide a dinner or a racing plate. On the four occasions when 'the ffree plate' was ordered there was but a small bench, with Sir William Pennington in the chair, but at the Carlisle Sessions in 1701, when the dinner was substituted, it is evident Sir William was out-voted, no less than nine justices being present. Again, when the 'dinner' order was discharged in favour of the 'plate' in 1702, the Sessions was attended only by Sir William Pennington, Sir Richard Musgrave, Robert Carleton and William Gilpin. With regard to the discontinuance of silver plate as prizes, it may be mentioned here that 'George I. was no racer, but he discontinued silver plate as prizes, and instituted the *King's Plates*, as they have been since termed, being 100 guineas paid in cash' (*Quarterly Review*, July, 1833, p. 386).

ventured to forecast the 'good sport' that was likely to be had at Workington in April, 1687, when seven horses were to run, 'one of Sir John Lowther's, Mr. Curwen's, Mr. Davison's, Mr. Lowther's, Charles Bannister's, Jack Aglionby's, and one from Cockermouth.'[1]

Racing at Burgh was invested with a new interest when the 'Barony Cup' came to be reckoned among the prizes for competition on this course. The barony of that name passed by purchase to the Lowther family in 1684,[2] and soon after that date we find record of the gift of this cup. It is said that it was originally given by the lords of the barony 'upon their respectively coming of age.'[3] But this is not in accordance with more recent custom, for during the nineteenth century it had been always given shortly after a new lord succeeded to the estates. Six of these cups are known to be in existence at the present time. The oldest, a cup of silver, inscribed with the legend, 'The gift of the Right Honourable Richard Lord Viscount Lonsdale, run for on Burgh Marsh ye 10th 8br. 1712,' is now in possession of the representatives of the late Mr. Oliphant Ferguson, Broadfield House, in the parish of Dalston, having been won by one of that gentleman's ancestors. We meet with no other instance of the 'Barony cup' till 1804, though it is very probable that other cups may have been run for between 1712 and that date.[4] The first cup of the nineteenth century was won by a horse said to have been purchased while drawing a coal cart at Dearham. It is of massive silver and bears the inscription 'Given by Willm. Viscount Lowther to be run for on Thursday, 3rd May, 1804, on Burgh Marsh. Won

[1] *Rydal Hall MSS.* pp. 92, 373 (Hist. MSS. Com.).

[2] Thomas Denton, 'Perambulation of Cumberland,' MS. f. 70.

[3] Hutchinson, *History of Cumberland*, ii. 509, Carlisle, 1794.

[4] Among the muniments at Lowther there is an undated petition to Sir James Lowther, baronet, signed by twenty of 'the inhabitants of Brough and the neighbouring towns,' asking him to postpone the races on the marsh till after harvest. The petitioners 'apprehended that the races at this season, being time of harvest, will be attended with damages, the high tides having overflow'd and sanded the low ground, and the numbers of cattle being confined on the high ground, being the race ground, and the number of people attending the Races will in all probability make the cattle break into the cornfields adjoining the Marsh.' Mr. William Little, the earl of Lonsdale's agent, is of opinion that 'the petition was probably presented between 1757 when Sir James Lowther came of age and 1784 when he was raised to the peerage.'

by Mayson Hodgson's C. Mare.' This is the veritable cup of which Anderson wrote :—

The cup was au siller, and letter'd reet neycely,
A feyne naig they've put on't, forby my lword's name.

It is now in possession of Miss Ruth Blaylock, Rindal House, Burgh-by-Sands, who inherited it from Miss Hodgson, daughter of the winner. It was not until forty-one years afterwards that another 'Barony Cup' was run for. About twelve months after the death of William, Earl of Lonsdale, the new earl gave 'an elegant cup value fifty guineas for horses foaled within the barony and the bona fide property of a free or customary tenant at the time of starting. Heats, one mile and a quarter.' This event excited, say the newspapers of that time, an extraordinary and widespread interest. There was a general holiday in Carlisle and it was estimated that no fewer than 15,000 people were present at the races on Burgh Marsh. While only four horses competed in 1804, nine ran for the cup in 1845. The prize was carried off by Mr. Oliphant's 'Lady Eleanor' in the final heat by a couple of lengths. The cup is inscribed : 'The gift of the Right Honourable William, Earl of Lonsdale, run for on Burgh Marsh, April 9th, 1845, and won by George Henry Hewitt Oliphant's chestnut mare 'Lady Eleanor.' This cup is also at Broadfield House, the winner being the late Mr. Oliphant Ferguson's father. Events of the same nature took place in 1873 and 1876, the winner in the former year being Major Browne's horse, 'The Crow,' and in the latter year the cup was won 'in a canter by Lady Brown,' the property of Mr. R. Hodgson of Beaumont, in whose family it is still preserved. Ten horses competed for the cup in 1876. The last 'Barony Cup' was run for in 1883, when the present Earl of Lonsdale succeeded to the title. In this year the cup was changed for a shield valued at 100 guineas. The shield, of beautiful pattern and embossed with sporting scenes, bears the inscription, 'The Burgh Barony Cup, the gift of the Right Honourable Hugh Cecil, Earl of Lonsdale, for horses, &c., the bona fide property of free or customary tenants of or resident in the barony. Won by Mr. Thomas Robinson's Harmony.' It is now in the possession of Mr. R. B. Hetherington of Carlisle, and 'Harmony' still browses on the marsh at Burgh. It should be noticed that the 'Barony Cup' has no connection with the race meetings annually held in that parish. They take place on different courses, the race for the cup being held on the marsh and the annual steeplechases on a course now marked out by posts in the fields to the north of the parish church.

In the eighteenth century hunt meetings were often held at Penrith, Wigton, Egremont, and elsewhere, the Hunters' Plate, sometimes of the value of 50 guineas, given by the gentlemen of the county, being a much coveted prize. These meetings were always enlivened by cockfights and concluded with a ball. There is some vestige of the same custom surviving at the present day in what is called 'the point to point race' at the end of the hunting season, but it is a feeble affair, and creates little interest. It cannot be denied that the sporting instinct of Cumberland has undergone a great change within living memory. With the exception of the competition for the 'Burgh Barony Cup,' which of course takes place only at long intervals, there is little or no racing rivalry among horse breeders in the county. The horses entered annually on the Swifts at Carlisle or at Burgh by Sands are supplied for the most part by professional sportsmen from a distance. Racing in Cumberland cannot be any longer considered a county institution. The local features are well nigh obliterated.

WILDFOWLING

There is probably no English county, not even excepting Norfolk, in which the gun is more generally used for killing wildfowl than Cumberland. In earlier days the capture of duck and wigeon was often effected by the use of snares, still remembered in the neighbourhood of the Solway Firth under the name of 'wiles.' But a heavy muzzle-loader was for many generations the favourite weapon of the Cumbrian 'statesman' when he went 'on t' moss to look for a brace of teal maybe or a couple of snipe.' The progress of agriculture has drained many of the marshy meadows which formerly afforded 'smittle spots' for 'fowl,' but the enthusiasm for killing wildfowl is still very strong. Good shooting can be obtained on many loughs and tarns inland as well as on the better known lakes, but the estuaries of the coast are naturally the chief hunting grounds of our wildfowlers. The marshes of the Duddon, of the Irt, Mite and Esk are not without their attraction for wildfowl, but the most famous shooting quarters of the wildfowler are to be found upon the Solway Firth. Punt-gunners have exercised their craft upon the tideways of this great basin of brackish water for upwards of a hundred years, Port Carlisle and its neighbourhood having been their chief headquarters. It would be easy to dilate upon the experiences of such veteran gunners of the last generation as 'Bill the Shooter,' once of Gretna, or the late Mr. Borrowdale of Glasson; but it may be better that I should tell my own plain unvarnished tale of wildfowling just as I have followed it, year in and year out, for upwards of thirty years without a break.

I was brought up on the Solway Firth among a race of natural wildfowlers, who had inherited a passionate love of this sport from their forefathers. There were no punt-guns in our primitive hamlet, but nevertheless I very early cherished an ambition to acquire one. The idea did not find favour with my elders, and my youthful resources being meagre I had to commence my sporting career with a very doubtful outfit. The first punt that I became the proud owner of had been built for a man of fourteen stone, and was far too heavy for a young slight lad to handle easily. It had however the merit of being a very safe craft. My gun, on the other hand, was of slender calibre, and as I was ignorant of the tricks which a light gun is likely to play when too heavily loaded, I not unfrequently ran some risk of losing her overboard. The lock belonged to an old musket brought back from the Crimean war; the trigger required a strong pull, an unsatisfactory thing in any fowling-piece, but especially in a punt-gun, the lanyard of which the owner is accustomed to pull with his teeth. Sometimes this weapon was too stiff to be fired, and sometimes my teeth were extracted by its vagaries, so that I was thankful to exchange it for a safer and more trustworthy weapon. The first punt that I built for myself proved a great success. I used her for seventeen successive winters. She measured 17 feet in length and 2 feet 8 inches in breadth. The punt that I now use is of the same dimensions. This little craft enables me to explore the waters of the Solway Firth under a variety of circumstances, and though, as a professional wildfowler, I am obliged to shoot for the market, my greatest pleasure lies in studying the habits of the birds that I find swimming and diving in the tideway. A thorough knowledge of the locality in which he works is indispensable to the wildfowler. Owing to the strong ebb and flow of the tides, the strength and swiftness of which can only be realized by those whose calling brings them into daily contact with them, the punts-man needs to exercise constant alertness. One constant and ever increasing danger to punts-men lies in the number of stakes, broken and otherwise, which are left by fishermen in the bottoms of the channels. A puntsman of my acquaintance was thrown out of his punt in consequence of its striking one of these sub-merged stakes. It happened to be ebb tide, and he was able to hold on until the water had become sufficiently shallow to enable him to get ashore in safety. But the risk of a punt striking such an obstacle in the dark is very great.

The spring and neap tides have a marked influence upon the movements of wildfowl. The gunner has to learn by experience in what particular position he is likely to find the birds that he is in pursuit of, at daybreak. Not only so, but he has to outwit the caution of the most wary and suspicious wildfowl. An incident which happened during the daytime may be related here. I had occasion to leave my punt at the edge of a narrow channel, and as it did not matter whether she remained fast or not I omitted to throw out the anchor. After I had walked two or three hundred yards towards the marsh where some barnacle geese were feeding, I saw a flock of thirty or forty barnacles come and settle on the water edge, about 150 yards below where my punt was lying. The intervening ground was level, so that it was impossible for me to return to the punt unobserved. Presently I saw my punt drift off into the current. I watched her with no small interest as she gradually neared these shy creatures. I was much surprised to see them sit until the punt, *without the gunner*, was within forty yards of them before they showed any signs of uneasi-ness. Had I remained on board the little craft they would not have allowed her to approach within a hundred yards of them. The quieter the movements of the puntsman and the more he keeps out of sight while 'setting to' fowl, the better are his chances of success. Another important qualification of the fowler is the power of estimating distances correctly. Water and sand are both decep-tive with regard to distance. I remember firing eleven shots at wigeon one stormy day with a ten-bore muzzle loader, heavily charged, and only killing one bird. As soon as I saw it fall it dawned upon me that I was shooting at too great a distance. At certain times wildfowl are extremely restless without any apparent reason. Manœuvre as cleverly as you may, they will not sit long enough to

allow you to approach within range. Under such circumstances it is best to leave them alone, for if you get a shot at all it will probably prove a long one, resulting only in your wasting more ammunition in retrieving three or four winged birds, while on the other hand you may have scared other wild-fowl, that under more favourable conditions would offer good sport. I have long observed that fowl of the night-feeding kinds are most easily approached at daybreak. Like most other creatures with well-filled stomachs, they are inclined to be sleepy. After taking a morning bath they settle down, and are not so easily disturbed as at other times. But the gunner who wishes to take advantage of this circumstance must be willing to rise early, for he must get into his punt between four and six in the morning and push out in the dark for a distance of two or three miles, until he reaches the spot where he expects that the wildfowl will alight at daybreak. An inti-mate knowledge of the currents of the tide-way is indispensable in order to secure even partial success.

Punting upon the Solway Firth in foggy weather calls for the exercise of a more than ordinary degree of caution. At such a time the fowler can safely reckon upon getting near enough to the objects of his pursuit if he can find them without losing himself, but the latter performance is by far the easier of the two. When certain species of wildfowl have settled during the prevalence of fog they are very loth to stir, but if once they become alarmed and take wing they are a long time before they settle again. My mode of pro-cedure in such a difficulty is to steer the punt into a current which takes a fixed course and drift with it to the place where I expect to find fowl, with everything ready to shoot, the lanyard fixed to the trigger being held between the teeth. This means that the gunner occupies a sitting position, with both hands at liberty to keep the punt in the required position, ready to fire the instant that the birds appear in sight. On 1 Novem-ber, 1892, a very foggy day, I allowed my punt to drift with a strong flood-tide to the place where I expected to find geese. There I lay in a 'setting' position, straining eyes and ears to catch the least indication of their whereabouts. The flap of a wing gave me the required information. Presently about thirty geese loomed out of the mist within easy distance. To get the gun to bear upon them was only the work of a few seconds. After the smoke cleared off there was a sight to make a puntsman glad and 'put him in a splutter,' as we say in Cumberland. Three or four birds were pinioned, and one made off in one direction, its fellow in another. It was no easy matter to keep the cripples in sight until they could be stopped with a shoulder gun, especially as the inrushing tide was covering acres of level sand, while thick fog hung all around. However I managed to gather up fifteen geese and lost another. It is an axiom of first rate importance that the gunner must never allow himself to lose sight of the punt in a mist, unless it has previously been secured to a bank where her owner is certain of finding her on his return. I have known men to be bewildered in the fog and to leave their punts, expecting that they could grope their way home on foot, with the result that they lost their punts and failed to find their way, and had to remain upon the marsh until they attracted the attention of their friends by firing their shoulder guns.

Punt-gunning by moonlight in foggy weather is not a commendable practice, and can only be carried out with safety under certain special conditions, e.g. when both tide and moon are favourable. I have, however, enjoyed good sport with barnacles on a foggy night; indeed, on one particular evening I killed eighteen of these geese at three shots. The best chance that ever offered itself I missed by having an empty gun. But there is the risk of getting uncomfortably near other fowlers in thick weather. I have had more shots flying about my head than seemed at all desirable, and if my big gun had happened to have been fired in the line of the flight-shooter who fired in my direction, the consequences would have proved serious. But though the sport of shooting on foggy nights is not devoid of an element of danger, there is, nevertheless, a peculiar fascination in being out in the midst of wildfowl by moonlight, whether the weather be dense or clear. I have only, however, found shooting on the water answer on the flood-tide up to high water. As soon as the water begins to ebb the fowl are left upon the marsh or mud flats, which are as a rule upon a dead level, scores of acres being covered at high water with ten or twelve inches of water, which ebbs off very quickly. The risk of being left stranded on these mud flats on a misty winter night is not worth running, and one experience of this kind is sufficient in a lifetime. On the Solway Firth the most favourable time for night-fowling is from 10 p.m. to 3 a.m. The night must be calm, as you depend almost entirely upon the cries of the fowl to direct your course.

Barnacle geese are the birds that offer the best night-shooting upon the Solway Firth, but only on odd occasions can they be found sufficiently closely packed together to offer the chance of a raking shot. I have made good bags of mallard occasionally during the night, but only during hard frost. Mallard do not frequent the salt marshes of the Waver and Wampool, unless previously driven from their customary feeding grounds by sharp frost. One evening in 1892, when a heavy fall of snow was followed by severe frost, I started from home about 9 p.m., the moon and tide being favourable, with the intention of shooting barnacle geese, as I knew that these birds were in the neighbourhood. I had only proceeded about two miles up the marsh when a shore-shooter fired a shot at the geese. I then saw that my prospects of sport were poor, so turned homewards; shortly after, I shot a goose with my shoulder-gun out of the flock disturbed by the shore-shooter.

After proceeding another hundred yards, I moored the punt and listened. A wild duck called in a manner that indicated that she was not alone. Dropping into position as quickly and noiselessly as possible, I 'set to' where the sound came from, and could soon hear the ducks feeding on the only piece of green ground in the neighbourhood. At first only one or two fowl were visible, but I gave a low call and the birds left the dark ground and entered the water. After giving a loud shout I fired, and picked up nine mallards. Shortly after this I heard geese alighting on the marsh about a quarter of a mile from where I was. It being ebb tide, it was useless to try to get near them with the punt. After making her fast, I took the shoulder-gun and tried to stalk them. After a long perspiring crawl I managed to get to what seemed to be a proper distance for shooting purposes. The edge of the marsh happened to be very rough and slippery, hence the instant that I pulled the trigger I fell down, both barrels going off together. As the gun was a ten-bore muzzle loader, loaded with 6 drachms of powder and 2 ounces of shot to each barrel, I felt strange sensations for a few seconds. Before ascertaining how the geese had fared I looked for the gun, thinking to myself that if the birds had been hit as hard as I had there must be some fowl to pick up. Sure enough I gathered four geese, making a total bag for the evening of five geese and nine mallards.

I now propose to enumerate some of the different species of wildfowl which I have shot upon the Solway Firth.

Bewick's Swan. The punt-gunner has, of all men, the most numerous opportunities of observing the movements of these birds, both in flight and when resting on the sands of the Solway Firth. When they arrive upon the estuary they almost invariably alight on the sand and then walk into the water to wash and dress their spotless white plumage. They appear to visit the estuaries in the daytime almost exclusively. Although I have tramped about the shores of the Solway at all hours of the night for upwards of thirty years, it has only been my privilege to hear the notes of wild swans in the night-time on three different occasions. The first instance occurred at an unusual season of the year for swans to visit tidal waters, namely, in the month of July. Three of us were crossing the sand on our way to Anthorn to fish, when we were startled by hearing an unusual sound about a quarter of a mile off, in the direction of a scaur well known to us. The hour was between one and two on a Monday morning. None of us could make out what the strange sound could be. I have never heard it since. It resembled the short loud hiss of a steam engine when blowing off steam, and we concluded (while making our way in the direction from which it came) that it must be a stranded whale, and were already discussing the best method of securing and disposing of the animal, when to our disappointment we saw a large white swan rise off the scaur. To what species it belonged I cannot say. Its voice in the night sounded anything but canny, and had we not distinctly seen the bird we should have felt persuaded that some strange animal must be in the neighbourhood. Another night, about the middle of February, 1901, having occasion to take observations of the weather before retiring to rest, I was delighted to hear in the darkness the well known musical notes of the Bewick's swan uttered by birds flying over the houses towards the sea. At daybreak on the following morning, while drifting with the flood-tide, I got within thirty yards of five Bewick's swans, which I conjectured must have been the birds which I had heard in the darkness the previous night. I did not attempt to shoot them, as I expected to find either geese or wild duck in the vicinity. Of all the species of web-footed birds that have fallen to my gun, swans are the least difficult to approach in a punt unless you come across one or two odd birds that have already been shot at, in which case they seem to understand the nature of the suspicious-looking object which is gradually drifting towards them, and make off to some safer quarter. During thirty years' punt-gunning and shore-shooting I have only killed eight wild swans;

but then I never searched specially for them, and usually spared them when found. But on the first day of March, 1901, being my last shot on the last day of the open season, I killed five Bewick's swans, three old birds and two cygnets, out of a herd of thirty, which is the largest I have met with. It would have been easy to have killed double the number, had I felt anxious to do so. The morning was wild and showery, with a keen east wind blowing. The position in which I found the birds was all that could be wished for. All seafowl when exposed in the water set head to wind. Had not the water been shallow and the punt looking right in the wind's eye, I could not have kept her from filling with water. The swans were packed close together, with five cygnets in the rear. They allowed me to approach as near as was desirable, and in the hope of securing a pinioned bird, I allowed them to open out, wishing to take them as they rose upon the wing. The report of my gun so alarmed them that at first sight it seemed as if I had killed half the flock. They floundered and splashed on the water in their haste to escape, calling loudly to one another. I never was anxious to shoot swans, and after what I saw of these, I am less desirous of doing so than I was previously. After their first alarm had abated they soon discovered that some of their companions were missing, and returned to the spot, calling piteously to their dead mates to rejoin them, and evidently wondering why they failed to do so. These birds do not as a rule stay long upon the Solway, the food procurable upon the marshes being less palatable than the roots and fibres of aquatic plants obtained in loughs inland. Bewick's swans were more numerous upon the Solway Firth during the winter of 1892–3 than at any other time within my recollection. On 3 December, 1892, I saw two flocks of Bewick's swans on the wing at one and the same time ; the first herd consisted of twenty-four birds, the other of twelve. On 2 January, 1893, I observed five birds of the same species. On 2 February I saw two birds. On 11 March that year I observed eleven Bewick's swans ; they were flying due east.

Whooper Swan. This bird visits the Solway Firth less frequently than its smaller relative. I have never shot a whooper, but I observed five birds of this species on 22 January, 1892. No doubt I may have met with others when in pursuit of duck, but these were the only whoopers that I carefully identified.

Polish Swan. Whether this bird deserves to rank as a separate species or only as a variety of the mute swan is a matter of opinion. It occasionally visits the Solway Firth. Four Polish swans were shot upon the waters of the Solway Firth in. January, 1892, and. of this number one was shot by myself on the fifteenth of the month. It was a male and weighed 18 lb.

Grey Lag Goose. The grey lag is seldom present in any numbers upon our marshes; only once have birds of this species afforded me sport when punt-gunning. On 21 December, 1900, when shooting with another punt-gunner, I came across a gaggle of about twenty birds, which having satisfied their appetites upon the marsh were now resting high and dry upon a mud bank. We had to wait a considerable time for the tide to float our punts near the geese, but before we could approach within range the flood-tide reached the fowl and drove them in a thin line before our guns. My mate's gun missed fire. I killed four birds, one of which was afterwards preserved for the Carlisle Museum. These grey lags had apparently no previous experience of powder and shot; certainly they were remarkably tame. Some few years earlier a gaggle of six birds of the same species appeared upon the Solway marshes. The punt-gunner who first fell in with them had an opportunity of killing all six, but his gun happened to miss fire. He fell in with them a second time and killed one of their number. The other five remained in the vicinity about a fortnight, but were quite unapproachable. I tried to stalk them on several occasions, but they had learnt wisdom by the misfortune of their companion, and were not to be outwitted.

White-fronted Goose. This species, like the last, is an uncommon visitor to the Solway Firth. Early in January, 1890, a gaggle of nine grey geese arrived in our neighbourhood. On the sixth of the month I observed these birds alight upon the marsh, and managed, after a good deal of exertion, to cross a stretch of rough water and enter a narrow creek. I waited in the punt until the tide lifted her above the level of the marsh. Being then within easy distance of the geese, I fired and bagged nine white-fronted geese of various ages. This was a red-letter day. I have shot single birds on one or two occasions, but have never killed any number except on the occasion just referred to.

Bean Goose. Hitherto the most plentiful goose upon the marshes near Skinburness has been the bean goose. This bird, though a common winter visitor, affords but indifferent sport to the wildfowler, who too often experiences the bitter truth of the Cumbrian adage, 'Thee's gone on a wild goose chase.'

Bean geese are easily shot, however, if found near the water. They are very partial to the same certain patches of the marsh, and may be found upon the same ground for several successive winters. The old race of wildfowlers used to say that it was useless to go out shooting wild geese upon the marsh before midnight. I am inclined to think that they were not far wrong. These geese as a rule fly inland at daybreak, returning to feed upon the marshes during the night and early morning.

Pink-footed Goose. Large flocks of pink-footed geese have latterly frequented Rockliffe Marsh, but this bird is curiously local in its preferences. I have never shot any birds of this species with my punt-gun, and have only killed odd birds with the shoulder-gun. A bird which I shot on 22 January, 1891, only weighed 4 lb. 14 oz., but another was shot on Rockliffe Marsh which turned the scales at 8¼ lb.

Brent Goose. Small gaggles of brent geese visit the foreshores of the Solway Firth, but I can only recall a single occasion upon which I met with a large flock of these birds.

Barnacle Goose. The most abundant goose upon the marshes of the Solway Firth is the barnacle goose. Birds of this species usually arrive in the neighbourhood of our estuaries about the first week of October and remain until the middle and sometimes the end of April. When almost every other species of wildfowl has left the Solway, either on account of persecution or severe weather, the barnacle goose is still present in sufficient numbers to call forth the skill and defy the craft of the wildfowler. I imagined for many years that it was useless to attempt to shoot barnacle geese from a punt in daylight. I still find it a difficult feat, except when performed under certain special conditions. On 22 January, 1901, while waiting until the tide should float my punt out of a creek into which I had managed to get unobserved, I saw a flock of 250 or 300 of these geese fly off the marsh and settle upon a mud bank near the spot where I lay concealed. Presently they commenced to walk in my direction. By the time that the tide raised the punt above the level of the creek-edge, the geese in the rear were passing at too great a distance to admit of much execution being done, but as it was a case of taking this chance or none I fired and bagged half a dozen birds. The best shot at these birds which I ever enjoyed was obtained on 12 December, 1892. Starting between five and six in the morning, in company with another punt-gunner, we worked our way up the estuary, but meeting with two small flocks of geese in flight, we concluded that these birds had all left their feeding grounds. We therefore separated, proceeding in opposite directions. We had not parted more than fifteen minutes when I observed a dark line in the distance between the approaching daylight and myself. I immediately settled into position and soon discovered that the dark object was a flock of barnacle geese. I shaped my course to a scaur which was strewn with large stones two or three feet high, knowing that if once I could gain the shadow of these stones the rest would be comparatively easy. Working nicely within range of about 150 geese, I soon placed a pound of number one shot in their midst, and had the satisfaction of bagging thirty-eight birds, besides two cripples which I secured the following morning. My friend, the late Rev. H. A. Macpherson, informed me of a tantalizing experience that befell a local wildfowler named Smith in January, 1895, when the Wampool and Waver were full of floating ice. He donned a white shirt and white cap, covered his punt with snow, and paddled down the Wampool an hour before the tide had ceased to ebb. At first the ruse seemed likely to succeed, for he fell in with a flock of barnacle geese, but just as he had worked within about 80 yards of the birds his punt went aground upon a great block of ice. He tried to push forward and he attempted to retreat, but he found his punt was fast. Even then he might have killed a few birds, but he wanted to rake the whole flock. He therefore made up his mind to wait for the tide to flow. When the tide turned it moved his punt, but only turned her round, so that the gun pointed up stream, while the birds were now behind him ; before he could right her position the entire gaggle of geese rose off the sands and flew away. The unsuccessful fowler expressed an opinion that had his efforts prospered he would have made ' sic a *mollment* of them !' Thomas Peal killed sixteen barnacle geese with his shoulder-gun upon Newton Marsh, 7 February, 1894, in two shots. A westerly gale was blowing at the time with heavy rain. The wildfowler wormed his way on foot up the creeks until he got close to the birds, killing nine birds at one shot and seven at another. He returned home at the end of the day with nineteen dead geese and one winged bird. It rarely happens that such a large bag of these geese is made during the day, but the late Alfred Smith, an enthusiastic sportsman and good naturalist, made some very good bags on Rockliffe Marsh. He and three brother

gunners together shot seventeen barnacle geese on that marsh one evening in November, 1883. He often related how on a certain memorable occasion he crawled a long distance along the side of the Eden, in pursuit of a flock of these geese. Unfortunately, just as he got within range of the birds, he stepped into a dangerous quicksand, from which he extricated himself with the greatest difficulty. In the struggle to release himself his gun became choked with wet sand, and he had the mortification of observing the birds at close quarters without being able to bag one of their number.

Mallard. The bird which affords the best sport to the wildfowler in Cumberland is the mallard or common wild duck, and I rejoice to say that this bird appears to be upon the increase. On referring to my notes I find that the number of wild duck which fell to my gun in the winter of 1900–1 exceeded the bags of previous seasons by the substantial majority of sixty-five. For many years these birds were less plentiful upon the Solway Firth than wigeon. The time at which mallards arrive varies with the particular season. In some years my best bags have been secured between the middle and end of November. In 1900, on the other hand, mallard were more numerous during the month of February than they had ever been before, at least in my own experience. The immense extent of sand which is exposed at low water makes it difficult for the wildfowler to get a shot at any large flocks which may be present. Again, at high water there are so many *small* bunches of wild ducks scattered about that it is very difficult to reach the *big* flocks without alarming these outposts, which if disturbed communicate their alarm to the main bodies. I have met with so many reverses in shooting mallard that I now make it my rule to shoot the first small bunch that comes within range, as half a dozen mallards in the punt are worth a dozen on the water. The most difficult bird to retrieve when pinioned is a female wild duck. If the water happens to be rough the chances are that, when once she has gone under, you will never see her again, for when she rises to the surface to breathe her body will be still submerged and only her bill will appear. The mallards which frequent the shores of the Solway Firth in hard weather may often be seen at the entrance to small runners of water, in which they obtain small shell-fish. The dietary of those that I have opened has generally proved to consist of small and decayed potatoes, grain, beans, worms, and minute species of shellfish.

Wigeon. Wigeon used at one time to afford first-class shooting on the Solway marshes, both to the flight-shooters and punt-gunners. The numbers of these birds have fallen off latterly, probably owing to the incessant persecution to which they are subjected. I find however that when the feeding ground is really good, wigeon are still fairly numerous. The finest sport that I ever obtained with wigeon was in the winter of 1890–1, that of 1900–1 being our next best season. The fact is that, barring excessive shooting, such as scares birds away, wigeon will be found wherever new marsh is being formed. The largest bag that I procured last winter consisted of twenty-eight birds.

Pintail. This handsome duck occurs almost annually, but only in very small numbers. I met with twenty individuals in six seasons and have shot a few old males in very perfect livery.

Gadwall. The gadwall is one of the rarest of the wildfowl that visit the Solway Firth. I have very seldom met with it. One of the finest old drakes that I have ever seen was a bird which I shot out of a bunch of wigeon, 8 January, 1892. I have killed others with my shoulder-gun when flighting over the marshes, but the bird just mentioned was procured with the punt-gun.

Various Wildfowl. I have of course shot many teal, shovelers, scaup, tufted ducks, common scoters, goldeneyes, pochards, sheldrakes, and at rare intervals a few velvet scoters and long-tailed ducks upon the waters of the Solway Firth. In some years large numbers of scaups and common scoters congregate in Silloth Bay. Goldeneyes are more numerous on the higher reaches of the Solway Firth than in my own immediate neighbourhood. They are sometimes killed in fair numbers by the Port Carlisle punt-gunners. Smews and goosanders rarely visit the Waver or Wampool, but the red-breasted merganser is not uncommon in the winter season.

FOULMART HUNTING

Hunting the foulmart[1] (*Putorius putorius*) was once a popular sport in many districts in the county. As there was no need for the employment of horses, the expenses connected with it were so moderate that they were within easy reach of almost everybody. A good stick and a stout pair of legs may be named as the chief articles of equipment for the day's recreation. When the fashion for this sort of hunting arose, the sport came natural and ready to the hand of the Borderer whose ancestors had been accustomed to track the moss-troopers across the wastes of Bewcastle and the Debatable Land with the aid of sleuth-hounds kept for that purpose. The Border freeholder, who farmed his ancestral acres and acted as his own gamekeeper, was notoriously partial to good hounds, so that the formation of a pack in any village or countryside was not a difficult process, especially if the movement was started, as it often was, on the principle of co-operation. At all events the foulmart was destined for almost a century to afford pastime to a

large number of people throughout the county. The history of the sport cannot be said to date back to any antiquity. Up to the middle of the eighteenth century the foulmart was reckoned as vermin and ranked with the raven, the falcon, the fox, the badger or brock, to be shot or trapped as occasion offered, and a reward was ready for the slayer when his head or his skin was presented to the authorities of the neighbouring parish. In the accounts of several parishes in the county the churchwardens are credited with varying sums which they paid over as head money for the slaughter of these animals. As late as 1794, Dr. John Heysham had nothing to say of the foulmart as a beast of venery, though he mentioned that the otter was 'frequently hunted by hounds trained for the purpose.' Its characteristic qualities in the eyes of that eminent naturalist seemed to have been confined to its predatory or destructive habits. 'It preyed by night,' he said, 'and was extremely destructive to poultry and young game of all kinds; in winter it approached the villages where it committed great depredations in farmyards.'[2] A zoological observer,[3] who visited Keswick in 1803, has stated that 'the foul and sweet marts (as is the provincial expression for the

[1] The foulmart is so named from the strong odour of its scent to distinguish it from the clean mart or sweetmart. It is sometimes called the polecat. It was known in Dr. Heysham's time as the 'fitchet or foulmart.' In the vernacular it is usually pronounced 'foomat' with a decided accent on the first syllable. James Clarke tells us that Roger Ascham called it 'the fumart' (*Survey of the Lakes*, p. 193, ed. 1789).

[2] Hutchinson, *History of Cumberland*, i. 2, 'Catalogue of Cumberland Animals.'
[3] *Observations chiefly Lithological.*

marten) are very common here, and are valuable on account of their skins. The first sells for eightpence in the market, and the latter for four shillings and sixpence.' In these circumstances it is open to question, in the absence of actual evidence, whether the foulmart was viewed as an object of sport before the close of the eighteenth century. We have not noticed any record of it. Be that as it may, from the oral testimony of persons still living, we can carry back the traditions of foulmart hunting as a sport till within a few years of 1800. For instance, Mrs. Stordy of Thurstonfield, now in her eighty-seventh year, the wife and mother of foulmart hunters, remembers well that the sport evoked the enthusiasm of that district when she was 'quite a little girl.' From the evidence before us we may conclude that this form of pastime was a creation of the nineteenth century. Old sportsmen used to look back to the 'fifties' and 'sixties' as the halcyon days of foulmart hunting in Cumberland. As the practice has been extinct for ten years or so, it may be said that the sport was peculiar to the Victorian era. One never hears nowadays of a hunt. The animal is very scarce and the keenest huntsmen shake their heads when you suggest the possibility of the revival of the recreation.

It is a debatable point among sportsmen whether the night or early morning was the best time for hunting the foulmart. The advocates of a 'good moonlight night' contend that as the 'quarry' was only abroad between sundown and sunrise the practice could not be reckoned a sport unless there was a possibility of seeing the game and killing it before it reached its lair or hiding place. It was under the encouraging light of the moon, they say, 'that the drag was hottest, and the pace was breakneck' as the hounds gave tongue that they were in touch with the game. Our inquiries lead us to the belief that most of the hunting in Cumberland was done in the early hours of the morning. The scent remained on the ground from eight to ten hours, and at certain times of the year, or on a damp morning, for a much longer time. The months 'with the "r's" in them.' that is, the months from September to April, were considered the best. But the month which ranked foremost was April, for it was then the foulmart left the heaviest 'drag' behind him: it was the rutting season when 'hob,' or the dog foulmart was apt to wander a great distance during the night in search of a mate. It was the habit of John Peel, the famous Cumberland foxhunter, as soon as

the hunting season was over, that is, about the end of March, to pick out half a dozen of the older deep-toned foxhounds and to continue his sport in hunting the foulmart till the middle of May. This mighty hunter was in favour of employing the slow hounds of his pack for the purpose. In the depth of winter, when the weather was too cold for otter hunting, some of the hounds were turned on to the foulmart with more or less success. But the more experienced sportsmen say that hounds should be trained specially for the foulmart, as foxhounds and otter hounds never become experts in this kind of sport. Any hound with a good nose may afford a pleasant outing to the generality of people, but 'sport' can only be obtained by the employment of the foulmart hound. The number of hounds varied according to the nature of the ground and the idiosyncrasy of the huntsman. Some authorities advocate as many as eight couples; but as a rule it had been found that two couples with a good terrier were quite sufficient to make satisfactory sport.

The genius of the foulmart hound was tested to the best advantage when the trail was struck 'heel-way,' that is to say, when the hounds took up the scent and ran in the direction from which the 'quarry' had come, and not in the direction in which it had gone. In morning hunting this contingency was always possible. If hounds accustomed to hunting the otter or the fox were employed, one might follow the chase for hours and find at the finish that he had arrived at the spot in which the foulmart had slept through the previous day.

Mr. Henry C. Howard has recorded some curious incidents [1] which illustrate the ludicrous aspect of the sport. He relates that 'the hounds on being let out of the kennels struck a drag at once, and a long run ensued, finishing on Skiddaw, or, as he should perhaps have said, beginning there, as it was from Skiddaw that the quarry had started on her wanderings: so the return journey had to be undertaken, and on arrival at the kennels the foulmart was discovered actually lying under the building from which the hounds had set off in the morning!' One day at Isel, so Mr. F. Wybergh informed him, a foulmart bolted out of a stone-heap, and was immediately killed. Directly afterwards the hounds went on the scent for a distance of four miles over the Haigh, nearly to Cockermouth, and straight back to the same stone-heap where they had killed in the morning, thus killing

[1] *The Badminton Magazine of Sports and Pastimes,* May, 1900, No. 58, pp. 524-31.

the beast first and hunting it afterwards. On another occasion Mr. Wybergh, at the request of a lady living near Arkleby, brought his hounds with the view of destroying a foulmart which was making 'sad work' among her young ducks. The hounds headed off from a cat-hole in the barn close by, and, after a long run at a good pace, they returned to the same cat-hole. The hay in the barn was then moved, and Mr. Wybergh had the satisfaction of killing the largest foulmart he ever saw. From these incidents it may be gathered that the training of the foulmart hound became an object of the first consideration.

Mr. Norman Stordy of Thurstonfield, whose family has been foulmart hunters since hunting came into fashion, says that no hound would be considered worth keeping unless he could recover himself and follow the scent 'toe-way.' It was an elementary principle of the sport that a good hound was never deceived in his direction. If he happened to strike the foil or scent 'heel-way,' he would soon return to the trail and follow it where it was hottest.

Old hunters are not agreed on the length of time that the scent will lie on the ground in favourable weather. We have one tale, vouched for on good authority, that the same foulmart was hunted for three days in succession, men and dogs resting at night and taking up the drag on the following morning, till at last the beast was found in a stone drain and slaughtered. But a run of eight hours was sufficient to glut the appetite of most sportsmen. The late Mr. John Jennings of Thornby Villa, who hunted the fox in company with John Peel, once took the drag of a foulmart at Miller Moss, to the west of High Pike, and ran it to Sowerby Row, and from thence onwards to Middlesceugh, where it was dug out of a hole by the road side, thus covering a distance of about twenty miles, or eight miles as the crow flies. One of the greatest disappointments Mr. Stordy ever had, as well as one of the best day's sport he remembers, was on the occasion of a run from Fisher's Gill, where his hounds came upon the trail, through Aikton and Drumleaning to Oulton Moss. After two hours' work at a brisk pace, the foulmart when dug out was discovered to be a bitch with only half a tail! As females were exempt from slaughter, no trophy remains to signalize his triumph on that occasion. It was no unusual experience for hunters to follow the trail from daybreak, or 4.30 a.m., till late in the afternoon, when men and dogs were obliged to desist from exhaustion.

The natural features of the country were so well adapted to the habits of the foulmart that it would be difficult to say in which district it abounded most. It was found almost everywhere. Old people of the fell-sides say that they were so plentiful at one time that the farmers had to shut their doors in order to keep them out. In the low-lying tract to the west of Carlisle, stretching to Maryport and Silloth, so full of marsh and moss, rough ground and damp woods, the foulmart bred in abundance. This district was perhaps the most notable in the county for this kind of sport. Several packs of hounds hunted indiscriminately over that area. There were one or two packs at Carlisle, and packs' at Thurstonfield, Wigton and Aspatria. There does not appear to have been any understanding between the sportsmen as to a division of territory, though the Aspatria hounds usually threw off in the neighbourhood of Allonby. In the central district, the pack kept by the Rev. C. H. Wybergh, for fifty years vicar of Isel near Cockermouth, enjoyed a sporting reputation second to none in Cumberland. In the south-west, packs hunted in Ennerdale and Eskdale, and in the east, at Alston, but they do not appear to have been as well established as those which hunted in the great plain of the county. We believe that Mr. Stordy's was the last pack to go out of existence.

It is little wonder that foulmarts have become very scarce in the county when we consider the numbers killed during one hunting season. It is said that the late Mr. Isaac Stordy was responsible for an average of fifteen a year with the Thurstonfield pack alone. Mr. Coward, a notable sportsman in Carlisle, could remember a 'kill' of thirty-nine in one season in the neighbourhood of that city. If we are to believe reports from Wigton and Aspatria, the destruction of foulmarts in these districts was fairly equal in proportion. But the authorities are not quite agreed on the actual causes of the scarcity. The late Rev. H. A. Macpherson, who has collected much valuable information on the natural history of the animal, inclined to the belief that it was the introduction of the steel trap and the employment of professional trappers in game preserves.[1] On the other hand, Mr. Henry Howard was of opinion 'that the great number of rival packs which were kept for some years between Carlisle and Silloth must very considerably have reduced their number, as, from what I could learn, very few days passed without one or

[1] *Fauna of Lakeland*, pp. 27–35.

more packs being out on the war-path, each one desirous of scoring over his rivals ; and it seems rather curious that the sport should have dropped out all at once, after being carried on for a number of years, during which time the country was very much over-hunted, and there appear to have been as many hounds as hunters.' [1] We owe the present scarcity of the animal probably to a combination of both of these causes. The foulmart still roams after sundown beneath the hedgerows and along the 'soughs' in the lowland tracts, of which Abbeyholme is the centre, but neither hound nor sportsman follows the drag. The numbers are too few, and their whereabouts are too uncertain to make it worth while to organize a hunt. What was once a ruling passion has completely passed away.

SWEETMART HUNTING

The hunting of the mart, sweetmart, cleanmart, cragmart, or pine marten (*Mustela martes*) —for the animal is known locally by all these names [2]—bears a certain resemblance to the hunting of the foulmart except in the nature of the country in which the sport is obtainable. The sweetmart is a denizen of our mountainous districts and frequents the precipitous slopes which form the picturesque valleys of Eskdale, Wasdale, Ennerdale, and Borrowdale. It is also found on the hills in the neighbourhood of Keswick and Ulleswater, while individuals have been seen in recent years on the sides of High Pike and Carrick. If his malodorous kinsman was an object of veneration among sportsmen in the plains of Cumberland, the mention of the sweetmart to the dalesman makes his eye to kindle and his tongue to speak of many adventures by fell and field.

During a portion of the eighteenth century the sweetmart, like the foulmart, was classed as vermin and included in churchwardens' lists as a destructive beast to be exterminated in the public interest. Its name does not figure so often in those accounts owing perhaps to its distribution being confined to a more limited area as well as to the circumstance that in many of the mountain parishes the annual expenditure of the churchwardens has not been handed down to us. But there can be no doubt that its death warrant had been issued and a price set on its head. In the manor of Greystoke it was customary for the bailiff to keep dogs for the purpose of destroying foxes and other vermin which infested that neighbourhood, for which protection the tenants were obliged to pay a certain quantity of oats, a manorial rent, which went by the name of 'foresters' corn.' [3] In process of time the custom became obsolete, though the lord of the manor continued to exact the payment. In consequence the vermin began to increase, and farmers and graziers suffered heavy losses during the lambing season from their depredations. At a vestry meeting called to consider the situation some of the inhabitants were of opinion that the lord should be compelled to keep the hounds as he received their corn for that purpose, 'but the more general opinion was, that since damage was done every night and immediate relief must be had, it was better to hire men to destroy the vermin than risk the precarious issue of a tedious and expensive suit at law.' It was resolved to levy a cess on the parish and to draw up a schedule of rewards to be offered for the slaughter of 'these noxious animals.' For many years afterwards, we are told, this decree remained in force and the following prices were paid by the authorities of that parish : 'To the taker or killer of a fox, 10 groats ; of a fox's cub, 3 groats ; of an eagle, 5 groats ; of a marten, 3 groats ; of a wild cat, 2 groats ; of a raven, 1 groat.' How the new statute of parish law was first carried into execution will be best described in the words of a competent eye-witness, whose father was a tenant of the manor. 'They procured,' he said, 'the swiftest foxhounds from the mountainous environs of Keswick, etc.; skilful sportsmen were also hired to attend with guns and every other engine for the destruction of these annoyers. Whitsun week, A.D. 1759, was

---

[1] *Badminton Magazine*, May, 1900, p. 530.

[2] Manwood, writing at the close of the sixteenth century, names the species 'the marterne or martron, as some old foresters or woodmen do call them, being the fowerth beast of chase, whereof we have no great store in these forests on this side Trent, but yet in the county of Westmerland in Martendale there are many' (*A Treatise of the Forest Lawes*, p. 26). Clarke calls it 'the marten,' or 'martern' (*Survey of the Lakes*, pp. 30, 193, ed. 1789). It is now generally known as 'the mart,' though the reappearance of 'martern' under its old form unexpectedly occurs in the churchwardens' accounts of Martindale, a parish in Westmorland on the Cumbrian border, in the years 1825–6 (*Fauna of Lakeland*, p. lxx.).

[3] This manorial tribute was common in many places in the county.

fixed upon for the attack, when I myself was an eye-witness to the death of twelve foxes within the week. The sum total of vermin destroyed was fifteen foxes, seven badgers, twelve wild cats, and nine martens (called here, by way of distinction, clean marts) besides a prodigious number of foulmarts, eagles, ravens, gleads, etc. The wiles and policy of the foxes were truly astonishing, such as jumping from the rocks upon trees covered with ivy, where they would sometimes conceal themselves and defeat their pursuers; at other times they ran just within the edge of Ulleswater, so that no scent remained.'[1] It was probably out of this organized effort for self-protection that the practice of hunting the vermin as a sport arose in that district. The sudden change of public opinion with regard to the sweetmart, the foulmart and the fox during the latter half of the eighteenth century is very striking. It was during that period in later times that these animals ceased to be regarded as vermin and came within the category of sport. The sporting name is still ' the varmint,' almost certainly the survival from a more prosaic time. Whether or not the tenants of Greystoke learned to respect the animal for its sporting qualities and imbibed their sporting inclinations from the orgies of 1759, certain it is that very soon after we have record of the sweetmart as a beast of venery. Richardson, writing before 1794 of the fauna in the neighbourhood of Ulleswater, stated that the sweetmart occasionally afforded good sport to the hunters in the woods and about the rocks, adding that its skin was held in high estimation.[2]

The hunting of the mart, so keenly enjoyed by the dalesmen, must be reckoned a feature of Cumberland sport during the nineteenth century, though it appears to have been practised more frequently in the sister county of Westmorland where the animal was more widely distributed. We have no certain evidence to show whether hounds were kept exclusively for this sort of hunting. It is probable that the packs in the dales were composed of foxhounds and employed to hunt foxes, marts, polecats and badgers indiscriminately as occasion offered. While Mr. W. A. Durnford was out with the Wasdale hounds in 1879 he witnessed a mart hunt on Yewbarrow, a mountain about 1,000 feet in height overlooking Wastwater. In the graphic account of his experiences on that early morning he says it soon became evident that something was on foot as they commenced the ascent. The hounds showed manifest signs of excitement, examining every nook and stopping at every crevice to take in the scent. Suddenly an old dog gave tongue and the whole pack was quickly off in full cry up the face of the mountain raising a chorus which resounded from crag to crag across the valley below. As the beast was soon discovered to be a mart, men and dogs settled down to the chase. At one time, continues the sportsman, we were clambering on hands and feet up a perpendicular precipice, at another, crawling through a narrow crevice between two high boulders; now running across a sea of stones, which gave way at every step and rendered it impossible even to think of standing still; now stepping from ledge to ledge, and trusting one's life to the sturdy alpenstock with which each one had armed himself before setting out. The hounds were in the meantime clambering up with an agility which would astonish their relations further south, resembling a party of squirrels rather than members of the canine race as they vied with one another in their anxiety to be to the fore.

After an hour of that sort of work, the mart took refuge in a crevice in the face of a rock, from which the huntsmen smoked him out with the aid of grass, gunpowder and an old newspaper. As soon as the smoke reached the beast it bolted from a hole a short distance off. Away it went again with dogs and men in hot pursuit. Presently taking refuge in some loose boulders, the terriers were set to work and from the ' bield ' it was soon dislodged. But it was the beginning of the end. The ' quarry ' escaped to a plateau on the summit of the mountain broken only by some fragments of rock which afforded no shelter. It was evidently making for the Pillar Mountain which stood out in the distance, a notable stronghold for birds and beasts of prey, and which, if once reached, would afford a certain protection. Bravely the little creature raced on, staking life on its swiftness of foot. On the level ground however it had no chance, though it managed to head its pursuers for about a mile after leaving the rocks. The hounds alone were present at the death.[3]

The sport was not always accompanied by the element of danger while men and dogs

---

[1] James Clarke, *Survey of the Lakes*, pp. 29, 30, (ed. 1789).
[2] Hutchinson, *History of Cumberland*, i. 448.

[3] For the picturesque narrative of which we have made a short summary see the *Field*, Dec. 6, 1879. The article has been reproduced in the *Zoologist* of 1891 and in the *Fauna of Lakeland* (1892).

followed the chase on the screes and lower fells with which the lake country abounds. It is not every sportsman who has had the exciting experience so vividly described by Mr. Durnford. A mart hunt is oftener a much tamer affair. A stiff run along a ridge of fell, or down a rough gill, or up a rocky surface, with the deep bay of the dogs in his ears, has sufficed for many a hunter. Sometimes the animal takes refuge in a tree at a critical moment, but its favourite hiding-place is a crevice in a rock or in a heap of boulders. When closely pursued on a level its mode of running is by a series of leaps, often covering six feet at a bound. It is not often that marts visit the valleys, except during the breeding season when they come down to the woods in April and May to have their young. During the first week of the latter month in 1886 a fine specimen was captured by the Blencathra hounds in the vale of Naddale near Keswick.

Local naturalists are not quite agreed on the distribution or scarcity of the sweetmart in the county, but it is safe to say that it is not now as plentiful as it used to be. From information gathered in the autumn of 1901 in Eskdale and Keswick, the two centres of hill hunting, we learn that it is only now and again that the trail of a mart is crossed. In some of the fell districts it is exceedingly scarce, if indeed it can be said to exist at all. The last individual found on Black Comb was killed as far back as 1847. But on the less frequented or more inaccessible hills in the central districts the mart still roams and sportsmen are still keen on a hunt if a fox fails to put in an appearance.

NORTH COUNTRY TRAIL HOUNDS AND TRAILS

> Hark ! on the trail I hear
> Their doubtful notes, preluding to a cry
> More nobly full, and swell'd with ev'ry mouth.
> *Wm. Somervile.*

Hound dog trail matches do not, as far as we are enabled to judge, date back to the earlier times of wrestling. Litt in his *Wrestliana* does not once mention the subject. If we had the means of arriving at a knowledge of its origin we should in all probability find that soon after coming into vogue it became in most instances an important item in the programme for filling up a day or two's amusement along with wrestling, jumping, etc. Keswick races or wrestling for a lengthened period held a high place in public estimation, and the local hound dog trails were considered the most celebrated of any in the north. Great was the rivalry amongst breeders and trainers. A large concourse of spectators, both residents in the town and neighbourhood and strangers from all the distant parts of Cumberland, Westmorland and north Lancashire, assembled to witness the keen contests. The ground was highly favourable for testing the capabilities of the very best dogs, and many a severely contested trial was witnessed by the anxious crowd. Not unfrequently betting in small sums was brisk, particularly in the second day's race, when an estimate could be formed of the speed, hunting qualities and endurance of the contending animals. There was at one time running at these meetings a celebrated hound from Threlkeld Hall. It was not unusual to hear some one exclaim, 'I hear t'ho dog and he's leading,' and sure enough soon after 'Rattler' would come tearing in first. This same 'Rattler' ran a 5 mile match for £10 at Caldbeck—celebrated for its breed of trail hounds—against Gilkerson's 'Butler.' The conditions were to win and draw on each mile. Two persons were stationed—hidden from the dogs—at the end of each mile to certify which was first. 'Rattler' won the first, second, third and fifth mile.

Then came the far-famed 'Flan' meeting, rapidly assuming greater proportions and offering richer prizes than had previously been given at the best patronised meetings. It would be difficult in any part of the country to select a better course—barring a straightforward one—than that usually selected at Flan, particularly for some twenty years after the meeting was established. To begin with there was a 4 mile run on the slopes of a vale nearly straight, then crossing the vale and climbing to the summit of a heathy common. Then followed right on end to the winning point 4 or 5 miles of good going moor ground. As many as thirty-two dogs have started, and the number frequently ranged from twenty to thirty. It was a really beautiful sight to see a score and a half high couraged and resolute dogs all brought to the post in perfect condition and witness their frantic efforts to be slipped when the trailer came within a field or two of the appointed ground where the struggle commenced. The barking, the howling, the struggling would suggest the idea of a lot of dogs gone furiously mad, and when let slip such was the eagerness to get away that not one gave mouth. There was usually a prize for the first mile, and it was in this short run that dogs like Alpin's 'Tuner'— one of the fastest—distinguished themselves. The course—10 to 12 miles—was usually run in from twenty-six to thirty minutes, a pace that no horse—trained hunter or racer —over similar ground could have maintained, and nearly double the speed of a good pedestrian on level turf. It was in running up to the winning post, facing the crowd and noise without slackening, that dogs as eager and well trained as Devonshire Square 'Towler' and Alick Wallace's 'Tipler,' sire and son, snatched victory from more forward animals and got placed first by the judges.

Yorkshire dogs were for several years at the Flan keen and frequently successful competitors against the northern hounds. Sometimes they defeated the whole lot. On one occasion a bitch from Saddleworth named 'Bounty,' to the complete dismay and discomfiture of both Cumbrians and Westmorlanders, won on both days, carrying off not only the head prize but a round sum in bets. 'Finder,' another Yorkshire dog, at that time from the neighbourhood of Oldham, won two days together at Cartmel, 6 miles from the Flan, beating some of the best dogs going. 'Swinger' from Sheffield was a first rate dog, and frequently distinguished himself both in the north and in the 10, 12 and 14 mile matches on the Yorkshire moors. The Yorkshire trails were mostly straight on end, and the dogs not slipped till the trailer had been gone an hour and in some cases much more.

The longest trail we have any knowledge of was run a few years before the 'Flan' meetings were given up. The length of the chase was at least 25 miles, all over enclosed ground with scores of stiff fences. The start took place from Swathmoor near Ulverston; thence all down the east coast to Roose, a village close by the sea; and then past the rising town of Barrow. Thence to the west side of Furness the trail was continued in a somewhat circuitous direction to Kirkby Ireleth and thence to the starting place. A noble looking dog called 'Ringwood,' bred by the late Henry Rauthmell, Hutton Bridge End near Kendal, had the credit of pulling off the chief prize. He was from a good stock — the Devonshire Square 'Towler'—and cut out the work for the whole of this unexampled trail by keeping a lead the whole distance from 30

to 100 yards. This picking up the scent and keeping a lead hunters know is hard work. The same dog a fortnight after ran a match for £20 against a Whitehaven dog named 'Nudger.' The chase was from Ulpha to Bootle, places fully 10 miles asunder, and over a rough mountainous track the whole distance. 'Ringwood' won all the way easily. Unfortunately this fine foxhound took to worrying sheep and had to be destroyed. Of his breeder, the late Mr. Rauthmell, it may be said that no better sportsman has lived in Cumberland.

At Mardale, at the head of Hawes Water, one of the wildest, most solitary and secluded dales or districts in the whole of the mountainous region of the north, Mr. Rauthmell with his usual train of followers on one occasion stopped for a whole week. In that time nine foxes were killed. But the excellent sport on that occasion was marred by an unhappy incident. On the drag of a fox with a burning scent through some precipitous screes between High Street and Mardale, when in momentary expectation of Reynard bolting, up jumped a sheep. The pack under a sudden excitement broke out and worried to a serious amount. It must be borne in mind as part excuse that they were at the moment in a fever of expectation and were becoming impatient. They had then been bred— principally by crossing with Devonshire Square 'Towler'—to such a pitch of high courage as to render them dangerous in such a crisis as unfortunately occurred. Mr. Rauthmell, with the promptitude and decision that distinguished him, had the offenders shot in order to prevent further destruction, for he well knew a hound once guilty is likely to continue in the same fault, and that there is no safe remedy but death.

When Mr. Rauthmell gave up keeping the hounds they were taken in a covered conveyance to York. One named 'Ruler' found its way back to Hutton, a distance of 115 miles, through a perfectly strange country. The dog was sent away a second time and again returned home. 'Ruler' was allowed for the rest of his life to remain at Hutton, and from frequently going out with Mr. Rauthmell when he was shooting he became nearly as good as a pointer as he had previously been in the chase, and would retrieve either game or rabbits.

The same breed of dogs can be trained to run with fire and resolution an inanimate trail. No wonder therefore that the Duke of Beaufort, when he made the great match for one thousand guineas to run ten dogs 4 miles over the Beacon course at Newmarket against five thoroughbred horses, carrying eight stones and a half, should resort to the northern trail hound. A high authority, the *Field*, said that the duke's 'sole chance in the forthcoming great match was in his adoption of the northern trail hound instead of the true foxhound.' This dictum we strongly protest against, and think ample testimony may be easily produced to prove the most successful trail dogs that have ever existed were true foxhounds. Many a cross has been attempted by sanguine breeders to bring out a dog capable of contending against and beating the foxhound at trail running. All such efforts have been given up as failures. Hunting determination in a ten or twelve miles chase, dogged perseverance to run a scent till the end is accomplished, and a fine sense of smelling to aid the work, are not to be found except in very rare and exceptional cases out of the true foxhound breed. Half-bred dogs are as a rule useless for trail hunting. With a breast high scent they may run 4 or 5 miles, but will then generally give in.

The following are a few more instances of good foxdogs and successful trailers. Sixty years ago the late Mr. John Todd of Waterhead, Gilsland, had a large, pure-shaped, resolute dog called 'Towler.' He was for years regularly hunted with the Gilsland pack. He is still spoken of by those who recollect and have heard stories recounted of his marvellous speed and stoutness as by far the best trail dog throughout all the north country in his day. Twenty years later Mr. Todd had another 'Towler.' No better foxhound at all points was ever slipped from a couple. To form an estimate of his capabilities for a trailer it is sufficient to state that at six and seven years old he several times defeated the celebrated 'Brampton bitch' while in her prime.

'Tipler,' a dog bred and kept at Swaits near Gilsland, ran several 10 and 12 mile matches. His speed and endurance were so extraordinary that he won them all with ease. This dog was the admiration and boast of both old and young foxhunters throughout the country in which he hunted. He was considered the most certain and reliable dog that ever chased a fox over the wild moors and hills of the north. It was 'Tipler' when the 'arvel' was being drunk that had the credit of securing many a brush.

The late Mr. Holmes of Colees—a genuine foxhunter of the 'olden time'—had a 'Towler' considered to possess extraordinary speed on a trail and highly esteemed as a persevering dog after live game. This gentleman understood dog trailing and foxhunting well, and scouted the idea that half-bred dogs could compete successfully with the pure bred foxhound.

There was another noted 'Tipler' which we must not omit noticing. It belonged jointly to John Paterson and Alick Wallace, both of Carlisle; was a big, resolute, spotted dog standing 24 inches high with a well developed large head, broad chest, and somewhat long body. The career of this trail hound for the three years he lived was distinguished by startling incidents. One was perfectly astounding, as the reader will see below. When once fairly settled on a trail and warmed to his work 'Tipler' was a wonderfully persevering dog; he would rush without a stop or pause through the thickest hedge or 'face any mortal thing.' He could always be depended upon for coming in at a rattling pace and mostly finishing off a clear winner. During a brief career in east Cumberland he started frequently amongst the best dogs, and on trails varying in distance from 5 to 12 miles in almost every instance carried off the chief prize. On one occasion Alick 'carried' his favourite westward to Cockermouth. Trail hunts took place on two successive days, 'Tipler' won the first day and ran next to Gilkerson's 'Butler' on the second day. The first day's trail was one of the most spirited runs ever witnessed. Fifteen prime dogs started, and when they approached the goal, the umpire was obliged to mount a fence in order to decide which dog made the first spring to clear it, three of the foremost running neck and neck, or rather nose and nose, for a considerable distance. Returning by way of Wigton he encountered a good field on two days and was again victorious, thus scoring to his credit three important chases and a good second place. This was in 1839.

We now come to a strange accident which put an end to a brilliant career and might easily have proved fatal. Some sports were advertised to be held at Elijah Kennedy's, Warwick Bridge. 'Tipler' in first rate condition went to contend in the trail and started full of vigour and life, but never returned within sight of the winning post. Alick, who had charge of the dog on that day, to use his own words, 'laited it an' better laited it' until he was completely worn out. On reaching home long after nightfall he was half broken-hearted at his loss. By daybreak on the following morning both John Paterson and Alick were astir to renew the search, and at length succeeded in finding the lost dog among some brackens and long grass close to the dry arch of Wetheral bridge on the Corby side of the river Eden. Their joy was great at the discovery, but soon gave place to sad and bitter feelings when the state of the poor brute became apparent. It had leapt the battlements of the railway bridge and fallen a height of 100 feet ! Both fore legs were so violently strained by the fall that it could not crawl from the spot, and had lain all night in extreme agony It is a marvel that any life was left after such a fall. Had it occurred nearer the middle of the bridge, and the tumble been into the rough bed of the river, death would in all probability have been the result. Alick and his sorrowing companion carefully lifted the dog into a plaid and carried it home with as much care as if they had been bearing a lame child. Various reports got into circulation respecting 'Tipler's' leap over Wetheral viaduct. Some persons would have it that an attempt was made to stop the dog, and that he cleared the battlements of the bridge to avoid being caught. Another account was that the trail had been treacherously dragged over the battlements in order to destroy the dog. The owners however did not give credit to either statement. They were under the impression that the man Harding, who ran the trail, stopped on the bridge to rest and unwittingly did the mischief which nearly cost the dog its life. The accident or wilful injury—whichever it was—to 'Tipler' did not end fatally, but he never recovered sufficiently to run another race. On recovery 'Tipler' was turned to the stud and was the sire of some noted dogs, Devonshire Square 'Towler' being one of them.

Probably no dog trail match ever created greater interest throughout a wide district in the north than the great 12 miles on end match between the 'Brampton bitch' and a pure bred foxhound called 'Ranger,' which Mr. Todd of Waterhead got from the Haydon Bridge pack. The greatest pains were taken by both parties to bring their dogs to the post in first rate condition. A peculiarity of this match was a stipulation that both hounds should have a companion dog, one they had been accustomed to run with, in order to make or assist the running. 'Damsel,' a bitch belonging to Mr. Thompson, started for this purpose with Mr. Todd's 'Ranger,' and Gilkerson's 'Crowner' with the Brampton bitch 'Ruby.' The first trial from Waterhead to Kershope Head turned out undecisive. The running hounds got so close to the trailers that they had left the trail before arriving at the goal. A fresh

start had therefore to be made, and the parties agreed to run directly back from Kershope Head to Waterhead. Mr. Todd's 'Ranger' led and did the leading work in the two long chases with the exception of about a mile, middle way, in the second start. He galloped in winner at the finish, full of resolution and courage and immediately flew at a 'grew' belonging to Mr. Hedley of Bewshaugh, and would have made short work in worrying 'long tail' had not assistance been at hand. The time taken to run over the last 12 miles was twenty-five minutes and a half, very fast indeed considering the rough country and that they had done 11 miles previously.

Mr. Routledge of Devonshire Square farm, midway between Penrith and Carlisle, had a 'Towler' by Alick Wallace's 'Tipler.' This dog hunted the fox regularly till he was eight years old. He began to run trails when eighteen months old and continued for upwards of six years, winning regularly two out of three. He was an extraordinary good dog at finishing off or coming in, frequently defeating three or four in the last 200 yards. He appeared a strongly made, big dog—speedy and with plenty of stamina, good muscular legs and hard wiry hair—capable of withstanding from morning till night the piercingly cold sleety rains of the Cumberland hills. We have no particular data to go by, but entertain the impression he won more trails than any other dog. He won a match for £40 on Shap Fells that caused considerable sensation at the time. His opponent was 'Nudger' from Ulverston but Yorkshire bred, a weedy animal in appearance when beside 'Towler.' The race was a straight 10 miles over some very rough ground. It was altogether a hollow affair. 'Towler' led from the first and came in a winner fifteen minutes before 'Nudger' made his appearance. There was some talk of foul play—that the beaten dog was caught and held. No evidence was however forthcoming to substantiate any such allegation. On an open common stopping a dog when in full cry is no easy matter. Moreover, Mr. Routledge's well known reputation as an honourable sportsman gives the lie to such a supposition. The probability is, as a good judge at the time stated, that 'Nudger,' finding himself outpaced and likely to be left, had made a wrong cast, intending, as dog trailers term it, to 'cheat,' and for a time got lost thereby. When 'Towler' ran at the Burgh Marsh races in 1845 he was not so fortunate. The Border dogs gave him and the best hounds of Cumberland and

Westmorland a decisive beating. It was a capital trail run at a speed to shut up middling ones. Well known dogs such as Jeremiah Wilson's 'Laddie' and Fletcher Pearson's 'Stormer,' in their own neighbourhood considerable favourites, came in nowhere, beaten off in fact, and after the first mile clean out of the hunt altogether. The winner on this occasion was 'Black Towler,' a very superior fast dog bred by Jim Morley, weaver, at Holme Head, Carlisle ; the second Mr. Hodgson's (of Aikton) 'Darter.' The former was one of a litter of four out of J. Green's 'Crafty' and got by 'Haydon' from the Haydon Bridge pack. They were considered by far the best ever bred in one litter. Besides 'Black Towler' there was another 'Towler,' a 'Tipler,' and 'Rattler.' Morley was an extraordinary character in his way about trail dogs, so enthusiastically attached to the sport that frequently after attending to his trade for

twelve hours he would devote hour after hour ' in the season of the year' till midnight and often till one or two in the morning in running breaking-in trails for young dogs. This was Jim's special delight, and he 'waad ha' gane anywhere' to see a good trail.

In conclusion, it may be interesting to institute a comparison between the hounds of the north and the south. For this purpose we must refer again to the 12-mile match run near Gilsland in twenty-five minutes and a half over a *rough country*. In a famous match at Newmarket between two dogs owned by Mr. Barry and two belonging to Mr. Meynell, the time for 4 miles was a few seconds over eight minutes. Bearing in mind that the Gilsland run was three times as long as the other, which was over the best going ground in England, we should probably be correct in concluding that the northern hounds were the faster.

OTTER HUNTING

The early history of the hunting of the otter (*Lutra vulgaris*) in Cumberland is enveloped in much obscurity.[1]

A search of parish registers has failed to discover that the otter was on the list of vermin for whose destruction churchwardens paid rewards ; but as such head money, ranging from sixpence to a shilling a head, was offered at Kendal, in the neighbouring county of Westmorland, in 1731–70, it seems probable that a similiar practice prevailed in some parts of Cumberland. At any rate, gamekeepers regarded otters as 'noxious animals.' Nine killed in one year (1821–2) by Robert Cowen, gamekeeper to Sir Wilfrid Lawson, are so catalogued in the *Carlisle*

[1] We have failed to find references to otter hunting in Cumberland in the early records of sport. It may be mentioned however that a 'master of the otter hounds' was reckoned among the officers of the king's household from an early period. In the Wardrobe Account of 18 Edward I., John le Oterhunte has an allowance 'pro putura octo canum suorum lutericiorum.' Edward IV. had a pack of otter hounds which, like the packs of harriers and buckhounds, was composed partly of running hounds and partly of greyhounds. By letters patent dated 18 July, 1461, the 'office called oterhunte' was granted to Thomas Hardegrove for life (*Select Pleas of the Forest*, p. 145, ed. G. J. Turner, Selden Society). It is evident that otter hunting was at one time the sport of kings.

Journal of 8 June, 1822, in a list of vermin which he had destroyed in twelve months. The hunting of the otter with hounds had however already begun. There appears in Hutchinson's *History of Cumberland* a description by Richardson of otter hunting from a boat on Ulleswater at the end of the eighteenth century; and in an obituary notice of Thomas Fenton, aged 77, published in the *Carlisle Journal* of 26 July, 1823, otter hunting is mentioned among the diversions of that 'veteran sportsman.' It may be further stated that Dr. Heysham in his natural history notes in 'Hutchinson,' written towards the end of the eighteenth century, remarks that 'the otter, although not numerous, is an inhabitant of almost all our rivers and lakes, and is frequently hunted with hounds trained for the purpose.' Otter hunting with hounds in Cumberland may therefore be carried back to the last decade of the eighteenth century, and probably it was practised before that period.

In the first half of the nineteenth century otter hounds were kept in small numbers in different parts of the county, and used for hunting both otters and foulmarts. About 1830 otter hounds were kept at Isel Vicarage near Cockermouth, and were hunted for nearly thirty years by the vicar, the Rev. Hilton Wybergh. They did not number at first more than half a dozen, one of the pack being, strange to say, a Newfoundland dog, and some of them were kept at Brayton by Sir Wilfrid Lawson, one of the vicar's brothers. As time went on the strength of the pack increased. There were hounds of good blood among them, notably 'Swimmer' and 'Stormer' (painted on wood in 1830 by Mr. John Hartley and now in the possession of Mr. Francis Wybergh); and 'Guider,' which Mr. Francis Wybergh describes as by far the best hound he ever saw. 'Guider,' like 'Stormer,' was sired by a foxhound. There was 'Marjery' too, which later was the mother of nearly the whole of a kennel of sixteen. The pack varied in number; but ten couples may be taken as its full strength. One of its earliest notable runs was on 17 September, 1837, when an otter was dragged from Bassenthwaite Beck into the side of Dash waterfall, over a hilltop adjoining Skiddaw, and down the watershed of the river Ellen. It was killed in that river close to the famous hunting and coaching hostelry at Cock Bridge. This run was interesting as proving that otters migrate from one river to another —a fact in natural history which has often since been demonstrated on the Scottish border. The Rev. Hilton Wybergh was a very keen sportsman, and his otter hunting country was very extensive. Near home he had that splendid otter river, the Derwent; also the Cocker and the Ellen. Further away, south of Whitehaven, the Ehen, Irt, Mite, Esk and Duddon; in Westmorland the Eden, Eamont and Lowther rivers, and Haweswater furnished good sport. In Scotland the pack hunted the Tweed, the Annan (best of all), Esk, Leader, Lyne, Kirtle, and Æ; and he even went to Ireland (in 1857) and hunted the Liffey. No list of fixtures was published in the newspapers; but the word was passed round among enthusiasts when and where the meets were to take place. For what may be called 'home meets' a very convenient arrangement was adopted. Upon a suitable morning William Stordy, who lived at Isel Vicarage and hunted the pack for twenty-five years, would take a few trusty hounds down to the river at Isel Bridge to ascertain if an otter had been afoot there during the night or early morning. If the 'foil' could be struck, young Mr. Francis Wybergh would be dispatched upon his pony to Cockermouth, six miles away, to rouse the local sportsmen, who lost no time in getting to Isel. The largest otter ever killed by these hounds scaled 29 lb. Some most exciting sport was shown from time to time, and Mr. Francis Wybergh relates that upon a certain day of many incidents an enthusiast said to him, 'Oh! Mr.

Frank, this is far too much for yan man to see!' Otters were plentiful in the district, and the Rev. Hilton Wybergh had the unique experience one winter's morning of seeing three of them from his own bed. In spring, from March till about the end of May, foulmarts were hunted. The hounds were kept together until 1857, when they were disposed of to Mr. Newton of Devonshire, none of the breed remaining in Cumberland.

Dr. Hildebrand, a Carlisle medical practitioner, had a small pack of his own between 1830 and 1840; several hounds were kept in Carlisle about twenty years later by butchers, who joined forces occasionally in the summer months and hunted the Eden and the Lyne; and about 1860 Mr. John Irving, miller, of Maryport, had a small pack. It was not however till 1863, when the Carlisle Otter Hunting Club was established, that otter hunting became a popular sport. The Carlisle pack was composed of ten couples of hounds, with a few terriers, which had before been in private hands in the district. They included Mr. Irving's contingent; and 'Carlisle Thunder,' a celebrated specimen of the breed, was at their head. The owner of this patriarch of the pack was Mr. Robinson Carr, butcher, who was chosen as the first Master; his deputy being Mr. William Robinson, also a butcher, who contributed 'Lame Swimmer,' 'Major' and 'Rally,' three hounds of the same strain. Both the Master and the Deputy-Master were experienced otter hunters; and William Sanderson, afterwards celebrated as 'Sandy,' was appointed huntsman. Sandy, who at this time was thirty years of age, was a butcher by trade, but he had been an otter hunter since he was a lad. He had hunted with the Rev. Hilton Wybergh, and had graduated in the sport under Dr. Grant and Mr. Lomax, two keen sportsmen, who hunted on the Scotch side of the Border. Sandy had been a sprint runner in his day, and was endowed with courage, patience and great physical endurance. His knowledge of the habits of the otter amounted almost to instinct; and he had abiding faith in his well trained hounds. The hunting territory of the new club comprised the Eden and its tributaries within a range of about twenty-five miles; the Esk, the Annan, and the Nith, with their tributaries on and across the Border; and at times visits would be paid, on invitation, to Ayrshire, and Roxburghshire, and to the Lune. In one year the north of Ireland was hunted. The success of the Carlisle Otter Hounds was immediate, and in a very few years they had established a high reputation throughout the kingdom. Under the skilful guidance of Sandy, excellent sport was afforded to large 'fields,' which varied in number from 200 at the first meet, in April, 1864, to twice that number when a selection of the pack co-operated with a section of Dr. Grant's pack in June, 1865, at Penton. The spectators as a rule travelled on foot, the only exceptions being when two or three landed proprietors, such as Sir Frederick Graham of Netherby and Mr. Johnson of Castlesteads, rode over to meets in their neighbourhood. Occasionally ladies joined the hunt. Such large crowds might have been embarrassing but for the powerful though quiet influence of Sandy, in whom the spectators had implicit confidence. 'Keep back,' he would say to any who were over eager; 'leave the hounds alone; they are far wiser than a man; they can tell us far more than we can tell them.'

On a very good day—of course there were often 'blanks'—the sport was exciting from the first moment when, on nearing the river, the huntsman released his pack with the cry 'Seek for him!' and the hounds raced to the water side. Perhaps even at this early stage 'Thunder' would throw up his head with a loud 'Boo!' and proclaim that the otter had been there. Sandy at once recognizing the voice would shout, 'Ha, lad! That's him,' regardless of grammar in the excitement of the moment; adding quietly to those around him, 'That's the otter; that hound never told a lie.' Nor was 'Thunder' the only George Washington in the pack. Now the other hounds would nose the drag and join in a canine chorus, which, to Sandy's ears, sounded 'like a peal o' bells.' The spectators at once arouse themselves, fearing to miss any incident in the hunt. Some run along one bank of the river; others wade across to the other side. But suddenly the music stops, the scent having failed, and a quiet interval is only relieved by the crack of the huntsman's whip calling to order a young hound that had been 'running riot' after a rabbit. The old hounds however are still hard at work on both sides of the river, or wading and swimming, trying to hit off the 'foil' again by nosing every exposed stone, and trying to 'wind' the game on the water flowing past them. The huntsman makes sure that he is not running a 'heel drag' by examining stretches of sand by the river side for pad prints, distinguishing the footing of the otter from that of a hound by its five toe marks. The otter has swum to one of his favourite holts half a mile away behind the root of an old ash tree, with subterranean retreats higher up the river bank. 'Major' and 'Lame Swimmer'—both famous for 'marking'—have discovered the fact, and with loud voice proclaim it to their associates, who give a responsive 'boo!' and hurry up to the spot. Now comes the chance for the terriers. One of the gamest of them is introduced into the hole, and, if fortune favours the field, a distant underground scuffle is heard, and the otter with a rapid rush bolts into the river, perhaps (as happened at Wetheral in June, 1869) with both a hound and a terrier hanging on to his tough hide. At this point a crisis comes. The hunters form lines across the river, both above and below the hole from which the otter has been dislodged, in the hope of intercepting his progress; but sometimes he succeeds in making his way under bushes at the river side and escaping unseen. If however the water into which he bolts is a deep pool he swims away below the surface pursued by the pack, a line of air bubbles, or 'bells' as they are called, marking his progress. As he tires the 'bells' become more numerous, and he begins to put his head out to look about and take breath. The appearance of his head is the signal for a loud 'Hoo!' and waving of hats on the bank, and the hounds rush forward in maddened frenzy. Should they succeed in reaching him his moments are numbered, despite his slipperiness, the toughness of his hide, and the superiority of his swimming and diving powers. But he may succeed in emerging from the pool, getting away, and gaining another favourite stronghold higher up the river. This time the refuge leads into a drain with ramifications in the field above. Some of the field jump upon the earth to try and frighten the otter out; but that failing, spades are procured from a neighbouring farmhouse, the drain is cut say twenty or thirty yards from the river, a terrier put in, and the otter driven out into the river, and probably 'into the jaws of death.' But perhaps—as often happens—he has retired to an impregnable cross drain, there to remain until his pursuers have departed.

It is important to notice that with the establishment of strong packs changes in favour of the otter have been made in the rules of the hunt. From the description of the otter hunt in Ulleswater at the end of the eighteenth century it appears that the hunter was armed with 'otter grains' (bearded spears), with which he continued to strike the otter whenever it put its head above water to take breath. The use of the spear is also shown in Landseer's well known picture, and in older illustrations of the sport; but it has now been completely abandoned, otter hunters only carrying hazel poles like alpenstocks to assist them in wading in the river. Shortly after the establishment of the Carlisle pack, ' tailing the otter,' that is, holding him by the root of the tail to assist the hounds in worrying him—a hazardous proceeding for the tailer—has also been forbidden. The code sets forth that 'no attempt must be made to seize or strike the otter, or to interfere with him with poles, sticks, or otherwise, at any period of the hunt.' From twelve to fourteen otters are killed in a season by the Carlisle hounds, the bitches varying from 13 lb. to 18 lb. in weight, and the dogs scaling from 17 lb. to 28 lb., and in one notable instance, in which the otter was drowned, 31 lb.

In 1866 Mr. Robinson Carr resigned the mastership, and Mr. John C. Carrick of Carlisle was appointed to the office, which he held until 1877, when he was succeeded by Mr. James Steel of Eden Bank, Wetheral, who undertook the responsibilities until 1883, when Mr. Carrick resumed them. In 1893 Major Arthur Mounsey-Heysham, a keen local sportsman, not only undertook the mastership but bought the hounds. He resigned in 1901, when Mr. James W. Graham of Carlisle succeeded to the office. The palmy days of the pack were in the twenty years during which the incomparable Sandy was huntsman. One of the most celebrated hunts at that time was on 29 June, 1869. The meet was at Newby Bridge, near Irthing Foot, at six o'clock in the morning. A drag was struck almost immediately. The quest continued up the Eden beyond Corby Castle, one or two strongholds being visited on the way, and the otter was found ensconced behind his entrench-

ments at Cooey's Nab, below Cotehouse Island. He was ejected, and a water hunt, full of exciting incidents, ensued between that point and Corby Castle. It did not end till nearly nine o'clock at night, when the otter, a 24 lb. dog, was killed near the salmon coops. Much of this triumph of skill and endurance was due to Sandy, who always looked upon this hunt as one of his finest exploits. Sandy remained huntsman for fourteen years longer, when failing health compelled him to retire. His death, in March, 1886, was tragic and pathetic. He was then huntsman of the Brampton Harriers. The meet was at Seathill, Irthington, and after the hounds had been in full cry for twenty minutes Sandy was missed. Shortly afterwards a labourer crossing a field near Freelands found him lying dead on his back. His hunting whip was grasped in one hand, and a favourite terrier was seated on his chest. Thus this famous huntsman died in harness, the music of the hounds which he loved so well being the last sounds that fell upon his ears. His successors as huntsmen of the Carlisle Otter Hounds were first of all Jim Pattinson, who gave place to Ned Park, who is now hunting the Brampton Harriers. Park was followed by Tom Parker, who held the office till his death in 1899, when his son 'Young Tom' succeeded to the vacant place. The pack still flourishes (1902) but a rival has appeared in Dumfriesshire, and packs have been established at Cockermouth and at Egremont, which hunt the rivers of their respective districts, so that the county of Cumberland, from the Scottish Border to the boundary lines of Lancashire and Westmorland, is now fully covered.

ANGLING

To the angler Cumberland offers a field both wide and varied, for her rivers, lakes and streams are many in number, and are fairly well stocked with both migratory and non-migratory Salmonidæ, also in some instances with several species of coarse fish.

The Eden, with its tributaries, forms the most important river-system of Cumberland, and runs through this county from near Langwathby, where it is augmented by the Eamont, for a distance of about twenty-five miles to the Solway Firth. It is, however, to the sister county of Westmorland that the Eden owes its origin, for it rises near Kirkby-Stephen and runs through the county town of Appleby, whence it flows until it enters Cumberland. The Eden is also indebted to Westmorland for the contributions of the river

Lowther, a tributary of the Eamont, and the former pretty little river is the favourite spawning ground of Eden salmon.

The rivers Irthing, Petterill and Caldew are also tributaries of the Eden and run into it in the neighbourhood of Carlisle.

The rivers Wampool and Waver also run into the mouth of the Solway but they are of no great importance, and in the north-eastern corner of the county the small river Line discharges into the Border Esk.

The other rivers of Cumberland spring from the Lake and Fell district of the county and discharge their volumes into the sea at various points along the west coast. These are the Derwent, the Ellen, the Ehen, the Calder, the Irt, the Esk and the Duddon.

The lakes, Bassenthwaite, Derwentwater,

Ulleswater, Wastwater, Ennerdale, Crummock, etc., supply one or other of the rivers above mentioned, and afford sport of various kinds, and it is probable that by cultivation this might be greatly improved.

Salmon are plentiful in the Eden, for large numbers are captured annually by the nets in the Solway, in the tidal waters of the river, and in its upper reaches so far as Armathwaite Bay or Weir. Considerable numbers of these fish are caught by rod and line from Armathwaite downwards, and a few are killed in the water between that village and the junction of the Eamont with the main river, and in the Eamont itself.

It is difficult to obtain trustworthy returns of the salmon captured by the nets in the Solway and in the lower waters of the Eden, but to give some idea of what sport the river might afford, were it preserved for rod-fishing, I may say that, in a recent good year for salmon, over a length of twelve miles of water, six miles of which were netted, more than one thousand fish were taken in the spring season, and the rods probably accounted for about one hundred and fifty in addition.

In the Eden there are both spring and autumn runs of salmon, the precise dates of which are determined by the rainfalls, and it is scarcely necessary to mention that these do not always occur at times best suited to the open season for rod-fishing, viz. from 16 February until 15 November inclusive.

Salmon are also fairly plentiful in the Derwent, the Ehen, etc., but there is practically no spring run of fish in any of the west-coast rivers ; a few odd fish may ascend earlier or later, but July, August and September are the best months for salmon fishing in these rivers.

Sea-trout and its grilse, the herling, ascend most of the Cumberland rivers during the late spring and summer months, but at the present time these fish do not run up the Eden in any numbers beyond a few miles above Carlisle.

Bull-trout and grayling are both very scarce, but the brown trout flourishes in nearly all the rivers and in many of the lakes of Cumberland, and although the average weight is not great, they are very handsome fish, and when in good condition show excellent sport. An odd fish weighing from 4 lb. to 6 lb. is now and again captured in the Eden, and no doubt a few such fish exist in the deep pools in the Cumberland portion of the river, but the average weight of the trout killed by the rod in the middle and lower waters would probably be rather under than over ¼ lb., which is rather curious, as in a big river, exceedingly well supplied with food, one would expect a higher average weight.

A good many trout from 1 lb. to 2 lb. in weight may be observed jumping the weirs in the time of autumn floods, and likely enough these might be killed during the season by spinning, but this is not a method much practised for trout in Cumberland.

The rivers which discharge their volumes by the west coast contain very few coarse fish, but the Eden breeds a good many pike, and vast numbers of chub (locally called the skelly), while dace, eels, lampreys, etc., are not uncommon ; but, as might be expected, they are not much fished for where the Salmonidæ are fairly plentiful. It would be much to the advantage of the ova and young of the Salmonidæ if the Fishery Board and others interested were to make regular raids upon these coarse fish, which in this county are worthless.

The Cumberland rivers, like all those whose watersheds are partly under cultivation, have altered much of recent years by reason of the effect of the system of land drainage which has been prosecuted by the farmers. Year after year tracts of mire and bog disappear, and crops of various kinds replace heather, whins and bracken ; with the result that the rainfall, instead of filtering gradually through the soil and thence by way of the becks into the tributaries and main rivers, now runs off the channelled land as water from a duck's back. Thus the volumes falling from the clouds are retained in the rivers for a much less space of time than was formerly the case, and for a far shorter period are they available for the requirements of fish life.

A definite quantity of water will provide the necessities for the existence of the Salmonidæ over and over again, if at regular intervals it be recharged with the gas abstracted and be permitted to free itself from that returned. These operations are performed naturally by the agency of falls and swift runs which aërate the water, and by the action of aquatic vegetation, so in many instances the effect of land drainage in hurrying the rainfall to the sea may be compensated for by opening up the higher reaches of rivers and lakes, where such exist.

It can scarcely be doubted that this modern treatment of the rainfall has considerably influenced the salmon as regards the times at which they ascend rivers, the Eden for example, and if no fresh fields be opened up, so as to permit the fish to distribute themselves over a larger area of water, instead of being crowded together within a space which has become insufficient for their needs, it is obvious that disease will be cultivated and the stock of fish will be reduced to a number that the decreased volume of water is able to support.

There is another influence at work which is most disastrous in its effects upon fish life and fish reproduction in our rivers and estuaries, viz. the pollution of the water by sewerage and refuse from manufactories, etc. The present conditions of many of our rivers from these causes are bad enough, but with increasing population, unless new measures are adopted, they are certain to grow worse.

The Eden running into the sea by the straits of the Solway Firth is an object lesson providing the most convincing proof of the damage that sewerage inflicts upon a fishery, and its insanitary condition at the present time reflects discredit on the authorities of Carlisle and the district.

A mass of filth is poured into the river within a short distance of Carlisle, contaminating air and water alike. Lower down it surges to and fro with the tides, being continually augmented by the refuse from the city drains, and what obstruction it causes to running fish may be imagined from one fact alone, viz. that those netting below the main bulk of it are not anxious for its removal.[1]

Several autumn floods are required to sweep away the sewerage and settlement which collect below Carlisle while the Eden is low during the summer months. Thus the ascent of autumn salmon is retarded and the fish sicken with disease, while later on in the year much of the ova shed upon the lower beds is suffocated through the want of pure water.

After a series of floods in the spring or in the autumn, which unfortunately occurs but seldom, the fish are less languid and pay more heed to the angler's lure. Again, of the bulk of the fish sickened by the sewerage below, some few will take the fly after becoming recruited in health, while resting for a week or two in the purer middle waters, having partly shaken off the effects of the poison or disease, but large numbers die.

Even within recent times angling for both salmon and trout was obtainable in Cumberland for quite a small annual payment, and

[1] Since these lines were penned a statement was semi-officially made at the meeting of the Eden Fishery Board held in Carlisle in October, 1902, to the effect that the town council of Carlisle had plans in their possession for treating the sewerage of the city, and this scheme they hoped to carry out at a cost of £60,000. There would thus seem to be some chance that this question may be dealt with before long.

fair good fishing it was ; but, in the Eden at all events, many of the rods fished for the markets rather than for sport, and I once saw a man kill a spring fish of 28 lb. and take it forthwith by train to Carlisle, where he sold it for 2s. per pound and was again fishing the pool within little over two hours.

According to my judgment but few of such professionals were good salmon anglers, for many of them tried to bully fish into taking by continual casting over them, and when playing a fish they proceeded more as if the market value of the salmon than the fish itself were on the hook.

At trout-fishing on the contrary many of them were first-rate hands, they fished more freely and were not in such awe of the quarry. In the use of the fly, the creeper and the clear-water worm the old hands were expert, and it was not uncommon for a rod to creel 20 lb. to 25 lb. weight of trout between the hours of 7 p.m. and early morning in the summer months.

Until it became illegal, fishing with the otter, or 'jacking' as it was called, was practised on the Eden, and to within recent years some of the old hands were using their big jacking-reels for fly-fishing.

Circumstances have much changed upon the Eden and the other rivers during the last twenty years, as elsewhere, and there is very little fishing now to be obtained as described above upon small payment, and what little there may be is overfished.

Angling rents on the Eden and on the other rivers of the county are about on a par with those of the best rivers of Scotland as compared with the number of fish taken by the rod, and the rents paid for trout-fishing are very high also ; however one obtains a vast amount of walking, a great deal of casting and unlimited opportunities of wearing out good gut and flies in the attempt to lure ' dour ' fish into taking.

Legislation administered with a firm hand might easily improve the situation and without much delay, but at present the fact is not to be denied that the salmon of the Cumberland rivers are very bad takers.

This trait in their character has unfortunately led to the indiscriminate and selfish use of baits, both natural and artificial, by some who, upon finding that they do not obtain sufficient fish (I do not use the word sport advisedly) for their money, become desperate and pelt the pools from morn until eve with baits mounted upon compound tackle. Even before the water has had time to fine down after a flood this class of angler weights his baited cast with heavy leads, he casts the lot at right angles across the stream of the pool and permits the combination to grovel across the bed of the river, the water being so thick the while that the fish cannot discern the engine in time to shift away from its path. This class of angler like the sewerage of Carlisle can be easily dispensed with.

I have been told by old men who have passed their days upon Eden's banks that some forty to fifty years ago the river was more an autumn than a spring one as regards salmon-fishing, but it is difficult to reconcile these statements with the evidence given by an old man in a recent lawsuit concerning fishery rights on the river, and as the incident was not without humour is worth relating.

The old man of about eighty years was summoned to give evidence, and on account of his extreme age and deafness was invited to afford testimony from the well of the court. In the course of examination he stated that he and his mate, in the olden times, while netting a pool of the Eden, captured ninety-nine salmon in one night's fishing. The catch was certainly a very large one and the number of fish seemed somewhat peculiar. In cross-examination by eminent counsel, questions were put to the witness, in the usual professional tone, which seemed to imply that his memory was possibly defective. Failing to catch counsel's words the old man raised both hands to his ears, and the question gained emphasis by repetition. Without a moment's hesitation the old fellow replied more or less in these words : ' A remember eet weel—me an' Jim had been feeshin' a' neet, an' Jim says to me, " We've gotten ninety-nine feesh, an' we maun hae aneether to mak' eet a 'underd," an' we wrought on for foor moortal 'oors, but we could na'.' It was a distinct score for the veteran, who was then permitted to retire.

It is difficult to imagine that these could all have been fresh-run fish, and the probable explanation is that in those days they were not so particular about kelts.

The Cumberland rivers, including the best of them, the Eden, will not yield a big bag of salmon under existing conditions ; indeed five or six fish is the most I have known taken by a rod in one day, and this has happened only under peculiarly favourable conditions of water and weather.

I killed five fish one day with the fly but they only averaged 11 lb., which is very low for the river, as I should put the average weight of the fish falling to the rod in February, March and April at about 17 lb. to 18 lb., and in the autumn some 2 lb. to 4 lb. higher.

I do not claim to possess records of fish taken throughout the length of the Eden, but at about the above spring average I have known four fish killed by a rod in a day upon a few occasions, many times have I known of three fish in a day, but probably most anglers fishing in this river would be contented with the average of one fish a day ; indeed the probability is that in a month's fishing, upon sufficient water to occupy the day, fifteen fish would be a fair bag, and twenty a very good one.

A few years since, upon 8 November, I killed a cock fish of 38 lb., and soon after lost another of about the same size when close to the bank, and then landed a spring fish of 17 lb., which shows how early upon occasions will the spring fish ascend the river, and this was not a solitary instance.

The largest fish I have known killed on the Eden was a cock fish of 56¼ lb. in the back-end with an artificial minnow just above Warwick Bridge, and he was a very fine fish in fair condition.

The scenery around a watershed, the growth of timber, shrubs and wild flowers upon the banks, together with the resident and migratory bird-life, add so much to the enjoyment of angling, that without these adjuncts the sport is bereft of a considerable amount of its charm. No complaint however can be made of the Cumberland rivers and lakes in these respects, for their scenery is delightful, as it tells the tale of the seasons by its foliage and feathered inhabitants.

The angling is also interesting in itself, for the bluff sandstone crags and wooded banks call for all methods of casting, and the sunken rocks which line many a pool demand expert handling of the fish when hooked.

The weather is often uncommonly wild and rough for the first four months of the year in Cumberland, and frost, cold winds, snow and sleet are pretty certain to take their turns until May arrives ; indeed many a time has my line been frozen in the rings of the rod as the ' helm-wind' swept down from the fells.

The opening day of the season is of peculiar interest to the salmon-fisher, for he puts up his rod with the knowledge that, whether the fish have been lying in the pools for a day or a month, they at all events have not seen a fly or bait since they left the sea.

The rod seems a trifle heavy, those submerged rocks to be covered in the cast appear somewhat distant, the fly does not shoot forth and drop upon the ripple with quite its usual easy grace, and as he wades with the rushing stream around his waist, the angler's eyes are rather dazed by the light and the movement of the water, while the awkward wading places he treats with more respect than is his wont. He is merely a little out of practice, and within the space of an hour or so he can scarcely credit that the rod has for so long been laid aside.

The temperature and weather in Cumberland may vary much in different seasons, but at some time or another during the spring months, even in a somewhat sheltered valley like that of the Eden, the angler is sure to encounter rough winds bearing rain, hail, sleet, or snow, and he should be clad accordingly. The gusty blasts come hard and stiff as they strike up the valley direct from the eastern fells, and although there is a fair show of fish in the water most of them will ignore the best efforts of both head and hand, contenting themselves with occasional graceful leaps above the surface of the pools. Yet by careful and diligent fishing the angler should pick up an odd fish or two now and again, and under the circumstances should not be altogether dissatisfied; indeed my experience is that one rarely fails to get one chance a day whatever the weather and water may be like.

To-day as he walks to the water the air seems rather softer, and of wind there is so little that it is difficult to tell whence it springs. The sky is completely cloud-covered, and as he descends the steep brow of the hill below appears in excellent trim, and he remarks to his companion : 'If fish don't take to-day they never will!' As the angler reaches the pool the air has become yet milder, and fearful that the sun may penetrate the clouds he splices his rod in haste, runs the line quickly through the rings and loops on the well soaked cast and fly.

One cast—two casts—three casts—when, as the fly is hanging almost straight down stream, the surface of the water is agitated, and in the turmoil a few inches of a dorsal fin for an instant catch the eye, and immediately the tip of a tail cleaves the surface and disappears. The line draws almost imperceptibly, the rod-top tells no tale, and the fisher, with that restraint and confidence acquired by long practice, allows a second or so to elapse ere he moves a muscle. Those seconds seem as minutes, but the sand surely runs from the glass; a sharp, firm strike bends the rod down to the hand, and the line is tight indeed. The dreaded sunlight permits of no dallying, and with scant ceremony the fish is run up the gravel strand —a fine fresh run salmon of near upon 20 lb.

There is no time to waste, so the fly speeds forth again, and at the very third cast it is taken savagely under water with no surface rise. A powerful fish indeed, but the best of single gut permits of his being rattled up the strand ere he scarce appreciates his dilemma ; his weight is 18 lb.

A slight rift in the clouds now gives passage to feeble golden rays, and without delay the jock-scot is again dismissed upon its errand.

Twice does the double-hooked 3/0 complete its course unmolested, but, curious to relate, again at the third time of asking it is arrested in its progress over those sunken moss-begrown rocks. This time the fish fairly races at the fly, and before any strike is possible the impetus of his rush lifts him high above the pool's surface. There is a moment of doubt and suspense, but fortunately the fly is fast, and so it remains until released from his jaw as he rests upon the green sward, side by side with his brothers in misfortune, the three weighing 20 lb., 18 lb. and 21 lb. Three fine spring fish killed in nine casts within the space of forty minutes, whereas the previous week of hard fishing had only yielded a like result. Such was the luck of salmon fishing upon the Eden, and I hope may be again. The last fish was not hooked a moment too soon, for as he came to bank the river was aglow with sunlight and further attempt was useless until eventide.

Towards the end of March the days are getting long, and the sun grows in power, so, even with the water in order, it is not good to fish during the mid-day hours, unless indeed the weather be dull. Better sport will probably be enjoyed with the trout rod, for on or about the 22nd of the month the March-browns will come sailing down the necks of the pools to meet their fate in the slower running water lower down.

The seasons differ much as regards trout-fishing. The trout are there sure enough, but during long spells of cold dry weather they feed upon the bed of the river, and when the water is low and fine they are extremely difficult to lure with the fly, lying as they do in the flats rather than in the streams, at the early part of the season.

In three or four hours' fishing I have often landed only about half a dozen trout, while upon other days I have in the same time killed from two to four dozen, averaging about $\frac{1}{2}$ lb., and in addition have returned to the water ten or twelve smaller fish.

The March-brown continues to rise until nearly the middle of April, but soon after that fly-fishing for trout becomes for a while rather uncertain sport, for all the best fish will be hunting among the stones for the creeper (the pseudo-imago of the stone-fly) as he shifts his position while wending his way towards the banks, where he will emerge as the perfect winged fly.

The creeper is fixed upon two hooks mounted above one another and back to back upon a strand of gut, and the bait is cast up stream mostly in thin water, sometimes only six inches deep, and so long as the creeper season lasts the fish will scarcely look at ought else.

Later on, should the water be favourable, nice baskets of trout may be killed with the olive and the blue duns when the sun is off the water, but when June arrives, trouting is mostly confined to early and late hours, and those who do not object to night-fishing can make good bags with the 'bustard' (or artificial moth) in warm weather.

As a matter of fact, most of the proprietors and lessees do not fish the Eden hard for trout, and generally give it up when they have creeled a dozen or so, but upon a few occasions I have tried out of curiosity to see what I could do, and in 1902 in the week or two previous to Whitsun-week, I killed in three days forty-seven, fifty, and fifty-six trout, averaging over ½ lb. apiece, and also returned to the river ten to twelve a day, but the conditions in each instance were exceptionally favourable.

The fifty-six trout were killed on the Friday before Whitsun Day; they weighed 32 lb., and were caught in heavy rain between the hours of 11.30 a.m. and 3.30 p.m.

In June, July and August the sea-trout and herling ascend the Cumberland rivers, but these sharp-sighted fish do not take well in the daytime. They show excellent sport in the summer evenings and nights.

In the Derwent and in the other rivers of the west coast of Cumberland there is really no spring run of salmon. These fish make their appearance in June and July and afford good sport into September. By the end of September in Cumberland the summer salmon fishing and sea-trout fishing are practically over, and the brown-trout are getting soft in condition; thus in this county the angler's remaining chance of sport with the rod is centred in the 'back-end' salmon fishing, which entirely depends upon the rainfall.

In an autumn attended by continual rain I have known excellent sport enjoyed on the Eden with fresh-run clean fish, but for the last four or five years very few of such have ascended the river to any distance above Carlisle until after the annual close-time has commenced. With 16 November the close-time for the latest of the Cumberland rivers commences, and the rods are laid aside until the winter's floods shall have scoured the river's banks and bed of summer growth and have obliterated the angler's footprints from the waterside.

The river Eden with its excellent tributaries, headed by such grand lakes as Ulleswater and Haweswater, is a system peculiarly constituted by nature to provide the necessities of a successful salmon fishery, and the area at the command of fish could be vastly increased at comparatively small expense. In the year 1900 a hatchery was erected near Armathwaite by private subscription of some few riparian owners and lessees. The house and ponds were constructed so as to hatch out 500,000 ova, and rear the resulting product, and since that date it has continued to do good work; the enterprise should soon increase the number of adult fish which ascend the river.

COURSING

Until the beginning of the nineteenth century there does not appear to have been any public coursing in Cumberland.[1] Owners of greyhounds ran friendly matches on each other's lands, but the sport was in no sense organized nor was there any breeding record kept. It is very difficult, therefore, except in very few cases, to trace a dog's pedigree back to the end of the eighteenth century. The literature of the sport commenced in 1828 with a book published by Mr. Thomas Goodlake, a south country enthusiast, and annual records were initiated by Mr. Thomas Thacker in 1840 and continued by him for some years.

[1] One of the earliest references to greyhounds in Cumberland appears to be in the Pipe Rolls (see *V.C.H. Cumb.* i. 389), where it is stated that in the fourth year of the reign of King John, Allan Wastehouse received a sum of £109 15s. 8d. as the wages for eighteen months of himself and four attendants. This included the care of a stud of ten dogs, called 'leporarii.' Greyhounds under one name or another, such as 'canes de mota,' 'currentes canes,' etc., are not unfrequently mentioned in the early historical records of Cumberland. A search through the Monastic Chartularies, Close Rolls and Forest Eyre Rolls relating to the county might be worth the labour to those accustomed to such investigation. For instance, greyhounds, locally known as 'strakurs,' were used by Cumberland sportsmen for poaching hares on the king's demesnes as early as 1287.

Mr. Thacker also compiled a code of rules; but it was not until 1858 that the sport was authoritatively regulated by a code which, with alterations from time to time, is now in force. The official Stud Book was instituted in 1881. But before that time strong clubs were in existence at Workington and Whitehaven; the latter club being chiefly supported—till its dissolution close upon 1870 — by the Lowther family, and the latter by the Curwens, being then succeeded by the short-lived West Cumberland Club. In the south-west of the county too there was plenty of coursing when the Whitehaven and Workington Clubs were full of life, and at Cockermouth General Sir Henry Wyndham, M.P., permitted meetings on the Castle estate for many years. But Cockermouth as a coursing centre was most noted for the Bridekirk meeting, held on the magnificent grass land of Mr. Henry Teshmaker Thompson's Tarnities estate from 1854 until 1873, when his successor, Colonel Green-Thompson, withdrew the necessary permission. The Bridekirk Cup, the principal stake at this meeting during the nineteen years referred to, was one of the chief coursing prizes of the season, and the thirty-two competing greyhounds embraced the pick of the celebrities of the kingdom. It goes without saying therefore that the break up of the Bridekirk meetings was a blow to coursing in Cumberland; indeed, it was the beginning of the decadence that culminated with the Ground Game Act of 1880, and now, unfortunately, the Border Union Meeting on the Netherby estate remains alone in its glory. In the eastern part of the county, moreover, there was at one time or other an abundance of coursing, which the Hares and Rabbits enactment tended to abolish. In this connection prominence may be given to the Brampton Club, the home of which was on the Naworth estate. The club in question existed for some thirty years, and in its palmy times very many greyhounds whose blood courses through the veins of latter day Waterloo Cup winners graduated on the Naworth estate, which, it is interesting to add, can claim the distinction of being the oldest coursing country in Cumberland from a historical point of view.

The Border Union country has for many years past been second in importance only to the Waterloo Cup in Lancashire, the prize that everybody, fortunate enough to possess a first-class greyhound, is ambitious to win. The Border Union, however, like its prototype, was commenced on very humble lines as far back as 1850, but as time rolled by, the Netherby Cup increased in reputation, and for the greater part of the half-century its sixty-four competitors have included the pick of the kennels in England, Ireland and Scotland. Luckily the Ground Game Act has not exercised the deterrent effect so severely felt in every other part of the kingdom, for the sufficient reason that the Netherby tenantry, to a man almost, co-operate in the heartiest manner with the managing committee. Indeed it is a singular fact that the committee is to a great extent composed of the farmers. And it is fitting that the Border Union Meeting should be held on ground that for coursing purposes cannot be excelled anywhere, covering as it does magnificent stretches of grass and seeds, perfectly level, and practically clear of stones, its locality extending from the outskirts of Longtown to Gretna on the banks of the Esk. There are also two less important meetings held on the Netherby estates. In some other parts of England, as well as in Ireland, the exigencies arising out of the Ground Game Act led to the introduction of another form of coursing in the shape of inclosures, in which the hares are really confined, and liberated from their covert one by one as required. This was never more than an imitation of the ancient pastime, in many respects contemptible by comparison, and it is creditable to the instincts of Cumbrian and Scottish coursers that no attempt has ever been made to plant this abomination in the Border county.

In the old days when public coursing was flourishing from end to end of the county it may be imagined that the breeding of greyhounds was a necessary means to an end. In consequence the best blood north and south of the Border was ever being minlged and disseminated, and the present day result is that the lines of long past Cumbrian canine notabilities are to be found in the pedigrees of all the winners of valuable stakes, not only in the United Kingdom, but in Australia, New Zealand and the United States, where coursing has for several years past been a popular pastime. Nowadays however Cumberland is almost destitute of breeding studs, the only one worthy of the designation being Stonerigg near Carlisle, belonging to Mr. Thomas Graham, originally a Dumfriesshire courser, who for many seasons past has bred winners by the score. Here and there also a farmer breeds on a small scale for the London sale ring, young greyhounds reared on the breezy and health-giving lands of Cumberland invariably commanding a profitable market. In this connection too several of the principal kennels in the south of England supply team upon team of young puppies for Cumberland 'walks'; indeed, the farmers' wives and daughters on the Border have a reputation second to none for their care and upbringing of greyhounds, and quite naturally they watch the public careers of their whilom charges with the deepest interest.

As will be readily inferred, Cumberland has the credit of producing a long array of famous greyhounds during the sixty years public coursing has been carried on in the county. The palm of superiority, from every point of view, must undoubtedly be accorded to 'Judge,' bred in 1852 by the Rev. John Fox of St. Bees, and owned by his friend Mr. Henry Jefferson of Rothersyke near Egremont. Mr. Jefferson was the owner of running greyhounds as far back as 1840, winning cups at Whitehaven, Workington and elsewhere. 'Judge' was by Mr. Jefferson's own dog 'John Bull' (by Jebb's 'Lodore' out of 'Jane'), and his dam was Mr. Fox's 'Fudge' (by 'Oliver Twist' out of 'Fairy,' by the celebrated Cockermouth dog 'Carronade' out of 'Gamut,' another of Mr. Fox's kennel). 'Judge' was therefore a thorough Cumberland bred dog. He was a red dog, and when a puppy he divided a stake at Workington, besides winning the Altcar Club Cup in Lancashire. In the same year he ran in the Waterloo Cup, and was beaten in the third round by the eventual winner, Lord Sefton's 'Sackcloth.' In his second season however 'Judge' commenced by winning the Bridekirk Cup, and then attained the pinnacle of fame by securing the Waterloo Cup, as the representative of Mr. (now Sir Thomas) Brocklebank, whilst the following year he again made a bold bid for Waterloo Cup honours, running second to 'Protest' after an 'undecided,' and for the second time representing Mr. Brocklebank. 'Judge's' peculiarity—a very rare one—was that he required little or no training ; in other words, he trained himself into condition. As an instance of his wonderful constitution, he had only been about a week in hand prior to winning the Bridekirk Cup, and at the close of the ordeal was fit to run on, in spite of the stout hares. During his famous running career it is a singular fact that 'Judge' in three of his five defeats was vanquished by the ultimate winner after 'undecideds.' In one instance he went to slips three times with 'Bright Idea' in the Champion Cup at Biggar, in Lanarkshire, whilst he had to be drawn lame after an 'undecided' with the Lancashire bitch 'Jael,' winner of the Druid Cup on the Wiltshire Downs. From the foregoing it will be gathered that 'Judge' was at home in any country, and it will suffice to add that in all he won twenty-eight courses out of thirty-three. At the stud Mr. Jefferson's wonderful greyhound was equally successful. He was the sire of three

Waterloo Cup winners, namely 'Clive,' 'Maid of the Mill' and 'Chloe,' the second referred to being a Cumberland bitch, of whom more anon. To wind up our reference to 'Judge,' his stout blood is to be found in at least three-fourths of the Waterloo Cup winners down to the present day. His pedigree traces back to the latter part of the eighteenth century. In 'Judge's' earlier times his progenitors were decidedly in-bred, a circumstance that would be carefully avoided in these latter days, in contradistinction to a hundred years ago when people were not so particular.

At this stage it will be appropriate to introduce Sir Thomas Brocklebank as a prominent Cumbrian courser, the more so that he was a contemporary of Mr. Henry Jefferson, the Rev. John Fox and many others who were pillars of the pastime in the early 'forties.' Of that worthy school he is the only representative left, and from 1847 down to the present time he has been actively engaged in coursing pursuits all over the kingdom. During his long career Sir Thomas Brocklebank has bred and run many first-class greyhounds that have done him suit and service at the meetings of the Altcar and Ridgway Clubs, and many other clubs in different parts of the country, not omitting the Waterloo Cup and the Whitehaven and Workington Clubs of the old days. He was also a prominent member of the National Coursing Club during a long period of years. Sir Thomas Brocklebank's most notable greyhounds have been 'Border Boy,' 'Britomart,' 'Beer,' 'Bowfell,' 'Beeswing,' 'Brigade,' 'Bacchante,' 'Bishop,' 'Burlador,' 'Bière,' 'Black Veil' and 'Border Song.' He bred them all with the exception of 'Border Boy,' bought as a puppy in 1850, and 'Brigade,' given to him by his friend Mr. Henry Jefferson, also when a puppy, in 1866. 'Britomart' won the Altcar Club Cup in 1852, 'Bowfell' was second for the Waterloo Cup in 1862, and nineteen years later 'Bishop' occupied the same tantalizing position, whilst the brilliant 'Brigade' (a grand-daughter of 'Judge' through her dam 'Java') reached the last four at Waterloo, when the Irish wonder, 'Master McGrath,' was victorious. Subsequently 'Brigade' divided the Altcar Club Cup and won the Bridekirk Cup. But 'Bacchante's' record was, if anything, of higher merit than any of the foregoing greyhounds, as she ran second for the South Lancashire Stakes (Ridgway Club), won the Waterloo Purse, won and divided the Altcar Cup, and was runner-up for the Craven Cup over the historical Ashdown country. 'Bacchante's' greatest performance, though unsuccessful, was when she met the celebrated 'Bab at the Bowster' in the fifth round of the Great Scarisbrick Cup at Southport. The course was one of the longest ever witnessed in that most severe country, and the greyhounds were a match in every attribute but speed, which eventually left the Scotch bitch mistress of a trying situation. 'Beer' and 'Beeswing' were daughters of 'Bacchante,' the former of whom divided two Craven Cups, and her sister was the winner of an Altcar Cup and a Lytham Cup. During later years 'Burlador' divided the Carmichael Cup (in Lanarkshire), and 'Black Veil' and 'Border Song' respectively won their veteran owner the much appreciated Corrie Cup in Dumfriesshire. Sir Thomas Brocklebank may truly be described as the 'father of coursing,' not only of his native county of Cumberland, but also of the United Kingdom. 'Carronade,' although located in Cumberland, was of Scotch lineage, but the property of Mr. William Bragg, a solicitor in Cockermouth, and agent to General Wyndham, successively M.P. for the old borough and for West Cumberland. 'Carronade's' blood runs through many Waterloo Cup winners, inclusive of 'Judge' and 'Fullerton,' the latter of whom bears the great distinction of having divided and then won in three consecutive years. 'Carronade's' sire was 'Carron,' descended from one of the Duke of Gordon's celebrities about 1821, and 'Carron' ran a sensational match in 1840 for £100, the result of a challenge to 'All Scotland,' but was defeated by the Earl of Eglinton's 'Waterloo.' Mr. Bragg was a keen courser, a winner of many prizes in West Cumberland and a member of the Workington and Whitehaven Clubs, having thus been intimately associated with Mr. Fox, Mr. Jefferson, Captain John Harris, Dr. Anthony Peat, Mr. Thomas Falcon, Mr. Joseph Lindow, Captain Spencer, Mr. Thomas Dalzell and Mr. Richard Smith, the latter also a Cockermouth sportsman of the old school and a manufacturer in the town. Travelling much, in conjunction with his business his greyhounds ran successfully at the most important meetings on both sides of the border, and from the year 1840 until his death, some fifteen years later, he must have acquired a valuable collection of plate. Recurring to Mr. Henry Jefferson and to the Rev. John Fox, the owner of 'Judge' had also the celebrated 'Jacobite,' bred however in 1854 by Mr. Fox. 'Jacobite' was by the Nottingham dog 'Bedlamite,' and his dam was 'Florence,' a daughter of 'Carronade' and 'Gamut'; but 'Jacobite' early passed into the hands of a Scottish courser, Mr. John Gibson, for whom he won many stakes, and subsequently increased his fame at the stud. Others of Mr. Jefferson's winning

greyhounds were 'Jim-along-Josey,' 'Jeremy Diddler,' 'Jeu d'Esprit,' 'Jester,' 'Judy,' 'Jeannie Deans,' 'Johnny Newcome,' 'Jericho,' 'Jane,' 'Jack o' Lantern,' 'Jock,' 'John Bull' (sire of 'Judge '), 'Java' (winner of the Waterloo Plate), and 'Imperatrice' (a daughter of 'Java '), who was the dam of the Lancashire wonder, 'Bed of Stone.' The Rev. John Fox retired from coursing comparatively early, but between 1840–50 he was very successful in all parts of the country.

A well known greyhound in Cumberland about 1845 was Mr. John Rogers's 'Crofton,' winner of several prizes, and whose name is prominent in the pedigrees of many notabilities, inclusive of 'King Lear' and 'Maid of the Mill,' winners of the Waterloo Cup. 'Crofton' was one of the fastest greyhounds of his time. He was named as a compliment to the Brisco family, of whom Sir Robert, prior to succeeding to the baronetcy, was an active Cumberland courser. Sir Robert's first greyhound of note was 'Beau Cœur,' whelped in 1838, and bred at Crofton. Sir Robert Brisco won no fewer than five Whitehaven Cups in the early 'forties.' Captain Joseph Spencer's kennel of greyhounds flourished in 1846 till a dozen years later. He will not readily be forgotten as the owner of 'Sunbeam,' a son of 'John Bull' and Mr. Fox's 'Fleur-de-Lys.' 'Sunbeam' began his career by winning a stake at Altcar; he ran second for the Bridekirk Cup and Altcar Club Cup, also won the Clifton Cup at Lytham and the Douglas Cup at Biggar, and within a few days carried off the Bendrigg Cup, one of the leading prizes of the time in Westmorland, where, by-the-bye, there is now no public coursing. But 'Sunbeam's' historical feat was his defeat in the deciding course of the 1857 Waterloo Cup by 'King Lear,' a keen disappointment for Cumberland, as the dog's chance was considered second to none. The year following 'Sunbeam' ran into the last four of Neville's Waterloo Cup. There were old coursers however who considered 'Seagull' a better greyhound than 'Sunbeam,' both as a public performer and at the stud. 'Seagull' was by 'Bedlamite—Raven,' and was bred in the south of England; in fact, before he came into Cumberland had run under the name of 'Reveller.' It will be sufficient to say that 'Seagull' won for Captain Spencer two Altcar Club Cups, the Biggar Cup, the Whitehaven Cup and the Scottish Champion Cup, truly a brilliant record, and reflecting no little credit on the West Cumberland courser as a judge of a good greyhound.

The border name of Hyslop has for many years been associated with coursing in Cumber-

SPORT ANCIENT AND MODERN

land and farther afield. Five brothers were born and bred on the Denton Hall farmstead-ing of Lord Carlisle, and they were all coursers of the old-fashioned stamp, breeding and run-ning their greyhounds to some substantial pur-pose. The eldest of them, Mr. John Hyslop, now more than fourscore years, makes a point of attending the Border Union, while the two youngest, also veterans, still breed and run a few dogs now and again. The other two brothers died some years ago. Mr. John Hyslop was for many years honorary secretary of the old Brampton Club, and fifty years ago officiated as judge at the Border Union meet-ing. But it is with the many good greyhounds that sprang from Denton Hall that we have now to deal. Two of the earliest winners were ' Young Eve ' and ' Harpoon,' by ' Eden ' out of ' Old Eve,' and ' Harpoon ' in the same season carried off the Scottish Champion Cup as well as a valuable stake at Workington. The next to bring lustre to Denton Hall was ' Hue and Cry,' winner of the Brougham Castle Cup in 1859, and in a year or so the future famous brood bitch ' High Idea ' was to the fore. She was however in due course eclipsed by her son ' Strange Idea ' (by ' Car-dinal York '), who opened his career by win-ning the Brampton Puppy Stakes, and he won the Waterloo Plate on the occasion of the first of ' Master McGrath's ' three Waterloo Cup victories. It was at the stud, though, that ' Strange Idea ' made a name, and not only were his fine speed and brilliancy transmitted to future Denton Hall winners, but to grey-hounds all over the country, and at the present day there is scarcely a greyhound of note in this country, as well as in Australia and America, in whose pedigree the ' Strange Idea ' line is not to be found. The ' Car-dinal York—High Idea ' combination included ' Lion's Share,' who divided the Brampton Cup ; ' Bright Idea,' second for the great Bothal St. Leger in Northumberland ; and ' No Idea,' who divided the Bridekirk Cup. ' Confidence ' was another great performer, she was a winner at Brougham and at Bramp-ton, and divided the Bridekirk Cup with Sir Thomas Brocklebank's ' Brigade.' ' Strange Idea's ' best success at the stud however was a bitch called ' Covet,' a daughter of the Northumberland ' Curiosity,' and given to the Messrs. Hyslop for the stud fee. A lucky bargain it was too, as the bitch com-menced when very young by running to the end of a Sapling Stakes at Brampton, where she also shared the Puppy Stakes. In a month only from this ' Covet ' was taken to Bothal, where she divided the St. Leger of 143 puppies, and then changed hands for £200, the new owner being the Lancashire courser, Mr. James Spinks, who renamed the bitch ' Sea Cove,' under which name she divided the Hardwick Cup in Shropshire, and then won the Waterloo Cup. This string of successes, it is interesting to know, was achieved when the bitch was a puppy. She was not by any means a fast greyhound, as a matter of fact she was led by ' Confidence ' in a private trial prior to the Waterloo Cup. The last of the really good greyhounds owned by the Denton Hall triumvirate was ' Hermit,' who created a memorable surprise when he turned the tables on Lord Haddington's ' Horn-pipe ' in the final course for the Stainburn Cup at Workington. ' Hermit ' had been previously run to death almost, and went to the encounter a thoroughly distressed greyhound, whereby the issue appeared a certainty for the Scotch bitch. However the unexpected happened, as it often does in coursing, as after ' Hermit ' had been led to the hare he resolutely set to work when the opening came, and finished the winner.

Captain Dees was a prominent member of the Whitehaven Club in its palmiest days, and his successes on Lord Lonsdale's ground were simply marvellous. On two occasions a brace and once three of his greyhounds were left in for the Whitehaven Cup, which required to be won three times in order to become the permanent property of a member. It took Captain Dees seven years to accomplish the feat, and the details are so interesting that they are here given : 1859, Captain Spencer's ' Seagull ' ; 1860, Mr. Lindow's ' Lizard ' ; 1861, Mr. (now Lord) Brougham's ' Belle of Eamont ' ; 1862, Captain Dees's ' Ewesdale ' beat his ' Duke ' ; 1863, Captain Dees's ' Detector,' his ' Duke ' and his ' Ewesdale ' divided ; 1864, Mr. Blackstock's ' Beckford ' ; 1865, Mr. A. Thompson's ' Ticket of Leave' ; 1866, Captain Dees's ' Doctor ' beat his ' Dean Swift.' ' Duke,' it should be added, was by ' Seagull,' ' Detector ' by ' Judge,' and ' Doc-tor ' and ' Dean Swift ' by ' Ewesdale.' ' Dé-butante,' a sister of ' Detector,' won the Border Union Puppy Stake in 1863, and ' Ewesdale ' won the Bridekirk Cup in the same year.

The name of Mr. G. A. Thompson, owner of ' Ticket of Leave,' recalls another prominent Brampton courser. At one time he was honorary secretary of the old Bramp-ton Club, and he started as an owner of greyhounds in 1853 by running second for the Club Cup with ' Telemachus.' Two years after Mr. Thompson was victor-ious in the Brampton Cup with ' Titmouse,' who also ran second for the Caledonian Cup to ' Jacobite,' whilst she divided the year following. 'Tearaway,' a son of 'Telemachus,' also carried off the Carmichael Stakes at the same meeting. 'Tearaway' and 'Truth' subsequently shared the Sefton Stakes at Altcar, and the former followed it up with the Altcar Club Cup, whilst 'Tearaway's' brother 'Tempest' won the Bridekirk Cup. From this Mr. Thompson all at once got together a strong kennel of high class greyhounds that could win stakes when pitted against the best in all countries. It would be tedious to name the half of them, and it must suffice to observe that 'Tullochgorum' (brother to 'King Death,' winner of the Waterloo Cup in 1864) as a puppy ran second for the Sefton Stakes, and in his second season won the Brampton Cup and divided the Bridekirk Cup. 'Tullochgorum's' Bridekirk success was the subject of winter controversy round many a farm fireside for years after. 'Theatre Royal' was another great greyhound. She was by 'Cardinal York' out of 'Meg of the Mill' (a celebrated Longtown bitch), and after earning herself a name when a sapling, the following season won the Challenge Bracelet on Salisbury Plains, as well as running second at Sundorne in Shropshire. In her next season 'Theatre Royal' won the Altcar Cup, divided the Douglas Cup with 'Cauld Kail,' and reached the penultimate stage of the Waterloo Cup, won by 'Brigadier.' And 'Trovatore' (by 'Ticket of Leave' out of 'Touchwood') was yet another of Mr. Thompson's brilliant performers. She won the Brownlow Cup in Ireland and the Lytham Cup, divided the Caledonian Stakes, and was put out in the decider for the Douglas Cup by 'Lancaster.' Further, Mr. Thompson acquired the famous brood bitch 'Princess Royal,' a full sister to 'Theatre Royal,' just before his retirement from coursing through ill-health ; indeed he died at Nice almost on the eve of 'Master McGrath's' second Waterloo Cup victory.

Memories of the Bridekirk Cup are closely associated with the name of Mr. John Blackstock of Hayton Castle, who was practically the founder of the meeting. As an owner of greyhounds he had achieved something more than a fair share of success at Bridekirk and other important meetings in different parts of the country. He began by running second to 'Judge' with his bitch 'Bartolozzi' for the Bridekirk Cup of 1854. 'Judge' and 'Bartolozzi' were subsequently mated, and the produce included two greyhounds that speedily gained Mr. Blackstock fame, namely 'Bridegroom' and 'Maid of the Mill,' who made their first appearance at Southport, the dog running second to 'Derwentwater' for the Scarisbrick Cup after three 'undecideds,' and

the bitch winning the Southport Stakes. 'Maid of the Mill' followed up this creditable *début* with a stake at Brougham, and she found more than her match in 'Annoyance' in the 'decider' for the Bridekirk Cup, but was not long after victorious in the Waterloo Cup. 'Belle of the Moor,' a daughter of 'Bridegroom,' also won amongst other stakes the Netherby Cup, and 'Beckford,' another scion of 'Bridegroom,' carried off a second Bridekirk Cup. 'Beckford' was the fond hope of all Cumberland for the Waterloo Cup of 1864, but he failed to survive the first round, winning however the Purse the year following. By common consent Mr. Blackstock's most brilliant greyhound was 'Belle of Scotland' (a daughter of 'Maid of the Mill'), though a more unfortunate one never went to slips, as after running unsuccessfully all over the kingdom she managed to divide the Netherby Cup, soon after which she went to the stud. In 1871 'Belle of Lorne' divided the Bridekirk Cup.

One of the greatest greyhounds ever associated with coursing in Cumberland was 'Cauld Kail.' Although bred on the Scotch side of the river Liddel and full of Cumberland blood, 'Cauld Kail' was subsequently the property of Mr. William Forster of Stonegarthside, also on the banks of the Liddel and almost opposite the place of the dog's nativity. 'Cauld Kail's' earliest successes were at Brampton, where he divided the Cup, and at Hawick and Lockerbie, where he also shared the Stobs Castle Stakes and the Castlemilk Stakes. Next greatly fancied for the Waterloo Cup, won by 'Brigadier,' his colours were lowered in the second round, after two 'undecideds,' by 'Blue Eye,' but the following month, in the more congenial Scottish National country, he divided the Douglas Cup (fifty-eight entries) with 'Theatre Royal.' A second division of the Stobs Castle Stakes, and, strange to say, again with 'Princess Royal,' ended 'Cauld Kail's' winning successes, and he went to the stud. His immediate progeny won valuable stakes in England, Ireland and Scotland, including the Waterloo Cup, and one of them, a Cumberland-bred dog, named 'Royal Water,' after dividing a stake at Lockerbie, changed hands for £150, went to Australia in 1874, and shortly after landing won the Waterloo Cup, a stake of the same dimensions and value as that in England. At the present day, like 'Judge' and 'Strange Idea,' the blood of 'Cauld Kail' runs in the veins of the majority of the very best greyhounds. Reverting to Mr. Forster, however, he was subsequently the possessor of many winners of valuable stakes. Included in these was 'Fortuna' (by 'Cardinal York' out of 'Meg'), who won the Jedburgh St. Leger, divided the Biggar Stakes with 'Wigton Lass' (bred in the same kennel as 'Royal Water '), ran up for the Sundorne Cup (Salop), and divided the Bridekirk Cup with 'Princess Royal.' 'Fairy Glen' (grand-daughter of 'Cavalier,' a celebrated son of 'Cauld Kail') won Mr. Forster his third Corrie Cup, whilst the last really good one at Stonegarthside was 'Fugitive' (by 'Cock Robin' out of 'Fortuna'), whose record as a puppy was signalized by dividing the Wig-townshire St. Leger and the Border Union Derby, also running into the semi-finals of the Waterloo Cup, when he was put out by 'Magnano,' the winner, and a son of 'Cauld Kail.' In his second season 'Fugitive' divided the Netherby Cup.

In the 'fifties'. and 'sixties' the Cumber-land farmers had a notable representative courser in Mr. George Carruthers, the then tenant of Gale Hall near Penrith. Mr. Carruthers' name will go down to posterity as the owner of the third Cumberland Water-loo Cup winner. This was 'Meg,' not bred in the county, by-the-bye, but in Dumfries-shire, by Mr. John Jardine, her sire being Lord John Scott's 'Terrona,' and her dam 'Fanny Fickle,' both full of the best Cumber-land blood. A slow greyhound, 'Meg' never-theless was quick in seizing openings, and once behind a hare stayed there. It was these valu-able qualities that won her the Netherby Cup, whilst she ran second next year and was put out by 'Johnny Cope.' It was only a month after this reverse that the Cumberland bitch succeeded in winning the Waterloo Cup. 'Bonus,' her brother, won the Brougham Cup, and ran second to 'Tullochgorum' for the Brampton Cup, and to 'Beckford' for the Bridekirk Cup. Many old coursers however unhesitatingly point to 'Crossfell' as the best of Mr. Carruthers' greyhounds. He was a son of the Scotch celebrity 'Canaradzo' and the Waterloo Cup heroine 'Meg.' 'Cross-fell,' within a month of dividing the Brampton Cup, won the Great Scarisbrick Cup (sixty-four entries) in Lancashire, and the year following, when the stake had been doubled in number of entries, he was defeated in the last four by the invincible 'Bab' at the Bowster. Mr. Carruthers also owned 'Canzonette,' her daughter 'Coupland Lass,' and several other winning greyhounds.

With the decadence of coursing in Cumber-land the references to its greyhounds towards the close of the nineteenth century are neces-sarily few and far between, and it must suffice to remark that the one and only kennel of note remaining worthily upholds the prestige of past years. The Stonerigg Kennel in fact produced another Waterloo Cup winner in 1897, that is to say, 'Gallant,' who is owned by a native of Cumberland, resident in the county of Durham, but was trained in Cum-berland. 'Gallant's' sire is 'Young Fullerton,' a brother of the great 'Fullerton,' and his dam 'Sally Milburn,' so that he is full of the best Cumberland blood of bygone days, and at the stud the performances of 'Gallant's' stock are substantial evidences of his great value as a sire.

GAME COCKFIGHTING

Seventy or eighty years ago cockfighting was one of the most popular sports in the country. If not admired, yet it was toler-ated by all ranks, and eagerly followed by a numerous class, both high and low, rich and poor, from the nobleman with his hundreds of carefully bred and carefully treated birds to the peasant with his one favourite, proudly strutting before his thatched cottage. Boys at nearly all public schools were brought up and initiated into all the mysteries of cock-fighting. Clergymen of our national religion, when the offices of minister of the Church and school teacher were combined, frequently officiated as high priests at the Shrovetide gatherings, nay, made the practice a means to increase their stipends. Most towns had their annual mains of two, three, or four days' fighting. County was arrayed against county, or district against district, sometimes for extravagant sums. Most villages, parti-cularly throughout the northern part of the kingdom, had their Shrovetide cockfights, when mains and single matches were fought. A main might consist of any un-even number of birds agreed upon ; a match, of two birds. The stakes might be in the main, say £1 in each battle, £10 the main, the result of the latter being governed by a majority of wins. Schools throughout all parts of the country had their 'captain matches,' a ridiculous and senseless arrange-ment, which yearly brought into existence hundreds of youthful cockers. Masters and pupils were often more conversant with the points, qualities and colours of cocks than with grammar or arithmetic.

Farmers throughout the country were be-sieged with solicitations and offers of remun-eration varying from 2s. 6d. to 4s. a year for 'cock walks.' Huts too might often be seen dotted over fields erected purposely for 'walks.'

A popular nobleman in the southern part of Lancashire had hundreds of game-cocks out at walk at the same time, and it was quite a usual thing with him to have a clause inserted in his farm leases stating that the tenant must walk a game-cock for his lordship, just as in many parts of the country nowadays tenants are often required to walk puppies for the master of the hounds hunting the district.

A singular illustration of school fights in the neighbourhood of Carlisle is afforded by a donation made by a Mr. Graham of a silver bell, weighing 2 ounces, upon which is engraved 'Wrey Chapple 1665,' to be fought for annually on Shrove Tuesday by cocks. About three weeks previous to the eventful day the boys assembled and selected as their captains two of their schoolfellows whose parents were willing to bear the expenses incurred in the forthcoming contests. After an early dinner on Shrove Tuesday the two captains, attended by their friends and schoolfellows, who were distinguished by blue and red ribbons, marched in procession from their respective homes to the village green, where each produced three cocks, and the bell was appended to the hat of the victor, in which manner it was handed down from one successful captain to another.

In 1836 the cockfighting of Wreay was put down by the Rev. R. Jackson, and superseded by a 'hunt,' which from the first obtained a degree of celebrity to which the 'captain battles' never had any pretension. For some time after cockfighting was nominally put down it still went on, and usually took place while the hunt was in progress, and wrestling and other games were held. Schools in adjoining villages had holiday for 'Wreay hunt.' At the present time there are the ordinary village sports at Wreay, and there may be a 'hound trail'; but for hunting the district is dependent upon neighbouring packs. The 'Wreay bell' has been lost for some twenty-five years, and all efforts to trace this interesting relic have failed. When won at the Shrove Tuesday cockfights the owner usually allowed it to be kept at the village inn, and the probability is that it has been stolen.

At Sedburgh School an annual payment of a guinea was made by each pupil to the master for 'cock money.' Scholars at the Penrith Grammar School also paid 'cock money' annually, and indeed the practice obtained in many schools in the north.

There were unfortunately many instances of cockfighting a great deal more deplorable than village school fights at Shrovetide. In most of the secluded dales the clergymen, from their connection with the schools, were the principal abettors of cockfighting. Drinking was a regular accompaniment of rural cocking, and the two bad practices combined tended to destroy the usefulness of Church ministers in districts which required better teaching and example. A cockpit was formerly connected with Bromfield Church, near Wigton, where cockfighting was frequently carried on after church service on Sundays, with what effect on the congregation we may imagine.

The late Chancellor Ferguson, in an article on 'Cockfighting' in the *Transactions of the Cumberland and Westmorland Antiquarian and Archæological Society* (ix. 366–82), writes : 'It is possible that the "gentlemen of the sod" who fought their mains on Sunday in a churchyard cock-pit may have had some qualms of conscience to gulp down ; if any such existed at Alston in Cumberland, the old maxim of the end justifying the means would be used for their alleviation, for there was " an endowed grammar school, rebuilt in 1828, among the holiday sports of which in the olden time was that of a main of fighting cocks for a prayer-book at Easter. Some of the books thus won are yet in possession of some of the surviving scholars." ' The Chancellor further says that this Sunday cocking was not peculiar to the north of England.

It is related of a certain sporting parson that while dozing in his pulpit during a collection he suddenly woke up, and cried out in a voice loud enough to be heard by the whole congregation, 'I'll back t' black cock—black cock a guinea—damn me ! '

But keen as was the interest in school fights and local mains the more important mains were mostly fought in towns, and drew large and sometimes fashionable crowds. Cocks intended to fight in a main, say at Liverpool, Carlisle, Penrith, or Ulverston, were usually weighed, matched, and their colours and marks taken down three days before fighting. Occasionally they weighed and fought off the scale. This mode of procedure was however exceptional. The 'main' was sometimes only a day's fight, but generally lasted three or four. By mutual agreement each contending party was bound to weigh-in a certain specified number of birds, thirty or forty for three or four days' fighting. The weight agreed upon would be mostly from about 3 lb. 14 oz. to 5 lb. 4 or 6 oz., and the contracting parties must weigh the whole number of birds they agree to fight within the specified weight. Those of equal weight were appointed to contend against each other, and 1 or 2 oz. difference in weight according to agreement was not a hindrance to their being 'main' battles. When a greater difference in weight occurred they were termed 'bye' battles. Entrance to the cockpit was charged pretty high in order that the receipts might realize something towards the expenses and keep out the 'rough' element. The distinctive marks and colours of each cock after being weighed were entered in a book with so much particularity as almost to render it impossible to substitute another in place of the one whose description was recorded. The book was produced when the cocks were brought into the pit ready and eager for action. For seven or eight days before the cocks were weighed they were subjected to a course of physicking and spare regimen. They were sparred amongst thickly strewn straw with 'muffles' on in place of gloves, tied over their shortened spurs to prevent injury ; about two or three sparrings were usually given in the course of their training. This not only got them into practice and improved their wind, but also rendered them eager, so that they would commence fighting at once on being put down, since in a match a cock that walked round his opponent and crowed would probably be struck by the other cock before he had begun fighting. Too much sparring had a contrary effect, and would destroy their courage. These proceedings were watched by the experienced feeder with the greatest care, and were intended to clean out and purify the system, and to reduce the weight of each bird as much as was thought prudent prior to strong food being given. Some feeders and trainers reduced their cocks more than others, and in consequence were enabled when pitted against their opponents to show a bigger looking bird. This system without great care and judgment was liable to be attended with bad consequences. Full strength and vigour—fighting pitch—could not be got up before fighting time, and the battle was sometimes thus sacrificed through want of stamina. After weighing, instruction and description duly registered, they were hurried from the weighing room to their own numbered pen, and served with a most generous and nourishing feed. This first good meal since being penned consisted of fresh warm new milk and 'cock loaf,' a rich bread made with great care from fine flour, eggs, milk, sugar, and sometimes a few currants thrown in. After this first meal the feeding was continued with the same prepared bread, whites of eggs, barley sugar, and many curious compounds which the feeder might think requisite. Great attention was paid to cleanliness and having the straw in their pens changed constantly. The skill and judgment of the feeder had to be continually on the alert during the preparation and feeding for the important day of battle. Some hardy constitutioned thriving birds will jump up into condition much more readily than others, and have to be fed accordingly ; indeed each bird in the pen required careful watching, no two being treated exactly alike. It was astonishing how readily a well walked, sound constitutioned pen of two-year-old cocks recovered and gained flesh after a violent reducing process when they came to have good feed at regular intervals. Successful feeding, the making the cock fight cool, right in his wind, ready with the spur, and to wear well could not be achieved without much study and long experience. The success too must be on at the right time, for it is a well-known fact that the cocks only remained in full and complete fighting trim for a few hours. At noon they might be capable of splitting a thread, and in four hours unable, in cocking phraseology, to 'hit a pair o' barn doors.'

As an instance of the hold that cockfighting had over educated men it may be mentioned that one of its most enthusiastic followers was John Wilson, sometime Professor at Edinburgh. Before his drawing-room at Elleray was completed there was a main fought in it, a pit being fitted up with sods from the adjacent ground.

A match which illustrates this question of management was the big meeting at Chester, when an Ulverston gentleman met a party of Chester gentlemen for £50 a battle and £1,000 the main. The Ulverston man took with him some of the finest cocks ever put down in a pit. One half were black red beezers bred by a Mr. Robert Towers of Force Forge in High Furness. Their splendid condition made the fight a one-sided affair. At the end of four days' fighting the Ulverston gentleman retired from the pit with a majority of sixteen in his favour, and returned home the winner of a very large sum.

The scene at any of the more important meetings was usually most exciting. The pit erected for the purpose had every convenience for a numerous body of spectators and was generally excessively crowded. The betting amongst such a host of spectators, almost all betting men, was astounding ; thousands of pounds changed hands at the conclusion of each match. Notwithstanding the immense amount of betting, disputes seldom occurred, and if a disagreement did arise, a summary settlement was soon effected by the appointment of a referee in whose judgment both parties had confidence. A defaulter rarely appeared in the numerous assembly. The loud bawling of anxious bettors, the frantic efforts to get on the odds or hedge previous bets, as the advantage in fighting swayed from one to the other of the panting and exhausted birds, was deafening. Most of our readers probably do not know what 'poundage' means. It is a bet when taken up of £10 to 5s. If not taken up before forty is deliberately counted, the match is concluded in favour of the cock backed at such long odds. The offer of such a striking difference—£10 to a crown—is generally resorted to for the purpose of bringing a battle to an end. A betting man named Clarke—a small tradesman and one of the yeoman class, residing at Broughton, a small market town on the confines of west Cumberland and north Lancashire—used to win the 'poundage' about once every season for a great number of years. He probably won the long odds oftener than any other betting man in the habit of attending cockfights. But he was such a judge as was seldom met with. He had, owing to his acumen, a singularly successful career in the betting arena. He could detect what is termed a 'throat' in its earliest stages with remarkable celerity and certainty. A 'throat' is inflicted by and arises from a deep body blow. The unfortunate recipient of the deadly stab bleeds internally, and in a majority of cases soon after the infliction of the wound dies. In most cases when the effects of the blow are fully developed there is a loud ruckling in the throat and attempts to void the blood. The serious nature of the injury is then quite plain even to a novice. All cocks immediately after receiving the blow may be seen by a close observer to draw in the neck and make a gasp as if for breath. Mr. Clarke being quick to see the fatal signal would frequently get on a round sum before it was noticed by others. He would often drop on a half awake bettor when a cock was knocked down and deprived of the use of its legs. There is a great difference in the condition of a bird when the legs are stretched out stiff and when they can yet be drawn under the body. In the former state it is all 'up,' but in the latter, when the legs are not quite useless, a vicious cock will occasionally administer a blow that seals the fate of its standing antagonist. A thoroughly good judge like Mr. Clarke was alive to these and other important indications which will frequently occur during the progress of a pro-

tracted fight. Mr. Clarke had at one time a breed of game cocks which, judging from appearances, seemed to be without any perceptible fault. They were thoroughly true game—stood cutting up without any flinching whatever; but were unable to inflict any return injury on their adversary. They were tried time after time, and invariably lost. It did not matter who the feeder was, the upshot was always the same. Ten or a dozen were thus sacrificed before it was discovered or surmised that they had no proper fighting leg action. They could not in striking get their legs apart so as to make the blow have any damaging effect. After so signally failing in brown reds Mr. Clarke tried a breed of white game, and they turned out exceedingly well, in fact were thoroughly determined game, wary scientific fighters, quick and sure with their spurs, and with no end of endurance.

The big cockfights were usually an accompaniment to the race meetings at the larger towns. Ulverston without the attraction of a race meeting could keep up with éclat its annual three days' cockfighting on a raised pit in the large assembly room. The opposing party to the Ulverstonians was generally a Mr. Benn, a celebrated breeder in west Cumberland, and a few friends. For generations the name of Benn appeared in the annals of northern cockfighting. The Mr. Benn alluded to as an opponent to the Ulverston gentlemen resided at Middleton Place near Bootle, and for a quarter of a century bred some of the best game cocks in the kingdom. His brown reds—well known and feared throughout a wide district—were big slashing muscular hard-feathered birds, capable at any time of worrying a moderate antagonist and by their prowess occupying a conspicuous position in the Ulverston and other mains. Previous to breeding brown reds, Mr. Benn had for three or four years a lot of beautiful-looking, gay-plumaged birds. They were white with yellow or straw-coloured saddles. When in tip-top condition, eyes bright, sparkling, and feathers shining like silver, they made a showy, slashing fight, hitting whenever they lifted a leg, but if ever so little off fighting pitch, they were not to be dreaded. A gentleman, looking admiringly at one of his black reds just about to be set down to engage its white and yellow foe, exclaimed, 'Yan'l see my cock will strip every feather off the white one's back,' and sure enough in a short time the surface of the pit was strewn with white feathers. To illustrate the amazing power there is in the stroke of a gamecock, we may remark that one of those white and yellow birds sent its spur clean through a deal board three quarters of an inch thick, that formed an edging to the raised pit. The following is a return of the last main fought at Ulverston in 1828. By advertisement it was announced that 'a grand main of cocks was to be fought at Ulverston on the twenty-ninth, thirtieth and thirty-first of May between the gentlemen of Lancashire and Cumberland. William Woodcock feeder for Lancashire and Addison for Cumberland. A pair of cocks to be in the pit each day at ten o'clock.' The fighting took place in the forenoon and afternoon of each day, and was decided as follows :—

	Woodcock Main Byes	Addison Main Byes
Thursday forenoon	4 – 1	2 – 0
„ afternoon	3 – 0	3 – 0
Friday forenoon	5 – 0	1 – 1
„ afternoon	3 – 1	3 – 0
Saturday forenoon	4 – 0	2 – 1
„ afternoon	3 – 1	3 – 0
	22 – 3	14 – 2

The superior training of Woodcock's birds gave them a decisive victory.

At the time that this main was fought, cockfighting was at its height in Ulverston and the neighbourhood comprised in all that large district known as Lonsdale north of the Sands.

Besides the Shrovetide fighting in Lonsdale North, open mains for stakes varying in amount from £1 to £2 were fought at Dalton, Kirkby Lonsdale, Bouth, Arrad-Foot, etc. Nearly every village in fact had its annual 'open main.' Within a circumference of ten miles round Ulverston thousands of cocks must have been slaughtered yearly. Arrad-Foot, two miles from Ulverston, was the most celebrated of these local meetings. From 80 to 100 cocks were penned in the early part of February and prepared for fighting. The feeders most in request were Askew, Redhead and Braithwaite, all three men of considerable ability and skill in bringing out cocks in fighting condition. Redhead in one main against Askew made a consecutive winning run of thirteen. We are not aware that such a long unbroken run has been paralleled. No feeder that ever pitted a cock could make his birds kill quicker than Redhead. It was marvellous how quickly they could take away life. They appeared to be fighting quite easily. No loud crack with the wings— almost noiseless, in fact—but sure after two or three meets to stretch out their adversary if not stone dead yet in the throes of death. At Whitsuntide, on the race day at Arrad-Foot, a 'stag main' was for several

years fought. The parties to the meeting were gentlemen of Hawkshead *versus* Ulverston, Redhead feeder for the latter and Nash the former. The fighting was in a large empty barn on a raised pit. This meeting attained great popularity and drew together a numerous assemblage of sporting characters.

The *Carlisle Patriot* by advertisement announced a long main of cocks to be fought at Aspatria on 17, 18, 19 and 20 March, 1819, between the gentlemen of Abbey Holme and the gentlemen of Carlisle, for 5 guineas a battle and 50 guineas the main, Glaister feeder for Abbey Holme and Kirk for Carlisle. The result of this great fight was as follows: —

	Kirk Main Byes	Glaister Main Byes
First day	5 – 0	8 – 2
Second day	7 – 1	6 – 1
Third day	8 – 2	5 – 0
Fourth day	8 – 0	4 – 0
	28 – 3	23 – 3

It will be seen from the above that Carlisle came off victorious by five in the main.

The late Chancellor Ferguson, in his article on cockfighting in the *Transactions of the Cumberland and Westmorland Antiquarian and Archæological Society*, writes : ' It is said that the Earl of Surrey and Sir James Lowther, in 1785, erected the cockpit, which up to 1876 stood in a court on the west side of Lowther Street, Carlisle. At that time these two eminent personages were quarrelling over Carlisle elections as bitterly as they could, and their combining to do anything is very odd ; probably they each gave a handsome subscription by way of influencing the cock-fighting interest at some election. Mr. Fisher of Bank Street, Carlisle, possesses a picture of it in oils painted by H. St. Clair in 1873, and an interesting model to scale by Bellamy. It was octagonal, 40 feet in diameter, the walls 12 feet high, and it was 45 feet in height to top of the octagonal roof. In 1829 it was occupied by Messrs. Burgess & Hayton as a brass and iron foundry, and afterwards was well known as 'Dand's smithy.' It is now a portion of the premises occupied by a cabinet maker. It rose to be, and continued for a long series of years, a most attractive gathering place, and much more aristocratic in its character than any other in the county. The most distinguished individuals who honoured the Carlisle meetings with their patronage and presence were the Duke of Norfolk and the Earl of Derby. The first main we can glean any account of in the Carlisle pit was a sixteen cock main in 1804. It was a hard contested fight, and won by a cock belonging to 'humpy back't Thompson.' An important main came off at Stanwix, Carlisle, on Tuesday and Wednesday, 29 and 30 March, 1828. The feeders engaged for the occasion were Russell and Newton. This great contest, for 20 guineas a battle, was got up by the gentlemen of east Cumberland against those of the western part of the county. Russell fed for the west, and was victorious at the conclusion of the fighting by three main battles. The weighing in had not been very even, for several matches fell into byes, which were in most instances won by Russell. The gentlemen of east and west Cumberland had another meeting at Oulton near Wigton on 6, 7 and 8 April, 1836. According to the advertisement in the *Carlisle Journal*, the stake amounted to £50 the main and £2 a battle. The eastern gentlemen, fully determined if possible to retrieve their laurels, engaged a celebrated feeder from the southern part of the kingdom named Weightman. The western were fortunate in securing the services of the rising feeder Brough. The main was fought out with the bitterest determination. Brough, speaking of the fighting afterwards, said, 'Fwok sed 'et Weetman was niver bet afoor, but I dud gin 'im a dressing.' Soon after this main, signs that this public cockfighting was tottering to its fall began to manifest themselves. In the year following the Oulton meeting, Isaac Armstrong of Powhill was sent to the house of correction at Carlisle by J. Dand, Esq., for fourteen days with hard labour 'for aiding and assisting in a fighting of cocks at Kirkbride in March.' The editor of a Carlisle paper expressed a hope that this example would be the means of putting an end to the cruel and demoralizing practice of cockfighting, which had so long prevailed in many of the country towns of Cumberland.

While cockfighting was rife, and for many years before it was suppressed, there were throughout Cumberland, Westmorland and north Lancashire numerous cockfighting contests called 'bull fights.' At that time bull beef was not so good or tender or so readily saleable as the three or four year old highly bred shorthorns of the present day. The old English long horned breed of bulls six or seven years of age were a tough lot and difficult to dispose of, even in the then scantily supplied meat markets. A rump steak ever so carefully cooked required strong jaws and sound teeth to masticate it. Farmers therefore resorted to the popular announcement of cockfighting to turn the carcass into pounds, shillings and pence. Their friends and neighbours were invited to enter the cocks, match them, and fight for the bull beef cut into half quarters. The price put on was generally a trifle over market value. By this means farmers were enabled to realize something more than the threepence per pound which butchers could afford to give in those days.

From all information that can be gathered, Kirk the publican and Russell seem to have been by far the most popular and successful feeders in Cumberland in the early part of the last century, as Brough and Bailey were at a later period. Brough and Bailey were the last two of the celebrated Cumberland feeders, and may be classed as equals to the Potters, Gillivers, Hines and Woodcocks of southern fame. Brough—originally a pupil of Glaister, who lived near Abbey Holme—was in great request as a feeder. He had frequently engagements in London, Newmarket, Birmingham, Staleybridge, Manchester, Glasgow and other places. In Brough's various encounters at the places we have mentioned his skill and experience in a majority of instances brought him off victor. He always set his birds himself, and would not allow any one else to act for him in this way. In the eighteenth century it was usual for the same persons to feed the cocks and set them in a contest; afterwards the tendency was for the professions of 'feeders' and 'setters' to become distinct; women were sometimes 'feeders.' When a man set his own birds of course he had to have an assistant to bring them to him in the pit. A Carlisle man whose real name was Carruthers, but better known locally as 'Dick the Daisy,' had a great reputation for many years for setting cocks or acting as 'pitter' at a main. He was reckoned one of the best men of his day in this capacity, and was often engaged months beforehand by the principals in a match.

In 1846 a main was fought at the Dandie Dinmont without much pretence of concealment, a coach and four taking the sportsmen out from Carlisle. 'Dick the Daisy' was one of the setters on that occasion. 'Within the last twenty years a gentleman in Carlisle, now dead, kept his cocks in a sodded attic in his house, and fought them within the city.' A friend of the writer tells him that cockfighting was carried on in various parts of Carlisle till quite recently, and that he remembered a large room above an hotel in Scotch Street into which cartloads of turves were taken and laid on the floor for the purposes of cockfighting. In the *Carlisle Journal* of 17 April, 1868, the following obituary notice appeared : 'In this city on the 11th inst., Mr. Richard Bailey, the celebrated cock-feeder, at the ripe age of 77 years.'[1]

When Dick died his admirers subscribed and put up a monument to him in Carlisle cemetery, on which were graven the tools of his art, a pair of cock-spurs. It is to be regretted that this interesting tomb has been defaced and the spurs taken off.

Cockfighting was carried on openly for many years in the surrounding villages after it was given up in Carlisle itself. At Thurstonfield the annual cockfight took place openly on Carlin Saturday (a fortnight before Easter); at Great Orton Easter Monday was the day, and Moorhouse also had its annual day. Among the noted breeds remembered in Cumberland are the 'Jean's my darling,' formerly kept by the Wills of Burgh; the 'Birchin Greys,' formerly kept by Adam Honnam of Cobble Hall; the 'Robespierres,' kept by the Riggs of Moorhouse—a bird which used to fight about 6 lb. and which was never known to flinch. Brough, speaking of a breed they had at Abbey Holme, says they were the best he ever saw or knew. They were hardly ever beaten. He would often point proudly to a stuffed hen of this famous breed, called 'Daisy,' which hung on his cottage wall. All bred from this hen were prize winners except in one single instance. Brough had also a breed of white cocks; twenty out of twenty-three proved winners of first class prizes.

At Dalston near Carlisle there existed a famous and highly successful breed known as 'black-reds,' and the Dalstonians are to this day called 'black-reeds.' It is a proverbial saying with them, 'While I live I'll craw.'

For two years a breed of singular fighters were in the neighbourhood of Dalton bred by Mr. William Simpson, Pennington Mill. They were a good hard-feathered black-red with tawny saddle. On being set down to fight, instead of 'setting to' face to face they always made a wheel at 3 or 4 yards distance, and swooping down on their opponents caught them on the broad side a shooting blow. If not successful at the first attempt the same manœuvre would be repeated till a crippler was dealt, and then they would finish off in front. We have alluded to Mr. Clarke's breed that were unable to use their

legs with any effect, and we have another instance of a breed that could but wouldn't fight. J. Woodburn, Esq., Thurstan Ville near Ulverston, had the trouble of rearing a breed of muffed game-cocks. They were true unflinching game—good shaped and feathered, quite likely to turn out fighters, but when pitted would only jump up and down without striking out a blow, and in this manner would suffer cutting up without flinching. A correspondent writes: ' Of men of repute as "pitters" memory recalls the following names: John and Edward Bivens, Thomas Coupland, William Kendall, T. Chapman, Thomas Seward, Robert Steel, Bell Burton, William Duke, John Dymond, Myles Butcher, John Johnson and Richard Gelderd, the latter the owner of one of the biggest game-cocks we remember. He was named "Ben Caunt," after the professional prize-fighter, and he went through many battles before he met his fate.' Ben's dead weight was 9 pounds, and my informant ' had a share in his eating.' A gamecock that had been fed for fighting and fallen in battle was considered a great luxury, and no breed of fowls excels them for the table, the flesh being beautifully white, short in fibre, and extremely delicate.

A proof that in Cumberland the old connection between education and cockfighting is not wholly severed is found in the fact that the seal of the Dalston School Board displays a fighting-cock, a Dalston 'black-red,' in the act of crowing, though unfortunately they have omitted to add the motto 'Dum spiro cano,' or the still more appropriate and ringing one 'While I live I'll crow,' both of which were suggested, we understand.

An old 'setter' well known in the north remarked to the writer in the course of conversation that he had no preference in colour. He had handled black-reds, bright-reds, piles, and the white one above mentioned, and found good and game birds in all. He thought it a great pity that the sport was dying out, for we had no substitute to show to the rising generation in what real pluck, courage, stamina and endurance really consisted. In gamecocks all these existed in the greatest perfection, and he thought no man could prove a coward after seeing how game-cocks acquitted themselves.

[1] A friend of the writer has spoken lately to Mr. Tyson of Grinsdale who remembers Bailey, and has seen him 'pit' cocks. He says nothing pleased Dick Bailey better than this. He became so excited when a bird was fighting that he would follow

the strokes with his fists, imitating the actions of the bird. If there were any feathers in the mouth he would blow them out, as it was against the rule to pick them out with the hands.

WRESTLING

In the north, up to within quite recent years, wrestling formed a part of almost every youth's education. None but those who have attended such wrestling rings as Carlisle or Grasmere can realize with what enthusiasm the sport is regarded in the Border counties.

In writing of wrestlers and wrestling it is proposed to confine the account mainly to doings which are within the memory of those now living. The sport is of course a very old one, but there are few evidences from which to construct its early history.

It seems strange that a harmless sport like wrestling should have ever been looked upon with disfavour by a considerable portion of the community and classed with sports like bull-baiting and cockfighting; but that this was so in the time of the Puritan, the following curious extract will abundantly testify. It is quoted from ' *The Agreement of the Associated Ministers and Churches of the Counties of Cumberland and Westmorland.* London : Printed by T. L. for Simon Waterson, and are sold at the sign of the Globe in Paul's Churchyard, and by Richard Scot, Bookseller in Carlisle 1656 ' :—

All scandalous persons hereafter mentioned are to be suspended from the Sacrament of the Lord's Supper, this is to say—any person that shall upon the Lord's Day use any dancing, playing at dice, or cards, or any other game, masking, wakes, shooting, playing, playing at football, stool ball, Wrestling : or that shall make resort to any Playes, interludes, fencing, bull baiting, bear baiting : or that shall use hawking, hunting, or coursing, fishing or fowling : or that shall publikely expose any wares to sale otherwise than is provided by an Ordinance of Parliament of the sixth of April 1649. These Counties of Cumberland and Westmorland have been hitherto as a Proverb and a by-word in respect of ignorance and prophaneness : Men were ready to say to them as the Jews of Nazareth, can any good thing come out of them.

Early in the last century back-hold wrestling was more practised and held in higher estimation in the borders of Cumberland, Westmorland and Northumberland than in any other place in England or Scotland. Almost every village had its annual wrestling competition, wherein the prizes consisted chiefly of belts, sometimes of silver cups, leather breeches and so forth. Gradually scientific methods came to be introduced, and it is urged by many that this has tended to increase the system of ' barneying.' No doubt this, however deplorable, is true to a certain extent in spite of the vigilance of competent judges.

Among the most celebrated places for wrestling meetings in the past was Melmerby, one of the best types of fellside villages in Cumberland. For a century, and probably much longer, Melmerby commenced its annual two days' sports on old Midsummer day—that is, on 5 July. The wrestling took place on that part of the green known as the cockpit, where many a doughty champion has been sent sprawling at full length on his back. Although the amount given in prizes was small, the entry of names was always large,. from sixty to seventy being the average number, while more than fourscore men have contended at various times. By being held at the season of the year when the days were longest Melmerby Rounds were invariably attended by vast concourses of spectators. The Alstonians used to muster remarkably strong, the miners and others coming over Hartside in considerable droves from that town and from the neighbouring villages of Nenthead and Garrigill Gates. So great became the celebrity of the Melmerby ring that first-rate wrestlers have frequently travelled as far as thirty and forty miles to throw and be thrown upon its village green. Buying and selling was a thing unknown. One friend might give way to another sometimes, but as a rule it was purely the honour of becoming victor for the time being that stimulated the competitors. Owing to the establishment of spring and ' back-end ' fairs in the village for the sale of cattle, sheep, etc., it was thought better to abolish the annual rounds. Accordingly this ancient gathering came to an end about the year 1850.

Langwathby, also a typical ·Cumberland village like its twin sister Melmerby, was another great centre for wrestling. The Langwathby Rounds, unlike those at Melmerby, were held annually in winter, on New Year's Day and the day following. Yeomen, farmers and husbandmen from the neighbouring hamlets were the principal ·competitors. The sports took place, as a rule, in a field close to the village, which belongs to Mr. John Hodgson ; but on some few occasions they were held on the opposite or western side of the river Eden. The prizes given were of small value but great honour. During the early part of the last century a narrow leathern belt of meagre appearance or a pair of buckskin breeches was almost the only trophy given for wrestling. In the year 1816, when James Robinson won, a couple of guineas was the full amount offered, and this sum, we suppose, was never exceeded till many years after. The Langwathby Rounds continued to flourish as long as they were almost entirely confined to the villagers and the rural population. But when the meetings became larger, owing to the increased value of the prizes offered, they were gradually swamped by unruly characters from the towns, and finally had to be given up about the year 1870.

It may be interesting to notice here a curious and remarkable old custom at which, towards the latter end of the eighteenth century and the early part of the nineteenth, wrestlings and a variety of other sports were much patronized. The celebration of bridewains or bidden weddings was extremely popular in Cumberland. All the people of the country side were invited. For the amusement of the spectators assembled prizes were given for sports of various kinds, as will be found described in the graphic dialect poem of John Stagg, the blind bard :—

Some for a par o' mittens loup't,
Some wrustl'd for a belt :
Some play'd at pennice-steans for brass :
And some amaist gat fell't :
Hitch-step-an-loup some tried for spwort,
Wi' many a sair exertion :
Others for bits o' 'bacca gurn'd,
An sec like daft devarshon
Put owre that day.

If any reader wishes for a full description of the various incidents and details connected with this old wedding custom, he is recommended to consult Stagg's poem of 'The Bridewain,' from which the preceding lines are quoted. The people of the district were generally invited to these weddings by public advertisement, specimens of which still exist in the files of one or two of the earliest local newspapers.

Ancient sports were formerly held upon Stone Carr near Greystoke. They existed for many years previous to 1787, and a leathern belt was the usual prize for wrestling. The Sunday following victory, the champion might be seen marching to church decorated with the belt, and on the Sunday following, showing off at another neighbouring church.

Early in the last century there still used to be held meetings on 10 July on the top of High Street, a mountain near Haweswater in Westmorland. It was customary on that day for the shepherds of the mountain sheep farms to hand over to the rightful owners the stray sheep they had collected. After this business had been gone through, a dinner was set out, and then commenced wrestling and other sports. These meetings were discontinued about sixty or seventy years ago.

Previous to the year 1809 the wrestling in the vicinity of Ambleside and throughout the Lake circuit in general was considered very inferior to that usually witnessed about Penrith and the greater part of Cumberland. It was probably through a laudable desire to remedy this deficiency and to bring this manly exercise into more general estimation that Professor Wilson, then residing at Elleray, who was devoted to athletic amusements through a conviction of their utility, by his own liberality and example promoted the donation of a larger sum of money to wrestle for at the annual sports, near Ambleside in the year 1809, than had ever been known at any preceding period in that part of Westmorland. Among the competitors for this liberal prize was Thomas Nicholson of Threlkeld in Cumberland, who afterwards attained such distinction at Carlisle. Nicholson was the winner of this prize, throwing a distinguished wrestler of the name of Dixon and the two well known wrestlers Rowland and John Long. Owing however to the introduction of evil practices, wrestling in the Windermere district has completely disappeared.

It was followed in the days of its prosperity rather in an amateur than a professional spirit. This is particularly exhibited in the case of Jonathan Rodgers, who, after many local successes and other more important ones against such men as Joseph Parker of Crooklands and Richard Chapman of Patterdale, gave up wrestling and became the respected and prosperous tenant farmer of Brothereldkeld, his birthplace, in the vale of Eskdale.

After the resuscitation of the Ambleside wrestlings by Mr. Wilson in 1809 it is somewhat remarkable to note the large number of first-rate lake-side wrestlers that came out ; and it may not be amiss to bestow a passing notice on the foremost. The celebrated Windermere champion, John Barrow, flourished in the wrestling ring in the early part of the last century. William Litt, the author of *Wrestliana*—one whose judgment may be relied on—pays him a deserved compliment when he rates him as 'the most renowned wrestler of this period,' and 'a match for any man in the kingdom.' He stood fully six feet and weighed fourteen stone. His favourite chip was the inside stroke—indeed it was generally considered he invented the inside chip, and that William Richardson of Caldbeck in Cumberland, better known locally as 'Belted Will,' got it from Barrow. Most assuredly the pair grassed scores with it, and were quite as clever as Adam Dodd, who won for many years in succession at Langwathby, was with the outside stroke. After Barrow, Miles and James Dixon of Grasmere were the prominent men about Windermere. Before the Dixons had retired the two Longs —Rowland, commonly called Roan, and John, the one a giant in size and strength and the other a big burly man—figured in the ring; then, most renowned, in the galaxy, William Wilson of Ambleside. When full grown he was quite six feet four inches high, straight, and as lithe as a willow wand, and at twenty-two he weighed from fourteen to fifteen stone, with a good reach of arm and a finely developed muscular frame. As a hyper, or 'inside striker' as Litt calls him, he displayed superb form. For three or four years he stood unmatched and irresistible in this particular stroke, and since his day no man has appeared worth calling a rival to him except William Jackson of Kinneyside.

In 1818 he and Tom Richardson showed some remarkably good play in the ring at Keswick, which for a time was justly entitled to be considered the most important wrestling gathering in the north. Wilson gathered his men quickly and cleanly, and threw them as fast as he came to them. Coming against Richardson in the final fall, he lifted him from the ground with the intention of hyping, but failing to hold his man firmly, Tom turned in, and after a considerable struggle managed to bring him over with the buttock. After this tussle Wilson always spoke of Richardson as being 'swineback't,' meaning thereby that his back was extremely slippery and difficult to hold from the nature of its peculiar roundness.

Wilson again attended the Keswick gathering in 1819, and it proved memorable above all others in his wrestling career. Although he did not succeed in winning the chief prize this year, he nevertheless distinguished himself ten times more than the victor who did by throwing the man with whom no one else had the shadow of a chance. We refer to his struggle with John McLaughlan of Dovenby, more than two inches taller than Wilson, and at that time five or six stones heavier. As a prelude to this fall 'Clattan' (the name McLaughlan was commonly known by) took hold of Wilson in the middle of the ring in a good natured sort of way and lifted him up in his arms to show how easily he could hold him. No sooner was he set down than Wilson threw his arms around Clattan's waist and lifted him in precisely the same way, a course of procedure which greatly amused the spectators. After these preliminaries had been gone through, the two men were not long in settling into holds, each having full confidence in his own powers and his own mode of attack. A few seconds however decided the struggle of these two modern Titans. No sooner had each one gripped his fellow than, quick as thought, Wilson lifted Clattan from the ground in grand style and hyped him with the greatest apparent ease, a feat that no other man in Britain could have done. This fall is still talked of at the firesides of the dalesmen of the north—cottars, farmers and 'statesmen' —as one of the most wonderful and dazzling achievements ever witnessed in the wrestling ring. As will be seen below, McLaughlin was only beaten in the final round so late as 1828.

Returning to the next Keswick meeting, Wilson found no difficulty in walking through the ranks of 1820. Here he met William Richardson, 'Belted Will' of Caldbeck, in the final round and threw him with ease. Litt says 'Richardson had not the shadow of a chance with him.' This testimony is exceedingly significant and says much for Wilson's powers as a wrestler. 'Hoo 'at thoo let him hype the i' that stupid fashion, thoo numb divel, thoo?' said Tom Richardson ('Dyer') reproachfully to the loser of the fall, while the latter was engaged in putting his coat on. 'What, he hes it off, an' that thoo kens as weel as anybody,' was the sturdy reply. 'I cudn't stop him, ner thee nowder, for that matter, if he nobbut gat a fair ho'd o' thee.' So far as we have been able to ascertain, the year 1822 was the last one in which Wilson figured in the ring. If this be correct, his wrestling career will be limited to four or five years' duration at the utmost. No doubt the wasting disease from which he suffeted was the principal cause of his early retirement from a sport which he only regarded as a means of recreation and pastime.

Among other famous lake-side wrestlers were Tom Robinson, the schoolmaster; Richard Chapman, George Donaldson, Joseph Ewebank and Joseph Sargeant, the two last being Haweswater lake-siders; William Jackson, an Ennerdale lake-sider; and Thomas Longmire —men whose names and deeds will be cherished as long as 'wruslin' is a household word in the north. At present there is not one man of note now wrestling on the immediate borders of Windermere, Ulleswater or Derwentwater.

The experiment of giving handsome money prizes, first tried at Ambleside for two years, was followed up at the Carlisle races, where the first annual wrestling on the Swifts took place in the month of September, 1809. The successful establishment of the great northern wrestling meeting was due principally to the endeavours of Mr. Henry Pearson, solicitor, Carlisle. Previous to this period wrestling in the immediate vicinity of Carlisle was in no very great estimation. It was seldom witnessed, and consequently could not be duly appreciated; and it was probably owing to this circumstance that there was not any wrestler of celebrity, either in the city itself or within some miles of it; therefore, notwithstanding the novelty of such an exhibition on the Swifts and the very handsome sum subscribed, the competitors were not usually numerous.

The gentlemen of Penrith, well aware of the universal satisfaction the revival of this truly British amusement had given to all ranks at Carlisle, determined to adopt the same means of increasing the popularity of the ensuing races at that town; and Dr. Pearson, brother to Mr. Pearson of Carlisle, exerting himself in the business, it was attended with corresponding success. As Penrith was deemed a kind of central position between Carlisle and Ambleside, and situated in a much more noted country for wrestling than either of them, the competitors for that prize were more numerous than at the other places.

The wrestling at this meeting seems to have awakened an interest in the sport, for in the following year two purses of gold were offered as prizes, and an immense multitude was drawn to the ring. Thomas Nicholson, the winner of the previous year, whose success at Ambleside has already been mentioned, again won the first prize, and William Richardson of Caldbeck obtained the second. Wrestling had now been fairly set going, and in October, 1811, it was announced that athletic sports in Cumberland were to be revived. A prize of twenty guineas was to be offered, and from the terms of the announcement it would appear that wrestling had formerly been a favourite pastime, but that either from want of money or of wrestlers it had for a time been allowed to decline. Later on we find the sport patronized at Carlisle by the Duke of Norfolk, the Marquis of Queensberry and the Earl of Lonsdale, the buttock and cross-buttock in those days being the favourite 'chips.'

Tom Nicholson owed the high position he attained in the wrestling ring not to overpowering strength and weight, but to what lend the principal charm to back-hold wrestling—science and activity. He stood close upon six feet: lean, muscular, with broad and powerful shoulders; had remarkably long arms, reaching, when at full length and standing perfectly upright, down to his knees. His weight never exceeded thirteen stone. He accidentally dislocated his shoulder in 1812 and thereafter acted as umpire.

From about 1827 to 1840 or so, the interest in wrestling, not only in Carlisle but all over Cumberland and Westmorland, continued to increase; the prizes were more tempting, the entries at the different meetings more numerous, and the scientific attainments of the athletes became more and more apparent, till at Wigton in 1839 the all-weight prize was the largest entry ever known in England, either before or since, there being 256 competitors.

From 1822 up to 1836 the most prominent names in wrestling annals were those of William Cass, John Weightman, George Irving, John McLaughlan, John Liddell, William Robinson of Renwick, T. Richardson, James Little, John Fearon, Robert Watters, Tom Todd, and Joseph Robley of Scarrowmannock, who is credited with being the originator of the swinging hype, a *modus operandi* he used for many years with considerable effect in east Cumberland.

For great size and well proportioned figure, combined with amazing strength and activity, John Weightman was one of the most remarkable men ever bred in Cumberland. Born at Greenhead near Gilsland in 1795, he was brought up at the quiet pastoral village of Hayton near Brampton, where he continued to live until the time of his death. From a physical point of view he was a wonder, being endowed with tremendous bodily strength on the. one hand and the agility of a cat on the other. He stood fully six feet three inches high and weighed from fifteen to sixteen stone. Possessing a good reach of arm and formidable power in the shoulders, he invariably beat his elbows into the ribs of an opponent, which vice-like pressure was so terrific in its results that many strong men were glad to get to the ground in order to escape his punishing hug. Notwithstanding the facility with which prizes might have been gained, it was only on rare occasions that Weightman attended the great annual gathering at Carlisle, and yet he was champion in three different years in the ring there, which speaks volumes for his wrestling powers.

There have been many good men in the north who have not been fortunate enough to win the chief prize at Carlisle though they were second to none in wrestling ability. Such was Tom Todd, who was a most accomplished and scientific wrestler. He could buttock cleanly, hype quickly, and excelled in most other chips. Weighing and watching his opponent's movements narrowly, he seemed to anticipate what was coming and prepared accordingly, both for stopping and chipping. In taking hold, like most good wrestlers, he stood square and upright; but in consequence of having a very peculiarly shaped back, like half a barrel, it was next to impossible to hold him. At the Carlisle meeting of 1822 he made a gallant but unsuccessful struggle to carry off the head prize. Being engaged as a gamekeeper in the service of the Earl of Carlisle on the Naworth estates, he entered himself under the assumed name of 'John Moses of Alston.' Todd distinguished himself much by throwing several dangerous hands, of whom may be specially mentioned John Fearon of Gilcrux, seventeen stone weight; John Liddell of Bothel, a fourteen and a half stone man (winner of the head prize at Keswick a few weeks previously, where he finally disposed of William Cass of Loweswater); and Robert Watters of Carlisle, a light weight, but an accomplished scientific wrestler. In the final fall however with Cass the weight—sixteen stone—and strength of the Loweswater champion proved too much for twelve and a half stone.

Turning to more recent times—times within the recollection of those now living—we find the character of the sport well sustained. Richard Chapman, William Jackson, Robert Gordon, George Donaldson, Thomas Longmire, Robert Atkinson, Joseph Sargeant, Joseph Ewebank, J. Milburn, Jonathan Thomlinson were—although some of the above were really only about eleven stone—a few of the chief competitors for the heavyweight prizes during the next sixteen or eighteen years, while the same period was noted for its long list of accomplished light weights, including Jonathan Whitehead, George Donaldson, Joseph Harrington, Joseph Halliwell, Walter Palmer, John Watters, W. Glaister, Thomas Roper and many others. As far back as 1841 we find old Jack Ivison, who only died recently, winning laurels within the cords. Roper was a fine wrestler, and his winning the celebrated match with Joseph Harrington of Keswick stamped him as one of the best men of his day at his weight. This match for £5, the best of five falls, came off on the morning of 17 October, 1845, at Penrith

and terminated in favour of Roper, who won the first two falls, Harrington the third, and Roper the fourth. Harrington, Halliwell and Ben Cooper were the three best right leg strikers of their day and right side buttockers.

Jonathan Thomlinson of Embleton, who carried off the chief prize at Carlisle in 1834, was just about the same size and weight as his exceedingly clever predecessor and near neighbour, Tom Nicholson. Though he did not occupy as prominent a position in the wrestling world as William Jackson, Dick Chapman, George Donaldson and a few others, he was considered by good judges an exceedingly clever scientific wrestler, and if he had gone about from place to place, week after week and year after year, like many others, we should without doubt have had to credit him with a much larger list of victories.

Those interested in wrestling are probably familiar with the names and exploits of many Bampton scholars. In the latter part of the eighteenth century, Abraham Brown, a Bampton scholar, and one of the most accomplished wrestlers that ever stepped into a ring, invented and brought into practice buttocking, one of the most effective chips a clever wrestler resorts to for bringing down an antagonist. It was a Bampton scholar under twenty years of age who, in 1827, vanquished the herculean Weightman at Penrith. At Bampton, the 'swing' was brought out and made to do surprising execution, and we much doubt if any one has appeared during the last century who could 'swing' so effectively as the Bamptonian, Joseph Sargeant. Another famous Bamptonian was Joseph Ewebank. In height he measured five feet ten inches and a half, and generally stript close upon fourteen stone weight. He was a good all-round wrestler, excelling most particularly with the buttock and striking with the left foot. His demeanour in the ring was quick and unobtrusive; at work without any delay and a determination to win honestly, if at all. This fine old wrestler left a good representative behind him in his son Noble Ewebank, also a Bampton scholar, and still hale and hearty. He was good all round, but perhaps his favourite chips were the hype and striking outside with the right foot. He carried off the chief prize at Carlisle in 1858, and won at many other meetings about this time, often being successful against Richard Wright and William Jameson, who were the most prominent heavy weights of the period. He was a finer wrestler than either, but not so successful against Jameson as against Wright, the fact being that Jameson was too heavy and strong for him, and withal quite as active. He threw Wright at Ulverston, Carlisle, Kendal, Barrow, and five times at Lancaster. Wright only threw Ewebank once, and that was at Jedburgh. Ewebank was also successful at Newcastle, Carlisle, Barrow, and at Lancaster he twice carried away the prizes. He won the prize for the last sixteen standards at Morecambe, and at Liverpool divided the stakes with Longmire.

In the ring on the Swifts, Richard Chapman of Patterdale, the most extraordinary middleweight wrestler that ever existed, gained a distinguished position, not by towering height, not by extraordinary strength and weight, but by sheer force of activity, science and clearsighted shrewdness. When with exulting shouts he was hailed victor at Carlisle in 1833, he was not nineteen years old, weighed no more than twelve stone six pounds and measured five feet ten inches. When the Carlisle wrestling of 1840 was over he had gained the chief prize four times. No one hitherto had attained this proud position.

Robert Gordon of Plumpton, who won the all-weight head prize at Carlisle twice and came second five times, never exceeded five feet ten inches in height, his general wrestling weight being only eleven and a half stone. If there had been in his day eleven stone wrestling he would have had no difficulty in training to the weight provided he could have been induced to change a pair of heavy cloth trousers for the light garments in which wrestlers weigh at the present day. In appearance he was a thin, spare, angular sort of man, carrying very little flesh, big-boned, and remarkably strong about the shoulders and body. His limbs however were so light and shapeless that he never cared to roll his trousers above the calf of his leg. He had a cautious and peculiar way of getting hold, or rather he had a peculiar way of slipping his hold and getting into what he considered a favourite position. This mode consisted in keeping well clear of his opponent, and to wriggle down on one side of him. This he generally effected from possessing vast power in the shoulders and arms, and having such a lithe slippery back that scarcely any one could hold him. His iron grip was so powerful that a short struggle enabled him to attain his object and quietly pull his antagonist over the knee or fairly drag him to the ground. Very few men, or only at odd times, could hinder Gordon from getting them into this fatal position. He rarely lifted his man, but when he did so the fall was mostly an awkward one.

Like Tom Nicholson, Dick Chapman, William Jackson and other celebrated wrestlers, Gordon appears to have been as good

when about twenty years old as during the remaining portion of his career ; and like William Richardson of Caldbeck—' Belted Will '—he was not once thrown in the first year of his public wrestling.

In 1844 at Penrith he wrestled up with Robert Atkinson of Sleagill. Both of the final falls were severely contested, 'Sleagill' viciously gripping and gripping again as if he would squeeze the very life out of his wiry opponent. All however of no avail. He had to succumb twice in succession to an eleven and a half stone man.

At Carlisle in 1846, although not in good feather this year, William Jackson the fouryear champion came again for the express purpose of carrying off the head prize for the fifth time. When drawn against Gordon in the fourth round the latter expressed a desire to give way to his formidable rival without a struggle. His mind quickly changed, however, when told by the umpires ' there would be no money for him at all unless he went into the ring and did his best.' ' Wey ! if that's to be t'game, than I'll russel him ! He can only throw me ! ' In the betting large odds were offered—as much as six to one, and up to ten to one on Kinneyside. Old Will Glen of Calthwaite staked enthusiastically against his neighbour, and seemed much chagrined at finding himself £10 out of pocket by the fall. The men were no sooner in holds than, quick as lightning, Gordon got into his favourite position. Jackson tried hard to neutralize his opponent's tactics by drawing him up, but his utmost efforts were futile. The advantage already gained was used so quickly and effectually that before the champion could effect any change he was literally dragged to the ground in spite of all the efforts used. Immense cheering greeted the fall and for some time a perfect furor raged in all parts of the ring.

On 8 October, 1851, the great match for the wrestling championship of all England and £300 between Jackson and Atkinson took place at the Flan near Ulverston. This event caused a greater sensation in all wrestling circles than any contest on record in the north, and has ever since been a theme of conversation among the natives of Cumberland and Westmorland. The contest came off in a spacious ring lying to the north of the town of Ulverston, in the presence of about 10,000 persons. On the afternoon previous great numbers arrived from London, Liverpool and Manchester, and on the morning of the contest farm servants, farmers' sons and others, on foot, poured into the town from all points. The great majority from Westmorland came by special train. The Cumbrians were taken up by special train at Carlisle and the intermediate stations between that city and Whitehaven. This train, when it left Whitehaven, was swelled to near forty carriages, and was drawn part of the way by three engines, and part by four. Notwithstanding these efforts, it was an hour and a half behind time, and the passengers had difficulty in reaching the wrestling arena (about four miles from the station) in time to see the great match.

One o'clock was the time stated for the two competitors to enter the arena, and shortly after that hour they began to 'peel off.' Atkinson, a native of Sleagill, Westmorland, winner in 1847 of the chief prize at Carlisle, whose weight on this occasion reached about eighteen stone, appeared in excellent condition and full of confidence as to the issue of the contest. His brawny frame and colossal dimensions were a theme of general comment, and elicited expressions of astonishment and wonder from a large number of sporting men, who had congregated to witness the contest. Jackson, as is well known, was a native of Kinneyside, a mountainous district bordering the lake of Ennerdale in Cumberland. He had carried off the head prize for four successive years at Carlisle, and at the numerous other places where he had wrestled he almost invariably came off victorious; but he had retired from the ring several years before this great contest, and there is no doubt he made a mistake, as was said at the time, in again appearing before the public to contend for that which he had before so honorably won—the championship of England. Jackson's appearance in the ring was the signal for the most rapturous cheering. His dignified and manly deportment, his strict integrity and honesty of purpose, and, still more, his previous achievements, had drawn to his standard a numerous host of warm admirers. He weighed about fourteen stone and a half, but the disparity in the bulk of the men was strongly marked when they placed themselves in a position for 'play.' At starting, betting was five to four and £30 to £20 on Jackson for the match, and five to four on the first fall in his favour. The match was the best of five falls. Jackson only gained the second fall, the first, third and fourth, going to Atkinson, who thus became wrestling champion of England.

After William Jackson had retired from wrestling the most prominent man for many years was Thomas Longmire of Troutbeck near Windermere. His wrestling career for public prizes commenced when only seventeen years old. During a week's holiday at

Whitsuntide, wrestling was the absorbing game to be followed. His first belt was won at Crook near Kendal, the second at Flookburgh near Cartmel, the third at Arrad-foot near Ulverston. These winnings at three different places in one week, where he would have to face strong local rings, are sufficient proofs that when only seventeen years old he possessed extraordinary science and strength. Longmire won the chief prize at Carlisle in 1854 and 1855. In the latter year in the final wrestle up he came against the celebrated William Robley of Egremont. It was Cumberland against Westmorland,· and the best man in each county to contend for the championship. The betting round the immense ring—lined nine or ten deep with anxious spectators—ranged five and six to four on Cumberland. They quickly got hold, and soon a loud cheer from thousands proclaimed 'Longmire's won,' a quick resolute back heel having stretched his antagonist on the turf. They had soon hold again, and the Westmorland champion put in one of his grand cross buttocks. Both went to the ground and the umpires amid a storm of disapprobation decided 'a dog fall.' It was the general opinion Longmire ought to have had the fall. He did not attempt to interfere, but stood quiet and collected at the side of the ring, and when called on again stepped in and met the cheer of the multitude with characteristic modesty. In the third attempt, as soon as they had hold the whole of the surging mass all round the immense circle became quiet 'as Billy Watson' lonnin' of a lownd summer neeght,' till the Cumberland representative went down with an admirable outside hype, when a wild scene of congratulation and confusion ensued.

At nearly the close of Longmire's career in 1859, at Lancaster, his old opponent Dick Wright of Longtown turned out to contest the last falls, and parried two attempts with an outside stroke, but got brought to ground with a third attempt. In the second fall the winner resorted to his favourite swing, sent his opponent spinning with great velocity and grassed him. Later in the year they met once more at Talkin Tarn, and Wright again suffered defeat. It may be remarked the fact of so repeatedly overcoming the best Cumbrian in his prime is enhanced, if the reader will bear in mind that Longmire was nearly forty years old, had contested for twenty years in public rings, and was long past the prime of wrestling days. At this same Talkin Tarn entry, before becoming entitled to the head prize, he had to throw Thomas Roper, James Pattinson, William Jameson and

Thomas Kirkup, as well as Dick Wright. Though many people might think otherwise it is a remarkable fact that good wrestlers very rarely hurt one another, and Longmire was no exception to this rule, for in his over twenty years' experience he was never once hurt.

Of the many matches that took place about this period none created more interest than the one for £100 and the championship of the light weights (eleven stone) between Jonathan Whitehead of Workington and Thomas Davidson of Castleside, on 19 August, 1856, at Botchergate, Carlisle. Whitehead, one of the oldest wrestlers in the ring, and one of the most celebrated of his class, was about thirty-seven years of age, five feet nine or ten inches in height, finely proportioned, and had at his command a store of science which few if any of his competitors could equal. Davidson, on the other hand, was comparatively young in years, but had earned for himself a well-merited reputation as a crack wrestler. He was somewhat less in stature than Whitehead, was about twenty-six years of age, and possessed strength, activity, and wrestling capability which it required the utmost exertions of his opponent to overcome. Whitehead, after a struggle lasting rather more than two hours, gained three against Davidson's two falls, and so won the match.

For about a dozen years after Longmire had retired from wrestling, the most prominent men in the Cumberland and Westmorland rings were Richard Wright, Noble Ewebank, William Hawksworth, William Jameson amongst the heavy weights; and in the long list of middle and light weights to the fore as successful competitors during this period, the following were at the top of the tree: James Pattinson, Jim Scott, William Rickerby, Ralph and Tom Powley, Joseph Allison, W. Lawson, W. Park, George Graham, John Graham (of Carlisle), Ben Cooper and Harry Ivison.

Richard Wright of Longtown, during his career of something approaching to twenty years, had but one or two equals in the wrestling ring as a crack heavy-weight wrestler. He was good all round, but his favourite move was a peculiar twist off the chest or breast stroke. There is nothing particularly clever about the manœuvre; the assailant has merely to grasp his man firmly, twist him suddenly to one side and as suddenly to the other; but it requires great development of the chest in order to accomplish it successfully. It is very difficult to meet, and time after time has foiled the best men in England. Wright's career extended from 1855 to 1875, and he succeeded in carrying off the chief prize at Carlisle no less than six times during this period.

In the above list of wrestlers the two most powerful men of their weight were James Pattinson (eleven stone) of Weardale and William Jameson of Penrith. James Pattinson was a marvel; like George Donaldson of a previous generation he had very long arms, reaching well below his knees when standing erect, and so strong was he that it was said he could hold Dick Wright, the champion heavy weight, and that if they had had a match the betting would have been in favour of Pattinson. Noble Ewebank has often said to the writer, 'I dreaded Pattinson as much or more than any man I ivver met in the ring.' When Pattinson contested for the chief prize at Carlisle in 1859, he came against William Hawksworth of Shap in the final wrestle up, one of the strongest heavy men of the day, and won. As to William Jameson, he was one of the most remarkable men, for strength and activity combined, who has appeared to compete for prizes in the wrestling rings of the north. He won the championship at Carlisle no less than five times, and in the opinion of some men who were well able to judge, he could have won for ten years running if he had been so minded, so active and powerful was he, but he was not so keen about winning as his principal opponent, Dick Wright.

On Monday, 26 August, 1872, the great wrestling match for the eleven stone championship of the world and £100, between William Rickerby of Carlisle and Ralph Powley of Longlands, took place in the circus, William Brown Street, Liverpool, in the presence of a large concourse of spectators, and resulted in a victory for Powley. Few events in the annals of wrestling have provoked a wider and more general interest than this affair did, both men being so well known as first-class athletes; and moreover their merits were equally divided, having previously met six times and obtained three falls each.

The *Carlisle Journal* in a report of the match remarked: 'There cannot be the slightest doubt in the world but that the best man at the weight won the match. Rickerby was overmatched throughout. But though beaten he was not disgraced. He wrestled as well as ever man could do; but Powley could worry him in taking holds, the Longlands man having a longer reach, and nature having moreover endowed him with a queer back to get hold of. The second fall was perhaps the best of the three, and it was

A HISTORY OF CUMBERLAND

in this bout that most science was displayed on both sides. The hype was Rickerby's instrument of warfare, but he was unable to bring over his opponent, and the fatal click, which Powley knows so well how to use, sealed Rickerby's fate, even in this fall. The long and short of it is that though Rickerby is a good game wrestler, Powley is a better at eleven stone. The three wrestles were honest and genuine and will long live in the memory of all who saw them. Powley's great length however served him well, and he won, and won well, indeed. A word now for the fallen. Rickerby is a great wrestler, but he requires that which he can never have—namely, an inch more arm reach and two inches more length to his legs—in order to enable him to throw a man like Powley at eleven stone. As it is, Powley is, and has proved himself to be, the champion eleven-stone man in the world. After the match, Rickerby, in good-hearted style, admitted he was fairly beaten.'

We now come to the time when George Steadman and George Lowden came to the front, closely followed by William Blair of Solport Mill, one of the greatest buttockers ever known, Edward Norman of Carlisle and Hexham Clark. Steadman, who has held the championship about thirty years, retired from the ring in August, 1900, after winning the chief prize at the Grasmere sports. Blair and Norman retired some years ago, and it is said that Lowden will not appear in the wrestling ring any more as a principal, consequently Hexham Clark becomes champion, and well worthy is he of the position.

In conclusion we may say that wrestling, compared with what it was in its palmy days, has latterly, it cannot be denied, lost some of its interest for the people, even in the district where it has held supremacy as an out-door sport for generations. Youths, it is true, still practise it in the dales and on the fell sides, and it takes its place regularly in the programme of most athletic meetings in the two counties. Nevertheless it appears to be incontestably relaxing its hold upon the public, partly, no doubt, owing to the fact that 'barneying' becomes so frequent when men gain the top of the tree, that legitimate sport disappears just at the stage when it would be most interesting : but also, we imagine, from other causes, traceable to the principle embodied in the maxim 'other times, other

manners.' Twenty or thirty years ago it was a very different matter. The tastes of the people then were simpler ; and it was no wonder in the days before the immense modern development of field sports of all kinds—cricket, football, horse-racing, etc.—that exhibitions of prowess by noted wrestlers of Penrith, Carlisle and elsewhere should have stirred the towns and villages of Cumberland and Westmorland to their depths.

The compilation of the above article is chiefly based on voluminous manuscript notes made by the late Jacob Robinson of Ulverston and the late George Coward of Carlisle. Very many thanks are due to Mr. J. H. C. Colton of Carlisle for enabling me to acquire these notes, and also to Mr. Thomas Coward of Carlisle for kindly revising the article on 'Hound Dog Trailing,' on which subject he is an acknowledged authority. The local newspaper files have materially aided my labours in a variety of ways. Besides supplying many passing incidents, I have found them, in some instances, exceedingly useful in the way of verifying facts and correcting dates, added to which I am indebted to a multitude of narrators, who with never-failing willingness have supplied the items of the various events chronicled.

While the feats of many well known wrestlers are to be found in the article on 'Wrestling,' the names of others equally well known are necessarily omitted, and little or no allusion is made to those who competed only in the rings of north Lancashire, Westmorland and elsewhere outside Cumberland, of whom there have been many of marked ability in the past. The following list of local works on wrestling have been largely quoted from : *Wrestliana :* an Historical Account of Ancient and Modern Wrestling by William Litt, Whitehaven (R. Gibson. 1823). Second edition of the above (reprinted from the *Whitehaven News*) by Michael and William Alsop, 1860.

Wrestliana : A Chronicle of the Cumberland and Westmorland Wrestlings in London, since the year 1824. By Walter Armstrong (London : Simpkin, Marshall & Co. 1870).

Famous Athletic Contests, Ancient and Modern, compiled by Members of the Cumberland and Westmorland Wrestling Society (reprinted from the best authorities) (London : F. A. Hancock. 1871).

Great Book of Wrestling References, giving about 2,000 different prizes from 1838 to the present day, by Isaac Gate, twenty-five years Public Wrestling Judge (Carlisle : Steel Brothers. 1874).

Wrestling and Wrestlers, by Jacob Robinson and Sidney Gilpin (London : Bemrose & Sons, Limited ; Carlisle : G. & T. Coward).

FOOTBALL

ASSOCIATION

The modernized Association game is a recent development in Cumberland. A century or so ago the 'football play,' with its rude rough-and-tumble tactics, existed and flourished amongst the villagers in certain districts. Then, from the time the ball was thrown down in the churchyard until it reached its goal—a distance of two or three miles perhaps —every inch of ground was keenly contested by almost the entire male population of the rural villages ; and in some cases even by the other sex.

About 1874 occasional games of Association football were played in the 'Border City,' but no organization attempted ; 'the real football,' as far as Cumberland is concerned, dates from the late 'seventies.' The Carlisle Club was the first of its kind apart from school football, and was formed on 8 September, 1880, two years after the formation of the Denton Holme Club in the same city. United efforts at Carlisle were immediately followed by the formation of Wigton Club in September 1880, and the Workington and Distington Clubs a short time later.

The organizations named were the original members of the Cumberland Football Association, which was established at Wigton in the year 1884. Progress was at first slow. It took the novitiate clubs a long time to persuade the hard-headed Cumbrians that football was a health-giving game to be admired and fostered. In January, 1886, there were seven Association clubs in the county, but only four affiliated. But the game had come to stay, and it gradually gained ground until in the season of 1899–1900 the Cumberland Association had a record membership of forty-two clubs.

The season of 1885–6 saw the inauguration of the Cumberland Cup Competition, which has done much to advance the game locally. The Carlisle men were the first winners, their victory over Workington being challenged without avail by the losers on the novel ground 'that the referee gave his decision before being appealed to by the umpires !' Workington's revenge came later, for, winning the much-coveted trophy the following season, they retained possession until 1891–2, when it was gained by the Moss Bay Exchange, another Workington combination which held it for two years. In 1893–4 the cup again found a home in Carlisle, but

was brought back the next year to Workington by the Black Diamonds. From that period the trophy remained in the Cumberland 'Ironopolis,' until the season 1900–1, when Shaddongate United, the then premier Carlisle club, was successful. During this time Workington has registered four more wins, and the Black Diamonds one. Frizington White Star were the holders in 1901–2.

With a view to encouraging the rising talent, the Cumberland Shield Competition was inaugurated in 1889. It has fully answered its purpose, thirty or more teams competing annually for the coveted trophy. So keen is the competition, that no club has won the shield more than twice, as will be seen from the following list of champions : Season 1889–90, Arlecdon ; 1890–1, Moss Bay Exchange ; 1891–2, Black Diamonds ; 1892–3, Imperial Rovers ; 1893–4, Wigton Harriers ; 1894–5, Workington ; 1895–6, Black Diamonds ; 1896–7, Workington ; 1897–8, Frizington White Star ; 1898–9, Shaddongate United ; 1899–1900, Frizington White Star ; 1900–1, Cockermouth Crusaders ; 1901–2, Scalegill Rovers ; 1902–3, Moss Bay Exchange.

It is interesting to trace the development of the league system in Cumberland. A 'West Cumberland Association League' was formed about 1890, but had a brief and precarious existence. At a meeting held at Cockermouth 24 March, 1894, the league was reformed under the title of 'The Cumberland League' and its scope extended. The following eight clubs claimed membership : Imperial Rovers (Workington), Cockermouth Crusaders, Black Diamonds, Carlisle City, Moss Bay Exchange, Workington, Keswick and Wigton Harriers. The league commenced working the following season. The Workington men proved the champions, and retained the position during the three following seasons. In the seasons of 1898–9 and 1899–1900, however, the seaport club more than met their match in Frizington White Star, an organization in the iron-ore mining district which had been making bold but unsuccessful bids for the cup. The abstention of Keswick from league football in recent years, and the limited number of senior clubs, somewhat checked the interest in the annual competitions ; but at the meeting of 1900 a revival appeared to have taken place, for four new clubs (three of whom had been working under the auspices of the Junior League) joined the senior ranks and brought up the number of competing clubs to ten, the largest entry up to date. The present members are Frizington White Star, Workington, Black Diamonds, Moss Bay Exchange, Carlisle Red Rose, Shaddongate United, Wigton Harriers, and Keswick. The league has a promising future, being in touch with the four divisions into which the county is divided.

At the annual meeting of the league held 30 May 1896, at the Commercial Hotel, Workington, a junior division was formed of the following eight clubs : Maryport, Wigton Harriers, Cockermouth Crusaders, Harrington, Workington Reserves, Moss Bay Reserves, Black Diamonds Reserves and Imperial Rovers Reserves. Harrington was the first winner. The season following (1897–8) the composition of the Junior League underwent a great change. Of the original clubs only four—Cockermouth, Wigton, Harrington and Moss Bay—remained. Maryport had succumbed to the strong opposition of the Rugby code, the Imperial Rovers had followed suit, and Workington and Black Diamonds withdrew their reserve teams. Frizington White Star Reserves, Wheatsheaf Rovers (a junior Workington club) and Arlecdon were included, and made up a complement of seven clubs, of which Cockermouth proved the champion with 16 points out of a possible 20, having only once suffered defeat. At the annual meeting in 1898 the Frizington Rovers were admitted members, but as the Moss Bay Reserves retired, the number of competing clubs remained the same. After a keen competition Frizington White Star was declared champion, a performance which that team might have repeated the following season, but owing to a variety of causes the fixtures were not completed. In the latter season new blood had been admitted with the West Seaton, Distington and Scalegill Clubs, whilst Harrington and Wheatsheaf Rovers had gone under, succumbing to the inevitable. The Junior League, weakened by the promotion of three of its most prominent clubs to the 'upper house,' collapsed, but its place has been taken by a similar organization.

In October of the Diamond Jubilee year a meeting was held at the King's Arms Hotel, Wigton, ' to consider the question of forming a Cumberland Thursday Association League, with a view to furthering the interests of mid-week football.' It was unanimously decided that such a combination be set on foot. The original clubs were few in number : Aspatria Agricultural College, Carlisle .Thursday, Workington Thursday and

Wigton Harriers Thursday. Workington proved the first champions in 1898–9, and repeated the success the following season, when interest was added to the competition by the inclusion of Midland United, a Carlisle organization. The following season the committee failed to carry on the Thursday League.

Other competitions which have done much to maintain the interest in the game in Workington have been the Workington Infirmary Shield Competition and the Workington Town Championship, which have usually excited the keenest encounters amongst the borough clubs.

No organization has better answered the purpose for which it was formed than the Carlisle and District Charity Shield Competition, which came into being in 1890 with the object of encouraging the game amongst junior clubs or teams. In a great measure due to the hon. secretary, Mr. J. A. McLean, the competition has been a success from the beginning, and there is now an average annual entry of over twenty clubs. The winners are : 1890–1, Eden Vale ; 1891–2, West End Rangers ; 1892–3, Carlisle Red Rose ; 1893–4, Carlisle City ; 1894–5, Willow Holme Mission ; 1895–6, Shaddongate United ; 1896–7, Carlisle Red Rose ; 1897–8, Shaddongate United ; 1898–9, Carlisle Red Rose ; 1899–1900, Shaddongate United ; 1900–1, Shaddongate United ; 1901–2, G. and S. W. Rovers.

The Association game in the east of the county will probably be further advanced by the Carlisle and District Junior League, formed 28 August 1900, to operate in a twelve mile radius of the ' Border City.' The original members were Dalston, Wigton, Burnfoot Star, G. and S.W. Rovers, Carlisle Red Rose, Cummersdale Hornets, N.B.R. Loco., West End, Shaddongate United, Grassing Athletic, Caxton and Longtown. Cummersdale Club was the first winner, and N.B. Loco. the second.

In West Cumberland the Egremont Division Junior League was formed the same month, consisting of Frizington White Star, Frizington Rovers, Keekle, Scalegill Rovers, St. Bees and Arlecdon. The first-named was champion in 1900–1, and in 1901–2 Scalegill Rovers.

The Cumberland Junior Medal Competition, during its brief existence under the Association's maternal wing, did much to foster rising talent.

In the earlier years of the Cumberland Football Association each affiliated club was entitled to representation on the Executive

Committee, but as the number of clubs multiplied this method grew too cumbersome in its working, and an efficacious departure was made when the system of club representation — under which the interests of the county might occasionally be overlooked — was abolished and divisional representation substituted. For this purpose the county was grouped into four divisions, each of which is represented by two independent men elected at the annual meeting. In 1904, there are about fifty affiliated clubs, but of this number fourteen, although affiliated direct, are connected with the Carlisle and District Charity Shield and do not take part in any of the county competitions.

Any record of Cumberland Association football would be incomplete without allusion to that pioneer of the game, Mr. F. J. Hayes of Workington. He was one of the first representatives on the Association, has ever since its formation occupied a seat on the Executive Committee, and has for several years impartially filled the post of chairman, succeeding in that capacity the late Mr. G. Hetherington of Wigton. In this direction may be mentioned the good work done by the secretaries of modern times : Mr. R. K. Malone of Workington, who on his departure to the west of Ireland—far removed from the haunts of the dribbling code—relinquished the secretarial duties to Mr. R. Graham, then of Workington and now at Ebbw Vale. Mr. Graham was in turn succeeded by Mr. J. C. Ellis of Grasslot, Maryport, who at the time of writing carries out the duties.

West Cumberland has ever been the hotbed of the Association game, but the eastern clubs have been gradually asserting themselves. In the season of 1893–4, when Carlisle City brought back the cup to the ' Border City' after seven years' absence, and the Wigton Harriers carried the shield eastwards for the first time, the west county clubs received warning that they must look to their laurels, and, roused to greater activity, they still succeed in more than holding their own. The admission of the Workington Club to the Lancashire League in the season of 1901–2 introduced a better class of football into the district, and aroused greater interest in Association rules. At the present time almost all the players are amateurs, professionals being practically unknown in the north-west county.

RUGBY

The Rugby Union game in Cumberland is a product of the last thirty years. The earliest trace of any real organization for the development of football under that code is to be found in 1870. In that year the Carlisle Club had not only a local habitation but a name which it has actively maintained up to the present time. Carlisle's enterprise before long received the flattery of imitation in outlying parts of the county. In 1876 the Whitehaven Club was already making a reputation as a staunch supporter of Rugby football. A little later Workington followed suit, initiating a movement which very soon found plenty of support in the western division. So rapid indeed was the development in that district that by the commencement of 1882 a silver challenge cup, mainly the result of a subscription from the western clubs, had been instituted. The inauguration of the cup competition necessitated an organization of some sort to control it. The outcome was the establishment of a county club which was in time to become the Cumberland County Rugby Football Union as it is to-day. In connection with this county club two names deserve to be remembered with gratitude. The Rev. J. W. Wainwright of Aspatria was elected the first president, but the credit of the initial work in the main belongs to J. E. Birkett of Workington and E. G. Mitchell of Maryport, who did active service as vice-president for several years. At the time the number of clubs of any influence was limited. The County Union in fact had a constituency of only seven clubs. These were Carlisle, Aspatria, Eden Wandeters, Maryport, Workington, Whitehaven and Cockermouth, and these seven at the outset alone competed for the challenge cup which fell into the hands of Aspatria at the first contest in 1883. This club won again in 1885, Whitehaven having proved successful in the intermediate season. Aspatria's second victory was of the greater merit from the fact that in 1885 the county club had received considerable accession to its strength by the addition of Millom, Penrith and Wigton, among other clubs. So far Rugby football had gone on steadily increasing its area as well as its influence. But it had difficulties in store for it. Carlisle won the cup in 1886 only to secede from the county club with two others of the most influential clubs, namely, the Eden Wanderers and Whitehaven.

Meanwhile Cumberland as a county had been making history. Matches had been arranged and played with Northumberland, Durham and Westmorland. Fortunately too the withdrawal of the three clubs just mentioned did not give rise to prolonged anxiety. For a time it looked as if the rupture would have serious effects in retarding if not altogether checking the extension of the game. The restoration of diplomatic relations was due in a great measure to the patriotic efforts of two stalwart supporters of Rugby football. The one, R. Westray of Carlisle, took office as president; the other, C. J. Lewthwaite of Cockermouth, became honorary secretary of the county club on its resuscitation, or rather on its commencement of a new career in 1887. With the two workers already mentioned, J. E. Birkett and E. G. Mitchell, as vice-presidents, the Cumberland Union had the advantage of four keen and enthusiastic workers for its principal officers. Under their auspices a great impetus was given to the game throughout the county.

By 1888 Cumberland indeed had gained so materially in strength that the Rugby Union paid it the compliment of allotting it a representative on the committee of the national body. By this time the supremacy in club football had passed away to the western district. Millom was able to gain possession of the challenge cup and to retain it for the two succeeding years. In the interim the area over which the Union itself had control had naturally been extending in proportion as the game grew in public favour.

The immediate result of the elevation of the county to a seat on the Rugby Union was an extension of the programme to be undertaken by the Cumberland Fifteen. From the very outset the Lancashire executive had extended the hand of fellowship to their neighbours, a kindly act which did much to encourage the Cumbrians when they really needed encouragement. Lancashire's example was soon followed, with the result that before long Cumberland's match list included fixtures with Cheshire, Northumberland, Westmorland, South of Scotland and Cambridge University. The addition of these important fixtures naturally brought with it a corresponding increase in the influence of the County Union. In 1887 the clubs affiliated could almost have been counted on the fingers. By 1892 no less than twenty-six acknowledged Cumberland's jurisdiction. The institution of a challenge shield for the advancement of junior players in 1889 had perhaps a good deal to do with this increase. The new competition proved an undoubted success, so much so that in 1892 no less than twenty teams had entered to contend for the possession of the trophy. Just about this period Millom was undoubted champion of the Cumbrian clubs.

Thrice victorious for the challenge cup, this club not only scored a "double first" in 1889 by landing both cup and shield, but after an interval of a year won the latter again, as also in the following spring of 1892. Millom's record between 1887 and 1892 was indeed one of the most remarkable features of Cumberland football in the earlier days of the Union. In only one season during this period was the team without one or other of the two trophies. Both were missed in 1890, and that season, oddly enough, Egremont rivalled Millom's performance of the previous spring in securing the shield as well as the cup. In the earlier days of the County Club, Cumberland's record, as was only to be expected, was one of but partial success. At the commencement of the 'nineties,' Lancashire was quite in the forefront of Rugby Union counties, and the Cumbrians were thought to have done well at Whitehaven in February, 1890, in having only 7 points, the entire score of the match, registered against them by the Lancashire Fifteen. But the men of Cumberland were apt pupils, and the practical experience they were gaining in meeting players, who were at that time of a better calibre, soon bore fruit.

The close of the season of 1893 gave some conclusive evidence of the reality of the progress made under the new régime. In the County Championship the Bordermen had run out winners of the North Western Group and tied with Yorkshire for possession of the blue ribbon of the sport. The season's record for a hitherto obscure county was remarkable. After defeating Cheshire and Westmorland and drawing with Lancashire, the Cumbrians vanquished Cambridge University, South of Scotland, Middlesex and Devon. But one try indeed was registered against them, obtained on the Corpus ground by Cambridge University, and this was the only occasion upon which Cumberland had her line crossed during the whole of the seven matches. The final contest with Yorkshire, coming as it unfortunately did within two or three days of the arduous tour of over 1,000 miles, with its severe encounters, naturally found the Border team somewhat stale; anyhow it fell an easy victim to the fresh and more vigorous Yorkshiremen. The position however was an honourable one in standing next to a county which had for some years monopolized the honour of being declared champion. The succeeding season, if producing a less prominent position for the county team than in the preceding year, found the clubs more than maintaining their progress in inter-club fixtures. Perhaps the chief point of interest in this season (1893-4) was the memorable Forsyth and Boak case, in which the Cumberland and Yorkshire Unions found themselves involved in a lengthy and costly inquiry as to whether these two players had been improperly induced to desert the Border county for the purpose of assisting in the operations of the Huddersfield Club. In consequence of the decision being in favour of the complainants, the suspension of the Huddersfield Club afforded one of the earliest instances of punishment inflicted by the Rugby Union in the interests of amateur sport. The advent of the season 1894-5 gave promise of a more pleasing departure, in which the Border county more than sustained the advance already accomplished. A series of brilliant performances against Durham, Lancashire, Westmorland, Midland Counties and Devon found Cumberland contesting once more with Yorkshire the honour of being declared champion county of England. A splendid struggle at Manningham, when a kick at goal was the narrow margin by which Cumberland had to yield in favour of Yorkshire, was the result. As an indication of the relative merits of the two rivals, it ought to be remembered that at this time Yorkshire was untouched by those secessions to northern unionism which afterwards so seriously decimated her ranks, a circumstance which had a most material bearing on the severity of the test to which Cumberland was subjected. Following upon an uneventful interval the operations of 1896-7 witnessed a surprising revival of the county's previous good form. Victories were gained over Durham, Cheshire, Lancashire, Yorkshire and Westmorland, with a draw against the Northumbrians. The net result was the attainment of the *third* time of the position of champion of the north, with the honours attaching to another final contest for premier county. One of the most remarkable incidents of this tournament was that, as on a previous occasion, Cumberland had not permitted one of the counties named to cross her goal-line. The final test for chief honours against the southern champion (Kent) was played at Carlisle in April 1897, when the Kentish men secured a well deserved victory.

Up to this time Cumberland had maintained its normal strength of about sixteen senior clubs. The following season however was destined to see a change, as no less than four of these clubs cast off their allegiance to the Rugby Union and espoused professionalism. Notwithstanding the disadvantages attaching to such a loss, Cumberland continued to

hold a strong position amongst the other counties, and in 1898-9 succeeded in defeating Yorkshire, Durham, and Cheshire, drawing with Lancashire, and succumbing to Northumberland only. The following season, that of 1899-1900, had to be met under very discouraging auspices. Reduced to a membership of only three clubs—Aspatria, Carlisle, Penrith—Cumberland had to face a situation of no ordinary difficulty. The position however only served to rouse the executive to the occasion, and to its credit be it said that notwithstanding this serious reduction of numerical strength, the county Fifteen secured victories over Cheshire, Lancashire and Yorkshire, a draw with Durham, and only sustained reverse in the closing contest against Northumberland. A tie for the northern championship being thus recorded between Cumberland and Durham, a second encounter had to be undertaken, in which, by a goal to nil, Durham secured the advantage. As the latter subsequently defeated the southern champion (Devon) by a substantial score, the practical result of the season was to place Cumberland —in order of merit at least—next to the champion county, notwithstanding the severity of the ordeal which it had been called upon to undergo.

During those successful competitions with other counties it was only to be expected that the Bordermen should find their way into the English team. These selections were confined almost exclusively to the forward division, a department in which the county had uniformly excelled. Foremost amongst those securing international caps was James Davidson, captain of the Aspatria and county teams, who with his brother Joseph, and J. H. Blacklock of the same club, shared with Knowles of Millom the honour of representing Cumberland's best forwards at that period. The challenge cup has furnished a stimulus to local effort with varying results. The Aspatria club has supplied the best record in connection therewith, having carried off the trophy in 1883, 1885, 1891, 1892, 1896 and 1899. Millom won in 1887, 1888, 1889; Maryport in 1893, 1894; Seaton in 1895, 1897, 1898; the remaining contests being awarded to Whitehaven in 1884, Carlisle in 1886, and Egremont in 1890. The challenge shield has been won no less than four times by Millom, namely in 1889, 1891, 1892 and 1895; by Workington in 1897 and 1898; by Egremont in 1890; Whitehaven Recreation in 1893; Maryport in 1894; Wath Brow in 1896; and Highmoor Rovers in 1899. The temporary discontinuance of these two competi-

FORESTRY

CUMBERLAND cannot be considered one of the well-wooded counties of England, as the aggregate of woods and plantations according to the latest official returns for 1895 amounts only to 35,054 acres, out of a total area of 970,161 acres (of which 11,533 are water). This indicates woodlands to the extent of about 3·6 per cent. of the total area, which is considerably under the average percentage for the whole of England (5·4 per cent.). No less than 261,158 acres consist of mountain and heath land used for rough grazing. The only other county which contains more of such poor land than Cumberland is the adjoining county of Northumberland (with 469,719 acres), and if the similar class of land in Westmorland (208,426 acres) be added to these other two, the three mountainous northern frontier counties contain no less than 939,303 acres out of the gross total of 2,289,662 acres of mountain and heath lands in the whole of England.

The county is rich in the variety of its scenery and its surface, and it shows great variations as to its climate. Towards the east and south-west its surface is diversified by high rugged sterile mountains, fissured with gullies abounding in waterfalls and fringed with woodlands, and divided by deep and narrow fertile valleys, often with lakes; the northern and north-western districts are low and flat, or else gently undulating; while the central portion consists of elevated ridges, hills, and fertile valleys. On the coast the climate is mild and temperate though rather moist, but in the mountain region it is variable and wet, especially during the summer months and the early autumn. The rainfall varies from about 30 to 35 inches in the Carlisle and Wigton districts, amounting to about 50 inches a year at Whitehaven on the west coast, and even attaining the maximum for Europe of 244 inches measured at the Styhead Pass (1,600 feet) in 1872. The mountain region comprises more than one-third of the county and includes some of the highest elevations in England. There are 10 peaks of over 2,500 feet in height, four of which exceed 3,000 feet (Scaw-fell Pike, 3,210; Scaw-fell, 3,162; Helvellyn, 3,118; and Skiddaw, 3,054).

Throughout the greater part of the mountain region the soil consists of a black peaty earth, often spongy and wet, which extends into the moors and commons in the eastern part of the county. On the lower hill-sides, there is often a cold, stiff, wet clay, which also frequently forms the subsoil on the lowlands, consisting mostly of dry loams well suited for farm crops.

A HISTORY OF CUMBERLAND

Whether the wooded tracts of Cumberland were originally 'forests' in the legal and technical sense of having been afforested and brought under the jurisdiction of the Justices in Eyre, foresters, and minor officials, or whether they were merely called 'forest' after the manner still customary of using the words *forest* and *woodland* as more or less synonymous terms, does not seem clear from any of the works published concerning the history and antiquities of this county.

The actual afforestation or afforestations made to the south of Carlisle probably date from the reign of Henry II., who had a passion for this exercise of the royal prerogative, though they may possibly be older. According to the perambulation of 1300 (29 Edward I.) there was only one royal forest in Cumberland, i.e., one forest in the true sense of the term ; and this was the forest of Englewood or Inglewood. This was a large tract of more than 150 square miles, stretching south-wards, south-west and south-east from close to the city of Carlisle away to a distance of about 16 miles, and with a breadth of about 10 miles. It included the woodlands of Inglewood between the Caldew and Petterel rivers, those of West Ward to the south of the Wampool, part of what is now Greystoke Park, and Plumpton Park between the Petterel and the Eden, together with all the tillage, pasturage and waste lands lying within the boundaries perambulated and detailed in the record.[1]

Soon after this, the inhabitants of 'Penreth Sakeld at Soureby,' within the Inglewood Forest, petitioned the King that their lands were wasted by the Scots and their corn destroyed by 'the wild beasts of the forest,' and on 26 October 1301 letters patent were issued granting them the perpetual privilege of common of pasturage for all their cattle within the said forest in as ample a manner as the prior of Carlisle, and William English, and other tenants holding similar privilege by royal grant ; and this right of user was granted 'without interference by our-selves or our heirs, justices, foresters, verderers, regarders, agistors, bailiffs, or any other of our other officials of the forest.'[2] Tithes in the forest of Inglewood had previously been granted by King Edward I. to the prior and canons of Carlisle in a deed dated 5 December 1293.[3]

The only other sanctuaries for game of any considerable size left in the county (and probably still partially wooded) was what is known as the 'forest of Copeland,' afterwards called Egremont, lying to the south of the four lakes (Thirlmere, Derwentwater, Crummock Water, and Ennerdale Water) towards the south-western corner of the county, Geltstone or Geltsdale forest (including Breirthwaite or Tarnhouse Forest) south-east of Castle Carrock, and Nichol forest in the north-east of the county. These were, however, not *forests* but *chases*. Thus, the barony of Copeland was granted by Ranulph de Meschines to his brother William, who built the Castle of Egremont and made various grants of

[1] This perambulation has been printed by Nicolson and Burn, *Hist. of Cumb.* ii. 522
[2] See transcript of original grant given in Nicolson, *op. cit.* i. 315.
[3] Ibid. p. 546.

lands subject to the reservation of his baronial rights of the chase as to hunting 'hart and hind, wild boar, and their kinds.' So, too, with regard to Nichol Forest in Eskdale ward. This was in the barony of Lyddale, and was granted by Ranulph de Meschines to Robert de Stutevill, from one of whose successors in the reign of King John, Nicholas de Stutevill, the hunting ground there 'received the name of Nichol forest which it bears to this day.'[1]

A survey of the oak trees in most of the royal forests was made about 1565. In an inquisition held in 1588 concerning the chase specified as the 'Foresta de Breirthwaite,' also known as Tarnhouse forest or Tindale forest and adjoining the chase or 'forest of Geltesdale,' it was said that 'there are, within the said forest, certain boundes or dales of haye ground, &c. do amount unto 874 acres; and there are also in other waste, heath, and barren ground, within the said forest, above a thousand acres.' But nothing is said of woodlands, which evidently were non-existent. These so-called *forests* of Geltstone or Geltsdale and Breirthwaite had been given to the priory of Hexham, but when Henry VIII. dissolved the religious houses they were granted to the barons of Gilsland. About a hundred years ago Geltsdale forest is described as a considerable tract of mountainous land, chiefly heathy pasture, with some extensive birch and alder woods in the lower parts.[2]

Another timber survey was ordered to be made in 1608 throughout all the 'forests, parks, and chases belonging to His Majesty,' but in this there is no mention of any timber belonging to the Crown, or over which it had any lien under the forest laws, in any part of the four northern counties. Probably only partially wooded near the base of the hills, the woodlands once existing in the forest of Inglewood and in the chases (locally known as forests) seem to have been gradually cleared and completely 'wasted' or 'assarted' to tillage and pasturage by this time. Plumpton Park, formerly the demesne land of the Crown, had meanwhile been alienated. On 26 April 1625 Charles I. granted in fee and perpetuity, 'all that the park or land of Plumpton, within the forest of Inglewood, containing by estimation in meadow, pasture, and arable ground 2,436 acres, and common of pasture in the forest of Inglewood to the same appertaining'[3]; so apparently the park of Plumpton was then as unadorned with timber as the forest of Inglewood had become. The manor and town of Penrith had been granted in 1397 to Ralph Nevill, Earl of Westmorland. It was forfeited in 1459, and again in 1471, when it was granted to Richard, Duke of Gloucester, and became attached to the Crown in 1483. In 1616 'the Honour of Penrith, with its rights, members, and appurtenances,' were demised in trust for Charles, Prince of Wales; and in 1671 they were granted by Charles II. as part of Queen Catherine's

[1] Nicolson and Burn, *op. cit.* ii. 464.
[2] Britton and Brayley, *Beauties of England and Wales*, 1802, iii. 138.
[3] Nicolson and Burn, *op. cit.* ii. 419, 420.

jointure. In 1696 they were granted by William III. to William Bentinck, first Earl of Portland. Subsequently the Duke of Portland contested the title of the Crown, holding that the rights in Inglewood forest went with the franchise of the Honour; and he won the lawsuit that resulted. On page 3 of the Schedule attached to the *First Report of the Commissioners appointed to enquire into the State and Condition of the Woods, Forests, and Land Revenues of the Crown,* 1787, Sir James Lowther, bart., is shown as holding under lease from the Crown (1) 'the Manor and Forest of Ennerdale, and all the Mines and quarries within the said Manor' for 99 years or three lives from 1765 at a rental of £20 17s. 8½d. and one-tenth of the profits on mines and quarries; and (2) 'the Forest of Inglewood, with all Rents, Courts, Royalties, Mines, Quarries, Privileges and appurtenances thereto belonging' for 99 years or three lives from 1767 at a rental of 13s. 4d., plus one-third of the profits of the lands and one-tenth those of the mines; but a note adds that this estate is now lost to the Crown and the lease invalid, the contest regarding it having been 'finally determined at the Summer Assizes for Cumberland in 1776' in favour of the Duke of Portland. This manor and the forest of Inglewood were afterwards sold by the Duke of Portland to the Duke of Devonshire in 1787.[1] In 1873, all the land held in this county by the Crown consisted merely of 8½ acres; but even in 1788 there were no Crown woodlands in any of the northern counties of England.[2] The forest of Inglewood declined to the lowest possible level of an absolutely treeless condition in 1825.

On Wragmire Moss, until the year 1823, there was a well-known oak, known as *the last tree of Inglewood forest,* which had survived the blasts of 700 or 800 winters. This 'time honoured' oak was remarkable . . . as being a boundary mark between the manors of the Duke of Devonshire and the Dean and Chapter of Carlisle; as also between the parishes of Hesket and St. Cuthberts, Carlisle; and was noticed as such for upwards of 600 years. This 'gnarled and knotted oak,' which had weathered so many hundred stormy winters, was become considerably decayed in its trunk. It fell not, however, by the tempest or the axe, but from sheer old age; this happened on 13 June 1823. If not of late years as beautiful in its foliage, nor presenting such a goodly assemblage of wide-spreading and umbrageous branches, as some other celebrated oaks, yet it was an object of great interest, being the veritable last tree of Inglewood forest.[3]

[1] In this great seignorial franchise, the forest of Inglewood comprises many parishes within the wards of Leath and Cumberland. Hesket, near the western border, is the scene of an interesting survival of the old forest court of freeholders, long after the abolition of the courts in royal forests by the Act of 1817. 'The forest or Swainmote courts for the seigniory are held annually on the Feast of St. Barnabas the Apostle (June 11), in the open air, on the great north road to Carlisle. The place where the courts are held is marked by a stone table placed before a thorn called *Court Thorn,* beneath whose branches unnumbered annual courts have assembled. The tenants of upwards of twenty mesne manors attend here, from whom a jury is impannelled and sworn; of which, Dr. Todd says, anciently the Chamberlain of the City of Carlisle was foreman. Here are paid the annual dues to the lord of the forest, compositions for improvements, purprestures, agistments, and puture of the foresters' (Jefferson, *History and Antiquities of Leath Ward,* 1840, page 205).
[2] See *The account of the several Woods, Forests, Parks and Chases* under the Surveyor General of His Majesty's Woods and Forests, Appendix No. 1, Third Report of Commissioners, &c., 1788, p. 55.
[3] Jefferson, *op. cit.* p. 206.

FORESTRY

Early in the nineteenth century the only places where even some poor scattered remnants of the original woodlands still existed were the deer-parks at Greystoke, Gowbarrow, Muncaster and Crofton, and the former deer-parks at Cockermouth, Naworth, Brampton, Isel, Brayton, Castlerigg, Ulpha, Millom, Crookdake and Netherhall. But on some of the estates a good deal of planting was done, sometimes of oak and other hardwoods in the valleys, or of larch and pine on the hills. Perhaps one of the best wooded of these during the early part of the eighteenth century was the manor of Castlerigg, which along with other estates in Cumberland had been granted to Greenwich Hospital after the attainder of the Earl of Derwentwater in 1715, for in 1777 it is spoken of as having been 'replenished with a prodigious quantity of tall stately large oaks; all which the trustees of Greenwich Hospital have cut down and sold, but within a few years past they have made some small plantations.'[1] These plantations here mentioned are still standing and consist chiefly of oak trees of large dimensions interspersed with other hardwoods, while they also contain a few very fine larch trees girthing up to ten feet at breast-height. Among the latter those known locally as 'the Twelve Apostles' are splendid specimens of the growth of larch under favourable conditions.

None of the 35,054 acres of woods and plantations in Cumberland, are owned by the Crown. They are all to be found on private estates, and consist chiefly of ornamental woodlands near the residences of the landowners, of game covers, or else of woods planted for the two-fold purpose of growing timber for profit and of giving shelter to the lower pastures in windswept localities. Along the outer edges on the windward side of such plantations the growth of larch and pine is exceedingly poor, being dwarfish, stunted, and bent by the wind. But under the shelter of the outer fringe the growth of the conifers has usually been satisfactory, and some of the plantations (chiefly of larch, with pine and spruce fir), formed in blocks varying up to about 200 acres in extent about the middle of last century, have yielded very satisfactory returns both directly in timber and indirectly in improved grazing. Formed on land of inferior quality and situated at a considerable elevation—worth in fee-simple only about £1 an acre—larch plantations (with pine, and spruce on the poorer and moister parts), then made at a cost of £2 an acre (on hillsides having good natural drainage), have in some instances, where care was bestowed not only on their formation but also on their subsequent treatment, yielded remunerative thinnings almost every year (the thinnings being done in annual sections, and repeated about every five years or so) from about seven years after planting; while the crop still on the ground, and practically mature and ready for felling whenever clearance may seem to the proprietor desirable, is worth from £50 to £60 an acre, according to the local market demand. Though such crops, of course, show neither the same large cubic contents nor the same money value per acre as if the plantations

[1] Nicolson and Burn, *op. cit.* ii. 80.

501

had been kept in close cover, yet it is not improbable that actuarial calculations would prove that under the given local circumstances this system of treatment with early thinnings (and with pasturage in the woods worth at least five shillings an acre per annum) has perhaps been more remunerative than any more scientific sort of treatment of the woods would have proved, unless the production of timber for profit had formed the main object desired by the landowner.

In planting for either shelter or profit in Cumberland there can be no doubt that conifers are likely to prove the most successful. For shelter the evergreen Scots pine and Douglas fir will be most effective, while a mixture of larch will add to the profit. Taken as a whole, the climate and the physical conditions of the county are far more suitable for coniferous than for hardwood crops of timber, even though a fine growth of oak and other broad-leaved trees (beech, sycamore, elm, etc.) is often to be found in the lower situations, more especially when well sheltered, as, for example, around the shores of Derwentwater.

In many cases, however, the mistake has been made of raising pure or almost pure plantations of larch on the hillsides, and often on soil and situations not satisfying its natural requirements in important respects, in order to reap the advantage derivable from this fine timber as compared with the less valuable pines and firs. The result of this has only too frequently resulted in the fungous canker disease getting a firm foothold among the young poles, thus spoiling their growth and destroying their utility, and rendering it impossible for them ever to develop into valuable stems. So prevalent has the canker disease consequently become in many parts of the county, since about the year 1840, that the formation of mixed crops seems to hold out the best promise of raising sound larch timber, the larch being, of course, judiciously favoured at the different times of thinning. Even though apt to lose its top from wind when grown in single specimens, Douglas fir is likely to prove a very valuable tree for mixing along with larch, although the assistance of Scots pine will usually be required on the poorer classes of land. Some of the finest larch in the county is to be found growing among the old oakwoods where they were probably planted first of all as 'nurses,' and then subsequently allowed to stand and form part of the main crop.

During the course of last century planting of oak was often undertaken on hillsides, with such want of success that sometimes hardly a tree remains to mark the site of the plantation. It is only on the lower and richer lands that the oak plantations can be said to have done well. Even there the growth of the trees, originally planted with a view to supply crooks and ship-building timber, is not usually of the straight, clean description that now fetches the best market price ; and on such lands being replanted, mixed conifer crops are likely to prove more profitable than broadleaved trees.

Owing to the heavy rainfall and the stiff soil and subsoil in many parts of the county, drainage is often necessary before planting can be carried out with any reasonable chance of proving successful. This adds considerably to the expense of planting, which is further increased greatly by the necessity for wire-fencing against rabbits. The earlier plantations of fifty to a hundred years ago had not this difficulty to contend with, and this alone makes a very considerable difference in the cost of fresh plantations nowadays.

'The New Domesday Book' or *Parliamentary Return of Owners of Land in England and Wales*, 1873, giving the acreage and rental value of the lands held by the various owners, expressly states that in the details compiled 'no account is taken of those waste lands, the area of which could not be ascertained, of woods other than saleable *underwoods*,' etc., and no other statistics have ever been collected or published either officially or unofficially ; hence no statement can be made as to the total extent of the oakwoods, larchwoods, etc., on individual estates or even throughout the county generally. Most of the woods are to be found on the largest estates, which are owned by the Earl of Carlisle (Naworth Castle), the Earl of Lonsdale (Lowther, Castle), Sir Richard Graham, bart. (Netherby Hall), H. Howard, esq. (Greystoke Castle), and Lord Leconfield (Cockermouth Castle).

From an arboricultural point of view the Netherby estate, the property of Sir Richard Graham, bart., on the river Esk about ten miles north of Carlisle, is one of the most interesting in the county. The property consists of 26,000 acres, of which about 2,800 acres are plantations—exclusive of ornamental clumps, park, timber and hedgerow trees—comprising about 1,000 acres from 100 to 150 years old, 1,300 acres from 50 to 90 years, and about 500 acres under fifty years of age. These woods are all enclosed with fencing aggregating about 300 miles in length. Although not more than 150 to 200 feet above the sea-level, most of the land planted was not worth more than five shillings to seven shillings and sixpence an acre for agricultural occupation, and drainage, preparatory to planting, cost about seven shillings an acre. The usual plan followed was to cut open drains, $2\frac{1}{2}$ feet wide at top and 2 to $2\frac{1}{2}$ feet deep, at a distance of 8 to 12 yards according to the degree of wetness of the land.

The better tracts were planted with a mixture of oak, ash, elm, sycamore, larch, silver fir, Scots pine, spruce, and a few lime, maple, chestnut, and horse chestnut, while the black-topped or peaty lands were planted with Scots pine, spruce, and birch. February and March were found to be the best months for planting, all the larger-rooted hardwoods being set in pits of about 12 to 14 inches square and one foot deep, while smaller-rooted hardwoods and conifers were simply notched into the ground. The plants were put in 3 to $3\frac{1}{2}$ feet apart (3,556 to 4,840 per acre), and the whole cost of planting seldom exceeded £5 an acre. Where hares and rabbits were numerous, the plantations had to be specially protected by wire-netting for six to eight years, and in such cases of course this added very materially to the cost of protection.

Thinning operations were usually begun at about 12 or 13 years and repeated every four or five years till the plantations were 30 years of age, after which they were continued every six or eight years for other 30 years. To ensure regularity, the thinnings of the old and the young woods were so arranged that the whole area would be gone over at least once every seven years.

During the twenty-eight years from 1855 to 1883, in which 800 acres were planted but had not yet become old enough to yield appreciable returns, the receipts obtained from the woodlands averaged £1 10s. 11d. an acre, while the expenditure on them was £0 12s. 4d. per acre, thus showing an average income of £0 18s. 7d. per acre from land whose agricultural value varied, as already mentioned, from five shillings to seven shillings and sixpence an acre. This is, of course, not net profit or rental yielded by the land, because it includes the annual interest payable on the capital locked up in forming the plantations; but then, on the other hand, it does not give any indication of the capital represented by the growing crops of timber. Taking the whole wooded area of 2,800 acres into consideration, the average receipts have been £1 2s. 1d. per acre, the expenditure £0 8s. 5d. an acre, and the income £0 13s. 8d. per acre, while the crops still left to mature are estimated as worth from about £40 to £60 an acre. Insufficient as these data are for showing with anything like actuarial exactness the precise amount of profit annually accruing from these investments in growing timber on the Netherby estate, they nevertheless afford a tolerably clear proof that the plantations have been profitable in themselves, while at the same time the woodlands have also been indirectly of further benefit in improving adjoining arable land through the shelter from wind afforded to it.

The woods on the Greystoke Estate, the property of H. C. Howard, esq., are also of considerable extent. They amount altogether to about 1,860 acres, of which 701 acres are old woods planted between 1746 and 1814, 294 acres planted from 1826 to 1850, 334 acres planted between 1852 and 1880, and 531 acres of recent plantations formed from 1881 to 1900. The largest plantations are those of the year 1808, when 200 acres were planted. The woods now consist generally of a mixture of larch, sycamore, ash, oak, birch, beech, alder, spruce and Scots pine; while the general treatment accorded to them consists in simply clear-felling a given area of woodland every year, and replanting a corresponding acreage of recently cleared land or of other land which it is desired to bring under wood. Planting is done both in autumn and in spring, whenever the weather will permit. The plantations of the last ten years have amounted to 360 acres, or an average of 36 acres a year.

The woodlands on the Brayton estate, the property of Sir Wilfrid Lawson, bart., aggregate 1,503 acres. About three-fourths of these are old woods of uncertain age, mainly consisting of mixed hardwoods (though principally of oak) and often interspersed with Scots pine and larch ; the remainder are young plantations formed between 1870 and 1892, and consisting chiefly of mixed hardwoods with Scots pine, spruce and larch as nurses, or else of mixed Scots pine and larch. Only in one instance has larch been planted almost pure in 30 acres of a plantation (of 115 acres) formed during 1882 to 1884. The largest wooded tract on the estate consists of a compact block of 694 acres of old mixed hardwoods, with some Scots pine and larch, in the parish of Isel.

In the old plantations dating from the active period of arboriculture towards the end of the eighteenth century and the beginning of the nineteenth, the chief aim seems to have been the growth of oak for shipbuilding, and this object was apparently sought to be attained by growing it along with sycamore, beech, ash and larch. In the younger plantations formed during the last thirty years larch has been largely planted along with Scots pine, spruce and birch, probably with a view to securing a very quick growing and early maturing crop ; but the larch has unfortunately become much affected with the cankerous disease due to the fungus *Peziza Willkommii*, so that a great many of them have had to be cut out. In some instances these premature clearances have been so extensive as to necessitate the replantation of such parts with Scots pine. In this locality the cultivation of birch pays fairly well, the wood being much in demand for making the soles of clogs.

The method of management adopted with regard to the older woods is the customary British system of thinning the crops. This is done regularly, the oak-trees being peeled and the bark sold to local tanners. The price of bark has during late years ranged from £4 5s. od. to £5 os. od. a ton, which, though nothing like so favourable to growers as in past times, is higher than the recent prices obtaining in many of the other parts of England. Sometimes a few acres of hardwoods are clear-felled and replanted with Scots pine, spruce and birch, while shoots are allowed to spring up from oak-stools and are afterwards cut for their bark and the small wood they yield.

Pit planting is the method usually practised on the Brayton estate, but **T** shaped *notching* (with close planting at about three feet apart, or 4,840 per acre) is occasionally adopted when planting on grass land. Blanks are filled during the first and second years, and early thinnings commence at from 15 to 20 years, after which they are repeated every six to eight years. Where the ultimate crop is intended to consist of hardwoods, these are of course specially favoured during the thinnings, and occasional pruning is also done to repair defects in the way of forked growth.

But some of the smaller estates also possess woodlands of an extremely interesting character. In this respect none surpass the old oak-woods and the more recent larch plantations on the Castlerigg and Derwentwater estates, the property of R. Dykes Marshall, esq., by whose father they were acquired on the sale of the forfeited Derwentwater property by the trustees of Greenwich Hospital. Some of the oak plantations made by the trustees during the eighteenth century, when the outlook was very gloomy for the maintenance of the supply of timber for the navy, are now fine specimens of typical, old-fashioned English arboriculture.

Though comparatively small in extent, the woods and plantations on the Castlerigg and Derwentwater estates show how well pleasure and profit can be combined for the owner under a continuity of careful, well considered and methodical management. The woods (645 acres) comprise 28 acres of ornamental plantations and shelter-belts, 181 acres of woods treated partly for ornament and partly for profit by a system of selection fellings (such as were also included within the term *thinnings*, under the old-fashioned system of British Arboriculture), and 406 acres of plantations of different ages (but mostly mature or approaching full maturity) treated purely upon commercial principles. Careful estimates made in 1900 show that these 406 acres are now (after heavy regular thinnings carried out periodically) stocked with 44,019 trees, containing 458,371 cubic feet of timber.

In the old woods, aggregating about 350 acres in extent and consisting mainly of crops of oak formed about 100 and 150 years ago, when oak for shipbuilding seemed likely to be able to command a high price in future, the timber may now be regarded as fully mature. Measurements made from borings showing the annual rings of several of the trees prove that they have taken from 15 to 21 years to increase by one inch in radius (or $6\frac{2}{7}$ inches in girth), and the rate of growth is not at all likely to increase now. Some survivors of the larch apparently put out to nurse the oak are now splendid trees, girthing up to 7 and even 8 feet, and in one case attaining a circumference of 10 feet at breast-height.

The chief of the conifer plantations is a block of 200 acres (Coomb Wood), an outlying plantation formed in 1846–8, of larch with slight admixture of spruce in moist parts and Scots pine in exposed places. Here the rate of growth ascertained from the stems showed that they have taken from 10 to 16 years to increase by the last inch of radius (or $6\frac{2}{7}$ inches in girth), representing a current increase of over 3 per cent. on the trees now forming the crop. Methodical and carefully kept estate accounts show (1) that this plantation was made at a cost of about £2 an acre (there being then no necessity for expensive wire-netting against rabbits) on land the fee-simple of which was not more than £1 an acre, and (2) that from a very early age this wood, being periodically thinned in sections, has yielded thinnings almost regularly year by year. As for some years past these thinnings have really been of the nature of partial clearances of the maturing (and nearly mature) crop, which have thus already liquidated a portion of its capital value, the stock of 53 to 55-year-old timber is not so large per acre as it otherwise would have been ; but, as the grazing (of good quality) in the now rather open wood is let along with other pasture land at about five shillings an acre, this of itself forms an improved income from what the land could possibly have yielded for pasturage in the condition it was in before planting. The well kept estate accounts consequently prove that this compact block of plantation of about 200 acres has been a very profitable and beneficial investment to the landowner.

One of the great dangers to which investments of capital in the production of timber must be exposed in a county with the configuration and other physical conditions of Cumberland is windfall and other damage by heavy winds. Many of the plantations suffered severely in the gales which occurred towards the end of 1883 and the beginning of 1884, and again in the heavy storms of the autumn of 1893 ; but a year seldom passes without damage having to be recorded to a greater or less extent. Protection can to some extent be afforded by felling only against wind. Even, however, with this danger being kept in view, Cumberland is still one of the counties of England best suited for the profitable growth of coniferous timber ; and with the present outlook in regard to the maintenance of future supplies of the building wood required in such enormous quantities as is now the case in Britain, this class of woodland crop is what holds out the best promise of profit in time to come.

There is a good market for timber in Cumberland. Well-grown ash is in demand for coach-building and agricultural implements ; while oak, beech, larch and sycamore, if of good size, can be readily disposed of to buyers coming from Newcastle, Lancashire, and Yorkshire.[1]

---

[1] *The Journal of the Board of Agriculture*, vol. vii. No. 1, June 1900, page 8.